A Companion to Hegel

Blackwell Companions to Philosophy

This outstanding student reference series offers a comprehensive and authoritative survey of philosophy as a whole. Written by today's leading philosophers, each volume provides lucid and engaging coverage of the key figures, terms, topics, and problems of the field. Taken together, the volumes provide the ideal basis for course use, representing an unparalleled work of reference for students and specialists alike.

Recent books in the series (a full list appears at the back of this book):

Forthcoming:

A Companion
to Hegel

Edited by

Stephen Houlgate and Michael Baur

A John Wiley & Sons, Ltd., Publication

This edition first published 2011

Blackwell Publishing was acquired by John Wiley & Sons in February 2007. Blackwell's publishing program has been merged with Wiley's global Scientific, Technical, and Medical business to form Wiley-Blackwell.

Registered Office
John Wiley & Sons Ltd, The Atrium, Southern Gate, Chichester, West Sussex, PO19 8SQ, United Kingdom

Editorial Offices
350 Main Street, Malden, MA 02148-5020, USA
9600 Garsington Road, Oxford, OX4 2DQ, UK
The Atrium, Southern Gate, Chichester, West Sussex, PO19 8SQ, UK

For details of our global editorial offices, for customer services, and for information about how to apply for permission to reuse the copyright material in this book please see our website at www.wiley.com/wiley-blackwell.

ISBN: 978-1-4051-7076-5 (hardback)

Library of Congress cataloging-in-publication data is available for this title

A catalogue record for this book is available from the British Library.

This book is published in the following electronic formats: ePDFs 9781444397147; Wiley Online Library 9781444397161; ePub 9781444397154

Set in 10/12.5 pt Photina by Toppan Best-set Premedia Limited
Printed in Malaysia by Ho Printing (M) Sdn Bhd

1   2011

Contents

Notes on Contributors

Michael Baur is Associate Professor of Philosophy and Adjunct Professor of Law at Fordham University. He holds a PhD in Philosophy from the University of Toronto, and a J.D. from Harvard Law School. He is the translator of Fichte's *Foundations of Natural Right* (2000), Series Editor of "Cambridge Hegel Translations" (Cambridge University Press), and Associate Editor of the *Owl of Minerva: Journal of the Hegel Society of America*. His areas of research include German Idealism, the philosophy of law, and contemporary continental thought. He has published articles on a wide range of thinkers, including Aristotle, Aquinas, Kant, Fichte, Hegel, Heidegger, Adorno, and Gadamer.

Frederick C. Beiser is Professor of Philosophy at Syracuse University. He is the author of *The Fate of Reason* (1987), *Enlightenment, Revolution and Romanticism* (1992), *The Sovereignty of Reason* (1996), *German Idealism* (2002), *The Romantic Imperative* (2003), *Hegel* (2004), *Schiller as Philosopher* (2005) and *Diotima's Children* (2009). He has edited two collections on Hegel, *The Cambridge Companion to Hegel* (2002), and *The Cambridge Companion to Hegel and Nineteenth-Century Philosophy* (2008). He is currently finishing a book on German historicism.

Robert Bernasconi is Edwin Erle Sparks Professor of Philosophy at Pennsylvania State University. He was previously for over twenty years Moss Professor of Philosophy at the University of Memphis. He is the author of *The Question of Language and Heidegger's History of Being* (1985), *Heidegger in Question* (1991), and *How to Read Sartre* (2006). He has published numerous articles on such figures as Kant, Hegel, Levinas, Derrida, and Fanon, and he has written extensively within the field of political philosophy and critical philosophy of race.

John W. Burbidge, FRSC, is Professor Emeritus at Trent University, Canada. He is the author of *On Hegel's Logic* (1981), *Hegel on Logic and Religion* (1992), *Real Process: How Logic and Chemistry Combine in Hegel's Philosophy of Nature* (1996), *The Logic of Hegel's Logic: An Introduction* (2006), *Hegel's Systematic Contingency* (2007), and *The A to Z of Hegelian Philosophy* (2010). He has been President of the Hegel Society of America and is currently Honorary President of the Hegel Society of Great Britain.

Judith Butler is Maxine Elliot Professor in the Departments of Rhetoric and Comparative Literature and the Codirector of the Program of Critical Theory at the University of California, Berkeley. She is the author of *Subjects of Desire: Hegelian Reflections in Twentieth-Century France* (1987), *Gender Trouble* (1990), *Bodies That Matter* (1993), *The Psychic Life of Power* (1997), *Excitable Speech* (1997), *Antigone's Claim: Kinship Between Life and Death* (2000), *Precarious Life: Powers of Violence and Mourning*

(2004), *Undoing Gender* (2004), *Who Sings the Nation-State?* (2008) (with Gayatri Spivak), *Frames of War: When Is Life Grievable?* (2009), and *Is Critique Secular?* (2009) (with Talal Asad, Wendy Brown, and Saba Mahmood). She is active in Jewish Voice for Peace and is presently the recipient of the Andrew Mellon Award for Distinguished Academic Achievement in the Humanities.

Andrew Chitty is a Lecturer in Philosophy at the University of Sussex. He has published on Hegel, Marx, E.V. Ilyenkov, and Alan Gewirth, and is coeditor (with Christopher Bertram) of *Has History Ended? Fukuyama, Marx, Modernity* (1994) and (with Martin McIvor) of *Karl Marx and Contemporary Philosophy* (2009). He is a founding member of the Marx and Philosophy Society. He is currently working on a monograph on freedom and sociality in the thought of Marx.

Daniel O. Dahlstrom, Chair of the Department of Philosophy at Boston University, is the author of *Das logische Vorurteil* (1994), *Heidegger's Concept of Truth* (2001), and *Philosophical Legacies: Essays on the Thought of Kant, Hegel, and Their Contemporaries* (2008). He has published numerous articles and has translated works by Mendelssohn, Schiller, Hegel, Feuerbach, and Heidegger. A former President of the Metaphysical Society of America and currently Presiding Officer of the Heidegger Circle, he is the editor of *Interpreting Heidegger: New Essays* (2010) and the cotranslator (with Klaus Brinkmann) of Hegel's *Encyclopedia Logic* (2010).

Karin de Boer is Lecturer in Philosophy at the University of Groningen, The Netherlands. Her areas of interest include Kant, Hegel, Heidegger, tragedy, metaphysics, and contemporary French thought. She is the author of *Thinking in the Light of Time: Heidegger's Encounter with Hegel* (2000) and *On Hegel: The Sway of the Negative* (2010), as well as numerous articles on modern and contemporary continental philosophy. She is the editor (with Ruth Sonderegger) of *Conceptions of Critique in Modern and Contemporary Philosophy* (2011).

Katerina Deligiorgi teaches philosophy at the University of Sussex. She is currently completing a monograph on *The Scope of Autonomy: Thinking About the Morality of Freedom with Kant, Schiller, and Hegel*. She is the author of *Kant and the Culture of Enlightenment* (2006) and the editor of *Hegel: New Directions* (2006). She has been editing the *Bulletin of the Hegel Society of Great Britain* since 2007.

Alfredo Ferrarin is Professor of Theoretical Philosophy at the University of Pisa. He is the author of *Hegel and Aristotle* (2001), *Artificio, desiderio, considerazione di sé. Hobbes e i fondamenti antropologici della politica* (2001), *Saggezza, immaginazione e giudizio pratico. Studio su Aristotele e Kant* (2004), and over 30 articles on ancient and modern philosophy. He is the editor of *Congedarsi da Kant? Interventi sul Goodbye Kant di Ferraris* (2006), *Passive Synthesis and Life-world* (2006), and *La realtà del pensiero. Essenze, ragione, temporalità* (2007). He co-organized the Eleventh International Kant Congress in Pisa in May 2010.

Cinzia Ferrini is a Lecturer in the History of Philosophy at the University of Trieste and a Humboldt Fellow. She is the author of *Guida al "De orbitis"* (1995), *Scienze empiriche e filosofie della natura* (1996), and *Dai primi hegeliani a Hegel* (2003), the editor of *Eredità kantiane* (2004) and *Itinerari del criticismo* (2005), and has contributed two essays on "Reason" to the *Blackwell Guide to Hegel's "Phenomenology"* (2009). Her essays in English on Kant's and Hegel's philosophies of nature have appeared in journals such as *The Owl of Minerva* (1988), *Hegel-Jahrbuch* (1991), *Archiv für Geschichte der Philosophie* (2000), *Philosophia Naturalis* (1994), *Bulletin of the Hegel Society of Great Britain* (1999, 2007), and *Hegel-Studien* (2004, 2010), and in a number of collections and proceedings. She currently serves on the Board of the Academia Europaea.

Peter C. Hodgson is Charles G. Finney Professor of Theology, Emeritus, Divinity School, Vanderbilt University. He is the author, in recent years, of *Winds of the Spirit* (1994), *God's Wisdom* (1999), *Christian Faith* (2001), *The Mystery Beneath the Real* (2001), *Hegel and Christian Theology* (2005), and *Liberal Theology* (2007). He is the editor and translator (with R. F. Brown and J. M. Stewart) of Hegel's *Lectures on the Philosophy of Religion* (1984–1987), of Hegel's *Lectures on the Proofs of the Existence of God* (2007), and (with R. F. Brown) of Hegel's *Lectures on the Philosophy of World History* (forthcoming).

Stephen Houlgate is Professor of Philosophy at the University of Warwick. He is the author of *Hegel, Nietzsche and the Criticism of Metaphysics* (1986), *An Introduction to Hegel: Freedom, Truth and History* (1991, 2005), and *The Opening of Hegel's Logic* (2006). He is the editor of *Hegel and the Philosophy of Nature* and *The Hegel Reader* (both 1998), *Hegel and the Arts* (2007), and *G.W.F. Hegel: Elements of the Philosophy of Right* (2008). He served as Vice-President and President of the Hegel Society of America and was editor of the *Bulletin of the Hegel Society of Great Britain* from 1998 to 2006.

Catherine Malabou is Professor of Philosophy at the University of Paris Ouest-Nanterre and will be Professor of Philosophy in the Centre for Modern European Philosophy at Kingston University from 2011. She is the author of *The Future of Hegel: Plasticity, Temporality and Dialectic* (English translation, 1985), *What Should We Do With Our Brain?* (English translation, 2005), and *Plasticity at the Dusk of Writing* (English translation, 2009).

Frederick Neuhouser is Professor of Philosophy at Barnard College, Columbia University. He is the author of *Rousseau's Theodicy of Self-Love: Evil, Rationality, and the Drive for Recognition* (2008), *Actualizing Freedom: Foundations of Hegel's Social Theory* (2000), and *Fichte's Theory of Subjectivity* (1990). He is an editor of *The Journal of Philosophy*.

Angelica Nuzzo is Professor of Philosophy at the Graduate Center and Brooklyn College, City University of New York. Among her publications are *Representation and Concept in the Logic of Hegel's Philosophy of Right* (in Italian, 1990), *Logic and System in Hegel* (in Italian, 1996), *System* (in German, 2003), *Kant and the Unity of Reason* (2005), *Ideal Embodiment. Kant's Theory of Sensibility* (2008), and the edited volume *Hegel and the Analytic Tradition* (2009). Her numerous essays on German Idealism and Modern Philosophy appear in journals such as the *Journal of the History of Philosophy*, *Metaphilosophy*, *Journal of Philosophy and Social Criticism*, *Deutsche Zeitschrift für Philosophie*, *Hegel Studien*, and *Fichte Studien*.

Brian O'Connor is Associate Professor of Philosophy at University College Dublin. He is the author of *Adorno's Negative Dialectic* (2004), *Adorno: The Routledge Philosophers* (2011), and papers on the German Idealist and Critical Theory traditions. He is the editor of *The Adorno Reader* (2000) and (with Georg Mohr) of *German Idealism: An Anthology and Guide* (2007).

Terry Pinkard is a Professor at Georgetown University in Washington, DC. He is the author of *Hegel's Phenomenology: The Sociality of Reason* (1994), *Hegel: A Biography* (2000), and *German Philosophy 1760–1860: The Legacy of Idealism* (2002). He is the editor of and wrote the introduction for *Heinrich Heine, On the History of Religion and Philosophy in Germany and Other Writings* (2007).

Thomas Posch is Senior Scientist and Lecturer at the Institute of Astronomy of the University of Vienna. He holds a PhD in Philosophy (2002) and one in Astronomy (2005). His current research topics include the history of astronomy, the philosophy of nature and the role of solid particles in the cosmic matter cycle. As well as publishing numerous papers on these subjects, he has edited several lecture transcripts of, and anthologies on, Hegel's philosophy of nature. Combining astrophysics and the humanities, he recently edited a book entitled *Das Ende der Nacht* (*The End of Night*) (2010), which examines the history and the dramatic effects of turning night into day through the ever-growing excessive use of artificial illumination.

Paul Redding is Professor of Philosophy at the University of Sydney. He is the author of *Hegel's Hermeneutics* (1996), *The Logic of Affect* (1999), *Analytic Philosophy and the Return of Hegelian Thought* (2007), and *Continental Idealism: Leibniz to Nietzsche* (2009).

John Russon is Professor of Philosophy at the University of Guelph. He is the author of *The Self and Its Body in Hegel's Phenomenology of Spirit* (1997), *Human Experience: Philosophy, Neurosis, and the Elements of Everyday Life* (2003), *Reading Hegel's Phenomenology* (2004), and *Bearing Witness to Epiphany: Persons, Things, and the Nature of Erotic Life* (2009). He is the coeditor (with Michael Baur) of *Hegel and the Tradition: Essays in Honour of H. S. Harris* (1998), (with John Sallis), of *Retracing the Platonic Text* (2000), and (with Patricia Fagan) of *Reexamining Socrates in the Apology* (2009). He is also Director of the Toronto Summer Seminar in Philosophy.

John Sallis is the Frederick J. Adelmann Professor of Philosophy at Boston College and a regular Visiting Professor at the Universität Freiburg. He is the founding Editor of *Research in Phenomenology* and the author of many books, including, most recently, *Shades: Of Painting at the Limit* (1998), *Chorology* (1999), *Force of Imagination* (2000), *On Translation* (2002), *Platonic Legacies* (2004), *Topographies* (2006), *The Verge of Philosophy* (2007), and *Transfigurements: On the True Sense of Art* (2008).

Sally Sedgwick is Professor of Philosophy and Affiliated Professor of Germanic Studies at the University of Illinois at Chicago. Her publications include numerous essays on Kant and Hegel, and the monograph *Kant's Groundwork of the Metaphysics of Morals: An Introduction* (2008). She is the editor of the volume *The Reception of Kant's Critical Philosophy: Fichte, Schelling, and Hegel* (2000) and she has under review a book on Hegel's critique of Kant's theoretical philosophy. In the academic year 2009–2010, she was President of the Central Division of the American Philosophical Association.

Allen Speight is Associate Professor of Philosophy at Boston University. He is a recipient of Fulbright, DAAD, Berlin Prize and NEH Fellowships and is the author of *Hegel, Literature and the Problem of Agency* (2001) and *The Philosophy of Hegel* (2008). He is also coeditor and translator (with Brady Bowman) of *Hegel: Heidelberg Writings* (2009), the first volume to appear in the new series of Hegel translations published by Cambridge University Press. He currently serves as Director of the Institute for Philosophy and Religion at Boston University and is editor-in-chief of the series *Boston Studies in Philosophy, Religion and Public Life* (Springer).

Robert Stern is Professor of Philosophy at the University of Sheffield. He has written widely on Hegel and German Idealism more generally, including *Hegel, Kant and the Structure of the Object* (1990) and *Hegel and the "Phenomenology of Spirit"* (2002), while a collection of his papers has been published under the title of *Hegelian Metaphysics* (2009). He was the editor of *G.W.F. Hegel: Critical Assessments* (1993). He is currently President of the Hegel Society of Great Britain.

Jon Stewart is Professor at the Kierkegaard Research Centre at Copenhagen University. He is the author of *The Unity of Hegel's Phenomenology of Spirit* (2000), *Kierkegaard's Relations to Hegel Reconsidered* (2003), *A History of Hegelianism in Golden Age Denmark* (2007), and *Idealism and Existentialism* (2010). He is the editor of *The Hegel Myths and Legends* (1996), *The Phenomenology of Spirit Reader* (1998), *Miscellaneous Writings by Hegel* (2002), and *Kierkegaard and His Contemporaries* (2003). He has translated *Heiberg's "On the Significance of Philosophy"* (2005) and *Heiberg's Speculative Logic* (2006) into English. He is the editor of the series *Kierkegaard Studies: Sources, Reception and Resources, Texts from Golden Age Denmark*, and *Danish Golden Age Studies*. He is a member of The Royal Danish Academy of the Sciences.

Jere O'Neill Surber is Professor of Philosophy and Cultural Theory at the University of Denver. He is the author of numerous books and articles in the areas of nineteenth- and twentieth-century Continental Philosophy and contemporary cultural critique. He has been a visiting professor at such institutions as the Johannes-Gutenberg-Universität, Mainz, and Katholieke Universiteit, Leuven; he serves on the editorial boards of several journals; and he has been Vice-President and Program Chair of the Hegel Society of America.

Kenneth R. Westphal is Professorial Fellow at the University of East Anglia. He is author of *Kant's Transcendental Proof of Realism* (2004), *Hegel's Epistemology* (2003), *Hegel, Hume und die Identität wahrnehmbarer Dinge* (1998), "From 'Convention' to 'Ethical Life': Hume's Theory of Justice in Post-Kantian Perspective" (*The Journal of Moral Philosophy*, 2010) and "Mutual Recognition and Rational Justification in Hegel's Phenomenology of Spirit" (*Dialogue*, 2010). His current projects are "Hegel's Critique of Cognitive Judgment: From Naïve Realism to Understanding" and "Moral Constructivism Modern Style."

Robert R. Williams is Professor Emeritus of Germanic Studies, Philosophy and Religious Studies at the University of Illinois at Chicago. He is the author of *Schleiermacher the Theologian* (1978), *Recognition: Fichte and Hegel on the Other* (1992), and *Hegel's Ethics of Recognition* (1997), and the editor of *Beyond Liberalism and Communitarianism:*

Studies in Hegel's Philosophy of Right (2001), the translator (with Claude Welch) of I. A. Dorner's *Divine Immutability* (1994), and the translator of *Hegel's Lectures on the Philosophy of Spirit 1827–8* (2007). He was Vice President of the Hegel Society of America from 1998 to 2000 and President from 2000 to 2001. He is currently completing a book entitled *Tragedy, Recognition and the Death of God: Studies in Hegel and Nietzsche*.

Richard Dien Winfield is Distinguished Research Professor of Philosophy at the University of Georgia, where he has taught since 1982. He is the author of *The Just Economy* (1988), *Reason and Justice* (1988), *Overcoming Foundations: Studies in Systematic Philosophy* (1989), *Freedom and Modernity* (1991), *Law in Civil Society* (1995), *Systematic Aesthetics* (1995), *Stylistics: Rethinking the Artforms After Hegel* (1996), *The Just Family* (1998), *Autonomy and Normativity: Investigations of Truth, Right and Beauty* (2001), *The Just State: Rethinking Self-Government* (2005), *From Concept to Objectivity: Thinking Through Hegel's Subjective Logic* (2006), *Modernity, Religion, and the War on Terror* (2007), and *Hegel and Mind: Rethinking Philosophical Psychology* (2010), and *The Living Mind: From Psyche to Consciousness* (2011).

Allen W. Wood is Ward W. and Priscilla B. Woods Professor at Stanford University. As of 2011–2012, he will be emeritus at Stanford and will be Ruth Norman Halls Professor at Indiana University. He has taught at Cornell University (1968–1996) and Yale University (1996–2000), and held visiting appointments at the University of Michigan (1973), the University of California at San Diego (1986), and Oxford University (2005). He is author of numerous books and articles, chiefly on ethics and on the German idealist tradition from Kant through Marx.

Chronology of Hegel's Life and Work

1770   March 20: Friedrich Hölderlin born in Lauffen am Neckar. August 27: Georg Wilhelm Friedrich Hegel born in Stuttgart. Ludwig van Beethoven and William Wordsworth are born in the same year.

1775   January 27: Friedrich Wilhelm Joseph von Schelling born in Württemberg.

1776   American Declaration of Independence.

1777   Hegel enters the Stuttgarter Gymnasium.

1781   First edition of Kant's *Critique of Pure Reason* is published.

1783   September 20: Hegel's mother dies.

1784   Hegel transfers to the Stuttgarter Obergymnasium.

1785   Hegel begins writing a diary, partly in Latin. Kant's *Groundwork for the Metaphysics of Morals* is published.

1787   Second (revised) edition of Kant's *Critique of Pure Reason* is published.

1788   Kant's *Critique of Practical Reason* is published. October: Hegel and Hölderlin begin studies in theology and philosophy at the Tübinger *Stift*. During their time at the *Stift* the two students develop a close friendship with one another and with Schelling (after he enters the *Stift* in 1790).

1789   July 14: The storming of the Bastille in Paris marks the beginning of the French Revolution, which is greeted with enthusiasm by students at the *Stift*.

1790   Hegel receives his M.A. degree. Kant publishes his *Critique of Judgement*.

1792   Fichte's *Critique of All Revelation* appears.

1793   Louis XVI is guillotined. Hegel graduates from the Tübinger *Stift*. Autumn: He takes up a position as private tutor with the family of Captain Carl Friedrich von Steiger in Bern. Kant publishes *Religion within the Bounds of Reason Alone*.

1794   Fall of Robespierre. Fichte begins to publish his *Foundation of the Entire Science of Knowledge*.

1795   Schiller's letters on the *Aesthetic Education of Man* are published. Hegel works on "The Life of Jesus" and on "The Positivity of the Christian Religion." Kant publishes "Towards Perpetual Peace."

1796   Hegel (or Schelling or Hölderlin) writes the *Earliest System-programme of German Idealism.* Napoleon campaigns in Italy.

1797   January: Hegel moves to Frankfurt am Main to take up a position as private tutor which Hölderlin had arranged for him with the family Gogel. Summer/ autumn: Hegel drafts fragments on religion and love.

1798   Schelling becomes Professor of Philosophy at Jena on the recommendation of Johann Wolfgang von Goethe. Hegel works on Kant's *Metaphysics of Morals.* Napoleon campaigns in Egypt.

1799   January 14: Hegel's father dies. Hegel writes the "Spirit of Christianity and Its Fate" and works on Sir James Steuart's *Inquiry into the Principles of Political Economy.*

1800   Schelling publishes his *System of Transcendental Idealism.* September: Hegel completes his "System-fragment." From 1800 to 1802 Hegel works on (but does not complete) his extended essay, "The Constitution of Germany."

1801   January: Hegel joins Schelling at the University of Jena. He begins lecturing as an unsalaried lecturer (*Privatdozent*) on logic and metaphysics. His first publication, an essay entitled *The Difference between Fichte's and Schelling's System of Philosophy*, appears. He completes his dissertation, *On the Orbits of the Planets.*

1802   Hegel lectures on natural law. He begins publication of the *Critical Journal of Philosophy* with Schelling. Publication continues until the summer of 1803 when Schelling leaves Jena. Essays by Hegel published in the journal in 1802 and 1803 include *Faith and Knowledge, The Relation of Scepticism to Philosophy,* and *On the Scientific Ways of Treating Natural Law.*

1803   September: Hegel prepares a manuscript known as the "System of Speculative Philosophy," which includes material on the philosophy of nature and the philosophy of spirit.

1804   February 12: Kant dies. December 2: Napoleon crowns himself Emperor.

1805   February: Hegel is appointed Extraordinary Professor of Philosophy at Jena through the help of Goethe. May 9: Schiller dies.

1806   July: Hegel draws his first regular stipend at Jena. October: He finishes the last pages of the *Phenomenology of Spirit* during the night before the battle of Jena (in which Napoleon's army defeats the Prussian troops). Earlier, during the day before the battle, he sees Napoleon riding out of the city on reconnaissance.

1807   *Phenomenology of Spirit* is published. February 5: Christiana Burckhardt (*née* Fischer), Hegel's landlady and housekeeper in Jena, gives birth to his illegitimate son, Ludwig Fischer. (Ludwig is raised in Jena by the sisters-in-law of Hegel's friend, the publisher Karl Friedrich Frommann, until he is taken into Hegel's own home in 1817.) March: Hegel moves to Bamberg to become editor of a newspaper. Autumn: A period of reform begins in Prussia, initially under Freiherr von Stein, then under Karl von Hardenberg. This lasts until 1813.

1808   November: Hegel moves to Nuremberg to become rector of the Ägidiengymnasium. One of his tasks at the Gymnasium is to teach speculative logic to his pupils.

1811   September 15: Hegel marries Marie von Tucher (born 1791).

1812   Napoleon's Russian campaign. Volume 1 of the *Science of Logic* (the Logic of Being) is published. June 27: Hegel's daughter Susanna is born. She dies on August 8.

1813   June 7: Hegel's son Karl is born. Volume 2 of the *Science of Logic* (the Logic of Essence) is published. Søren Kierkegaard, Giuseppe Verdi, and Richard Wagner are born.

1814   January 29: Fichte dies. September 25: Hegel's son Immanuel is born.

1815   Napoleon is defeated at Waterloo.

1816   Volume 3 of the *Science of Logic* (the Logic of the Concept) is published. Hegel becomes Professor of Philosophy at the University of Heidelberg. At Heidelberg he lectures on the history of philosophy, logic and metaphysics, anthropology and psychology, political philosophy, aesthetics, and the *Encyclopaedia*.

1817   The first edition of the *Encyclopaedia* is published. Hegel becomes co-editor of the *Heidelberg Yearbooks* and in that journal publishes his "Proceedings of the Estates Assembly in the Kingdom of Württemberg 1815–1816."

1818   May 5: Karl Marx is born in Trier. Hegel is recruited by the Prussian Minister for Religious, Educational and Medical Affairs, Karl Siegmund Altenstein, to become Professor of Philosophy at the University of Berlin, where he remains until his death.

1819   August/September: The Karlsbad Decrees are passed, authorizing press censorship and closer surveillance of universities in Germany. In the period of crackdown shortly before the decrees are passed, one of Hegel's students, Leopold von Henning, is arrested.

1820   October: *Philosophy of Right* published (dated 1821).

1821   Hegel lectures for the first time on the philosophy of religion. May 5: Napoleon dies.

1822   Hegel travels to the Rhineland and the Low Countries, where he sees paintings by Rembrandt and van Dyck. In Berlin he lectures for the first time on the philosophy of history.

1824   The Brockhaus *Konversationslexikon* includes an account of Hegel's life and philosophy. Hegel visits Vienna where he attends several operas by Rossini.

1826   Hegel founds the *Yearbooks for Scientific Criticism.*

1827   The second edition of the *Encyclopaedia* is published. Hegel visits Paris, where he sees Molière's *Tartuffe* and an operatic version of *Oedipus at Colonus.* He also sees the central section of the van Eyck Altarpiece in Ghent and paintings by Memling in Bruges. October: He visits Goethe in Weimar on the way home to Berlin.

1830   Hegel is Rector of the University of Berlin. The third edition of the *Encyclopaedia* is published. The July Revolution occurs in France.

1831   January: Hegel is awarded Red Eagle Third Class by Friedrich Wilhelm III of Prussia. August 28: Ludwig Fischer dies in the East Indies. November 14: Hegel dies in Berlin (probably of a chronic gastrointestinal disease) without learning of his son's fate. December 24: A contract is signed by Hegel's wife, students, and friends for the publication of his collected works.

1832   March 22: Goethe dies.

1835   D. F. Strauss's *Life of Jesus* is published, marking the beginning of a split between
–6   Left, Right, and Middle Hegelians.

1841   Schelling is called to the University of Berlin by Friedrich Wilhelm IV to counter the influence of Hegelianism. L. Feuerbach's *The Essence of Christianity* is published.

1843   June 7: Hölderlin dies in Tübingen.

1848   Marx and Engels publish the *Communist Manifesto.*

1854   August 20: Schelling dies in Switzerland.

G.W.F. Hegel: An Introduction to His Life and Thought

STEPHEN HOULGATE

Georg Wilhelm Friedrich Hegel (1770–1831) is one of the giants of the European philosophical tradition. Indeed, in the eyes of many the depth and sophistication of his thought are matched only in the work of Plato, Aristotle, and Kant. Hegel's texts and lectures are by no means easy to read, but his influence on the modern world has been profound and wide-ranging. His thought helped spawn Marxism, existentialism, American pragmatism and the critical theory of the Frankfurt School; his philosophy of religion has left its mark on theologians, such as Karl Barth, Hans Küng, and Rowan Williams; he was considered by Ernst Gombrich to be the "father" of art history;[1] and he continues to provide inspiration to many contemporary philosophers, including Judith Butler, John McDowell, and Robert Brandom.

Hegel is worth studying, however, not just because of the influence he has exercised, but also because of the intrinsic merits of his thought. He has challenging and profound views on thought and being, nature and natural science, consciousness and language, human freedom in society and the state, and on history, art, religion, and the history of philosophy.

The bulk of the chapters in this collection examine aspects of Hegel's mature thought, which is set out in the *Phenomenology of Spirit* (1807) and the texts and lectures Hegel produced in the years following the *Phenomenology*'s publication. All of the principal parts of Hegel's system are covered in this collection, including the philosophy of nature and philosophy of subjective spirit, which are often overlooked in studies of Hegel. The collection also includes a chapter on Hegel's early writings that brings out the exploratory character of his work in the late 1790s and early 1800s, and eight chapters that explore the ways in which some of the most significant post-Hegelian thinkers have engaged both sympathetically and critically with Hegel's ideas.

The chapters in this collection have been written by scholars from Europe, North America, and Australia, and bear witness to the fact that the significance of Hegel's thought is recognized worldwide. They also reflect a wide variety of different approaches to Hegel. No single "orthodox" interpretation of Hegel's thought is presented here, but

A Companion to Hegel, First Edition. Edited by Stephen Houlgate and Michael Baur.

together the chapters provide a rich and multifaceted study of one of the richest and most multifaceted philosophies in the European tradition.

Hegel's Life

Hegel was born on August 27, 1770 in Stuttgart in the duchy of Württemberg and died on November 14, 1831 in Berlin, probably due to a gastrointestinal disease (though he was thought at the time to have succumbed to cholera).[2] He was the first of seven children to be born to Maria Magdalena Hegel and her husband, Georg Ludwig, a secretary at the court of Duke Karl Eugen. His sister, Christiane, who committed suicide in 1832, was born in 1773, and his brother, Georg Ludwig, who was lost serving in Russia with Napoleon in 1812, was born in 1776. The four remaining children of the Hegel family all died in infancy.[3]

Hegel began at the local German school when he was just three years old, moved to the Latin school at five, having already been taught the first declension in Latin by his mother, and entered the Stuttgarter Gymnasium when he was six or seven.[4] In September 1783 his mother died, the following year he transferred to the Stuttgarter Obergymnasium, and in 1785 he began a diary that he wrote for at least eighteen months in German and Latin.[5] His reading at this time included Rousseau, Klopstock, Lessing, Wieland, and Moses Mendelssohn, and his interests also encompassed history, Greek, Latin, and trigonometry, to which he appears to have devoted both Saturday and Sunday mornings.[6] Hegel was not, however, an utter bookworm but, as a teenager, enjoyed the company of young women and loved to dance (though he was said by his sister to be a somewhat "awkward" [*linkisch*] dancer).[7] He also developed a lifelong fondness for playing cards.[8]

In 1788 Hegel entered the theological seminary or *Stift* in Tübingen, becoming friends with Friedrich Hölderlin, who would go on to become one of Germany's greatest poets, and (after 1790) with Friedrich Wilhelm Schelling, who would go on to become one of Germany's greatest philosophers. (The three friends famously shared a room at the *Stift*, though there were at least seven other students in the room, too.)[9] Hegel had joined the *Stift* with the intention of contributing to the development of a new, "enlightened" religion. During his time there, however, he abandoned this aim in favor of leading what Terry Pinkard calls "an independent life as a 'man of letters.'"[10] What prompted Hegel's change of heart was partly his growing aversion to the theological orthodoxy and "supernaturalism" of teachers, such as Gottlob Christian Storr, and partly his enthusiasm, shared by Hölderlin and Schelling, for the French Revolution of 1789. As Pinkard puts it, Hegel came "to identify the French Revolution with moral and spiritual renewal" and the overthrow of theological orthodoxy, and, under the influence of his admiration for ancient Greece, he began to equate the new, revolutionary age "with the coming reign of beauty and freedom."[11]

Upon leaving Tübingen in 1793, Hegel took up a post in Berne as a private tutor (or *Hofmeister*) to the family of Captain Carl Friedrich von Steiger. While in Berne he read Gibbon's *Decline and Fall of the Roman Empire* and probably studied the work of Adam Smith. He also devoted himself assiduously to the study of Kant, Fichte, and Schelling (who by this time was already making a name for himself in philosophical circles).[12] In the provincial setting of Berne, however, Hegel felt isolated from intellectual and literary activity, and in a letter of August 1795 he tells Schelling rather plaintively "how much good it does me in my solitude to hear something from you and my other friends from time to time."[13]

Knowing that Hegel was unhappy in Berne, Hölderlin managed to find a position for him in Frankfurt as private tutor to the family of the wine merchant, Johann Noë Gogel, and Hegel took up his new post in January 1797.[14] While in Frankfurt Hegel was able to enjoy a richer cultural life than he had been able to enjoy in Berne, attending the theater "at least once a week" and delighting especially in the opera (seeing Mozart's *Magic Flute* and *Don Giovanni* in March 1797).[15] He read the works of Schelling, Plato, and Sextus Empiricus; in August 1798 he began an intensive study of Kant's *Metaphysics of Morals*; in 1799 he worked through a German translation of Sir James Steuart's *Inquiry into the Principles of Political Economy*; and, according to Walter Jaeschke, he made his first forays into the philosophy of nature. Hegel was also able to renew his personal and intellectual contact with Hölderlin and may well have read the latter's novel, *Hyperion*, when it was published in 1797.[16]

By the end of his stay in Berne, Pinkard maintains, "Hegel was beginning to redescribe everything in terms of the basic notions of Kantian ethical theory." Indeed, in Hegel's essay, "Life of Jesus," written in 1795, Jesus emerges, in Pinkard's words, "as one of the foremost exponents of Kant's 'religion of morality.'"[17] During the years in Frankfurt, however, Hegel came more under the influence of Schelling and Hölderlin. As a result he sought to overcome some of the characteristic dichotomies of Kant's thought: Karl Rosenkranz, for example, reports that Hegel strove to unite the Kantian concepts of "legality" and "morality" in a "higher concept" which he called "life" or, later, "ethical life" (*Sittlichkeit*).[18] Hegel also began to reflect more on the philosophical foundations of Kantian (and Fichtean) thought and of his own project of "educating the people." As a consequence he started to develop his own philosophical *system* and to turn his mind toward theoretical, rather than directly practical, concerns. As he puts it in a letter to Schelling, written in November 1800, "in my scientific development, which started from [the] more subordinate needs of man, I was inevitably driven toward science [*Wissenschaft*], and the ideal of [my] youth had to take the form of reflection and thus at once of a system."[19] This does not mean that Hegel suddenly lost interest in transforming modern political and religious life; but he came to believe, as he wrote to his friend, Immanuel Niethammer, in 1808, that "theoretical work accomplishes more in the world than practical work." "Once the realm of representation [*Vorstellung*] is revolutionized," Hegel declared, "actuality [*Wirklichkeit*] will not hold out."[20]

In January 1799 Hegel's father died, leaving him an inheritance that was modest but enough to open the possibility of his abandoning the life of a private tutor.[21] In January 1801 Hegel then joined Schelling at the University of Jena, where he worked initially as an unsalaried lecturer (*Privatdozent*), paid only by the students whom he could attract to his lectures.[22] While at Jena Hegel defended his dissertation "On the Orbits of the Planets" (1801), published several significant essays, including *The Difference between Fichte's and Schelling's System of Philosophy* (1801), and lectured on logic and metaphysics, natural law, philosophy of nature, philosophy of spirit, and the history of philosophy.[23] He also completed his monumental introduction to his philosophical system, the *Phenomenology of Spirit* (1807), which contains some of his most famous and influential analyses, including the "master / slave" dialectic, the account of the "unhappy consciousness," and the examination of revolutionary consciousness (which is now understood to lead of necessity to terror).

Hegel famously finished the last pages of the *Phenomenology* "in the middle of the night before the battle of Jena" and had to send earlier installments of his manuscript by courier through French lines to Niethammer in Bamberg (who then passed them on to the publisher).[24] On the day before the battle, October 13, 1806, Hegel saw Napoleon – "this world-soul" (*Weltseele*) – riding out of the city on reconnaissance, and he commented: "it is indeed a wonderful sensation to see such an individual, who, concentrated here at a single point, astride a horse, reaches out over the world and masters it."[25] Hegel retained an enduring respect for Napoleon throughout his life and in particular welcomed the introduction into parts of Germany of the Napoleonic Code, which, in Clark Butler's words, was "unambiguously revolutionary" in the still relatively feudal German context, even if it was "conservative" in comparison to the ideals of the French Revolution itself.[26]

In Jena Hegel made the acquaintance of Goethe, and it was Goethe who finally secured a small salary for him in 1806, well over a year after he had been made "Extraordinary Professor of Philosophy."[27] By February 1807, however, Hegel was "virtually penniless." He had also fathered an illegitimate son, Ludwig Fischer, by his housekeeper and landlady, Christiana Charlotte Burckhardt (*née* Fischer).[28] He was in urgent need, therefore, of finding more lucrative employment. Opportunity came in the form of a newspaper editorship in Bamberg, which Hegel took on in March 1807. By November 1808, however, Hegel had moved to Nuremberg, where he became rector of the Ägydiengymnasium. In Jena and later in Heidelberg people remarked on Hegel's "tormented lecture style"; in Nuremberg, by contrast, "his students remembered him as an inspiring teacher." He was also known especially for his concern and care for students in financial hardship.[29]

Hegel's great philosophical achievement in Nuremberg was the completion and publication of his three-volume *Science of Logic* (1812–1816), a work of formidable complexity that presents his speculative logic. The most significant event in his personal life was his marriage in September 1811 to Marie von Tucher, the daughter of a prominent Nuremberg family.[30] A month after the wedding Hegel wrote to his friend, Niethammer, of his newly found happiness: "on the whole – apart from a few modifications still to be desired – I have now reached my earthly goal. For what more does one want in this world than a post and a dear wife?"[31] The Hegels' first-born child, a daughter, Susanna, died in August 1812, just six weeks old. A son, Karl, was then born in June 1813 and a second son, Immanuel, was born in September 1814.[32] (Karl edited and published the now familiar second edition of Hegel's lectures on the philosophy of world history in 1840.)

Among the "few modifications" that Hegel still desired, even after his marriage, was a secure, salaried position teaching philosophy at a university. In the autumn of 1816, at the age of 46, he finally fulfilled his desire by becoming Professor of Philosophy at the University of Heidelberg. There he lectured on the history of philosophy, logic and metaphysics, anthropology and psychology, political philosophy, and aesthetics, and in 1817 he published the first edition of his *Encyclopedia of the Philosophical Sciences*.[33]

In the spring of 1817 Hegel and his wife took Hegel's illegitimate son, Ludwig Fischer, now ten years old, into their household in Heidelberg. Ludwig had previously been brought up in an orphanage in Jena run by the sisters-in-law of Hegel's friend, Karl Friedrich Frommann, and in April 1817 Hegel describes to Frommann the pleasure that both he and his wife now take in his son. Hegel writes that Ludwig "gives evidence of a good mind. He is now attending the local gymnasium, which to be sure could be better. But I am most surprised at how much Latin he has learned this past winter."[34] Ludwig's own recollections of his time in Heidelberg were, however, somewhat less positive: "I lived always in fear of, but never with love toward, my parents – a relationship that necessarily produced a constant tension that could never do any good."[35]

In 1818 Hegel left Heidelberg to become Professor of Philosophy at the University of Berlin. During his years in Berlin Hegel published his *Elements of the Philosophy of Right* (1820) and two further editions of his *Encyclopedia* (1827, 1830). He also gave lectures on the whole of his philosophical system, including philosophy of nature, philosophy of history, aesthetics, philosophy of religion, and the history of philosophy. It was through these lectures above all that Hegel exercised influence on his contemporaries.

Hegel became a prominent public figure in Berlin during the 1820s, socializing with politicians, such as Johannes Schulze, a minister in Karl Siegmund Altenstein's ministry for "Religious, Educational and Medical Affairs," and with leading figures in the arts, such as the opera singer Anna Milder-Hauptmann, who was admired by Beethoven and Goethe.[36] There was, however, little public engagement with Hegel's *philosophy* during his lifetime (in marked contrast to the public interest shown in the thought of Kant, Fichte, and Schelling). Many of Hegel's colleagues at the University of Berlin, such as Schleiermacher, were actively hostile to Hegel's philosophy, and the broader educated public did not devour Hegel's published works with any great enthusiasm. (Walter Jaeschke notes that the first edition of Hegel's *Phenomenology*, published in 1807 with a print run of only 750 copies, was still available in 1829, the year in which Hegel was made rector of the university.)[37] What influence Hegel did exercise was confined principally to his lectures, which were attended by, among others, Ludwig Feuerbach, David Friedrich Strauss, and the young Felix Mendelssohn.[38] Only after Hegel's death in 1831 did his influence spread, aided by the new edition of his works (including revised versions of his lectures) produced by his friends and by the critical reception of those works by figures such as Feuerbach, Marx, and Kierkegaard.

In the 1850s Rudolf Haym asserted that Hegel's philosophy was the "scientific home of the *spirit of the Prussian restoration*."[39] In this way Haym helped to popularize the idea that Hegel is authoritarian, reactionary, and hostile to the cause of modern freedom: the now familiar "philosopher of the Prussian state." The charge frequently leveled against Hegel in the more immediate aftermath of his death, however, was that his philosophy was *at odds* with the principles of the Prussian restoration. Hegel's strongly monarchist opponent, Karl Ernst Schubarth, published a work in 1839 entitled *On the Irreconciliability of Hegel's Doctrine of the State with the Supreme Principle Governing the Life and Development of the Prussian State*, and, in my view, Schubarth is much closer to the truth than Haym and those influenced by him.[40]

5

During his years in Berlin Hegel was, indeed, an employee of the Prussian state (since all university professors, including opponents of Hegel, such as Schleiermacher, were state employees), but it is important to note that he was called to Berlin by a *reform-minded* minister in the Prussian government, namely Altenstein. Furthermore, Hegel never became close to King Friedrich Wilhelm III or to the party of restoration that surrounded him; nor did he have any special influence on the government. Indeed, unlike many colleagues, Hegel was never made a Privy Councillor.[41] Hegel was thus by no means as closely associated with the reactionary figures in the Prussian state as Haym (and others, such as Karl Popper) would have us believe.

On the contrary, Hegel sympathized deeply with the advocates of reform, and his distance from, indeed opposition to, the party of restoration is evident from his scathing criticism of one of the latter's chief philosophical spokesmen, Carl Ludwig von Haller. Haller, Hegel tells us, maintains that it is "the eternal, unalterable, ordinance of God, that the mightier rules, must rule, and will always rule." In Hegel's view, however, this exhibits Haller's "virulent hatred of all laws and legislation, of all formally and legally determined right," and so shows him to be at odds with the principles of modern freedom that Hegel himself endorses.[42] Popper accuses Hegel of proclaiming the "doctrine that *might is right*."[43] Hegel's criticism of the party of restoration, however, is precisely that *it* equates might with right by defending power and privilege against the modern insistence on the primacy of freedom, right, and law.

In March 1819 the playwright August von Kotzebue was murdered by Karl Ludwig Sand, a member of the student fraternity, or *Burschenschaft*, at the University of Erlangen. Prompted by the Austrian Foreign Minister, Metternich, the governments in Germany and the federal parliament in Frankfurt responded to the murder by passing, in August and September 1819, the "Karlsbad Decrees," under which universities became subject to more and more repressive scrutiny. Censorship was increased, and lecturers or professors who were suspected of promoting "demagogical," or in other respects "liberal," tendencies ran the real risk of losing their posts. In the period before and after the passing of the Karlsbad Decrees not only Hegel himself, but also some of his students, fell under suspicion. In July 1819, for example, one student, Leopold von Henning, was arrested on the basis of comments in letters sent to him and was held for seven weeks. Then, in December 1819, Hegel's choice for his teaching assistant, Friedrich Wilhelm Carové, was denounced as a subversive and thereupon advised by Altenstein to leave Berlin.[44] Hegel clearly felt under threat himself and in October 1819 wrote to his friend, Friedrich Creuzer:

> I am about to be fifty years old, and I have spent thirty of these fifty years in these ever-unrestful times of hope and fear. I had hoped that for once we might be done with it. Now I must confess that things continue as ever. Indeed, in one's darker hours it seems they are getting ever worse.[45]

Hegel's fears were by no means unjustified, and at the time of Carové's denunciation he was precariously close to being denounced himself.[46]

Although Hegel was charged by Haym with supporting the conservative and reactionary policies of the Prussian state, he was in fact strongly opposed to the party of restoration that instigated those policies, and after 1819 felt (with justification) threatened by them. He has also been charged with preparing the way for twentieth-century totalitarianism,[47] when in fact he was profoundly hostile to nationalistic political violence and deeply committed to the rule of law and respect for freedom and rights. Hegel's commitment to law, freedom, and right was not merely a personal preference, but a commitment firmly rooted in his systematic philosophy. For the remainder of this Introduction I will give an – all too brief – account of the central themes of that philosophy.

Logic and Phenomenology

Hegel's philosophy has been, and is still, interpreted by commentators in widely differing ways. Some see Hegel as completing Kant's project of establishing the transcendental conditions of human cognition; others see him as continuing the work of *pre*-Kantian philosophers, such as Spinoza, by showing us what *being* is in itself. Some see Hegel as a deeply religious, indeed profoundly Christian, thinker; others concur with Robert Solomon's judgment that Hegel is "the precursor of atheistic humanism in German philosophy."[48] Some, as I noted above, see Hegel as a political reactionary; others see him as a dedicated advocate of human freedom. My aim here is not to try to do justice to the manifold ways in which Hegel's thought has been understood. I propose, rather, to provide a brief sketch of Hegel's system as I understand it, and to leave it to readers to explore other interpretations, many of which are represented in this collection, by themselves.

The first work published by the mature Hegel is his *Phenomenology* (1807). On my reading, however, phenomenology does not form part of Hegel's philosophy proper, but provides a systematic introduction to that philosophy – "the way to Science," as Hegel puts it.[49] Hegel's philosophy proper starts with speculative logic, which is set out in fully developed form in the *Science of Logic* (the so-called Greater Logic) (1812–1816, 1832) and in abbreviated form in the first part of the *Encyclopaedia* (the so-called Lesser Logic) (1817, 1827, 1830).

Speculative logic provides an account of the pure categories of thought, such as "being," "cause," "substance" and "object" (rather than empirical concepts, such as "tree" or "chair"). Some commentators thus take Hegel to be doing no more in his logic than showing us what it is to *think* properly. To my mind, by contrast, Hegel's logic unfolds the categories through which the fundamental forms or ways of *being* are disclosed. Speculative logic, therefore, is at the same time a fully-fledged ontology or metaphysics that tells us a priori what there is (and must be), in a manner akin to that of Spinoza in the *Ethics*.[50] In such logic, as Hegel puts it, "being is known to be the pure concept [*Begriff*] in its own self, and the pure concept to be true being." The "element" of speculative logic is thus not just thought, but the "unity" of thought and being.[51]

Speculative logic discovers the basic categories of thought (and forms of being) by rendering explicit what is implicit in the thought of *pure being*. In this way, logic discloses the categories and forms that are immanent in pure being itself. An important result of Hegel's immanent logic is that each form of being proves to be inseparable from its *negation*; indeed, it proves in a certain respect to *be* its own negation. This result sets Hegel at odds with previous metaphysicians, such as Plato and Spinoza, whom in other ways he resembles. For Plato, each form is simply itself and can never also be "opposite to itself," and for Spinoza "the definition of any thing affirms, and does not deny, the thing's essence."[52] Each form or thing, therefore, is what it is, and nothing in what it is makes it *not* be what it is. For Hegel, by contrast, each category, in being what it is, proves at the same time to be, and so to be one with, its negation. Indeed, right at the start of his logic Hegel claims that pure being and pure nothing *vanish* into one another of their own accord; each is thus "in its own self the opposite of itself."[53] This process of becoming, or proving to be, one's own opposite, simply by being what one is, is what Hegel understands by *dialectic*.[54]

Hegel's logic reveals that each category must be thought together with its negation if it is to be thought properly. As the logic proceeds, however, the precise character of the categories under discussion and of their relation to their negation alters. Categories in the first book of the *Science of Logic* – the "doctrine of being" – retain a certain independence from their negation, even though each also proves to be inseparable from that negation: to be *something*, for Hegel, is at the same time to be *other* than something else, yet it is also to be simply what it is – something *of its own* – quite apart from any relation to what is other than it.[55] By contrast, categories in the sphere of essence lack such independence and are thoroughly bound to their opposites: being a "cause," for example, is nothing but being the "cause-of-an-effect"; the one has no meaning apart from the other.[56]

In the sphere of the "concept," concepts (and ways of being) are neither partially independent of, nor thoroughly bound to, their negations but *continue to be themselves* in and through their negations. The *universal*, for example, continues to be itself through *particular* individuals.[57] It is a genuine universal, therefore, only to the extent that it particularizes, individuates, and thereby *determines* itself. When being is understood explicitly to be, not just "something," or the "cause" of certain "effects," but the process of self-determination, it is understood to be what Hegel calls "the absolute Idea [*Idee*]."[58] This Idea is what speculative logic shows being ultimately to be: being, for Hegel, is not just a realm of monads (as it is for Leibniz), nor is it endlessly striving will (as it is for Schopenhauer), but it is in truth the very process of free self-determination itself. As such, being is *reason* (*Vernunft*) or *logos*.[59]

Hegel's speculative logic discloses what he understands to be the true nature of being itself, and in that sense it continues the project of pre-Kantian metaphysics and ontology. Such logic is, however, a distinctively *post*-Kantian enterprise for two reasons. On the one hand, speculative logic tells us about being by setting out the fundamental *categories of thought* in and through which the character of being is disclosed, and, in Hegel's view, it is above all Kant's great merit to have focused philosophical attention on those categories (even though Kant himself did not accept that being could be known through categories alone). As Hegel puts it, it was Kant's critical philosophy that "turned *metaphysics* into *logic*," that is, into the explicit study of *thought*.[60]

On the other hand, Kant's promotion of the idea of philosophical critique prompted Hegel to take such critique to its logical conclusion. In Hegel's view, that means taking nothing for granted in advance about thought or being, except for the bare idea that thought discloses being. Hegel's logic is a *post*-Kantian logic-cum-metaphysics, therefore, because it begins by setting aside all determinate presuppositions about philosophical method, the structure of specific categories, and the nature of being itself.[61]

Speculative logic does not assume (with Aristotle and most of the tradition) that philosophy should avoid contradiction, or (with Kant) that concepts are "predicates of possible judgments," or (with Spinoza) that "whatever is, is either in itself or in another."[62] On the contrary, Hegel insists that speculative philosophy should eschew all such assumptions and be "preceded by *universal doubt*, i.e., by total *presuppositionlessness* [*Voraussetzungslosigkeit*]."[63] Speculative logic may begin, therefore, with nothing but the utterly indeterminate and empty category of "pure being"; to start with anything more determinate than this – for example, with the idea of possibility, or substance, or "will" – would presuppose too much about being at the outset and so violate the modern, post-Kantian requirement that thought be thoroughly self-critical. (The bare idea that thought discloses being is not itself to be regarded as a mere presupposition, by the way. For Hegel, it is the idea we are left with when we *suspend* the unwarranted assumption made by abstract, "reflective understanding" that thought and being are quite *separate* from one another.)[64]

In the *Science of Logic* Hegel maintains that nothing is required in order to begin speculative logic except "the resolve [*Entschluss*], which can also be regarded as arbitrary, that we propose to consider thought as such" and the readiness to "rid oneself of all other reflections and opinions whatever."[65] Hegel also argues, however, that the standpoint of speculative logic cannot be *justified* unless it can be shown to emerge "in consciousness."[66] Is Hegel being inconsistent here? I think not. His position, as I understand it, is this: philosophical thought can begin to think speculatively simply by setting traditional conceptions of thought and being to one side and starting with the indeterminate category of pure being. Doing so, however, will appear quite unjustified to ordinary, *non*-philosophical consciousness that is not moved by the spirit of modern self-criticism and that rejects the idea that we can know the nature of being simply by thinking about it. The standpoint of speculative philosophy will appear justified to ordinary, non-philosophical consciousness only if that standpoint is shown to be made necessary by the commitments of such consciousness itself. The task of Hegel's *Phenomenology of Spirit* is precisely to show this to be the case.[67]

On this interpretation, the *Phenomenology* does not present Hegel's own understanding of the world directly. It examines an array of alternative views of the world, or "shapes" [*Gestalten*] of consciousness,[68] and shows that they are led *by their own experience* to mutate into one another and eventually into the standpoint of speculative philosophy. The viewpoints examined in the *Phenomenology* count as shapes of *consciousness* because they assume a certain "antithesis," or contrast, between the knowing subject and the object known. Sense-certainty, for example, distinguishes between itself – *this* I – and its object – *this, here, now* – and perception distinguishes between itself and the *things* it encounters.

Hegel writes that "the standpoint of consciousness which knows objects in their antithesis to itself, and itself in antithesis to them, is for Science [i.e., speculative philosophy] the *other* [*das Andere*] of its own standpoint."[69] This is because speculative philosophy understands being to be disclosed in and through the categories of thought and not to be something "over there" to which we have to gain access, as it were, from "over here." The aim of phenomenology, therefore, is to show that the antithesis in consciousness between itself and its object is progressively undermined in the course of its experience and eventually gives way to the position of speculative philosophy which "unites the objective form of truth and of the knowing self in an immediate unity."[70]

In the course of the *Phenomenology* Hegel describes many shapes of consciousness that have emerged at certain points in human history, including, for example, the consciousness of "absolute freedom" (manifest in the French Revolution). Other shapes are more abstract and less easy to locate historically, including sense-certainty and perception, and some are found principally in works of art, such as the "ethical order" (encountered in Sophocles' *Antigone*). Some shapes are theoretical, some practical, some aesthetic, some religious; some are shapes of individual consciousness, some "shapes of a world."[71] What connects each shape to the next one, however, is always the same thing, namely the *experience* that is made by each shape or, rather, that logically *should* be made if the shape is to be true to its own conception of its object. Phenomenology is thus a systematic account of the logically necessary experience of consciousness, an account that starts with the simplest shape of consciousness – bare sense-certainty – and leads eventually to the standpoint of speculative philosophy. As such, phenomenology justifies that standpoint to non-philosophical consciousness (or to philosophers wedded to a non-philosophical view of things).

Philosophy of Nature and Spirit

If phenomenology precedes speculative logic, what follows such logic in Hegel's system is the philosophy of nature. The latter is made necessary by the fact that self-determining reason, or the Idea that being proves to be, is not purely and simply what it is but is itself "the negative of itself."[72] Such reason thus necessarily takes the form of *unreason*, more specifically, Hegel claims, the "unreason of externality."[73] According to Hegel's metaphysics, therefore, what actually *exists* is not pure reason or logos alone, but being that is wholly *external* to itself. Such being, we are told, is *space* (which is itself inseparable from *time*). Reason, for Hegel, is inherent in space and time, and indeed in nature as a whole, but it is inextricably mixed with its negation: *contingency*. Such contingency may be explicable from the point of view of natural science, but from the perspective of philosophical reason it is non-rational. It thus constitutes what Hegel calls "the *impotence* of nature": nature's essential inability to be completely rational.[74]

Significantly, Hegel notes that "this impotence of nature *sets limits* to philosophy." Hegel is sometimes accused of trying to explain absolutely everything through the workings of the dialectic, but this is clearly not his ambition. On the contrary, he insists that "it is quite improper to expect the Concept [*Begriff*] to comprehend – or as it is said, construe or deduce – these contingent products of nature."[75] In Hegel's day, apparently, over 60 species of parrot were known;[76] it is certainly not the task of philosophy, however, to explain why this should be the case.

The task of philosophy is, rather, to work out what is made necessary by the reason inherent in space and time themselves. Hegel argues that such reason requires there to be motion, gravity, light, electricity, magnetism, and physical, chemical, and organic matter. Together these phenomena thus constitute what philosophy understands by the term "nature." Hegel is not concerned with the temporal processes that produce these phenomena. He is not seeking to explain the genesis of matter and gravity, or the genesis of life; that is for natural science to explore. The philosophy of nature aims to show why it is *rational* for these phenomena to occur (whatever their more precise causes might be). Philosophy, for Hegel, is thus not in competition with natural science. Indeed, philosophy draws on science for a full understanding of the phenomena whose rationality it demonstrates (and, contrary to popular myth, Hegel was very knowledge-able about the science of his day).[77]

This is not to say that the philosophy of nature leaves natural science completely unaffected. Hegel is especially critical, on the basis of his philosophy of nature, of what he sees as a tendency toward reductionism in contemporary science. The challenge, he contends, is not to efface the differences between phenomena such as electricity and magnetism by reducing them to one single, undifferentiated phenomenon, but to rec-ognize that their unity (which he by no means disputes) is a unity of *different* phenom-ena. "Formerly," he writes,

> magnetism, electricity, and chemism were treated as wholly separate and uncorrelated, each being regarded as an independent force. Philosophy has grasped the idea of their *identity, but* with the express *proviso* that they also are *different*. Recent ideas in physics seem to have jumped to the other extreme and to emphasize only the *identity* of these phenom-ena, so that the need now is to assert the fact and manner of their distinctiveness.[78]

Hegel is often accused (by critics such as Deleuze) of privileging identity over differ-ence.[79] It is clear, however, that his philosophy of nature leads him to insist on the qualitative *differences* between natural phenomena that, in his view, contemporary science has come to regard as identical.[80]

The philosophy of nature ends with an account of organic life. With life, Hegel maintains, matter in space and time becomes explicitly self-determining, self-moving, self-replicating. Since reason is understood by philosophy to be the process of self-determination, one can say that matter is most rational when it is alive.

The next part of speculative philosophy is the philosophy of subjective spirit, or what one might also call "philosophy of mind." In this part of his philosophy Hegel seeks to understand what is made necessary logically when life becomes conscious and self-conscious, that is, when life becomes *spirit* (*Geist*). Once again, Hegel's aim is to not explain the temporal genesis of consciousness – the natural processes that lead to the emergence of consciousness – but to show that logically – according to the demands of reason – spirit involves specific activities of mind. To be properly "spiritual," in Hegel's view, is not only to experience sensation and feeling, but also to participate in activities of mind (or to exhibit capacities of mind), such as consciousness, self-consciousness, intuition, representation, language, memory, thought, and will.

Hegel shows that these activities or capacities are distinguished from one another by the degree of freedom and self-determination they manifest. In intuition the mind "*finds itself* determined" in a certain way (by what is given to it in sensation); in thought, on the other hand, and especially in inference, "the intellect *determines content* from itself."[81] The will, too, is free "in giving itself the content," that is, in setting itself ends which it seeks to realize in the world.[82]

In the philosophy of objective spirit, Hegel then examines the specific ways in which the free will gives itself objective expression, or rather *must* give itself objective

11

expression if it is to count as truly free. The truly free will, Hegel argues, must assert its right to own and exchange property and must engage in action to fulfill its aims and satisfy its intentions. More controversially, Hegel claims that true freedom also requires life in a family, in civil society and its constituent institutions, and in a constitutional state. Such a state is one in which the powers of the state – the crown, the executive and the legislature – are clearly distinct, if not wholly separate, from one another, and in which the citizen can trust that his or her "interest, both substantial and particular, is contained and preserved in another's (i.e. in the state's) interest and end."[83] Hegel defends his view that true freedom is inseparable not only from right, but also from a rational political constitution, in the *Elements of the Philosophy of Right* (1820). This work makes it clear, therefore, that Hegel's commitment to freedom and right – and his hostility to the Prussian "restoration" – is not just a personal one, but one that is grounded in the very concept of freedom itself (and ultimately in the speculative philosophical understanding of being).

The philosophy of right tells us what true freedom is, what freedom must be. It concludes with the idea that humanity does not understand the true nature of freedom from the very start, but gradually comes to understand freedom's true nature in and through *history*. As Hegel famously puts it, "world history is the progress of the consciousness of freedom – a progress whose necessity it is our business to comprehend."[84] The stages in the development of the consciousness of freedom are summarized in this equally well-known passage:

> the different degrees of knowledge of freedom – firstly, that of the Orientals, who knew only that *one* is free, then that of the Greek and Roman world, which knew that *some* are free, and finally, our own knowledge that *all* human beings as such are free, that *the human being* as *human being* [*der Mensch als Mensch*] is free – supply us with the divisions we shall observe in our survey of world history.[85]

With the changes in human understanding of freedom, Hegel contends, come changes in the social and political constitution of the state. The Greeks and Romans, who knew only "that *some* are free," thus sanctioned slavery, whereas we in the Christian era, who proclaim the freedom of *all* human beings and maintain that "slavery is unjust in and for itself,"[86] develop modern constitutional states that – in principle, at least – guarantee the rights of all citizens.

History, for Hegel, does not culminate in a single state that exhibits all the features set out in the philosophy of right. It culminates in a group of modern Western European states, including "Denmark, the Netherlands, England, Prussia" (and to a lesser extent France), whose constitutions, while not completely rational, are nonetheless rational enough to be seen as embodiments of the idea of true freedom.[87] The idea of freedom set out in the philosophy of right is thus not realized perfectly in any one modern state, in Hegel's view, but nor is it a mere ideal against which modern states are to be judged. It is, rather, the idea of freedom that is embodied in modern constitutional states *to a greater or lesser degree* (and that can thus always be embodied more adequately).

The last part of Hegel's philosophy is the philosophy of absolute spirit, which comprises the philosophies of art, of religion, and of the history of philosophy itself. Absolute spirit, for Hegel, is spirit that has come to understand its own absolute nature. Such understanding is set out most clearly in speculative philosophy, in which, as we have seen, spirit is understood to be organic life – indeed, *being itself* – that has achieved self-consciousness and freedom. As Hegel puts it in the Preface to the *Phenomenology*, spirit is "substance" that has become "subject."[88] Essentially the same understanding of spirit, Hegel contends, is present in religion, specifically in Christianity. Religion, however, expresses that understanding of spirit in what Hegel calls "representational," rather than purely conceptual, terms. Whereas speculative philosophy talks of *being*, or the *Idea*, becoming self-conscious in humanity, Christianity talks of "God" becoming "incarnate" in the figure of Jesus Christ and then, after Christ's death, becoming "Holy Spirit" within human beings. In Hegel's view, the form of religious expression differs from that of philosophical understanding; the content, or fundamental truth, that is expressed is, however, the same in both cases.[89]

Since Hegel's death, many have questioned whether his account of Christianity is compatible with orthodox Christian faith. Some have bemoaned the fact that Hegel appears to allow no place for a genuinely personal God and have thus maintained that he misunderstands Christianity; others have highlighted the fact that Hegel places love and forgiveness at the heart of Christian faith and so have found great profundity in his understanding of Christianity.[90] Whatever the truth may be, it is clear that Hegel himself thought that his account of Christianity and indeed his philosophy as a whole are quite compatible with Christian faith. As he puts it in a letter written in 1826 to the theologian Friedrich August Tholuck, "I am a Lutheran, and through philosophy have been at once completely confirmed in Lutheranism."[91] There are readers of Hegel – including Feuerbach and Marx – who think that learning from Hegel means rejecting religion. For Hegel, however, this is seriously to misunderstand the relation between philosophy and religion. In his view, philosophy not only shows the content of Christianity (properly understood) to be true, but it also shows that it is necessary for human beings to know and understand that content both through philosophical concepts *and* through the representations of faith.[92] In Hegel's view, the truth may be most clearly articulated in philosophical concepts, but humanity cannot live by concepts alone.

Hegel argues that art also gives expression to our understanding of being, reason, and freedom.[93] It differs from philosophy and religion by rendering reason and freedom *visible* or *audible* in a medium that is accessible to the *senses*. Specifically, art gives expression to freedom through wood, stone, color, or sound (the sound of music or of language). The sensuous expression of freedom is what Hegel understands by *beauty*, the creation of which is thus, for him, the principal purpose of art. Since he thinks that our understanding of freedom develops through history, he thinks that art, too, develops from its early "symbolic" form in ancient India and Egypt through the "classical" art of ancient Greece to the "romantic" art of the Christian era (which includes, among other things, medieval and Renaissance painting and the dramas of Shakespeare and Goethe). Put very simply, symbolic art intimates a "spiritual" meaning that it never fully expresses, a meaning that thus remains hidden or obscure in various ways. Classical art, by contrast, presents the perfect fusion of spirit and body, in which free spirit manifests itself fully in bodily shape and posture (as in the sculptures of Phidias or Praxiteles). Romantic art is the most complex of the three

13

forms of art, since it gives expression to inner subjectivity that both lies *beyond* what is visible and reveals itself *in* what in visible. Whereas classical sculpture *embodies* free spirit, romantic art is thus like a *face* that allows the character and feeling within to shine through.[94] (Hegel's criticism of late eighteenth- and early nineteenth-century Romantics, such as Friedrich Schlegel and Novalis, is partly that they betray this idea of romantic art and turn back to more symbolic modes of expression.)[95]

Hegel is thought by some to have asserted that art "ends" or "dies" in the modern world.[96] In fact, he claims only that modern art is no longer capable of fulfilling art's highest task, namely that of giving adequate expression to our deepest *religious* beliefs. Art fulfilled this task in ancient Greece (and to an extent in the medieval period), but in the modern period – the period since the Reformation – art has largely lost its religious function and has become more secular and human-centered. It has become a separate and distinctive form of "absolute spirit" that complements but is – or, at least, *should be* – subordinate to religion (and to philosophy). Since Hegel's death much of the debate about the status of art has been influenced by his views on art (or by what those views are mistakenly thought to be); so much so, indeed, that without Hegel's contribution the hugely important work of Heidegger, Adorno, and Danto on modern art would be unimaginable.

Hegel's system of philosophy ends with his account of the history of philosophy. Needless to say, the Greeks, especially Plato and Aristotle, loom large in Hegel's account; so also do the early moderns, such as Descartes, Spinoza, and Leibniz, and Hegel's contemporaries, Kant, Fichte, Jacobi, and Schelling. But Hegel also considers Indian philosophy in some depth, as well as the thought of less well-known European thinkers, such as Jakob Böhme.

According to Hegel, the history of philosophy culminates in speculative philosophy, as he understands it. Yet his account of the history of philosophy also *presupposes* speculative philosophy. Not only does Hegel assume that philosophy, as a mode of spirit, progresses toward consciousness of spirit's freedom, but he also contends from the outset "that the *historical* succession of the systems of philosophy is the same as the succession in the *logical* derivation of the Idea's conceptual determinations" in the *Science of Logic*.[97] This would appear to make Hegel guilty of vicious circularity. It does not do so, however, if one recalls that speculative philosophy itself begins by setting to one side all unwarranted presuppositions about thought and being. Hegel's account of the history of philosophy presupposes a conception of spirit that is itself the product of a thinking that embraces "*presuppositionlessness*" in the interest of being thoroughly self-critical and free.[98]

Hegel's claim to be thinking "without presuppositions" has been challenged by subsequent critics, such as Feuerbach, Schelling, Kierkegaard, Heidegger, and Gadamer; though it has also been defended by other, more recent, commentators.[99] Whether they are critics or defenders of Hegel, however, it is evident to most who take the time to study his texts and lectures in detail that his philosophy provides one of the richest, most subtle, and most challenging accounts of the natural and the human world that we have. The chapters that follow in this collection bear witness to that extraordinary richness and subtlety.[100]

Notes

1   Ernst H. Gombrich, " 'The Father of Art History.' A Reading of *Lectures on Aesthetics* of G. W. F. Hegel (1770–1831)," in *Tributes: Interpreters of our Cultural Tradition* (Ithaca, NY: Cornell University Press, 1984), 51–69.

2   Terry Pinkard, *Hegel. A Biography* (Cambridge: Cambridge University Press, 2000), 659.

3   Pinkard, *Hegel*, 661; *Hegel: The Letters*, trans. Clark Butler and Christiane Seiler (Bloomington: Indiana University Press, 1984), 272; *Briefe von und an Hegel*, ed. Johannes Hoffmeister, 4 vols. (Hamburg: Felix Meiner, 1952–1961, 1977), 4.1: 10–12.

4   Pinkard, *Hegel*, 4; Walter Jaeschke, *Hegel-Handbuch. Leben, Werk, Schule* (Stuttgart: J. B. Metzler, 2003), 1; H.S. Harris, *Hegel's Development. Towards the Sunlight, 1770–1801* (Oxford: Clarendon Press, 1972), 3. Jaeschke claims that Hegel probably started at the Gymnasium in 1776, whereas Harris gives the date of Hegel's entry as 1777.

5   *Briefe von und an Hegel*, 4.1:13; Jaeschke, *Hegel-Handbuch*, 1; *Dokumente zu Hegels Entwicklung*, ed. Johannes Hoffmeister (Stuttgart-Bad Cannstatt: Frommann-Holzboog, 1974), 6–41.

6   Jaeschke, *Hegel-Handbuch*, 1–2; *Dokumente zu Hegels Entwicklung*, 41.

7   *Dokumente zu Hegels Entwicklung*, 394.

8   Pinkard, *Hegel*, 248, 463.

9   Jaeschke, *Hegel-Handbuch*, 6–7.

10 Pinkard, *Hegel*, 17.

11 Pinkard, *Hegel*, 35, 50.

12 Pinkard, *Hegel*, 45, 53, 58.

13 *Hegel: The Letters*, 43.

14 Jaeschke, *Hegel-Handbuch*, 14–15.

15 *Hegel: The Letters*, 59.

16 Jaeschke, *Hegel-Handbuch*, 16, 18. A second volume of *Hyperion* was published in 1799; see Ulrich Häussermann, *Friedrich Hölderlin mit Selbstzeugnissen und Bilddokumenten* (Reinbek bei Hamburg: Rowohlt, 1961), 162.

17 Pinkard, *Hegel*, 60.

18 Karl Rosenkranz, *Georg Wilhelm Friedrich Hegels Leben* (1844) (Darmstadt: Wissenschaftliche Buchgesellschaft, 1977), 87.

19 Pinkard, *Hegel*, 85–86; *Hegel: The Letters*, 64.

20 *Hegel: The Letters*, 179.

21 Jaeschke, *Hegel-Handbuch*, 18.

22 Pinkard, *Hegel*, 106.

23 Jaeschke, *Hegel-Handbuch*, 21.

24 *Hegel: The Letters*, 80, 114. Hegel sent the manuscript of the Preface to the *Phenomenology* to Bamberg on January 16, 1807; see Jaeschke, *Hegel-Handbuch*, 25.

25 *Hegel: The Letters*, 114.

26 *Hegel: The Letters*, 158–159; Jaeschke, *Hegel-Handbuch*, 34, 45.

27 Jaeschke, *Hegel-Handbuch*, 24.

28 Pinkard, *Hegel*, 230; Jaeschke, *Hegel-Handbuch*, 26.

29 Pinkard, *Hegel*, 279, 281, 371.

30 Pinkard, *Hegel*, 295–296.

31 *Hegel: The Letters*, 255.

32 *Briefe von und an Hegel*, 4.1: 100–106.

33 *Briefe von und an Hegel*, 4.1: 108, 110–111.

34   Jaeschke, *Hegel-Handbuch*, 26, 39; *Hegel: The Letters*, 434.

35   Jaeschke, *Hegel-Handbuch*, 40.

36   Jaeschke, *Hegel-Handbuch*, 41, 47; Pinkard, *Hegel*, 516.

37   Jaeschke, *Hegel-Handbuch*, 502–503.

38   Jaeschke, *Hegel-Handbuch*, 47, 52; *Hegel in Berichten seiner Zeitgenossen*, ed. Günther Nicolin (Hamburg: Felix Meiner, 1970), 392.

39   *Materialien zu Hegels Rechtsphilosophie*, ed. Manfred Riedel, 2 vols. (Frankfurt am Main: Suhrkamp Verlag, 1975), 1: 366.

40   *Materialien zu Hegels Rechtsphilosophie*, 1: 249; Jaeschke, *Hegel-Handbuch*, 510, 520.

41   Jaeschke, *Hegel-Handbuch*, 45.

42   G.W.F. Hegel, *Outlines of the Philosophy of Right*, trans. T. M. Knox, ed. Stephen Houlgate (1952) (Oxford: Oxford University Press, 2008), 231–232 [note to §258 Remark]; G.W.F. Hegel, *Grundlinien der Philosophie des Rechts*, ed. Eva Moldenhauer and Karl Markus Michel (Frankfurt am Main: Suhrkamp Verlag, 1970), 402–403.

43   Karl Popper, *The Open Society and its Enemies*, 2 vols. (1945) (London: Routledge, 1966), 2: 41.

44   Pinkard, *Hegel*, 435–450; Jaeschke, *Hegel-Handbuch*, 42–45.

45   *Hegel: The Letters*, 451.

46   Pinkard, *Hegel*, 448.

47   See, for example, H.C. Graef, "From Hegel to Hitler," *Contemporary Review* 158 (July-December 1940): 550–556. For a brief discussion of Graef's article, see also Stephen Houlgate, *Hegel, Nietzsche and the Criticism of Metaphysics* (Cambridge: Cambridge University Press, 1986), 4.

48   Robert C. Solomon, *From Hegel to Existentialism* (Oxford: Oxford University Press, 1987), 57.

49   G.W.F. Hegel, *Phenomenology of Spirit*, trans. A. V. Miller (Oxford: Oxford University Press, 1977), 56; G.W.F. Hegel, *Phänomenologie des Geistes*, ed. Eva Moldenhauer and Karl Markus Michel (Frankfurt am Main: Suhrkamp Verlag, 1970), 80.

50   See Stephen Houlgate, *The Opening of Hegel's Logic. From Being to Infinity* (West Lafayette, Ind.: Purdue University Press, 2006), 115–143.

51   G.W.F. Hegel, *Science of Logic*, trans. A. V. Miller (Amherst, NY: Humanity Books, 1999), 60. For the German text of this passage, see G.W.F. Hegel, *Wissenschaft der Logik*, ed. Eva Moldenhauer and Karl Markus Michel, 2 vols. (Frankfurt am Main: Suhrkamp Verlag, 1969ff.), 1: 57.

52   Plato, *Phaedo*, trans. David Gallop (Oxford: Oxford University Press, 1993), 60 [103b]; *A Spinoza Reader. The Ethics and Other Works*, ed. Edwin Curley (Princeton: Princeton University Press, 1994), 159 [EIIIP4Dem]. See also Houlgate, *The Opening of Hegel's Logic*, 42–44.

53   Hegel, *Science of Logic*, 106; *Wissenschaft der Logik*, 1: 112.

54   See G.W.F. Hegel, *The Encyclopaedia Logic. Part 1 of the Encyclopaedia of Philosophical Sciences with the Zusätze*, trans. T. F Geraets, W. A. Suchting, and H. S. Harris (Indianapolis, Ind.: Hackett Publishing, 1991), 128 [§81]; G.W.F. Hegel, *Enzyklopädie der philosophischen Wissenschaften im Grundrisse (1830). Erster Teil: Die Wissenschaft der Logik. Mit den mündlichen Zusätzen*, ed. Eva Moldenhauer and Karl Markus Michel (Frankfurt am Main: Suhrkamp Verlag, 1970), 172.

55   See Hegel, *Science of Logic*, 116–119, 122: "although they essentially refer to each other or are as a being-for-other, they too count as *qualitative*, as existing on their own account"; *Wissenschaft der Logik*, 1: 125–127, 131.

56   See Hegel, *Science of Logic*, 559; *Wissenschaft der Logik*, 2: 224.

57   See Hegel, *Science of Logic*, 602: "*continues* itself"; *Wissenschaft der Logik*, 2: 276.

58 Hegel, *Science of Logic*, 824: "self-determination or particularization"; *Wissenschaft der Logik*, 2: 549.

59 Hegel, *Science of Logic*, 39: "the logos, the reason of that which is"; *Wissenschaft der Logik*, 1: 30. See also Houlgate, *The Opening of Hegel's Logic*, 115–116.

60 Hegel, *Science of Logic*, 51; *Wissenschaft der Logik*, 1: 45. See also Hegel, *The Encyclopaedia Logic*, 81–82 [§41 and Addition]; *Enzyklopädie. Erster Teil: Die Wissenschaft der Logik*, 113–114.

61 See Houlgate, *The Opening of Hegel's Logic*, 24–28.

62 Immanuel Kant, *Critique of Pure Reason*, trans. Paul Guyer and Allen W. Wood (Cambridge: Cambridge University Press, 1997), 205 [B 94]; *A Spinoza Reader*, 86 [EIA1].

63 Hegel, *The Encyclopaedia Logic*, 124 [§78 Remark]; *Enzyklopädie. Erster Teil: Die Wissenschaft der Logik*, 168. See Houlgate, *The Opening of Hegel's Logic*, 29–53.

64 See Hegel, *Science of Logic*, 45, 69–70; *Wissenschaft der Logik*, 1: 38, 68–69, and Stephen Houlgate, "Hegel's Logic," in *The Cambridge Companion to Hegel and Nineteenth-Century Philosophy*, ed. Frederick C. Beiser (Cambridge: Cambridge University Press, 2008), 120–121.

65 Hegel, *Science of Logic*, 69–70; *Wissenschaft der Logik*, 1: 68.

66 Hegel, *Science of Logic*, 48; *Wissenschaft der Logik*, 1: 42.

67 See Stephen Houlgate, *An Introduction to Hegel. Freedom, Truth and History* (1991) (Oxford: Blackwell, 2005), 48–66.

68 Hegel, *Phenomenology of Spirit*, 265; *Phänomenologie des Geistes*, 326.

69 Hegel, *Phenomenology of Spirit*, 15 (translation modified); *Phänomenologie des Geistes*, 30.

70 Hegel, *Phenomenology of Spirit*, 491; *Phänomenologie des Geistes*, 589.

71 Hegel, *Phenomenology of Spirit*, 265; *Phänomenologie des Geistes*, 326.

72 G.W.F. Hegel, *Philosophy of Nature. Being Part Two of the Encyclopaedia of the Philosophical Sciences (1830)*, trans. A. V. Miller (Oxford: Clarendon Press, 1970), 13 [§247]; G.W.F. Hegel, *Enzyklopädie der philosophischen Wissenschaften im Grundrisse (1830). Zweiter Teil: Die Naturphilosophie. Mit den mündlichen Zusätzen*, ed. Eva Moldenhauer and Karl Markus Michel (Frankfurt am Main: Suhrkamp Verlag, 1970), 24. See also Houlgate, *An Introduction to Hegel*, 109.

73 Hegel, *Philosophy of Nature*, 17 [§248 Remark]; *Enzyklopädie. Zweiter Teil: Die Naturphilosophie*, 28. See also Houlgate, *An Introduction to Hegel*, 111.

74 Hegel, *Philosophy of Nature*, 22–23 [§250]; *Enzyklopädie. Zweiter Teil: Die Naturphilosophie*, 34.

75 Hegel, *Philosophy of Nature*, 23 [§250 Remark] (emphasis added); *Enzyklopädie. Zweiter Teil: Die Naturphilosophie*, 35. See also Houlgate, *An Introduction to Hegel*, 112–115.

76 Hegel, *Science of Logic*, 682; *Wissenschaft der Logik*, 2: 375.

77 Hegel, *Philosophy of Nature*, 6–7 [§246 and Remark]; *Enzyklopädie. Zweiter Teil: Die Naturphilosophie*, 15. See also Houlgate, *An Introduction to Hegel*, 115–121.

78 Hegel, *Philosophy of Nature*, 170 [§313 Remark]; *Enzyklopädie. Zweiter Teil: Die Naturphilosophie*, 211–212.

79 See, for example, Gilles Deleuze, *Difference and Repetition*, trans. Paul Patton (London: Athlone, 1994), 49–50.

80 See Houlgate, *An Introduction to Hegel*, 120–121, and the chapters by Thomas Posch and Cinzia Ferrini below.

81 G.W.F. Hegel, *Philosophy of Mind*, trans. William Wallace and A. V. Miller, rev. Michael Inwood (Oxford: Clarendon Press, 2007), 177, 204 [§§446, 467]; G.W.F. Hegel, *Enzyklopädie der philosophischen Wissenschaften im Grundrisse (1830). Dritter Teil: Die Philosophie des Geistes. Mit den mündlichen Zusätzen*, ed. Eva Moldenhauer and Karl Markus Michel (Frankfurt am Main: Suhrkamp Verlag, 1970), 246, 285.

17

82 Hegel, *Philosophy of Mind*, 206 [§469]; *Enzyklopädie. Dritter Teil: Die Philosophie des Geistes*, 288.

83 Hegel, *Outlines of the Philosophy of Right*, 240, 259 [§§268, 273]; *Grundlinien der Philosophie des Rechts*, 413, 435–436.

84 G.W.F. Hegel, *Lectures on the Philosophy of World History. Introduction: Reason in History*, trans. H.B. Nisbet (Cambridge: Cambridge University Press, 1975), 54; G.W.F. Hegel, *Vorlesungen über die Philosophie der Weltgeschichte*. Band 1: *Die Vernunft in der Geschichte*, ed. Johannes Hoffmeister (Hamburg: Felix Meiner, 1955), 63.

85 Hegel, *Lectures on the Philosophy of World History. Introduction: Reason in History*, 54–55 (translation modified); *Vorlesungen über die Philosophie der Weltgeschichte*. Band 1: *Die Vernunft in der Geschichte*, 63.

86 Hegel, *Lectures on the Philosophy of World History. Introduction: Reason in History*, 184; *Vorlesungen über die Philosophie der Weltgeschichte*. Band 1: *Die Vernunft in der Geschichte*, 226. See also Houlgate, *An Introduction to Hegel*, 187.

87 G.W.F. Hegel, *Vorlesungen über die Philosophie der Weltgeschichte*. Band 2–4, ed. Georg Lasson (Hamburg: Felix Meiner, 1923, 1976), 933.

88 Hegel, *Phenomenology of Spirit*, 10; *Phänomenologie des Geistes*, 23.

89 Hegel, *Philosophy of Mind*, 267 [§573 Remark]; *Enzyklopädie. Dritter Teil: Die Philosophie des Geistes*, 379. See also Houlgate, *An Introduction to Hegel*, 244–249.

90 See *Materialien zu Hegels Rechtsphilosophie*, 1: 250, and Houlgate, *An Introduction to Hegel*, 249–254.

91 *Hegel: The Letters*, 520; see also 531–532.

92 Hegel, *Philosophy of Mind*, 267 [§573]: "cognition of the necessity of the *content* of the absolute representation, as well as of the necessity of the two *forms*"; *Enzyklopädie. Dritter Teil: Die Philosophie des Geistes*, 378.

93 For an overview of Hegel's philosophy of art, see Stephen Houlgate, "Introduction: An Overview of Hegel's Aesthetics," in *Hegel and the Arts*, ed. Stephen Houlgate (Evanston, IL: Northwestern University Press, 2007), xi–xxviii, and the entry on "Hegel's Aesthetics" in the Stanford Encyclopaedia of Philosophy (http://plato.stanford.edu/entries/hegel-aesthetics/)

94 For Hegel's extensive account of the three forms of art, see G.W.F. Hegel, *Aesthetics. Lectures on Fine Art*, trans. T.M. Knox, 2 vols. (Clarendon Press: Oxford, 1975), 1: 299–611; G.W.F. Hegel, *Vorlesungen über die Ästhetik*, ed. Eva Moldenhauer and Karl Markus Michel, 3 vols. (Frankfurt am Main: Suhrkamp Verlag, 1970), 1: 389–546, 2: 13–242.

95 Indeed, according to Hegel, Friedrich Schlegel contends that "in every artistic representation an allegory is to be sought." See Hegel, *Aesthetics. Lectures on Fine Art*, 1: 312; *Vorlesungen über die Ästhetik*, 1: 404.

96 See Houlgate, "Introduction: An Overview of Hegel's Aesthetics," in *Hegel and the Arts*, xxii–xxiv.

97 G.W.F. Hegel, *Lectures on the History of Philosophy. 1825–6. Volume 1: Introduction and Oriental Philosophy*, trans. Robert F. Brown and J. M. Stewart (Oxford: Clarendon Press, 2009), 176 (my emphases); G.W.F. Hegel, *Vorlesungen über die Geschichte der Philosophie. Teil 1: Einleitung in die Geschichte der Philosophie, Orientalische Philosophie*, ed. Pierre Garniron and Walter Jaeschke (Hamburg: Felix Meiner, 1994), 27.

98 Hegel, *The Encyclopaedia Logic*, 124 [§78 Remark]; *Enzyklopädie. Erster Teil: Die Wissenschaft der Logik*, 168.

99 See, for example, Richard Dien Winfield, *Reason and Justice* (Albany, NY: SUNY Press, 1988), 136–143; William Maker, *Philosophy Without Foundations. Rethinking Hegel* (Albany, NY: SUNY Press, 1994), 85–86, and Houlgate, *The Opening of Hegel's Logic*, 29–53. On the criticisms levelled at Hegel by the figures mentioned, see Houlgate, *The Opening of Hegel's Logic*, 54–59, 73–79, 88–98, 103–109.

100 I wish to express my considerable gratitude to my coeditor, Michael Baur, not only for his very helpful comments on this introduction, but also for the invaluable assistance he has provided in preparing all of the chapters in this collection for publication. Editing this volume has been a genuinely cooperative activity, and I cannot thank Michael enough for his diligence, efficiency, and good humor throughout the editing process. I would also like to extend thanks to David Gadon for his indispensable work in helping to compile the index for this volume.

Part I

Early Writings

1

Religion, Love, and Law: Hegel's Early Metaphysics of Morals

KATERINA DELIGIORGI

Hegel's concern with the moral choices of concretely situated individuals, which was once thought to cast doubt on the very possibility of formulating a Hegelian ethics, is now regularly viewed as the expression of a genuine ethical stance; 'Hegelian' has come to mean attentive to the social and political context in which moral agency is exercised.[1] So a Hegelian ethics is an ethics that emphasizes context, history, community, and the roles and relations that give substance to our moral life. This is often defined in contrast to the ambition, associated with Kant's moral philosophy, to provide a metaphysics of morals, to engage, that is, in an abstract interrogation of the a priori possibilities of moral agency. And yet, this is precisely the project that occupies Hegel in the period from the late 1790s to the early 1800s. In these early works, he engages deeply with the problems that arise for moral agency from the incompatibility between the order of reason, which is shaped by laws that give expression to human freedom, and the order of nature, which is shaped by laws of physics that describe the causal relations between natural phenomena.

Hegel's continuing engagement with the metaphysics of morals is easy to miss because the ostensible themes of his early writings are not in any obvious way 'moral.' Among the works discussed here, "The Positivity of the Christian Religion," the "Love" fragment, and the essay "On the Scientific Treatment of Natural Law," the first two belong to the so-called 'theological' writings and the third addresses a key topic of modern political philosophy.[2] The passage from religion to politics is generally seen as marking different stages in Hegel's ongoing search for a model of a modern ethical community – a modern *Sittlichkeit*.[3] On this reading, the strong bonds and sense of belonging fostered in religious communities explain Hegel's early interest in religion. If we take a step back, however, to consider the context in which the theological writings took shape, a more complex picture emerges. "The Positivity of the Christian Religion," given this title by Hegel's editor, Herman Nohl, was written in 1795 and 1796, with a final part written in 1800 that contains a revision of the original preface. It remained unfinished. The "Love" fragment dates from 1797 to 1798. The dates are significant in

A Companion to Hegel, First Edition. Edited by Stephen Houlgate and Michael Baur.
© 2011 Blackwell Publishing Ltd. Published 2011 by Blackwell Publishing Ltd.

situating these pieces in a distinctively German philosophical tradition of religious-theological debate. Appreciating Hegel's participation in this debate will help with identifying the *moral-metaphysical* concerns of these early pieces.

The intellectual environment in which Hegel composed these pieces is saturated with debates about the continuing role of religion in human life in light of the aspiration to organize one's life on rational principles. Fichte's *Attempt at a Critique of All Revelation*, at first thought by many to be authored by Kant, appeared anonymously in 1792, and then in Fichte's name in 1800. Kant's own *Religion Within the Limits of Reason Alone* appeared in part in 1792, then fully in 1793, with a revised version coming out the following year. Fichte and Kant follow on the steps of an earlier generation of German *Aufklärer* who sought to show that religious content can be claimed by enlightened reason and reshaped in accordance with rational moral ideals. The idea that a rationally vindicable human *telos* is compatible with a divinely commanded one is mainly associated with Lessing.[4] He argued that the moral message of revealed religion, laid bare and freed of its external historical manifestations, chiefly its cultic form, is directly accessible by reason; in effect revelation and reason share the same truth. What is left unresolved, however, is what we might call the 'hermeneutic' question: how does one identify what is to count as 'external'? Unless a satisfactory answer can be found to this question – and what may be satisfactory for the philosopher may not be so for the believer – the assurance that religion and reason are compatible will be in vain. A sobering lesson from the history of biblical hermeneutics is that what in each case counts as authoritative interpretation reflects concerns traceable to the context of appropriation of the purportedly authentic message.

It is directly to these difficulties that Hegel addresses himself when at the very beginning of the "Positivity" essay he writes about the different 'methods' of treating Christianity and distances himself both from those who submit religion to the test of 'reason and morality,' and from those who appeal to the authority of tradition, 'the wisdom of centuries' (*ETW* 67; 152). Hegel can do so because his own approach is primarily diagnostic: he does not set out to defend a particular interpretation of the truth of the religious message; he is interested rather in analysing what is at stake in modern, morally oriented investigations of Christianity. Hegel's analysis is explicitly located within a post-Kantian moral universe. His aim is to show how, for a modern audience grappling with the compatibility of reason and religion, the life of Jesus and his teaching make vivid key concerns about the nature of moral commands and the way in which these are taken up by finite human agents. Hegel's guiding insight is that the hermeneutic question, which can be posed with reference to the religious message, can also be posed with reference to the moral law itself: which of our substantive moral commitments genuinely represent the moral law, and which are merely 'external,' a matter of habit and conformity to 'positive' practices? The question is an urgent one because it concerns the kinds of commands that may legitimately be thought to have authority over us. Allied to this is the problem that the purer our conception of the moral law is, the more difficult it becomes to identify with any certainty any specific duties as authentic expressions of it.

Note that Hegel's approach to the moral law is indirect: he offers a diagnostic analysis within a *religious* context of the problems of modern *moral* metaphysics. That he undertakes this diagnosis within a religious context is not simply a matter of historical accident. Though he certainly shares the view of his contemporaries that religion raises distinctive problems for a purely rational morality, he is also concerned (as we shall see below in Section 1) to identify the brittle points of a conception of agency that takes its law from a transcendent authority. In this part of his argument, his chief interlocutor is not Lessing, but Kant.

Kant's project of a 'critique' of reason, which sets limits to reason's cognitive power, was taken to caution against rationalist immodesty. On the other hand, in his moral philosophy, Kant insists that reason is sufficient as moral legislator and indeed necessary for the achievement of true morality and the genuine exercise of our freedom. In short, moral agency is a rational agency, and rational agency gives its proper meaning to free agency. God's existence, though explicitly postulated within the practical sphere, appears to be a matter of subjective need – the need to assure ourselves that the natural universe we inhabit is not hostile to reason's moral commands, and that happiness is proportionate to morality. Although, as Kant says, this "hope ... first arises with religion," rational morality also has to address this need (*Rel* 87; VI:131). The need for assurance does not arise only out of a natural human concern with happiness but also out of the desire to view our moral ends as realizable. Kant treats this topic in *Religion* when he interprets the biblical announcement of the advent of God's kingdom here on earth in terms of the achievement of an 'ethico-civil' union, or an 'ethical commonwealth' (*ein ethisches gemeines Wesen*) (*Rel* 86; VI:130). What is left out of this hopeful prospect is an account of how nature, which for Kant himself as well as for his naturalistically minded contemporaries is explicable according to its own laws, might be amenable to the demands of a rational morality, which Kant states takes its cue from pure reason alone.[5] It is just such an account that Hegel seeks to elaborate in his early works, starting, as we said earlier, with what appears to be the more tractable problem of how a purely rational moral command – the moral law – can find expression in the kinds of practices and substantive commitments that make up the moral world in which we find ourselves.

One of the advantages of foregrounding Hegel's moral-metaphysical concerns is that it becomes possible to address a cluster of issues that Hegel saw as related: reason in relation to morality, to freedom, and to nature, and the metaphysical and historical conditions for the realization of moral agency. Each of these topics forms a discrete element of a philosophical tradition dominated by Kant, which Hegel inherits and with which he engages critically, but also largely constructively and synthetically. To unpack the cluster, we may start with reason itself. The notion, mainly owed to Kant, that reason is an active determining force in our moral lives means that reasoning is not just a matter of instrumental satisfaction of whatever ends we happen to have, but rather that it can help us identify ends that are morally worthy. Obviously, this process of evaluation of ends would be empty if we were not in position to put into practice what we rationally choose. So, as Kant admits, we need to assume freedom in order to think of rational agency in the first place. But a more interesting conception of freedom emerges from the idea that we are free insofar as we can give rational shape to our lives through the appropriate *choice of ends*. When it comes to identifying some content as 'free' and so as 'rational' and 'moral,' however, we find that it is easier to provide a negative definition: we are free to the extent that we manage to exclude anything that can appear as given – not only natural inclinations and received opinion but also previously endorsed maxims that are part of our own personal history. The danger with this entirely negative conception of rational freedom is that it commits us to permanent self-testing: nothing is taken on trust, not even our own earlier testimony. Apart from other inconveniences, such as the onset of moral paranoia, this absolutist version of the demand for rational vigilance presents us with the task of identifying what is effectively a philosophical chimera, a self-authenticating insight that is capable of instructing us in a direct and epistemically sound way about what is morally right. Even assuming we had access to such action-guiding intuitions, we would not be able to tell why any specific norm rightly commands assent and is not just a matter of ad hoc conviction. It is important to note that Kant's test for what can be universalized is in part conceived to free us from such chimerical pursuits. What remains a problem for Hegel is that within the Kantian critical framework, it is difficult to identify with any confidence a specific content – *this* action, *this* end – that is rational and free in the requisite sense.

The problem of rational content, as becomes evident already in the "Positivity" essay, is for Hegel symptomatic of the metaphysical gap that separates pure practical reason and nature. One of the ways he formulates this question in "Positivity" is to ask how the deliverances of pure practical reason can be felt in our lives – how we, natural and also socially situated beings, heed reason's commands. He offers a tentative answer in the "Love" fragment when he entertains the thought that reason can be naturalized, and so not only speak to us through feeling but also be active through our natural desires. The problem with this solution is that the identification of feelings, say love, to explain how it is possible for nature to conform to reason runs the risk of making reason altogether redundant. In a fully closed naturalistic system, it is nature that determines us "to judge as well as to breathe and feel" (Hume 1949:183). Hegel is sufficiently committed to the Kantian (or more generally rationalist) view of reason to be dissatisfied with such an outcome. So although he remains throughout his career sympathetic to various naturalizing options, his chief concern is to show that these are compatible with an emphatic conception of rational agency. As we saw, a key obstacle in thinking about reason's activity in shaping our ends is a strictly negative notion of rational freedom that remains at a further remove from the actual commitments and actions that make up our moral lives. It is to address this problem that Hegel turns to consider the conception of freedom that must be presupposed for rational agency. This is the topic of the "Natural Law" essay.

Hegel holds that the worldly shape of practical reason is not mysterious; it is the shape of ethical life, *Sittlichkeit*. What he wants to show is that 'ethical' is not just an empty honorific title for events following a natural causal pattern, and that the events that make up a life can be recognized as actions brought about by agents who have both an understanding of their freedom and the capacity to act on such understanding. The "Natural Law" essay is an attempt to show that ethical life – and so human life – is the product of freedom. Of the three works considered here, it is the only one that Hegel prepared for publication. It appeared in consecutive issues of the *Critical Journal* in 1802 and 1803. Thematically, the essay is situated within the natural law tradition, that is, a tradition of enquiry that seeks to identify the principles of right that should form the basis of legislation, irrespective of whatever 'positive' law is in force in particular legislatures. Methodologically, it stands out from other writings of this period because of

Hegel's stated ambition to treat his topic 'scientifically.' For Hegel's readers, this would have signalled the adoption of a mode of argumentation, broadly based on Kant's transcendental method, where the emphasis is placed on the a priori deduction of the philosophical concepts applicable to the problem at hand.[6] The essay contains a highly abstract, almost geometrical treatment of empirical natural law theories followed by a discussion of the practical philosophies of Kant and Fichte, and a lengthy analysis of ethical life. Hegel's account of ethical life, 'deduced' a priori from the notion of freedom, represents at once a synthesis of freedom and nature, and, significantly, an explicit acknowledgment of a necessary gap between the two. This acknowledgment suggests that there is no further to go with the metaphysical investigation of the problem of agency. The "Natural Law" essay can be seen then as completing the philosophical task that Hegel sets himself in these early works, namely to offer a metaphysics of morals by describing the utmost bounds of this type of analysis.

Though written at different periods of Hegel's early development, coinciding with his stay in Berne (1793–1796), Frankfurt (1797–1800), and Jena (1801–1807), these three pieces show a consistent preoccupation with the fundamental possibilities of human agency. They also display a degree of philosophical experimentation that is not often associated with Hegel. Accordingly, the aim of the present chapter is to show the philosophical openness of the early works, their deep engagement with moral-metaphysical questions, and to identify the elements of a philosophical propaedeutic that although situated outside Hegel's system, nonetheless informs the 'Hegelian' ethics of the mature philosophy.

1. Religion: A Moral-Metaphysical Interpretation of 'Positivity'

"The aim and essence of all true religion, our religion included," Hegel states, "is human morality" (*ETW* 68; 153). The claim that religious teaching is in its essence moral teaching seems to follow on the tradition of Lessing's and Kant's writings on religion. But there is something new here. The key term is 'human morality.' Hegel asserts that when it comes to appraising the 'worth' and 'sanctity' of religious prescriptions with respect to obligations, we have a 'measure': human morality (*ETW* 68; 153.). Yet Hegel gives no definition of 'human morality.' On a Kantian interpretation, 'human morality' means the commands of morality as they apply to the will of finite rational beings like ourselves, for whom moral propositions take a categorical and imperatival form. However, we can also think of 'human' as a modifier of morality, and so as signifying a morality that is consonant with our humanity, or 'adapted to the moral needs of our spirit' (*ETW* 76; 159).[7] In the first case, moral concepts are what they are without regard for who *we* are, so 'human morality' is about how these concepts are known by us and how they shape our actions. In the second case, human feelings and interests are seen as continuous with morality, so it is human nature that provides the starting point for the discussion and development of moral concepts. The two interpretations are clearly in tension. Hegel does not reveal which one he favors. On the contrary, the moral terms he uses to articulate his criticism of the positivity of Christianity – and also his criticism of Judaism as a 'positive' religion – draw equally on both conceptions of human morality. That Hegel does not resolve this ambiguity is not a sign of indecision on his part. It is the upshot of his indirect approach to the discussion of morality and religion. For Hegel, religion is a topic of vital moral interest from a post-Kantian perspective precisely because its study can contribute to a diagnosis of the difficulties with a conception of agency that takes its law from a transcendent authority.

Characteristic of Judaism, and also of Christianity in its 'positive' stage, is the requirement of rigid adherence to given laws and rituals. This description can be made to fit a number of critical diagnoses. To understand what exactly is amiss with positivity, we need to look at the detail of Hegel's criticism. Close examination of both wording and claims reveals that he draws on two distinct sets of arguments: Kant's analysis of heteronomy and Schiller's analysis of self-alienation. The opening reference to 'mechanical slavery' (*ETW* 69; 153) echoes Kant, who, in his essay "What is Enlightenment?" describes 'dogmas and formulas' as "mechanical instruments ... [that] are the ball and chain of man's immaturity" (II:36). In a lengthier and more explicitly Kantian reference, Hegel contrasts unfavorably the man who, compelled by "fear of his Lord's punishment," bears the yoke of a law that he "has not given by himself, by his reason" (*ETW* 80; 161), with those who show "disinterested obedience to ... the moral law" (*ETW* 85; 165). Disinterested obedience expresses "the spirit of acting from respect for duty, first because it is a duty and secondly also divine command" (*ETW* 99; 176).[8] It is finally worth mentioning in this context Kant's own distinction between authentic *cultus* and *cultus spurius*, that is, between a church based on pure rational faith, which promotes a 'religion of pure reason' with a practical universal core, and a 'pseudo-service' that preaches salvation through "allegiance to the historical and statutory element of ecclesiastical faith" (*Rel* 141; VI:184). So on the Kantian interpretation, positivity is a combination of immaturity, moral heteronomy, and *cultus spurius*. The normative assumption motivating this criticism is that we should be able rationally and freely to obey the law, without further interest or regard. But a 'Schillerian' interpretation is also available. A clue is given early on in the essay, when Hegel laments the transformation into 'lifeless machines' of those who renounce the life of feeling (*ETW* 69; 153). This is reminiscent of Schiller's description of the predicament of those who, bereft of "living understanding ... imagination and feeling," are condemned to bare existence as 'lifeless parts' of the 'ingenious clockwork' that is modern collective life (*AE* 35; XX:323).[9] Reading on, it becomes clear that Hegel sees the link between feeling and the voice of conscience as a vital one. He emphasizes the importance of "free virtue springing from man's own being" (*ETW* 71; 154) and draws attention to the role of love as '*complementum*' of the law (*ETW* 99; 176). On the Schillerian reading, positivity signifies affective self-alienation, a cutting off of ourselves from the very resources that animate our moral life. The normative assumption here is that we should restore the moral role of feeling and affect. Hegel uses both Kant and Schiller because he wants to establish from the start that avoiding 'positivity' is not a matter of emphasizing the purity of practical reason over mere habit and positive law because pure reason itself can become 'positive,' issuing commands that are experienced precisely as external only. This is the first step to an analysis of why this problem of positivity recurs, and the answer has to do with a certain conception of rational agency.

The Kantian and Schillerian elements of Hegel's criticism of positivity reflect the ambiguity of the measure Hegel chooses to judge religious practice: 'human morality' is compatible both with recognition of our rational agency, which demands 'struggle against inclinations' (*ETW* 70; 154), and with recognition of the value of a 'virtuous disposition,' which demands the collaboration of reason and inclination. Not only do we have two moral ideals in play, but one, Schiller's, was explicitly formulated in response to perceived flaws in the Kantian one. To see how Hegel is able to use both, we need to look beyond the substantive positions of each and examine how each perspective allows different aspects of rational agency to come to view. From the Kantian perspective, reason is an active force in our lives precisely to the extent that it is not caught up in any of the other, natural and social, forces that shape our conduct. From the Schillerian perspective, it matters urgently for the vindication of reason's role to show that nature is hospitable to rationally determined value. Rational activity and natural receptivity then form the two sides of the metaphysical picture Hegel seeks to describe. Here is how he states the problem:

> The assertion that even the moral laws propounded by Jesus are positive, i.e, that they derive their validity from the fact that Jesus commanded them, betrays a humble modesty and a disclaimer of any inherent goodness ... in human nature; but it must at least presuppose that man has a natural sense of the obligation to obey moral commands (*ETW* 73; 157).

Jesus' purpose, Hegel claims, was to "restore to morality the freedom which is its essence" (*ETW* 69; 154). How and why, then, was freedom compromised and turned into the servitude of 'positivity'? Hegel initially shows Jesus as confronting a pragmatic problem about authority because at that historical juncture an appeal to pure practical reason was simply unavailable, and the appeal to 'God's will' was an expedient answer to the need to invoke a higher authority (*ETW* 76; 159). Accepting the moral laws Jesus teaches on the authority of God requires that Jesus be accepted as the Son. So is set in place a structure of authority that encourages patterns of obedience that in due course transform moral religion into 'positive' religion (*ETW* 77; 159).

Alongside this pragmatic story, Hegel offers a more interesting moral analysis that goes to the heart of the problem of rational agency. He argues that the people's acceptance of Jesus as their teacher and of his command as binding is a sign of modesty and a "disclaimer of any inherent goodness ... in human nature" (*ETW* 73; 157). This structure of top-bottom authority is not a contingent feature of the particular set of moral laws contained in Jesus' teaching. 'God's will' stands for a transcendent moral authority that performs a function similar to that of pure practical reason: it is a voice we may heed but not a voice we may contain and fully encompass. This is why even though Jesus himself speaks out of a living sense and feeling of morality, he commands that his teachings be recognized as God's will. The invocation of God's will is a way of saying that there is such a thing as objective moral value and so moral commands necessarily appear to us in a categorical and imperatival form, and without regard to our predisposition to hear or heed them. Indeed, this autonomy of morality is essential to the claim that we freely assent to its commands. And yet, Jesus' teaching presupposes in his audience a capacity for receptivity to moral laws, and so an element of 'predisposition,' possibly a 'natural sense of the obligation to obey' (*ETW* 73; 157). The ambiguity we identified originally in the notion of human morality is now tied explicitly to a specific view of rational agency. Hegel is persuaded by the Kantian view, which he also attributes to Jesus, that moral commands appear as having the requisite authority and so are binding on us finite rational beings to the extent that they appear as categorical, and so he emphasizes the link between the authoritativeness of moral commands and their transcendent origin. However, Hegel also suggests that positivity is a structural feature of this conception of morality. The Schillerian view, signalled here with the references to moral predisposition and to natural moral sense, is attractive but not problem free either: first it is not obvious how the naturalization of moral reason can be reconciled with the categorical character of its laws, and second, this process of domestication of the divine voice is itself not immune to the problem of positivity since what thus becomes second nature, familiar, and ordinary is precisely absorbed in the given, the habitual, and so the 'positive.'

Hegel's analysis of the fate of Jesus' teaching provides further illustration of this moral double-bind. Jesus grafts his moral lessons onto existing codes and uses parables to show that he speaks of everyday, familiar, common things. This strategy fails to the extent that the authorities of the time recognize the startling *novelty* of his message. A different failure awaits when Christianity becomes institutionalized and 'positive.' Transformed into a daily ritual, an unthinking gesture or habit of words, its teachings lose their startling character. Hegel's account of this failure of ordinariness and of extraordinariness creates the context for a fresh understanding of his criticism of positivity. He does not see his task as consisting in the rational reconstruction of religious content, that is, the extraction of some moral essence from the 'positive' historically accreted extraneous matter. He adopts an indirect approach to show that the problem of positivity as it arises for the divinely commanded moral message *also* arises for a modern morality that aspires to autonomy. The basic difficulty, as Hegel states it in the context of Jesus' teaching, stems from the impossibility of reconciling the extraordinariness of Jesus' message – its practical rational purity, which commands respect – with the need for the teaching to be familiar so that it may touch ordinary human lives.

Though overall Hegel's aim in 'Positivity' is diagnostic and cautionary, the essay offers some intriguing anticipations of the socialized conception of agency developed in later works in the brief discussion of the different types of moral agency Hegel associated with Antigone, Jesus, and Socrates. He presents Antigone as subject to 'invisible' and 'unstated' laws she is free to obey or not (*ETW* 155; 222). What moves her to act is her vivid awareness of the law. While she experiences herself as bound by the law, her adherence to it is a matter of a free act; this is why, Hegel explains, she can break one law to obey another (*ETW* 155; 222). Drawing a tentative link between moral freedom and tragic agency, he suggests that Antigone's free law-abidingness appears as wanton disregard for the law. The solitariness of an agent who sets herself outside the *polis* is contrasted to both Jesus and Socrates, whose agency is realized within a community of like-minded individuals. In the case of Jesus, this is the community of his disciples. The disciples follow Jesus and his teaching because they love him (*ETW* 81; 162). So they love virtue because they love him. The inversion is familiar from post-Humean accounts of desire: we do not desire something because it is good, it is good because we desire it. So although Jesus and his disciples form a virtuous community, the love that binds this community together appears contingently motivated. Things stand differently with Socrates's pupils (*ETW* 82; 163). Hegel presents them not as disciples but as free citizens, members of a *polis* who are shaped by a culture of public virtue; they love Socrates because they love virtue. It would seem then that Hegel recommends this virtuous community for having a comparatively solid foundation. Socrates's fate should, however, warn us against drawing conclusions too quickly from this highly schematic treatment of socialized agency. Nonetheless, the lengthy and sympathetic treatment he reserves for classical forms of citizenship suggests that one way of doing full justice to the idea of a human morality is by articulating conditions under which the moral agent is recognized as moral in community with others. The "Love" fragment describes the possibility of such recognition but also a different way of thinking about morality.

2. Love: Outline of an Ethical Relation

The "Love" fragment begins with a description of loss:

> [E]ach individual loses more and more of his worth, his pretensions, and his independence … for a man without the pride of being the centre of things the end of his collective whole is supreme, and being, like all other individuals, so small a part of that, he despises himself (*ETW* 303; 278).

The cause of the loss remains somewhat mysterious. Hegel relies here on a discussion that is no longer part of this fragment.[10] It is possible, however, to reconstruct this analysis of loss from what remains. When the collective to which he belongs expands, the individual loses the sense that he is a valued member of the collective, and so his very individuality fades. Thus, Hegel writes, "equality of rights is transposed into equality of dependence" (*ETW* 302; 378). Although this could plausibly form part of a political or social analysis of dispersal and alienation, the immediate context of Hegel's remarks is religious: he speaks of the changing relation of a member of a cultic community to the 'ruling Being' (*ETW* 303; 378). This religious context allows us to build on the previous analysis of positivity. Whereas the "Positivity" essay examines from an external standpoint the genesis, character and effects of 'positive' religious structures, the "Love" fragment shifts to an internal perspective, showing what it *feels* like to be under such structures. It is by building on this individual experience that Hegel ventures to resolve the moral-metaphysical issues that occupy him. There are certain continuities with the earlier piece, especially in the use of terms such as 'living' and 'dead' to describe the changing relation of the individual subject and his world. Nonetheless, there is no explicit connection made in this fragment between the stages of this changing relation and the history of Christianity. The analysis of subjective experience is conducted in an abstract philosophical idiom that describes the evolving relations of a subject with respect to other subjects, to objects, and to God. For all these relations, Hegel uses a single term, 'love.'[11]

Love is at first presented as a form of loss. This is an elaboration of the individual experience of loss with which the fragment begins. Love-as-loss is a relation in which "something dead forms one part of the relationship" (*ETW* 303; 378). We can think of this as the subject's love for something dead, and use the resources of the analysis of positivity to fill in this relation. The individual who is subject to positive religious structures – and who therefore entertains a positive conception of the divine – experiences divine authority as mere fact. God's will is not the animating force of the worshipping community; it is reduced to a set of rules the individual obeys insofar as he is part of the community. 'Love' expresses his ongoing dependence on such authority, his desire to be guided, his need to view his daily relations to the social and natural world as divinely sanctioned. Speaking more abstractly, we might say that love is the continuing endeavor to make one's life meaningful. How, then, can love have something dead as part of it? We can think of the positive authority of law or of God as the dead element – we might want to say, for instance, that the subject is tied to the dead letter of the law. Note however that the 'something' that is dead is not a fixed position. And it is this that allows the relation of love-as-loss to develop. 'Something dead' describes also the way the subject relates to objects and perhaps also to other subjects *as* objects: "he is an independent unit for whom everything else in the world is external to him" (*ETW* 303; 378). In his daily interactions, the individual encounters his environment as made up of a multitude of changeable and perishable objects. Contrasting with this experience of daily loss, and to some extent compensating for it, is the conviction that the totality of entities, the world itself, is God's eternal creation.

Continuing the dialectic of this relation, Hegel invites us now to consider the subject's relation to himself: "his God is there, as surely as he is there" (*ETW* 303; 378). The necessity that binds the subject to God is experienced as conditional on self-awareness – on the *subject's* continuing being. But this is hardly reassuring for the subject, who is originally defined in the fragment by the experience of his utter unimportance. So it happens that the subject himself can occupy the position of 'something dead.' This is not because he realizes the contingency of his existence; this is not news to him. Rather it is because he realizes the contingency of his bond to God:

He exists only as something opposed [to the object] and one of a pair of opposites is reciprocally condition and conditioned. Thus the thought of self *must* transcend its own consciousness (*ETW* 304; 378, emphasis added).

The force of this 'must' is presented as if coming from subjective experience: "the individual cannot bear to think himself in this nullity" (*ETW* 304; 378). So self-transcendence is experienced as a spiritual need by a subject who is painfully aware of his nullity. However, Hegel wants to show that this subjective experience has an objective side to it. He wants us to see the love-as-loss relation as inherently unstable, so what 'must' be transcended is the basic incoherence that lies at its heart. The love-as-loss relation both affirms and denies the necessity of God's presence in the life of the individual. God's presence is necessary ontologically, as guarantee of the world's being; it is also necessary ethically for the conduct of daily life, and for the guidance one seeks and receives. This necessity vanishes with the subject's discovery of his own contingency. There is an interesting parallel here with the interpretation of individual self-abasement in the "Positivity" essay. A sign of modesty it may be, but the denial of goodness in human nature contributes to the problem of receptivity to the moral law. In the "Love" fragment, Hegel focuses on the problem of knowledge of God (rather than of the moral law). From the subject's ontological condition as *ens creatum*, Hegel draws the conclusion – or perhaps indicates that the conclusion can be drawn by a subject who finds himself in this situation – that the subject's cognitive powers cannot convincingly establish relations of necessity.[12] The subject cannot *know* God's necessity with any certainty, he can only be certain of his need to know, a need that stems precisely from his 'nullity.'

As the position of 'something dead' is taken up by various objects (people, God, things in the world) and the subject himself, the love-as-loss relation is exhausted. At this point Hegel indicates that a new relation of love can emerge if the original experience of nullity can be re-described. This remains a highly abstract and quite formal exercise. So although Hegel refers to individual experiences of loss, dependence, and love, he draws on these familiar psychological states to hunt a metaphysical quarry, a noncorrosive re-description of 'nullity.' This turns out to involve a basic relativizing move: "there is no determinant without something determined and vice versa" (*ETW* 304; 378).[13] The central idea is that "nothing is unconditioned; nothing carries the root of its own being in itself ... each is only relatively necessary; the one exists for the other" (*ETW* 304; 378). This idea allows dependence to be thought of as a relation of reciprocal sustenance between "living beings who are alike in power"; this, Hegel says, is "true union, or love proper" (*ETW* 304; 378).

Having reached this stage of Hegel's analysis, we can see how the permutations of the love-as-loss relation relate to the subject's search for an absolute foundation for his life. Under conditions of positivity, this search leads to the frustrating realization that the bond to God withers to mere subjective need. It is at this juncture that Hegel presents the problem from a different perspective thus offering a kind of resolution. Let us consider again the 'something dead.' One way of understanding the attraction of this metaphor for Hegel is that it can be used to describe both something burdensome (the 'dead letter' of the law) and something whose loss may be mourned (the loss of relations of reciprocity and recognition possible in a small community of believers). It also conveys the inertness attributed to mere matter – the world viewed as object – and, by extension, the normative opacity of nature (i.e. of nature conceived as mere matter). So the human subject encounters a world that is fundamentally indifferent to his spiritual or moral interests. This is very significant for Hegel's analysis of love and for his solution to the spiritual-moral predicament that love is meant to address. Hegel suggests that the encounter with the world as a dead object is the result of adopting an absolutist perspective in spiritual and moral matters, which amounts to sheltering spiritual and moral value in a wholly other world that is not determined by our human interests. This other world (of absolute value) can sustain human practical ambitions and hopes but at the cost of the now familiar problem of lack of interaction with the world that human beings inhabit and familiarly experience. Hegel proposes to resolve the problem through a relativizing move: the absolutist perspective is recognized as absolute *with respect to* the claims (moral, spiritual) it enables us to raise and appropriately redeem. This satisfies the demand, repeatedly asserted in "Positivity," that moral commands be categorical. However, and this is crucial, we gain access to the absolutist standpoint, and so recognize the moral command as categorical, only through ordinary practical experience and in response to specific practical needs. If we translate 'love proper' into moral-metaphysical terms, the claim that "each is only relatively necessary" (*ETW* 304; 378) suggests that each perspective, including the absolutist moral one, is only relatively necessary. More broadly, the relativizing move introduces the thought that claims are always relative to particular frameworks, which of course does not mean that claims raised within a particular framework are necessarily relativistic. This is what enables Hegel to write that in love "the separate does still remain, but as something united and no longer as something separate; life ... senses life" (ETW 305; 379).

This structural solution is just one of those offered in the "Love" fragment. 'Love' for Hegel is a term of art, but it is never just that. It is also a feeling that founds an ethical relation of mutual reciprocity. The apparent simplicity of a felt emotion, which is directly involved in how we treat (some) others, opens the prospect of a continuity between nature and morality. Scattered references throughout the early writings to 'moral sense,' and to 'moral disposition' as the '*complementum*' of the law, and to love as the '*pleroma*' of the law indicate a persistent attraction to the idea of a naturalized moral reason.[14] In the "Love" fragment, Hegel devotes sufficient space to the phenomenology of love, a "mutual giving and taking" whereby the "giver does not make himself poorer" (ETW 307; 380), to make this interpretation plausible.[15] Here love is not presented merely as a perfection of virtue but rather as the natural basis from which virtue can develop; love holds the key to the transformation of desirous subjectivity into ethical intersubjectivity. Significantly, what Hegel describes is a noncognitive form of ethical responsiveness to another human being: the loved one is 'sensed,' Hegel writes, as worthy of love. Philosophically, 'love' is a seamless union of ethics and affect. But as we shall see in the "Natural Law" essay, what blocks the path of the naturalization of moral reason is Hegel's concern that this is a reductivist position, which does not leave any room for freedom.

3.   Law: Death and Absolute *Sittlichkeit*

In "Natural Law," Hegel announces at the outset his 'scientific' intentions by framing the essay as the search for a single concept that can explain and also metaphysically ground the relations between reason and nature. Formally, this single concept is aptly characterized as 'absolute' (NL 417; 55).[16] This search for the absolute has, however, interesting unexpected outcomes, among them a radical and unflinching Kantian moral metaphysics.

Early on in Hegel's discussion of empirical theories of natural law, the question arises whether the scientific treatment of natural law permits the designation of law as 'natural.' Hegel's interrogation of the relation between 'law' and 'nature' raises the suspicion that there is a fundamental lack of sympathy between the projects of scientific and empirical natural law. It is interesting therefore that Hegel starts by praising the empiricists' respect for experience – especially what he calls 'intuition' (NL 57–58; 419).[17] What he faults is their methodology. He focuses his criticism on perhaps the only feature that is common to those theories that he indiscriminately treats under the label 'empirical,' namely the use of counterfactual 'state of nature' arguments. He argues that such hypotheses are formed from psychological, economic, or political observations made within the civil state, and that there is no independent methodological justification for the features chosen in each instance. This procedure is flawed and cannot yield philosophically and scientifically robust results because we have no reason to think that what is identified as fundamental in the explanation of the formation of civil society is indeed so. Empirical theories, Hegel concludes, take "the forms in which the fragmented moments of organic ethical life [*Sittlichkeit*] are fixed as particular essences and thereby distorted" (*NL* 66; 427). Because empirical theories combine explanatory with normative aims, the same methodological problem affects their normative claims. The set of natural characteristics identified in any particular theory as fundamental play a role in the account given within that particular theory of what the well-ordered *Sittlichkeit* should look like. Because these visions of postcontractual ethical life take their bearings from what was identified as 'natural,' Hegel argues, the ethical becomes 'contaminated' (*verunreinigt*) by the natural. Features such as atomism, property, or individual rights, which turn out to be central to the normative content of such theories, cannot be accepted as normatively 'natural' because the procedure that identifies them is faulty; 'the natural which would have to be regarded in an ethical relation as something to be sacrificed, would itself not be ethical and so least of all represent the ethical in its origin' (*NL* 66; 427).[18]

Hegel's criticism of empiricism is, however, not just methodological. What concerns Hegel is the way in which empirical treatments of natural law deal with the problem of receptivity to norms. Insofar as empirical natural law theories seek to show how individuals come to recognize the authority of the state and be bound by its laws, they seek to show how an ethical relation between human beings is possible. The establishment of contractual relations forms a central part of this account. At the same time, recognition of contractual relations depends on receptivity to norms, minimally on acceptance by the contracting parties of the very idea of a contract. But, the founding of this ethical relation precisely depends on recognition that the state of nature must be left behind and so on a view of nature as "something to be sacrificed" (*NL* 66; 427). At the same time, this ethical possibility must also be somehow recognized as natural, as inherent in the state of nature. On the one hand, Hegel is critical of the notion of 'nature' invoked in empirical theories because it fails in its main explanatory task, which is to show how the ethical relation of the recognition of contractual bounds is possible. On the other hand, he wants to hold onto the idea of necessity conveyed by the designation 'natural,' the idea of a necessity that is not local, relative to specific legislatures and thus 'positive,' but rather attaches to the very notion of law.

What Hegel calls 'a priorism' promises to do justice precisely to this notion of necessity (*NL* 70; 431). The specific application of a priorism that interests Hegel relates to Kant's and Fichte's attempts to vindicate their respective models of rational agency. Again, despite references to Kant and to Fichte, his concern is with the basic normative picture that emerges out of transcendental argumentation, not with the detail of Kant's or Fichte's practical philosophies.[19] This is how Hegel summarizes this basic picture:

> It is possible for right and duty to have reality independently as something particular apart from individuals, and for individuals to have reality apart from right and duty; but is also possible that both are linked together. And it is absolutely necessary for both possibilities to be separate and to be kept distinct [...], and the possibility that the pure concept and the subject of right and duty are *not* one must be posited unalterably and without qualification (*NL* 84; 442).

35

The key element in this picture is that it is pure reason – what Hegel calls here 'the pure concept' – that issues the demands of right and duty. In the *Critique of Practical Reason*, Kant claims that the moral law "exhibits us in a world that has true infinity," because it reveals "a life independent of all animality and even of the whole world of sense" and a destination that is "not restricted to the conditions and limits of this life but reaches into the infinite" (V:162). On Hegel's interpretation, this revelation of our moral personality –the 'subject of right and duty' – depends on an absolute unalterable separation – 'without qualification' – between the ordinary reality of the world of sense and the pure reality of right and duty. That Hegel speaks here of the 'reality' of the pure concepts of right and duty suggests that he wants to draw a close connection between this analysis of how the ideas of right and duty appear to us and where they might be located metaphysically.

Kant's discussion of spontaneity provides a useful context here. Human beings, Kant argues in the *Groundwork*, have a capacity that separates them 'from all other things,' and this is "a spontaneity so pure that [this capacity] goes far beyond anything in sensibility ... and because of this we regard ourselves as belonging to the two worlds" (IV:450–52). For Hegel, the problem is precisely our dual citizenship, so to speak. It is tempting here to import the relativizing move Hegel proposes in the "Love" fragment so we can think of belonging to two worlds as meaning simply that we must consider the claims that are permissible and possible within each conceptual framework. This is not a path Hegel is prepared to take in this essay; "it is absolutely necessary," he writes, "for both possibilities to be separate and to be kept distinct" (IV:450–52). Interestingly, this blocking of the relativizing move allows a more positive assessment of Kantian and of Fichtean a priorism. The emphatic articulation of rational agency Hegel finds in a priorism enables him to introduce to the discussion the idea of a necessity that is purely ethical – that pertains only to right and duty.

To understand the next step of Hegel's analysis of a priorism, which paves the way for his own rather striking conclusion, it is important to appreciate how 'infinity' is linked to 'freedom.' Already, as we saw in the quotation from the *Critique of Practical Reason*, Kant claims that the moral law shows our belonging to a world that has true infinity, and that this belonging is credited to our capacity for pure spontaneity. Whereas for Kant spontaneity understood as transcendental freedom is a condition for practical freedom, that is, the infinity revealed to us through the moral law, Hegel uses 'freedom' to encompass both spontaneity and infinity. This enables him to focus directly on how freedom should be understood for moral agency to be possible. So the problem of how to establish the compatibility between the order of reason and the order of nature, successively reinterpreted in terms of our receptivity to morality and then our belonging to the worlds of freedom and of sense, is now recast in terms of understanding freedom for finite organic beings. And the natural fact that all organic beings have to face is death. For Hegel then, giving an adequate account of freedom is a matter of showing how individuals deal with this natural fact. The key claim is that "[f]reedom itself (or infinity) is ... the negative and yet the absolute" (*NL* 91; 448). Hegel establishes the connection between freedom and 'the negative' in a lengthy and rather repetitive argument to the effect that freedom is not mere choice between options and so is not merely a matter of choosing between doing A or its opposite (*NL* 89f; 447f). Choice depends on a possibility that is not itself among the available options, or in Hegel's words, 'determinations.' It is this possibility, which is enabling but not manifest, that Hegel calls 'the negative' to underline the need to distinguish qualitatively between freedom as enabling condition for the exercise of choice and the practical freedom of doing A or −A. The enabling condition, which both Kant and Fichte term 'transcendental,' remains unknowable.

Having established this connection between infinity and freedom, Hegel claims that the 'negatively absolute, pure freedom' appears as 'death' (*NL* 91; 448). How are we to understand this sudden identification of an unknowable, yet practically and metaphysically necessary, condition for the possibility of particular choices with the naturally ever-present possibility of annihilation of each and any particular choice? Death, a natural phenomenon, would seem to provide the link between freedom and nature. The connective step is this: "by his ability to die the subject proves himself free and entirely above all coercion (*Zwang*)." The reference to the 'ability to die' is not a reference to a property of mortality that human beings possess *qua* natural beings. It is a reference to a choice – a choice that is the enabling condition of all other, particular choices. The ability to choose death suggests that human beings can choose something that is a natural possibility (the fact of mortality) against nature (since nature instructs creatures to do all in their power to survive). The individual who is able to confront death in this way, that is, see death as a choice and not as mere fact, acts purely as a free being 'above all coercion.' Thus nature (the fact that we are natural creatures who die) is used to overcome nature (as we are also creatures who can go freely to meet our death). The revelatory power of confronting our mortality already acknowledged in Kant's analytic of the sublime in the *Critique of Judgement* (V:269–70) is taken here as the key to a moral metaphysics: it is by confronting the necessity of death that the necessity of freedom is realized. The possibility that death can be a choice for an individual allows Hegel to draw a connection between freedom and nature but also between individual and collective. The communal confrontation with death is the conceptual link that allows him to 'deduce' the socio-political concept of 'absolute ethical life.'

The prospect of death, now as a possibility for a plurality of agents acting in cooperation, produces bonds among members of the community but also justifies their communal life under laws, thus enabling them to realize their freedom within an ethical whole. In effect, Hegel presents *war* as constitutive of absolute ethical life (*NL* 93; 450). This is not a pragmatic claim about how people come together when confronting a common enemy, it is a moral-metaphysical claim that results directly from Hegel's analysis of freedom in terms of the human ability to confront death.[20] Hegel interprets war – the empirical fact of war – in light of his interpretation of freedom to show that real historical communities have an ultimately metaphysical foundation in freedom. Thereby, although Hegel devotes most of his positive argument to describing the life of the members of the ethical whole, the rational life of institutions, principles of legislature and structures of political economy, the key to it all is the 'negatively absolute,' the pure freedom that appears as 'death.' The choice of death makes manifest the possibility of choice as such. From this, Hegel draws the conclusion that ethical life requires continuous confrontation with nature; that is to say the natural imperative of survival is 'confronted' when death (which is itself a natural, organic necessity) is confronted as a choice.

A number of points can be raised against this analysis of *Sittlichkeit*. Whatever its precise metaphysical status – and here some commentators detect in Hegel's references to 'ethical nature' (*NL* 66; 427, and 73–4; 433–4) undisclosed and possibly untenable Spinozan metaphysical commitments – it can be argued that as a political model it is archaic and so, irrelevant to modern societies, and with its emphasis on the organic structuring of ethical life, fails to protect modern freedoms.[21] Often allied to this worry is the concern that Hegel abandons the ambition to justify specific action-guiding norms and in doing so reduces the practical domain to the object of merely theoretical observation and description. The complaint is that a philosophical account of how human beings are capable of leading an ethical life cannot just be a matter of offering a description of the practices in which they engage, however sophisticated such a description may be.[22] Both sets of arguments can be plausibly prosecuted. There is indeed a naturalizing tendency in all the early works. Furthermore, Hegel is committed to the idea that to be free is to be able to subjugate one's self to norms, and he thinks that we have no other way of grasping this than through some account of the practices of ethical life. What enables Hegel to interpret these practices *as* ethical, however, is his analysis of freedom as a metaphysical condition for the founding of an ethical community. It is an analysis of freedom that depends on a complex 'confrontation' with nature, not mere absorption of the ethical into the natural. Similarly, although it is true that Hegel does not concern himself with issues of normative justification, he is no mere observer of communal habits. Rather, he is concerned to ground them on an account of *pure* freedom.

Hegel's analysis of freedom as the choosing of death is intended to show that it is pointless to seek guarantees of a fit between our rational and natural interests. What remains is the daily struggle to realize our freedom, the outcome of which we are in no position to prejudge. Hegel uses the word 'fate' to designate this surprisingly Kantian solution (*NL* 105; 460).[23] He explains fate by describing what he calls its 'picture,' which is to be found in Aeschylus's *The Eumenides*. The picture shows the litigation in the Areopagus over Orestes's fate, which is decided when Athene intervenes in the proceedings. Orestes' release through Athene's vote is 'fate,' because it exceeds normal expectations. At the same time, his release is not wholly miraculous because Athene intervenes within the established mechanisms of justice, namely the Areopagus court, and submits herself to the court's voting procedures. Hegel's picture is Kantian because it shows that as moral agents we can have no guarantees of safe conduct; metaphysically, the opposition between reason and nature is real, and so it appears to us as 'fate.'

This sobering conclusion brings to an end Hegel's metaphysical propaedeutic. It is extensive, detailed, and takes us in different directions, initially in the direction of a socialized agency in "Positivity," of a naturalized agency in "Love," and, in the "Natural Law" essay, of the practices that make up 'ethical life.' But it is not these anticipatory elements of later positions that make these pieces of lasting interest. Rather it is the way in which these different possibilities are presented as issuing from a systematic examination of the ways in which we seek to make moral sense of ourselves as natural and rational creatures. Through the different layers of Hegel's analysis and criticism of positivity, we gain an understanding of the difficulties of seeking to articulate a human morality– of the questions that motivate the metaphysical analysis of morality and of the problems that beset such analysis. A central question concerns the recognition of moral demands, typically of the moral law, by finite rational beings. The "Love" fragment represents an attempt by Hegel to address this issue in ways that do not fall foul of the problems identified in his earlier diagnostic essay. In that respect the structural solution he offers is of considerable interest since it consists in recognizing the role of the absolute practical standpoint within a specific sphere of human action; the suggestion is that absolute claims form part of our ordinary practical discourse. This very sketchy proposal gives way to the more systematic treatment of law in the "Natural Law" essay. Here Hegel gathers together all the elements of the post-Kantian discussion of the relation between reason, nature, and freedom to offer a striking interpretation of freedom as the choosing of death, which consists in basically showing that we may assert our rational freedom only to the extent that we are in position to confront nature. This fundamental confrontation gives meaning to our attempt to make moral sense of ourselves as rational and natural creatures.

Notes

1   Doubt about the possibility of a Hegelian ethics is discussed in Walsh (1984:11, 55). Recent studies that emphasize the social and political aspects of Hegel's ethical thought are Neuhouser 2000, Franco 1999, and Hardimon 1994; see also Schnädelbach 2000 and Siep 1992:81–115. The subjective/intersubjective dynamic is explored in Patten 1999 and, within a broader philosophical context, in Pippin 2005. Wood's exclusive focus on ethics and Quante's on action are the exceptions (Wood 1990; Quante 2004). For the use of 'Hegelian' as identified here, see Eldridge 1989. The habitual distinction between morality and ethics is not directly relevant to the present discussion, though see Wood 1990:131 and Pippin 1999.

2   On the suitability of the 'theological' label, see Walker 1997 and 2006. For an account of Hegel's early development, see Pinkard 2000; see also Beiser 2005 and Bienenstock 1992. The philosophical context is given in Di Giovanni 2005, Pinkard 2002, Ameriks 2001, Beiser 1992, and H. S. Harris 1972.

3   Examples include Beiser 2005 and Wood 1990. The aim of this chapter is not to give an overall account of Hegel's early development. However, because of the emphasis I place on moral metaphysics, a general account is implied that is at variance with prevalent interpretations, so I do not treat the nature-reason relation as a version of 'romantic' concerns, as Beiser recommends (Beiser 2005: 11 and 13); see also Wood 1990:202–205. The discussion presupposes a more positive engagement with the Enlightenment inheritance than Beiser allows, closer to the account given in Pinkard 2000:58–75. Finally, against the tendency to identify a hiatus in Hegel's early development between an early Kantian stage and one under Fichte and Schelling's influence that coincides with a sharp turn away from Kant (Wood 1990:127–129; Geiger 2007:26–27), I follow Harris in arguing for continuity; though unlike Harris, who sees this in terms of the search for an organic unity of life (Harris 1972:233), I interpret it in terms of Hegel's engagement with moral metaphysics.

4   Lessing articulates this position in "The Christianity of Reason" (1753), "On the Origin of Revealed Religion" (1764), and "The Education of the Human Race" (1777–1780) (see Nisbet 2005). The religious-theological debate starts with the *Aufklärer* and the 'popular philosophers,' continues with Kant, Schiller, Fichte, Schelling, Hegel, and the early romantics, and revives with Nietzsche and the Young Hegelians.

5   Di Giovanni describes aptly the broader issue in terms of the tension between post-Enlightenment positivism and humanism (Di Giovanni 2005:1–6). Kant is keenly aware of the moral peril of leaving the nature-reason divide as an open chasm. But while he is able

in his historical writings to offer interesting accounts of the prospects for the realization of political goals, his commitment to moral autonomy leaves little scope for a positive account of moralized nature.

6   The post-Kantian development of transcendental arguments is examined in Ameriks 2001. On interpretative issues concerning Kant's transcendental procedure, see Stern 1999 and 2000.

7   Kant himself opens *Religion* with a reference to what he calls the 'pessimists' and the 'optimists' about morality (*Rel* 15; VI:21).

8   See also *ETW* 85; 165–166. The relevant references to Kant are to the *Groundwork of the Metaphysics of Morals* IV:440–444; also the Preface to the first edition of *Religion* (*Rel* 3–4; VI:18). As with questions of law, so with religion the usual contrary to 'positive' is 'natural.' The Roman and specifically Ciceronian idea of a universal natural law is philosophically motivated by the search for natural order and politically by the need to discover principles of governance that are plausibly shareable over a large empire inhabited by people with different legal traditions and customary laws. Hegel's discussion of the methodological flaws of empirical natural law, discussed in Section 3 below, are anticipated in the extensive debates occasioned by the reception of Aquinian natural law in the Catholic Church about what is to count as natural (a good reference remains D'Entrèves 1951).

9   The entire Sixth Letter from *On the Aesthetic Education of Man* is relevant here because Schiller is using Kantian themes to articulate his criticism of the separation of reason from feeling and to promote an ideal of human wholeness. Hegel appears to quote directly Schiller when he talks of 'moral superstition' (*ETW* 71; 154): Schiller describes the modern vacillation between "unnaturalness and mere nature, between superstition and moral unbelief" (*AE* 29; XX 321). Hegel's criticism of a "life spent in monkish preoccupation with petty, mechanical, trivial usages" (*ETW* 69; 153) echoes Schiller's criticism of 'monkish asceticism,' which is a position that according to Schiller represents a misunderstanding of the Kantian position. This criticism is developed in "On Grace and Dignity," and Kant responds to it in *Religion* (*Rel* 18–19; VI:23–4).

10   "But the wider this whole ... extends., the more an equality of rights is transposed into an equality of dependence (as happens when the believer in cosmopolitanism comprises in his whole the entire human race), the less dominion over objects granted to any one individual, and the less of the ruling Being's favor does he enjoy. Hence each individual loses more and more of his worth, his pretensions, and his independence" (*ETW* 303; 378).

11   Standard interpretations tend to focus on the motif of romantic love; see Habermas 1999:140. The concept of 'love' is of course laden with religious and philosophical meanings. It is likely that Hegel draws from a range of sources to present a relationship that combines an explicit ethical dimension (from the Christian usage of *agape*), a cognitive rational dimension (from the Platonic conception of the rational soul's erotic attraction to the good), and a natural dimension (from orectic and conative interpretations). An epistemic dimension is explored in Schiller's "Philosophy of Physiology" of 1779, where he claims 'love' as a principle of truth if the aim of our cognitive endeavors is to attain 'unity' between knower and known.

12   See also: "That the world is as eternal as he is, and while the objects by which he is confronted change, they are never absent, they are there, and his God is there, as surely as he is here. This is the ground of his tranquility in face of loss ... but, of course, if he never existed, the nothing would exist for him, and what necessity was there for his existence?" (*ETW* 303; 378).

13   The text is ambiguous here on whether God is also to be included in this 'vice versa.' At first God appears as sustaining the new relation of love. However, as Hegel elaborates this new relation, especially its procreative aspect, God appears to dissolve into it (cf. *ETW* 307; 381).

14 The references are respectively from "Positivity" (*ETW* 99; 176) and from "The Spirit of Christianity and Its Fate" (*ETW* 213–216; 266–268).

15 Hegel quotes Shakespeare "The more I give to thee, The more I have" (*ETW* 307; 380). Aspects of this relation develop into the concepts of 'recognition' and of 'letting-go' in the *Phenomenology*. Recognition is structurally similar to love: "it is only when the 'I' communes with itself in its otherness that the content is known conceptually" (*PS* 486; 583) 'Letting-go' is characteristic of the 'self' who is capable of releasing itself (*entlassen*) from its possessive desire and grant its object 'complete freedom' (*PS* 492; 590). An early treatment of the epistemic features of recognition can be found in the "Scepticism" essay, where an encounter between incommensurable philosophical standpoints is presented as a suspension of reciprocal recognition that leaves the philosophical as "two subjectivities in opposition" (Harris and di Giovanni 1985:253, 276).

16 Characteristic of 'science' is what Franks calls 'derivation monism' (Franks 2005:17); see also Jamme and Schneider 1990. Again, the interpretation given here departs in significant ways from those that are based on reconstructions of Hegel's substantive criticisms of Kant and of Fichte; see for example Franco 1999:60–61.

17 "[T]his thing styling itself 'philosophy' and 'metaphysics' has no application and contradicts the necessities of practical life" (*NL* 430; 69). Empiricism concentrates on the facts of our existence, and its scientific ambition is to found and vindicate a this-worldly unity; see Cruysberghs 1989:116, and Cristi 2005:65–67. In the *Lectures on the History of Philosophy*, Hegel praises Hobbes for he "sought to derive the bond which holds the state together, that which gives the state its power from principles which lie within us, which we recognize as our own" (316). Hegel argues that the emergence of modern natural law itself as a universal and unchanging principle that limits and informs the stipulated order of positive law, is the expression of and reaction to a specific socio-historical state of affairs (op.cit., 809ff.); see also *NL* 57; 418, and 58; 419. He allies this with the possibility of immanent critique. If empiricism were true to itself, he claims, it would "treat the mass of principles, ends, laws, duties and rights as not absolute but as distinctions important for the culture through which its own vision becomes clearer to it" (*NL* 69; 430).

18 This is a Rousseauian point as Hegel acknowledges in the *Philosophy of Right* (§258), where he describes Rousseau as a pivotal figure in natural law theories for making freedom the principle of state formation; in the *Lectures on the History of Philosophy*, Hegel credits Rousseau with the idea that "man possesses free will, and freedom is what is qualitatively unique in man. To renounce freedom is to renounce being human" (527). See also Honneth 1992:204; and Wylleman 1989:15.

19 Clearly there are here anticipations of criticisms Hegel develops in later works (see *NL* 76; 436); interpretations of "Natural Law" that follow this path are Wood 1990 and Franco 1999. See also Bonsiepen 1977.

20 The role of war in Hegel's thought is a matter of controversy (see Stewart 1996: 131–180). Geiger treats it as paradigmatic of the shocking act of founding an ethical community (Geiger 2007).

21 See Riedel 1984:69, Franco 1999:65–66, and Horstmann 2004. On the problem of organicism, see Henrich 1971:27 and Wahl 1951:185.

22 See Claesges 1976, esp. 61, and Cruysberghs 1989:90; see also Chiereghin 1980.

23 "Tragedy consists in this, that ethical nature segregates its inorganic nature (in order not to become embroiled in it) as a fate and places it outside itself" (*NL* 105, 460). See also Deligiorgi 2007. I would like to thank Stephen Houlgate, Jason Gaiger, and Nicholas Walker for their very useful comments on earlier versions of this chapter.

References

All references in the main text to the English translations listed below are followed by references to the relevant German edition given after the semicolon.

ETW   Hegel, G.W.F. *Early Theological Writings*, trans. T. M. Knox, with an introduction and fragments translated by R. Kroner. Chicago: University of Chicago Press, 1948.

Hegel, G.W.F. *Hegels Theologische Jugendschriften*, ed. H. Nohl. Tübingen: J.C.B. Mohr, 1907.

NL   Hegel, G.W.F. *Natural Law. The Scientific Ways of Treating Natural Law, Its Place in Moral Philosophy, and Its Relation to the Positive Sciences of Law*, trans. T. M. Knox, introduction by H. B. Acton. Philadelphia: University of Pennsylvania Press, 1975.

Hegel, G.W.F. "Über die wissenschaftlichen Behandlungsarten des Naturrechts, seine Stelle in der praktischen Philosophie und sein Verhältnis zu den positiven Rechtswissenschaften," in *Jenaer Kritische Schriften* II, ed. Hans Brockard and Hartmut Buchner. Hamburg: Felix Meiner, 1983.

PS   Hegel, G.W.F. *Hegel's Phenomenology of Spirit*, trans. A. V. Miller with analysis and forward by J. N. Findlay. Oxford: Oxford University Press, 1977.

Hegel, G.W.F. *Phänomenologie des Geistes, Werke* 3. Frankfurt am Main: Suhrkamp Verlag, 1986.

Hegel, G.W.F. *Lectures on the History of Philosophy* trans. E. Haldane. New York: Humanities Press, 1968.

Rel   Kant, I. *Religion Within the Limits of Reason Alone*, trans. Theodore M. Greene and Hoyt H. Hudson. Harper and Row: New York, 1960.

Kant, I. *Kants gesammelte Schriften: herausgegeben von der Deutschen Akademie der Wissenschaften* (formerly *Königlichen Preußischen Akademie der Wissenschaften*), in 29 vols. Walter de Gruyter (formerly Georg Reimer): Berlin and Leipzig, 1902.

AE   Schiller, F. *On the Aesthetic Education of Man in a Series of Letters*, trans. Elizabeth M. Wilkinson and L. A. Willoughby. Clarendon Press: Oxford, 1982.

Schiller, F. *Schillers Werke. Nationalausgabe* vol. XX, ed. Lieselotte Blumenthal and Benno von Wiese. Weimar: Hermann Böhlhaus Nachfolger, 1943.

Secondary Sources

Ameriks, Karl. *Kant and the Fate of Autonomy*. Cambridge: Cambridge University Press, 2001.

Beiser, Frederick C. *Enlightenment, Revolution, and Romanticism. The Genesis of Modern German Political Thought, 1790–1800*. Cambridge Mass.: Harvard University Press, 1992.

Beiser, Frederick C. *Hegel*. New York and London: Routledge, 2005.

Bienenstock, Myriam. *Politique du Jeune Hegel. Iéna 1801–1806*. Paris: Presses Universitaires de France, 1992.

Bonsiepen, Wolfgang. *Der Begriff der Negativität in der Jenaer Schriften Hegels*. Bonn: Bouvier Verlag, 1977.

Chiereghin, Franco. *Dialettica dell'Assoluto e Ontologia della Soggettività in Hegel. Dall'Ideale Giovanile alla Fenomenologia dello Spirito*. Trento: Pubblicazioni di Verifiche, 1980.

Claesges, Ulrich. "Legalität und Moralität in Hegels Naturrechtsschrift," in Ute Guzzoni, Bernhard Rang, and Ludwig Siep, eds., *Der Idealismus und seine Gegenwart. Festschrift für Werner Marx zum 65. Geburtstag*. Hamburg: Meiner Verlag 1976, 53–74.

Cristi, Renato. *Hegel on Freedom and Authority*. Cardiff: University of Wales Press, 2005.

Cruysberghs, Paul. "Hegel's Critique of Modern Natural Law," in Wyleman 1989: 81–115.

Deligiorgi, Katerina, ed. *Hegel: New Directions*. Chesham: Acumen, and Montreal & Kingston: McGill-Queen's, 2006.

Deligiorgi, Katerina. "Modernity with Pictures: Hegel and Géricault," *Modernism/Modernity* 14:4 (2007): 607–623.

D'Entrèves, A. P. *Natural Law. An Introduction to Legal Philosophy*. London: Hutchinson's University Press, 1951.

Di Giovanni, George. *Freedom and Religion in Kant and His Immediate Successors. The Vocation of Humankind 1774–1800*. Cambridge: Cambridge University Press, 2005.

Eldridge, Richard T. "The Phenomenology of Moral Consciousness: Principle and Context, Kant and Hegel," in *On Moral Personhood Philosophy, Literature, Criticism, and Self-Understanding*. Chicago: University of Chicago Press 1989, 26–67

Franco, Paul. *Hegel's Philosophy of Freedom*. New Haven and London: Yale University Press, 1999.

Franks, Paul W. *All or Nothing: Systematicity, Transcendental Arguments, and Skepticism in German Idealism*. Cambridge, Mass.: Harvard University Press, 2005.

Geiger, Ido. *Hegel's Critique of Kant's Moral and Political Philosophy*. Stanford: Stanford University Press, 2007.

Habermas, Jürgen. "From Kant to Hegel and Back Again – The Move Towards Decentralization," *European Journal of Philosophy* 7, no. 2 (1999): 129–157.

Hardimon, Michael O. *Hegel's Social Philosophy. The Project of Reconciliation*. Cambridge: Cambridge University Press, 1994.

Harris, H. S. *Hegel's Development, Toward the Sunlight 1770–1801*. Oxford: Clarendon, 1972.

Harris, H. S., and George Di Giovanni. *Between Kant and Hegel. Texts in the Development of post-Kantian Idealism*. Albany: SUNY Press, 1985.

Henrich, Dieter, *Hegel im Kontext*. Frankfurt am Main: Suhrkamp, 1971.

Honneth, Axel. "Moral Development and Social Struggle: Hegel's Early Social-Philosophical Doctrines," in Honneth et al. eds. *Cultural-Political Interventions in the Unfinished Project of Enlightenment*. Cambridge, Mass.: MIT Press, 1992.

Hume, David. *A Treatise Concerning Human Nature*, ed. L. A. Selby-Bigge. Oxford: Clarendon, 1949.

Jamme, Christoph, and Schneider, Helmut, eds. *Der Weg zur System. Materialien zum jungen Hegel*. Frankfurt am Main: Suhrkamp, 1990.

Neuhouser, Frederick. *Foundations of Hegel's Social Theory: Actualizing Freedom*. Cambridge, Mass: Harvard University Press, 2000.

Nisbet, H. B., ed. *Lessing. Philosophical and Theological Writings*. Cambridge: Cambridge University Press, 2005.

Patten, Alan. *Hegel's Idea of Freedom*. New York: Oxford University Press, 1999.

Pinkard, Terry, *Hegel: A Biography*. Cambridge: Cambridge University Press, 2000.

Pinkard, Terry. *German Philosophy 1760–1860. The Legacy of Idealism*. Cambridge: Cambridge University Press, 2002.

Pippin, Robert B. "Naturalness and Mindedness. Hegel's Compatibilism," *European Journal of Philosophy* 7, no. 2 (1999): 194–212.

Pippin, Robert B. *The Persistence of Subjectivity: On the Kantian Aftermath*. Cambridge: Cambridge University Press, 2005.

Priest, Stephen, ed. *Hegel's Critique of Kant*. Oxford: Clarendon, 1987.

Quante, Michael. *Hegel's Concept of Action*, trans. Dean Moyar. Cambridge: Cambridge University Press, 2004.

Riedel, Manfred. *Between Tradition and Revolution*, trans. W. Wright. Cambridge: Cambridge University Press, 1984.

Schnädelbach, Herbert. *Hegels praktische Philosophie*. Frankfurt am Main: Suhrkamp, 2000.

Siep, Ludwig. *Praktische Philosophie im Deutschen Idealismus*. Frankfurt am Main: Suhrkamp, 1992.

Stern, Robert, ed. *Transcendental Arguments. Problems and Prospects*. Oxford: Oxford University Press, 1999.

Stern, Robert. *Transcendental Arguments and Scepticism: Answering the Question of Justification.* Oxford: Oxford University Press, 2000.

Stewart, Jon. *The Hegel Myths and Legends.* Evanston, Ill.: Northwestern University Press, 1996.

Wahl, Jean A. *Le Malheur de la Conscience dans la Philosophie de Hegel.* Paris: Presses Universitaires de France, 1951.

Walker, Nicholas. 'Hegel's Encounter with the Christian Tradition' in Michael Baur and John Russon, eds., *Hegel and the Tradition: Essays in Honour of H. S. Harris.* Toronto: University of Toronto Press 1997, 190–211.

Walker, Nicholas. "The Gospel According to Immanuel," in Deligiorgi 2006: 193–206.

Walsh, W. H. *Hegelian Ethics.* New York: Garland, 1984.

Wood, Allen W. *Hegel's Ethical Thought.* Cambridge: Cambridge University Press, 1990.

Wylleman, A., ed. *Hegel on the Ethical Life, Religion and Philosophy.* Leuven: Kluwer Academic Publishers and Leuven University Press, 1989.

Part II

Phenomenology of Spirit

2

The Project of Hegel's *Phenomenology of Spirit*

JOHN RUSSON

You would never discover the limits of soul, should you travel every road, so deep a logos does it have.

— Heraclitus, fragment 45

Hegel's *Phenomenology of Spirit* was and remains a revolutionary book in the history of philosophy. It continued and developed what Kant called his own "Copernican Revolution" in philosophy, simultaneously speaking authoritatively to the questions that animated the tradition of philosophy that it inherited, and opening up the lines of analysis and inquiry that continue to fuel the tradition of philosophy that developed after it.[1] I want here to describe the distinctive project of this book: the project of phenomenology. A unique characteristic of Hegel's project is that the method of phenomenology is itself shaped by what it reveals. Understanding Hegel's project will thus require a consideration of both the methodological principle that animates the book and, in broad outline, the central results of that method insofar as they shed light on the concrete significance of that principle. I will begin by describing the basic principle of Hegel's phenomenology – the principle of scientific passivity – and the beginning of the project of phenomenology. I will then turn to considering how that method is shaped by what it reveals. Hegel's project is a development of the project Kant pioneered, and in discussing what the method reveals, I will draw on Kant's *Critique of Pure Reason* to establish the most fundamental point about experience, namely, that it is inherently characterized by the experience of infinity. From here, and broadly in continuing dialogue with Kant, I will consider the dimensions of infinity that Hegel reveals within experience, identifying the distinctive way in which Hegel shows experience to be inherently characterized by a conflict of infinities, most especially the conflict of the infinity of substance and the infinity of subjectivity. Investigating the infinity of subjectivity will allow us to see that the phenomenological method demands that one be a participant and not simply an observer, and that this in turn entails that one's

A Companion to Hegel, First Edition. Edited by Stephen Houlgate and Michael Baur.
© 2011 Blackwell Publishing Ltd. Published 2011 by Blackwell Publishing Ltd.

embrace of the project of phenomenological description be as much practical as theoretical. In conclusion we will see that the project and method of phenomenology is
ultimately to bear witness in vigilant openness to the unacknowledged absolutes that
leave their trace in finite experience, a project realized in conscience, absolute knowing,
and the project of phenomenology itself.

Hegel's Project of Phenomenology

Hegel describes the *Phenomenology of Spirit* as "the science of the experience of consciousness."[2] This work is a description of the form(s) experience takes, and the special
project of the work is to let experience itself dictate the form in which the description
unfolds. Hegel's objective is to be simply the medium through which the form of experience is able to present itself: his philosophy aims, that is, to be a philosophy without an
author.[3]

In this desire to give voice to reality rather than to his own private perspective,
Hegel's objective – the objective of philosophy – is basically the same as the objective of
the artist or the religious person. The religious person aims to make him or herself open
to being led by the divine, and to remove his or her own agency from the central position in his or her experience: "not my will, Lord, but thine be done" (*Luke* 22:42; cf.
John 5:30).[4] The artist, similarly, wants his or her artwork to be a revelation of truth,
a new form in and through which human experience can be articulated, rather than
merely a presentation of private interests: as Michelangelo says, "Every block of stone
has a statue inside it and it is the task of the sculptor to discover it."[5] The philosopher,
likewise, aims not to present mere "opinions," but to articulate for others a compelling
revelation of the nature of things. As Hegel says in the "Preface,"

> It is customary to preface a work with an explanation of the author's aim, why he wrote
> the book, and the relationship in which he believes it to stand to other earlier or contem-
> porary treatises on the same subject. In the case of a philosophical work, however, such
> an explanation seems not only superfluous but, in view of the nature of the subject-matter,
> even inappropriate and misleading.[6]

Like the artistic and the religious person, the philosopher is not putting forth his or her
"own" ideas, and the book is not strictly his or her "own" work, but is more like an act
of devotion, inviting the truth itself – "the absolute" – to show itself.[7] In short, all – the
artist, the religious person, and the philosopher – aspire to a stance of passivity, and
Hegel's *Phenomenology* is thus a project of passivity. To let experience show itself, then,
the philosopher must approach experience simply with the question, "What is the
immediate given form of experience?" or, perhaps more clearly, "What appears?" The
task, that is, is simply to describe the immediate form, simply to describe the appearing
as it appears.[8]

How might we describe the immediate form of experience? If we just open ourselves
to the observation of the fact of our own experiencing, what can we say? Shall we
simply say "there is" or "now"? Will that simple term – "now" or "is" – be sufficient to
articulate the character of our experience? This is where Hegel's phenomenology

begins, namely, with the attempt simply to announce the fact of experience – "now." As Hegel explains,

> The knowing which is first or immediately our object can be nothing other than that which is itself immediate knowing, *knowing of the immediate* or *of being*. We must ourselves also be immediate or receptive, and alter nothing in it as it presents itself and, in apprehending, hold ourselves back from conceptualizing.[9]

In fact, however, what the *Phenomenology* demonstrates in its actual enactment of this project of description is that the immediate form of experience is not so easy to describe. Let us see how this is so.

Hegel's work is a work of phenomenology: a description of the happening of experience. Just as one must have sight in order to appreciate a discussion of colors, so in general must one have the experience under discussion if the phenomenological description Hegel gives is to be meaningful. For that reason, one must oneself *enact* the experience he or she is describing in order to recognize the sense and the force of his or her claims. One must be a participant in this work, not just an observer. To understand and appreciate Hegel's claims about the experience of "now," one must oneself have that experience in front of one, and so, to begin, the reader must him- or herself attend to experiencing simply this moment, now. What Hegel notes in his description of this experience is that the now is itself not experienced as an isolated instant, but is experienced as a passage: it is experienced as coming into being and passing away in a temporal flow.[10] But the notion of "passage" is more complex than the notion of "is" – it is becoming, a motion defined as "from … to," and not just an unqualified immediacy of being. What we see here is that, if we try to describe experience simply in the terms of unqualified immediacy – if we use a simple term such as "is" or "now" or "here" – we under-represent the character of that experience, and *the experience of the "now" itself reveals this*. Our approach to receptiveness – our attempt to describe the experience without introducing an intervening interpretation – allows our object to reveal itself to us in such a way that *it* demonstrates the insufficiency of our own initial approach to it, demonstrating that it is *becoming* and not simply *being* as our initial apprehension implies. The project of phenomenology seems initially to demand a "hands off" approach, but, in enacting that project, we find out *from the object* that this attitude is inadequate to it. The "hands off" approach is in fact a tacit presumption that the object must be simple "being," and does not allow the object to appear on its own terms as becoming: apprehending the object as becoming goes hand in hand with a transformation of perspective, a transformation in what one is prepared to recognize. From this, we learn two important lessons about the method and project of the phenomenology.

The first lesson we learn from our attempt to describe the experience of "now" is that the project of phenomenology itself comes to be defined through its enactment. In other words, it is only through its realization that the real meaning of the originating intention can be determined. Thus Hegel remarks in the Preface:

> For the real issue [*die Sache selbst*] is not exhausted by stating it as an aim, but by carrying it out, nor is the result the actual whole, but rather the result together with the process through which it came about. The aim by itself is a lifeless universal, just as the guiding

tendency is a mere drive that as yet lacks an actual existence; and the bare result is the corpse which has left the guiding tendency behind it.[11]

Just as experience itself cannot be understood except through participating in the happening of experience, so the project of phenomenology cannot be understood except through working through its actual unfolding.

The second lesson from our description of the now is that, in order to relate to experience so as to "let it be," one must make oneself *appropriately* receptive, and this is not the same as the removal of perspective. The object, in other words, demands of us that we be active in certain ways in order to receive it, in order to be passive. This passivity, however, is not an abandonment of intelligence, effort, or learning, but is rather a passivity enabled by the most rigorous engagement.[12] The project is to allow experience to show itself, but this "letting show," this releasing of the inherent form, is not itself immediately within one's power. One must learn how to apprehend what shows itself. Though it is indeed one's own experience that is to be described – and thus in principle one *has access to* the object, obviating the skeptical concerns that typically accompany projects of knowledge – it is not the case that one automatically *has insight into* one's own experience, into oneself.[13] For this reason, being passive is the same project as developing the rigorously answerable attitude of the scientist, for one is called upon to make one's perception conform to the demands made by the object under study. This is Hegel's stance as the "author" of the *Phenomenology of Spirit*: "[t]o help bring philosophy closer to the form of science ... – that is what I have tried to do."[14] Holding himself responsible to the highest scientific standards of comprehensiveness and rigor, he endeavors to make manifest the self-presentation and self-movement – the dialectic – of experience itself.[15] This scientific passivity amounts to an acceptance of the givenness of experience: "scientific cognition ... demands surrender to the life of the object."[16] The philosopher, that is, must be open to what experience itself presents, whether it meets his or her expectations or not.[17] Based on what we have already learned through the first enactment of the method in relationship to the "now," we can say something in outline of what this adequate receptivity involves.

The form of our experience is not adequately captured by a simple term such as "is" or "now" because our experience is always inherently complex. What we experience is not just an indeterminate, immediate field of being, but a world of diverse things. That world is complex, for it comprises many things in their complex relations with each other;[18] those things, too, are themselves inherently complex, being simultaneously discrete, autonomous individuals, differentiated from each other, and assemblages of different properties.[19] The world of our experience is not adequately captured by a single, simple term such as "is" – by what Hegel calls a "logic of immediacy" – but requires more complex terms that name relations, terms such as "thing" (which implies a relation of thinghood and properties) or "appearance" (which implies a relation of inner essence and outer show) – what Hegel calls a "logic of reflection."[20] And there is a further complexity to experience, in that the world of our experience is always *appearing to* us, it is there *for* us. Though explicitly an experience of consciousness – the awareness of an other, of an object – our experience is always implicitly an experience of self-consciousness – an awareness of ourselves as experiencers in our awareness of the object.[21] "What appears" in appearance is simultaneously the world and our awareness of it. Adequately describing what appears then requires a logic of reflection to adequately characterize the nature of the object – "*substance*" in the language of the Preface – but, beyond that, it requires what Hegel calls a "logic of the concept" to characterize this way in which the fabric of experience is *subjectivity* itself; that is, it will require terms that express a relationship in which something relates to itself in relating to what is opposite to it.[22] Experience is simultaneously the explicit appearing of an object and an implicit appearing of a subject, a simultaneity of substance and subject, the significance of which we go on to pursue in greater detail below.

The immediate form of experience, then, only shows itself to one who is prepared to recognize relations of "reflection" and of "the concept," and not just situations of immediacy. The immediate form of experience, then, does not itself appear immediately, but shows itself only to a developed onlooker. What this project seems most immediately to require is a stance of nonintervention, a stance of noninterpretation in which one "clears one's mind" of any structures, plans, or expectations, but such a stance is in fact a stance without intelligence, a stance *unable to recognize* intelligence when it sees it. To see the world in its rationality, one must look at it rationally.[23] The ongoing process of the *Phenomenology* describes experiences in which these logics of reflection and concept are inherently at play (what the experience is "in itself") but are not acknowledged as such (not what the experience is "for itself"). The description notices how this disparity that characterizes the experience (the disparity between what it is in itself and what it is for itself, or, as Hegel sometimes says, the disparity between its concept and its actuality) manifests itself within the process of experience itself. In other words, the phenomenology bears witness to the ways in which particular forms of experience themselves demonstrate, through their own process, the inadequacies internal to their own makeup. The simple description of experience thus offers the phenomenological observer an education into the nature of experience to the point at which the immediate form of experience can be adequately described. This education into the proper description of experience itself comes through the progressive attempt to describe the immediate form of experience and the discovery within experience that the form of experience exceeds the terms of the description. In other words, it is through the *attempt* made by a given form of consciousness to describe experience that one is taught by experience how one *needs* to describe experience. The *Phenomenology of Spirit* offers an education into how to describe experience by allowing its reader the opportunity to learn the lesson enacted by each shape of consciousness, and thus to see the rationale for the development of different shapes of consciousness, even if that realization is not explicitly made within those shapes of consciousness themselves (a project completed when the phenomenological experience itself becomes the experience under description).[24]

The project of phenomenology as Hegel understands it is a handing of oneself over to experience in order to learn from it what its nature is. This project of phenomenology had already been pioneered by Kant. Though Kant's work does not follow this same route of allowing the process of describing experience to educate itself, he had in fact already made the phenomenological description of experience the core to his argument in the *Critique of Pure Reason*, especially in his study of the role of "intuition" in experience. Through a brief consideration of Kant's study we can see particularly clearly that the simple description "now" hides within itself a complexity – a richness of "mediation," in Hegel's language – that the simplicity of the mere term "now" does not adequately express. As with Hegel, so with Kant we will see that the fabric of experience is the co-occurrence of substance and subject. More specifically, what we will learn from Kant is that "what appears" is always infinite, a lesson that Hegel's phenomenology in turn will take up and develop more fully.

Kant and the Infinite Within-and-Without Experience

Kant's philosophy emerges naturally from a simple phenomenological observation: the object of our experience is given in experience *as* something not defined by our experience. To understand this, let us engage in a simple exercise in thinking: let us distinguish between what we mean when we say that something is "real" and what we mean when we say that something is "imaginary."

When we merely imagine ourselves to be at the beach, we experience ourselves as having the power to modify at will the character of our imagined beach experience. At will, I can change the beach in my imagination from sandy to rocky, the atmosphere from sunny and dry to cloudy and humid, the time from late evening to early morning, and so on. Also, the beach in my imagined experience will have only as much of its sensuous character filled in as I in fact imagine – I may not, for example, imagine the scent of the water, the temperature of the air, or the color of the clothes I am wearing. Further, the relation of the beach situation to the "rest of the world" is left unspecified. I focus on it in isolation, and there is no answer to the question, "And what's over there?" unless I have in fact specified it to myself. These characteristics are sufficient to allow us to distinguish what we experience as "imaginary" from what we experience as "real."

When we experience ourselves as *really* at the beach, it is not up to us to decide whether it is hot or cold, sunny or cloudy, early or late. On the contrary, these characteristics of the situation are forced upon us. Again, the real object has all of its sensuous features filled in without gaps, regardless of whether we happen to be attending to them.[25] Further, unlike the imagined object for which its relationship to the rest of the world is left undefined, the real object is seamlessly integrated with all other things in reality.[26] The real object is sensuously saturated, and has definite characteristics that answer to its own internal reasons, without reference to our will, and stands in definite relation to all other things, again according to reasons internal to "the nature of things" in general, without reference to our will. In short, the form of the imaginary object answers to our will, whereas the form of the real object is something to which our will must answer: it is something that must be *known*, something that is the proper object of *science*, whereas the object of imagination is a matter of fantasy.

We can now ask, "How do we experience the world that is the normal object of our experience?" The answer is that we experience it *as* something real, not *as* something imaginary. Whether or not the world ultimately *is* an independent reality or, instead, is a figment of our imagination is not here at issue. The question is simply *how we experience it*. We *experience* it *as* something real. The object of our experience is given in experience *as* something not defined by our experience. Empirically, the object of our experience is *real*. This *description of our experience* is the sole fact from which Kant's philosophy (in the *Critique of Pure Reason,* at least) emerges. His philosophy is only the rigorous description and analysis of various aspects of this fact. Let us pursue a few of these aspects.

We noted above that something we experience as "real" is something we experience as seamlessly integrated with everything else that is real, such that they form a single fabric: "the" real, "reality." Perceptually this is manifest in the fact that whatever part of the world we experience here and now is experienced *as* participating within a space and time that go on infinitely beyond the determinate specificity that we are presently experiencing. Space, as Kant notes, is experienced as "an infinite, given magnitude."[27] Again, whether or not space *ultimately is* such, *within our experience* space is *given as* infinite: we experience space *as* going on forever (and the same for time).

Here, in this observation about space, we see again a way in which the object of our experience is experienced *as* not defined by our experience. Indeed, the object of our experience is experienced precisely as exceeding our experience. We experience space *as* real and *as* infinite, and therefore as something not defined or exhausted by our finite experience of it. We find ourselves exposed in principle to the infinite space in which we are situated. From this observation about the form of our experience, Kant draws an important epistemological point.

Since the very form of the object of experience is that it exceeds our experiences of it, that object cannot be simply the sum of those finite experiences. If our finite experiences were the sole source of our knowledge, then we would know the object to be exactly defined by the sum of those experiences. In that case, we would never experience the object *as* infinite. We *do* thus experience the object, however, and therefore that experience must have some source other than the finite history of our specific experiences. Said otherwise, this openness to the experience of space could not have been *learned*: it must be *inherent to* our experience to experience the object in this way, for, otherwise, we could never come upon the experience we actually do have. This Kant describes by saying that the form of our experience of space – the fact that any *specific* experience of space (and all our experiences are that) is always given as contextualized by participation in the infinitude of space – is an a priori rather than an a posteriori dimension of our experience.[28] It is a *condition* of our finite experience of space, not a *result* of it, that it be situated in infinite space. Space, Kant says, is a "transcendental" – that is, pervasive and inherent – condition of our experience.

To call this knowledge of space as infinite "transcendental" is simply to say in different words what we already said above: to say that the infinitude of space is *empirically real* is *only* to describe the form of our experience, and not to say anything about the "ultimate nature" of reality as such, of reality beyond any possible experience or "in itself." As well as being empirically real, then, space is "transcendentally ideal," that is, we are describing structures *internal to the happening of experience,* not "transcendent" realities beyond experience.[29]

This distinction between real "within experience" and real "in itself" pertains to our approach to ourselves as subjects of experience as well as to the objects of experience. Our reality is the ("first person") reality of *experiencing*: we are not objects but subjects, those *for whom* experience is happening. We also experience ourselves as bodies, as things of a piece with the world, in space. As Kant says, describing the a priori character of the experience of space,

> [T]he presentation of space must already lie at the basis in order for certain sensations to be referred to something *outside me* (i.e., referred to something in a location of space *other than the location in which I am)*.[30]

The space of which I have an a priori experience is a space *that contains me. Empirically,* we are situated *within the world:* I am one thing among many. At the same time, however, we are subjects *for whom* the appearing of reality is happening. In that sense the world – the *real* that is the object of our experience – is *in us* inasmuch as we are the act of experience, the fact of the happening of appearing. "I," then, names simultaneously and equivocally the form of the whole of our experience and one thing within our experience. "I" is the very *form* of all our experience in that there is experience only as it is experienced as "my experience," that is, I experience the appearing *as* appearing, that is, *as* for me, and "I" is thus the *transcendental* – pervasive and inherent – form of the unity of *all* experience.[31] For this reason, this transcendental "I" can be found only by *thinking,* since it could never be identified with any determinate object of experience.[32] But "I" is also the name for a specific thing in the world. "I" is always experienced as both in the world and the form of the world. Though "I" is always experienced as a finite specificity – this empirical self, here and now in this world – that experience is itself necessarily contextualized by its being defined by a sense of "I" – *itself* – that is the form of experience as such. Like space, however, this *transcendental* "I" is not a *transcendent* reality – an independently existing reality beyond experience that fabricates experience – but is only the form of meaningfulness *inherent within* all experience.[33]

In sum, our experience is always a finite situatedness – a "being in the world," as Heidegger describes it – that inherently involves an infinity of substance (reality) and subject that is its form.[34] There are two important points here. First, I exist *as* an inherently finite crystallization of what is inherently infinite. Second, the form of this finite enactment of the infinite is that I always experience myself as one thing among others located here *in* a real spatial world, while simultaneously experiencing that world as *in* my experience. In neither case, though – neither in the case of the containing real nor of the containing I – are we considering a causal thing-in-itself beyond experience. Instead, these are forms *inherent to experience,* and *they are forms that must be acknowledged in any accurate description* of experience. We can only describe, not account for the constitution of, experience. It is *given* as this happening of meaning and we can describe its form, but we can never get beyond this.

We began with the project of describing the form of experience: "What's happening?" or "What appears?" With Kant, we have seen that our experience always takes the form of a specific, finite experience within which a deeper, a priori character manifests itself. That deeper form is itself the appearance of the infinite. That infinite is both *within* finite experience, inasmuch as it is inherent to it as a form *of* experience, and it is *outside* experience, in that the very sense with which it is given – to intuition, in the case of space, to thought in the case of the "I" – is "beyond." In fact, the specific experience is the site for the co-occurrence of – our inherent exposure to – two such infinites "within-and-without": the infinite beyond of the real, the spatial, causal "is" within which we are contained, and the infinite beyond of the "I," which is the form of all appearing, that within which the very experience of the real is contained. Hegel's

Phenomenology began by asking whether "now" adequately describes the form of experience. What we saw already is that "now" always appears as the site of co-occurrence of substance and subject, and now, with Kant, we have seen that these are infinites and that the method of phenomenology, therefore, is a witnessing to infinity. What we will now explore is how each of these infinites contests with the other for the claim of ultimacy.[35] This infinite contestation is the form of experience, and describing this properly is the project of Hegel's *Phenomenology of Spirit*.

The Phenomenology of Infinite Conflict

It is the very character of experience to present us with a "real," and this is precisely experienced as an imperative within experience. Within our experience we are claimed – held answerable to – the demands of an object that does not itself answer to the terms of our subjectivity: *within* experience it is *given as* infinite in itself, both in its spatial extension and in its causal interiority: the object is *given as* "*without*," as infinitely exceeding us in its providing on its own both the domain of its existence (the spatial domain in which, indeed, we too are contained) and the causal principles of its existence. The very nature of the object, then, as it is *given*, challenges any attempt we might make to treat it as "merely mine": *it* calls us to science, to answerability to it, whether we explicitly acknowledge this or not. As does Kant's analysis in the *Critique of Pure Reason*, Hegel's analysis in the "Consciousness" section of the *Phenomenology* similarly culminates in the description of the inherent infinity of the real and its imperative force.[36]

At the same time, however, Kant's correct description of the infinite claim of the object does not end the question of the nature of what appears. With Kant, we have seen that the "I" is necessarily already insinuated within any appearance as its overarching form. We are called, that is to say, to recognize ourselves as what is *really* appearing in any appearance. Though the given nature of the real calls us to knowledge of its infinite, independent nature, we are also claimed by the nature of the "I," and the claim of the "I" is in tension with the claim of the real object. Kant himself recognized this tension. It is the central concern of the "Third Antinomy" from his study of the "Dialectic of Pure Reason," and it is the organizing principle behind the larger articulation of his philosophy in the relationship between the *Critique of Pure Reason* and the *Critique of Practical Reason*.[37] It is the force of this claim that is worked out through the section called "Self-Consciousness" in Hegel's *Phenomenology*.

Appearance, by its nature, is *for* me, and I feel the imperative force of this as desire, as the sense that the real is the site for the satisfaction of my subjectivity.[38] In acting from desire, the significance of experience comes from me: my desire is expressed in the world, and thus I impinge upon the real as much as the real impinges upon me. In opposition to the stance of knowing in which my subjectivity is answerable to taking its determination – its form – from the object, in answering to desire I experience the object as rightly receiving its determination from my subjectivity.[39] Just as the character of the real is given in experience, so too is this sense of "mineness" given: it is not something I "make," but is rather the experiential precondition for there being any "I," any "making." It is thus just as much a given form – indeed an infinite form – by which

55

I am claimed as is the form of space or the form of causality. And yet, even though these desires are "me," it is nonetheless the case that I *find out* the nature of my desires, the nature of my singular subjective perspective, by being exposed to it.

We exist in a state of exposure: this is the basic form of experience recognized by both Kant and Hegel. By exposure, I mean the way that we are unprotectedly in contact with an outside that defines us but that exceeds our grasp, an infinity that claims us without our having the option to refuse, a constitutive imperative to which our experience is answerable. With Kant, we notice that we are always spatial, always wrapped up in a space that in magnitude infinitely exceeds us – we could never "gather this experience up," so to speak – and that in essence is inherently opaque to us, that is, it is an intuition, an immediate given determinateness that is impenetrable to our insight. We are always exposed in space. With Hegel, we notice that we are exposed in further ways, and, furthermore, the dimensions of our exposure are in tension with each other. Desire – the experience of our singular subjectivity – is one such dimension, one such domain of opaque, alien determination. We find ourselves compelled by desires as imperatives to which we are internally answerable, having neither insight into their source nor the ability to control their emergence: the "heteronomy" of the will, as Kant describes it, "it" as Freud describes it. In desire, we experience ourselves as subjected to an alien authority, even as that authority is given as our very self. The "I," our most intimate "self," is itself, in other words, something to which we are beholden, something with which we find ourselves confronted. It is in exploring the claims of desire that constitute the "I" that further dimensions of our exposure reveal themselves.

The progress of the phenomenological method is the progressive unearthing of more and more fundamental "infinities," more fundamental "absolutes," that characterize, contextualize, or constitute our experience. Though I will not pursue the study of it here, such an unearthing occurred throughout the "Consciousness" section. Hegel's phenomenology here is, in fact, somewhat richer than Kant's, witnessing within-and-without the infinitude of sensuous multiplicity the emergence of the infinitude of the thing, as well as witnessing within-and-without the domain of things the emergence of the infinitude of the real as such that Kant acknowledged. Within the domain of meaning opened up by desire, which will be our concern in this section, Hegel witnesses within-and-without the infinitude of sensual multiplicity the emergence of the infinitude of other self-consciousnesses, and, further, he witnesses within-and-without the domain of others the emergence of the infinitude of the "Other" as such. With any infinite (as Kant showed in the *Critique of Pure Reason*), our experience of it is an *exposure* and not something *learned*. In other words, it is something that can be described and discussed only by someone who actually participates in the experience. Thus, with the "now," the "thing," and the "real," and also with "others" and "the Other," we can understand Hegel's phenomenology only if we first recognize within our own experience the exposures he is describing. In this domain of desire the conflict of these infinites is not merely a conceptual matter, but a matter of the most intimate, living practicality, and the phenomenological acknowledgment of this conflict – the phenomenological method itself – becomes as much a practical as a theoretical affair.

In the discussion that is perhaps most definitive of the *Phenomenology of Spirit*, Hegel first considers a particular way in which we are exposed, a particular desire that claims us: we are exposed to others, and we desire to be acknowledged by them. Appearance has an inherently intersubjective form. We experience ourselves as already in a world, already subject to the perspectives of others. Experience is "for" us in the sense that we are the subjects of our own experience – we are having our experience – but we precisely experience this world that is for us (and, furthermore, ourselves) as "for" others: we are perceived as much as we are perceiving. For this reason, *our own* identity is from the start dual – *we* are both subject and object, perspective on the world and thing within the perspectives of others. We experience ourselves, in other words, as insufficient on our own to account for our own identity: we experience ourselves as dependent on others to let us know who we are. Our experience is characterized by a *constitutive* desire for recognition by others, itself a desire that conflicts with other desires.

This desire for recognition is the primary imperative that drives the development of our identities, and the bulk of the *Phenomenology of Spirit* is devoted to describing this development.[40] At the most personal level, we seek the recognition of our immediate companions in order to establish a sense of our self-worth. Our basic sense of self is established only in dialogue, only in a negotiation between our own immediate sense of our primacy – we are, after all, always at the center of our own experience – and the sense of our secondariness in the eyes of others (who, of course, experience themselves at the center of their own experience). The sense of ourselves as equal participants in a shared world with which we normally live is itself a developed view, a view accomplished through this negotiation. Indeed, this is perhaps Hegel's most distinctive contribution to our philosophical heritage: the *Phenomenology of Spirit* demonstrates that the sense of ourselves that we typically live with – a coherent sense of ourselves as independent agents, coherently integrated with the human and natural world – is an achievement (indeed, a complex negotiation with the conflicting infinities of reality, desire, and others) and not our "given" state.[41] The achieving of this coherent, integrated sense of self is accomplished only through interpersonal negotiation, and Hegel demonstrates, in his descriptions of the "struggle to the death" and "master and slave," the ways in which we can fail to cooperate in allowing each other to live as equal selves. Hegel's book reveals that violence and power struggles do not exclusively obtain in the relations between fully developed selves – between "egos" – but that such violence and struggles for power are inherent to and constitutive of the very concept of self-conscious experience. In describing these power struggles that characterize the dialectic of recognition by which we cooperatively establish our sense of ourselves, Hegel's *Phenomenology* also demonstrates (in keeping with the demand of phenomenology that it bear witness to the intrinsic dialectic of the experience under observation) that such situations of unequal recognition reveal their own inadequacy and point, from within themselves, to the need to establish a situation of equal recognition.

Our experience is inherently intersubjective, that is, "what appears" is "other people." We saw above that what it takes to recognize "now" was a perspective attuned to a more sophisticated rationality than simply the "logic of immediacy." Analogously, Hegel's description here points to the complex demands of recognizing another person. Recognizing another person *as such* requires understanding, compassion, and respect, and these attitudes themselves can be meaningfully enacted only in a shared context of communication (language) and cooperative living (law): if, for example, we do not understand language, we cannot appreciate what another person presents; if we do not establish a context of law, another person cannot come into his or her being as a person. There are, in other words, perceptual, behavioral, and material conditions that must be met in order for the other person to be able to appear as such. With this recognition we see that the project of phenomenology itself comes to impinge upon us practically as well as theoretically. What the object prescribes for its adequate recognition – what it takes for us to carry out our project of description – is our practical acceptance of our answerability to the demands of other persons.

This situation of equal recognition – the situation of a cooperative enactment of a situation in which we each recognize ourselves and others as an integrated community of equals – is what Hegel calls "*Geist*," "spirit," "the I that is we and the we that is I."[42] It is this domain of "spirit" that provides the fundamental context for the bulk of our experience – it is our basic "home" – and, as the title "Phenomenology of Spirit" suggests, it is the primary project of the book to describe this reality of "spirit," this definitive character of our experience.[43] The *Phenomenology* is as much the recognition of an ongoing imperative to realize this community as it is a description of its already accomplished form.

The dialectic of recognition establishes the fundamental parameters of our identity. Identity, however, is always something "reflected" in Hegel's language, that is, it is always something turned back on itself, something defined as a kind of response or interpretation. The identity may be the "truth" of something, but precisely by being the truth "of something" that truth points to a something of which it is the truth, that is, it points to the immediacy of which it is the truth, of which it is the essence.[44] It is indeed in inhabiting an identity that we first experience ourselves as someone specific and determinate in relation to others. Yet in inhabiting this identity, we can also experience a sense that "this is not enough," that something in us has been betrayed. We can precisely experience ourselves as living from an immediacy that is lost in our established identities, the immediacy of our singularity as a desiring being. There is, then, within identity, always a voice calling that very identity into question, and calling us to an originating source beyond the neatly resolved, systematic character of our social identity. The experience of the challenge to the limits of our established identity can also take the form of an experience of a "higher calling," a sense of the possibility of a meaning beyond even desire and community. This sense that the identity established in the dialectic of recognition is circumscribed by a higher calling is described by Hegel in the dialectic of what he calls "the Unhappy Consciousness."[45]

A community – spirit – is always realized in a determinate and therefore limited form. It is through the collective embrace of a particular language and the historical establishing of laws and other institutions that a system of equal recognition is realized, but such laws and language are always determinate, always the specific institutions of *this* community, and therefore inherently finite, that is, inherently exclusive of other communities and other individuals.[46] As developed, integrated members of such a community, we can experience the limitations of this finitude, and, though our community is itself a way of answering to our exposure to others – it is a way of being open to others and thus a fulfillment of the project of equal recognition – we can, like Socrates, Mohammed, or Luther, recognize that in establishing a settled way of doing things it also encourages a complacency and a closedness to other possibilities. Within our identities, we can precisely experience a call from beyond our identities, that is, we can recognize an exposure to an infinite not adequately realized by our finite identities.[47]

58

What Hegel calls "Unhappy Consciousness" is the recognition of this exposure to a source of meaning that in principle will never be addressed adequately by any finite system of identity: beyond the other that is the infinite real object, beyond the other that is the infinity of desire, beyond the other that is another infinite self-consciousness, we are exposed to the other "as such," the other that is the infinite giving power behind experience as such.

These different imperative infinites – the infinity of the real, of singular subjectivity, of others, and of the Other – all conflict; that is, practices of recognizing one are not automatically practices of recognizing the others, and our experience is the space of contestation between these different principles. The lives of individuals testify to the fact that these demands do not automatically speak with a single voice but instead invite us – tempt us, perhaps – to various ways in which we can commit ourselves one-sidedly to one or the other of these definitive dimensions of meaning; such one-sided lives are found in the rational agents of "Pleasure and Necessity," "Virtue and the Way of the World," "The Spiritual Animal Kingdom," in "Ethical" agents such as Antigone and Creon, in "Cultured" agents such as the "Noble Consciousness," the "Wit," and the "believing consciousness," in moral agents such as the "Hard-Hearted Judging Consciousness," and in other figures described throughout the *Phenomenology*.[48] The imperative the phenomenology puts upon us is to enact in our experience a reconciliation of these imperatives. The later sections of the *Phenomenology of Spirit* – Reason, Spirit, Religion, Absolute Knowing – deal with various experiences that are precisely attempts to acknowledge the necessity of the reconciliation of the infinities of consciousness with the infinities of self-consciousness and to enact this reconciliation. Ultimately, the demand will be realized in an experience that, operating within the terms of the real, realizes the imperative to community while also answering to the imperative of "the Good as such" – the divine, the Other – and this within the imperative to be a finite, desiring, singular self.

Finally, with this experience of Unhappy Consciousness, we have returned to the standpoint with which the project of the *Phenomenology* begins. Phenomenology is the project of bearing witness to the given dimensions of meaning, the parameters of experience that can only be described, not deduced, a project that itself produces the recognition that our nature as self-conscious subjects – as experiencers in a real world of other people – is fulfilled only in giving ourselves over to the project of giving voice to the self-presentation of the absolute.

Hegel and Witnessing to the Traces of Unacknowledged Absolutes

So let us return now to Hegel's phenomenology and to the simple question, "What is the immediate form of experience?" or "What appears?" What is the given form of experience? On the one hand, we undergo our experience as knowers, that is, we experience the world as presented to us as an object. This world floods our senses, is itself articulated into a manifold of independently existing things, and holds itself together as a single unity. This is the world to which our cognition answers – our consciousness is to be determined by it. On the other hand, we are subjects, and our subjectivity floods our experience, articulated into the manifold desires that give meaning to the things of the world, defining the terms of the unity of our experience. Within this world of desire, the gaze of the other floods in upon us, and we are constitutively drawn to answer to it and to participate in a world of language, companionship, community, tradition, and law. Within our experience as members of the community, we are called beyond the finite determinateness of our established human world to realize the possibilities that exceed that world, an experience often identified as the flooding in of the divine. Our experience is shaped by the contestation of these inexhaustible, infinite dimensions of experience to which we are inherently exposed, these irreducible dimensions of meaning within our experience.

The world is the setting in which we are torn by the imperative force of all these many directions – called to objective knowledge, drawn to self-interested action, commanded to answer to the needs of others, and summoned to bear witness to the Other – and these different imperatives conflict, each claiming absolute authority. Our experience is the ongoing negotiation with these multiple, given absolutes to which we are intrinsically exposed. Kant's *Critique of Pure Reason* focuses on the infinity that is constitutive of the imperative of objectivity that operates within our experience of ourselves as knowers. And as Kant began to acknowledge in his *Critique of Practical Reason*, in all these other dimensions as well, in our experience of ourselves, of others, and of the Other, we experience comparable infinites – irreducible and unsurpassable dimensions of our experience that are given in experience as exceeding our experience – and Hegel's *Phenomenology*, in describing the self-showing of experience, particularly reveals, displays, and demonstrates the overlaying of these mutually conflicting infinites, these mutually conflicting imperatives.

Our experience always takes the form of answering to the commanding force of an absolute, of an infinite that gives itself as self-authoritative, and the various experiential stances we adopt – now studying the object, now satisfying our desires, now caring for others, now worshipping the divine – are necessarily selective, one-sided enactments of a reconciliation of these conflicting demands that necessarily relativizes and contradicts these absolutes *qua* absolute. Inasmuch as these absolutes are given as intrinsic and pervasive to all experience ("transcendental"), they make their "presence" felt even in those experiences that do not adequately answer to them. *Within* any one-sided enactment of reconciliation, then, a voice of dissatisfaction will express itself: a one-sided experience carries within itself the challenge to its own form, a self-critique in which an indwelling infinite leaves a trace of its insufficient acknowledgment. Thus the thing of perception, which, in its negativity and determinacy is not acknowledged by sense-certainty, shows itself to be implied in the very fact that sense-certainty can recognize passage, that is, can recognize the "of" of the property;[49] or again the "One" of reality as such betrays its essentiality in the unacknowledged but presupposed holding of the many things together in a common field;[50] or the authority and autonomy of another self-consciousness shows itself in the very fact that the master seeks the recognition of the slave in the first place.[51] Hegel's description brings to light the presence within experience of the traces of unacknowledged absolutes that bespeak the insufficiency of the stance of experience to live up to its own intrinsic demands. The success of Hegel's method is its recognition that it is the nature of experience to be this texture of self-opposition:[52] this is not a situation to be *corrected* but is rather the very character of the situation within which we must make meaningful lives.

Our own experience, ultimately, is a finite embrace of these conflicting infinites. Our experience will always be the determinate form of holding them together in an attempted reconciliation. The project of the *Phenomenology* is to unearth the ways in which different determinate forms of experience are one-sided and do not adequately acknowledge one or another of these essential dimensions of meaning.[53] Where does the phenomenology conclude? We have already anticipated the answer to this question in our discussion of the imperative to the reconciliation of the contesting infinites. The phenomenology concludes in the experience that is the acceptance that we are always one-sided appropriations of an infinite that exceeds us and claims us. This acceptance is described in the *Phenomenology of Spirit* as the moral stance of conscience and the philosophical stance of absolute knowing.

The project of the *Phenomenology* points, ultimately, to the stance of conscience, as the self-conscious embrace of the stance of finite answerability to these infinite claims. It is the conscientious agent who recognizes what we have recognized in this analysis, namely, that what is without is within – we are *intrinsically* called to an answerability to the outside. The conscientious agent knows him- or herself to be a singular desiring self, irreducible to any other, but knows him- or herself to be answerable to others. The conscientious agent knows him- or herself to be a member of a community and answerable to it, but also knows this membership to be finite, and therefore to be guilty of realizing inadequately the imperatives of the other and of the Other. The conscientious agent knows that his or her conscience must be enacted within the demands of the real. In short, the conscientious agent recognizes him- or herself in others and makes his or her finite situatedness a site of hospitality to others within-and-without, while simultaneously forgiving him- or herself for the necessity of his or her limitations and forgiving others for their own.[54]

An enactment of conscientious commitment, "absolute knowing" is the ultimate methodological acknowledgment of answerability to the given, and the methodical enactment of this in dialectical, phenomenological method itself. Absolute knowing is this experiencing of ourselves as the agents of the real, as the ones who speak on behalf of the absolute: we are "certain of being all reality" in the sense of recognizing our infinite indebtedness, and recognizing that the absolute must speak here and now.[55]

Conclusion

In the "Transcendental Dialectic" of the *Critique of Pure Reason*, Kant demonstrated that reason unaided by intuition produces conclusions about the nature of reality that do not carry cognitive weight despite their seemingly compelling argumentative force. In his discussion of the "Antinomies of Pure Reason," in particular, he demonstrates the insufficiency of purely discursive constructions – trying to "reason" to ultimate conclusions about the nature of reality – by showing the contradictions these rational arguments produced. Equally compelling arguments can be made, for example, to defend the necessity of free will and the necessity of determinism. Though each side taken by itself seems compelling, seeing the equally compelling character of the argument for the opposed side reveals that reason cannot settle the matter.

In these cases of purely rational argument, we try to *deduce* what reality *must* be like, without any intuitive support for the conclusions we reach. In this way, these rational constructions differ fundamentally from Kant's own method in the "Transcendental Aesthetic" or the "Analytic of Principles," in which he follows the essentially phenomenological method discussed in the section above on "Kant and the Infinite Within-and-Without Experience." This phenomenological method does not speculate about a reality beyond the limits of intuition – it does not *construct* a model of experience – but instead *starts from* the given form of experience, with the imperative to discern its intuitive character, and then to describe the logic *inherent to* it. This is surely a method that requires a great deployment of thought, but it is thought aimed, not at fabricating a model, but at recognizing what is already at play within experience. In this way, the indubitability of what is revealed is assured by the given intuitive ground of those revelations, in contrast to the dubitability that attaches to the contradictory results of purely rational argumentation.

Kant rightly demonstrates that, so to speak, intuition "trumps" discursive *construction* here. Sound philosophical method must think *from* the "found" meaningful forms within experience. That is why Hegel's own method can only be a method of exhortation, and never deduction: Hegel can describe experiences, but it is only the reader's own recognition that he or she is participating in such an experience that gives him or her access to the phenomenon that is the sole source of meaning here.[56] And this is the form Hegel's writing typically takes: he initially describes the phenomenon in question, and only then proceeds to investigate what is revealed in the characteristic process of development of that experience.[57] Like Kant, then, Hegel rejects the method of deduction, and his "method" is at root a method of "intuition": it is a method that requires the most rigorous thought, but it is thought that holds itself answerable to the ways in which experience *reveals its own determinate forms,* ways that can never be predicted but must be experienced. Beyond Kant, however, what Hegel shows is that it is not merely unaided reason that produces contradictions. On the contrary, these indubitable intuitions themselves conflict.

Kant argued that attempting to use reason alone to reach metaphysical conclusions produces contradictory results. In the case of the conclusions of merely rational construction, we can dispense with them as mere temptations. What Hegel shows, however, is that these intuitions that are constitutive of our experience – the infinites to which we are exposed – themselves conflict. In the case of conflicting intuitions we are not free to reject the contradictory results, for *they claim us.* The conflict of intuitions is not evidence of an error in method; rather, it is evidence of a conflict – a contestation – that is definitive of the very nature of meaning, the very nature of experience. The conflict of intuitions is not an error, but is the lived imperative to enact a reconciliation between them within experience.[58] Such a reconciliation, however, is not a removal of the tension, but an embrace of the tension that does not one-sidedly disavow one aspect of the tension. The tension is final – it is constitutive of the nature of experience – and our imperative is to enact forms of experience that acknowledge the equal claim of each side. So, finally, there is the tension between the call of knowing and the call of acting, tension between the call of the I and the call of the we, tension between the infinite call of the beyond and the specific call of this community. We exist as these tensions, as the mutual contestation of these infinities, these absolutes.

Notes

1 On Hegel as completing Kant's "Copernican Revolution," see Hans-Georg Gadamer, "Hegel's Inverted World" in *Hegel's Dialectic: Five Hermeneutical Studies*, P. Christopher Smith (trans.) (New Haven: Yale University Press, 1976), and Robert C. Solomon, "Hegel's *Phenomenology of Spirit*," Chapter 6 of *The Age of German Idealism (Routledge History of Philosophy*, Volume 6), ed. Robert C. Solomon and Kathleen M. Higgins (London and New York: Routledge, 1993), 181. See also H. S. Harris, *Hegel's Ladder I: The Pilgrimmage of Reason* (Indianapolis: Hackett, 1997), 3–4, on the relationship between Kant's philosophy and the emergence of the project of the *Phenomenology of Spirit*. See especially p. 4: "The *Phenomenology* begins with a justification of the Kantian theoretical philosophy of Understanding; then, after a critical destruction of Kant's practical standpoint (in *Phenomenology* IV-V), we come to a 'history of mankind' (in Chapter VI) which establishes the absolute (or 'divine') standpoint." This interpretation resonates strongly with I what I will say below.

2 G.W.F. Hegel, *Phänomenologie des Geistes*, ed. H.-F. Wessels and H. Clairmont (Hamburg: Felix Meiner Verlag, 1988), 68, 28; translated into English by A. V. Miller as *Phenomenology of Spirit* (Oxford: Oxford University Press, 1977), paragraphs 88, 36. Subsequent textual references will be given to the paragraph number of the English translation (M) and to the pagination of the German text (W/C). All translations of this work are taken from Miller's text.

3 See M71, W/C 52–53.

4 Compare the definitive sense of "Islam": "The word *Islam* means 'the willing and active recognition of and submission to the Command of the One, Allah'" (David Waines, *An Introduction to Islam* (Cambridge: Cambridge University Press, 1995), 3). Compare also the notion of "bhakti" – devotional self-surrender – in the Shvetashvatara Upanishad, and of central importance to the Bhagavad-Gita. Karen Armstrong, in *The Great Transformation: The Beginning of Our Religious Traditions* (Toronto: Vintage Canada, 2007), helpfully discusses the etymology of this word in a way that underlines the logic of this relation to the absolute: "The word *bhakti* is complex. Some scholars believe that it comes from *bharij*, "separation": people become aware of a gulf between them and the divine, and yet, at the same time, the god of their choice slowly detached himself from the cosmos he created and confronted them person to person. Other scholars believe that the word relates to *bhaj* – to share, participate in – as the yogin in Shvetashvatara becomes one with Lord Rudra" (p. 430). The ambiguity in the etymology nicely captures the different dimensions that characterize one's adopting the position – as artist, religious person, or philosopher – of giving voice to the absolute. Hegel's explicit study of this relationship is found in the section of the *Phenomenology* entitled, "The Unhappy Consciousness"; see especially M210, for the discussion of the threefold logic of this relationship.

5 Compare as well, "In every block of marble I see a statue as plain as though it stood before me, shaped and perfect in attitude and action. I have only to hew away the rough walls that imprison the lovely apparition to reveal it to the other eyes as mine see it."

6 M1, W/C 3.

7 For the theme of art, religion, and philosophy as the forms of consciousness of the absolute, see Hegel, *The Philosophy of Mind, Being Part III of the Encyclopaedia of the Philosophical Sciences*, trans. William Wallace (Oxford: Clarendon Press, 1971), Sections 553–577. See especially Section 572.

8 Hegel's phenomenology is thus a form of empiricism. Compare Tom Rockmore's discussion of Hegel's "tertiary empiricism," in *Cognition: An Introduction to Hegel's Phenomenology of Spirit* (Berkeley: University of California Press, 1997), 197.

9   M90, W/C 69.

10 M106–107, W/C 75.

11 M3, W/C 5.

12 When a disdain for rigorous thinking is put forth as an attempt "to philosophize in a true and holy manner," "when [such minds] give themselves up to the uncontrolled ferment of substance [and] imagine that by drawing a veil over self-consciousness and surrendering understanding they become the beloved of God to whom He gives wisdom in sleep, ... what they in fact receive, and bring to birth in their sleep, is nothing but dreams" (M10). Giving oneself over to the subject matter is not as easy as simply abandoning oneself, for this lack of rigor produces only what is arbitrary.

13 See M83, W/C 64 for the idea that we already possess the object of our investigation. See also M26–7, W/C 19–22: "[T]he individual has the right to demand that science should at least provide him with the ladder to this [scientific] standpoint, should show him this stand-point within himself. ... Science must therefore unite this element of self-certainty with itself, or rather show *that* and *how* this element belongs to it. ... It is this coming to be of *Science as such* or of *knowledge*, that is described in this *Phenomenology* of Spirit."

14 M5, W/C 6.

15 M1–29, W/C 3–24, basically articulate the project of the phenomenology from the point of view of science. See also M17, W/C 13–14, on the insufficiency of the individual stand-point: "In my view [Es kömmt nach meiner Einsicht], which can be justified only by the exposition of the system itself ... [welche sich durch die Darstellung des Systems selbst rechtfertigen muß ...]."

16 M53, W/C 39.

17 On the theme of the openness integral to Hegel's project, compare Catherine Malabou's discussion of Hegel's concept of "plasticity" throughout *L'avenir de Hegel: Plasticité, Temporalité, Dialectique* (Paris: Vrin, 1996), translated by Lisabeth During as *The Future of Hegel: Plasticity, Temporality, Dialectic* (New York: Routledge, 2005). See also the online review of this book by William Dudley, *Notre Dame Philosophical Reviews*, October 5, 2006.

18 M134–135, 145, W/C 94–95, 102.

19 M113–114, W/C 80–81.

20 On the logic of immediacy or being, see Stephen Houlgate, *The Opening of Hegel's Logic: From Being to Infinity* (Purdue University Press, 2005). For the logic of immediacy as it first emerges in Hegel's *Logic*, see Dieter Henrich, "Anfang und Methode der Logik," in *Hegel im Kontext*, ed. Dieter Henrich (Frankfurt am Main: Suhrkamp Verlag, 1971), 73–94; for the logic of reflexion as it first emerges in Hegel's *Logic*, see Dieter Henrich, "Hegels Logik der Reflexion. Neue Fassung," in *Die Wissenschaft der Logik und die Logik der Reflexion*, ed. Dieter Henrich, *Hegel-Studien*, Beiheft 18 (Bonn: Bouvier Verlag, 1978), 203–324. M37 and 48 discuss the nature of logic in relation to the *Phenomenology*.

21 This is what Fichte identifies as the first principle of experience; see Johann Gottlieb Fichte, *Science of Knowledge*, ed. and trans. Peter Heath and John Lachs (Cambridge: Cambridge University Press, 1982), Part I, "Fundamental Principles of the Entire Science of Knowledge," Section 1, "First, Absolutely Unconditioned Principle," 94–102.

22 M17, W/C 13–14, and M37, W/C 28–29, discuss the project of the *Phenomenology* in terms of the recognition of truth as both substance and subject. See also M26, W/C 19, for the notion of "pure self-recognition in absolute otherness," and the discussion in M54, W/C 41, of "pure self-identity in otherness." On the logic of the concept, see Jean Hyppolite, *Logique et Existence* (Paris: Presses Universitaires de France, 1952), translated into English by Leonard Lawlor and Amit Sen as *Logic and Existence* (Albany: State University of New York Press, 1997). Hyppolite's construal of the concept as "sens" and "love" (*Logic and Existence*, 4–5, 19) is accurate and helpful. Note, too, his claim (*Logic and Existence*, 170–171) that

the Doctrine of Being corresponds to the Transcendental Aesthetic, the Doctrine of Essence to the Transcendental Analytic, and the Doctrine of the Concept to the Transcendental Dialectic. Compare also Jean Hyppolite, *Genèse et Structure de la Phénoménologie de l'Esprit de Hegel* (Paris: Éditions Montaigne, 1946), Volume 1, pp. 142–148. For an introduction to Hegel's logic in general, see John Burbidge, *The Logic of Hegel's Logic: An Introduction* (Broadview Press, 2006).

23 See G.W.F. Hegel, *The Philosophy of History*, trans. J. Sibree (New York: Dover, 1956), 9–11, especially 11: "To him who looks upon the world rationally, the world in its turn presents a rational aspect."

24 See M87, W/C 67–68, on phenomenology as the perspective that recognizes the transitions between different stances of consciousness. See M796–8, W/C 521–523, on the completion of the project in the stance of the phenomenologist who recognizes the lesson *of the path of description* undertaken in the *Phenomenology of Spirit*.

25 This is the substance of Kant's discussion of the importance of the "mathematical" categories in the "Axioms of Intuition" and the "Anticipations of Perception" in *Critique of Pure Reason*, A160/B199, A162–176/B202–218. The mathematical categories basically correspond to what Hegel calls a logic of immediacy or "being."

26 This is the substance of Kant's discussion of the importance of the "dynamical" categories in the "Analogies of Experience" and in the "Postulates of Empirical Thought" in *Critique of Pure Reason*, A160/B199, A176–235/B218–294. The dynamical categories basically correspond to what Hegel calls a logic of reflection or "essence."

27 *Critique of Pure Reason*, A25/B39–40.

28 *Critique of Pure Reason*, A20–22, 26/B34–36, 42.

29 *Critique of Pure Reason*, A28/B24.

30 *Critique of Pure Reason*, A23/B38 (emphasis added).

31 *Critique of Pure Reason*, A106–108, 116, and B131–132. This is also Fichte's "first principle"; see note 21, above.

32 Because the transcendental "I" is accessible only to thought and has no empirical presentation, Kant himself refuses to designate this an "intuition." Fichte, on the contrary, describes this recognition as precisely an "intellectual intuition" because its significance has the character of something *found*, rather than something constructed. Like Fichte, I will use the language of "intuition" to describe the recognition of the transcendental "I."

33 This is the focus of the "Paralogisms of Pure Reason."

34 My language of "substance" and "subject" here is drawn from Hegel, not Kant. While Kant explicitly associates "infinity" with space, this is not his language in his own discussion of what he calls "substance," and it is not obvious that he would choose this term as a description of the pure "I."

35 Compare Fichte's second principle of all experience: *Science of Knowledge*, "Second Principle, Conditioned as to Content," 102–105.

36 M160–165, W/C 114–119. I have developed my interpretation of Hegel's description of "Consciousness" in "Reading: Derrida in Hegel's Understanding," *Research in Phenomenology* 36 (2006): 181–200. For a sustained study of the relationship of Hegel's philosophy to Kant's epistemology, see Robert B. Pippin, *Hegel's Idealism: The Satisfactions of Self-Consciousness* (Cambridge: Cambridge University Press, 1989).

37 *Critique of Pure Reason*, A444–453, B472–481.

38 M166–167, W/C 120–122. On the nature of desire, see David Ciavatta, "Hegel on Desire's Knowledge," *The Review of Metaphysics* 61 (2008): 527–554.

39 See M174, W/C 125–126. This language is how Schelling describes the situation in *System of Transcendental Idealism (1800)*, Introduction, Section 3, "Preliminary Deduction of Transcendental Philosophy."

40 See M178–185, W/C 127–129 for the definitiveness of recognition for the dialectic of self-consciousness. On the primacy of the theme of recognition (*Anerkennung*) for Hegel's *Phenomenology*, see Robert R. Williams, *Recognition: Fichte and Hegel on the Other* (Albany: State University of New York Press, 1992), and Andreas Wildt, *Autonomie und Anerkennung: Hegels Moralitätskritik in Lichte seiner Fichte-Rezeption* (Stuttgart: Klett-Cotta, 1982).

41 Compare Richard Dien Winfield, "Commentary on Hegel's Concept of *Geist*," in *Hegel's Philosophy of Spirit*, ed. Peter G. Stillman (Albany: State University of New York Press, 1987), 22: "Hegel understands consciousness to be the very concrete structure that can only be conceived as the embodied awareness of a living individual inhabiting a world of nature common to others."

42 M177, 351, 439, W/C 127, 235–236, 288–289. See also M69, W/C 50–51.

43 M440, 352, W/C 289–290, 236. J. N. Findlay, *Hegel: A Re-examination* (London: George Allen and Unwin, 1958), 39–47, helpfully interprets Hegel's notion of *Geist* as a descendent of Kant's transcendental ego, as I am arguing here; while I think Findlay's account is imperfect, it nonetheless contains considerable insight.

44 G.W.F. Hegel, *Science of Logic*, trans. A. V. Miller (New York: Humanities Press, 1976), 389: "The truth of *being* is *essence*."

45 See Jean Wahl, *Le malheur de la conscience dans le philosophie de Hegel* (Paris: Rieder, 1929), on the ultimacy of unhappy consciousness, and also H. S. Harris's comprehensive discussion of this section of the *Phenomenology* in *Hegel's Ladder I*, 395–436. For a useful discussion of this history of the interpretation of Unhappy Consciousnes in French philosophy that is misrepresentative of Hegel but helpful in its understanding of the French interpreters of Hegel, see Bruce Baugh, *French Hegel: From Surrealism to Postmodernism* (New York: Routledge, 2003).

46 M354, W/C 236–237.

47 See M355, 441, W/C 237, 290.

48 These figures appear, respectively, in M360–366, 381–393, 397–418, 464–476, 500–526, 531–537, 661–669, W/C 240–244, 251–259, 261–277, 304–316, 331–348, 352–355, 434–440.

49 M107, 113, W/C 75, 80–81.

50 M134–5, W/C 94–95.

51 M192–193, W/C 133–134.

52 See M89, W/C 68.

53 Compare the idea, discussed in M24, W/C 18, that the method of dialectic is such that the "refutation" of a position is the same as its "development" into its own truth.

54 M669–671, W/C 440–442. For the interpretation of Hegel's descriptions of conscience and forgiveness, see Jay Bernstein, "Confession and Forgiveness: Hegel's Poetics of Action," in *Beyond Representation: Philosophy and Poetic Imagination*, ed. Richard Eldredge (New York: Cambridge University Press, 1996); "Conscience and Transgression: The Exemplarity of Tragic Action," in *Hegel's Phenomenology of Spirit: A Reappraisal*, ed. G. K. Browning (London: Kluwer, 1997), 79–97; and Shannon Hoff, "Law, Right, and Forgiveness: The Remains of Antigone in the *Phenomenology of Spirit*," in *Philosophy Today* 50 (2006): 31–38. See also Kym Maclaren, "The Role of Emotion in an Existential Education: Insights from Hegel and Plato," *International Philosophical Quarterly*, 48 (2008): 471–492.

55 M793–8, W/C 519–523. For an interpretation of Hegel's conception of absolute knowledge, see John Burbidge, "Hegel's Absolutes," *Owl of Minerva* 29 (1997): 23–37. On the theme of the self-showing of the absolute, compare Hyppolite, *Logic and Existence*, 74. On the theme of enacting the absolute here and now, compare the discussion of "Here is your Rhodes, here is your jump" in G.W.F. Hegel, *Elements of the Philosophy of Right*, trans. Allen W. Wood (Cambridge: Cambridge University Press, 1991), 21.

56 Compare Fichte, *Science of Knowledge*, p. 91: "The Science of Knowledge should in no way *force* itself upon the reader, but should *become a necessity* for him, as it has for the author himself." Compare William Maker, "Does Hegel Have a Dialectical Method?" *Southern Journal of Philosophy* 20 (1982): 75–96.

57 He contributes the recognition that the next phenomenon lives up to the logic of the last; we must do the same, recognizing in our own experience that we are already have an intuition of the phenomenon Hegel points to that resolves the contradiction of the preceding shape of consciousness. Hegel cannot supply this recognition for us; what he can do is educate our expectations, preparing us for this recognition, exhorting us to acknowledge what is already appearing, and inspiring us to be open to self-transformation.

58 Compare Fichte's third principle of all experience: *Science of Knowledge*, "Third Principle, Conditioned as to Form," 105–119.

3

Self-Consciousness, Anti-Cartesianism, and Cognitive Semantics in Hegel's 1807 *Phenomenology*

KENNETH R. WESTPHAL

1. Introduction

This chapter seeks to answer two questions important to understanding the aims, structure, results and significance of Hegel's analysis of "Self-Consciousness" in the 1807 *Phenomenology*. Franco Chiereghin (2009, 55–58) notes the apparent oddity that Hegel explicates his own concept of thought (*Denken*) only after examining the Lord and Bondsman (in §A), in the introduction to §B, "The Freedom of Self-Consciousness." Chiereghin explicates Hegel's concept of thought and provides several important reasons why Hegel explicates his concept of thought at this specific juncture. Here I aim to augment Chiereghin's answer to the question, why Hegel explicates his concept of thought only at this juncture, in order to answer a further question: If Hegel's 1807 *Phenomenology* is to examine – and indeed to establish – the reality of absolute knowing[1] by examining a "complete" series of forms of consciousness (*PhdG* 56.36–7/¶79), why and with what justification, if any, does he omit the familiar Cartesian ego-centric predicament, according to which we know our own thoughts, feelings and sensory contents, though nothing about any physical or natural world "outside" ourselves?[2]

Answering these questions requires examining, if briefly, Hegel's semantics of singular cognitive reference (§2) and how he presents and justifies this semantics in "Consciousness" (§3) and in §A of "Self-Consciousness" (§4). These points afford an illuminating answer to the second question, why the Cartesian ego-centric predicament does not appear in the series of forms of consciousness examined in the 1807 *Phenomenology* (§5). Here I cannot reconstruct Hegel's analysis in "Self-Consciousness" in detail; instead I highlight some important aspects of Hegel's analysis which have not yet received their due.[3] Here I can provide only a conspectus; I submit that it becomes much more telling when we consider in detail the experiences of the relevant forms of consciousness, for as Harris notes (1997, 1:54), Hegel's phenomenological " 'Science of experience' is meant to be the remedy for 'formalism' of *all* kinds."

A Companion to Hegel, First Edition. Edited by Stephen Houlgate and Michael Baur.
© 2011 Blackwell Publishing Ltd. Published 2011 by Blackwell Publishing Ltd.

2. Hegel's Semantics of Singular Cognitive Reference

Analytic philosophy began by raising semantics, as the analysis of conceptual or linguistic meaning and reference, to the rank of first philosophy, thus supplanting both prior claimants to that rank, metaphysics and epistemology respectively. Following Gettier's (1963) devastating critique of contemporaneous, anti-naturalistic epistemology – an epistemology which rested entirely on conceptual analysis and hence dismissed concerns about our actual cognitive functioning – analytic philosophy has developed a variety of significant criticisms of Cartesianism. Yet the aim of analytic philosophy to supplant epistemology through semantics persists, for example, in the work of Davidson and Brandom.

Yet all of these interesting developments have occurred while disregarding that the first great anti-Cartesian was Kant, who already recognized that resolving key epistemological issues requires a sound semantics of specifically *cognitive* reference to particular spatio-temporal objects or events.[4] The centrality of cognitive semantics to Kant's *Critique of Pure Reason* is evident in statements such as this:

> It is possible experience alone that can give our concepts reality; without it, every concept is only an idea, without truth and reference to [*Beziehung auf*] an object. Hence the possible empirical concept was the standard by which it had to be judged whether the idea is a mere idea and thought-entity or instead encounters its object in the world. (*KdrV* B517, tr. Guyer and Wood)

Following Tetens, Kant means by the "reality" of a concept the real possibility of its referring to one or more specifiable spatio-temporal objects or events (henceforth: "particulars"). Kant's express attention to the issue, whether our concepts can or under what conditions they do "connect" or refer to (*sich beziehen auf*) objects, indicates his central concern with issues of singular reference, *i.e.* determinate reference to specific particulars. Kant's contention that our concepts can only be referred to specific particulars in cognitive judgments in which we identify those particulars indicates his concern with specifically *cognitive* reference to particulars. Kant's critique of Leibniz in the "Amphiboly of the Concepts of Reflection" shows that descriptions alone cannot secure singular cognitive reference because no matter how specific or detailed a description (or analogously any combination of concepts in a proposition or judgment) may be, this conceptual specificity alone cannot determine whether this description is empty, definite or ambiguous because it refers to no, only to one or to several particulars. Whether a description refers at all, and if so, to how many particulars, is equally a function of the contents of the world. Accordingly, securing singular *cognitive* reference requires also locating the relevant particulars within space and time. Locating these particulars requires singular sensory presentation, either directly (simple perception) or indirectly (observational instruments).

One central result of Kant's "Transcendental Aesthetic" and "Amphiboly" is nicely formulated by Evans:

> [T]he line tracing the area of [ascriptive] relevance delimits that area in relation to which one or the other, but not both, of a pair of contradictory predicates may be chosen. And

69

that is what it is for a line to be a boundary, marking something off from other things. (Evans 1985, 36; cf. 34–37)

Evans' analysis shows that specifying the relevant boundary for the use of either member of a pair (or set) of contrary (*i.e.*, mutually exclusive) predicates is only possible by specifying the region relevant to the manifest characteristic in question, and vice versa, where this region will be either co-extensive with or included within the spatio-temporal region occupied by some particular. Hence predication requires conjointly specifying the relevant spatio-temporal region and some manifest characteristics of any particular we self-consciously experience or identify. I shall call this the "Evans Thesis."

Kant recognized that these conjoint specifications may be rough and approximate. More importantly, he recognized that spatio-temporal designation of, and ascription of manifest characteristics to, any particular are *conjoint, mutually interdependent*, specifically *cognitive* achievements which integrate sensation ("sensibility") and conception ("understanding"). Both are required to sense, to identify and to integrate the various characteristics of any particular we sense into a *percept* of it, which requires distinguishing it from its surroundings by identifying the spatio-temporal region it occupies along with at least some of its manifest characteristics.[5] Integrating the sensed characteristics of any one particular, and distinguishing them from those of other particulars in its surroundings, requires perceptual synthesis which is guided in part by a priori concepts of "time," "times," "space," "spaces," "I," "object," "individuation" and "cause."[6]

Hegel recognized the great importance of Kant's semantics of singular cognitive reference. He further recognized that most of Kant's central results in the *Critique of Pure Reason*, both theoretical and practical, can be justified by Kant's cognitive semantics without invoking Kant's transcendental idealism. Indeed Hegel argues for Kant's semantics of singular cognitive reference far more directly than Kant, beginning in "Sense Certainty" with his internal critique of putative aconceptual knowledge of particulars, now familiar as Russell's "knowledge by acquaintance."[7]

3. Hegel's Justification of His Semantics of Singular Cognitive Reference in "Consciousness"

Hegel develops his semantics of singular cognitive reference beginning in "Sense Certainty."[8] Sense Certainty holds that sensation is sufficient and conception unnecessary for our knowledge of spatio-temporal particulars, for example, the night, this tree, that house. All it claims about any particular it knows is that "*it is*" (*PhdG* 63.17/¶91). It cannot articulate any more specific claim without conceding the role of concepts within sensory knowledge. However, the abstractness of its cognitive claim reveals that Sense Certainty can be neither a commonsense nor a tenable view. Because its cognitive claim is so abstract, it is falsified by the passage of time, during which either sensed particulars themselves change or we shift the focus of our sensory attention. Obviously we all know how to distinguish among and to designate various particulars and our various sensory experiences of them. So doing, however, requires our possession and competent use of concepts of "time" and of "times," that is, periods of time during which any particular is experienced. Hegel makes analogous points about the roles of the concepts "space" and "spaces" (regions of space) by considering a shift in attention from a tree to a house (*PhdG* 65.24–30/¶98). We know how to distinguish trees from houses and how to keep track of their respective locations and viewings. Hegel's point is that this commonsense know-how is not merely sensory; it requires competent (if implicit) use of the concepts of "space" and "spaces" (regions of space) to designate and mentally coordinate the locations of the various particulars we sense on various occasions.

To maintain its core view Sense Certainty now (in the second phase of its phenomenological examination) maintains that within the context of each of its *own* cognitive claims, its knowledge of its object is immediate, direct and aconceptual (*PhdG* 66.7–8, .12–15/¶¶100, 101). Regarding this retrenchment Hegel observes that one person claims "I see a tree" while another claims "I see a house, not a tree" (*PhdG* 66.17–19/¶101). Both claims are equally legitimate, and yet "one truth vanishes in the other" (*PhdG* 66.21/¶101). Why? These two claims appear inconsistent with each other only if one fails to distinguish among subjects of knowledge who make various claims. This is Hegel's point: the strictly aconceptual, entirely sensory model of knowledge of particulars espoused by Sense Certainty provides neither an account of, nor even a basis for, our doing what we all commonsensically do, namely, to distinguish our own perceptual claims from those of others, in part by self-reference using the first-person pronoun "I." This capacity is not, Hegel here shows, simply sensory; it is also a conceptual ability based in our recognizing that any specific use of the term "I" in sensory knowledge is significant and can be understood only by recognizing that its use presumes that the speaker serves as the point of origin of an implicit spatio-temporal framework, reference to which is required to identify the relevant spatio-temporal region designated by the speaker when designating sensed particulars. In this way, Hegel makes the complementary point about "I" which he made previously about "this," "now" and "here."

Sense Certainty attributes these difficulties to its attempt to export its cognitive claims to others outside its own cognitive context. Accordingly in the third phase of its phenomenological examination it holds that aconceptual sensory knowledge of any particular is possible only within any one specific cognitive episode in which it senses that particular, which can be designated solely by ostensive gesture, without using token demonstrative terms (specific uses of, *e.g.*, "this," "that," "now"), nor any other concepts (*PhdG* 67.27–30/¶106). Sense Certainty now grants equal priority to the object and to itself as cognizant subject and stresses that the key point is the direct, immediate cognitive relation it (purportedly) has to its object (*PhdG* 67.12–15/¶104). By disregarding other subjects and other instances of knowledge and by seizing upon any one particular cognitive connection, Sense Certainty proposes to avoid problems with spatio-temporal scope and to obtain immediate, aconceptual knowledge of some one sensed particular. Hegel's main critical point is that scope problems are neither avoided nor resolved by recourse to ostensive gestures. The punctual here and now neither contains nor specifies any sensed particular, while any extended here and now which can contain or designate a sensed particular requires specifying conceptually the relevant region of space and period of time in which that particular is located and sensed, where any region of space contains an indefinite plurality of punctual "heres" and any period of time contains an indefinite plurality of momentary, vanishing "nows" (*PhdG* 68.29–33/¶108). In our sensory knowledge ostention cannot be pointilistic, though if sense certainty is tenable it must be (*PhdG* 68.18–20/¶107). Our cognitive use of ostention, too, has sense only within a presupposed, implicit yet conceptually structured spatio-temporal framework within which the cognizant subject occupies the point of origin.[9]

In conclusion Hegel considers one last, desperate effort by exponents of aconceptual sensory knowledge of particulars (i.e., naive realists) to preserve the mutual independence of sensation and conception in our sensory knowledge of particulars (Westphal 2002/2003b). To designate the spatio-temporal particulars she claims to know, the naive realist now describes them. Beginning with the hopelessly indefinite "absolutely individual thing," which indifferently describes any and every "individual thing," she then improves this with, for example, "this bit of paper," though any and every bit of paper is a "this bit of paper"; then she embarks upon the infinite task of exhaustively describing any one particular. Yet no matter how extensive and specific is her description, by itself no description determines whether it is empty, definite or ambiguous. To resolve this problem, the consciousness under observation finally combines its linguistic descriptions with demonstrative reference, thus conceding that *both* are required for, and both are integrated within any actual instance of sensory knowledge of spatio-temporal particulars (*PhdG* 70.21–29/¶110). Once it recognizes the roles of both sensation and conception (including both demonstrative reference and descriptive attribution of sensed qualities) in our sensory knowledge of particulars, the observed consciousness admits the ineliminable role of predication in sensory knowledge and advances to Perception.

Hegel's examination of Perception further supports his semantics of singular cognitive reference by showing that the relation "thing-property" is distinct and irreducible to the quantitative relations "set-member" and "one-many," or to the relation "product-ingredient." Two key aspects of any one perceptible thing, its unity and its plurality of properties, are interdependent; there is no unitary thing without its plurality of properties and there are no properties without some unitary thing to which they are proper. Something is a perceptible thing if and only if it unifies a plurality of properties, and conversely: something is a plurality of properties if and only if they are unified in some one thing. Hegel's demonstration of this conclusion involves showing that only by identifying its properties can we identify any one thing, and conversely, only by identifying that one thing can we identify a plurality of sensed qualities as *its properties*. Hegel thus joins Hume and Kant in recognizing that our perceptual knowledge must solve what in contemporary neuro-psychology is called the perceptual "binding problem": How do we determine whether one and the same particular (instead of several) stimulates, for example, different receptors in the retina, or stimulates different receptors in different sensory modalities? This problem must be solved in order for us to engage in predicative judgments, which are required for perceptual knowledge in the ways identified by Kant, Hegel and Evans, who show that predication requires distinguishing any one sensed particular from its surroundings by identifying its spatial boundary by discriminating some of its manifest characteristics from those of other particulars surrounding it. Hegel's justification of the transition from "Perception" to "Force and Understanding" recognizes, as does Kant, that only through competent (if implicit) use of causal judgments can we identify manifest, sensed characteristics as properties of some one thing which causally integrates and manifests them.

The conclusion to these aspects of Hegel's critique of Sense Certainty and of Perception is tantamount to the Evans Thesis, which concerns predication, a central component of perceptual knowledge. To this thesis Hegel adds that these conceptual abilities are enabled by our possession and competent use of a series of specifically a priori concepts, including "time," "times," "space," "spaces," "plurality" (number and individuation), "I" (oneself) and "object" (thing). Like Kant, Hegel embeds Evans' semantic thesis in a richer epistemological context, because they recognize the distinction between the semantic content of concepts or terms as such (roughly, their intensions or connotations) and the specifically *cognitive* significance concepts or terms (singly or in combination) obtain when they are referred to spatio-temporally localized particulars. This second semantic element is cognitive because only when referred to localized particulars can thoughts, statements or judgments *be* either true or false, and either justified or unjustified. Neither descriptions nor concatenations of concepts (propositions) are even candidates for truth or falsehood unless and until they are referred to specific, localized particulars. This is a key reason why philosophy of language cannot supplant epistemology, and why contemporary philosophers should take very seriously Kant's and Hegel's semantics of singular cognitive reference.

In "Force and Understanding" Hegel makes two key points which are based, in part, on his semantics of singular cognitive reference and which link this semantics with his concept of thought. First, Hegel contends – rightly, I submit – that the very concept of "law-like relations," and likewise the very concept of "force," both require inter-defined factors into which causal phenomena can be analyzed.[10] Hegel contends that adequate scientific explanation provides the sole and sufficient grounds for determining the constitutive characteristics of the objects and events in nature, by providing maximally precise, quantified specification of their constitution, parameters and interrelations, including interactions. An adequate scientific explanation justifies ascribing causal forces to material phenomena because so far as logical, metaphysical or mathematical necessities are concerned, natural phenomena could instantiate any mathematical function whatsoever, different functions at different times or no such function at all. The fact that a natural phenomenon exhibits a mathematical function indicates, as nothing else can, that something in that phenomenon is structured in accord with the mathematical function it exhibits. That "something" is the structure of the causes which generate that phenomenon. Though we may be mistaken about the laws governing the causal structure of phenomena, this is a matter to be determined by empirical investigation, not by metaphysical speculation nor by empiricist skepticism.[11]

Hegel justifies realism about causal forces in part by using his semantics of singular cognitive reference to rule out various empiricist and infallibilist objections to causal realism which stress various "logical gaps" involved in causal realist interpretations of scientific theories. According to these critics, logical gaps in a line of scientific reasoning count as gaps in the cognitive justification (purportedly) provided by that scientific reasoning. Hegel's point to the contrary is that treating logical gaps as cognitive, justificatory gaps presumes infallibilist models of justification which are suited only to formal domains, and not at all to the non-formal domains of empirical (whether commonsense or natural-scientific) or moral knowledge. In non-formal domains mere logical possibilities have no *cognitive* status because they lack reference to any localized particulars. Thus in principle they cannot provide counter-examples to justificatory

73

reasoning in non-formal domains. This basic point of Hegel's semantics of singular cognitive reference undercuts a broad swath of considerations widely held to support anti- or non-realism about causal forces (cf. below, §5).

Furthermore, Hegel's analysis of the integration of general laws with the specific laws they subsume, through the successive re-introduction of specific systems of particulars and their initial conditions, has an important cognitive-semantic component. Hegel contends that statements of general scientific laws, such as Newton's three laws of motion, are expressly and necessarily abstractions. As abstractions, they lack determinate semantic and cognitive content or significance because they lack determinate reference to localized spatio-temporal particulars. Statements of general laws of nature acquire truth values only when they are referred to localized particulars through their complement of more specific laws, theoretical auxiliaries, system parameters, initial conditions, instrumentation and observational or experimental techniques. This important conclusion is a direct implication of Hegel's semantics of singular cognitive reference, according to which neither concepts or descriptions (propositions), nor uncontextualized use of token demonstrative terms, alone suffice for cognitive reference to particulars. Instead, only by integrating conceptual content with contextualized use of token demonstrative terms can we obtain determinate cognitive reference to any particulars.[12]

4.   "Self-Consciousness," Thought, and the Semantics of Singular Cognitive Reference

The basic point of Hegel's explication of thought at the beginning of §B of "Self-Consciousness" is that the content of a thought about an object is instantiated in that object, and nevertheless is *thought*, so that this object is not foreign to the cognizant subject, but rather is the object thought about by that self-conscious subject.[13] This point may appear to be a trivial corollary to Hegel's semantics of cognitive reference. Indeed Hegel states this point already in the penultimate paragraph of "Force and Understanding" (*PhdG* 101.25–7, 101.30–5/¶164). This raises a double question: Why has Hegel not established his cognitive semantics at the end of "Consciousness," and why does he postpone his explication of thought to §B of "Self-Consciousness"? Part of the answer is that in "Consciousness" Hegel demonstrated his semantics of singular cognitive reference and his explication of thought to his philosophical readers, though not yet for the forms of consciousness observed within the *Phenomenology*.

Though correct, this answer is not especially helpful. An adequate answer requires considering Hegel's transitions from "Consciousness" to "Self-Consciousness" and from the latter to "Reason." In the penultimate paragraph of "Force and Understanding" Hegel states the following about consciousness and self-consciousness:

> The necessary progression from the preceding forms of consciousness, to which its true was a thing, something other than itself, expresses just this, not only that the consciousness of a thing is possible only for a self-consciousness, but indeed that this alone is the truth of those forms. However, only for us is this truth available, not yet for the [observed]

consciousness. Initially self-consciousness has become for itself, not yet as unity with consciousness as such. (*PhdG* 102.1–7/¶166)

Here Hegel restates and claims to have demonstrated – to us his readers – the Kantian point that our self-consciousness is necessary for our consciousness of objects. He also claims that the observed form of consciousness now to be introduced as Self-Consciousness does not recognize that human self-consciousness requires consciousness of objects. This suggests that Self-Consciousness mistakes a necessary condition for our consciousness of objects – that we are self-conscious – for a sufficient condition of our consciousness of objects. This indeed is the initial claim to self-sufficiency made by Self-Consciousness.

When introducing Self-Consciousness as an observed form of consciousness Hegel first states his own (Kantian) view:

[I]n fact self-consciousness is the reflection out of the being of the sensible and perceived world, and essentially the return out of *other being*. (*PhdG* 104.7–10/¶167)[14]

Here Hegel adds the complement to his previous claim (that self-consciousness is necessary for our being conscious of objects), that our consciousness of objects is necessary for our being self-conscious. This is Hegel's counterpart to the conclusion of Kant's Refutation of Idealism,[15] though he argues for it by appeal to his semantics of singular cognitive reference, without invoking transcendental idealism (nor Kant's analysis of time-determination). Hegel's method involves establishing his own positive claims through strictly internal, phenomenological critique of forms of consciousness which espouse and seek to substantiate claims opposed to Hegel's. The Thesis of Self-Consciousness is that our self-consciousness does not depend upon our consciousness of particulars; instead, our own self-consciousness suffices to account for the whole range of our experiences of particulars. This is the (purported) "self-sufficiency" of self-consciousness announced in the title of §A of "Self-Consciousness," viz.: "The Self-Sufficiency and Self-Insufficiency of Self-Consciousness; Lord and Bondsman." Though less idiomatic than the standard English rendering, this translation is more literal and more accurate; "independence" and "dependence" too readily connote the social dynamics of the initial struggle for recognition and of the Lord and Bondsman, while distracting us from the circumstance that Hegel discusses these idealized social relations within the context of this more basic issue regarding the purported sufficiency of our self-consciousness to account adequately and exhaustively for our manifest consciousness of particulars, stressed in Hegel's introductory discussion of "The Truth and Self-Certainty" of Self-Consciousness.[16]

Hegel states this core position of Self-Consciousness in these terms:

Through that first moment [of "other-being, *as a being*, or as a *distinguished moment* ... for" self-consciousness], self-consciousness is as *consciousness*, which for it contains the entire breadth of the sensed world; yet at the same time it is as related only to the second moment, the unity of self-consciousness with itself; and herewith it [viz., the entire sensible world] is for self-consciousness something persisting, but which is only *appearance*, or a distinction

KENNETH R. WESTPHAL

which *in itself* lacks being. This opposition between the appearance of this distinction and its truth has, however, only the truth, namely the unity of self-consciousness with itself, as its essence. ... (*PhdG* 104.14–23/¶167)

Hegel reiterates this point in the remainder of this paragraph, where he also indicates that Self-Consciousness aims to substantiate its self-conception as self-sufficient unto itself, even in view of its rich range of sensory experience of the world, so that it can substantiate its fundamental self-identity (*PhdG* 104.24–31/¶167), which it presumes to require the independence of the world of which it is conscious.

This "Self-Sufficiency Thesis," as I shall call it, Hegel must refute in order to establish, both for observed forms of consciousness and for his readers, his concept of thought and his semantics of singular cognitive reference. Hegel designates the self-proclaimed self-sufficiency of self-consciousness with Fichte's phrase, "I am I" (*PhdG* 104.13/¶167). Yet Hegel's use of Fichte's phrase does not restrict Hegel's examination of Self-Consciousness to Fichte's views, nor does it indicate that Hegel examines specifically Fichte's views. Though there are many Fichtean themes and elements in Hegel's examination of "Self-Consciousness" (Chitty 2007, Redding 2008), only in his earliest writings did Fichte venture anything so strong as this Self-Sufficiency Thesis.[17] This is to say, Hegel sets his own agenda in the *Phenomenology of Spirit*; other philosophical views are arrayed as exemplary forms of consciousness espousing the opposed views Hegel critically examines. Even when Hegel shares some of Fichte's issues and aims, most centrally, to demonstrate that theoretical reason is rooted in practical reason,[18] Hegel must devise his own demonstrations of these theses in accord with his much more subtle and stringent standards of justification (cf. Westphal 1998).

It is important to note that the Self-Sufficiency Thesis examined in "Self-Consciousness" is but the first of a series of such theses examined also in "Reason" and "Spirit." This series includes "Stoicism," "Skepticism" and "The Unhappy Consciousness" from §B of "Self-Consciousness" (Chiereghin 2009), the self-sufficiency of rational thought proclaimed as "The Certainty and Truth of Reason" (Ferrini 2009a), the three forms of consciousness considered in "The Actualization of Rational Self-Consciousness through itself" and the three considered in "Individuality which is Real in and for itself" (Pinkard 2009), especially in "The Animal Kingdom of the Spirit." It includes the dogmatic self-assurance of both Creon and Antigone and the presumed sufficiency of rule by edict both in "Legal Status" (J. B. Hoy 2009) and in "Absolute Freedom and the Terror" (Stolzenberg 2009, 203–204). It includes the Enlightenment individualism and the struggle between the Enlightenment and Faith examined in "Self-Alienated Spirit: Enculturation and its Realm of Actuality" (Stolzenberg 2009), along with the varieties of moral individualism examined in "Law-Giving Reason," "Law-Testing Reason" (D. C. Hoy 2009) and "Morality," especially in "Conscience" (Beiser 2009). These forms of presumed individual rational self-sufficiency have precursors in the problem of *petitio principii* and the Dilemma of the Criterion in Hegel's Introduction and to an extent in the second and third phases of "Sense Certainty" (above, §3).[19]

This dense series of distinct individualist theses cannot be examined here, but they are important to note in order to identify the specific aim of Hegel's critique of the Self-Sufficiency Thesis examined in "Self-Consciousness."[20] This thesis, Hegel reiterates at the beginning of §A, is that Self-Consciousness is self-sufficient because it "is enclosed

76

within itself, and contains nothing that is not due to itself" (*PhdG* 110.4–5/¶182). At the outset of the first phase of his phenomenological examination of Self-Consciousness Hegel restates this thesis in these terms:

> Initially self-consciousness is simple being-for-itself, self-identical by the exclusion of eve-rything *other from itself*; to it, its essence and absolute object is *I*; and in this *immediacy*, or in this *being* of its being-for-itself, it is an *individual*. Whatever other object is for it, is as inessential, marked with the character of the negative. (*PhdG* 110:35–111.2/¶186)

Here Hegel characterizes the Self-Sufficiency Thesis in terms broad enough to include the ego-centric predicament, which recalls his strategic reason for considering here this radical view of self-consciousness, namely, to demonstrate that our self-consciousness is possible only if we are also conscious of independently existing particulars (and, ultimately, of other rational agents); I shall call this the "General" Self-Sufficiency Thesis. The range of versions of the Self-Sufficiency Thesis relevant here is suggested in "The Certainty and Truth of Reason," where Hegel associates Fichte's "I am I" not only with Descartes but also with Luther and the rise of natural science.[21] To look ahead in this way helps focus the original question: How, in what way(s) and to what extent does Hegel justify (or at least aim to justify) his own conception of thought by the begin-ning of §B of "Self-Consciousness," and what remains to be done to develop his account of thought into an initial form of Reason?

Answering this question is facilitated by restating the Thesis of Self-Consciousness in this way: in being aware of particulars, Self-Consciousness is only aware of itself; or self-conscious awareness of objects is nothing but a mode of self-consciousness.[22] Very briefly, "Self-Consciousness" examines several practical attempts to substantiate this General Self-Sufficiency Thesis; "Reason" then examines several theoretical attempts to substantiate the same general thesis. Hegel aims to show that, though highly instruc-tive, none of these attempts justifies the General Self-Sufficiency Thesis, nor any specific version of it. Hegel further aims to show that we can be solely aware of ourselves in our awareness of the world, not in the form of Self-Consciousness, but only once we attain the level of Spirit, indeed, the developed, "mediated" form of Spirit presented in "Absolute Knowing."[23]

In this regard two reasons Hegel introduces "desire" into his examination of the general Self-Sufficiency Thesis are especially important. First, experienced particulars appear to exist and have their own characteristics regardless of anyone's self-conscious awareness of them. In view of their apparent independence, Self-Consciousness desires to substantiate its General Self-Sufficiency Thesis. Second, at the outset we have no account of Self-Consciousness's capacities or abilities. Because Self-Consciousness has a task to do (namely, to substantiate the General Self-Sufficiency Thesis despite the apparent independence of the world it experiences), it must be practical. Desire is the most elementary practical structure of human agency. Hegel's phenomenological examination of forms of consciousness must begin with the simplest version of a form of consciousness; only by identifying its manifest shortcomings does it justify more sophisticated successor versions which are then examined. The most direct and simple way to address the apparent independence of particulars is to destroy the evidence of their independence by consuming them (cf. *PhdG* 107.27–8/¶189).

KENNETH R. WESTPHAL

At this point one must wonder, how could this simple point about consumption have anything to do with the philosophical issues with which we began, and especially with the putative ego-centric predicament? Hegel's phenomenological method is designed to challenge his readers with such questions; they are Platonic exercises we must master in order to understand Hegel's *Phenomenology*.[24] Fans of the ego-centric predicament will dismiss Hegel's appeal to desire and consumption as irrelevant. In effect, Hegel's challenge is to ask: Irrelevant to what, or to whom? As did Kant, Hegel realized that to be adequate, a theory of knowledge must be true *of us*; we seek and need to understand *our* knowledge, not that of other kinds of beings. In effect, the Cartesian ego-centric predicament demands that our cognitive capabilities be proven to be trustworthy in any possible environment before trusting them in our own environment. To the contrary, Kant and Hegel sought (in their different ways) to identify our basic cognitive capacities and their attendant incapacities in order to determine the scope, limits and character of human knowledge. Though important traces of the role of our embodiment in enabling us to be self-conscious can be found in Kant's epistemology, Fichte and Hegel (in their different ways) made this a central philosophical task.[25] Hegel undertakes part of this task in "Self-Consciousness." As concerns the ego-centric predicament, part of Hegel's strategy is to develop some key features of a tenable philosophical anthropology which show that the ego-centric predicament is literally inhuman because its model of and presuppositions about knowledge don't hold of human beings (see below, §5).

Desire introduces elementary classification and hence nascent conceptualization of the world, for desiring distinguishes objects which satisfy a desire from those which do not. The experience of desire also teaches a rudimentary lesson in realism: Objects satisfying desires are not conjured up just by desiring them. Those objects exist and have characteristics (*e.g.*, being nutritive, providing shelter) independently of their being desired, while obtaining and using them requires effort. Self-consciousness as desire is wholly inadequate, for it achieves its ends only by destroying its means (the desired object); hence it cannot sustain its own self-consciousness without depending upon both a plethora of new desires and a steady supply of independently existing desired objects to destroy (*PhdG* 107.33–108.6/¶175). Desire is thus shown not to be the essence of self-consciousness, as initially conceived in accord with the Self-Sufficiency Thesis (*PhdG* 107.38–9/¶175).

Desire-fulfilment, like wish-fulfillment – whether the wish that physical objects were not independent of Self-Consciousness, or that its desires were automatically fulfilled by nature – requires willing rather than wishing, and yet Self-Consciousness seeks (wishes, desires) to uphold its Self-Sufficiency Thesis, that it alone is self-sufficient. The awareness of other self-conscious beings, of other persons, is an obvious objection to the Self-Sufficiency Thesis, because awareness of another person is awareness of someone other than oneself who has his or her own thoughts, experience, plans, decisions, and activities, and so is not simply a mode of one's own self-consciousness (*PhdG* 110.35–111.3/¶186). This sets the stage for another attempt to destroy counterevidence to Self-Consciousness's Self-Sufficiency Thesis: the Struggle unto Death. Hegel argues that self-consciousness both requires and is not reducible to biological existence by arguing from the contrapositive. Fighting unto death shows that neither combatant, as a self-conscious being, can simply be identified with a biological organism; it shows that as self-conscious beings we are not merely natural beings, that prestige is a social,

78

not merely a biological, phenomenon. It also shows conversely that as self-conscious beings none of us is independent of biological organisms, namely our own bodies (*PhdG*112.5, 112.21–22/¶¶188, 189).

Yet whoever slays the other self-consciousness again confronts the affront to its Self-Sufficiency Thesis posed by the recalcitrance of natural objects of desire. This motivates another attempt to destroy counter-evidence of another agent's self-sufficiency: the subjugating battle for mastery. The Lord holds the Self-Sufficiency Thesis, claiming that all things are modes of his self-awareness. If he destroys or denies the existence of the subjugated Bondsman, he again confronts the problem of the independence of desired objects from his desires; if he recognizes the Bondsman as another person, he must repudiate his Self-Sufficiency Thesis. The Lord's solution is to use the Bondsman to grapple with recalcitrant objects while denying his self-sufficiency; both parties take the Bondsman as a mere extension of the Lord (*PhdG* 113.10–13/¶190). Yet the Lord solves only part of the problem of desire: by using the Bondsman he evades the independence of desired objects from his desires for them. He does not solve the problems that desiring depends on desired objects for its satisfaction, nor that the satisfaction of a desire terminates that desire (and so terminates that bit of his self-consciousness). The Lord's sense of self-sufficiency (his "being for himself") thus depends both on the recurrence of his desires and on the continuing availability of objects to satisfy them promptly. The Lord's sense of self is thus fleeting and dependent, and thus not genuine self-sufficiency.

The Bondsman must work on independent objects, some of which he cannot directly consume; rather he must transform them and serve them to the Lord. Regarding technique, the Bondsman's formative activity is self-directed and the artifacts he produces are testimony to his enduring skills and efforts. Thus he constructs monuments to his own ingenuity (*PhdG* 115.3–11/¶195). The Bondsman triumphs over the independence of particulars by learning how to use them as raw materials and to make them into artifacts. His designs and efforts are permanent, relative to the transitory character of objects used as raw materials (*PhdG* 115.14–19/¶196). He becomes genuinely self-directing by developing and exercising his control over antecedently independent objects. He finds his initial designs actually embodied in his artifacts, yet his designs are not foreign to him even though they have become embodied. Thus he solves the original aim of self-consciousness: to be conscious of oneself in being conscious of objects. However, this success requires acknowledging the initial independence and recalcitrance of objects as raw materials, and recognizing that the Self-Sufficiency Thesis is tenable only within a very restricted domain of objects, namely one's own artifacts. This destroys the generality and hence the tenability of this version of the Self-Sufficiency Thesis (*PhdG* 116.3–5/¶196).

At the start of §B, "Freedom of Self-Consciousness," Hegel expressly contrasts the outcome of the Lord's experience with that of the Bondsman by crediting the Bondsman with attaining – genuinely, if implicitly and immediately – the level of thought (*Denken*) because the forms of the Bondsman's artifacts are the same as his intelligent designs for them (*PhdG* 117.20–4/¶197). The core idea of "thought," according to Hegel, is that it is structured by concepts, that is, specific forms of thinking instantiated in specific, localized particulars (*PhdG* 117.30–118.12/¶197). Achieving the level of thought results in a new form of Self-Consciousness which is "free" because the particulars it conceives are not foreign others but are cognitively transparent to it, so that

79

in conceiving a particular, Self-Consciousness remains within itself while having that particular for itself even though that particular is numerically distinct from it (*PhdG* 117.3–6, 117.8–12/¶197).[26] Now that the observed consciousness of the Bondsman has in fact attained a concept, Hegel can explicate here his conceptions of thought and of genuine concepts (*Begriffe*). Hegel stresses that this point is essential for understanding his ensuing discussion of Stoicism, Skepticism and the Unhappy Consciousness (*PhdG* 117.12–5/¶197).

Yet the unity of this new form of Self-Consciousness with its object is merely immediate (*PhdG* 117.12–18/¶197). Hegel equates this initial form of free Self-Consciousness with Stoicism, which stresses the "*pure universality*" of thought (Hegel's emphasis); accordingly, Hegel claims, Stoicism is only the concept of freedom, rather than living freedom, because this concept lacks "the fullness of life" (*PhdG* 118.13–15/¶200). The Stoic dictum to "follow nature" subverts the autonomy (and hence the freedom) of thought because it attempts to derive the proper content of thought from an allegedly given nature (*PhdG* 118.22–24/¶200). Insofar as Stoic autonomy avoids this problem, it must determine the content of thought entirely a priori. In so doing, however, it can generate only edifying platitudes, though no criterion of truth. Hence it fails literally to come to terms with the details of everyday reality and so fails to substantiate Self-Consciousness's Self-Sufficiency Thesis (*PhdG* 118.27–31/¶200).

Whereas Stoicism was only the concept of freedom, Pyrrhonian Skepticism, Hegel claims, realizes the concept of freedom.[27] Hegel here uses, indeed stresses, the term "*Realisierung*" (not "*Verwirklichung*," actualization). Tetens defined the term "*realisieren*" to mean "to show that a concept has an object" (cf. above, §2). His definition became common philosophical usage, and was adopted by Kant (Westphal 2004,133). Hegel indicates that the Pyrrhonist is a counterpart to the Bondsman, who actually works on particulars. The Pyrrhonist works by attacking any and all claims to know reality, purporting (*inter alia*) that particulars lack reality, being, truth and knowability because they are neither self-sufficient nor stable. By appealing to the diversity of opinions on any topic and to the Dilemma of the Criterion (Westphal 1998), Pyrrhonists purport to make apparent that all the distinctions drawn by theorists are merely their own conceptualizations (*PhdG* 119.3–25/¶202).

Hegel's attributions clearly allude to the Trope of Relativity, which relies on the Parmenidean "ontological" conception of truth, according to which something is true only if it is unchanging, constant and so eternally self-identical (cf. *PhdG* 120.7, 120.11/¶204). Because this trope can be used against any and all particulars, Pyrrhonism achieves the comprehensive scope lacking from the Lord's desire and consumption and from the Bondsman's artisanship, and it appears to substantiate its independence from and its superiority over the world of appearances, both natural and social. If particulars can be shown not to be self-sufficient, then, perhaps, they are no threat to Self-Consciousness's Self-Sufficiency Thesis. In this way, Pyrrhonism produces its certainty of its own freedom and being-for-self (*PhdG* 120.7–9/¶204). Skeptical *ataraxia* (unperturbedness) is to provide "unchangeable and *truthful*" self-certainty (*PhdG* 120.18–9/¶204; Hegel's emphasis).

For present purposes the most important problems facing Pyrrhonism developed by Hegel are these. Hegel judiciously notes that the Pyrrhonist may exhibit various inconsistencies without admitting to any of them. This is true of observed forms of consciousness generally and is one of Hegel's key reasons for distinguishing between them and our point of view on them as phenomenological observers (Westphal 1989, 103–108). Hegel notes that rather than exhibiting an "unchangeable and truthful" form of self-consciousness, by its own Parmenidean conception of truth as unchangeable being, the Pyrrhonist him- or herself is utterly changeable and hence untruthful because he or she unhesitatingly proposes "not-A" when counter-balancing "A," and just as readily proposes "A" when counter-balancing "not-A," for any claim "A" whatsoever. Though Pyrrhonists purport dispassionately to continue seeking the (Parmenidean) truth, they conduct their lives – non-committal though they may be – according to mere semblances, whether natural or social. Because above all Pyrrhonism is supposed to be a dispassionate, healthy way of life, these practical tensions are grave internal problems. By attaining *ataraxia* only through the *epoché* (suspension) of others' claims to knowledge, Pyrrhonism shows that its proclaimed self-sufficiency is a sham: as in the case of the Lord's desires, Pyrrhonism's most basic method depends upon a steady supply of cognitive claims to neutralize. Though Pyrrhonists artfully avoid uttering any commitment to any claim or truth, their own skeptical practice exhibits repeated and unquestioning reliance upon the Parmenidean conception of truth, the Trope of Relativity and the Dilemma of the Criterion. Judged by Pyrrhonism's Parmenidean notions of truth and knowledge, in practice Pyrrhonists are committed to these principles, even if they expressly disavow them and (in effect) strategically appeal to their opponents' implicit acceptance of them. Their behavior, their skeptical way of life, is thus deeply at odds with their artful non-utterance of theoretical or factual commitments (*PhdG* 120.16–121.22/¶205).

A very important criticism of Pyrrhonism is latent in Hegel's text, though Hegel clearly intends it. Only by presuming the Parmenidean conception of truth can the Trope of Relativity reduce everything we experience to mere appearance because what we experience, like our experiences themselves, changes and varies. In the introductory section to "Self-Consciousness" Hegel notes that "*being* no longer has the significance of the *abstraction of being*" (*PhdG* 105.25–6/¶169; Hegel's emphasis). The "abstraction of being" rejected here, subsequent to "Consciousness," is the abstract cognitive claim criticized in "Sense Certainty" that any purportedly known object simply "is." This undifferentiated sense of "is" is tantamount to the Parmenidean conception of truth. Hegel's critique of Sense Certainty shows that this conception of truth *qua* changeless being can be referred to no particulars, to nothing we experience nor to any of our experiences, and thus has no genuine cognitive significance. For this reason Pyrrhonism fails to achieve genuine thought because it fails to refer any of its own ideas (representations, *Vorstellungen*) to particulars; it fails to *realize* any of its presumptive concepts. In this regard, like Stoicism, Pyrrhonism fares worse than the Bondsman. This is an important example of the kind of Platonic exercise Hegel's *Phenomenology* poses and requires us to master in order to understand his issues, analyses and results. Consequently, Pyrrhonism too cannot sustain Self-Consciousness's Self-Sufficiency Thesis; both its thought and its way of life are entirely dependent on a world independent of it, from which it alienates itself due to its unquestioned presumptions about truth, relativity and criteria of justification.

Because the Pyrrhonist is aware of its Parmenidean conception of truth *qua* changeless being and also of a welter of what it regards as mere appearances, while also

81

exhibiting the inconstancy of its own skeptical thought and behavior, it contains and exhibits (though does not expressly connect) the two sharply contrasting poles of unchanging ultimately real being and evanescent particularity. The integration of these two poles, Hegel claims, is essential to "the concept of spirit." The Unhappy Consciousness advances beyond Skepticism because it is aware of both of these poles within itself, though it does not know how to integrate them, whence its unhappiness (*PhdG* 121.23–39/¶206). Yet it improves on both Stoicism and Pyrrhonism because it "brings and holds together" pure thought and particulars, though without reconciling these two poles (*PhdG* 125.12–4/¶216). Significantly, Hegel here distinguishes "pure thought," which is not referred to specific particulars (Hegel speaks generically of "*Einzelheit*"), from his own explication of (genuine) thought which does refer to particulars (*PhdG* 125.22–9/¶217).

Aware that it satisfies no criteria of self-sufficiency, the Unhappy Consciousness ascribes self-sufficiency to a transcendent, alien "unchangeable being," the divinity (*PhdG* 122.11–30/¶208). Ultimately through the mediator or pontiff (i.e. bridge), the inessential Unhappy Consciousness totally alienates its thoughts, deeds and guilt to the (presumptive) essential, unchangeable being, who thus acquires the particular characteristics of the individual devout self-consciousness, to whom in principle it is thus no longer alien or transcendent (*PhdG* 130.9–131/¶228–30). This is Self-Consciousness's "turning point" towards spirit; here is the first indication to the observed consciousness and to us, Hegel's readers, that the content and effectiveness of spirit is due to our own activities.[28] I stress Hegel's dative case here ("to whom") because this point is not yet explicit for Unhappy Consciousness. Significantly, Hegel presents this point as a symbolic one: to the Unhappy Consciousness this implicit reconciliation is a representation (*Vorstellung*) and not yet even a pure concept (lacking reference to particulars) of Reason. Because its object presents to it its own individual deed and being as being and deed *per se*, it is a representation of Reason, as "consciousness's certainty, within its individuality, of being absolute *in itself*, of being all reality" (*PhdG* 131.30–1/¶230).[29]

This is tantamount to the Thesis of Reason, the next major section of Hegel's *Phenomenology*, "Reason." Though Hegel's introduction to this section, "The Certainty and Truth of Reason," contains a panegyric on reason and its (purported) comprehensive identity with all reality triumphantly proclaimed by Fichte's phrase, "I am I" (*PhdG* 104.13/¶167), Hegel's introduction to "Reason" encompasses the entire Modern Age, including Luther, Descartes, Bacon and the entire scientific revolution (Harris 1997, 1:447–73; Ferrini 2009a). Historically, the transition from "Self-Consciousness" to "Reason" thus marks the transition from Mediaeval Christian Faith to the Modern Age of Enlightenment, early to late, as is borne out by Hegel's ensuing discussions of theoretical and practical reason.[30] This observation allows us to understand why Hegel's transition to "Reason" turns on a merely implicit, symbolic representation and also why the various forms of Reason seek to uphold a series of more intellectual forms of the General Self-Sufficiency Thesis. That more versions of the Self-Sufficiency Thesis must be critically examined, not only in "Reason" but also in "Spirit," indicates that by the end of "Self-Consciousness" Hegel has not completed his case for his Kantian thesis that we can be self-conscious only if we are conscious of particulars.[31]

5.   Hegel's Interim Critique of the Ego-Centric Predicament

If ultimately Hegel can show that our self-consciousness depends upon our conscious-ness of particulars, then he can dismiss the Cartesian ego-centric predicament. Yet if Hegel does not complete his case for this Kantian thesis by the end of "Self-Consciousness," what bearing does "Self-Consciousness" have on the ego-centric predicament? Three important points can now be made.

Hegel's point that in principle the Parmenidean conception of truth lacks cognitive reference to particulars entails that skeptical hypotheses based on it are cognitively transcendent, idle speculations that lack cognitive standing and so cannot justify reject-ing (or "defeating") any actual evidence or justification we have for believing as we do in the existence of spatio-temporal objects. This point holds *mutatis mutandis* also for the Cartesian *malin genie*, the "evil deceiver hypothesis." In principle this hypothesis too cannot be referred to particulars and so is a cognitively transcendent idle speculation lacking any implications for our knowledge of particulars. Likewise, the notion that the particulars we perceive may vanish when they are not perceived by any or all of us, in principle lacks cognitive significance because it cannot be referred to any localized particulars.

Similarly, it is simply a truism that as a matter of logic all of our perceptual beliefs could be as they are even if they were all false. To think that this truism is relevant to our perceptual knowledge presupposes that empirical justification must conform to the deductivist requirements of *scientia*, according to which evidence sufficient for knowl-edge entails the truth of what is known. (This entailment relation requires eliminating all logical gaps in any line of justificatory reasoning.) This supposition is symptomatic of profound misunderstanding of the manifold roles of logically contingent facts and principles in cognitive justification in non-formal domains such as empirical knowl-edge. This idea, like Cartesian skepticism generally, presumes that mere logical possibili-ties suffice to block cognitive justification, even in non-formal domains. This presumption assimilates logical gaps to cognitive gaps in any justificatory evidence or reasoning. Thus Cartesian skepticism assimilates all non-formal domains of knowledge to the deductivist, infallibilist model of *scientia*. However, this model of justification – like the notion of "provability" – is only definable, and thus only defensible, within formal domains of knowledge.

In contrast to this, Hegel (like Kant) is a fallibilist about empirical justification; according to this view, evidence sufficient for knowledge (in non-formal domains) strongly indicates, though does not entail, truth. The Cartesian skeptic's "standards" for empirical knowledge are not "too stringent," as has been often been said. Rather, they are entirely inappropriate to the non-formal domain of empirical knowledge. Hegel's semantics of singular cognitive reference entails that counter-arguments or counter-examples to justificatory evidence or reasoning in the non-formal domain of empirical knowledge require, not mere logical coherence, but positive, identified counter-evidence, where such evidence requires cognitive reference to spatio-temporally localized particulars (which alone can be the source of relevant evidence). Hence the deductivist, infallibilist ideals of justification presumed by Cartesians – and in this,

83

empiricism in the analytic tradition remains deeply Cartesian – is altogether ill-suited to the non-formal domains of empirical and moral knowledge. Moreover, examining the *Meditations* using Hegel's method of determinate negation through internal critique reveals that Descartes' analysis is infected not by one but by five distinct, vicious circularities, that it cannot refute Pyrrhonian skepticism and that it is subject to the Dilemma of the Criterion (Westphal 1989, 18–34).[32]

Hegel also realized that the Pyrrhonian Dilemma of the Criterion shows that the foundationalist model of justification embedded in the model of *scientia* can neither refute nor evade Pyrrhonian skepticism in non-formal domains because the foundationalist model of justification cannot avoid *petitio principii* against those who dispute the particular premises or the particular derivation rules used in any foundationalist line of justificatory reasoning, or who dissent from the foundationalist model of justification itself (Westphal 2008b/2009c/2010c, 2010a).

The Cartesian ego-centric predicament presupposes both the foundationalist, deductivist model of *scentia* and its appropriateness to non-formal domains of knowledge. All this is symbolized by Descartes' *malin genie*. Hegel's semantics of singular cognitive reference, developed in "Consciousness" and "Self-Consciousness," shows that this seductive symbol of skepticism is in principle a cognitively transcendent, idle speculation. In "Consciousness" and "Self-Consciousness" Hegel refutes the epistemological presuppositions of the ego-centric predicament; hence he can disregard that predicament and need not criticize it directly. Hence he need not include the ego-centric predicament among the forms of consciousness examined in the *Phenomenology*.

6. Conclusion

"Self-Consciousness" contributes *inter alia* to establishing Hegel's semantics of singular cognitive reference, which provides a powerful critique of Cartesianism in epistemology. Hegel's explication of thought and his cognitive semantics provide the basis for introducing and developing "the category" (in "Reason"), which then forms the point of departure for "Spirit."[33] Against the Self-Sufficiency Thesis that all our awareness of particulars is nothing but modes of our self-awareness, Hegel argues in "Observing Reason" that after the scientific revolution, much of our awareness of particulars is possible only through scientific investigation of independently existing natural phenomena (Ferrini 2007, 2009b). Thus our scientific consciousness of natural phenomena depends entirely on our awareness of particulars which are not merely modes of our self-awareness, where our awareness of particulars involves conceptually structured thought in the form of categories.[34] "Observing Reason" thus greatly augments and specifies Hegel's justification of causal realism in "Force and Understanding" (Westphal 2008a), thereby undermining the generality and hence the tenability of the Self-Sufficiency Theses both of Self-Consciousness and of Reason. These conclusions suggest some of the important ways in which Hegel seeks to show that skepticism and subjective (or "one-sided") idealism are symptoms of profound self-misunderstanding. Understanding human knowledge requires understanding who we *are*, not who we might be or who we might think we are. Epistemologists, too, must heed the inscription at Delphi: "Know thyself!"[35]

Notes

1 *PhdG* 58.13–14/¶81; cf. *PhdG* 25.16–17/¶29. Hegel's 1807 *Phenomenology* is designated by the acronym of its German title ("*PhdG*") and cited according to Hegel (1980) by page. line numbers. Paragraph numbers of Pinkard's translation (Hegel 2008) follow a slash: "/¶*n*." All translations from Hegel are my own.

2 Beiser (2005, 174–91) contends that Hegel's analysis of the Lord and Bondsman aims to refute solipsism, an important component of the ego-centric predicament. Critical reservations about Beiser's analysis are developed by Stern (forthcoming) and Westphal (2008b/2009c/2010c), §3.3.

3 Here I set aside Hegel's Intersubjectivity Thesis (that we can only be self-conscious if we are self-consciously aware of other self-conscious agents) and all other issues in 'Self-Consciousness' to focus on Hegel's concept of thought and his cognitive semantics. For comprehensive discussion of Hegel's introduction to and §A of "Self-Consciousness," including its important social dimensions, see Neuhouser (1986, 2009), Siep (1992), Bykova (2009a, §3.2), Chitty (2007), Redding (2008, forthcoming) and, as always, the relevant sections of Harris (1997); on Hegel's Intersubjectivity Thesis see Westphal (2008b/2009c/2010c, 2010a).

4 See Westphal (2007a, 2004), respectively. For a précis of Kant's cognitive semantics, see Westphal (2007b, 2007c). Bird (2006) explicates substantially the same semantic theory within Kant's *Critique of Pure Reason*.

5 In the second edition Deduction (§26) Kant stresses identifying the spatial "form" (*Gestalt*), hence the boundary, of a perceived house (*KdrV* B162).

6 These concepts are a priori because they cannot be defined or acquired in accord with concept empiricism; instead they are presupposed for identifying any particular, including any particular sensory quality, on the basis of which alone we can either define or learn empirical concepts. "Cause" enters this list because, Kant argues, causal judgments are discriminatory and we can only individuate particulars by identifying some of their causal characteristics (Westphal 2004, §§22, 23, 36–39, 62).

7 In Westphal (2000) I examine in detail and defend Hegel's justification of the Evans Thesis in "Sense Certainty"; in Westphal (2009b) I examine some of the role of Hegel's semantics of singular cognitive reference in "Consciousness" and "Self-Consciousness." Though my discussion in §3 relies on these previous analyses, it also augments them. In Westphal (2010b) I defend Hegel's critique of Russell's "knowledge by acquaintance"; in my (2005) I show how Hegel's critique of "Sense Certainty" holds of Hume; in my (2002/2003b) I show how it holds against several of Hegel's German contemporaries. All of these support my attribution to Hegel of this specific form of cognitive semantics.

8 Hegel's chapter titles are set in quotes, e.g.: "Sense Certainty"; the corresponding form of consciousness is designated with capitals without quotes, e.g.: Sense Certainty; the core philosophical view espoused by a form of consciousness is designated by the relevant phrase, though without quotes or capitals, e.g.: sense certainty.

9 How one can understand something both implicitly and yet conceptually appears puzzling on the nominalist presumption that concepts and their understanding can be exhaustively specified by the use of terms, that is, words. Hegel rejects nominalism in part by justifying the legitimate cognitive use of a range of a priori concepts which are generated, as it were, spontaneously by the human mind. These issues require careful consideration which cannot be provided here; their proper understanding is facilitated by Pinker (1994), Wolff (1995) and Hanna (2006).

10 *PhdG* 93.7–94.28/¶¶152–4; cf. Westphal (2008a).

11 On Hegel's responses to various forms of skepticism, see Westphal (2002/2003a or 2003).

12 It suffices for Hegel's purposes to show that this conclusion is correct and is justified; the issue of how we are able to integrate these two factors within successful acts of cognitive reference can be addressed properly only after Hegel demonstrates, in the 1807 *Phenomenology*, that philosophy is competent to know the truth.

13 *PhdG* 116.30–117.12/¶197; see Chiereghin (2009, 55–8) for detailed discussion of Hegel's explication of thought; cf. Westphal (1989), 164–5.

14 Cf. Bykova (2009a), 267–9, 275–7.

15 Kant: "The mere, though empirically determined consciousness of my own existence proves the existence of objects in space outside me" (B275); see Westphal (2006).

16 Please recall note 3 above regarding the scope of the present analysis.

17 *E.g.*, "For everything else to which it should be applied it must be shown that reality is transferred to it *from the I*" (Fichte 1971, 1:99, KRW tr.); Although "presentation in general" can be thought possible only "on the assumption of a check occurring to the infinitely and indeterminately active reaching out of the self," "Yet according to all of its determinations the I should be posited altogether through itself, and hence completely independently from any possible not-I" (Fichte 1971, 1:248–9, KRW tr.).

18 See Bykova (2008a, 2008b, 2009b).

19 See Westphal (2009b), §6; (1989), 164–88; de Laurentiis (2009), Bykova (2009a).

20 Noting this series suggests why Hegel can only fully articulate and justify his own Intersubjectivity Thesis at the very end of "Morality." Quante (2009) very nicely explicates the Intersubjectivity Thesis announced at the end of "The Truth and Self-Certainty" of Self-consciousness (*PhdG* 108.29–31/¶176), though he does not recognize how Hegel further explicates and justifies this thesis, on which see Westphal (2010a).

21 See Ferrini (2009a), 72–5; Harris (1997), 1:447–73.

22 These terms closely follow Hegel's own in the first paragraph of "Self-Consciousness": "However, what was not achieved in the previous relations [of consciousness to its objects] is now achieved, namely a certainty which is identical to its truth, for the certainty itself is its object and consciousness is to itself the true. Of course a being-other is also involved herein: consciousness distinguishes something, though for consciousness it is also at the same time not distinguished" (*PhdG* 103.11–16/¶166).

23 Cf. Stolzenberg's (2009) account of the Principle of Consciousness and the Principle of Spirit in Hegel's analysis of Enlightenment and Faith. Looking ahead to "Spirit" is not to look too far; Hegel states that the Intersubjectivity Thesis in "Self-Consciousness" presents his readers with "the concept of spirit" and that "Self-Consciousness" provides the "turning point" in consciousness becoming spirit (*PhdG* 108.35–109.3/¶177). On "Absolute Knowing" see de Laurentiis (2009); on developed Spirit see di Giovanni (2009) and Bykova (2009a).

24 Cf. *Theatetus* 162; Hegel (1802), *GW* 4:207.15–25, 211.20–28/(2000) 327–8; *Enz.* §81Z2.

25 On Fichte's analysis of embodiment, see Nuzzo (2006) and Zöller (2006).

26 On Hegel's view of freedom as being by oneself see Hardimon (1994), 112–4.

27 For a concise summary of the main principles of Pyrrhonism see Westphal (1989), 11–16. Hegel's present discussion directly concerns pyrrhonian rather than Cartesian skepticism, which is discussed below (§5).

28 *PhdG* 108.35–109.3/¶177, cf. di Giovanni (2009), Bykova (2009a).

29 For detailed discussion of the "Unhappy Consciousness" see Chiereghin (2009, 64–70) and Burbidge (1992).

30 See Ferrini (2009b), Pinkard (2009) and D. C. Hoy (2009).

31 Westphal (2003, §§16–20) examines Hegel's case against some still-standard Enlightenment views about individual cognitive self-sufficiency.

32 The other two paradigmatic attempts to assimilate empirical knowledge to the deductivist requirements of *scientia* are the empiricist attempt to reduce talk of physical objects to talk of sense data and Kant's transcendental idealism. Both strategies fail in this regard; see Westphal (1989), 47–67, 230–2, and (2004), *passim*.

33 *PhdG* 134.24–30ff, 238.6ff/¶¶235, 437; cf. Westphal (2009b) §6; (1989), 164–77.

34 *PhdG* 191.6–9, 193.20, 238.3–7, .14–17; cf. Ferrini (2009b).

35 I gratefully thank John Burbidge, Marina Bykova, Franco Chiereghin, Robert Stern, and Stephen Houlgate for their helpful comments on drafts of this paper. I am especially grateful to all the contributors to *The Blackwell Guide to Hegel's Phenomenology of Spirit* (Westphal 2009a) for consolidating and greatly enriching my understanding of Hegel's first masterpiece. I thank Andrew Chitty for kindly sharing his illuminating 2007 ms. with me.

References

Beiser, Frederick C., 2005. *Hegel*. London, Routledge.

Beiser, Frederick C., 2009. "Morality in Hegel's *Phenomenology of Spirit*." In: Westphal (2009a), 209–225.

Bird, Graham, 2006. *The Revolutionary Kant*. LaSalle, Ill., Open Court.

Burbidge, John, 1992. "'Unhappy Consciousness' in Hegel's *Phenomenology*: An Analysis of Medieval Catholicism?" In: J. Burbidge., *Hegel on Logic and Religion* (Albany, State University of New York Press), 105–18.

Bykova, Marina F., 2008a. "On Fichte's Concept of Freedom in the *System of Ethics*." *Philosophy Today* 52:3–4:391–398.

Bykova, Marina F., 2008b. "Fichte's Doctrine of Self-Positing Subject and Concept of Subjectivity." *Fichte-Studien* 32:129–139.

Bykova, Marina F., 2009a. "Spirit and Concrete Subjectivity in Hegel's *Phenomenology of Spirit*." In: Westphal (2009a), 265–295.

Bykova, Marina F., 2009b. "The Self as the World Into Itself. Towards Fichte's Conception of Subjectivity." In: *Fichte, German Idealism, and Early Romanticism, Fichte-Studien* Supplementa 7:131–147.

Chiereghin, Franco, 2009. "Freedom and Thought: Stoicism, Scepticism, and Unhappy Consciousness." In: Westphal (2009a), 55–71.

Chitty, Andrew, 2007. "Identity with the Other in Hegel's Dialectic of Recognition." Unpublished ms. delivered to the *Hegel Society of Great Britain* annual meeting in Oxford, September 2007.

Ferrini, Cinzia, 2007. "Hegel's Confrontation with the Sciences in 'Observing Reason': Notes for a Discussion." *Bulletin of the Hegel Society of Great Britain* 55/56:1–22.

Ferrini, Cinzia, 2009b. "Reason Observing Nature." In: Westphal (2009a), 92–135.

Ferrini, Cinzia, 2009a. "The Challenge of Reason: From Certainty to Truth." In: Westphal (2009a), 72–91.

Fichte, Johann Gottlieb, 1971. *Grundlage der gesammten Wissenschaftslehre* (1794), rpt. in: I. H. Fichte, ed., *Johann Gottlieb Fichtes Sämmtliche Werke* (Berlin, DeGruyter), 1:83–328.

Fichte, Johann Gottlieb, 1982. *The Science of Knowledge, with the First and Second Introductions*. Trans and ed. P. Heath and J. Lachs, Cambridge, Cambridge University Press; includes pagination of Fichte (1971).

Gettier, Edmond, 1963. "Is Justified True Belief Knowledge?" *Analysis* 23.6: 121–23.

Giovanni, George di, 2009. "Religion, History, and Spirit in Hegel's *Phenomenology of Spirit*." In: Westphal (2009a), 226–245.

Hanna, Robert, 2006. *Rationality and Logic*. Cambridge, Mass., MIT Press.

Hardimon, Michael, 1994. *Hegel's Social Philosophy: The Project of Reconciliation*. Cambridge, Cambridge University Press.

Harris, H. S., 1997. *Hegel's Ladder*, 2 vols. Cambridge, Mass., Hackett Publishing Co.

Hegel, G. W. F., 1802. "Verhältniss des Scepticismus zur Philosophie, Darstellung seiner verschiedenen Modificationen, und Vergleichung des Neuesten mit dem Alten." *Kritisches Journal der Philosophie* 1.2:1–74; rpt. in *GW* 4:197–238.

Hegel, G. W. F., 1807. *Phänomenologie des Geistes*. Bamberg and Würzburg, Goephard; W. Bonsiepen and R. Heede, eds., in *GW* 9.

Hegel, G. W. F., 1968–. H. Buchner and O. Pöggeler, eds., *Gesammelte Werke*, Rheinisch-Westfälischen Akadamie der Wissenschaften and Deutsche Forschungsgemeinschaft (Hamburg, Meiner); cited as "*GW*."

Hegel, G. W. F., 2000. "The Relation of Scepticism to Philosophy," rev. ed. H. S. Harris, tr., in: trans. and ed. H. S. Harris and G. di Giovani, *Between Kant and Hegel: Texts in the Development of Post-Kantian Idealism* (Cambridge, Mass., Hackett Publishing Co.), 311–362.

Hegel, G. W. F., 2008. *The Phenomenology of Spirit*, trans. T. Pinkard. Draft bi-lingual translation in PDF format; cited by paragraph (¶) numbers provided by the translator corresponding to *GW* 9. Posted by the translator at: http://web.mac.com/titpaul/Site/About_Me_files/Phenomenology%20of%20Spirit%20(entire%20text).pdf

Hoy, David Couzens, 2009. "The Ethics of Freedom: Hegel on Reason as Law-Giving and Law-Testing." In: Westphal (2009a), 153–171.

Hoy, Jocelyn B., 2009. "Hegel, *Antigone*, and Feminist Critique: The Spirit of Ancient Greece." In: Westphal (2009a), 172–189.

Laurentiis, Allegra de, 2009. "Absolute Knowing." In: Westphal (2009a), 246–264.

Neuhouser, Frederick, 1986. "Deducing Desire and Recognition in Hegel's *Phenomenology of Spirit*." *Journal of the History of Philosophy* 24.2:243–262.

Neuhouser, Frederick, 2009. "Desire, Recognition, and the Relation between Bondsman and Lord." In: Westphal (2009a), 37–54.

Nuzzo, Angelica, 2006. "The Role of the Body in Fichte's *Grundlage des Naturrechts* (1796–97)." In: D. Breazeale and T. Rockmore, eds., *Bodies, Rights and Recognition* (Dartmouth, Ashgate), 71–89.

Pinkard, Terry, 2009. "Shapes of Active Reason: The Law of the Heart, Retrieved Virtue, and What Really Matters." In: Westphal (2009a), 136–152.

Pinker, Steven, 1994. *The Language Instinct: How the Mind Creates Language*. New York, W. Morrow & Co.

Quante, Michael, 2009. "'Der reine Begriff der Anerkennung'. Überlegungen zur Grammatik der Anerkennungsrelation in Hegels *Phänomenologie des Geistes*." In: H.-C. Schmidt am Busch and C.F. Zurn, eds., *Anerkennung* (Berlin, Akademie), 91–106.

Redding, Paul, 2008. "The Independence and Dependence of Self-Consciousness: The Dialectic of Lord and Bondsman in Hegel's Phenomenology of Spirit." In F. Beiser, ed., *The Cambridge Companion to Hegel and Nineteenth Century Philosophy* (Cambridge, Cambridge University Press), 94–110.

Redding, Paul, forthcoming. "The Role of Work within the Processes of Recognition in Hegel's Idealism." In: N. H. Smith and J.-P. Deranty, eds., *New Philosophies of Labour: Work and the Social Bond* (Leiden and Boston, Brill).Pre-print available from the author's website: http://www-personal.arts.usyd.edu.au/paureddi/Redding_Hegel-rec&work.pdf

Siep, Ludwig, 1992. "Der Freiheitsbegriff der praktischen Philosophie Hegels in Jena." In: L. Siep, *Praktische Philosophie im Deutschen Idealismus* (Frankfurt am Main, Suhrkamp), 159–171.

Siep, Ludwig, 2006. "Die Bewegung des Anerkennens in Hegels *Phänomenologie des Geistes*." In: O. Pöggeler and D. Köhler, eds., *G. W. F. Hegel: Phänomenologie des Geistes*, rev. ed. (Berlin, Akademie), 109–129.

Shklar, Judith, 1976. *Freedom and Independence: A Study of Hegel's Phenomenology of Mind*. Cambridge, Cambridge University Press.

Stern, Robert S., forthcoming. "Is Hegel's Dialectic of Self-Consciousness in the *Phenomenology* a Refutation of Solipsism?" *British Journal of the History of Philosophy* (in press).

Stolzenberg, Jürgen, 2009. "Hegel's Critique of the Enlightenment in 'The struggle of the Enlightenment with Superstition'." In: Westphal (2009a), 190–208.

Westphal, Kenneth R., 1989. *Hegel's Epistemological Realism*. Dordrecht, Kluwer.

Westphal, Kenneth R., 1998. "Hegel's Solution to the Dilemma of the Criterion." Rev. ed. in: J. Stewart, ed., *The Phenomenology of Spirit Reader: A Collection of Critical and Interpretive Essays* (Albany: State University of New York Press), 76–91.

Westphal, Kenneth R., 2000. "Hegel's Internal Critique of Naïve Realism." *Journal of Philosophical Research* 25:173–229.

Westphal, Kenneth R., 2002/2003a. "Die Vielseitigkeit von Hegels Auseinandersetzung mit Sceptizismus in der *Phänomenologie des Geistes*." *Jahrbuch für Hegel-Forschungen* 8/9:145–73.

Westphal, Kenneth R., 2002/2003b. "Analytischer Gehalt und zeitgenössische Bedeutung von Hegels Kritik des unmittelbaren Wissens." *Jahrbuch für Hegel-Forschungen* 8/9:129–43.

Westphal, Kenneth R., 2003. "Hegel's Manifold Response to Scepticism in the *Phenomenology of Spirit*." *Proceedings of the Aristotelian Society* 103.2:149–78.

Westphal, Kenneth R., 2004. *Kant's Transcendental Proof of Realism*. Cambridge, Cambridge University Press.

Westphal, Kenneth R., 2005. "Hume, Hegel, and Abstract General Ideas." *Bulletin of the Hegel Society of Great Britain* 51/52:28–55.

Westphal, Kenneth R., 2006. "How does Kant Prove that we Perceive, not merely Imagine, Physical Objects?" *Review of Metaphysics* 60:781–806.

Westphal, Kenneth R., 2007a. "Consciousness and its Transcendental Conditions: Kant's Anti-Cartesian Revolt." In: S. Heinämaa, V. Lähteenmäki, and P. Remes, eds., *Consciousness: From Perception to Reflection in the History of Philosophy* (Dordrecht, Springer), 223–243.

Westphal, Kenneth R., 2007b. "Kant's Anti-Cartesianism." *Dialogue* 46.4:709–715.

Westphal, Kenneth R., 2007c. "Proving Realism Transcendentally: Replies to Rolf George and William Harper." *Dialogue* 46.4 (2007):737–750.

Westphal, Kenneth R. 2008a. "Force, Understanding and Ontology." *Bulletin of the Hegel Society of Great Britain* 57/58:1–32.

Westphal, Kenneth R. 2008b. "Hegel'in Tinin Görüngübilimi'nde Karşıhkh Onanma ve Ussal Gerekçelendirme." ("Mutual Recognition and Rational Justification in Hegel's *Phenomenology of Spirit*.") *MonoKL* 4–5:212–230. (Excerpt of Westphal 2010c.)

Westphal, Kenneth R., ed., 2009a. *The Blackwell Guide to Hegel's Phenomenology of Spirit*. Oxford: Wiley-Blackwell.

Westphal, Kenneth R., 2009b. "Hegel's Phenomenological Method and Analysis of Consciousness." In: Westphal (2009a), 1–36.

Westphal, Kenneth R., 2009c. "Mutual Recognition and Rational Justification in Hegel's *Phenomenology of Spirit*." *Dialogue* 48.4:1–47. (Slightly revised English version of Westphal (Вестфал) 2010c)

Westphal, Kenneth R., 2010a. "Urteilskraft, gegenseitige Anerkennung und rationale Rechtfertigung." ("Judgment, Mutual Recognition and Rational Justification.") In: H.-D. Klein, ed., *Ethik als prima philosophia?* (Würzburg, Königshausen and Neumann), 171–193.

89

Westphal, Kenneth R., 2010b. "Hegel, Russell, and the Foundations of Philosophy." In: A. Nuzzo, ed., *Hegel and the Analytical Tradition* (New York: Continuum), 174–194.

Вестфал К.Р., 2010c. «Сужление, взаимное признание и рационалъное обоснование». In: Н. В. Мотрошилова, рел, *"Феноменология луха"* Гегеля в контексте современного гегелевеления, отв (Москва: «Канон+» РООИ «Реабилитация»), 195–219.

Zöller, Gunter, 2006. "Fichte's *Foundations of Natural Right* and the Mind-Body Problem." In: D. Breazeale and T. Rockmore, eds., *Bodies, Rights and Recognition* (Dartmouth, Ashgate), 90–106.

4

Spirit as the "Unconditioned"

TERRY PINKARD

The chapter on "Spirit" in Hegel's 1807 *Phenomenology of Spirit* comes after a lengthy and, at first glance, rather puzzling set of preceding chapters. Starting the book with themes that would be familiar to any contemporary student in an epistemology course (sensing, perception, the knowability of explanatory constructs, etc.), Hegel then quickly moves to a discussion of mastery and servitude, followed by sections on some ancient philosophies (such as stoicism) and on early Christianity. Those discussions then set the stage for a very long chapter on "Reason," which involves lengthy discussions of the nature of the natural world, the adequate explanation of that nature, and the nature of psychological explanation, as well as untagged references to various literary works and contemporary cultural disputes, and finally concludes with something that vaguely, but only vaguely, resembles a discussion of some problems contained in the alleged formalism of Kantian ethics. All that is to set the stage for a further, even longer, chapter simply titled "*Geist*" (Spirit).

It is thus no wonder that all those chapters have given rise to a virtual industry of commentators trying to make sense of them and the order in which they are put. Therefore, before beginning one's remarks on one particular section – and a particularly long one at that – it helps to step back and think about some of the general themes that are at play in the work as a whole. At least in doing so, one can make it clear to the reader what suppositions are guiding the interpretation being put forth.

Spirit, Metaphysics, and the "Unconditioned"

As with so many things that have to do with Hegel, it is worth returning, however briefly, to Kant to get a hold of what Hegel would be trying to accomplish. Kant begins the *Critique of Pure Reason* with some of the most famous lines in philosophy:

A Companion to Hegel, First Edition. Edited by Stephen Houlgate and Michael Baur.
© 2011 Blackwell Publishing Ltd. Published 2011 by Blackwell Publishing Ltd.

> Human reason has this peculiar fate that in one species of its knowledge it is burdened by questions which, as prescribed by the very nature of reason itself, it is not able to ignore, but which, as transcending all its powers, it is also not able to answer. The perplexity into which it thus falls is not due to any fault of its own.[1]

He concludes the paragraph a few lines later with the sentence: "The battle-field of these endless controversies is called metaphysics."

The perplexity of which Kant speaks has to do with reason's need to go beyond the bounds of experience in order to arrive at answers about the "unconditioned," that which would complete the various series constituted by our claims to know something about the world and ourselves. However, once rational inquiry goes beyond possible experience and tries to speak of the world as it is apart from all the conditions under which we finite human beings can experience it – of things in themselves, as Kant phrases it – it loses all its anchors and finds itself floating around in a sea of antinomies, that is, mutually contradictory assertions for which equally good arguments can be made. Since we know that the world as it exists "in itself" cannot itself be self-contradictory, we thus know that pure reason cannot know what things in themselves are but can only know the various conditioned things of our own experience. The demonstration of these contradictions – in what Kant calls the "battlefield" that is metaphysics – constitutes in Kant's terms a *dialectic*, and it demonstrates to us how our knowledge must be restricted to the realm of possible experience (with "transcendental" – or what Kant also calls "critical" – philosophy stepping in to replace the traditional "metaphysics"). That is, it demonstrates that we can know nothing about things-in-themselves (apart from all conditions of possible experience) and can only know things as they must appear to us. However, reason, since it seeks a grasp of the whole of reality, cannot be satisfied with that restriction and thus, by its own hand, condemns itself to its own eternal "perplexities."

Although many have since been intrigued by Kant's sharp distinction between knowledge of appearances and the impossibility of knowledge of things-in-themselves, it seems that about the only person who ever completely accepted it was Kant himself. Indeed, a large measure of the backlash to and development of Kantian philosophy had to do with rejecting that distinction. Indeed, just as Kant predicted at the end of the *Critique*,

> we shall always return to metaphysics as to a beloved one with whom we have had a quarrel. For here we are concerned with essential ends – ends with which metaphysics must ceaselessly occupy itself, either in striving for genuine insight into them, or in refuting those who profess already to have attained it.[2]

In the third of the big critiques – the *Critique of Judgment* – Kant himself helped to pave the way for the idea that there might be alternative ways of grasping the unconditioned, particularly through the experience of beauty. There he noted that the experience of beauty – precisely by giving us an experience of "purposiveness without a purpose" (a sense of goal-oriented direction for which the goal nonetheless cannot be stated) – offered us the indeterminate concept of the "indeterminate supersensible substrate of appearances,"[3] something that would itself be "neither nature nor freedom and yet [would be] linked with the basis of freedom."[4] This was heady stuff, and the generation of early Romantics found this bait too sweet to resist and immediately set themselves to work on theories about how it was art, not philosophy, that allowed us a nondiscursive grasp of things-in-themselves.

Hegel's *Phenomenology* is his first great work in which he puts his famous (or, depending one's point of view, infamous) dialectic to work, and it is Kant whom Hegel often credits with reviving the dialectic in his sense.[5] What Hegel thinks he can show in the *Phenomenology* is that something like Kant's dialectic can be put to work in much the same way Kant intended it but reach importantly different results. First, Hegel agrees with Kant that what reason tries to do is grasp things-in-themselves – which Hegel in his own special jargon simply abbreviates as *the* "in-itself" – and that when it does so, it runs into contradictions. But this is not a demonstration, so Hegel argues (or, rather, he uses his entire system to build his case), that we cannot grasp "the in-itself." It shows, rather, that when we assert that something inherently limited – or, in Hegel's terms, "finite" – is also exhaustive of the whole, we necessarily run into contradictions. We grasp what exists in itself only when we grasp the infinite "whole" in terms of which we make sense of our assertions about "the unconditioned." Or, to put it in slightly different terms, the attempt at explicating what is ultimately authoritative for us in our reason-giving practices itself fails when it takes something limited, some "part," to be authoritative for those practices.

To take an example: Hegel starts the *Phenomenology* with a discussion of "sense-certainty," the idea that we can have an unconditional grasp of distinct objects of experience (what we sense as this, right here, right now); what is problematic about such "sense-certainty" is not the idea that we grasp single things here and now, but the assertion that this is the truth itself – that is, that such "sense-certainty" is an unconditional or "immediate" grasp of things. It is this assertion of its unconditional truth that provokes our reflection on it, which in turn reveals the contradictions inherent in taking something like the singular object of sense certainty to be something we could know without having to know anything else. The failure of reflection on "sense-certainty" to make good on its claim to grasp the "unconditioned" does not show that we cannot know the "in-itself"; rather, it is indicative of something else, namely, that the "truth is the whole," that is, that it is only in comprehending the way in which all such claims are embedded in other claims that we can get a knowledge of what things are "in themselves." Thus, in each case of Hegel's version of the dialectic, there is the assertion of something "finite" as "the unconditioned" (what Hegel calls throughout the *Phenomenology* simply "the object" of that part of the investigation), and the contradictions involved in that supposition that lead one to realize that the assertion could not be what it started out to be but instead had to be something else (such as, "it is not the object of sense-certainty that is the unconditioned; it is the object of perception which is the unconditioned").

The thesis that the truth is the whole is moreover not anything that can be assumed from the outset. First, at the outset there cannot be any a priori proof that taking any specific "finite" thing – something whose limits are set by factors or things distinct from it – as the "unconditioned" will necessarily turn out to be so self-undermining. *That* something is taken as unconditionally binding and turns out to be self-undermining can only be established after the fact – after it is has been shown to be self-undermining.

Second, it cannot be assumed from the outset that we will actually end up with anything at all that can be shown to be unconditional in this demanding sense; it may well be (or at least as far as we know when we start out) that Kant was right and that our reflective powers are not able to answer the questions we put to them. (To generalize this point: There can be no a priori method that Hegel would be applying that would guarantee that contradictions will always result from looking at finite things as the unconditioned, nor can there be any guarantee that such contradictions will ever be finally resolved; the proof, as it were, can come only by following out all the steps.)[6]

Now, before Hegel has reached the "Spirit" chapter, he has taken himself to have already shown that several lines of thought have exhausted themselves as attempts to articulate "the unconditioned" – or what Hegel, following Schelling's lead, took to calling the "absolute." Neither the grasp of the object of sense-certainty nor that of the objects of perceptual experience can consistently be made out to be grasps of "the unconditioned." Nor could the supposed intellectual grasp of a world, as it were, behind the curtain of appearance, which would consist of a priori determinable forces, fill that bill.[7] What seemed to be at work in all those attempts was not so much a grasp (sensory or intellectual) of a singular object as the unconditioned but instead a grasp of our own grasp of the object, of how it was not our direct awareness of things but our reflective consciousness that has pushed us into those self-undermining stances.[8] We come to understand that we do not merely *take* things to be such and such; we also take *ourselves* to be taking those things to be such and such; or to use Robert Brandom's terminology, we are not merely immediately "taking things in" but are *undertaking* commitments. What looked like a full absorption in something like the immediately grasped objects of sense-certainty or perception in fact involves a kind of distance between our grasp of those objects and the capacity (which is not always exercised), as Kant so famously phrased it, of the "I think" to accompany all my representations; that means that we are subject to norms, even if we are not reflectively attending to those norms all the time. Hegel's thesis is that what at first seems straightforward and obvious (and non-normative) begins to lose its grip on us as we reflect on it and see the various problems involved in trying to specify those norms without contradiction or paradox.

As such reflective creatures, we are also embodied creatures, relating to the world around us in terms of satisfying needs and desires. As such, our relation to our own desires, however, is like our relation to the objects of perceptual experience; it is guided by norms, and the subject can always (but does not necessarily) come face to face with a gap between his or her given desire and how he or she is to take that desire (as something to be postponed, to be rejected, resisted, given into, etc.) – that is, to put it in more contemporary terms, the subject can take (or reject) his or her desires as reasons for action. To the extent that the self-conscious subject can relate to its own animal embodiment as a source of reasons, or so Hegel also takes himself to have shown, such subjectivity requires a form of sociality; other objects in the world may physically resist one's using them to satisfy desire, but other agents can demand that one give reasons for what one is doing, and that introduces a new dynamic in the dialectic – not merely the reflectively encountered paradoxes of, say, perceptual experience but the "negations" that other embodied subjects make of our fundamental claims to be entitled to do what we do. This leads to a struggle over recognition, not only over the principles of recognition but even over the principles that are to regulate the principles themselves.

Since at the outset there are no such principles, authority can be established only by a brute act of will; one agent becomes master, the other the slave, a state of affairs that in turn produces its own breakdown since the master now finds his or her authority to be coming from recognition by someone whom he or she in turn recognizes as lacking the authority to confer such recognition.

The internal failures of mastery and servitude in all its various forms lead to the conclusion that the "unconditioned" cannot lie in de facto intersubjective relations of power but in something more like the unforced force of the better argument, that is, in *reason* itself (the title of a long chapter in the *Phenomenology*). Reason, to put it in Kantian terms, both is the faculty that grasps the unconditioned and is itself, particularly in its practical form, the unconditioned. (Kant, for example, holds that the categorical imperative gives us an unconditionally valid duty, and that our grasp of it through practical reason is itself unconditional.) However, this is reason as "taken up" by individuals who then apply the unconditioned standards of pure (or pure practical) reason to themselves in their very contingent and "conditioned" state. This too generates a set of antinomies: reason is supposed to unconditionally generate various sets of unconditional duties or commands, but these putatively unconditional duties themselves collapse under the kinds of mutually exclusive commitments that any such assertion of unconditional commitments as applied to flesh and blood (conditioned) agents necessarily involves.[9] The dependence of rational agents on each other in terms of their giving and asking for reasons pushes "reason" to the point where, in its own unconditional self-critique, it comes to realize that it is, as a standard taken up by "conditioned" individuals who are themselves taken to be completely self-reflective and metaphysically cut off from each other, empty and paradoxical.

Thus, the self-study of reason – Kant's idea of reason's "self-knowledge" as a critique of pure reason that amounts, in his own words, to a "tribunal which will assure to reason its lawful claims, and dismiss all groundless pretensions, not by despotic decrees, but in accordance with its own eternal and unalterable laws"[10] – pushes reason itself to consider the conditions under which it can be realized. Part of the force of the "Reason" chapter is thus to exhibit – in Hegel's German, *darstellen* – a general Hegelian thesis about meaning to the effect that the way in which a concept is put into practice (or "realized" or "worked out"[11]) makes a difference to the meaning of the concept (or to put it in non-Hegelian terms, that "meaning" and "use" are distinguishable but not separable, i.e., that "meaning" cannot be determined apart from use *but* is nonetheless not identical with use).[12] Moreover, as this thesis itself comes to be put into practice in the *Phenomenology* – from its first presentation in the "Consciousness" chapter up until the end of the "Reason" chapter – it becomes clear that it is also a social and historical thesis about how forms of life cannot understand the basic commitments they have collectively undertaken – most importantly, those commitments to what counts for them as the "unconditioned," as what is ultimately authoritative for them – until those commitments have been put into practice and then worked out within the various institutions and other arrangements that hold that form of life together.[13]

The commitments of a form of life – the social facts that structure it – must be seen in terms of what it was that, as it were, people thought they meant (or what in Hegel's terms they "abstractly" meant) and what they turned out to have meant.

Spirit as Positivity

Thus, Hegel begins the "Spirit" chapter by remarking that what he had earlier called "*the* category" – the most basic concept of the "unconditioned" – had turned out to be "reason" itself, but that, as it was put into practice, it became clear that "reason" requires its realization in a set of institutions and practices that form the "substance," or what Hegel later calls the "second nature," of the individual: a set of psychological dispositions, social skills, and tacit knowledge. Without such a realization, the concept of reason would be indeterminate; to see reason as the "unconditioned" would in effect amount only to a generalized picture of an individual agent who "either legislates arbitrary laws, or who supposes that he has those laws as they exist in and for themselves solely within his own knowledge, and ... takes himself to be the power which passes judgment on them."[14] Thus, the failure of that conception of reason makes it seem that at first the "unconditioned" could in fact only be our own social mindedness itself as it articulates itself in institutions and practices that flesh out the concept of reason; reason, or so we might put it, at first seems like the merely "positive" rules structuring a community's shared, intersubjective self-awareness of what the community is; and what the community is becomes revealed by how its ground-level commitments work out in practice.

Part of this thesis about spirit in its initial appearance is also intended to exhibit Hegel's general theses about "positivity" and "negativity," two key terms in Hegel's specially constructed vocabulary. The *negative* of anything is its limit, what distinguishes it from something else, that is, the point where it either ceases to be what it is or where it ceases to exercise the authority it otherwise has; in Hegel's idiosyncratic jargon, all "finite" things thus are what they are only in terms of their distinction from something else; they are what they are by virtue of the relations they entertain with their "other." (This is true both of finite "things" and of finite "norms.") A major point of Hegel's claim is that what at first seems only to be a "positive," factual sense of negativity – claims of the form "this is not that" or claims of the form such as "this is what society requires of you" or "this is the positive law in force" – in fact cannot ultimately be made intelligible without some further understanding of negativity as normative, that is, as the normative setting of the boundary itself between the normative and non-normative. That in turn demands that we develop a concept of self-relating negativity, that is, of a "negativity" that sets its own limits, which is the kind of normative self-distinction that *subjects*, not substances, carry out as they set their own normative limits to themselves instead of having the normative limits set by something external to the space of reasons itself. Spirit, as a form of life, has a positivity to it in that the norms governing its members have a kind of force in terms of being embodied in sets of psychological dispositions and social skills on the part of the agents in that form of life; but it also has a *negativity* in that the agents within these different forms of life are not merely blind rule-followers but also develop principles for criticism of the rules, which at first are themselves part of the very "positivity" of the form of life itself.

This distinction, obvious as it is, is sometimes overlooked by those who read Hegel – at first, not implausibly – as holding something like the view that since (Kantian) practical reason divorced from social practice is empty, we therefore have a duty to abide by the principles and codes embedded in our own form of life (thus making Hegel into a version of Bradley's "my station, my duties" *avant la lettre*). Hegel's point, however, is different; it is that although we are all ultimately children of our own time and thus cannot leap out of it to make judgments in terms of some nonembedded set of principles, our form of life can itself nonetheless be irrational in a profound way, such that the hold the positive norms have on us – via our second nature and set of socialized dispositions – can itself begin to abate; the norms lose their hold on us because of the deep level of tensions and contradictions at work in their one-sided presentation of the "unconditioned." When such a waning of attachment becomes more clearly evident, those norms gradually cease to be genuine norms and instead come to be seen as something more like merely positive social rules whose bindingness is now merely a matter of power, of lack of alternatives, or something similar.

The chapter on "Spirit" thus begins with a treatment of what Hegel calls "true spirit." What makes that form of life "true" is that the conception of the "unconditioned" embedded in that form of life – the world (or nature) as a purposive whole in which each part has its proper role to play – seems to be almost perfectly mirrored in the positive rules of its own civic life, and that the positive social rules contain no contradictions within themselves. Indeed, such a form of human life seems to embody Kant's own conception of beauty as exhibiting purposiveness without a purpose; even though no individual participant can state the purpose that the cosmos as a whole serves, there is nonetheless the feeling (or at least a kind of tacit grasp) that there is indeed such a purpose and that the spontaneously produced harmony that comes about when each does what is required of him or her is more or less the proof that the purpose is being realized. Further proof is that in those cases where the harmony is thrown out of kilter by someone violating the requirements of his or her station in life, punishment – either divine or human – restores the social world to its original harmony by visiting on the wrongdoer the equivalent harm he or she has done to the harmony of the whole.

Such a unity between "positivity" and "negativity" – that is, between social facts and norms – is undone when the most basic conceptions of what is unconditionally required of such agents come into contradiction with each other. Hegel takes Sophocles' *Antigone* to exhibit the most basic and submerged contradiction in that form of life. Antigone is presented with (1) the unconditional duty to obey her uncle, Creon, who has forbidden her to give her dead brother the required burial rites, (2) the unconditional duty to perform those rites, and (3) the unconditional prohibition against making up her own mind about where her duties lie. Thus, whatever she does is wrong under some aspect, and not only does the unconditionality of the first two requirements make a compromise difficult, but the unconditional demand that she *not* make up her own mind about them makes it logically impossible for her to avoid the dilemma. The Greek form of life (in this admittedly idealized form) thus pushes and provokes its members to adopt a reflective, quasi-autonomous stance toward their duties while at the same time forbidding it, and the undoing of Greek life lies in the way that the imposition of such incompatible deep commitments leads to its norms losing their hold on its members.

The form of life that both takes up the remnants of the Greek spirit and replaces it is that of Roman legality, within which the individual agent takes a more distanced stance toward the "positivity" of the social substance. Just as the Greeks were self-consciously absorbed into their form of life (and their corresponding lots in life), Romans (on this equally idealized interpretation) are self-consciously at one step removed from the empire, in which the only shared commitments among its inhabitants are the set of Roman laws and nothing further.[15] Understanding, however tacitly, that the positive (legal) rules of social order may indeed be at odds with those of others or with other requirements of, say, family life or the life of one's clan – such that one cannot rationally expect a harmony to emerge spontaneously from each if one simply follows the requirements embedded in one's lot in life – the Roman finds something like stoicism to be the philosophical and lived expression of what his or her form of life has already brought to pass. The logic of that kind of experience gives rise to the idea that the only unconditional requirement is that one seek self-sufficiency, that is, that one endeavor to need as little from others or other groups as possible.[16]

In this way, the outcome of Roman legality in part replays the end of the "master-servant" dialectic of the "Self-Consciousness" chapter of the book, which has to do with a "struggle for recognition" between two agents, that is, a struggle over which of them is either to acknowledge or to confer a normative status on the other.[17] (The other agent in the struggle is experienced not so much as being an obstacle to be overcome – like a river to be forded – but as a challenge to one's own claim to any authority.) Since authority is not a natural feature of human beings, it must be something achieved, and thus where there is no antecedent agreement about who or what has authority, one or the other of them will simply have to establish authority; thus, without any further authoritative principles for doing so, the initial establishment of authority will have to be done by fiat, by an act of will. In Hegel's scenario, one of the two agents is willing to risk his or her life to set up the standards of authority (i.e., his or her own standards), whereas the other person, out of fear for life, opts for accepting the rule of the former; one becomes the master, the other the servant (or slave). The master thus seeks a form of self-sufficiency, an ability to dominate others, that is, to normatively compel them while being normatively compelled by nobody else.[18] The failure of such self-sufficiency – since, according to the master's fiat, the slave on whose recognition the master depends cannot have the authority to confer that recognition – results in the realization that self-sufficiency, which itself requires domination of others, can itself only be a one-sided and unsatisfactory conception of freedom as self-direction, and that this ultimately requires a conception of freedom as something that moves beyond self-sufficiency while incorporating parts of it.[19]

If an agent seeks self-sufficiency (or if he or she understands freedom to be the realization of self-sufficiency), then such an individual can be ruled only by an even more powerful individual who has the power to impose obedience on him. Thus, the logic of a form of life based on self-sufficiency – which is, as it turns out, the very logic of the Roman empire itself – pushes it to the idea of a single ruler (an emperor) who can, godlike, simply impose his or her will on others. Of course, the way in which such an emperor must understand him- or herself – namely, as an instance of supreme self-sufficiency, the point at the very top of the pyramid of power – is itself fundamentally deceptive for all the reasons that all forms of domination over others is flawed. (The only way out of that logic would be to construe the sovereign power, as Hobbes later did, as a kind of corporate individual; but the state of Roman legality did not have the European early modern conception of particular persons as moral *individuals* and hence that move was not open to them.)

Alienation

The failure of empire results in the gap between "positivity" and "negativity" being opened up in the Roman world, which in turn led to the medieval world that followed the empire's collapse. Mere social rules were now seen as not necessarily carrying their own authority with them. In light of that new understanding, the interpretation of such authority came to concern itself with the way in which the always potential normative gap between the results of self-conscious reflection and the givens of the surrounding world from that point onward had to open up in a way that henceforth could not be retracted.[20] This thus forms a sphere of spirit that is fundamentally alienated from itself in that it knows that whatever authority it acknowledges as the limits (the "negative") of its own authority is also something that is equally limited by itself; the post-Roman subject is in a way the continuation of the slave in the dialectic of mastery and servitude who eventually comes to understand that although powerless, he or she participates in the practice of his or her own domination by granting the master's authority. This subject is thus alienated in that he or she knows him- or herself to be both powerless and powerful (a condition that makes the subject unintelligible to him- or herself). This alienation of spirit plays itself out, so Hegel argues, in the complicated dialectic of early modern Europe as it passes from its medieval corporate understanding of the different estates in society to the idea of an absolutist monarch. The crux of the passage from competing systems of authority to absolute monarchy emerges in the so-called absolute distinction between aristocrats, who in their self-sufficiency are suited for rule, and the commoners (especially the emerging *bourgeois* of early modern town life), who by virtue of their own commitment to self-interest and their dependency on others for their livelihood are fit neither to represent themselves in state institutions nor to govern. However, the aristocrats' pretense of self-sufficiency collapses under the unifying impulses of monarchs (who are themselves faced with the option of either increasing the wealth and size of their realms or being gobbled up by more powerful neighbors). The monarchs eventually transform the aristocrats into a court whose very existence depends on the kind of recognition they receive from each other and most particularly from the monarch himself. In addition, the absolute distinction between aristocrats and commoners itself collapses under the weight of the newly ennobled merchant class that often now commands more wealth than the older aristocracy.

The result is the development of acute alienation; as we might put it, what started out as a political practice in early modern Europe eventually came to be understood as merely a game kept in existence by thoroughly alienated actors. If the "unconditioned" comes to be seen as that which individuals can – by utilizing resources solely within their own powers – affirm for themselves, then their interaction can only be that of keeping a tally on each other.[21] Each takes what he or she thinks is true and keeps a tally on the others, and social life becomes a play over who gains the authority to set what the standards are for "scoring" each other. In such conditions, it becomes clear to each player in the game that what therefore counts in setting the rules are matters of power and interest, not genuine truth. The main character of Diderot's short piece, *Rameau's Nephew*, encapsulates this stance: the character (a musician)

99

openly avows that he is in fact more authentic than those who profess a deeper authenticity than him because he self-consciously has no deeper commitments than to bow to the commitments of those more powerful than him, that is, to bend his will to what the market demands of him, to flatter those who need flattering, and to say whatever it takes to get ahead in this world. The world of the nephew is, to use the technical philosophical term that the philosopher Harry Frankfurt has given for such things, a world of bullshit.[22]

This lands the participants of the courtly world of *Bildung* – of the self-conscious shaping of one's self and desires in terms of the "positive" rules of the culture of reciprocally "keeping a tally" that surrounds them – in the contradiction of claiming unconditional truth for something that in its own terms has no truth. It is the unconditional demand to adhere to the fully contingent rules of the social formations around oneself – and de facto of the accepted tastemakers of the time – and to strive to change those contingent rules into those serving one's own contingent interests.[23] The "truth" of the world divided between the "noble" and the "base," and of the flattery and vanity of the court culture surrounding that way of life, is thus, to put some Hegelian jargon to use, pure positivity. That the participants in that way of life understand that the world of reciprocally "keeping a tally" is itself without truth – that it is merely a matter of social coordination amid grabs for power and influence – is itself a reflection of the way in which this kind of self-conscious distancing from the positive rules of the social order is at work – or, in Hegel's jargon, is actual, *wirklich* – in this life.

At the same time that the participants in the world of "cultural formation" find themselves to be caught in the tension involved in holding fast to the idea that the only unconditional truth is that there is no unconditional truth, others find themselves committed to the idea that truth must be something that transcends the pure positivity of keeping a tally. This takes two forms: first, an emotionalist faith in God's ultimately providing guidance for us that is not in any way a matter of social positivity, and, second, a belief that some kind of intellectual rational insight is possible such that we can grasp the truth in a way that transcends all contingent practices altogether. Both embody a commitment to an abstract conception of truth that is not explicable in any terms having to do with any de facto practice at all.

What is most striking about Hegel's claim here is the way in which he argues that, although historically both of these camps took the other to be its enemy, both were actually two sides of the same coin, two virtually identical but nonetheless formally different reactions to the alienated, "tally keeping" world of courtly culture, each of which took the other reaction to be its opposite.[24] ("Pure insight" is for its adherents the intellectual rejection of the truth as apprehended by "faith," whereas "faith" is for its adherents the emotionally religious rejection of the truth as apprehended by the detached intellectuality of "pure insight," and each realizes that the other takes itself to be the rejection of its other.) The problem is that there is no real content within either side's conception of the "unconditioned." Each sees the "truth" that transcends "keeping a tally" in such abstract terms that "truth" cannot serve to rule in or rule out any (or very much) particular content, and thus one ends up once again in a form of life displaying what looks like a set of Kantian antinomies.

Rational Insight, Utility, and Freedom

"Pure insight," the detached intellectual grasp of "the truth," is worked out in the practices of the European Enlightenment, and "faith" is worked out in the practices (both Protestant and Catholic) of the emotionalist religions and sentimentalism that accompanied the Enlightenment. (Hegel offers up an extended argument about how such "faith" inevitably loses its battle with Enlightenment since it tacitly accepts the basic premises of the Enlightenment's worldview and thus tries to play the Enlightenment's argumentative game on the Enlightenment's own terms, but that argument will be put to one side here.) Since the Enlightenment sees the truth as grasped intellectually, and since it seeks to have some more material result than simply the rejection of the sentimental pieties of faith, it seeks to find some kind of "given" in experience that can anchor all other claims to knowledge. (Thus, the opening chapter of the *Phenomenology* on "sense-certainty" is revealed to be one of the key moves made by such Enlightenment thought when it seeks the "unconditioned" in experience as something that can be known absolutely without our having to know anything else.[25]) It is a long story in Hegel's text, but the failures of such claims to immediate knowledge lead to the idea that "the truth," if it is to have any content, must be that which is useful to us; that is, they lead to a concept of utility, the general idea that all deliberation about final purposes comes to an end in some kind of conception of what objectively produces the greatest amount of some good (perhaps that of human happiness, assuming that it can be measured precisely enough).[26] This conception of "utility as grasped by rational insight" is, for the Enlightenment, what counts as the "unconditioned."

However, what this conception of utility marks is the more basic idea that, fundamentally, we cannot be called to obedience to some law that we cannot ourselves understand and against which our sinful, fallen natures make us naturally susceptible to revolt – in sharp contrast to the claim that was made in medieval Europe and that emerged as one of the flashpoints in the struggles over the Reformation and Counter-Reformation in early modern Europe. Rather, we must see it for ourselves, must see ourselves as setting all our particular laws and customs in light of what a disinterested and detached intellectual grasp of the truth would give us. Hegel characterizes this conception as "absolute freedom," the idea that the community cannot be subject to any authority except that which it itself establishes as rational and that no de facto practice can make any claim to authority except by being submitted to the standards supposedly implicit in such a view of reason. However, since the only standard available to such a detached view of reason is that of utility (of producing some maximal amount of goodness as viewed impartially), utility comes to be the rule in the course of the French Revolution, where (on Hegel's account) the "general will" is, as Rousseau describes it, always tending to utility. However, since such a "general will" must be implemented by finite, contingent agents, those who are carrying out the implementation are in turn inevitably seen only as members of a particular faction implementing its own partial views instead of those of the impartial general will. The result of the imposition of the standard of utility is the Terror, the execution by the "humane" standards of the guillotine of those whose further existence is of no use or even

101

dangerous to the social whole, with the result being that of "the coldest, emptiest death of all, having no more meaning than does chopping off a head of cabbage or swallowing a mouthful of water." The Republic is, of course, never fully cleansed of such dangers, and thus one faction is always being overthrown by another, with each new one claiming to be the true embodiment of the impartial general will.[27]

Hegel's point about the Terror should not be confused with the familiar conservative complaint about the Terror's savagery being the inevitable result of cutting oneself free from all traditional restraint; Hegel was and remained throughout his life a supporter of the Revolution. His point was rather that the logic of "absolute freedom," when cut off from any more concrete conception of how to realize it, certainly cleared the way for something like the Terror. The proponents of the Terror took themselves only to be impartially applying a determinate meaning to concrete circumstances; they were prey to the fantasy that in matters of "infinite" concern – in matters that depend on our allegiance to some conception of the "unconditioned" – we can have a determinate meaning that is antecedently fixed prior to its instantiations and for which we need only look to instances in the actual world. Those dissenters who were dangerous to the survival of the Republic were thus seen as diseases to be excised, a result of the disinterested application of a principle to the situation. (Not for nothing was Robespierre, the architect of the Terror, called "the incorruptible," the embodiment of virtue itself; his coolness in expunging the malignancies in the Republic was evidence of his impersonal attitude in applying the principle.) Part of what was so desperately misguided about the Terror was its one-sided conception that all that was at stake was the disinterested application of an already determinate principle. The deeper conflict between living subjects having a point of view on the world and those same subjects taken as objects to be arranged in the optimal order had to remain invisible from within the outlook shared by Robespierre and his cohorts.

The Moral Worldview as the Culmination of the Positivity and Negativity of Spirit

What was true in the Revolution was the conception of freedom as obeying a self-instituted law that was only redeemable by appeal to reason. For that, however, what was required was not the principle of utility as the final end that structures all deliberation but something more like the Kantian universal will, where the limits to the will are set not by the external and hopelessly abstract concept of utility but by the rationality implicit within the concept of a free will itself (which supposedly in Kantian theory results in a conception of all agents as ends in themselves who are never to be used merely as means). The practical, social background of the Kantian system – what Hegel calls the "moral worldview" – understands the normative limits of the will to be set not by the merely positive rules of the social order (or even "the Republic") but by what is involved in an idealized order in which each agent is both sovereign (as the unconditional lawgiver) and subject (as unconditionally subject to the moral law). This is, of course, Kant's kingdom of ends, the moral successor to Rousseau's political conception of the general will. However, the moral worldview, whose motivational force lies in its existence as the practical complement to the political upheaval of the Revolution – that is, as the other side of the coin to the Revolution's conception of "absolute freedom" – is itself burdened with a very similar problem to the problems bedeviling "absolute freedom" itself. It assumes that an individual subject can arrive at a determinate meaning – a moral principle that it can use to form or to test maxims – and then apply it in action; this once again assumes there to be a sharp distinction between the meaning of the principle and its realization, a distinction that cannot be sustained (or so the central thesis of Hegelianism goes); or it retreats into an equally sharp distinction between inner intentions and outward actions, a distinction that when put into practice makes the moral worldview unlivable.

The moral worldview culminates in a confrontation between two "beautiful souls." The confrontation takes place between two agents who each have accepted a basic Kantian point: it is impossible for us to have any theoretical grasp of the world as it might be apart from the conditions under which we must experience it, but we can genuinely grasp "the unconditioned" through our practical reason. In the use of practical reason, we experience ourselves as bound by the unconditional duty to act according to the terms set by an unconditional moral command. (Or, to put it another way, for the moral worldview, the only metaphysics that actually provides us with a genuine grasp of the unconditioned is the metaphysics of morals.) Such a moral worldview also demands that all agents seek therefore a purity of motive on their own part, however much they have to acknowledge that no finite human being ever achieves such a purity of heart. Each must, that is, unconditionally try to submit all of his or her proposed maxims to the moral law, and each must unconditionally try to the best of his or her ability to formulate the moral law in the best way possible. Now, not only is this unconditional moral requirement potentially at odds with virtually all the other contingent features of one's life (both one's own needs, desires, personal commitments, and the contingency of the world itself in which such actions are realized), its problems are further compounded by the kind of heightened self-consciousness in which during and after the eighteenth century the agents of the moral worldview found themselves enmeshed, namely, that "we" are now acutely aware of the finitude, or contingency, of our standards – one thinks in particular of Hume's challenge to the traditional views on the matter – and of the equal necessity of justifying those standards. Put more generally: the philosophical confrontation between Kant and Hume – or, to put it even more generally, the worry about whether there are any categorical imperatives at all and whether the only imperatives that can work are hypothetical – was itself anchored in a social and existential worry about whether there was any true grasp of the "unconditioned" at all – a worry that played itself out in the very concrete religious and moral disputes that are treated in the final sections of the "Spirit" chapter.

This confrontation that Hegel stages between the two "beautiful souls" is another exhibition – a *Darstellung* – of Hegel's more general and ambitious thesis about the nature of conceptual content. As such an exhibition, it is the existential enactment of a more general theory of conceptual content that has been in the process of development throughout the entire *Phenomenology*. In the confrontation between the "beautiful souls," each agent experiences the tension between his or her own individual desires and his or her other commitments. Each sees that his or her only grasp of the unconditioned is, as it were, to be found in the purity of the agent's own heart, his or her own unconditional assent to submit all of his or her maxims to the test of the moral law. By adopting such a stance, each thus finds him- or herself in the same position as the other,

103

as each of the two beautiful souls is in effect the authority-conferring self – or, in a less orthodox Kantian mode, is the self who submits him- or herself to the unconditional authority of reason – but who is equally as well a contingent, situated self who is seeking to establish just what that authority requires. Moreover, each is convinced that since it is the authority of reason itself to which one is submitting, each has within him- or herself all the resources necessary for determining just what it is that impersonal reason requires. Given that setting, the enactment quickly splits into two different understandings of what unconditional duty requires, a split that itself stems from two different understandings of what moral judgment requires in the conditions of the acceptance of such unconditional duty. Each makes a judgment as to what is required of him or her; one agent sees the purity of his motive as preserved in his actions despite the contingency of their realization (i.e., he sees that, irrespective of how his deeds might appear to others or what shape they might take in the contingent world, the purity of his motive remains intact); the other agent sees the purity of her motive as lying solely in her capacity for moral judgment itself and not in action at all. One of them thus acts and takes this action to preserve the beauty of his soul, provided he adopt something like an ironic stance toward his actions (or, more likely, toward the consequences of those actions, matters for which he is not fully in control); the other, on the other hand, does not act and instead takes the beauty of her soul to be evidenced by her very refusal to sully herself with the impurity of the world. Each thus also necessarily thinks of the other as a hypocrite: she who thinks of her own purity as lying in her refusal to act and thereby sully herself thinks of the other as only pretending to be pure while acting in such a way as to produce deeds of less than absolute moral worth, whereas the acting person must see the protestations of the judgmental (but not acting) agent as only the attempt to cover up with all her moral talk her inability to do the right thing.

Ultimately, each comes to see him- or herself *in* the other as each comes to admit that, in Kant's terms, he himself or she herself is radically evil, that is, each comes to understand that he or she cannot easily pry apart the contingency of his or her own situated perspective (and thus his or her own individuality, or "self-love") and his or her demand for a unconditional justification of his or her actions. Without this acknowledgment on the part of each that both for their own parts have good reasons to suspect the other of dissembling, of hypocrisy, or of saying and doing what he or she does out of merely strategic considerations, and without this acknowledgment also becoming mutual, the slide into a destructive moralism itself becomes unlivable since the logic of such a moralism imposes demands for purity that cannot be acknowledged by the other or, ultimately, by oneself. In Hegel's staging of the confrontation, this awareness of the identity of each within a larger whole in turn leads each of them to forgive the other, since both come to see that neither was, as it were, without sin (i.e., radical evil). It is in that way that the dialectic of beautiful souls can be said to be the existential enactment of the conceptual dialectic between the unconditional demands of reason and our contingent situatedness, and, in following out the terms of Hegel's theory of conceptual content, such an enactment precedes the conceptual grasp of what has been enacted.

This culmination of "Spirit" thus emerges as the "truth" of this confrontation between two moralistic beautiful souls; however, it is "spirit" as a form of sociality that has come to understand its own limits as lying between its demand for a grasp of the unconditioned and the necessary situatedness of any agent. There is no determinate meaning of any basic principle or claim that can be established and understood outside the ways in which it is realized, and therefore no such principle that is completely transcendent to all its institutional realizations and to the problem of finitude confronting any agent. This sets the stage for the problem Hegel will meet head-on after the *Phenomenology*, namely, to determine what, if any, sort of institutions and practices are compatible with such a comprehension of this very basic tension at the heart of all modern, "reflective" conceptions of agency. In effect, that is to ask how such an abstract understanding of the unity of the unconditioned and conditioned – of the unconditional necessity of submitting all our claims to reflective justification together with the fact of our own contingency and the perspectival nature of all our conceptual contents – is to be realized in a way that does not impose incompatible commitments or unlivable requirements on those who must live within those institutions and practices. Certainly, Hegel did not think that any political organization could fully live up to that demand (although he clearly thought some were better than others).

The rest of the *Phenomenology* tries to show how what Hegel came to call "absolute spirit" as the self-reflection of the human community on what ultimately, "unconditionally" mattered to it was the only appropriate response to that open-ended requirement. Thus, the rest of the *Phenomenology* after the "Spirit" chapter focuses on art, religion, and philosophy, the only practices where those two demands – of the unconditioned and the conditioned – come into sharper focus and where the antinomies provoked by the institutional demands of a way of life and those of freely self-directing individuals are not so much in play. Only in art, religion, and philosophy is our timeless grasp of our own contingency and temporality more sharply and self-consciously worked out, quasi-paradoxically, in a time-bound manner. However, just how that part of the story goes would have to be the subject for another chapter.

Notes

1 Immanuel Kant, *Critique of Pure Reason*, trans. Norman Kemp Smith (London: Macmillan and Co., 1964), 7 (Avii).

2 *Critique of Pure Reason*, 664–665 (A850/B878).

3 See Immanuel Kant, *Critique of Judgment*, trans. Werner S. Pluhar (Indianapolis, Ind.: Hackett Publishing Company, 1987), §57.

4 See *Critique of Judgment*, §59.

5 For example, one passage among others: G.W.F. Hegel, *Wissenschaft der Logik*, ed. E. Moldenhauer and K. M. Michel, 2 vols. (Frankfurt am Main: Suhrkamp Verlag, 1969), vol. 1, p. 52: "Kants dialektische Darstellungen in den Antinomien der reinen Vernunft verdienen zwar, wenn sie näher betrachtet werden, wie dies im Verfolge dieses Werkes weitläufiger geschehen wird, freilich kein großes Lob; aber die allgemeine Idee, die er zugrunde gelegt und geltend gemacht hat, ist die Objektivität des Scheins und Notwendigkeit des Widerspruchs, der zur Natur der Denkbestimmungen gehört: zunächstd zwar in der Art, insofern diese Bestimmungen von der Vernunft auf die Dinge an sich angewendet werden; aber eben, was sie in der Vernunft und in Rücksicht auf das sind, was an sich ist, ist ihre Natur. Es ist dies Resultat, in seiner positiven Seite aufgefaßt, nichts anderes als die innere Negativität derselben, als ihre sich selbst bewegende Seele, das Prinzip aller natürlichen und geistigen Lebendigkeit überhaupt." ("Thus, Kant's expositions in the antinomies of pure

reason, when closely examined as they will be at length in the course of this work, do not indeed deserve any great praise; but the general idea on which he based his expositions and which he indicated is the objectivity of the illusion and the necessity of the contradiction which belongs to the nature of thought determinations: primarily, it is true, with the significance that these determinations are applied by reason to things in themselves; but their nature is precisely what they are in reason and with reference to what is intrinsic or in itself." Hegel, *Science of Logic*, trans. A. V. Miller [London: Allen and Unwin, 1969], 56.)

6 The idea that Hegel's thought proceeds along the lines of a method of "thesis-antithesis-synthesis" is thus not only textually false, it is undone by Hegel's own conception of how dialectic is supposed to work.

7 The phrase "'curtain' of appearance" is Hegel's own rather acerbic description of this view. See G.W.F. Hegel, *Phenomenology of Spirit*, trans. A. V. Miller (Oxford: Oxford University Press, 1977) (henceforth: *PhG*), ¶165.

8 *PhG*, ¶165: "what is present is the gazing of the inner into the inner... *self-consciousness*. It turns out that behind the so-called curtain, which is supposed to hide what is inner, there is nothing to be seen unless *we* ourselves go behind it, in precisely in the same way that it is seen that there is supposed be something behind the curtain which itself can be seen"

9 Putting it like this, of course, is in effect stating Hegel's conclusion as if it were the argument itself. Hegel himself offers the entire "Reason" chapter as a kind of exhibition of how these contradictions in taking reason to be the "unconditioned" play out in practical life when they are worked out, or realized, in various situations, ranging from Faustian quests for power, reliance on the "heart" as the source of rational law, Shaftesburyian assertions of virtue as lining up with the harmony of the world order, all the way up to the pretenses and collapse of a kind of theatrical presentation of one's true self and true interests in what Hegel calls the "spiritual kingdom of animals" (very likely a reference to the popular series of prints by various artists of animals dressed in the high style of bourgeois society that were so popular across Europe).

10 *Critique of Pure Reason*, 9 (Axi-xii).

11 Hegel's various terms for this have to do with plays on "*realisieren*" and "*verwirklichen*" (which seem to be synonymous for him) and "*ausführen.*"

12 See Robert Pippin, "Concept and Intuition: On Distinguishability and Separability," *Hegel Studien* 40 (2005): 25–39, where the key Hegelian use of the "distinguishable but not separable" thesis is fleshed out.

13 This thesis about conceptual content does become more and more a feature of explicit argumentation as Hegel develops his thoughts in his later works and lectures. The *Phenomenology* is, in his own words, simply the "ladder" one climbs to attain the kind of high-altitude vantage point at which the thesis begins to appear. The *Encyclopedia* is Hegel's more explicit set of arguments for this thesis; it remains a matter of dispute, however, whether the *Phenomenology*'s *Darstellung* is more persuasive than the more systematic arguments of the *Encyclopedia*.

14 *PhG*, ¶437; the phrase "second nature" is taken from the later *Philosophy of Right*. See G.W.F. Hegel, *Elements of the Philosophy of Right*, ed. A. W. Wood, trans. H. B. Nisbet (Cambridge: Cambridge University Press, 1991), paragraph 151.

15 See *PhG*, ¶476: "He is that substance as the *positive* universal, but his actuality is to be a *negative*, universal *self.*"

16 See *PhG*, ¶479.

17 The struggle over recognition is also a struggle over the status of self-consciousness itself. In *PhG*, ¶178, Hegel notes, "Self-consciousness exists *in* and *for itself* because and by way of its existing in and for itself for an other; i.e., it **exists only as a recognized being**" (emphasis in boldface added).

18   See Henry S. Richardson, *Democratic Autonomy: Public Reasoning About the Ends of Policy* (Oxford: Oxford University Press, 2002), for the discussion of domination as normative compulsion (where he makes this point against Philip Pettit's influential non-normative conception of domination).

19   Thus, the chapter on mastery and servitude in the *Phenomenology* is titled as being about self-sufficiency, *Selbstständigkeit*, and the successor chapter is titled as being about the "freedom of self-consciousness."

20   Thus, in *PhG*, ¶483, Hegel notes, "The ethical substance kept the opposition enclosed within its simple consciousness, and it kept this consciousness in an immediate unity with its essence. For that reason, the essence for consciousness has the simple determinateness of *being*, towards which consciousness is immediately directed and whose ethos it is.... However, the spirit whose self is the absolutely discrete self has in its own eyes its content confronting it as an equally hard actuality, and the world bears the determination of the external, that is, the negative of self-consciousness." His use of the phrase "the opposition" here refers to the basic opposition between all forms of merely positive authority and genuine authority (i.e., to the opposition between the non-normative and the normative). He also speaks of "the distinction" (*der Unterschied*, which could also be rendered as the "difference") as that between subjects (as loci of entitlements and commitments) and objects.

21   I have used "keeping a tally" rather than the term "scorekeeping" to set it off from Robert Brandom's use of "scorekeeping" to explain how conceptual contents can be both perspectival *and* shared and to show how one generates a conception of objectivity out of his inferentialist account of meaning (Brandom, *Making It Explicit: Reasoning, Representing, and Discursive Commitment* (Cambridge, Mass.: Harvard University Press, 1994)). Brandom explicitly rejects the idea that scorekeeping in his sense could only be a matter of *mere* coordination among viewpoints; if it were mere coordination, then it would be a form of the "regularism" that he criticizes in the first part of *Making It Explicit*. However, it seems that his account of scorekeeping at the end of *Making It Explicit* falls exactly into the trap he cautions against at the beginning of the book, since it is a matter that rests on factual deontic "attitudes," what people in fact do in keeping score. There is obviously more to be said about Brandom's nuanced position on this point, but that would be another chapter in itself. On the "regularism" inherent in Brandom's own antiregularist position, see Robert B. Pippin, "Brandom's Hegel," *European Journal of Philosophy* 13 (2006): 381–408.

22   For a more nuanced discussion of the concept, see Harry Frankfurt, *On Bullshit* (Princeton: Princeton University Press, 2005). Do note that although I talk about the alienated world as a world of bullshit and as a world of "keeping a tally," this should not be taken to imply, to suggest, wink at, or even to hint that I also think that Robert Brandom's discussion of "score-keeping" is an instance of bullshit, or that it leads to it, or that it even stops just short of being bullshit. Brandom's work is both important and admirable. That I also think that Hegel's conception of truth and Brandom's own conception of truth diverge in ways that show Hegel's own views to be better is a separate topic for another time.

23   Thus, in the concluding paragraph of this discussion (*PhG*, ¶525), Hegel notes, "From the aspect of the return into the self, the *vanity* of all *things* is its *own* vanity, that is, it *is* itself vain. It is the self existing-for-itself, which does not merely know how to evaluate and how to chatter about everything but which also knows how to convey wittily the fixed essence of actuality as well as the fixed determinations posited by judgment, and it knows how to speak of them in their *contradictions*. This contradiction is their truth."

24   See *PhG*, ¶541.

25   See *PhG*, ¶552.

26   See *PhG*, ¶561.

27   *PhG*, ¶590.

Part III

Logic

Thinking Being: Method in Hegel's Logic of Being

ANGELICA NUZZO

In Hegel's *Science of Logic*, the problem of "method" does not appear thematically until the last chapter.* This could lead one to assume that in its first logical sphere, the Logic of Being, we should still be far from methodological concerns. However, from early on in the history of Hegel interpretation, critics and interpreters of this work have focused primarily on methodological questions. How can the Logic begin with no presuppositions when it presupposes the *Phenomenology of Spirit* or, at the very least, the language of which it makes use? How can the Logic proceed immanently, as it promises, without being in effect a sort of dialectical 'trick' that progressively discloses what it has initially hidden or, alternatively, without claiming a creativity difficult to justify outside of a problematic metaphysical framework? And what are we supposed to make, even granting the assumption of such immanence, of the many 'anticipations' of later logical forms that appear throughout the Logic of Being? These are just a few of the questions that interpreters have heretofore explored for the most part accurately even if they have not settled them. I will not repeat or address these questions directly here.[1]

On the other hand, the question, of what 'method' is in Hegel's speculative-dialectical logic deserves special attention – if only because of the unconventional use that he makes of this concept. Since the last chapter of the *Science of Logic* dedicated to the absolute Idea presents the absolute Idea itself as "absolute method," we can legitimately assume that herein lies the answer *in* the Logic to the question of method.[2] For within the Logic, this is the place where method is taken up *thematically* by the logical discourse, that is, the place where Hegel offers a metareflection on or theorization of the issue of method. What is intriguing, however, is the further question: What is the

---

* Citations from Hegel's *Wissenschaft der Logik* are from G.W.F. Hegel, *Werke in zwanzig Bänden* (=TW), ed. Eva Moldenhauer and Karl Markus Michel (Frankfurt am Main: Surhkamp Verlag, 1986); citations from other works are from G.W.F. Hegel, *Gesammelte Werke* (=GW), ed. Reinisch-Westfälischen Akademie der Wissenschaften in Verbindung mit der Deutschen Forschungsgemeinschaft (Hamburg: Felix Meiner, 1968ff.).

---

method *of* the Logic itself? That is, what is the method that Hegel de facto employs in developing logical thinking throughout its different forms and spheres even before coming to address the issue thematically at the end of the work? What is the method *used* by Hegel in his Logic that shapes the logical development itself? And what is the relation between the method that is *used* and the method that is *thematized?*[3] This broad question is scarcely explored in the literature, and it is not evident to what extent Hegel himself intends to address it in the chapter on the absolute Idea. Obviously, I have no pretensions to answering it fully within the space of this chapter. Here I will only begin to tackle the issue within the more limited horizon of the Logic of Being (and even within it, I will only take a few examples into account). My first aim is to argue that this question matters for the Logic of Being *more than for all other spheres of the Logic.* My second aim is to offer an *example* of how to approach the problem of reconstructing the method of the Logic of Being.

The Problem: Perspectives on Method, Or, How to Approach Being

In presenting the "absolute method," Hegel suggests that only at the end of the logical development does it become clear that what has been the forward-moving *advance* of the process of determination is truly a *return back* to the beginning. In addition, only at the end does it become clear that the two opposed directions in which the logical development has moved – the "retrogressive grounding of the beginning" and the "progressive further determining of it" – "coincide and are the same."[4] This, Hegel explains, is the "circle" of the method.[5] Once the standpoint of the end has been gained, the thematization of method leads Hegel to revisit the beginning of the Logic with a different knowledge or in a different perspective.[6]

Following the suggestion of the method's "circle," I propose to read the movement of the first sphere of the Logic starting from the end of the work, or from the perspective of the end having finally been achieved – that is, with the consciousness that has been gained once the entire logical development has come to its conclusion. Since such consciousness first arises, on Hegel's view, with the thematization "of absolute method," I will call such consciousness or knowledge *methodological.* I will distinguish the *methodological* perspective on the movement of being from the *immanent* development itself – the former indicating the approach to being that comes back to it once the Logic has reached its final chapter and the latter characterizing the internal movement of being that does not take into account the implications of its advancement for the system of logic as a whole (at the beginning no knowledge that the advancement of determination is a retreat to the ground is involved).[7] My aim is to bring to light what such a change of perspective – namely, the change of perspective brought about by the choice to begin the Logic again once the end has been achieved – reveals with regard to the method employed by Hegel in structuring the dialectical-speculative process of being.

The Logic of Being is the beginning of the Logic as a whole. Its question is: What is being when being is (immanently) the beginning? In the chapter on the absolute Idea, Hegel presents the "beginning" as a "determination" of *method.* The question here is: What is the beginning, when being is the first, most radical instance of such (methodological) beginning?[8] I will investigate what the Logic of Being reveals about the method

112

used by Hegel in this sphere once it is considered as a beginning, this time in the methodological or thematic sense discussed at the end. The task is to find the relation between those two questions on the basis of the method's "circle." I contend that the Logic of Being provides the first "example" of what Hegel presents thematically as the "beginning," that is, a moment of method. I claim that this can be established only once the perspective of the end is assumed, and I suggest that in positioning the first sphere of the Logic within the larger systematic whole, such a reading offers an important insight into the way in which the logical advancement is made de facto.[9]

Although the method is thematically absent (and only operative *in fieri*, as it were) if the sphere of being is viewed in its isolation from what follows, the method comes to the foreground once the Logic of Being is read against the background of the entire Logic, that is, from the perspective of the end, as Hegel invites us to do at the height of the absolute Idea.[10] Thus, to be able to 'see' method in the Logic of Being, we should consider being from the perspective of the end, that is, against the entire development of the Logic. In this perspective, we will be able to detect in the overall development of being the formal character that the chapter on "absolute method" thematizes as proper to the beginning as such. On the other hand, however, I want to push this claim further and maintain that the methodological thematization of the beginning as a moment of "absolute method" can take place only on the basis of the preceding movement that begins with being – the movement from which the "absolute Idea" as "absolute method" results. It is only because the beginning, which being makes or rather is, successfully advances the logical process to further determination – namely, eventually, to the highest form of the "absolute Idea" – that the beginning becomes a moment of method. To put this point differently: only an *immanent* beginning that can produce an advancement able to be at the same time a retreat to the ground is a *methodological* beginning or the beginning as a moment of the "absolute method."[11]

My suggestion is that we must attempt this – at once prospective and retrospective – methodological reading of the Logic of Being if we want to give a satisfactory answer to the problem of the *immanence* of thinking in the first logical sphere, that is, more precisely, to the question of *how immanence is presented* by Hegel in the actual shaping of the logical process. On first consideration it seems that such a task is simply proposed by the *interpreter* who, having come to the end of the Logic and learned about the moments of method, decides to revisit the Logic of Being and ask how such a beginning relates to what is said at the end of the work. However, I will suggest that an additional reason for embracing such a perspective is internal to the text of the Logic of Being, and is provided by a series of passages in which Hegel himself seems to be assuming the methodological perspective of the end. In this chapter I attempt such an interpretive change of perspective in order to give an account of some of these passages in the Logic of Being. I will show that Hegel himself endorses such a methodological standpoint. In this latter claim, my interpretation differs from those readings that tend to underline Hegel's appeal to either "external reflection" or the anticipation of later logical forms in constructing the logical advancement. My contention is that Hegel's introductory claims regarding the need for the Logic to develop immanently do not offer a complete account of how the logical development is actually construed – or better, they do not in themselves answer the question of how Hegel de facto *presents* such immanence. In bringing to the fore the 'methodological' perspective of the end, I will offer a more complex picture of how Hegel de facto proceeds in shaping the logical movement. Hegel's overall procedure, I will argue, is immanent-*cum*-methodological. If viewed in this perspective, the exclusive alternative between immanence and external reflection no longer holds. There is a reflection that is methodological and accompanies the immanent development of the logical forms. Hegel's actual practice in setting out the immanent movement of being is interwoven with methodological reflections that are integral to the unfolding of the logical forms themselves.

Although it develops immanently, that is, in a first approximation, without external intervention (be this the work of an external reflection, the reference to consciousness or a transcendental subject, or the intervention of a final purpose at which the movement is aiming), the Logic of Being includes claims that belong thematically to the level of discourse proper to the end. The focus on method in the sense that Hegel gives to it at the conclusion of the Logic allows me to account for a puzzling difficulty that we encounter in the development of being and which constitutes the focus of this chapter. In the first sphere of the Logic, Hegel repeatedly insists on the difference between the immanent development of the logical determinations, the function of anticipatory considerations, and the intervention of "external reflection." And yet against Hegel's reassurance to the contrary, both reflection and anticipation seem to play an indispensable role in Hegel's account of the generation of the progressive determinations of being out of the radical immediacy and indeterminacy of being-nothing with which the beginning is made. Such a role becomes even more relevant in the second edition of the Logic of Being. How then will we account for the presence of reflection – a function that seems alien to the immanent movement of the Logic in its inception and thematic only at the level of essence – in Hegel's account of the initial progression of being? It is precisely in articulating an answer to this question that I will pursue the issue of the method of Hegel's Logic of Being.

In what follows, I offer a contextual reading of the last chapter of the Logic and of some crucial passages from the first sphere of being (Quality) in light of the questions raised above. I thereby offer an "example" of what logical method is, more generally, in Hegel's speculative dialectic and, more specifically, of the way in which in Hegel's presentation being-thinking actually begins the immanent movement of its internal determination.

To sum up: (i) I will first assume the *interpretive methodological* position disclosed by the last chapter of the Logic in order to read some moments of the opening sphere of being – taking 'methodological' to indicate an account of the "beginning" as a determination of "absolute method;" (ii) I will then distinguish such a perspective from the *immanent development* of the sphere of being – namely, the development that advances by referring neither to some consciousness presiding over the process, nor to the anticipation of what is to follow, nor to the broader logical system as a whole; (iii) finally, I will analyze some of the passages in which Hegel, having distinguished the immanent movement of determination from the working of external reflection, contrary to his own reassurance, seems to appeal to such reflection. Herein I propose to read such passages as an example of Hegel's own endorsement of the methodological perspective disclosed by the end of the work. The answer to the initial question concerning the method that Hegel de facto *employs* in shaping the movement of the Logic of Being will be provided by a combination of the three steps or elements in my account, just summarized above: that method is immanent-*cum*-methodological. Moreover, I will argue that if, as I do in this chapter, we take the term "method" in the strict sense that Hegel confers on it in the last chapter of the Logic, the immanent movement of logical determination (which Hegel himself calls "method" in the introductory writings to the Logic) fulfills *only in part* the description of *"absolute* method" since it lacks the dimension of (methodological) consciousness. In short, I contend that immanence is a necessary but not a sufficient description of the method actually employed throughout the Logic. Thus, on the view that I am here proposing, the overall movement of the Logic can be summed up as follows: Hegel conceives of a purely immanent development that eventually leads to the absolute Idea; from the perspective of the absolute Idea (or "absolute method") Hegel (and we) can then look back at the development of the Logic as a whole and discern its systematic structure (e.g., beginning/advancement/end); furthermore, we see that Hegel's *actual practice* in setting out the immanent development is not itself purely immanent because he combines the immanent unfolding of the categories with *methodological* reflections. Indeed in his actual practice, such methodological reflections form part of the presentation of the "immanent" development itself.

In the first section I discuss the *"Vorbegriff"* – the "preconcept" or introductory notion – of method that Hegel offers in the preface to the *Science of Logic*. In the second section, I analyze some passages from the chapter on the absolute Idea in which Hegel presents the idea of "absolute method." Finally, in the last part of the chapter, I come to more specific considerations regarding the way in which the immanence of the movement of determination is presented in the initial steps of "Determinateness (Quality)."

1.   Hegel's "Vorbegriff" of Logical Method

In the preface to the second edition of the *Science of Logic*, in introducing the general idea of his work, Hegel offers a *preliminary* reflection on logical method that parallels the considerations that the *Encyclopaedia* entitles *"Vorbegriff"* or "preconcept" of the Logic.[12] Like all the remarks that Hegel generally places in the introductory writings to his works, these considerations do not belong to the proper development of the discipline.[13] Hegel contends that what distinguishes speculative-dialectical logic from traditional logic and from Kant's transcendental logic is not so much the "content" (*Gehalt und Inhalt*) but the "method," that is, the way in which the content is dealt with in its exposition. In particular, Hegel argues that although traditionally logic has treated its content as a "dead" unmoved material, and therefore has arranged it in an arbitrary and external way, the task of his work is to "infuse life into the dead limbs of logic," hence to treat those "limbs" according to their own "spirit."[14] The problem of method is the problem of how to think of a self-generating living movement. This movement is the inner necessary process of determination of thinking itself. This is the true content of the Logic. At stake is both the issue of thinking and presenting the dynamic of a movement (and not, for example, a static set of categories), and the issue of thinking and presenting a movement whose order and determination unfolds following its own internal laws (or its own "soul" or "spirit"). In this regard, the method and its content are said to be identical.[15] To think according to a movement and not according to fixed determinations or positions is to present the movement of thinking itself (or thinking itself as a movement).

Traditional logic assumes its content as historically given and ready at hand. The only way to infuse life into such content is to find the "method" that alone can trans-form logic into "pure science." However, Hegel observes that in the present state of the discipline, logic has not yet found its "scientific method."[16] And yet the paradox already raised in the introduction to the *Phenomenology* is that method can neither be separated from that *of which* nor that *for which* it is method; hence it cannot be given beforehand and be simply applied as an external instrument to a given material.[17] Ultimately, to find the true scientific method is to deal with an utterly new content.

"The exposition of what alone can be the true method of philosophical science falls within the treatment of logic itself; for the method is the consciousness of the form of the inner self-movement of the content of the logic."[18] In this passage Hegel gives us an insight into the sense in which the method is identical with, but also the sense in which it is different from, the logical movement.

In one respect the true method is one with the movement of the *entire* Logic itself; method is that which generates the movement and thereby the content of the Logic. On this premise, it seems that no 'treatise on method' can be formulated *in abstracto* or that no method can be theorized outside of or before its practice. Nonetheless, concrete "examples" of such method can still be provided. In the *Phenomenology*, Hegel explains, he has offered an "example" of the true method in considering a "more concrete object, which is consciousness."[19] Awareness of its being an example *of method,* however, is displayed only *after* the science of phenomenology has run its course.[20] What we have in the Logic is another example of method, which arises when attending to the most abstract of all objects: pure thinking itself. Within this project, in turn, the Logic of Being provides the very first example of logical method in which pure thinking is taken in the most abstract and immediate of all its determinations, namely, in the utter indeterminateness from which all successive determination arises. Thus, the example of the Logic of Being is the most fundamental example of logical method. In analogy with the case of the *Phenomenology,* however, we can assume that awareness of its being an example *of method* will emerge only at the end of the science.[21] Once again, the "*preconcept*" of method does not belong to the development of the Logic itself.

In another respect, the passage quoted above suggests that the method is *distinct* from the movement that it generates. Offering a preliminary definition that will be confirmed in the last chapter of the Logic, Hegel recognizes a moment of "conscious-ness" proper to method and a formal character that is obtained by appealing to the form/content distinction: method is "the consciousness *of the form of the inner self-movement of the content* of the logic."[22] The consciousness of form proper to the method is awareness of the dynamic nature of the logical content: method is the form of the "self-movement" of the content. It is precisely this *consciousness* that distinguishes that self-movement from its form. Indeed it is consciousness that sets the movement apart and considers it as an "example" of method. To be sure, the consciousness belonging to method is not the same subjective finite consciousness that the *Phenomenology* takes as its concrete object and follows throughout the complete series of its oppositions up to Absolute Knowing. The Logic begins only once such finite consciousness (and the necessary opposition belonging to it) has been left behind once and for all.[23] What then is the "pure" consciousness proper to logical method, and how is such consciousness present in the Logic of Being?[24] To answer these questions, we need to look more closely at Hegel's account of method itself.

If method is the exposition of a movement *as movement*, the question of how "advancement" is achieved becomes crucial.[25] There are two features that Hegel considers in the preliminary concept of method – also called explicitly "dialectic"[26] – (i) determinate negation and (ii) immanence or, in an alternative formulation, the consideration of things "in-and-for-themselves" (i.e., without reference to metaphysical substrates or subjective representations).[27]

(i) Determinate negation is presented as "*das Einzige*" – the one and only necessary point – through which to attain the dynamic progress of the Logic.[28] The "system of concepts," Hegel suggests, must be built according to this principle. Determinate negation implies recognition that negativity and contradiction are always determinate and as such determining. That is to say, first, that they are the negation of and contradiction in determinate contents; and second, that the concept resulting from negation contains in itself that which has been negated as the determinate basis on which the successive movement is built. In Hegel's dialectical method, negation is thus not absolute (though absolute negation and contradiction are thematic moments of the logical development itself). The opening and first advancement of the Logic of Being offer the first "example" of this principle. Significantly, both the exposition of this principle in the introductory preconcept of method and its first exemplification in the inception of the movement of being are distinct from the thematic account of contradiction and its principle at the level of the Logic of Essence. The latter does not belong to the methodological account that I am pursuing here. (It constitutes, instead, the specific content of the *Wesenslogik*).[29]

(ii) Immanence or the consideration of things "in-and-for-themselves," the second feature of method, is introduced as an indirect justification in support of the "one and only point" that is determinate negation. In formulating this second feature, Hegel conveys, at one and the same time, the method's perfectibility and incompleteness, and the inescapable necessity of its truth: "I could not pretend that the method, which I follow in this system of logic – *or rather, which this system follows in itself (an sich)* – is not capable of greater completeness, of greater elaboration in detail."[30] Since in one respect the method is identical with the movement of thinking in the Logic, it ultimately erases the author's presence (and his arbitrary choice), becoming one with the development that the logical system follows "in and of itself." In this way, Hegel also seems to sidestep the issue of the method *used* in the logical presentation, or rather seems to reduce it to the modality in which logical determination proceeds immanently. This point requires some explanation (or, at least, some exemplification), for it sounds indeed like a shift in the burden of proof from the author to the logic itself, which thereby acquires a life of its own. Hegel's point is that to the extent that pure thinking follows *its own* movement whereby the logical process is produced, instead of being forced to fit into prearranged schemes (tables of categories, various external purposes, etc.), it will prove its own truth. This method, Hegel declares forcefully, is "*the only true one*" although it can still be perfected and made more stringent in the details.[31]

The "truth" of the method is indeed a peculiar truth. It does not consist in its being given once and for all – the method is not a fixed scheme or instrument; rather it can and should be perfected – but in its being indistinguishable from its object and content, "for it is the content in itself *(in sich)*, the dialectic which it possesses within itself *(an ihm selbst)*, which moves it on"[32] (from which the method's perfectibility follows). If we connect this passage with the previous description of method – in which Hegel brings in the distinction of form and content, suggesting that though content is that which displays an inner self-movement (or indeed, as now claimed, "dialectic"), form is that of which there arises "consciousness"[33] – we can conclude that when the truth of method is at issue, at stake is *the way in which form and content correspond or are adequate to each other*. Hegel suggests that such adequacy is only then fully reached, when the content, as living content, in its inner dynamism gives and follows its own inner method or is ultimately one with it, that is, when the content shaped by its own internal negativity (or dialectic) is moved on through determinate negation to further determination. "It is clear that no exposition can be taken as scientifically valid, which does not pursue the course of this method ... for this is the course of the subject matter itself [*Gang der Sache selbst*]."[34] This is Hegel's first explanation of the method's immanence, which is ultimately one with the proof of the method's truth. But where and how does the "consciousness of the form" of such movement arise? Because of its merely introductory function, the preconcept of method does not offer further hints as to the way in which the inner self-movement of the content and the consciousness of its form are achieved. This will be the issue directly addressed by the thematic chapter on "absolute method" at the end of the Logic. As we will see, although immanence is first displayed in the opening of the Logic of Being, the identity of method and truth is eventually reached at the end of the Logic.

The two points that Hegel makes in the preconcept of method support each other: (i) determinate negation requires (ii) immanence, and immanence produces advancement precisely through a negation that functions as determinate negation. It is this view of method that places "dialectic" – heretofore considered, even by Kant, only as a "part" of logic – in a thoroughly new perspective and accords it a chief function in generating the movement of determination.[35] On Hegel's view, dialectic is not just a part of the Logic but is its pervasive underlying dynamic structure. Although the material of the Logic is inherited from the tradition, its formal integration into a whole is not, so the new problem that speculative logic (and specifically its method) is called on to solve is a problem of dynamic "order," that is, how to produce the "inner necessary connection" of the systematic whole, how to "immanently generate the differences," and how to achieve the "transition" among successive determinations and spheres of determination.[36] This is the methodological problem of the dynamism of the logical progress as it appears in the introduction to science, that is, before its actual beginning.

Hegel contrasts the immanence of dialectic with the procedures of "external reflection" *(äußerliche Reflexion)*[37] at work in all traditional expositions of logic. External reflection resorts to "deduction" as justification of the determinations arbitrarily anticipated in the division of the whole. This is the instrumental procedure that treats its object as a dead, unmoved material and considers negation as the dissolution of contents into nothingness. The necessity it provides to the logical exposition is, in turn, a merely external necessity that has no connection to the nature and specificity of the content under consideration but is entirely the product of an external thinking activity that organizes the exposition from without according to external presuppositions and purposes. Herein the only movement is that of reflection, which, however, remains utterly separated from its content, unable to fully grasp it in its specific nature. On Hegel's view, the shortcomings of external reflection ultimately stem from its inability to consider the determinations of thinking in their "purity" – which is instead the proper task of the Logic as the science of pure thinking. For the form when thought precisely "in its purity, contains in itself (*in sich selbst*) the capacity of determining itself,"[38] since it contains the negativity which moves it on to further determination. External reflection can present (and indeed deduce) thinking's own determinations only insofar as they are not taken as pure conceptual forms but are anchored in some more concrete representation (on this view, for example, "nothing" cannot be thought in its purity and becomes the representation of the "void"),[39] or, as Kant paradigmatically put it, in an "I think" that as thinking "subject" must be able to accompany all our representations, thereby becoming the reference point on which the entire logic and all use of the understanding ultimately depends.[40] Traditional metaphysics offers just another version of this inability to consider the form of thinking in its purity or "in-and-for-itself." In this case, however, thinking's determinations – which are, at the same time, determinations of being – are anchored in presupposed metaphysical "substrates" (being, for example, is *ens*).[41] In both cases, thinking and being are deprived of movement: determination does not occur as a development through negativity and does not produce a necessary logical order.

Summing up the results of the previous analysis and relating them to the two other systematic places in reference to which I will discuss the issue of method in the Logic, we can distinguish the following:

(i) in the "preconcept" of method, Hegel offers a first, introductory characterization of the "only true method" of logical science. This is a notion of method outlined *before the beginning* of the science and hence still *external* to the Logic. As such, it does not itself belong to its development. Hegel proposes determinate negation and immanence as fundamental features of such method and establishes two points. On the one hand, he insists on the coincidence between method and the logical development of the content. On the other hand, appealing to the distinction between form and content (yet, without further elaborating on it) he sees method as possessing – over and above the content – the "consciousness of the form" (of the content's own self-movement).

(ii) When the Logic of Being properly begins, we have the presentation of the immanent movement of being, which according to the preconcept is to be taken as an "example" of the method. In following such movement there is neither thematic mention, on Hegel's part, of "method," nor is there a "consciousness" of the overarching *systematic structure* in which the movement is inscribed.[42]

(iii) Such consciousness, or method as "form" – and precisely as the "form-determination" of the entire logical development – emerges only at the end, in the chapter on the "absolute Idea." There Hegel thematizes "absolute method" for the first time, and confirms the points made in the introductory "preconcept" and summarized in (i). The thematization of method at the end of the Logic *results from* the preceding immanent development of the logical content – (see ii) – in the sense of being the *proven truth* of the fully accomplished practice of immanence. It is at this level, namely, only after the logical content has been entirely displayed in its inner movement that the *consciousness* of such movement arises, and the *form* of the process is presented in terms of the complete logical "system." To this I will turn in the next section.[43]

2. Absolute Method and the Truth of Being

It is only at the very end of the Logic that Hegel tackles thematically the issue of method. At this point, Hegel confirms the determinations of method discussed in its "preconcept," lending them retrospective force with regard this time to the internal movement of the whole that now reaches its conclusion in the form of a "system of totality."[44] The "absolute method" is presented by Hegel as the *formal* side of the "absolute Idea," which, viewed retrospectively, is the result of the entire previous logical process.[45] The development of this formal side is now responsible, in a new final step, for bringing the entire course of the Logic to the form of an overarching systematic structure, whereby the end is finally reached. While the "absolute Idea" has in itself the content developed throughout the Logic and is the final "truth" of such content, the "absolute method" is declared to be the "form-determination" of the Idea. As such, it shows how this content is arranged to give the Logic the form of a "system of totality." It is from the height of the "absolute Idea" conceived as "absolute method" that I propose to read some crucial methodological moments of the first division of the Logic of Being. Accordingly, this reading will place the Logic of Being within the systematic totality that logical method constitutes at the end. Let us then look at the way in which the last chapter can help us in this inquiry.

Considered as the result of the entire preceding logical development, the "absolute Idea" is presented as the only true being: "the absolute Idea *alone* is *being* ... , truth that knows itself, and is all truth."[46] As the last moment of the Logic, the absolute Idea is introduced by appeal not only to the immediately preceding development ("theoretical" and "practical Idea," "life") but to the very first logical form, namely being.[47] At this point, being achieves the dimension of its ultimate truth, and the form of self-knowledge and awareness proper to the Logic.[48] Herein we discover that since the Idea is the one and only object or content of philosophy, all determinations of thinking-being developed throughout the Logic are determinations of the Idea and are contained within it. The absolute Idea is the ultimate 'horizon' of all logical thinking and being – the same ultimate horizon that "pure being" is at the beginning of the process (and *as* the beginning of the process). At the end of the Logic, the Idea's realized truth replaces the initial sheer immediacy of being. However, as true being, the absolute Idea is not yet complete or, alternatively, being as Idea is not yet entirely determined. The Idea – and thereby the true being that the Idea alone is – must still be presented as "absolute method." This is the topic of the last chapter of the Logic.

Hegel uses the distinction between "form" and "content" to establish both the relationship between the previous movement and the Idea, and the relationship between the absolute Idea and the absolute method.[49] The absolute Idea, being one with the entire process of the Logic is, as such, nothing but the "self-movement" of thinking taken in its pure logical formality. Since the pure form of thinking, fully developed to reach the "absolute Idea," is the "content" of the logical science (a content that is in turn merely formal if compared with the 'real' sciences), the absolute Idea "has itself as infinite form for its content."[50] Although form and content are one in the absolute Idea (their identity constituting precisely its absoluteness), unlike the content, which has been the object of the previous development, the way in which the Idea is *form* has not yet come to the fore. Hegel observes that the absolute Idea has not yet appeared in its pure "form determination" (*Formbestimmtheit*), that is, as "method."[51] This is the side that the last chapter will develop. Method is the form of the absolute Idea and concerns the 'modality' in which the content is known and systematically organized so as to constitute the totality of the logical science. In other words, Hegel distinguishes a *form* and a *content* of the absolute Idea: the content is the entire preceding development of the Logic (this, in turn, is formal in the generic sense of concerning the pure form of thinking); the form is the aspect that needs now to be developed – this is the "method."

The Logic, which begins with being, is the development of the "determinateness" of the Idea, the production of its content. But Hegel now suggests that such determinateness has in addition a formal side, namely, "method." Hence, the task of the last chapter is to develop not a new content-determination of the Idea (for there is nothing that can be added to it in this regard) but its "form-determination," namely, its being "absolute method."[52] The need to carry out this further task is the first result of which there is now (i.e., for the first time) methodological consciousness. As Hegel suggested in the preconcept of method, method is the "consciousness of the form of the inner self-movement of the content."[53] Although the previous logical development has produced the entire self-movement of the content and is now complete, what still needs to be developed is the "consciousness of the form" of such movement – and this is what Hegel here calls "method."[54] The presentation of such reflective consciousness whereby content achieves its completed form-determination is the topic of the last chapter of the Logic. At this point, "method"[55] for Hegel is not the development of a new content-determination of the absolute Idea but the retrospective consideration (retrospective because all content has already been achieved) of the entire logical content from the perspective of its "form-determination," that is, *with the 'methodological consciousness' of its position within a totality that now displays the form of a system*. Thus, in his discussion of "absolute method," Hegel presents first the formal moments of "beginning," "advancement," and "end" in order to position the preceding contents within the whole precisely *as* "beginning," "advancement," or "end." Second, he shows that the entire course of the Logic – under the aspect of both content and form – now constitutes a "system of totality."[56]

We can now see in what sense the immanent movement of determination throughout the Logic *differs* from what Hegel calls thematically the "absolute method" reached only at the end. Although it is in the position of immanence before the conclusion of the process that the sphere of being is developed, starting from its initial immediate indeterminateness, to further qualitative determination and so on, the absolute method repositions the Logic of Being within the whole logical development, producing the 'methodological consciousness' of the place that this sphere occupies within the overall comprehensive "system" of logic. The Logic of Being, with regard to the "form-determination" of method (namely, the distinction between beginning, advancement, and end), is the beginning of the totality; that is to say, the sphere of being is the *beginning of method*. The Logic of Being is thereby characterized by its place within the systematic whole, *which was not in sight from the position of immanence*. This I take to be the "consciousness of the form" of the logical content, namely, the positioning of a logical structure not simply within a linear advancement but within the completed systematic form of the logical whole.

In his first definition Hegel presents "method" both as a "modality of being that is determinate in and for itself" *and* as a "modality of cognition."[57] As the former, method is the "substantiality of things" – it is properly their animating "soul." In this way, the method replaces the metaphysics of substrates already criticized in the preconcept of the preface. The Logic of Being tackles the same problem: how to develop being in its successive determinations without reverting to metaphysical substrates. Immanence is in both cases at issue. The end of the Logic tells us that "method," that is, the immanent soul and moving principle of thinking-being is the answer. As a modality of cognition, on the other hand, the absolute Idea as absolute method raises the subjective universality of finite knowledge (presented in the Idea of Cognition) to the truth and concrete universality of the Idea.[58]

In presenting the method as the "soul" of the content, Hegel claims that "method" is the inner "activity of the concept" itself. However, although the concept has been developed in its determinations throughout the Logic, method *as such* emerges only at the end. It follows that in addition the "*difference* of the method from the concept as such" must be drawn.[59] Within the immanent development (or "in itself") the concept appeared "in its immediacy." It is only at the end that the methodological awareness or reflective "cognition" (*Wissen*) that the method itself involves allows us to consider the place that the "concept" occupies within the whole.[60] If in the position of immanence (or in the concept taken "in itself" in its "immediacy") we want to speak of "reflection" – that is, Hegel explains, of the "concept that considers [the concept]" – then we have to say that such reflection, along the way, "fell within *our* knowing."[61] On Hegel's view, however, the "absolute method" *overcomes* the difference that throughout the Logic still separates the immediate and immanent development of the concept from the reflective awareness of a cognition that heretofore "fell within *our* knowing."[62] The absolute method as the form-determination of the "absolute Idea" in which the entire content of the Logic is present[63] involves the reflected knowledge of this very content in its completed self-movement, namely, knowledge of its position *within a whole* (and not only in relation to what precedes). In the absolute method, all logical determinations are 'reflected,' known, and finally brought to consciousness: method is "this knowing itself" (*dies Wissen selbst*),[64] namely, the final convergence of our knowing and the immanent movement of thinking. Thus, it is here that we find the full explanation of the claim that "method is the consciousness of the form of the inner self-movement of the content of the logic."[65]

Method is not only consciousness of form, but also *form itself* (indeed, the highest "form-determination" of the absolute Idea and thereby the systematic form of the entire Logic); yet it is not an "external form" (*äusserliche Form*) applied to given contents or in which different contents are arbitrarily made to fit. It is instead the "absolute form" (*absolute Form*) in which all possible logical content is immanently produced in its truth, that is, more properly, is shown in its "untruth" and necessary "transition" into its opposite.[66] Set against merely external reflection, the method requires a consideration of "things in and for themselves," that is, in their immanent "soul" and moving principle.[67] Logical method is a way of attending to things – or better, to the determinations of thinking-being in their purity. It is thereby meant to bring forth "what is immanent in them, *and to bring this to consciousness.*"[68] What comes to consciousness at the end of the Logic is the absolute *form*, or absolute method, of the whole. As absolute form, method is thus "the absolute foundation and last truth"[69] of the entire Logic. Significantly, the initial sphere of being is characterized by an analogous determination that places the unity of being-nothing as the "first truth" that as ultimate foundation of all that follows is established as the irrevocable basis of the entire movement once and for all.[70] In the "circle" of method, the conclusion of the advancement in the process of determination is a return back to the beginning that appears now as the ultimate ground.[71] Owing to the circularity of the logical process whereby the end is a return to the beginning, being and method – the first and the last truths of the Logic – share an analogous structural definition, that is, an analogous position within the "system of totality;"[72] the task of the Logic of Being is to *begin* the logical process, and the task of "absolute method" is to *end* it.[73] The end is achieved as the thought of being as *content* becomes the idea of being as *form* (the form of the "beginning" as determination of method), indeed as the "absolute form"[74] in which all content or being is immanently produced and inscribed in its truth.

The moments of the "absolute method" – the moments of its "form-determination" – are "beginning," "advancement," and "end."[75] As Hegel comes to give a direct account of these moments, the entire Logic is reframed according to the structures of method. We can now see in what sense the question that Hegel poses by way of introduction, "With What Must the Science Begin?" is truly a question of method. The Logic of Being addresses the first determination of method – "beginning" – thereby offering the chief "example" of it. The spheres of Essence and Concept also begin, but it is the method of Being that properly constitutes their "beginning" insofar as the methodological moment of the beginning is at stake. With regard to "content," the beginning is "the immediate"; with regard to "form" it is "the abstract universal."[76] In retrospect, however, both immediacy and abstract universality are the methodological or formal coordinates that guide the movement of the sphere of being throughout its determinations. They are not only the *content* of the movement of being as immanently developed ("being, pure being" as the immediate; indeterminateness as the very determination of being).[77] But they are the *form* proper to the entire sphere of being – its specific methodological *form-determination* or the "element" of its presentation (immediacy is *the way in which* the transition from Being/Nothing to Becoming is achieved). Hegel insists that the immediate at stake in the beginning *of method* is not the immediate of representation or sensible intuition but the beginning *of thinking.*[78] The Logic of Being is the beginning of thinking (and of thinking's own being) – it is both the inception of pure thinking as such, namely, of the process that gives thinking its actuality or being (independently of a presupposed transcendental 'I think') and is the sphere that displays the first determinations that being presents to thinking when thinking approaches being in its utter purity (and not in relation to presupposed metaphysical substrates). Moreover, being is not the beginning of a *deductive* logical process because being is the most universal and most abstract thought: from its utter emptiness (or nothingness, as it were) there is nothing to deduce. Being is rather the beginning of the "realization of the concept." This is the "goal and task" pursued by the further development *of cognition*.[79] It does not, however, lie in the beginning as a presupposition of the entire process. The program of the Logic of Being is precisely to develop the connection between the indeterminateness and immediacy of being and the immanent beginning of the process of determination leading on to the "realization of the concept" – a process that is not already inscribed in the beginning and yet arises from it, or better, begins in and from it. Viewed as a moment of the method, the beginning has no other determination than that of being "the simple and universal."[80] It is precisely this determination taken "in itself" – namely, in its constitutive lack[81] or negativity and immediacy, and not, however, in its being enforced by "external reflection"[82] – that leads the process on to its advancement. Methodologically, as "beginning of the advancement,"[83] the universal of thinking discloses the meaning of the "concrete totality"[84] even though the beginning is only the simplest abstraction.

3.   The Method of the Logic of Being

If read in light of both (i) the "preconcept" of method offered in the preface to the Logic and (ii) the relationship that the "absolute method" establishes with the sphere of being at the very end of the work, the Logic of Being appears different from how it would appear if read simply as its opening sphere in its isolation from the whole. In particular, in the new perspective disclosed by the end, it becomes possible to see the methodological grain that in Hegel's actual practice sustains the immanent determination-process of being. Here, once again, I understand by 'methodological' the "consciousness of the form of the inner self-movement of the content" explained above in relation to Hegel's presentation of the "absolute method."

It is certainly true that the *immanence* of the development is comprehensible even without reference to the end of the Logic. Such immanence, however, is not properly "method" (in the specific thematic sense that Hegel gives to this concept) before the end of the development is reached.[85] And when the thematization of "absolute method" is achieved, immanence is only part of the meaning of "method." As explained above, what I propose here is an *interpretive* perspective on the development of logical content that first, addresses the issue of how the process of being appears if read with the knowledge of "method" gained at the end and second, accounts for some passages of the Logic of Being in which Hegel himself seems to endorse such a perspective. My claim is that if read with the knowledge of the end some passages of the Logic of Being show, along with their immanent significance (the "immediacy" of the "in itself" of which Hegel speaks in drawing the difference between "concept" and "method"),[86] a broader systematic meaning that arises when a certain determination is placed within the overall logical process that is not visible from the position of immanence. Consciousness of such additional systematic meaning is *not necessary* for the Logic to advance immanently, but it is important not to mistake such additional meaning for the intervention of the "external reflection," criticized by Hegel as the opposite of immanence.

124

The question that I am here pursuing is the following: What are we to make of those passages of the Logic of Being in which Hegel seems to step out of the immanent movement of determination and offer reflections, anticipations, and systematic remarks that somehow add to the determination immanently derived? Can Hegel's idea of "absolute method" help us in answering this question? I suggest that what we have in these cases is not an external intervention of reflections or anticipations but rather the "reflection" proper to "absolute method" itself or proper to the content determinations when taken up in the "form" disclosed by the "absolute method."[87] In other words, Hegel himself is here doing what the interpreter who endorses the perspective of the end and turns back to the Logic of Being does. I will raise the further question of the relation between such methodological reflection and the position of immanence.

In this last section, I analyze a few moments of the Logic of Being with regard to the issues discussed by Hegel in the chapter on method with regard to (i) the relation between the form and content of the process, (ii) the problem of reflection on the logical determinations of being (or the role of reflection in the progressive determination of being), and (iii) the immanence of the development once the problem at stake is that of producing the beginning of a movement that is forward moving as much as retreating into the ground of its foundation.[88] My interest is to pinpoint in the development of being the presence of logical method – the "method" that becomes visible only once the end of the Logic has been achieved. To this end I introduce a third methodological notion of "reflection" in addition to the criticized "external reflection" as a mental act intervening from the outside on the one hand, and to "external reflection" as content-determination thematized in the sphere of Essence on the other.[89] I designate as 'methodological reflection' the reflection that belongs in Hegel's view to "absolute method," namely, to the perspective that in repositioning logical determinations within the achieved whole of the system of logic discloses a "knowing" (*Wissen*) of their connection in such a whole that is essential to those determinations. If such knowing or reflection is not referred to "method" (in the sense that method has in the last chapter), that is, to the already constituted totality of the Logic (which obviously happens only at the end), it appears, as Hegel maintains, to "fall within *our* knowing" and to be distinct from and external to the immanent movement.[90] In other words, although the process develops immanently, *we* may reflect on the position that a certain determination occupies in the overall logical order. This, however, is only "our" knowledge because the Logic has not yet developed to a complete system. At the end by contrast, "absolute method" achieves precisely that backward-looking reflecting on the whole, thereby giving the whole the "form" of a "system of totality." I suggest that on a 'second reading' of the immanent development, we encounter passages in which a 'methodological reflection' positions the obtained determination within the logical whole exactly in the same way in which "method" does this in the last chapter. If we do not recognize the reference to "absolute method," we may mistake those passages for an illegitimate intervention of the criticized "external reflection."

Thus, my claim is that when reflection appears in the passages of the Logic of Being that I examine below, what we have is neither the external intervention of an already given structure of order as in the traditional expositions of logic criticized by Hegel, nor an anticipation of reflection as a moment of the Logic of Essence. Reflection – just like the reference to a "for us" that is ultimately "posited" (*gesetzt*)[91] – is the reflection of "absolute method." What we are presented with in the Logic of Being is the workings of *methodological reflection* – a reflection that in the inception of the Logic is "external" only insofar as it belongs to being as the "beginning" that is thematized *at the end* as a determination of "method," but is, truly, *"internal"* and *"pure reflection"*[92] – reflection internal to the de facto process of immanent determination itself.

Three general points can be established with regard to the program of the Logic of Being. First, its task is to think being out of its most radical indeterminateness and immediacy as the movement of progressive determination in which thinking itself is directly involved. At no point is thinking external to the process as, for example, is the 'we' of the *Phenomenology*. Thinking is one with being that becomes in the process. The being of thinking is this same progressive movement of determination out of thinking's own radical indeterminateness and immediacy in which being is in its most abstract universality. Second, the process in which thinking acquires its being and being becomes thought develops 'out of itself' or, owing to the radical indeterminateness and immediacy of being-thinking, 'out of nothing.' No presupposition is given on which to build the first sphere of being – neither the ontological substrates of metaphysics nor the representations of the omnipresent 'I think' of transcendental philosophy or of a phenomenological consciousness can be counted on. But also, more generally, all those presuppositions are lacking by which logical thinking may be set in motion – such as language, a primitive set of rules, axioms or definitions, or what may be taken as the traditional ready-made tools of the method. Speculative logic is the first sphere of the system of philosophy, and as such, it is absolutely presuppositionless.[93] In it alone the rules of thinking are first established. Third, the movement of being out of pure indeterminateness and immediacy is the movement in which determinateness and mediation – first as quality, then as quantity, and finally as measure – emerge as they are posited as spheres of being. The qualitative determination of being is the process in which being is reflected, distinguished, and posited in itself.[94] The problem at this point is how Hegel's claim that the sphere of quality does not rest on presuppositions and develops immanently can be reconciled with the language that articulates quality in terms of reflection, positing, and difference. Does not this language presuppose or rather anticipate what is still to come, namely, the Logic of Essence with its reflection, positing, and difference? In discussing a few paradigmatic cases, I argue that within the sphere of being, reflection is neither the criticized external reflection of traditional logic, nor an anticipation of contents proper to essence but the specific *method of being*.

3.1 Unity of Being and Nothing: "First Truth" and "Last Truth"

The utterly immediate and indeterminate first movement of being establishes the unity of being and nothing as becoming.[95] In the remarks Hegel offers some crucial observations that place this first, still very poor result within the entire development to come. Here we have an example of Hegel's endorsement of the standpoint of the end of the Logic – the presence of "method" in the Logic of Being.[96] The "unity of being and nothing," Hegel suggests in the first remark, is the "first truth" of the Logic.[97] We have seen above that from the standpoint of "absolute method" – which reconsiders the logical development in terms of "beginning," "advancement," and "end" – what is at stake is the "last truth" of the Logic and the way in which the "absolute Idea" is the truth of "being."[98] My present suggestion is that the remark that declares the unity of being and nothing to be the "first truth" of the Logic belongs to the same level of discourse as the "absolute method." Hegel positions an immanently achieved determination (the "unity of being and nothing") within the overall logical movement by declaring it to be the "first truth" of a series to come, i.e., by positioning it as the "beginning of the advancement" precisely in the sense developed by the "absolute method."[99] It is indeed the *consciousness of method* (not an external consideration or anticipation) that declares the unity of being and nothing to be the first logical truth. It thereby "brings to consciousness"[100] the position that this result occupies in the "system of totality" that the logical process ultimately constitutes. In other words, the movement of being develops immanently from pure being-nothing to becoming. At this point, however, only the perspective of the "method" can tease out of this determination its meaning for the further logical development. Precisely because it is the "first truth," being-nothing is seen as forming "once and for all the basis [*zugrunde liegt*] and element of all that follows."[101] It is to this still utterly indeterminate basis that the "absolute method" views the logical process as returning in its forward movement of determination. Although this unity remains the firm basis of the successive process, the process itself is the "retrospective foundation of the beginning."[102] The true foundation is only at the end in the absolute ground that is also the "last truth" of being.

Furthermore, Hegel declares the unity of being and nothing to be the "element"[103] in which the entire successive movement will take place. Just as the absolute Idea contains all logical determinateness "in itself,"[104] the method frames the first result of becoming as the pervasive element in which all logical determination is minimally inscribed. The immanent movement of the Logic is enclosed by these two methodological points – by pure being and the absolute Idea as the first and the last truths of the Logic. Since the thought of an 'outside' of being as well as an 'outside' of the absolute Idea is utterly meaningless (for all determination is a determination within the element of being-nothing and is determination of the Idea), no reflection can be placed outside of the logical process. Moreover, Hegel adds that to claim that the unity of being and nothing is the "first truth" and "element" of all that follows implies that "all further logical determinations" (and even "all philosophical concepts") will be "examples of this unity."[105] It should be recalled that in the "preconcept" of method, Hegel presents the phenomenological development as an "example"[106] of the dialectical-speculative method. Now, at this initial stage of the movement of being he declares all logical forms to come to be "examples" of the unity of being and nothing. Notably, this can be done only once such unity is brought to methodological consciousness, that is, once its function in the overall logical process is brought to light. And this confirms the peculiar perspective from which these remarks are drawn, which is the perspective of the "method."

To sum up: I distinguished two different levels at which Hegel's own presentation of the first movement of the Logic of Being takes place: the level of immanence that attains the "unity of being and nothing," and the perspective on being disclosed by the consciousness of "method" achieved at the end of the Logic, which declares such unity to be the "first truth" of the entire Logic.[107] One may indeed argue that the methodological consideration is *not necessary* in order to proceed immanently in the development of being – which is the reason one finds this consideration in a Remark. Such consideration, however, does not belong to a merely external reflection or anticipation. Having

127

pursued in this discussion the question of what procedure Hegel uses de facto to present the Logic of Being, we can now see that the answer is immanence-*cum*-methodological reflection. This combined perspective is, I submit, the 'method of being.' In other words (i) immanence is not coextensive with the "method" followed de facto by the Logic of Being; (ii) Hegel's remarks concerning the systematic validity of the first result of the movement are not simply external considerations that can be left aside or ignored but belong to the method used in the presentation of being.

3.2 Transition to Becoming: The "Pure Reflection of the Beginning"

In the third remark to the first movement of being, Hegel discusses Jacobi's critique of Kant's a priori synthesis of self-consciousness. Jacobi's critique raises the issue of the "transition" – on his undialectical view, utterly impossible – from an abstract first term to a further determination. Hegel uses Jacobi's argument to bring to light an important methodological dimension of the "transition" from being-nothing to becoming achieved by dialectical logic. The problem, on Jacobi's view, is twofold. At issue is both "what (*was*) brings determinateness into the indeterminate," and "how" (*wie*) the indeterminate ever comes to determination.[108] The first problem, Hegel suggests, is answered by Kant's synthesis of self-consciousness but has no place in speculative logic, which develops immanently and does not require the external, subjective intervention of an 'I think'. For in such logic, the problem of "what" brings determination into the process is already answered by the dialectical structure of indeterminateness. More important is the second question, which, if taken seriously and brought a step further than Jacobi does, is a question of method, that is, of the "modality" (*Art und Weise*)[109] in which determinateness is immanently produced de facto from within the indeterminate. However, in order to answer this question, the framework of Jacobi's objection to Kant must be abandoned, and appeal must be made to the claim of "absolute method": the indeterminate and immediate at stake in the beginning *of method* is not the immediate of representation or sensible intuition (to which, instead, Jacobi and Kant hold fast) but the beginning *of thinking*.[110] At issue in the opening of the Logic is the beginning *of thinking*, i.e., a *discursive* beginning. But this point becomes clear only once the beginning is viewed from the perspective of the method. It is from the standpoint of "method" then that Hegel contends that the transition from indeterminateness to determination is made because indeterminateness is itself the very determinateness of being.[111] Since such a transition implies process, it is discursive and not intuitive, but since it belongs to indeterminateness itself, it excludes the externality of Kant's 'I think.' In other words, in this remark Hegel offers an *additional* perspective on the route from being to *Dasein* – a view that is attained precisely by reframing the first movement of being-nothing in terms of the beginning *of method*, by reflecting on it, as it were, from a standpoint that is internal to the Logic itself. As in the former example, I want to point out how Hegel's discourse proceeds here on two different levels: that of the immanent movement and that of the methodological reflection. The latter is *not necessary* for the former to accomplish its result, but it is not an external, merely subsidiary remark either. The methodological perspective is necessary to frame the immanently attained result within the logical whole, and this, in turn, provides the inner systematic answer to the critics of the beginning.[112]

Endorsing the methodological perspective, Hegel can bring to light the peculiar "reflection" with which the first logical transition is achieved. To be sure, Hegel observes that "in the *pure reflection of the beginning* (*in der reinen Reflexion des Anfangs*) as it is made in this logic with being as such, the transition is still concealed (*ist der Übergang noch verborgen*)."[113] Yet viewed from the standpoint of the method of being, where the visibility of the different stages of the process is at issue (the beginning is the beginning of an advancement), Hegel can claim that the pure immediate being that constitutes the beginning of thinking is a reflected position or is itself pure reflection – "the pure immanent reflection of the beginning." However, what we have here is not subjective external reflection but objective "pure reflection."[114] The latter does not contradict the immediacy of being but truly expresses its being the *beginning* of thinking. Since in the pure reflection of the beginning being "*is posited* (*gesetzt*) only as immediate, nothing emerges in it only immediately."[115] That is, since in its pure reflection the beginning is posited as utterly immediate, the transition to nothing is not itself *posited* in it but is simply and immediately made – between being and nothing there is no true *transition* from one determination to another. Starting from *Dasein* and then in all successive, more concrete logical determinations, by contrast, "there is already *posited* (*gesetzt*) that which contains and produces the contradiction of those abstractions and therefore their transition."[116] It is precisely the reflected dimension of the first indeterminate determinations of being that allows one to detect the way in which the advancement is made, that is, the way in which the "transition" is "posited" (or rather, is precisely *not* "posited") in them. The language of reflection and positing thus expresses the point of view of the method of being: it is neither an anticipation of essence nor the intervention of an extra-logical subjective reflection. It is a reflection conducted from within the Logic itself, namely, from its end.

3.3   *Dasein: Immanent Process or Our Reflection?*

At the beginning of the chapter, "*Das Dasein,*" in developing the first moment, "*a. Dasein überhaupt,*" Hegel offers some crucial considerations with regard to the methodological notion of reflection at play in the first sphere of being.[117] *Dasein* issues from becoming in an immediate way as the simple oneness or "being one" of being and nothing – the same convergence or oneness of being and nothing that becoming is, now, however, mediated by becoming itself. Thus, leaving becoming "behind" as its "mediation," *Dasein* "appears as a first (*ein Erstes*),"[118] the beginning of the new movement in which "determinateness" acquires consistent being. *Dasein* is in the form of an immediate and entails two unilateral moments separated only by the different logical phases in which they appear as thematic in the development. It is precisely in the space of this difference that reflection plays a role in the presentation of *Dasein*. *Dasein* "is *first of all* in the unilateral determination of being."[119] However, it also contains the other determination of nothing, which it *then* displays in contrast to the former. *Dasein* is *being* which hosts in itself a "non-being." When instead the whole movement is considered from the negative side of *non-being*, determinateness emerges: "*Non-being* taken up into being in such a way that the concrete whole is in the form of being, of immediacy, constitutes *determinateness* as such."[120] Hegel presents *Dasein* and determinateness as two unilateral sides of the "concrete whole" that now replaces the abstractness of pure being-nothing. The former is being affected by non-being; the latter is non-being bent to the "form of being" and its immediacy. Methodologically, what we have here is the beginning *of the de facto advancement* of the determination-process of *Dasein*. In the chapter on method, Hegel expresses this moment by claiming that "the *concrete totality* constituted by the beginning has, as such, in itself *the beginning of the advancement and development.*" For, in the concrete the immediate hosts in itself a difference that brings the universal to a reflection into itself. To which he adds, significantly, "*[T]his reflection is the first step of the advancement.*"[121] As in the case of *Dasein*, the beginning of determination as first advancement is no longer pure abstraction but is a "concrete whole" or "concrete totality."

Given that my present concern is the methodological aspect of this development, the question here regards the status of Hegel's presentation of *Dasein* – or, once again, the different levels of discourse on which such presentation takes place. It seems that the characterization of *Dasein* and determinateness just offered is an immanent characterization since it follows, as Hegel repeatedly stresses, from its direct derivation from the previous movement of becoming. And yet, after introducing in a methodological observation the notion of "external reflection" and contrasting it with the immanent consideration of the logical contents, Hegel does not hesitate to claim that the fact "that the whole, the unity of being and nothing, is in the unilateral determinateness of being is an external reflection."[122] What is "external reflection" at this point of the development of *Dasein*, why is it invoked, and what does it accomplish in the movement of determinateness?

At stake is the relationship between, and the divergent methological status of, the following two claims:

(i)   "*Non-being* taken up into being in such a way that the concrete whole is in the form of being ... constitutes *determinateness* as such."[123]

Non-being is present in the concrete whole of *Dasein* in such a way that being still is, or does not vanish in the immediate fashion in which it disappeared in becoming: now non-being is present as determinateness that *is*. This is indeed an immanent characterization of *Dasein* as the content of the present logical stage;

(ii)   "The whole is likewise in the form, that is, *determinateness*, of being, ... a sublated, negatively determined being."[124]

Hegel thereby characterizes the further development of (i): in the concrete whole, the determinateness of being is a negative, "*aufgehoben[e]*" determinateness. *Dasein* is a *negatively* determined being. Unlike the first, this claim does not belong to the immanent presentation of the logical content. This is not *Dasein* as "a first" that immediately issues from becoming and from which a new development starts. It is rather this very advancement itself. The fact that the form of being in *Dasein* turns into a negative determinateness is that which carries the process on; it is not the beginning but a further "advancement" – it is, at this stage, a movement that is "not yet."[125] In fact, after presenting (ii), Hegel adds that the concrete whole is negatively determined being "for us in our reflection (*für uns in unsere Reflexion*), it is *not yet posited* as such in itself (*noch nicht gesetzt an ihm selbst).*"[126] What is posited in *Dasein* itself is only (i), namely, that non-being is taken up into being to constitute determinateness. That such determinateness is itself negative and *aufgehoben* constitutes instead a reflected determinateness – a determination that is posited by our reflection and therefore, at this stage, has the status of a "*not yet.*" However, since it is through this reflection that the advancement is made and presented, the conclusion is that what is not yet posited and falls in our reflection becomes de facto the immanent force that drives the process on. Once again, there is no 'outside' of the process; but there is a methodological difference between different stages of the process.[127]

To elucidate this situation, Hegel discusses a general methodological point. If speculative logic must think of its forms dynamically, then in all concepts the distinction must be drawn between "*posited*" and "*not yet posited determinateness,*"[128] that is, between different stages of the development that characterizes a certain concept. The de facto dynamism of the dialectical process lies precisely in the movement from posited to not-yet-posited determination. Reflection is the methodological function that achieves this transition. Hegel claims that "only that which is *posited* in a concept belongs in the consideration of its development (*entwickelnde Betrachtung*), belongs to its *content.*"[129] Methodologically, as determinations of thinking, all logical forms are "posited" or purely reflected when viewed *in the systematic place* in which they are thematically derived (as contents). In the immanent development, what is posited as content is that which a determination is *immediately* 'in itself' – *Dasein* is precisely that which its expression says it is, as Hegel explains appealing to the word's etymology.[130] But since in the de facto dynamism of the logical process a content's being posited leads to its further determination, each posited determinateness always already presents the side of (or turns into) a "not yet posited determinateness" – the determinateness to which the first eventually leads. This, however, when as yet only the immediately posited determinateness is at stake as *content,* "belongs to our reflection"[131] and indicates the *form* that such determinateness as content displays in the process (this time as it is no longer immediately 'in itself' but as sublated).[132]

Hegel distinguishes two alternative meanings or uses of "our reflection." On the one hand, such reflection "concerns the nature of the concept itself"[133] and differs from it only methodologically, that is, as regards the place or stage in which it intervenes in the process: at a certain stage, a determination pertaining to the "nature of the concept" may be "not yet posited" and nonetheless be thematized by "our reflection." On the other hand, "our reflection" may be concerned with extrinsic considerations and anticipations.[134] Unlike the reflection that belongs to the nature of the concept, the latter sense of reflection is excluded from the logical consideration. This is the point that Hegel makes in the "preconcept" of method. Thus, with the distinction between immanent movement and our reflection, Hegel distinguishes two connected phases of the logical process. The result of such distinction, however, is the opposite of the assumption of a subjective reflection (our reflection viewed as external) that allegedly sets the process in motion from without. Rather, Hegel's suggestion indicates that *our reflection is always already immanent in the presentation of the process* and operative in different moments as reflection on what is "not yet" posited – hence that it is not really "our" reflection but is rather, as becomes clear at the end of the Logic, the very consciousness of method or the pure reflection proper to all logical forms when considered methodologically with regard to the beginning, advancement, and end of the movement. It is precisely in this sense that Hegel in the preface presents the method as "the method, which I follow in this system of logic – *or rather, which this system follows in itself*."[135] Within the Logic, reflection does not belong to us but to the logical forms themselves. And yet, such reflection plays itself out at two different levels separated by the consciousness of method, once as "our" reflection and once as the reflection proper to the absolute method.

Hegel's reference to a non-subjective reflection proper to logical forms themselves reveals the complex character of Hegel's *actual practice* in structuring the logical process. For, what Hegel actually presents us with is not the simplified alternative between an immanent self-generating process and the external intervention of a subjective reflection. Passages such as the ones analyzed offer a more complex picture that should ultimately lead us to rethink the role of logical immanence in Hegel's dialectic. What he de facto does is weave together with immanence a methodological perspective that as such, becomes thematic only at the end of the process. The notion of a reflection proper to logical forms themselves must be understood in this way. If we focus exclusively on the immanence of the movement, and we miss the methodological dimension of the process, the only way to read Hegel's reference to "reflection" is to discard it either as an external intervention or as an illicit anticipation of what follows. What interests me here is, once again, the way in which Hegel in fact presents the logical process in its making.

In the last chapter of the Logic, Hegel claims that the "method" under consideration is nothing but the immanent "movement of the concept itself," whose nature is already known to us from what precedes.[136] Alternatively, he contends that what constitutes the method "are the determinations of the concept itself and their relations" that now become determinations of method.[137] In other words, method has been there all along but '*not yet*' *as method*. There is in fact "a difference of the method from the concept as such,"[138] and such difference is explained precisely in terms of the position that reflection has in relation to the immanent logical development. The passage is parallel to that of "*a. Dasein überhaupt*" analyzed above. "The concept when it was considered by itself appeared in its immediacy; the reflection, or the concept that considered it, fell within our knowledge."[139] Before reaching the end of the Logic the distinction between the immanent, immediate consideration of the logical content and its reflective, methodological dimension – a separation that accounts for the fact that the process is not yet concluded – is expressed by the presence of "our reflection" or "our knowing." "The method is this knowing itself, for which the concept is not merely the object but is knowing's own subjective activity."[140]

Conclusion

In this chapter I have offered only the beginning of a consideration of the way in which Hegel's speculative dialectical method is at work within the Logic of Being. In analyzing the account of "method" that Hegel offers before the beginning of the Logic (in what I called the "preconcept") and in the conclusion of the work, I have drawn a distinction between the immanent movement of the content and the "method." I have argued that the former is not coextensive with the latter. The "absolute method" adds to the immanent movement of the content "the self-consciousness of the form" of such movement. On this basis, I have proposed a reading of a few passages of Quality from the standpoint of the "absolute method." At issue was the way in which the consciousness of method is at work before reaching its absolute and conclusive dimension but also the way in which an account of the declared immanence of the process can be given that confirms both the use that Hegel makes of reflection in crucial passages of the Logic of Being, and his explicit rejection of a reflection intervening in the process from the outside. I have suggested that reflection plays a fundamental methodological role in *presenting* the immanent movement of the initial determinations of being, and that this reflection is both the "pure reflection" belonging to all logical forms as forms of thinking, and the methodological reflection of the logical "not yet" – "our reflection," as it were – with which the advancement in the process is made de facto. Ultimately, the two forms of reflection coincide in the methodological consciousness achieved by the absolute method.

Notes

1   See Stephen Houlgate, *The Opening of Hegel's Logic* (West Lafayette, Ind.: Purdue University Press, 2006) for a *summa* of the discussion. I have discussed some of the early criticisms of Hegel's logical beginning (by Trendelenburg and Schelling, in particular) in "Pensiero e realtà nell'idea hegeliana della Logica come fondazione del sistema della filosofia," in: *Discipline Filosofiche*, 5, 1995, 1, 141–160.

2   I have explored this problem in "The End of Hegel's Logic: Absolute Idea as Absolute Method," in *Hegel's Theory of the Subject*, ed. David G. Carlson (London: Palgrave Macmillan, 2005), 187–205.

3   The difference between the method *of* the logic or the method *used* by it, and the method *thematized* in the logic is the same difference, to adapt an example provided by Hegel himself, that runs between the (unreflected, unconscious) presence of grammar in the language used by a speaker and the thematization of grammar in a treatise on the grammar of a specific language. The distinction that I propose can be brought back as a variation to the old medieval distinction (taken up again by Peirce) between *logica docens* and *logica utens*. Interesting in this connection (from medieval logic to Peirce) are the questions of method, critique, and whether or not one can assume a sort of unreflected or unconscious use of logic.

4   TW 6, 570; see also 5, 71.

5   The method "thus winds itself into a circle" (TW 6, 570).

6   Minimally, the acknowledgment that the beginning that is progressively determined is the ground to which logical thinking retreats.

7   TW 6, 570. In this first, general determination, 'methodological' and 'immanent' refer to the topological standpoint assumed by the interpretation. Accordingly, 'methodological' is the view that is placed at the end of the work and that from this refers back to the beginning; 'immanent' is the perspective that follows the development step by step with no 'whereto' in sight. The former is a circular, and the latter is a linear reading.

8   TW 6, 553.

9   I do not claim, however, that the Logic of Being must assume this perspective in order to develop immanently. I claim that, interpretatively, to assume this perspective allows one to see a different and additional aspect of the Logic of Being – the aspect that I call "methodological."

133

10 TW 6, 549.

11 However, in the beginning of the logic – or in the position of immanence – we don't know that such beginning is the ground in which the movement retreats.

12 Henceforth I render Hegel's technical term *"Vorbegriff"* as "preconcept" (with its variants preconceptual, etc.). The use of this term for the reflections in the preface to the *Science of Logic* is mine. In a general sense, "preconcept" simply means 'introductory' concept, which is therefore external to the scientific development itself. The term has no reference whatsoever to a possible intuition (as coming before the concept). See my "Das Problem eines 'Vorbegriffs' in Hegels spekulativen Logik," in *Der "Vorbegriff" der Wissenschaft der Logik in der Enzylopädie von 1830*, ed. Alfred Denker, Annette Sell, and Holger Zaborowski (Freiburg: Karl Alber, 2010), 84–114 for an exhaustive account of Hegel's use of this term as well as of the systematic problems that he tackles with this notion (among others, the problem of an 'introduction' to the science).

13 Accordingly, these remarks cannot be normative for the development of the science itself. Their validity, Hegel often observes, is merely "historical."

14 TW 5, 48; the claim is repeated in the introductory pages of the *Begriffslogik*, TW 6, 243, and is already in the preface of the *Phenomenology*, TW 3, 37. The idea that logic treats its material as "dead *(todtes)*" has been entertained by Hegel since his reflections on Logic and Metaphysics in the early *Systementwurf I*; see GW 7, 111f.

15 See TW 50: "[Die Methode ist] von ihrem Gegenstande und Inhalte nichts Unterschiedenes."

16 TW 5, 48.

17 See TW 3, 68. Hegel opposes here the view of method as *"Werkzeug"*; see also TW 6, 552, according to which the instrumental conception of method is proper to finite cognition.

18 TW 5, 49.

19 TW 5, 49; also Enz. §25 Anmerkung, and the general seminal study by Hans Friedrich Fulda, *Das Problem einer Einleitung in Hegels Wissenschaft der Logik* (Frankfurt am Main: Vittorio Klostermann, 1965). More recent literature is discussed in my "Das Problem eines 'Vorbegriffs,'" cited above).

20 This is the case precisely at the beginning of the *Encyclopaedia* (see the references given in the preceding footnote). Hegel does seem to endorse the Greek etymology of metodos – meta odos: "after the road."

21 See the discussion in the next section below.

22 TW 5, 49, emphasis added.

23 See Walter Jaeschke, "Äußerliche Reflexion und immanente Reflexion. Eine Skizze der systematischen Geschichte des Reflexionsbegriffs in Hegels Logik-Entwürfen," *Hegel-Studien* 13 (1978): 85–117.

24 We will come back to this question below when discussing the presence of reflection in the development of being.

25 Indeed, the issue of the beginning is as important as that of the advancement or, as Hegel puts it in the method-chapter, methodologically the beginning is the beginning *of an advancement*. See TW 5, 48: "Das Einzige, um den wissenschaftlichen Fortgang zu gewinnen. ..."

26 TW 5, 50–51.

27 Given my present objective, I will dwell on the latter more than on the former.

28 Jaeschke points to the insufficiency of Hegel's characterization of this principle. See "Äusserliche Reflexion und immanente Reflexion," cited above. Hegel's considerations, however, must be understood precisely in the framework of a preconcept of method.

29 Briefly put, at stake here is the distinction between thematic and operative concepts.

30 TW 5, 50, emphasis added.

31 TW 5, 50, emphasis added. See David Kolb, "The Necessities of Hegel's Logics," in *Hegel and the Analytic Tradition*, ed. A. Nuzzo (London, New York: Continuum, 2010), 40–60,

which addresses the problem of how the claim of the truth and necessity of the method can be reconciled with the variations not only of content, but also of order, that Hegel introduces in the different editions of the Logic (both the *Wissenschaft der Logik* and the *Encyclopaedia* logic).

32 See TW 5, 50.

33 See TW 5, 49 discussed above.

34 TW 5, 50.

35 See TW 5, 51; also Enz. §79 Anmerkung.

36 TW 5, 51.

37 TW 5, 50.

38 TW 5, 61.

39 See, e.g., TW 84f., including the mention of the use of representation.

40 See KrV B131–134, footnote.

41 TW 5, 61.

42 Exceptions are the passages discussed in the last section of this chapter. For this, see below.

43 In the last section I will ask how (ii) the immanent movement looks if we assume (iii) the perspective of the absolute method, namely, the *consciousness* of the method that arises only at the end. In the first section I have suggested that this gesture is both an interpretive decision taken in the aftermath of the method's circularity (the end return on the beginning – see above), and a move that Hegel himself seems to make in crucial passages of the Logic of Being.

44 TW 6, 569.

45 See TW 6, 548, the "absolute idea" "has been obtained" from the previous development; and 550: content is the entire development of the logical science; form is the "method" that the last chapter of the Logic sets out to address. See my "The End of Hegel's Logic: Absolute Idea as Absolute Method," cited above.

46 TW 6, 549.

47 TW 6, 548f.

48 *Erkennen, Wissen,* and *Bewusstsein* are all determinations of method; as such, however, they do not entail a psychological dimension, nor do they refer to a psychological subject or consciousness.

49 The entire TW 6, 550, is argued in these terms.

50 TW 6, 550. This is not very different from 'thinking that thinks itself' in Aristotelian fashion.

51 TW 6, 550.

52 TW 6, 550: "The determinateness of the idea and the entire course followed by this determinateness has constituted the object of the logical science, from which course the absolute idea itself has issued for itself. For itself, however, the absolute idea has shown to be this, *that determinateness does not have the shape of a content but exists only as form.* ... Therefore what remains to be considered here is not a content as such but the universal aspect of its form – that is the method." (Miller translation, 825, slightly revised; emphasis added).

53 TW 5, 49 discussed above.

54 This is also the first thematic occurrence of this term; see TW 6, 550, quoted above.

55 I am using here the term "method" in the very specific sense that Hegel gives to it in this last chapter of the Logic, not generically, in a common-sense way. If I refer to the "preconcept" of method discussed above, it is to confirm the points that Hegel made there in light of this more specific meaning.

56 The logical process does not become a "system" until the end. I have developed the different steps of Hegel's argument in this last chapter in "Absolute Idea as Absolute Method," cited above.

57 TW 6, 551.

58 TW 6, 552.

59 TW 6, 552. Notice that this articulation of the relationship between concept and method as identity (the method is "soul" of the content because it is the activity of the concept itself) and "difference" (there is an *Unterschied* between method and concept) confirms the interpretation of the passage about the "preconcept" in which Hegel both identifies the true method with the logical process and distinguishes it from such process as the "consciousness of the form" of it (see above). In 6, 552, Hegel distinguishes the two respects as the sides of "universality" and "particularity" of the method.

60 TW 6, 552.

61 I will suggest below that this "our knowing" is the perspective of a reading of the immanent development after the end has been achieved.

62 TW 6, 552. In this sense, I do not think that it is true that in the *Wissenschaft der Logik* (in contrast to the earlier view of *Systementwurf II*), the "Spannung zwischen der tatsächlichen Darstellung und dem Methodenbewusstsein ausgeglichen [ist]" (see Walter Jaeschke, "Äusserliche Reflexion und immanente Reflexion," 117, 112). This is indeed the case in the absolute method; not, however, in the development-process of the Logic. The interesting point concerns precisely the transition to the position of absolute method.

63 See the argument developed above in commenting on TW 549–550.

64 TW 6, 552.

65 TW 6, 49.

66 TW 6, 551.

67 TW 6, 557: this is precisely what Plato's dialectic requires; see also 560 in reference to "dialectic."

68 TW 6, 557, emphasis added. Significantly, Plato's dialectic is mentioned as an example in this connection.

69 TW 6, 551.

70 TW 5, 86. See the discussion of this passage in the last section.

71 TW 570.

72 TW 6, 569.

73 Notice that by "absolute method" I mean the last moment developed in the chapter, "Absolute Idea," in the *Science of Logic*. The task of this last moment is specifically to bring the entire logic (as a "system") to its end.

74 TW 6, 551.

75 For an analysis of these moments, see my "The End of Hegel's Logic," cited above.

76 TW 6, 553: "Weil er der Anfang ist, ist sein Inhalt ein Unmittelbares, aber ein solches, das … die Form abstracter Allgemeinheit hat."

77 See TW 5, 104: "Unbestimmtheit ist aber das, was die Bestimmtheit [des Seins] ausmacht."

78 TW 6, 553, the former makes, for example, the beginning of the *Phenomenology* or of the *Critique of Pure Reason*. In TW 5, 82–83, the distinction between intuition and thinking is not yet drawn. Such distinction is a distinction that only the consciousness belonging to method is able to draw. In the immanent position of *Sein-Nichts*, intuition and thinking are the same pure, indeterminate being that is nothing. Interestingly, in the vast literature on this initial passage of the Logic Hegel's mention of intuition and thinking is never accounted for (see the positions discussed in Houlgate, *The Opening of Hegel's Logic*, chapter 14). For another direction, however, see Anton Friedrich Koch, "Sein – Wesen – Begriff," in *Der Begriff als die Wahrheit: Zum Anspruch der hegelschen "Subjektiven Logik,"* ed. Anton Friedrich Koch, Alexander Oberauer, and Konrad Utz (Paderborn: Schoenig, 2003), 17–30, 18–20.

79 TW 6, 554.

80 TW 6, 554.

81 TW 6, 555: it is *"mangelhaft,"* suggests Hegel.

82 TW 6, 555.

83 TW 6, 556.

84 TW 6, 555.

85 Throughout the process one may well bring in Hegel's own considerations on immanence and method in the "preconcept." In so doing, however, one steps out of the position of immanence and reflects, as it were, on it. It is indeed "our reflection" that considers this.

86 See TW 6, 552.

87 See the passage discussed in the previous section: TW 6, 552.

88 See TW 6, 570.

89 Jaeschke distinguishes the last two meanings of external reflection also terminologically as *"äusserliche Reflexion"* and *"äussere Reflexion"* (Hegel himself is not so consistent in this distinction; see "Äusserliche Reflexion und immanente Reflexion," 90). However, Jaeschke does not seem satisfied with the explanatory force that this distinction provides in accounting for Hegel's actual use of reflection in the *Seinslogik*, for example. Moreover, he suggests that these two meanings do not overlap with the distinction between operative and thematic logical concepts (94). Clearly, they cannot overlap if "external reflection" in the non-thematic sense is taken only in the sense of the criticized mental activity.

90 TW 6, 552.

91 TW 5, 122.

92 See TW 5, 104.

93 See, in general, Houlgate, *The Opening of Hegel's Logic*, chapter 3.

94 See for example, TW 5, 122f., the beginning of the section, *"c. Etwas."*

95 An accurate commentary on these sections is found in Houlgate, *The Opening of Hegel's Logic*, 263–283.

96 Once again, I use "method" neither in the generic sense of the term, nor in the sense of the method de facto used by Hegel, but in the technical sense that the term displays in the last chapter of the logic.

97 TW 5, 86.

98 TW 6, 551.

99 TW 6, 556: the beginning is "Anfang des Fortgehens und der Entwicklung."

100 TW 6, 557.

101 TW 5, 86.

102 TW 6, 570.

103 TW 5, 86.

104 TW 6, 549.

105 TW 5, 86.

106 TW 5, 49.

107 Notice that I do not call the perspective of immanence 'method.' This is what Hegel does in the "preconcept" and here *only*.

108 TW 5, 100.

109 TW 5, 100, compare with 6, 550f.

110 TW 6, 553.

111 See TW 5, 104.

112 The importance that Hegel attributed to these remarks is confirmed by his extensive reworking of these sections in the second edition of the Logic of Being.

113 TW 5, 104, emphasis added.

114 "Both external and internal reflection" ultimately reach exactly the same result: in its indeterminateness being is nothing. (TW 5, 104).

115 TW 5, 104.

116 TW 5, 104.
117 Jaeschke underlines the importance of these considerations for the problem of external reflection in the Logic (see "Äusserliche Reflexion und immanente Reflexion," 93, note).
118 TW 5, 116.
119 TW 5, 116, emphasis added.
120 TW 5, 116, see also the "concrete totality" with regard to the beginning of method in TW 6, 570.
121 TW 6, 556, emphasis added.
122 TW 5, 117.
123 TW 5, 116.
124 TW 5, 116.
125 TW 5, 116–117: "noch nicht" recurs frequently in these few pages. Spelled out in the terminology that Hegel introduces in presenting the "absolute method," what we have here is the distinction between the analytic and the synthetic moment of the "method" (TW 6, 557).
126 TW 5, 116, emphasis added.
127 TW 6, 557.
128 TW 5, 116–117. Properly speaking, Hegel does not distinguish between posited and not posited determinateness, as Jaeschke suggests ("Äusserliche Reflexion und immanente Reflexion," 93, note), but between determinateness that is posited "in itself" and determinateness that is "not yet posited."
129 TW 5, 117, emphasis added.
130 TW 5, 116.
131 TW 5, 117.
132 A determination is considered as 'content' when it is taken as the immediate thematic result of the process (it is the 'what' at which the process arrives); it is considered as 'form' when it indicates the modality in which a certain determination is present in the process (it is the 'how' through which such determination obtains). In the reconstruction of this passage, I have used the distinction drawn in the "absolute method" chapter (between the development of logical contents before the end of the Logic and the consideration of such development in the method) to shed light on Hegel's remarks on reflection in the first section of *Dasein*. In his presentation of method, Hegel draws a distinction between the "concept" immanently obtained as content in the subjective logic, and the concept as the reflected, conscious form present in all preceding logical determinations as their "soul." Although the former is taken "in its immediacy" and "reflection" "[falls] in *our* knowledge," in the second "method is this knowledge itself" and this very reflection (TW 6, 552 commented on in section 2 above). See Hegel's own rendering of this in TW 5, 116: *Dasein* initially coming from becoming has "die Form von einem Unmittelbaren"; the whole is "in der Form, ... des Seins ... ein aufgehobenes."
133 TW 5, 117, must be read along with TW 6, 552, in which exactly the same language occurs.
134 TW 5, 117. We may recognize in this distinction a "relict" of the two meanings of reflection with which Hegel has been struggling in the versions of logic before 1807. See the detailed account of these logics by Jaeschke, "Äusserliche Reflexion und immanente Reflexion," 96–117, 110 in particular.
135 TW 5, 50, emphasis added.
136 TW 6, 551.
137 TW 6, 553.
138 TW 6, 552.
139 TW 6, 552.
140 TW 6, 552.

6

Essence, Reflexion, and Immediacy in Hegel's *Science of Logic*

STEPHEN HOULGATE

The doctrine of essence, by Hegel's own admission, is the most difficult part of speculative logic.[1] Much of this difficulty is due to the fact that Hegel equates the essence of things with the movement of "reflexion" (*Reflexion*).[2] Even by Hegel's notorious standards, the concept of reflexion is formidably hard to understand: reflexion, he tells us, is simply the "*movement from nothing to nothing and thereby back to itself*" (SL 400 / LW 14). If we are to appreciate what is distinctive in Hegel's conception of essence, therefore, we must explain why, in his view, essence turns out to be reflexion, and how reflexion itself gives rise to further concepts, such as identity and difference.[3]

From Being to Essence

Hegel's *Science of Logic* is the study of the fundamental categories of thought and being. It is thus a work of both logic and ontology, that is to say, it sets out "the science of logic which constitutes metaphysics proper" (SL 27 / LS 6).[4]

The *Logic* begins with the category of pure, indeterminate being and proceeds to render explicit what is implicit in such being. In the first part of the book – the doctrine of being – Hegel demonstrates that being entails determinacy, finitude, infinity, quantity, and measure (*Maß*). These different "ways" or "dimensions" of being are derived by Hegel from the initial category of pure being itself and are thereby shown to be inherent in being as such. It is not an accident, therefore, but it lies in the very nature of being, that there are finite, quantifiable things. Similarly, it lies in the nature of thought that we think in terms of "finitude" and "quantity." Hegel's *Logic* thus discloses the categories that are inherent in, and so made necessary by, thought itself. It also discloses how those categories are to be understood, if we are to follow the demands of thought (and being).

Hegel argues that the categories (and ways of being) that are derived in the doctrine of being turn into one another "dialectically": something is itself *other* than what is

---

A Companion to Hegel, First Edition. Edited by Stephen Houlgate and Michael Baur.
© 2011 Blackwell Publishing Ltd. Published 2011 by Blackwell Publishing Ltd.

other than it, and infinity that is bounded by finitude is itself a *finite* infinity. Hegel points out, however, that the categories developed in the first section of the doctrine of being – the sphere of quality – also retain a certain immediacy that distinguishes them from one another: even though every something is other than something else, there is still an immediate difference between being *something* and being *other*.[5] Indeed, the whole sphere of being can be described (with some qualification) as the realm of *immediacy* – the realm in which each category retains a character of its own, and in that sense remains *itself*, even though it turns into its opposite.

Yet as the doctrine of being proceeds, this immediacy is progressively undermined. Indeed, by the end of this first part of the *Logic* being proves to be the sphere in which there is in truth *no* simple immediacy after all. As Hegel writes, we come to see "that being in general and the being or immediacy of the distinct determinatenesses ... has vanished" (*SL* 385 / *LS* 431). How does this occur?

At the close of the section on quality Hegel demonstrates that quality makes quantity necessary: being quantifiable is thereby shown to be an intrinsic feature of what there is. In the section on measure, Hegel then points out that quantity in turn gives rise to changes in quality: if water is heated beyond a certain point, for example, it ceases being a fluid and turns into steam (see *EL* 171 / *EWL* 226 (§108 addition)). Quality and quantity turn out, therefore, not simply to be different from, and indifferent to, one another, but each proves to be what it is "*through the mediation* of the other" (*EL* 173 / *EWL* 229 (§111)). In this way, each proves to be dependent on the other. This means that neither quality nor quantity is in truth *simply and immediately* what it is. Qualitative categories, such as something and other, are initially understood to be immediately distinct. It now becomes apparent, however, that there is in truth no simple immediacy in the sphere of being, because both quality as a whole and quantity as a whole arise *through* and *thanks to* one another.

As such, Hegel argues, quality and quantity form a unity – a single realm of self-relating being – in which they are contained as *non-immediate* moments. The true nature of being is thus not simple immediacy, as we first thought; being is, rather, a unity constituted by relative, non-immediate moments, each of which is *not* the *non*-immediacy that the other one is (or, to put it another way, each of which is the *negation* of the *negation* that the other one is). When it is thought as such a unity of negative moments, Hegel writes, "being or immediacy is *essence*" (*EL* 173 / *EWL* 229 (§111)). Note that the word "essence" (*Wesen*) does not refer to something that is supposed to lie beyond or behind being. It is the name Hegel gives to *being* itself when the latter proves to be not simple immediacy, but the unified, self-relating sphere of non-immediacy or "negativity."[6] Essence, for Hegel, is what being proves to be of its own accord, what being itself proves to be *in truth*. Accordingly, the first sentence we read in the doctrine of essence is: "the *truth* of *being* is *essence*" (*SL* 389 / *LW* 3).

Essence and Seeming

Hegel's doctrine of essence does not begin with our ordinary conception of essence as the "inner nature" of things or their underlying "substrate." It begins with the conception of essence that emerges at the end of the doctrine of being, and it proceeds by rendering explicit what is implicit in that conception. Hegel's aim is thus to *discover* – without assuming in advance that we already know – what essence entails, what the sphere of non-immediacy proves to be.[7] What emerges in Hegel's account may or may not correspond to our familiar conceptions of essence. It will, however, be the truth about essence and will serve (if necessary) to correct our familiar conceptions. As we shall see, Hegel maintains that essence, when understood properly, proves to be *reflexion*.

The essence of being, for Hegel, is not – or at least not initially – necessity or possibility, but rather *non-immediacy*.[8] Once the essence or truth of being has been understood in this way, however, being's initial immediacy cannot be regarded as anything but an "illusion" (*Schein*). Being is initially understood to be the sphere of immediacy; now, however, being has proven to be the sphere of non-immediacy; that initial immediacy, therefore, can be no more than what being initially *seems* to be (see *SL* 395 / *LW* 9).

Yet there is a problem lurking in what we have just said: for the contrast between the essence of being and being's illusory immediacy confers a certain *immediacy* on the essence itself. The essence is understood to be *this*, rather than *that* – to be the *essence*, rather than what is merely illusory; but that means that the essence proves to be immediately what it is, rather than what it is not. The essence of being, however, is precisely *non-immediacy*. It cannot be the case, therefore, that the essence of being is immediately distinct from and other than being's illusory immediacy, for in the sphere of essence (as it arises from the doctrine of being) *there is no simple immediacy*.[9]

Hegel's account of the relation between essence and illusory immediate being (or seeming) traces the changes that are forced on essence by its thoroughly "*negative nature*" (*SL* 397 / *LW* 11). These changes gradually undermine the initial immediate difference between essence and seeming. Essence first changes from being that which is simply distinct from all seeming immediacy to being that which is responsible for all seeming immediacy. That is to say, essence comes to be understood as that which *itself* projects the illusion of immediate being, that which *itself* appears in the guise of immediate being. Illusory immediate being, or seeming, ceases thereby to be something distinct from essence and comes to be seen as essence's *own* seeming or the "*seeming of the essence itself*" (*der Schein des Wesens selbst*) (*SL* 398 / *LW* 12). From this point of view, the sphere of immediacy described in the doctrine of being is simply what the essence itself initially *seems* to be.

Yet this still preserves an immediate difference between the essence and its own seeming. That difference is finally eliminated when essence is understood to be nothing but *the very process of seeming itself*. At that point, there is no longer anything to essence beyond, or other than, its seeming: there is nothing that essence is *immediately* apart from seeming. Essence as it is in truth, therefore, is not simply distinct from seeming, nor is it that which seems; it is the very process *of* seeming – the process of seeming to be immediate being and of seeming to be distinct from such seeming immediacy. That is to say, essence is the movement from one seeming to another, from seeming to seeming, or "the seeming of itself within itself" (*das Scheinen seiner in sich selbst*) (*SL* 398 / *LW* 13). Earlier, Hegel equated seeming or illusory being with "the immediacy of *non-being*" (*SL* 397 / *LW* 11): an illusion is not just nothing, but is "something" with a character of its own; yet at the same time it is not something real, it consists precisely in that which does not exist, that which is not, that which "is" utter *non-being*. The movement from seeming to seeming is thus the movement from non-being to non-being or, as Hegel also puts it, "*from nothing to nothing*" (*SL* 400 / *LW* 14). When essence is understood as the sheer movement of seeming, therefore, it is understood as the movement of *reflexion*.

This account of the emergence of the idea of reflexion is highly simplified.[10] However, it serves one important function: to show that essence must be understood as reflexion if its sheer *non-immediacy* is to be taken seriously. For Hegel, being is the sphere of immediacy and essence is the sphere of non-immediacy. That means that the essence of being cannot itself be something immediate. It thus cannot be *something other* than being, or indeed *something other* than being's seeming immediacy. All essence can "be" is the very movement of seeming itself, the movement from one seeming to another and thus from non-being to non-being. We now need to examine what (if anything) emerges from the idea that essence is reflexion.

Reflexion

Robert Pippin reads Hegel's discussion of reflexion as an account of "thought's reflective activity."[11] Thirty years ago, however, Walter Jaeschke pointed out that Hegel in the *Logic* is discussing neither the reflective activity of consciousness nor that of the understanding, but rather "reflexion as such" (*Reflexion überhaupt*).[12] The *Logic*, according to Jaeschke, is an "ontology of the concept," not a study of various forms of subjective thought. Reflexion as such, as it is thematized in the *Logic*, must thus be an *ontological* structure, not just an operation of the mind. This understanding of reflexion is, in my judgment, correct: reflexion is what being itself proves to be at a certain point in its logical development.[13]

As noted above, reflexion is defined by Hegel as the "*movement from nothing to nothing*" (*SL* 400 / *LW* 14). Strictly speaking, however, reflexion is not just the movement *from* one negative *to* another, but is also the movement of a negative that is utterly *self-negating*. Let us consider briefly why this should be. Essence is the movement of seeming – of seeming to be immediate being (the sphere of quality, quantity, and measure) and of seeming to be distinct from such seeming immediacy. It does not, however, move from one seeming to another arbitrarily, but is driven from one to the other by the logic of non-immediacy. Since there is no simple immediacy in the sphere of essence, essence cannot be anything immediate. It cannot, therefore, *be* simple, immediate being, but can only *seem* to be; nor can it *be* immediately distinct from such seeming immediacy, but can only *seem* to be that, too. By virtue of its non-immediacy, essence thus negates whatever immediate form it takes and reduces the latter to mere seeming immediacy; and precisely by negating itself in this way it moves from one seeming to another.

Essence is non-immediacy, or the *negative*, that can never be simple, immediate being, and can never be simply and immediately the *non*-immediacy that it is either. It is so lacking in immediacy, therefore, that it is utterly *self-negating*. As such, it is nothing but the movement of its own mere seeming. That movement of seeming is thus the movement of "absolute negativity" (*SL* 399 / *LW* 13) that Hegel calls *reflexion*.

This is without doubt a strange and unusual conception of essence. It appears to be far removed from our more familiar ways of conceiving essence as "ground" or "substrate." If Hegel is right, however, it is the conception of essence that we are forced to adopt if we take seriously the idea that the essence of things is *not* simple immediacy.[14]

Positing and Presupposing

We turn now to consider Hegel's account of the "logic" of reflexion itself. What follows from the very idea of sheer negativity, of the self-negating, "reflexive" negative? Hegel notes that in negating itself the reflexive negative does not cease being *negative*. On the contrary, it reinforces itself and becomes doubly negative. In so doing, Hegel writes, the negative relates to, and coincides with, *itself*. In coinciding with itself, however, the self-negating, reflexive negative comes to exhibit the very quality it is supposed to lack: for it comes to exhibit simple "equality with itself" or *immediacy* (*SL* 400 / *LW* 15). The negative that coincides with itself is purely *self-relating*, and so is just itself, not something else. In this sense, it enjoys immediacy. The paradox here is that the negative comes to enjoy immediacy precisely because it *lacks* immediacy. The reflexive negative is not simply and immediately negative, because in the sphere of essence there is no simple immediacy. The reflexive negative is, therefore, utterly self-negating: it is the negative that is *not* just the negative that it is. Yet precisely because it is self-negating, it relates to itself, coincides with itself, and thereby acquires the *immediacy* that consists in being "equal with itself," being nothing but *itself*.

This paradox, however, is not quite as sharp as it appears, since we are talking here of "immediacy" in two subtly different senses. The reflexive negative lacks any *simple* immediacy, but it acquires what Hegel calls "reflected [*reflektierte*] immediacy" (*SL* 397, 524 / *LW* 11, 154).[15] Such reflected immediacy is still immediacy: it consists in being what one is, being oneself, and in that sense is not utterly distinct from simple immediacy. But it is immediacy that is *produced* by the movement of reflexion rather than simply *there*. This immediacy evidently has a place in the sphere of essence, whereas all other, simple immediacy has been exposed as illusory (at least for the moment).

Hegel emphasizes that the reflexive negative acquires immediacy not by becoming something else, but by coinciding with itself in negating itself. The reflexive negative acquires immediacy, therefore, by doubling back or *turning back* on itself. Hegel introduces the idea of the "turn back" (*Rückkehr*) with these words: "*Die Beziehung des Negativen auf sich selbst ist also seine Rückkehr in sich.*" In Miller's English translation this reads: "the self-relation of the negative is, therefore, its return into itself" (*SL* 401 / *LW* 15). Yet the word "return" in the English version is subtly misleading, for it leads us to think that the negative becomes *once again* what it once was. Hegel's point, however, is that by "turning back" or recoiling on itself, the negative comes to exhibit an immediacy that it did not previously enjoy. It comes to *acquire* immediacy in the very movement of turning back on itself. In turning back on itself, the reflexive, utterly self-negating, negative turns *into* a self-relating negative – a negative that is *immediately itself* – for the first time. In that sense (and in that sense alone), the reflexive negative can be said to turn back ... *into* itself.

The immediacy that arises in this way is not pure and simple immediacy, since it is the *result* of the self-negating of the negative. The name that Hegel gives to such

143

reflexive immediacy is "posited being" or "positedness" (*Gesetztsein*). Posited immediacy is not simply immediate, precisely because it is *posited by*, and so *results from*, the negative's self-negation.[16]

There is also a second immediacy associated with reflexion. This is the immediacy *of* the very movement of self-negation, of reflexion, itself – the immediacy of the movement of *positing* (*Setzen*). This movement exhibits immediacy because it does not relate to, or become, anything other than itself: at this stage in the *Logic*, the movement of reflexion is all that there is. Accordingly, Hegel writes, reflexion is "*positing* in so far as it is immediacy as a returning movement" (*SL* 401 / *LW* 16).

Note that with the concept of reflexion the concept of essence undergoes an important transformation. At the start of Hegel's account, the concept of essence served to reduce immediacy to mere illusion or *Schein*: if the truth or essence of being is non-immediacy, then the immediacy of being with which we began (in the doctrine of being) can be no more than seeming immediacy. With the emergence of the idea of reflexion, however, essence becomes *productive*, rather than *destructive*, of immediacy. It is now understood to *posit* immediacy – to bring it into being – in a movement that Klaus Schmidt names "creatio ex nihilo."[17] Subsequent conceptions of essence as the "ground" or "cause" of being will be indebted to (and indeed be versions of) the idea of reflexion as the positing of positedness.

The problem, however, is that the immediacy that is posited is not immediacy in an undiluted sense. It is immediacy that negates or "sublates" itself due to the fact that it is the result of, and so is *mediated* by, the movement of positing. Posited immediacy always refers *back* to the reflexivity that gives rise to it.[18] It bears the clear mark of its indebtedness for all to see, and in that sense is not properly immediate.

Not only is the immediacy of posited being a mediated, and therefore "sublated," immediacy, but so also is the immediacy of positing itself. This is because such positing is not pure, unmediated positing, but also the *presupposing* of an immediacy from which all positing begins (or at least appears to begin). Dieter Henrich maintains that presupposing is the positing of something as quite *independent* of all positing.[19] The problem with this interpretation, however, is that what is presupposed acquires independence, in Hegel's account, only for *external* reflexion. Presupposing, as a moment of reflexion in its initial "absolute" form, is not the presupposing of what is independent of reflexion. It is, rather, the presupposing of what is simply and immediately *negative* (and wholly dependent on reflexion itself).

This is suggested in particular by the following lines: "immediacy emerges simply and solely as return and is that negative which is the illusion of the beginning that is negated by the return" (*Die Unmittelbarkeit kommt überhaupt nur als Rückkehr hervor und ist dasjenige Negative, welches der Schein des Anfangs ist, der durch die Rückkehr negiert wird*) (*SL* 401 / *LW* 16). Let us look a little more closely at what Hegel is saying here.

Hegel first reminds us that immediacy arises only in and as the movement of "return," that is, in the movement wherein the reflexive negative turns back on, and so relates to, itself. He then goes on, however, to attribute immediacy to the negative that is the "illusion of the beginning that is negated by the return." So, on the one hand, immediacy is said to *arise with* the movement of return, but, on the other hand, it is also said to constitute that from which the movement of return *seems to begin*. What is that from which the movement of return seems to begin? What is the apparent starting point that is then negated in the movement of return? Surely, it must be the *negative* itself. What appears to happen in the movement of return is that an initial simple negative is negated with the result that immediacy emerges. This, however, is only what *appears* to happen, for we know that the reflexive negative never is simply negative but is self-negating *from the start*. The reflexive negative is *always* self-negating, and only as such does it negate itself *into* being a self-relating negative that exhibits immediacy.

In truth, in the movement of reflexion there is no simple negative at the outset that is then negated, leading to the emergence of immediacy. Hegel suggests, however, that in the movement of self-negation the negative is posited *as* the simple negative that is negated, leading to the emergence of immediacy. That is to say, the simple negative is placed *by reflexion* before the immediacy that results or, in other words, is presupposed as the origin of the process through which immediacy results. The process of positing, therefore, is not purely the process of positing, for it is at the same time the process of *presupposing* the simple, immediate negative, the negation of which gives rise to affirmative immediacy. Such affirmative immediacy thus arises as one side of a contrast: for as the reflexive negative negates itself, it comes to coincide with itself immediately, *as opposed to being simply negative*. The reflexive negative never was simply and immediately negative, but in the process of negating itself it posits itself *as* initially simply negative in contrast to the immediacy that emerges. The reflexive negative, one might say, thus *comes to have been* simply negative in the very movement in which it *turns into* affirmative immediacy.

The simple, immediate negative that is presupposed by reflexion is thus nothing but a posit of reflexion itself: it appears to come first, but it actually owes its "prior" status to the very movement of reflexion to which it appears to give rise. Hegel confirms this point in the following lines: "the immediacy that reflexion, as a process of sublating, presupposes for itself is purely and simply a *positedness*, an immediacy that is *in itself* sublated, that is not distinct from the return-into-self and is itself only this movement of return" (*SL* 402 / *LW* 17).

Hegel claims that the processes of positing and of presupposing are one and the same: positing is itself the movement of *presupposing*, and presupposing in turn is the pre-*positing* of what is presupposed. In each case, therefore, what is posited or presupposed is explicitly *dependent* on the process of reflexion: it is a positedness that necessarily points back to the reflexion that posits it. Understood in this way, reflexion is unable to give rise to genuinely independent immediacy. Hegel goes on to argue, however, that reflexion must give rise to such independent immediacy, because it must presuppose an immediacy that is *external* to it.

External and Determining Reflexion

I claimed above that Henrich's account of presupposing is problematic. What is presupposed in absolute reflexion is not something *independent* of reflexion, but something explicitly *negative* – the immediate negative posited by reflexion as that from which reflexive positing appears to begin. Henrich's account of presupposing serves very well, however, to explain the transition from absolute to external reflexion. Henrich's argument goes like this: insofar as reflexion is not purely and immediately itself, is not pure positing, it must presuppose that which is *not* itself reflexive, that which is *not* merely posited by reflexion. It must presuppose the "negative" of reflexion. However, to the extent that what is presupposed really is the *negative* of reflexion, really is *non*-reflexive, it must be *non-negative* (since reflexion itself is utterly negative). The negative character of what is presupposed and its negative relation to reflexion must, therefore, themselves be negated. Accordingly, what is presupposed by reflexion as non-reflexive must be presupposed as wholly affirmative, immediate, and independent of reflexion. As Henrich puts it: "That which is posited is no longer only the negative of the positing essence. Its negative character is itself negated. It is posited as independent and is thereby precisely *pre*-posited, *pre*-supposed."[20]

This account, in my view, does not apply to presupposing as it occurs within the sphere of absolute reflexion. It explains perfectly, however, why reflexion must become external reflexion.[21] If reflexion presupposes "the negative of itself" (*SL* 403 / *LW* 17), then what it presupposes must itself be wholly non-reflexive and *non-negative*. It must, therefore, be affirmative, immediate, and independent of reflexion. It must thus be presupposed (or posited) by reflexion as falling *outside* reflexion and so as not posited by reflexion at all.

With the emergence of external reflexion essence undergoes another significant transformation. We have already seen that essence becomes productive, rather than destructive, of immediacy when it proves to be reflexion. Absolute or positing reflexion, however, produces no more than posited being. That is to say, it gives rise to being or immediacy that is explicitly dependent on reflexion. Absolute reflexion thus behaves rather like Nietzsche, who can never let things be what they are by themselves, but always insists that what we relate to are *our* interpretations and *our* evaluations.[22]

When it becomes external reflexion, however, reflexion posits or presupposes genuine, free-standing immediacy. Yet reflexion is still not understood explicitly *to produce* free-standing immediacy through its *own* reflexive activity. This is because such immediacy is presupposed by reflexion as falling *outside* reflexion. It is presupposed by reflexion, therefore, as that which is not posited by reflexion at all but *found* by it. External reflexion itself posits immediacy, insofar as it places such immediacy outside itself. In so doing, however, external reflexion suppresses the fact that *it* posits immediacy as lying outside it. As Hegel puts it, "reflexion, in its positing, immediately sublates its positing and thus has an *immediate presupposition*" (*SL* 403 / *LW* 18).

In his further analysis of external reflexion, however, Hegel emphasizes that such reflexion is *itself* responsible for positing its own immediate presupposition. External reflexion presupposes or preposits immediacy, but negates (or suppresses) its own activity of positing insofar as it sets itself in relation to an immediacy that is external to it. In doing so, however, reflexion remains the activity of *positing*: it actively *sets* immediacy outside itself as its presupposition. As Hegel writes, external reflexion is "immediately equally a *positing*" (*SL* 403 / *LW* 18).

This is not to say that what is presupposed by external reflexion is merely *posited* being and so not genuinely immediate after all. That would be to reduce external reflexion once again to absolute, positing reflexion. We have seen, however, that reflexion cannot remain absolute. The logic of reflexion itself requires it to become external: reflexion must presuppose its own negative; but the negative of reflexion is immediacy, so reflexion must presuppose free-standing immediacy that is not merely posited being.

146

Hegel's recognition that external immediacy is nonetheless reflexively *posited* immediacy does not, therefore, undermine its status as genuine immediacy and reduce it once more to merely posited being. Rather, it takes us forward to a new conception of immediacy (and of reflexion). In the section on absolute reflexion, immediacy is understood merely to be posited by reflexion and so not to be properly immediate. In the section on external reflexion, by contrast, immediacy is understood to be genuinely immediate but to fall outside reflexion. Now immediacy is understood to be genuine immediacy *and* reflexively posited *at one and the same time*. Being reflexively posited or constituted does not, therefore, prevent such immediacy from being genuinely immediate, but is precisely what establishes it *as* genuine, free-standing immediacy. This dramatically alters the relation between reflexion and immediacy, for immediacy and reflexion now can no longer be thought simply to fall *outside* one another. If immediacy is reflexively constituted *as* free-standing immediacy and *in* its free-standing immediacy, then it must be reflexive *in itself* without reference to any reflexion that differs from it and stands in relation to it. In other words, reflexion must now be understood to reside within free-standing immediacy itself, to be immanently constitutive of it, and, indeed, to be identical to it. In Hegel's words, "the immediate is ... *the same as* reflexion [dasselbe, *was die Reflexion ist*]," and reflexion is "the immanent reflexion of immediacy itself" (*SL* 404 / *LW* 19). When reflexion is understood in this way, it is understood to be "determining reflexion" (*bestimmende Reflexion*).

There is a tendency among some readers of Hegel to see in him what Wilfrid Sellars calls "that great foe of 'immediacy.'"[23] This view of Hegel finds support, of course, in Hegel's critique of Jacobi.[24] It also finds support at the start, at least, of Hegel's account of essence in the *Logic*. Hegel's account of reflexion reveals, however, that he is not as hostile to immediacy as some of his readers have claimed. It is true that at the start of his doctrine of essence Hegel shows simple, unmediated immediacy to be an illusion, but his account of reflexion demonstrates that he accepts that there is *mediated, "reflected" immediacy* in the world. Indeed, he argues that such immediacy is a necessity, since reflexion – which is the truth of being – necessarily gives rise to immediacy. Furthermore, reflexion gives rise not just to quasi-immediacy or "positedness" but to genuine, free-standing immediacy. The negativity or reflexivity that forms the essence of things does not, therefore, reduce all immediacy to mere illusion. On the contrary, it turns out to *constitute* genuine, independent immediacy itself.[25] The idea of an immediacy that is constituted by *negativity* is bound to strike many readers as strange. Yet Hegel has shown that the idea of such immediacy is made necessary *by the very idea of essence itself*.

Identity and Difference

Posited being is immediacy that results from, and points back to, the movement of reflexion that gives rise to it. External immediacy is immediacy that is presupposed by reflexion as falling outside it. The new immediacy that has now emerged differs from these two in one important respect: it no longer *refers back* to reflexion that is prior or external to it, but it is *one with* the very movement of reflexion itself. It is the self-relation and "equality with itself" that is directly established *by* the self-negating, reflexive

147

negative, the self-relation that the reflexive negative itself constitutes in its very self-negating. Such immediacy thus consists in simple self-relation *without reference to anything other than or beyond itself*. It does not depend on or point back to any prior positing, but stands alone as independently subsisting immediacy. Yet it is not simple immediacy, such as we encountered in the doctrine of being, since it is reflexively constituted, and so immanently reflexive, immediacy. Such simple, reflexive immediacy, that is not pure and simple immediacy, is named by Hegel *identity*. Qualitative being, as described in the doctrine of being, is subject to change and destruction; the essence of being, however, is identity (or, which is the same thing, self-identity), that is, relating to oneself and remaining oneself in the very movement of self-negation or, as Hegel himself puts it, being "self-equal in its negativity" (*SL* 411 / *LW* 27).

Identity is thus what Hegel calls "the *immediacy* of reflexion" (*SL* 411 / *LW* 27). As such, it is never simply given, but is constituted, or constitutes itself,[26] through the movement of self-negation. Identity, in other words, is being or immediacy that establishes itself through *not just being negative*. Indeed, identity can be said to *consist* ultimately in not just being negative, since it is nothing but the self-relating *of* the self-negating negative. From this point of view, Hegel writes, identity is identical with reflexion itself or "absolute negation" – "the negation that immediately negates itself" (*SL* 412 / *LW* 28). Another way of putting the point is to say that identity is nothing but *difference*.

Note that Hegel's initial claim is *not* that identity is explicitly different from difference and for that reason is nothing but difference itself. Identity at first does not stand in relation to anything besides itself and so does not yet differ from difference; it is nothing but difference because *within itself* it is nothing but reflexion and self-negating negation. The difference in which identity consists is thus not a differing from anything *else*, but what Hegel calls "self-related" or "absolute" difference (*SL* 413 / *LW* 28).

As wholly self-relating, such difference differs from nothing but *itself*. In differing from itself, however, difference is necessarily difference *that is not just difference*. Indeed, it is precisely in *not* just being difference that difference constitutes *identity*. Hegel's point, however, is that difference constitutes identity by being sheer self-relating *difference*. Identity, understood as consisting in reflexion and negation, is thus nothing but absolute difference as such.

Identity, therefore, proves to be "difference that is identical with itself" (*SL* 413 / *LW* 29). At the same time, difference is wholly negative, whereas identity is affirmative self-relation. Difference, therefore, is the *negation* of identity, or "absolute *non*-identity," and identity in turn must be the negation of difference. This sets identity in a *twofold* relation to difference. On the one hand, as we have seen, identity is one with difference: "identity … is *in its own self* absolute non-identity." On the other hand, identity is also different from difference: identity is "identity as against non-identity" (*SL* 413 / *LW* 29). To put it another way, identity is the whole that includes *both* identity and difference, but it is also *one* side or "moment" of a relation to difference. Furthermore, identity is the one in being the other: identity includes difference as that which is *not* itself identity, that which utterly different from identity. It is in this way that identity comes to be, not just identity alone, but what Hegel calls the "*determination*" (*Bestimmung*) of identity: identity that is itself identity-rather-than-difference.

Identity is initially understood to be sheer self-relating identity, with nothing outside it to which it relates. In the course of Hegel's account, however, identity has proven to be identity only "in contrast to absolute difference" (*SL* 413 / *LW* 29). This means that identity has now to be understood both as what Hegel calls "posited being" (*Gesetztsein*) and as "reflexion into itself." Identity has proven to be identity only in relation to and in contrast with difference; that is to say, it is what it is *thanks to* and *by virtue of* that relation of contrast; or, to put it another way, it is *posited* as identity *by* that relation of contrast. On the other hand, thanks to that contrast with difference, identity is precisely *identity* – "simple equality with itself" (*SL* 413 / *LW* 29) – rather than difference. As such, identity is reflected by that contrast back into *itself* and its own simple self-relation. The contrast with difference does not, therefore, turn identity into a wholly relational structure, but enables it to be *identity*, that is, simple *self-relating* being. If identity were turned into a wholly relational structure, it would be reduced to that-which-differs-from-difference, and so would collapse into difference altogether. Identity, however, is not destroyed by the contrast with difference, but is constituted by it *as identity*. Hegel himself puts the point as follows: identity "posits itself as its own moment, as positedness, *from which it is the return into itself*" (*SL* 413 / *LW* 29, emphasis added).

It is at this point that identity proves to be *explicitly reflexive*. Initially, the inherent reflexivity of identity is, as it were, immersed in the affirmative self-relation in which identity consists. At the end of Hegel's account, however, identity has emerged as constituted by being the explicit "negation of negation," that is, by explicitly differing from difference. To repeat, however: this contrast with difference allows identity to be genuine, self-relating *identity*, that is, to be "reflexion into itself," not just posited, relational, "differentiated" being. This contrast must, therefore, set identity in relation to difference that is itself sheer, self-relating *difference*. Such "absolute" difference will turn out to have a structure similar to that of identity.

Absolute difference is difference taken purely by itself: "*self-related*, therefore *simple* difference" (*SL* 417 / *LW* 33). Such difference, Hegel tells us, is to be distinguished from "otherness" (*Anderssein*), which arises in the doctrine of being. Otherness is a relation in which something stands to something *else*; difference, by contrast, is not a relation of one thing to another, but is the negative that is reflected wholly into *itself*: "the *simple not*" (*das* einfache Nicht) that stands by itself, without relation to anything beyond or outside itself. This simple "not" is what *makes* the difference between A and *not*-A and so what allows there to be two things that are *other* than one another.

Difference that is wholly self-related cannot, however, be pure and simple difference, since in relating to itself it must *differ from itself* and thereby negate itself. Self-relating, self-negating difference must, therefore be *identity*. Yet identity is *not* difference. Sheer difference that is not just difference thus necessarily includes identity, but it includes identity *as that which it is not*. Difference is thus the whole that unites difference with identity, and yet at the same time it stands in *contrast* to identity. Moreover, it is the one in being the other: difference is in irreducible *union* with identity and therein is *one side* of a relation to identity. Difference sets itself in relation to identity in this way because it is reflexive, and so self-negating, and so not just itself. As Hegel puts it, "difference and also identity make themselves into a *moment* or a *positedness*, because, as reflexion, they are negative relation-to-self" (*SL* 417–418 / *LW* 34).

In relating to and differing from identity, however, difference continues to be *itself*. That is to say, in that relation difference remains *difference* rather than identity, just as identity remains *identity* rather than difference. Hegel points out that both difference and identity are a "positedness," since each is posited as what it is by virtue of its contrast with the other, but he adds that "in this positedness each is *self-relation*" (*SL* 418 / *LW* 35). Each remains *itself*, therefore, precisely in not just being itself but standing in relation to the other.

Together difference and identity thus constitute a relation of two different moments, each of which is distinguished by being wholly self-related and so identical with itself. This relation of two separate, self-related identities is named by Hegel "diversity" (*Verschiedenheit*). Diversity is reflexively constituted immediacy in the more developed form of reflexively constituted *otherness*.[27] It is the relation between two moments that are *other* than one another, not just because each is immediately what it is, but because each is reflected into itself, and so identical with itself, in not-just-being-itself-but-relating-to-its-negative.

Diversity

It is crucial to recognize that diversity is reflexively constituted, and that, conversely, reflexion (or the essence of things) must take the form of diversity. Reflexion, as we have seen, necessarily constitutes identity. It constitutes identity, however, as relating to itself in negating itself, and so in not just being itself, and so in relating to difference. It constitutes difference in a similar way. Reflexion thus constitutes identity and difference as two self-relating, self-identical moments that differ because they are *separately* self-relating. Diversity is itself thoroughly reflexive, because it is difference that consists *not* in simple difference but in having separate identities, and it is identity that consists *not* in simple identity but in difference-as-separateness.

The two moments that constitute diversity are identity and difference. As separate, diverse moments, however, they are both reflected into themselves and so wholly *self-related*. As such, Hegel writes, "they are *in the determination of identity*, they are only relation-to-self" (*SL* 418 / *LW* 35). As *diverse* moments, therefore, they are not related to one another, or determined with respect to one another, *as* identity and difference, but are simply *separate identities*. These diverse moments are thus, as Hegel puts it, "indifferent" to the determinate difference between them.

Hegel's point here is a significant one: insofar as things are thought of as "diverse," they are not understood to be *intrinsically* different or identical: they are just thought of as various separate things. Whatever difference or identity there may be between them must, therefore, be what Hegel calls an "external" difference or identity. External identity, Hegel explains, is "likeness" (*Gleichheit*) and external difference is "unlikeness" (*Ungleichheit*). Diverse things may, therefore, be like or unlike one another, but as diverse they are not intrinsically either. They are alike or unlike from the external point of view of a third party that *compares* (*vergleicht*) them, a point of view to which the diverse things themselves are quite "indifferent" (see *SL* 419–420 / *LW* 36–37).

It is important to stress that likeness and unlikeness are *external* characterizations of the diverse. As such, they fall outside the sphere of "reflexion into self" that constitutes the diverse themselves. Accordingly, likeness and unlikeness are not themselves constituted by "reflexion into self." This means that they do not acquire an "identity" through an irreducible relation to one another, and so are not reflected back into themselves *by* the other. On the contrary, each one has a certain *immediacy* of its own: each one just *is* what it is in its own right and is *not* the other one. Each one is thus applied separately to the diverse by external, comparative reflexion. The diverse are judged to be like one another *or* unlike one another, or they are judged to be alike in *this* respect but unlike in *that* respect; they are not, however (at least not initially), judged to be alike *insofar as* they are unlike, and vice versa. As Hegel puts it, therefore, "likeness and unlikeness appear as mutually unrelated. ... *Likeness* is related only to itself, and similarly *unlikeness* is only unlikeness" (*SL* 420 / *LW* 37).

The emergence of the ideas of likeness and unlikeness represents another important turning point in the doctrine of essence: for it is the first time that the movement of reflexion has given rise to immediacy that is genuinely *non-reflexive*, rather than mediated and reflected. That is to say, it is the first time that reflexion has given rise to the immediacy found in *the doctrine of being*. Hegel makes this clear in these lines from the second paragraph on opposition:

> *Likeness* and *unlikeness* are the self-alienated reflexion; their self-identity is not merely the indifference of each towards the other distinguished from it, but towards being-in-and-for-itself as such, an identity-with-self over against the identity that is reflected into itself; it is therefore *immediacy* that is not reflected into itself [*die nicht in sich reflektierte Unmittelbarkeit*]. The positedness of the sides of the external reflexion is accordingly a *being* [*Sein*], just as their non-positedness is a *non-being* [*Nichtsein*]. (*SL* 424 / *LW* 42)

We saw earlier that (non-comparing) external reflexion also set itself in relation to immediacy that was non-reflexive and so fell outside reflexion itself. But such non-reflexive, external immediacy was itself *presupposed* by external reflexion and so was just as much reflexively posited being as it was genuine, free-standing immediacy (see *SL* 403–404 / *LW* 18–19). This then led on logically to the idea of immediacy that is reflexively constituted *as* free-standing immediacy and *in* its free-standing immediacy, immediacy that is *immanently* reflexive.

What has now emerged, however, is subtly different from what we encountered before. The external immediacy that emerges with diversity does not just fall outside presupposing reflexion, but it falls outside *reflexively constituted immediacy*. It is thus a further immediacy *beyond* reflexive immediacy, an immediacy that by being explicitly *non-reflexive* returns once more to the immediacy of being. With diversity, therefore, reflexion gives rise not just to "the otherness as such of reflexion" (*SL* 418 / *LW* 35), but also to the immediacy that consists in simply *being* this and *not* being that. Some words of qualification are, however, required here.

Earlier in this chapter it was stated that in the sphere of essence *there is no simple immediacy*. This is still true, if by "simple immediacy" we mean immediacy that is not generated by reflexion in any way at all. We have now seen, however, that *reflexion itself* gives rise to the simple, non-reflexive immediacy found in the sphere of being. It does so by negating or "sublating" itself and turning itself into that which falls *outside* itself and its own reflexive immediacy. That is to say, reflexion produces simple, non-reflexive immediacy by becoming wholly external to itself.[28] Identity and difference are both reflected back *into* themselves by their relation to the other, and in this way reflexion constitutes a sphere of "reflexion into self" (namely, diversity); at the same time, however, reflexion sets itself *outside* this sphere of "interiority" (as external identity and difference, or "likeness" and "unlikeness"). It is this activity whereby reflexion *externalizes* itself in the very process of constituting "inner" identity that produces the immediacy of *being* – likeness and unlikeness that are each immediately what they are and not the other – alongside reflected immediacy.

Reflexive and Non-reflexive Immediacy

Readers familiar with Hegel's doctrine of essence will know that the simple distinction between likeness and unlikeness is undermined in the course of the analysis of diversity. This occurs for the following reason: the diverse are wholly indifferent to likeness and unlikeness; in that respect, however, they are quite *unlike* those determinations; likeness, as the likeness of the diverse, is therefore the likeness of that which is quite unlike likeness itself; unlikeness, too, as the unlikeness of the diverse, is the unlikeness of that which is quite unlike unlikeness (but for that reason also just like it) (see *SL* 421 / *LW* 38–39). In this way, likeness and unlikeness prove to be determinations of the diverse themselves: the diverse, *as diverse*, are both unlike and like likeness and unlikeness. Furthermore, likeness and unlikeness themselves prove thereby to be inseparable from, and reflexively mediated by, one another: neither, it turns out, is simply what it is, but each is only *thanks to* the other.

The fact that the diverse are now *intrinsically* characterized by likeness and unlikeness means, in Hegel's view, that it now belongs to their very identity to be "like" and "unlike" *one another*. That is to say, each is just like the other in having its own "positive" identity, but each *within itself* is also *unlike* the other, is *not* the other, and so is the "negative" of the other. Understood in this way, the diverse prove to be not just diverse after all, but intrinsically *opposed* to one another. Reflexively constituted identity thus turns out to be identity that is established in and through opposition; indeed, as the argument proceeds, such identity turns out to be thoroughly contradictory, as well.

Now with the undermining of the simple distinction between likeness and unlikeness, it would seem that the immediacy of being that has just been generated by reflexion should disappear again completely. This, however, is not the case, since without that simple immediacy there would be no opposition (and so no contradiction either). If opposition involved only reflexive immediacy without the simple immediacy of *being* and *non*-being, each side of the supposed opposition would simply be reflected back into *itself* by the other (like identity and difference), and we would be back in diversity again.[29] What produces genuine opposition is the fact that each side within itself explicitly *excludes* the other as "a self-subsistent *being*" (*SL* 426 / *LW* 45), and so is defined internally as *not* being what the other outside it *is*.

Identity and difference are reflected *back into themselves* by their intrinsic difference from one another; that intrinsic difference gives them separate, self-relating identities and so makes them simply diverse. By contrast, the positive and the negative – the two sides of an opposition – are not just diverse, but incorporate their difference from, and *exclusion* of, one another *explicitly within* their own identities: each within *itself* is explicitly *not* what the other *is*. This renders each side contradictory, since each thereby *includes* within itself the very negative of itself that it must *exclude* in order to be itself (see *SL* 431 / *LW* 50–51). Without the simple, immediate, and determinate distinction between *being* and *not being*, however, no exclusion could occur, for neither the positive nor the negative could consist in explicitly *not being* – and thereby shutting out – the other "self-subsistent *being*";[30] and without such internal exclusion there could be no contradiction in the identity of either one. This is not to deny that opposition and contradiction are thoroughly *reflexive* structures, involving both "reflexion-into-self" and relative, "posited" identity. It is to point out, however, that simple, non-reflexive immediacy is also a crucial component of these structures.

One should not be surprised by the reappearance of simple immediacy in the realm of reflexion: for reflexion is precisely the movement of the self-*negating* negative. It is thus not just the movement of producing reflexive immediacy in its various guises, but also the movement of negating or "sublating" itself into the *non-reflexive* immediacy of being. As the logical development of reflexion proceeds the non-reflexive immediacy generated by reflexion continues to play a significant role. The idea of an existing thing, for example, includes the moment of "*non-reflected immediacy*" that sets the thing in relation to what is *other* than it (*SL* 484 / *LW* 109). Indeed, the whole sphere of "existence" (*Existenz*), for Hegel, is the "restoration of *immediacy* or of *being*" (*EL* 192 / *EWL* 252 (§122)). Existence is reflexive, since it is not simply there but *emerges* from a ground; but it also incorporates the immediacy of being, and so is not just the sphere of identity and difference but is equally "exposed to the becoming and alteration of being" (*SL* 488 / *LW* 113).[31]

The categories of "necessity" and "substance" represent the explicit unity or identity of the two forms of immediacy, and indeed of reflexion as such and being. Absolute necessity is understood by Hegel to be being that is "*because it is*": nothing outside it grounds it, but it is absolutely necessary *within itself*. Such necessity is reflexive insofar as it has a *ground*: it is *because* it is. At the same time, it has its ground within itself and its own being, and so is in fact simple immediacy: it *is* quite simply because it *is*. It is thus "as much simple immediacy or *pure being* as simple reflexion-into-self or *pure essence*; it is this, that these two are one and the same" (*SL* 552 / *LW* 188).[32]

With the idea of "substance," Hegel maintains, we reach "the final unity of essence and being" within the doctrine of essence (*SL* 555 / *LW* 191). Substance is being or "self-relation" that is identical not only with its reflexive "positing of itself" (*Sich-selbst-Setzen*) but also with all that it posits itself to be, that is, with the totality of its own accidents (see *SL* 554–555 / *LW* 190–191). Expressed in the language of Spinoza, substance is not only *causa sui* but is also identical with the system of its own modes.[33] This unity of being and essence thus points forward logically to the sphere of the concept (*Begriff*), in which the "universal" *continues* itself throughout its "particular" forms and in this way particularizes and individuates *itself*.[34]

Reflexion and the Concept

In the sphere of being categories immediately pass over into one another: something, for example, immediately proves to be *other* than something else. In the sphere of essence, by contrast, reflexion *generates* immediacy and is thus, in Richard Winfield's words, the "privileged determiner" of what there is.[35] As we have seen, reflexion does so in various ways: by presupposing such immediacy, constituting it immanently, or giving rise to it by externalizing itself. Once being proves to be the "concept," however, *reflexion ceases to play this determining role*, for being ceases to be that which is "produced" or "constituted" and proves to be wholly *self*-determining and *self*-developing. Soon-Jeon Kang claims that "reflexion functions ... as the general method of the whole Logic" and even "underlies [*zugrunde liegt*] the developments of the logic of the concept."[36] This, however, is not the case, since being-as-concept *determines and develops itself* and so has nothing "underlying" (or "grounding" or "constituting") it. Reflexion does not itself determine the development in the logic of the concept; rather, it is a moment (with the immediacy of being) *of* that development. This is made clear in these lines from the section on the universal concept:

> *Being* ... has become an *illusory being* or a *positedness*, and *becoming* ... has become a *positing*; and conversely, the *positing* or reflexion of essence has sublated itself and has restored itself as a being that is *not posited*, that is *original*. The Concept is the interfusion of these moments. (*SL* 601 / *LB* 33)[37]

It turns out, therefore, that reflexion is not the fundamental *source* of all immediacy after all, but is in fact a moment *within* being-as-concept. Something of the strangeness of Hegel's concept of reflexion thus disappears when we reach the logic of the concept: for it is no longer the case that everything is grounded in sheer *negativity*, but self-negating negation is itself revealed to be a moment of what there truly is. Reflexion taken by itself is, indeed, the movement of absolute negation, and it produces the determinations we have seen, such as identity and difference. The truth, however, is that reflexion does not constitute (or ground) the whole, but, like the immediacy of being, is but one aspect of that whole.

It is important to note that reflexion *turns itself* into the thoroughgoing "unity of *being* and *essence*" that is being-as-concept (*SL* 596 / *LB* 28) – a unity that is even deeper than that found in substance, since it is one in which reflexion has given up its determining role. In so doing, reflexion turns itself *qua reflexion* into a *moment* of that thoroughgoing unity. Reflexion does this because it is the process of self-negation and so constantly turns itself into that which is *not simply reflexive*. Reflexion negates itself by constituting reflexive immediacy, by becoming external to itself in the form of simple immediacy, and by becoming a moment of being-as-concept. This latter transition from the logic of essence to the logic of concept is itself prefigured in the process in which reflexion shows itself to be constitutive of, and immanent in, immediacy, that is, constitutive of *identity*.

Reflexion is initially the activity of positing and presupposing, on which posited and presupposed immediacy depends. It is that activity to which such immediacy points back. This idea of essence as *active* in relation to what *depends* on it survives in the later concept of "cause." This contrast between active reflexion and dependent immediacy is, however, subtly undermined when reflexion is understood to be immanent in and identical to immediacy itself. At that point – the point at which identity arises – reflexion ceases being prior to and different from immediacy and becomes *one with* immediacy itself. As Christian Iber puts it, reflexion becomes the "*immanent movement of the Sache selbst*."[38] Indeed, one can say that reflexion becomes a *moment within* immediacy.

Yet at the same time, reflexion is *wholly constitutive* of – and so wholly *determines* – reflected immediacy, and in that sense is not merely one "moment" of it. To become just *one* moment of being, reflexion must give rise to an immediacy that is itself *non*-reflexive and simple, and then go on to form a thoroughgoing unity with such non-reflexive immediacy. Thus, although the transition from essence to the concept is indeed prefigured in the constitution of identity, that transition cannot actually occur until reflexion has given rise to, *and thoroughly united itself with*, the immediacy of being. The emergence of simple, non-reflexive immediacy in diversity – in the form of likeness and unlikeness – is thus not just a minor event in the logical development of reflexion that can be safely overlooked. It is a crucial stage in the process whereby reflexion turns itself into a moment of "the unity of *being* and *essence*" that is the concept.

Conclusion

At the start of the logic of essence, Hegel writes that "the *truth* of *being* is *essence*" (*SL* 389 / *LW* 3). The true character of essence then turns out to be reflexion. Reflexion in its initial, "absolute" form has priority over the being that it posits: it is the active positing of such being. The lesson of the logic of reflexion, however, is that reflexion does not preserve its initial form because it is intrinsically self-negating and self-sublating. As it develops logically, therefore, reflexion undermines its own priority and authority and reveals itself (together with the various "determinations" to which it gives rise) to be a *moment* of being-as-concept. In this way, the logic of reflexion, and the logic of essence as a whole, serve to prove that the truth of being is *not* just essence or reflexion after all but the concept (and eventually the Idea).

Notes

1   See Hegel, *EL* 179 / *EWL* 236 (§114 remark). I have occasionally altered the English translations of Hegel's texts throughout this chapter.

2   In this chapter I have spelled "reflexion" with an "x" (rather than "ct") to indicate its ontological character and its proximity to the term "reflexive." I understand "reflection" (with "ct") to be a special operation of thought, as in Lockean or Kantian "reflection."

3   Note that there is no separate discussion of reflexion in the *Encyclopaedia Logic*, though the term "reflexion" is used throughout the doctrine of essence in that work. Reflexion is discussed in detail by Hegel only in the *Science of Logic*.

4   For a more detailed discussion of the relation between logic and ontology in Hegel's *Science of Logic*, see S. Houlgate, *The Opening of Hegel's Logic. From Being to Infinity* (West Lafayette, Ind.: Purdue University Press, 2006), chapter 6. See also S. Houlgate, "Hegel's Logic," in *The Cambridge Companion to Hegel and Nineteenth-Century Philosophy*, ed. F. C. Beiser (Cambridge: Cambridge University Press, 2008), 117–124.

5   See also Hegel, *SL* 123 / *LS* 119: "in the sphere of quality, the differences in their sublated form as moments also retain the form of immediate, qualitative being relatively to one another."

6   See J. Burbidge, *On Hegel's Logic. Fragments of a Commentary* (Atlantic Highlands, N.J.: Humanities Press, 1981), 64: "*essence* does nothing but signify the process by which the

concept of *being* cancels its own immediacy in thought." See also M. Baur, "Sublating Kant and the Old Metaphysics: A Reading of the Transition from Being to Essence in Hegel's *Logic*," *The Owl of Minerva* 29 (1998): 147: "The movement from being to Essence cannot be a movement which is imposed from without, but must result instead from the internal inadequacy belonging to the sphere of Being itself."

7   See S. Houlgate, "Review of G. M. Wölfle, *Die Wesenslogik in Hegels "Wissenschaft der Logik"* (Stuttgart-Bad Cannstatt: Frommann-Holzboog, 1994)," *Bulletin of the Hegel Society of Great Britain* 32 (1995): 45–46.

8   See D. G. Carlson, *A Commentary to Hegel's Science of Logic* (Basingstoke: Palgrave Macmillan, 2007), 251, 266: "essence is non-being and nothing more." Peter Rohs makes explicit use of the term "non-immediacy" (*Nicht-Unmittelbarkeit*) to understand reflexion, which, as we shall see, is what essence proves to be; see P. Rohs, *Form und Grund. Interpretation eines Kapitels der Hegelschen Wissenschaft der Logik*, Hegel-Studien Beiheft 6 (Bonn: Bouvier Verlag, 1982), 57.

9   See Hegel, *SL* 399 / *LW* 13: "both the unessential and illusory being, *and also the difference of essence from them*, derive solely from the fact that essence is at first taken as an *immediate*, not as it is in itself, namely, not as an immediacy that *is* as pure mediation or absolute negativity" (emphasis added).

10   For more detailed accounts, see D. Henrich, "Hegels Logik der Reflexion. Neue Fassung," in *Die Wissenschaft der Logik und die Logik der Reflexion*, ed. D. Henrich, Hegel-Studien Beiheft 18 (Bonn: Bouvier Verlag, 1978), 203–324, and C. Iber, *Metaphysik absoluter Relationalität* (Berlin: de Gruyter, 1990). See also S. Houlgate, "Hegel's Critique of Foundationalism in the 'Doctrine of Essence,'" in *German Philosophy since Kant*, ed. A. O'Hear (Cambridge: Cambridge University Press, 1999), 25–45.

11   R. Pippin, *Hegel's Idealism: The Satisfactions of Self-Consciousness* (Cambridge: Cambridge University Press, 1989), 201. A similar position is adopted by Béatrice Longuenesse. See B. Longuenesse, *Hegel's Critique of Metaphysics*, trans. N. J. Simek (Cambridge: Cambridge University Press, 2007), 51: "reflection is the process by which thought ... brings to unity the multiple determinations it finds within itself."

12   W. Jaeschke, "Äußerliche Reflexion und Immanente Reflexion," *Hegel-Studien* 13 (1978): 89.

13   Thus the categories or "determinations" generated by reflexion "must be present in every experience, in everything actual, as in every concept" (*SL* 440 / *LW* 60). As noted above in note 2, I use "reflexion" to refer to the ontological structure (and consider "reflection" to refer to the operation of the mind).

14   See Longuenesse, p. 52: "Essence is negation as the superseding of all immediacy, including its own."

15   See also Henrich, p. 274. Michael Baur defines reflected immediacy as "immediacy which is only by means of its negation", and he reminds us that seeming (*Schein*) is also understood by Hegel to be such reflected immediacy ("Sublating Kant," pp. 150–151, 154). Hegel himself connects the two forms of reflected immediacy in his account of reflexion: "This immediacy which is only as *return* of the negative into itself" – the new immediacy that emerges with reflexion – "is that immediacy which constitutes the determinateness of illusory being [*Schein*]" (*SL* 401 / *LW* 15). In the case of seeming, however, emphasis is placed on the fact that it *lacks* simple immediacy and consists in *nothing but differing* from essence, i.e., that it is "negative or *determinate* in regard to [essence]" (*SL* 398 / *LW* 12). In the case of the new reflected immediacy, by contrast, emphasis is placed on the fact it is "immediacy as the sublating of the negative" (*SL* 401 / *LW* 15) and thus the *affirmative product or result* of reflexion. The new reflected immediacy can itself be considered "illusory" to the extent that it, too, lacks simple immediacy, but it is not *merely* illusory, since it is affirmative, self-relating being that is explicitly *produced* by reflexion.

16 Hegel gives distinctive expression to the idea that posited immediacy is the *result* of reflexion – i.e., of the self-negating negative – by saying that it is to be understood as "*return from a negative*" (Rückkehr aus einem [Negativen]) (*SL* 401 / *LW* 15).

17 K. J. Schmidt, *Georg W.F. Hegel. Wissenschaft der Logik – Die Lehre vom Wesen* (Paderborn: Schöningh, 1997), 50.

18 See Hegel, *SL* 406 / *LW* 21: "for what is posited is only as sublated, as a relation to the return-into-self."

19 See Henrich, p. 279, and also Iber, p. 152.

20 Henrich, p. 278: "*Das Gesetzte ist nicht mehr nur das Negative des setzenden Wesens. Sein negativer Charakter ist selbst negiert. Es ist als unabhängig, und eben das heißt* voraus-*gesetzt.*"

21 George di Giovanni claims that Hegel's text does not itself explain why immediacy should become external to reflexion. In my view, however, Henrich's account provides precisely the explanation that di Giovanni thinks is missing. See G. di Giovanni, "Reflexion and Contradiction. A Commentary on Some Passages of Hegel's *Science of Logic*," *Hegel-Studien* 8 (1973): 152.

22 See S. Houlgate, "Power, Egoism and the 'Open' Self in Nietzsche and Hegel," *Journal of the British Society for Phenomenology* 22 (1991): 120–138.

23 W. Sellars, *Empiricism and the Philosophy of Mind*, with an Introduction by Richard Rorty and a Study Guide by Robert Brandom (Cambridge, Mass.: Harvard University Press, 1997), 14.

24 See Hegel, *EL* 108–122 / *EWL* 148–165 (§§61–75).

25 Needless to say, I do not share Franco Cirulli's view that Hegel's talk of immanent reflexion is merely "ironic." See F. Cirulli, *Hegel's Critique of Essence: A Reading of the Wesenslogik* (London: Routledge, 2006), 49.

26 Hegel describes identity at one point as "this pure constitution [*dieses reine Herstellen*] from and within itself" (*SL* 411 / *LW* 27).

27 See Hegel, *SL* 418 / *LW* 35: "Diversity constitutes the otherness as such of reflexion."

28 See Hegel, *SL* 420 / *LW* 36: "external reflexion is, as such, external to itself."

29 See Hegel, *SL* 425–426 / *LW* 44: "Further, however, this mere positedness is simply reflected into itself. ... The two sides are thus merely diverse [*verschiedene*]." In this respect the two sides would both be purely positive. Without the simple immediacy of *being* and *non*-being, the two sides could also both be purely negative. This, however, would be due not to their reflexive immediacy – to their being "reflected into themselves" – but to their being moments of a single contrast, i.e., to their both being *posited* by that contrast as not-one-another (see *SL* 425 / *LW* 43–44: "The determinations which constitute the positive and negative ... are, in the first place, absolute *moments* of the opposition").

30 See Hegel, *SL* 426 / *LW* 45: "But the other of itself, the negative, is itself no longer a positedness or moment, but a self-subsistent *being* [Sein]; thus the negating reflexion of the positive is immanently determined as *excluding* from itself this its *non-being* [Nichtsein]."

31 Reflexive and non-reflexive immediacy are both present in the relation between the "inner" and the "outer," as well: "the *inner* is determined as the form of *reflected immediacy* or of essence over against the *outer* as the form of *being*" (Hegel, *SL* 524 / *LW* 155).

32 See also S. Houlgate, "Necessity and Contingency in Hegel's *Science of Logic*," *The Owl of Minerva* 27 (1995): 37–49.

33 On Hegel's concept of substance in relation to Spinoza and Kant, see S. Houlgate, "Substance, Causality, and the Question of Method in Hegel's *Science of Logic*," in *The Reception of Kant's Critical Philosophy: Fichte, Schelling, and Hegel*, ed. S. Sedgwick (Cambridge: Cambridge University Press, 2000), 232–252.

34 See Hegel, *SL* 602 / *LB* 35: "The universal ... , even when it posits itself in a determination, *remains* therein what it is. ... It is not dragged into the process of becoming, but *continues*

itself through that process undisturbed and possesses the power of unalterable, undying self-preservation." Whereas the concept continues to be itself *in* the other, a determination of reflexion (such as "identity") is reflected *back* into itself *by* the other; a determination of reflexion appears *in* the other only as negated and, as it were, pushed out of the other back into itself. (A determination of being, such as "something," simply *becomes* the other.) See *EL* 306 / *EWL* 391 (§240). Substance points forward to the concept, because, even though it is reflected *back into itself* by its accidents (and so is the *power* over them), it also posits itself as, and so is *identical with*, its accidents. See *SL* 556 / *LW* 192: "Substance, as this identity of the reflexive movement [*des Scheinens*], is the totality of the whole and embraces accidentality within it, and accidentality is the whole substance itself"; see also Houlgate, "Substance, Causality, and the Question of Method in Hegel's *Science of Logic*," p. 235.

35   R. Winfield, *From Concept to Objectivity: Thinking Through Hegel's Subjective Logic* (Aldershot: Ashgate, 2006), 36.

36   S.-J. Kang, *Reflexion und Widerspruch, Hegel-Studien* Beiheft 41 (Bonn: Bouvier Verlag, 1999), 145.

37   For my account of the principal differences between these two parts of the *Logic*, see S. Houlgate, "Why Hegel's Concept Is Not the Essence of Things," in *Hegel's Theory of the Subject*, ed. D. G. Carlson (Basingstoke: Palgrave Macmillan, 2005), 19–29.

38   Iber, p. 191. See also T. M. Schmidt, "Die Logik der Reflexion. Der Schein und die Wesenheiten," in *G.W.F. Hegel: Wissenschaft der Logik*, ed. A. F. Koch and F. Schick (Berlin: Akademie Verlag, 2002), 109.

Abbreviations

EL   G.W.F. Hegel, *The Encyclopaedia Logic. Part 1 of the Encyclopaedia of Philosophical Sciences with the Zusätze*, trans. T. F. Geraets, W. A. Suchting, and H. S. Harris (Indianapolis, Ind.: Hackett Publishing, 1991).

EWL   G.W.F. Hegel, *Enzyklopädie der philosophischen Wissenschaften im Grundrisse (1830). Erster Teil: Die Wissenschaft der Logik. Mit den mündlichen Zusätzen*, eds. E. Moldenhauer and K.M. Michel (Frankfurt am Main: Suhrkamp, 1970).

LB   G.W.F. Hegel, *Wissenschaft der Logik. Die Lehre vom Begriff (1816)*, ed. H.-J. Gawoll (Hamburg: Felix Meiner, 2003).

LS   G.W.F. Hegel, *Wissenschaft der Logik. Die Lehre vom Sein (1832)*, ed. H.-J. Gawoll (Hamburg: Felix Meiner, 2008).

LW   G.W.F. Hegel, *Wissenschaft der Logik. Die Lehre vom Wesen (1813)*, ed. H.-J. Gawoll (Hamburg: Felix Meiner, 1999).

SL   G.W.F. Hegel, *Science of Logic*, trans. A.V. Miller (Amherst, N.Y.: Humanity Books, 1999).

7

Conceiving

JOHN W. BURBIDGE

1

One of the continuing puzzles in Hegelian scholarship is why Hegel discusses formal logic within the third and culminating book of his *Science of Logic*, on the concept (*Begriff*). On the one hand, he suggests that the concept incorporates the many determinations already discussed in the *Logic*; on the other hand, the formalism of traditional logic abstracts from all concrete content. The concept seems to be the culmination of Hegel's desire to integrate all the many facets of our experience into a single world view, yet in developing its primary characteristics, he looks only at the bare bones of reasoning: connecting subject to predicate, or inferring some trivial, but reliable, conclusion from abstract premises.

The response of many interpreters is to focus on the comprehensive quality of the concept, while minimizing the role of formal logic. Charles Taylor provides an initial illustration of this approach:

> Our basic ontological vision is that the Concept underlies everything as the inner necessity which deploys the world, and that our conceptual knowledge is derivative from this. We are the vehicles whereby this underlying necessity comes to its equally necessary self-consciousness. Hence the concept in our subjective awareness is the instrument of the self-awareness of the Concept as the source and basis of all, as cosmic necessity.[1]

By shifting from the lower to the upper case, he distinguishes the Concept (with a capital C) – an ontological entity governing the operation of the whole cosmos – from the concept (in lowercase), which represents only the subjective tools of our thinking, the means whereby we come to know and understand that reality.

A Companion to Hegel, First Edition. Edited by Stephen Houlgate and Michael Baur.
© 2011 Blackwell Publishing Ltd. Published 2011 by Blackwell Publishing Ltd.

The same distinction between upper and lower case can be found in earlier commentators. W. T. Harris, in 1890, ruefully pointed out that

the use of the expression *Begriff*, ordinarily translated notion or concept, is unfortunate and misleading. If he had called this third part person or personality, the student would have seen the drift of the entire system.[2]

He was followed in 1910 by J.M.E. McTaggart:

When we examine the categories which have the titles of Notion [Concept], Judgment and Syllogism, it is evident that, in spite of their names, they do not apply only to the states of our minds, but to all reality. ... They must therefore, if there is to be any validity in the process, apply to the same subject as the categories of Essence and the Idea, which admittedly apply to all reality.[3]

In 1948 G.R.G. Mure turned back from equating Concept with all reality to Harris's earlier appeal to personality:

For Hegel the logical movement of the Notion [Concept] is illustrated *par excellence* in human self-consciousness; in that self-identity, that complicity of the whole person in all phases of a subject's activity, upon which depend equally, for example, a man's coherent thinking and his moral conduct.[4]

And in 1958, John Findlay tried to combine the two:

The Notion [Concept] is accordingly one with a man's thinking being, the same universal thinking nature in all, but individualized in this or that thinking being.[5]

Our final witness is E. E. Harris, who, in 1983, wrote:

The Concept is the system or whole determining itself in thought; that is, the system conscious of itself as such, and so specifying itself in and through the thinking process. Thus it is the concrete universal, which is a self-differentiating whole, the system self-constituted as an individual totality. It is Concept, Spirit, the Absolute conscious of itself as subject.[6]

To be sure there have been other voices. Robert Pippin, for example, says that Hegel is following a Kantian project – of articulating those concepts that we require whenever we think in a rigorous way about any possible object whatever and then exploring their categorical commitments; but because Hegel does not accept Kant's distinction between the world as it is in itself and the world of experience, his categories simply define "the world" as such.[7]

Hegel himself has provided the impetus for this variety of interpretations. In the introduction to the *Science of Logic*, he notes that logic as a discipline cannot simply presuppose a method, since its subject matter is the process of thinking itself, and any method is simply an expression of that thinking.[8] But at the same time, such thinking is not abstract and formal, focused simply on the activity of thinking. It also has to take account of the content being thought. Many interpreters (perhaps overly influenced by the tradition of British empiricism) have assumed that such content can come only from our encounters with the world. Whenever Hegel gives an illustration about how a concept is used, or an example of how it may be applied in practice, it is assumed that this application fleshes out the specific content of the term being discussed. When Hegel offers 'I' as the best example of a genuine "concept," Taylor, W. T. Harris, and Mure are led to assume that Concept (with a capital) primarily refers to the dynamic of self-consciousness.

What these commentators have missed is a warning Hegel introduces when he talks about the subject matter of logic: the *content* of its process of thought. He explicitly rejects the presupposition that the subject matter of thought must always be something found in the world, and that thought on its own is empty. For, he says, thought can think about its own thinking and the rules it follows. Indeed, it is *this* content that provides the proper subject matter for any science of logic.[9] This suggests that, when Hegel talks about "the concept," he is primarily discussing the process of conceiving – that rational dynamic by which we comprehend and understand. There is no need to refer to some metaphysical reality. The intellectual process of conceiving may well find concrete embodiment in what Kant has called the transcendental unity of apperception, or the 'I.' But we can understand that embodiment correctly only if we have first considered what the act of conceiving on its own involves.

Once we make this move, we are no longer surprised when Hegel, in the final volume of his work, looks at the workings of traditional logic: the discipline that has formalized the results of careful and correct thinking, and spelled out the forms of judgments and syllogisms. Nor should we be surprised that it is precisely at this point that he explores the way we abstract universals from concrete content.[10]

This is the approach I adopt in my reading of the section on the subjective concept. But I do not limit myself to a simple exposition of Hegel's text. If he is exploring the way *all* thinking can understand its own operations, and he is not merely speculating about his own distinctive vision of the universe, then his analysis should be able to take account of developments in logic since his time. For symbolic logic, too, is not an arbitrary system. It was designed and developed as a way of coming to terms with the way thought functions, and many of its insights have led to revisions and clarifications of traditional logical concepts. With this in mind, I shall develop a dialogue between Hegel's text and more recent developments, and suggest that Hegel's chapter on the subjective concept can be read as a sophisticated philosophy of logic, one that shows why certain forms of judgment and syllogism are required, and why each must then be supplemented by more complex symbols.

2

In the first two books of the *Logic*, Hegel has been analyzing concepts that we use for anything whatsoever, whether material things, thoughts, or creative fictions. We start by thinking something that has no specific defining characteristics but just is, or at least can be: what we could call "being." From this beginning we are led eventually to the basic relationships involved in defining anything whatever: the relationship between a substance and its properties, or between cause and effect. Careful reflection on the relation of cause and effect, however, reveals that something can be a cause only if it is in some way incited to action by some other substance upon which it in due course works its effects. There is, then, a reciprocal interaction between two "substances." So we come to the thought of a double transition, from the one substance over to another that it incites to action, and from that other, now made causally effective, back to the original one.

Over the years Hegel came to stress the critical importance of such double transitions. In the second edition of his *Encyclopaedia of the Philosophical Sciences* of 1827, he introduces a paragraph devoted exclusively to this kind of move in the midst of the second step of his philosophical method (§241): "The development of this sphere becomes a return into the first, just as the first is a transition into the second. Only by way of this doubled movement does the difference achieve its due, in that each of the two differentiated [terms] considered on its own reaches its fulfillment, and thereby activates itself to become united with the other. Only the self-sublating of the onesidedness *of both on their own account* keeps the unity from becoming onesided."[11] And he returns to the theme while revising the first book of the larger *Science of Logic* in 1831. In noting that the analysis of quantity has led him back to quality, even as the original analysis of quality had led into magnitude and number, he writes: "That the totality be *posited*, there is required the *doubled* transition, not only that of one determination into its other, but equally the transition of this latter, its return into the first. Through the first [transition] the identity of the two is only present *implicitly*; – quality is contained in quantity, which nonetheless remains only a onesided determination. That this latter, in an inverted way, is equally contained in the first – is equally present only as sublated – emerges from the second transition – the return into the first. This remark concerning the necessity of the *doubled* transition is of great importance for the whole of the scientific method."[12]

Double transitions connect two items or terms, bringing them together into a synthesis; terms and transitions belong in the same context. Under the term "reciprocity" – which names this kind of interaction between two causes each inciting the other – they become the explicit focus of attention in Hegel's study of pure thought at the end of his second book on "The Doctrine of Essence," just as he is preparing the move to his discussion of "The Concept."

Hegel calls on Kant to explicate and clarify the transition to this third level of logical discourse. By referring to the transcendental unity of apperception, he sends us back to the passage in the *Critique of Pure Reason* where Kant introduces the pure concepts of the understanding.[13] There Kant distinguishes the syntheses introduced by the transcendental imagination from the unity provided by conceptual understanding. "By *synthesis* in its most general sense," writes Kant, "I understand the act of putting different representations together, and of grasping what is manifold in them in one [act of] knowledge."[14] This, he adds, is the mere result of the power of imagination, drawing on the multiple content of intuition. In contrast, "the concepts which give *unity* to this pure synthesis, and which consist solely in the representation of this necessary synthetic unity, furnish the third requisite for the knowledge of an object; and they rest on the understanding."[15]

This sharp distinction between the syntheses of imagination and the unity provided by the understanding continues throughout the Transcendental Deduction of the

Categories in the first edition, though it was blunted in the second edition. It becomes, however, critical to understanding what Hegel is doing as he moves into the third book of his *Logic*.

The first thing to notice is that Hegel, by developing his analysis of reciprocal interaction, has shown that imagination is not the sole source of synthesis. Thought itself, by recognizing that it has moved back and forth between two distinct determinations, has effectively "grasped a manifold in one act."

Second, when we focus on the simple unity involved in the act of understanding, rather than on its content, we find that it collapses the diversity of those double transitions into a single integrated concept. In other words, the synthetic pattern of pure reciprocity sets the stage for thought to recognize its distinctive unifying role in conceiving, when it unites (as Kant has suggested) these double movements into simple, self-contained concepts. The task of the third Book of the *Science of Logic* is to explore what happens once this is done.

Third, we can understand what is going on in this move by recalling Hegel's remark, early in the *Science of Logic*, on the German word *Aufhebung* (sometimes translated "sublation"). This comment comes just at the point where, in "coming-to-be" and "passing-away," thought has distinguished between two kinds of becoming that function as a double transition: moving from nothing to being and from being back to nothing. For Hegel this double process collapses into a new single concept, which he calls *Dasein* (misleadingly translated as "determinate being"). The unity introduced by this act dissolves, retains, yet transforms, the distinctive characteristics of the original terms in the reciprocal interaction. In other words, the conceptual operation of integrating into a simple unity the multiplicity of a double transition is the specific referent for the process called *Aufhebung*, a technical term of great importance for Hegel's system.

Fourth, Hegel follows Kant in ascribing this act of uniting syntheses – of generating concepts – to the work of understanding. While he at times decries the work of those who rely solely on the understanding and miss both the dynamic of dialectical transitions and the reflective, or speculative, work of synthesis, he nonetheless continues to assert that understanding is critical to the working of the scientific method. By fixing its integrated concepts and holding them fast, it provides the necessary conditions for the dialectic to do its work.[16] While the "activity of dissolution is the power and work of the *understanding*," it is nonetheless "the most astonishing and mightiest of powers, indeed the absolute power."[17] So we should not be surprised that Hegel starts the body of his chapter on "The Concept" with the statement: "The faculty of conceiving in general tends to be identified with the *understanding*."

Frequently, the understanding is contrasted with judging and inferring in that it focuses on individual, abstracted concepts. But Hegel suggests that it needs to be applied more widely to the processes by which we abstract concepts from singular objects of reference, conjoin singulars and concepts in judgments, and draw inferences. To be sure, the power of fixation and death (as Hegel suggests in the Preface to the *Phenomenology*) can be found in all things; it is the key not only to decay but also to development and growth. But it is found first and foremost in the understanding as conceiving – the power of pure abstract thought.

3

We turn now to the chapter on the Subjective Concept.

In the previous section, we have seen that the act of conceiving integrates a dynamic synthesis of reciprocal interaction into a simple unity. As containing all the various moments of that complexity, its product is general and *universal*. But at the same time this concept is made into something distinctive by the specific elements that have reacted to each other, so it is also a *particular*. In addition, as one unified integration, it is equally individual or *singular*.

But conceiving does not just generate a unified concept. It seeks to render that thought more precise by identifying its determinations; by defining it, the understanding distinguishes it from other similar concepts. The concept now becomes one among many particulars, all of which are included within some more general universal. At the same time, understanding isolates this general concept, which covers the common features that its various determinate species or particular kinds share. In both of these processes, the strictly universal abandons key elements of its determinate content to the particular species and, now isolated on its own, becomes abstract and fixed.[18] The particulars, on the other hand, for all their specific determination, retain an element of universality.

But the process of definition and determining goes further; for each particular universal can in its turn be defined more precisely by identifying its constituent species. To escape the residual generality that such particular concepts retain, thought seeks to render it fully determinate by referring to something singular and individual. It cancels its own generalizing character and appeals to a strictly referential act that points beyond itself. In this way the process of conceiving moves over dialectically to its alien opposite – a singular that cannot be conceived[19] but simply indicated or referred to as a "this." In this move it has left behind all universal thought, which has become, as a result, ever more abstract. Each – the singular as well as the universal – has become fixed, having isolated itself from the dynamic of pure thinking; each has become, in a strange way, a simple object of reference.

In this discussion of the function of understanding or conceiving, Hegel has outlined the way pure thought has moved from simply integrating a dynamic synthesis into a conceptual unity to isolating pure abstract universality on the one hand and the recalcitrant singulars to which thought can only refer on the other. He is showing that the universal functions and individual objects of reference that pure logic, whether traditional or symbolic, likes to manipulate are not simply presented to us as irreducible starting points, but are in fact the result of a complex process of thinking, in which the terms we use initially to understand anything whatsoever become the object of our attention and so refined into their discrete and contrasting elements: the abstract generality of a thought, and the singular instances to which they refer. Far from being the starting points for a philosophy of logic the singulars of pure reference are themselves the result of a prior logical operation.

What Hegel has done is to provide the initial stages for a philosophy of logic, an explanation of the way the basic terms of logic emerge. By so doing he will then be able to show why logic takes the next step – from concepts to judgments and propositions.

It is because one and the same activity of conceptual thinking both identifies singulars and abstracts universals that thought is justified in considering how they are related one to another. That relation finds expression in the act of judging, or forming propositions.

4

Unlike the tradition represented by Aristotle through to Kant, Hegel does not just list the set of judgments. He shows instead how the various forms of judgment are required; for each articulates a relationship that was implicit, but not expressed in the previous form. At first, we have simply a singular object of reference and an abstract universal. Judgment picks up the fact that both emerge from a prior relationship and affirms that the singular inheres in, or is subsumed by, the universal. This becomes the positive judgment, *S is P*, more accurately represented in symbolic logic by Ab, which says that a general function A is instantiated in the singular b. Such a judgment presupposes, but does not expressly state, that the subject and the predicate are to be of two quite different orders. To express this, we need to introduce a further kind of judgment – one that captures the difference between singulars and universals. For that we need a negative judgment: *S is not P*. Unfortunately, the traditional form does not translate directly into symbolic form for it contains an ambiguity: the negative judgment can be pointing either to a contrary or to a contradictory. For when we say "this is not green" we usually imply that it is nonetheless colored, since green is a contrary of red and blue and gray. But we could be saying that it is simply not true that this predicate is appropriate at all, so that the whole statement is false, the contradictory of what is true.[20] Symbolic logic might be able to avoid this ambiguity by adopting, for the contrary sense, a simple bar (rather than the tilde ($\sim$) used for strict negation) and placing it either in front of (or over, as in $\bar{A}b$) the predicate symbol: $-Ab$, *S is non-P*.[21]

However, we may well want to use a negative judgment to say something more radical: to simply deny that the subject and the predicate are related, as if we were to say "the current exchange rate between dollars and pounds is not black." To capture this we have to negate the whole sentence, and not just the predicate: *it is simply not the case that S is P*, or *S is-not P*. Symbolic logic has represented this sharp contrast between what is and what is not by using the tilde as in $\sim Ab$.

In the tradition from Aristotle to Kant, this latter kind of negative judgment was called an indefinite or infinite judgment. Once again we find that it has its flaws. For such judgments affirm nothing at all; they completely abandon any implicit relationship between singular and universal, which was what judgments were supposed to express.

Kant, following the tradition, had called these three judgments qualitative; Hegel, drawing on earlier discussions in the *Logic*, calls them judgments of determinate being (here Miller translates *Dasein* with "existence"), since (as we found with the negative judgments) the predicates implicitly lead thought over to their contraries, just as "something" leads to the thought of "other." Once we have pushed this analysis to its limits, however, and discover that we have reached the dead end of a judgment that conveys no positive information at all, we are led to reflect back over the process as a whole and consider what its most critical moment was. This, in fact, lies in the recognition that the first form of the negative judgment distinguished among contraries – several particulars that share a common universal. While the judgment was negative, it nonetheless implied some kind of positive relationship between the subject and the general context within which the predicate functions. Since this context lies below the surface structure as its underlying foundation, it represents what is *essential* to the formation of meaningful judgments. Because the infinite judgment does not take this context into consideration, it leads to its dead end. So the next set of judgments will consider the role the subject plays in the kind of judgment that explores *essential* relations, which Kant and the tradition called judgments of quantity and which Hegel calls "judgements of reflection."

With respect to these judgments of quantity, Hegel starts once again with *This S is P.* This time the focus is not on how the subject is simply qualified by its predicate, but rather on how the essence of a singular subject is captured by the predicate universal. Symbolic logic has several versions of this kind of proposition: on the one hand we can reuse our original Ab, or alternatively we can adopt the Boolean symbol for class membership: $a \in F$, which says that a belongs to the class F. The latter has the advantage of stressing the kind of essential relationship that is to hold between subject and predicate, since we use the language of classes to capture what is distinctive about their members, and not contingent and accidental properties.

Having introduced the thought of essential relation, however, we realize something is missing. For classes are not limited to having only one singular member; they have a more general reference. We can initially suggest this through a particular judgment: *Some S are P.*

Modern logic symbolizes the indefinite range of "some" by using $(\exists x)$ Fx: "*there is at least one x such that x is F.*" This form by itself, however, is not able to capture all that is expressed by the traditional particular judgment, for the subject, S, is not just an indefinite individual but, like P, a class. To represent the suggested intersection of the two classes, S and P, symbolic logic uses the symbol for conjunction (which will emerge only later in Hegel's analysis). This gives us $(\exists x)$ $(Cx.Fx)$: *There are some x's, which being C's are also F's.* At this point we could again adopt Boolean algebra and introduce the symbol for class intersection: $C \cap F$, which says that the two classes C and F overlap.

As we might expect, reflection soon notices something not adequately expressed by the particular judgment. The predicate is a universal, but the subject is only a particular selection from the indicated set. This means that there is nothing to indicate that the relationship between subject and predicate is indeed essential. To capture that feature we need a universal subject as well – one that incorporates all members of the class under consideration: *All S are P.* Symbolic logic at this point draws on the symbol for conditional judgments (again introduced later in Hegel's text), as well as the symbol for all possible instances of a variable, to provide us with (x) $(Cx \supset Fx)$: *For all cases of x, if it is C it is also F.* In Boolean terms, we have class inclusion: $C \subset F$, the class C is included within the class F.

If the first set of judgments showed how a predicate implicitly refers to its more general context, the second set focuses on the subject: it shifts from a singular to a particular selection to all members of a class. The analysis ends with a universal class related to a universal context. Since universals are the function of understanding and thought, and do not involve specific reference to any particular singular, we have in fact introduced a relationship that holds simply between concepts. Judgments of relation, or what Hegel calls "judgments of necessity," focus on conceptual relationships that hold between terms that are themselves concepts. In symbolic logic, then, we can dispense with the need for implicit reference to members of a class through the use of variables, and adopt symbols that capture the way universals incorporate their particular instances into a totality. *p,q,r* have been used to represent propositions in which subject and predicate have been integrated into a unit; they can thus serve our purposes at this stage of our analysis.

Since in the subject we are now talking about the specified class as a whole, we can omit the term "all" and simply talk about "the crow" as a universal concept; the predicate on the other hand must be something to which that subject concept is inherently related. The most obvious candidate for this would be its proximate genus – the universal under which it, as a particular, is included. So we have the categorical judgment form: *S is P* but it is now used to say things like "The crow is a bird." In translating this into symbolic form, we need to take account of the fact that "crow" and "bird" are simply coupled by a copula. This coupling is captured with the symbol for conjunction *p.q: p and q.*

The difficulty with the straightforward categorical judgment is that it does not make explicit the necessity of the connection between subject and predicate. For that we need a judgment form – the hypothetical – that spells out how the two terms are necessarily related: *if p then q*, represented symbolically as $p \supset q$.

While we have gained a necessary relationship, however, we have lost the assertive force of the categorical judgment, since the *if-then* relationship is conditional on whether the antecedent *if* actually obtains or not. So we need a judgment form that both articulates a necessary relationship and asserts it as actually the case. This double demand is satisfied by the disjunctive judgment: *U is either P or Q or R.* It not only makes an assertion, but it also spells out that particular classes are necessarily included in a more universal one. Symbolic logic, because it lacks any means for representing restricted ranges for its symbols, treats the universal as referring to all that is – or what is true. Using the symbols for class membership mentioned in the previous discussion of judgments of reflection, it can represent disjunction as $(x) (Bx \lor Cx \lor Dx)$: *For any x whatever, it will be either B or C or D.* In propositional calculus it is represented more simply as $(p \lor q \lor r)$: *either p or q or r.*

In the course of exploring the various sets of judgments, we have elaborated on the role of the predicate, then that of the subject, and thirdly the kind of relation that holds between them. Once all three have been fully developed we can bring them together into a synthesis, and legitimately unite them into a single judgment or proposition. All such acts of uniting, we have seen, are the work of conceiving and understanding. So the final set of judgments is called judgments of conceiving by Hegel.

We start from the realization that a disjunctive judgment, by articulating all the appropriate subcategories, is simply making an assertion. It is ascribing a necessary relation to the world. Assertion, however, introduces a new dimension into our consideration of judgments – the status the proposition has in relation to the context in which it is uttered or thought – the mood of the verb that conjoins subject and predicate. So we need to move on to consider the various forms of modal judgment.

167

For the simple act of assertion ("this *is* the case") symbolic logic uses the symbol ⊢: ⊢*p: p is the case*. Yet any act of assertion is ultimately contingent. And contingency introduces doubt. So the only thing that can be affirmed with confidence is the possibility of what is said. "This *may be* the case," symbolized by ◊*p*. To overcome that indecisiveness we would have to go back into the subject and predicate and develop the particular sense of each as well as the nature of the connection that holds between them. Once we do that, the connection is no longer problematic, but necessary, and we have an apodictic judgment: "This *must be* that," or □*p*.

With this Hegel has completed his discussion of all the judgment forms identified by the traditional logic of his time – those Kant used as the foundation for his categories. We have found him introducing each form to make explicit a relationship that was only implicit in the previous one; to acknowledge its partiality; or to capture a structure of mutual relation that had been found to hold – between a predicate and its contrary, between a universal subject and a universal predicate, or between a judgment and the actual state of affairs. This reflection on the various forms identified their particular characteristics and pointed toward others in a progressive, reasonable development.

We have also found that we can apply Hegel's analysis to more contemporary logical terminology. To be sure, we have had to move back and forth between Aristotelian, Boolean, lower functional, and propositional logics. But we have done enough to illustrate how Hegel's approach might be expanded to provide a systematic setting for the judgment forms adopted by contemporary logical theory.

For Hegel the task of a *Science of Logic* is not simply to list the judgment forms and concepts (which, after all, he took over from the tradition). Rather, he was primarily interested in showing how they can be placed within a systematic structure, in which by identifying one form and reflecting on its strengths and shortcomings we can move to another that rectifies its weaknesses. He is creating a rational connection that links them all into a rational sequence. This is the proper way of developing a fully systematic philosophy of logic.

5

This approach is extended in the subsequent chapter of the *Science of Logic* on inferences and syllogisms. The necessity expressed in an apodictic judgment cannot emerge out of nowhere. Something has to mediate the link between subject and predicate. In Hegel's analysis, subject, predicate, and mediator are all moments within a single conceptual activity of inference, so that the various functions of universal, particular, and singular come to be distributed among them. Mediation occurs, however, at two levels. On the one hand each formal syllogism has in both its premises a middle term that can justify linking the subject and predicate in the conclusion. On the other hand, each inference involves a mediating conceptual activity, whether a particular dialectical transition, an individual reflective synthesis, or a universal process of understanding.[22] On this basis, Hegel organizes his discussion of inference according to three triads. Each set of three inferences is governed by one of the mediating activities of conceptual thought; within each set we have syllogisms that formally identify the middle term as particular, individual, or universal.

We start, then, with formal syllogisms, where the inferential activity involves particular transitions, in that thought moves over from one term to its counterpart. Here Hegel looks at the traditional Aristotelian syllogisms. (Apart from Boolean algebra, there has been little interest in these syllogisms in symbolic logic since they require the use of particular subclasses as well as universal classes, whereas symbolic, mathematical logic works only with singulars and abstract universals.)

The first syllogistic form has a particular subclass as the middle term, which is to link an indicated singular with an abstract universal.[23] At the same time, to establish necessity, it has to include a moment of universality in the intermediate class. As a result, transitions move easily from singular to particular and from particular to the universal; and we have the Aristotelian 'Barbara' form of syllogism: "Alice [singular] is blonde [particular]; all blond [particular] people are beautiful [universal]; so Alice [singular] is beautiful [universal]."[24]

In this syllogism there is something unresolved about the major premise: "all blonde people are beautiful." The universal subject suggests a necessary relationship between being blonde and being beautiful, but this has not itself been justified. So we need a syllogism that establishes a link between *particular* subclasses and *universal* abstractions. The term thus left to serve as a mediating term is the indicated *singular*. But while any singular can be qualified by some more general particular or universal, to produce two premises: "Alice is blonde" and "Alice is beautiful," that singular on its own cannot justify an independent link between the two predicates. All we can say is that in this instance the two classes intersect. So we are left with a conclusion that is particular, as in the Aristotelian form 'Datisi': "Alice is blonde; Alice is beautiful; so some blonde people [or, in logical terms, "at least one blonde person"] are beautiful."[25]

In this second argument form we have lost the universal necessity that inferential mediation was supposed to provide. To remedy this we introduce a third form in which the universal term is to serve as the middle. But the fact that we can pass over from a singular to a universal ["Alice is beautiful"] or from a particular subclass to a universal ["Blonde people are beautiful"] can tell us nothing positive about the relationship between the singular [Alice] and the particular [being blonde]. If, however, the particular subclass is *excluded from* the universal class and vice versa, then we are able to draw the conclusion that the singular is also excluded from that particular class. So the major premise and the conclusion do not affirm, but deny, any positive linkage, and so must be negative judgments. So we end up with the Aristotelian form 'Cesare': "Alice is beautiful; no blonde people are beautiful; so Alice is not blonde."[26]

Since the role of negatives is to exclude, they generate abstractions that lack concrete content. As we gradually remove all determinate significance, we end up with the most banal of abstract universals that can then be linked together in a purely quantitative syllogism: where two universals are both equal to a third one, they are equal to each other. Such geometric axioms work because we have abandoned all determinate content (such as fingers, toes, and days) and have left only their abstract quantity (or number) remaining. ("The number of digits on my hand is the number of working days in a week; the number of toes on my foot is the number of working days in a week; so the number of digits on my hand is the number of toes on my foot.")

The inferences that rely on the particularity of dialectical transitions have ended up with the barest of abstractions. But reflection on this suggests that we might resolve the problem were we to adopt a different mediating strategy and work instead with the concrete, or the singular. Reflective thought thus turns to the mediating activity of synthesis – a singular act that brings together the two extremes. With this Hegel moves from his qualitative syllogisms, or syllogisms of determinate being, to his syllogisms of reflection.[27] Once again, the particular forms that implement this kind of mediation, use particular, singular, and universal middle terms.

Hegel starts this section with a form rather like the 'Barbara' syllogism identified earlier. But here the focus is not on the transition from subject to predicate in the two premises, but on the collected universality of the particular middle term: *All* deciduous trees shed their leaves in the fall; this oak is a deciduous tree; so it will shed its leaves in the fall.[28] This argument works because the middle term "deciduous trees" is made a universal in the major premise, so it already includes any particular instance, such as the oak of the minor premise. But this means that we have not really moved to something new in the conclusion. Once we know that the oak is deciduous, there is nothing new to learn. The inference is empty. A useful argument would need to justify the universal premise, where *all* of a particular subclass is included in the predicate class.

The inference that accomplishes this task is induction. There we collect together a number of individuals and find that (for example) each one is a tulip flower, and also originates from a bulb. From this we generalize to the conclusion that all tulips originate from bulbs.[29] Whereas the earlier inference was so necessary that it became trivial, however, this inference is bedeviled with contingency. For, as we saw in the 'Datisi' syllogism, the intersection of two characteristics in the same individual does not establish any universality; expanding the number of individuals does not overcome this limitation, since one can never be sure that the same conjunction will occur the next time around. To remedy this we need an inference that justifies connecting just these individuals in just this way.

Hegel finds that arguments from analogy try to satisfy this requirement. Because all the tulip flowers (a collected set of individuals) have the same relationship between petals, stem, and flowers (a general set of properties), they will be similar in the kind of seed from which they develop (an additional particular property). More recent reflection on scientific reasoning has identified at this point a broader classification of inferences, generally called "reasoning to a hypothesis." Some individual state of affairs, or set of things, has a wide range of properties and characteristics. From this we try to find a general explanation that will show why it has just the particular character it does. Unfortunately, in both arguments from analogy and reasoning to a hypothesis all pretense of necessity has been lost. For there is an innumerable set of possible explanations for any set of conditions; and analogies can focus on inessential as well as essential features.

Inferences that rely on a reflective synthesis turn out to be inescapably affected by contingency.[30] But reasoning was supposed to justify the necessity of an apodictic judgment. Necessity can emerge only where the mediating logical operation is a conceptual universality that determines how the various components are to function with respect to each other. So Hegel turns to a third triad of syllogisms, which he calls the syllogisms of necessity; and again we have three forms, where particularity, singularity, and universality mediate.

In the first form, we find ourselves back with a version of the 'Barbara' syllogism. This time, however, the focus is not on the "all" of the major premise, but on the particular significance of the middle term. It has to be a substantial genus that determines both the way its general characteristics are specified and what kind of individuals it can subsume: "Humans are mortal; Lionel is human; so Lionel is mortal."

The simple assertion of the major premise in this categorical syllogism does not tell us how and why mortality follows from the middle term "being human." Since its conceptual significance is not a part of the logical form, the latter on its own cannot ensure necessity. For that we need to find an operator that, as a singular, brings together the two terms in the necessary synthesis. This is found in the conditional "if/then." "If something revolves around a star in a regular orbit, then it is a planet; Mars is something that revolves around the sun in a regular orbit; so Mars is a planet." This is a version of modus ponens, one of the two primary syllogisms of symbolic logic: "$p \supset q$; p; so q."[31]

The if-then operator in modus ponens spells out a necessary connection, but the hypothetical form represents a singular act of synthesis and can be adopted for all kinds of implications that never in fact could occur: "If the moon is made of green cheese, then I am a monkey's uncle." As symbolic logic has made clear, a hypothetical inference holds as long as either the consequent (predicate) is true or the antecedent (premise) is false.[32] When this is applied to modus tollens – the negative counterpart of modus ponens – we can produce the intended inference: "I am not a monkey's uncle, so the moon is not made of green cheese." In other words, there are all kinds of abstract hypothetical inferences that involve no necessary conceptual connection between antecedent and consequent.

To avoid such strange results, we need an argument form in which formal structure and conceptual content are integrated. The disjunctive judgment, as we have seen, is designed to spell out the particular species that fit under a universal genus: "All material things in the world are either animal, vegetable, or mineral." From this we can draw several inferences: "This cube of salt is neither animal nor vegetable, so it must be mineral"; or alternatively, "This shell is the skeleton of an animal, so it is neither vegetable nor mineral." Thus we have a disjunctive syllogism, where the universal "material things," together with its species, are integrated by the all-encompassing operator "either-or" to produce a necessary inference.

In symbolic logic, as we have seen, a disjunction starts from the broadest universal: truth. So it can dispense with spelling out the universal's mediating role in the syllogistic form: "$p \lor q \lor r$; $\sim q$ & $\sim r$; so p."[33]

In a disjunctive syllogism we have, in the major premise, a universal that is differentiated into its particular species; in the minor premise some singular state of affairs requires the rejection of a set of these particulars; so we are left with one particular species in the conclusion. (Alternatively, the fact that one particular species can be affirmed requires the rejection of its contraries.) This formal structure captures the dynamic we originally saw in the act of conceiving: understanding particularizes a universal into its particulars, then abstracts its own conceptual role to leave an individual object of reference. There remains nothing implicit that needs to be given formal expression. If understanding brings all of this together and then collapses this synthesis into a simple unity, it has the thought of something that is self-contained and unmediated by anything outside it. To this new concept we can give the name "objectivity."

Hegel will go on to show that whenever we understand objects conceptually we continue to use patterns that reflect the forms of traditional logic. We will fix singulars and associate them with abstract universals, discover that the two sides are related as contraries, and explore the network of mediating transitions that connect them into a complex, but single pattern. For the world itself is not completely fluid. Things and entities become fixed; they pass nonetheless over into something else; and by taking account of their past, they develop into more complex integrated structures.

In his philosophy Hegel frequently talks about patterns of three syllogisms. In doing so he is not simply selecting three from the total sequence of ten that he has studied in this chapter. He is referring rather to the three kinds of mediation: the mediation that happens when something simply passes over and disappears into its opposite or counterpart; the mediation that happens when, through a singular act of reflection, past and present are brought together into a synthetic perspective; and the mediation that happens when, from the standpoint of a unified whole, we can understand why the various components have played the role they have, and why they fit within a single perspective.

All reality, Hegel wants to suggest, is structured by this kind of dynamic. And so the judgments and syllogisms of formal logic, for all their abstraction, have a role to play in spelling out how the universe is constituted. They are tools we use in fixing, and so understanding, the world. And they are successful because they capture the way things in the world become individuated; how they nonetheless pass away into other things; and yet how they are integrated into larger wholes. Nonetheless each form is faulty because it presupposes much that it does not explicitly articulate. And so we always pass over to other related forms until we have the whole picture. Each point of understanding or fixation expands as it initiates dialectical transitions and speculative syntheses. When we integrate the formal analysis of concepts and conceiving with the full range of our experience over time, then we are on the way to transforming our thinking from being a bare philosophy of logical forms into a description of all reality. If we wish, we can leave behind the language of (subjective) conceiving altogether, and start to talk about the ultimate dynamic inherent in the universe – something we might deign to call the "Concept."

Unfortunately, such talk ultimately betrays Hegel's project. For it underplays the important role that understanding, with its fixity, abstraction, and formalism, has in crystallizing and promoting development. Without it, there is nothing for dialectic to react against; without it, there are no distinctive terms to be synthetically related by speculative thought; and without it, there can be no integration of such syntheses into new conceptual unities. In other words, it is only because the understanding, with its formal logic, marks the culminating stage of all rational thought that the *Science of Logic* can take the place of what traditionally was called metaphysics.

Notes

1   Charles Taylor, *Hegel* (Cambridge: Cambridge University Press, 1975), 299–300.
2   W. T. Harris, *Hegel's Logic: A Book on the Genesis of the Categories of Mind* (Chicago: Griggs, 1890), 349.

3   J.M.E. McTaggart, *A Commentary on Hegel's Logic* (Cambridge: Cambridge University Press, 1910), 190. McTaggart is particularly puzzled by the turn to formal logic: "This will enable us to explain why the divisions of Subjectivity drew their names from formal logic. The reason is not that these categories apply only to the subject-matter of formal logic, but that the procedure of formal logic involves the validity of these categories in a way in which it does not involve those which come later in the chain" (p. 191). We should note that some of the older commentators, such as McTaggart, Mure, and Findlay, prefer Wallace's "Notion" when translating the German *Begriff*.

4   G.R.G. Mure, *A Study of Hegel's Logic* (Oxford: Clarendon Press, 1950), 158.

5   J. N. Findlay, *Hegel: A Re-examination* (London: George Allen & Unwin, 1958), 223.

6   Errol E. Harris, *An Interpretation of the Logic of Hegel* (Lanham, MD.: University Press of America, 1983), 224.

7   Robert B. Pippin, *Hegel's Idealism: The Satisfactions of Self-Consciousness* (Cambridge: Cambridge University Press, 1989), 91: "Whatever else Hegel intends by asserting an 'Absolute Idealism,' it is clear by now that such a claim at the very least involves Hegel in a theory about pure concepts, and about the role of such concepts in human experience, particularly in any possible knowledge of objects, but also in various kinds of self-conscious, intentional activities. Moreover, his account of this role is clearly committed to the priority of such a conceptual element. Throughout his mature system, his general term of art for such a nonempirical and supposedly 'spontaneously self-moving' condition is 'the Notion' (*der Begriff*) and, simply put, his claim is that the Notion originally determines the possibility and character of human experience. ... There is, in Hegel's final position, no possible *contrast* between our conceptual framework and 'the world,' and hence no such limitation."

8   "But not only instruction about the scientific method, but also the very *concept* of *science* in general belongs to its content, and indeed constitutes its final result. So what it is cannot be presupposed, but its whole discussion develops this knowledge of itself only as its final stage, and as its completion. Similarly its object, *thinking*, or more determinately *conceptual thinking*, is essentially handled within it; its concept is generated in the course of its development, and thus cannot be put forward in advance" (my translation). G.W.F. Hegel, "Introduction" to *Wissenschaft der Logik*, vol. 21 of *Gesammelte Werke* (Hamburg: Meiner, 1985), 27. Compare *Hegel's Science of Logic*, trans. A. V. Miller (London: Allen & Unwin, 1969), 43.

9   "For since thinking and the rules of thinking are to be its object, it thus has its proper content immediately at hand. There it also has that second requirement for cognition, a material about whose constitution it should concern itself." Ibid. 28; compare Miller's translation, p. 44.

10   Despite Errol Harris's claim that the concept is the concrete universal.

11   G.W.F. Hegel, *Enzyklopaedie der philosophischen Wissenschaften*, 2. Auflage, vol. 19 of *Gesammelte Werke* (Hamburg: Meiner, 1989), 179. The paragraph is retained in the third edition: see G.W.F. Hegel, *The Encyclopaedia Logic*, trans. Geraets, Suchting & Harris (Indianapolis: Hackett Publishing Company, 1991), 306.

12   Hegel, *Wissenschaft der Logik*, 2. Auflage, in vol. 21 of *Gesammelte Werke*, 320; compare *Hegel's Science of Logic*, trans. A. V. Miller, 323. Double transitions function throughout the logic. Consider the shift from being to nothing and from nothing back to being in its very first chapter.

13   "§10, "The Pure Concepts of the Understanding," Section 3 of the chapter on "The Clue to the Discovery of all Pure Concepts of the Understanding," from Immanuel Kant, *Critique of Pure Reason*, A76-83/B102–109.

14   Immanuel Kant, *Critique of Pure Reason*, A77/B103. The English rendering is taken from the translation by Norman Kemp Smith (London: Macmillan, 1953), 111.

15   A79/B104; Kemp Smith, 112.

16 See §§79–82 in the *Encyclopaedia Logic*.

17 G.W.F. Hegel, *Phänomenologie des Geistes*, vol. 9 of *Gesammelte Werke* (Hamburg: Meiner, 1980), 27; compare *Hegel's Phenomenology of Spirit*, trans. A. V. Miller (Oxford: Clarendon Press, 1977), §32, 18.

18 Notice how abstraction and fixity become the theme of Hegel's discussion under "the particular concept": *Wissenschaft der Logik*, Band 2, vol. 21 of *Gesammelte Werke*, 40–43; *Science of Logic*, 608–612.

19 Notice that Hegel calls this section simply "The Singular" in contrast with the earlier "Universal Concept" and "Particular Concept."

20 As in "the number three is not green."

21 There seems to be some discrepancy between the terminology adopted by Kant and that used by Hegel. For Kant, the negative judgment involves strict denial; whereas the infinite judgment limits the range of the predicate but allows it to extend over other contraries. Because standard symbolic logic works with either full truth or absolute falsity and nothing else, it sees no value in such a limited sense of negation. Nonetheless, the use of the simple negative as a contrary was explored by both Rudolf Carnap and Gilbert Ryle in their essays on "category words."

22 These operations have already been analyzed in the three Books of the *Science of Logic*: dialectical transition in the Doctrine of Being; reflective synthesis in the Doctrine of Essence; and conceptual understanding in the Doctrine of the Concept.

23 The reader is reminded that, in traditional logic, the middle term is found in both premises, but not in the conclusion.

24 Aristotle's first figure.

25 Aristotle's third figure.

26 Aristotle's second figure.

27 Recall that the logic of determinate being involves becoming or transition; whereas the logic of reflection is found in the discussion of essence – of speculative syntheses between reciprocal terms.

28 Symbolic logic calls this Universal Instantiation.

29 This would be Existential Generalization; but the limits imposed on both it and Universal Generalization reflect the contingencies that may jeopardize this kind of reasoning.

30 Because the reflective inferences (other than the trivial first form) introduce contingencies, they do not appear in symbolic logic, though they have become the focus of interest in philosophy of science.

31 Strictly speaking, to represent the cited syllogism, we need to introduce variables: (x) $(Rx \supset Px)$; Rm; so Pm.

32 As in the example suggested, people often use a hypothetical judgment to assert the impossibility of the antecedent: "If God had meant us to fly, he would have given us wings."

33 The necessity does not find complete expression in symbolic logic, since the operator $\vee$ allows for its two related terms both to be true; so that the other deductive form "$p \vee q \vee r$; p; so $\sim q$ & $\sim r$" is not valid.

Part IV

Philosophy of Nature

8

Hegel and the Sciences

THOMAS POSCH

1.   Introductory Remarks

When dealing with Hegel's *Philosophy of Nature* and in particular with the sections of his *Encyclopaedia* entitled "Mechanics" and "Physics," it is virtually impossible to ignore the harsh criticism that this part of his system has faced over the past two centuries. Hegel was fully aware of the opposition faced by idealist philosophy of nature (especially in the latter's Schellingian form), even though this opposition had by no means reached its zenith in the first quarter of the nineteenth century. In the Addition to §244 of the *Encyclopaedia* of 1830, we find the following statement:

> It may certainly be accepted as *indisputably* true ... that the *philosophy of nature* in particular is suffering from a very considerable lack of favour. ... [L]ooking at the way in which the *Idea of the philosophy of nature* has exhibited itself in recent times, one might say that in the first gratification which its discovery has afforded, it has been grasped by fumbling hands instead of being wooed by active reason, and that it is by its suitors rather than by its detractors that it has been done to death.[1]

It is likely, however, that Hegel did not expect scientists and philosophers to condemn his *own* version of *Naturphilosophie*, soon after his death, as an example of "an external formalism," of "a notionless instrument for superficiality of thought and unbridled powers of imagination,"[2] much in the way he had criticized the philosophies of nature produced by Schelling and, especially, Schelling's followers. Yet this condemnation is exactly what ensued.[3] One example may suffice to demonstrate the extremely negative attitude toward all philosophy of nature that prevailed just a decade after Hegel's death. In 1842, the mere remark that "this is philosophy of nature" was enough to motivate

---

A Companion to Hegel, First Edition. Edited by Stephen Houlgate and Michael Baur.
© 2011 Blackwell Publishing Ltd. Published 2011 by Blackwell Publishing Ltd.

Johann Christian Poggendorff (1796–1877) to reject studies by Robert J. Mayer (1814–1878) and later by Hermann von Helmholtz (1821–1894) on the principle of energy conservation and to refuse their publication in the renowned *Annalen der Physik*.[4]

James Hutchison Stirling (1820–1909), one of the first apologists for Hegel in Great Britain, has given quite an accurate description of the impression Hegel's *Philosophy of Nature* may leave on the impartial reader who is unfamiliar with Hegel's distinctive terminology:

> I have before me not an active, sensible, intelligent man, with his wits about him, looking at *the thing* in a business-like manner, and treating it so on the common stage of education and intelligence as it is now, but an out-of-the-way sort of body, a mooning creature with a craze, who, in pure ignorance, non-knowledge, non-education, non-intelligence, simply impregnates a mist of his own with confused figures of his own, that have no earthly application to the business in hand – as a Jacob Böhm[e] or other mere stupid dreamer might do. That any reputable persons of the usual education and position, should be caught with such self-evident, gratuitous, muddle-headed nonsense, fills me with ... surprise, regret, sorrow. ...[5]

Though he is, of course, being ironic, Stirling is referring to certain passages from Hegel's paragraphs on the solar system, which William Whewell (1794–1866), in an essay from 1849, had argued were indeed nonsensical.[6] Whewell had done this, as Stirling rightly observes, on the basis of his own, very inadequate translations of selected paragraphs of the Hegelian *Encyclopaedia*.

Generally speaking, Hegel's *Philosophy of Nature* – much more than most great books in the history of Western thought – has been the subject of a lively debate as to whether it makes sense at all.[7] How can this be explained? Why did Hegel's *Philosophy of Nature* (especially his "Mechanics" and "Physics") attain this strange position in human history, characterized by such a gulf between its apologists and its detractors?

Those who consider Hegel's "Mechanics" and "Physics" to be an insignificant aberration of the human mind perceive Hegel to be a philosopher who does not accord due respect to the wealth of knowledge that is based on physico-chemical experiments and astronomical observations; they argue that Hegel generally did not care much about scientific insights that had been or must be obtained a posteriori. One of the historical roots of this perception is to be found in Hegel's early work, written to obtain the *venia legendi* at the University of Jena in 1801: the *Dissertatio philosophica de orbitis planetarum*. At the end of this short book, Hegel had famously dared to question the hypothesis that a planet was "missing" between Mars and Jupiter. As any modern reader, working with some diligence, can verify by reading the original Latin text, *De orbitis planetarum* does not contain any a priori judgment stating that no planet or celestial body, revolving about the sun between Mars and Jupiter, can possibly exist. Rather, Hegel formulates a careful if-clause, saying that *if* a series based on the numbers proposed by Plato in his *Timaios*[8] somehow reflects the true order of the planetary orbits, *then* there is no need to look for a planet between Mars and Jupiter.[9] As Craig and Hoskin[10] have pointed out, there is hardly anything outrageous in this statement, and it was certainly not meant as an a priori proof of the nonexistence of the minor planets, which, starting precisely in 1801, were discovered by Giuseppe Piazzi (1746–1826) and other astronomers to be orbiting the Sun between Mars and Jupiter. Nevertheless, researchers such as Franz Xaver von Zach (1754–1832) and Matthias Jakob Schleiden (1804–1881) claimed that Hegel had "dialectically annihilated" the minor planets.[11] Since there are many examples of similar judgments by scientists as well as philosophers, it is not at all astonishing that corresponding prejudices against the author of *De orbitis planetarum* (and later of the *Encyclopaedia*) became very common among scholars of all disciplines and the general public.

But the myth of the dialectically annihilated asteroids, influential though it was, would not have been sufficient to establish so deeply rooted an aversion to Hegel's philosophy of nature as the one that actually emerged. There had to be a *more substantial* point to Hegel's (and partly also to Schelling's) philosophy that provoked the resistance of so many erudite minds. There had to be some Hegelian standpoint or starting point that significantly distinguished his philosophy from Kant's: for, throughout the nineteenth century, the latter was respected by at least a very significant number of scientists. Why was Kant respected? Probably because Kant, famously stating that conceptions without intuitions were empty *seemed to limit* the range of justified philosophical 'constructions' *much more strictly* than Schelling and Hegel did after him. John Burbidge explains the underlying problem concisely:

> Any philosophy of nature has a fundamental problem: How can the thinking of philosophy do justice to the facts of experience? Kant presented the challenge in a definitive way: thought involves concepts, and concepts, being general, express only possibilities. In sensation we encounter facts, and facts are singular and actual. ... [W]here thought follows its own logic it can construct consistent theories, but these have no truth unless one can show how concept and fact correspond. In other words, explanations of nature are impossible without some point of contact between thought and ... experience.[12]

Even though Hegel did indeed largely recognize the latter point in his philosophy of nature,[13] many of his opponents pretended that he did not. While Hegel, in his own eyes, aimed at a philosophy that is *to a degree* a priori but also close to what he considers to be concrete phenomenal reality, his critics perceive his system – especially in his discussion of subjects that are also treated by the empirical sciences – to be *much more thoroughly* a priori than Kant's and much more abstract. This may be due to a specific aspect of Hegelian thinking that Burbidge, again, characterizes thus:

> philosophical thought, following the cognitive demands of the logic [i.e., Hegel's *Science of Logic*], could construct a model to represent the basic organization of matter, and then show how natural processes reproduced this conceptual structure. In other words ... , the idea could derive natural principles by means of pure thought and then confirm its conclusions with reference to what actually happened in nature. This derivation using construction and proof would lead to a genuine cognition of nature.[14]

It is this very question of how to get from "pure thought" to "what actually happens in nature" that lies at the heart of many attacks against Hegel and his followers. The standard argument against Hegel – illustrated above by the "dialectically annihilated asteroids" – is that he intended to *derive* the structure of space, time, motion, matter, of the properties of light, electricity, magnetism, chemical elements, the essence of organisms (eventually including human beings, their history, etc.), *completely and utterly from pure reason*, referring to empirical data where they somehow matched his ideas, but ignoring them where they did not. This immediately leads to the question of how Hegel *really* derives the basic terms and concepts of his philosophy of nature.

2. The 'Construction Principles' of Hegel's Philosophy of Nature

The opening paragraphs of the second section of the philosophy of nature, entitled "Physics," provide important hints as to how any philosophy of nature should derive its basic terms. In the remark to §276, which deals with light, Hegel states: "that which is immanently philosophical is the inherent necessity of [the] *Conceptual determination*, which then has to be illustrated by *some* natural existence *or other*."[15] In the same sense, the addition to §275 begins thus: "The a priori *Conceptual determination* of light is now the *primary* consideration. In the second instance we have to discover the mode and manner in which this conceptual determination occurs in our sensuous perception."[16] These phrases may seem hardly intelligible without illustration. Consider the conceptual determination of light. Light, says Hegel in the main text of §275, is *"pure self-identity*, unity of *intro-reflection* [*reine Identität* mit sich, als Einheit der *Reflexion-in-sich*]."[17] Now even this concrete example of a 'conceptual determination' may still appear enigmatic. It becomes more transparent when we add the following phrases from the addition to §274:

> We enter logically into the sphere of essence. This is a return into self in its other; its determinations appear within each other, and intro-reflected in this way, now develop as forms. These forms are identity, diversity, opposition, and ground [*Identität, Verschiedenheit, Gegensatz, Grund*]. This is therefore an advance upon the primary immediacy of matter.[18]

Taken together, this means that *light* – the first phenomenon considered in the *second* section of Hegel's philosophy of nature, "Physics" – corresponds conceptually to the category of *self-identity*. Accordingly, then, all phenomena treated in "Physics" correspond to categories developed in the sphere of *essence*, that is, in the second section of the *Science of Logic*. Much in the same way, Hegel had pointed out in the first section of his *Philosophy of Nature* that time is "intuited becoming,"[19] that is, that there is a correspondence between the category of *becoming* and the phenomenon occurring "in our sensuous perception" as *time*. As a first approximation, it may thus be said that all categories developed in the *Science of Logic* have their respective counterparts in the *Philosophy of Nature* (and also in the *Philosophy of Spirit*); moreover, the succession of the logical categories and of their respective counterparts is roughly the same. On closer examination, however, we find subtle differences between content, structure, and the arrangement of the categories developed, respectively, in the *Science of Logic* and in the two subsequent parts of Hegel's system;[20] but such a closer examination would lead too far astray here. Suffice it to say that without any such differences, the *Philosophy of Nature* would be nothing but an unnecessary repetition of the *Logic*.

The basic point in the present context is that the following two-step construction scheme seems to underlie Hegel's *Philosophy of Nature*.

1. The basic conceptual content of the *Philosophy of Nature* is derived from the categories developed in the *Science of Logic*, under the 'boundary condition' that nature is "the Idea in the form of otherness" or "externality."[21]

2. Hegel makes numerous and ubiquitous references to the sciences and to common-sense-perception of natural phenomena. They are to be understood – in the light of §§246, 275, and §276 of the *Encyclopaedia* – as (mere) illustrations of the way "in which the conceptual determinations occur empirically."

Though these two points may give the impression that Hegel – largely in the way referred to in the Introductory remarks above – aims at an *entirely* a priori and hence "nonempirical" account of all natural phenomena, this is not true for the following reasons.

(a) As Carl Siegel rightly observes, a priori knowledge – as conceived by Schelling and also by Hegel – does not preclude reference to experience: as Siegel puts it, Schelling's and Hegel's a priori is nothing other than *conceptual* necessity.[22] What does 'conceptual necessity' mean, according to Hegel? We may call a natural law conceptually necessary in the Hegelian sense if it reveals a structure or a relationship of concepts that corresponds to the basic principles of the *Science of Logic*. For example, the existence of natural motions is conceptually necessary in the sense that motion represents the unity of space and time that is derived dialectically at the start of the *Philosophy of Nature* in accordance with the development at the start of *Logic of Being*. That motion is the unity of space and time is evident from the fact that velocity – the basic quantity characterizing motion – is a relation between the length of a path and a corresponding duration. Within "Organics," Hegel argues that it is conceptually necessary that (higher) animals do not eat all the time – or that they have, as he puts it, "interrupted intussusception": their nonpermanent eating corresponds to their individualized, or rather self-individualizing, relation with individuals and with inorganic nature. This contrasts with the behavior of plants that nourish themselves (if possible) without break and that do not yet represent fully individualized organisms.

The analysis of Kepler's laws in §270 of the *Encyclopaedia* provides another, much more intricate example. Hegel starts by arguing that space and time have to be considered as two qualitatively distinct moments of planetary motions. Kepler's third law – which states that the squares of the orbital periods of any two planets are proportional to the cubes of their distances from the sun – is the mathematical formulation of the particular (quantitative and qualitative) relation between space and time in the case of planetary motion. Concerning the "conceptual necessity" of elliptical orbits, Hegel's reasoning is this: Since we know (a posteriori from Kepler's third law) that space and time are not merely exchangeable parameters in celestial motions (as they are, e.g., in unaccelerated rectilinear motion: $s = $ const. $\cdot\ t$, $t = s\ /$ const.), it would not fit the level of complexity reached in celestial mechanics to conceive the planetary orbits as circular, since a circle is defined by one and only one quantity, namely its radius, and in the mathematical description of the motion of a body on a *circular* orbit the spatial coordinate (e.g., the position angle ϕ) and time coordinate t are precisely exchangeable parameters, linked with each other again by a simple linear function: $\phi = $ const. $\cdot\ t$. So the geometrical description of circular motion as $\phi = $ const. $\cdot\ t$ would be largely the same as that of rectilinear motion (cf. above). Only if the speed of a body on a circular orbit were periodically to increase and decrease, would the situation be different. As for this possibility, however, Hegel holds that, even though "it is ... conceivable ... that a uniformly increasing and decreasing motion should take place in a circle," this conceivability is only an *"abstract representability,"* since there is no reason why the speed of a body moving along a line that is completely isotropic should increase and decrease at specific, but geometrically equivalent points of its orbit. (The term "abstract representability" (*abstrakte Vorstellbarkeit*) is the Hegelian opposite of conceptual necessity.) Only in the case of an *elliptical* orbit do space and time cease to be merely exchangeable parameters, because here the function describing the time-dependence of the radius vector of a planet is a complex nonlinear equation (Kepler's equation) that cannot be inverted in any analytic way. Hence, for the motion of a planet along an elliptical orbit, space and time are no longer exchangeable parameters. In this sense, the elliptical orbits of the planets (described in Kepler's first law) are conceptually necessary in the light of the totality of Kepler's laws. This highly complex example illustrates that Hegelian conceptual necessity is closely linked to systematical coherence (namely of a set of basic laws, logical structures, or metaphysical assumptions).

It is important to note with respect to the above examples that we do not have to find Hegel's analysis entirely convincing in order to see what Hegel means *formally* by conceptual necessity. More specifically, the main point to be made about conceptual necessity is that it does not preclude reference to experience. On the contrary, conceptual necessity "justifies" the content of empirical laws or observations; it is their "rationalization" by means of dialectics.

(b) As far as the *details* of natural phenomena are concerned, Hegel does *not* claim that philosophy should aim at deriving all of them a priori, that is, at proving that all natural phenomena necessarily present themselves in the way they do. In several passages (e.g., the end of the extensive addition to §270), Hegel expressly states that it is impossible for a philosophy of nature to account for all the details of natural processes and phenomena.[23] The same skepticism toward a complete a priori deduction within the domain that has traditionally been called *ontologia specialis*[24] occurs in the Preface to the *Philosophy of Right*, where Hegel criticizes Plato and Fichte for their ambition to demonstrate the necessity of particular positive laws, social institutions, and so on – an ambition that he calls "super-erudition" *(Ultraweisheit).*[25]

The property of nature that makes it impossible for spirit to comprehend everything in it as necessary or to derive all its features even has a well-known proper name in Hegel's system: it is called "the impotence of nature" (*die Ohnmacht der Natur).*[26] This term reflects the fact that any – even the most sophisticated – system of classification of natural genera and species, as well as any attempt to find basic forces, pure substances, and so on – in short, each and every systematization of nature – is confronted with transitional phenomena, borderline cases, and exceptions that do not occur in pure logic. Hegel fully acknowledges this:

> This impotence on the part of nature sets limits to philosophy, and it is the height of pointlessness to demand of the Concept that it should explain, and as it is said, construe or deduce these contingent products of nature, although the more isolated and trifling they are the easier the task appears to be.[27]

In other words, Hegel does recognize that contingency or chance plays an essential role in the realm of nature, and he holds that philosophy should, for this very reason, refrain from any attempt to deduce *all* features of the material world from a priori principles.

It is, however, still a matter of debate whether the "impotence of nature" – together with the limitations of our knowledge about nature at any given time – inhibits an a priori conceptual account of nature *altogether* or merely limits it. It seems to me that the second option, according to which at least the "structure or skeleton of the *Philosophy of Nature* is developed purely conceptually,"[28] is more likely to describe what Hegel actually does.[29] Nevertheless, it may be that any present-day philosophy of nature should go one step further, in a direction only foreshadowed but not fully realized by Hegel: "to provide [only] a flexible framework which organizes in an intelligible way, and is wholly *relative* to, the scientific knowledge of a given time, and which changes with future scientific discoveries" – as Houlgate puts it.[30]

3. The Content of Hegel's "Mechanics" and "Physics" in Outline[31]

Although a wealth of secondary literature on Hegel's "Mechanics" and (to a lesser extent) on his "Physics" has been published especially since 1970, texts giving an *overview* of these sections' contents are still rare. The aim of the present section is to fill this gap and to pave the way for a discussion of selected problems (Section 4).

3.a. "Mechanics"

It has been mentioned above that *externality (Äußerlichkeit)* – or, as Hegel sometimes puts it, *extrinsicality (das Außereinander)* – represents the *basic conceptual element* – we could also say, the boundary condition – under which everything in nature exists.

The first concept we encounter in the *Philosophy of Nature*, *space*, is nothing other than the immediate realization of nature's basic determinateness. This also is stated in a passage from Hegel's *Lectures on the Philosophy of Spirit*:

> All that is natural is spatial, time already being higher, already initiating inwardness; spatiality is nothing other than something extrinsic, everything having place in space, where everything is affirmative, determinate, and does not interfere with anything else. Space is the subsisting of all things, where each is indifferent to the others. This is the abstract absolute determinateness of nature, extrinsicality.[32]

This passage presents two insights at once. The first is that spatiality, *qua* basic element of any natural existence, is externality, and that externality means, initially, a mode of mere *co*existence in which nothing "interfere(s) with anything else." The second insight – only implicitly contained in the above lines – is that *time* is fundamentally different from space. By *not* being a mode of mere coexistence, time is the "now" that *excludes* any other "now," in contrast to space, which in its immediacy is the "here" that *does not interfere* with other "heres."

While we are used to speaking of them as merely two *different* concepts, or *different* coordinates – the spatial coordinates x,y,z versus the time coordinate t – Hegel makes clear at the beginning of his "Mechanics" that it is not satisfying philosophically merely to distinguish these concepts without asking about their *relation* to each other.[33] When asking about this relation, we find that space is on the verge of the *transition* into time. This can be seen by considering the infinitesimal element of space: the point. The point is the negation of space, more precisely of spatial extension. But it is more than that. The point is intuited negativity, the intuited exclusion of others (other points). As such, it is *in nuce* what the *moment* of time is in a more concrete way. Hence it makes sense to claim that there is a transition from space to time, and to illustrate this transition with the concept of the (geometrical) point. Conversely, there is also a 'transition' from time to space. Time becoming spatial is *motion*. While time is a sequence of "now, now, now," motion is a sequence of the form "now here, then there, then there." Motion, as Hegel puts it, is the unity of space and time, posited in the logical form of time (i.e., in a negative form). Alternatively, motion may be called the unity of space and time in an 'ideal' form, because motion is something immaterial (even though moving objects are not immaterial). Matter, by contrast, is the unity of space and time posited in the logical form of space (i.e., in a positive form or in a 'real' form).[34] By reference to the law of conservation of momentum ($p_{total} = \Sigma\, m_i v_i = $ const.), Hegel tries to show that mass (the basic quantitative unit of matter) and velocity (the basic quantitative unit of motion) have the same effect and must therefore be closely related conceptually: a piece of matter, hitting another one that has twice its mass, will, if it is thereby brought to rest in an elastic collision, transfer only half of its velocity to the second one. Also due to the same law of conservation of momentum – or, as Hegel would say, due to the exchangeability of the factors 'mass' and 'velocity' – a mass of 6 pounds traveling at 'speed 4' has the same impact on another object as a mass of 8 pounds traveling at 'speed 3.'[35]

With this example, we have already entered the second section of "Mechanics," entitled "Finite Mechanics." This section treats *inert matter* as subject to different kinds of *motion* that cannot be sustained for long, but come to an end: *impact* and *free fall*.[36] Of course, according to classical mechanics, cases are conceivable in which an impact gives rise to a rectilinear motion that does *not* come to an end in time – namely in the case of the absence of any friction or forces acting at a distance. However, Hegel considers this case of infinite, unaccelerated rectilinear motion to be an empty abstraction (and indeed, such a motion does not occur on Earth). Impact and fall, in the way we encounter them in terrestrial nature, constitute "finite" – first of all in the sense of temporally limited – processes. Moreover, they require for their realization initial conditions that are contingent and extrinsic to the moving bodies themselves (in many textbook cases, these initial conditions are artificially produced). The free fall of a body, for instance, requires its being elevated to the starting point of fall, and this is a merely external and contingent condition.

The subject of what Hegel calls "Absolute Mechanics" is the motion of celestial bodies – more specifically, the motion of bodies in a solar system. Why does Hegel make the motions of celestial bodies a wholly distinct *stage* of his "Mechanics," instead of considering them merely as motions in a field of force under specific boundary conditions, as is done in classical mechanics? First, because the motions of bodies in

184

the solar system appear as temporally infinite (at least on time scales accessible to us). This infinity is, according to Hegel, more than a result of the boundary condition 'absence of friction,' since it is also connected with *forms* of motions that are entirely different from terrestrial ones, that is, from ones in which friction generally plays a dominant role. Phenomenally, there *is* a significant difference between natural motions observed under terrestrial conditions and the motions of the planets. The motions of bodies in the solar system appear to us as self-sustaining infinite motions. They proceed along closed orbits that are described mathematically (to close approximation) by conic sections and have an exact periodicity over extremely long times – a fact that contributed to establishing astronomy as a science very early in human history. This phenomenal and epistemological distinction between celestial and terrestrial natural motions is reflected in Hegel's distinction between "finite" and "absolute" mechanics.

With respect to the categories developed in the *Logic of Being*, Hegel observes that matter becomes "qualified matter" in being considered as a system of internal relations. The qualification, however, lies so far just in the different forms of motion, or, as John Burbidge puts it: "mechanics talks about how movement [we may add: and *only* movement] particularizes matter."[37] The qualification thus remains relatively extrinsic to the members of the solar system themselves; the Sun, for example, does not by itself exhibit any essential relation to all the bodies revolving around it. The categorial development – the main driving force of the philosophy of nature – must hence proceed to a kind of qualification that does not just consist in distinct shapes of trajectories of 'mass points.' It must proceed to a sphere where every individual part of a considered whole *shows* its being related *to* the whole. As Hegel puts it: "what the solar system is as a whole, is what matter has to become in particular."[38]

3.b. "Physics" and the Transition to "Organics"

The subject of *Physics* is matter that is about to find its individual form: "Bodies are now subject to the power of individuality."[39] Mechanical matter (matter as it is considered in Hegel's "Mechanics," but also in the corresponding parts of modern textbooks on classical mechanics) is not yet individuated since among its many (qualitative and quantitative) properties, only its mass, velocity, acceleration, and so on come into play. This is also why within large parts of classical mechanics, material entities can be considered as *point masses*. Only their *ways of motion* with respect to other bodies are relevant. By contrast, what we are confronted with in the second section of the *Philosophy of Nature* is the *process* by which bodies strive for individuation and "qualification," strive to be constituted as qualitatively specific entities, with their qualities lying in themselves, not in their motion.[40]

3.b.1

In its immediacy, material individuality manifests itself as *light* and *dark*. Light itself is but the simplest *universal* quality of nature; Hegel calls it the "abstract self of matter."[41] As mentioned above in Section 2, light is also paralleled with the logical category of pure *self-identity*.[42] When light actually takes the form of an individual material body, it appears as the Sun, or, more generally speaking, as a star. Hegel introduces a slight categorial difference between the Sun and the stars. While the concept of a star is light as an individual natural body (in its mere immediacy), the concept of the Sun is the star as "moment of a totality" (i.e., of a solar system; §275).[43]

On the basis of his *Logic of the Concept*, Hegel distinguishes four moments of the solar system: the *Sun* (corresponding to the notion of universality), the dependent "bodies of opposition" (*satellites* and *comets*) (corresponding to particularity), and the *planets*, which, by virtue of their being individual subcenters of motions, correspond to concrete singularity. The idea that particularity has *two* counterparts in the solar system – satellites and comets – has its root in Hegel's conviction that nature is the sphere of difference or otherness. In Hegel's words: "The second term [i.e., particularity] ... appears in nature as a duality, for in nature the other must exist itself as an otherness."[44]

Our paradigm of a planet is the Earth. From §280 on – after the further discussion of the solar system within "Physics" – Hegel's *Philosophy of Nature* is devoted to terrestrial nature.[45] This is to some extent a vestige of the historical development of Hegel's thought, since in the fragmentary systems developed up to 1804/1805 in Jena, Hegel seems to have divided the *Philosophy of Nature* mainly into the "Solar System" and the "Terrestrial System,"[46] still corresponding to the Aristotelian distinction between supralunar and sublunar worlds.

On Earth, what the ancients already recognized as the basic conceptual moments of inorganic nature are the four elements. They are also called "physical elements" in the *Encyclopaedia*. The four "physical" elements are, famously, air, fire, water, and earth. Hegel calls the physical elements "universal natural existences, which are no longer independent, and yet are still not individualized."[47] He is fully aware of the fact that already during his time "[n]o educated person, and certainly no physicist or chemist is ... permitted, under any circumstances, to mention the four elements."[48] However, he holds that these do represent a necessary, basic stage of the concept of nature, prior to the more sophisticated system of the *chemical* elements.[49] The irreducible function of the four elements, according to Hegel, lies in their being moments of the "becoming of the universal individual" – the Earth.[50] (The question of how this may be translated into present-day philosophy will be briefly discussed below.)

Air again represents the moment of universality (as light does in the previous sphere); in the context of matter's striving for individuality, air is a negative moment: it is "negative universality against the specific" and has the power of dissolving the latter, as becomes evident for example from wind-supported erosion processes and various chemical processes supported by the presence of air.[51] Fire and water, by contrast, represent the moment of particularity within the physical elements. *Fire* can be said to radicalize the shape-dissolving power of air: it is "the consumption of another which simultaneously consumes itself."[52] With respect to *water*, Hegel stresses the dissolving power that it has as well, but he emphasizes even more its "neutral" character and its "shapelessness," which is its capacity to take on any shape.[53] *Earth* or "terrestrialness" (*Erdigkeit*) represents the moment of singularity. It is the concretized "concept of individuality,"[54] or, as Hegel puts it in a manuscript from his Jena period: "Earth, as the reduction of the elements, stands in a passive relationship to itself, and is therefore determinateness in itself."[55]

Instead of speaking of four physical elements, it might be better to speak – given the background of nineteenth- and twentieth-century physics – of the four basic aggregate states of matter: the gaseous, plasma, liquid, and solid states. It might be said, furthermore, that the gaseous, liquid, and solid states are more abstract 'versions' of air, water, and earth, respectively. The correspondence between fire and the plasma state of matter is more difficult to show.[56] But recalling that the four elements were introduced by Hegel as moments of the becoming of the universal individual (the Earth) strengthens the case for the aggregate states, since we know today that planet formation does indeed involve phase transitions from the gaseous to the liquid, solid, and plasma states of matter.

Returning to Hegel's "Physics," its first section concludes with the meteorological process. It is understood by Hegel as a process of the four physical elements, which are in its course perpetually transformed into one another. *Process* here turns out to be more fundamental than any self-contained subsistence. However, Hegel goes too far in holding that water, for example, is not conserved materially in the process of evaporation, but wholly *transformed* into the element air. It could, of course, be said of the *aggregate states* that the one is completely transformed into the other, but this cannot be said of the *substance* (namely, water) that is subjected to the process of evaporation. I shall come back to this problem below in Section 4.b.

3.b.2

In the second section of Physics, entitled "Physics of Particular Individuality," Hegel treats specific gravity, cohesion, sound, and heat. This section is best understood by taking a closer look at its last stage. The conceptual determination of *heat* is "matter's restoration ... to formlessness."[57] Heat thus clearly represents a negative moment of the process of matter's (self-)formation. This negative moment – which has its counterpart in the second law of thermodynamics (not yet known to Hegel, of course)[58] – paves the way for a more than merely mechanical individualization of natural bodies. Phenomenologically, the "negativity" of heat – as well as of sound – appears in their generating *internal vibrations* of bodies that may lead to their disaggregation.

Hegel's concept of heat is in remarkable accordance with the kinetic theory of gases, developed in nineteenth-century physics, insofar as both are based on the conviction that "heat is simply a *modal condition* of matter."[59] This wording anticipates similar ones that we are used to finding in physics textbooks only since the second half of the nineteenth century, that is, since Maxwell. In Hegel's own lifetime, by contrast, most scientists still viewed heat as a particular substance (the so-called *caloric*).[60]

3.b.3

In the third section of Physics, entitled "Physics of Total Individuality," form becomes immanent to matter in a way that no longer depends on gravity. The first concept that we encounter in this section is *shape*, which appears as "spatial assemblage of material being" or as external spatial limitation of bodies.[61] Most strikingly, shape manifests itself in nature in the formation of crystals (though, of course, noncrystalline objects in nature also have shape). "The form which deploys itself in crystallization," says Hegel, "is a mute vitality, which is active in a truly remarkable way within that which is purely mechanical."[62] This is not to say that crystals were little organisms; but in crystallization and crystal growth, matter *tends* toward a specific shape – depending on its chemical composition and other factors – and hence teleological categories do come into play here.[63]

Magnetism, which we have become accustomed to consider as an epiphenomenon of electric currents, is also treated as a phenomenon related to shape in Hegelian physics. The characteristic feature of magnetism is polarity, where the poles do not have any subsistence of their own.[64] Magnetic polarity is even *defined* as a relation between two indivisible entities that cannot be separated from each other – at least not without splitting up again into poles. It still holds true for contemporary physics that no magnetic monopoles have been found.

In *electricity* we are confronted with a different kind of polarity, namely one that *is* characterized by the relative subsistence of the respective poles.[65] This relative subsistence of the electric poles corresponds to the existence of bodies (as well as ions and elementary particles) with positive and negative electrical charges. Terms such as "anions" and "cations" or – much earlier in the history of physics – "resinous electricity" and "vitreous electricity" – have been coined to account for the duality of electrical charges. At the same time, electricity is more of a *process* than magnetism, whence Hegel speaks of the "electric movement" (*das elektrische Bewegen*) that is able to neutralize differences as well as to create them, or, in logical terms, to posit as identical the differentiated as well as to differentiate the identical.[66]

Electricity finally passes into the *chemical process*. Under the heading of "chemism," the latter figures also as an important section of the *Science of Logic*. There it is considered in the middle section of the *Logic of the Concept*, namely as one of the three forms of "objectivity," which are mechanism, chemism, and teleology. Even though "chemism" as treated in the *Science of Logic* is not identical with the "chemical process" as analyzed in the *Philosophy of Nature*, the very fact that Hegel names the whole second sphere of objectivity in the Logic "chemism" points to its outstanding significance, in marked contrast to Kant's neglect of chemism in comparison with mechanism and organism. Generally, the relations between objects in Hegelian chemism can be characterized in the following way: objects that differ chemically have their respective essential characters expressly and only by virtue of their *difference* from each other, and are driven by the absolute urge to merge and reach a neutral unity thereby.[67] Within Hegelian "Physics," the chemical process is the point of culmination of the categorial development. By virtue of the drive to integrate opposite substances into a whole, the chemical process already has a structure that is analogous to life; if it were able to rekindle and reproduce itself after having come to its end, it could in fact be said to *be* life.

> The chemical process ... displays the dialectic by which all the particular properties of bodies are drawn into transitoriness. ... It is therefore solely the being-for-self of infinite form which endures, the pure incorporeal individuality which is for itself, and for which material subsistence is simply a variable. The chemical process is the highest expression of inorganic being ... ; [it] constitutes the transition to the higher sphere of the organism. ...[68]

So in the chemical process, nature is just about to reach the categorial stage of life, which manifests itself as subjectivity, that is, as an inner being that dissociates its interior from its exterior. Since, however, the world of living organisms is beyond the scope of the present chapter,[69] my overview of Hegel's Mechanics and Physics concludes at this point.

4.   Problems Inherent in the Sciences According to Hegel

Even though – as we have seen – Hegel holds, on the one hand, that any philosophy of nature should be in accordance with the results of the respective contemporary sciences, he holds, on the other hand, that there are severe problems inherent in the general methods of the sciences. To be sure, these problems largely do not appear *within* scientific work itself; they occur rather when scientific results and methods are taken – without the critical guidance of philosophy – as a basis for constructing a *world-view*. The following features of science appear especially problematic to Hegel in this respect:

- The annihilation of *qualitative differences* in the course of scientific progress (Section 4.a below)
- The *atomistic* consideration of nature (Section 4.b)[70]
- The search for *dynamical laws* of nature and their being preferred to phenomenological laws (Section 4.c).[71]

4.a.   *The Sciences' Annihilation of* Qualitative Differences

Like Kant, Hegel is fully aware that scientific work *necessarily* involves abstraction and mathematization. He is far from considering this to be per se a problematic feature of the sciences. He concedes that scientific descriptions of natural phenomena are fundamentally mathematical and abstract. Abstractness is, of course, also a feature of philosophical views of nature:

> The more thought predominates in ordinary perceptiveness, so much the more does the naturalness, individuality, and immediacy of things vanish away. As thoughts invade the limitless multiformity of nature, its richness is impoverished, its springtimes die, and there is a fading in the play of its colours. That which in nature was noisy with life, falls silent in the quietude of thought; its warm abundance, which shaped life itself into a thousand intriguing wonders, withers into arid forms and shapeless generalities, which resemble a dull northern fog.[72]

Gerd Buchdahl called these phrases some of Hegel's truly memorable formulations.[73] They certainly are; and they make clear that Hegel is *not* opposing the abstractness of any (scientific or philosophical) view of nature. What he is opposing is rather the *annihilation of qualitative differences* within the realm of nature as a result of scientific work, or rather as a result of a specific style of scientific work. Hegel's contention is that a proper understanding of the essence of nature is impossible if the human intellect puts "everything on the same level," that is, if it does not take into account the categorial determinateness of the individual stages of nature.[74] Broadly speaking, new levels of determinateness emerge, according to Hegel, not merely through aggregation or the summation of parts, but through new *modes of relation* that add new qualities to the parts. In the addition to §286 of the *Encyclopaedia*, Hegel's criticism of reductionist approaches in the sciences is expressed in the following way:

> The attempt is made to put everything on the same level. *Everything* can of course be treated from a chemical point of view, but everything can also be treated from a mechanical point of view. ... When bodies are treated at one stage, this does not exhaust the nature of other bodies however, as for example when vegetable or animal bodies are treated chemically.[75]

It cannot be denied that there is a deep truth in these claims. Hegel defends the old view of nature as a system of qualitatively distinct stages, as it was understood to be in the concept of the *scala naturae* or the "great chain of being."[76] The idea of a *scala naturae* ascribes – as noted by Arthur Lovejoy – three basic features to the universe: *plenitude, continuity,* and *gradation*. The principle of *plenitude* states that the universe exhibits the greatest possible diversity of kinds of existence. According to the principle of *continuity,* the universe is composed of an infinite series of forms, each of which shares with its neighbor at least one attribute. According to the principle of *gradation,* finally, this series ranges in hierarchical order from the barest type of existence to the most perfect conceivable entity (i.e., God).[77] While Hegel evinces some skepticism toward the principle of continuity,[78] he does defend the view that nature has a hierarchical order and represents a *system of forms*.[79] At the same time, he rightly points out that 'modern' science tends to overlook or to doubt the existence of qualitative differences in nature.[80] Especially when new tools, proving powerful in the mathematical treatment of natural phenomena, are developed (such as Newton's concept of force or – after Hegel's death – the concept of energy conservation), it regularly happens that nature is seen almost exclusively in the light of these. Formulations such as the following then typically prevail: "The whole realm of nature is governed by forces, the differences consist *only* in the respective kinds of acting forces," or "Energy conservation governs *all* natural processes, both in the inorganic and in the organic world," or "The struggle for existence creates *all* forms in nature." In his *Philosophy of Nature,* Hegel shows quite a pronounced hostility toward this *type* of view (some of them, of course, had not been explicitly developed during his lifetime), each of which tries to reduce the full range of the *scala naturae* to one or to very few of its stages.

This *antireductionism* is one of the chief strengths of Hegel's philosophy of nature[81] – and moreover of his system in general. One might argue, of course, that science would be impossible without some sort of reductionism.[82] However, given that the specific stages or principles *to which* – more or less successfully – the complexity of nature is reduced vary significantly in the course of history,[83] it is necessary to point out the limited validity of any particular version of reductionism.[84] This is precisely what Hegel does, even though his attacks are, unfortunately, in several instances focused too much on Newton's particular model of reducing natural phenomena to forces.

Furthermore, it is worth pointing out – even though it cannot be demonstrated here in detail – that Hegel's criticism of reductionist world-views paves the way for a nonreductionist philosophy of mind. Only by conceiving a hierarchical system of categories, within which it is illegitimate at *any* point to explain a more complex level *wholly* in terms of basic levels (i.e., to call them "nothing but" arrangements or combinations of

190

the basic levels), can Hegel elaborate a philosophical "anthropology" and "psychology" in a nonreductive way.[85] By contrast, a philosophy of mind that tries to oppose the reduction of mind to mere properties of matter *without* a general concept of qualitatively distinct ontological levels deprives itself of strong points that Hegel has to make, one of which is still to follow below.

4.b. *The Atomistic View of Nature, Or, Why Hegel Would Have Preferred Quarks to Atoms*

Hegel's criticism of the atomistic view of nature is motivated by his antireductionist orientation. This is of course consistent since *philosophical atomism* is a *prototype of reductionism*. According to Hegel, atomism fails to grasp the essence of *natural unities* such as planets, solar systems, plants, and animals. All these natural unities are more than mere sums of their parts; conversely, their parts exist only as "sublated" (*aufgehoben*) and as transformed moments of qualitatively new entities.[86] In contrast, on the basis of atomism, "all union becomes merely mechanical; ... the united elements nevertheless remain remote from one another."[87]

As for the atoms and molecules conceived by eighteenth- and nineteenth-century physics in particular, we find the following statement in the Remark to §298 of Hegel's *Encyclopaedia*:

> Wherever the question of material *parts* arises, one should not think of them as atoms or molecules, i.e. as separated and self-subsistent, but as merely quantitatively ... distinguished, so that their *continuity* is essentially inseparable from their *distinctness*.[88]

It is hence *not the physical atom in itself* that Hegel considers as a problematic concept, but rather its being conceived as "separated and self-subsistent." The background is the following: Hegel tends to argue that *all entities* (everything that can actually be thought, i.e., that can be thought in a *coherent* manner) exist exclusively by virtue of their relatedness to other entities. Hence he ultimately denies the existence of entities that are per se – independently of their relations to others – ultimate building blocks of reality.

This attitude has its merits both within the theory of state – where it makes intersubjectivity a more suitable starting point than mere individuality – and the philosophy of nature. However, in the latter domain the way in which Hegel elaborates it is not always convincing.

For example, when treating the meteorological process, Hegel states: "Rain comes, so to speak, out of dry air."[89] He opposes the view according to which water droplets or water vapor are contained in the air as a necessary precondition for rain. On the contrary, he holds that rain is an example of a real transformation of (dry) air into water within the process of the elements. In the same context, he even goes so far as to dispute the extraterrestrial origin of meteorites, which he considers as solid precipitates of the atmosphere. Processes such as precipitation of rain out of entirely dry air would seem to us miraculous today – and even more so the formation of meteorites in the Earth's atmosphere. However, these issues were still matters of debate among scientists in the first quarter of the nineteenth century.[90] Hegel's views on these subjects show that he did *not* have anything in mind like a 'principle of mass conservation' in closed systems.

191

This is precisely because of his skepticism toward regarding material atoms as self-subsistent, imperishable building blocks of nature. The Hegelian idea of nature leaves more room for a 'creatio ex nihilo' (or rather a 'creatio ex concepto') than for any sentence such as: 'The number of atoms in a closed volume remains constant over time.'

Are we forced to say, in the light of today's scientific views, that Hegel's critical attitude toward atomism has been altogether falsified? Certainly not. Rather, the crux is the *specific level* at which Hegel thinks that atoms represent mere moments or easily transformable entities. Within the meteorological process, atoms – and even water molecules – largely act as indissoluble compounds; hence on *this* level, Hegel was too optimistic about their being 'mere moments.' In stellar interiors, by contrast, atoms are in fact mere 'moments' of nuclear processes that transform them into one another and that even transform mass into energy. Indeed, due to the transformation of mass into energy, we cannot say that the number of atoms remains constant over time in a (hypothetically) closed volume element inside a star. This is, of course, only a particular case, insufficient as an example in favor of Hegel's theory. However, the smallest units of present-day elementary physics, *quarks*, provide an additional argument. Quarks are conceived as elementary particles that do *not occur at all as self-subsistent natural unities*. Quarks build up matter only by occurring in different combinations – or, as we might put it in a Hegelian way, by virtue of different modes of relatedness.

Should today's standard model of elementary particles stand the test of time, this would interestingly imply a late confirmation of the Hegelian axiom 'relatedness first,' since this standard model involves a theory of matter in which at least some of the smallest basic units, the quarks, have no self-subsistence in nature and can be transformed into one another (by means of the so-called weak interaction).

4.c.   *Phenomenological Versus Dynamical Laws of Nature – Or, Why Hegel Prefers Kepler to Newton*

One of the most fundamental points of disagreement between Hegel and modern scientific approaches to nature concerns the role of *forces* in the description and (especially) explanation of natural phenomena. This is equivalent to saying that *dynamical laws* of nature – natural laws involving force terms – are something against which Hegel has a point to make, even though they turned out to be a powerful tool in science.

It is generally known that Kepler – whom Hegel admires and praises very much for finding the three laws of planetary motion – also used the term 'force' repeatedly in his oeuvre, and speculated about a magnetic origin of the forces keeping the planets in their orbits around the Sun. However, no force terms enter explicitly into the three Keplerian laws. Furthermore, Kepler's laws are not meant to be *universal* natural laws, but rather *laws of particular phenomena* – though, as we know today, very widespread ones, namely planetary motions. Kepler's laws have not yet led to a unified description of terrestrial and celestial motions. By contrast, Newton's law of gravitation is both a law explicitly containing a *force term* and a *universal* law of nature. It encompasses, for example, Kepler's third law and Galileo's law of free fall. And – what is more – it was formulated by Newton in the course of a *quest for basic forces* on which *all* natural phenomena were suspected to depend. "The whole burden of philosophy," says Newton in the Preface to the first edition of his *Principia*, seems to consist in this – from the phenomena of motions to investigate the forces of nature, and then from these forces to demonstrate the other phenomena. ... I am induced by many reasons to suspect that they [i.e., the phenomena of nature] may all depend upon certain forces by which the particles of bodies, by some causes hitherto unknown, are either mutually impelled towards each other, and cohere in regular figures, or are repelled and recede from one another. These forces being unknown, philosophers have hitherto attempted the search of Nature in vain; but I hope the principles here laid down will afford some light either to this or some truer method of philosophy.[91]

Hence, it is quite appropriate to call Kepler's laws "phenomenological laws," while Newton's law of universal gravitation may be termed a "dynamical [=force-based] law." Other dynamical laws include Coulomb's law of electrostatics and Maxwell's equations, while an additional example of a phenomenological law is Snell's law of refraction. Hegel indeed uses this terminology in his *Lectures on the History of Philosophy* when writing that Newton "set the *laws of forces* in the place of the [Keplerian] *laws of phenomena*."[92] Now while scientists are generally used to having higher esteem for dynamical laws than for phenomenological ones (mainly due to the higher degree of universality characterizing the former), Hegel has the opposite preference, as has already been observed, for example, by Buchdahl[93] and Falkenburg.[94] According to Hegel, the main problem inherent in the description of nature by means of dynamical laws is the *explanatory power* that is claimed for them. On the one hand, Newton assigns a very strong 'physical' meaning to forces by saying – as cited above – that they are the entities on which *all* natural phenomena (probably) depend. On the other hand, at the end of his *Principia*, in the *Scholium generale*, Newton famously declares that he does not have any real explanation for the properties of gravity and does not wish to frame any hypotheses.[95] Hegel finds it very dissatisfying that every physical explanation should be based on forces that in turn are declared to be essentially inexplicable. His suggestion on this point, as put forward in the lectures on the philosophy of nature from 1825/1826, reads thus: "If nothing ought to be determined physically [as Newton pretends], then the term 'force' should be totally omitted."[96] Interestingly, this suggestion has also been made by physicists who had almost certainly not read Hegel. Heinrich Hertz, in the introduction to his *Principles of Mechanics*, calls (Newtonian) forces "needless auxiliary wheels" and stresses – much in same way as Hegel – that forces are usually *not* subjects of experience.[97] The development of nineteenth- and twentieth-century physics in fact led partly to the replacement of the concept of force by the concept of energy and partly to the 'geometrization' of forces that we encounter in the General Theory of Relativity. None of these developments were aimed at or influenced by Hegel, but they were motivated by criticisms of the concept of force that have remarkable similarities with Hegel's; this is one more motivation for continuing to take the latter seriously today.

5. Conclusions

Hegel's *Philosophy of Nature* has been criticized throughout the past 200 years for its alleged nonconformity with essential results of the sciences. Many authors considered this part of his encyclopedic system to be the weakest one, and partly for reasons that sounded convincing to the impartial reader.

Starting around 1970, the attempt has been made to re-examine the relation between Hegel and the sciences in a thorough way, questioning and avoiding earlier prejudices. Nowadays – even though many statements on *individual* topics contained in the *Philosophy of Nature* may seem to contrast even more strongly with current scientific views than at the time they were written – it can be seen more clearly that Hegel did have serious points to make against specific aspects of scientific methods (or of *the* scientific method). These points include Hegel's criticism of the annihilation of qualitative differences in nature, his criticism of various kinds of science-based reductionism, and his idea that replacing phenomenological laws (having explicitly restricted domains of validity) with universal dynamical laws of nature does not in every respect constitute progress. Some of these problems have also been highlighted by scientists who lived several decades after Hegel and who were not directly influenced by him – a fact that may be interpreted as "independent confirmation" of Hegelian views on the sciences.

Generally, however, Hegel aimed at a philosophy of nature in *accordance* with the results of science. Its task would be to answer questions such as "What is nature?" "What is the relation between space and time?" "What is life?" or, more specifically, "How can the realms of nature be structured based on a predefined system of categories (developed in the *Science of Logic*) so as to proceed, in a nonreductive way, from lower to higher levels of complexity?" One may possibly object that these questions cannot be answered at all. But hardly anybody would dare to say that they have been or will soon be answered by the sciences themselves.

Of course, we do not have to consider the Hegelian answers to the above questions to be authoritative, but ignoring them means – to say the least – the loss of valuable tools for finding adequate answers.[98]

Notes

1   *Hegel's Philosophy of Nature*, ed. and trans. with an Introduction and Explanatory Notes by Michael J. Petry. (London and New York: Allen and Unwin, 1970), vol. 1, p. 191 (=*Encyclopaedia of the Philosophical Sciences in Outline*, §244, addition).

2   Note that these are Hegel's words against Schelling and his disciples (ibid.).

3   Cf. Karl Rosenkranz, *Hegel's Naturphilosophie und die Bearbeitung derselben durch den italienischen Philosophen Augusto Vera* (Berlin: Nicolaische Verlagsbuchhandlung, 1868; reprinted Hildesheim: Georg Olms, 1979), 13: "It may be said that the prejudice against Hegel's philosophy in Germany has nowhere reached the same resoluteness as it has with respect to his philosophy of nature" (my translation).

4   H.-J. Treder, "Zum Einfluß von Schellings Naturphilosophie auf die Entwicklung der Physik," in *Natur und geschichtlicher Prozeß*, ed. H. J. Sandkühler (Frankfurt am Main: Suhrkamp, 1984), 327.

5   James Hutchison Stirling, Lectures on the Philosophy of Law, Together with Whewell and Hegel, *and* Hegel and Mr. W. R. Smith: A Vindication in a Physico-mathematical Regard (London: Longmans, Green, 1873), 70.

6   Cf. W. Whewell, "On Hegel's Criticism of Newton's Principia," *Transactions of the Cambridge Philosophical Society* 8, Part V (1849): 696–706.

7   Michael J. Petry, in the Introduction to his edition of *Hegel's Philosophy of Nature*, states: "There can be very few works of this importance that have remained so completely unappreciated for so long." (loc. cit., vol. 1, 114.)

8   Cf. Plato, *Timaeus*, 34b–36d.

9   Cf. Hegel, *Dissertatio Philosophica de Orbitis Planetarum*, ed. and trans. by Wolfgang Neuser (Weinheim: VCH Verlag, 1986), 138: "Quae series si verior naturae ordo sit, quam illa arithmetica progressio, inter quartum et quintum locum magnum esse spatium, neque ibi planetam desiderari apparet." ("If this series [i.e., the one from Plato's *Timaeus*] really does give the true order of nature as an arithmetic series, then there is a great space between the fourth and fifth places where no planet appears to be missing." Translation: David Healan.)

10 E. Craig and M. Hoskin, "Hegel and the Seven Planets," *Journal for the History of Astronomy* 23 (1992): 208–210.

11 Cf. Matthias Jakob Schleiden, *Schelling's und Hegel's Verhältnis zur Naturwissenschaft* (Leipzig: Engelmann, 1844), 41: "In 1801, Hegel had dialectically annihilated the asteroids. In 1801, Ceres was discovered, in 1802, Pallas was discovered" (my translation).

12 John W. Burbidge, *Real Process. How Logic and Chemistry Combine in Hegel's Philosophy of Nature.* (Toronto: University of Toronto Press, 1996), 15.

13 Cf. *Hegel's Philosophy of Nature*, loc. cit., vol. 1, p. 197: "It is not only that philosophy must accord with the experience nature gives rise to; in its *formation* and in its *development*, philosophic science presupposes and is conditioned by empirical physics" (*Encyclopaedia of the Philosophical Sciences*, §246, Addition).

14 John W. Burbidge, loc. cit., 21.

15 *Hegel's Philosophy of Nature*, ed. Petry, loc. cit., vol. 2, 17. I have taken the liberty of replacing "Notional determination" with "Conceptual determination." The original term is "Begriffsbestimmung."

16 Ibid., 12. Again, "Notional determination" has been replaced with "Conceptual determination."

17 Ibid.

18 Ibid., 11. In Petry's translation, we find the term "variety" for the German word "Verschiedenheit," but "diversity" is probably a more adequate translation.

19 *Hegel's Philosophy of Nature*, ed. Petry, loc. cit., vol. 1, p. 230 (*Encyclopaedia of the Philosophical Sciences*, §258).

20 For example, a dialectical step contains normally three moments in the sphere of Logic and in the sphere of spirit, whereas it can contain four – in some cases even five – moments in the nature, as stated in the Addition to §248: "In nature taken as otherness, the square or tetrad also belongs to the whole form of necessity, as in the four elements, the four colours etc.; the pentad may also be found, in the five fingers and the five senses for example; but in spirit the fundamental form of necessity is the triad. The second term is difference, and appears in nature as a duality, for in nature the other must exist for itself as an otherness. Consequently, the subjective unity of universality and particularity is the fourth term, which has a further existence as against the other three. In themselves the monad and the dyad constitute the entire particularity, and the totality of the Notion itself can therefore proceed to the pentad" (*Hegel's Philosophy of Nature*, ed. Petry, loc. cit., vol. 1, p. 211).

21 *Hegel's Philosophy of Nature*, ed. Petry, loc. cit., vol. 2, p. 205: "Nature has yielded itself [i.e., at the end of the *Science of Logic*] as the Idea in the form of *otherness*. Since the *Idea* is therefore the negative of itself, or *external to itself*, nature is not merely external relative to this Idea (and to the subjective existence of the same, spirit), but is embodied as nature in the determination of *externality*." (An alternative way of translating the last phrase is: "Externality constitutes the determination in which nature as nature exists.") On the relation between "Idea in the form of otherness" and "externality," see William Maker,

195

"The Very Idea of the Idea of Nature, or Why Hegel Is Not an Idealist," in: *Hegel and the Philosophy of Nature*, ed. Stephen Houlgate (Albany: State University of New York Press, 1998), 12.

22   Carl Siegel, *Geschichte der deutschen Naturphilosophie* (Leipzig: Akademische Verlagsgesellschaft, 1913), 220.

23   Hegel – according to the edition prepared by Michelet – says in the concluding passage of the Addition to §270: "Philosophy has to proceed on the basis of the Notion, and even if it demonstrates very little, one has to be satisfied. It is an error [!] on the part of the philosophy of nature to attempt to face up to all phenomena. ... philosophy need not be disturbed if the explanation of each and every phenomenon has not yet been completed" (*Hegel's Philosophy of Nature*, ed. Petry, loc. cit., vol. 1, p. 281).

24   As for the term *ontologia specialis* in relation to Hegel's system, cf. Dieter Wandschneider, who correlates the *Science of Logic* with the traditional *ontologia generalis* and both *Philosophy of Nature* and *Philosophy of Spirit* with the traditional *ontologia specialis* (Dieter Wandschneider, "Die Stellung der Natur im Gesamtentwurf der Hegelschen Philosophie," in *Hegel und die Naturwissenschaften*, ed. Michael J. Petry (Stuttgart – Bad Cannstatt: Frommann-Holzboog, 1987), 33–64, esp. 38). It is particularly within *ontologia specialis* that a priori deductions become problematic. Hegel himself uses the term "Realphilosophie" as equivalent of *ontologia specialis*.

25   Cf. Hegel's *Philosophy of Right*, trans. T. M. Knox (Oxford: Oxford University Press, 1942), 11: "Plato might have omitted his recommendation to nurses to keep on the move with infants and to rock them continually in their arms. And Fichte too need not have carried what has been called the 'construction' of his passport regulations to such a pitch of perfection as to require subjects not merely to sign their passports but to have their likenesses painted on them. Along such tracks all trace of philosophy is lost, and such super-erudition it can the more readily disclaim since its attitude to this infinite multitude of topics should of course be most liberal."

26   Cf. Hegel's *Philosophy of Nature*, ed. Petry, loc. cit., vol. 1, 215 (§250): "The *impotence* of nature is to be attributed to its only being able to maintain the determinations of the Notion in an abstract manner. ..."

27   Ibid. (§250 remark). Again, Petry's translation has been modified here: "Notion" has been replaced with "Concept."

28   Stephen Houlgate, "Introduction" to *Hegel and the Philosophy of Nature*, ed. by Stephen Houlgate (Albany: State University of New York Press, 1998), xiii–xiv: "Some argue that the structure or skeleton of the *Philosophy of Nature* is developed purely conceptually, but that the flesh, as it were, is derived from empirical observation and sientific experimentation and analysis. On this view, Hegel is led to the very idea of nature by the *Science of Logic*, develops the conceptual structure of nature a priori from the initial determination of nature as abstract externality, and then 'maps' natural phenomena as described by science on to the various conceptual determinations that arise. ... Others argue, however, that scientific discoveries themselves condition, and perhaps even determine, the development of Hegel's conceptual account of nature." Cf. also Houlgate's extensive disussion of this point in his *An Introduction to Hegel* (Oxford: Blackwell, 2005), 115–121.

29   Cf. Also William Maker, loc. cit., 19–20: "Hegel articulates a philosophy of nature which ... provides an a priori account of nature, not as it is given in all its specificity (as that must fall beyond systematic thought), but in terms of delineating and accounting for the general features of givenness as such."

30   Ibid.

31   Organics – the third part of the *Philosophy of Nature* – will not be covered here since it is the topic of Cinzia Ferrini's contribution to this volume.

32   *Hegel's Philosophy of Subjective Spirit*, ed. and trans. Michael J. Petry, vol. 1: Introductions (Reidel: Dordrecht/Boston, 1978), 37.

33   Cf. Hegel's *Philosophy of Nature*, ed. Petry, loc. cit., vol. 1, p. 229 (Addition to §257): "Space and time are generally taken to be poles apart: space is there, and then we *also* have time. Philosophy fights against this mere 'also'" ("dieses *'Auch'* bekämpft die Philosophie"; translation emended). Note that this may even be considered as a definition of dialectic philosophy, according to which thought "fights" against the ordinary representation insofar as the latter considers concepts and things as orginally independent from or external one to another, relations between them being mere epiphenomena. Philosophical thought, at least after Hegel, has to invert this order.

34   Cf. Hegel, *Vorlesung über Naturphilosophie Berlin 1821/22* [Manuscript Uexküll], ed. Gilles Marmasse and Thomas Posch (Frankfurt am Main: Peter Lang, 2002), 42: "Beide [=Materie und Bewegung] sind ein und dasselbe; die Verschiedenheit beider besteht nur darin, daß die Materie eben die Wahrheit des Raums und der Zeit ist, und zwar gesetzt auf einfache, selbst unmittelbar ruhende Weise, in der Weise des Raums. Dies Resultat nun gesetzt in der Form des Prozesses oder der Zeit, ist die Bewegung." ("Matter and motion are the same; their difference is just the following: matter is the truth of space and time, posited in a simple, immediate, quiescent way – in a spatial way. This result, posited in a processual form, or in a temporal form, is motion.")

35   Cf. *Hegel's Philosophy of Nature*, ed. Petry, loc. cit., vol. 1, p. 248 (Addition to §265; note that Hegel speaks of "force" here where he should actually speak of "impact").

36   In §214 of the 1817 edition of his *Encyclopaedia*, Hegel thus says: "This motion [i.e., motion as considered in finite mechanics] transforms itself for itself into rest."

37   John Burbidge, *Real Process. How Logic and Chemistry Combine in Hegel's Philosophy of Nature*, loc. cit., 111.

38   *Hegel's Philosophy of Nature*, loc. cit., vol. 1, p. 282 (Addition to §271; translation emended).

39   Ibid., vol. 2, p. 9 (Addition to §272). On the meaning of "individuality" in Hegel's Philosophy of Nature, see the illuminative comment by John Burbidge in *Real Process*, loc. cit., 109–111.

40   To cite, once again, John Burbidge: "the middle section on physics stands between nature considered abstractly or universally and nature considered as integrated, singular organisms. The characteristics described are ways of differentiating among natural entities. Physics is nature particularized" (Burbidge, *Real Process*, 110).

41   *Hegel's Philosophy of Nature*, loc. cit., vol. 2, p. 17 (§276).

42   How does pure self-identity relate to individuality? The human self, or the I, may be taken as a conceptual model illustrating this. The I is in the sphere of spirit what light is in the sphere of nature: reflective self-identity, which, *in* its reflection, marks the beginning of individuality. Cf. ibid., 13: "This [i.e., the concept of light] is pure intro-reflection which, in the higher form of spirit, is the ego. The ego is infinite space, the infinite equality of self-consciousness with itself, the abstract and empty certainty of myself, and of my pure self-identity. The ego is merely the identity of my own attitude as subject, to myself as object. Light corresponds to this identity of self-consciousness, and is the exact image of it."

43   Since we know today that many – probably most – stars have planets around them, we may even more expressly say that the difference between stars and suns is merely one of the respect in which we regard it (i.e., as self-sustaining natural source of light or center of a planetary system). Note, however, that Hegel already envisaged the same kind of difference.

44   *Hegel's Philosophy of Nature*, loc. cit., vol. 1, p. 211 (Addition to §248).

45   Cf. Hegel's *Philosophy of Nature*, loc. cit., vol. 2, p. 31 (§280 Remark): "We now come to stand upon the Earth ... , which is not only our physical, but also spiritual home."

46   G.W.F. Hegel, *Jenaer Systementwürfe II: Logik, Metaphysik, Naturphilosophie*, ed. Rolf-Peter Horstmann. (Hamburg: Felix Meiner, 1982), VI.

47   Hegel's *Philosophy of Nature*, loc. cit., vol. 2, p. 34 (§281 Remark).

48   Ibid.

49   Cf. ibid., 33, where Hegel speaks of the chemical elements as "volatilized into chemical abstraction" (§281 Remark).

50   Ibid., 35 (Addition to §281).

51   G.W.F. Hegel, *Naturphilosophie. Die Vorlesung von 1819/20* [Manuscript Bernhardy], ed. Manfred Gies (Napoli: Bibliopolis, 1982), 48.

52   *Hegel's Philosophy of Nature*, loc. cit., vol. 2, p. 38 (§283).

53   Cf. G.W.F. Hegel, *Naturphilosophie. Die Vorlesung von 1819/20* [Manuscript Bernhardy], loc. cit., 49: "als formlos schließt es alle Form in sich." See also Vorlesung über Naturphilosophie Berlin 1821/22 [Manuscript Uexküll], loc. cit., 101: "gleichgültig gegen die Gestalt, ist das Wasser … die Möglichkeit verschiedener Gestaltungen."

54   Cf. G.W.F. Hegel, *Naturphilosophie. Die Vorlesung von 1819/20* [Manuscript Bernhardy], loc. cit., 49: "Begriff der Individualität überhaupt."

55   *Jenaer Systementwürfe II. Logik, Metaphysik, Naturphilosophie*, ed. Rolf-Peter Horstmann (Hamburg: Felix Meiner, 1982), 292: "Die Erde als das Redukt der Elemente ist passiv sich auf sich selbst beziehend, und damit selbst Bestimmtheit."

56   In fact, many natural plasmas (e.g., the solar wind) are hot; the plasma state of matter is also a "dissolved" or "dissolving" one insofar as electrons are detached from atomic nuclei in plasma.

57   Ibid., 82 (§303).

58   The second law of thermodynamics has been formulated, in different versions, by Lord Kelvin (Sir William Thomson, 1824–1907), Rudolf Clausius (1822–1888) and others. I'm here not referring to any particular version of this law, but to its consequence that in closed natural systems, entropy will always increase with time, which in many cases leads to an increase of disorder with time, which in turn corresponds to transitions from form to "formlessness."

59   Ibid., 85 (§304, Remark). Hegel refers to the experiments with the heating of bodies by friction, carried out by Benjamin Thompson (1753–1814) Count Rumford.

60   Cf. Thomas Posch, "Die Rezeption der Hegelschen Lehre von der Wärme durch C. L. Michelet und K. R. Popper," in *Wiener Jahrbuch für Philosophie* 34 (2002): 143–158. See also Thomas Posch, Die "Mechanik der Wärme," *in* Hegels Jenaer Systementwurf von 1805/06: Ein Kommentar vor dem Hintergrund der Entwicklung der Wärmelehre von 1620 bis 1840 (Aachen: Shaker Verlag, 2005).

61   *Hegel's Philosophy of Nature*, loc. cit., vol. 2, p. 96 (§310).

62   Ibid., 96 (Addition to §310).

63   In fact, Hegel calls the crystal the "quiescent end" (daseiender Zweck [télos]); ibid., 114 (Addition to §315).

64   Cf. ibid., 99 (§312).

65   As Hegel puts it: "The two poles [that we had in magnetism] as existing separately from each other, each pole carried by an individual body, this is electricity" (G.W.F. Hegel, *Vorlesungen über Naturphilosophie Berlin 1825/26* [Manuscript Dove], ed. Karol Bal et al. (Hamburg: Felix Meiner, 2007), 154 (my translation)).

66   Cf. ibid.: "This is the electrical movement: to posit identical the different and to differentiate the identical" (my translation).

67   Cf. Addition to §200 of Hegel's *Encyclopaedia* (section on "Chemism"). In the *Science of Logic*, Hegel points out the applicability of the category of chemism also to love and friendship. This merely illustrates that chemism, according to Hegel, is indeed a very general

form of object relation; it is *not* meant as a reductionist consideration of love and friendship.

68   *Hegel's Philosophy of Nature*, loc. cit., vol. 2, p. 222 (Addition to §336).

69   As for the transition to Organics and the idea of Life, see Chapter 9 in this volume.

70   Haering, in an essay from 1931, already pointed to Hegel's opposition to the former two tendencies of modern science. Cf. Thomas Haering, "Hegel und die moderne Naturwissenschaft ["Hegel and Modern Science"]: Bemerkungen zu Hegels Naturphilosophie," in *Philosophische Hefte* 3, no. 1/2 (1931): 71–82. While Haering, however, fully affirmed Hegel's positions in this regard, I shall try to take up a more differentiated stance.

71   The third point has been highlighted, *inter alia*, by Buchdahl and Falkenburg. Cf. Gerd Buchdahl, "Conceptual Analysis and Scientific Theory in Hegel's Philosophy of Nature," in *Hegel and the Sciences*, ed. Robert S. Cohen and Marx W. Wartofsky (Dordrecht: Reidel, 1984), 13–36; Brigitte Falkenburg, "How to Save the Phenomena: Meaning and Reference in Hegel's Philosophy of Nature," in *Hegel and the Philosophy of Nature*, ed. Stephen Houlgate (Albany: State University of New York Press, 1998), 97–135.

72   *Hegel's Philosophy of Nature*, vol. 1, p. 198 (§246 Remark).

73   Buchdahl, loc. cit., p. 19. Buchdahl refers to Miller's translation of the Remark to §246, in which the essential phrase reads: "The rustle of Nature's life is silenced in the stillness of thought."

74   As for the term "stages," cf. §249 of the *Encyclopaedia*: "Nature is to be regarded as a *system of stages. ...*"

75   *Hegel's Philosophy of Nature*, loc. cit., vol. 2, p. 43 (Addition to §286). Cf. ibid., vol. 1, p. 201: "The current philosophy is called the philosophy of identity. It might be much more appropriate to apply this name to this kind of physics, which simply dispenses with determinateness. It is a fault in physics that it should involve so much identity, for identity is the basic category of understanding" (Addition to §246).

76   For the history of the concept of *The Great Chain of Being*, cf. Arthur Lovejoy's study with this title (Cambridge, Mass.: Harvard University Press, 1936). However, Hegel does not play a particular role in Lovejoy's version of the story of this concept.

77   Cf. *The New Encyclopaedia Britannica*, 15th edition (Chicago: University of Chicago Press, 2005), vol. 5, p. 442.

78   Cf. Michael J. Petry, *Hegel's Philosophy of Nature*, vol. 1, pp. 214–215: "The old saying, or law as it is called, 'non datur saltus in natura' is by no means adequate to the diremption of the Notion. The continuity of the Notion with itself is of an entirely different nature" (Addition to §249).

79   See also Michael J. Petry, *Hegel's Philosophy of Nature*, vol. 1, Introduction, pp. 21–40, Section "Levels, Hierarchies and Spheres."

80   Ibid., 30.

81   Cf. Thomas Posch, "Hegel's Anti-reductionism: Remarks on What Is Living of His Philosophy of Nature," *Angelaki: Journal of the Theoretical Humanities* 10, no. 1 (April 2005): 61–76.

82   As for a contemporary definition of antireductionism, cf., e.g., John Polkinghorne: "[Physics] pulls things apart into smaller and smaller pieces. We have learned all sorts of worthwhile and interesting things this way. The question is whether or not it is the only way to learn what things are *really* like. In the end, are we just immensely complicated collections of quarks, gluons, and electrons? People who answer 'Yes' to this last question are called reductionists. In their view, the whole reduces simply to a collection of the parts. They are sometimes also called 'nothing butters', for they believe we are 'nothing but' collections of elementary particles. Those ... who do not share this view are called antireductionists." See John Polkinghorne, *Quarks, Chaos and Christianity* (New York: Crossroads Publications, 1996), 51.

83 For example, Aristotle notoriously considers the living organism and its entelechy a sort of paradigm for the description of natural phenomena; Newton uses mechanical forces as a paradigm of his physics; several physicists of the nineteenth century assigned a similar role to the concept of energy (as mentioned above).

84 Cf. Richard Kroner, *Von Kant bis Hegel*, vol. 2, loc. cit., p. 249: "Der Philosophie fällt daher das Wächteramt zu, kraft dessen sie jeden Uebergriff einer empirischen in eine andere Disziplin, bzw. in die Philosophie selbst, zu verhüten und die *Grenzen der Wissenschaften* mit kritischer Strenge zu schützen hat." ("It is hence up to philosophy to prevent the encroachment of any one empirical discipline into another or into philosophy itself; it is up to her to guard the *limits of individual sciences* with critical rigor.")

85 On Hegel's Philosophy of Mind, cf. Chapter 10 in this volume.

86 It is in the same context that Hegel holds that the *evolution of species* is not properly understood (or rather, that evolution is not a useful concept at all) if understood merely as the sum of a huge number of tiny steps.

87 G.W.F. Hegel, *Lectures on the History of Philosophy 1825–6*, Vol. 2: Greek Philosophy, ed. Robert F. Brown (Oxford: Oxford University Press, 2006), 92. Hegel goes on to say there, treating Leucippus and Democritus: "The bond between [the atoms] is only external; it is a combination, for there is no actual union or unity."

88 *Hegel's Philosophy of Nature*, loc. cit., vol. 2, pp. 66–67, emphasis added.

89 Ibid., vol. 2, p. 46. As for the context in which the meteorological process is treated in the Philosophy of Nature, see above, Section 3b.

90 For example, the Swiss geologist and meteorologist Jean André Deluc (1727–1817) still denied the extraterrestrial origin of the meteorites; so did the German physicist Johann Tobias Mayer (1752–1830). Cf. Petry's more extensive notes in this subject in *Hegel's Philosophy of Nature*, loc. cit., vol. 2, p. 278.

91 *Sir Isaac Newton's Mathematical Principles of Natural Philosophy*, ed. F. Cajori (Cambridge: Cambridge University Press, 1934), xvii–xviii.

92 G.W.F. Hegel, *Lectures on the History of Philosophy*, trans. E. S. Haldane and Frances H. Simson (London: Kegan Paul, Trench, Trübner & Co., 1895), vol. 3, p. 323, emphasis added.

93 Cf. Gerd Buchdahl, "Conceptual Analysis and Scientific Theory in Hegel's Philosophy of Nature," loc. cit., 20, 25. (Buchdahl explicitly speaks of Hegel's "preference for the use of phenomenological theory-types.")

94 Cf. Brigitte Falkenburg, "How to Save the Phenomena": loc. cit., 114; ibid., 132, n. 3. Kenneth Westphal, however, stresses that we should not go so far as to say that Hegel rejected forces or dynamical laws altogether: see his essay "Force, Understanding and Ontology," *Bulletin of the Hegel Society of Great Britain* 57/58 (2008): 1–19, especially section 5 with n. 14.

95 *Sir Isaac Newton's Mathematical Principles of Natural Philosophy*, ed. Florian Cajori, loc. cit., 547: "But hitherto I have not been able to discover the cause of those properties of gravity from phenomena, and I frame no hypotheses; for whatever is not deduced from the phenomena is to be called an hypothesis; and hypotheses, whether metaphysical or physical, whether of occult qualities or mechanical, have no place in experimental philosophy."

96 G.W.F. Hegel, *Vorlesungen über Naturphilosophie Berlin 1825/26*, Manuscript Dove, l.c., 68 ("Wenn nichts physikalisch bestimmt werden soll, so wäre der Ausdruck 'Kraft' wegzulassen"). In other words, Hegel argues that describing motions in a way exemplified by the Keplerian laws (where exclusively spatio-temporal quantities occur) is preferable to using dynamical laws (that introduce unexplainable explanatory principles).

97 Cf. Heinrich Hertz, *The Principles of Mechanics Presented in a New Form*, trans. D. E. Jones and J. T. Walley (New York: Dover Publications, 1956), 11–12: "It cannot be denied that in very

many cases the forces which are used in mechanics for treating physical problems are simply sleeping partners [Hertz's original expression is "leergehende Nebenräder," i.e., "needless auxiliary wheels"], which keep out of the business altogether when actual facts have to be represented. In the simple relations with which mechanics originally dealt, this is not the case. ... But it is otherwise when we turn to the motions of the stars. Here the forces have never been the objects of direct perception; all our previous experiences relate only to the apparent positions of the stars. Nor do we expect in future to perceive the forces. The future experiences which we anticipate again relate only to the position of these luminous points in the heavens. It is only in the deduction of future experiences from the past that the forces of gravitation enter as transitory aids in the calculation, and then disappear from consideration. Precisely the same is true of the discussion of molecular forces, of chemical actions, and of many electric and magnetic actions. And if after more mature experience we return to the simple forces, whose existence we never doubted, we learn that those forces which we had perceived with convincing certainty, were after all not real."

98 I wish to express my gratitude to Stephen Houlgate and to Ken Westphal for their thorough review of the original manuscript of this chapter.

References

Alexander, Samuel. "Hegel's Conception of Nature." *Mind* 11, no. 44 (1886): 495–523.

Buchdahl, Gerd. "Conceptual Analysis and Scientific Theory in Hegel's Philosophy of Nature." In *Hegel and the Sciences*, ed. R. S. Cohen and M. W. Wartofsky (Reidel: Dordrecht, 1984), 13–36.

Burbidge, John W. *Real Process: How Logic and Chemistry Combine in Hegel's Philosophy of Nature* (Toronto: University of Toronto Press, 1996).

Craig, Edward, and Michael Hoskin. "Hegel and the Seven Planets." *Journal for the History of Astronomy* 23 (1992): 208–210.

Falkenburg, Brigitte. "How to Save the Phenomena: Meaning and Reference in Hegel's Philosophy of Nature." In *Hegel and the Philosophy of Nature*, ed. Stephen Houlgate (Albany: State University of New York Press, 1998), 97–135.

Haering, Theodor. "Hegel und die moderne Naturwissenschaft: Bemerkungen zu Hegels Naturphilosophie. "*Philosophische Hefte.*" 3, no. 1/2 (1931): 71–82.

Hegel, G.W.F. *Jenaer Systementwürfe II: Logik, Metaphysik, Naturphilosophie*, ed. Rolf-Peter Horstmann (Hamburg: Felix Meiner, 1982).

Hegel, G.W.F. *Dissertatio Philosophica de Orbitis Planetarum*, ed. and trans. Wolfgang Neuser (Weinheim: VCH Verlag, 1986).

Hegel, G.W.F. *Naturphilosophie: Die Vorlesung von 1819/20*, ed. Manfred Gies, in cooperation with K.-H. Ilting (Napoli: Bibliopolis, 1982).

Hegel, G.W.F. *Vorlesung über Naturphilosophie: Berlin 1821/22*, ed. Gilles Marmasse and Thomas Posch (Frankfurt am Main: Peter Lang, 2002).

Hegel, G.W.F. *Vorlesungen über Naturphilosophie: Berlin 1825/26*, ed. Karol Bal, Gilles Marmasse, Thomas Posch, and Klaus Vieweg (Hamburg: Felix Meiner, 2007).

Hegel, G.W.F. *Lectures on the History of Philosophy*, trans. E. S. Haldane and Frances H. Simson (London: Kegan Paul, Trench, Trübner & Co., 1895).

Hegel, G.W.F. *Lectures on the History of Philosophy*, Vol. 2 (Greek Philosophy), ed. Robert F. Brown (Oxford: Clarendon Press, Oxford, 2006).

Hegel, G.W.F. *Hegel's Philosophy of Nature*, ed. and trans. with an Introduction and Explanatory Notes by Michael J. Petry, 3 vols. (London and New York: George Allan and Unwin), 1970.

Hegel, G.W.F. *Hegel's Philosophy of Right*, trans. with notes by T. M. Knox (Oxford: Clarendon Press, 1942).

Hegel, G.W.F. *Hegel's Philosophy of Subjective Spirit*, ed. and trans. with an Introduction and Explanatory Notes by Michael J. Petry, 3 vols. (Dordrecht and Boston: Reidel, 1978).

Hertz, Heinrich. *The Principles of Mechanics Presented in a New Form*, trans. D. E. Jones and J. T. Walley (New York: Dover Publications, 1956).

Houlgate, Stephen. *An Introduction to Hegel* (Oxford: Blackwell, 2005).

Kroner, Richard. *Von Kant bis Hegel.* Vol. 2: Von der Naturphilosophie zur Philosophie des Geistes, 4th edition (Tübingen: Mohr Siebeck, 2007).

Lovejoy, Arthur. *The Great Chain of Being: A Study of the History of an Idea* (Cambridge, MA: Harvard University Press, 1936).

Maker, William. "The Very Idea of the Idea of Nature, or Why Hegel Is Not an Idealist." In *Hegel and the Philosophy of Nature*, ed. Stephen Houlgate (Albany: State University of New York Press, 1998), 1–27.

The New Encyclopaedia Britannica, 15th edition (Chicago, Ill.: University of Chicago Press, 2005).

Newton, Isaac. *Sir Isaac Newton's Mathematical Principles of Natural Philosophy and his System of the World*, trans. Andrew Motte, 1729, revised, and supplied with an historical and explanatory appendix by F. Cajori (Cambridge: Cambridge University Press, 1934).

Polkinghorne, John. *Quarks, Chaos and Christianity: Questions to Science and Religion.* (New York: Crossroads Publications, 1996).

Posch, Thomas. "Die Rezeption der Hegelschen Lehre von der Wärme durch C. L. Michelet und K. R. Popper." *Wiener Jahrbuch für Philosophie* 34 (2002): 143–158.

Posch, Thomas. "Hegel's Anti-reductionism: Remarks on What Is Living of His Philosophy of Nature." *Angelaki: Journal of the Theoretical Humanities* 10, no. 1 (2005): 61–76.

Posch, Thomas. *Die "Mechanik der Wärme" in Hegels Jenaer Systementwurf von 1805/06: Ein Kommentar vor dem Hintergrund der Entwicklung der Wärmelehre von 1620 bis 1840* (Aachen: Shaker Verlag, 2005).

Rosenkranz, Karl. *Hegel's Naturphilosophie und die Bearbeitung derselben durch den italienischen Philosophen Augusto Vera* (Berlin: Nicolaishe Verlagsbuchhandlung, 1868; reprinted Hildesheim: Georg Olms, 1979).

Schleiden, Matthias Jakob. *Schelling's und Hegel's Verhältnis zur Naturwissenschaft* (Leipzig: Engelmann, 1844).

Siegel, Carl. *Geschichte der deutschen Naturphilosophie* (Leipzig: Akademische Verlagsgesellschaft, 1913).

Stirling, James Hutchison. *Lectures on the Philosophy of Law. Together with Whewell and Hegel, and Hegel and Mr. W. R. Smith: A Vindication in a Physico-mathematical Regard* (London: Longmans, Green & Co., 1873).

Treder, Hans-Jürgen. Zum Einfluß von Schellings Naturphilosophie auf die Entwicklung der Physik. In *Natur und geschichtlicher Prozeß*, ed. H. J. Sandkühler (Frankfurt amd Main: Suhrkamp, 1984), 326–334.

Wandschneider, Dieter. "Die Stellung der Natur im Gesamtentwurf der Hegelschen Philosophie." In *Hegel und die Naturwissenschaften*, ed. Michael J. Perry (Stuttgart: Frommann-Holzboog, 1987), 33–64.

Westphal, Kenneth R. "Force, Understanding and Ontology." *Bulletin of the Hegel Society of Great Britain* 57/58 (2008): 1–29.

Whewell, William. "On Hegel's Criticism of Newton's Principia." *Transactions of the Cambridge Philosophical Society* 8, Part V (1849): 696–706.

9

The Transition to Organics:
Hegel's Idea of Life

CINZIA FERRINI

My aim in this chapter is to place Hegel's view of organic life in its philosophical and historical context, that is, to highlight its distinctive theoretical features and to examine them against the background of the approaches, achievements, and trends of the empirical sciences of his time.[1]

I focus first on what Hegel understands to be the conceptual structure or logical form of life. Then I examine the transition, through chemical processes, from the sphere of the inorganic to that of the organic. I shall show that this transition, as Hegel conceives it, is a *logical* one that hinges on conceptual inner necessity, not a *natural* one in which chemical processes actually give rise to living organisms at specific points in time. I claim that Hegel holds neither the vitalistic view that organic life 'emerges' from an essentially lifeless matter by means of the sudden appearance of a natural productive power of generation (*Lebenskraft*), nor the hylozoic view that nature in its temporal existence is everywhere really alive in all its parts.

1. General Characteristics of the Concept of Natural Life

In her long entry on 'life' (*Leben*) in the recent *Hegel-Lexicon*, Annette Sell examines diachronically and systematically the wide range of Hegel's analyses of life and their associated standpoints. At the end of her entry, Sell summarizes the religious, aesthetic, spiritual, political, practical, logical, and natural meanings of Hegel's concept of life from *The Early Theological Writings* to the 1831 *Science of Logic*: life, in her view, is "the movement characterised by division and reintegration into unity," which expresses the dynamic "relationship of individual and universal [*von Einzelnem und Allgemeinem*]" (Sell 2006a, 305).

A Companion to Hegel, First Edition. Edited by Stephen Houlgate and Michael Baur.
© 2011 Blackwell Publishing Ltd. Published 2011 by Blackwell Publishing Ltd.

In other words, the structure of life can be summed up as follows: life begins from an essential though abstract principle, distinguishes or particularizes its components, and then reintegrates these real divisions within the original essential principle to form a concrete living individual. Note that, on Hegel's view, this is also the very dynamic of 'conceiving' or the very form of pure conceptual thinking (Burbidge 2008, 50–51). In this respect, the philosophy of nature is a sort of 'applied logic,' the task of which is to *recognize* the pure and abstract determinations of thought (studied in the *Logic*) in the shapes of mind-independent nature. This is especially so in the case of living things. Living things as such (i.e., a certain existent dog) come to be and pass away (W8, §24Z[2]: 84), but they have a permanent essence or substantial form (i.e., a determinate genus or species) that conforms to the syllogistic, conceptual process of linking the extremes of the universal (animality) and the singular ('this' dog) through the middle term (*its* particular species and variety). Indeed, Hegel understands the totality of the animal organism as the "living universality" (*lebendige Allgemeinheit*) of the concept, which passes syllogistically through its three determinations of shape (*Gestalt*), assimilation as opposition and relation to otherness (the inorganic nature of its environment), and genus (W9, §352: 435).

Hegel also contends, however, that this syllogistic linkage is in general "a universal form of *all* things [*eine allgemeine Form* aller *Dinge*]" (W8, §24Z[2]: 84),[2] and in the 1823/1824 philosophy of nature, he explains that, although the "basic form" (*Grundform*) of qualitative natural bodies (organic and inorganic) is to appear to be merely coexisting, this mutual externality is only a "semblance" (*Schein*). What *essentially* rules the appearance of natural things – and is the sole concern of the philosophy of nature – is the syllogistic process of the concept as "the master that keeps singularities together" (Hegel 2000, 90; Ferrini 2002, 70–74). This is not to say that everything in nature is really alive in all its parts; yet even an inorganic planet that is *part* of a mechanical system of heavenly bodies exhibits 'to the eye of the concept' (i.e., to thought or 'ideally') that syllogistic reintegration into unity that is distinctive of living processes.[3]

To translate the conceptual structure of life into the concrete terms of natural shapes, therefore, it suffices to recall that in the 1819/1820 *Philosophy of Nature* Hegel declares that

> life is *essentially* organism. In the organism the form is this unity, and at the same time these parts of the form are not parts but *members* [*Glieder*], they are ideal. (*Vorl*.16, 139.31; emphasis added)

Hegel uses the word 'ideal' here in a special, and somewhat unusual, sense (Houlgate 2005, 162–163). To say that the parts of an organism are 'ideal' is not to say that they are perfectly formed or merely illusory or transcendent; instead, Hegel's point is that in truth the parts are mutually related as interdependent *moments* of *one* whole. Hence their real differentiation and division is *ideally* and *necessarily* reintegrated into the unity of their common purpose, namely, the conservation of the organism in a state of functional activity, directed so as to cause feedback from the outside world.[4]

In the 1821/1822 *Philosophy of Nature* Hegel further explains how this 'ideal,' conceptual structure of life, as the 'organic' movement of division, determination, and reintegration into the unity of universality and singularity, makes explicit a fundamental characteristic of life: the fact that life preserves a differentiated 'self-form.' Indeed, Hegel says that, as "the process of leading the members back to identity," life must be *individuality* (Hegel 2002, 168).[5] It is through this purposive process that the individual living organism acquires, preserves, and transmits by reproduction the form of a *self*.

Finally, in the opening paragraph of "Organic Physics" Hegel introduces life by referring to the 'self-related *negative* unity' that natural individuality has become. This is to say that life is the circular infinite process of determining itself to particularity or finitude (*Besonderheit oder Endlichkeit*) and equally *negating* this and returning into itself, so that at the end of the process it re-establishes itself to begin anew (W9, §337: 337). Within this frame, and from the standpoint of Hegel's generally dynamic conception of the universal forms of all natural things, "Mechanics, " "Physics," and "Organic Physics" will show increasing degrees of self-determination and self-preservation (subjectivity) and decreasing degrees of externality and contingency (separation, isolation).

2. The Path to the Individualization of Matter

In the section on "Mechanics" Hegel discusses three kinds of movement: uniform motion that results from external thrust and is expressed by the simple relation of space to time, relatively free motion (where motion accelerates uniformly, due to gravity), and absolutely free motion (the movement of orbiting planets in the solar system).[6] These three stages of "Mechanics" show how a relatively homogeneous matter passes from passivity to activity, from being set in motion by external thrust to having the principle of motion within itself.[7] Since matter is defined in "Mechanics" as essentially composite, consisting entirely of discrete parts which all tend toward a center (Hegel 1980, 48), it is still characterized above all by "essential externality" and is still governed by gravity: it has thus not yet become properly self-determining (W9, §272Z: 109). Consequently, as Hegel notes in 1819/1820, in this sphere the organism "does not allow itself to occur [*geschehen*]"; that is to say, organisms cannot be produced by purely mechanical or gravitational motion (*Vorl.*16, 139.18).[8]

Having said this, the *structural form* of the organism already begins to appear in the 'ideal' point of unity that governs the movement of free, independent material parts in the solar system: the sun in relation to the orbiting bodies that carry the principle of motion (gravity) in themselves (see Chapter 8 in this volume, Sections 3.a and 3.b.1). Yet by being confined to a central body in relation to the merely mechanical motion of mutually external and independent bodies, the solar system is merely the "first organism," that is, only "the organism of mechanism" (W9, §337Z: 339).

"Physics" deals with 'real' matter, that is, in Hegel's terms, with matter that has a certain inner *form* and comes to manifest that form. This inner form endows bodies with *individuality* (and a distinctive *quality* or specificity) that bodies lack in so far as they are understood as purely mechanical bodies (or mere quantities of matter). In the Addition to the opening paragraph of this Section we read that:

> The bodies now come under the power [*Macht*] of individuality. What follows is the reduction of the free bodies under the power of the individual point of unity, which digests

[*verdaut*] them. Gravity, as the inward essence of matter, only inner identity, passes ... into the manifestation of essence. (W9, §272Z: 109)

"Physics" begins with what Hegel calls "matter in its first qualified state": light as matter's general and abstract appearance to and for others (not for itself) (W9, §275, §275Z: 109, 113; see Chapter 8 in this book, Sections 2 and 3.b.1).[9] Yet Hegel claims that light is implicitly '*self*-determining,'thus announcing a dimension that is characteristic of the concept of 'life.'[10] In the *Philosophy of Nature* of 1805/1806 (GW8, 108.5–8) we find a clear assessment of how and why with the physical dimension of light we reach the universal form of 'life': the key notion is the *thorough* co-penetration of *all* the parts of a transparent body (i.e., a glass, a crystal) by *a unity* of presence and actuality.

Famously, from the time of *De orbitis* (Hegel 1801, 8.2–4) to the *Encyclopaedia* (W9, §320Z: 246), Hegel always criticizes the statement in Newton's *Opticks* that "the whiteness of the Sun's light is compounded of all the primary colours mixed in due proportion" (Bk. I, Pt. 2, Prop. 5, Theorem 4). He also criticizes Newton's interpretation of the experiments that involve the resolution of light by "grating" and the forming of the spectrum by a prism, charging him with understanding the nature of light as a "composite" (*Zusammensetzung*).[11] Hegel seems to draw on the experimentalism of Rohault, a Cartesian physicist, whose *Traité de physique* he could have well read in Tschugg's Library during his Berne period (1793–1796). According to Rohault, light was an "elementary matter" and colors were only "pure modifications" of that fundamental unity (Ferrini 1995, 105–106). Hegel underscores (W9, §320: 241–248) that this 'elementary matter' is an original unity capable of division into luminosity and darkness (à la Goethe's *Farbenlehre*). It is still, however, a unity of space, externality, and generality, which thoroughly co-penetrates all the parts of a transparent body (i.e., a prism) in an external, *simple* way:[12] in the *Science of Logic*, Hegel's originally *colorless* light is an example of pure indifferent (abstract) *sameness* in spatial extension, that is, of pure quantity (W5, 214). Hence, this condition of unity is not yet that of "the singular [*einzelne*] self," as is the case with organic nature or the self-conscious I at the higher level of the philosophy of spirit. Yet since the spectrum of colors that light displays results from its inner principle of differentiating *itself* when it thoroughly permeates the material structure of the body it illuminates (i.e., the prism), light, though simple, is no longer the kind of unity that governs the motion of parts that remain *external* to their center.[13]

In the sphere of its *qualitative* particularization (*Besonderung*), hetereogeneity, and finitude, matter develops as its 'self-form' determines it to an increasing degree and comes to be more explicitly *the point of unity* of all the material components of a body. This is why "Physics" offers a reappraisal of the system of the heavenly bodies. What was merely understood as a 'mechanical organism' is now determined as the manifestation of a *thoroughgoing* unity – the wholly universal, 'cosmic' *life* in which all living nature participates. This life is constituted by the *union* of the mechanical connections between heavenly bodies governed by gravity with their physical relation that is governed by the Sun's light, that is, matter in the condition of unity (W9, §279Z: 130)[14]. Indeed, only when matter is regarded as *inwardly self-determining*, and the sun is no longer understood as a mere center of motion, but *also* according to its higher determination as a *star*, "as self-sustaining natural source of light" (see Chapter 8 in this book, Section 3.b, n. 43), which illuminates all the planets and is the source of life, do we have light as the complete master of gravity that holds the gigantic members of heavenly bodies within a unity that has the principle of difference within itself and is *immanent and actively, thoroughly present* (W9, §337Z: 339). Otherwise stated, here we 'comprehend' the *syllogism* of the sun (as the moment of universality), the comets, and the moon (which represent the moment of particularity), and the singularity of the planets (the moment of the reflection in itself, the unity of universality and particularity) (W9, §279Z: 129–130; see Chapter 8 in this volume, Section 3.b).[15]

The highest point achieved in the sphere of "Physics" is fully individualized matter (*Vorl*.16, 139.6–7).[16] That is to say, the culmination of the physical drive to subjugate the particularity of parts or properties to the unity of selfhood is the individuality of the chemical body (W9, §337Z: 339). I shall contend that this key point helps us to understand the conceptual necessity of nature's leap from the inorganic to the organic realm.

3. Chemistry and Individuality: The Appearance and Disappearance of Life

The dynamic process through which universal matter is further particularized and qualified can thus also be seen as the necessary drive to make the unity of individuality, or 'selfhood,' in matter manifest. The content of "Physics" thereby becomes what Hegel calls "total *free* individuality" (W9, §273: 110; emphasis added). The last sphere of "Physics" treats different kinds of *chemical* process (W9, §§326–336: 287–336), in which the 'inner necessity' of the activity and movement of individuality and being-for-self is countered by the outward division and mutual indifference of the chemical products (W9, §335: 333).[17]

The standpoint of chemistry presupposes the individuality of a body (the point of unity that contains the difference of the various material components within itself) and then tries to split it up, and by decomposition seeks to liberate its different constituents (W9, §281Z: 135). However, in the effort to reach what is simple, chemistry actually destroys individuality (W9, §281Z: 135), whose unity cannot come into existence. Chemical bodies possess a certain unity, insofar as they are individuals, but the chemical *process* itself is as yet devoid of identity, since it depends on externally given circumstances and so does not 'return into' itself: it does not *renew* and *reproduce* itself of its own accord. Since self-renewal and self-reproduction constitute the distinguishing 'infinity' of vital activity, their absence constitutes what Hegel calls the 'finitude' of the chemical process (*Vorl*.17, 167.27–29).[18]

Thus, the reintegration into unity and the mastering of externality that characterizes life are not fully manifest, but can only 'shine through,' in the spontaneous energy of some kinds of chemical process (W9, §335: 333); or, at most, the distinguishing feature of life may appear only *momentarily*, as "a flash" (*Augenblick*: W9, §336Z: 335) in the immanent activity of combustion (which Hegel calls the 'fire process': W9, §331: 318–321). This is why, when Hegel writes that "indeed [*zwar*], in general the chemical process is *life*" (W9, §335: 333), he also immediately warns the reader that life is only *potentially* (*an sich*) present in chemistry. Insofar as the chemical process is determined by conditions that are already *outwardly* at hand, it cannot begin again unless those conditions are encountered once more. Once the process is completed, therefore, any further activity ceases, unless external factors cause a new process to begin. The beginning and end of the chemical process thus *fall apart*, in the sense that the end of the process does not of itself lead back to the beginning and initiate the process once more.[19] In this respect, chemical processes fall short of what is required for life. Furthermore, by contrast with the transformation of nutrients into blood through bile and gastric juice in the higher forms of animal life, the chemical combination and decomposition of salts shows only the instability of any character and that the chemical process is not able to bring about any thorough and enduring internal transformation of the chemicals concerned. In combination, two original matters give rise to a new matter that wholly replaces their difference, but in decomposition it is the product that loses its individuality, with the return of the constituents to their initial identity; hence, the chemical process involves continuity and external sameness:

> When I decompose a salt, I obtain again the two matters which had combined to form it; with this, the salt is also grasped conceptually [*begriffen*], and the matters within it have not become something other, instead they have remained the same. (W9, §365Z: 484)[20]

Further implications can, however, be drawn from the fact that at least a sign of the *entelechia*[21] of life can be discerned, for instance, in combustion, namely the presence of an "initial self-determination of the concept from within itself in its realization,"[22] that is, an immanent drive to posit a determinateness (in ignition) and also to negate it, to be in opposition to it (in the consuming of the flammable elements) (see W9, §335: 333).[23] Hegel states that if the products of the chemical process were spontaneously self-renewing, they would be life (ibid; see Chapter 8 in this volume, Section 3.b.3), thus claiming that, in this regard (*insofern*), "life is a chemical process made to be perennial." That is, life is nature expressing itself as a characteristic unity of infinity and finitude:

> As existing, this unity is the determination of life, and it is towards this that nature drives [*treibt*]. Life is present at hand [*vorhanden*] in itself [*an sich*] within the chemical process; but the inner necessity is not yet an existent unity. (W9, §335Z: 334)[24]

Yet in the Addition to §335 Hegel comments that, though there is, indeed, a "glimpse" (*ein Anschein*) of vitality in the chemical process, this hint "gets lost in the product" (ibid.).[25] Hegel's comment entails the rejection of any thought of a naturally spontaneous (*aus sich*) transition from the inorganic to the organic. Such a transition does not occur because *chemical processes come to a dead end in their products.*[26]

Hegel is here not advancing the vitalistic thesis that life 'emerges' from lifeless individualized matter as a mere product or consequence of the physical and chemical complexity of matter's structure, and as something new.[27] Rather, Hegel claims that there is a natural drive to make manifest the point of unity of individuality, or 'selfhood,' in matter. The drive is to determine an individual in relation to a center that has the form of the self (W9, §337: 337). This is nothing but the qualitative manner in which specific individual *subjects* live and have their being.

This self-form is *logically prior* to these physical and chemical conditions, for it is inwardly and essentially present in matter starting from its more abstract individualized shapes and therefore does not depend on them. Starting from 'the organism of mechanism' and the thoroughly co-penetrating self-identity of light, Hegel has consistently argued that, despite appearances, 'Organics' is the *logical basis* of the preceding stages ("Mechanics" and "Physics"). That is to say, life is 'ideally' (i.e., for our thought) the unity and original truth of those stages. Hegel does not hold, therefore, that organic life 'emerges' in nature and in time *from* (or because of) the processes characterized in the preceding stage. Hegel's philosophy of nature moves systematically and dialectically through nature's *coexisting*, qualitatively distinct and mutually external stages (*Stufenleiter* or *scala naturae*; see Chapter 8 in this book, Section 4.a), leaving no room for any thought of a 'historical' development of nature (W9, §249: 31;Verra 2007, 67–68).

The problem of clarifying Hegel's transition from inorganic to organic nature through chemism is thus not solved by a 'naturalistic reading,'[28] since chemical processes do not renew themselves on their own and thereby give rise to organic life. Moreover, such a reading, by appealing to what emerges through actual natural processes, leaves a further question unanswered: since Hegel characterizes chemical phenomena as acting and reacting by passing through different states and determinations *without maintaining themselves as differentiated particulars*, how can we understand his claim that the continuous variation and alteration of the bodies' material existence leads to the manifestation of *free* individuality (announced in §273), and provides a *necessary* 'transition' (W9, §336Z: 334) to the new sphere of "Organics" (W9, §336: 334), resulting in the "real totality of the body" which *is* a living individual (W9, section 337: 337)? I will address the issue of the contradiction inherent in chemical individual substances in Section 4, and the issues of necessity and freedom in Sections 5 and 6, respectively.

4. Contradiction in Chemicals

To begin to answer this question, note that Hegel calls chemical substances 'bodily individualities' or 'individualised bodies' (*Körperindividualitäten*) (W9, §334Z: 331): they are singular individuals that through their cycle of changes *acquire their own particular, specific character*. This process produces individualized bodies but also *negates their immediacy*. Indeed, chemicals challenge any cognitive attempt to determine their proper (e.g., acidic or basic) and stable nature, for they *do not maintain their difference, that is, their individuality*, when they enter into chemical processes.[29] As remarked above, in combination, the two original constituents disappear in the neutral product, but in decomposition the salt then loses its character. In his 1809 *L'idées sur l'acidité*, Avogadro had introduced the concept of the 'relativity' of acids, according to which a substance that is acidic in respect to another substance can be basic in respect to a third one. He proposed a scale of relative acidity and alkalinity, which emphasized that "the term acid denotes only an accidental property and should not be used without qualification" (Morselli 1984, 150). In the *Philosophy of Nature* of 1825/1826, Hegel makes clear that this contradiction within chemical individuality between the identification of a matter and the relativity of its transitory properties is what becomes *posited* in the chemical process. As Hegel puts it, in the chemical process "the real immediate exists as not immediate" (*Vorl.*17, 168.59–61), that is to say, the properties that immediately identify a certain chemical substance here and now as *this* (rather than *that*) prove to be relative: the results of a series of mediations.[30] The interesting point here is thus to clarify why the sphere of "Physics," with chemistry, does not naturally and immediately evolve into "Organics" on its own, though Hegel speaks here of a 'transition,' and to examine the role played in that transition by the finitude of the chemical product.

To recapitulate: Hegel does not claim that life is to be conceived as springing from or originating in a process of *physically* qualified (individualized) matter that as such is *essentially* alien to the logical *form* of life.[31] Note, however, that he does not incline toward any form of hylozoism, either. Hegel clearly distances himself, for example, from the metaphysical philosophy of nature of his time that holds that all matter is alive. Such metaphysical philosophy of nature follows Jacobi's pronouncement that "Everything in nature lives. Nothing is completely dead" (Rühlig 1998, 360). In the *Ideen* Herder, too, advocated the existence of a "living, organic force," which he called the "mother of all formations on earth." Though the origin and essence of this *"genetische Kraft"* were unknown to him, he claimed to recognize its presence and generative effects everywhere in nature. He regarded nature as living and endowing itself with organic parts "from the chaos of a homogeneous matter" (*HSW*, XIII, 273–274; see Proß 1994).[32] One should also note that in 1805 Oken published his *Die Zeugung* on the primary causes of generation. In his view, the basic constituents of higher vegetable and animal organisms are not inorganic elements but elementary organic units, that is, lower but specific and primordial organisms *(Infusorien)* present from the moment of creation, which constitute the higher (vegetable and animal) living bodies as members of a system ruled by an internal and living organizing principle (Oken 2007, 142).[33]

In the *Encyclopaedia*, Hegel emphatically rejects the presupposition of the *temporal existence* of anything like a "life-in-general" that then divides into plants, animals, and human races, and dismisses such a presupposition as "a representation of the empty force of imagination" (*W*9, §339Z: 349). In the Jena period he had already maintained that

> the concept ... is not the discourse on a general life of nature in the sense that nature is living everywhere;[34] rather it speaks of the essence of life. Nature is to be grasped [*begriffen*] and explained in the moments of its actuality or totality, and these moments have to be shown. (*GW*8, 119.10–13)

Furthermore, Hegel does not claim that the transition from the inorganic to the organic is to be thought of as due to an actual natural capacity *of* the inorganic to evolve or arrange itself into an organic formation,[35] for our philosophical consideration of the chemical product must account precisely for the *loss* from that product of any glimpse of vitality. Moreover, we have seen how, in contrast to organisms, in differentiated chemicals the essential nature of a body does not pass into external existence while at the same time negating its finitude and returning into itself through an infinite, perennial, self-stimulating and self-sustained process (cf. *W*9, §352Z: 436). That is to say, chemicals, unlike organisms, neither *reproduce* themselves through their own activity, nor conserve themselves in a state of functional activity, nor do they have the capacity of adapting themselves to an indefinite number of changing circumstances.

In purely formal terms, the proper logical determination through which to conceive the chemical object in its truth is 'the singular not yet determined as different' (GW12, 149.3–6) that proves itself to be "altogether [*schlechthin*] related to what is other" (W8, §200Z: 357). Chemicals, in other words, are both separate from and essentially related to one another. The crucial point, however, is that in the *Logic* Hegel places the thought-determination "Teleology" (W8, §§204–212) immediately *after* "Chemism" (W8, §§200–203) and before "The Idea of Life" (W8, §§216–222). On my reading of the Addition to §335, this means that chemical matter is understood to be unable to arrange its parts from within according to a self-maintaining internal purposiveness. It also means that the formal character of chemicals is directly subordinated to the next higher logical determination of 'external' finality or purposiveness. In the *Encyclopaedia Logic*, finite purposiveness is defined as "an *externally* posited form in the pre-given material." The achieved end is therefore an object "which is once more a means or a material for other purposes, and so on *ad infinitum*" (W8, §211: 366).

That this suggests a certain 'disposition' of chemical bodies to be subjugated by an alien power (W9, §337: 339) is further clarified in the following paragraph, where Hegel writes that both mechanical and chemical processes take place "under the lord-ship [*Herrschaft*]" of a purpose that simply subsumes and adapts from the outside the material at hand as a means to the end to be achieved, thus overcoming the appearance (*Schein*) that the content of the mechanical or chemical object is independent of the concept that is expressed in the purpose (W8, §212: 366).[36]

By contrast, it is not possible to understand truly *organic* nature in terms of external, finite teleology: life is the immediate union of a subjective, internal purpose with its objective realization. Hence, to be ontologically (and internally) committed to ends and purposes is something that, for us, belongs to the very concept of life (see Burbidge 2007, 118).

5. The Necessary Limits of the Inorganic

The finitude of the chemical process means that, *in concreto*, the relations among the body's sensible properties are unstable: on the one hand, the body's configuration (*Gestalt*) has no *real* unity because of the variation of the reactions it undergoes, due to the change of the reagent, so that even its allegedly most profound and stable determination fails to be preserved and the true individuality of the body does not *exist* in any one of its states.[37] On the other hand, the diversity of the reagents in these reactions entails an affinity between them; the essential nature of the acid and the alkali or base – that is, the fact that they are *related* to one another – is thus already present in that diversity. These two aspects together show that the chemical bond is the mere *possibility* of different affinities and different products, for the chemical reaction between substances is nothing but the action of moments that in themselves remain *different and separated* (Hegel 1959, 350; see Burbidge 2007, 115)[38] and may show different degrees of affinity with other substances. The necessary limit of all inorganic nature – whether

211

mechanical or physical, connected through space or affinity, ruled by efficient causality or external finality (Langthaler 1992, 157–158) – is thus constituted by the structural absence of a bond that purposively realizes the existence of a whole, that is, the absence of an essential (ideal) internal unity that unfolds by connecting its parts as the truly active, actual ground that rules external necessity.[39] Consider the following passages:

> Plants. Leaves, blossoms, roots thus bring the plant into evidence and go back into it; and that which they effect [bewirken] is already present as such a universal, as the singular seed. ... Nature has its means within itself, and the means are also ends. This end in nature is its *logos*, the truly rational.[40]
>
> As its own product, animal life is self-purposive, that is, at the same time both end and means. The end is an ideal determination, which is already previously present, and since the realizing activity which then occurs must conform to the determination present at hand, it brings forth nothing different. The realization is just as much the return-into-itself. (W9, §352Z: 436)
>
> The chemical product does not seem [scheint] to have itself so present at hand – acid and base; in the chemical, a third appears to come forth. But the universal, the essence of these, is their connection (Beziehung) – affinity – and this connection is the product; this connection is present in the product only as a thing, a reified concept [dinglicher Begriff] – as possibility.[41]
>
> The syllogism of the organism is not the syllogism of *external purposiveness*, for it does not stop at directing its activity and form against the external object, but makes an object out of this process itself, which because of its externality, is on the verge of becoming mechanical or chemical. (W9, §365: 482)

Because of the presence of the 'essential' bond (that is chemical affinity), the inorganic in our account verges on the organic, though the individual elements (the acid and the base) remain distinct. Since they are *not* related to the unity of an end, and not animated by any immanent, permanent activity, their product cannot resist the dominion of external purposiveness and being used only as a means. Indeed, their unity falls in a third substance that is not itself a process, but rather the inert thinghood that results from their reaction with one another: this is why in a chemical product we can no longer recognize any trace of proper vitality.[42]

6. The Path to the Free Individuality of Life

To answer our question about why the dialectic of chemical processes makes the existence of life conceptually necessary, we must still clarify how can we equate life with the stage of the 'total *free* individuality.' Indeed, that "Physics" ends with the positing of a total 'free' individuality within its own sphere is a point that still requires elucidation, since even the most recent interpreters have focused on the fact that either *we* look upon or interpret the chemical process *as* a totality or we look upon the dimension of freedom as mere independence from external causes in organic self-production.[43]

At the real level of the concrete formations of nature, the living being is a self-maintaining unity and as such is an end in itself. In chemical transformations, by contrast, what a body *is* is given by the whole cycle of its possible changes and reactions with other bodies. Hegel remarks, however, that in this case the 'totality' of the reactions is present *only* as a sum (*nur als Summe vorhanden*) and not as "infinite return into itself" (*W9*, §336Z: 335), not as concrete totality[44]: iron, for instance, has no single universal character, for it is the circle of the specific reactions that constitutes the universal specificity of particular bodies. Hence in processes like oxidation (or neutralization for salts), the substance 'iron' remains the same matter only conceptually or in itself (*an sich*), "though *not* in the mode of its existence" (ibid.).

In my view, Hegel contends here that in the very real process in which its properties prove to be relative, chemical matter *itself* reveals "the stability" of its point of unity *as a form*. That is to say, to the question of how any chemical substance is identified and posited according to its individual form or essential (ideal) nature through the process in which its finite and unstable properties are shown to be relative, Hegel replies that the immediately present transitoriness of the properties *presupposes something really persistent*, though not present to observation, in relation to which their change can be determined.

To summarize, therefore, Hegel makes the following claims. (1) Through the chemical process, in which all the material properties of the chemical prove to be transitory and relative, something really persists. (2) This something is nothing but the 'point of unity' of the properties or the 'ideal form' of the chemical substance. (3) This persistent 'something' has no permanent *sensible* characteristics, and so it cannot be perceived as a sensuous thing, though its *real* unity can be identified within the chemical process by the knowing subject.

Consider that at the outset of the discussion of "Observing Reason" in the 1807 *Phenomenology* Hegel claims that, in the course of understanding the natural world, reason is driven to contradict its opinion that the content of the empirical sciences is warranted because it is found to be immediately present to observation and to be something opposed to the knowing subject, as a mere 'fact' of experience (*GW9*, 38, 28–30). Hegel's claim proves itself in chemistry, when he treats the case of the scientific identification of chemical elements within compounds. Hegel refers to "purified matters" (*GW9*, 144.25–26) such as oxygen, heat, and positive and negative electricity. These are natural matters that exist for themselves, but their proper chemical nature has been identified only through artificial experimental conditions of production and isolation from compounds.[45] The further *conceptual* issue for Hegel is that they are consciously posited by working scientists in an 'ideal' manner, according to their own true and objective essence. Hegel calls them "non-sensuous things of sense" or "incorporeal and yet objective being" (*GW9*, 144.30–31; Ferrini 2007, 13–14; see Ferrini 2009, 103–105).

Moreover, the way in which he interprets the scientific investigation of such pure conditions of chemical matters shows that this investigation amounts to *liberating* consciousness from the external necessity of deriving truth solely from existing sensuousness (Ferrini 2007, 14–15). The point returns in the introductory paragraphs of the *Encyclopaedia*: the *form* in which the variety of the empirical content is offered to the experiential sciences is said to be the form of immediacy, of something simply found, of a manifold of juxtaposed shapes altogether contingent, while at the same time they carry with them the stimulus to overcome (*besiegen*) such form and to elevate *(zu erheben)* that content to the necessity of the concept (*W8*, §12: 56).[46]

213

In the 1821/1822 *Lectures on the Philosophy of Nature* Hegel states that in the chemical process, "the activity is not the activity of the one [*des Eins*] itself," so that an alien power (*eine fremde Macht*) can master the chemical product (Hegel 2002, 167). Correspondingly, in the 1830 *Encyclopaedia Logic*, he makes clear that, from the standpoint of our practical use of nature and finite purposiveness, any alleged material 'independence' of the chemical object, as the real that stands over against the ideal, as the negative of the concept, has already evaporated in the chemical process itself:

> since the accomplished purpose is determined *only* as means and material, this object is already posited at once as something that is in-itself null and only ideal. (W8, §212: 366)

Right at the outset of the new sphere of "Organic Physics" Hegel links the actual human use of the chemical product according to external purposes (and the consequent *positing* of the mere ideality of it) to the idea (set out in the *Phenomenology*) that the objective 'ideality' of the purified matters represents liberation from sensuousness, and also to the stimulus to overcome the immediacy, manifoldness, and contingency of the empirical content by elevating it to the internal necessity of the concept. Indeed, the two lines converge in the concept of the individuality of the body itself that has been *freed* from its material existence, from its "prose" (W9, §336Z: 334). Introducing the new sphere of organics, Hegel claims that it represents an elevation to the "poetry" of nature (ibid.), because the parts no longer lack their "spiritual bond" (W8, §38Z: 110).[47] Hegel writes: "as the ideality we have had in the chemical process is *posited* [*gesetzt*] here, the individuality is *posited* [*gesetzt*] in its freedom" (W9, §337Z: 339, emphasis added). The chemical process points forward logically to life, therefore, because the *material finitude* of the particularized body, what its natural being '*is*,' fails to endure in that process, as we have shown in Sections 3–5.

In this respect the transition to "Organic Physics" should not be understood as produced merely by *our* reflective assessment of chemical phenomena that considers them as a totality. What has been shown through the *dialectic* of chemical reality is that the thought of the 'object' as what is 'independent from the subject' and stands over against the concept proves without remainder to have been a semblance (*Schein*), because the independent material subsistence of the properties of chemical phenomena turns out to be "*in itself null*" (emphasis added), that is, not illusory but completely limited, finite, and transitory, even as regards what is allegedly their most profound sensible characteristic:

> In the chemical process, the body changes itself not superficially, but on all sides: every property is lost, cohesion, colour, lustre, opacity, sound, transparency. Even specific gravity, which seems the deepest and simplest determination, does not hold out. ... Brittleness, solidity, smell and taste also disappear; it is this ideality of the particular [*des Besonderen*] that is here expounded. (W9, §336Z: 334–335)
>
> Now, however, while the chemical process just exposes the dialectic through which all the specific properties of bodies are thrown into transience ... what alone persists is the infinite form that exists for itself [*die für sich seiende unendliche Form*], the pure incorporeal individuality which is for itself, and for which material subsistence is utterly a variable. (W9, §336Z: 336)

7.   Conclusion

To recapitulate: (1) In chemical processes, chemical objects acquire their properties, but in turn they reveal the transience of all of their alleged 'fundamental' material characteristics. (2) The demise (*Untergang*) of the chemical body's particular material configurations – which nevertheless exhibits the nature of the chemical substance itself – shows, at the same time and through the whole set of processes, the persistence of the ideal side of that specific finitude: what is stable in the individuality of chemicals such as 'iron' is nothing but the point of unity of their properties. (3) The conceptual point at issue for Hegel is that *for thought* the acquired material properties cease to define the substance of the chemical. The chemical substance comes to be identified as 'point of unity,' and its properties 'conceived' as momentary appearances, reintegrated into the essential unity of a persistent coordination of the parts (the bond or connection: *Beziehung*). (4) The transition from the inorganic to the organic realm is not a natural transition occurring at the immediate level of existence: chemicals do not of their own accord give rise to life. The third feature of the thought of chemical matter just mentioned points forward *logically* to life, in which this 'point of unity' is an *explicit* and manifest feature of the purposive process through which a natural object unfolds itself as a self-maintaining individuality. (5) This internal purpose is nothing but the *life* of corporeal individuality, which, governing its differentiation into 'members' that are not merely 'parts,' is 'conceived' as immediately active and therefore as achieving immediate existence through a *double* move: on the one hand, nature "reaches the being-there [*Dasein*] of the concept" (W9, §336Z: 336), on the other hand, the infinite form – the concept – achieves the reality of matter. (6) This implies that an *elevation* (*eine* Erhebung) from sensuousness, negation, and mediation is *the truth* of mechanical, merely spatial continuity and the physical, external connection of real, material, sensible existence (W8, §12: 56).[48] (7) In immediate nature, life is what Hegel calls "the soul [*Seele*] of the individuality" (W9, §336: 336) or "spiritual bond" as an immediate, undivided, unitary existence, that is, a kind of objectivity in which the internal necessity of the form is purposively self-determining. (8) Life is therefore *causa sui* (*Vorl.*17, 169.5–6), Spinoza's 'adequate' concept, that which reproduces itself originating from itself.[49]

In this way Hegel's philosophy of nature passes over to the rational thought of a different kind of natural object, organic life, in which different elements (e.g., bud, blossom, and fruit) are not understood as mutually exclusive determinations, but truly 'comprehended' as what Hegel calls "vanishing" differences, because they *really* are reciprocally necessary moments of the organic phenomenon of a plant (Harris 1983, 444; Ferrini 2009, 105)[50]. With the transition from inorganic to organic nature, the "real totality of the body" is the negative processual unity of individuality (the whole that determines itself through differentiation and negation of the apparent independence and mutual externality of its parts) raised to "the *first* ideality of nature" (W9, §337: 337; emphasis added). In 1825/1826, Hegel emphasizes this determinate negative or dialectical moment, calling it the "inward source [*Quellpunkt*] of the transition" (*Vorl.*17, 168.60–61). Moreover, with this double-sided move Hegel achieves the task sketched in §12 of the *Encyclopaedia*: philosophy gives to the concrete and determinate, but also immediate and contingent, content of the experiential sciences (the a posteriori) "the most essential shape [*Gestalt*] of the *freedom* of thinking (or: of what is a priori) as well as the *validation* [*Bewährung*] of *necessity*" (W8, §12: 58). What has been achieved is not merely the abstract idea of life to which scientific thought can rise through its tools, observation, and description of phenomena and conditions (Cuvier 1829, 79), since it is the *Idea itself* that has come to life.[51]

Notes

1   Research on this chapter was made possible by the financial support of the 2009 University of Trieste Research Funds (FRA), which allowed me to pursue extensive studies at the British Library and the Berlin Staatsbibliothek. All translations, both from primary and secondary sources, are my own with the exception of Hegel 1980.

2   It should be noted that here Hegel uses the term 'universal' not in the traditional formalistic logical sense of 'common to all,' but in his own rational, speculative sense of the proper immanent, innermost persistent substance of things. So the genus (*Gattung*) constitutes the specific essentiality, the 'universal form' of an individual animal: "If we were to deprive a dog of being-an-animal [*das Tiersein*] we could not say what it is. Things in general [*überhaupt*] have a persisting, inner nature, and an external otherness ... their essentiality, their universality [*Allgemenheit*], is the kind, and this cannot be grasped simply as something that is in common" (W8, §24Z[1]: 82).

3   For instance, chemistry is 'comprehended' to be (a) the last extreme of the syllogism of shape (*Gestalt*) which has as its first term only the abstract activity of magnetism (the mere concept of the totality of form: the moment of universality), then (b) the middle term of electricity (the moment of particularity), split into the two 'moments' of the particularization of the *Gestalt* within itself (positive electricity) and of the opposition to its other (negative electricity), and finally (c) the concrete reality (the singularity) of the self-realizing dynamic of the chemical process (W9, §326Z: 288).

4   See Haldane and Haldane 1883, 56: "It would thus appear that the parts of an organism cannot be considered simply as so many independent units, which happen to be aggregated in a system in which each determines the other. It is on the contrary *the essential feature of each part that it is a member of an ideal whole*, which can only be defined by saying that it realises itself in its parts, and that the parts are only what they are in so far as they realise it. In fine the relations of life are not capable of reduction to the relations of mechanism" (emphasis added).

5   Compare Hegel's definition of the organic in 1805–1806: "the organic is the self, the force, the unity of its own self and its negative. Only as this unity has it force upon that one, and the connection makes *actual* what is *in itself* [*an sich*]" (GW8, 109.21–24).

6   This systematic subdivision already appears in the 1812/1813 *Encyclopaedia*; see *Vorl*.15, 105.21–28 and 232.

7   As early as 1801 Hegel 'conceived' "nature through reason," which means to 'conceive' it in terms of truth, inwardness, immanence, and necessity, according to the principle of identity that posits difference within itself. From this speculative standpoint he criticized the Kantian metaphysical foundation of the law of inertia that understands its object as an inert matter always moved by an external impulse, i.e., by a force impressed from without which is alien to matter itself (see Hegel 1801, 22.26–23.3 and Kant, AA IV, 543–545).

8   Note that Schelling (SSW 1, 388; see Beiser 2002, 484; Schelling 1992, 124–125, see Freiberger 1997, 147–148) draws no distinction between living and nonliving "organization" in nature: since in the whole of organic nature intelligence must intuit itself as active,

every stage of nature must possess 'life,' i.e., "an inner principle of motion within itself." See Moiso (1986) for a detailed account of the relation between individuality and quality in Schelling's and Hegel's approaches to physics and chemistry.

9   Cf. also *Vorl*.15, 107.22–29 and pp. 232–233; Hegel 2000, 136, and *W*9, §275Z:112ff.

10   See *W*1, 382–383 for the spiritual and religious (John 12:36) significance of the identity of light and life.

11   See Petry's note to 137,5 Hegel 1970b II, 353–354, and note to 139,20 Hegel 1970b II, 355–356.

12   See Falkenburg 1993, 539: "light is not only present in luminous matter, but also spreads throughout space. ... Hegel's abstract notion of light, rather than bringing out this distinction, tends to unify the two aspects."

13   In the 1823/1824 philosophy of nature, Hegel remarks that "blue and green," because diverse, seem to exist independently of one another, but at the same time they cannot be divided, as can acid and base: each of them possesses not just its own being, but, at the same time, also the being of the other (Hegel 2000, 90).

14   See Falkenburg 1993, 539: "Since light is identified with luminous matter, it is *embodied in the sun*."

15   On the (quadruple) "essential syllogism of the solar system," see Filion 2007, 194–198. In the Addition to section 353, Hegel draws a parallel between the "syllogism of the solar system" and the moments of the animal's conformation: sensibility, irritability, and reproduction (*W*9, 438).

16   Burbidge warns the English reader to distinguish between *Individuum* and *Das Einzelne*, often translated with "individual," for: "*Das Einzelne* is a logical term for the singular object of reference and stands in relation to concepts, both universal and particular" (Burbidge 1996, 109). On the difference between the "real individual" of the "Physics" (which exhibits the being-in-itself of a natural individuality) and the living individual of the "Organics" (which exhibits itself as life in the form of singularity, *Einzelheit*), see De Vos 2006, 274.

17   Renault 2002, 128–135 has shown how Hegel supports the autonomy of chemistry against the attempts to integrate it into a physics of molecular attraction (Berthollet) or into a general theory of the dynamical process (Schelling), when he conceives chemistry as the synthesis of magnetism and electricity and as the "moment of totality," thus rejecting any natural transition among the stages of the section "Physics." Engelhardt has pointed out how Georg Friedrich Pohl (1788–1849), who taught mathematics and physics, shared with Hegel this general interpretation of magnetism, electricity, and chemism as different forms of divided and conjoined activities (Engelhardt 1976, 122–123).

18   See Houlgate 2005, 163–164.

19   As Filion 2007, 314 puts it: "The spatial separation still maintains its rights" in the chemical process.

20   Cf. *W*9, §281Z, 135: when the individual under consideration is something neutral, as a salt, then chemistry is successful: "it manages for itself to exhibit the sides themselves, since the unity of the difference is only a formal unity, which collapses on its own." But when the chemical decomposition regards something organic, "then it sublates not only the unity, but also what one wants to know": the organism.

21   See *Vorl*.8, 76,53–54: "this that we call end [*Zweck*], *telos*, is the *energheia*, efficacy [*Wirksamkeit*], Aristotle's *entelechia*." Cf. *Phys*. II 8; see Ilting 1987, 354–356. For an account of Hegel's appropriation of Aristotle's notion of constitutive inner finality (*Selbstzweck*) as the true concept of 'life' and his divergence from Kant's regulative assessment of it, see Frigo 2004.

22   *W*9, §335: 333: *eines anfänglichen Selbstbestimmens des Begriffs aus sich in seiner Realisation*. Hegel's original does not seem adequately rendered in the standard English translations. Cf.

Hegel 1970a, 269: "There is a rudimentary self-determination of the Notion from its own resources in its realization"; and Hegel 1970b, II 219: "In this realization of itself the Notion displays the beginnings of a spontaneous self-determination."

23 Note that in the course of the exchange of letters on chemical matters between H. Döbling and Goethe (December 7, 1812), Döbling sent to the latter Prof. Döbereiner's 1811–1812 report about his research on inflammable bodies and kinds of combustion, where the author criticized Lavoisier's approach and endorsed the electrochemism of Goethe, Winterl, Ritter, and Davy. Interestingly enough, Döbereiner wrote that on his view those *Feuererscheinungen* could be neither the results of a simple mutual compenetration of dead matters nor a mere change of the state of matter; rather, they made apparent the presence of something of *spiritual nature, wholly active and conditioning the becoming of matter* (original text reprinted in Renault 2002, 45).

24 According to Filion 2007, 313, the "defect" of inorganic nature consists in the impossibility of assembling and coordinating the chemical process into one unity.

25 W9, §335Z: 333: *verlorengeht*. Miller renders this term as 'destroyed' (Hegel 1970a, 269).

26 See Burbidge 1996, 185: "The transition here is not one that happens in nature. Hegel stresses that chemical processes on their own do not convert into organic ones; they continue to be finite and discrete." On the basis of the text of the Remark to §335 (the Addition to §335 is disregarded), Filion 2007, 315, advances the possibility of a "radical ontological argument, where there are the natural phenomena themselves which can teach the working scientist." The evidence for this move appears clearly once the working scientists dismiss their prejudices and "open themselves to reality, as it produces itself in nature." For a 'naturalistic' reading that views the "internal motor of the concept," i.e., the principle of determinate negation, as grounded in the description of life and derived "directly from what nature does," see also Hahn 2007, 26–33.

27 This is in the same vein, for instance, as Lloyd Morgan's and Samuel Alexander's later theory of the "emergence" of life, which was criticized by Haldane (Haldane 1931, 38–39).

28 See Hahn's account: "Organics first operates at the immediate level of unconscious nature, accepts its basic structure, and then exposes its contradictions on its own terms ... by making explicit in human awareness nature's affinity for human reason from a standpoint already immanent in nature" (Hahn 2007, 33–34).

29 In Ferrini 2009, note 37, 120, I show that from the time of his writing of the *Phenomenology*, Hegel referred to J. J. Winterl's 1804 *Darstellung der vier Bestandtheile der anorganischen Natur.* Winterl sets up the empirical problem constituted by the proper definition of what is an acid and what is a base for the host of distinguishing marks that come together. He concludes that those marks may give a likely indication of this or that nature of bodies, but do not provide anything determinate, for there is a border line beyond which the acidic or basic characters disappear in the same body. Cf. Burbidge 1996, 189.

30 On the thought of life as the thought of being in its contradictions in Hegel, as the factor of circulation and fluidity of the system, and in comparison to Schelling's view of contradiction as the "poison" of life, see Bensussan 2007. Note that by exhibiting the degrees (*Stufen*) of concrete natural existences as totalities Hegel distinguishes the systematic philosophical consideration of nature from the merely empirical one. The latter provides only the degrees of the determinations (W9, §326Z:290).

31 Cf. the parallel passage in W9, §343Z, 372: Hegel makes clear that the concept of life, that is, life *an sich*, is everywhere, though this is *not* the case with the real life, "the subjectivity of the living being," in which each part *exists* as endowed with life.

32 In the Addition to §339, Hegel seems to refer to positions such as that of Herder when he remarks: "in general one expounds the production of the living as a revolution out of chaos, where vegetable and animal life, organic and inorganic had been in *one* unity." (In his note

to 23,8, Hegel 1970b III, 229, Petry sees here a reference to Caspar Wolff's *Theoria generationis*.)

33 Poggi recalls the criticism leveled in 1838 by C. G. Ehrenberg's *Die Infusionsthierchen als vollkommene* (sic) *Organismen* (Leipzig: Voss) against the alleged simple structure of the *Infusorien*, which supported creationism (Poggi 2000, note 35, 536).

34 Note that in the second half of the seventeenth century, French naturalists were committed to the "law of uniformity" between inorganic and organic nature. For instance, Robinet had spoken of a *suc*, a solution of minerals and salts in ground water, as the universal fluid that caused transportation, deposit, alluvial beds, evaporation, etc. (Robinet 1761, Ch. XIV:286–290), as well as of the "generation" of stones from stones and from metals to metals (in this regard in perfect analogy with plant and animal reproduction) in terms of "development of intussusceptions," thus claiming the existence of *germes fossiles* (Robinet 1761, Ch. XIV:290–291). Hegel owned a copy of Robinet's work (Neuser 1987, entry 183, 492).

35 As Pinkard 2002, 271, puts it, summarizing the tenets of §249 and the Zusatz: "Hegel did not think that a proper *Naturphilosophie* ... would show how 'mechanical' systems evolve into or produce non-mechanical, organic systems by virtue of some metaphysical force or vitalist principle pushing nature forward, nor did he think that it would be at all instructive to see all the natural forms as evolving from others or emanating out of some set of Platonic Ideas."

36 See W6, 444–445: "Thus, the mechanical or chemical technique, through its character of being externally determined, on its own presents itself to the end relation." For a thorough analysis of this sentence, which examines the logical significance of the use of the term *Technik* for the *concepts* of 'mechanism' and of 'chemism,' focusing on their transition to teleology, cf. Sell 2006b.

37 Cf. Davy 1840, 69–70: "it is a general character of chemical combination, that it changes the sensible qualities of bodies. ... Bodies possessed of little taste or smell often gain these qualities in a high degree by combinations. ... The forms of bodies, or their densities, likewise usually alter; solids become fluids, and solids and fluid gases, and gases are often converted into fluids or solids."

38 According to Marmasse 2008, 290–291, on Hegel's view the return into itself that distinguishes the autonomy of the organism in respect to the chemical product and its inner finality is to be conceived on the basis of "the sole resources of nature." The self-mediation is "perfectly authorized by the principles of the systematic progression of nature" and "does not require a spiritual activity."

39 The authoritative entry "Vie" (Life) by M.G.L. Duvernoy in Vol. 58 of the *Dictionnaire des sciences naturelles* (1829), edited by Frédéric Cuvier, espoused the view that the binding activity of "forces," which combine the atoms of the living bodies, and make their molecules close and keep them united, is of a nature utterly different from the work of chemical affinities: "celles-ci font entrer les molécules organiques dans de nouvelle combinaisons, *après les avoir décomposées dans leurs élémens, dès que ces molécules ne sont plus soumises à l'action de la vie*" (Frédéric Cuvier 1829, 80–81, emphasis added).

40 Hegel 1959, 349. A similar passage is found in GW8, 110.1–4.

41 Hegel 1959, 345–346. See Frigo 2004, 27–28.

42 In his 1799 *Erster Entwurf*, Schelling offered an alternative way to cognize finite products: starting from his primary view of nature as *natura naturans*, i.e., as absolute activity, they were regarded as *Scheinprodukte* and *Hemmungen*, namely, apparent products and obstacles to the display of its ceaseless operational activity, which could be adequately grasped only through the notion of "infinite product" (SSW 3, 15). On Schelling's concept of nature as universal organism and on his theory of life, see Beiser 2002, 515–523 and 538–544.

43 In the chemical process taken as a systematic whole, Houlgate sees the reason why life is "made logically necessary (in Hegel's distinctive sense of 'logical necessity') by chemistry" (Houlgate 2005, 164). This reading draws from Burbidge 1996, 186: "this transition in the philosophy of nature is, then, the product of a reflective assessment of chemical phenomena that considers them as a totality." Burbidge 2007, 115, writes that although in chemical process we have not reached the full concept of 'life,' when we look at all chemical processes as a totality "we reach something that does resemble" the concept of organism discussed in the *Logic.*

44 According to Filion 2007, 313, the "defect" of inorganic nature consists in the impossibility of assembling and coordinating the chemical process into one unity. On Burbidge's view, to individuate the set of chemical processes as a whole and to think about their unity both belong to the way 'nature is understood to be'; this feature marks the move to organic nature (Burbidge 1996, 186).

45 Humphry Davy, in the "Historical View" that introduces his 1812 *Elements of Chemical Philosophy,* recalls that it was Pierre Bayen, in 1774, who showed that mercury converted into a calx or earth, by the absorption of air, and could be revived without the (external) addition of any peculiar principle of inflammability (i.e., Stahl's phlogiston, which was supported by Cavendish, Kirwan, and Priestley; see Davy 1840, 28). After Priestley's 'phlogistic' determination of the chemical nature of the air produced from metallic calxes ('phlosisticated air'), Lavoisier showed instead in 1775 that Priestley had isolated one part of the air, a gas, that supports flame and respiration (which he afterward named oxygen), and another part that does not ('azote': "no life," renamed 'nitrogen' in 1790); and Lavoisier thus passed from the imaginary existence of a peculiar principle and of its external intervention to an 'immanent' account of the chemical process and activity of combustion.

46 Hegel 1959, 350, quotes Aristotle's view that the end is a higher principle than matter, and comments that indeed the end is the true ground, i.e., what moves, and by no means does it deal with (external) necessity, though it is able to restrain external necessity in its own power: "it does not let it go freely for itself, hinders external necessity." In the parallel passage in the *Lectures on the History of Philosophy,* edited by Garniron and Jaeschke, in place of the last phrase in the Glockner edition (*es,* i.e., *das Bewegende,* what moves, *die äussere Nothwendigkeit hemmt*), we find a stronger statement of the powerful autonomy of purposive self-determination that rules external necessity: *sondern es selbst regiert* (*Vorl.*8, 78.192).

47 In the *Philosophy of Nature* of 1805–1806, though Hegel treats "the universal life of Earth" within the sphere of "Physics," he already holds the view that chemistry (as well as mechanics) is subordinated to life, to the extent that the conceptual bond among parts rises from the lower level of external purpose and thinghood to the higher one of internal finality and spirituality (*GW*8, 110, 10–14). See also the Addition to §348: "Observation slips out of the rough hands of chemistry that kills the living and arrives to see only that which is dead, not what is alive" (*W*9, 420).

48 Hegel refers to Goethe's *Faust* and uses a restatement of poetic intuition in the philosophy of nature to make intelligible the same unity of the individual necessitated by the concept. In doing so, he avoids the pitfalls of romanticism, for he places poetic intuition under the power of thought (cf. also *GW*5, 372.12–373.7); in a passage in the Addition to §365, Hegel points to a reappraisal of what implicitly conforms and corresponds to rational speculation in terms of a "rational instinct" that answers the call of the more powerful concept (*W*9, 483).

49 See Cuvier 1800, 7: "La vie ne naît que de la vie."

50 See the following 1826–1827 passage of Hegel's *Lectures on the Philosophy of World History:* "The nature of the substance remains concealed from the senses, just as the hand cannot perceive the nature of colour; and the understanding, which comprehends the finite world,

cannot perceive it either. The motley confusion of all the shapes and phenomena of existence contains the truth within itself, and it is the eye of the concept which penetrates the exterior and recognises the truth. And it is philosophy which purges the understanding of such subjective conceits" (Hegel 1980, 210).

51   *W9*, §337: 337. On the relation between *ousia* and *tode ti*, cf. Aristotle, *Cat.* 5, 3b10.

References

Abbreviations

AA: *Kants Werke.* Akademie-Ausgabe. Berlin: Walter de Gruyter, 1968.

AA IV: *Metaphysische Anfansgründe der Naturwissenschaften* (1786), 465–566.

GW: Hegel, G.W.F. *Gesammelte Werke.* In Verbindung mit der Hegel-Kommission der Rheinisch-Westfälischen Akademie der Wissenschaften und dem Hegel-Archiv der Ruhr-Universität Bochum. Hamburg: Meiner, 1968.

GW5:   *Schriften und Entwürfe (1799–1808).* Ed. Manfred Baum and Kurt Rainer Meist, with the assistance of Theodor Ebert, 1998.

GW8:   *Jenaer Systementwürfe III (1805/1806).* Ed. Rolf-Peter Horstmann, 1976.

GW9:   *Phänomenologie des Geistes (1807).* Ed. Wolfgang Bonsipien and Reinhard Heede, 1980.

GW12:   *Wissenschaft der Logik. II: Die Subjective Logik (1816).* Ed. Friedrich Hogemann and Walter Jaeschke, 1981.

HSW: Herder, Johann Gottfried. *Sämtliche Werke.* Ed. Bernhard Suphan. Hildesheim: Georg Olms Verlag, 1967 (reprinted in 1981).

XIII: *Ideen zur Philosophie der Geschichte der Menschheit.* Part I, 1784; Part II, 1785.

SSW: Schelling, F.W.J. *Sämtliche Werke.* Ed. K.F.A. Schelling. Stuttgart: Cotta, 1856–1861.

SSW 1:   1792–1797, 1856.

SSW 3:   1799–1800, 1858.

Vorl.:   G.W.F. Hegel. *Vorlesungen.* Ausgewählte Nachschriften und Manuskripte. Hamburg: Meiner.

Vorl.8:   *Vorlesungen über die Geschichte der Philosophie 3. Griechische Philosophie* II. Plato bis Proklos. Ed. Pierre Garniron, and Walter Jaeschke, 1996

Vorl.15: *Philosophische Enzyklopädie.* Nürnberg 1812/1813. Nachschriften von Christian Samuel Meinel, Julius Friedrich Heinrich Abegg. Ed. Udo Rameil, 2002

Vorl.16: *Vorlesungen über die Philosophie der Natur.* Berlin 1819/1820. Nachgeschrieben von Johann Rudolf Ringier. Ed. Martin Bondeli, Hoo Nam Seelmann, 2002.

Vorl.17: *Vorlesungen über die Philosophie der Natur.* Berlin 1825/1826. Nachgeschrieben von Heinrich Wilhelm Dove. Ed. Karol Bal, Gilles Marmasse, Thomas Posch, and Karl Vieweg, 2007.

W: Hegel, G.W.F. *Werke in zwanzig Bänden.* Ed. Eva Moldenhauer and Karl M. Michel. Frankfurt am Main: Suhrkamp Verlag, 1970.

W1:   *Frühe Schriften.*

W5:   *Wissenschaft der Logik I.*

W6:   *Wissenschaft der Logik II.*

W8:   *Enzyklopädie der philosophischen Wissenschaften im Grundrisse (1830) I. Mit den mündlichen Zusätzen.*

W9:   *Enzyklopädie der philosophischen Wissenschaften im Grundrisse (1830) II. Mit den mündlichen Zusätzen.*

Works Cited

Beiser, Frederick. *German Idealism: The Struggle against Subjectivism, 1781–1801*. Cambridge, Mass. and London: Harvard University Press, 2002.

Bensussan, Gérard. "La vie comme contradiction: De Hegel à Schelling." In *Hegel-Jahrbuch* 2007: *Das Leben denken, Zweiter Teil*, ed. Andreas Arndt, Paul Cruysberghs, and Andrzej Przylebski in cooperation with Frank Fischbach. Berlin: Akademie Verlag, 2007.

Burbidge, John W. *Real Process: How Logic and Chemistry Combine in Hegel's Philosophy of Nature*. Toronto: University of Toronto Press, 1996.

Burbidge, John W. *Hegel's Systematic Contingency*. Houndmills, Basingstoke, U.K.: Palgrave Macmillan, 2007.

Burbidge, John W. *Historical Dictionary of Hegelian Philosophy*. 2nd edition. Lanham, Md.: Scarecrow Press, 2008.

Cuvier, Frédéric. *Dictionnaire des sciences naturelles, dans lequel on traite méthodiquement des differens êtres de la nature ... suivi d'une biographie des plus célèbres naturalistes/ par plusieurs professeurs du Museum national d'histoire naturelle et des autres principales écoles de Paris* (1816–1830). Vol. 58, Vert-Vy. Ed. Frédéric Cuvier. Strasbourg and Paris: F. G. Levrault, 1829.

Cuvier, Georges. *Leçons d'anatomie comparée*. Vol. 1. Recuillies et publ. sous ses yeux par C. Duméeril. Paris: Beaudoin [An VIII], 1800.

Davy, Humphry. Elements of Chemical Philosophy as Regards the Laws of Chemical Changes (1812). In *The Collected Works of Sir Humphry Davy*, Vol. 4, ed. John Davy. London: Smith, Elder. Cornhill, 1840.

De Vos, Lu. "Individuum." In *Hegel-Lexicon*, ed. Paul Cobben, Paul Cruysberghs, Peter Jonkers, and Lu De Vos. Darmstadt: Wissenschaftliche Buchgesellschaft, 2006.

Engelhardt, Dietrich von. *Hegel und die Chemie: Studie zur Philosophie und Wissenschaft der Natur um 1800*. Wiesbaden: Guido Pressler Verlag, 1976.

Falkenburg, Brigitte. "Hegel on Mechanistic Models of Light." In *Hegel and Newtonianism*, ed. Michael J. Petry. Dordrecht: Kluwer, 1993.

Ferrini, Cinzia. *Guida al* De orbitis planetarum *di Hegel ed alle sue edizioni e traduzioni*. With the collaboration of Mauro Nasti De Vincentis. Bern, Stuttgart, and Wien: Haupt Verlag, 1995.

Ferrini, Cinzia. "Framing Hypotheses: Numbers in Nature and the Logic of Measure in the Development of Hegel's System." In *Hegel and the Philosophy of Nature*, ed. Stephen Houlgate. Albany: State University of New York Press, 1998.

Ferrini, Cinzia. "Being and Truth in Hegel's Philosophy of Nature." *Hegel Studien* 37 (2002): 69–90.

Ferrini, Cinzia. "On Hegel's Confrontation with the Sciences in 'Observing Reason': Notes for a Discussion." *Bulletin of the Hegel Society of Great Britain* 55/56 (2007): 1–22.

Ferrini, Cinzia. "Reason Observing Nature." In *The Blackwell Guide to Hegel's* Phenomenology of Spirit, ed. Kenneth R. Westphal. Oxford: Wiley-Blackwell, 2009.

Filion, Jean-François. *Dialectique et matière: La conceptualité inconsciente des processus inorganiques dans la philosophie de la nature (1830) de Hegel*. Lévis: Les Presses de l'Université Laval, 2007.

Freiberger, Erich D. "The Genesis of Hegel's Concept of Life: A Translation of the 1803 and 1805 Jena Lectures on the Organic with an Historical Introduction and Commentary." Ph.D dissertation. Boston College, 1997.

Frigo, Gian Franco. "Aristoteles' Einfluss auf Hegels Naturphilosophie." In *Logik, Mathematik und Natur im objektiven Idealismus: Festschrift für Dieter Wandschneider*, ed. Vittorio Hösle and Wolfgang Neuser. Würzburg: Königshausen & Neumann, 2004.

Hahn, Songsuk Susan. *Contradiction in Motion*. Ithaca, N.Y., and London: Cornell University Press, 2007.

Haldane, J. S. *The Philosophical Basis of Biology (The Donnellan Lectures, University of Dublin, 1930)*. London: Hodder & Stoughton, 1931.

Haldane, J. S., and Haldane, R. B. "The Relation of Philosophy to Science." In *Essays in Philosophical Criticism*, ed. Andrew Seth and R. B. Haldane, with a Preface by Edward Caird. London, Longmans, Greens, 1883.

Harris, H. S. *Hegel's Development: Night Thoughts (Jena 1801–1806)*. Oxford: Clarendon Press, 1983.

Hegel, G.W.F. *Dissertatio philosophica de orbitis planetarum*. Jena: Prager, 1801.

Hegel, G.W.F. Vorlesungen über die Geschichte der Philosophie. In *Sämtliche Werke*. Jubiläumsausgabe in zwanzig Bänden. Vol. 18.II, ed. Hermann Glockner. Stuttgart: Frommann, 1959.

Hegel, G.W.F. *Philosophy of Nature* (1830). Trans. A. V. Miller. Oxford: Clarendon Press, 1970a.

Hegel, G.W.F. *Philosophy of Nature*. 3 Vols. Trans. Michael J. Petry. London/ New York: Allen & Unwin/Humanities Press, 1970b.

Hegel, G.W.F. *Lectures on the Philosophy of World History*. "Introduction." Trans. H. B. Nisbet. Cambrdige: Cambridge University Press, 1980.

Hegel, G.W.F. *Vorlesung über Naturphilosophie Berlin 1823/24* (Nachschrift von K.G.J. von Griesheim). Ed. Gilles Marmasse. Frankfurt am Main: Peter Lang, 2000.

Hegel, G.W.F. *Vorlesung über Naturphilosophie Berlin 1821/22* (Nachschrift von Boris von Uexküll). Ed. Gilles Marmasse and Thomas Posch. Frankfurt am Main: Peter Lang, 2002.

Houlgate, Stephen. *An Introduction to Hegel: Freedom, Truth and History*. Oxford: Blackwell, 2005.

Ilting, Karl.-Heinz. "Hegels Philosophie des Organischen." In *Hegel und die Naturwissenschaften*, ed. Michael J. Petry. Stuttgart-Bad Cannstatt: Frommann-Holzboog, 1987.

Langthaler, Rudolf. *Organismus und Umwelt: die biologische Umweltlehre im Spiegel traditioneller Naturphilosophie*. Hildesheim: Georg Olms Verlag, 1992.

Marmasse, Gilles. *Penser le réel. Hegel, la nature et l'esprit*. Paris, Kimé, 2008.

Moiso, Francesco. "Die Hegelsche Theorie der Physik und der Chemie in ihrer Beziehung zu Schellings Naturphilosophie." In *Hegels Philosophie der Natur*, ed. Rolf-Peter Horstmann and Michael J. Petry. Stuttgart: Klett-Cotta, 1986.

Morselli, Mario. *Amedeo Avogadro: A Scientific Biography*. Dordrecht: Reidel, 1984.

Neuser, Wolfgang. "Die naturphilosophische und naturwissenschaftliche Literatur aus Hegels privater Bibliothek." In *Hegel und die Naturwissenschaften*, ed. Michael. J. Petry. Stuttgart-Bad Cannstatt: Frommann-Holzboog, 1987.

Oken, Lorenz. *Die Zeugung* (1805). In Lorenz Oken, *Gesammelte Werke*, Vol. 1. Frühe Schriften zur Naturphilosophie, ed. Thomas Bach, Olaf Breidbach, and Dietrich von Engelhardt. Weimar: Verlag Hermann Böhlaus Nachfolger, 2007.

Pinkard, Terry. *German Philosophy 1760–1860: The Legacy of Idealism*. Cambridge: Cambridge University Press, 2002.

Poggi, Stefano. *Il genio e l'unità della natura. La scienza della Germania romantica (1790–1830)*. Bologna: Il Mulino, 2000.

Proß, Wolfgang. "Herders Konzept der organischen Kräfte und die Wirkung der Ideen zur Philosophie der Geschichte der Menschheit auf Carl Friedrich Kielmeyer." In *Philosophie des Organischen in der Goethezeit. Studien zu Werk und Wirkung des Naturforschers Carl Friedrich Kielmeyer (1765–1844)*, ed. Kai Torsten Kanz. Stuttgart: Steiner, 1994.

Renault, Emmanuel. *Philosophie chimique. Hegel et la science dynamiste de son temps*. Pessac: Presses Universitaires de Bordeaux, 2002.

Robinet, Jean B. R. *De la Nature*. Amsterdam: E. van Harrevelt, 1761.

Rühling, Frank. "Anorganische Natur als Subjekt: Zum Problem des geologischen Organismus in Hegels Jenaer Naturphilosophie." In *Hegels Jenaer Naturphilosophie*, ed. Klaus Vieweg. München: Fink Verlag, 1998.

Schelling, F.W.J. *Das System des trascendentalen Idealismus*. Hamburg: Felix Meiner, 1992.

223

Sell, Annette. "Leben." In *Hegel-Lexicon*, ed. Paul Cobben, Paul Cruysberghs, Peter Jonkers, and Lu De Vos. Darmstadt: Wissenschaftliche Buchgesellschaft, 2006a.

Sell, Annette. "La technique mécanique ou chimique dans la *Science de la logique*." In *Logique et sciences concrètes (Nature et Esprit) dans le système hégélien*, ed. Jean-Michel Buée, Emmanuel Renault, and David Wittmann. Paris: L'Harmattan, 2006b.

Verra, Valerio. "Storia e seconda natura in Hegel." In *Su Hegel*, ed. Claudio Cesa. Bologna: Il Mulino, 2007.

Part V

Philosophy of Subjective Spirit

10

Hegel's Solution to the Mind-Body Problem

RICHARD DIEN WINFIELD

The Traditional Dilemma

The subjectivity of mind has always posed a challenge for theorists. At every level, what mind is reflects how it relates to itself, whether as a psyche that is what it feels itself to be, a conscious subject treating its own mental content as the appearance of a world it confronts, or an intelligence that intuits, represents, or thinks by relating to its determinations as both mental and objective. The reflexive self-activity pervading mental life has always eluded those who confine themselves to categories of being and of essence, where terms are determined, respectively, through negation by an other or by being posited by some determiner.[1] In each case, the autonomy of subjectivity remains inscrutable, for what is determined by contrast with an other or by being posited by something else cannot be determined by itself.

So long as objectivity is presumed to lack the self-determined character of subjectivity, mind seems condemned to be an ineffable entity standing apart from tangible reality. The material world, considered as conditioned by chains of external necessity, where each factor is determined by something else, offers little foothold for mind, whose subjectivity seems so incongruent with objectivity. Yet, if mind cannot retain its subjectivity without opposing objectivity as an independently determined, incommensurate factor, we are left with an implacable divide between mind and body, and mind and world, whose resulting difficulties have made "Cartesian dualism" an untouchable option.

Beyond Mind-Body Dualisms

The dilemmas of mind–body dualism are manifold.

To begin with, conceiving mind as something separate from body raises insurmountable epistemological problems. Solipsism becomes unavoidable, for if mind can be

---

A Companion to Hegel, First Edition. Edited by Stephen Houlgate and Michael Baur.

without anything nonmental, nothing in mind can secure a bridge to what lies beyond. Mind is left communing with itself, stuck in meditation, for no mental feature is inherently connected to something other, and the incommensurability of the nonmental makes interaction an insoluble mystery.

Yet even solipsism's sole certainty of self-knowledge is doubtful when the individuality of the self has no real foothold in the physical world. First, as Kant argues in his "Refutation of Idealism,"[2] the very temporality of mental life becomes inexplicable if mental contents have no abiding background to manifest the temporal unity of their succession. If all mental contents are temporally successive, only the appearance of something *nonmental* can provide a persisting backdrop sufficient to connect past, present, and future in the flow of self-awareness. Consequently, self-awareness is impossible without awareness of enduring objects other than the self, objects that are spatially and temporally ordered.

Further, if mind stands in relation to nothing but its own mental content, there is no basis for individuating the self and uniting the diversity of mental content into *a* mind. As Strawson argues in *Individuals*, mental contents cannot belong to an individual mind unless it can be tied to a nonmental factor exclusive to it. Given that bodies in space-time constitute the minimal materiality irreducible to logical determinacy – the least that material existence can *be* – what provides an exclusive nonmental mooring individuating mind is none other than the unique spatio-temporal itinerary of a body inherently connected to mind and its mental activity. Even if, to paraphrase Kant, all mental content must be able to be accompanied by the representation "I think," that representation is purely abstract, lacking any individuating content that could tie mental content to one mind rather than another.[3] As Hegel has shown in his analysis of "Sense Certainty" in his *Phenomenology of Spirit*, "I" applies to any subject just as "here" and "now" refers to any time and place.[4] Without a unique embodiment, mind has no individuating anchor with which to unite the temporal flow of mental contents into a single awareness.

That connection between mind and body must be evident to mind itself, but this is impossible within the framework of mind–body dualism, which leaves inexplicable any interaction between mind and its own or any other body. Only if mind is embodied in a body in which it experiences itself as uniquely active, can mind relate to itself as an individual subject and through this self-relation be *a* mind of its own.

Although mental embodiment may not require linguistic intelligence, to have self-knowledge, mind must make propositional claims to the extent that knowledge involves judgment. Judgments, like the concepts they contain, cannot be mentally realized apart from language, for judgments connect individuals and particulars to universals and only words can express the purely intelligible conceptuality of universality, which transcends the particularities to which images are confined. Language, however, cannot be private since one cannot employ some intuition as a sign for a generalized representation with any assured communicability without recognizably participating in an ongoing practice in which others make the same connection. Accordingly, mind cannot have self-knowledge without access to the conditions of linguistic interaction, which, as Sellars argues,[5] involve relations between individual minds who cannot appear to one another and make and comprehend communicable utterances unless they are embodied. Mental contents must be given some physical expression before they can be perceived by others, and communicable signs cannot be formed unless interlocutors can indicate to one another materially what common expressions they are using and to what commonly observable objects they refer. Only then can interlocutors move on to communicate purely universal meanings and converse philosophically. Thus, unless individuals possess bodies over which they have some control, they will have no way of coming to participate in discursive rationality.

All such interaction between mind and physical reality and between mind and other minds is precluded if mind and body are inherently separate. Sensation becomes doubly mysterious since a purely immaterial mind can have neither an intelligible connection to bodily sense organs through which physical objects make themselves manifest nor any way of otherwise being affected by material things. Although causal relations between sense organs and physical objects cannot themselves enable sensations to refer to what produce them unless there are physically induced modifications of sensibility to which mind can relate, mind has nothing with which to apprehend phenomena. Conversely, worldly action becomes unthinkable since the mind–body dualism leaves incomprehensible how a mind can affect a body of its own and thereby anything else. With no way of having a tangible object-like presence distinguishable from other objects nor any way of making its own activity appear to itself or to others, mind can hardly be self-aware, let alone aware of other things and other minds.

The Failed Remedies of Spinoza and Materialist Reductions

Insofar as mental reality cannot be retained by denying matter, the impasse of Cartesian dualism can hardly be resolved by following the immaterialist route pioneered by Berkeley, for whom existence consists in being perceived. Given the dilemma of the immaterialist option, a solution to the dualist impasse has instead been sought in two closely linked rescue strategies, one invoking a parallelism between mental and physical reality, and another eliminating the immateriality of mind by reducing mind to matter.

Spinoza pioneers the first remedy in his *Ethics*. He there removes the dilemma of accounting for interaction between mind and body by depriving both of any independent substantiality and then recasting them as modes of the one substance that is both thought and extension, and whose unity ensures their thoroughgoing correlation.[6] The stumbling block of Spinoza's solution is the absence of any resources for individuating finite minds and for securing the correlation of any particular mental state with any particular object or any corporeal condition of an aware individual. Both problems are closely interrelated. By being reduced to different modes of the same substance, both mind and body are rendered phenomena that are externally determined in the endless causal chain of conditioned events.[7] Deprived of the independence and autonomy of substance whose self-sustaining "conatus" Spinoza otherwise acknowledges,[8] mind and body are left exclusively determined by efficient causality. This precludes any final causality or self-activity on which Spinoza's own theory of emotion, virtue, and freedom depends.[9] Whereas each mental state is caused by a preceding mental event, each physical condition is determined by antecedent physical events. Psychological necessity runs its own course alongside physical necessity, each involving occurrences that are indifferent to what kind and import or what type and end anything mental or corporeal

229

might have.[10] Each event, be it psychological or physical, is caught in a blind succession of external conditions where no factor has any intrinsic relation to any other. As a consequence, there is no more basis for grouping together certain mental states as those of a single mind than for treating successive physical conditions as belonging to a particular finite body. Although Spinoza does subject bodies to laws governing the motion of matter,[11] these laws cannot individuate the bodies they rule in common. Whatever particular mass, density, or other features bodies possess must be given apart from laws that apply to all bodies equally, but no resource is available to account for these individuating factors. This is all the more true in Spinoza's case, for whereas other early modern philosophers from Locke through Kant treat individual bodies as particular *substances*, Spinoza cannot avail himself of that category to give bodies a persisting identity.[12] Where every mental and physical occurrence is a mode with no abiding independent being of its own, neither minds nor bodies can be individuated.

This naturally prevents any mind from being aware of itself as an individual, let alone from having any individual body as its own, despite Spinoza's assurances to the contrary. Any connection between corporeal events and mental events is equally problematic since no causal chain can cross over the parallel streams of necessity. That these streams are modes of the same substance may provide a global unification. Yet that unification provides no basis for connecting any specific physical event with any specific mental occurrence. Spinoza may suggest that particular physical and mental occurrences are different expressions in different attributes of the same event, but he has nothing to offer as their common bearer other than the one substance that underlies everything without exception. How then are coexisting corporeal events to be parceled out to one coexisting mental happening rather than another? Even if only one physical occurrence and one mental event were simultaneous, what could allow them to be ascribed to a single finite phenomenon somehow expressed in both the attributes of thought and extension? The one substance may encompass all mental and physical occurrences, but all that is left are the modes themselves in their parallel conditioned successions. Given these difficulties, there is no accounting for how one could sense objects impinging upon one's sense organs or be aware of acting in the corporeal world. Both require that mind somehow be able to relate to itself as embodied.

Those who seek to reduce mind to matter might seem to escape these dilemmas by supplanting dualism with a physical monism and dispensing with the halfway house of dual modalities of a single substance. The problem remains, however, of how to explain away mental life, which remains incongruent with the mechanism of material nature even if reduced to an epiphenomenal show. With physical reality subject to the exclusive governance of efficient causality, there is no room left for either goal-directed behavior or the self-activity where something independently acts upon itself rather than being externally impelled to affect something else. Yet not only do ends figure prominently in desires, emotions, and intentional conduct, but mind pervasively appears to involve reflexivity, where the psyche, consciousness, and intelligence all owe their distinctive character to how mind acts upon its own determinations. As Hegel details throughout his account of mind under the rubric of "Subjective Spirit," every form of mental awareness involves a self-relation determinative of mental content. The psyche is what it feels itself to be, registering feelings that cannot be without being felt. The psyche relates to its feelings as determinations of its own psychic field, not yet distinguishing them from itself as sensations of an objective world.[13] By contrast, consciousness is aware of objects by taking what it feels to be not itself but determinations of a unified domain from which it has extricated itself as a subject confronting objectivity.[14] Intelligence for its part has intuitions, representations, and thoughts by relating to its various mental contents as both products of its own activity and as determinations of objects.[15] In each case, mind acts upon itself, constituting a type of awareness whose characteristic mental content cannot be apart from that form of reflexivity. Whether these mental shapes be regarded as reality or as phenomenal illusion, how they can be reduced to blind material necessity is just as inscrutable as explaining the interaction of separate substances of mind and body.[16]

The problem does not reside in some fundamental incompatibility between physical and chemical processes, and the goal-directed and self-active character endemic to much and/or all mental activity. As Hegel has shown in his analyses of mechanism, chemism, teleology, and life in the *Science of Logic*,[17] the external determination of mechanical and chemical process is precisely what allows them to be enabling constituents of artifacts and living things that have dimensions irreducible to physics or chemistry. Both mechanical and chemical relations depend upon some external condition to get underway, such as an impulse in mechanical motion or a catalyst to precipitate chemical reactions. As a consequence, they can be instigated by something else that may act mechanically or chemically upon objects but do so as part of a process having a different type of initiation and result. An end, for example, is distinct from an efficient cause in that what it brings into being is not something different from itself and devoid of any intrinsic relation to it. Rather, an end gets realized, relinquishing the subjectivity of being merely a prospective goal and gaining fulfillment in an objectification with the same content. An end, however, as something yet to be realized, cannot immediately be its own fulfillment. If it were, the end would have no subjective character, and there could not be any teleological *process*. Something must therefore mediate the end's realization, a means that works upon objectivity to make the end objective. That working upon objectivity is external to objectivity and therefore constitutes a mechanical or chemical process. Nevertheless, the objective realization of the end achieves something unlike mechanism or chemism. Instead of resulting in a movement or chemical reaction different from the starting point, the fulfillment of the end arrives at the same content subjectively present in the unrealized end. So long as the fulfillment of the end depends upon a means separate from it and an intervening process that imposes the end in an independently given object, teleology is external, generating a product like an artifact, which embodies the end by extinguishing the process by which it has been realized.

Teleology becomes internal, constituting the process of life, when physical and chemical processes are incorporated in a self-sustaining objectivity, which is an end in itself by continually reproducing the activity in which it consists, being both means and end at once. Mechanical motions and chemical reactions still come into play wherever factors get acted upon by something else, such as when one part of an organism affects another, or when an organism sustains itself by assimilating material from its external environment. These causal relations now unfold within an encompassing process of a radically different character. Here determiner and determined are not distinct since the self-sustaining life process acts upon itself. Action depends on nothing external since the organic process is self renewing. Ends are always objective since the life process already realizes what it continually brings about, and that objectivity is for its own sake since it acts to reproduce itself. Moreover, since what life is thereby determines its own ongoing process, that process is intrinsic to its specific nature and not indifferent to it, as are the laws of matter that govern all things, whatever their type or import.

All these features appear much more amenable to mind and its subjective self-activity than the debilitating dualism of separate mental and physical substances, the parallelism of mental and physical modes, or a reduction to matter. Can the mind–body relation be resolved by conceiving mind in terms of life?

Dilemmas of the Aristotelian Solution

Aristotle points toward such an escape from dualistic difficulties by conceiving mind as inherently embodied, identifying the psyche as the principle of life animating the living organism. As such, the psyche never confronts the problem of bridging any gap between itself and the world, or more specifically, between itself and the body with which it perceives and acts.

Aristotle's solution, however, suffers from two flaws.

First, when Aristotle conceives the self-activity of the organism, and by implication, the principle of the psyche animating the body, he falls back upon categories of technique that involve the very separation between active agency and passive recipient material that is ingredient in mind–body dualism.[18] Likening the organism to a doctor who cures himself,[19] Aristotle employs the external purposiveness of artisan activity to characterize the internal purposiveness of life's self-sustaining process. Artisan activity is externally purposive insofar as its end is preconceived by the artisan, who imposes it upon a given material, making a product that does not contain the activity producing it but rather, results from that activity's completion. By contrast, life sustains itself by containing the activity by which its unified organic process is maintained and reproduced. Because the living organism has within itself (a) its end, (b) the material in which that end is realized, and (c) the process of that realization, life's telos is internal. This internal teleology cannot be captured by Aristotle's example of a self-treating doctor. An ailing doctor may certainly impose the lost form of health upon himself by using his craft. Nevertheless, the doctor's own medical intervention is not part of the ongoing self-activity of his healthy existence. That existence is self-sustaining without the purposive intervention of medical craft, which only enters in when health is threatened. Consequently, when Aristotle uses the external teleology of craft to explain the internal teleology of life, he inserts mind (that of an artisan) into the organism in a way that is extraneous to its ongoing process.[20]

This difficulty is complemented by a converse problem. By identifying the psyche with the principle of life, Aristotle reduces mind to organic unity, leading him to ascribe a psyche to all life forms, including plants. Although mind may well be something alive, that does not entail that all life possesses mind. Life minimally involves an entity differentiated into complementary organs that serve as means and ends of one another, reproducing the self-sustaining whole to which they belong. As such, the living organism can not be constructed by mechanically assembling preexisting parts, contrary to the reveries of human or divine "intelligent design." Because the organs of the organism exist only within the complementary functioning of a self-sustaining whole, the living thing can never be produced as an artifact, issuing from an exercise of technique imposing form upon some pre-existing material. Instead of being made, the living organism grows and reproduces, generating its form and matter internally. Yet in doing so, the living organism need have no indwelling focal point that could be distinguished from its physiological organs as a mind.

Plato reveals this in his preliminary analysis of the "City of Pigs" in the *Republic*.[21] Whereas an economy can sustain itself through the complementary occupations of a division of labor, the unity of the whole is not the aim of any of the particular trades comprising its organs. In such a "City of Pigs," limited to organic interdependence, no ruling function is exercised for no agency imposes the unity of the whole upon its constitutive elements. To paraphrase classical political economy, the economic law of market interdependence operates behind the backs of all without being enacted by anyone. Mind, however, adds to life a factor that relates itself to the entirety of the organism, be it through feeling, consciousness, or intelligence. As the activity of rule, which is exercised by something within the body politic that nevertheless acts upon the whole, mind relates to the organism to which it brings feeling, awareness, and intentional control in a way very different from the way in which merely physical organs complement one another. Plato distinguishes the unity of the body politic from that of an economic order by revealing how the body politic depends upon a ruling element that realizes the unity of the whole in virtue of knowing what that unity is and purposefully sustaining it. By analogy, the psyche relates to the body by being that element of the embodied self that determines its totality in function of being aware of who it is.[22]

Hegel's Conceptual Breakthrough for Comprehending the Nondualist Relation of Mind and Body

In drawing his analogy between polis and soul, Plato points toward a logical difference that Hegel makes thematic for comprehending the nondualist relation of mind and body. Mind and body are not related as one particular to another, be it as independent substances or as different organs of an organism. Rather, mind and body are related as the *universal* that relates to the *particular* by overarching and containing it.[23] The universal cannot be at one with itself without having the differentiation that particularity affords. Particularity, however, is not simply something different from universality. It is rather an otherness that is no less united with the universal that pervades it. Otherwise, the particular is not the instantiation of the universal, but just something that the universal is not. In that case, "third man" problems are inevitable, for some extraneous factor must be introduced to connect universal and particular, which, as itself an extraneous addition, calls for further mediation without end.[24]

Moreover, particularity is not an appearance of the universal, nor is the universal the essence or ground of the particular. Plato makes the mistake of subsuming the particular and universal under such categories of the logic of essence by treating particulars as phenomenal, deficient replicas of the universal idea, which figures as their true essence. Yet determinations that are posited by some prior determiner always lack the independent being belonging to what determines them. Particulars, however, are not mere posits. As differentiations immanent in the universal, they must share the same intrinsic being that allows them to be the universal's own determinacy. The universal *determines itself* in the particular, rather than positing something else with a derivative, conditioned existence. That is what allows the universal to have individuality with an intrinsic differentiation that is determined in and through itself. It is also what allows particulars to be individuals, exhibiting the same independent being endemic to self-determination.

Mind, inherently embodied, will exhibit the true relation of the universal and particular by being at one with itself in the body, provided the body in its distinction from mind is so determined that it comprises the necessary vehicle of mind's own actuality. Then, mind, while not being just another bodily organ, will still exist nowhere else than in the body. Even though a central nervous system will enable the animal to both feel as a unitary self and move itself as a unitary subject of action,[25] mind will thereby pervade the organism as a whole and therefore not be seated just in the brain or in any other particular location within the body. This omnipresent subjectivity is precisely what gives mind its inwardness and "ideality," leaving it situated within the body it inhabits but infusing it in its totality. Similarly, the universal, by differentiating itself in particularity, relates to particularity as a specific differentiation falling under its own encompassing unity, which now has the universal and the particular as its differentia. So mind, relating to itself in the body, will equally relate to the body in a relationship contained within the whole that mind comprises.

That relation will not make bodily alterations *effects* caused in whole or part by the mind. Categories of essence cannot apply to the relation of mind and body. If they did, mind would have a prior immaterial existence of its own of which the body is a mere semblance. Yet mind cannot have an individual unity, temporality, or any specifically mental content without embodiment. Hence, the physical realization of mind cannot be posited by mind, for mind cannot posit anything without already being embodied. For this reason, the mind's relation to the body never consists of mind being a cause of bodily events. That would reinstate a mind–body duality wherein mind would act upon not its embodied self but a body different from itself. Mind must instead be thought of as being self-cause, *developing* as something encompassing the body and the bodily processes of the mind-endowed individual. Only as self-cause of an embodied unity, that is, as self-determined, can the mind be the cause of something else, namely effects generated by the influence of its corporeal actions upon other things, whether inorganic objects, plants, or animals with varying degrees of mental endowment.

Limits of Searle's Parallel Proposal

John Searle alludes to something seemingly similar, describing mind as both realized in the brain and having the brain as its enabling condition. The principal false assumption plaguing dualism and reductive materialism, namely, that the subjectivity of consciousness cannot belong to the physical world, is overcome, according to Searle, by recognizing that brain processes cause our conscious states and that consciousness is itself a biological phenomenon.[26] Subjective states of mind are no more than higher-level features of the brain just as digestion is a higher-level feature of the stomach. That consciousness has an irreducible first-person being is just a fact about nature rather than a metaphysical puzzle.[27]

Searle's account asserts that life and mind go together, but how and why mind requires biological realization remains largely unexplained. Can one really equate how mind supervenes upon the brain with how digestion is a "higher-level" feature of the stomach? The stomach, like any organ, can hardly be detached from its function since the different parts of an organism are means and end to one another in virtue of their complementary functionality, and no organ can continue to be what it is apart from that organic unity. This certainly applies to the brain, as part of the nervous system, which sustains itself as an organ of the animal by facilitating the sensibility and irritability by which the animal interacts with its environment, thereby enabling nutrition and reproduction, and allowing the other organs to function and jointly uphold both the whole individual and the entire species to which they all belong. Although injury or disease can debilitate the nervous system and reduce the animal to a vegetative state, it would be a mistake to presume that the nervous system can be fully operative as a brain in a vat. In that example, the brain is ripped apart from a living organism and somehow connected to an electro-chemical mechanism, which supposedly keeps it functioning as before. Yet, that supporting electro-chemical mechanism is itself inanimate and therefore must be set in play and controlled by some agent that can hardly be just a brain in a vat. Even if such a brain were to embody a mind, that mind would not relate to that brain as digestion relates to the stomach. Mind may be embodied in an animal organism, but its relation to the organism is not identical to that of the function of a single organ to that organ. If it were, the mind–body relation would revert to the organic unity of the "City of Pigs," undercutting the subjective centrality of mind.

That subjectivity is further jeopardized by Searle's employment of efficient causality in characterizing how the brain makes mind possible, and how the mind affects the body. If the brain is the cause of the mind, the brain has no intrinsic connection to mind, for an effect may owe its existence to its cause, but otherwise cause and effect are indifferent to one another, so long as causality is solely efficient and not formal or final.[28] As effect of the brain, mind is something separate, and its difference from the brain leaves undetermined why mind has the psychological features that distinguish it from neurological activity. The same duality reenters when mind is considered the cause of effects in the body,[29] rather than as something always embodied that acts upon its own embodiment. It is thus no accident that Searle allows for the possibility of consciousness being caused and sustained by an artificial brain fashioned out of inanimate materials just as a heart can be replaced by an artificial machine that pumps blood.[30] Since function is kept separate from the material in which that function is carried out, it has the external teleology of an artifact, rather than the internal teleology of a self-realizing form that cannot be apart from the living material it encompasses.

Mind is not the property of the brain or even of the entire nervous system. Still, mind cannot be had by plants because only animals have sensibility and irritability, together with the nervous system these functions involve. These physiological features endow the animal organism with a degree of self-related activity without which the subjective

235

centrality of mind cannot introduce itself. Yet mind still relates to itself as embodied in the entire animal organism, rather than as belonging to a particular organ or physiological system among others. Particular features of the nervous system may be associated with specific activities of mind such that, for example, damage to certain brain areas can be correlated with certain mental deficits. Nevertheless, the mind feels, senses, thinks, and acts always in and through its own body as a whole.

For just this reason, the mind can never act upon its body as if the body were an object apart that could suffer the effects of mental causality. Just as the body does not cause the mind, so the mind does not affect the body. Precisely because the mind is inherently alive and encompasses the animal organism in its entirety, categories of efficient causality cannot apply. Nor, however, is the relation of mind and body revealed by employing the categories of external teleology, appropriate to artifacts, to which Searle reverts in describing the "higher level" of mind as something imparted by an external function that artificial "brains" could fulfill.

The Self-Development of Embodied Mind

The solution to the mind–body problem hinges upon recognizing that mind does not act upon the body as cause of effects but rather acts upon itself as an embodied living subjectivity. As such, mind develops itself, progressively attaining more and more of a self-determined character. This progressive self-formation is endemic to mind. Hegel logically captures this process in further characterizing mind in terms of the Idea, whose process unites concept and objectivity in and through themselves, bringing into being the inherent correspondence in which truth resides. This characterization allows Hegel to speak of the embodied mind as coming to exhibit the truth of the Idea, where body and mind unite objectivity and subjectivity, leaving the dead body something "untrue," lacking that unifying process. [31]

This process of self-formation has a definite beginning. Even though mind always engages in reflexive self-activity, at the outset mental process must have a natural character, that is, a given determinacy through which it relates to itself. This given determinacy constitutes what Hegel aptly calls the anthropological dimension of mind,[32] to the extent that mind is from the start encumbered with a natural species being involving a physiological body with its own specific metabolism, sensory apparatus, and way of sustaining itself within its encompassing biosphere. Although we may be born as homo sapiens, mind need not share in that species being, which as contingently given has features extraneous to mind per se. Mind, however, must have some given species being through which mental life can be self-active, necessitating that mind has a natural endowment upon which it can proceed to individuate itself through its own activity.

Mind's being encumbered with "natural," given determinacy is logically prefigured by how, as Hegel shows in his *Logic*, the self-determined determinacy of the concept arises from something else, namely the reciprocity into which the logic of essence reverts. Although the concept emerges logically when the difference between determiner and determined is overcome, the self-determined determinacy that results has not given itself its own character. Rather, it arises from that antecedent process, leaving the concept with an initial form of self-determination that has not yet fully determined

236

itself.[33] Consequently, the concept must come to mediate its own determination, which it can only do through further development that progressively renders every determination of the concept something determined by conceptual factors. This occurs first in judgment, where the factors of the concept (universality, particularity, and individuality) are *immediately* determined by one another through the copula "is" (e.g., the particular or individual *is* the universal).[34] The syllogism then overcomes judgment's immediate determination by providing a mediating term, enabling the determination of one concept term by another to be mediated by a third (e.g., the individual is the universal by virtue of its particularity).[35] Objectivity removes the abiding difference between the mediating term and the two terms it connects, allowing individuals to be so completely self-mediated that their external relations are completely indifferent to their individuality.[36]

Hegel delineates the mental analogue to this progressive self-determination in conceiving the successive ways in which the always embodied mind cultivates itself to become more and more thoroughly what it has determined itself to be. The succession of these mental way stations has a dual significance. On the one hand, it comprises an ordering of structural constitution, where preceding shapes are prerequisites for those that follow, either as temporally prior developments or as component constituents. On the other hand, because the latter stages presuppose the earlier ones, mental processes can appear independently in a temporal development. In other words, if, following Hegel, mind involves successive mental processes of the psyche, consciousness, and intelligence, then the psyche can emerge without consciousness or intelligence; consciousness must involve the psyche but can exist without intelligence; and intelligence can emerge after the development of psyche and consciousness but not without either. These possible independent temporal realizations can involve distinct species arising in evolutionary succession and/or existing simultaneously with different mental endowments, distinguished by their greater or lesser inclusion of the various shapes that must always incorporate those that structurally precede them. The succession can also take the form of the mental maturation of an individual, whose mind undergoes a temporal development of its own. In every case, at every stage the self-formation applies to a mentality that has its own physiological dimension. Each stage in the self-cultivation of mind therefore comprises a specific mind–body unity.

Mind, as initially self-active with a given animal species being, minimally does nothing more than immediately register the determinations of its nature, feeling them as a psyche consisting in merely the feeling of its own natural determinacy.[37] That natural, "anthropological" endowment involves both its own internal physiological process and its interaction with the surrounding biosphere. Mind as psyche has nothing with which to determine further its own feeling other than the immediate feeling activity in which it solely consists. In the absence of any other mental resources, this added determining can itself only occur immediately, as the "natural" automatic result of prior engagements in feeling. Given the immediacy of these prior engagements, they can only impact upon current acts of feeling by rendering them immediately distinct from other acts that have no relation to those prior acts. That immediate distinction cannot involve positing new felt qualities for their introduction would require some mediating discrimination to qualitatively differentiate them. Since immediate feeling has no power of comparison to discriminate between felt contents, any distinctiveness

237

acquired by such contents must reside simply in a nonbeing or suspension of the feeling concerned, which adds no new determinations to it but only involves mind's relative withdrawal from it. This can occur when feelings that resemble some antecedents thereby get psychologically sequestered from those that do not have any relation to prior acts of mind. Such is the course of habituation, where mind becomes inured to feelings that resemble others that precede their registration. Since feelings are bound up with bodily activities, habituation allows mind to detach itself from both certain repeated feelings and repeated corporeal behavior by not attending to them in its current psychic field. These repeated feelings and behavior can now proceed without mind having to be immediately immersed in their process. In this way, mind and body become simultaneously transformed through the functioning of the psyche, which has now begun to refashion itself. What occurs is not an act of mind upon the body, as if categories of essence such as cause and effect applied. Since mind is always embodied, the transformation is not an effect upon something else but rather, a self-development or cultivation, where the psyche gives its specific mind–body unity a character determined by its own self-activity, encompassing physical, chemical, and biological processes.

That concrete self-determination continues apace with the emergence of consciousness. As Hegel argues, once the psyche has succeeded in detaching itself as a disengaged standpoint from its feeling and its embodiment, it can confront some of its feelings as sensations of an independently given objectivity and give expression to others in corporeal behavior that mind can recognize as both occurring in the world and being its own activity.[38] This allows mind to individuate itself as an embodied subject in the world of which it is conscious. Thanks to this embodiment, mind can confront its own awareness as something objective. Doing so, however, depends upon a cultivation of mind's own embodiment, so that it recognizably exhibits the subjectivity of the consciousness to which it is uniquely connected. This cultivation is not entirely an affair of the individual consciousness in isolation from others. An animal may confront its own subjectivity in a purely negative fashion by consuming an object of desire, thereby revealing itself in the negation of an independent object. Yet to have a positive objectivity that reveals the self, consciousness must confront consciousness itself as something independently other. This other reflects consciousness itself by being another consciousness, rendering both minds particular exemplars of consciousness in general, which recognize each other's distinct individuality. Hegel characterizes this relation as one whose participants show their desire for the desire of one another.[39] This manifestation must involve corporeal activity both expressive of desire and related to the desire of the other for otherwise it remains purely internal and private. Recognition always involves embodied selves conscious of other living minds and self-conscious as living minds both sharing in what is universal to consciousness and individuating themselves from others. Since recognition applies to subjects manifest to one another in and through their bodies, the universality of consciousness equally involves a commonality in physical behavior, which need not as yet take the form of linguistic interaction.

The emergence of linguistic intelligence depends neither on any causal movement upon the individual mind nor on mind acting upon the body. Rather, it arises through a self-development that embodied mind undergoes in conjunction with others. The psychological precondition of theoretical intelligence, whether intuiting, representing, or thinking, is the achievement by consciousness of the universal self-awareness that recognizes itself in objectivity and treats its mental determinations as equally objective.[40] This requires a physical interaction with others, with mind encompassing bodies trained so as to give recognizable expression to the consciousness of one another. Linguistic interaction cannot occur until individuals are in a position to fashion and use perceivable signs so as to participate in a shared practice of communication. At one and the same time, this physical–mental linguistic habituation allows mind to access the intersubjectivity of rational discourse and to behave physiologically as an embodied rational individual.

Accordingly, action never involves the mystery of mind acting upon the body, where categories of essence, such as cause and effect, enter in to raise the specter of a disembodied soul. Intelligence becomes practical by instead acting upon its ever embodied self. The individual agent articulates purposes and intentions that may involve pictorial representations and/or words as well as the physiological dimension they involve, and realizes these purposes and intentions through behavior that may cause other things to occur but which itself comprises a self-determination of the individual agent. Reasons do not "cause" the action that ensues. Rather, the action *qua* action already has intentions ingredient in it. If instead, the individual just moved its body without intrinsic purpose, the movement would be an intentional act only relative to external observers who imparted their aims to what occurs.

The self-determination of action is, however, only formal at the outset. In exercising choice, the agent employs a "natural" form of willing that is not determined by its act but constitutes the given capacity to choose which provides the enabling condition of each and every choice. That capacity involves the ability to represent ends and focus on one rather than another, and the physical skill to achieve whatever ends are chosen. Although these arise from the physiological as well as psychological maturation and cultivation of the individual, they are still preconditions of choice rather than products of the volition with which they are connected. Similarly, the ends inherent in action are first given by desire and contingent circumstances rather than being determined by willing. The will only opts for one or another of these given aims, exercising a volition whose form and content are equally externally determined rather than self-determined. Even when practical intelligence reflects upon its aims and seeks their universal fulfillment in the pursuit of happiness, that encompassing goal remains bound to whatever desires the individual happens to have.

Only when individuals interact so as to exercise rights can will obtain both a form and content determined by willing. Hegel shows this in its most minimal form in explicating the recognition process of property ownership, with which the *Philosophy of Right* systematically begins. Individuals will into being their own form of agency as owners by first making known to one another that their wills exclusively inform their own bodies. This requires coordinated action accompanied by coordinated recognition of the significance that the parties to the interaction ascribe to their conduct. Once more, only embodied selves who have achieved the universal self-transformations of intelligence can give themselves the form of agency of owners and will a content, property, that is determined by will, rather than externally given. On that basis, persons can use that recognized embodied agency to lay claim recognizably to external factors that have yet to be informed by anyone's will, establishing alienable property that can then figure in contractual relations.

239

These developments push beyond the domain of philosophical psychology to that of ethics, where philosophy addresses the reality of self-determined agency. By resolving the mind–body problem, Hegel has provided not only a viable framework for the philosophy of mind but also the enabling conditions of ethical theory.[41]

Notes

1 Hegel provides a systematic account of these two types of categories in the successive sections of his *Science of Logic* entitled "The Logic of Being" and "The Logic of Essence." The categories of the Logic of Being are generally determined through contrast with one another, where each term is equiprimordial and has its own character in virtue of what it is not. By contrast, the categories of the Logic of Essence involve two-tiered relations where one term has priority over the other, in some respect determining it. Such categories of essence include essence and appearance, a thing and its properties, a whole and its parts, ground and grounded, substance and accident, and cause and effect. See G.W.F. Hegel, *Science of Logic*, trans. by A. V. Miller (New York: Humanities Press, 1976), 79–385, 389–571.

2 Kant, Immanuel, *Critique of Pure Reason*, trans. Paul Guyer and Allen W. Wood (Cambridge, U.K.: Cambridge University Press, 1998), B274–279, 326–329.

3 P. F. Strawson, *Individuals: An Essay in Descriptive Metaphysics* (London: Methuen, 1979), 82.

4 G.W.F. Hegel, *Phenomenology of Spirit*, trans. A. V. Miller (New York: Oxford University Press, 1977), 58–66.

5 Wilfrid Sellars, *Empiricism and the Philosophy of Mind* (Cambridge, Mass.: Harvard University Press, 1997).

6 Spinoza, *Ethics*, Part II, Propositions 1, 2, and 7, in Spinoza, *Complete Works*, trans. Samuel Shirley (Indianapolis: Hackett, 2002), 245, 247.

7 Spinoza, *Ethics*, Part I, Proposition 28, p. 233, Part II, Proof to Lemma 3, p. 252, Proposition 48, 272.

8 Spinoza, *Ethics*, Part III, Propositions 6 and 7, p. 283, and Proposition 28, 293.

9 Spinoza, *Ethics*, Appendix to Part I, 239–241.

10 Spinoza, *Ethics*, Part III, Proposition 2, 279–280.

11 Spinoza, *Ethics*, Part II, Proposition 13, Lemmas 1–7, 252–255.

12 "Bodies are distinguished from one another in respect of motion-and-rest, quickness and slowness, and not in respect of substance" (Spinoza, *Ethics*, Part II, Proposition 13, Lemma 1, 252).

13 G.W.F. Hegel, *Hegel's Philosophy of Mind: Part Three of the Encyclopaedia of the Philosophical Sciences* (1830), trans. William Wallace and A. V. Miller (Oxford: Oxford University Press, 1971), addition to §402, 88–92.

14 Hegel, *Philosophy of Mind*, §412–413, additions to §412–413, 151–155.

15 Hegel, *Philosophy of Mind*, §440, addition to §440, 179–181.

16 Even if one invoked the blind necessity of evolution to account for the *genesis* of "reflexivity," such as in the emergence of animal life from plant life, that emergence does not account for the reflexive *actuality* of mental processes, whose self-activity remains irreducible to mechanism.

17 G.W.F. Hegel, *Science of Logic*, trans. A. V. Miller (New York: Humanities Press, 1976), 711–774.

18 So Aristotle writes in Chapter 8, Book II, of his *Physics*, "If the ship-building art were in the wood, it would produce the same results by nature." *Physics* 199b 28–29, in *The Complete*

Works of Aristotle, ed. Jonathan Barnes (Princeton: Princeton University Press, 1984), Vol. 1, p. 341.

19 Aristotle continues, "If, therefore, purpose is present in art, it is present also in nature. The best illustration is a doctor doctoring himself; nature is like that." *Physics* 199b 29–30, in *The Complete Works of Aristotle*, Vol. 1, p. 341.

20 Similarly, Aristotle distinguishes between the active and passive intellect, where the active intellect acts upon something else, its passive counterpart, which is thereby not self-active, but determined from without. Once more categories of craft enter in, with the passive intellect receiving form imposed upon it by the artisanship of the active intellect. See Aristotle, *De Anima*, Book III, Chapter 5, 430a10–26, *The Complete Works of Aristotle*, Vol. 1, p. 684.

21 Plato, *Republic*, Book II, 369b–372d, in Plato, *Complete Works*, ed. John M. Cooper (Indianapolis: Hackett, 1997), 1008–1011.

22 As Michael B. Foster points out in his critical evaluation of the *Republic* in *The Political Philosophies of Plato and Hegel*, Plato still makes use of categories of craft to comprehend rule, even though these are incompatible with the reflexivity of rule. Thus Plato is compelled to divide the polis and the soul into ruling and ruled components, although ruling parts of the polis and the soul still rule over themselves. See Michael B. Foster, *The Political Philosophies of Plato and Hegel*, 1–71. Plato, like Aristotle, lacks the conceptual resources to conceive self-rule, which is shown when Socrates argues that the soul must be divided into separate ruling and ruled parts because self-control is inconceivable, given that it requires that patient and agent be one and the same. See Plato, *Republic*, Book IV, 430e–431a, *Complete Works*, 1062.

23 Hegel, *Philosophy of Mind*, addition to §389, 33. In the *Philosophy of Right*, Hegel further characterizes the relation of soul and body in terms of the Idea, where the body figures as objectivity, and the soul figures as the concept, with the embodied soul exhibiting the truth of the Idea, whereas a dead body is "untrue." As we shall see, this further characterization underlies the self-determining cultivation endemic to mind. See Hegel, *Elements of the Philosophy of Right*, trans. H. B. Nisbet (Cambridge, U.K.: Cambridge University Press, 1991), Addition to §21, 53.

24 In his dialogue *Parmenides*, Plato lays out the crux of the "third man" problem as follows: "But if like things are like by partaking of something, won't that be the form itself?" "Undoubtedly." "Therefore nothing can be like the form, nor can the form be like anything else. Otherwise, alongside the form another form will always make its appearance, and if that form is like anything, yet another; and if the form proves to be like what partakes of it, a fresh form will never cease emerging" (132e–133a). See Plato, *Complete Works*, ed. John M. Cooper (Indianapolis, Ind.: Hackett, 1997), p. 367.

25 This centrality is what distinguishes the sentience and irritability of animals from the sensitivity and tropism of plants, which always operate locally, involving just a particular part of the organism, without achieving the unification constitutive of subjectivity.

26 John R. Searle, *Intentionality: An Essay in the Philosophy of Mind* (Cambridge, U.K.: Cambridge University Press, 1983), ix.

27 See John R. Searle, *Mind, Language and Society: Philosophy in the Real World* (New York: Basic Books, 1998), 50–52.

28 This is why Hume insists that one cannot derive any causal (e.g., efficient) relation from the concepts of objects. To do so would require formal causality, and more specifically, the derivation of necessary differentia from the genus, which ancient metaphysics privileges.

29 This is evident in Searle's acceptance of the "causal efficacy of consciousness" in repudiating the epiphenomenalist reduction of mind. See Searle, *Mind, Language and Society: Philosophy in the Real World*, p. 58. See also Searle, *Intentionality*, 265.

30 Searle, *Mind, Language and Society: Philosophy in the Real World*, 53.

31 Hegel, *Elements of the Philosophy of Right*, trans. H. B. Nisbett (Cambridge, U.K.: Cambridge University Press, 1991), Addition to §21, 53.

32 Hegel, *Philosophy of Mind*, §387, p. 25; Addition to §387, 27; §391, 35–36.

33 Hegel provides an account of this development in Chapter 1, "The Notion of Subjectivity," in the *Science of Logic*, 600–622.

34 Hegel details the stages of this development in Chapter 2, "The Judgment of Subjectivity," in the *Science of Logic*, 622–663.

35 Hegel details the stages of this development in Chapter 3, "The Syllogism of Subjectivity," in the *Science of Logic*, 664–704.

36 Hegel details this development in his account of the emergence of the immediate form of Objectivity, Mechanism. See Chapter 1, "Mechanism of Objectivity," in the *Science of Logic*, 711–726.

37 Hegel, *Philosophy of Mind*, §401, 75–77.

38 Hegel, *Philosophy of Mind*, §412, 151, Addition to §412, 151–152.

39 Hegel, *Philosophy of Mind*, §430–435, 170–176.

40 Hegel, *Philosophy of Mind*, §436–437, 176–178.

41 The above discussion has benefited from helpful and relentless comments from Stephen Houlgate.

11

Hegel's Philosophy of Language: The Unwritten Volume

JERE O'NEILL SURBER

Introduction

It is impossible to work through Hegel's great corpus of writings without noticing the ubiquity of the theme of language. It announces itself in the first decade of the nineteenth century in his Jena lectures, the text of which constituted the initial drafts of what would later become his 'system,' and it appears with regularity up to his last lectures in Berlin in the 1820s, which set out his 'mature system' as outlined in the *Encyclopaedia of Philosophical Sciences*. At times Hegel offers quite extended discussions of various linguistic themes, at others merely brief references or asides. His more extended presentations of linguistic ideas tend to appear especially at some of those points most pivotal for the dialectical unfolding of his systematic thought, such as the famous opening sections of the Jena *Phenomenology* and the crucial transition from representation to thought in the Berlin *Encyclopaedia*. Other important extended reflections on language occur in his lectures on aesthetics and religion. To these can be added several important speeches and essays, especially the address of 1809 on the importance of the study of classical languages in the Gymnasium curriculum and his reviews in the 1820s of works by Hamann and Wilhelm von Humboldt. Were these to be joined with the various brief passages, asides, footnotes, and '*Zusätze*' pertaining to language scattered throughout his works, the result would constitute a fair-sized volume.

In the time since Hegel's death, his preoccupation with linguistic issues and their importance for the broader trajectory of his thought has often been noted by many of his attentive readers. Especially beginning after the Second World War, there was a 'first wave' of serious attempts to bring together Hegel's diffuse texts on language, view them as a whole, and, so far as possible, reconstruct in a more systematic format the implicit 'philosophy of language' at work in Hegel's texts.[1] Of course, all this has taken place against the background and, in part, as a response to the so-called linguistic turn that

A Companion to Hegel, First Edition. Edited by Stephen Houlgate and Michael Baur.
© 2011 Blackwell Publishing Ltd. Published 2011 by Blackwell Publishing Ltd.

dominated so much of the philosophical thought of the twentieth century, both in the Anglophone countries and on the European continent. More recently, the importance of Hegel's linguistic ideas has become apparent in the range of thinkers who have commented, often critically and sometimes polemically, on one or another of Hegel's texts concerning language – a list that would include Gadamer, Habermas, Hyppolite, Ricoeur, Derrida, Deleuze, Lyotard, Nancy, and Zizek.[2] Currently, a 'second wave' of self-standing and comprehensive approaches to Hegel's linguistic thought seems to be emerging that not only continues the earlier project of reconstruction but attempts to show how this can provide important insights for addressing contemporary issues in logic, epistemology, and the philosophy of language.[3]

Despite all this, one rather obvious question has yet to be seriously posed: Why did Hegel himself not write a 'Philosophy of Language'? Given that the theme of language was a crucial element running through his thought, why did he not choose to develop his ideas on language into a philosophical statement that could stand beside his philosophies of art, religion, politics, and history? Another way to phrase this would be: Why did Hegel not present language as a (relatively) independent 'moment' within his broader systematic project? Hegel's 'philosophies' of art, religion, politics, and history are, in fact, more detailed elaborations of 'moments' of his overall system. Why, then, did Hegel not see language as also being such a determinate moment that would be amenable to a more detailed treatment?

In response to my question, some scholars might immediately reply that, though he did not write a self-standing work or series of lectures devoted exclusively to this theme, he did, in fact, offer a treatment of language in his "mature system" of the 1820s, a discussion that appears in the "Subjective Spirit" section of the third division of the *Encyclopaedia of Philosophical Sciences*, "The Philosophy of Spirit."[4] Part of my task in this chapter will be to suggest that his treatment there neither fairly represents something approaching the comprehensive account of language that we might be led to expect from his earlier discussions of language, nor is it even entirely consistent with views expressed elsewhere in his writings.

Beyond this more local issue regarding the status of his treatment of language in the 'Berlin system,' the broader question that I am posing is by no means peripheral but goes to the heart of Hegel's idea of philosophy as a systematic enterprise, his own view of the historical significance of his project, and our assessment of both. Nor is it as straightforward a question as it may appear at first glance. Rather, it requires some detailed consideration of several significant aspects of Hegel's philosophical activities and motivations. My general claim in this chapter is that Hegel himself came to realize that articulating a 'Philosophy of Language' was at odds with the idea of system that he had adopted, continuously maintained, and resolutely pursued since his first philosophical writings. The fact that he did not compose such a work (or perhaps set of lectures) was neither an accidental omission, a matter of historical anachronism, nor a judgment on his part that language just was not a central philosophical concern. Rather, I will suggest that it was a deliberate choice in favor of a systematic conception of philosophy and against a project that would serve to disrupt the general economy of his systematic enterprise. It is in light of this choice that Hegel must be read as bringing to completion one epoch of philosophy and laying the foundations for the next, which remains our own to this day.

1.   Hegel's Linguistic Inheritance

To begin, it is crucial to recognize that the idea of a 'philosophy of language' was by no means something entirely novel or unknown to Hegel, that it was not only a real possibility by Hegel's time but had several important precedents within the general milieu and, more specifically, within the immediate tradition in which he was working.

In a broad sense, philosophical reflection about language already occupied a central place in classical thought in such works as Plato's *Cratylus* and various of the logical writings of Aristotle. It was continued within the Roman texts on rhetoric and, in the Middle Ages, was treated under the general heading of the 'theory of intentions.' In the early modern period, it was often associated with the 'Port-Royal School' of logic and, in the seventeenth and eighteenth centuries, appeared as a central theme within the philosophies of such diverse thinkers as Hobbes, Locke, Condillac, Hume, and Rousseau. So intertwined were philosophy and linguistic ideas through most of the tradition that it is impossible to write a history of philosophy without reference to linguistic ideas (and vice versa, as many recent histories of linguistics clearly demonstrate[5]).

Despite claims about a 'linguistic turn' that have dominated many twentieth-century (mainly Anglophone) accounts of the recent history of philosophy, it would probably be more accurate to say that this is, in fact, a second 'linguistic turn,' the first commencing in the mid-eighteenth century with Rousseau's essay on the origins of language (1754) and Herder's famous "Prize Essay" (1772), which was a partial defense of Rousseau's naturalistic (as opposed to theological) view of language. The *'Ursprungsfrage'* posed by Herder dominated much of the discussion within German-speaking academic circles in the last three decades of the eighteenth century and ultimately attracted the attention of Kant, who was quite familiar with Herder's views and even wrote a major review of Herder's work.

Despite the importance of Kant's philosophical revolution for the 'second,' twentieth-century 'linguistic turn,' it is ironic that Kant himself tended to view the explosion of interest in language, both philosophical and empirical, that characterized his own epoch as being of little or no interest to the practitioner of the new 'transcendental' style of philosophizing that he had pioneered. On Kant's view, linguistic matters must always fall on the side of the empirical and merely contingent and had nothing of value to teach the 'transcendental philosopher' who was concerned solely with the necessary and universal structures of experience and thought.[6] However, within his own lifetime, Kant's dismissal of language as a serious philosophical theme came under fire from three quite different perspectives that nonetheless agreed on one point: that reflection on language was a central philosophical task that directly affected the very conception of the enterprise of philosophy itself. These reactions formed the immediate background of Hegel's linguistic thought.

The earliest approach was that of Hamann, who regarded language as the ultimate and inexhaustible horizon within which all experience and thought, including the philosophical, occurs. At the most fundamental level, language is a dynamic living organism that serves as a sort of 'spiritual storehouse' of human experience, thought, and history. In direct opposition to Kant's critical attempt to elucidate the basic underlying structures of experience and thought independently of the (for Kant) 'merely empirical' features of language, Hamann asserts, in his first responses to Kant's Critical Philosophy written even before the *Critique of Pure Reason* was published, that there can be no position 'outside language' from which such a philosophical project as that of Kant could be launched. Rather, all philosophy, including and especially that of Kant, can only be a specific, partial, and finite mobilization of the infinite and inexhaustible resources provided by language itself. In a sense that anticipates views later associated with Heidegger and Gadamer, Hamann views language as 'speaking through us' rather than as some sort of mere arbitrary means or device that we utilize to express ourselves or communicate with others. With respect to philosophy, this implied, for Hamann, a strict identity between thought and language: thinking is always and irreducibly linguistic and language is the living repository of thought.[7]

Schelling, the seminal influence on Hegel's first forays into philosophy, articulated a similar view of language, though in the new terminology of post-Kantian philosophy. In his *System of Transcendental Idealism* (1801), Schelling developed a philosophical viewpoint whereby the fundamental task of philosophy consisted in the articulation of the relations between a self existing in a world (a 'Subject-object') and a world that included selves within it (an 'Object-subject'). For Schelling, the actuality of this relation was none other than language, which he calls "the absolute Subject-Object." Language is at once the medium by which subjectivity expresses itself and becomes objective, and the objective transpersonal realm that permits subjects to emerge and define themselves. Schelling also refers to language as the "ultimate work of art" within a section where he argues that the artwork, in general, lies beyond philosophical articulation and is, nonetheless, our privileged access to 'the Absolute.' In what follows, I will refer to such views of language as those of Hamann, Schelling, and also some of the Romantics (especially Friedrich Schlegel) as 'Concrete Organism' (henceforth CO) views.[8]

The second philosophical approach to linguistic issues in the period preceding Hegel was that proposed by Fichte in his monograph on language of 1795.[9] Fichte clearly and directly challenges Kant's dismissal of reflection on language as 'merely empirical' and yet, in his way, remains 'true to the spirit if not the letter' of Kant's thought by attempting to show that language can be treated within the scope of a broadly 'transcendental' approach. This involves 'scientifically deducing' (in Fichte's own distinctive version of this term) the various basic elements of language (words and other 'lexematic units') and their larger-scale grammatical combinations (e.g., sentences) from the self-positing activities of consciousness. In contrast to CO views, Fichte's 'transcendental view' (henceforth T) maintains that language and its determinations are *products* of the activity of consciousness as it posits an empirical world in opposition to an empirical self. Rather than viewing language as the organic medium out of which various specific possibilities of thought are actualized, he views consciousness as the 'ground for the possibility' of there being such a medium of expression.

Three features of Fichte's discussion deserve special note. First, since consciousness and its positing activities constitute the a priori ground of language itself, Fichte must oppose any claim that thought (or reflection) and language are, in some sense, identical. Rather, as Fichte's discussion makes clear, language not only originates as a product of reflection but develops by the repeated acts of reflection that must intervene at every stage of its development and elaboration. Second, this in turn implies that the basic elements and structural features of language will, in effect, mirror or strictly corre- spond to the intuitions and categories elucidated by transcendental philosophy. As Fichte presents it, it is precisely the task of a 'speculative grammar' to demonstrate how the basic units and structures of language strictly parallel the universal and necessary structures of consciousness at their most fundamental levels. Third, such a 'non- identical parallelism' of language and thought implies not only, *pace* Kant, that the study of linguistic structures can yield insights into the basic 'transcendental structure' of consciousness, but also that transcendental philosophy requires (and will always have available) corresponding linguistic determinations for the articulation of its own project. In this sense, Fichte's view of language is the precursor of many later 'tran- scendental' approaches to language such as those of Frege, Husserl, and perhaps even the 'logicist' program of the early Wittgenstein.

Although Hamann was the first to introduce the term, the third, 'metacritical' approach (hereafter M) was most closely associated with and developed in some of the later writings of Herder and his circle.[10] Rejecting some of the more extravagant and mystical claims of Hamann on behalf of language, though drawing some inspiration from his early responses to Kantian transcendental philosophy, Herder developed a critical viewpoint that was both naturalistic and skeptical in orientation. While he could agree with Hamann that all thought presupposed a 'linguistic medium' for its concrete articulation, Herder viewed language not as some concrete totality but as a diverse set of human historical and cultural practices always evolving in response to natural human needs and desires. Although he did not yet use the term 'ordinary lan- guage,' he was firm in maintaining that the native element of language was that of natural communicative human activity. Anticipating Wittgenstein by almost 150 years, Herder's 'metacritique' was an indictment, first, of Kantian transcendentalism and, by extension, of all speculative philosophy, on the grounds that any distinctively philosophical language was, at best, an artificial and unnecessary reflection and, at worst, an outright confusion of the natural language of 'sound human reason.' In fact, Herder went so far as to state explicitly that all true philosophy was ultimately *"Sprachkritik,"* the critique of philosophical language that had lost touch with its own origins in natural human perceptions, desires, activities, and their native means of expression.

If the CO approach to language tended to view thought and language as, in some sense, identical, and the T approach suggested a strict though nonreductive parallelism of the two, the M approach tended ultimately to reduce thought to language. When we turn to Hegel's views on language, it is important to understand, from the outset, that the nature of language, and hence of philosophical language, was already a highly contested field when Hegel began his philosophical career, that there was no commonly accepted view of philosophical language that he could presuppose in articulating his own philosophical viewpoint. One could then fairly expect that Hegel would, at some point, address these issues. However, as I hope to show, despite the many discussions and references to language found in Hegel's works, no resolution of these issues was forthcoming. Rather, I will suggest that Hegel tended to vacillate between two conflict- ing views of language that, he came to realize, could not be squared within the limits of systematic philosophy as he understood and pursued it.[11]

2. Hegel's Early View of Language in the Jena Period (1804–1806)

While Hegel occasionally refers to language in the course of discussing other matters in his early writings, his first extended discussions of language occur in his lectures on logic and metaphysics at Jena in the middle years of the first decade of the nineteenth century.[12] These lectures provide the initial sketches of what would become his 'mature system' in the 1820s. In his notes for these lectures, the so-called *Jenaer Systementwürfe*, his account of language is clearly influenced by Schelling, who had secured him a teaching position and collaborated with him on several projects earlier in the decade. At the crucial point of transition from Nature (or 'Objectivity') to Spirit ('Subjectivity'), Hegel explicitly invokes language as the medium by which this is accomplished. Referring to language as "the first potency of consciousness," he presents it as a dynamic 'subject-object' with dual aspects. On the one hand, language is the external-ized existence of the interior realm of experience and thought and thus serves to make Spirit 'objective.' On the other, it is equally that external medium by which conscious-ness is capable of grasping and internalizing the exterior realm of Nature, of appropri-ating Nature 'for itself.'

Hegel notes, anticipating later discussions, that language is capable of being both an 'externalization of inwardness' and an 'internalization of externality' because it possesses both spatial and temporal aspects. As articulated in physical sounds and fixed in writing, it exists in what Kant called the spatial form of 'outer sense'; as produced by the activities of consciousness, however, it equally involves the form of time governing 'inner sense.' As Schelling would also hold, as product of consciousness, language is spatial and 'objective'; as process of articulation it is temporal and 'subjective.' This 'dual aspect' permits language to serve as the vehicle for both internalizing the external spatial realm of Nature and externalizing the internal temporal realm of Spirit.

In the Jena lectures, Hegel also introduces a distinction that he will later rework extensively. This concerns the difference between 'signs' (*Zeichen*) and 'names.' At this point in his linguistic thought, he regards signs as more or less 'abstract' and formal elements of the structure of language that serve to classify and to organize sensory experience into more determinate conceptual structures. By contrast, he views names as specific and singular linguistic elements, possessing their own determinate 'content' and providing links between consciousness and its objects based on the process of 'naming.' Signs, that is, point toward concepts, while names are directed toward their respective experiential objects. Here, he seems to suggest that language is composed of signs and names, which, so to speak, constitute the 'warp and woof' of 'textuality' (in its etymological meaning of 'weaving') or, in other terms, the 'conceptual form and experiential content' of language itself.

At this early stage in his linguistic reflections, Hegel's view, closely following Schelling's lead, is clearly associated with those who regarded language as a 'concrete totality' (CO views). Here there is no hint of any tendency to consider language 'tran-scendentally,' and no metacritical suspicions about language seem to come into play. While language does make an appearance at a few other points in these early manuscripts, for instance, in the subsequent discussions of intersubjectivity, social and political considerations ('Objective Spirit'), and religion, Hegel's general perspective remains governed by the themes discussed above.

3. Language in the Jena *Phenomenology of Spirit* (1807)

Hegel's project of a 'phenomenology of spirit' represented a new departure in comparison with his earlier attempts to outline a philosophical system. In particular, it signaled a decisive break, both intellectually and personally, with Schelling, whom Hegel had come to associate with the Romantics' 'unscientific' approach to philosophy that merely postulated 'the Absolute' (like a 'shot from a pistol') without accounting for the individual's access to it. The task of his phenomenology was, as Hegel put it in the Preface, precisely that of providing "a ladder to the standpoint of Science" by demonstrating, through all of Spirit's specific stages of development, that "Substance is essentially Subject."[13]

For such a project, his earlier treatment of language, derived from Schelling, as a sort of pre-existent 'Subject-Object' not only proved inadequate to the complexity of his new task but seemed to be the linguistic counterpart of the merely postulated, abstract, and internally indeterminate 'Absolute' that Hegel famously referred to as "the night in which ... all cows are black."[14] In the course of this work, Hegel explicitly discusses language on several occasions, introducing a set of novel insights that reveal the distance his linguistic reflections had moved from those of Schelling.

3.1. Language and Sense-Certainty

The importance of the role played by language in the Jena *Phenomenology* is evident from the opening sections entitled 'Sense-Certainty' and 'Perception.'[15] At the most rudimentary level at which a 'subject' confronts an opposing 'object' and attempts to articulate its 'certainty' that 'being is the purely individual and particular,' a mere 'this and that,' this very linguistic expression undermines the subject's own intentions. Hegel notes that linguistic determinations are necessarily universals, not particulars – words such as 'individual,' 'particular,' 'this,' and 'that' apply indifferently to any object and fail to designate any single object in its concrete specificity. As a result, whereas the subject meant to claim that being was just whatever specific object was presented in its sensory experience, the linguistic expression of this claim defeated its 'certainty' in specific sensory experience through the fact that the linguistic statement of the claim immediately involved the very universals that sense-certainty intended to deny. Here, as elsewhere in the *Phenomenology*, the linguistic formulation of an intended view or interpretation of an object that is presumed to stand over against a subject ends up saying more and something other than is originally meant, and thereby serves as the 'dialectical engine' that moves the 'subject' to assume another position or viewpoint with regard to the 'object.'

What is decisive here in Hegel's deepening understanding of language is his implicit realization that language itself cannot adequately be viewed as some 'pre-existent Subject-Object,' but involves a 'performative' dimension on the part of the subject itself. To view language as a 'Subject-Object' is treat it as itself a sort of higher-order 'object'

249

(or 'organism,' as Schelling sometimes puts it), an approach that fails adequately to recognize that its 'life-force' is its concrete performative deployment by a 'subject.' More generally, when Hegel takes up language at various points in the *Phenomenology*, it is never as some 'concrete totality' whose general features he attempts to describe, but always as playing specific roles at various stages in the unfolding of consciousness on its path to the 'Absolute standpoint.'

3.2. Language and 'Spirit'

Much further along in the *Phenomenology*, but certainly well prepared for at earlier stages, Hegel writes,

> Here again, then, we see language as the existence of Spirit. Language is self-consciousness existing *for others*, self-consciousness which *as such* is immediately *present*, and as *this* self-consciousness is universal.[16]

Once more, this seems directed against such CO views as those of Hamann, Schelling, and his own earlier perspective. Language now appears not as some 'objective Subject-Object' that the individual subject somehow 'plugs into' or mobilizes for its own purposes but as both constituting the very 'self' of the subject's own *self*-awareness and as that self's existence for other self-conscious selves.

As in the preceding point, Hegel's emphasis remains on the active engagement of the subject in linguistic activity that both constitutes the existence of the subject as self and yet also takes the subject beyond itself, revealing the 'truth' of the self, beyond the sphere of its own self-consciousness, as universal Spirit.

3.3. 'Truth' as Embedded in Language

Just as "language ... is the more truthful"[17] in relation to the intended meaning of the attitude of sense-certainty or individual self-consciousness, so, in other passages throughout his works, Hegel seemed to relish pointing out instances where specific words or phrases convey philosophical 'truths' that typically go unnoticed in their ordinary usage. Hegel's favorite example of this was the word 'Aufheben,' which, he liked to point out, contained within its meaning the essential features of his conception of dialectic: to raise up, to cancel or negate, and to preserve.[18] To adapt one of Hegel's own famous phrases, he had, by the time of the *Phenomenology*, come to recognize a 'cunning of language,' a capacity of language to 'bespeak the truth' or 'disclose the rational' quite apart from its ordinary, unreflective, and debased usages.

In this connection, Hegel, in the Preface, touches briefly on a theme to which he will return in more detail later in his career.[19] He notes that, to ordinary nonphilosophical understanding, the mode of expression and basic terms employed by the 'scientific philosopher' will often seem "inverted" and opposed to ordinary usage. His point is not that philosophy requires some specialized or contrived terminology and usage of its own, but that the philosopher utilizes and consciously deploys the 'truth' contained in ordinary discourse of which nonphilosophical consciousness is unaware. In a sense that contains at least the seed of a response to the Metacritics, Hegel suggests that

250

'ordinary language' implicitly contains all the resources necessary for speculative philosophy on the condition that it is approached in a way that attends to the 'truth' that
lies within, thus liberating this 'truth' from the obscurations besetting its nonphilosophical employment. The philosopher, that is, must trust language while realizing
that the potencies of language are not exhausted, and generally obscured, in ordinary
usage.

3.4. The 'Speculative Sentence' (Der spekulative Satz)

The Preface to the *Phenomenology* also contains a remarkable and widely debated
passage in which Hegel introduces the notion of the 'speculative sentence.'[20] To understand the importance of this passage for Hegel's linguistic thought, we must recall that
Hegel composed the Preface after the body of the *Phenomenology* itself was completed.
Although Hegel placed it at the beginning of the work, its 'standpoint' is clearly that
reached at its conclusion, as Hegel himself notes on several occasions in the Preface
itself. I want to suggest that the introduction and discussion of this quite unprecedented
idea is best read as Hegel's 'linguistic introduction' to his next major project, *The Science
of Logic*, which otherwise contains very little explicit discussion of linguistic matters.
My conjecture here is that, having achieved the standpoint of 'absolute knowing' (the
fully mediated identity of subject and object) in the *Phenomenology*, and then explained
the implicitly 'speculative character' of language in the Preface, Hegel felt confident
that he had laid a sufficient foundation for proceeding with his treatment of logic
without further need for the sort of ongoing linguistic reflection required by the
Phenomenology. As Hegel reminds us on several occasions,[21] all the propositions or
sentences (*Sätze*) of logic are 'speculative,' which means that his discussion of the
'speculative sentence' applies to the *Science of Logic* in whole and in part.

Put briefly, Hegel begins by pointing out that logic has traditionally taken its basic
'unit' (and, by extension, that of all rational discourse) to be the predicative judgment,
'S is P.' Logic then proceeds to treat judgments as pure forms indifferent to any determinate content, catalogues their various types, and explicates the formal relations that
obtain among them. Hegel associates this purely formal approach with the Understanding
(*Verstand*), whose function, as we know from Kant, is to make formal distinctions and
'fix' the elements so distinguished.

However, as Hegel often insists, even for Kant, Understanding is a manifestation,
albeit limited, of thinking or Reason (*Vernunft*) itself. Hegel especially emphasizes that
'speculative thought' can never be purely formal, that it has its own determinate 'conceptual content.' Further, speculative thought, for Hegel, is always a "fluid" movement
or progression among concepts. It is the Understanding that abstracts the 'conceptual
content' from this natural movement of thinking and freezes it into the discrete forms
of 'propositions,' thus converting logic into a sort of external manipulation of
forms from which all truth and life have been drained.

In response to this, Hegel once more affirms his trust in concrete language against
the 'empty formalism' of traditional logic. Whenever the 'Ss and Ps' of the formal judgment are replaced by actual words, we come to realize that the 'subject' is not simply
identical with the 'object,' as the 'is' of the formal copula would seem to assert, but that
the two stand in an internally complex relation involving difference and mediation as

well as identity. For instance, to say that "A dog is a mammal" is at once to bring the two terms into a relation of identity, to differentiate them (here, as species and genus), and to 'protend' their relations to other concepts (here, perhaps, the 'higher-order concept' of 'vertebrate'). To abstract all content from the sentence and view it as expressing a discrete formal identity obscures and conceals the complex thought-movement involved when a concrete linguistic example is chosen. Perhaps Hegel's sense here is better captured by speaking of a 'sentence viewed speculatively' than of a 'speculative sentence,' which might suggest that it is a particular kind of sentence to be distinguished from others.

However, the main point, consistent with our earlier discussions, is that this 'speculative movement' is not something imported into language from outside, some 'content' that thought injects into the forms of logic or some activity that a 'thinker' performs on language. Rather, this 'fluid movement' is the very essence of language in its concrete occurrence. Once more, and in the most universal sense, language turns out to be 'truer' than the empty forms of logic and its abstract notion of 'logical truth.'

When Hegel turns to composing the *Science of Logic*, he insists on exactly this point: that logic as he develops it is not some alternative formal construction or a mere reworking of a 'theory of categories.' It is, rather, the fluid and concrete movement of concepts themselves expressed in linguistic sentences understood speculatively and not merely formally.[22] In a sense, it is Hegel's most forceful expression of trust in the truth embedded in concrete language and his ultimate act of liberating this truth from viewpoints that would eviscerate language, leach away its life, and freeze it into empty specimens for detached observation.

To summarize, Hegel's view of language in the Jena *Phenomenology of Spirit* (and, as I have argued, in the *Science of Logic* as well) had clearly moved beyond the view of language as a 'posited concrete totality' that he had inherited from Schelling, though without entirely breaking with it. Perhaps it would be most accurate to say that he had significantly enriched this view by emphasizing the 'performative' aspect of language, the variety of concrete ways in which the subject engages with and deploys language, and the fact that language, as concretely existing Spirit, possesses a truth and cunning of its own, beyond the intentions of any individual subject, that allows it to serve, when properly attended to, as the universal and objective vehicle for speculative thought. To repeat Hegel's own dictum, "Language is the existence of Spirit," the form in which Spirit achieves objectivity and truth across all its dimensions.

4. Language in Hegel's 'Mature System' (*The Encyclopedia of Philosophical Sciences*) (1818–1830)

Prior to Hegel's assuming his position at Berlin in 1818, it is difficult to determine his degree of familiarity with the works of other thinkers concerned with language (beyond those of Schelling). However, during his years at Berlin, it is clear that he became increasingly interested in the various discussions of linguistic issues that had become ever more prominent in German intellectual circles since the last decades of the eighteenth century. Not only did he begin to deal with language at considerable length in most of the lectures presenting and amplifying parts of what he came to call the

'Encyclopaedia of Philosophical Sciences,' but, in the 1820s, he wrote two lengthy and detailed reviews of works by Hamann and W. von Humboldt, projects that must have cost him considerable time and effort in the midst of a full schedule of lecturing and other administrative responsibilities. Specific references in his lectures on the philosophy of spirit reveal that, by this time, he had also become familiar with Herder's *Metakritik* and the heated debates surrounding it.[23] His lectures on the philosophy of art, especially the sections dealing with literature, show that he had some knowledge of the linguistic thought of the Romantics, and those on the philosophy of religion suggest that he was acquainted with developments in textual hermeneutics. By this last phase of his career, then, it is clear that language was no longer a topic (albeit an important one) that arose in the course of his broader philosophical projects but one that he had come to view as a central philosophical theme in its own right, one that demanded its own 'place' within the philosophical system presented in his *Encyclopaedia*.

Hegel's single most detailed and explicit discussion of linguistic issues is contained within the first major section of the philosophy of spirit (the third division of the Encyclopedia) entitled "Philosophy of Subjective Spirit." This section is divided into "Anthropology," "Phenomenology," and "Psychology," and the last has, as its divisions, "Intuition," "Representation," and "Thought." It is within the section entitled "Representation" (and virtually coextensive with it) that Hegel assigns language its systematic place. Given Hegel's earlier discussions of language, this 'systematic place-ment' of language is surprising on several scores. First, Hegel's positioning of his discussion of language within 'Psychology' seems, in comparison with his earlier views, something of a reversal (or at least limitation) of perspective, since Hegel had previously emphasized the ubiquity and 'objectivity' of language. Instead, here it is explicitly relegated to an aspect of 'Subjective Spirit.' Second, linguistic considerations are entirely absent as an explicit theme from the immediately preceding section on 'Phenomenology,' an omission striking to any reader of the earlier work of this title, even granted the differences between the two projects pursued under this heading. Finally, the delimitation of the explicit discussion of linguistic issues to 'Representation' and their exclusion from 'Intuition' and 'Thought' signals what seems to be a complete break with the CO approaches of Hamann and Schelling. In fact, as the ensuing discussion will show, Hegel's approach to language in his mature thought adopted a sort of 'transcendental (T) form,' though one well advanced beyond Fichte's earlier attempts in this direction.

Before we consider the details of Hegel's discussion of language in the philosophy of subjective spirit, it is important to see exactly what this is designed to accomplish in the broader context of his mature thought. By this point in his career, Hegel seems to have concluded, possibly through his own encounter with Hamann's and Herder's *Metakritik* and the views of Humboldt, that any approach that overstated the role of language in thought and experience, that amounted to a 'panlinguisticism,' threatened to reduce thought and experience to language, an event that would signal the reduction of speculative thought to *Sprachkritik* or *Sprachtheorie*. To make it clear that this was not his own view while remaining true to his earlier insights about the crucial philosophical role played by language, Hegel came to see the systematic place of language as cognate and intimately intertwined specifically with his treatment of the 'psychological faculty' of representation (*Vorstellung*). As he presents this in the philosophy of subjective spirit, each of the various aspects or 'moments' of the 'transcendental faculty' of

253

representation both produce and are, in turn, mediated and linked together by specific significational or linguistic functions, yielding a sort of parallel series of 'representational faculties' on the one side and 'linguistic counterparts' on the other. Put in other terms, the transcendental analysis of representation is accompanied by and coordinated with a sort of 'transcendental linguistics' reminiscent of the 'transcendental grammar' sketched by Fichte in his essay on language of 1795. It is this entire account, then, that effects the crucial transition from 'intuition,' now viewed by Hegel as 'pre-linguistic' and closely associated with sensory images and feeling, to 'thought,' which moves exclusively in the 'post-linguistic' realm of concepts freed of all sensory, imagistic, and merely contingent linguistic restrictions.

Hegel's systematic discussion of language commences with intuition and its immediate sensory images, moves through the various 'transcendental functions' of representation and their significational counterparts, and concludes with thought and its pure concepts.

4.1.   Intuition: Sensuous Image (Bild)

Unlike Kant (at least in his theoretical philosophy), Hegel tends to associate intuition with 'feeling' and claims that, "in intuition, I was immersed in immediate being."[24] Like Kant, however, Hegel now (and unlike his view in the Jena *Phenomenology*) insists that intuition is 'non-discursive,' that it does not yet involve the universality (and hence 'objectivity') of concepts. It is 'pre-conceptual' and thus 'pre-linguistic.' However, as a capacity of human cognition, it involves a drive to express itself and this expression is the 'image.' As Hegel puts it,

> The intelligence, as positing intuition inwardly, posits the content of feeling in itself, in its own space and time, and so the content [of feeling] becomes an image. Image = when the given, which is in the form of immediacy, has sensible content.[25]

The image, that is, is entirely based on and reiterates the 'immediately given (sensuous) content' of intuition. In one sense, the image appears as merely another intuition, but, in another, it has disengaged itself from the subject's mere 'immersion in given content' and "is taken [abstractly] out of the space and time in which it was, and now exists in my space and my time."[26] Hegel goes on to claim that "image means that the intuition is mine" and that "it no longer possesses the complete determinacy or the uniqueness determined by all points [of context] that are possessed by the intuition." The sensuous image, that is, is a copy of the intuition on which it is based, but exists not in the externality of the sensuously given but within the subject itself. Freed from the 'external' conditions of space and time, it becomes a possession of the subject that the subject can voluntarily reproduce within its own 'psychic space and time' and communicate to others through, perhaps, gestures or drawings.

4.2.   Recollection (Erinnerung): Psychic Image (or Representation Proper)

Hegel emphasizes the root-meaning of the term *"Erinnerung"* (to 'internalize' or 'make inner') in defining "recollection proper" as "the inwardizing of the image in the intelligence, not the disappearance from, but the complete immersion of the image in the intelligence and its connection with an intuition that belongs to me."[27] The internalized or 'psychic' image, that is, is Janus-faced: on one side, it remains connected to the original intuition of which it is a copy; on the other, it has become a possession of the subject, which "can for the first time repeat the intuition as it were,"[28] though "in my space and my time."

Recollection thus effects a separation of the 'psychical order' of images that can be freely recalled from the immediately experienced sequence of intuitions. Freed from the sensuous particularity of intuition, the 'psychic image' "is supported [no longer by its context but] by itself."[29] (Hegel sometimes refers to the 'psychic image' as a "representation" in the narrow sense of something that is 'made present again within consciousness.') For Hegel, the most important result of this is that "the image that belongs to me has acquired the determination of the universal."[30] It is, of course, not a 'universal' in the sense of an idea or concept, but it permits a certain degree of generality so that, for instance, one might draw the image of 'a cat' (in a nonspecific, generic sense) rather than 'the cat that I see here on my sofa.'

4.3. Reproductive Imagination (Reproduktive Einbildungskraft): Abstract Representation

Put simply, whereas the function of recollection is, as Hegel famously puts it, to "bur[y] the image ... in the pit of my consciousness,"[31] that of the reproductive imagination is to retrieve images, now freed of their particular intuitional contexts, so that they are "capable of being expressed."[32] Hegel emphasizes here that, just as Recollection had bestowed a certain sort of universality (or, perhaps better, generality) on the image, the Reproductive Imagination, in calling forth images, makes them "objective to the intelligence, and so the intelligence knows of the object it has reproduced." Hegel sometimes refers to the general and objective image as an 'abstract representation,' which he regards as the proper designation for what some empiricists such as Locke called 'ideas.'[33] This result of the working of the Reproductive Imagination brings us to the threshold of the point where signification proper begins to intervene in Hegel's account.

4.4. Productive Imagination (Produktive Einbildungskraft or Phantasie): Signs

Taking over the 'abstract representations' produced by the Reproductive Imagination, the Productive Imagination varies and places them in diverse combinations. It is "a free connecting of representations, a presentation that connects the image to the explication of its proper sense – its proper sense is the universal – as processed representation."[34]

To demonstrate how 'sense' emerges, Hegel refers to the symbol as the simplest example of the working of the Productive Imagination. An 'abstract representation,' which is still a sort of image, can be paired or associated with another. When this occurs, as when an image of a fox is associated with, say, an image of Odysseus, then the former can be said to function as a symbol for the latter. Hegel tells us:

Symbol is an image, the content of an intuition, but it no longer has a simple, natural sense; rather it has a second sense. The one is the immediate sense of intuition, the second is the [symbolic] sense. In the symbol as such, the intuition as such according to its proper essential content, is the same as what the meaning, the sense is.[35]

Like the role of the image with respect to intuition and recollection, the symbol has a dual aspect: on the one hand, it is an internalized, recollected image; on the other, it has a 'second sense' arising from its 'productive pairing' with another image or representation.

Expanding and generalizing on such a simple example, Hegel explains the 'sign' as the result of "the drive of externalization" implied in the productive capacity of the Imagination. A sign arises when some "external immediate [means]," itself spatial and temporal (Hegel mentions "a sound, a tone, a color"[36]), is associated by the Productive Imagination with an [internal] 'abstract representation.' When this happens a 'second sense' or 'meaning' of the sign is produced. A sign, therefore, always possesses a dual aspect: "The one is the meaning, the sense of the sign, that which is represented; the other is that which represents."[37] Later 'structural linguistics' would call these the 'signified' and the 'signifier.' Even further anticipating a cardinal point of this later linguistic approach, Hegel also claims, in a Remark to paragraph 458 of the *Encyclopaedia*, that the sign differs from the symbol in that the relation between 'signifier' and 'signified' is completely arbitrary, that is, unlike the case of the symbol and that which it symbolizes, there is no intrinsic connection between the sign itself and its meaning.

4.5. Sign-Making Imagination (Zeichen machende Phantasie): Words and Language

Although Hegel sometimes seems to elide this 'faculty' with the Productive Imagination, he does, in fact, clearly present it as a third form of Imagination, especially in the 1830 outline of the *Encyclopaedia*.[38] The contrast seems to be that, whereas signs are the result of the operation of the Productive Imagination, the 'Sign-Making Imagination' takes these still somewhat discrete signs and places them in various combinations so that they become integral parts – words – of the higher unity of language. As Hegel states, "Immediate things [and here I read him as meaning intuitable signs] acquire a second existence in and through language."[39]

There follows a lengthy and somewhat digressive discussion about the relative advantages of spoken versus written language and, with respect to the latter, about hieroglyphic versus alphabetic forms of writing. We can summarize Hegel's conclusions briefly by noting that he regards "the sign whose externality is time, namely, sound and language" as "much more appropriate to intelligence"[40] and that, of written forms of language, alphabetic systems, which are more directly connected with spoken language, have a decisive advantage by way of simplification and capacity for expressing abstract ideas.

4.6. Memory (Gedächtnis): Names

To understand Hegel's complex discussion of the crucial final moment of Representation, it is well to observe that the root of the word he employs (*Gedächtnis*) is *denken*, thinking, which will be the next major moment of his presentation. Not to be confused with Recollection (*Erinnerung*), whose primary task is to 'inwardize' the images derived from intuition, Memory operates at the furthest remove (within Representation) from all images. Hegel explains:

> First the object is preserved in the intelligence as image. Like the object, the image has an immediate sensible quality. The name is a second mode [of existence] of the sensible as it has been produced by the intelligence. The name is the determinate existence of the content so that we do not need the image at all; we do not need to bring the image of the content before us.[41]

As noted above, words are linguistic signs that still retain an 'imagistic element' alongside their sense or meaning. On the one hand, names have no such connection and are free of any sensual, imagistic, or representational component. On the other hand, "we have the entire content while we have the name before us,"[42] though without having to imagine the content itself. In the name, the entire 'content' of intuition and meaning is stripped away, leaving us in the purified realm of 'meaningless signs.'[43]

Hegel calls that faculty dealing exclusively with names "Mechanical Memory." As he notes, "It appears miraculous that the spirit, this essential freedom at home with itself, relates to itself externally in its [own] inwardness in an entirely mechanical way."[44] And yet, Hegel says that it is "of the greatest importance in relation to thought" to realize that it is precisely this complete detachment from the sensuousness of the image and its particularities that first makes genuine thinking possible. As any reader of Hegel will immediately understand, it is only at the most extreme point of alienation, of the abject emptiness of meaning, that 'Thought,' a new form of truth and objectivity, can arise.

It is quite clear that Hegel's systematic treatment of language in the Berlin *Encyclopedia* represents a dramatically different approach from that of his earlier writings. While Hegel continues to assign language a vitally important role in his overall philosophical project, it is now much more restricted in scope than in his earlier writings. Certainly within this more limited range, novel ideas did emerge. For one, Hegel clearly saw that any discussion of language required expansion to include the broader theme of signification, which some might interpret as a 'semiotic turn.' For another, his later account was much more attentive both to the constituent elements of language as well as to broader linguistic issues such as the relation between spoken and written language. The discussion was, as well, enriched by Hegel's own study of the growing body of writings involving empirical and historical linguistic research. Finally, he had clearly rethought his earlier views on the important distinction between signs and names, attributing to the latter a crucial role in preparing the ground for conceptual thought. But missing in the later account was his earlier insistence on the *performative* dimension of language; the powerful idea of the 'speculative sentence' as the underlying engine of the fluid, dialectical movement of thought; and the crucial role played by language in the constitution and objective expression of subjectivity in its *entire* range.

5. The Philosophy of Language: The Unwritten Volume

We return now to our original question concerning why Hegel did not compose a philosophy of language to stand alongside his other 'philosophies' of art, religion, politics (*Recht*), and history. Language was clearly a central concern for Hegel throughout his career; there were already numerous precedents for such a project; and there were more than enough ideas in his writings that could be fashioned into such an account. Based on our review of the course of Hegel's thought about language, I suggest two closely related reasons for his not pursuing such a project, one more specific and the other more general.

First, Hegel's thought about art, religion, politics, and history seemed to develop fairly continuously from earlier rudimentary insights and ideas. That is, these projects tended to grow 'organically' so that their later 'self-standing' treatments were more elaborated and detailed presentations that remained consistent with the earlier views from which they developed. However, Hegel's thought about language was an anomaly in this respect. Not only did his basic philosophical approach to language alter over his career from a CO to a ramified T perspective, but, on the one hand, this gave rise to new insights that in no way represented developments of earlier ideas, and, on the other, some prominent earlier themes seemed to drop out of his account. As a result, if one considers the entire range of Hegel's writings on language, it is quite impossible to discover some single or even dominant 'philosophy of language' in his works. Hegel was certainly a thinker who was sufficiently acute and self-conscious to realize that, given the discontinuous path of his own thought about language, the attempt to compose a self-standing philosophy of language would likely be tantamount to 'squaring a circle.'

Second, with the arguable exception of history, Hegel's other 'thematic philosophies' were themselves expansions of discrete 'moments' of his comprehensive philosophical system. However, Hegel had realized early on that language was a ubiquitous philosophical issue in some sense coextensive with systematic philosophy itself, and his later reading of metacritical texts surely reinforced this view. Still, when it came time to present his entire system of philosophy, the project itself required that he assign language a determinate place within it. The path that he chose was to treat language as a key component within a sort of 'transcendental psychological account' of representation. In a sense, Hegel turned a theme that he had long acknowledged as philosophically relevant to every part of philosophy into a more limited, even subjective 'moment' of his overall systematic thought.

In the final analysis, it was Hegel's commitment to the aim of articulating a comprehensive system of philosophy that militated against his attempting to formulate a self-standing philosophy of language. To have done so would have produced a work that could only be either a sort of rewriting of the system itself in a linguistic idiom (which might well have precipitated a second so-called linguistic turn in philosophy a century before it in fact occurred) or an 'extra-systematic' and likely fragmentary exploration of linguistic issues that could have no specific systematic location (thus threatening the very idea of a comprehensive philosophical system to which Hegel had long been committed.) In fact, if the history of philosophy since Hegel has taught us anything, it is that language is central to the very being of philosophy as (at least minimally) a form of discourse, but that any attempt to state *in language* the relation between philosophy and its linguistic medium must remain partial and fragmentary. In this respect, as in so many others, it may be that Hegel's real importance in the history of philosophy is not just his actual accomplishment but what this, at the same time, prevented him from pursuing. Many works bearing the title "Philosophy of Language" have appeared since Hegel, attesting to the importance of the work that he did not write, but it may be that Hegel's decision to remain committed to his comprehensive systematic project was precisely what was necessary to give birth to a new era of philosophy.

Notes

1   Among the more important of such studies are Bruno Liebrucks, *Sprache und Bewusstsein* (Frankfurt/M.: Akad. Verl.-Ges., 1964–); Josef Simon, *Das Problem der Sprache bei Hegel* (Stuttgart: Kohlhammer, 1966); Werner Marx, *Absolute Reflexion und Sprache* (Frankfurt/M.: Klostermann, 1967); Theodor Bodammer, *Hegels Deutung der Sprache* (Hamburg: Meiner, 1969); and Daniel Cook, *Language in the Philosophy of Hegel* (The Hague: Mouton, 1973).

2   Among this group, most of the references to Hegel's linguistic ideas occur in the context of broader discussions and do not amount to anything approaching a comprehensive treatment of the topic. The two most extended and frequently cited, though by no means comprehensive, discussions are Jean Hyppolite, *Logic and Existence*, trans. L. Lawlor and A. Sen (Albany: SUNY Press, 1997), and Jacques Derrida, "The Pit and the Pyramid: Introduction to Hegel's Semiology," in *Margins of Philosophy*, trans. A. Bass (Chicago: University of Chicago Press, 1982).

3   Jere O'Neill Surber, ed., *Hegel and Language* (Albany: SUNY Press, 2006), presents the proceedings of a scholarly conference, held in 2002, dedicated specifically to this theme. Two of the participants have since published book-length works on this topic: Jeffrey Reid, *Real Words: Language and System in Hegel* (Toronto: University of Toronto Press, 2007), and Jim Vernon, *Hegel's Philosophy of Language* (New York: Continuum, 2007).

4   There are several versions of this text, which mainly consists of Hegel's outlines and notes for his lectures in Berlin from 1817 to 1830. All are highly condensed and somewhat fragmentary. However, two much more complete handwritten transcripts by students attending Hegel's lectures were made available in 1994, and these have recently been translated by Robert R. Williams as *Lectures on the Philosophy of Spirit 1827–8* (Oxford: Oxford University Press, 2007) (hereafter LPS). This volume contains a much more detailed and coherent presentation of Hegel's mature thought on language and will serve as the basis for my later discussion of this topic. Cf. William's excellent introduction to this volume for both information regarding the complex history of these texts and an overview of the systematic context in which Hegel's mature discussion of language occurs.

5   R. H. Robins, *A Short History of Linguistics* (Bloomington: Indiana University Press, 1967), is a concise but very useful resource for gaining an overview of the interactions between philosophical thought and linguistic theory in the European tradition.

6   For Kant's most explicit statement of his overall attitude toward language, see *Kants Werke*, Akademie-Textausgabe (Berlin: 1968), IV, 322–323. The most comprehensive study of Kant's view of language is Jürgen Villiers, *Kant und das Problem der Sprache: Die historischen und systematischen Gründe für die Sprachlosigkeit der Transzendentalphilosophie* (Konstanz, 1997). This volume also contains much valuable information about the historical background of linguistic thought in the pre-Kantian German tradition. On this topic, the reader

may also wish to consult Jere P. Surber, "The Problems of Language in German Idealism: An Historical and Conceptual Overview," in O. K. Wiegand et al. (eds.), *Phenomenology on Kant, German Idealism, Hermeneutics and Logic* (The Netherlands: Kluwer, 2000).

7   For a more extended discussion of Hamann's writings and role in the debates about language contemporaneous with Kant, see the Introduction and relevant chapters by Jere Surber in *Metacritique: The Linguistic Assault on German Idealism* (Amherst, N.Y.: Humanity Books, 2001).

8   The most helpful general discussion of Schelling's linguistic thought is Jochem Hennigfeld, "Schellings Philosophie der Sprache," *Philosophisches Jahrbuch* 91 (1984). See also Surber, "The Problems of Language in German Idealism," for a somewhat different approach together with additional references concerning various aspects of Schelling's linguistic ideas.

9   An English translation of this monograph, together with background and additional bibliographical materials, extensive notes, and a much fuller discussion of issues mentioned in the present chapter, can be found in Jere Paul Surber, *Language and German Idealism: Fichte's Linguistic Philosophy* (Atlantic Highlands, N.J.: Humanities Press, 1996).

10   Translations of and commentaries on some of the key documents of the 'metacritical tradition' (as well as representative texts of some of its opponents) can be found in Surber, *Metacritique*. This volume also contains additional bibliographical resources.

11   The reader may wish to consult the Editor's Introduction to Surber, *Hegel and Language*, for another account, from a somewhat different perspective, of Hegel's major texts on language.

12   These early texts can be found in G.W.F. Hegel, *Gesammelte Werke*, ed. Der Rheinisch-Westfälischen Akademie der Wissenschaften (Hamburg, 1968ff.), Bd. VI, 277–296 and Bd. VIII, 185–196. See Thomas Sören Hoffmann, "Hegels Sprachphilosophie," in Tilman Borsche (ed.), *Klassiker der Sprachphilosophie* (München, 1995), for a more extended discussion of these texts.

13   *Hegel's Phenomenology of Spirit*, trans. A. V. Miller (Oxford: Oxford University Press, 1977), pp. 16ff. (hereafter HPS). The reference to the "shot from a pistol" is on p. 16.

14   HPS, p. 9.

15   HPS, pp. 58–79.

16   HPS, p. 395.

17   HPS, p. 60.

18   For one among several passages where Hegel presents this, see *Hegel's Science of Logic*, trans. A. V. Miller (Amherst, N.Y.: Humanity Books, 1969), p. 107.

19   See HPS, pp. 15ff.

20   The relevant passage is HPS, pp. 38 ff. The most extensive study of Hegel's notion of the 'Speculative Sentence' is Günter Wohlfart, *Der Spekulative Satz* (Berlin: de Gruyter, 1981). For a fuller presentation of the view of this matter provided in the present essay, see J. P. Surber, "Hegel's Speculative Sentence," in *Hegel-Studien*, Band 10 (1975).

21   E.g., see HPS, pp. 40ff. The Introduction to the *Encyclopaedia of the Philosophical Sciences* also develops this point at length.

22   See Hegel's Introduction to the *Science of Logic* where he rejoins the discussion commenced in the Preface to the *Phenomenology of Spirit*, reiterating and expanding its main points regarding speculative and non-speculative views of the proposition or sentence.

23   For more background on Hegel's engagement with contemporaneous discussions of language, see Jere Surber, "Hegel's Linguistic Thought in the 'Philosophy of Subjective Spirit': Between Kant and the 'Metacritics,'" forthcoming in the proceedings of the 2008 biennial meeting of the Hegel Society of America, held in Columbia, South Carolina (October 24–26, 2008).

24 LPS, p. 214.
25 LPS, p. 215.
26 LPS, p. 216.
27 LPS, p. 217.
28 LPS, p. 218.
29 LPS, p. 216.
30 LPS, p. 217.
31 LPS, p. 217.
32 LPS, p. 218.
33 Cf. LPS, pp. 219ff.
34 LPS, p. 222.
35 LPS, p. 222.
36 LPS, p. 224.
37 LPS, p. 224.
38 Cf. G.W.F. Hegel, *Enzyklopaedie der philosophischen Wissenschaften 1830* (Hamburg: Felix Meiner, 1969), p. 368.
39 LPS, p. 225.
40 LPS, p. 224.
41 LPS, p. 230. See the translator's introduction to LPS, pp. 33ff. Jim Vernon, in *Hegel's Philosophy of Languge* (London and New York: Continuum, 2007), also offers a detailed and lucid discussion of the role played by *Gedächtnis* in the form of 'mechanical memory' as a basis for the transition from Representation to Thought. Cf. pp. 73ff.
42 LPS, p. 232.
43 Cf. LPS, p. 233.
44 LPS, p. 234.

Part VI

Philosophy of Right

12

Hegel on the Empty Formalism of Kant's Categorical Imperative

SALLY SEDGWICK

Hegel tells us that Kant's supreme practical law or categorical imperative is an "empty formalism." As such, the law lacks sufficient content to ground or justify our various practical obligations. Although Kant employs the law to derive particular duties, he is able to do so, on Hegel's account, only with the help of additional assumptions or content.

Typically, Kantians dismiss these charges as products of misinterpretation. Some claim that Hegel misunderstands how it is that Kant intends us to derive particular duties from the supreme moral law. They take him to attribute the view to Kant that we can determine what morality demands of us in particular instances without attending to the concrete specifics of the case at hand. Deriving particular duties, on this reading, is merely a matter of subjecting the concepts of the moral law to analysis. Others fault Hegel for narrowly focusing on Kant's first formulation of the moral law, the formula of universal law (hereafter "FUL"). They suggest that it is because he ignores Kant's further formulations and their relation to the first that he fails to appreciate all that FUL implies. Still others assert that Hegel's empty formalism critique can be traced back to his misunderstanding of FUL itself. They insist that even if we consider FUL in isolation from Kant's other formulations, it is not empty of content, as Hegel contends.

The interpretation of Hegel's critique I defend in this essay is more charitable. I rely on the following two assumptions: First, I assume that we make a mistake if we restrict our attention to the few passages in which Hegel explicitly attacks the categorical imperative. As will become apparent in Section 1, those passages are far too vague and uninformative to support a reliable interpretation of his empty formalism critique. My interpretation here thus draws on features of Hegel's rejection of Kant's larger philosophical commitments. I take it to be significant, for example, that he discovers empty formalism not just in the categorical imperative but in Kant's account of laws of reason more generally – in the theoretical as well as practical domain.[1] Second, I assume that in charging the categorical imperative with empty formalism, Hegel's complaint is not

---

A Companion to Hegel, First Edition. Edited by Stephen Houlgate and Michael Baur.
© 2011 Blackwell Publishing Ltd. Published 2011 by Blackwell Publishing Ltd.

so much that Kant singles out the wrong law as the supreme guide of conduct, or formulates the law too abstractly. Rather, he means to call into question the special status Kant awards the law. Kant insists that the categorical imperative is universally and necessarily valid. It has this validity, he argues, precisely because it derives from pure practical reason. On my reading, it is Kant's conception of the nature of human reason and its laws that is the ultimate target of Hegel's charge that the categorical imperative is an empty formalism. The fact that Kant presupposes content in his applications of the moral law is evidence in Hegel's view that the law lacks the universality and necessity Kant awards it.

After beginning in Section 1 with a review of passages in which Hegel formulates his critique of the categorical imperative, I move on in Section 2 to examine a common strategy for defending Kant against it. The strategy seeks to establish that the categorical imperative can adequately determine our particular obligations without presupposing content. In Section 3, I explain why this strategy would not be successful in Hegel's eyes. Beginning in Section 4, I defend Hegel's charge that Kant presupposes content in his applications of the moral law, and suggest that he has a plausible case to make against Kant's claim that the law is universally and necessarily valid.[2]

1

Two texts in which Hegel's empty formalism objection is particularly explicit are his Natural Law essay of 1802 and *Philosophy of Right* of 1821. My aim in this section is simply to summarize Hegel's remarks on the categorical imperative in these works briefly and with little commentary. This will prepare the way for our critical assessment beginning in Section 2.

First, a preliminary note: Although Hegel intends his critical remarks in both of these texts to apply to the categorical imperative as the supreme law of right *and* of morality, he draws his examples of its emptiness from Kant's moral philosophy. For the sake of economy, I restrict myself in what follows to his discussion of Kant's moral philosophy.

In the essay on Natural Law, Hegel tells us that in Kant's practical philosophy, the "essence of the pure will and of pure practical reason is to abstract from all content" (435f.;76).[3] Pure practical reason abstracts from content in that it makes into its "highest principle" "no more than the form or fitness of the maxim of the will" (435; 75). Pure practical reason in other words requires that the will's maxims have a certain *form* if they are to count as morally permissible. Although any given maxim has a "content" in that it "includes in itself a determination," the pure will is itself supposed to be "free from determination"; it legislates merely that our maxims have a certain *form* (435; 75). Because we want to know "what right and duty are," Hegel writes, practical legislation must "have a content"; however, practical legislation is precisely what this system cannot provide (435f.; 75f.).

Paraphrasing a passage from the *Critique of Practical Reason*, Hegel provides the following formulation of the categorical imperative: the "maxim of your will must at the same time be valid as a principle of universal legislation" (436; 76).[4] A maxim expresses a principle of intention. What the categorical imperative commands, according to this formulation, is that we act only on those maxims that could be willed by *all* rational agents. Hegel charges that this principle lacks sufficient content to adequately distinguish morally permissible from morally impermissible maxims.

We get some clues to the reasoning that leads Hegel to this conclusion from his remarks on a passage from the second *Critique*, in which Kant discusses a case of a man who comes into possession of a deposit for which there is no proof.[5] Quoting the passage almost verbatim, Hegel notes that the man considers whether to deny having received the deposit in order to "increase [his] property by all safe means" [436; 77].[6] The man asks himself whether his maxim to deny having received the deposit can be universalized without contradiction. Hegel interprets Kant to argue along the following lines: The universalized maxim would effectively allow that "anyone may deny having received a deposit for which there is no proof." If made into law in this way, "such a principle would ... destroy itself because it would then be the case that there would be no deposits." On the basis of this reasoning, Kant concludes that the maxim cannot be universalized without contradiction.

The problem with Kant's analysis, Hegel goes on to insist, is that it does not explain *why* the non-existence of deposits produces a contradiction:

> Were there no deposits, that would contradict other necessary determinations ... But other aims and material grounds are not supposed to be brought into consideration. Rather, the immediate form of the concept is supposed to decide the validity of either the first or the second claim [either the impossibility or the possibility of deposits]. But as far as form is concerned, one of the opposed determinations is just as good as the other (436f.; 77).

Hegel's point here seems to be this: Although the universalized maxim would indeed destroy the institution of making deposits, this does not by itself establish that the maxim is morally impermissible. The test for universalizability in other words lacks sufficient content to explain why the non-existence of deposits is self-contradictory. Moreover, the failure of the test is not limited to this case alone. The fact that the test lacks content is responsible for its more *general* inadequacy in distinguishing morally permissible from morally impermissible maxims, in Hegel's view. As he puts it, there is "nothing that cannot be made in this way [i.e., by means of this test] into a moral law" (436; 77).

Hegel defends his claim about the more general inadequacy of the test by drawing our attention to a case in which its application would seem to lead to highly counterintuitive results. In this case, the test appears to condemn a maxim that most of us would judge to be not just morally permissible but obligatory. The maxim in question is to help the poor. In common with all maxims, Hegel writes, this maxim has a content in that it refers to a specific thing and expresses some specific aim. But if universalized, the maxim turns out to be self-contradictory; its content is therefore "cancelled" (439; 80):

> Were it thought that the poor are to be generally helped, then either there would be no more poor or nothing but poor and no one left to help them ... Thus, as universalized, the maxim cancels itself [*hebt sich selbst auf*] ... Should poverty remain in order that the duty to help the poor can be practiced, then (in light of the remaining poverty) the duty to eliminate poverty is not fulfilled (439; 80).

On Hegel's rendering, the maxim to help the poor destroys or 'cancels' itself, when universalized, for precisely the same reason that the maxim to deny having received a deposit does. If the man in the deposit example tries to universalize his maxim to deny the deposit, what gets 'cancelled' is the aim or purpose of his maxim. Universalization undermines the maxim's aim because fulfillment of the intention to deny having received the deposit depends on the practice of making deposits. If the maxim to help the poor is universalized, then likewise its aim or purpose is cancelled. Its aim is cancelled because, once again, universalization undermines a condition on which the fulfillment of the maxim depends. If the maxim to help the poor is universalized, then either poverty itself is abolished, or those intending to give aid are no longer able to do so (because everyone will have given their money away). As in the deposit case, the maxim can only achieve its aim if it is not universally adopted. The universalization test thus yields the counterintuitive result that even the maxim to help the poor is ruled out on moral grounds. We get counterintuitive results, Hegel claims, with "infinitely more" maxims. Universalization has the effect of "cancelling" them (439; 80).

Hegel reformulates these points 20 years later in §135 of his *Philosophy of Right*. He tells us there that Kant's "moral standpoint" is an "empty formalism" unable to justify an "immanent theory of duties" or a "transition to the determination of particular duties." In requiring of us no more than the "absence of contradiction," the categorical imperative cannot determine whether any particular "content" is or is not a duty. "On the contrary," Hegel writes, "all wrong as well as immoral modes of action can be justified." If we derive from our application of the moral law the conclusion that it is a contradiction to commit theft or murder, he says, this is only because we rely on assumptions not implied by the law itself. We in other words presuppose some content – in this case, that property and human life should exist and be respected. As he puts it,

[A] contradiction can only occur with a content that is presupposed as an established principle. Only in relation to such a principle is an action either in agreement or in contradiction. But the duty that is supposed to be willed, not on account of a content but only as such, is the duty that is formal identity and that excludes all content and determination.

2

Before we turn our attention to efforts to defend Kant against these charges, I want to make two general remarks about the passages we have just considered. Note first that in the Natural Law essay, Hegel writes that it is the "essence of the pure will and of pure practical reason to abstract from all content" (435; 76). He thus identifies as empty and formal not just the supreme moral law of Kantian practical reason but Kantian practical reason itself. In the *Philosophy of Right*, Hegel likewise singles out more than the categorical imperative for attack. His remarks on the categorical imperative are part of a larger critique of the Kantian "moral standpoint" and its "formal" conception of human subjectivity.[7] So although the specific passages we reviewed in Section 1 might lead us to suppose that Hegel was narrowly concerned to convince us of the inadequacy of Kant's supreme practical law, his objections are in fact more far reaching. As I suggested in my introduction, he traces the empty formalism of the categorical imperative back to defects in Kant's account of the faculty of pure practical reason.

Regarding Hegel's remarks on the categorical imperative in particular, we should furthermore note that in the passages we reviewed he considers just one (or two versions of one) of Kant's formulations of the law. In the Natural Law essay, he restricts his discussion to the universal law formulation. In the *Philosophy of Right,* he begins by characterizing the moral law as commanding the absence of contradiction, but then turns his attention to what he refers to as its "more concrete" representation as the requirement of universalizability. Hegel never mentions Kant's further formulations of the law. In both texts, his point is that the categorical imperative is empty and formal when expressed as requiring either universalizability or absence of contradiction.[8]

In both discussions, Hegel's explicit complaint is that Kant's supreme moral law is inadequate to its intended task; it cannot serve to guide the determination of particular duties. Formulated as the requirement of universalizability or of absence of contradiction, the law fails to distinguish morally permissible from morally impermissible maxims. Kant is of course convinced that the law may be applied to guide our conduct in specific instances, and he shows us by means of a number of examples how this application is to be carried out. In Hegel's view, however, Kant's own efforts to apply the law only reveal the fact that he has to presuppose content.[9] In deriving particular duties, Kant in other words relies on more than the test for absence of contradiction or universalizability. Were the categorical imperative really as formal as Kant claims it is, it would lack the resources to guide its own applications. It would indeed be empty, according to Hegel.

I now turn to consider some typical responses to Hegel's critique. As I mentioned earlier, one line of response focuses on his failure to consider Kant's further formulations of the categorical imperative – formulations which, as Kant writes in the *Groundwork,* bring the law "closer to intuition" and thereby offer us a more informative expression of what it commands (436).[10] Here the response is that in ignoring Kant's further formulas, Hegel's effort to convince us that the categorical imperative is an empty formalism rests on an incomplete or superficial rendering of it.

The question of how Kant intends us to understand the relation of FUL to the other formulas is one we will eventually have to address. We will also need an explanation at some point for Hegel's exclusive attention to FUL. For reasons that will become apparent later, I am going to postpone discussion of these two issues until I have considered a different strategy of response to his empty formalism critique. The strategy I have in mind singles out Hegel's interpretation of FUL and seeks to convince us that he misunderstands the way in which that formula is to be applied as a test. Against Hegel, the claim is that once we have at our disposal a *proper* interpretation of that formula, we can indeed demonstrate its efficacy in determining duty. Even without the help of the other formulas, we can employ FUL to discover our concrete obligations in at least in some instances.[11]

It is important that we be clear about what is being claimed here. When it is charged against Hegel that the FUL test (properly interpreted) is sufficient to determine some of our duties, part of what is implied is that the test can do so *without presupposing content.* The idea is that, if the test is correctly applied, then any rational agent will be able to use it to discover what morality requires in specific cases. By employing the test, any rational agent will have the means for distinguishing maxims that are practically permissible from those that are not. The claim, then, is that application of the law does not presuppose content in the following sense: It is not that we first assume some substantive conception of morality, or of what makes a rational will a good will, and then rely on that conception to guide our employment of the moral law. Rather, a conception of what duty specifically requires of us *first emerges* from any rational will's applications of FUL.[12]

Why do these Kantians wish us to understand the test for universalizability in this way? Why, in other words, do they set out to establish that, for Kant, the FUL test does not presuppose content? To answer this question we need to remind ourselves of the particular status Kant awards the moral law. He claims that the law is valid necessarily. This means that it is valid transhistorically, valid for all time. Kant also claims that the law is valid universally. It is therefore supposed to bind all rational natures without exception. The law enjoys this kind of status, on his account, precisely because of its formal nature.[13] So if it can be demonstrated that the law is not the formalism Kant claims it to be, then he loses his basis for asserting its universal and necessary validity. The Kantians set out to establish that the FUL test does not presuppose content because they seek to secure the universal and necessary validity of the moral law.

We can examine this strategy of defense by considering how these Kantians respond to Hegel's treatment of the deposit case. The man in financial difficulty seeks to increase his property by any safe means. He reflects upon the morality of denying receipt of a deposit for which there is no proof. Kant tells us that the man's maxim cannot be universalized without contradiction because universalization would destroy the practice of making deposits. As we saw, Hegel responds to this reasoning by asking: Where is the contradiction in the absence of deposits? A contradiction is committed, he says, only if we presuppose that the system of making deposits ought to exist.

Kantians respond by pointing out that the contradiction with which Kant is concerned here is not in the absence of deposits. That is, Kant's claim is not that the absence of the institution of making deposits is self-contradictory. Instead, the contradiction is between the man's maxim and its proposed universalization. The man wishes to escape difficulty by engaging in deception: he will deny receipt of a deposit for which there is no proof. On the one hand, his maxim affirms the practice of making deposits in that he wills to receive a deposit. On the other, his universalized maxim would effectively destroy the system of deposits.[14] The universalized maxim is self-contradictory because it asserts in effect that the practice of making deposits both ought and ought not to exist. In willing the maxim as universal law, the man in other words wills both the existence and the non-existence of the practice. It is as if, in willing the maxim as universal law, he misunderstands what the concept of making a deposit implies. Kant says of cases like this that the universalized maxim cannot "even be *thought* without contradiction" (424).[15]

On this interpretation, then, there is a contradiction not in the nonexistence of deposits, as Hegel suggests, but in the will of the agent who expects to be able to engage in the practice of making deposits when no such practices exist. The argument against Hegel is that the self-contradictory nature of the universalized maxim can be demonstrated without presupposing that there ought to be a system of making deposits.

270

Is this response to Hegel's critique successful? Can it plausibly be argued that FUL is sufficient for determining some of our duties without presupposing content? In Hegel's treatment of the deposit example, he indeed charges Kant with presupposing that deposits ought to exist. But *why* does he direct this charge at Kant? This is the crucial question. As we know, one proposed answer is that he claims that Kant presupposes content because he misunderstands where the contradiction is supposed to occur. On this analysis, Hegel makes the mistake of assuming that a contradiction arises between the universalized maxim (such as the maxim to deny having received a deposit for which there is no proof) and some presupposed good (the practice of making deposits). But since Kant does not in fact presuppose that the institution of deposits ought to exist, his defenders tell us, Hegel is at fault for locating the contradiction in the wrong place. What is contradicted, according to Kant, is not some presupposed good, but the aim expressed in the agent's maxim. If the maxim to deny having received a deposit for which there is no proof is universalized, what results is a contradiction in the agent's willing.

But is it true that Hegel locates the contradiction in the wrong place? If we return to our presentation of his critique of Kant in Section 1, especially in the Natural Law essay, we discover that the evidence in support of this charge is inconclusive. The man in the deposit case seeks to increase his property by all safe means. He considers whether he can universalize his maxim to deny having received a deposit for which there is no proof. He discovers that, if universalized, his maxim would, as Hegel puts it, "destroy itself" since the system of making deposits would cease to exist. The man thus discovers that the aim stated in his maxim is incompatible with the universalization of his maxim. Hegel does not specifically indicate that the contradiction in this case is in the agent's willing, but nothing about his treatment of the example *rules out* this kind of analysis. Universalization has the effect of undermining the man's aim, the aim specified in his maxim. Universalization thus contradicts the man's *willing*.

It is not obvious, then, that Hegel charges Kant with presupposing content only because he misunderstands where Kant locates the contradiction. But if Hegel's charge does not rest on this kind of mistake (and thus cannot be dismissed for this reason), we need to find some other explanation for it. What other basis for his objection could there be? The alternative interpretation I defend here proceeds along the following lines: Hegel charges Kant with presupposing content because he thinks that the FUL cannot by itself determine duty *even if* we agree that the contradiction with which Kant is concerned is in the agent's willing. So even if we locate the contradiction in the agent's willing, we are still warranted in charging Kant with presupposing content, in Hegel's view.

We can derive support for this latter interpretation if we think about why both in the Natural Law essay and in §135 of the *Philosophy of Right*, Hegel follows his remarks about the deposit case with a discussion of the maxim to give aid to the poor. As is the case with the maxim to deny having received a deposit, if we universalize the maxim to aid the poor, our maxim "destroys" or "cancels" itself; Hegel says that its purpose cannot be achieved. Either there would be no poverty left or so much poverty that no one would be in a position to provide aid. Hegel's point is that if we rely on nothing other than the test to determine whether universalization produces a contradiction, we are forced to conclude not just that the maxim to deny having received a deposit fails the test, but by the same reasoning, the maxim to give aid fails the test as well. In *both* cases, universalization undermines the aim specified in the agent's maxim. So if we rely on the universalization test alone, we have to live with the unsatisfactory result that Kantian moral theory obliges us not just to avoid acts of deception but also to refrain from helping the poor. We can avoid this result, in Hegel's view, only by conceding that the universalization test by itself does not allow us to distinguish morally permissible from morally impermissible maxims. And if we concede this, then we also have to grant that in judging the maxim to deny having received a deposit to be morally impermissible, Kant himself relies on more than the FUL test. In Hegel's terms, he relies on some presupposed content.

Remember that on the line of interpretation we have been considering (the line pursued by certain defenders of Kant), the FUL test is supposed to be sufficient to determine the moral status of at least some of our maxims. The test can, for example, adequately identify the contradiction that results when an agent tries to will the maxim to deny having received a deposit for which there is no proof. The claim is that FUL is able to identify the contradiction without additional assumptions or content – without presupposing some particular conception of the good, or without relying on a morality-laden account of rational willing. But if our above discussion is on target, FUL is *not* sufficient as a test of the morality of this maxim – at least not the representation of FUL we have been examining. For on the account of FUL we have just reviewed, there is no way to explain why the maxim to deny having received a deposit turns out to be morally impermissible, in Kant's view, and the maxim to give alms to be morally obligatory.[16] On the account of FUL we have been considering, *both* maxims, when universalized, contradict the agent's willing.

We can add to these conclusions a further reason for rejecting the claim that the FUL test is adequate for deriving particular duties. This further argument nowhere appears in Hegel's remarks on the categorical imperative, but it gives us another means of supporting his attack on the FUL formulation of the moral law. Consider the deposit example again. A contradiction is supposed to result when the man tries to universalize his maxim. According to the line of interpretation we have been considering, a contradiction results because if the maxim were universalized, the institution of making deposits would cease to exist, and the man would be unable to achieve his purpose. The further reason for rejecting the claim that the FUL test is sufficient becomes obvious as soon as we notice just how incomplete this rendering of Kant's reasoning is. When universalized, the maxim to deny having received a deposit produces a contradiction in the man's willing, and FUL commands us to avoid such contradictions. On this interpretation of the test, all that was supposed to be of consequence in determining morality is that there be no contradiction in the agent's willing. Morality, according to this representation of the FUL test, is simply a matter of not contradicting our ends; no restrictions are placed on *which* aims or ends are morally relevant. In the deposit case, the man aims to increase his property. But if all we have at our disposal is the foregoing interpretation of FUL, then nothing prevents us from carrying out our analysis as follows: Universalization conflicts with the aim specified in the man's maxim; the man therefore ought not to act on his maxim. He ought not to act on his maxim because doing so would interfere with his objective – in this case, to increase his property. To appreciate the problem with this interpretation of FUL, we need merely note that it offers us no means of distinguishing Kant's test for morality from a prudential test. On this interpretation, we ought not to act on those maxims that when universalized, conflict with our ends – and since no restrictions are placed on which ends are of moral significance, this injunction may *include* empirical ends or ends of inclination (such as happiness). However, given the great lengths to which Kant goes in the *Groundwork* and elsewhere to distinguish his moral theory from a merely prudential theory of the good, it is clear that something crucial is missing from this rendering of FUL.

4

To summarize the results of our discussion so far, formulated as FUL, the categorical imperative is empty and as such insufficient for determining duty. We arrived at this conclusion on the basis of two arguments. The first was that if the categorical imperative commands nothing more than that we avoid self-contradiction, then it is not possible to explain how Kant can maintain both that the maxim to deny having received a deposit is morally impermissible and that the maxim to aid the poor is morally obligatory. In each case universalizing the maxim under consideration produces a contradiction in the agent's will. Mere reference to contradiction alone thus leaves mysterious the different moral status Kant awards the two maxims. The second argument drew attention to the fact that the requirement that we not act on those maxims that when universalized contradict the ends of our willing places no conditions on which of our ends are morally relevant. If morality requires nothing more than that we not contradict our ends, *whatever those ends happen to be,* we are left with no way to distinguish Kant's test from, for example, a prudential test for morality.

Our next question is whether a more adequate interpretation of FUL is available – one that better captures what Kant has in mind by it. Minimally, we need an explanation for why he holds that we have a duty both to help the poor and not to engage in acts of deception. If the FUL is not sufficient to determine duty (if, as Hegel claims, it is "empty" because "formal"), then what further content needs to be brought in?

The thesis I defend in this section is that Kant indeed brings in additional content – that he does not *expect* us to be able to understand all that he intends by the FUL test in the absence of further assumptions. In effect, then, I lend support to Hegel's claim that Kant presupposes content in his own applications of FUL. This will complete one important step in our task of providing a sympathetic reading of Hegel's charge that, in the absence of this added content, Kant's FUL is an empty formalism. But this is only a single step: even if we succeed in establishing that Kant needs to supplement the requirement that we avoid self-contradiction with further assumptions, it does not follow from this that his supreme practical law is defective. Nor does it follow that there is something fundamentally misguided about his general moral standpoint or conception of practical reason. Clearly, Hegel intends his empty formalism charge as an expression of criticism. In Section 5, I provide some indication of why he believes criticism is warranted.

Relying once again on the *Groundwork*, we can support the thesis that Kant introduces content if we carefully attend to the way in which his discussion in that text progresses. Early on in section I of that work, his first references to the concept of duty are accompanied by very little explanation. Gradually, however, he reveals his specific understanding of the concept. The same can be said with regard to his first explicit formulation of the categorical imperative, which appears in section II. His initial highly abstract formulation of the moral law as FUL is followed by a number of others. and the others, he tells us, are formulations of the "same law" (436). Kant thus seems to acknowledge that FUL is in need of supplementation – that it does not by itself satisfactorily express all that he has in mind by the supreme moral law.

We can get some sense of the kind of content Kant introduces by taking a closer look at these discussions. Kant's preliminary reflections are contained in the first pages of section I, in which he introduces the concept of a good will. There, he tells us no more than that a good will acts "from duty" (400). When he moves on to clarify what he means by duty, his initial remarks are once again quite uninformative. He describes duty as the "necessity of an action from respect for law" (400). The determining principle of a good will, in his words, is "mere conformity to law as such" (402).

These comments tell us nothing about the nature or content of the law to which the good will conforms. But Kant proceeds to elaborate. The actions of the good will conform to "*universal* law" (402; emphasis added). He conveys this point more clearly in section II, where he writes that duty requires that our maxims conform to the "universality of a law" (421). These comments suggest that on Kant's account, the maxims of a good will conform to law in that they share with law a certain feature, namely, universal validity. He highlights this feature in section II when he gives us his first explicit formulation of the categorical imperative as FUL: *"act only on that maxim through which you can at the same time will that it become a universal law"* (421).

Already in section I of the *Groundwork*, then, Kant identifies the maxims of a good will as maxims that are universalizable. But this still does not tell us very much. For one thing, we need to know *for whom* our maxims are supposed to be universalizable. Kant turns his attention to this question in section II. The grounds that determine the maxims of a good will, he writes there, are valid "for every rational being as such" (413). So to say that the maxims of a good will are universalizable just means for Kant that they could be willed by all rational natures.

So far, then, we know that a good will respects duty, and that the maxims of a good will are maxims that could be willed by "all rational natures." But we now need an answer to a further question: *which* maxims qualify as maxims that could be willed by every rational being? Which are in other words consistent with ends or interests that all rational natures share?

In effect, we are seeking a more complete answer to a question Kant posed in section I:

> [W]hat kind of law can that be, the representation of which must determine the will ... if the will is to be called good absolutely and without limitation? (402).

Kant indeed has more to say in section II of the *Groundwork* about the precise nature of the ends of rational wills. Once again, his remarks are initially quite uninformative.

We learn first that the universally valid end that duty commands is represented as "*in itself* good" (414). An end is "in itself" or "practically" good, he claims in these passages, only if it determines the will "objectively" or "by means of representations of reason." Only then, he says, are its grounds valid "for every rational being as such" (413). If the will is determined by some "subjective" end, deriving not from reason but from the "feelings and propensities" of human nature, it will not serve to ground principles or laws that are truly "objective," principles or laws that are valid for all rational wills (425). The reason for this is that "feelings and propensities," on Kant's account, are features of our empirical natures and as such contingent. Therefore, if we are going to discover an end that is "good in itself," good for all rational wills, we therefore cannot rely on a merely empirical account of the contingent motivating forces of human nature.[17]

Since we cannot appeal to experience in our effort to discover the end that qualifies as an object of universal respect for rational natures, Kant proposes that we focus our attention elsewhere. He asks us to consider what is implied by the very *concept* of the will of a rational being.[18] What he discovers in that concept is the following:

> The will is thought as a capacity to determine itself to act in conformity with the *representation of certain laws*. And such a capacity can be found only in rational beings (427).

Here at last, Kant identifies the end that for rational nature has absolute rather than merely conditional worth and that thus qualifies as an object of universal respect. The end that is of value "in itself" and not merely as a "means" to be "used by this or that will at its discretion" turns out to be nothing other than the will of a rational being (428). The will of a rational being is "objectively" and "unconditionally" valuable, he tells us here, because it has the unique capacity to "determine itself" by acting "in conformity with the *representation of certain laws*."

It is not until we reach these later pages of section II of the *Groundwork*, then, that we learn precisely what is required by the command that we act only on maxims that can be universalized without contradiction. This was not obvious at the outset. When we first encountered Kant's definition of duty as the conformity of our maxims to universal law in section I of the *Groundwork*, we did not know for whom our maxims were supposed to be universalizable. Moreover, we had not yet encountered his argument linking universal ends with ends that are "objective" and as such, unconditionally valid. Nor were we familiar with Kant's strategy for identifying universalizable or objective ends. We needed to follow further steps in his discussion to learn from his analysis of the concept of a rational will, in section II, that the universal or objective end of a rational will is rational nature itself. Only then did it become clear, in addition, that rational nature itself is our objective or unconditional end, on his account, because of its possession of a certain capacity: the capacity to act in conformity with a law it gives itself (431).

Kant's discussions in sections I and II of the *Groundwork* therefore lend support to the thesis that not even he expects us to be able to derive from FUL alone a fully satisfactory understanding of his test for moral worth. FUL commands that we act only on maxims that can become universal law. This command does not by itself specify which maxims qualify as universalizable. We get that further specification, as we have just seen, only with the help of additional assumptions – assumptions about who we are as rational natures and about the unconditional ends of all rational natures. Kant provides this elaboration as his discussion in section II unfolds. In this way, he renders more precise what FUL commands.

As for his further formulations of the categorical imperative in section II – they serve this function as well. The further formulas, Kant says explicitly, are not additional moral laws; as we noted earlier, he tells us that they are further expressions of the "same law." By means of them, it is possible to bring the supreme moral law "closer to intuition."[19] The formula that has come to be identified as the "formula of humanity" gives expression to the claim we discussed above that the object of unconditional worth is rational nature itself, including human rational nature: "So act that you use humanity, whether in your own person or in the person of any other, always at the same time as an end, never merely as a means" (429). The so-called "formula of autonomy" specifies what it is about rational nature that is worthy of unconditional respect. As we saw, Kant identifies as the object of unconditional respect the capacity of rational nature to give itself law. This idea is conveyed in the formula that commands us to act only on the maxims of a "will that could at the same time have as its object *itself as giving universal law*" (432; emphasis added). With this formula, Kant makes explicit his view that what qualifies the will as an object of universal respect is its capacity to give law to itself, its "autonomy."

We know from our earlier discussion that, for some Kantians, the FUL is sufficient for deriving at least some of our duties. These Kantians hold that if we locate the contradiction for which the law tests in the right place, we can demonstrate that the FUL test can determine duty without presupposing content. They tell us that, on Kant's account, the contradiction that results when we try to universalize morally impermissible maxims arises not in the relation between the universalized maxim and some presupposed good, but in the will of the agent. But as I noted in my concluding remarks in Section 3, even if we grant that the contradiction that results from the universalization of a morally impermissible maxim is to be discovered in the agent's willing, this leaves out an important feature of what FUL (or *any* of Kant's formulations of the moral law) is intended to test *for*. If we merely say that the universalized maxim to deny having received a deposit for which there is no proof would thwart the agent's willing, we leave open the possibility that the aim or end that is thwarted – the end (the good) that Kantian morality is ultimately supposed to promote and protect – is nothing other than that of the agent's happiness. If we are to avoid this result, as Kant would surely want us to, we need to add further specification to our interpretation of the test.

We are in a position to do just that, now that we have reviewed some of the additional content Kant introduces in the *Groundwork*. It is now possible to explain what we could not explain before, namely, why he holds that we are both morally obligated to help the poor and prohibited from denying a deposit for which there is no proof. The categorical imperative test commands not just that we avoid contradictions in our willing, but that we avoid contradictions in our willing *of a particular kind*. It is not that, on Kant's account, morality prohibits us from acting on maxims that, when universalized, inconvenience us or make our lives less pleasant. Rather, morality prohibits us from acting on maxims that, when universalized, thwart or contradict ends we share with all rational agents. As we now know on the basis of the further assumptions we have just reviewed, Kantian morality requires us to refrain from acting on maxims that undermine the capacity of rational agency to act from the law that it gives itself. In short, the categorical imperative commands us to respect autonomy.

With the help of these additional assumptions, we can move on to provide a more adequate account of Kant's treatment of specific duties. When it comes to the question of why one must give aid to the poor, we now know that this question is a specific instance, on Kant's account, of the more general question: in what way does indifference to the plight of the poor contradict or thwart autonomy? We know that Kant's answer has to be roughly this: I am morally required to give aid not because my failure to do so is incompatible with my personal objectives – not even because my failure to do so conflicts with the happiness of humanity as a whole. I am required to give aid, rather, because my not doing so undermines a condition upon which the exercise of practical agency or autonomy depends. The same kind of reasoning allows us to explain Kant's claim that morality prohibits us from denying having made a deposit for which there is no proof. Once again, the key question is: in what way does such an act of deception thwart rational ends? The answer, in essence, is that the exercise of autonomy is possible only in a context of mutual trust.

5

I have been arguing that an accurate understanding of Kant's supreme moral law is available to us only if we bear in mind a number of assumptions that cannot simply be read off his expression of it as FUL. These include assumptions, for example, about the beings for whom morally permissible maxims are supposed to be universalizable, beings who share objective ends owing to the fact that they possess the faculty of practical reason and are therefore capable of a special kind of freedom. As the discussion in the *Groundwork* unfolds, Kant gradually brings these assumptions into the foreground. It thus gradually becomes clear that if we are to appreciate all that he means to imply by FUL, we need to take this additional content into account.

But even if we grant this point about the role of additional content, why should we follow Hegel in concluding that Kant's moral theory is defective? Expressed as FUL, the categorical imperative initially seemed too thin to guide the derivation of particular duties. Now that we understand its reliance on background assumptions, however, we are in a position to appreciate just how rich a principle it really is. So what reason is there for inferring that the law's reliance on content is evidence of its deficiency?

We can answer this question by once again recalling the motivation of those who defend Kant against the charge that the categorical imperative presupposes content. Their worry is that if the law presupposes content, then it is not the formalism Kant claims it to be. If it is not the formalism Kant claims it to be, then Kant is without means of demonstrating its *universal* and *necessary* validity. At stake then, is the special status Kant awards the categorical imperative – as the eternally binding supreme practical principle for all rational natures.

Hegel focuses on the most abstract formulation of the moral law, FUL, because he can thereby most easily make his case that Kant's own applications of the law are possible only with the help of presupposed content. He draws our attention to Kant's reliance on presupposed content in order to encourage in us doubts about the moral law's purported universality and necessity. As our analysis in Sections 3 and 4 revealed, FUL cannot be applied without invoking background assumptions about who we are as rational natures, about our unconditional or objective ends, and about our capacity to give ourselves law. And this is not all. Pushing our analysis of Kant's commitments back further, we discover that the assumption that we can give ourselves law depends in turn upon the presupposition that we possess a special kind of freedom or self-causation. This "transcendental" freedom, as Kant calls it, is what allows us to rise above the determinations of nature and initiate a causal series from a standpoint outside time.[20] If we believe ourselves warranted in thinking of ourselves as free in this radical sense, it is because we have embraced a further Kantian assumption, namely, the transcendental idealist assumption that objects appearing to us in space and time are not things in themselves.

In charging that Kant presupposes content, Hegel hopes to direct our attention to the long list of substantive philosophical commitments Kant relies on in his applications of the supreme moral law. He thereby hopes to reveal the *particularity* of the very system of practical obligation Kant insists is universally and necessarily valid. Hegel's larger objective is to call into question the Kantian thesis that we possess a faculty of pure reason that can rise above history and bind us unconditionally.[21] For Hegel, the categorical imperative and the conception of practical reason upon which it rests are artifacts of a unique moment in the dialectical journey of human reason – a moment he believes modern consciousness has progressed beyond.[22]

Notes

1 For one bit of evidence that this is the case, see, e.g., §54 of Hegel's *Encyclopedia Logic*, where he writes that Kantian practical reason does not "get beyond" the formalism of Kantian theoretical reason.

2 I have defended Hegel on this issue elsewhere, most recently in "The Empty Formalism of the Categorical Imperative: Hegel's Critique Revisited," *Internationale Zeitschrift für Philosophie* 16, no. 2 (2007): 5–17, and some years ago in "Hegel's Critique of Kant's Empiricism and the Categorical Imperative," *Zeitschrift für philosophische Forschung* 50, no. 4 (1996): 563–584. Once upon a time, I argued in favor of the very reading of Hegel I am calling into question here. See, e.g., my essay "On the Relation of Pure Reason to Content: A Reply to Hegel's Critique of Formalism in Kant's Ethics," *Philosophy and Phenomenological Research* 49, no. 1 (1988): 59–80.

3 The first page reference to this work is to "Über die wissenschaftlichen Behandlungsarten des Naturrechts, seine Stelle in der praktischen Philosophie und sein Verhältnis zu den positiven Rechtswissenschaften," in volume 4 of Hegel's *Gesammelte Werke*, ed. H. Büchner and O. Pöggeler (Hamburg: Felix Meiner Verlag, 1968). The second reference is to the English translation of this piece by T. M. Knox in *G. W. F. Hegel: Natural Law*, ed. H. B. Acton (University of Pennsylvania Press, 1975). Although I cite the Knox translation, translations of Hegel's texts here are my own.

4 The passage Hegel paraphrases is from Part I, Book I, Chapter 1, paragraph 7.

5 I have made a minor alteration to Kant's example. Kant tells the story as if he (and not "a man") were the subject.

6   *Critique of Practical Reason*, Part I, Book I, Chapter 1, paragraph 4 Remark.

7   *Philosophy of Right* §§132, 136, 137.

8   While Hegel tells us in *Philosophy of Right* that the requirement of universalizability is a more concrete representation of the law, he also goes on to say that it amounts to nothing more than the requirement that we avoid contradiction.

9   For passages in which Hegel explicitly charges Kant with "presupposing" or "smuggling in" content, see the Natural Law essay (423; 60) and *Philosophy of Right*, §135.

10 *Groundwork of the Metaphysics of Morals*. The page reference in parentheses is to the Royal Prussian (later German) Academy edition of Kant's works, *Kants gesammelte Schriften*, vol 4. (Walter de Gruyter & Co., 1900–). I occasionally make slight modifications to Mary Gregor's translation in the *Practical Philosophy* volume of the series *Cambridge Edition of the Works of Immanuel Kant*, ed. Paul Guyer and Allen W. Wood (Cambridge, U.K.: Cambridge University Press, 1996).

11 This claim is compellingly argued by Christine Korsgaard, e.g., in her essay, "Kant's Formula of Universal Law," reprinted in her collection, *Creating the Kingdom of Ends* (Cambridge, U.K.: Cambridge University Press, 1996), pp. 77–105. Korsgaard sets out to demonstrate that FUL is sufficient to handle at least some cases. Other cases can be successfully treated, she says, but only with the help of Kant's further formulas. (I should note that she intends her discussion as a response not to Hegel in particular but to the "Hegelian" critique.) I discuss Korsgaard's essay in greater detail in "The Empty Formalism of the Categorical Imperative: Hegel's Critique Revisited."

12 This account of what it means to assert that the FUL may be applied without presupposing content is endorsed, e.g., by Korsgaard in "Kant's Formula of Universal Law," p. 80.

13 One passage in which Kant is particularly explicit in linking the "formal" or "pure" nature of the supreme moral law to its universal and necessary validity is in the Preface to the *Groundwork* (389).

14 The following question arises at this point: just how much deception must occur before the system of deposit-making ceases to exist? Or, how much deception must occur before the aim expressed in the agent's maxim becomes "inconceivable"? In effect, these are questions about the precise meaning of Kant's universalization test. Sometimes he seems to suggest that the test requires us to ask a question like this: what if everyone were to engage in deception about the receipt of a deposit at the same time? At other times, however, he suggests a weaker test: what if it were universally *permissible* for everyone to engage in such acts of deception? (Evidence that he intends this weaker interpretation may be found in the *Groundwork* at (422) and in the *Critique of Practical Reason* at (69).) Note that the weaker interpretation is sufficient to result in the destruction of the institution of deposit making, provided that enough people engage in acts of deception. How many have to actually act on it to destroy the institution of promising? Kant does not tell us. In the spirit of Kant, however, we might say that even a single false promise damages the delicate fabric of trust without which institutions such as promising and deposit making could not exist.

15 The same kind of analysis applies in cases in which the contradiction that results when we try to will a morally impermissible maxim is of a weaker variety. On Kant's account, some morally impermissible maxims can be thought but not "willed" without contradiction (424). He discusses the case of a man for whom things are going well who adopts the maxim to be indifferent to the welfare of others. In this case, the contradiction that results when the man tries to universalize his maxim is not conceptual or logical. In this case, that is, universalization of the maxim does not entail the destruction of the practice of indifference; the man can continue to practice indifference, presumably, even if others do as well. But although universalization does not destroy the practice, it nonetheless results in a contradiction in the man's willing. This is because universalization of his maxim would likely make

it more difficult for him to maintain his indifference to others. As Kant notes, the man might find himself in situations in which he would need help from others.

16 Kant discusses the duty to be "beneficent" to "those in need" in his *Doctrine of Virtue*, Part II of the *Metaphysics of Morals*, §§29–31. See also his references to this duty in the *Groundwork* (423, 430).

17 Returning to a central theme of his Preface, Kant writes in these paragraphs of section II that, "everything empirical is ... wholly unsuitable to the purity of morals, where the proper worth of an absolutely good will ... consists just in the principle of action being free from all influences of contingent grounds" (426).

18 Kant indicates that this is his strategy at (426). If there is a "necessary law for all rational beings," he says, "then it must already be connected (completely a priori) with the concept of the will of the rational being as such."

19 *Groundwork* (436). There are more than two further formulas, but in the service of economy I mention only two here.

20 Kant writes that when reason acts freely, it acts "without being determined ... by external or internal grounds temporally preceding it in the chain of natural causes" (*Critique of Pure Reason*, A 553/B 581).

21 In *Philosophy of Right*, for example, Hegel argues that modern philosophy has superseded the idea of a will whose freedom is supposed to consist in abstracting away "every limitation, every content" given either "through nature" or in some other way (§5).

22 I wish to thank Stephen Houlgate and Michael Baur for suggesting ways to improve the clarity of some of my discussions in this chapter.

13

The Idea of a Hegelian 'Science' of Society

FREDERICK NEUHOUSER

My purpose in this chapter is not to set out the content of the "science" of modern society that Hegel claims to have achieved in his *Philosophy of Right* (1821) but to articulate the *idea of science* that informs his theoretical project in that text and in his social philosophy in general. My task, in short, is to explain the kind of intellectual enterprise a Hegelian science of society takes itself to be. Doing so will involve addressing two fundamental issues: what the principal *aim* of Hegelian science is, and what *method* it employs to achieve its aim.

Even though Hegel does not distinguish social science from social philosophy – for him *Wissenschaft* and (true) *Philosophie* amount to the same thing – his theoretical aspirations in the *Philosophy of Right* have been influential in shaping the projects of later social theorists. Hegel's idea of a science of society shares deep affinities with a long tradition of social theorists – a tradition initiated by Smith and continued by Marx, Durkheim, and the Frankfurt School – whose theories straddle the boundary between empirical social science and normative philosophy. What these theories have in common is a vision of the good social order grounded in both a detailed, empirical understanding of how existing institutions function and a commitment to normative criteria that are (in the broadest sense) ethical. Although Hegel's science of society is more thoroughly permeated by philosophical concerns than his followers', its accounts of the distinctive institutions of the modern social world – the family, civil society, and the constitutional state – rely heavily on empirical knowledge of contemporary social reality. Articulating Hegel's own social-scientific aspirations will help to make clear his continuing relevance for social theorists today who seek an empirically grounded understanding of society but reject the ideal of a purely explanatory, "value-free" social science that looks to the natural sciences for its model of scientific objectivity.

The Aim of Hegel's Science of Society

Of the two aspects of Hegel's science of society that I investigate here – its aim and its method – the former is by far the easier to pin down. For Hegel tells us plainly what the

A Companion to Hegel, First Edition. Edited by Stephen Houlgate and Michael Baur.
© 2011 Blackwell Publishing Ltd. Published 2011 by Blackwell Publishing Ltd.

aim of his science is, namely, to comprehend reality, or "actuality" (*Wirklichkeit*) – to comprehend what is present and real (*PhR*, p. 20)[1] – in a manner that results in our *reconciliation* with the very reality that science comprehends (*PhR*, p. 22).[2] In taking this position Hegel denies that the aim of science is exclusively theoretical *or* practical, at least in the ordinary senses of those terms. That is, its aim is not primarily to explain social phenomena, whether this consists in accounting for their origin or in laying bare (as Marx purports to do for capitalist society) their "laws of motion." Nor is it science's chief aim to guide human action, whether by prescribing social policy, directing individuals how to live their lives, or providing a blueprint for social transformation. Instead, Hegel insists, science restricts itself to comprehending what is (*PhR*, p. 21), where the comprehension at issue is quite different from both the understanding delivered by the natural sciences and the causal explanations that belong to ordinary experience.

The key to articulating the idea of science that informs Hegel's account of modern society lies in understanding the ideal of reconciliation – what it consists in and why it is needed – as well as its relation to the type of cognition ("scientific," "philosophical," or "speculative") that produces it. More specifically, we need to ask what kind of comprehension Hegel has in mind if comprehending modern society is to have the effect of reconciling us to it. The first thing to say about such comprehension is that it is the product of reason (*Vernunft*) rather than understanding (*Verstand*). As Hegel tells us in the Preface to the *Philosophy of Right*, the aim of a science of society is "rational insight," which consists in "comprehending and presenting" the social order as "an inherently rational entity" (*ein in sich Vernünftiges*) (*PhR*, p. 21). Seeing what it is for science to comprehend something as inherently rational will occupy us for the remainder of this chapter, but one thing it certainly involves is showing its object to be *good* – and, so, worthy of affirmation.

Clearly, recognizing the connection between the rational and the good is essential for understanding science's ability to reconcile us to the object of its comprehension. (When on the seventh day of Creation, God looked back at his work and "saw that it was good," he engaged in what for Hegel counts as the paradigm of rational insight.) Recognizing this connection also makes it clear that, whatever else a science of society involves, it is an inherently normative enterprise. To comprehend modern society as rational is to see it as good, and this insight is the basis for the affirmative attitude at the core of reconciliation. It is important to note that despite the normative character of Hegelian science, the attitude it adopts to reality is not prescription but *affirmation*: embracing as good a state of affairs that (in some sense) already exists. As Hegel famously claims, science's aim is not to "instruct" society as to "how it ought to be" (*PhR*, p. 21).

Yet reconciliation involves more than simply affirming the real as good. This can be seen by returning to the example of divine affirmation alluded to above. For even though God affirms his Creation as good, it would be odd to say that he is thereby reconciled to it. This is because reconciliation entails, in addition to affirmation, a movement out of – an overcoming of – an estrangement (or alienation) from the affirmed object that God has not experienced in creating the world.[3] Hegel's claim, then, that a science of modern society seeks to reconcile us with our world implies that before such a science has been achieved, we are alienated from that world. In this context, alienation refers to a subjective estrangement from the social world that derives from a feeling or judgment that that world fails to constitute a "home," that it is alien or inhospitable to one's deepest aspirations.

Hegel often characterizes modern alienation as grounded in the perception that our social participation – the obligations that laws and social institutions impose on us – is not a source of fulfillment but a "dead, cold ... shackle" (*PhR*, p. 17). The metaphor of the shackle provides a clue to the form alienation takes in modern society, as well as insight into the value its inhabitants prize most highly: modern individuals tend to perceive their social world as alien and inhospitable because they regard it as restricting their freedom, where freedom consists in (various forms of) *individual* sovereignty over one's own activity. One conception of individual sovereignty that plays a prominent role in defining modernity's predicament is the "great obstinacy" – one "that does honor to the human being" – of refusing to acknowledge the validity of laws that one fails to see for oneself as "justified by thought [or reason]" (*PhR*, p. 22). As we shall see below, this conception of freedom – "moral freedom" – is the most important contribution of modern European culture to the progress of humanity. But this contribution brings with it a dilemma for modernity: how is the sovereignty of individual moral subjects compatible with the demands of social life, which seems to require its participants to recognize various authorities – the state, the laws of the market, the norms of family life – beyond their own consciences?

The idea that reconciliation is the proper aim of modern science – that it is rational for us to affirm the "present and real" social world – is itself in need of explanation. It represents another respect in which Hegel's science of society is tailored to (what it takes to be) the distinctive predicament of modernity. In other words, Hegel's view is not that reconciliation with the social world is the appropriate aim of science in all historical circumstances. On the contrary, reconciliation is called for only in modern (Western) society, and this is because that society already is, in its basic outline, rational and good. In historical circumstances in which this is not true – in all premodern societies, for example – affirming the existent world is not rational. In the *Philosophy of Right* the idea that the modern social world is already essentially rational can easily appear to be an unjustified, even outrageous presupposition. For Hegel himself says that a science of society "takes as its point of departure the conviction" that "what is actual (*wirklich*) is rational" (*PhR*, p. 20). A statement like this serves as a reminder that Hegel's science of society is situated within a comprehensive philosophical system and that its location in that system makes it (to some degree) parasitic on a philosophy of history that views history as following a necessary course of rational progress.

Rather than attempt to defend this philosophy of history, it will be more fruitful for us simply to acknowledge this "presupposition" of Hegel's science of society without letting it distract us from our task of articulating the kind of comprehension Hegelian science seeks to provide. It is possible to proceed in this way because the *Philosophy of Right* presents its own argument for the rational character of modern society that can be grasped independently of presuppositions concerning the identity of the rational and the real. Contrary to received wisdom concerning the Hegelian method, the success of his social-scientific enterprise – demonstrating the rational character of modern society – is not guaranteed from the start, and this is made evident by the difficulties Hegel himself runs into in attempting to square some of the real problems of his social world – poverty, for example – with his claim that modern society is rational.

283

This account of the aim of Hegel's science of society leaves unanswered the more difficult question of how – by what method – it seeks to achieve its aim. The remainder of this chapter will be devoted to two issues related to Hegel's method: What must be comprehended about modern society in order for rationally warranted reconciliation to be science's result? And how does Hegel's science proceed in order to deliver this comprehension?

The Method of Hegel's Science of Society

To some extent we already know what Hegel thinks science must demonstrate about its object in order for us to be reconciled to it: modern society must be shown to be "inherently rational" (or good). More specifically, we know that overcoming the alienation of modern individuals requires ridding them of the notion that the demands of society are "shackles" on their freedom. This connection between freedom and reconciliation is hardly accidental. On the contrary, freedom, for Hegel, makes up the entire content of the rational and the good[4] (although, as we shall see, freedom is not exhausted by the individualistic conceptions of freedom that alienated social members have in mind when they perceive their social order as restraining their freedom). The fundamental claim of Hegel's science of society is that a single idea – freedom[5] – provides the conceptual resources science needs to comprehend the whole of modern society as "inherently rational": what makes social institutions rational (or good) is that they play an indispensable role in "realizing" freedom (PhR, §4). Yet Hegel's view is considerably less straightforward than this claim suggests. This is because the conception of freedom that informs his science is extremely complex; articulating its content and demonstrating its unity are tasks of considerable philosophical difficulty.[6]

Before articulating the conception of freedom underlying Hegel's science of society, it will be helpful to look briefly at a specific example Hegel gives of a social science other than his own that performs a reconciling function. The science Hegel refers to is political economy in general, but as his remarks make clear, Adam Smith's *Wealth of Nations* is the principal text he has in mind. Political economy, Hegel says, starts out from a multitude of individual acts, the aim of which is the satisfaction of particular, contingent needs. What makes political economy a science is that it

> explains the relations and movements of the masses in their qualitative and quantitative ... complexity. ... [In] science *thought* extracts from the infinite multitude of details with which it is initially confronted the simple principles of the thing, the understanding that works within it and governs it. ... To recognize in the sphere of needs this manifestation of rationality that is present in the thing and active within it has ... a reconciling effect, but this is also the field within which understanding ... gives vent to discontent and moral dissatisfaction. (PhR, §189A)

A number of points made here illuminate Hegel's idea of a science of society. First, Smith's science (like Hegel's) is grounded in empirical reality. It starts out from the needs and activities of real individuals and takes as its object an already existing social institution – what Smith calls "commercial society" – within which those needs and activities are regulated and harmonized. This empirical starting point is important, for it implies that despite the normative character of Hegel's science, it does not aspire to give an a priori account of the good society in the manner of, say, Rousseau, whose aim is to establish the principles that *ought* to govern society, not those that are in fact at work in the world.

The second relevant feature of Smith's social science is that, although it begins with an empirical reality that appears endlessly varied and complex, it goes on to find within that reality a small number of principles that render its multitude of movements intelligible. What initially appears as an infinite number of arbitrary economic transactions is revealed by the law of supply and demand to be a coherent, surveyable system of economic cooperation. As Hegel describes it, political economy devotes itself to uncovering "the laws underlying a mass of contingent occurrences" by showing that "this proliferation of arbitrariness, ... this apparently scattered and thoughtless activity, is subject to a necessity that arises of its own accord" (PhR, §189Z). A science of society, in other words, comprehends by discovering a systematic unity within its manifoldly complex object.

Finally, Smith's political economy anticipates Hegel's science of society in that the unity it finds in its object has more than a theoretical significance: the laws of political economy do more than explain how commercial society functions; they also have "a reconciling effect." This is because what Smith's science reveals is how a market economy promotes the individual and collective well-being of its participants; hence, in comprehending its object, political economy shows it to be good. One reason that Hegel holds up Smith's political economy as a model for science is that it does not regard the project of explaining commercial society as fundamentally distinct from that of evaluating it. But there is even more that Hegel's normative science of society borrows from political economy, which can be seen by recalling some of the specific normative claims Smith makes in defending the free market.

Most obviously, Smith finds commercial society to be good because the unregulated market promotes certain collective – or, in Hegelian jargon, "universal" – goods: a decent level of material well-being for workers, the lowest sustainable prices of necessary commodities, and greatly increased social productivity. But beyond pointing out the collective benefits of commercial society, Smith also exposes its social *structure* – that is, the relation between individual economic agents (with divergent particular ends) and the functioning of commercial society as a whole. Smith's most famous claim about the market economy concerns precisely this issue, and what it asserts about the structure of commercial society is what Hegel calls "the interpenetrating unity of universality and individuality"[7] (PhR, §258A). The unity at issue here is the harmony between individual and collective interests that Smith finds in a market economy, where individuals need pursue only their own particular ends in order for the collective good to be achieved. The structure Smith attributes to commercial society is one in which the collective good is achieved only through the satisfaction of particular ends, and, conversely, the satisfaction of particular ends depends on the flourishing of the economy as a whole (PhR, §184Z).

What makes a society with such a structure rational for Hegel is not merely that it efficiently satisfies its members' material needs. Beyond this, such a society is rational because it allows for – indeed, requires – the flourishing of particularity, or difference

285

(*PhR*, §184). (For Smith the principal source of this particularly is the increasingly specialized division of labor that a free market economy engenders.) In other words, a society that exhibits an "interpenetrating unity of universality and individuality" achieves collective ends not by squelching diversity but by fostering it and then bringing it into a harmonious, purposeful arrangement, thereby preserving the qualitative richness that diversity implies.

A more important reason Hegel is impressed by Smith's account of the market lies in its effects on its members' *freedom*. Smith argues that a free market promotes its participants' freedom, and for him, too, this is part of what makes commercial society good: the absence of laws or traditions that restrict an individual's free choices, especially to dispose of his or her own labor as he or she sees fit. Although Hegel accepts this point, he is more interested in a further sense in which commercial society promotes freedom. Because a free market so effectively harnesses the forces of self-interest to promote the well-being of all, it achieves the collective good of a group through the free (uncoerced) activity of its individual members. Since individuals realize universal ends by pursuing their own particular ends, they are able to promote the good of the whole by following only their own wills and, hence, freely. In other words, the structure of commercial society is important to Hegel because it responds to the basic problem his science of society aims to solve: the perceived opposition between the demands of social life and the freedom of its participants. What Smith's political economy shows – and what accounts for a large part of its "reconciling effect" – is that when production and exchange are structured by the free market, economic activity is not plagued by an irreconcilable conflict between fulfilling social obligations and remaining free.

Yet, despite this considerable overlap, Hegel's science of society goes beyond Smith's in significant ways. This is reflected in Hegel's remark that because political economy remains at the level of the understanding, it gives rise not only to affirmation but also to "discontent and moral dissatisfaction"; only the comprehension of *reason*, in other words, can effect a complete reconciliation with what is. Rather than focus on Hegel's controversial view that existing social reality already is essentially rational, it will be more fruitful to examine instead what, beyond Smith's science of the understanding, Hegel thinks a genuine science of society ought to deliver: What more is involved in comprehending society through reason?

One way of distinguishing reason from the understanding is to say that the latter proceeds analytically, emphasizing distinctions among its objects, whereas the former is synthetic, seeking a fundamental unity in what to the understanding appears as discrete, unrelated phenomena. In other words, reason seeks a more thoroughgoing *systematicity* in the world it comprehends than is visible to the understanding. The principal deficiency of political economy, as Hegel sees it, is that it is insufficiently systematic, and it is this lack of systematicity that accounts for the discontent – the less than perfect reconciliation – it engenders. Seeing how Smith's account of economic life falls short of true systematicity will open the way to understanding what Hegel thinks a genuine science of society must accomplish.

Before doing this, it is worth pausing to survey some implications of Hegel's critique of Smith. The charge that political economy is insufficently systematic means that Smith's treatment of commercial society is not so much false as incomplete. This is important because it implies that what reason tells us about its objects will not be fundamentally discontinuous with the understanding's grasp of the same phenomena. Instead, what distinguishes these two modes of cognition is mostly a difference in scope, or comprehensiveness, rather than radically divergent conceptions of how commercial society works or what its goodness consists in. Since what Hegel calls the understanding is in turn closer than reason to common sense – and, so, closer to the views that actual social members have of their institutions – Hegel is committed to the position that the normative standards in terms of which ordinary individuals tend to evaluate their social institutions will approximate to or be continuous with those employed by science. This has two important consequences. First, it means that a science of society does not seek its evaluative criteria in some "pure" normative realm outside the consciousness of society's participants (i.e., science's norms come not from outside but from within the object it comprehends). Second, the rational transparency that science must produce for social members if it is to succeed in reconciling them to their world will not involve a radical re-education – requiring them to espouse completely new and unfamiliar values – but only less fundamental changes in consciousness that enable them to see how the various aspects of their complex social world work together, better than common sense apprehends, to realize values they already prize.

The most obvious respect in which political economy falls short of true systematicity is that it is insufficiently comprehensive: its object is not society as a whole but only one of its parts, commercial or, as Hegel calls it, "civil" society. Hegel's science, in contrast, will comprehend the whole of modern society, which includes not just civil society (the sphere of market-governed production and exchange) but two other institutions as well: the nuclear family and the constitutional state. One reason political economy yields discontent rather than full reconciliation is that its restricted scope leads it to uncover problems in its object of study that, when the latter is viewed in isolation from the family and the state, appear irresolvable. Examples of this are what Hegel recognizes as the inevitable but irrationally "contingent" consequences of an unregulated market economy: poverty, unemployment, and extreme inequality (*PhR*, §§185, 200, 230–245). These evils cannot but evoke "discontent and moral dissatisfaction" as long as civil society is considered in abstraction from the rest of society. This is because the spheres of society that political economy leaves out of view play important roles in ameliorating these economic evils, and precisely this – the way each social sphere helps to make up for the deficiencies of the others – constitutes a large part of what makes them a "system." Families, for example (along with corporations), cushion the blows that unlucky or ill-equipped participants in the market economy are bound to endure (*PhR*, §§ 238, 252). More important, the state acts to alleviate poverty, to keep necessities affordable and in ample supply, and to put a check on inequalities that threaten to undermine the moral fiber of society (*PhR*, §§ 235–236, 244–245).[8] Another way in which civil society's relation to the rest of society matters for reconciliation concerns the one-sidedness of the "subjective disposition" (the set of attitudes, or frame of mind) that civil society encourages in its participants. If civil society were the totality of social life, then the only social relations individuals would know would be contractual interactions grounded in mutual self-interest. The egoism of civil society – a positive phenomenon when properly circumscribed – appears less destructive and hollow when one realizes that its two companion spheres foster very different attitudes to fellow

287

social members: in both the family and the state individuals learn to regard others' good as internal to their own (*PhR*, §§158, 268).

For Hegel the most important respect in which political economy falls short of true systematicity is captured in the charge that it fails to grasp the *single principle* that underlies the various elements of society and makes the latter a unified, fully intelligible thing. To understand the kind of unity Hegel thinks a science of society ought to reveal, it is helpful to recall a passage from the *Philosophy of Right* that locates the main failing of contemporary social "science" in its tendency

> to base science not on the development of the Concept in thought but on immediate perception and contingent imagination; and likewise, to reduce the complex inherent articulation of the ethical [*des Sittlichen*], i.e., ... the architectonics of its rationality – which, through determinate distinctions between the various spheres of public life ... and through the strict proportions in which every pillar, arch, and buttress is held together, produces the strength of the whole from the harmony of its parts – to a mush of "heart, friendship, and enthusiasm." (*PhR*, pp. 15–16)

According to this passage, a science of society must be based on the "development" in thought of a single principle – "the Concept" (*der Begriff*) – which enables science to grasp its object as a complex but unitary whole that exhibits a "harmony of parts" akin to the unity found in a Gothic cathedral (or a work of art more generally). (This is the same unity earlier referred to as "the interpenetrating unity of universality and individuality.") Moreover, finding this unity in social reality is precisely what it is to comprehend the latter as "inherently rational" (and, so, to reveal it as good). We already know that, in the case of society, the single principle in terms of which science will comprehend its object is freedom (though we have yet to say what, more specifically, freedom consists in). This implies that the central task of Hegel's science of society will be to comprehend how the family, civil society, and the state, taken together, constitute a genuine *system* of institutions in which all parts are shaped by and dedicated to a single rational purpose: the realization of freedom.

We must now say more precisely what it means for a science of society to "develop" this single principle of freedom and how, in doing so, it shows its object to be a harmoniously ordered, thoroughly intelligible reality. This description of the task before us implies that systematicity enters into Hegel's science in two places: first, the principle, or "Concept," of freedom undergoes some "development" (in thought) that issues in a complete, or fully adequate, conception of freedom; and second, the entity in the world that embodies this principle of freedom is itself a system – a complexly ordered set of complementary institutions that, together, serve the unitary end of making freedom real. In articulating this vision of systematicity it is important not to confuse 'systematic' with 'a priori.' As we noted above, Hegel does not aim to construct, from scratch, a picture of the ideal social world that can then serve as the standard against which existing social reality is measured. Instead, he begins by acquainting himself with how the institutions of his time actually function, and only then, once empirical reality has been attended to, can science undertake a systematic comprehension of its object. At the same time, science's empirical engagement with its object is guided by the "conviction" (*PhR*, p. 20) that the existing social world, as varied and chaotic as it initially appears, is informed by a single principle that, once uncovered, reveals the systematic intelligibility of that world:

> the rational ... becomes actuality (*Wirklichkeit*) by entering into external existence; it emerges in an infinite wealth of forms, appearances, and shapes and surrounds its core with a brightly colored covering in which consciousness at first resides, but which only the Concept can penetrate in order to find the inner pulse and to detect its continued beat within the external shapes. (*PhR*, pp. 20–21)

The "inner pulse" that reason finds at the core of existing social reality is, of course, "the Concept" (of freedom), and our task now is to understand how this undertaking fits together with the conceptual component of Hegel's scientific project – the "development" of the idea of freedom.

One way of reconstructing the method of Hegel's science of society is to return to the *Wealth of Nations*. In this context it is helpful to think of Smith's political economy as including not only an account of how the free market functions but also an investigation into the ideals, including freedom, that make commercial society intelligible to an observer (as purposive and good) and motivate its actual participants. In uncovering the ideals at the core of existing institutions, Hegel's science goes beyond Smith's in that it finds not just one type of freedom at work but three: *personal*, *moral*, and *social* freedom.[9] Each of these types of freedom grounds one of the *Philosophy of Right*'s major divisions: personal freedom is the basis of "Abstract Right" (*PhR*, §§34–104); moral freedom is the topic of "Morality" (*PhR*, §§105–41); and social freedom is the concern of *Sittlichkeit*, or "Ethical Life" (*PhR*, §§142–360). Since Hegel's science attempts to show how all three forms of freedom are realized in modern society, it is necessary to say a word about what each consists in.

Of the three types, personal freedom is the easiest to explain, as well as the closest to the kind of freedom Smith finds in a free market economy. This freedom consists in the free (undetermined) choosing of ends. Persons are conceived of as having drives and desires that are capable of motivating them to act, but they are persons in virtue of the fact that they are not *determined* to act on the drives and desires they happen to have. Persons have the ability to reject some of their desires and to embrace others: they are able to "step back" from their given inclinations and to decide which to satisfy and how precisely to do so (*PhR*, §12). The doctrines of abstract right are arrived at by considering how the social order must be structured if personal freedom is to be realized by all its members. Hegel's answer is that personal freedom is realized when an individual exercises control over a set of will-less entities, or "things" (*PhR*, §42), that constitute his *property*. Over that specific portion of the external world the person has unlimited sovereignty, including the right to be unimpeded by others in the pursuit of his or her chosen ends. The purpose of abstract right, then, is to define and protect for each person an exclusive domain for action that is subject only to his or her own choosing will, and it accomplishes this by ascribing to persons a set of rights guaranteeing them the liberty to be unimpeded by others in doing as they please with their property – their lives, their bodies, and the material things they own.

Moral freedom is a more complex freedom appropriate to what Hegel calls the moral subject. Moral subjects are free not because they simply choose (arbitrarily) which of

289

their desires they want to act on but because they choose in accordance with principles that "come from themselves." More precisely, moral subjects set ends for themselves in accordance with their own understanding of what is (morally) good. (Kant's autonomous agent, who determines his actions by consulting what his own reason – via the categorical imperative – tells him to do, is the paradigm of a moral subject.) The freedom attributed to moral subjects is more complex than that of persons not only because it involves willing in accordance with normative principles but also because those principles are "the will's own" in the sense that moral subjects are able to reflect rationally on the principles they follow and, on that basis, to affirm, reject, or revise them. One way social institutions are implicated in the realization of moral freedom derives from the requirement that moral subjects be bound only by principles they themselves recognize as good. This implies that the rational social order must satisfy the most important right of moral subjects (*PhR*, §132), namely, that all dictates governing their lives, including the laws and norms of social life, be accepted and affirmed as good by the subjects whose actions they govern. It is not enough, however, that social members *in fact* regard their social order as good; moral freedom also requires that their attitude be rationally defensible, that the social order they affirm be genuinely *worthy* of affirmation. A social order that realizes moral freedom, then, must be able to withstand the rational scrutiny of its members. A society that prohibits rational criticism, or whose appearance of goodness could not survive such questioning, might win the actual assent of its members, but it would fail to satisfy the demands placed on it by the ideal of moral freedom.

In contrast to personal and moral freedom, where the emphasis is on the free individual conceived of as independent of others, social freedom consists in certain ways of belonging to and participating in the three principal institutions of modernity. The starting point for Hegel's conception of social freedom is his understanding of the freedom citizens enjoyed in the ancient Greek city-state. According to him, citizens in ancient Greece had so deep an attachment to their polis that their membership in it constituted a central part of their identities. For them, participating in the life of the polis was valuable for its own sake (not simply as a means to achieving other, egoistic ends), as well as a source of the projects and social roles that were central to their understanding of themselves. Hegel regards the subjective relation Greek citizens had to their polis as a kind of freedom for two reasons. First, the fact that they did not regard the good of their community as distinct from their own enabled them to obey the laws that governed them – laws directed at the collective good – without experiencing those laws as external constraints. Second, the classical polis was the source of a distinctive and deep satisfaction for its members. It provided a social framework that gave meaning to their lives and served as the primary arena within which, by fulfilling their roles as citizens, they achieved a "sense of self" through the recognition of their fellow citizens.[10]

These three types of freedom are the result of what Hegel takes to be the systematic "development" of the concept of freedom in thought. As my references to ancient Greece suggest, it is possible to interpret this "development" as not only a logical,[11] but also a *historical* process: the three freedoms that Hegel's science takes as the "inner pulse" of modern society represent three distinct conceptions of freedom that modernity has inherited from the past. Hegel endorses this reading of his project by identifying each type of freedom with a particular historical era in which it dominated. According to this view, personal freedom comes to us from the ancient Roman legal practice that recognized all free citizens of the empire as *personae*, bearers of specific personal and property rights. Moral freedom, in contrast, is a product of modernity. It first appears in the theology of the Reformation (in the view that God's word is present in the hearts of all believers), but it is most fully articulated in the Enlightenment, especially in Kant's conception of an autonomous moral subject, bound only by principles that derive from his or her own rational will.

Implicit in this historical understanding of freedom's "development" is the view that, as inheritors of this tradition, we moderns could not regard a social order that excluded any of these forms of freedom as fully rational (or satisfying). From this perspective, the systematically rational social order can be defined as one that fulfills its members' aspirations to be free in all three of these senses. Hegel's science of society, then, is an attempt to show that the three institutions of modernity, working in concert, can accommodate each of these ideals. One way of formulating its central claim would be to say that what makes the modern social world rational is that it integrates the freedom of ancient Greece with the two types of freedom that succeed it historically. Modern institutions achieve this integration in two respects. First, modern social members have a subjective relation to their social order that is similar to the one Greek citizens had to theirs but also crucially different: in the modern world having identity-constituting attachments to one's community is compatible with conceiving of oneself as an *individual* – that is, as a *person* with rights and interests separate from those of the community, and as a *moral subject* who is entitled to pass judgment on the goodness of social practices. Second, the institutions within which modern individuals achieve their identities (and, so, their social freedom) also promote personal and moral freedom by bringing about the social conditions (explained below) without which those freedoms could not be realized.

With the thought of a social world in which personal, moral, and social freedoms are realized for all we have arrived at a general characterization of what it means for the family, civil society, and the state to constitute a *system* of freedom. It is time to make this idea more concrete by bringing together a number of points already touched on in order to present a more coherent picture of the kind of systematicity Hegel's science of society aims to find in its object. As we know, the essential aim of such a science – to comprehend the entire social order as "inherently rational" – is to show how the three institutions of modernity cooperate to realize freedom in all its forms and for all social members. This aim includes a number of tasks, which fall into three categories:

(1) Rational social institutions *promote collective well-being* by providing social arenas within which their members can satisfy their basic physical, emotional, and spiritual needs. One way of making this point is to look at human needs from the perspective of society as a whole. If we think of the social order as analogous to a biological organism, it becomes clear that, at the very least, a rationally organized society must have at its disposal the materials and capacities required for its own reproduction. This thought brings into view an important piece of what makes the structure of modern society rational for Hegel, namely, that each of its spheres exercises a distinct function necessary for society's material reproduction: the family furnishes society with human individuals; civil society supplies the material goods needed for the sustainment of life; and the state carries out the function of coordinating the two spheres (in that its legislation aims, in part, at shoring up the two subordinate institutions and ensuring that neither flourishes at the other's expense).

It is just as important, however, to view the satisfaction of human needs from the perspective of individuals. From this point of view, too, rational social institutions promote collective well-being. That civil society furthers the material well-being of its members is obvious, for the economic cooperation it facilitates enables humans to produce the goods they need to survive and to achieve a degree of material comfort and luxury (*PhR*, §§191Z, 195). Here Hegel accepts the substance of Smith's claim that the free market[12] – where society's work is not centrally coordinated but undertaken by independent agents motivated only by their own gain – is a highly efficient way of organizing production and ensuring maximal output. But beyond material well-being, members of civil society achieve a "spiritual" good as well: the self-esteem and recognition from others that come from fulfilling one's needs through one's own labor (*PhR*, §§244–245). (The family, grounded in sexual love and the love between parents and children, satsifies the emotional and erotic needs of its members while also providing them with social roles – spouse and parent – that, like the roles assumed in civil society, are sources of self-esteem and social recognition.)

In addition, rational social institutions promote their members' well-being in a way that, at the same time, realizes freedom (in all its relevant senses). The ways rational institutions realize personal, moral, and social freedom can be grouped into two categories, which correspond to the second and third tasks of Hegel's science of society:

(2) Rational social institutions *encourage the expression of personal, moral, and social freedom*; that is, they furnish individuals with the social space they need to realize their conceptions of themselves as persons, moral subjects, and members of particular social groups. Civil society, for example, allows individuals opportunities to act – to acquire and dispose of property – as they choose (personal freedom) and to work out and express their own conceptions of the good life (moral freedom). Participation in the state, too, involves the exercise of moral freedom insofar as citizens play a role in crafting legislation in accordance with a shared, publicly acknowledged conception of the collective good.[13]

The most important respect in which rational institutions are sites for the expression of freedom concerns the ways they foster social freedom by providing individuals with particular identities that make social participation both free (uncoerced) and personally satisfying. Because in the rational social order individuals' self-conceptions are linked to the particular social roles they occupy, their social participation is not only voluntary but also an activity through which they express their particular identities. To say that individuals find their identities in these social roles is to say, first, that they regard the ends and projects they have by virtue of occupying those roles as their most important, life-defining aims; and, second, that in carrying out these roles they win their "sense of self" – their self-esteem and recognition from others. Although Hegel acknowledges many differences among the family, civil society, and the state, he takes these institutions to share one basic feature: each functions by fostering among its members a distinctive kind of particular identity that makes it possible for them to subordinate their purely private (egoistic) interests to collective ends and to do so willingly, without experiencing the social need for such behavior as an external constraint on their wills.

Hegel's idea is that individuals can work freely for the collective good, insofar as doing so is also a way of giving expression to a particular identity they take to be central to who they are. This means that participation in the family, civil society,[14] and the state can be both universally beneficial and particularly satisfying, since to act on the basis of one's identity as a family member, as the member of a profession, or as a citizen is at the same time to work for the good of the whole.

Part of what makes modern society *systematically* rational is that the distinct identities acquired in its three major spheres are complementary. This means that each sphere corresponds to one of the three "moments" that, for Hegel, are essential to any rationally ordered whole. These moments – immediate unity, difference, and mediated unity[15] – refer to what I earlier called the *structure* of social institutions. Thus, the family counts as an instance of immediate unity because love is the bond that unites its members and makes it possible for them to have a collective will, each regarding the good of the family as his or her own good. Civil society represents the moment of difference because its members participate in it as independent individuals who work and trade in order to satisfy their own particular needs. The state, in contrast, embodies mediated unity since it consists in a public realm where laws are framed in accordance with a shared conception of the collective good. The state incorporates the "difference" of civil society because citizens enter the political sphere as particular individuals whose family ties and positions in civil society provide them with divergent interests. Because the moment of difference is not to be suppressed by the state but incorporated into it, its unity cannot be grounded in immediate feeling or any purely natural bond (such as blood). Rather, the tie that binds citizens in the state arises through a collective act of reason – through the making of laws that are universally binding, explicitly known, and consciously endorsed through public reflection on the common good (*PhR*, §270).

The thought behind the claim that a rational society allows its members to develop and express all three types of identities is that each type has a distinct value for individuals and that possessing them all is essential to realizing the full range of possible modes of selfhood. To miss out on any of these forms of social membership, then, is to be deprived of one of the basic ways of being a self and hence to suffer an impoverishment of one's life (in this one respect). This is because membership in each sphere brings with it a distinct kind of practical project with distinctive satisfactions and rewards. While family members engage in shared projects defined by the good of others to whom they are attached through love, civil society is the sphere in which individuals are free to choose how to pursue their own good and to enter into voluntary relations with others. Membership in the state is important because it provides citizens with attachments that round out and enrich their otherwise merely particular lives. In contrast to the other spheres, the state allows its members to acquire a universal identity (one shared with all other citizens) that approximates the ideal of moral subjectivity. For in the state, citizens – constituted as a single body – determine themselves in accordance with universal principles legislated by their own public reason.

(3) Rational social institutions *secure the social conditions necessary for achieving personal and moral freedom*, primarily through the *Bildung* – the formation or education – of its members into agents who possess the subjective capacities required of persons and moral subjects. By its very nature, *Bildung* must take place unconsciously and involuntarily – "behind the backs" of those who undergo it. This is because the subjective

293

capacities freedom depends on are acquired only through a disciplinary regimen, such as labor (the form of discipline distinctive to civil society) or subjection to the will of a higher authority (the basis of discipline in the family). The fact that individuals submit to the process of formation only out of necessity makes the family and civil society especially well-suited to carrying out *Bildung*'s tasks. For individuals belong to the family, for example, not out of choice but because their neediness – the physical and emotional dependence of children, the sexual neediness of their parents – leaves them no other option. Human neediness, then, guarantees that individuals will take part in the family (and civil society), and, when rationally ordered, these institutions both alleviate that neediness and put it to work in the service of freedom.

There are many respects in which rational social institutions are instruments of *Bildung*. Here, one example from civil society will indicate the general thrust of his view. The formative effects of civil society have their source in the fact that its members' productive activity takes place within a system of cooperation marked by a division of labor (*PhR*, §187). Since in such a system no one can satisfy his or her needs through his or her labor alone, members of civil society must learn to tailor their activity to take into account the needs, desires, and perceptions of other individuals. In other words, labor in civil society is informed by a recognition of the subjectivity of others, including a recognition of the necessity of letting others' ends enter into the determination of one's own actions. For this reason civil society helps to form its members into moral subjects. Although labor in civil society is not itself moral action (since it is motivated by egoistic ends), it cultivates in individuals a subjective capacity that moral action requires, namely, the ability to discern, and to determine one's activity in accordance with, the ends of others.

Comprehension versus Critique

Critics of Hegel often object that his science of society, with its emphasis on comprehending what is, has no resources for *criticizing* existing social reality. This charge, however, is based on a misunderstanding. To see this, it is sufficient to note a frequently overlooked feature of his view, namely, that the society described in the *Philosophy of Right* has never existed in the form in which Hegel presents it. Despite Hegel's reputation as an apologist for the Prussian state, the institutions he endorses are not identical to those of nineteenth-century Prussia. It is precisely here – in the disparity between existing institutions and those that are "actual" in Hegel's technical sense – that the possibility for social criticism lies. For Hegel's science provides the resources for seeing where existing institutions do not fully measure up to what they should be and for thinking about how they can be made to conform to their own (immanent) rational principles.

That the critical potential of Hegel's science is so often overlooked is due to a natural misunderstanding of his claim that science's aim is to reconcile individuals with the actual world. But that reconciliation is compatible with social criticism directed at the reform, as opposed to the radical overhaul, of existing institutions. Criticism and reform are consistent with the spirit of Hegel's science, insofar as they aim at transforming institutions so as to conform more faithfully to the rational principles already implicit in their existent practices. This is just to say, in Hegelian jargon, that the proper object of our reconciliation is *Wirklichkeit*, not mere existence (*Existenz*). Applied to the social world, *Wirklichkeit* refers to existing social reality as reconstructed in thought – thought that aims to clarify and bring into harmony the basic principles underlying the various existing social orders that typify Western European modernity. As such, *Wirklichkeit* is a purified version of existing reality that is more fully rational than any particular existent social order but that is not for that reason independent of, or out of touch with, the existing world. Thus, the normative standards that a Hegelian science of society brings to bear on the existing world are "actual," and not merely ideal, in that they are not externally imposed on, but already belong to, the existing object of criticism.

The idea that a science of society can both comprehend and criticize its object has had a large influence on Hegel's successors, many of whom have found the specific normative standards that Hegel's science employs compelling, while rejecting his claim that modern institutions satisfy them. When contemporary social theorists criticize society for fostering anomie, lacking transparency and intelligibility, failing to provide its members with meaningful work, and destroying social structures that give individuals a sense of identity, they are continuing the part of Hegel's project that can be called immanent critique: assessing the goodness of social institutions by holding them up to normative standards internal to the practices being assessed. It is important to see that to say that a certain ideal is internal to a social institution – implicit in its existing practices – does not imply that the ideal is *realized*, or even realizable, by that institution. For Hegel (and his followers), norms are internal to an existing institution in the sense that its functioning depends on participants having an implicit conception of its value and purpose. Thus, it is possible – and many of Hegel's successors have taken this route – to follow Hegel in searching for the norms of critical social science within existing practices but to deny that the existing social world can accommodate those ideals. Such a project can appropriate many aspects of Hegel's science of society while denying that, in the modern world, reconciliation is the appropriate response to comprehension.

Notes

1   "*PhR*" refers to page (p.) or paragraph (§) numbers in *Elements of the Philosophy of Right*, ed. Allen W. Wood (Cambridge: Cambridge University Press, 1991) (hereafter PhR). Hegel's remarks (*Anmerkungen*) are indicated by "A" and his additions (*Zusätze*) by "Z."
2   Hegel's conception of reconciliation is explored by Michael O. Hardimon, *Hegel's Social Philosophy* (Cambridge: Cambridge University Press, 1994).
3   Presumably, Hegel does think of the first six days of Creation as *Geist*'s "externalization" in which God, absorbed in His work, "comes out of Himself" only to return to Himself on the seventh day with the insight that what He has created is good. Still, this externalization is not alienation since it does not involve God's subjective alienation from what He has created.
4   The relation between freedom and the good is complex. At times (*PhR*, §130) Hegel implies that freedom (though here, only *personal* freedom) is merely one component of the good; the other is well-being (*Wohl*). Yet in its most comprehensive sense freedom includes well-being. In other words, a society is not completely "free" unless it provides for the basic well-being of all its members. I discuss this issue in Frederick Neuhouser, *Foundations of Hegel's Social Theory* (Cambridge, Mass.: Harvard University Press, 2000), 237–239.

5   More precisely, it is *practical* freedom – freedom realized through action – that is central to Hegel's science of society. Hegel distinguishes this from speculative freedom, which is the reconciliation, or overcoming of alienation, that results from comprehending society scientifically.

6   I attempt this in Neuhouser (2000); see also Alan Patten, *Hegel's Idea of Freedom* (Oxford: Oxford University Press, 1999).

7   Here I use 'individual' and 'particular' interchangeably. Although in the *Logic* Hegel distinguishes individuality (*Einzelheit*) from particularity (*Besonderheit*), in other contexts he ignores the distinction.

8   Hegel actually attributes these functions to the police, which belongs to civil society rather than the state. Still, these goals must make up part of what rational legislation, the province of the state, aims to achieve. In any case, the general point holds that the state is charged with overseeing and putting checks on the other two spheres insofar as the health of society as a whole requires it (*PhR*, §§260–261).

9   Hegel sometimes calls the latter "substantial" freedom (*PhR*, §§149, 257).

10 Strictly speaking, this constitutes only the "subjective" component of social freedom. The latter has an "objective" component as well, which has two parts: first, the institutions individuals embrace must objectively promote their personal and moral freedom; second, the social order as a whole – not just the individuals who comprise it – must realize a kind of "self-determination," insofar as it constitutes a teleologically organized, self-sustaining system. I discuss these issues in Neuhouser (2000), chapters 2–5.

11 The logical "development" is to be found in the *Philosophy of Right*'s extended "dialectical" argument for the claim that the three conceptions of freedom constitute a single ideal and that only a freedom with this three-fold structure is completely adequate to the core idea of practical freedom: the idea of a wholly self-determining will. I sketch this logical argument in Neuhouser (2000), 27–32.

12 But governmental intervention via "the police" is needed to facilitate the exchange of goods, care for public health, and ensure the quality of the commodities necessary for life (*PhR*, §§235–236).

13 Admittedly, average citizens hardly take part in the making of laws; still, the state's legislative body is designed to make the legislative process sufficiently transparent that citizens can see their laws as rational and affirm them as (if they were) products of their own wills (*PhR*, §§314–315).

14 In civil society professional identities imbue labor with more than instrumental significance and serve as the basis for bonds of solidarity among members of the same profession. Although Hegel largely accepts Smith's point about the role of egoism in a free market economy, he also holds that civil society fosters certain forms of association – the corporations – in which relations among individuals go beyond self-interest.

15 These moments can also be called universality, particularity, and individuality, but when Hegel refers to the Concept in the context of *Sittlichkeit* (*PhR*, §§157–158, 181), he employs the terms I use here.

14

Hegel's Political Philosophy

ALLEN W. WOOD

> To comprehend *what is* is the task of philosophy, for *what is* is reason. As far as the individual is concerned, each individual is in any case *a child of his time*; thus philosophy, too is *its own time grasped in thoughts*. It is just as foolish to imagine that any philosophy can transcend its contemporary world as that an individual can overleap his own time, or leap over Rhodes. (PR Preface, pp. 21–22)

These words were written by Hegel with the direct intention that his political philosophy should be understood in light of them. Hegel's political thought is above all an attempt to grasp the political institutions of his own time rationally, to comprehend them. Compared to any philosopher of any age, moreover, Hegel was uncommonly well equipped to do this. Many who do not know Hegel's philosophy well, but have been deterred from making its closer acquaintance by Hegel's abstract terminology and his willing embrace of metaphysics, may think of him as a philosopher detached from the affairs of common life, unfamiliar and unconcerned with the affairs of practical politics. Nothing could be farther from the truth.

When Hegel's academic career was interrupted in 1807 owing to Napoleon's victory at the Battle of Jena (an event that he welcomed, despite its immediate effect on him), it is significant that his first nonacademic job was editor of a newspaper in Bamberg. Throughout his life, Hegel followed closely the political developments all over Europe, not only in the German states, but in France and England as well. As we will see below, his philosophy of the state as presented in *Elements of the Philosophy of Right* (PR, §§257–329) was an attempt to bring his philosophy to bear on some of the chief political issues of his day.

For just this reason, however, it is particularly distorting to read Hegel's theory as an attempt to respond to the political options of *our* age and the issues *we* most care about. We have most to learn from Hegel by attending to some of the *problems* he raises, which usually show deep insight into the moral and spiritual life of modern society, and the contradictions and dilemmas we face on account of them. Hegel's solutions to the problems may often be outdated, untenable, or even morally objectionable, and easily

A Companion to Hegel, First Edition. Edited by Stephen Houlgate and Michael Baur.

dismissed. But the problems themselves are usually still with us in some form, and Hegel's reflections on them are usually well worth our attention.

The "rational state" as Hegel describes it in this work is decidedly an early nineteenth-century European political institution, and the political issues Hegel takes up are the issues of his own day. Hegel declares that it is not his intention to describe the state as it "ought to be" (PR Preface, pp. 12, 22), but his state includes a number of features that did not exist in his time, or at any time, though it may have been reasonable for him to hope that existing states (such as the Prussian state in which he lived) might soon adopt them. Hegel's political stance was always that of a moderate or cautious progressive in relation to the options of his time. He was certainly no radical, but the all too common depictions of him as a "conservative," "quietist," or "reactionary apologist" are equally off the mark.

Political Events Surrounding Publication of the *Philosophy of Right*

Hegel's publication of the *Philosophy of Right* was itself in a sense a political act. According to some, from its first appearance down to the present day, it was even a shameful or a dastardly act. For this reason, even before we begin to say anything about the contents of Hegel's political philosophy, it is necessary to relate the facts, and indicate some of the options available for their interpretation.

Hegel's university career, which began at Jena in 1801, was interrupted, as already mentioned, in 1807. He made his living first as newspaper editor, then as headmaster at a Nuremberg Gymnasium (secondary school). By the time he returned to university teaching as a professor at Heidelberg in 1816, he had published not only the *Phenomenology of Spirit* (1807) but also both volumes of the *Science of Logic* (1812, 1813, 1816). He was called to Heidelberg to replace J. F. Fries, whom he had earlier known at Jena, and who was Hegel's lifelong enemy, not only philosophically but personally. Only two years later, Hegel was appointed to the prestigious chair in philosophy at the Humboldt University in Berlin, whose only previous occupant had been Fichte.

Hegel's appointment at Berlin itself had political significance. Ever since the defeat of Prussia by Napoleon, there had been a reform movement within the governing elite in Prussia, first under Chancellor Karl Freiherr vom Stein (1808–1810) and then under Chancellor Karl August von Hardenberg (1810–1822). This reform movement aimed at abolishing serfdom in Prussian territories and reorganizing the Prussian system of state ministries. By 1817, there was a movement afoot to open the upper levels of the state bureaucracy and the army to the middle class (only the nobility had ever been eligible for these positions). There were also plans to introduce representative institutions (an "Estates assembly") in Prussia, and also to provide a written constitution. Hegel was appointed in Berlin largely through the influence of two men who were partisans of these reforms: Interior Minister Wilhelm von Humboldt and Education Minister Karl von Altenstein. It is likely that when he arrived in Berlin, Hegel brought with him a draft of the *Philosophy of Right*, which was an expansion of the section on "objective spirit" from the first version of his *Encyclopedia of the Philosophical Sciences* (1817), the text Hegel had written for his university lectures. A comparison of the

298

contents of the *Philosophy of Right* with the constitutional plans drafted by Humboldt and Hardenberg around this time shows that Hegel's conception of the "rational state" resembles closely the Prussian state as it was to have become under these plans.

Two crucial political events, however, derailed the Prussian reform movement, and also led Hegel to postpone publication of the *Philosophy of Right*. The first was a festival held by the German student fraternities (*Burschenschaften*) in October 1817 at the Wartburg in Eisenach. The occasion was a celebration of the tricentennial of the Lutheran Reformation, and at the same time the fourth anniversary of the victory over Napoleon at Leipzig. About five hundred students from a dozen German universities took part. This was one of the earliest expressions of the kind of "student dissent" that has become familiar since then in Europe and other places around the world. In an age where the powers that be were still terrified by the memory of the French Revolution, the German authorities perceived the students as a direct threat to them. Hegel's enemy Fries gave a prominent speech at the Wartburg Festival, which Hegel denounces in the Preface to the *Philosophy of Right* (PR Preface, pp. 15–19). But a number of prominent participants also had ties to Hegel. (His brother-in-law and several of his friends were participants; Hegel's friend Lorenz Oken was as prominent as Fries among the professorial mentors at the festival; and the founder of the "General German Student Fraternity" was Hegel's student Karl Ludwig Carové, whom Hegel later tried unsuccessfully to appoint as his assistant at Berlin.) So Hegel had good reason to take a self-protective stance regarding the Wartburg Festival.

The even more decisive event came in March 1819 when the reactionary writer August von Kotzebue was assassinated by a student, Karl Ludwig Sand, who believed him (probably correctly) to be a Tsarist agent. Sand was a follower of Karl Follen, a student of Fries, who had advocated a "theory of individual terror," according to which such deeds were noble if carried out from political motives.[1] The murder of Kotzebue became a *cause célèbre* for the reactionary faction in Prussian politics. It led Prussia, relatively liberal among the post-Napoleonic restoration states, to join in the Carlsbad Decrees, later in 1819 imposing censorship on academic publications (such as the *Philosophy of Right*) and the removal of academic "demagogues" from their professorships (this included Fries, from his professorship in Jena, though it was restored to him in 1824). The Carlsbad Decrees prompted the resignation in protest of Wilhelm von Humboldt from the Prussian government; Chancellor Hardenberg, better entrenched and more pragmatic than Humboldt, remained in office until 1822. But the reform era in Prussia was over.

Hegel's relation to this history has often been seen exclusively in terms of his obvious attempt to placate the Prussian censors in the Preface to the *Philosophy of Right* (which was finally published in October 1820, though it is dated 1821). It is certainly unattractive and unedifying to witness his denunciation of Fries at the time of his persecution, as well as his evident attempts to persuade the now ascendant Prussian reaction that it had nothing to fear from his book. Some of Hegel's own closest academic friends, such as the rationalist theologian Heinrich Paulus, Fries' colleague at Jena, denounced the *Philosophy of Right* as a mere conservative apologetic.[2] Fries himself famously declared that "Hegel's metaphysical mushroom has grown not in the gardens of science but on the dunghill of servility."[3] This image of Hegel's political philosophy persists in many quarters even to the present day.

It might be open to us to blame Hegel for cowardice in adopting a self-protective stance in the *Philosophy of Right* rather than putting himself on the line in defense of academic freedom. But before we are too quick to judge Hegel, we ought to keep in mind that Hegel's position as a recent academic appointee at Berlin was vulnerable enough. Several of his own students were imprisoned under the Carlsbad Decrees, and he had taken steps to protect them, though in most cases not with much success: he laid out the equivalent of three months' pay to have one of them, Gustav Asverus, released on bail, but Asverus was not released until 1826. It is certainly true that the contents of the *Philosophy of Right* contain nothing dangerous or subversive. Indeed, since Hegel largely defends the position of the Prussian reform movement, much of what he said had until quite recently been the official position of the king and his chief ministers. At the same time, Hegel advocates progressive reforms on such matters as public jury trials, eligibility for governmental offices and the officer corps, the transformation of Prussia from an absolute to a constitutional monarchy, and the creation of representative institutions. His position on all these issues was diametrically opposed to that of the reactionaries, whose views, however, were destined to prevail. It is therefore utterly impossible to reconcile the detailed contents of the *Philosophy of Right* with the virtuously ubiquitous myth of popular intellectual history that Hegel was a partisan of the Prussian reaction or an apologist for the Prussian state in the form it actually existed in his day.

Freedom, Right, and Ethical Life

Hegel's philosophy of right is based on a theory of the human good as the self-actualization of spirit. Hegel claims that the essence of spirit is freedom (PR, §4). Hegel's concept of freedom is a variant on the Kantian and Fichtean theories of freedom as autonomy and as the self-determination of the I. For Fichte, the relation of the I to the not-I is initially negative – the not-I resists the striving of the I – but the essential being of the I is a tendency to wholeness, unity, agreement, which therefore means bringing the not-I into agreement with the I by transforming it according to the I's ends or practical concepts (SL 4:71, 9093, SW 6:298–305) – a process Fichte takes to be infinite and never finally achievable (SL 4:131, 150, 229). Hegel's reaction to these doctrines is to say that freedom must not be conceived as activity in opposition to objectivity or otherness, but rather as the achievement of harmony or agreement between the rational agent and otherness. His preferred formula for freedom, therefore, is "Being with oneself in another" (*Beisichselbstsein in einem Andern*) (PR, §23, cf. PhG ¶ 799, EL §24A, EG, §382,A). By this Hegel means that we achieve freedom when something that counts as "other" in relation to our own agency comes to be in harmony with it, for example, as an enabling condition of it or a fulfillment of its aims. Then this "other" no longer limits us or poses any resistance to our agency, and it is this unlimitedness of agency that constitutes its freedom. Since Hegel thinks we do achieve such freedom in many different ways, he does not see the striving of freedom as infinite (hence insatiable, and in a sense pointless, as it seems to him it is in Fichte). But he agrees with Fichte that the truly free will is the will that wills its own freedom "merely for freedom's sake" (SL 4:139) or "the free will that wills the free will" (PR, §27). The free will does this when it "cancels the contradiction between subjectivity and objectivity" (PR, §28) by relating itself to some existent other in which it is "with itself" in the sense just explained.

This leads Hegel to his formula for "right" (*Recht*), which is the fundamental conception of the *Philosophy of Right* as a whole: "*Right* is any existence in general which is the *existence* of the *free will*" (PR, §29). The importance of this highly abstract and technical notion of "right," for this work as a whole, and for an "ethical theoretic" interpretation of it, cannot be overemphasized. And both the structure and the development of the *Philosophy of Right* are to be comprehended by understanding the kinds of "existence" that are the "existence of the free will," the corresponding kind of free will that gives itself existence (or is "with itself") in them, and the developmental series of these forms as Hegel presents them systematically.

The first stage of the theory is Abstract Right, in which the free will is determined 'immediately' as a 'person' (an abstractly and arbitrarily free agent) confronting an external world of mere things (PR, §§34–39). The right (existence of the free will) corresponding to this relation is *property* (PR, §§40–41). The second stage of the system is morality (*Moralität*), in which the free will is an individual *subject*, whose task it is to bring its particular aspect into conformity with its universal aspect (PR, §§105–113), and whose *right* (existing freedom) consists in actions – external events in the world that are imputable to the subject (PR, §§115–122) and aim at the subject's well-being (PR, §§123–128) and also at the universal moral good (PR, §§129–140).

The spheres of abstract right and morality, however, are for Hegel abstractions from the true existence of the free will, which is *ethical life* (*Sittlichkeit*) (PR, §142). Here the subjectivity of the will is in harmony with a social world of customs, whose rational norms constitute the true content of the universal will that was left as an empty form at the stage of morality. In effect, ethical life, on its objective side, consists of a rational social order in which shared, collective action realizes the welfare of individuals and the moral good (PR, §§144–145). But ethical life also refers to a subjective side, which is the consciousness that individual agents have of this social order, which becomes something real and existent only through their actions (PR, §146). Hegel is often thought to have conceived this subjective side of ethical life only as something unreflective, an attitude of uncritical obedience to social customs. In fact, however, he thinks of it as admitting also of rational reflection, both in the form of the (one-sided) insight into finite benefits for individuals and groups of social institutions and also the (philosophical) comprehension of their rational worth as valuable in themselves; ethical self-consciousness consists at least as much in these developed forms as in the more immediate and unreflective ones (PR, §147). The ethical free will is most truly free, or "with itself" in its other (which here comprises the objective social institutions) when it rationally comprehends them and participates in them rationally and knowingly. As we shall see presently, this point is essential to understanding Hegel's conception of the state (or political institutions) in general.

It is also important to emphasize that ethical life for Hegel represents a rational standard of social life, not just the empirical description of some set of customs or folkways that might happen to exist. "Ethical life" as presented in the *Philosophy of Right* is Hegel's attempt to display the rationality of modern social life, where the standard of rationality lies in the comprehensive knowledge of itself that spirit has attained at this point in history, and the manifold ways in which its nature is actualized by modern institutions – including, for example, the self-conception of modern individuals as *persons* with rights and as moral *subjects*. The whole point of the *Philosophy of Right*, in fact, is that the ethical truth contained in public laws and morality should come to be rationally "comprehended" and hence "also gain a rational form and thereby appear justified to free thinking" (PR Preface, p. 11).

The Family and Civil Society

Hegel divides modern ethical life into three basic institutions: the family, civil society, and the state. The family, according to Hegel, is the institution that expresses the unity of spirit *(Geist)* at the level of immediate *feeling*. The determination of the free will corresponding to the family is not that of an independently existing person but that of a "member" *(Glied)*, and its immediate way of "being with itself" in others is *love* (PR, §158). The foundation of the family is marriage (PR, §§161–165), with the partitioning of sexual roles, with the family as the woman's special vocation *(Bestimmung)* (PR, §166). Marriage is the union of two persons into a single one (PR, §167), while the man's role is to be the administrator of the family's common resources, and also the representative in the public realm of its personality (PR, §171). Hegel conceives the family as the bourgeois nuclear family, not the feudal extended family – the "clan" or "kinship group" *(Stamm)*, whose traditional status in premodern societies Hegel sees as waning – a social development he welcomes (PR, §177). This conception of the modern family is dictated by the crucial importance of the distinctively modern social institution – "civil society" *(bürgerliche Gesellschaft)* (PR, §§182–256).

Prior to Hegel, the Latin term *societas civilis* and its cognates in modern languages ('civil society,' *bürgerliche Gesellschaft, société civile,* etc.) were generally taken to refer to the political state.[4] Hegel's distinction between 'civil society' and the 'state' in fact represents a change in the conception of the institutions to which *both* terms refer – a point that is crucial to the understanding of Hegel's political philosophy.

The basis of civil society is a distinctively modern way that people relate to one another in their economic life. Individuals in the modern world understand themselves as particulars existing on their own, freely determining their own way of life. This is the source of the modern conceptions of the *person* (in the sphere of abstract right) and of the *subject* (in the sphere of morality). At the same time, both these spheres involve universal standards – of arbitrary freedom, property, and mutual recognition in the sphere of right, and of responsibility, welfare, the good, and conscience in morality. The fact that individuality also involves certain normatively regulated relations to others is what makes civil society a species of ethical life at all (PR, §§182–186).

We may consider civil society in terms of the Hegelian concept of right as the existence of freedom, and the variations in the corresponding relation between the conception of the *free will* and the corresponding *existence* or "otherness" in which the will is "with itself." The free will simply as a member of civil society *(bürgerliche Gesellschaft)* in general is the 'citizen' *(Bürger)* in the determinate sense of the French word *bourgeois* (as distinct from *citoyen*, who is instead a member of the political state). But there are three levels of this bourgeois existence: as a member of the economic realm properly speaking, the "system of needs," as a person before the law in the system of justice, and as a member of a determinate branch of civil society, to which Hegel gives the name "corporation" (*Korporation*) (PR, §188). Each corresponds to a way in which the bourgeois is "with himself" or achieves freedom in relation to a determinate institutional form in civil society.

The greatest contribution of Adam Smith's *Wealth of Nations* was to show how the relations between people in what he called "commercial society" express and also actualize a certain conception of human individuality and dignity that is characteristically modern and that corresponds to values such as individual freedom and personal independence that belong to post-Enlightenment culture. According to Hegel, people receive education (*Bildung*) for this new kind of society from the *labor* they do in civil society (PR, §187). This labor makes them part of a "system of needs." Adam Smith's "commercial society" is not accurately depicted as equivalent to more recent economic conceptions such as "the market" or "the capitalist economy." Still less is Hegel's civil society reducible to anything like them. In Hegel's view, the division of labor educates each person to a distinctively different way of life, and to a determinate social group, for which he uses Fichte's term "estate" (*Stand*) (PR, §201). For Hegel, there are three basic estates: the "substantial" (rural, agricultural) estate, the "formal" (urban manufacturing and commercial) estate, and the universal (or civil service) estate (PR, §202). Especially in the "formal" estate, people achieve a determinate sense of identity and honor (*Standesehre*) through being a specific kind of professional or tradesman (*Gewerbsmann*) (PR, §§252–253).

In this connection, Hegel shows remarkable insight into some of the contradictions involved in the inequality and poverty in civil society (PR, §§243–249). Poverty is a serious problem because it brings to light a large class (*Klasse*) of people who (now in Marx's words rather than Hegel's, but the thought is entirely Hegelian) are *in* civil society but without being *of* civil society. For properly speaking, to belong to civil society is to have the determinate social identity pertaining to an estate, and to belong to what Hegel calls a 'corporation' (*Korporation*). This term refers not to the limited liability firm but to something more like a guild or professional organization, which both takes collective responsibility for performing a determinate service in civil society and also serves as a kind of "second family" to its members, providing them with economic security and a determinate ethical home in civil society (PR, §§250–256).

The fact that one's identity as a professional or tradesman and membership in a corporation are essential features of membership in civil society points to the fact that civil society for Hegel is not the accidental result of the interaction of isolated individuals but a form of *ethical life*. This is even clearer in Hegel's treatment of the two institutional features of ethical life that others tend to view as functions of the *state*. The first of these is the "administration of justice," the system of law enforcement, civil and criminal law, and the courts (PR, §§209–229). The other is the administrative system Hegel calls the 'police' (*Poliziei*) (PR, §§230–240). In Hegel's day, this term did not refer only to the activities of law enforcement but included the provision of all kinds of public services that regulate and enable the functioning of civil society – from road repair and street lighting to the regulation of the economy to providing for poor relief. Thus Hegel formulates the meaning of 'police' in his lectures as "the state, insofar as it refers to civil society" (VPR19 187).[5] Both the administration of justice and the police, to be sure, belong under the legal and administrative functions of what Hegel will call the 'state,' but in his view their activities are not political, but are rather activities of civil society and within civil society.

Hegel's Concept of the State

"The state is the actuality of the ethical idea – the ethical spirit as substantial will, *manifest* and clear to itself, which thinks and knows itself and implements what it knows in so far as it knows it" (PR, §257). Hegel's jargon, especially combined with pompous sounding pronouncements of what may be unfamiliar philosophical ideas, often leaves us puzzled as to what he is saying. So let's look at the parts of the above assertion, and try to figure it out. An *idea* is a concept that gives itself external or objective existence (EL, §213). The *ethical*, as we have seen, is the unity of subjective consciousness with rational social institutions. And *actuality* is anything that has developed its nature so that it corresponds to its concept, the concept expressing that nature (EL, §6, 142). So the state is the externally existing social institution that fully expresses the nature of social institutions in their most rational form. From what Hegel says in PR §257, it is plain that this complete actuality has a lot to do with the way the objective side of the ethical – the social institutions, their rationality – is perceived or known by the subjective side, or the ethical consciousness of individuals. The state is complete ethical actuality. This contrasts with the spiritual unity of the family, whose scope is restricted and not universal, and whose consciousness is merely the immediate form of that unity, present in the love of family members for one another. It contrasts also with the kind of universal rationality present in civil society, for this is not present as knowledge in the consciousness of individuals. As members of civil society, they participate in it as concrete persons and subjects with their own particular ends, or at most with the consciousness of their estate and their corporation, which (as Hegel emphasizes) falls short of being a universal consciousness (PR, §256). The highest freedom of individuals lies in their "patriotism" or "political disposition" (PR, §268). But Hegel understands patriotism less as a "willingness to perform extraordinary sacrifices and actions" for the sake of the state than as "that disposition which, in the normal conditions and circumstances of life, habitually knows that the community is the substantial basis and end" (PR, §268R). For Hegel, our lives as individuals become meaningful, and we achieve freedom, when we devote ourselves to a rational end beyond our own self-interest that is shared with others but also takes care of our own rights, subjective freedom, and welfare as parts of it. The state is the highest rational end of this kind.

Thus Hegel rejects the idea that the state is there only to serve the interests of individuals – he thinks this is an error that results from the failure to distinguish the state from civil society (PR, §183). But it is equally false that Hegel thinks of the state as something to which individuals must sacrifice either their individual welfare or (especially) their freedom as persons with rights or subjects determining their own path in life. He accepts the claim that the end of the state is the happiness of its citizens (PR §265A), insisting on the complementary proposition that the state itself is the precondition of their welfare (PR, §261A). The entire strength of modern states, in his view, consists in the fact that their principle "allows the principle of subjectivity to attain fulfillment in the *self-sufficient extreme* of personal particularity, while at the same time *bringing it back to substantial unity* and so preserving this unity in the principle of subjectivity itself" (PR, §260).

What is distinctive about the state, then, is on the objective side that it represents the most complete unity of the ethical spirit as something universal. Its laws and norms are the highest ones for individuals, "whose highest duty is to be members of the state" (PR, §258). On the subjective side, the state also represents these norms in their fully conscious and rational form as something consciously known and *willed* (PR, §§256–258, R). These two claims about the state are likely to be unfamiliar to us, and we may even feel profound resistance to them. To the first claim, we may object that surely our duties to the state are duties to a community of limited scope. Duties to the state are in that sense not genuinely "universal" at all. Other duties, more truly universal in scope – to humanity in general, to the general happiness of all sentient beings or the supreme principle of morality, or duties to God – surely take precedence. Our reaction to the second claim may be not so much resistance as simply puzzlement. Why should we think that the *state* is the locus of any special sort of consciousness or knowledge of rational principles and norms? We tend to think of the state instead as a sort of *enforcement mechanism* for certain basic norms – those protecting the personal security and the rights of individuals or guaranteeing the general conditions of human cooperation. The idea that it is more than this, and especially that its special function is in some sense *cognitive* (a locus of some unique kind of social knowledge that liberates) seems not only false (and perhaps politically dangerous), but downright bizarre.

I raise these questions and objections not only because I consider them natural, but also because I myself share them, and I am even inclined to press them after I believe I have fully appreciated what Hegel's response to them is. So I do not think that response is in the end a satisfactory one. Nevertheless, I think not only that it deserves a fair hearing, but also that we may have something to learn from it.

Hegel's answer to the first complaint, I think, is that duties to some community, principle, or divine entity beyond the state *might* take precedence over duties to the state if we had determinate duties of this kind, which would presuppose that we had a determinate ethical identity in relation to some larger community or rational principle or divine being that has a concrete existence and can make rational claims on us that transcend those of the state. But – Hegel asserts – *there is no such community, principle, or supernatural entity* and *we have no such corresponding ethical identity*. We actualize universal values, and achieve true community, only concretely, in a real social union with others: "Union as such is itself the true content and end, and the vocation of individuals is to lead a universal life" (PR, §258). The largest and most universal union with others that we can actually live and experience is, in Hegel's view, that of the state. Any larger supposed community – the human species, all sentient creation, the Kantian realm of ends – all these are mere abstractions, not real social unities in relation to which we have a genuine identity. Our conception of ourselves in relation to these abstractions, as abstract rational agents or citizens of the world, is too thin an identity for us ever to feel at home in relation to it – the airy conceptions of "rational being" and "citizen of the world" provide us with no living ethical identity.

I think that Hegel's position here was perhaps quite reasonable in its own day, when it was still possible to see nation-states as communities independent of one another, social wholes representing the highest actual form of human unification that might be the source and locus of the largest practical identities of individuals, the identity that lays claim to the most universal values and standards. But this position seems to me no longer tenable in a human world of global interdependency and an ever-expanding world culture. We can still learn something about our modern predicament, however, from Hegel's conception of the problem of achieving ethical identity, even if we cannot accept Hegel's answer to the problem, and even if the lesson for us must be the bleak and unconsoling one that Hegelian ethical identity is no longer within our reach.

Hegel's response to the second objection is easy enough to grasp as soon as we understand his response to the first and also appreciate the high calling Hegel assigned to the law, and especially to acts of legal codification, as found in the Institutes of Justinian (referred to countless times in the *Philosophy of Right*), the Prussian General Legal Code, and the Napoleonic Code. The state for Hegel is the most universal form of real human community. Laws, Hegel thinks, articulate on the level of explicit reason the terms of this association, and a legal code articulates these terms in a fully explicit and systematic form (PR, §§211, 215–216). If the highest form of freedom for individuals is "being with oneself" in social institutions in the form of explicit rational awareness, then rational comprehension of the laws of the state turns out to be the highest form of freedom: "The state is the actuality of concrete freedom" (PR, §260). This conclusion follows only if we accept several distinct ideas and theses that may seem implausible to us. But there is no doubt that Hegel found them compelling, and together they do lead directly to the conclusion he drew from them.

The Rational Structure of the State

For Hegel, the structure of the state is determined by the *constitution*. Hegel favored a constitutional form of monarchy (over the absolutism of the Prussian state under which he lived), but he thought of the constitution of the state as arising from the inherent rationality of historical conditions, not as a scheme contingently devised by legislators (PR, §273R).

For Hegel, the rational structure of many subject matters, including the structure of freedom, follows the three "moments of the concept:" universality, particularity, and individuality (EL, §§163–192). Hegel draws this triad from traditional logic: they were the forms of judgment that led to Kant's three categories of quantity. Here as elsewhere, Hegel invests traditional logical or metaphysical categories with what could be called a cultural or even "existential" significance. "Universality" refers to the moment of the free will in which it detaches itself from determinate contents (PR, §5); in "particularity" it identifies with some contents, while rejecting others (PR, §6); and with "individuality" it fully determines its identity as the free individual it is (PR, §7). Hegel uses the same device in presenting the rational structure of the state: universality corresponds to the *legislature*, particularity to the *executive*, individuality to the *monarch*, who represents the personality of the state (PR, §273).

We might tend to think of any such divisions within the state as there as "checks and balances" – limiting the possible abuse of one center of authority by the correcting influence of another. If so, then Hegel is aware of the problem that motivates us here, but he rejects our solution to it. A rational constitution, he thinks, will not be set up on the assumption that there will be abuses and conflicts, but rather in a way that avoids or minimizes them. Where one interest might tend to assert itself too much, the rational constitution must place it in close conjunction with other interests that moderate its influence. "The constitution," he says, "is essentially a system of mediation" (PR, §302A). In effect, wherever elements within the state threaten to conflict, Hegel sees the constitution as inserting between them a mediating element that has something in common with both sides and has the effect of defusing the potential conflict.

The monarch, for instance, possesses the ultimate power of decision in the state, but makes these decisions under the advice of ministers in the executive, who must implement them. For this reason, Hegel says, the particular character of the monarch is of no significance (PR, §280A). If the constitution is stable, the monarch "often has nothing more to do than sign his name" (PR, §279A). But this name is important, Hegel thinks, because in the modern world, where the personality and subjectivity of individuals is the supreme principle, the actions of the state itself should be seen as the actions of an individual person (PR, §279). If this person is to represent the state, he must be distinct from the ministers who make difficult and controversial political decisions, so that the symbolic state sovereignty in the person of the monarch should remain inviolable and above the decisions for which ministers and politicians can be held accountable (PR, §284). If actions of the government are unpopular, it is the ministry that bears the brunt of the criticism, while the monarch, who personally represents the unity of the state, remains above the fray. For this reason, however, the ministry, which is in touch with political realities, has strong motives that the monarch should not make decisions that the population will find difficult to accept. We may see in this an argument in favor of the present-day "figurehead" monarchies in the Netherlands, Denmark, Sweden, or the United Kingdom, and also of "symbolic" presidencies, as we find in Germany and Israel, and an argument against systems, such as the United States or France, where the president is both the symbolic head of state and also has great political power.

Perhaps the paradigm illustration of Hegel's "mediating" approach to the distribution of state power lies in his conception of the legislative function. Hegel advocates representative institutions in the form of an "Estates" assembly (something proposed in the constitutional plans of Humboldt and Hardenberg, but never accepted in Prussia during Hegel's lifetime). But he thinks of the Estates not as itself the entire legislative process, but rather as a legislature complementing the monarchy as "the power of ultimate decision" and executive power as the "advisory moment" (PR, §300). He criticizes those who would exclude members of the executive from legislative bodies (as happened in the Constituent Assembly in France) (PR, §300A). In his early lectures, Hegel even sees a rather close connection between the executive and the Estates, envisioning majority and opposition parties in the Estates and claiming that the "ministry must be in the majority in an Estates assembly" (VPR17 187) – thus already suggesting something rather like parliamentary systems as they still exist today.

The Estates itself is viewed as a "mediating organ" standing between the government (the executive) and the people (PR, §302). Hegel favors a bicameral legislature, with an "upper house" made up of hereditary (rural, agricultural) nobility (PR, §306), and a "lower house" drawn from the urban bourgeoisie, representing corporations. The upper house thus mediates between the (hereditary) monarchy and the lower house of the Estates (PR, §§305–307).

Representative Institutions

It is important to Hegel that the lower house of the Estates should consist of deputies of corporations (which in his time would have included municipalities as well as professional and trade associations) rather than being elected at large from geographical districts. This feature of Hegel's conception of political representation must strike us as an innovation, but in fact on this point it also follows the (never implemented) constitutional proposals of Stein, Humboldt, and Hardenberg (though closer in detail to the first two than to the third). This is yet another indication that the *Philosophy of Right* represents the position of the Prussian reform movement.

It is important to Hegel that members of the Estates should have a certain expertise in political affairs. He thinks that in the upper house this will be secured by the fact that their position is hereditary, and they will have been educated for it from birth (PR, §307). In the case of the lower house, it is "the aim of elections to appoint individuals who are credited by those who elect them with better understanding of matters [of universal concern] than they themselves possess" (PR, §309). The deputies should have "disposition, skill and knowledge of the institutions and interests of the state and civil society," acquired through "the actual conduct of business in *positions of authority* or *political office*" (PR, §310). Deliberations in the Estates, moreover, should aim at the common good of the state, and not merely the sectional interests represented by the deputies, so their constituents should not send them with anything like a *mandat impératif* (PR, §309).

It is illuminating to compare Hegel's views on representative institutions with those of a later nineteenth-century figure with whom he might be thought to differ considerably, but with whom he in fact has much in common: John Stuart Mill. For both Hegel and Mill, one of the primary functions of political representation is *education* of the public in political matters (PR, §315; cf. Mill, pp. 114–115).[6] For both, it is important that individuals should know what their government is doing, and understand the reasons for it. This is even essential to the *freedom* achieved by the state, since it enables citizens to grasp the state's actions in rational thought and judgment, as well as giving them occasion to exercise their own subjective judgments about political matters in the form of public discussion and public opinion (PR, §§315–317). Mill and Hegel also see representative bodies as keeping those who govern informed about public opinion, and aware that their deeds are being watched and judged by the citizenry (PR, §307; VPR17 187; Mill, pp. 74, 81–82).

Pretty clearly, for both philosophers, the real power of the state is supposed to reside in a professional class of government officials, not in representative bodies. Neither philosopher is fundamentally a democrat; neither (to put it bluntly) *trusts the people.*

The motivation in the two cases is slightly different, however. For Mill, the source of the mistrust is the thought that the uneducated masses will enforce their ignorant prejudices on the more educated and enlightened, and even violate the rights of individuals in the name of these (Mill, pp. 118–119). For Hegel, the worry is that "the people" may be constituted as an unstructured rabble; it is essential, in contrast, that in electing deputies civil society "acts as *what it is*" (PR, §308R) – that is, that what is represented should be determinate social identities, professions, and dispositions having a specifiable rational place, and assignable interests, within the structure of civil society.

Clearly, Hegel values social differentiation, as part of the subjective freedom of modern society, in which individuals may choose between determinate and satisfying ways of life. For this reason, however, he not only tolerates but even wants to encourage certain forms of social inequality that many of us now find objectionable. Further, he sees no objection to these inequalities finding political expression, so that some people, and some social positions, have a greater voice than others in determining the interests and policies of the state. Here is a point on which Mill, writing a generation later, expresses thoughts we might have, but that Hegel does not share: "It is a personal injustice to withhold from anyone ... the ordinary privilege of having his voice reckoned in the disposal of affairs in which he has the same interest as other people" (Mill, p. 131). Hegel, however, sees the matter quite differently:

> The notion that all individuals ought to participate in deliberations and decisions on the universal concerns of the state – on the grounds that they are all members of the state and that the concerns of the state are concerns of everyone, so that everyone has a right to share in them with his own knowledge and volition – seeks to implant in the organism of the state a democratic element *devoid of rational form*. (PR 308R)

For Hegel, it is more important that all the potent political interests belonging to the rational structure of the state be taken into account than that everyone should have a voice. The attempt to give everyone an equal voice by permitting them to vote in large elections even seems to him to undermine the freedom of the state by making the outcome something distant, impersonal, and contingent, alienating the citizens from the state instead of enabling them to achieve their "being with themselves" (or their *freedom*) in relation to it. Further, Hegel argues, if the aim of representative institutions is to promote the common interest rather than particular or factional interests, large elections in which everyone has a vote so watered down as to be meaningless tend to achieve just the reverse of what they are supposed to:

> As for mass elections, it may also be noted that in large states in particular, the electorate inevitably becomes indifferent in view of the fact that a single vote has little effect when numbers are so large, and however highly they are urged to value the right to vote, those who enjoy this right will simply fail to make use of it. As a result, an institution of this kind achieves the opposite of its intended purpose [*Bestimmung*], and the election comes under the control of a few people, of a faction, and hence of that particular and contingent interest which it was specifically designed to neutralize. (PR, §311R)

It would be just as untenable today to deny the truth of what Hegel says here as to accept his conclusion that one may legitimately reject the principle of universal

309

suffrage. Thus here again, Hegel's political philosophy provides us with insights into political problems more than with solutions to them that we can still take seriously.

In this way, Hegel's political philosophy may turn out to be "its own time grasped in thought" in more than one way – or rather, 'its own time' may be understood as having more than one referent. Hegel grasped his own time in a broad sense, one that still includes our time as well, when he expounded and expressed the values and spiritual needs of the modern world and some of the political requirements they lay down. These values include personal rights and subjective freedom, but they also include the need for a human community with shared ends and purposes on a large scale, and a community experienced and comprehended rationally rather than merely felt or accepted as a matter of custom and tradition. In his attempt to describe a rational state that gives actuality to these needs and values, however, the time he grasped was for the most part only the early nineteenth century, with what we now regard as only a limited understanding of these values, and with a set of political and cultural institutions, issues, and problems many of which have since been radically transformed or have disappeared entirely. As reflective historians of Hegel's time, we ought to admire the depth of his understanding of his time, taking that term in the narrower sense. In the broader sense, however, Hegel defines a set of cultural problems that are still with us and to which we do not yet have any clear solutions.

Abbreviations

Hegel's writings are cited using the following system of abbreviations:

Werke   G.W.F. Hegel, *Werke*. Theorie Werkausgabe. Frankfurt: Suhrkamp, 1970. Cited by volume.

EG   G.W.F. Hegel, *Philosophy of Spirit*, trans. W. Wallace and A. V. Miller. Oxford: Oxford University Press, 1977. Cited by paragraph (§) number. Werke 12.

EL   G.W.F. Hegel, *The Encyclopedia Logic*, trans. T. F. Geraets, W. A. Suchting and H. S. Harris. Indianapolis: Hackett, 1991. Cited by paragraph (§) number. Werke 10.

PhG   G.W.F. Hegel, *Phenomenology of Spirit*, trans. A. V. Miller. Oxford: Oxford University Press, 1975. Cited by paragraph (¶) number in this translation. Werke 3.

PR   G.W.F. Hegel, *Elements of the Philosophy of Right*, trans. H. B. Nisbet, ed. A. Wood. Cambridge, Eng., Cambridge University Press, 1991. Cited by paragraph (§) number; the Preface, by page number in this translation. Werke 7.

VPR   *Vorlesungen über Rechtsphilosophie*, ed. K.-H. Ilting. Stuttgart: Frommann Verlag, 1974. Cited by Volume:page.

VPR17   *Die Philosophie des Rechts: Die Mitschriften Wannemann (Heidelberg 1817–1818) und Homeyer (Berlin 1818–1819)*, ed. K.-H. Ilting. Stuttgart: Klett-Kotta, 1983.

VPR19   *Philosophie des Rechts: Die Vorlesung von 1819/1820*, ed. D. Henrich. Frankfurt: Suhrkamp, 1983.

Fichte's writings are cited using the following system of abbreviations:

GNR   Fichte, *Foundations of Natural Right*, trans. Michael Baur, ed. F. Neuhouser. Cambridge: Cambridge University Press, 2000.

SL   Fichte, *System of Ethics*, trans. D. Breazeale and G. Zöller. Cambridge: Cambridge University Press, 2006.

SW   *Fichtes Sammtliche Werke*, ed. I. H. Fichte. Berlin: de Gruyter, 1970. Cited by volume: page number.

Notes

1 See K. G. Faber, "Student und Politik in der ersten deutschen Burschenschaft," *Geschichte in Wissenschaft und Unterricht* 21 (1970); Karl Alexander von Müller, *Karl Ludwig Sand* (Munich: C. H. Beck, 1925); and Richard Preziger, *Die politische Ideen des Karl Follen* (Tübingen: Mohr, 1912).

2 H.E.G. Paulus, Review of the *Philosophy of Right, Heidelberger Jahrbücher für Literatur* 1821; reprinted in Manfred Riedel, *Materialien zu Hegels Rechtsphilosophie* (Frankfurt: Suhrkamp Verlag, 1975), pp. 54–55.

3 See the letter from Fries to L. Rödiger, dated January 6, 1821: "Ich habe im Augenblick wenig Lust [etwas gegen Hegel zu schreiben], und Hegels metaphysischer Pilz ist ja nicht in den Gärten der Wissenschaft, sondern auf dem Misthaufen der Kriecherei aufgewachsen" (Günther Nicolin, ed., *Hegel in Berichten seiner Zeitgenossen* (Hamburg: Meiner, 1970), p. 221).

4 See Manfred Riedel, *Between Tradition and Revolution*, trans. Walter Wright (Cambridge: Cambridge University Press, 1984), pp. 132–137.

5 See G. C. von Unruh, "Polizei, Polizeiwissenschaftg und Kameralistik," in K.G.A. Jeserich, Hans Pohl, and G. C. von Unruh (eds.), *Deutsche Verwaltungsgeschichte* (Stuttgart: Deutsche Verlagsanstalt, 1983), pp. 388–427. Fichte sometimes uses the term *Polizeistaat* ("police state") and with no negative connotations whatever (GNR 3:292–303). This is not because he is a fan of police power and hostile to individual rights – on the contrary, Fichte's views about personal liberty and privacy are often quite radical in the libertarian direction. It is rather because he strongly believes in the responsibility of the state to regulate the economy and provide for public goods that Hegel would consider to belong to "civil society." But Hegel thinks Fichte goes too far in this direction (VPR19 152, VPR17 139, VPR 4: 190–191.)

6 John Stuart Mill, *Considerations on Representative Government* (Indianapolis, Ind.: Bobbs-Merrill, 1958). Cited as "Mill," by page number.

Part VII

Philosophy of History

15

"The Ruling Categories of the World": The Trinity in Hegel's Philosophy of History and The Rise and Fall of Peoples

ROBERT BERNASCONI

In the nineteenth century and well into the twentieth century, Karl Hegel's edition of his father's *The Philosophy of History* served as the standard introduction to his thought. If this work is still sometimes used for the same purpose today, it is only after the Introduction to these lectures has been isolated from the main body of the text and issued in a separate edition in spite of Hegel's famous warnings about prefaces and introductions.[1] In this chapter I will explain why I believe that studying *The Philosophy of History* in its entirety is still a good way to learn about some of the central concepts of Hegel's philosophy. In particular, I will show that the organizing structure of these lectures lies in his somewhat heterodox account of the Trinity (O'Regan 1994), but I will also explain that the Trinity supplies more than a structure. *The Philosophy of History* is in a sense a history of the emergence of the Trinity within history.

In the first part of this chapter I will outline some of the textual issues that make it impossible for scholars to have confidence in the edition edited by Karl Hegel, which is the only edition of the whole of the lectures that has been translated into English (VPG). It is unreliable even though it remains indispensable. Regrettably, the lack of a complete critical edition of all the surviving student notes of Hegel's lectures on the philosophy of history means that I will be forced from time to time to focus almost as much on the textual sources for our knowledge of these lectures as on the philosophical issues they raise, but it is better to face these issues head on than to be misled as a result of a failure to attend to them.

In the second and third parts of the chapter, after some general remarks on the philosophy of history as a theodicy, I shall piece together the evidence that shows that Hegel organized his lectures on the philosophy of history around his idiosyncratic concept of the Trinity and the related concept of reconciliation. I will try to show how Hegel faces the problem of finding an order and a meaning in human affairs under the rubric of finding reason in history. Giving a full reading of the lectures in all their detail in this light is beyond the scope of this chapter, but there are sufficient indications to

A Companion to Hegel, First Edition. Edited by Stephen Houlgate and Michael Baur.
© 2011 Blackwell Publishing Ltd. Published 2011 by Blackwell Publishing Ltd.

show that this would be a fruitful avenue for future research. I will address in the second part Hegel's statements from the various versions of the Introduction about the Trinitarian structure before locating in the third part how Hegel actually presents that structure in the course of his reading of history.

Finally, I will turn to the implications of this theodicy for what Hegel has to say about race. I will show that Hegel's belief in the existence of the various races left him with an insoluble problem, as it was already for Kant, precisely with respect to the demands of a philosophy of history. Kant's conviction that only the White race possessed all the talents put in question the historical role of at least some of the other races that in his view lacked the full range of talents possessed by the White race. Hegel's account of the nature of race was significantly different from Kant's, but the fact that he saw peoples, and not races, as the primary agents of history should not hide the fact that in his view history proper was the preserve of the White race. Kant's problem of the world historical role of, for example, Native Americans and Africans, and not only them, was thus left unresolved by Hegel. I will also examine Hegel's belief in the efficacy of race mixing, which seems to have gone largely unnoticed hitherto even though it anticipates in certain important respects the significance of race mixing to other nineteenth-century philosophers of history. However, there is also a puzzle about why Hegel presents the Germans as a pure race in this context. This too marks out an area for possible future research.

Textual Problems

In 1955 Johannes Hoffmeister produced a new edition of the German text of Hegel's introductory remarks to the lectures on the philosophy of history that superseded all previous editions.[2] However, as he was the first to concede, he was forced to rely more heavily on Georg Lasson's edition of the Introduction than would have been appropriate for a proper critical edition (VPW viii–ix/6). [3] Furthermore, Hoffmeister decided not to attempt a revision of the remainder of the lectures on history, so Lasson's text from 1919 remained the best available (Hegel 1988). Lasson's text was considered to be preferable to the two previous editions, the first prepared by Eduard Gans in 1837 (Hegel 1837), followed by Karl Hegel's edition in 1840 (VPG). However, judged by modern standards, all of these editions are grossly inadequate.

To understand the relative merits of the various editions, one needs to know something about the considerable battle after Hegel's death over his legacy that took place in the context of the publication of his complete works. Hegel had published very little during more than 12 years as Professor of Philosophy at the University of Berlin. He had concentrated on preparing his lectures. After his death a group calling themselves "The Friends of Hegel" used student lecture notes and where available, Hegel's own manuscripts to assemble editions of the lectures. Hegel's first lecture course dedicated exclusively to the philosophy of history was in 1822–1823. Until then he had addressed this theme only as part of his lectures on the philosophy of right (V 1: 256–265/306–315 and V 14: 198–206), but from that point on, he would return to it every other year until his death, a total of five times in all. The challenge that confronted the editors was that every time Hegel took up the task, his emphasis changed, and even the order in which he presented the material was altered (VPG: xxiii/xiii). But whereas today we want to see an edition in which each of the lectures is kept separate so that the development of Hegel's ideas is clearly visible, as is the case with Walter Jaeschke's superb edition of the *Lectures on the Philosophy of Religion* (V 3, V 4, and V 5), the "Friends of Hegel" saw their task differently. They sought to write the books that Hegel himself had not written, and in this way they gave shape to Hegelianism as a doctrine rather than as a work in progress.

When Gans presented the first edition of the lectures on history in 1837, he said only a little in his Introduction about the editorial principles he employed to weave the materials at his disposal into a single whole, but he acknowledged that he had access to at least some of Hegel's manuscripts for the whole course and not just the Introduction, and that he had made them his starting point (Hegel 1837:xx). He also noted that it was not until Hegel gave the lectures for the last time that he offered an extensive treatment of the Middle Ages and Modern Times (Hegel 1837:xx–xxi). Not everybody was happy with Gans' edition. In 1840, only three years later and barely a year after Gans' death, Karl Hegel produced another edition, which as the only version translated into English and the one most often included in collections of Hegel's works remains to this day the best known.[4]

Karl Hegel gave some indications as to why it was so important to him to produce another edition. He directly contradicted Gans's assertion that he had used the philosopher's manuscripts as the basis for the lecture course as a whole (VPG xxii–xxiii/xii–xiii). Karl Hegel also emphasized that his new edition made greater use of the notes from the two earliest courses, which he described as more comprehensive and richer (VPG xxii/xii). Ironically, his concession that Gans had "succeeded in presenting the lectures much as they were delivered in the winter of 1830–31" (VPG: xx/xi) would, if we were confident that he was right, make Gans' edition more valuable to us now than the one he replaced it with, but in fact this claim cannot be sustained, and the value of Gans's edition is that he used sources that have since been lost. Karl Hegel seems to have been more interested than Gans in providing the reader with direct statements about the principles governing the organization of the material, but by mixing notes from different years, he in fact only succeeded in distorting our sense of how those principles were reflected in the material presented. Indeed, Lasson's edition, whose advantage is mainly that it included a great deal of material that had not been published previously, merely exacerbates the problem for the very same reason.

It was not until 1996 that it finally became possible for scholars to see how Hegel himself presented his lectures. In that year, the student notes for Hegel's course in 1822–1823 were finally published (V 12). It was the first – and to date, only – integral edition of any set of lectures on the philosophy of history from a given year. Although to date they remain largely ignored by scholars, they should now be the first point of reference for any scholarly study of Hegel's own thought on this topic as opposed to a study of his influence. However, they cannot be the exclusive reference point. On their own, they do no more than provide a snapshot of how Hegel thought of the philosophy of history the first time he taught the course. We have no alternative but to learn what we can from the other editions even though we recognize that they were edited according to principles that we would reject out of hand today. Close examination of the 1822–1823 lectures suggests that Gans, Karl Hegel, and Lasson all felt free to take individual sentences from one context and move them elsewhere. Indeed, my suspicion is that these editors not only freely changed the context but also felt free to create a new context for them by writing new sentences of their own. Gans' edition is largely forgotten, but so long as readers of Hegel believe they can rely only on the standard editions of Karl Hegel and Lasson, their conclusions are built on sand.[5]

The Trinitarian Structure within the Introduction to the Philosophy of History

The relative lack of scholarly attention to Hegel's courses on the philosophy of history together with the absence of a critical edition like that which we have for the *Lectures on the Philosophy of Religion* is not altogether surprising. The philosophy of history as a discipline has fallen into disrepute, and Hegel is partly to blame. Whereas many in the mid-nineteenth century found in these lectures what Hegel intended – a theodicy in the sense of a justification of God that makes sense of suffering and reconciles thought to the existence of evil (VPW: 48/42 and VPG: 547/457) – his claim that no people ever suffered wrong unjustly (V 1: 257/307), which should always have been considered outrageous, has never seemed as scandalous to Western eyes as it does today.

To understand why the philosophy of history became one of the central areas of philosophy at the beginning of the nineteenth century and would remain so until the end of the Second World War, one must turn back to Kant's "Idea for a Universal History with a Cosmopolitan Purpose." In spite of the fact that Hegel was a consistent opponent of Kantian cosmopolitanism, this short text set the stage for Hegel. One might say that Kant called for a future philosophy of history (Kant 1998:30–31/Kant 1991:53) and that Hegel answered the call. He shared Kant's feeling of indignation at the apparent lack of law in human affairs, a lack that contrasted sharply with the lawfulness visible in nature (Kant 1968:17–18/Kant 1991:42). Kant sought an answer by turning from the perspective of the single individual to that of the human species (Kant 1968:18/Kant 1991:42), and his essay is saturated with the language of natural history, the language of germs (*Keime*) and capacities (*Anlagen*). He insisted that an arrangement in nature that does not fulfill its purpose contradicts the teleology of nature, and his claim that nature unwittingly guides individuals and entire peoples toward their goal (Kant 1968:18/Kant 1991:42) stands midway historically and theoretically between Adam Smith's "invisible hand" and Hegel's "cunning of reason" (VPW 105/89; Veto 1998). Nevertheless, Kant remained puzzled that earlier generations had to work and sacrifice themselves for later generations without seeing any benefits for themselves (Kant 1968:20/Kant 1991:44).

Hegel believed that this problem that Kant left unresolved could be addressed only to the extent that individuals saw themselves not in their particularity but in their universality. This was one task of the *Phenomenology of Spirit*: "The task of leading the individual from his uneducated standpoint to knowledge had to be seen in its universal sense, just as it was the universal individual, self-conscious Spirit, whose formative education had to be studied" (PG: 24/16).[6] The lectures on the philosophy of history necessarily chart the same course although, of course, they do so in a more directly historical way. Hegel was in effect saying that it was only by adopting the standpoint of what he called "worldspirit" (*Weltgeist*) that one left behind the more particular viewpoint that might lead one to believe that one was abandoned by history. One saw reason operating in history only insofar as one took a broad perspective: "the principles of the national spirits (*Volksgeister*) in their necessary progress are themselves only moments of the universal spirit" (VPW: 75/65). So it was in terms of the progress of universal spirit that Hegel attempted to make sense of the rise and fall of peoples. In Hegel's view, earlier generations worked not so much for later generations, as Kant thought, but rather to further the development of universal spirit as such, to which – and this is the important innovation – both earlier and later generations belong. However, although Hegel addressed Kant's problem of the sacrifices that earlier generations made for later generations in this way, he seems, as I shall show below, to have left intact, and perhaps even exacerbated, Kant's tendency to see the existence of non-White races as making sense only insofar as they served the interests of the White race. One should not underestimate the extent to which such questions were the preoccupation of the philosophy of history in the late eighteenth century and throughout the nineteenth century, and the extent to which the various answers that were given directed the racial policies and imperial ambitions of White nations throughout the world (Bernasconi 2005).

Nevertheless, before exploring this issue, one must first be clear what Hegel means by spirit. The communitarian conception of spirit has become popular in the English language literature on Hegel as part of an effort to secularize Hegel or see Hegel as offering a secularized version of Christianity, but this conception is simply not adequate to the task of addressing the problem of the rise and fall of peoples in the way that Hegel proposed. Study of the lectures shows that Hegel employs a specifically *Trinitarian* conception of spirit to address this task. This conception is visible at the end of the chapter on Religion in *Phenomenology of Spirit*, but it is a misleading guide if it is not appreciated that the same pages are supposed to illustrate the inadequacy of picture thinking (*Vorstellung*) (PS: 418–421/473–478). To the extent that the Trinity is pictured as three persons in one, it is a childlike idea, as Hegel explains elsewhere (V 5: 127/193–194). The fact that he presented the Spirit as coming after the death of Christ in what one might call a Pentecostal moment indicates the sense in which Hegel does legitimate a certain communitarianism, albeit the communitarianism of a religious congregation (*das Gemeinde*) (e.g., V 12: 421). However, this representation does not guide Hegel's speculative idea of spirit so much as the Trinity does. One place where he develops his Trinitarian idea of spirit is in his lectures on the philosophy of religion from 1831: "The abstractness of the Father is given up in the Son – this then is death. But the negation of this negation is the unity of Father and Son – love, or the Spirit" (V 5: 286/370; see also Hodgson 2005:127–140).

The lectures on the philosophy of history are another place where Hegel sets out a speculative account of the Trinity, and indeed one where he was less immediately vulnerable to theological attack than he was in his lectures on religion. The most comprehensive study of the doctrine of the Trinity in Hegel has relatively little to say about its role in the lectures on the philosophy of history precisely because of concerns about the reliability of the text of these lectures (Splett 1965:94), but the publication of Hegel's 1822–1823 lectures enables us to approach the question of how Hegel understood the Trinitarian structure of history with greater confidence. A good starting point is Hegel's declaration, in the context of a discussion of how the idea of spirit corresponds to what the Christian church represents as the doctrine of the Trinity, that the moments of spirit are the ruling categories of the world. He warns us, however that as categories they are only determinations of the understanding and that they can be grasped in their truth only when brought together as a unity as moments of the concept of the spirit (V 12: 421–422). This is what the Trinitarian structure of thought speculatively seeks to do.

One relatively economic way of showing both (a) how Hegel thinks his Trinitarian conception of spirit speculatively, and (b) the way he relates it to the task of understanding the rise and fall of peoples, is by examining his attempt to explain the central but seemingly paradoxical idea that "spirit is only as its own result." The phrase appears to be absent from Gans's edition, but it is introduced by Karl Hegel in the form, "Spirit is essentially the result of its own activity" (VPG: 97/78). The fullest discussion of this idea is to be found in Lasson's edition of the Introduction (Hegel 1930:35), which was faithfully reproduced by Hoffmeister (VPW: 58/50), and in the 1822–1823 lecture course (V 12: 30). The context of the remark is the same in both texts: the human being as spirit is not an immediate existence, but is essentially turned in upon itself. Hegel highlights the mediating movement of spirit: "... its activity consists in transcending and negating its immediacy and turning in again upon itself."[7] In the course of trying to clarify this movement, Hegel offers a series of illustrations organized around the speculative proposition: "spirit is only as its own result." There is the example of a plant which grows from a seed only to produce more seeds. There is also the example of education through which human beings shake off what is merely natural. In addition, both editions include what Hegel called the most sublime example, the Trinitarian nature of God, albeit he conceded that God cannot be considered an *example* of spirit, or of anything else, since God is universal truth (VPW: 58/51). God the Father is a universal power enclosed within itself, but in the Son God divides into two. However, insofar as God knows Himself in this other, He is Spirit, not as a third person, but as "this self-having, self-knowing, unity-having, being-at-home-with-itself-in-another" (V 12: 32). It is as this whole that spirit is its own result.

However, Hegel in 1822–1823 offers another illustration of spirit as its own result. He explains that the activity of a people is the execution of its principle, but that in this process it gives rise to the principle of another people (V 12: 31).[8] One may recall here Hegel's elucidation of the dialectic in the Introduction to the *Phenomenology of Spirit* where the experience that is undergone with one object gives rise to a new one (PS: 60/55). In an effort to make this idea persuasive in the context of the lectures on the philosophy of history, Hegel has recourse to the natural metaphor of seeds, which he then applies to the birth and death of peoples, their rise and fall. The life of a people in relation to its principle can be understood as the ripening of a fruit that then serves as the seed (*Same*) for another people (V 12: 31). Hegel makes a comment that is a clear echo of Kant: whereas in nature the species makes no progress, in the human world it is different as there is progress there (V 12: 38–39). It is on this basis that Hegel thinks of the death of a people positively. He even suggests a little later that what appears to be the natural death of the spirit of a people can also be seen as a form of suicide that allows for the new to arise (V 12: 47). This too is what it means for spirit to exist as its own result.

One should not be surprised by the role Hegel gives to the Trinity. It was appealed to by philosophers such as Friedrich Schelling and Carl Eschenmayer to show how speculative thought elevates itself beyond the static categories of the understanding (Schelling 1965:147–148 and 223–224; Eschenmayer 1803:36–37). However, Hegel distinguished himself from Schelling and Eschenmayer in the more specifically speculative way that he took up the challenge of thinking the Trinity. Some time between 1804 and 1806, Hegel wrote a short text on the Trinity using a diagram of a triangle of triangles (Magee 2001:104–110). Unfortunately, this text no longer survives, but we have a report of it from Karl Rosenkranz, and while much of it is obscure, it is clear that Hegel already saw the Trinity as a way of comprehending evil, much as he would do some 20 years later in his lectures on world history: the passage of the Son through the Earth is conceived as the overcoming of evil, and when the Son steps aside, this opens the way to the Spirit. Rosenkranz explained that the Trinity cannot be conceived in such a way that the Spirit is both the unity of the other two and a third person with the same independence as the other two persons because this would make problematic the relation between Father and Son (Rosenkranz 1844:161/Harris 1983:186). "What was only a mixture [*eine Vermischung*] is through this Spirit absolutely one with God, and as he is cognizant of himself in it, so it is cognizant of itself in God" (Rosenkranz 1844:164/Harris 1983:188). With the Son the Earth is consecrated, and with the Spirit the Earth becomes one with God and the Son.

The Trinitarian Structure in History

The place in the main body of the lectures on the philosophy of history where Hegel's focus on the Trinity comes to the fore most clearly is his account of the transition from the Roman world to the Germanic world, but it is not the same in all editions. Gans in 1837 provided only a very brief introduction to the Germanic world, a mere two and a half pages (Hegel 1837:353–355), and his text stops short at the very point where in Karl Hegel's edition, in whose version the transition runs to six and a half pages, the three periods of the Germanic world are identified as specifically belonging to the Trinity. In the first period, which culminates in Charlemagne and corresponds to the kingdom of the Father, the spiritual and the secular are merely different aspects or sides (VPG: 418/343). In the second period, which coincides roughly with the Middle Ages and corresponds to the Kingdom of the Son, these two sides have transformed into an opposition between a theocratic Church and a State constituted as a feudal monarchy (VPG: 418–419/344). Finally, the third period from the Reformation to Hegel's own day, corresponding to the Kingdom of the Spirit, finds the two sides reconciled (VPG: 420/345). We are told next that the Trinitarian structure of the Germanic world is a repetition of three earlier periods: the Persian Empire with its substantial unity, the Greek world with its ideal unity, and the Roman world, where we already find the unity of the universal in the form of the hegemony of self-conscious thought (VPG: 420–421/345–346). This whole discussion with the parallel structures was taken over by Lasson for his edition with only a few, relatively minor additions (Hegel 1988a:757–767).

If we now turn to the text of the 1822–1823 lecture course, we find that the Trinitarian structure that brings together the Persian, Greek, and Roman worlds is already there in its essentials, even if the Trinity is not named at that point. We find three kinds of unity – substantial unity, ideal unity, and universal unity – together with the phrase "the hegemony of self-conscious thought" (V 12: 447–449). Nevertheless, even though the Trinity is not mentioned specifically here, the 1822–1823 lecture course provides an account of the Trinitarian structure of the Roman world that is lacking from the other editions. The major part of Hegel's discussion of the final period of the Roman world is in all editions devoted to Christianity, but there are great differences between the editions. The Trinitarian structure of world history is least pronounced in the Gans edition. His focus is more on the general theme of the reconciliation between the divine and the human, the speculative identity of God and man: "God is man and man is God" (Hegel 1837:330). However, we already find there a clear statement of the Trinity as a principle: "God is spirit in that he becomes known as the Trinity, and world history is developed in terms of this principle" (Hegel 1837:331). This principle is described as "the axis of the world," as well as "the *goal* and the *starting point* of history [*Bis hierher und von daher geht die Geschichte*]." He adds a little later in the paragraph: "God is Spirit insofar as he is known as Triune" (Hegel 1837:331).

Karl Hegel's edition takes up this discussion and rewrites it to make it more precise: "God is thus recognized as *Spirit* only when known as the Triune. The new principle is the axis on which the History of the World turns" (VPG: 388/319). However, Karl Hegel saw the need to introduce further clarification of the structure of the Trinity: "If Spirit be defined as absolute reflexion within itself in virtue of its absolute duality – Love on the one hand as comprehending the Emotional [*Empfindung*], knowledge on the other hand as Spirit – it is recognized as *Triune*: the 'Father' and the 'Son' and that duality (*Unterschied*) which essentially characterizes it as 'Spirit'. ... For Spirit makes itself its own opposite – and is the return from this opposite into itself." (VPG: 393–394/324).[9] In this context, too, Hegel affirms the positive role of pain and misery as necessary for the mediation of the unity of man with God (VPG: 394/324), thereby confirming the connection between the Trinity and theodicy on Hegel's account.

However, if we look at how the 1822–1823 lecture course proceeds and compare it with Karl Hegel's text, we receive a clear indication of how only the former unveils Hegel's true meaning.[10] Hegel here identifies "the ruling categories of the world" as first, being for itself, as the determinacy of finitude, and second as belief in infinitude, the universal (V 12: 422–423). Furthermore, it is explicitly stated in the 1822–1823 lectures that these categories are as such determinations of the understanding that lack truth until they are brought together into unity. Hegel associates the first category with the hard service of the Roman world, where religion has the character of finite purposiveness (V 12: 423). In the Roman world, the individual is sacrificed to universality (V 12: 116). This is one of Hegel's recurrent themes: in the Roman Empire, the individual citizens are detached from the interest of the state and must surrender to abstract universality (VPG: 251/204). This abstract universality is embodied in the arbitrary will of a finite Emperor (V 12: 417) whom, nevertheless, Hegel presents as corresponding structurally to what is known representationally as God the Father. In this vein he even calls the Roman Emperor "the God of the World" (V 12: 424). The sacrifice of the individual to the universal in the Roman world, although imperfect from the perspective of spirit, nevertheless is a crucial anticipation of the sacrifice that world history imposes as the condition of any theodicy.

Hegel's treatment of infinity as the second category is still more striking. Although he initially finds it reflected in certain philosophical tendencies in the ancient world such as Stoicism, Epicureanism, and Skepticism in the form of infinite freedom and universality (V 12: 424), he soon comes to focus on the way in which it was also exhibited in the infinite range and free universality of the Orient, specifically in what he calls Eastern intuition (V 12: 425). This enables him to highlight the way Roman infinitude and Eastern intuition come together among the Jews, and he specifically references the way in which East and West are both represented among the Jews of Alexandria (V 12: 426). Nevertheless, what is important in this context is not the meeting of East and West as such, which had already happened in Egypt in an enigmatic way (Bernasconi 2007), but the fact that for the Jews, God is One. Hegel insists that it was with this determination that God first becomes a world historical principle (V 12: 425) although this happened only when the world's longing that God reveal himself in human form had been fulfilled, thereby opening up an intuition of the reconciliation of God and humanity (V 12: 427).

However, what it means for God to be a world historical principle becomes apparent only when these two categories of finitude and infinite freedom are united as being in and for itself (V 12: 423). This happens through reason, as Hegel had already set out in *Faith and Knowledge*, but here, as in the *Lectures on the Philosophy of Religion*, this process is referred to the emergence of the Trinity within history. Hegel writes that the knowledge of God possessed by Christians is the key to world history in the sense that it allows one to see the nature of the essence of God unfolded in its particular element (V 12: 23). Knowledge of history is knowledge of God, and knowledge of God is knowledge of the Trinity as seen by reason. But Hegel goes further than saying that in Christianity God is revealed as spirit (V 12: 31). Hegel's aim is to show how through the course of history the Trinity revealed itself in the sense that insight into the Trinity is a product of history as a product of spirit. Hegel is not merely saying that the Trinitarian categories can be used to organize history. He is saying that in history the Trinity becomes self-conscious as spirit and without this process the individualistic viewpoint that he is attempting to overcome is left intact. At very least, the Trinity provides the model for thinking beyond the particularity of specific peoples as temporal stages in a historical process to seeing them as "moments" of a conceptual whole. He insists that, insofar as reason itself is Trinitarian and reason governs history, the Trinity governs history. And it is because the Trinity is in the process of discovering itself at work in history that its different aspects appear differently at different times.

This emerges in the way Hegel continues his account. Within the Roman Empire, the law-governed (*gesetzmässig*) character of the state is put into movement by pure arbitrary subjective individuality. This struggle of abstract universality against particular subjectivity determines the transition to Germany, where subjective singularity emerges as the victor and accomplishes a reconciliation between the two, albeit initially only in the secular realm. Hence the Germanic world is characterized at the outset by an opposition between the secular and spiritual worlds, and it is the task of that world to reconcile these two (V 12: 117). It does this in the context of the relation of church and state (VPG: 417/343). That is to say, the historical relation between secular and

323

spiritual is ultimately posed in institutional form, and it is in this respect that Hegel locates the superiority of Protestantism over Catholicism. As the Middle Ages was the kingdom of the Son, so the kingdom of the Spirit began with the Reformation (Hegel 1988a:881). But Hegel insists that this reconciliation – a reconciliation between secular and spiritual, rather than between Protestant and Catholic – needs to be thought in terms of the speculative Trinity. Hegel's *Lectures on the Philosophy of Religion* help clarify the significance he gives to the Trinity: "it is only as what is called 'triune' that God is God as spirit" (V 5: 79/III 143), and the Trinitarian aspect of reconciliation is reconfirmed in the Preface to the second edition (1827) of the *Encyclopedia*, where Hegel argues against August Tholuck in these terms: "How can the doctrine of reconciliation – which Tholuck seeks so energetically to bring to our feeling in the essay under discussion – have more than a moral sense (or, if you like, a pagan sense), how can it have a Christian sense without the dogma of the Trinity?" (Hegel 1989:14n/Hegel 1991:13n).

Nevertheless, the notion of reconciliation cannot do the work required of it unless it is accompanied by the related notion of sacrifice. Through sacrifice the individual alienates him- or herself from property, will, and emotions, and becomes conscious of the state as the site of freedom (VPW: 124/104). Sacrifice is also central to Hegel's account of the Trinity: it is through the sacrifice of the Son that, according to the narrative, the spirit arrives. In Hegel, it is the sacrifice of the particular individual to the universal that leads to the realization of the universal spirit and in terms of which Hegel sought to overcome the Kantian divisions between peoples and generations. Hegel explained this in his lectures on religion: "'To sacrifice' means to sublate the natural, to sublate otherness. It is said: 'Christ has died for all.' This is not a single act but the eternal divine history: it is a moment in the nature of God himself; it has taken place in God himself" (V 5: 251/327–8). We have already seen this approach at work in Hegel's treatment of the Roman world. That the individual sacrifices him- or herself is perplexing unless that individual recognizes him- or herself in that to which he or she is sacrificed. Hegel's reading of history is an attempt to broaden the terms of that recognition. His claim is that when the individual can recognize him- or herself in the universal, that individual is reconciled to history with all its suffering and sacrifice. However, the mediating term here is the world historical people. Each world historical people has one task to perform within the successive stages of world history (VPG: 180/148). It performs this task through its activity and the institutions it builds. This is its substantiality, its way of making a world (V 12: 45). Its satisfaction resides in realizing its ends, but once that is accomplished, it wastes away and dies (V 12: 46). Nevertheless, its contribution remains, and insofar as it belongs as a people to universal spirit and recognizes itself therein, it shares in that resolution. But can that be said of all peoples, all races?

The Role of Race in History

What Hegel called "the ruling categories of the world" were, as we have seen, categories of the understanding that prove from the perspective of reason to be more properly conceived of as "moments" of his Trinitarian concept of spirit. The relation between these two forms of presentation operates by a kind of doubling of the text that is reminiscent of the way that a first reading of the *Phenomenology of Spirit* presents the book in the form of a narrative and that it is only on a second reading that its logical or conceptual necessity becomes clear (Bernasconi 1999). Nevertheless, within Hegel's philosophy of history, the category of race seems not to be fully integrated into the conceptual structure provided by the Trinitarian conception of spirit. Indeed, it seems on occasion that it is race, not spirit, that is a ruling category of the world. This is not far fetched. In a manuscript that seems to be roughly contemporaneous with the first lecture course on the philosophy of history, Hegel acknowledged that questions of racial origins were the concern of understanding, but that questions of race could nevertheless not be excluded from the philosophy of spirit altogether (Hegel 1990).

The initial problem that gave rise to the philosophy of history was how to locate meaning and order in a history that was characterized by the seemingly chaotic rise and fall of peoples. Kant's answer was to posit a cosmopolitan history. Kant recognized that there was a problem in calling each generation to sacrifice itself for future generations. I have shown how Hegel sought to address that same problem by understanding such sacrifice to be a moment in the process whereby the Trinitarian spirit comes to consciousness of itself. But there was another problem that arose in the context of Kant's philosophy of history of which Hegel seems to have been less aware than Kant. It arose, for example, in response to Herder's *Ideas on the Philosophy of the History of Mankind*. Kant wrote: "Does the author really mean that, if the happy inhabitants of Tahiti, never visited by more civilized nations, were destined to live in their peaceful indolence for thousands of centuries, it would be possible to give a satisfactory answer to the question of why they should exist at all, and of whether it would not have been just as good if this island had been occupied by happy sheep as by happy human beings who merely enjoy themselves?" (Kant 1968: vol. 8, 65–66/Kant 1991:219–220). Similar concerns were expressed by Kant in the *Critique of Judgment* (Kant 1968:vol. 5, 378/Kant 1987:258). The problem arose from the fact that according to Kant's own views on race, the non-White races could never participate fully in the final purpose of humanity because only the White race had all the talents (Bernasconi 2002:158). Of course, asking the non-White races to sacrifice themselves for the White race was not a great stretch for a philosopher like Kant, who accepted the institution of slavery as he did throughout the 1780s (Bernasconi 2002:149–152).

Even though his racial theories were significantly different from those of Kant, a similar problem arose in Hegel's philosophy of history. Since in Hegel's view only the Caucasian peoples are world historical in the sense of participating in what he called history proper, he only succeeded in justifying the misfortunes of the Caucasian race. Everyone is familiar with Hegel's exclusion from history of Africans and Native Americans, but the range of exclusion is broader (Bernasconi 1998; Hoffheimer 2005). Persia marks the entry of the Caucasian race into history, whereas the Chinese and Indians both belong to the Mongolian race (Hegel 1837:176. VPG: 211/173). If, as we have seen, the vanishing of peoples is productive, those peoples who do not vanish, like the Chinese and Indian, show no progress. This is why Hegel says that the Persians are "the first historical people": theirs was "the first Empire that passed away" (VPG: 211/173). Or, as he already explained in the 1822–1823 lecture course, "we first enter into world history proper with this empire," thereby placing China and India outside world history (V 12: 233). They are "the mere presupposition of moments whose combination must be awaited to constitute their vital progress" (VPG: 141–142/139, translation modified; see Bernasconi 2000:182–183). The combination is not a physical one produced by mixing. Continuous history has not yet begun. The combination is conceptual. Hegel devotes so much time to China and India partly because he seems to have been genuinely interested in them but also for pedagogic reasons. Karl Hegel explained: "In proceeding to treat of China and India, he wished, as he said himself, only to show by example how philosophy ought to comprehend the character of a nation; and this could be done more easily in the case of the stationary nations of the East, than in that of peoples which have a *bona fide* history [*eine wirkliche Geschichte*] and a historical development of character" (VPG: xxi/xi). In other words, if one wants to know what "substantial unity" means, one should look to China and India.

Contemporaries recognized the racial aspect of Hegel's philosophy of history. Ludwig Buhl, a close member of Hegel's circle, published anonymously a book on Hegel's philosophy of history in 1837. In it he maintained that in general only the Caucasian race (*Rasse*) is worthy of history (Buhl 1837:37), and in the context of the Persians he acknowledged that "races come, races go, in the same way that leaves fall and come forth anew" (Buhl 1837:55). This was clearly intended as his own version of Hegel's account of the rise and fall of peoples, but by using the metaphor of leaves rather than seeds, Buhl failed to capture Hegel's point that there is continuity in spite of the change over time. That Buhl used the term "race" here where Hegel used the word "*Volk*" is probably less significant than it might seem: both terms are being used to refer to subdivisions of the Caucasian race.[11] Another Hegelian reading of history, that by Friedrich Liebe, also emphasized how with the Persian's history passed from the Mongolian race to the Caucasian race (Liebe 1844:103). This indeed is why, when Hegel gives his account of the Trinitarian structure of the Germanic world as repeating earlier epochs, he references the Persian, Greek, and Roman worlds (VPG: 420/417): the Trinitarian structure is correlated with the history of the Caucasian race. So the question is whether by excluding all but the Caucasian race from being agents of world history and by excluding Africans and Native Americans from history altogether, Hegel has not effectively excluded them from the solution that he proposed to Kant's problem. In other words, does not Hegel sacrifice the African on the altar of history as much as Kant sacrifices Africans, Tahitians, and Laplanders? No doubt there is more to be said on this point, but such a question is inevitably raised by a close reading of Hegel's attempt to answer Kant.

Finally, before closing this chapter I will raise one more question to which the secondary literature fails to provide an adequate answer. Indeed, the question is barely posed there: why does Hegel give such significance to the mixing of peoples in explaining their world historical significance until he came to the Germans?

It has previously been noted that Hegel expressed fairly standard views of the time that race mixing improved the lower stock (Hoffheimer 2000:38). However, little or no attention has been given to the fact that he also believed that the mixing of peoples, the uniting of differences of "blood," was a necessary condition for a people to have a claim to world historical significance (V 12: 319). Indeed, it was on this basis that he tried to explain his view that the Jews as a people were not a world historical people: they were unmixed, and to that extent their religion remained "silent and concealed," so its historical significance awaited spirit to run its course (V 12: 429). In the editions of both

Gans and Karl Hegel, remarks about race mixing are reduced to one or two sentences, but there are many more in Lasson and in the 1822–1823 lecture course.[12] The Greeks arise from a mixing of peoples (V 12: 319, 333, 368), and the same is true of the Romans (V 12: 394).

With his emphasis on mixing, Hegel anticipates the direction that the philosophy of history would take in Comte Joseph Arthur de Gobineau, for whom race mixing was also a necessary precondition of civilization even though it would also in time prove to be the source of the decline of civilizations (Gobineau 1983:173, 342–348). However, Gobineau was thinking of race mixing between the main races, whereas Hegel did not have in mind race mixing in that sense but mixing among peoples within the Caucasian race. The idea that race mixing led to sterility was rare in Hegel's time.[13]

Nevertheless, there is a remarkable exception to Hegel's rule that only peoples of mixed blood have world historical significance, and it is this that gives the topic its main interest. We saw earlier that Hegel insisted that world history follows the path of Protestantism and leaves Catholicism behind. In trying to explain why the Reformation took place in some countries rather than others, he pointed to the belief that Protestantism arose within the countries of pure stock, whereas the countries that remained Catholic were constituted from a mixture of Roman and Germanic natures (V 12: 445–446). The main source of Hegel's idea of the Germans as a pure race was Tacitus, who described the Germans on the basis of speculations about possible migrations as "indigenous and very slightly blended with new arrivals from other races or alliances" (Tacitus 1970:131. V 12: 453). They were "a race unmixed by intermarriage with other races, a peculiar people and pure, like no one but themselves, whence it comes that their physique, so far as can be said with their vast numbers, is identical" (Tacitus 1970:135–137).

The fact that Hegel saw history as culminating in the Germans as an unmixed race at first sight seems to make all the more puzzling the fact that he excluded the Jews from world historical status on the same grounds. But at least in this case Hegel gives a reason: the purity of the Jews meant that they lacked the dynamic principle for change and reconciliation that is characteristic of mixed peoples. The puzzle thus becomes why Hegel thought that history would culminate in a pure stock. Although attributing a belief in the end of history to Hegel is not entirely without problems, the fact is that Hegel in the 1822–1823 lectures announced that the Germanic world represented the fulfillment of Christianity. It is unlike earlier periods of world history where each world historical people relates to both earlier and later periods (V 12: 441). It seems that reconciliation serves as a kind of end, as it does at the end of the sixth chapter of the *Phenomenology of Spirit*.

The parallel that I have drawn between the *Philosophy of History* and the *Phenomenology of Spirit* can be extended, particularly as both texts can be understood to serve as a ladder to the system of science. If one thinks of the key to Hegel's *Phenomenology of Spirit* as lying in the final chapter, where Hegel reveals that the history of spirit that is set out in the sixth chapter provides the form of absolute knowing, whereas the seventh chapter, with its more systematic interpretation of religion, culminates in Christianity and supplies its content, one can then also see a parallel in the way that the lectures on the philosophy of history portray the coming together of two ways of apprehending the truth: in faith through the use of representation and in thought through reason (V 12: 421). Both texts not only portray but also enact a reconciliation between the secular and the spiritual. However, although the closing chapter of the *Phenomenology of Spirit* presents the coming together of actual spirit and religion in its conceptual necessity, it leaves the conditions of its occurrence unclarified. This lacuna is addressed in the Preface to the *Phenomenology of Spirit*, which was also intended as the Preface to the whole System of Science. *The Philosophy of History* fills out and completes Hegel's answer to that question of the preconditions for philosophy. No doubt Hegel could have been clearer that that was the case, but one suspects that if he was not, it was because he seems always to have run out of time at the end of each semester.

The question of the preconditions for philosophy was intimately bound up in Hegel's mind with the question of the end of history. That is why in the 1822–1823 Introduction to the lectures on the Philosophy of History, Hegel insisted that history is not about the past but about an eternal present (V 12: 15). Lasson in his edition, and following him, Hoffmeister, seems to garble this claim perhaps because he did not think to relate it to the parallel consideration in the *Phenomenology of Spirit*, where Hegel announced the annulment of time and history at the point it gives way to the concept (Hegel 1930:165. VPW 182/150).

One must understand that from early on Hegel was deeply impressed by the dangers of historical relativism. Some of the earliest expressions of Hegel's Jena philosophy were dominated by the concern that history as mere succession leads only to disillusionment and uncertainty (Hegel 1968:9/Hegel 1977:85–86). Similar ideas preface the lectures on the history of philosophy in the Berlin period (Hegel 1995:103). Hegel's answer is that even if there are privileged moments, the same spirit is at every moment operating. Alluding to this structure reveals that there is only one truth, not many rival competing truths. Hegel's solution in the lectures on world history is the same, and Hegel's presentation of the Trinitarian structure of world history as an answer to the rise and fall of (Caucasian) peoples must be seen in this light. It is not peripheral scaffolding. This makes it clear how all attempts to portray Hegel's philosophy as offering a secularized version of Christianity are reductive and undialectical: on Hegel's account of history, the secular and the spiritual are reconciled through the Trinity without either being diminished.[14]

List of *Abbreviations of Works by Hegel*

PS   *Phänomenologie des Geistes*, Werke 9, ed. W. Bonsiepen and R. Heede. Hamburg: Felix Meiner, 1980. Translated as *Phenomenology of Spirit* (trans. A. V. Miller). Oxford: Oxford University Press, 1977.

V 1   *Vorlesungen über Naturrecht und Staatswissenschaft*, ed. C. Becker et al. Hamburg: Felix Meiner, 1983. Translated as *Lectures on Natural Right and Political Science* (trans. J. M. Stewart and P. C. Hodgson). Berkeley: University of California Press, 1995.

V 3-5   G.W.F. Hegel, *Vorlesungen über die Philosophie der Religion*, ed. W. Jaeschke. Vorlesungen 3–5. Hamburg: Felix Meiner, 1983–1984. Translated as *Lectures on the Philosophy of Religion*, 3 vols., trans. Peter Hodgson. Berkeley: University of California Press, 1984–1985.

V 12   *Vorlesungen über die Philosophie der Weltgeschichte*, ed. K. H. Ilting, K. Brehmer, and Hoo Nan Seelman. Hamburg: Felix Meiner, 1996.

V 14   *Vorlesungen über die Philosophie des Rechts*, ed. E. Angehrn et al. Hamburg: Felix Meiner, 2000.

VPG   *Vorlesungen über die Philosophie der Geschichte*, Zweite Auflage, ed. K. Hegel. Berlin: Duncker und Humblot. Translated as *The Philosophy of History* (trans. J. Sibree). New York: Dover, 1956.

VPW   *Vorlesungen über die Philosophie der Weltgeschichte, Band I. Die Vernunft in der Geschichte*, ed. Johannes Hoffmeister. Hamburg: Felix Meiner, 1955. Translated as *Lectures on the Philosophy of World History* (trans. H. B. Nisbet). Cambridge: Cambridge University Press, 1975.

Notes

1   In the English-speaking world, the process of separating Hegel's Introductory remarks from the main text began in 1953, when Robert J. Hartman published a translation of the Introduction under the title, *Reason in History* (Hegel 1953).

2   Johann Hoffmeister's edition was translated into English in 1975 ((VPW). Unfortunately, Leo Rauch returned to the second edition of Hegel's lectures from 1840 for his *Introduction to the Philosophy of History* (Hegel 1988). His choice of text and his decision to omit Hegel's discussion of Africa undermines the value of his translation.

3   It should be noted that Hegel's surviving manuscripts of the Introduction have now been published separately in the Bochum edition of the Gesammelte Werke (Hegel 1995: 119–214). The same volume reproduces a manuscript of the lectures on the Orient which had previously been published by Lasson, but unfortunately no other sources survive (Hegel 1995: 221–227).

4   Gans died on May 5, 1839. The Preface to Karl Hegel's edition is dated one year and eleven days later!

5   On the surviving manuscripts of student notes for Hegel's five lecture courses on the philosophy of history, see Hespe 1991 and Grossmann 1996.

6   The first edition has "worldspirit" in place of "self-conscious Spirit," which makes my point even more clearly.

7   Lasson – and following him, Hoffmeister – has Hegel repeat this sentence (Hegel 1930: 35 and 50; (VPW: 57–58/50 and 73/63). It is not clear whether that means it was a favorite formulation of Hegel's or whether Lasson had forgotten that he had already used it while assembling the text from the multiple sources available to him.

8   The example is omitted by Lasson and, following him, by Hoffmeister, but it was in Karl Hegel's edition with only minor omissions, even though the overall account of the phrase is greatly abbreviated (VPG: 97/78).

9   The above two passages are also in Lasson's edition, but that edition seems to add little of importance on this topic (Hegel 1988a: 722 and 734).

10   Matters are even worse in Lasson's edition, which we can now suspect of introducing passages from the 1822–1823 lecture course into Karl Hegel's text, with additional materials from unknown sources (Hegel 1988a: 722–725; cf. VPG: 387–389/318–320 and V 12: 421–425). Indeed, a paragraph that begins by announcing the categories that rule the world supplies only two categories: the first, being determined in and for itself, which is the belief in finitude, and, the second, belief in universal infinitude (Hegel 1988a: 723), whereas the corresponding passage in the 1822–1823 lecture course makes clear that the ruling categories are threefold – as befits the Trinitarian structure – and quite different.

11   "Volk" was a higher category for Hegel than "Rasse." Indeed, he seems to have been inclined to believe that the former category was only well-suited to divisions within the Caucasian race (Hegel 1845: 73–74; Hegel 2007: 45; Bernasconi 2000: 187–188).
12   For example, contrast VPG: 373/306 and Hegel 1988a: 702.
13   Friedrich Ludwig Jahn had already in 1810 insisted that mixed peoples have little propensity for surviving as a nation, but this view which came to dominate at the end of the nineteenth century, as a result of the campaign by Josiah Nott beginning in the 1840s, was relatively unusual at this time, so far as I can tell (Jahn 1817: 20; Bernasconi 2010).
14   This chapter is dedicated to Amit Sen, with whom I have discussed Hegel and particularly Hegel's philosophy of history for more than a quarter of a century. Although we still see Hegel differently, this chapter is marked by those conversations from beginning to end. I would also like to thank Stephen Houlgate and Kristin Gissberg for their help preparing this chapter for publication.

References

Bernasconi, R. (1998). "Hegel at the Court of the Ashanti." In S. Barnett (ed.), *Hegel after Derrida*. London: Routledge, 41–63.

Bernasconi, R. (1999). "We Philosophers." In R. Comay and J. McCumber (eds). *Endings. Questions of Meaning in Hegel and Heidegger*. Evanston: Northwestern University Press, 77–96.

Bernasconi, R. (2000). "With What Must the Philosophy of World History Begin?" *Nineteenth Century Contexts* 22 (2): 171–201.

Bernasconi, R. (2002). "Kant as an Unfamiliar Source of Racism." In J. K. Ward and T. L. Lott (eds.), *Philosophers on Race*. Oxford: Blackwell, 145–166.

Bernasconi, R. (2005). "Why Do the Happy Inhabitants of Tahiti Bother to Exist at All?" In J. K. Roth, *Genocide and Human Right*. New York: Palgrave Macmillan, 139–148.

Bernasconi, R. (2007). "The Return of Africa: Hegel and the Question of the Racial Identity of the Egyptians." In P. Grier (ed.), *Identity and Difference*. Albany: SUNY Press, 201–216.

Bernasconi, R. (2010). "The Philosophy of Race in the Nineteenth Century." In D. Moyar (ed.), *The Routledge Companion to Nineteenth-Century Philosophy*. London: Routledge, 498–521.

Bernasconi, R. (2009). "After the German Invention of Race: Conceptions of Race Mixing from Kant to Fischer and Hitler." In T. Nagl and S. Lennox (eds.), *Remapping Black Germany*. Amherst: University of Massachusetts Press.

[Buhl, L.H.F.] (1837). *Hegels Lehre vom Staat und seine Philosophie der Geschichte*. Berlin: Forstner.

Eschenmayer, C. A. (1803). *Die Philosophie in ihrem Übergang zur Nichtphilosophie*. Erlangen: Walters.

Gobineau, Joseph Arthur, Comte de. (1983). *Essai sur l'inégalité des races Humaines*. In J. Gaulmier (ed.), *Oeuvres 1*. Paris: Gallimard.

Grossmann, A. (1996). "Weltgeschichtliche Betrachtingen in systematischer Absicht." *Hegel-Studien* 31: 27–61.

Harris, H. S. (1983). *Hegel's Development*. Vol. 2: *Night Thoughts*. Oxford: Oxford University Press.

Hegel, G.W.F. (1837). *Vorlesungen über die Philosophie der Geschichte* (ed. E. Gans). Berlin: Duncker und Humblot.

Hegel, G.W.F. (1845) *Encyklopädie der philosophischen Wissenschaften in Grundrisse. Dritter Theil. Die Philosophie des Geistes*. Werke 7.2. Berlin: Duncker und Humblot.

Hegel, G.W.F. (1930) *Die Vernunft in der Geschichte*, ed. G. Lasson. Leipzig: Felix Meiner.

Hegel, G.W.F. (1953). *Reason in History*, trans. R. J. Hartman. Indianapolis, Ind.: Bobbs-Merrill.

Hegel, G.W.F. (1968). *Jenaer Kritische Schriften*, ed. H. Buchner and O. Pöggler. Gesammelte Werke 4. Hamburg: Felix Meiner.

Hegel, G.W.F. (1977). *The Difference between Fichte's and Schelling's System of Philosophy*, trans. H. S. Harris and W. Cerf. Albany: SUNY Press.

Hegel, G.W.F. (1981). *Briefe von und an Hegel*, ed. F. Nicolin. Hamburg: Felix Meiner, 5 vols.

Hegel, G.W.F. (1988a). *Vorlesungen über die Philosophie der Weltgeschichte. Band II–IV*, ed. G. Lasson. Hamburg: Felix Meiner.

Hegel, G.W.F. (1988b). *Introduction to the Philosophy of History*, trans. L. Rauch. Indianapolis, Ind.: Hackett.

Hegel, G.W.F. (1989). *Enzyklopädie der Philosophischen Wissenschaften im Grundrisse (1827)*. Gesammelte Werke 19, ed. W. Bonsiepen and H.-C. Lucas. Hamburg: Felix Meiner.

Hegel, G.W.F. (1990). "Racenverschiedenheit." In *Schriften und Entwürfe I. (1817–1825)*. Gesammelte Werke 15, ed. F. Hogemann and C. Jamme. Hamburg: Felix Meiner, 224–227.

Hegel, G.W.F. (1991). *The Encyclopaedia Logic*, trans. T. F. Genaets, W. A. Suchting and H. S. Harris. Indianapolis, Ind.: Hackett.

Hegel, G.W.F. (1995). *Vorlesungsmanuskripte II. 1816–1831*, ed. W. Jaeschke. Gesammelte Werke 18. Hamburg: Felix Meiner.

Hegel, G.W.F. (2007). *Philosophy of Mind*, ed. M. Inwood. Oxford: Oxford University Press.

Hespe, F. (1991). "Hegels Vorleungen zur Philosophie der Weltgeschichte." *Hegel-Studien* 26: 78–87.

Hodgson, P. (2005). *Hegel and Christian Theology*. Oxford: Oxford University Press.

Hoffheimer, M. (2000). "Hegel, Race, Genocide." In *The Contemporary Relevance of Hegel's Philosophy of Right*, ed. T. Nenon. *Southern Journal of Philosophy* 29 (Supplement): 35–62.

Hoffheimer, M. (2005). "Race and Law in Hegel's Philosophy of Religion." In *Race and Racism in Modern Philosophy*, ed. A. Valls. Ithaca, N.Y.: Cornell University Press, pp. 194–216.

Jahn, F. L. (1817). *Deutsches Volksthum*. Leipzig: Wilhelm Rein.

Kant, I. (1968). *Werke*, Akademie Textausgabe. Berlin: Walter de Gruyter.

Kant, I. (1987). *Critique of Judgment*, trans. W. Pluhar. Indianapolis, Ind.: Hackett.

Kant, I. (1991). *Political Writings*, trans. H. B. Nisbet. Cambridge: Cambridge University Press.

Knox, R. (1851). *The Races of Men*. London: Henry Renshaw.

Liebe, F. (1844). *Sechs Vorlesungen über Philosophie der Geschichte*. Wolfenbüttel: Holle.

Magee, G. A. (2001). *Hegel and the Hermetic Tradition*. Ithaca, N.Y.: Cornell University Press.

O'Regan, C. (1994). *The Heterodox Hegel*. Albany: SUNY Press.

Rosenkranz, K. (1844). "Hegel's ursprüngliches System 1798–1806. Aus Hegel's Nachlass." In *Literarhistorisches Taschenbuch*, ed. R. E. Prutz, vol. 2, pp. 153–242.

Schelling, F.W.J. (1965). "Bruno." In *Werke* 3, ed. M. Schröter. Munich: Beck.

Splett, J. (1995). *Die Trinitätslehre G.W.F. Hegels*. Freiburg: Karl Alber.

Tacitus. (1970). *Germania*, trans. M. Hutton. London: Heinemann.

Veto. (1998). "La ruse de la raison." *Hegel-Studien* 33: 177–190.

16

Hegel and Ranke: A Re-examination

FREDERICK C. BEISER

1.   Ranke's Troubling Legacy

Without doubt, the most influential critic of Hegel's philosophy of history has been Leopold von Ranke (1795–1886). Today Ranke's critique of Hegel's philosophy of history has been largely forgotten, whereas those of Kierkegaard and Marx are still studied and even celebrated. However, from a broad historical perspective, Ranke's critique was more effective and devastating. For generations, it succeeded in completely discrediting Hegel's philosophy of history. Neither Kierkegaard nor Marx cast such a long, dark shadow. Kierkegaard would not become a famous name in German philosophy until the beginning of the twentieth century, long after the decline of Hegelianism; and Marx, in classical Hegelian fashion, would preserve as much of Hegel's legacy as he would negate. Ranke, however, condemned Hegel's philosophy of history wholesale on the grounds that it had the wrong method and so could not claim to be a science. For the nineteenth century, an age dazzled by the success of the growing empirical sciences, to deny scientific status to a philosopher's work was tantamount to a death sentence. All philosophy of history, of which Hegel's was the most outstanding example, became an intellectual pariah, as respectable as astrology or phrenology. It is no accident that some of Ranke's most famous students – Wilhelm Dilthey, Jacob Burckhardt, and Friedrich Meinecke – would later develop and propagate his criticisms of Hegel. Among professional historians in the United States, it was axiomatic for generations that Ranke had rightly condemned the philosophy of history, which had no place in the scientific discipline of history.

Ranke's reputation alone makes it impossible to ignore his critique of Hegel. Whether rightly or wrongly, Ranke has often been regarded as "the father of modern scientific history,"[1] and indeed as the founder of historicism itself.[2] At the very least, his many influential students saw him as the apostle of a scientific history.[3] As professor of history at the University of Berlin, first extraordinarius in 1825 then ordinarius in 1836, Ranke was in a powerful position to propagate the gospel of a scientific history. For

---

decades, he would hold lectures on modern history, which he would often begin with an account of historical method.[4] Ranke's influence rested on much more than his lectures, however. Having close connections with the Prussian government, he became, as editor of the *Historisch-Politische Zeitschrift,* one of the leading spokesman for its policies. Perhaps Ranke's most seminal role, however, was as the organizer of weekly seminars, whose purpose was to train future historians according to the new critical methods.[5] Among Ranke's students in these seminars were some leading historians of the next generation: Heinrich von Sybel, Georg Waitz, Wilhelm von Giesebrecht, and Jacob Burckhardt, to name a few.[6]

But world history is not always world justice, not even for Hegelians. If Ranke's criticisms of Hegel were successful, they were not accurate.[7] Ranke had discredited Hegel by attributing to him a deductive methodology that Hegel himself had explicitly repudiated. The irony is that Hegel shared many of Ranke's basic methodological principles, though Ranke made Hegel's methodology his model for how *not* to pursue history as a science. There are indeed fundamental philosophical differences between Hegel and Ranke, but they do not lie where Ranke had located them. On the whole, however, scholars have uncritically accepted Ranke's conception of Hegel's methodology.[8] As a result, they have failed to locate the real differences between Ranke and Hegel and to understand the issues dividing them. At the very least the Ranke–Hegel relationship stands in need of re-examination.

2. Ranke's Methodology

Before we reassess the Ranke–Hegel relation, we need at least a basic idea of Ranke's methodology. This is not so easy to acquire, however, because of some very deep-rooted misconceptions. For generations in the United States, Ranke has been perceived as a stern positivist, a hardheaded pedant who insisted that the chief purpose of history is to ascertain facts and nothing but the facts. Ranke became the Mr. Gradgrind of history: "Now, what I want is Facts.... Facts alone are wanted in life."[9] Like any caricature, this one has a grain of truth: Ranke did stress the importance of determining the facts and assessing the accuracy of sources. That was indeed the point of his critical method. It is necessary to emphasize, however, that Ranke – explicitly, emphatically, and repeatedly – rejected the view that the end of history consists in nothing more than ascertaining and collecting facts. He called this the chronological or antiquarian way of doing history, which he regarded as a much too narrow conception of the historical enterprise.[10] It was indeed important for the historian to determine facts and to assess sources; but it was no less important for him *to understand* these facts, *to explain* them by seeing them as part of a wider whole.

It is also true that Ranke wanted to defend the autonomy of history and to secure its status as a science independent of philosophy and theology. This would be a main theme of many lectures over the decades. It is important to see, however, that Ranke's conception of the autonomy of history was very different from that of positivism. There are three fundamental discrepancies. First, Ranke very much stressed the affinity of history with art, and he disapproved of those who wanted to conflate it entirely with the sciences.[11] For him, history was like art insofar as it had to form its materials into a meaningful and beautiful whole. Second, Ranke did not decry metaphysics, as the later positivists did, but made it the rationale for the study of history. The reason it was so important for him to investigate facts was that he saw each fact as "the appearance of the infinite."[12] While he rejected the traditional theological constraints upon history, he insisted that his own inquiry was based on a basic religious belief: "that nothing exists without God and nothing lives except through God."[13] Third, contrary to positivism, Ranke did not think that the chief end of historical inquiry consists in establishing general laws that one arrives at through induction as does the natural scientist. Rather, its ultimate goal lay outside the discursive domain entirely in a special kind of experience: the intuition of the individual, the perception of existence, the grasp of the infinite within the finite.[14] Ranke sometimes saw this goal in aesthetic terms: one should contemplate history as if it were a work of art, he wrote, "merely from joy in individual life, just as one enjoys a flower without having to think to which Linnaean order it belongs."[15]

No statement of Ranke has aroused more controversy than his famous dictum that the aim of the historian is not to instruct or moralize but simply to tell the truth "as it actually happened" (*wie es eigentlich gewesen*).[16] Ranke's dictum was a fundamental break with the Enlightenment tradition of "pragmatic history," which held that the aim of history is to provide moral lessons for future generations. Instead of judging the past and drawing lessons from it, Ranke insisted that the historian should be impartial and let the past speak in its own terms. Inevitably, that posed the difficult question whether the historian can ever attain such complete objectivity. That question has been the starting point of a long discussion in modern sociology, history, and hermeneutics, among whose participants have been Dilthey, Nietzsche, Weber, Heidegger, and Gadamer. Throughout this discussion the most common criticism of Ranke's dictum has been its naivete: that it is impossible for the historian to escape the standpoint of his own culture; that even to ask questions, and to select his subject matter, the historian has to begin with concepts and assumptions. While these criticisms make some valid points about the limits of historical objectivity, it is necessary to reply that they have really missed Ranke's basic point. Ranke was perfectly aware of the limits upon historical objectivity.[17] Never did he think that the historian could completely escape his own culture, and never did he assume that he could avoid all concepts and assumptions; still less was he asking for a pure knowledge of reality in itself, as if we could know a reality that existed apart from and prior to any human perspective. While Ranke did stress the importance of neutrality, of laying aside one's own values and bias, he also realized that this is a regulative ideal, an ideal that the historian could at best approach and never attain.[18] Ranke's basic point is simple but important: that the historian needs to check the reliability of his sources and to distinguish fact from fiction, truth from distortion and alteration.

The best illustration of his meaning here is given by his famous critique of Guicciardini's *Storia d'Italia*, which had been one of the most trusted sources about Renaissance Italy for generations.[19] When Ranke examined Guicciardini's history by comparing it to other sources, he found it full of inaccuracies, fabrications, and distortions. It was not an eyewitness account, as it was assumed to be, but a compilation from other sources; it pretended to cite verbatim speeches that were simply invented; and its chronology was a jumble. If Rankean objectivity in this sense is impossible, then so is accuracy in journalism. It is important to place Ranke's demand for objectivity in its context. It was a break with older habits of historiography that were happy to accept and hand down tradition; since history was part story and part instruction, facts were altered or embellished for the sake of entertainment and education. Ranke's work was directed against these habits; his basic motto was formulated by his teacher, Barthold Georg Niebuhr: "*Ewige Krieg der Kritik gegen die Überlieferung*" ("Eternal war of criticism against tradition"). Rightly, Ranke saw that the modern age, which had been so inspired and permeated by the ideals of the new sciences, demanded more than legend and tradition. Hence he declared: "We, in our place, have a different notion of history [than Guicciardini] ... naked truth without embellishments, thorough investigation of every single fact. ... By no means fiction, not even in the smallest details; by no means fabrications."[20]

Armed with these qualifications and caveats, we can now summarize, crudely but conveniently, Ranke's conception of scientific history. It consists in four basic principles.

(1) *Criticism.* The first task of the historian is to ascertain the credibility of his sources, to determine whether they are reliable bases of information. He should learn to distinguish fact from fantasy, reality from myth, embellishment and distortion; and he should give primacy to the evidence of eyewitnesses of, and participants in, the events rather than to later chroniclers. As Ranke put this principle: "Strict presentation of the facts, conditional and unattractive though it may be, is unquestionably the supreme law."[21]

(2) *Impartiality.* As far as possible, the historian should attempt to lay aside his own moral principles, political agenda, and religious beliefs, and he should try to understand the past in its own terms. The chief requirement of impartiality is self-renunciation: relinquishing one's own moral, religious, and political preconceptions, and immersing oneself in the life of the object; the historian must, as Ranke put it in some famous lines, "extinguish himself, so to speak, letting things speak for themselves."[22] Although Ranke stressed the importance of impartiality, he was quick to add that impartiality does not mean that the historian is amoral, a-religious; he insisted that he has a moral and religious standpoint all his own: that which attempts to do justice to all moral and religious standpoints in history.[23]

(3) *Primacy of Induction over Deduction.* The historian must begin from the examination of particular facts and derive general conclusions from them; he must never begin from general principles, which have some putative a priori warrant, and then apply them to the particular facts of history. Although history is not simply collecting facts, understanding facts should not mean ordering them according to preconceived general principles, whose legitimacy cannot be empirically established.[24]

(4) *Individuality.* The historian should treat each person, action, and epoch in history as an end in itself; he must never treat it as a mere means to some higher end, as a stepping stone in the progress toward some universal goal. As Ranke wrote in a much-celebrated sentence: "Each epoch stands immediately before God, and its value rests not at all on what comes from it but in its own existence, in its very self."[25] Ranke would make the individual the chief subject matter of history, and the perception of the individual its main purpose and reward. Whereas the philosopher sees the individual only as part of a greater whole or a process of development, the

335

historian attempts to grasp the infinite in each individual.[26] It was this principle of individuality that Meinecke would later make into the defining principle of historicism itself.[27]

3. The Secret Fellowship

Now that we have some idea of Ranke's method, we are in a position to compare it with Hegel's. The remarkable affinity between Ranke and Hegel – and the problems in the normal account of the differences between them – become immediately apparent when we realize that Hegel would have approved of all Ranke's basic principles. Let us take each of these principles in turn.

Regarding Ranke's first principle, it seems as if there is no affinity between Ranke and Hegel at all because, in the introduction to his lectures on world history, Hegel took issue with Niebuhr's critical history, which was the model for Ranke's own method.[28] Hegel had nothing but contempt for Niebuhr's method, which he saw as the most corrupt form of "reflective history." We will later have occasion to examine in more detail Hegel's attitude toward Niebuhr's critical method (Section 6). Suffice it to say for now that Hegel accepts the basic principle behind that method: that the historian should be critical of his sources and value facts for their own sake. As we shall later see, much of Hegel's critique of Niebuhr is immanent, that is, that Niebuhr violates his own standards by reading the historians' constructions into the past.

It should be clear that Hegel endorses Ranke's second principle. It was the heart of Hegel's phenomenological method, which he laid down in the *Phänomenologie des Geistes* and advocated for the philosophy of history,[29] that the philosopher should bracket all his preconceptions and follow "the immanent movement of his object itself." Both Ranke and Hegel stress that the historian should examine his subject in its own terms, according to its own standards and beliefs, and that he should not judge the past according to the standards and beliefs of his own age. Both disapproved of the pragmatic history of the Enlightenment tradition on these grounds; and both held that the only possible criticism is *internal*, that is, pointing out inconsistencies and the discrepancy between ideal and practice.[30] No less than Ranke, Hegel too insisted on the virtue of self-renunciation (*Enthaltsamkeit*), and his ideal of pure phenomenological observation (*reines Zusehen*) was the equivalent of Ranke's objectivity.[31] When Ranke wrote about the need for the historian "to immerse himself in his object" and "to grasp its inner necessity" he was using phrases that could have come directly from Hegel himself.[32]

No less explicitly and bluntly, Hegel also approves Ranke's third principle. Hegel too did not think that the philosophical historian should apply a priori principles to history, and he stressed that he should proceed more empirically, deriving his principles from the examination of the subject matter itself. It is almost as if we are reading Ranke when Hegel declares expressly in the introduction to his lectures: "We have to take history as it is; we must proceed historically, empirically."[33] Just as Ranke would have done, Hegel distances himself from the "*a priorischen Erdichtungen*" – ideas such as the *Urvolk* or *Naturstand* – that had been the stock-in-trade of philosophical history before him. In criticizing a deductive and a priori procedure, Hegel most probably has in mind the same target as Ranke: Fichte's method in the *Grundzüge des gegenwärtigen Zeitalters*.[34] As we shall soon see, Ranke saw Hegel as a Fichtean, not knowing that Hegel had explicitly distanced himself from Fichte's method long ago.[35]

Prima facie this similarity between Ranke and Hegel is exaggerated because, even though Hegel professes an empirical method, he still proceeds deductively or dialectically. We should take Hegel's empiricism *cum grano salis*, someone might say, because his normal practice follows no such principle. Anyone who reads a Hegelian text immediately sees that he constantly divides his subject matter into the moments of universality, particularity, and individuality, corresponding to the three aspects of the concept. These divisions are made *before* the examination of the subject matter; they are not its result. Where is the empiricism here? one might ask. Before making this objection, however, it is necessary to note a distinction that Hegel himself would often stress and that careless readers would often forget: that between the standpoint of the philosopher and the standpoint of the subject matter. Hegel argues that the standpoint of the philosopher has no a priori warrant, but that it stands in need of a posteriori confirmation from the self-examination, or what he calls the experience, of his subject matter. Applying this distinction to the present case, we should consider Hegel's conceptual divisions to be made from the standpoint of the philosopher, having only a provisional validity on their own because they are still waiting a posteriori verification from the inner experience of his subject matter. Whether Hegel actually makes good on this demand for a posteriori justification is a moot question; but the point here is that one cannot take his conceptual divisions of the subject matter as evidence for his belief in a deductive procedure.

Finally, regarding the principle of individuality, we shall soon see that this was the source of a major metaphysical difference between Hegel and Ranke. However, as far as its methodological implications are concerned, there is little difference between them. No less than Ranke, Hegel endorsed the principle of individuality. In his lectures he explicitly applied the concept of individuality to nations and epochs: "The national spirit is a natural individual, and as such blossoms, grows strong, then fades away and dies."[36] Like Ranke, Hegel insisted that the historian should study the individual for its own sake, focusing on its own internal logic, and bracketing all abstractions and generalizations about it. He stressed that each epoch, nation, and individual has to be treated as an end in itself, and it could not be taken only as a means for the realization of higher ends. Of course, there are many passages in Hegel's lectures where he seems to say just the opposite, where he appears to regard the individual, nation, or epoch only as a means, as an instrument for the achievement of world historical goals,[37] but these passages have to be balanced against many others where Hegel also insists that the individual, nation, or epoch are ends in themselves, having inviolable rights that have to be satisfied in world history.[38] There is no irreconcilable conflict between these passages, which derive from Hegel's organic conception of history, according to which every part of an organism is alternately and reciprocally both means and ends.

It might seem that, though Hegel and Ranke share the same basic methodological principles, there is still a fundamental difference between them regarding the ends or goals of historical inquiry. Whereas Hegel attempts to know the universal, the spirit behind an epoch, or the laws of world history, Ranke wants to know only the individual, a specific person, an action, or an epoch in all its detail. Indeed, as we have seen, Ranke would sometimes formulate the differences between philosophy and history in just these terms. However, scratch beneath the surface and one again sees more affinity than difference between Hegel and Ranke. Ranke himself would often stress that the chief goal of history is to know the "idea" (*Idee*) or "spirit" (*Geist*) behind each state or epoch, where the idea or the spirit is an organic whole that unites all aspects of a culture.[39] Each epoch or state has a characteristic nature, idea, or spirit that distinguishes it from all others, and this constitutes the fundamental force behind its development.[40] And, no less than Hegel, Ranke would stress the importance of having a universal history, whose task was to trace the stages and development of spirit throughout the various epochs of history. The structure of world history would be determined by the succession of these ideas.[41] While he denied that this succession is logical or rational, he affirmed its necessity all the same.[42] All that prevented Ranke from affirming the complete historical determinism he associated with Hegel was his uncertainty about the consequences for human freedom.[43]

The affinities between Ranke and Hegel seem less surprising when we realize that Ranke shared many of the basic metaphysical doctrines of the idealist tradition. As a student in Schulpforta and the University of Leipzig, he had studied Kant, Jacobi, Schiller, Fichte, and Schelling; and through the mediation of Fichte he had become deeply influenced by neo-Platonism, especially its doctrine that all sensible reality is the appearance of an intelligible form or idea.[44] In his early *Tagebücher* he had also espoused panentheistic views, according to which the divine nature, though not reducible to nature and history, is directly present within them.[45] These early metaphysical views were to prove decisive for the formation of Ranke's conception of history. The vocation of the historian, he wrote to his brother in March 1820, is to grasp the God who reveals himself in history:

> In all history God lives and dwells, and in history we know him. Every action, every moment, preaches his name, and most of all, I fancy, the fabric of the whole of history. He stands there like a hieroglyph, grasped and preserved in his most visible appearances, perhaps, so that he is not lost for future generations.[46]

The same conviction reappears in Ranke's 1831/1832 lectures on universal history, "Idee der Universalhistorie," the first statement of his mature conception of world history. Here Ranke declares that the work of universal history is based on the religious conviction of "the inner dwelling of the eternal in the individual." The task of the historian is to recognize in every existence "something infinite ... something eternal, something deriving from God."[47]

4. Hidden Differences

Given these methodological and metaphysical affinities between Hegel and Ranke, one is left wondering what, if any, were the differences between them. Such indeed are the affinities that Ernst Troeltsch concluded that Ranke's history is only a weakened, diluted version of Hegel's.[48] All that distinguishes Ranke's history from sociology and run-of-the-mill psychological history, he claimed, was its Hegelian themes.

Troeltsch was deliberately overstating the case, attempting to provoke people into rethinking entrenched views about Ranke's relation to Hegel. Though provocation has its point, he went too far in flattening the differences between Ranke and Hegel. *Pace* Troeltsch, there are indeed profound differences between Ranke and Hegel, even if they are rarely explicit. While they share a similar method and a similar conception of the object of knowledge, Ranke and Hegel differ sharply on at least two fronts: first, their epistemology, especially their views about the limits of knowledge; second, their meta-physics, especially their views about the ontological status of the individual. Let us examine each difference in a little detail.

Regarding their epistemology, Hegel believes, and Ranke doubts, that through the examination of historical particulars we can arrive at a systematic knowledge of the general plan of history. All the evidence received so far from the detailed study of par-ticular epochs, Ranke insists, is still not sufficient to warrant grand generalizations about the purpose of history in general. Ranke's greater skepticism, and indeed greater modesty, about achieving a universal or world history come clearly to the surface in the following passage from his 1831/1832 lectures:

> One sees how infinitely difficult it is with universal history. What an infinite mass! Such differing strivings! What difficulties we have even to grasp the individual! Since we do not know so many things, how do we even presume to grasp the causal nexus everywhere, let alone the essence of the whole? To resolve this task I regard as impossible. God alone knows world history. We know the contradictions ... but we can only divine, only approach from afar the whole itself.[49]

It is surely significant that Ranke himself saw the differences between the historical and philosophical schools in terms of their opposing views about the limits of knowledge. In the 1830s, when he was first forming his views about historical method and begin-ning his attack on the philosophy of history, he wrote this telling passage in his *Tagebuch:*

> The difference between the philosophical and historical school is solely that the former derives with a bold stroke forced conclusions from a flimsy and superficial knowledge of a few facts, whereas the latter attempts to grasp things in their particularity, investigates their specific characteristics and, mindful of the imperfections of tradition, only allows itself to have a feeling for the highest results.[50]

Ranke's skepticism about world history would abate somewhat in his later years. He seemed to think that history was making progress, and that it could approach closer to the ultimate goal of a universal history. However, he continued to stress, in true Kantian fashion, that universal history had to remain a regulative ideal, a goal that could be approached but never attained.[51]

The similarity with Kant here is not accidental. For Kant was indeed the ultimate source of Ranke's greater skepticism and epistemic modesty. Ranke's debts to Kant emerge clearly from his early *Tagebuch* entries, where he explicitly endorses Kant's cri-tique of knowledge. Ranke accepted Kant's argument that reason cannot give us knowl-edge of reality beyond experience, and he even declared that Kant had decisively settled the question about the limits of knowledge.[52] Ranke's constant insistence that universal history is an infinite task ultimately came from his adherence to the Kantian doctrine of regulative ideas. He could not accept Hegel's system of universal history because it made a constitutive principle out of a merely regulative idea whose sole purpose was to guide inquiry.

Regarding their metaphysics, Ranke departed from Hegel's rigorous holism and gave a greater ontological independence to the individual than Hegel. While Hegel's doctrine of the concrete universal means that the whole is prior to each of its parts, such that the identity of each individual depends entirely on its place within the whole, Ranke's principle of individuality means that the part is prior to the whole, such that the identity of each individual is, at least partially, independent of and irreducible to the whole. Although there is indeed a holistic tendency in Ranke's thinking – the same emphasis upon the organic unity of the idea – it is not so strict and drastic as in Hegel. It is a holism with a nonconceptual remainder. Each individual is for Ranke ultimately unique and singular, irreducible to the conjunction of its properties. It has a self-sufficient identity of its own not entirely formulable by its position in the whole. Such is the import of Ranke's famous declaration in his Berechtsgaden lectures that each epoch stands immediately before God, having a value that comes from itself alone. It emerges more explicitly much earlier, however, in Ranke's early 1831 lectures on universal history.[53] Here Ranke explains that his principle of individuality means not only that the historian should examine the individual for its own sake, but also that the individual is irreducible to universals. No amount of construction or deduction can in principle derive the individual, which transcends conceptual analysis and derivation.

The ultimate reason for Ranke's resistance to Hegel's holism was his belief in human freedom. Ranke feared that if every individual were nothing but a product of its relations within a whole, its actions would be a function of the laws governing it. There would be no space for what all freedom requires: the power to do otherwise. From an early age Ranke had endorsed the Kantian-Fichtean conception of transcendental freedom, which required that the self be independent of nature and the cosmos as a whole.[54]

These metaphysical differences between Hegel and Ranke are the source of further epistemological differences between them. Both Hegel and Ranke think that historical knowledge is about individuals, about what this or that person did on a specific occasion. However, they differ in their views about how such an individual is to be known. Since Hegel holds that the individual is fully expressible by its place within the whole, he thinks that historical knowledge, like all knowledge, should be discursive and systematic. Since, however, Ranke holds that the individual is self-sufficient, transcending its place within the whole, he maintains that historical knowledge should be immediate and intuitive. For Ranke, the ultimate end of history is to have an intuition of the particular, to perceive the individual in all its infinite depth. Some scholars write of this as Ranke's mysticism,[55] and so indeed it is. But it is important to see that it has a powerful pedigree and precedent: Jacobi's critique of reason. Ranke's conception of the aim of inquiry ultimately goes back to Jacobi, who was a decisive influence on his thinking in his early years. In his *Tagebuch* he fully endorsed Jacobi's famous slogan that the purpose of inquiry is "to disclose existence" (*Daseyn zu enthüllen*).[56] He too held with Jacobi: *Individuum est ineffabile* (the individual is ineffable).[57] Ranke simply applied these Jacobian dicta to the realm of history itself. The purpose of history is to have an insight into existence itself, to perceive the unique particularity of things. Ranke's great debt to Jacobi brings out, however, his distance from Hegel, who utterly rejected Jacobi's belief in the possibility of any kind of immediate knowledge.

5. Ranke's Polemic against Hegel

Whatever the fundamental similarities and differences between Hegel and Ranke, they were greatly obscured by Ranke's later polemics against Hegel. Flatly contrary to Hegel's express teachings in his lectures, Ranke saw Hegel's method in the philosophy of history as a priori deduction or construction. According to Hegel's method as Ranke describes it, the philosopher would begin from general principles, which had an a priori rationale, and then derive or explain the manifold data of history from them. Ranke would often contrast this *philosophical* method with the *historical* method: while the philosopher begins from the universal and descends to the particular, the historian starts from particulars and only gradually derives generalizations from them, which have only a problematic and relative validity.[58] In his 1839/1840 lectures on modern history Ranke will, for the first time, explicitly ascribe such a methodology to Hegel.[59] It is noteworthy that he formed his conception of philosophical method from Fichte, especially his *Grundzüge des gegenwärtigen Zeitalters*, which he explicitly cites in his 1831/1832 lectures.[60] For many years Fichte would be Ranke's model of the philosophical historian. Ranke knew his Fichte well, having studied him in detail since his Leipzig student years.[61] Rather than reading Hegel for his own sake, Ranke simply lumped him together with Fichte as a philosopher of history. Probably because of the influence of the Hegelian school, Hegel eventually replaced Fichte as Ranke's prime example of the philosophical historian.

It is unclear how much Ranke knew about Hegel's philosophy of history in the late 1820s and early 1830s, the period when he began to formulate his methodological views. Hegel's lectures on the philosophy of history began in 1822/1823, and continued when Ranke was in Berlin; but the text of his lectures, which were largely based on student notes, was not published until 1837. Hegel's mature conception of history appears, if only in very condensed form, in his 1817 edition of the *Enzyklopädie der philosophischen Wissenschaften*. Ranke knew about this work, but he scarcely read it. In his March 10, 1828, letter to August Varnhagen von Ense, Ranke admitted that he quickly glossed the *Enzyklopädie*,[62] though he was familiar with the early and later editions. To Von Ense he confessed a complete aversion to Hegel's writings. What content there was to Hegel's writings was only "the melody of depth," while the rest was "*eine Menge falsches, häßliches Zeug*" ("a bunch of false, abhorrent stuff"). Ranke borrowed the phrase "the melody of depth" from Friedrich Schlegel, an arch-enemy of Hegel.

After Hegel's death in 1831, Ranke's knowledge of Hegel grew, and his opinion of him began to mellow. Now that his own influence was growing as that of Hegel was waning he could afford to be more generous to his old foe. In his 1847 lectures on modern history, Ranke explicitly refers to, and summarizes portions of, Hegel's philosophy of history.[63] Here he even praises Hegel's "bold, gigantic attempt" to grasp all of world history through his dialectical method. It is an effort, he says, that deserves "much recognition." Later, in his 1867/1868 lectures on 'Neuere Geschichte,' Ranke spoke of "*der so reich begabte Hegel*" ("the so richly talented Hegel"), who had tried to explain world history with reference to a few leading events, such as the discovery of America or the French Revolution.[64] While Ranke criticizes this approach to history as too narrow, his praise of Hegel seems sincere. Toward his later years, he even stated

341

that the ideal historian should be a synthesis of the best of Niebuhr, who had a greater appreciation of the particular, with the best of Hegel, who had a better grasp of the universal.

Though Ranke's views on Hegel were maturing even in the late 1840s, there is little evidence of his growing wisdom in his chief polemic against Hegel, the first two lectures of his *Über die Epochen der neueren Geschichte*, which he delivered in 1854 in Berechtsgaden to Prince Maximillian of Bavaria.[65] In these lectures, despite having read Hegel, Ranke continues to interpret him as the epitome of a scholastic philosopher who has no appreciation of the empirical methods of history. Here Ranke makes two basic objections against Hegel's method, though both of them are misconceived. First, he claims that Hegel's method is deductive and a priori, forcing the facts of history into a Procrustean bed. Second, he complains that Hegel's method rides roughshod over historical individuality. Rather than treating each nation as an end in itself, Hegel's conception of progress, and the cunning of reason, makes him treat all epochs, nations, and individuals as mere means toward world-historical ends.

A careful look at Hegel's texts shows, however, that there is little warrant for either objection. What seems to justify the first is that Hegel states in his lectures that the philosophy of world history assumes that reason governs history, as if this were a presupposition that is justified elsewhere in his system.[66] This statement has led many scholars to assume that the philosophy of history presupposes Hegel's speculative logic, so that it seems as if the philosophy of history simply applies the principles of logic to history. But Hegel is very careful to correct that impression; for he states explicitly that he does not have to presuppose the principle that reason governs history, and that he has stated it only provisionally for expository reasons to give a general idea of his subject. He then declares explicitly and repeatedly that history must establish its fundamental principle by its own means, by an examination of the content of history itself.[67]

What seems to justify the second objection are the many passages where Hegel writes about the individual as a means toward the ends of reason. But, as we have seen, these passages have to be read in the wider context, because there are many other passages where Hegel writes about the need to treat each individual, age, and nation as an end in itself. In any case, it is inaccurate to regard Hegel as an uncritical champion of the idea of progress. For in his lectures he will distinguish many conceptions of progress and distance himself from the Enlightenment conception in ways that Ranke could only have admired.[68] Here again the apparent differences between Hegel and Ranke disappear on closer examination. Both Hegel and Ranke distinguished two senses of progress: progress toward some abstract ideal determined a priori apart from historical development; and progress according to some ideal inherent within the history of a nation. Both approved the latter and condemned the former.[69]

The reason historians have so happily accepted Ranke's account of Hegel's philosophical method is that they are guilty of a simple confusion: a conflation of the order of method with the order of being, or, in older scholastic terminology, the *ratio cognoscendi* with the *ratio essendi*. It is true that Hegel's ontology makes universals prior to particulars, and that his famous 'concept' or concrete universal is one that generates its own content. It then appears as if, following such an ontology, Hegel must proceed deductively, deriving particulars from universals. But this is a non sequitur. Crucial to

Hegel's entire philosophy is a distinction between the order of knowing and the order of being. This distinction means that although universals are prior to particulars in the order of being, they are posterior to them in the order of knowing. Hence the universal cannot be *known* by us a priori; rather, it has to be established only a posteriori, by examining the multiplicity of particulars and showing how each of them is impossible without the universal as a whole. What is first in order of being – the universal – then shows itself to be last in the order of knowing, where what is first is indeed the particular.

6. Hegel's Attack on Ranke and Niebuhr

It might seem as if the story of the Hegel–Ranke relationship is *per necessitatem* one-sided, as if the direction of critique had to go from Ranke to Hegel, not the other way round. Sheer mortality seems to dictate such one-sidedness: Ranke was twenty-five years younger than Hegel, who had been dead for decades when Ranke gave his Berechtsgaden lectures. Though Ranke and Hegel overlapped in Berlin for three years (1825–1827), Ranke was a minor *professor extraordinarius* and so, it seems, scarcely worth Hegel's attention. Sure enough, throughout his extensive correspondence, Hegel never mentioned the younger professor. Nevertheless, the assumption that the Hegel–Ranke relationship is one-sided is false. The remarkable fact of the matter is that Hegel knew Ranke all too well, and that he was very critical of his way of writing history.[70]

Once we place Hegel and Ranke in their historical context, this fact does not appear so strange after all. Such was the intellectual climate in Berlin in the 1820s that it was almost impossible for Hegel to ignore Ranke. When Ranke arrived in Berlin in 1825, the philosophical scene there was divided into two warring factions: "the philosophical school" revolving around Hegel, and "the historical school" centering around Savigny, Eichhorn, and Schleiermacher.[71] The hostilities between these parties were so intense that any partisan would be very interested to know the affiliation of a newcomer. Was he friend or foe? Should one welcome him or be on guard? Almost immediately, Hegel and his followers placed Ranke in the camp of the enemy. And one must admit: they knew their man! Although, when he first came to Berlin, Ranke frequented the literary salons of Rahel Levin and Henriette Herz, which were liberal and sympathetic to philosophers, his deeper loyalties were indeed with the historians. Ranke was not only on friendly terms with Schleiermacher, Eichhorn, and Savigny, but he was also the disciple of Niebuhr, who was one of Hegel's archenemies.

It was in this poisonous atmosphere that Hegel made one of his few recorded comments about Ranke. Under Schleiermacher's leadership, the historical school had achieved a great victory over Hegel in December 1827: they blocked his entrance into the *Akademie der Wissenschaften*. Smarting from that insult, Hegel retaliated by founding an academic society of his own, *Die Societät für wissenschaftliche Kritik*, whose main social purpose, it seems, was to snub members of the historical school. Predictably, the society consisted mostly of Hegelians, though a few non-Hegelians were added for appearances. When someone naively suggested adding Schleiermacher to their ranks, Hegel protested with the utmost vehemence. And when Ranke's name was put forward,

Hegel quickly quashed that proposal with a single damning sentence: "*Das ist nur ein gewöhnlicher Historiker*" ("He is only a mediocre historian").[72]

Given the animosities between the historical and philosophical schools, it was only natural for Hegel to want to defend his own approach to history in his lectures. History was the chief card his enemies were playing against him, and he wanted to show that here too he was master of the turf. Sure enough, in the drafts for the introduction to his lectures, Hegel engaged in an implicit critique of Ranke and Niebuhr. Amid his involved discussion of the various ways of writing history, there is a curious reference to Ranke.[73] The reference simply states the name 'Ranke' in parentheses. Georg Lasson, one of the first editors of the lectures, mistook the word for *Ränke*, and so missed its significance entirely; but Johannes Hoffmeister, a later editor, was able to determine from the handwriting and context that the word was indeed *Ranke*, the name of the historian.[74] The context of the remark makes it evident that Hegel had in mind Ranke's *Geschichte der romanischen und germanischen Völker 1494–1814*, which appeared in 1825.[75] This work and its sequel, *Zur Kritik der neueren Geschichtschreiber*, had made Ranke's name, and they also left no doubt about Ranke's intellectual affiliation. Here was a practitioner of Niebuhr's critical history who had applied his master's techniques to modern history. It was almost inevitable, then, that Hegel would want to take issue with him.

In his introduction Hegel cites Ranke's name as an example of a primitive form of what he calls *reflective* history, that is, that form of history where the narrator stands apart from the past and attempts to reconstruct it from documents; he constrasts such reflective history with *original* history, where the narrator is an eye witness, and so part of the historical process itself. The chief problem with all reflective history, Hegel thinks, is that "the writer approaches history in his own spirit, which is different from the spirit of the object itself." What matters is not so much how people in the past saw themselves but how the historian understands them. All reflective history therefore fails to get inside its subject matter; it forever sees the past from the standpoint of the observer rather than the actor. "When the [reflective] historian tries to depict the spirit of bygone times, it is usually his own spirit which makes itself heard."[76] Hegel thinks that Ranke's form of reflective history suffers from the problems of all reflective history, but he also adds that it has some special problems all its own. The purpose of Ranke's kind of reflective history, as Hegel explains it, is to avoid the dry abstractions of historical surveys by giving a faithful and lively picture of the times. Ranke rightly sees, Hegel implies, that the usual surveys of reflective history are too abstract and dry, missing all the vibrancy and immediacy of original history. However, Hegel suggests, Ranke's solution to this problem is inadequate. To compensate for the abstraction, Ranke piles detail upon detail, so that in the end one gets lost in them and fails to grasp the whole. His history provides "a colourful quantity of detail," though it does not see beyond it to "a whole concept, a universal end." The wealth of detail in Ranke's writing reminds Hegel of nothing more than Walter Scott's novels, and he adds that such narrative is better left to novelists than historians. Had Ranke known of Hegel's Walter Scott analogy, he would have felt it to be a cruel *ad hominem* point, for Ranke recollected that the reason he turned to history in the first place is that he found the *Mémoires* of Phillipe de Commynes more fascinating than Walter Scott's *Quentin Durward*.[77]

On the whole, Hegel's polemic against Ranke is limited to his misgivings about the narrative technique of the *Geschichte*. The broader point Hegel is making – that history cannot simply be a matter of determining the facts and becoming accurate about details – would have been strongly endorsed by Ranke himself. Indeed, in the introduction to the *Geschichte*, Ranke had insisted that understanding the unity and development of events is no less important than ascertaining facts themselves.[78] But Hegel's remark can be read as an internal critique that Ranke failed to achieve his own ideal of unity. It is noteworthy that Ranke himself, and most of his later critics, admitted this shortcoming.[79]

There is also in Hegel's drafts for the introduction a parenthical remark referring to Niebuhr's *Römische Geschichte*.[80] Hegel makes Niebuhr's critical history his example of the worst kind of reflective history. As Hegel explains it, critical history is essentially an examination of, and judgment upon, the credibility of sources. Its aim is to get down to hard facts and to remove all the accretions of tradition that have contaminated historical sources. But such history, Hegel charges, is only the history of history, not history itself.[81] The French have done critical history better than the Germans, he claims, because they write critical treatises and do not attempt to pass it off as history itself. As with Ranke, Hegel complains that Niebuhr does not live up to his own ideals. Rather than avoiding anachronism and sticking with the facts, critical history ends up reading the present into the past and creating all kinds of fictions of its own. A little later on in the introduction Hegel gives an interesting twist to his critique of the critical school: the critical historians, he claims, read their a priori constructions into history.[82] Here Hegel was turning Ranke's and Niebuhr's charge of a priori construction against them. It was they who were guilty of forcing the past to comply with a priori principles.

Hegel's polemic against Niebuhr has raised problems for Hegel scholars.[83] Could Hegel seriously mean to reject the value of the critical appraisal of sources? It seems as if Hegel's polemic is fueled more by partisan passions than any deeper disagreement. After all, Hegel agrees with Niebuhr and Ranke about the need for a close examination of evidence, about the dangers of a priori history, about the value of original history, and about the pitfalls of anachronism. If, however, we look carefully at Hegel's later remarks about Niebuhr in the lectures, the point of his criticism becomes clearer. These remarks show that Hegel had two basic objections to critical history. First, the critical historian was so intent on getting to facts alone that he discarded the value of legend and myth, which can also be of great value to the historian in understanding the beliefs and values of a past culture. Hence Hegel is happy to concede to Niebuhr that the story of Romulus is probably a myth and cannot be taken as a literal truth about the founding of Rome; however, the myth is still of great value because of what it tells us about "the Roman Spirit."[84] The problem with Niebuhr's critical history is for Hegel typical of all reflective history: it makes a too sharp separation between facts and narration of facts, between the *res gestae* and the *historia res gestae*, as if the former alone were history; but we cannot completely separate, Hegel believes, facts and narrative, because the narrative itself becomes part of history. So even if Thucydides versions of Pericles' speeches are not accurate, they are still of the utmost importance for what they tell us about ancient Greek culture.[85] Second, Niebuhr is so busy assessing and reasoning about the sources that he never gets down to the facts themselves. For this reason Hegel says that his work is more a history of the history of Rome rather than a history of Rome itself.[86] Sometimes, Hegel charges, what Niebuhr regards as a great discovery of fact is only a point of interpretation. His famous finding about the Roman agrarian laws – that they did not violate the sanctity of Roman laws regarding property but simply allowed the plebeians to use public lands usurped by the patricians – ultimately rests upon "a useless point of law" (*eine unnütze Rechtsfrage*).[87] For one could question whether the public lands, after having been in possession of the patricians for so long, were still public property. If one argues they were not public property, then the laws would have been violated after all.

Such, in sum, was Hegel's polemic against Niebuhr and Ranke. Although there were some serious points behind it, it does not reflect a fundamental difference in principle regarding their methodologies. Hegel's polemic is best seen as an *internal* critique of Ranke and Niebuhr, an argument for how they fail to meet their own methodological ideals. But Hegel does not question their methodological ideals themselves. He agrees with Niebuhr and Ranke about the need for a critical examination of sources, the primacy of original documents, the dangers of a priori history, and the importance of examining an age in the light of its own standards and values. Hegel differs from them chiefly about the extent to which these ideals can be achieved: he affirms, while Ranke and Niebuhr deny, that it is now possible to construct a philosophy of world history. The most interesting facet of Hegel's polemic is that it shows his extraordinary sensitivity to the methodological issues raised by the historical school. At the very least Hegel's brusque dismissal of the charge of a priori construction – and his willingness to turn it against the historians – show that there is something very wrong with the standard characterization of Hegel's methodology.

Summa summarum, the affinities between Ranke and Hegel are much greater than most scholars, and even Ranke himself, realized. Ranke and Hegel were at one regarding historical method and the goals of historical inquiry. Nevertheless, despite these affinities, there were still profound differences between them, specifically with regard to the ontological status of the individual and the limits of knowledge. The guiding spirit behind much of Ranke's thought was Kant's doctrine about the limits of knowledge and Jacobi's teaching about the value of intuitive insight into existence – two doctrines that Hegel had long fought against. Needless to say, much more needs to be said about the complex relationship between Ranke and Hegel. Their relationship is of great historical importance but also of great conceptual complexity. All we have attempted to do here is to get the discussion started and take it beyond the confusions of the past.

Notes

1   This was the epithet of Herbert B. Adams in "New Methods of Study in History," in *Johns Hopkins University Studies in History and Political Science* II (1884), p. 65. This view was very widespread in the United States and Britain during the late nineteenth and early twentieth century. On Ranke's reputation in the United States and Germany, see Georg Iggers, "The Image of Ranke in American and German Historical Thought," *History and Theory* 2 (1962): 17–40, and W. Stull Holt, "The Idea of Scientific History in America," *Journal of the History of Ideas* 1 (1940): 352–362. On Ranke's role in the development of history in Britain, see

Doris Goldstein, "History at Oxford and Cambridge," in *Leopold Ranke and the Shaping of the Historical Discipline*, ed. Georg Iggers and James Powell (Syracuse: Syracuse University Press, 1990), 141–153. Ranke's reputation in Britain was secured chiefly by Lord Acton, "German Schools of History," in *Historical Essays and Studies* (London: Macmillan, 1919), 344–392, and J. B. Bury, "The Science of History," in *The Varieties of History*, ed. Fritz Stern (Cleveland: Meridian, 1956), 210–223.

2   It was above all Friedrich Meinecke who promoted this conception of Ranke. See his *Die Entstehung des Historismus* (Munich: Oldenbourg, 1965).

3   See Meinecke's "Leopold Ranke," the *Beigabe* to *Die Entstehung des Historismus*, p. 585, which tells us that when Ranke died, he was regarded as *"der große Lehrer einer Wissenschaft."*

4   The introductions to these lectures have been collected and edited by Walther Fuchs and Volker Dotterweich. See their *Leopold von Ranke, Aus Werk und Nachlass* (Munich: Oldenbourg, 1975), volume 4. The most important for Ranke's methodological views is his 1831–1832 "Idee der Universalhistorie," IV, 72–89.

5   On the origins of Ranke's use of this method, see Edward Bourke, "Ranke and the Beginning of the Seminary Method in Teaching History," in *Essays in Historical Criticism* (Freeport, N.Y.: Books for Libraries Press, 1967), 265–274; and Gunter Berg, *Leopold von Ranke als Akademischer Lehrer* (Göttingen: Vandenhoeck & Ruprecht, 1968), 51–56.

6   On Ranke's school, see James Westfall Thompson, *A History of Historical Writing* (New York: Macmillan, 1942), II, 187–204; Heinrich von Srbik, *Geist und Geschichte von deutschen Humanismus bis zur Gegenwart* (Salzburg: Bruckmann, 1950), I, 293–325; Eduard Fueter, *Geschichte der neueren Historiographie* (Munich: Oldenbourg, 1911), 487–492; and G. P. Gooch, *History and Historians in the Nineteenth Century* (London: Longmans, Green, 1952), 98–121. Remarkably, Gooch does not mention Dilthey or Burkhardt.

7   As Duncan Forbes put it, Ranke's criticisms rested upon an "encyclopedic inattention to the texts." See his understandably choleric introduction to the Nisbet translation of *Lectures on the Philosophy of World History* (Cambridge: Cambridge University Press, 1975), p. xv.

8   This has been the case for even the best scholars. See, e.g., Herbert Schnädelbach, *Geschichtsphilosophie nach Hegel* (Freiburg: Alber, 1974), 34–47; Friedrich Jäger and Jörn Rüsen, *Geschichte des Historismus* (Munich: Beck, 1992), 34–40; Georg Iggers, *The German Conception of History* (Middletown: Wesleyan University Press, 1968), pp. 66, 77; and Theodor Steinbüchel, "Ranke und Hegel" in *Große Geschichtsdenker*, ed. Rudolf Stadelmann (Tübingen: Rainer Wunderlich Verlag, 1949), pp. 188, 196, 200. The most thorough study of the Ranke–Hegel relationship is still Ernst Simon, *Ranke und Hegel* (Munich: Oldenbourg, 1928), *Historische Zeitschrift, Beiheft* 15 (1928). Although Simon did note some of the important methodological affinities between Hegel and Ranke (pp. 125–126), he too conceives Hegel's methodology in essentially deductive terms as a progression from the general to the particular (pp. 124, 157–158). Despite its many other virtues, Simon's account is seriously out of date; he used the antiquated Lasson edition of Hegel, and the critical edition of the Ranke *Nachlass* appeared only in 1975.

9   Dickens, *Hard Times*, Book I, chapter 1.

10   See, e.g., the lectures "Geschichte der neueren Zeit" (1839–1840), and "Neuere Geschichte seit dem Westfälischen Frieden," in *Aus Werk und Nachlass*, IV, 134–135, 185.

11   See Ranke's "Idee der Universalhistorie," in *Aus Werk und Nachlass*, IV, 72–73. Ranke somewhat weakened the link between history and art in later lectures, when he would insist on the distinction between history and poetry. See the 1847 lectures on "Neuere Geschichte seit dem Westfälischen Frieden," *Aus Werk und Nachlass* IV, 188–189. The connections between philosophy, history, and poetry was an important topic for the young Ranke. See his *Tagebücher* I, 232–233, 233–234.

12   See his statement in "Idee der Universalhistorie," *Aus Werk und Nachlass* IV, 77.

13 Ibid., IV, 77.

14 Ibid., IV, 77, 78, 86, 87.

15 Ibid., IV, 88.

16 The phrase appears in the introduction to his *Geschichte der romanischen und germanischen Völker von 1494–1514*, in *Sämtliche Werke* (Leipzig: Duncker & Humblot, 1867–90), XXXIII, v–viii. Henceforth this work will be cited as SW.

17 This point has been argued by Leonard Krieger, *Ranke: The Meaning of History* (Chicago, Ill.: University of Chicago Press, 1977), 10–20.

18 See, e.g., Ranke's statement in *Analecten der englischen Geschichte*, SW XXI, 114.

19 Ranke's critique was in his *Zur Kritik neuerer Geschichtsschreiber*, which was published in 1824 as a critical appendix to his *Geschichte der romanischen und germanischen Völker*. It was the *Kritik* that secured Ranke's reputation and an appointment at Berlin. A later edition appeared in volume 33 of his *Sämtliche Werke*.

20 SW 33/34, 24.

21 See the introduction to the *Geschichte der romanischen und germanischen Völker*, SW 33, p. 6.

22 Self-extinction was another shibboleth of the Ranke school. It appears in his *Englische Geschichte, vornehmlich im Siebzehnten Jahrhundert, Sämtliche Werke* XVI, 103.

23 See "Einleitung zu einer Vorlesung über Neuere Geschichte," *Aus Werk und Nachlass*, IV, 295.

24 See "Geschichte der neueren Zeit," *Aus Werk und Nachlass* IV, 135.

25 From the "Erster Vortrag" to *Über die Epochen der neueren Geschichte, Aus Werk und Nachlass*, II, 59–60.

26 See "Idee der Universalhistorie," IV, 77.

27 See Meinecke, *Entstehung*, p. 595. Also see his later essay "Deutung eines Rankewortes," in *Zur Theorie und Philosophie der Geschichte*, ed. Eberhard Kessel (Stuttgart: Koehler, 1965), 140–152.

28 On Ranke's debt to Niebuhr, see Theodore Von Laue, *Leopold Ranke: The Formative Years* (Princeton, N.J.: Princeton University Press, 1950), pp. 14–15, 19–21.

29 That this is essentially Hegel's method in the philosophy of history I have argued elsewhere. See my "Hegel's Historicism," *Cambridge Companion to Hegel* (Cambridge: Cambridge University Press, 1993), 282–288.

30 See Ranke's statement in "Einleitung zur Historisch-Politischen Zeitschrift," in *Das politische Gespräch und andere Schriften zur Wissenschaftslehre*, ed. Erich Rothacker (Halle: Niemeyer, 1925), pp. 1, 2.

31 See the "Einleitung" to the *Phänomenologie des Geistes*, ed. Johannes Hoffmeister (Hamburg: Meiner, 1958), 72.

32 See Ranke's essay "Vom Einfluss der Theorie," *Sämtliche Werke* 49/50, 243–246.

33 See *Vorlesungen über die Philosophie der Weltgeschichte*, Band I, *Die Vernunft in der Geschichte*, ed. Johannes Hoffmeister (Hamburg: Meiner, 1970), 30. Henceforth I will cite this work as VG; I will also cite in parentheses the corresponding passage in the Nisbet translation, designated "N."

34 See Fichte's statement of method in *Grundzüge des gegenwärtigen Zeitalters*, in *Werke*, ed. I. H. Fichte (Berlin: Veit, 1845–1846), VII, 4–6.

35 Hegel criticized Fichte's deductive methodology in his 1801 *Differenzschrift* on the grounds that an abstract first principle cannot derive a concrete content. See Hegel, *Werke in zwanzig Bänden*, ed. E. Moldenhauer and K. Michel (Frankfurt: Suhrkamp, 1970), II, 61–65.

36 *Vorlesungen*, p. 67 (N 58).

37 Ibid., pp. 48–49 (N 43); 93 (N 80); 105 (89). These passages are stressed by Steinbüchel in his "Ranke and Hegel," pp. 182, 192, 194, as evidence for the fundamental difference between the two thinkers. But he underrates those passages where Hegel also says that the individual has to be treated as an end in itself. He notes these passages, p. 194, only to

dismiss them as evidence for a tension in Hegel's views. He fails to see how Hegel's organicism allows him to treat each individual as both means and end.

38 Ibid., pp. 82 (70); 106 (N 90); 137 (N 115).
39 See, e.g., "Geschichte des Mittelalters," and "Erster Teil der Weltgeschichte," in *Aus Werk und Nachlass*, IV, 141, 202.
40 See, e.g., *Epochen*, in *Aus Werk und Nachlass*, II, 58–59; and *Gespräch über Politik*, in Rothacker, pp. 25, 34.
41 See "Neuere Geschichte, seit dem Westfälischen Frieden," *Aus Werk und Nachlass*, IV, 191.
42 See "Neuere Geschichte seit dem Anfang des 17 Jahrhunderts," *Aus Werk und Nachlass* IV, 415.
43 See *Epochen*, *Aus Werk und Nachlass* II, 54–55.
44 On the importance of Fichte as a mediator of Neo-Platonic doctrine, see Krieger, *Ranke*, 50–51.
45 *Aus Werk und Nachlass* I, 142, 151–152, 154–155.
46 *Das Brief Werk*, ed. Walther Fuchs (Hamburg: Hoffmann und Campe, 1949), 18.
47 *Aus Werk und Nachlass*, IV, 77, 79.
48 See Ernst Troeltsch, "Über den Begriff einer historischen Dialektik," in *Historische Zeitschrift* 119 (1919), 421.
49 *Aus Werk und Nachlass*, IV, 83
50 Ibid., I, 237.
51 Ibid., IV, 297, 307, 411, 435.
52 *Aus Werk und Nachlass* I, 142–143, 146–147, 159.
53 Ibid., IV, 74–75.
54 See the early essay "Mensch und Natur," in *Frühe Schriften*, *Aus Werk und Nachlass* II, 223–232.
55 Von Laue, *Ranke*, pp. 43–44, 45.
56 Ibid., I, 152–154.
57 Meinecke would later make this dictum the motto of his *Die Entstehung des Historismus*. Thanks to Ranke's notebooks, we can see that the philosophical origins of this dictum goes back to Jacobi.
58 *Aus Werk und Nachlass* IV, 74–75, 76–77, 87.
59 Ibid., IV, 134.
60 Ibid., IV, 74.
61 Ranke took extensive notes in 1816–1817 on Fichte's *Das Wesen des Gelehrten* and *Die Anweisung zum seligen Leben*. See *Aus Werk und Nachlass*, I, 493–501.
62 See his March 10, 1828, letter to Karl August Varnhagen von Ense, in *Brief Werk*, ed. Walther Fuchs (Hamburg: Hoffmann und Campe, 1949), 148.
63 *Aus Werk und Nachlass* IV, 186–187.
64 Ibid., IV, 415.
65 Ibid., II, 53–83.
66 VG 28; N 27.
67 VG 30–31; N 29.
68 VG 149–150; N 124–126.
69 On Ranke's view of progress, see his "Über die Verwandtschaft und den Unterschied der Historie und der Politik," in SW XXIV, 280–293: "Political wisdom consists not so much in preservation as in progress and growth."
70 It is worth noting that Ranke met Hegel personally in the summer of 1831. See his letter to his brother Heinrich, end of April 1832, in *Neue Briefe*, ed. Bernhard Hoeft (Hamburg: Hoffmann und Campe, 1949), p. 171. Ranke was a friend of Hegel's son, Karl, and wrote about the father: "*Der Vater, den ich Sommer 31 kennengelernt, war doch gut und geistreich.*"

("The father, whom I met in the summer of '31, was nevertheless nice and entertaining").
The "*doch*" (nevertheless) is rich in meaning.

71 On these parties and their effect on Ranke, see Simon, *Ranke und Hegel*, pp. 16–119.

72 On this episode and the source of this remark, see Simon, *Ranke und Hegel*, pp. 81–83.

73 VG 17; N 18–19.

74 This important clue is overlooked by Simon, who used the Lasson edition. He writes that there is no reference to Ranke anywhere in the lectures. See *Ranke und Hegel*, p. 28.

75 This work was reviewed by Heinrich Leo, a student of Hegel's, in 1828 for the *Ergänzungsblätter zur Jenaischen Allgemeinen Literatur-Zeitung*. Ranke replied to the review in *Hallische Literaturzeitung*, in *Sämtliche Werke* LIII/LIV, 659–666. On this episode see Iggers, *German Conception*, pp. 65–69, and Simon, *Ranke und Hegel*, pp. 93–101.

76 VG 12; N 17.

77 Ranke, SW LIII/LIX, 61.

78 Ranke, SW XXX, vii.

79 In the introduction Ranke admitted that his treatment of the many particulars would seem "harsh, disconnected, colorless and tiring." Later historians have agreed with Hegel's assessment of Ranke's narrative. See, e.g., the opinions cited in Iggers, *German Conception*, p. 69, and Krieger, *Ranke*, pp. 107–108.

80 VG 20; N 22.

81 It is noteworthy that J. G. Droysen made the same point against the critical historians. See his *Historik: Vorlesungen über Enzyklopädie und Methodologie der Geschichte*, ed. Rudolf Hübner (Munich: Oldenbourg, 1960), 131–132.

82 VG 32; N 30.

83 See, e.g., Forbes, "Introduction," p. xvi; and George Dennis O'Brien, *Hegel on Reason and History* (Chicago, Ill.: University of Chicago Press, 1975), pp. 82–82. Ranke himself seems to have been puzzled by Hegel's criticism and replied to it in his "Neuere Geschichte, Seit dem Westfälischen Frieden," *Aus Werk und Nachlass*, IV, 185n. Ranke argued that even Hegel's original history is not possible without a critical history to certify his originality and authenticity.

84 Hegel, *Vorlesungen über die Philosophie der Geschichte*, Werkausgabe, XII, 360.

85 VG 7–8; N 13–14, 228.

86 *Vorlesungen*, XII, 342.

87 Ibid., XII, 368.

Part VIII

Aesthetics

17

Hegel and the "Historical Deduction" of the Concept of Art

ALLEN SPEIGHT

The notions of beauty and art acquire an important new philosophical status in the post-Kantian world. In the wake of Kant's 1790 *Critique of the Power of Judgment*, a host of claims, from Schiller to the Romantics, come to be made on behalf of the unifying power of beauty as a force that can harmonize the opposed realms of the rational and the sensible. Likewise, new claims are made on behalf of the distinct function – even sovereignty – now associated by some thinkers with artistic activity as an end in itself. Among the numerous retrospective accounts attempting to make sense of the important developments within this period is a remarkably brief section of the introduction to Hegel's *Lectures on Fine Art*, an account that, in the text of the "standard edition" of these lectures, bears the interesting title "Historical Deduction of the True Concept of Art."[1]

This title and the section that it heads raise a number of important philosophical questions worth exploring. On the historical side, the "true concept" of beautiful art that it is the task of this section to develop is a concept that Hegel seems to connect most directly to Schiller's definition of beauty as "freedom in appearance."[2] As Hegel and Schiller acknowledge, such a formulation can only have arisen in the context of a world construed in terms of the principles and oppositions of Kantian practical reason, but both Hegel and Schiller give it a significance that will mark a decisive departure from the context of Kant's aesthetics. A focus on this Schillerian formulation has implications for an understanding of Hegel's wider notion of absolute spirit, as well, since, as Terry Pinkard has recently put it, Hegel's triad of art, religion, and philosophy can be said to be concerned precisely with what it means to express freedom in the natural or material world.[3] Methodologically, there are also a number of important issues involved in the notion of an "historical deduction" of such a concept of art. It has recently been claimed, for example, that part of what is distinctive about Hegel's approach to art and beauty is its *narrative* structure.[4] What is the place of the so-called historical deduction within this larger narrative project? Despite a growing interest among scholars in Hegel's aesthetics, insufficient attention has been paid to this section

A Companion to Hegel, First Edition. Edited by Stephen Houlgate and Michael Baur.
© 2011 Blackwell Publishing Ltd. Published 2011 by Blackwell Publishing Ltd.

and the perspective it gives on the development of aesthetics from Kant to Schiller to Hegel.[5] In what follows, I will examine first the textual status of the deduction's claims (Section 1) and then look at its role within the philosophical argument of the Introduction to Hegel's *Lectures* (Sections 2–4). I conclude with some suggestions about how the re-examination of this section can be useful for getting a sense of Hegel's overall narrative and historical project in the philosophy of art (Section 5).

1.   The Textual Status of Hegel's "Historical Deduction"

We may well wonder about the title of this famous section itself. What is meant by the notion of an "historical deduction" in the context of Hegel's project in aesthetics and why does Hegel give it such a prominent role within the Introduction to the lectures? The use of the term "historical deduction" is certainly puzzling, if not problematic. Although Hegel speaks earlier in the Introduction to the *Lectures* about the difficulty of speculative philosophy's responding to the demand to "prove" the object of the philosophy of art and its more specific content, he does not otherwise speak in the lectures of undertaking a "deduction" in the proper sense.[6] Moreover, as has been frequently remarked, Hegel's philosophy of art clearly does not take as its aim to provide those particular deductions – of aesthetic judgments in general and judgments of beauty more specifically – which are so essential to the project of Kant's *Critique of the Power of Judgment*.

   As with many other issues at crucial points in the current text of the *Lectures*, scholarly questions about the text, and in particular the role of Hegel's editor Hotho, have arisen here.[7] Is the title "historical deduction" really Hegel's own, for example, or the suggestion of Hotho's? While that is a question that may never fully be answered, and certainly cannot at least be answered in the current state of scholarship, it is important here as elsewhere neither simply to ignore the long-standing status of the work of an editor who had at his disposal (as we do not) Hegel's own course notes, nor at the same time to neglect to see what a comparison of the extant transcripts and students' notes with the Hotho text might reveal. Recent publication of transcripts or student notes from three of the four lecture series Hegel gave on the philosophy of art in Berlin have given scholars a number of new insights into the construction of those lectures and have led to the questioning of certain formulations long thought to be Hegel's own.[8]

   In the case of the "Historical Deduction," it is important to notice the following facts:

(1)   Of the published versions of the student notes and transcripts of the lectures, those from the 1820–1821 lectures (by Ascheberg) and the 1826 lectures (by both Pfordten and Kehler) have sections in their introductions that trace at the same point the same development of the concept of art among the same figures as does the text of the *Lectures*. The 1823 transcript (made by Hotho himself) does not have such a section.

(2)   None of these transcripts or sets of notes gives the relevant section the title "historical deduction." (Although they take up the same historical figures, Pfordten and Kehler, for example, have instead the somewhat less imposing titles "*Geschichtliches*" or "*etwas Geschichtliches*.")

From these facts, we may draw the conclusion that, while the title of the "historical deduction" section may or may not deserve to have canonical status, it is nonetheless clear that during at least two of his four Berlin lecture series Hegel took his introduction to aesthetics to have the important *historical task* of placing his notion of the concept of art directly in the context of the development of post-Kantian notions of art and beauty. The currently available transcripts and student notes thus corroborate the impression that readers of the received text have drawn from Hegel's aesthetics for years. In light of this evidence, I propose that we examine the "standard edition" version of the section as a whole in terms of this task and – with an eye to why Hegel or his editor might have construed that task in terms of the search for a deduction's goal of showing the *validity* of a particular concept – see what the historical aims of this section offer with respect to that question.

2.   The Place of the "Historical Deduction" within the Argumentative Task of the *Lectures'* Introduction

If, then, we put aside for the moment the textual questions about this section and focus on its function within the "Introduction" of the "standard edition" of the text of the *Lectures,* what role is the "Historical Deduction" in fact playing? One possible key to the answer to this question lies in the stress (Hegel's or Hotho's) on the notion of *truth* in the philosophical construal of artistic beauty. The concern of the "Deduction" with giving a historical account of the derivation of the "true" concept of art is in fact situated within the larger trajectory of a project that clearly is intended philosophically to pull the question of Beauty – for all its apparent freedom – into the orbit of Truth. As any reader of the *Lectures* can attest, the numerous points of stress on the importance of Beauty's Truth in the Introduction as a whole are remarkable: art's vocation is "the *unveiling of truth* in the form of sensuous artistic configuration" (*die Wahrheit in Form der sinnlichen Kunstgestaltung zu enthüllen*); spirit alone, and not nature, is "the true that comprehends everything in itself," so that "everything beautiful is truly beautiful only as sharing in this higher sphere and generated by it"; art "liberates the true content of phenomena from the pure appearance and deception of this bad transitory world, and gives them a higher actuality."[9]

The tripartite structure of the development that the "Deduction" traces from Kant to Schiller to Romantic irony in fact stresses the importance of truth for understanding what is – or is not – achieved at each of these stages: while it is Kant's achievement both to have grounded philosophy's revolutionary turn in modern times and to have sketched the lines along which the opposed realms of reason and sensibility could be reconciled, the suggested Kantian reconciliation of these realms is "only subjective" and "not in and for itself true and actual" (*nur subjektiv ... nicht aber das an und für sich Wahre und Wirkliche selbst*)[10]; Schiller, by contrast, has moved forward from the terms of Kant's aesthetics to grasp a notion of unity that, "now, as the Idea itself, has been made the principle of knowledge and existence ... and become recognized as that which alone is true and actual" (*das allein Wahrhafte und Wirkliche*)[11]; and, finally, the notion of Romantic irony represents a falling away from this unity such that the substantial interests of the subject's "true earnestness" (*wahrhafter Ernst*) have been neglected.[12]

355

If the three moments of the "Deduction," then, articulate a historical development that fits within the overall task of the *Lectures'* "Introduction" to establish philosophy's interest in the concern for truth in beauty, how, more specifically, does Hegel's turn to a historical account help his overall argument? To answer this question, we need to examine more closely the internal connections between the argument of the "Introduction" as a whole and the development of the "Deduction."

The "Deduction" is situated between two key sections of the *Lectures'* "Introduction," both of which are central to Hegel's project of articulating the concept of beautiful art: (1) the sketch of "common ideas of art" (*gewöhnliche Vorstellungen der Kunst*), which concludes with an analysis of what can be taken to be the proper end (*Zweck*) of art, and (2) the general outline of the division of the study of philosophy of art itself, beginning with the universal consideration of what Hegel calls "the Ideal, or the Idea of the Beauty of Art."[13] Within this context, the "Deduction" is thus concerned precisely with the question of how art's "true" function can be assessed. And Hegel's answer to this question is that it is an essentially *historical or narrative task* to show what that true function is.

In examining how the historical task of the "Deduction" emerges from Hegel's discussion of the "common ideas of art" and serves as a bridge to the internal organization of his own "idea of the beauty of art," I will first examine Hegel's treatment of the central "common ideas" with an eye to their importance for the overall argumentative concern with the "truth of beauty" and then show how this treatment motivates Hegel's development of a historical and narrative account that runs from Kant to Schiller to Friedrich Schlegel.

3. The Three "Common Ideas of Art" and the Emergence of the Standpoint of the "Historical Deduction"

Hegel examines in this section of the "Introduction" three "common ideas," each of which has an important bearing on his consideration of the "truth of beauty." The first of the three "common ideas" is the notion that art is no natural product but the result of *human activity*. Under this heading, Hegel considers and rejects the notion that art is essentially *imitation* before turning to the more Romantic notion that art is the product of (he insists, a not merely natural) *talent or genius*. The more general conclusion developed in this section is that it is a "rational need" of humankind to recognize oneself and one's world within the productions of art. As Hegel puts it, things in nature are immediate and singular (*unmittelbar und einmal*), whereas it is in art that humankind as spirit "duplicates itself" in a product that both *is* and is *for-us*. So the first relevant truth-claim concerning art is that art's truth has a higher status than the only apparent immediate "truth" of nature.

The second of the three "common ideas" is that works of art are *for human beings'* sensuous nature (*Sinn*) and thus drawn from the sensuous sphere. As the discussion of the previous "common idea" moved from the examination of a precritical aesthetic stance (the imitation of nature as defining art's purpose) to a postcritical and Romantic one (the notion that talent or genius lies behind human aesthetic activity), so Hegel here moves from the Mendelssohnian claim that art's purpose is "to arouse feelings" to the concern with the specific feeling of beauty itself (and the taste and education required to experience it) and to the more Romantic claim that the whole depth of feeling involving art goes beyond what mere taste can evaluate and thus requires the fully spiritual and distinctly individual abilities of a true connoisseur (*Kenner*). While this section of the Introduction acknowledges some truth to the perspective from which art is seen in an essential connection to the sensuous, it argues, along the lines of Hegel's response to the first "common idea," that art is not *merely for* sensuous apprehension, but is more importantly to be appreciated spiritually. Thus the task of truth with respect to this "common idea" is that it is art's task to "liberate" the truth from an immediate reality that is only perceived to be true. But art's liberating activity cannot be compared directly either to practical or to theoretical intelligence: unlike the former (as Kant had argued) aesthetic appreciation does not involve a *desire* for a work of art, and unlike the latter it does not leave the individuality of the artwork behind in a universalizing conceptualization. A work of art involves "something ideal," Hegel says, but that ideal, as aesthetically experienced, must remain in some way embodied in a sensuous form (*das Sinnliche im Kunstwerk ist selbst ein ideelles, das aber, als nicht das Ideelle des Gedankens, zugleich als Ding noch äußerlich vorhanden ist*).[14]

It is the third of the three "common ideas" that contains within it the dialectical development that will directly lead to the standpoint from which the "historical deduction" will begin. The third "common idea" is that art is an *end in itself*. Hegel's exploration of this third common idea examines two conventional notions that he thinks can only produce *merely formal* considerations of art's purpose: the notion (discussed already in part under a consideration of the distinctly human artistic activity associated with the first "common idea") of the *imitation of nature* and the claim (similar to the second "common idea") that art's purpose is to bring closer to human sense or feeling "everything that has a place within the human spirit." Under the former consideration – a notion of the purpose of art that was already considered wildly out of date even in Hegel's own time – the objective side of beauty disappears in a consideration merely of whether something is a good imitation; for the second claim, Hegel does not deny that it has some validity, but questions what sort of definition of art's purpose can emerge from all of the contradictory and self-canceling elements of feeling within the human spirit.

What is instead required is a "higher and more universal, substantial end" for art, and this, Hegel thinks, has emerged from within a consideration of distinctively *moral* demands. Again Hegel examines first a precritical perspective, the general notion of art's "mitigation [*Milderung*] of the ferocity of desires," but this concern proves far too vague and the search for a more specific moral criterion for art's purpose looks instead to three aims in which there is some reference to a "criterion" (*Maßstab*) allowing the distinction of "pure" from "impure" elements. These three more criterially based moral aims are (a) the *purification* (*Reinigung*) of desires, (b) *instruction* (*Belehrung*), and (c) overall *moral improvement* (*moralische Vervollkommnung*), the last of which Hegel construes as a sort of synthesis of the first two moral aims. Despite the reference in the idea of purification to some criterion against which art could measure its progress, this idea retains the vagueness Hegel associates with the more general notion of the "mitigation" of desire's ferocity. The notion of instruction raises the difficulty Hegel will associate later in his *Lectures on Fine Art* with the temptations inherent in didactic poetry: the "instructional content" of works of art cannot be separated off as an "abstract proposition, prosaic reflection or universal teaching" of some sort without violating the unity of sensuous and spiritual elements that we have seen characterizes art in general – in such cases, the sensuous or pictorial shape of art becomes a "mere veil" (*bloße Hülle*).

With the question of the *moral utility* of art, Hegel recognizes, we have "come close to the boundary [*Grenze*] at which art is supposed to cease to be an end in itself" – a boundary that in fact is "most sharply marked" if art's relevance is measured by the "supreme aim and end" of moral improvement.[15]

In discussing this third candidate for art's moral purpose, Hegel acknowledges that in order to be clear about it one must inquire into the distinct historical standpoint from which such claims about the "highest end" are made. More specifically, Hegel sees a need to examine the oppositional terms of the moral world-view as an aspect of the general modern "culture of reflection" that he had had in his philosophical sights since his early Jena years. The moral world-view, as Hegel had argued at Jena, involves not merely a split between the universal will and sensuous natural particularity, but more broadly a "thoroughgoing cleavage" between an *absolute* and reality or existence. As at Jena, Hegel here grants that such an opposition has had "numerous forms" that have preoccupied philosophy over the years, but insists that it is in *modern life* that they are first "worked out most sharply and driven ... up to the peak of harshest contradiction."[16]

Philosophy's task in the face of such oppositions inherent in the reflective culture of modernity is to supersede them – in distinctively Hegelian terms, "to show that neither side possesses truth but that they are *self-dissolving* [*das Sichselbstauflösende*] and that truth lies only in the reconciliation and mediation [*die Versöhnung und Vermittlung*] of both and that this mediation is no mere demand but what is absolutely accomplished and ever self-accomplishing." It is from this philosophical standpoint – on which, Hegel famously insists, the sides do not lose their existence but exist *in* their reconciliation with each other – that it can be seen how the absolute moral demands of the modern culture of reflection have led to a new sense of what art's purpose must be. "Since this final aim, moral betterment, has *pointed to a higher standpoint,* we will have to vindicate this higher standpoint for art also."[17]

The higher and reconciliatory standpoint that has emerged from philosophy's consideration of the oppositions inherent in the moral world-view has thus yielded a new standpoint for art, one on which art does not serve any purpose beyond itself but rather reconciles opposites within itself. Art may be said to be *free*, then, precisely because it serves no external purpose but manifests in its works the reconciliation of oppositions. This important connection between art's reconciliatory function and its freedom leads to Hegel's conclusion that art is *true* which is *free alike in its means and ends:*

[A]rt's vocation is to *unveil the truth* in the form of sensuous artistic configuration, to set forth the reconciled opposition just mentioned, and so *to have its end and aim in itself, in this very setting forth and unveiling.* For other ends, like instruction, purification, bettering, financial gain, struggling for fame and honor, have nothing to do with the work of art as such, and do not determine its nature.[18]

We should note a number of important characteristics of Hegel's approach to the philosophy of art that can be glimpsed through the development of this claim about art's purpose. First, and perhaps most important, there is a distinctive sense in which Hegel can be said to uphold here a notion of art's autonomy or independence – precisely the sense in which art has no *other* or *external* end, even a high moral one, as its ultimate purpose. This commitment on Hegel's part (similar to that of a number of the Romantics) does not of course imply that art is autonomous in the sense that sensuous, artistic beauty is some sort of *independent realm* sealed off either from philosophical reflection or from the social norms and conditions that Hegel's philosophy of art is so concerned to make part of the new shape of post-Kantian aesthetic reflection.[19] But it is important to emphasize that Hegel does give art a distinctive *systematic place* that makes it reducible neither to ethics within the sphere of objective spirit nor to either of the other two moments of absolute spirit, religion, and philosophy.[20]

Second, although Hegel has made clear the distinct status of art vis-à-vis other realms of spirit, its essentially reconciliatory aim is expounded with an eye to important connections art shares with the moral and social. Hegel thus takes up in this context the two *practical* developments he had earlier marked as also crucially emerging from the oppositions representative of the Kantian moral world-view: (i) the realization, framed perhaps most famously in the "Morality" section of the Spirit chapter in Hegel's *Phenomenology of Spirit*, that it is the concept of *conscience* that is able to bring to an end, with a *concrete instance of moral action*, the divisions of the moral world, and (ii) the suggestion, framed in the *Philosophy of Right*, that the clear understanding of what is implied in the *modern concept of the state* represents an end that is at once substantial and universal in its relation to the multitude of individual moral purposes. Hegel picks up the concern with (i) in his discussion of art's reconciliatory function by noticing that this function of art "coincides immediately with the ingenuous faith and will that does have precisely this dissolved opposition steadily present to its view, and in action makes it its end and achieves it."[21] This appeal to conscientiously willed moral action as resolving in practice, as it were, the tensions inherent in the moral world-view will set up an important element of the account that the "Historical Deduction" will give of the relation between moral and artistic ends in its insistence – with Schiller but against Friedrich Schlegel – that there must be a "*genuinely* beautiful soul" that unites moral oppositions in its action and avoids the delusive claims Hegel connected with the "retreating" beautiful soul figure in Romanticism.[22] With respect to (ii), Hegel's appeal both in the section of the Introduction on the "common ideas" of art's purpose and in the "Historical Deduction" itself to the relation between the correct concept of art and the correct modern concept of the state is remarkable. In the "common ideas" section, it is precisely the need for a definition of a universal or substantial end for art that sets up the comparison: in both cases, the issue is how a single end (*Ziel*) can be the fundamental concept and final purpose (*Grundbegriff und letzten Zweck*) that holds together in some unity the multiplex shapes (*mancherlei Bildungen*) that allow the development of "all human capacities and individual powers": thus, "as with the concept of the state, so too with the concept of art there arises the need for a *common end* for its particular aspects, but also for a higher, substantial end."[23] As we will see in the following section, the center-point, in many ways, of the account Hegel gives of the origin of the concept of art in the "Historical Deduction" is Schiller's explication of the "true man" (*dieser wahrhafte Mensch*), who is "represented by the state" in a form that involves either the state's imposition of the universal on the individual or – more appealingly for an age concerned with the realization of human freedom – the possibility of the individual "raising himself" to the level of the universal by means of an "aesthetic education."

Third, and finally, as we have seen, the philosophical task of getting at the genuine concept of art is one that Hegel has now made clear involves an *essentially historical and narrative approach* to the philosophy of art. The *true* concept of art is something that has, in fact, only arisen in a specific historical context – the moment in which there is a need for resolution of the reigning oppositions of the age of reflection and morality. As Hegel puts it in the remarkable passage that opens the "Historical Deduction": "after all it was from this view [of the oppositions inherent in the moral world-view] that the *true reverence and cognition of art* [*die wahre Achtung und Erkenntnis der Kunst*] arose historically."[24] This claim, as we will see in the final section of this paper, raises some important questions about Hegel's historical commitments within the philosophy of art. But let us turn at the moment to the specific tasks Hegel has in mind in the "Historical Deduction" itself as a result of his consideration of the emergence of the demand for reconciliation within the moral world-view and the modern culture of reflection.

4. From Kant to Schiller to Schlegel: The Third *Critique*, the Culture of Reflectivity, and the Rise of the Concept of the Beautiful

In the "standard edition" of the text of the *Lectures*, the "Historical Deduction" section is divided into three parts: the first, devoted to Kant's third *Critique* and its importance; the second, devoted to Schiller, with a brief excursus on Winckelmann and Schelling; and the third, devoted to the Romantic construals of beauty in the brothers Schlegel, with a brief mention of Tieck and others in the Romantic movement. Hegel sketches these three moments as representing (i) the emergence of the *demand* for an essentially aesthetic reconciliation to the oppositions within Kant's world-view; (ii) the recognition – by Schiller, most prominently – of the notion of beauty as a moment of unity in which those oppositions are *actually* reconciled and the development – by Schelling particularly – of that notion as an explicitly developed philosophical concept (something that Hegel thinks implicit but not fully worked out in Schiller); (iii) the falling-away from the philosophical concept of that unity in the Romantic conception of irony.

Kant's Third Critique

Hegel's treatment of Kant's aesthetics in the "Historical Deduction" is a perhaps surprisingly limited account, consisting in a relatively brief description of the four moments Kant associated with aesthetic judgment: its disinterestedness, universality, purposiveness, and necessity.[25] My goal here is not to examine Hegel's treatment of these moments in the context of the larger reception history of the third *Critique*, but rather to focus on the use that he wishes to make of Kant in the context of the historical narrative of the post-Kantian concern with the concept of beauty. In this context, it must be emphasized that – despite the title of the "Historical Deduction" – Hegel does *not* in the main share Kant's concern with the importance of deducing aesthetic judgments and judgments of taste as part of an account of aesthetic experience more generally. Whatever the "Historical Deduction" is meant to do, it is not to provide a deduction of judgments of taste/aesthetic judgments. Instead, Hegel's interest in the achievements and limitations of the third *Critique* here are part of his situating of Kant within the larger historical narrative of the origins of the philosophy of art that he is tracing, the central emerging thematic of which is how "the Beautiful" becomes "Concept."

In his abbreviated account of the *Critique of Judgment,* Hegel stresses what he takes to be both the achievement and the insufficiency of Kant's approach to aesthetics: on the one hand, Kant "brought the reconciled contradiction [between reason and sense] before our minds," particularly in the unity of the intuitive understanding. Yet, on the other hand, Kant "makes this dissolution and reconciliation itself into a purely *subjective* one again, not one absolutely true and actual."[26] While the *Critique of Judgment* offers, then, "the starting point for the true comprehension of the beauty of art, yet only by overcoming Kant's deficiencies could this comprehension assert itself as the higher grasp of the true unity of necessity and freedom, particular and universal, sense and reason."[27]

Schiller on Beauty and Aesthetic Education

Many commentators have considered Schiller as a key transitional figure between Kant and Hegel, but the difficulty of construing both the exact nature of his debt to Kant and the inheritance he offers Hegel has remained a central issue in the literature. In what is still the classic treatment of Schiller's moral grounding of Kant's aesthetic terms, Dieter Henrich stresses Schiller's concern to focus on the *inwardness* of subjectivity and the *depth of potential meaning* involved in beauty – both moments within Kant's aesthetics but not as explicitly developed as the concern mentioned above with disinterestedness and objectivity. As Henrich points out, Schiller's particular concern is to derive these latter moments of beauty directly from an analysis of moral agency.[28]

Like Henrich, Hegel sees in Schiller's famous definition of beauty as "freedom in appearance" a development beyond Kant to a "genuinely actual" mutual formation (*Ineinsbildung*) of the rational and the sensuous and places the importance of that definition in the context of moral agency. Hegel cites the central image of the fourth of Schiller's *Letters on Aesthetic Education:*

> [T]he chief point from which Schiller starts is that every individual man bears within himself the capacity for ideal manhood. This genuine man, he holds, is represented by the State which he takes to be the objective, universal, and as it were canonical, form in which the diversity of individual persons aims at collecting and combining itself into a unity. Now he thought that there were two ways of presenting how man, living in time, might correspond with man in the Idea: on the one hand, the State, as the genus of ethics, law, and intelligence, might cancel individuality; on the other hand, the individual might raise himself to the genus, and the man of time ennoble himself into the man of the Idea.[29]

Like many passages in which Hegel quotes contemporary authors, this one involves an important but subtle reworking of the original text. Schiller's contrast between the

361

"man in time" and the "man of the Idea" had been set up within distinctly Kantian terms that stressed the relation between the "pure" and the "empirical" individual. Hegel takes over this concern with the relation between universal and individual not in these Kantian terms but rather in terms of the notion of the *true* or *genuine* man (*der wahre Mensch*) – an interesting correlation with the stress we have seen in this section and the *Lectures'* Introduction as a whole on the "true" concept of art.[30] As with his insistence in this section that *true* beauty of soul involves *actualization*, Hegel links the notion of the *true* man to the modern conception of the state. As suggested in the previous section of this essay, Hegel's appropriation of the aspiration behind Schiller's notion of "aesthetic education" in the context of his ethical and social philosophy involves a commitment on his part to show how individual feeling can be part of an objective normative order.[31] As the *Philosophy of Right* argues, the goal cannot be an ascetic *removal* or *denial* of desires, but rather a connection of desires to the unifying goal of ethical life.[32] Henrich's suggestion is right that Hegel developed grounds for the solution of the problem of "combining thought and pleasure" that detached these terms from the specific view of separate faculties that Schiller had inherited from Kant.

Friedrich Schlegel and the Concept of Irony

Hegel's claim is that what Schiller grasped in the unity of beauty has become the basis for the *concept of art* that Schelling and then Hegel have now elaborated: Schiller's unity "has now, as the *Idea itself,* been made the principle of knowledge and existence, and the Idea has become recognized as that which alone is true and actual."[33] The achievement that Hegel has so far signalled in his discussion – from Schiller's recognition of beauty's importance to its systematic conceptualization within German Idealism – has not, however, remained an unchallenged, once-and-for-all achievement. In fact, within the Romantic movement, Hegel holds, there has emerged a pulling-apart of the notion of beauty in the direction of irony and subjectivity.

The final section of the "Historical Deduction" seems to recapitulate territory familiar to readers of the account of the "beautiful soul" passage in the *Phenomenology of Spirit*. For our purposes, it is important to note that the unity achieved by Schiller's notion of beauty and Schelling's conceptual attempt to ground the *Idea* of art gave way historically to a moment that Hegel regards as both implicit in the unity itself and a degeneration therefrom – and that may correspondingly provide an interesting window onto how Hegel should be read in terms of his stance toward the post-Romantic and modernist elements of the art world that develops after his death.[34]

5.   The Problem of History and the Narrative Structure of Hegel's Philosophy of Art

How to assess Hegel's "Historical Deduction"? While we have acknowledged that the textual support for this title is not (and is not likely ever to be) definitive, we can still see that the section fulfills a "deductive" philosophical purpose of grounding the validity of the concept of art in a way that is consonant with the narrative and historical aims of Hegel's philosophy of art as a whole. As we saw, Hegel does not think it is possible in the context of an introduction to the philosophy of art as a specific discipline to derive the validity of the "true concept of art" other than by reference to the systematic place of that concept within the philosophical enterprise of his *Encyclopedia*. But that still leaves unaddressed within the scope of the lectures themselves the issue of why just this particular concept of art has emerged *as true* in *this particular historical context*.[35] From this perspective, the "historical deduction" might be said to have a function similar to that of the *Phenomenology of Spirit* in grounding the approach to Hegel's systematic position from within a historical development.

From what we have seen of the "historical deduction" of Hegel's concept of art, however, what conclusions can be drawn about the distinctively narrative or historical character of Hegelian philosophy of art? To some extent, Hegel's historical reflections here pose a question about how well they can be brought into the "official narrative" that will emerge in the section immediately following the "historical deduction," the organizational division of the work into the art forms of symbolic, classical, and romantic and the historically inflected account of the rise of the individual arts themselves. For starters, we might ask: how is it that the "true reverence and cognition of art" arose only after Kant with the philosophical recognition of the *concept* of art if, as every student of Hegel's aesthetics presumably knows, his official history has it that actual experience of – and reverence for – the beautiful in art was primarily characteristic of the ancient Greeks? How, in other words, should we square the claim in the "Historical Deduction" that it is only *now*, in the post-Kantian world, that we have a *true philosophical understanding* of art with the claim, made by Hegel elsewhere in the Introduction to the *Lectures*, that we are now quite beyond actually *venerating* works of art and in fact find that art has "*lost* for us genuine truth and life"?[36]

A complete answer to this question depends, of course, on the stance that one takes on the famous (and indeed perhaps overly discussed) topic of the "end of art" in Hegel's aesthetics.[37] But the reflections above on the "Historical Deduction" have led me to think that the narrative and historical character of Hegel's aesthetics has perhaps not been as yet fully explored and that, with an eye to doing so, we might start by distinguishing different ways in which historical or narrative conceptions are at play in Hegel's *Lectures on Fine Art*. On the basis of what I have said here, we might start at least by distinguishing *three* such levels of narrative or historical conceptions of the philosophy of art at work: the first level, attaching to Hegel's project of giving an account of the origins of the "true" concept of art, would be the "phenomenological" one of showing how the systematic position of Hegelian philosophy of art has emerged out of the context of its own age; the second level, a "formal" one showing that the opposition between the "classical" and the "romantic" that had become in Hegel's day so central to the concerns of Schiller, Friedrich Schlegel, and the Romantics in fact required another conceptual term – Hegel's notion of a preclassical "symbolic" – in order to be resolved; and the third level, a "material" one, showing how, from a philosophical conception of art in general a series of different *shapes* of artistic products might emerge.

If I am right, this means that what appears (at least in the light of the current state of scholarship on Hegel's philosophy of art) to have been Hegel's most fully developed organizational scheme for his work involves an associated historical task for each stage. On that scheme, the familiar tripartite division that Hotho ultimately settled upon for his edition of the *Lectures*, there is a transition from (i) the "universal" level of the Idea of Beautiful Art to (ii) the "particular" level of the symbolic, classical, and romantic art forms to (iii) the "individual" system of the arts of architecture, sculpture, painting, music, and poetry. Each of these narrative projects has the common aspect of showing how a philosophical stance has emerged *out of* an oscillating and self-canceling set of oppositions that "dissolve" into a speculative way of seeing them: the concept of art itself out of the oppositions of the moral world-view and the reflective culture of the modern age; the notion of the "art forms" out of the oscillating and unresolved tensions between "classical" and "romantic" that (as I have suggested elsewhere)[38] Hegel thought Schiller and to some extent Friedrich Schlegel had been unable to address; and the third, a way of seeing the individual arts themselves as the result of a dialectic of internal unity and external, multiform shapeliness.

The situation might be said to be similar to the three-level narrative structure of the *Phenomenology of Spirit* that Lukács and more recent readers of the *Phenomenology* have discerned, on which the result achieved in each of the first two narratives represents the need for *yet another* historical level of explanation and so the beginning of another narrative.[39] In the different context of the *Lectures on Fine Arts*, we might suggest something like the following: that it is only once one has seen the emergence historically in the post-Kantian world of the concept of art, and adopted its perspective on aesthetic issues, that one can start to see that the most widely current (if limited) narrative then in use concerning the historicality of art stands itself in need of further historical context. That current historical narrative, as championed by Schiller and the Romantics and to some extent by Friedrich Schlegel, held that the success of the Romantic movement lay precisely in its distinguishing itself from the past moment of the classical – and thus, among other things, opening up to contemporary enjoyment many works otherwise rooted in their time and place. From the perspective of Hegel's philosophy of art, we now see that "the classical" and "the romantic" are themselves terms that require a fuller historical perspective. And similarly, having taken the perspective on the *forms* of art that allows them to be seen as part of a larger historical progression, one can see the development of individual arts themselves as historically conditioned.

It is in this way that Hegel's historical approach makes a significant contribution to answering the question raised above: how is it that we have a true philosophical understanding of art only now that we are beyond venerating works of art? In answer to this question, Hegel shows first that a true understanding of art could only emerge out of the modern culture of *reflection*. He then shows that that true understanding itself brings with it – again as the distinctive product of modernity – the recognition that the veneration of art belongs to an earlier stage of "classical" art that occupied a specific place in the historical development of art but has now been superseded.

If we accept something like the tripartite reading set out here of the narrative project that Hegel is engaged with in the *Lectures on Fine Art*, then what the "Historical Deduction" achieves is a sort of clearing of the conceptual and systematic grounds for a new and specifically philosophical concern with art that will be characteristic of post-Kantian modernity. The historical task of this clearing of conceptual grounds is, then, achieved by attention primarily to the larger cultural and philosophical context of the modern world of reflectivity before we can turn to a consideration of the historicality of our actual experience of art itself – a consideration that specifically requires Hegel's two further historical narratives associated with the development of the art forms and the individual arts themselves.

The accomplishment in the "Deduction" of this first historical task of the *Lectures* not only grounds the account of art's independent existence as an end in itself in an understanding that can only have emerged from the tensions in post-Kantian idealism, but also offers for the future – more self-consciously than any of Hegel's predecessors – a richer potential grounding for an account of the shifts in historical norms of artistic creation and appreciation that will be very decisive for the understanding of important moments in post-Hegelian art. One might, of course, envision here at least two contrastive ways of viewing movements such as modernism, abstract expressionism, Dadaism, and postmodernism in light of this important section of the *Lectures*. On the one hand, one might view certain trends in modern and postmodern art as *degenerations* from the true concept of art – and Hegel gives a suggestive glance in that direction by the emphasis that we have seen him place in the third moment of the "Historical Deduction" on irony as a mode that slips away from the *true*. On the other hand, one might see in Hegel's sketch of art's increasing reflectiveness and inherent relation to the mode of its expression a greater openness to the way in which the truth of art must necessarily be realized within historical forms of practice and expression.

The narrative approach I have suggested leans more in the direction of this second alternative. For Hegel, individual art works and forms of art are what they (truly) are precisely *in* their modes of expression and those modes of expression have a historical manifestation and development: the artistic worth of a poem cannot be reduced to an "idea" taken as a separable piece of prose content that is merely illustrated with imagery and expressed in meter; lyric poetry, opera, and landscape painting are not natural kinds that can be construed apart from the specific histories of their practice. A work of art is, above all, as Hegel puts it elsewhere in the "Introduction" to the *Lectures*, a *question* – a question indeed in search of a true answer, but a truth that requires both spirit's historically inflected responsiveness and ongoing interpretation for its unfolding.[40]

Notes

1 Hegel lectured five times on the philosophy of art (in Heidelberg in 1818, and in Berlin in 1820–1821, 1823, 1826, and 1828–1829). Although Hegel had apparently planned before his death to publish his *Lectures on Fine Art*, the editing of what remained of his notes, together with the transcripts and notes of students who attended his lectures, fell to Hegel's student H. G. Hotho. The well-known textual difficulties in the publication of the text of these lectures by Hotho are discussed below. In this article when I cite the "standard edition" of the *Lectures on Fine Art*, I will be referring to the text of the lectures as edited by Hotho and printed in *G.W.F. Hegel: Vorlesungen über die Ästhetik*, ed. Eva Moldenhauer and Karl Markus Michel (Frankfurt: Suhrkamp, 1970), vols. xiii–xv and the current English translation, which relies on that edition: *Hegel's Aesthetics: Lectures on Fine Art*, trans. T. M. Knox (Oxford: Clarendon Press, 1975), volumes i–ii.

2 Schiller, letter to Körner (February 8, 1793, in Schiller, *Werke*, ed. Liselotte Blumenthal, Benno von Wiese, et al. (Weimar: Böhlaus, 1943), vol. 26, 183). Dieter Henrich suggests that this formulation may be seen as more broadly underlying *all* of Schiller's writings on

aesthetics, despite their internal differences (Henrich, "Beauty and Freedom: Schiller's Struggle with Kant's Aesthetics," in *Essays in Kant's Aesthetics*, ed. Ted Cohen and Paul Guyer (Chicago: University of Chicago Press, 1982), 244).

3 Terry Pinkard, "Symbolic, Classical and Romantic Art," in *Hegel and the Arts*, ed. Stephen Houlgate (Evanston, Ill.: Northwestern University Press, 2007), 8.

4 In addition to Pinkard's account of the successive development of moments of artistic agency through the symbolic, classical, and romantic art forms, see Robert Pippin, "The Absence of Aesthetics in Hegel's Aesthetics," in *The Cambridge Companion to Hegel and Nineteenth-Century Philosophy*, ed. Frederick Beiser (Cambridge: Cambridge University Press, 2008), 394–418.

5 Recent exceptions include Richard Eldridge, "Hegel, Schiller and Hölderlin on Art and Life" and Gregg Horowitz, "The Residue of History: Dark Play in Schiller and Hegel," both in *International Yearbook of German Idealism* 4 (2006), 152–178 and 179–198, respectively.

6 The other uses of the term *Deduktion* in the "standard edition" of the text of the *Lectures on Fine Arts* are both occasions where the mode of philosophical deduction in the proper sense is contrasted with what goes on in poetry: cp. LFA II.984, SW XV.254; II.1036, SW XV.318.

7 H. G. Hotho (1802–1873) took over Hegel's aesthetics lectures at the University of Berlin after his death and put together the three-volume *Lectures* for publication (first edition, 1835; second edition, 1842). Hotho had his own aesthetic interests, particularly in painting and music; he worked after Hegel's death in the painting gallery of Berlin's royal museum of art and published a number of his own contributions to art history. In editing Hegel's *Lectures*, Hotho had access to Hegel's own mansucript texts (unfortunately now lost) for both the first Heidelberg series of lectures and the Berlin series, as well as student transcripts and notes for the four lecture series in Berlin, including ones that Hotho himself had made during the lecture series of 1823 and 1826. A number of the extant sets of transcripts or notes have now been published: the set by Ascheberg for 1820–1821 (*G.W.F. Hegel: Vorlesung über Ästhetik Berlin 1820/21, Eine Nachschrift*, ed. Helmut Schneider (Frankfurt: Peter Lang, 1995)); the 1823 set by Hotho (*G.W.F. Hegel: Vorlesungen über die Philosophie der Kunst Berlin 1823 Nachgeschrieben von Heinrich Gustav Hotho*, ed. Annemarie Gethmann-Siefert (Hamburg: Meiner, 1998)) and the 1826 sets by Kehler ((*Georg Wilhelm Friedrich Hegel: Philosophie der Kunst oder Ästhetik, Nach Hegel. Im sommer 1826. Mitschrift Friedrich Carl Hermann Victor von Kehler*, ed. Annemarie Gethmann-Siefert and Bernadette Collenberg-Plotnikov with the help of Francesca Iannelli and Karsten Berr (Munich: Fink, 2004)) and Pfordten (*Georg Wilhelm Friedrich Hegel: Philosophie der Kunst Vorlesung von 1826*, ed. Annemarie Gethmann-Siefert, Jeong-Im Kown and Karsten Berr (Frankfurt: Suhrkamp, 2005)). Gethmann-Siefert's introductions to the above volumes situate the textual difficulties involved in editing this material in the light of Hegel's ongoing changes to the lectures as a sort of "work in progress." For a helpful English language discussion of the state of scholarship on the remaining materials, see Jason Gaiger, "Catching Up with History: Hegel and Abstract Painting," in *Hegel: New Directions*, ed. Katerina Deligiorgi (Acumen, 2006), 159–176.

8 Perhaps the most famous of these is Hegel's supposed claim that "art is the sensible manifestation or appearance of the Idea [*das sinnliche Scheinen der Idee*]," a phrase that does not appear in any of the extant student transcripts or notes, but only in Hotho's edition.

9 LFA I.55, SW XIII.82; LFA I.2, SW XIII.15 ("*der Geist erst ist das* Wahrhaftige, *alles in sich Befassende, so daß alles Schöne nur wahrhaft schön ist als dieses Höheren teilhaftig and durch dasselbe erzeugt*"); LFA I.9, SW XIII.22 ("*Den Schein und die Täuschung dieser schlechten, vergänglichen Welt nimmt die Kunst von jenem wahrhaften Gehalt der Erscheinungen fort und gibt ihnen eine höhere, geistgeborene Wirklichkeit*").

10 LFA I.60, SW XIII.89.

11   LFA I.63, SW XIII.91.

12   LFA I.65, SW XIII.94.

13   Hegel's organizational scheme for the *Lectures*, according to Hotho's text (which Knox's English translation follows), is the by now familiar tripartite structure of universal (the Idea of Beauty of Art or the Ideal), particular (the symbolic, classical and romantic art forms) and individual (the system of individual arts). Among the most interesting revelations to emerge from the recent scholarship on Hegel's aesthetics is that Hegel in his earlier lectures (prior to 1828–1829) actually had a *two-part* organizational scheme, under which the Idea of the Beautiful *and* the art forms were placed under the heading of "universal part" while the individual arts themselves came under the heading "particular part."

14   LFA I.38, SW XIII.59

15   LFA I.51, SW XIII.76

16   LFA I.54, SW XIII.79

17   LFA I.55, SW XIII.81; emphasis added.

18   LFA I.55, SW XIII.82; emphasis added.

19   There are a number of important related issues which I cannot address fully here, not the least of which concerns Hegel's position with respect to the possibility of there being any distinctive (if not "separable") cognitive "content" in aesthetic experience.

20   In fact, among the real achievements of Hegel's Berlin philosophy of art is its emergence *as* a separate item deserving of philosophical treatment. In Jena, the *Phenomenology of Spirit* had considered aesthetic issues explicitly under the heading of the "Religion *of Art*," and in Heidelberg, when Hegel initially published the systematic ordering of absolute spirit within the context of the *Encyclopedia* and gave his first lectures on aesthetics, art was still very much for him a part of a general discourse concerning the role of religion in the larger philosophy of spirit. (See Gethmann-Siefert, "Introduction" to *George Wilhelm Friedrich Hegel: Philosophie der Kunst Vorlesung von 1826*, 10–11.)

21   "*Diese Einsicht stimmt mit dem unbefangenen Glauben und Wollen unmittelbar zusammen, das gerade diesen aufgelösten Gegensatz stets vor der Vorstellung hat und ihn sich im Handeln zum Zwecke setzt und ausführt*" (LFA I.55, SW XIII.82).

22   Cf. Hegel, *Phenomenology of Spirit*, §§658–671. Despite his stress on the moments of unification represented by both conscientious action and artistic beauty, Hegel should not, I think, be taken to be endorsing the claim that beauty and art are to be construed simply as moments of beautiful conscientious action itself. His point is rather to place Schiller's concern about the relation between beauty and the beautiful soul in a perspective that bears important similarities to his discussion of the "beautiful soul" in the concluding part of the "Morality" section of the *PhG*'s Spirit chapter. In that discussion, as in the "Historical Deduction" that we are examining, Hegel makes clear that it is precisely the divisions of the moral worldview that lead to the Romantics' valorization of the "beautiful soul" and that *this* new concern with beauty requires yet another perspective on which beauty or art itself will have a new and philosophically distinct status. (In the *PhG*, of course, what the beautiful soul gives rise to is the new perspective of Religion, in which a distinct religious cult of artistic beauty will emerge; by the time of the Berlin *Lectures on the Philosophy of Art*, Hegel has already worked out an explicit place for art within his conception of absolute spirit.)

23   LFA I.48, SW XIII.72

24   LFA I.56, SW XIII.83.

25   Hegel also has accounts of the *Critique of Judgment* in the *Encyclopedia Logic* and in the *Lectures on the History of Philosophy*. For a comparison of these Hegelian treatments of the third *Critique* that takes into account diversions from Kant's own vocabulary and intentions, see Werner Euler, "Die Idee des Schönen: Hegels Kritik an Kants Theorie des ästhetischen Urteils," in *International Yearbook of German Idealism* 4 (2006), 91–123.

26 LFA I.57; SW XIII.84.

27 LFA I.60–61; SW XIII.89. Kehler's 1826 notes make this point even more vividly in their heralding of the transition from the discussion of Kant to the discussion of Schiller: *Die Kantische Ansicht ist der Ausgangspunkt. Das Höhere dagegen ist die Einheit der Notwendigkeit und der Freiheit – des Besonderen und des Allgemeinen, des Gemütlichen und Verständigen* (*Georg Wilhelm Friedrich Hegel: Philosophie der Kunst oder Ästhetik, Nach Hegel. Im sommer 1826. Mitschrift Friedrich Carl Hermann Victor von Kehler*, ed. Annemarie Gethmann-Siefert and Bernadette Collenberg-Plotnikov with the help of Francesca Iannelli and Karsten Berr, 18); emphasis added.

28 Henrich, "Beauty and Freedom: Schilller's Struggle with Kant's Aesthetics."

29 LFA I.62, SW XIII.90–91.

30 The variants in the transcripts and notes are interesting here: Kehler's 1826 notes have a conflation of the standard version "true" with Schiller's "pure" (*"dieser reine wahrhafte Mensch wird repräsentiert durch den Staat,"* 19), while Pfordten's 1826 notes simply continue Schiller's language (*"dieser reine Mensch wird repräsentiert ..."*).

31 The aspiration Hegel identifies as the underlying goal of the treatment of beauty in the *Letters on Aesthetic Education* – the "*actual* and *mutual* formation of the rational and the sensuous" – has obvious importance for the connection that Hegel comes to draw between emotional life and ethical rationality in his mature accounts of subjective and objective spirit. For Hegel, of course, the connection between feeling and rationality so crucial to his notion of freedom in the modern state is no longer primarily achieved by distinctly aesthetic means: the political goal of Schiller's aesthetic project, Hegel seems to think by the 1820s, has been achieved in a set of rational modern ethical institutions.

32 Cf. *Philosophy of Right* §§19–21 and *Philosophie des Rechts: Vorlesungen von 1819/1820*, ed. Dieter Henrich (Frankfurt: Suhrkamp, 1983), 64.

33 LFA I.62–63; SW XIII.91.

34 On the issue of the romantic and the post-romantic (and post-Romantic) in the context of Hegel's philosophy of art, see Martin Donougho, "Art and History: Hegel on the End, the Beginning and the Future of Art," in *Hegel and the Arts*, ed. Stephen Houlgate (Evanston, Ill.: Northwestern University Press, 2007).

35 The systematic function of art more properly is the task of Hegel's much briefer (and some-times neglected) account in the 1831 *Encyclopedia* (§§552–563). For a discussion of these paragraphs, see Angelica Nuzzo, "Hegel's 'Aesthetics' as Theory of Absolute Spirit," in *International Yearbook of German Idealism* 4 (2006), 291–310.

36 LFA I.11, SW XIII.25.

37 A subject that now merits its own bibliography: see my discussion in "Hegel and Aesthetics: The Practice and 'Pastness' of Art," in the *Cambridge Companion to Hegel and the Nineteenth Century*, ed. Frederick Beiser (forthcoming, 2009), n. 23.

38 See my "Was ist das Schöne der schönen Seele? Hegel und die ästhetische Implikationen der letzten Entwicklungsstufe des Geistes," in *Hegels Phänomenologie des Geistes: Ein kooperativer Kommentar zu einem Schlüsselwerk der Moderne*, ed. Klaus Vieweg and Wolfgang Welsch (Frankfurt: Suhrkamp, 2008), 504–519.

39 Georg Lukács, *The Young Hegel: Studies in the Relations between Dialectics and Economics*, trans. Rodney Livingstone (Cambridge, Mass.: MIT Press), 470–472, and more recently Michael Forster, *Hegel's Idea of a Phenomenology of Spirit* (Chicago: University of Chicago Press, 1998), 296–299.

40 *LFA* I.71; *SW* XIII.102.

18

Soundings: Hegel on Music

JOHN SALLIS

What sounds in music? What is sounded? What is music other than sound? Is it any-thing other than a sequence of sounds, of sounds sounding? Or does something also sound through it? Is something conveyed through the sounds that sound in it, as the look of a beautiful landscape may be conveyed through the colors of a painting or as, among the Greeks, a god could be made to appear through sculpted marble? On the one hand, the indisputably powerful effect of music would seem to attest to some such conveyance. How could music affect us so profoundly if in the end it were nothing but the mere sounding of a sequence of sounds? Yet on the other hand, there is nothing beyond music that its sounding would serve to present, nothing comparable to the landscape that the painting spreads before our eyes or to the figure of the god that the sculptor lets emerge from the marble.

Yet if music conveys nothing to us, could it be that music conveys us *to* something, that it carries us along, or rather draws us into a depth that we otherwise seldom fathom? Do the sounds of music serve to sound this depth, to take its measure, to let it resound? If the essence of music is to be determined as such a double sounding, every-thing will depend on the character of the depth that would be sounded by the sounds of music.

Hegel has no doubt but that the depth sounded by music is that of the self. In his words, most directly, "music makes the inner life resound in tones."[1] Yet it is not as though the inner life would otherwise go entirely unsounded, as if this depth required the advent of music in order to announce itself at all. States of the soul and feelings have natural forms of expression, as in a cry of pain, a sigh, a laugh. Yet in order to become music, these natural forms must be stripped of their wildness and crudeness and the feelings expressed must be linked to specific, determinate tones and relations between tones. Only in this way can the transition from nature to art, from natural outcry to music, be made. To be sure, Hegel does mention, precisely in this connection, the songs of birds, their delight as they put themselves forth in their songs. Nonetheless, Hegel will not allow these creatures with their songs to cross the threshold from nature

---

A Companion to Hegel, First Edition. Edited by Stephen Houlgate and Michael Baur.

to art. Though perhaps belied by his repeated, significant reference to bird songs, Hegel's insistence that there is no natural music is an index of the distance he takes from the *Critique of Judgment,* from its celebration of natural beauty.

Hegel was considerably less knowledgeable about music than he was, for instance, about painting. He readily admitted that his knowledge of musical theory and his acquaintance with the great musical works were limited and that limits were thereby prescribed for his philosophical treatment of music. At the outset of his account of music in the *Aesthetics,* he observes that one cannot enter into the particulars about music without running into technical matters concerning different instruments, different keys, etc.; and confessing that he is little versed in these matters, he excuses himself in advance for restricting his treatment to the more general points. Later in his account he reiterates his limitations in this regard, observing that a thorough treatment "would require a more exact knowledge of the rules of composition and a far wider acquaintance with the greatest musical works" than he possesses (*A* 2: 299/930). On the other hand, one should not make too much of Hegel's disclaimer, considering the extended discussion of harmonic intervals, scales, overtones, and so forth found in the relevant sections of the *Encyclopedia.*[2] Indeed Hegel's caustic comments about the theoretical insufficiencies of many practicing musicians could lead one to suppose that Hegel knew considerably more about musical theory than he took most musicians to know.

Hegel was also not a musician, not even an amateur. There is no evidence that he was practiced in any form of musical performance. Nonetheless, it is known that already at the time of his residence in Nuremberg he owned a piano; and during the Berlin period he is known to have held music evenings at his home.[3] Contemporary observers in Berlin report that after his lectures Hegel could often be seen hurrying over to the nearby opera house; it is known also that he regularly attended concert performances. In Berlin he was personally acquainted with a number of prominent musical figures including the most famous German singers. Above all, Hegel was enthusiastic for the soprano Anna Milder-Hauptmann, who is known to have been a guest in Hegel's home and who, in turn, extended her hospitality to Hegel. Milder-Hauptmann was especially celebrated for her roles in Gluck's operas, and it seems that Hegel never missed a performance.[4] The very positive estimation of Gluck's operas that Hegel expresses in the *Aesthetics* (see *A* 2: 315f./947) is perhaps not unrelated to his enjoyment of these performances.

It seems that it was in fact Milder-Hauptmann who recommended the Italian opera in Vienna when Hegel set out on his trip to the Austrian capital in 1824. Hegel's enthusiasm for the *bel canto* style of singing that he heard in Vienna seems to have been boundless. In a letter to his wife he writes: "There is no idleness in the singing and bringing forth of sounds, no mere recitation of lines, but rather the entire person is there in it. The singers ... generate and invent expression and coloration out of themselves. They are artists, composers as much as the one who set the opera to music."[5] Hegel's discovery of Rossini, in particular, made such an impression that he never faltered thereafter in his praise of Italian opera. His descriptions suggest that the performance he saw of *The Barber of Seville* was quite extraordinary. It seems that even Mozart's *Marriage of Figaro,* which Hegel saw two days later, paled somewhat by comparison, Hegel observing that "the Italian voices did not seem to have as many opportunities in this more restrained music to display those brilliant feats that are so sweet to hear."[6] As to Rossini, what Hegel admires most is that the music is preeminently for the voice. Having seen, the very next day, still another Rossini opera (*Corradino*), Hegel writes to his wife: "Now I completely understand why Rossini's music is reviled in Germany, especially in Berlin. For just as satin is only for ladies and *paté de foie gras* only for gourmets, so *this* music is created only for Italian voices. It is not for the music as such but for the singing *per se* that everything has been created. Music, having validity for itself, can also be performed on the violin, on the piano, etc., but Rossini's music has meaning only as sung."[7] Hegel had another opportunity to see a fine performance of Rossini when he traveled to Paris in 1827 and attended a production of *Semiramide* at the Italian theatre. Again his report to his wife is enthusiastic: "The opera was excellent in every respect, a performance as distinguished as the music was marvelous."[8]

Despite the enthusiasm with which Hegel attended musical and operatic performances, his acquaintance with the great musical works was, as he acknowledged, limited. This limitation is borne out if one considers the musical references given in the *Aesthetics*, and even more so if, from a textual-critical standpoint, one differentiates between Hegel's actual lectures (as preserved in transcriptions) and the text published by Hotho after Hegel's death. Yet what is most remarkable about Hegel's musical references is the fact that there is no mention whatsoever of Beethoven, neither in the lecture transcriptions nor in the published text of the *Aesthetics*. While it is true that by the time Hegel visited Vienna, Rossini had become much more the fashion, Beethoven continued nonetheless to be regarded throughout the European musical culture – and by younger composers such as Schubert and Schumann – as the greatest living composer. Furthermore, when Hegel arrived in Vienna in September 1824, he would almost certainly have heard reports about the great concert that had taken place at the Kärntnertor Theatre only four months earlier, the concert on May 7 at which the premier of Beethoven's Ninth Symphony was given. Whether Hegel actually heard any of Beethoven's music while in Vienna is uncertain, as the composer's name is not mentioned in any of the letters Hegel wrote during his stay in the city. Hegel is silent too about Schubert, who was also active in Vienna at the time of Hegel's visit. Had Hegel heard and taken to heart the final movement of the Ninth Symphony or some of the many songs that Schubert composed to poems by Schiller, then perhaps he would not have been so insistent on the inappropriateness of Schiller's poetry for being set to music.[9]

Hegel's taste in opera sometimes tended toward the banal and currently fashionable, especially following his discovery of Italian opera during his visit to Vienna. Even Hegel's son Karl expressed reservations about his father's musical preferences, and in his published recollections about his father's musical interests he felt obliged to remain completely silent about Hegel's enthusiasm for Rossini, stressing instead his father's liking for Gluck's operas.[10]

Yet Hotho played a much greater role in shaping what came to be communicated to posterity regarding Hegel's musical preferences and indeed regarding his philosophical approach to music. For Hotho had considerable expertise as regards music: he was active for many years as music editor for Cotta's *Morgenblatt* and in this capacity exercised considerable influence on the musical culture of Berlin. Since he was therefore very much in his element when it came to questions concerning music, it is likely to have seemed self-evident to him that in preparing for publication the portion of Hegel's lectures dealing with music he should take it upon himself to compensate for the deficiencies that, because of Hegel's lack of expertise, remained in the lectures. Thus seeking to improve on his teacher, Hotho produced a text that, especially in the account of music, deviates considerably from Hegel's own lectures.[11] Not only did Hotho fill out Hegel's statements and reformulate them more elegantly, but he also corrected Hegel's questionable musical taste by placing the emphasis on classical works by Mozart, Gluck, and Haydn. In addition, he realigned Hegel's account of music so as to force it to cohere with the system, effacing what traces there might have been of musical discoveries capable of challenging the systematic constraints. One sign of this realignment is the account, inserted at the very beginning, of the relation of music to all the other arts, an account not found in the lecture transcriptions. Another sign of Hotho's intervention is the sudden switch to first-person forms, as when the text, engaging in a discussion of musical instruments, continues: "I recall, for instance, that in my youth a virtuoso on the guitar had composed great battle music in a tasteless way for this trivial instrument" (A 2: 325/957). Not only the first-person form but also the very tone of the passage is foreign to Hegel's lectures.

What Hotho seems to have found especially difficult to understand or accept was Hegel's enthusiasm for Italian opera. To be sure, he did not suppress entirely Hegel's admiration for Rossini, which was probably so widely known that Hotho could have suppressed it only at the cost of discrediting his editorial practices. And so, instead, in a typical instance he begins with some positive generalities (perhaps taken from the lectures themselves), for instance, that Rossini's music is "full of feeling and genius, piercing the mind and heart," contrary to the belief that it is "a mere tickling of the ear," a suspicion Hotho raises by its very mention. Then comes explicit qualification: "even if it does not have to do with the sort of characterization beloved of our strict German musical intellect." Then comes still another reservation: "For it is true that all too often Rossini is unfaithful to his texts and with his free melodies soars over all the heights" (A 2: 317/949). Thus there is praise, to be sure, but not without several injections of poison, the contribution almost certainly of Hotho. Listen, by contrast, to Hegel himself in another of the letters from Vienna: "But with the Italians the sound is immediately free of longing, and the genuine ringing of naturalness is ignited and in full swing from the first moment. The first sound is freedom and passion. From the first tone they go at it blissfully with a free soul. The divine furor is at bottom a melodic stream that fills us with delight, penetrating and freeing every situation."[12]

Whatever deficiencies Hotho found in Hegel's musical taste, there was certainly no deficiency of contact with music and musicians during the Berlin period. Indeed there was one eminent, though still very young composer with whom Hegel had considerable personal contact. Felix Mendelssohn actually attended the 1828/1829 cycle of Hegel's lectures on the philosophy of art; furthermore Mendelssohn produced a transcription of the lectures in which reportedly he added some polemically humorous remarks of his own, especially concerning Hegel's thesis about the pastness of art.[13] It was at this time that Mendelssohn conducted the momentous performances of Bach's *St. Matthew Passion* at the Singakademie in Berlin, performances that not only revived this previously neglected masterpiece but indeed proved to be a turning point in the nineteenth-century revival of Bach's music at large. At both performances, on March 11 and 21,

1829, Hegel was present along with other such prominent guests as Schleiermacher, Droysen, and Heine.[14] Hegel also is known to have taken part in the social festivities associated with the performances.[15] In the *Aesthetics* there is a remark (presumably from Hegel himself) that, though probably preceding these historic performances, pays tribute to Bach and to the revival of his music: Hegel describes him as "a master whose grand, truly Protestant, robust, and yet, as it were, learned genius we have come only in recent times to admire completely" (*A* 2: 318/950).

One might imagine Hegel listening intently to the *St. Matthew Passion* as Mendelssohn conducted it in the Singakademie in Berlin. Hegel might well have had the text in hand, reading along in a kind of silent, interior enactment of what he heard. Yet he would not have been unresponsive to the place in which the performances were staged. The Singakademie was distinctively classical in its design. Its main facade resembled that of a Greek temple; its four columns were topped with Corinthian capitals upon which a typical entablature rested. Listening to the performance in this setting, Hegel might – one could imagine – have set about musing on the profound affinity between architecture and music that he had described in some detail in his lectures. One aspect of this affinity lies in the externality of form and content that architecture and music have in common. Just as in architecture the content cannot be made to command entirely the shape that is fashioned, so that architecture falls short of the classical unity achieved in sculpture; likewise in music as a romantic art this unity has been dissolved and the artwork itself remains apart from the inner life it would present. Hence, just as architecture surrounds the statue of the god with its proper columns, walls, and entablature, so music, expressing the element of feeling, accompanies a text or thoughts that, as determinate content, are not contained in the music.[16] In short, as architecture surrounds the god with his temple, so music surrounds enunciated spiritual ideas with melodious sounds expressive of feeling. Furthermore, both architecture and music produce their form, not from what exists (as in the more nearly mimetic arts of sculpture and painting), but rather by inventing them in accord with certain quantitative proportions, in one case, those pertaining to the laws of gravity and symmetry, in the other case, those pertaining to the harmonic laws of sound, the regularity of the beat, and the symmetry of rhythm. Hegel even draws a specific comparison between the columns of temples and the bar or beat as it functions in music (see *A* 2: 284/915). Thus he regards music as pairing the most profound feeling with the most rigorous mathematical laws. When these two moments are separated and music is freed of emotional expression, then, according to the *Aesthetics*, it acquires an architectonic character and becomes a musically regular building of tones (*Tongebäude*) (*A* 2: 264/894). As Hegel listened to Bach's great work there in the Singakademie, he might well have marveled that it was Bach's rare genius to have succeeded in creating a magnificent edifice of sounds that, precisely as such, expressed the most profound feelings.

One might imagine Hegel interrupting these musings in order to recall that, for all the affinity, the fact remains that architecture and music move in quite opposite realms, architecture remaining bound to heavy, visible matter, whereas music with its soulful tones liberates itself from space and matter. And yet one could imagine how the musings might resume as Hegel – continuing to listen intently to Mendelssohn's performance of Bach's great work – transported himself in imagination from the temple-like Singakademie to a magnificent Gothic cathedral, drawing perhaps on his memory of the great cathedral in Cologne, which, less than two years before, he had visited for the second time on his return trip from Paris. He might then have wondered whether, in such instances, a deeper affinity between architecture and music would not outweigh the apparent opposition between their realms. The affinity would lie in the commitment to verticality, to elevation. For as music elevates the soul and lets it soar upward, so it is with a Gothic cathedral: everything is constructed or contrived so as to deprive the stone of its massive heaviness and draw one's vision upward. As the *Aesthetics* declares: "There is no other architecture that with such enormous and heavy masses of stone ... preserved nonetheless so completely the character of lightness and grace" (*A* 2: 82/696). In the Gothic cathedral stone is deprived of its heaviness and made to soar.[17]

One might imagine Hegel entering the Cologne cathedral at the moment when Bach's Toccata and Fugue in D Minor begins to sound from the organ. Then, perhaps even more than at the historic performance in Berlin, he would have been struck by the profound affinity between architecture and music. Perhaps, too, he would have been set to musing on the interweaving of vision and audition that is indispensable for sensing this affinity. For he could not but have sensed how both the somber interiority of the sacred space and the upward thrust of the pillars and arches are matched by the walls of echoing sound intersecting at ever varying harmonic angles and the manifold tonalities ascending from the depths as those depths, too, continue to sound.

While music possesses an affinity in depth with architecture, the art to which it is most contiguous is painting. For this reason Hegel's account of music begins with the transition from painting to music.[18] Indeed the contiguity is almost such that no transition is needed. For there is a certain development in painting that almost turns it into music. Hegel calls this development "the magic of color"; it occurs at the point where shining becomes so prominent that the object begins to disappear and there remain only the compoundings of shinings, which are no longer tied even to figure. The objectivity of the painting's surface undergoes reduction to an objectless, figureless play of the shinings of color. While such surfaces "begin to pass over into the sphere of music" (*A* 2: 221/848), they remain nonetheless spatial; they continue to persist as surfaces over against the spectator. Thus, while beginning to pass over into the sphere of music, they stop short of the threshold. Passage over this threshold requires something else.

Music comes about only with the obliteration of such surface. From one point of view, the transition merely extends the reduction already effected in passing from sculpture to painting; whereas the previous passage required reduction from three spatial dimensions to two, now it is required that these two remaining dimensions, surface as such, be effaced. Yet, from another point of view, this passage is entirely different, for its effect is to eliminate spatiality as such. Once the spatiality of the artwork is entirely eliminated, then the work is no longer anything persisting over against the subject but is itself drawn back into subjectivity. This withdrawal into subjectivity brings to completion what with painting was already initiated: whereas in painting there remains a self-reposing, persistent object, a surface on which subjective inwardness is obliquely presented by way of traces of its withdrawal from objectivity, in music this surface disappears and even that by which subjective inwardness would be

374

presented is itself withdrawn into subjectivity. Thus, it can be said that music "even in its objectivity remains *subjective*" (*A* 2: 260/889).

Yet this passage by which music comes about is no simple negation, no mere cancellation leaving nothing behind. At this point in the text the word *Aufhebung* becomes prominent, for the pertinent operation is precisely that which this speculative word names. In the passage from painting to music, spatial objectivity is both cancelled as such and preserved as cancelled. With the advent of music something remains over against subjectivity; something is preserved in the place previously occupied by the painted surface, even though this place is stripped of its spatiality as such and retains only the character of being over against subjectivity. What comes to occupy this residual place, if only in being immediately displaced, is just music itself.

The *Aufhebung* through which this placement-displacement comes about is described as follows: "The *Aufhebung* of the spatial therefore consists here only in the fact that a determinate sensible material gives up its peaceful separateness, turns to movement, yet so vibrates [*erzittert*] in itself that every part of the cohering body not only changes its place but also strives to replace itself in its former position. The result of this oscillating vibration is *tone* [*Ton*], the material of music" (*A* 2: 260f./890). What the placement-displacement leaves in its wake is tone. Yet in the most succinct formulation, "Tone is to be considered only in its way of sounding."[19] Hence, what is produced by the *Aufhebung* of spatial objectivity, by the placement-displacement that it sets off, is sounding.

The other theoretical sense thus comes into play. Hearing is more ideal than sight, less directly linked to existing things to be apprehended in their independence. Whereas sight reveals how things look, apprehends their form and so discloses to some extent what they are, hearing is geared only to how things sound when they are struck or when they are made to vibrate. Thus it is that, as existent surfaces with their stable forms give way to internally vibrating things, hearing comes to replace sight.

What counts especially is the instability, the outcome of the double negativity. The first negativity is that by which every part of the object is displaced, this displacement being itself, in turn, negated by the striving of these parts to replace themselves in their original place. The operation of this double negativity is the internal vibration, the sheer instability itself that results in the sounding tone. In the formulation from the *Aesthetics*: "Since, furthermore, the negativity into which the vibrating material here enters is, on one side, an *Aufheben* of the spatial condition, which is itself again *aufgehoben* by the reaction of the body, therefore the expression of this double negation, namely, tone, is an externality that in its coming-to-be is annihilated again by its very existence and disappears of itself" (*A* 2: 261/890).

Yet the double negation and the sheer instability it releases cannot be entirely disengaged from the cohering body, from the spatial object. For tone can be produced only from such an object, only by setting such a thing vibrating. In fact, in the parallel and more elaborate treatment of sound that Hegel gives in the second part of the *Encyclopedia*, he explicitly links the quality of the sound produced to the character of the vibrating body: "The purity or impurity of sound proper [*des eigentlichen Klanges*] and its distinction from mere noise ... is bound up with the homogeneity of the vibrating body and also with its specific cohesion."[20] Furthermore, Hegel observes that because the vibration is a determinate negation of the specific forms of cohesion of the object and thus has these as its content, the sounds produced are also specified accordingly; and thus it is that the various musical instruments have their characteristic sound and timbre. As to the precise relation between the vibration of the object and the tone that sounds from it, there are passages that virtually identify these – as, for instance, the following from the *Encyclopedia:* "Sound proper is the reverberation [*Der eigentliche Klang ist das Nachhallen*], this unhindered inner vibration of a body, which is freely determined by the nature of its cohesion."[21] Thus music sounds from an instrument, from the vibrating strings of a violin or from the vibrating air column of a wind instrument or from the passage of breath across the vocal cords of a singer. Music sounds from these instruments so intimately, in a way so thoroughly bound up with the instrument, that there is hardly a difference between the vibration of the instrument and the tone that sounds from it. And yet, in sounding, the tone relinquishes entirely its objective existence and soars beyond the instrument by which it has been produced. No sooner does it sound than it disappears. As soon as it sounds for a subject, it is already gone and can only resound within the subject.

Not only is tone thus a vanishing moment, but it is also wholly abstract. In this connection the *Aesthetics* draws a distinction between, on the one hand, the way in which stone and color, the materials of sculpture and painting, respectively, can be given forms taken from the world of objects, thus portraying such objects in their enormous variety of forms; and, on the other hand, the incapacity of tone to be treated in this manner. To put it more directly, sculpture and painting are to some extent mimetic arts, whereas music is quite non-mimetic. Since music cannot portray objects, what remains for it to express is only the object-free inner life, abstract subjectivity, the self entirely empty of further content. In the formulation given in the *Aesthetics:* "Consequently the chief task of music consists in letting resound [*wiederklingen*] not the objective world itself, but, on the contrary, the way in which the innermost self is moved in its subjectivity and spirituality" (*A* 2:261/891).

According to this account there is nothing beyond music that its sounding would serve to present, nothing like the landscape evoked by the painter or the god called forth by the sculptor. Conveying nothing to us, music conveys us to ourselves, draws us into our own subjective depth, lets that depth resound and thereby be sounded. The sheer instability of tone as it momentarily hovers almost nowhere is indicative that, lacking any stability of its own, it is borne by the inner subjective life. As soon as a tone sounds, it vanishes, and the impression (*Eindruck*) made by it is inscribed not at the point where it is sounded but rather within. In the silence that supervenes as it is swept away, the tone goes on sounding (*nachklingen*) only in the depth of the soul.

At this point three sets of questions need to be formulated. They are questions that seek to confront Hegel's account with the actuality of music and thereby to mark – if still in the form of questions – certain limits of that account.

Without contesting the fleeting character of tone or the abstractness of music compared to painting and sculpture, there is need nonetheless to consider whether music is indeed so thoroughly assimilated to subjective interiority as Hegel maintains.[22] Is music in every instance so thoroughly non-mimetic that it can present nothing other than empty subjectivity? Leaving aside for the moment the forms such as song in which music is allied with poetry, focusing on purely instrumental music, even setting aside instances in which mere imitation of natural sounds such as bird songs are introduced into music, is there not still good reason to grant to music the power to present certain things in the world, even if in a way incomparable to those of painting and sculpture? How could Hegel have overlooked this power of music if he had heard the second movement of Beethoven's *Pastoral Symphony*, which, long before the bird songs enter near the end of the movement, will already have transported the attentive listener to the "Scene by the Brook," indeed will have done so by purely musical means. There are comparable examples from the Italian composers whom Hegel so admired, the storm, for instance, in Rossini's overture to *William Tell*. And though its expressive means goes beyond most, if not all, of the music of Hegel's time, there is perhaps no more convincing example of a musical presentation of nature than Debussy's *La Mer*. While it may be true that such works evoke natural phenomena by detouring, as it were, through subjectivity, that is, by evoking the very feelings that such a natural scene would evoke, still such music does succeed in presenting a natural scene rather than withdrawing entirely into resonant interiority.

A second question concerns the spatiality of music. The reduction of space is what both effects the transition from painting to music and, depriving music of place, prepares its assimilation to subjectivity. To be sure, it is acknowledged in the *Aesthetics* that the sounding is to an extent distinct from subjectivity: there is reference to "the beginning of a distinction between the enjoying subject and the objective work," which derives from the fact that the artwork "in its actually sounding tones acquires a sensible existence different from interiority." Yet this sensible existence is said to be purely transitory or ephemeral (*vergänglich*) (*A* 2: 275/905). Still, without contesting the instability of the sounding, it is relevant to observe that the sounding comes from somewhere, from the place where the instrument that produces it is located; and one might insist that this place retains a certain pertinence even after the tone that sounds there has passed. For the musical tones must at least traverse the space between the sounding instrument and the listener. Yet as it traverses this space, it will also spread throughout the surrounding space; and especially if that space is enclosed, the musical tones will reverberate, echo, resound, in a way that will add something to the tone produced by the instrument. In this resonating supplement a certain spatiality will become audible. Many composers have recognized the spatiality that in this way accrues to music and have sought to utilize this character to enhance their music: as in Gabrieli's antiphonal *Canzoni*, composed to be performed in San Marco Basilica in Venice, in which musicians are stationed at several different locations in such a way that the interplay between the differently spatialized musical tones can be incorporated into the very conception of the work. It is precisely this spatiality of music that prompts us to speak of edifices of sounds, a figure that points to a still deeper affinity between architecture and music.

A third set of questions brings the other two together. If the abstract subjectivity that music presents is not mere emptiness but rather, by its very indeterminateness, a broader, virtually unlimited opening onto the world, then it would seem that music's presentational capacity could be accounted for without, on the other hand, reducing the difference that sets music apart from painting and sculpture. Is it, then, in such a fashion – and not as mere emptiness – that the abstract subjectivity presented in music is to be understood? Furthermore, is it because music presents such an opening onto the world that spatiality flows back – in a distinctive form – into music itself? For much of the language used in speaking of music – oriented especially by the difference between high and low tones – suggests that music itself engages in a certain imitation of spatial figures.

The freedom that music enjoys is both distinctive and dangerous, setting music apart from the other arts while also exposing it to a unique threat of degeneration. Because music is released from all bonds to existent objects and their typical configurations, because, except as a vanishing moment, tone is nothing other than subjective, what counts for music is the proximity to inner life; to music, as to subjectivity, there belongs a tendency to detach itself from every determinate content. Or rather, to express it with the proper directionality, music can turn above and beyond any given content, soaring above everything that would bind it to determinateness. It is to this capacity for flight beyond content that Hegel refers in saying, according to a transcription of the 1823 cycle, that music is "for itself without content."[23] Furthermore, there is an appropriateness in representing this movement beyond content as a peculiar verticality, as a matter of flight beyond, of soaring beyond, every determinateness. Indeed it will turn out that this representation is more analogical than simply metaphorical.

The escape from content can become a flight of musical phantasy, which is itself an almost paradoxical hybrid, bound in its very freedom to the rigorous mathematical laws of musical form. The exercise of such phantasy can develop in such a way that liberation from restriction becomes virtually an end in itself, as, moving in a sphere where inventiveness and law, freedom and necessity, are almost perfectly blended, the composer develops and interweaves themes and counterthemes virtually without restriction, following up with his inventiveness the tonal possibilities delineated by the manifold of harmonic principles.

Yet when this tendency goes unchecked, it threatens to render music "completely spiritless,"[24] hence "empty, meaningless" (A 2: 271/902). Since spiritual content and expression is required for art as such, the overdevelopment of music in this direction broaches the danger that what is produced will cease altogether to be art, that it will degenerate into a mere display of skillfulness in handling the purely musical element, a kind of musician's music incapable of appealing to the general human interest in art. In the *Aesthetics* there is the suggestion that recent music has tended toward such overdevelopment, that it has retreated into the purely musical element, and that thereby it "has lost its power over the whole inner life" (A 2: 269/899). Yet even if this devaluation of recent music is indeed the verdict of Hegel himself[25] rather than an interpolation by Hotho, there is not the slightest indication as to which composers he might have had in mind. Rossini is almost the only composer Hegel mentions who could be considered contemporary, and his letters attest unmistakably to his admiration for Rossini. Even in those passages of the *Aesthetics* where other composers are mentioned by name, there is evidence of interpolations by Hotho,[26] though most of those included could hardly be considered recent. On the other hand, a century later, such overdevelopment of the purely musical element and the consequent restrictedness of appeal would become, in the view of many critics, the source of a profound crisis in music, one that, despite recent mutations and innovations, continues to determine much of our musical landscape.

To prevent music from succumbing to this threat, it would not suffice merely to limit the extent of the composer's development and interweaving of themes, figures, or motifs. Such a limit could not but prove in the final analysis arbitrary; and the insistence on such a limit could not but be countered by the observation that some of the very greatest composers, Bach, for example, were masters of contrapuntal inventiveness. What is required, rather, is that music not retreat into the purely musical element, that it not become isolated in a sphere that no longer admits the possibility of such spiritual presentation as constitutes the very essence of art as such. What is required is that music remain appropriately disclosive, that it remain, in its proper way, the sensible presentation of spirit. Its proper way to present spirit is by way of tones, by the configuring of tones in accord with the formal principles of music; and spirit, in the guise in which music, as a romantic art, would present, it is the inwardness of subjectivity.

A passage in the *Aesthetics* addresses this requirement quite precisely: the proper task of music is to present spiritually a certain content, not as this content occurs in consciousness in the form of a general idea, not as a determinate external shape either present to intuition or made to appear by art, but rather "in the way in which it becomes vital [*lebendig*] in the sphere of subjective inwardness" (*A* 2: 272/902). Thus, while tending to detach itself from all content, music has precisely as its task to adhere to a certain content so as to present it. This content to which music is to retain a certain bond is neither a general idea nor an external shape. It is, rather, the inner life itself, the inner life as such without further content, simply in its vitality (*Lebendigkeit*). Hence, the *Aesthetics* describes the task of music, considering it, first of all, quite independently of whether, as in song, it is allied with words and hence with ideas: "The difficult task assigned to music is to let this intrinsically veiled life and energy resound [*wiederklingen*] for itself in tones" (*A* 2: 272/902). At the most undifferentiated level, music presents spirit in its inwardness as such, presents it by way of the sounding of tones. Thus the *Aesthetics* explicitly identifies the content of musical expression as the inner life (*das Innere*) and its form as the purely transitory tones (see *A* 2: 275/906). What is decisive is that the sounding of tones lets the inward spirit resound in such a way that it is sounded in its depth. Through this complex of soundings, the inward spirit is presented, disclosed, as such.

As observed above, both the *Aesthetics* and the *Encyclopedia* seek to demonstrate that the sounding of tones originates from the vibration of a cohesive material. Indeed, even though the tones are capable of soaring beyond the material instrument that produces them, they are so closely allied to the vibratory motion that they are virtually indistinguishable from it, and in fact are identified with this motion in at least the one relevant passage cited above. One could, then, extend this identity to the receptive side, even though it must be acknowledged that such an extension is not explicitly marked in the relevant texts. Then, to say that the sounding of tones lets the inward spirit resound would mean that this inner life is set vibrating by the tones, or rather that the very reception of the tones is at once the energizing of inner life, whose movement, analogous to that of the vibrating instrument, takes the form of feeling.[27]

Such is, then, the task of music at the most undifferentiated level. Yet while music as such does not present spirit in the form of a general idea, music can – and readily does – come to be allied with words and ideas; indeed, as song it is always already allied with words and ideas. When this happens, then, according to the *Aesthetics*, music adds to these words and ideas, indeed redoubles them, casting them in another guise: for the task is "to immerse the ideas into this element" – that is, the element of music at the undifferentiated level – "in order to bring them forth anew for feeling" (*A* 2: 272/902). Far from superseding the soundings of music as such, the words and ideas are set to music, immersed in its soundings in such a way that they too begin to sound musically.

Although he sets aside the ancient tales about the all-powerfulness of music, Hegel grants that the power of music is elemental (*elementarisch*); and in order to account for this elemental power, he ventures an analysis of the connection between subjectivity and time, which he takes as the universal element of music.[28] At the undifferentiated level at which Hegel situates the initial account of music as it resonates in the inner life as feeling, there is as yet no separation between the inner feeling and an objective felt content. While at this level subjectivity is thus a unity, its unity is one not of subsistence, of mere perdurance, but rather of active self-unification. What happens in this process is that the subject makes itself its object, then cancels this objectivity in its otherness from the subject, and so, recovering itself in this other, affirms its subjective unity. Yet since nothing really objective is yet distinguished from the subject, there is no concrete determinate other from which, in recovering itself, the subject can become determinate. Thus its self-identity remains abstract and empty; it remains undifferentiated feeling.

What is decisive is that the same process is at the core of time. The juxtaposition of things in space, their three-dimensionality, is obliterated and drawn together into a point of time, into a *now*. But this point of time proves at once to be its own negation: as soon as this *now* is, it ceases to be and passes into another *now*. No true unity is established between the first *now* and the second *now*, for time is pure externality, that is, every *now* is outside every other *now*. Nonetheless, as with the undifferentiated feeling subject, a certain abstract, empty unity results, for the *now* always remains the same in its alteration. It is always now, every point of time is a *now*, and, regarded merely as points of time, the *nows* are entirely undifferentiated. Thus, in the case of time as in that of subjectivity, there is the same process: an empty positing of itself as other and then a cancelling of this otherness such that unity is restored. Furthermore, there is nothing that subsists in and through this process, nothing substantial; hence, in both cases there is nothing but the process, the very same process. Thus, not only does the subject prove to be in time, but, more fundamentally, the subject turns out to coincide with time; at this undifferentiated level of feeling, subjectivity is, like time itself, nothing but the positing of itself as other and the *Aufhebung* of this otherness. In the words of the *Aesthetics:* "The I is in time, and time is the being of the subject itself." Because of this identity and because time is the very element of tone, "tone penetrates the self, grips it in its barest existence, and sets the I ... in motion" (*A* 2: 277/908) – presumably, granted the extension ventured above, a vibratory motion in which the subject is displaced into its other only to return to itself, vibrating like the strings of a violin. Thus it is that music has elemental power.

One could say, then, that music is elemental, not by disclosing something elemental in nature, but rather by penetrating to the depths of the self so as to let the elemental within us resound. Yet if account were taken also of the distinctive spatiality of music, hence of a certain intervening or interpolation of a spatial moment within the operation of time and of the sounding of tones in time – as in the case of a tone that continues to echo after it has ceased actually sounding – then the question would be whether in sounding the elemental depths of the self music might also offer an intimation, however remote, of the elemental in nature.

Sounding is momentary. Even if a tone is extended in and through an echo, it soon vanishes. Unless it is sounded anew, it is replaced by silence. For this reason a musical composition requires repeated reproduction, or rather a musical work *is* only in being produced anew. Music requires performance. Furthermore, performance is not mere repetition, as if there were an original that had only to be repeatedly instantiated. Rather, the performer must animate the musical work, must lend his own inner life to the work. Such is, as the *Aesthetics* says, the deeper significance behind the necessity of performance: in performance "the expression must be the direct communication of a *living subject*, who puts into it the entirety of his own inner life" (*A* 2: 279/909).[29]

Sounding requires instruments capable of producing pure tones. Only one instrument is provided directly by nature: the human voice. All other instruments must be fabricated. Unlike the preparation of materials required in such arts as sculpture and painting, the fabrication of musical instruments is, for the most part, a complex process. In this respect music is – aside from song – the least natural art, the art that requires for its very means the most thorough transformation of natural materials of the most diverse sorts, wind instruments being fashioned from wood or metal shaped into a tube, strings being made from catgut or metal, percussion instruments from all manner of materials.

But the freest and most complete instrument, also the most natural, is the human voice. Its completeness stems from the fact that it combines the character of wind instruments and of string instruments: for the voice is breath flowing across the vocal cords. Most remarkably, the *Aesthetics* posits a perfect parallel between carnation and the human voice: just as the color of human skin (according to the analysis given in connection with painting) contains all the colors and so is the most complete color, so likewise "the human voice contains the ideal totality of soundings, which is merely spread out among the other instruments in their particular differences" (*A* 2: 291/922).[30] It is for this reason that the human voice blends most easily and most beautifully with other instruments. And yet, if in this respect music reaches its perfection in the human voice, it also undergoes a decisive displacement. For, in song, words and hence the ideas signified by those words are added to music. Even though, dipped in the element of music, the words and ideas are redoubled, nonetheless they draw music beyond the sphere in which its sounding presents and sounds the depths of undifferentiated inner life, that is, beyond the sphere of music simply as such. When music becomes song – and this it will of course always already have become – there is added to its subjectiveness the objective subsistence engendered by words and ideas.[31]

When music lets the inner life resound, there is a doubling, for in resounding it resounds *for itself*. While, on the one hand, the advent of song drives music beyond the pure sounding of inner life, it is, on the other hand, in the human voice that this doubling is most perfectly enacted. In the words of the *Aesthetics*: "At the same time, the human voice can apprehend itself as the tones of the soul itself, as the sound that the inner life has in its own nature for the expression of itself, an expression that it regulates directly. ... In song the soul sounds forth [*herausklingt*] from its own body" (*A* 2: 291/922). As the soul sounds forth, it hears itself immediately, and in that audition there is an immediate resounding that sounds the depths of the soul. To be sure, in playing an instrument, one hears the sounds produced, and, as with all music, those sounds resound in one's interiority. But there is lacking the immediacy that occurs when, as always in song, one hears oneself singing.

In music – and most immediately in song – the inner life sounds forth for itself. In this doubling, this apprehension of itself, it finds satisfaction. However, this satisfaction occurs only insofar as one does not simply remain immersed in the feeling that music engenders, in the passions and phantasies that pour forth in tones. In the words of the *Aesthetics*: "Music should lift the soul above this feeling in which it is immersed, make it hover [*schweben*] above its content, and so form for it a region where a withdrawal from this immersion, the pure feeling of itself, can occur unhindered" (*A* 2: 308f./940).[32] In the end everything depends on this elevation through which one comes to hover in the pure feeling of oneself, hearing oneself resound in a manner comparable to "pure light's vision of itself" (*A* 2: 309/940). That moment within music that engenders such elevation, letting one soar into the region of the pure feeling of self, constitutes the genuine song in a musical work.[33] For, above all, it is song, in which one hears oneself singing, that allows one to hover above in the pure delight of its sounding, as "the bird on the bough or the lark in the air sings cheerfully and touchingly just for the sake of singing" (*A* 2: 309/940).

Notes

This chapter first appeared in John Sallis, *Transfigurements: On the True Sense of Art* (Chicago, Ill.: University of Chicago Press, 2008). It is reprinted here with permission of the original publisher.

1 G.W.F. Hegel, *Ästhetik*, ed. Friedrich Bassenge, 2 vols. (West Berlin: Das europäische Buch, 1985), 2:310. Translated by T. M. Knox as *Aesthetics: Lectures on Fine Art*, 2 vols. (Oxford: Oxford University Press, 1975), 941. Further citations are indicated by *A*, followed by German and English pagination, respectively.

2 G.W.F. Hegel, *Enzyklopädie der philosophischen Wissenschaften im Grundrisse (1830)*. Zweiter Teil: Die Naturphilosophie, vol. 9 of *Werke in zwanzig Bänden* (Frankfurt a.M.: Suhrkamp, 1970), §§299–302. See especially the long *Zusatz* to §301.

3 See Otto Pöggeler, ed., *Hegel in Berlin: Preussische Kulturpolitik und idealistische Ästhetik. Zum 150. Todestag des Philosophen* (Berlin: Staatsbibliothek Preussischer Kulturbesitz, 1981), 240.

4 Ibid., 87.

5 *Briefe von und an Hegel*, ed. J. Hoffmeister (Hamburg: Felix Meiner Verlag, 1954), 3:56 (no. 479).

6 Ibid., 3:61 (no. 481). Rumor had it that Hegel actually preferred *The Barber of Seville* (which he calls Rossini's *Figaro*) over *The Marriage of Figaro*. Hegel is reported to have said that *The Barber of Seville* first conveyed to him a concept of comic opera (see Annemarie Gethmann-Siefert, "Das 'Moderne' Gesamtkunstwerk: Die Oper," in *Phänomen versus System, Hegel-Studien*, Beiheft 34 (Bonn: Bouvier Verlag, 1992), 179f.).

7 Hegel, *Briefe*, 3:64 (no. 481).

8 Ibid., 3:195 (no. 564).

9 In the published text of the *Aesthetics* it is said that "Schiller's poems ... prove very awkward and useless for musical composition" (*A* 2: 271/901). The same criticism is found already

in the 1820–1821 cycle of the lectures. Referring to the need for operatic poetry to be, as in Italian opera, somewhat mediocre (*mittelmässig*), Hegel says: "For the same reason very few of Schiller's poems are suitable for [musical] accompaniment" (Hegel, *Vorlesungen über Ästhetik. Berlin. 1820/21. Eine Nachschrift*, ed. Helmut Schneider (Frankfurt a.M.: Peter Lang, 1995), 281).

10   See Gethmann-Siefert, "Das 'Moderne' Gesamtkunstwerk," 176.

11   See ibid., 186, 198.

12   Hegel, *Briefe*, 3:71 (no. 483).

13   Gethmann-Siefert, "Das 'Moderne' Gesamtkunstwerk," 170f.

14   See Pöggeler, ed., *Hegel in Berlin*, 91.

15   Gethmann-Siefert, "Das 'Moderne' Gesamtkunstwerk," 172.

16   The treatment of the affinity between architecture and music is not found solely in the published text of the *Aesthetics*. Though it is only briefly introduced in the 1820–1821 cycle (*Vorlesungen über Ästhetik. Berlin. 1820/21*, 283), it does occur in the Hotho transcription of the 1823 cycle, as in this passage: "Music is similar to architecture in that it does not have its content in itself, and as architecture calls for a god, so does the subjectivity of music call for a text, thoughts, representations, which as determinate content are not in it" (*Vorlesungen über die Philosophie der Kunst. Berlin 1823*, transcribed by Heinrich Gustav Hotho, vol. 2 of *Vorlesungen: Ausgewählte Nachschriften und Manuskripte*, ed. Annemarie Gethmann-Siefert (Hamburg: Felix Meiner Verlag, 1998), 270).

17   See my analysis in *Stone* (Bloomington: Indiana University Press, 1994), 61–69.

18   Such a beginning is found not only in the text of the *Aesthetics* but also in both the Hotho transcription of the 1823 cycle (*Vorlesungen über die Philosophie der Kunst. Berlin 1823*, 262) and the Kehler transcription of the 1826 cycle. See Gethmann-Siefert, "Das 'Moderne' Gesamtkunstwerk," 191.

19   "Der Ton kommt nur als solcher in Betracht, nach der Weise seines Klanges" (*Vorlesungen über Ästhetik. Berlin. 1820 /21*, 278).

20   Hegel, *Enzyklopädie*, §300 Remark.

21   Ibid., §300 *Zusatz*.

22   In addition to the account in the *Aesthetics*, the following excerpted passage occurs in the transcription of the first (1820–1821) cycle of Hegel's lectures: "The most abstract, most formal interiority ... is the proper place of music" (*Vorlesungen über Ästhetik. Berlin. 1820/21*, 279). In a transcription of the third cycle, the following passage occurs: "Tone is the externalization of abstract inwardness" (*Philosophie der Kunst: Vorlesung von 1826*, ed. Annemarie Gethmann-Siefert, Jeong-Im Kwon, and Karsten Berr (Frankfurt a.M.: Suhrkamp, 2005), 216).

23   "für sich selbst inhaltslos." The phrase occurs in Hotho's transcription of the 1823 cycle (*Vorlesungen über die Philosophie der Kunst. Berlin 1823*, 265).

24   *Vorlesungen über Ästhetik. Berlin. 1820/21*, 288.

25   There are passages in the transcriptions that would support this supposition, for instance the following from the 1820–1821 cycle: "Especially in recent times music has become more independent; but what is natural is the music that accompanies song. To the extent that music becomes more independent, it loses its power over the mind" (ibid., 281).

26   See Gethmann-Siefert, "Das 'Moderne' Gesamtkunstwerk," 196.

27   In the philosophy of subjective spirit, Hegel describes the feeling soul in its immediacy as being set in vibration (*durchzittert*) (*Enzyklopädie*, §405).

28   All these themes are found already in the 1820–1821 cycle. According to the transcription, Hegel speaks of "the elemental power of music" and of "the connection of music with time" that results from the *Aufheben* of the spatial. He refers also to Orpheus, observing that the

civilizing effect of this legendary figure could not have been achieved "merely through tones" (*Vorlesungen über Ästhetik. Berlin. 1820/21*, 279f.).

29   According to a transcription of the third cycle, Hegel says that in singing, in particular, "the soul of the performing artist is more freely elevated; it is the free soul of the individual that one sees there before one's eyes" (*Philosophie der Kunst: Vorlesung von 1826*, 222).

30   This analysis is also found in the Pfordten transcription (ibid., 218f.).

31   Referring to the Kehler transcription of the 1826 cycle of lectures, Gethmann-Siefert notes that the advent of song both bestows on music an objective subsistence and draws it beyond the mere art of tones ("Das 'Moderne' Gesamtkunstwerk," 189).

32   There is a parallel passage in the transcription of the 1820–1821 cycle of lectures. Hegel speaks of how music arouses passions and expresses particular joys, sufferings, etc. Then he continues: "but at the same time the soul should lift itself into regions where it withdraws itself from this particularity." Music "does not merely draw us into this feeling, but rather the soul should rise above this, enjoy itself. It is the character of great music that it does not stream forth desiringly in a Bacchic manner but rather in such a way that the mind is also in itself soulful [*seelig*], like a bird in the air" (*Vorlesungen über Ästhetik. Berlin. 1820/21*, 289f.). It should be noted that in the text of the *Aesthetics* the description of this uplifting music is followed by a passage observing that music cannot rest content with such purity but must advance to the expression of the particularities of concrete inner life (*A* 2: 309f./940f.). However, in the transcription of the 1820–1821 lectures, the entire account of music concludes with the description of such pure music and makes no reference whatsoever to the need of an advance beyond it. Whether the insistence on this advance originated from Hegel himself or was interpolated by Hotho in order to "round out" Hegel's account is uncertain. In any case, even in the text of the *Aesthetics*, there is an indication of a still further advance that, formulated in terms of melody, leads to the preservation, within the particularization, of pure melody, which corresponds to the uplifting music described earlier and which in the later passage is designated as "the bearing and unifying soul" of music (*A* 2: 317/948).

33   See also *Vorlesungen über Ästhetik. Berlin. 1820/21*, 289f.

Part IX

Philosophy of Religion

19

Love, Recognition, Spirit: Hegel's Philosophy of Religion

ROBERT R. WILLIAMS

Despite the recent Hegel renaissance, or perhaps because of it, Hegel's philosophy of religion remains on the periphery of current interest. This may be due to (1) the collapse of Hegelianism in the early nineteenth century under the polemics of existentialist writers like Kierkegaard and Nietzsche; (2) the identification of Hegel's speculative theology with right-wing Hegelianism, itself a repristination of traditional theological metaphysics that Hegel criticized in his *Encyclopedia Logic:* and (3) the rise of professional philosophy as a secular discipline influenced by a positivistic reduction of philosophy towards philosophy of science that continues to shape the antimetaphysical bias of many professional philosophers.[1] Hegel observed that a similar philosophical consensus was already taking shape in his own time: "the doctrine that we can know nothing of God, that we cannot cognitively apprehend God, has become in our time a universally acknowledged truth, a settled thing, a kind of prejudice."[2] Far from celebrating such a view, Hegel criticizes it as the death of God: "It is no longer a grief to our age that it knows nothing of God; rather it counts as the highest insight that this knowledge is not even possible."[3] He adds that such antimetaphysics is not only antitheology, but also "the last step in the degradation of humanity."[4]

Viewed from the "degraded" anti- or nonmetaphysical temper that currently frames philosophy, Hegel is regarded principally as a transcendental philosopher in the Kantian or post-Kantian mold, or as a social and political philosopher (by readings that suppress the logical basis of the system or declare the latter superfluous for understanding Hegel's political philosophy).[5] If it is nevertheless acknowledged that Hegel does have theological interests, philosophers are unsure about what to make of these. Charles Taylor, who presents a 'large entity' interpretation of Hegel's absolute spirit, declares that despite Hegel's continued importance, Hegel's system is dead, *passé*, because "no one actually believes his central ontological thesis, that the universe is posited by a [cosmic] Spirit whose essence is rational necessity."[6] The discrediting of the cosmic spirit is at the same time a discrediting of theology as a branch of metaphysics. Robert Pippin, who develops a nonmetaphysical interpretation of Hegel, observes that

A Companion to Hegel, First Edition. Edited by Stephen Houlgate and Michael Baur.
© 2011 Blackwell Publishing Ltd. Published 2011 by Blackwell Publishing Ltd.

interpretations like Taylor's portray Hegel as a post-Kantian philosopher who nevertheless embraces theology and precritical metaphysics. This 'strange combination' makes
puzzling

> to the point of unintelligibility how Hegel could have been the post-Kantian philosopher
> he understood himself to be; that is, how he could have accepted, as he did, Kant's revela-
> tions about the fundamental inadequacies of the metaphysical tradition, could have
> enthusiastically agreed with Kant that the metaphysics of the 'beyond,' of substance, and
> of the traditional views of God and infinity were forever discredited, and then could have
> promptly created a systematic metaphysics as if he had never heard of Kant's critical
> epistemology. Just attributing moderate philosophic intelligence to Hegel should at least
> make one hesitate before construing him as a post-Kantian philosopher with a pre-critical
> metaphysics.[7]

Pippin rejects such a view of Hegel; he believes that "the left hegelians were right"[8] and
apparently believes that theology is synonymous with precritical metaphysics, that is,
those traditional views of God and infinity that Kant "forever discredited." So if Hegel
does have theological interests, then apparently he would be a post-Kantian philosopher with a precritical metaphysics.

In our contemporary situation, the interpretive alternatives for understanding the
theological aspect of Hegel's project are rather constricted: either it is assumed that the
left Hegelians like Feuerbach and Marx have shown theology to be reducible to anthropology, or Hegel's theology is acknowledged but treated as camouflage or disingenuous
because it is at variance with traditional Christian theology. The irony here is that
orthodox theology is often invoked by philosophers as a measure of Hegel's thought.[9]
Measured against that standard, Hegel's theological reconstruction appears to be an
ambiguously heterodox version of traditional Christianity. But since traditional
Christianity is on its way to becoming a fossil, heterodox interpretations of the fossil
are of interest chiefly to specialists and historians, constituting conversations that are
over as far as contemporary philosophical culture is concerned.[10] It seldom occurs to
anyone to challenge these alternatives or to consider the possibility that Hegel's project
is to provide a theological alternative to the 'bad infinite' transcendent theology of
right-wing Hegelians, and a philosophical alternative to the self-sufficient finitude of
left-wing Hegelians and antimetaphysics. Too philosophical for theologians, too theological for philosophers, and too metaphysical for both, Hegel's philosophy of religion
belongs to the endangered species of philosophical theology and liberal Protestant
theology.

Stephen Crites has pointed out that Hegel's system of philosophy is not merely compatible with speculative theology, it *requires* speculative theology in order to deal with
its fundamental problems, including the other, its incorporation in concrete universality, and its relation to good and evil. Hegel requires a speculative theology because his
philosophy has to treat the themes of negation, death, and resurrection.[11] That is one
reason why in *Faith and Knowledge* Hegel criticizes the alternatives of traditional metaphysics and modern philosophies of reflection, and points to the need for a speculative
Good Friday parallel to the historical Good Friday. Coming in for trenchant criticism
here are Kant's restriction of cognition to finitude and by extension, Kant's attack on
the theological proofs.[12] Also criticized here is Kant's treatment of God as a postulate

of practical reason that makes theology derivative from morality; elsewhere Hegel criticizes Schleiermacher's thesis that God is originally the referent of the feeling of utter
dependence.[13] All are rejected as half-truths and as the worst half of any truth they
may contain. This implies that both the right-wing and the left-wing Hegelian alternatives would be unacceptable to Hegel: Hegel's speculative theology is neither an other-
worldly *Jenseits* as the right-wing maintained, nor reducible to logical method and/or
naturalism and anthropology as the left-wing claimed.

Finally, lest anyone think that for Hegel religion is an optional topic that can be safely
set aside, consider that for Hegel every logical category may be regarded as a metaphysical definition of the absolute,[14] that religion is the consciousness of God in both the
subjective and objective genitive,[15] and that religion furnishes the fundamental speculative intuition of the system.[16] Lest anyone think that the religious–theological dimension in Hegel's thought implies that it rests upon precritical dogmatism and
authoritarianism, consider that he reconstructs Christianity as a religion of freedom in
the context of and as a consummation of a 700-page analysis of the history and philosophy of world religions. If Hegel's theology were intended merely as an exegesis of
an a priori divinely revealed deposit of eternal truth, no such contextualization and no
system of philosophy comprising logic, philosophy of nature, and philosophy of spirit,
would have been necessary for its understanding and interpretation.

In what follows I shall outline a progression in Hegel's thought: love, recognition,
spirit. His early intersubjective conception of love as a social infinite transforms the
kingdom of God from a union through domination into a vital living bond, a friendship
of soul embodying a divine spirit that unites and liberates its members.[17] Love as a social
infinite leads to his concept of mutual recognition and to his concept of spirit as arising
in and resulting from such mutual recognition. Spirit includes a conception of divine–
human community that is an embodiment of the true infinite that structures his speculative theology and his doctrine of absolute spirit. Thus the progression is love,
recognition, spirit. Love, recognition, and spirit are the concepts through which Hegel
appropriates and reconstructs Christian faith as a religion of freedom.

Hegel on Love: The Early Theological Writings

Hegel's most explicit treatment of love is found in his *Early Theological Writings*, especially the second of these unpublished treatises, "The Spirit of Christianity and Its
Fate."[18] This essay has as its underlying subject love, which it explores as (1) an emotion,
(2) as an ethical command – the love commandment, and (3) as an ontological principle, namely, the reunion of the separated.[19] In the latter sense love is the principle of
reconciliation, which Hegel conceives holistically. This holistic sense of love is contrasted with positivity, heteronomy, and alienation with the legal–penal vision of the
world and with Kantian morality.[20] Hegel reads morality against Kant not as genuine
autonomy but as a form of heteronomy, an internalized master–slave relation.

Hegel characterizes morality as tied to the imperative form, a form which implies
the domination of sensibility by reason, an inner cleavage between imperative–duty
and inclination–sensibility. The form of the imperative signifies an "ought," an unconditional command. Not only the Kantian duties but also divine command views of

morality are for Hegel essentially bound to the form of opposition. The Kantian virtues have the structure of an abstract universal (or master – the ought) and an abstract particular that must be constantly mastered because it fails to correspond with the ought.[21] Kantian virtue is founded on this fixed and rigid opposition such that if the opposition or the "ought" were to disappear, morality itself, constituted by such opposition, would cease. Thus the paradox: the realization of morality would constitute its disappearance.

This has important implications for thinking about reconciliation. For in the legal–penal vision of the world as Hegel understands it, the law is higher than man. In this framework there is no escaping the law. But the law as absolute admits no exceptions and cannot forego punishment; it cannot be merciful or it would cancel itself. So long as the law is supreme, the individual must be sacrificed to the universal – be put to death. Dualism is final. No reconciliation is possible.[22]

These views find expression in the classical royal metaphor for the relation of God to world. In this metaphor, God is regarded as a cosmic monarch and moral judge of the world, meting out rewards and punishments. Hegel criticizes the royal metaphor, finding in it a relation of master to servant, lordship and bondage, which implies that religion is essentially heteronomous and positive, that is, a form of domination.[23] Such alienation and heteronomy may also be present in relations to others and to community.

The totality of such dualisms yields the moral vision of the world with God as cosmic monarch and judge. The relation between law (duty) and individuals is condemnation: "if the law persists in its awful majesty, there is no escaping it.... The law cannot forgo punishment, cannot be merciful or it would cancel itself ... justice is unyielding; and so long as laws are supreme, so long as there is no escape from them, so long must the individual be sacrificed to the universal, i.e., be put to death."[24] In Hegel's view, morality, if it is not essentially condemnation, can easily turn into condemnation. Moreover Hegel shows that inherent in moralism and legalism, there is a reactive ressentiment-laden spirit which "needs an opposite, a reality from which it acquires its force."[25] Within the legal–penal vision and within the moral vision of the world, law and punishment cannot be reconciled, that is, they exclude reconciliation. However, they can be reconciled if *fate* can be reconciled. Hegel links the possibility of reconciliation to fate and the opposition constitutive of fate. More about this in a moment.

Love is not the law but the fulfillment of the law. As such, love is the transcendence of the opposition constitutive of morality. Hegel comments on the Sermon on the Mount and the love commandment. The love commandment is not a version of Kantian respect for law but rather the fulfillment of the law.[26] This fulfillment is a uni-fication of inclination with law wherein the law loses its form as alien, external law, or as a command/imperative. Hegel takes seriously the claim that love is the fulfillment of the law; he calls this fulfillment the pleroma. The pleroma or love as the fulfillment of the law displaces the moral concept of the human being as divided against itself with a restoration to wholeness and harmony in which reason and sensibility are united.[27]

The Sermon on the Mount does not teach reverence or respect for law but exhibits the pleroma, the fulfillment of the law that at the same time suspends it as law; love is higher than obedience to law because it makes law formally superfluous. Kant, however, misinterprets the love command as an imperative; he reduces it to a moral imperative to respect and revere that law that commands love. This leads to further confusion and reduction: love is confused with an emotion, an inclination that cannot plausibly be commanded, namely, a "liking to perform duties." This is reductive and wrong headed from Hegel's point of view because in love the thought of duty falls away and vanishes.[28]

Love is raised above the inner cleavage between duty and inclination, reason and sensibility. As the fulfillment of the law, love is not an abstract ought but actual, a modification of life, of existence.[29] Love is a union or synthesis in which the self ceases to be opposed, that is., the self ceases to be inwardly opposed to itself (duty–inclination) and ceases to be opposed to or estranged from its other. Love as the pleroma is a synthesis in which the law loses its (abstract) universality, and the subject loses its (abstract) particularity. Their opposition is replaced by agreement and harmony.

Love, as the pleroma, is a complex totality involving several mediations: (1) the fulfillment of the law (overcoming the abstract dichotomy of imperative and inclination); (2) the restoration or accomplishment of wholeness, overcoming the inner opposition of reason and sense, or more simply put, the fulfillment of human nature (overcoming its inner dichotomy between reason and sensibility); (3) the presupposition of intersubjective difference and the overcoming of hostility and alienation. Love is an intersubjective relation and union of different persons, the achievement of wholeness, community; and (4) the sum total of these mediations, or the achievement of the whole itself, which is freedom – freedom from internal constraint or from the internal master–slave relation, and freedom from external constraint or coercion by an other. Love as the reunion of the separate signifies that the self-relation (being-for-self) and relation to other (being-for-other) coincide. This coincidence is freedom, which is a being at home with self in the other. In this totality, the oppositions constitutive of morality are overcome and transcended.

Hegel takes up the question of reconciliation but in the context of tragic fate as an alternative to the legal–penal vision of the world. Unlike the latter, in which dualism is final, Hegel believes that fate has its basis in life and action. This contextualization means that opposition and dualism are not final but rather are moments within the life process. Paradoxical as it may seem, for Hegel fate holds out the possibility of reconciliation because "[i]n the hostile power of fate, universal is not severed from particular in the way in which the law, as a universal, is opposed to man or his inclinations. ... The trespass of the man regarded as in the toils of fate is therefore not a rebellion of the subject against his ruler [monarch], [or] the slave's flight from his master."[30]

In fate "[d]estruction of life is not the nullification of life, but its diremption, and [this] ... consists in transforming life into an enemy."[31] Hegel illustrates this by reference to tragedy: In his arrogance Macbeth "has destroyed indeed, but only the friendliness of life; he has perverted life into an enemy."[32] Macbeth's fate is his punishment, which "is the equal reaction of the trespasser's own deed, of a power which he himself has armed, of an enemy made an enemy by himself."[33] Macbeth's trespass against Duncan is a negation. It calls forth a corresponding second negation or punishment by fate. This second negation negates the original negation (the trespass) and reconciles the whole with itself. However, this reconciliation is tragic because the life Macbeth has destroyed is his own; through his trespass he has forfeited his own life. But note that in this very forfeiture there is a reconciliation. Macbeth's forfeiture of his life is retributive justice: in Macbeth's death, life has healed its wound. This reconciliation is tragic and bitter-sweet: before his demise, Macbeth longs for what he has lost.

Fate presupposes life and is a moment of life. This means that the dualism constitutive of the legal–penal vision of the world is not ultimate or final. This is crucial. Life as a vital and dynamic whole, can suffer disruption and yet heal its wounds. The severed, hostile life – the whole divided against itself – can return to itself again.[34] Opposition and conflict therefore are not final; as moments of life, they are rather the possibility of reunification and thus the possibility of reconciliation.[35] However, the reconciliation afforded by fate falls short of the reconciliation of love. Love moves beyond forfeiture, punishment, and negation to an affirmative reconciliation. Love is not only rooted in the power of life, it is a sensing of life in another. Hegel observes that since the enemy is sensed and felt as life, reconciliation is always possible. This sensing of life, a sensing which finds itself again in its other, is love, and *in love, fate is reconciled*.[36]

Since love transcends fate, it also transcends the imperatives and oppositions constitutive of morality. Love overcomes the might and division of objectification, it renounces coercion and domination. Love makes the imperative form of command and duty superfluous.[37] Hegel interprets Jesus as proposing "the higher genius of reconcilability (a modification of love) which makes [law] superfluous."[38] "For in love there vanish not only rights but also the feeling of inequality and the hatred of enemies."[39] Love is a readiness for reconciliation; having renounced coercion and domination, the spirit of reconcilability (*Versöhnlichkeit*) struggles to overcome the enmity of the other.[40]

The spirit of reconcilability is a true beauty of soul. Beauty of soul has as its negative attribute the highest freedom, which is "the possibility of renouncing everything."[41] Beauty of soul is a willingness not to insist upon one's rights but to let go of one's rights for the sake of reconciliation.

> Such a heart is open to reconciliation, for it is able forthwith to reassume any vital relationship, to re-enter the ties of friendship and love, since it has done no injury at all to life in itself. ... Forgiveness of sins, readiness to reconcile one's self with another, Jesus makes an express condition of the forgiveness of one's own sins, the cancellation of one's hostile fate. Both are only different applications. ... In reconciliation with one who hurts us, the heart no longer stands on the right acquired in opposition to the offender. By giving up its right, as its own hostile fate, to the evil genius of the other, the heart reconciles itself with him ... and the fate it had aroused against itself by its own deed has dissolved into the airs of night.[42]

When another injures us, Hegel believes s/he forfeits the very right s/he violates. The injured party acquires this forfeited right in the form of a legitimate retaliation or retribution against the offender. But if we seek reconciliation, we must resist the temptation to retaliate, for if we 'accept' this forfeited right, if we exercise our 'right of requital' in punishing the offender, we risk provoking and stirring up our own hostile fate. In forgiving, we forego this right of retaliation even though it is legitimate and justified. Even more important, by not insisting on its rights and by letting go even of rights acquired through forfeiture, love makes possible a reconciliation with the offender. In foregoing requital against an offense and the right of punishment acquired over another who injures, love manifests itself as a readiness for reconciliation.[43] Love recognizes the other not as a sin existent but as a living human being and affirms the other as intrinsically valuable in himself.[44]

Love participates in and directs the power of life towards the surmounting and overcoming of opposition and disunion. The opposition constitutive of morality cannot be final; rather "Opposition is the possibility of reunification. ... It is in the fact that even the enemy is felt as life that there lies the possibility of reconciling fate. This reconciliation is thus neither the destruction nor the subjugation of something alien. ... This sensing of life, a sensing which finds itself again, is love, and in love, fate is reconciled."[45] Again, "in love, life has found itself once more."[46]

Hegel contrasts the fullness inherent in reconciliation and liberation with the division, disunion, and asymmetry of lordship and bondage: "In contrast with ... reversion to obedience, reconciliation in love is a liberation; in contrast with the re-recognition of lordship and mastery, love is the cancellation of lordship in the restoration of the living bond, of that spirit of love and mutual faith which, considered in relation to lordship, is the highest freedom."[47] Yet love is not contrary to law, moral imperatives, virtues, and so on. Rather love, as the reuniting of the separate and estranged, lifts the virtues out of the sphere of opposition and purges them of ressentiment.[48] Love completes the virtues by constituting them as virtues without lordship (Herrschaft).[49] Love mediates and restores the whole.[50]

While it is true that love has an emotional aspect that cannot be commanded, love is not merely an emotion. In the Jewish and Christian traditions, love is commanded, a command at once ethical and religious, a command to love God and others. If love were simply an emotion, it could not be commanded, and all attempts to command and force it would produce only distortions and pathologies. But although love is a commandment, love itself pronounces no imperative, it is not a universal opposed to a particular.[51] Hegel observes that " 'Love has conquered' does not mean the same as 'duty has conquered,' i.e., subdued its enemies; it means that love has overcome hostility."[52] Only through love is the power of objectification broken, and through love the whole sphere of objectification [and separation] is broken through."[53] Again, "in love life finds itself as a doubling of itself and the union of this double."[54] Hegel provides an ontological analysis of love: love is the overcoming of estrangement; it is a reunion of what has been separated. Love presupposes the opposition that it mediates and overcomes.

This analysis of love has *theological* implications that point beyond the traditional monarchical metaphor, and beyond alienation and heteronomy: Hegel understands God *to be love* and to manifest his divinity in human love. Love is a unity of spirit, that is, divinity itself.[55] Hegel elaborates this in a discussion of the term "kingdom of God." He notes that the term "kingdom" usually "means only a union through domination, through the power of a stranger over a stranger."[56] Such a conception falls short of love as the reuniting of the separate wherein humans find themselves again in an other. Love is "a living bond which unites the believers; it is the feeling of the unity of life ... This friendship of soul, described in the language of reflection as an essence, as spirit, is the divine spirit, is God who rules the communion."[57] Love has profound theological significance – for God in truth *is love* – but this has been obscured by the monarchical metaphor and its moral vision of the world.

In the course of these analyses, Hegel takes up the question of whether love is inherently intersubjective. He asks whether love should be understood as self-love. He advances a striking claim, namely, that self-love is a meaningless (*sinnlos*) term. He observes that " 'Love your neighbor as yourself' does not mean to love him as much as you love yourself, *for to love oneself is a word without any sense.*"[58] The reason is that although the self can reflect on itself, oppose itself, and relate itself to itself, such oppositions are all *intrasubjective*. In these intrasubjective oppositions there is no serious otherness, no serious conflict. But love requires serious nonequivocal otherness; it requires an other capable of offering serious resistance. In short, love ontologically understood as a reuniting of the separate is a fundamentally *intersubjective* conception, a conception that presupposes different selves.[59] Hence love is not the appropriate term to name or designate an intrasubjective self-relation or being-for-self. Love is not self-love but a being-for-self in and for another.

Further, love presupposes the differences that it reconciles. It makes no sense to speak of reunion without separation and difference. However, although love presupposes the intersubjective other and otherness, that is, separate centers of agency, it is also the case that in love's reconciliation these separate centers are not eliminated but sustained and preserved. Love's union is not a collapse of love's double into an undifferentiated unity: "In love the separate does still remain, no longer as something separated, but as united."[60] "The beloved is no longer opposed to us; he is one with our being. We see only ourselves in him and yet he is not who we are – a miracle that we cannot comprehend."[61] What love cancels is not the other as such but only its foreign or hostile character.[62] Love's union is not reductive or homogenizing because love does not suppress or eliminate differences. On the contrary, love treasures and "seeks out differences and devises unions ad infinitum."[63]

The *Early Theological Writings* display love's complex intersubjective structure. On the one hand, love requires a real, nonequivocal other, irreducible to the self. It presupposes serious separation; as the principle of reconciliation, love presupposes opposition and conflict. On the other hand, love is ontologically the reunion of the separate. So the separation and otherness of selves that make conflict possible are not final barriers that make reconciliation impossible. When love reunites separate selves, it does not suppress but seeks out, cherishes, and affirms their differences. This analysis of love anticipates spirit and ethical life. The central insight that love is identity in difference, and difference in identity leads to the concept of mutual recognition, to Hegel's concept of spirit as resulting from mutual recognition, to the logical analysis of identity and difference, and to Hegel's conception of divine–human community in absolute spirit.

Recognition and Spirit: Hegel's Appropriation and Critique of Fichte

Fichte's account of recognition is his proposed solution to Kant's problem posed in the question "how do I know that I am free?" Fichte maintains that the consciousness of freedom is mediated by the summons (*Aufforderung*) of an other.[64] The term *Aufforderung* allows for a considerable range of translations: summons, invitation (e.g., to dance), appeal. Recognition is a response to such an appeal or summons, and what is recognized is that another has summoned me to freedom by limiting his own. The summons precedes my consciousness of freedom as its condition. This analysis of the summons in which the other takes priority over the subject is remarkable in an idealist program, which makes the subject central, if not foundational, and the condition of possibility for experience. Nevertheless, in several passages Fichte elaborates on the priority of the other. He suggests that the face of the other binds me by its very presence:

> at the basis of all voluntarily chosen reciprocal interaction among free beings there lies an original and necessary reciprocal interaction among them, which is this: the free being by his mere presence in the sensible world, compels every other freedom, without qualification, to recognize him as a person.[65]

This is a rich concept of summons and recognition that goes beyond what Fichte actually makes of it as the foundation of the concept of right. In this rich concept of recognition, "we are both bound and obligated to each other by our very existence."[66] Individuality is a reciprocal concept that can be thought only in relation to another and to community.

Further, Fichte maintains that the relationship between individuals is freely, mutually and reciprocally constituted. Because the relation is both the condition of freedom and the result constituted through freedom, coercion here is out of place. No party has or enjoys any absolute priority over any other. Such reciprocity is fundamental to the concept of recognition:

> Thus the relation of free beings to one another is a relation of reciprocal recognition through intelligence and freedom. One cannot recognize the other if both do not mutually recognize each other; and one cannot treat the other as a free being if both do not mutually treat each other as free. The concept established here is extremely important for our project, for our entire theory of right rests upon it.[67]

However, Fichte does not develop his account of recognition consistently within his *Rechtslehre*. He also maintains that despite being prevolitionally bound by an original and necessary reciprocity in which the free being obligates others by his sheer presence, living in community with others is also the result of a free and arbitrary decision. So freedom here is prior to the other. This contingent decision implies that living in community is optional because Fichte's theory "by no means asserts that such a community ought to be established."[68] Fichte explains that in the sphere of right, "each is bound only by the free, arbitrary decision to live in community with others, and if someone does not at all want to limit his free choice, then within the sphere of the doctrine of right, one can say nothing further against him."[69] These assertions threaten Fichte's account of freedom, recognition, and community with incoherence for they suggest that the summons, the other, and the prevoluntary communal ties, which are presented as quasi-transcendental conditions of freedom, are nevertheless conditional and dependent on a contingent and arbitrary decision to live within a certain community of right.

Moreover, despite Fichte's contention that recognition is fundamentally reciprocal and mutual, he also asserts that after mutual recognition "both recognize each other in their inner being, but *they are isolated, as before*."[70] Mutual recognition implies an intersubjective mediation of freedom that is supposed to bind the two parties together. Yet Fichte concedes that after such recognition the parties remain isolated as before.

395

No "we" results from mutual recognition. The parties remain isolated in spite of their relation.

This strange relation without relation, a relation that is external and leaves its relata as they were before, is a symptom of Fichte's failure to integrate recognition with his theory of right and punishment. Instead of showing that recognition grounds right and creates a community of freedom, Fichte displaces mutual recognition in favor of a coercive deterrence theory of right.[71] Implicit here is a grim vision of the state as a surveillance mechanism for deterring illegal behavior and punishing illegality with mechanistic necessity.[72] Hegel objects: "Fichte's state is centered on the police. ... no persons can go out without having their identity papers on them, and he deems this very important to deter crimes. But such a state becomes a world of galley slaves, where each is supposed to keep his fellow under constant supervision."[73]

Hegel criticizes Fichte for ignoring the intersubjective mediation of freedom in mutual recognition and for putting forth instead a vision of the state as a coercive mechanism: Fichte's *Natural Right* "really is an attempt at a consistent system which would have no need of the religion and the ethics that are foreign to it. ... In this way the externality of the units [comprising the state] is utterly fixed and posited as something absolute in and for itself; thereby the inner life, the rebuilding of lost trust and confidence, the union of universal and individual freedom, and ethical life itself, are made impossible."[74] In the *Difference* essay, Hegel criticizes Fichte's conception of the state as a mechanism for domination: "the state conceived by the intellect is not an organization at all, but a machine, and the people is not the organic body of a communal and rich life, but an atomistic, life-impoverished multitude. ... what binds them together is an endless domination."[75]

Hegel's criticisms of Fichte have implications for his appropriation and interpretation of the concept of recognition. He does not follow Fichte down the path of coercive right and the mechanistic conception of the state as an instrument of deterrence and coercion. Rather, he seeks to integrate his conception of love as the principle of reconciliation with Fichte's rich concept of mutual recognition. Contrary to Fichte, Hegel believes that the community of a person with others must not be regarded as a limitation of true freedom – for then community would be supreme tyranny. Hegel agrees with Aristotle that community is the enhancement and enlargement of freedom and selfhood. The highest community, he tells us, is the highest freedom.[76]

However, Hegel does not begin his analysis with the highest community or with reciprocal recognition; he begins with a worst case scenario, a pre-ethical Hobbesian state of nature, where trust has not been lost but is impossible. Under such conditions, individuals who are wholly external to each other at the point of zero mediation come into collision, that is, they enter the life and death struggle for recognition. Hegel's point in depicting this struggle is not to glorify violence but to show that it is self-defeating. The point is to leave the state of nature behind[77] by transforming the life and death struggle into a struggle for affirmative recognition, freedom, and liberation. In Hegel's famous account, the relation between master and servant is a transitional stage between the uncivilized state of nature and a civilized condition where mutual recognition holds sway. It is an unequal recognition where the victor of the struggle becomes lord, and the loser of the struggle preserves his life by surrendering his claims to recognition and becomes the servant. Hegel's analysis does not glorify such domination but shows that it merely replaces one contradiction – death – with another – the coercion of a free being. This coercion, enforced through the threat of death, contains within it the seeds of its own destruction: the goal for Hegel is not to replace one master with another but to get beyond mastery and domination.

In Hegel's initial account, the process of recognition is a double movement of two self-consciousnesses. Because that is the case,

> action by one side would be useless, because what is supposed to happen can only be jointly brought about by both. Thus the action has a double significance because it is directed against itself as well as against the other, but also because it is indivisibly the action of one as well as the other. ... Each is for the other the middle term, through which each mediates itself with itself and unites with itself; and each is for itself, and for the other, an immediate being on its own account, which is such only through this mediation. They recognize themselves as mutually recognizing one another.[78]

The result of such mutual recognition is spirit, the I that is a We and the We that is an I. The We, it should be noted, is not a machine but a spiritual organism. The difference is that in a mechanism the parts remain separate in spite of their relation; their relation remains external to them.[79] Fichte got as far as mutual recognition, but because he conceives mutual recognition through distorting mechanistic prejudices, he claims that people after recognition remain separate and isolated as before. Fichte's treatment of recognition falls short of the concepts of love and spirit. For Hegel, spirit is an organically interrelated totality. In such a totality relations do not remain external to its members or leave them unaffected; rather the whole is present in its members and exists in interdependence with them as their telos.[80]

The telos of the struggle for recognition is mutual recognition, a possibility which had been implicit all along. But owing to the struggle and violence which precede it, mutual recognition may emerge only in the shape of forgiveness, which Hegel characterizes as a mutual recognition that is the absolute spirit.[81] Here mutual recognition in its full and final shape is forgiveness; this has both religious and theological significance for Hegel.

So what has love to do with recognition? And what has recognition to do with love? And what does all of this have to do with religion and theology? To the first question, we have found that Hegel argues (1) that self-love is a meaningless concept because it lacks the serious intersubjective difference that love presupposes; (2) that love is the reunion of the separate; and (3) that love is essentially necessarily intersubjective. Love's intersubjective structure turns out to be mutual recognition. Love is a determinate affirmative intersubjectivity; it is not only the principle of marriage and family but also the basis of Hegel's theory of ethical life. It is also the being of God, who is love, and the objective foundation of reconciliation.

To the second question, Hegel's account of recognition begins with an immediate collision, a contradiction between raw selves that precipitates the life and death struggle. The struggle for recognition aims at overcoming that initial contradiction. But the resort to violence to compel recognition or to eliminate the other is counterproductive because what drives the struggle is the need to be recognized and legitimated by an other. Although the unequal recognition of master and servant suspends the initial violence, it resolves the original contradiction by propounding another, namely, the coercion of a free being and an asymmetrical, unequal recognition. Unless there is an alternative to mastery, the struggle for recognition would end in failure.

Is there an alternative? Hegel believes that there is, namely mutual recognition, in which each party gains recognition and independence through and by means of a certain dependence on the other, who must freely limit his own freedom and play the role of mediator. Note that a one-sided action is useless here. The drive towards recognition can be successful only if both parties freely and reciprocally play the role of mediator to the other. This paradoxical combination of independence (being-for-self) mediated by dependence (being-for-other) is a relation of mutual identity and difference, union and liberation, that Hegel analyzed as the intersubjective structure of love in the *Early Theological Writings*. What is recognition about? Although it may begin with struggle and exhibit unequal, asymmetrical shapes of lordship and bondage, its telos is love. Short of love's mutuality, which may include forgiveness, recognition presents only deficient modalities that fall short of actuality, self-realization, the "We."

What does this have to do with religion? Love is not merely the fulfillment of the intersubjective relation in a free mutuality, it is also the principle of reconciliation that Hegel first worked out in his *Early Theological Writings*. Love names the action of reconciliation that overcomes lordship and bondage, estrangement from others, and the estrangement of the self from itself inherent in the concept of moral duty (the internalized master/servant). Love embodies both a negative freedom and an affirmative freedom. Love exhibits a negative moment of freedom, which Hegel connects with self-sacrifice; this includes many religious practices, including not standing on the rights that one may acquire through the sins and trespasses of others. Love involves a readiness to let all these go for the sake of reconciliation.[82]

Love not only lets go of rights vis-à-vis the other, love embodies the affirmative freedom that affirms the other. Love completes the virtues by stripping out all one-sidedness and exclusiveness;[83] it aims not merely at community but at an inclusive community. Although love as the principle of the family is not without immediacy and parochialism, for love there are in principle no permanent outsiders or people permanently marginalized. Through his concept of mutual recognition in its full and final shape of love, Hegel appropriates and reformulates on an intersubjective basis Aristotle's insight that all the virtues are social – that the pursuit of virtue cannot be a solitary concern or affair. As the completion of the virtues, love affirms the other as coincluded in the end of each of the virtues. In the words of Martha Nussbaum, "one cannot choose ... excellent activities as ends in themselves ... without also choosing the good of others as an end. Deprived of this end, we lack not a part of our good but the whole."[84] This social conception of the virtues completed by love informs Hegel's reconstruction of the kingdom of God in the *Early Theological Writings*. No longer a heteronomous realm of lordship and bondage based on the power of a stranger over a stranger, the kingdom of God is an inclusive community united by love in which all oppositions, enmities, and rights are sublated in a "friendship of soul" that "is the divine spirit, is God who rules the communion."[85]

But we still do not yet have to do with Hegel's mature concept of religion as a domain of absolute spirit. The foregoing analysis has theological implications, but it has dealt more with Hegel's theological anthropology, or the domains of subjective and objective spirit, than with Hegel's concept of absolute spirit. Spirit is a social infinity, and the latter points to the true infinite. Hegel calls the true infinite the basic concept of philosophy.[86] The social infinite, or the We, points to the true infinite because in the We, being-for-self and being-for-other coincide in their difference, and individuals grasp themselves as ideal, relative to the whole of which they are members.[87] To get a more complete picture, we must turn now to Hegel's treatment of the finite–infinite relation in his *Logic* and *Philosophy of Religion*.

Hegel's Philosophical Theology: Love, Reconciliation, True Infinity

Stephen Crites points out that Kant's doctrine of the postulates exerted considerable influence on Fichte, Schelling, and Hegel because they saw in the postulates a way to get around the restrictions that Kant had placed on cognition and establish a new basis for philosophy that could expand it beyond the theoretical cognition of the sciences into art, morality, and religion, and enable it to become a genuine system of speculative philosophy. In particular, religious truth could be critically re-established as a requirement of praxis beyond the confines of empiricism and the old dogmatic rationalism.[88]

Recall that Kant's limitation of knowledge in order to make room for moral faith also results in the primacy of practical reason. The second Critique reopened certain metaphysical questions – which the first Critique had declared unanswerable – as interests of practical reason: freedom, immortality, and God. Kant maintains that God is a postulate of morality and moral action: when I act practically, I must assume that I am free (the first postulate) and that I am capable of realizing the telos of my action. I have to assume that "ought" implies "can." Otherwise morality would be impossible, and human nature, which in its rational aspect issues itself categorical imperatives and as agent seeks to carry them out, would be self-contradictory. Kant holds that it is morally necessary to postulate God to undergird the necessary assumptions of freedom: the inherent realizability of duty, and the achievement of moral worth through action conforming to duty. However, this moral and practical necessity remains subjective.

Nevertheless, in the doctrine of the postulates of practical reason, Kant explores the boundaries of cognition. Kant denies that practical reason's access to the supersensible through freedom is an illegitimate breach of the limits of cognition laid down in the first Critique. Practical reason does not breach the boundaries of cognition because the content of the postulates is qualified by their subjective form. This means that the content of any postulate expresses only a moral need of freedom; as such, it remains relative to the subject.[89]

Hegel criticizes Kant's treatment of the postulates as having only subjective validity and necessity. Hegel points out that if God were taken to be a postulate in this sense, God would have no being independent of the postulating subject.[90] God would be only an ideal that ought to be. For to postulate is a subjective act, and as Hegel observes:

> the only question is how to take this "subjective." Is it the identity of infinite thought and being, of reason and its reality that is subjective? Or is it only the postulating and the believing of them? Is it the content or the form of the postulates [that is subjective]? It cannot be the content that is subjective. ... Hence it is the form, or in other words, it is

something subjective and contingent that the Idea is only subjective.... Letting it rest there meets with universal approval, and what is approved is just exactly the worst thing about it, namely the form of postulating.[91]

The subjective form of the postulate makes its content relative to the postulating subject. If for that reason it is inferred that the content of the postulate – the identity of thought and being – is merely subjective, then the identity would not be what it is supposed to be but merely an identity yet to be constituted or actualized, that is, something that ought to be. The realization of the content of the postulate would be continually deferred; moreover, if moral striving ever achieved its goal of perfection, the postulates, including the God postulate, would no longer be necessary.[92]

Kant's doctrine of the postulates is compromised by two major limitations of the critical philosophy. First, Kant's sharp distinction between theoretical reason and practical reason introduces a "fundamental dualism into the heart of Kant's philosophy and signals that the whole is dominated by the bifurcating propensities of the understanding."[93] This dualism has to be overcome by a more robust, nonreductive interpretation of absolute identity, or the God postulate. Second, Kant's philosophy as dualism is dominated by its insistence on the absoluteness of finitude and of cognitive limits:

The fixed principle of this system of culture is that the finite is in and for itself, that it is absolute, and is the sole reality. ... The infinite and the finite are here not to be posited as identical in the idea; for each of them is for itself absolute. So they stand opposed to each other in the relation of domination. ... Because the antithesis between the infinite and the finite is absolute, the sphere of the eternal is incalculable, the inconceivable, the empty – the unknowable God beyond the boundary stakes of reason."[94]

The philosophy of finitude regards the absolute as an empty unknowable beyond, which reason both recognizes and from which it excludes itself. This self-exclusion of reason from the absolute makes theology impossible as the knowledge of God and leaves us instead with the knowledge of man.

The fundamental principle common to the philosophies of Kant, Jacobi and Fichte is ... the absoluteness of finitude. ... The one self-certifying certainty ... is that there exists a thinking subject, a reason affected with finitude ... Kant's so-called critique of the cognitive faculties, Fichte's doctrine that consciousness cannot be transcended ... Jacobi's refusal to undertake anything impossible for reason, all amount to nothing but an absolute restriction of reason to finitude, an injunction never to forget the absoluteness of the subject. ... In this situation philosophy cannot aim at the cognition of God, but only at what is called the cognition of man.[95]

Hegel believes that Kant's "philosophy of the postulates" is inadequate as far as the knowledge of God is concerned. On such a basis, it is possible to speak of a doctrine of religion but not a doctrine of God or a theology.[96] But this is the very point at issue.

Hegel does not deny Kant's intention to approach God through human freedom and praxis. But Kant's interpretation of the God postulate as subjective is reductive and indistinguishable from atheism. Even if Kant does not press the point that far, God as postulate would be derivative from morality. If the content of the God postulate were merely subjective, an 'ought,' we would arrive only at the spurious or leveled infinity.[97] This finitized infinite falls short of true infinity precisely because it is not actual. Moreover, it "is *supposed* to be unattainable. However, to be thus unattainable is not its grandeur but its defect, which is at bottom the result of holding fast to the *finite* as such as a *merely affirmative being*."[98]

Hegel corrects and extends Kant's approach to the God question through human freedom by distinguishing the content of the postulate from its subjective form and by suspending Kant's fundamental dualism (antithesis), a dualism that restricts the content of the postulate and cognition to a merely subjective validity: "On the contrary, the sole Idea that has reality and true objectivity for philosophy *is the absolute suspension of the antithesis. This absolute identity is not a universal subjective postulate never to be realized. It is the only authentic reality.*"[99] Hegel contends that the alleged subjectivity of the postulate is contradicted by the content of the postulate itself: God does not derive from human activity but is self-grounding, valid in and for itself: "This identity of thought and being is the very one which the ontological proof and all true philosophy recognize as the sole and primary idea."[100] The ontological argument rules out attributing to God the ontological status of a contingent being or an abstract possibility that is supposed to be unattainable, a mere ideal, or an 'ought to be.'[101]

If religion is taken seriously as a *sui generis* domain not reducible to morality or a postulate of morality, it requires a different interpretation of freedom and God than that afforded by Kant. Specifically Hegel holds that "Religion is ... not an invention of human beings, but an effect of the divine at work, of the divine productive process within humanity."[102] Religion has to do with praxis, but this is a divine–human praxis. The theological object can be described from the human side (the subjective form here is faith, religion), but it cannot be reduced to a postulate or constructed from the human side alone. Religion is faith *in God,* not faith in faith. Religion as a divine–human praxis requires the inversion of Kant's subjective morality-centered 'ontology' of the postulates: "Generally speaking, the highest independence of a human being is to know himself as totally determined by the absolute idea; this is the consciousness and attitude that Spinoza calls *amor intellectualis dei* [the intellectual love of God]."[103]

The philosophical theology in Hegel's *Philosophy of Religion* is not simply a theoretical discipline like the precritical *metaphysica specialis* that Kant discredited or a Kantian theory of theology as a postulate of practical reason but rather a critical discipline presupposing religion itself and investigating God as the object of religious practice:

> Our object ... is not just God as such; the content of our science is religion. ... To the extent that God is grasped as an essence of the understanding, God is not grasped as spirit; to the extent that God is grasped as spirit, however, *this concept includes the subjective side within it,* the side that is introduced into this concept when it is defined as religion.
>
> Our concern here is therefore *not with God as such or as object, but with God as he is present in his community.* It will be evident that God can only be genuinely understood in the mode of his being as spirit, by means of which he makes himself into the counterpart of a community and brings about the activity of a community in relation to him; thus it will be evident that *the doctrine of God is to be grasped and taught only as a doctrine of religion.*[104]

It is not the task of philosophy (or religion) to produce the content of religion, the theological object. "That would be like trying to introduce spirit into a dog by letting it see spiritual creations, or eat witty remarks ... or like trying to make a blind person see by telling him about colors."[105] The theological object cannot be produced by philosophy or religion because it "exists solely through itself and for its own sake. It is something absolute, self-sufficient, unconditioned, independent, free, as well as being the supreme end unto itself."[106] Furthermore, philosophy must presuppose religion: "there may be a religion without philosophy, but there cannot be philosophy without religion because philosophy includes religion within it."[107] However, for Hegel philosophy and religion are not opposed: he rejects double truth theories. An opposition between philosophy and religion would be symptomatic of the philosophies of finitude based on the understanding. But for Hegel speculative philosophy and religion are not exclusive. The philosophy of religion deals with the God who makes Godself the counterpart and spirit of a community.

Hegel's philosophy of religion is structured by a correlation between the human and the divine in which both are irreducible and yet related. This correlation means that "The principle by which God is defined for human beings is also the principle for how humanity defines itself inwardly, or for humanity in its own spirit. An inferior god or a nature god has inferior, natural and unfree human beings as its correlates. The pure concept of God or the spiritual God has as its correlate spirit that is free and spiritual, that actually knows God."[108] In this correlation between the divine and the human, Hegel is evidently claiming that in spite of the ontological difference, there is a common or shared principle: a God who is self-determining has as his correlate a free self-determining human being. This suggests that the divine and the human are correlated here in terms of a mutual self-recognition in other.

Does Hegel intend to assert that the divine–human correlation is like an intersubjective relation of mutual recognition? Yes and no. We have seen that mutual recognition is structured by reciprocity, and reciprocity presupposes not merely the freedom and independence of the parties but also that they are coequal and on the same level. Although the divine–human relation is mutual, this mutuality is qualified by the finite–infinite relation in which the transition from finite to infinite is ultimately grounded in the infinite itself. Reconciliation is a human need, not a simple human accomplishment. Hence, if it is to be actual, reconciliation must come to humans, and it is so celebrated in the cultus.

Further, Hegel thinks that finitude is a self-contradictory nullity: the being as such of finite things is to have the germ of their decease within themselves: the hour of their birth is the hour of their death.[109] This self-cancellation of finitude in its ontological indigence is reflected in and constitutive of religion and religious praxis. Sacrifice, including self-sacrifice, is the praxis of the self-sublation of finitude. For Hegel, religious praxis has ontological import, to wit, the nonbeing of the finite is the infinite. This does not mean simply that the finite has to die in order that the infinite can live, but that the finite in its living *and* dying is an ideal moment in the infinite process of self-diremption and return. With these important qualifications, the divine–human correlation is like mutual recognition, namely, a self-recognition in other and a being at home with self in another.[110]

Consider for example the Göschel aphorisms cited by Hegel: "God is God only insofar as he knows himself; his self-knowledge is further a self-consciousness in man and man's knowledge of God, which proceeds to man's self-knowledge in God."[111] Or in an alternative formulation in the *Philosophy of Religion*: "*God* knows himself in humanity, and human beings, to the extent that they know themselves as spirit and in their truth, know themselves in God. This is the concept of religion, that God knows himself in spirit and spirit knows itself in God."[112] Evidently Hegel is claiming that the divine–human relation, although not an 'ordinary' intersubjective relationship between equals, is nevertheless not unlike the structure of reciprocal-mutual recognition, in which being-for-self and being-for-other coincide in freedom. Thus the highest freedom and independence of human autonomy (being-for-self) and the highest dependence on another (being-for-other) coincide in theonomy. On both levels this coincidence is love. As love, God initiates an asymmetrical relation of reciprocity between God and humans. Here Hegel agrees with Spinoza that the love of humans for God is grounded in and enabled by God's love. Recall that love's asymmetry is the antithesis of mastery, lordship, and coercion. Religion in its consummate form is not merely self-knowledge in other; such self-knowledge in other is a relation of love and freedom: "This is also the meaning of the expression that God is love, i.e., knowing himself in an other of himself."[113] Love as the reunion of the separate, is not the principle of subjugation through power, coercion, and domination, but of reconciliation, liberation and freedom. God's love is the objective foundation of reconciliation and the presupposition of the human appropriation of reconciliation.[114]

These remarks show that the divine–human mediation is a complex dialectical one, at once intrasubjective and intersubjective. It is not to be understood in a one-sided, merely subjective way such that God is merely represented as a loving subject by the human side, but rather "the mediation is equally an objective mediation of God within himself."[115] Although God is not a being nor on the same ontological level as human finitude, God nevertheless divests and incarnates Godself, and incarnation means that the divine is not other than the human.[116] The philosophical expression of these claims is Hegel's doctrine of the true infinite, to wit, that the finite and infinite are not opposed, but identical in their differences and different in their identity. It is the doctrine of the true infinite that also distinguishes Hegel's position from Spinoza's *intellectualis amor dei*.

The true infinite is the union of finite and infinite in and through a process of dialectical mediation that involves both negation and negation of negation, or affirmation. On the side of God, Hegel interprets this double negation through the doctrines of the incarnation, the death of God, and his resurrection as spirit of the community. The incarnation involves a double kenosis: the self-divestment of the abstract substance devoid of self, and the self-divestment of the God-man in the form of a servant obedient to the point of death.[117] These double divestments constitute Hegel's theological interpretation of the death of God. The union of God and death in this supreme act of reconciling love is the central speculative intuition of Hegel's system.[118] Suffering and negation are 'in' God, part of God's life as love. However, the death of God is not final; rather it is a determinate first negation. Thus the death of God is rather the death of death, because God maintains godself in utter opposition. In this negation of negation, God is resurrected and transformed as Spirit in its community.

There is also a double negation of the human side of the true infinite, that is, the self-sublation of finitude. Hegel discusses this self-sublation in a passage in the 1824 *Lectures on the Philosophy of Religion* that is a commentary on the doctrine of the true infinite in the *Logic*. Again Hegel criticizes the Kantian position on the postulates for setting up an ideal in such a way that it is unattainable, and thus perpetuates a leveled, finitized infinite.[119] But if for Kant the infinite is continually deferred and never attained, the corollary of Kant's doctrine is that finitude itself is taken as absolute, a final irrevocable limit. This absolute finitude is the highest standpoint within reflection: it generates the spurious infinity. Having negated everything, and reduced all determinations to vanity,

> there remains this vanity itself, which does not vanish but still maintains itself. This acme
> of finitude ... has the semblance of renouncing the finite, but still maintains finitude as
> such even in the renunciation. [It is] pure thought as the absolute power of negativity. This
> standpoint that ... has dissolved all determinations – the self, the I that has arrived at
> absolute identity – is of the highest importance. It is the power of negativity which still
> maintains itself as the I, which only maintains itself by giving up all finitude, yet still
> retains (as its own self) this finitude and expresses it as infinity, as the sole affirmative.[120]

This subjectivity is absolute finitude. Absolute finitude is self-contradictory, for it both transcends all finitude and nevertheless perpetuates it. Such finitude is "the *negation as fixed in itself*, and it therefore stands in abrupt contrast to its affirmative."[121] Indeed, absolute finitude "is the refusal to let itself be brought affirmatively to its affirmative, to the infinite, and to let itself be united with it. Finitude is therefore posited as inseparable from its nothing, and is thereby cut off from all reconciliation with its other. ... The understanding persists in this *sadness of finitude* by making non-being ... imperishable and absolute."[122] As the highest level of reflection and the consummation of modernity and Enlightenment, this absolute self-sufficient finitude pushed to its peak of autonomy and independence is always on the verge of turning into evil.[123] This is not authentic religion but its perversion into idolatry and atheism. Given its refusal of reconciliation, no genuine religion is possible.[124]

In genuine religion this absolute finitude (negation) is itself negated, given up, surrendered, let go. Hegel writes: "This finitude, this I as finite, is a nullity which must be given up."[125] Such self-sacrifice, letting go, and self-transformation are constitutive of the religious standpoint and religious praxis, which Hegel describes as follows:

> I must recognize something objective, which is actual being in and for itself, which does
> indeed count as true for me, which is recognized as the affirmative posited for me; some-
> thing in which I am negated as this I, but in which at the same time I am contained as free
> and by which my freedom is maintained. ... But this is none other than the standpoint of
> thinking reason generally, and religion itself is this activity. ... in my recognition of [the]
> object, the universal, I do renounce my finitude. ... The universal counts for me as essence.
> ... this is the concrete, true relationship of the subjective I in religion, in which God, the
> absolute ... is the affirmative."[126]

Hegel describes here the achievement of the objective truth of finitude in and through a divine–human praxis, wherein our own nullity becomes manifest to us, but only as this nullity is itself negated, transformed, enlarged and affirmed by virtue of our inclusion and membership in the universal community. The presupposition of religious praxis "is that God alone is true actuality, that insofar as I have actuality I have it only in God. Since God alone is actuality, I should have my truth and actuality in God. That is the foundation of the cultus."[127] The cultus process of self-sublation and self-overcoming is like the consummation of the process of mutual recognition. The cultus is the recognitive, communal form of reconciliation. Here the human individual participates as a member of the spiritual community in which God is the affirmative objective foundation of reconciliation. The intersubjective mutual recognition between those who practice forgiveness is grounded in the cultus structure of the true infinite:

> The word of reconciliation is the objectively existent spirit, which beholds the pure knowledge of itself qua universal essence in its opposite ... a reciprocal recognition which is the absolute spirit. ... The reconciling 'Yes' in which the two I's let go of their opposed existence ... is God manifested in the midst of those who know themselves in pure knowledge."[128]

Included in that word of reconciliation, the reconciling 'Yes,' although not necessarily explicitly expressed, is the affirmation: "It is not the finite that is real, but the infinite."[129]

Hegel's concept of the true infinite is both indebted to and significantly different from Spinoza's. Hegel agrees with Spinoza that the starting point of both speculative philosophy and religion is the negation of finitude in the true infinite:

> When one begins to philosophize one must first become a Spinozist. For ... when we begin to philosophize, we must commence by bathing ourselves in the ether of the one substance, in which everything that we have taken as true disappears. This negation of all that is particular, to which every philosophy must have come, is the liberation of the mind and its absolute foundation.[130]

Kant and the philosophies of finitude, which issue "an injunction never to forget the absoluteness of the subject in every rational cognition,"[131] refuse to take this bath. For them "a denial of God seems so much more intelligible than a denial of the world."[132] They achieve not a true liberation but only the sadness of finitude, the negation fixed in itself; this is why their accounts of love, freedom, recognition, religion, and philosophy are one-sided and unsatisfactory. Second, Hegel agrees with Spinoza that the basis of the transition from finite to infinite can only be the infinite itself, as Spinoza asserts in his doctrine of the *amor intellectualis dei*. Reconciliation must come to humans rather than be produced or invented by them: the love of humans for God is included and grounded in the love of God for Godself. However, Hegel criticizes Spinoza's abstract substance for being the abyss of all determinations, including finitude, personality, and love itself.[133] Spinoza defrauds finitude and the difference of their due.[134] Spinoza's metaphysics of absolute substance is neither consistent with nor supportive of his doctrine of love, especially when we consider Hegel's insistence that love is essentially intersubjective and that self-love is a meaningless concept.

Hegel agrees with Spinoza that God's love is the foundation of human freedom and love, such that the highest human freedom and independence consists in knowing oneself as loved by God. Although Spinoza is right about God's love, Spinoza's metaphysics culminates (in Hegel's view) in a monist concept of substance that renders all determinacy external to substance (all determination is negation). Spinoza is not an atheist because he recognizes God alone as what truly is. But he conceives God only as abstract substance, and this lacks the principle of subjectivity, individuality, and personhood. Although substance is an essential stage in the development of the Idea, "it is ... only the idea in the still restricted form of necessity."[135] Spinoza's metaphysics of absolute substance undermines all distinctions in God and as impersonal fate, tends to undermine both freedom and love. Thus Spinoza's claims concerning the *amor intellectualis dei* are without foundation or expression in his concept of substance.

In contrast, the Christian doctrine of the trinity, with its immanent distinctions in God, corrects Spinoza's monism and makes the concept of God as love more plausible. Simply put, the immanent ontological distinctions mean that God negates Godself and becomes other as God's son, and God as spirit negates the negation and as love reconciles while preserving those distinctions. This immanent or ontological trinity means that God is not simply substance but also *subject*, and that God does not first become spirit or personal through human recognition, but rather is already personal and love in Godself. Divine personhood is a condition of God entering into personal–spiritual relations with what is other than God. It is also the condition of possibility of reconciliation: God is love, the conception of which is consummated in God's triune mode of being, the objective foundation and condition of divine–human reconciliation.

The latter reconciliation is the domain of the economic or inclusive trinity. Reconciliation underlies Hegel's analysis of Christianity as a religion of consolation:

> The Christian religion should be considered as the religion of consolation [*Trost*] and indeed, absolute consolation. ... Christianity asserts the doctrine that God wills that all humans should be saved [1 Timothy 2.4] and that means that subjectivity possesses an infinite value. More precisely ... the consoling power of the Christian religion consists in the fact that God himself is known as absolute subjectivity, and this subjectivity contains the moment of particularity within itself. Hence our particularity too, is recognized to be something that is not just to be abstractly negated; it must at the same time be preserved. ... The Christian God ... is not merely known, but utterly self-knowing, and not a merely imaginary personality, but rather the absolutely actual one.[136]

Since God is person, that is, spirit, to be related to God is not heteronomy or the death of one's freedom and personality but their condition. For Hegel human freedom is not simply autonomy, but theonomy. Autonomy is a drive towards independence and separation; autonomous freedom is a good that when absolutized becomes evil, that is, seeks mastery and lordship over others. In contrast, reconciliation points to a mediated freedom or theonomy. In the true infinite "in its passing into an other, something only comes together with itself; and this relation to itself in the passing and in the other is *genuine infinity*."[137] Divine personhood and divine love are reciprocally implicating concepts of the theological foundation of reconciliation. They correspond with and ground human personality, freedom, and liberation. And so we conclude this essay as we began it, with the concept of God's love as bestowing the gift of reconciliation, of a theonomous freedom, a being at home with self in another. Hegel puts the point like this:

> When we say "God is love," we are saying something very great and true. But it would be senseless to grasp this saying in a simple-minded way ... without analyzing what love is.

For love is a distinguishing of two, who nevertheless are absolutely not distinguished from each other. The consciousness of the identity of the two – to be outside myself and in the other – this is love. I have my self-consciousness not in myself, but in this other – and I *am* only because I have peace with myself. If I did not have such peace, then I would be a contradiction that falls to pieces.[138]

I believe that Hegel's interpretation of the love of God is absolute or objective idealism. This means that God is personal and that the finite has the ontological status of ideality, being relative to and a moment within the true infinite. The doctrine of God as true infinite is a doctrine of divine–human community, a social ontology – in theological terms, Spirit, the inclusive trinity. If absolute or objective idealism is metaphysics, then these claims are metaphysical, but it should be recalled that Hegel defines metaphysics simply as objective thought, and the prime, though by no means exclusive, example of objective thought is the concept of God – "that which can only be thought as existing."[139] This is not a precritical or dogmatic metaphysics of the sort that Hegel criticizes.[140] Nor can it be whittled down to a philosophy of finitude. Recall Hegel's outburst, directed at the reflective philosophies of finitude, to wit, Kant, Fichte, and Jacobi: truth is in a fine mess when all metaphysics and philosophy are mere things of the past, and the only philosophy that counts is no philosophy at all! Hegel intends his position to be an alternative to that. It is one that integrates form and content, method and ontology, in what he calls the realized concept, which he tells us includes the positedness of its determinations. "It is the idea which is the absolute first (in the method), and, as the [realized] end, is only the vanishing of the appearance that the beginning [of the logic] is something immediate, and that the idea is merely a [derivative] result. It is the recognition that the idea is the single totality."[141] Religion is an essential domain of absolute spirit because it makes explicit the reversal, both of perspective and in the order of things, wherein human beings do not apprehend themselves as the subject to which all objects are relative but instead find themselves measured and recognized as spirit. As thus reconciled, they grasp themselves as relative to and members within a larger whole, the ultimate community – the true infinite.

Notes

1   Positivism suppresses the fundamental problems of reason. See Edmund Husserl, *The Crisis of European Sciences and Transcendental Phenomenology*, trans. David Carr (Evanston, Ill.: Northwestern University Press, 1970).

2   G.W.F. Hegel, *Lectures on the Philosophy of Religion*, ed. Peter C. Hodgson, trans. Robert F. Brown, Peter C. Hodgson, and J. Michael Stewart (Berkeley: University of California Press, 1984), Vol. 1:86. Hereafter cited as LPR, followed by volume number and page number (e.g., LPR, 1:86).

3   LPR, 1:87.

4   LPR, 1:88.

5   See Frederick C. Beiser, "The Puzzling Hegel Renaissance," in *The Cambridge Companion to Hegel and Nineteenth Century Philosophy*, ed. Frederick C. Beiser (New York: Cambridge University Press, 2008). See also Alan W. Wood, *Hegel's Ethical Thought* (New York: Cambridge University Press, 1990), 4–8.

6   Charles Taylor, *Hegel* (Cambridge: Cambridge University Press, 1975), 538. For Hegel's critique of metaphysics, inclusive of theology, see his analysis of the first attitude of thought toward objectivity in *Encyclopedia Logic*, sections 26–36.

7   Robert Pippin, *Hegel's Idealism* (New York: Cambridge University Press, 1989), 7.

8   Robert Pippin, "What Is the Question for Which Recognition Is the Answer?" *European Journal of Philosophy*, 8:2 (2000), 161.

9   The further irony is that Hegel accuses the theologians of his own day of abandoning or surrendering the profound speculative truth of the theological tradition to such a degree that philosophy now believes itself excused from having to take theology – the God question – seriously. In such a cognitive wasteland, it is now Hegelian philosophy that must defend and conserve that ancient theological truth against its latter-day cultured philosophical and theological despisers. See LPR, 1, the three introductions (1821, 1824, 1827).

10 See Beiser, "The Puzzling Hegel Renaissance."

11 Stephen Crites, *Dialectic and Gospel in the Development of Hegel's Thinking* (University Park: Pennsylvania State University Press, 1998), 197, 219, 245.

12 G.W.F. Hegel, *Faith and Knowledge*, trans. Watler Cerf and H. S. Harris (Albany: SUNY Press, 1977), 94f. Hereafter cited as FK. It is worth noting that the last work that occupied Hegel before his death was a book on the "Proofs for the Existence of God." He was at work revising his lectures on the proofs as a book for which he had signed a contract when death claimed him. See G.W.F. Hegel, *Lectures on the Proofs of the Existence of God,* trans. Peter C. Hodgson (Oxford: Oxford University Press), 2007.

13 Friedrich Schleiermacher, *The Christian Faith,* trans. H. R. Mackintosh, J. S. Stewart, and B. A. Gerrish (Edinburgh: T&T Clark Publishers, 1999), §§4–5. Hegel's criticism of Schleiermacher is carried out in his foreword to Hinrichs's *Religionsphilosophie* (1822) and his *Lectures on the Philosophy of Religion* (1824).

14 G.W.F. Hegel, *The Encyclopedia Logic,* trans. T. F. Garaets, W. A. Suchting, and H. S. Harris (Indianapolis, Ind.: Hackett Publishing Company, 1991), §85. Hereafter cited as EL. See also LPR, 1:230.

15 LPR, 1:318: religion is "the self-consciousness of absolute spirit." See also 318n.

16 LPR, 3:125.

17 G.W.F. Hegel, *Early Theological Writings,* trans. T. M. Knox (Chicago: University of Chicago Press, 1948), 278. Hereafter cited as ETW.

18 ETW, 183.

19 For these distinctions, see Paul Tillich, *Love, Power, and Justice: Ontological Analysis and Ethical Applications* (Oxford: Oxford University Press, 1954). Tillich's discussion is heavily indebted to *Hegel's Early Theological Writings*.

20 For a discussion of positivity, see Georg Lukács, *The Young Hegel: Studies in the Relations between Dialectics and Economics,* trans. Rodney Livingstone (Cambridge, Mass.: MIT Press, 1976), 1–90.

21 ETW, 214; G.W.F. Hegel, *Der Geist des Christentums,* in Band 1 of *Werke in zwanzig Bänden,* ed. Eva Moldenhauer and Karl Markus Michel (Frankfurt am Main: Suhrkamp, 1970), 326.

22 ETW, 227.

23 Hegel here interprets Judaism as a religion of heteronomy and mastery; god as other than the world is its master; similarly, Abraham is related to the world and others only in the mode of mastery (ETW, 187) and this breaks the bonds of communal life and love (185). (In his later *Lectures on the Philosophy of Religion,* Hegel substantially revised this reading of Judaism.) Further, austere Kantian autonomous self-legislation in the concept of universal duty is interpreted by Hegel as an internalized master–slave, and thus as a form of heteronomy (ETW, 211; 214).

24 ETW, 226.
25 ETW, 229. Hegel's observation anticipates Nietzsche.
26 ETW, 212.
27 Possibly following the model of Schiller's *Spieltrieb* in contrast to the *Formtrieb* and *Stofftrieb*. See J.C.F. Schiller, *Letters on the Aesthetic Education of Man*, trans. Elizabeth M. Wilkinson and L. A. Willoughby (Oxford: Oxford University Press, 1982).
28 ETW, 213; SK, 1:325.
29 ETW, 212; SK, 1:324.
30 ETW, 229.
31 Ibid.
32 Ibid.
33 ETW, 230.
34 Ibid.
35 ETW, 232
36 Ibid.
37 ETW, 215.
38 Ibid.
39 ETW, 218.
40 ETW, 216.
41 ETW, 236.
42 ETW, 236–237.
43 Hegel anticipates the dynamics of nonviolence and nonviolent resistance to coercion and oppression.
44 ETW, 238: "For the sinner is more than a sin existent, a trespass possessed of personality; he is a human being, trespass and fate are in him. He can return to himself again, and if he does so, trespass and fate are under him."
45 ETW, 232.
46 ETW, 239
47 ETW, 241
48 ETW, 221, 225, 235, 236, 237
49 ETW, 246, 244.
50 ETW, 216
51 ETW, 247.
52 Ibid.
53 Ibid., translation corrected. For a critique of objectification, see Martin Buber's distinction between "I–Thou" and "I–It" in *I and Thou*, trans. Walter Kaufmann (New York: Scribner, 1970).
54 ETW, Fragment on Love, 305; translation corrected.
55 ETW, 247. I follow Paul Tillich, who corrects the prejudice that love is merely an emotion by pointing to figures in the history of philosophy and theology who develop an ontological conception of love (Empedocles, Plato, Aristotle, Augustine, and Spinoza). Spinoza's concept of the *amor intellectualis dei* grounds human love in the love with which God loves Godself. Tillich rightly observes that Hegel belongs in this tradition (*Love, Power, and Justice*, p. 4). That this is so is clear in Hegel's *Encyclopedia Logic*, §158, *Zusatz*, where he refers to Spinoza's intellectual love of God as the foundation of human freedom and love. Here in the ETW, Hegel's focus is rather on the concept of God as spirit of his community, but this is no less an ontological conception of God as love.
56 ETW, 278.
57 Ibid.
58 ETW, 247. Emphasis added.

59 Tillich, *Love, Power, and Justice* (pp. 6ff), appropriates and expounds Hegel's argument without acknowledging it.

60 ETW, "Fragment on Love," 305, translation corrected.

61 ETW, "Fragment on Love and Religion"; SK, 1:244.

62 Ibid. Life (in the subject) senses life (in the object).

63 Ibid., 307. This analysis implies that deconstructive readings of Hegel that identify love with identity and with the fusion of lover and beloved are erroneous. For as Hegel makes clear: (1) in love the other does remain but no longer as separate, i.e., alienated. Instead, the beloved is one with us. (2) Love does not objectify its object (unlike theory and practice). Thus love renounces and is beyond the active/passive postures of control, coercion, and domination constitutive of master and slave.

64 Johann Gottlieb Fichte, *Foundations of Natural Right*, ed. Frederick Neuhouser, trans. Michael Baur (Cambridge: Cambridge University Press, 2001). Hereafter cited as FNR, German edition and pagination as GNR.

65 FNR, 79; GNR, 85.

66 FNR, 45; GNR, 48.

67 FNR, 42; GNR, 45

68 FNR, p. 10; GNR, 10.

69 FNR, 11–12; GNR, 11.

70 FNR, 79; GNR, 85. Emphasis added.

71 FNR, section 13. See Ludwig Siep, *Anerkennung als Prinzip der praktischen Philosophie* (Freiburg: Alber, 1978).

72 FNR, 127; GNR, 142. Fichte writes, "if an arrangement could be found that would operate with mechanical necessity to guarantee that any action contrary to right would result in the opposite of its intended end, such an arrangement would necessitate the will to will only what is rightful; such an arrangement would re-establish security after honesty and trust have been lost, and it would render the good will superfluous for the realization of external right. ... An arrangement of [this] kind ... is called a law of coercion."

73 G.W.F. Hegel, *Lectures on Natural Right 1817–1818*, trans. J. Michael Stewart and Peter C. Hodgson (Berkeley: University of California Press, 1995), 212. Although Hegel concedes that some police supervision may be inevitable, he emphasizes that the purpose of such supervision "is that public life should be free" (ibid.).

74 G.W.F. Hegel, *Natural Law*, trans. T. M. Knox (Philadelphia: University of Pennsylvania Press, 1975), 85; SK, 2:471.

75 G.W.F. Hegel, *The Difference between Fichte's and Schelling's System of Philosophy*, trans. H. S. Harris and Walter Cerf (Albany: SUNY Press 1977), 148–149.

76 Ibid., 145.

77 See Hegel's *Encyclopedia Philosophy of Spirit*, §502.

78 G.W.F. Hegel, *Phenomenology of Spirit*, trans. A. V. Miller (Oxford: Oxford University Press, 1977), §§183–184. Hereafter cited as PhS. I agree with Paul Redding when he writes "'syllogism' simply is the logical term for the structure of recognition." See *Hegel's Hermeneutics* (Ithaca, N.Y.: Cornell University Press, 1996), 156n20.

79 *Hegel's Science of Logic*, trans. A. V. Miller (Atlantic Highlands, N.J.: Humanities Press 1969), 711. Hereafter cited as SL. This is why in Hegel's view, the windowless monad is an inadequate, defective conception. As self-enclosed, the monad is indifferent to its relations and determinacies. See SL, 714.

80 See Hegel, SL, 734–754.

81 PhS, §670.

82 ETW, 236–237.

83 ETW, 246.

84   Martha Nussbaum, *The Fragility of Goodness: Luck and Ethics in Greek Tragedy and Philosophy* (Cambridge: Cambridge University Press, 1986), 351–352.

85   ETW, 278.

86   EL, §95, R

87   According to Hegel, Fichte fails to appreciate, much less develop the affirmative aspect of community and recognition, and fails to attain the level of love as the principle of reconciliation, and of justice and ethical life. For Hegel, community is not the highest tyranny, but the highest freedom. The members of a love union grasp themselves as relative to that union. This grasping of oneself as relative to a higher union and totality has ontological implications, to wit, the ideality of the finite (EL, §95R). For an account of ideality as an ontological doctrine, see Stephen Houlgate, *The Opening of Hegel's Logic: From Being to Infinity* (West Lafayette, Ind.: Purdue University Press, 2005), 428–432, and Robert R. Williams, "Hegel's True Infinite," in *Tragedy, Recognition and the Death of God: Studies in Hegel and Nietzsche* (forthcoming).

88   Crites, *Dialectic and Gospel in the Development of Hegel's Thinking*, 34–51, 162–166. Crites is not the first or the only commentator to make this important point; see also Klaus Düsing, "Die Rezeption der Kantischen Postulatenlehre in den frühen philosophischen Entwürfen Schellings und Hegels," from *Das Älteste Systemprogramm: Studien zur Frühgeschichte des deutschen Idealismus*, Hegel-Studien 9, hrsg. Rüdiger Bubner (Bonn: Bouvier, 1973).

89   Cf. Kant's reply to Thomas Wizenmann's objection that it is fallacious to reason from a subjective need to the existence of the object that satisfies that need. Kant's reply is to distinguish the need of inclination that is subjective from the need of reason arising from the requirement of moral law, which is supposedly objective. That is the claim that interests Schelling and Hegel. But Kant here forgets his own point that moral necessity remains subjective. Thus not only does he not resolve Wizenmann's objection, he also flirts with a version of the double truth theory, or a "two reasons" theory. See Immanuel Kant, *Critique of Practical Reason*, trans. Lewis White Beck (Upper Saddle River, N.J.: Prentice-Hall 1992), 151n.

90   In *All or Nothing: Systematicity, Transcendental Arguments, and Skepticism in German Idealism* (Harvard University Press, 2005, 326–327), Paul Franks interprets early German Idealism as a continuation of Kant's postulates of reason. This is a correct reading of the Earliest System Program of German Idealism. However, Franks' discussion makes it appear as if German Idealism is simply a continuation of Kant's postulates, and not also a critique of Kant's postulates. For this side of the story, see Crites, *Dialectic and Gospel in the Development of Hegel's Thinking*, 34–51, 162–166. Franks' restricted account overlooks that in *Glauben und Wissen*, Hegel subjected the Kantian philosophy of the postulates to the criticism that it remains a subjective idealism and is incoherent because it fails to suspend its subjective form. Franks' reconstruction of German Idealism as a philosophy of postulates does not address Hegel's critique. Thus it appears to continue the "universal approval" of the subjective interpretation of the postulates that Hegel criticizes and that Hegel believes leaves philosophy not with all but with nothing.

91   FK, 95–96.

92   In the *Phenomenology of Spirit*, Hegel points out not only that the achievement of moral perfection would entail the disappearance of the 'ought' constitutive of moral consciousness, but also that the moral vision of the world is pervaded by a fundamental contradiction that it thoughtlessly evades by dissembling. Morality dissembles about God or the holy being that guarantees the connection of virtue with happiness "for that alone it holds to be sacred which it has itself made sacred. ... It is therefore just as little in earnest about the holiness of this other being. ... Such a purely moral being is ... a dissemblance of the facts

411

and has to be given up." PhS, §§626, 629. For Hegel, as for Nietzsche, the moral God is dead.

93 Crites, *Dialectic and Gospel in the Development of Hegel's Thinking*, 163.

94 FK, 60–61.

95 FK, 62, 64, 65; G.W.F. Hegel, *Glauben und Wissen*, in Band 2 of *Werke in zwanzig Bänden*, ed. Eva Moldenhauer and Karl Markus Michel (Frankfurt am Main: Suhrkamp, 1970),295, 298, 299.

96 Hegel, *Lectures on the Proofs of the Existence of God*, 66.

97 Hegel's term is *die schlechte Unendlichkeit*. *Schlecht* derives from *schlichten*, which means to level, to bring down. An infinite that is leveled is thus brought down to the finite; it is "fini-tized" *(verendlicht)*. See G.W.F. Hegel, *Wissenschaft der Logik* in Band 5 of *Werke in zwanzig Bänden*, ed. Eva Moldenhauer and Karl Markus Michel (Frankfurt am Main: Suhrkamp, 1970), 149. Hereafter cited as WL, followed by volume number and page number (SL, 137). Thus the *schlechte Unendlichkeit* is the *verendlichte Unendlichkeit* because as Hegel observes, it is a mere *Sollen* or 'ought to be'; it is opposed to the finite as a beyond. Fixed in this determination of the beyond-the-finite, it is not only not actual, it is not supposed to be actual and never meant to be actual (WL, 5:156; SL, 142).

98 SL, 149. The philosophy of finitude treats finitude as merely affirmative, and not as a nullity subject to inner collapse and self-sublation; hence it perpetuates the finite–infinite dualism it claims to overcome.

99 FK, 68. Emphasis added.

100 FK, 94.

101 On this issue, see the so-called second form of Anselm's argument in *Proslogion* 3. See also *The Many Faced Argument: Recent Studies on the Ontological Argument for the Existence of God*, ed. John Hick and Arthur McGill (New York: Macmillan, 1967), especially part II C.

102 LPR, 1:130 (1824).

103 Hegel, EL, §158Z; cf. Hegel's comments in the second preface to his *Encyclopedia Logic* on how to read Spinoza as a moral philosopher against the grain of his metaphysics of sub-stance (EL, 10).

104 LPR, 1:116. Emphasis added.

105 LPR, 1:89 (1821).

106 LPR, 1:84 (1821).

107 Hegel, EL, 1827 Preface, op. cit., 12.

108 LPR, 2:515 (1827).

109 SL, 129.

110 These terms also constitute for Hegel the meaning of freedom – *bei sich im anderen zu sein*.

111 G.W.F. Hegel, *Philosophy of Spirit* (1830), §564. Rendered into English as *Hegel's Philosophy of Mind*, trans. William Wallace (Oxford: Oxford University Press, 1971). For Hegel's 1829 review of Göschel's Aphorisms, cf. *Miscellaneous Writings of G.W.F. Hegel*, ed. Jon Stewart (Evanston, Ill.: Northwestern University Press, 2002), 401–429.

112 LPR, 1:465. (1831)

113 LPR, 1:465.

114 The appropriation is not a continuation of a struggle for recognition, nor does it imply a deferral of reconciliation. Hegel indicates that the last word is not the perennial struggle as in the Kantian philosophy, in which strife is unending and resolution is put off to infinity so that we must take our stand on the 'ought.' Here the contradiction is resolved, i.e., in God, and thus forgiveness is possible, and evil can be undone (LPR, 3:234–235).

115 LPR, 2:253 (1824).

116 PhS, §759. In LPR, Hegel observes that incarnation is a religious–theological conception that is found in Hinduism, in the Greek religion of art, as well as in Christianity. It is in

reference to its doctrine of divine human unity that Christianity is the consummate religion.

117 PhS, §785.

118 LPR, 3:125.

119 LPR, 1:292.

120 LPR, 1:296.

121 SL, 129–130.

122 SL, 130. Emphasis added.

123 G.W.F. Hegel, *Elements of the Philosophy of Right*, ed. Allan W. Wood, trans. H. G. Nisbet (Cambridge: Cambridge University Press, 1991), §§135–140.

124 LPR, 1:300 (1824)

125 LPR, 1:301 (1824)

126 LPR, 1:302–307.

127 LPR, 1:444 (1827). Hegel explains that "In the cultus ... God is on one side, I am on the other, and the determination is the including, within my own self, of myself with God, the knowing of myself within God and of God within me" (LPR, 1:443). These 1827 formulations predate the Göschel aphorisms cited above.

128 PhS, §§670–671.

129 SL, 149.

130 G.W.F. Hegel, *Vorlesungen über die Geschichte der Philosophie*, in Band 20 of *Werke in zwanzig Bänden*, ed. Eva Moldenhauer and Karl Markus Michel (Frankfurt am Main: Suhrkamp, 1970), 165. The English translation is available in G.W.F. Hegel, vol. 3 of *Lectures on the History of Philosophy*, trans. Elizabeth S. Haldane and Frances H. Simson (New York: Humanities Press, 1963) 257.

131 FK, 64.

132 EL, §50R.

133 Hegel, *Vorlesungen über die Geschichte der Philosophie*, op. cit., 20:164.

134 EL, §151 Zusatz.

135 EL, §151Z.

136 EL, §147 Z. This is a theological reason why slavery disappeared from Europe. Cf. EL section 163Z.

137 EL, 95. Emphasis in original.

138 LPR, 3:276 (1827).

139 EL, §§24, 50, 51R.

140 See Hegel's discussion of the "First Attitude of Thought Towards Objectivity," EL, sections 26–36.

141 EL, §243R.

20

Hegel's Proofs of the Existence of God

PETER C. HODGSON

1. Hegel's Discussion of the Proofs

Hegel's treatment of what he calls "proofs of the existence of God" is found principally in the *Lectures on the Philosophy of Religion* (1821, 1824, 1827, 1831) and *Lectures on the Proofs of the Existence of God* (1829). At the same time, the topic of the proofs is closely related to the *Science of Logic* (1812–1813, 1816). As Hegel conceives it, the whole of logic corresponds formally to the proofs; the subtext of the logic is theo-logic, as the additions from student transcriptions of Hegel's lectures on logic and metaphysics bear witness.[1] The first part of the logic, the "objective logic," is concerned with the transition from being and essence to concept (or from reality to thought as an ideal ground) and comprises a form of the cosmological proof of God. The second part, the "subjective logic," shows how the concept determines itself to objectivity, posits itself as real, and releases itself into nature and finite spirit, which is the same as the transition from the concept of God to God's existence, actuality, and activity: the ontological proof.[2] These transitions constitute two movements of thought, from finite to infinite and infinite to finite. The finite passes over of itself into the infinite, for its being is the being of the infinite; and the infinite passes over of itself into the finite, for its drive is to objectify or actualize itself in its other and make this other its own. This twofold passage, which follows from the logical definition of finite and infinite, is at the heart of religion. Near the end of the *Science of Logic* Hegel announced his intention to write further on the proofs in order to respond to criticisms based on "logical formalism," and thus, "by establishing their true significance, to restore the fundamental thoughts of these proofs to their worth and dignity."[3]

In addition to Hegel's specific writings and lectures on the proofs, to which we shall attend below, the topic of the proofs is engaged in other writings and lectures as well, for example, the introduction to the *Encyclopedia of the Philosophical Sciences*,[4] and the discussion of Anselm, Descartes, and Kant in the *Lectures on the History of Philosophy*.[5] The principal locus for the treatment of the proofs, however, apart from the *Lectures on*

A Companion to Hegel, First Edition. Edited by Stephen Houlgate and Michael Baur.
© 2011 Blackwell Publishing Ltd. Published 2011 by Blackwell Publishing Ltd.

the Proofs of the Existence of God, is the *Lectures on the Philosophy of Religion*. In the lectures of 1821, 1824, and 1831, the proofs are taken up in relation to specific religions as comprising the latter's "abstract" or "metaphysical" concept of God. The cosmological proof, according to Hegel, is implicit in the so-called religions of nature (including Asian religions) as well as Judaism and Greek religion. The teleological proof is implicit in Roman religion (and, according to the 1831 lectures, Greek religion). The ontological proof is the unique insight of Christianity. In the lectures of 1827 all the proofs are gathered into a single section of "The Concept of Religion" on "Religious Knowledge as Elevation to God," a section that anticipates the separate lectures of 1829.[6]

In the summer semester of 1829 Hegel delivered sixteen lectures on proofs of the existence of God concurrently with lectures on logic, drawing attention to the connection between the topics in the first of the lectures on the proofs. These lectures cover only introductory matters (lectures 1–9) and the cosmological proof (lectures 10–16), and they seem to represent a partial first draft of a work on the existence of God that Hegel intended to publish, an intention foreclosed by his untimely death in 1831. His lecture manuscript of 1829 was appended to the *Werke* edition (1832) of the *Lectures on the Philosophy of Religion* by the editor, Philipp Marheineke, together with a fragment "On the Cosmological Proof," which most likely dates from the time Hegel was completing the *Science of Logic*, and transcriptions of sections on the teleological and ontological proofs from the 1831 philosophy of religion lectures. This material provides the content of the recently published volume, *Lectures on the Proofs of the Existence of God*.[7] Because it has been largely ignored by previous literature on the proofs, it serves, along with the philosophy of religion lectures, as the principal resource for the present chapter.

2.   On "Proof" and "Existence"

Hegel's frequent attention to this topic and his thwarted publication plans indicate the importance he ascribes to proofs of the existence of God. He also makes clear, however, that the terms "proof" and "existence" as applied to God are problematic, or at least require clarification. With regard to "proof" he makes several points. The first concerns the *relationship between proof and faith*. Proofs of the existence of God have arisen out of the necessity of satisfying thought and reason and of overcoming the potential conflict between faith and reason. Faith, he remarks, is the presupposition that lies at the basis of all thought, but in free thought the presupposition becomes a result that is grasped conceptually. Such thought or "proof" does not remain outside its object (God) but occupies itself with it, is the proper movement of its nature (*Proofs* 1, 38–43).[8] A related point is that proofs comprise *"the elevation of the human spirit to God"* and express this elevation for thought. The elevation, which as we shall see constitutes the very essence of religion, entails intuition, imagination, feeling, and cultic practices as well as thought, and it is rooted in and necessary to the very being of humans as spirit. The portrayal of this necessity is what we call "proof" (*Proofs* 1, 43–44). Without faith and without the elevation as an existential reality, there is no proof. With Anselm, Hegel seems to be saying that proof is a form of "faith seeking understanding."[9] Religious elevation is not first accomplished by philosophical proof; rather the latter reflects on, proves and probes what is going on in religion, namely, the elevation of the human spirit to God. However, proof as such is a purely rational activity that proceeds not from concrete experience but from abstract categories such as "contingency" and "necessity" (*Proofs* 10, 94–95).

The second point Hegel makes about proofs of God is that they are not merely a subjective procedure on our part but *the proper movement of the object in itself* – the object in this case being the elevation of the human spirit to God, which is at the same time the return of God to godself. There is a kind of proof that is merely subjective, whose activity and movement take place only within ourselves and are not the proper movement of the thing considered – for example, scientific, geometric, and algebraic proof, or the proof that involves an "indicating" (*Weisen*), the pointing to something in experience, such as historical proof. But this is not genuine movement, and with this kind of proof we are unable, therefore, to reach the infinite, eternal, divine (*Proofs* 2, 45–50). True or proper proof (*Beweis, Beweisen*) entails *mediation*; it does not simply indicate or point to something (*Weisen*); it is itself a movement or transition (*Be-weisen*).[10] Mediation involves a relationship between things, a third term vis-à-vis two distinct sides, a third that brings them together. Just this is what is going on in a syllogism, or proof. The mediation at work in the proofs of God is not to be understood simply in a subjective way; rather "the mediation is equally an objective mediation of God within godself, an internal mediation of God's own logic." Only if the mediation is contained in the divine idea itself does it become a necessary moment, an objective activity on the part of the concept itself (*LPR* 1:408, 414–416; quotation from 2:253).[11] The true proof is God's self-proof or self-mediation.

The third point concerns the *inappropriateness of making God an object of "proof"* if, as is customary, proof is taken in the subjective rather than objective sense. The procedure we follow in an ordinary demonstration is not a process of the thing itself; the mediation through which we pass and the mediation in the thing are separate. It is simply inappropriate to make God into a result dependent on prior assumptions or conditions. The finite cannot be a foundation on which the being of God is demonstrated, for God is the nonderivative, the presupposition rather than the result. Despite this criticism, the elevation of the human spirit to God is not vacuous, for it involves something that is universal in human consciousness. Stripped of the form of demonstration, the cosmological and teleological proofs are nothing more than descriptions of the elevation to God. However, as we shall see, the elevation sublates or reverses itself: it negates the finite and affirms the infinite, which is not simply one aspect, one side of a polarity, but the whole (*LPR* 1:417–419, 422–425).

Finally, Hegel specifies the *genre* of the proofs. They are to be properly understood not as *historical* (an appeal to the views of others), nor as based on *consensus* (the specious claim that all humans everywhere have believed in some sort of deity), but rather as *metaphysical* or *philosophical*. The first two sorts of proof do not yield conviction, which entails the self-recollecting or self-inwardizing of spirit within itself. What is required for conviction is the witness of the spirit, not of external authorities. Metaphysical proof is "the *witness* of the *thinking* spirit," and "the object with which it is concerned exists essentially in thought" (*Proofs* 6, 69–73). However, the concept of God in the *metaphysics of natural theology* (Christian Wolff, A. G. Baumgarten) is wholly indeterminate; this metaphysics begins with empty possibility, simple, featureless identity, and it treats the concept, existence, and attributes of God as separate and abstract topics (*Proofs* 7, 75–8). By contrast, the *speculative concept of God* grasps God as utterly concrete, an organic unity of determinate qualities – qualities that are "ideal," posited and contained in the one concept (*Proofs* 7, 78–81). Among other things what this means is that God is properly conceived not as a metaphysical object, a supreme being or entity, but as the organic whole or subject in which everything of nature and spirit subsists and is mirrored. *God* is the mirror, the *speculum* (as well as what *is* mirrored in the elevation of consciousness); and what we shall call the "speculative reversal" qualifies Hegel's entire approach to the proofs.

Hegel devotes much less attention to the term "existence" than to that of "proof." In speaking of the "existence" of God, he is essentially adopting traditional language. Normally he uses the term *Dasein* but also refers to God's *Sein* or *Existenz*.[12] None of these terms is really adequate to God. *Sein* ("being") in Hegel's philosophical lexicon designates sheer immediacy, presence to self, and is the emptiest category, whereas "God" (or "absolute spirit") is the fullest. *Dasein*, normally translated "existence," designates determinate, finite being, being-there (*Da-sein*); while *Existenz* refers to something that is grounded and conditioned, not essential.[13] God"s being is in no way an immediate, limited, finite, conditioned being. Thus instead of talking of God's "existence" (whether as *Dasein* or as *Existenz*), it would be better, Hegel suggests, to say, "God and his being, his actuality [*Wirklichkeit*] or objectivity [*Objektivität*]" (*LPR* 1:417). It would indeed reflect Hegel's intention more accurately to speak of "proofs of the actuality of God."[14] *Wirklichkeit* also has the advantage of suggesting that what is involved is God's *Wirksamkeit* or "activity": God is at work in the proofs; God is pure act. "Objectivity" means that God's actuality is not a projection of human consciousness but rather stands over against consciousness (it is a *Gegen-stand*) even as it is known by consciousness. However, the term customarily employed by Hegel is *Dasein* – in the title of the lectures on the proofs and elsewhere – and there is a specific sense in which it *is* appropriate, as we shall see in connection with the ontological proof, to refer to the *Dasein Gottes*. In any event, *Dasein*, *Wirklichkeit*, and *Objektivität* must not be conflated in translation or in an analysis of Hegel's arguments.

3. The Proofs, Religious Elevation, and the Communion of Spirit

We have seen that Hegel views the proofs (at least the cosmological and teleological proofs) as the rational expression of the elevation of the human spirit to God. This "elevation" (*Erhebung*) is essentially what religion is about, its *Sache* or content, knowledge of which is not a subjective operation but an exposition of an objective movement (*Proofs* 1, 43–44; 5, 63). The elevation is "the driving power within us." It is not our own self-projecting power but a negative power that is generated by the affirmative, overreaching power of the absolute (*Proofs* 15, 127–131).

Related to this concept of religious elevation is what Hegel describes as a "speculative" discussion of "the self-consciousness of God and of the relationship of God's self-knowing to God's knowing in and through the human spirit," or of "God's self-knowing in humanity and humanity's self-knowing in God." This discussion is properly a topic for theology, which is not part of a philosophical treatment of the proofs. Yet Hegel

417

PETER C. HODGSON

offers a theological excursus to make the point that it is God's very nature to communicate godself to humanity. Christianity "teaches that God brought godself down to humanity, even to the form of a servant, that God revealed godself to humans; and that, consequently, far from *grudging* humanity what is ... highest, God laid upon humans with that very revelation the highest duty that they should *know God*." A related philosophical principle is that "it is the nature of spirit to remain fully in possession of itself while giving another a share of its possession." The hindrance in knowing God is not on God's part but ours, owing to caprice and false humility, an arbitrary insistence that the limits of human reason prevent knowledge of the infinite. "The more precise point is that it is not the so-called human reason with its limits that knows God, but rather the Spirit of God in humanity; ... it is God's self-consciousness that knows itself in the knowing of humanity" (*Proofs* 5, 64–68).

Thus the human elevation is generated by the divine descent; it is God's self-revelation or self-communication that is at work in humanity's knowledge of God. This is the speculative insight. Hegel returns to it toward the end of the lectures where he speaks of "the community and communion [*Gemeinschaft*] of God and humanity with each other," which is "a communion of spirit with spirit." "The spirit of humanity – to know God – is simply God's Spirit itself" (*Proofs* 14, 126). The communion of spirit with spirit is a theological version of the speculative concept of the relations between finite and infinite. The "true infinite" according to Hegel is not opposed to the finite but overreaches and includes finitude within itself.[15] What results is not "identity" but "organic life within God" (*LPR* 3:351). This is the condition of possibility for there being proofs of God.

4. The Multiplicity of Proofs and the One God

Hegel notes the historical fact of an empirical multiplicity of proofs (*Proofs* 8, 82–87). We should not be surprised by this diversity since with human interiority (to which alone God is present) there are "an infinite number of starting points from which it is possible and indeed necessary to pass over to God." Yet at the same time there is *one* God. The many predicates or attributes ascribed to God from the diverse starting points must not be separated in the divine subject as independent materials. Rather the multiple determinations are reduced to one in a higher unity, either the unity of an actual subject, the personal One (*der Eine*), or the unity of substance, the neuter One (*das Eine*). Both forms of unity are valid; God is both subject and substance.

Hegel proposes a reduction of the many proofs to three principal forms. While Hegel's argument is logical, the proofs arrived at are just the ones that have come to the fore in the history of religions and philosophy. The three proofs arise from two basic starting points: (1) the finite, which displays two distinctive aspects, namely the contingency of world events and the purposive connection of things; (2) the infinite, the concept of God (*Proofs* 8, 84). God is shown to be absolute necessity (causality), wisdom (freedom), and subjectivity (spirituality). The true proof arrives at one result, and thus it can be considered one proof that moves dialectically through three stages.

"One set of proofs passes over from *being* to the *thought* of God, or more precisely from determinate being [*bestimmtes Sein*] to genuine being [*wahrhaftes Sein*] as the being

418

of God; the other passes over from the *thought* of God, the truth in itself, to the *being* of this truth" (*Proofs* 9, 88). This distinction arises from the fact that the two categories, being (reality) and thought (concept), although opposite, are connected. Hegel explores in some detail the modes of connection between being and concept (*Proofs* 9, 89–91). The proper connection is that in which each preserves itself in the other and is exhibited in the other: reciprocity and mutual preservation transpire between them. This is seen clearly when the concept has the signification of God and being that of nature: without the reciprocity and preservation the result would be either pantheism (the disappearance of everything finite into the absolute divine substance) or atheism (the dissolution of God in the world).

As we have seen, three proofs arise from the two passages. The first starts out from a *contingent*, non-self-supporting being and reasons to a true, intrinsically necessary being; this is the proof *ex contingentia mundi*, or the *cosmological* proof. The second starts out from the *purposive relations* found in finite being and reasons to a wise author of this being – the *teleological* proof. The third makes the *concept of God* its starting point and reasons to the being of God – the *ontological* proof (*Proofs* 9, 92). The unique contribution of Hegel's *Lectures on the Proofs* is to show the logical progression from one proof to the next. A contingent thing can exist only if it has the ground of its being in an absolutely necessary being (the cosmological proof). Necessity, in turn, finds its truth in freedom, and freedom entails purposive relations. Given the ambiguity of good and evil in the world, finite purposiveness is true only if it has its ground in universal, divine purposiveness (the teleological proof). But the latter is not simply submerged in objectivity, as it is when as end or purpose it is merely the teleological determination of things (the objective concept). Rather it is for itself, self-mediating, the unity of objectivity and subjectivity, and as such it is the living idea, including within itself the transition into reality, becoming thereby spirit (the ontological proof) (*Proofs* 10, 98–100). In this way the cosmological proof passes into the teleological, and the teleological into the ontological; but then the ontological proof returns to the reality from which the first two proofs arise. A dialectical spiral (not merely a circle) inscribes itself between contingency/necessity, purpose/freedom, and concept/idea; and God is progressively disclosed as necessary being, wise author, and free spirit.[16]

5.   The Cosmological Proof

This proof presupposes the world in general (both natural and human) and its contingency in particular, from which it elevates itself to the region of the infinite, eternal, unchangeable, and necessary. Such predicates do not express the entire fullness of God, but God has at least these qualities. The elevation proceeds in terms of abstract categories, but "it is spirit in its innermost aspect, namely in its thought, that produces this elevation." The human heart will not allow itself to be deprived of its elevation to God by criticisms proffered by the understanding; the elevation is intrinsically necessary to spirit, and it is this necessity that proof grasps (*Proofs* 10, 93–96).[17]

The specificity of the goal to which we elevate ourselves depends on the specificity of the starting point. We could start from a specificity other than contingency, such as finite, existential being, and conclude with being itself, in which case God would be defined, as by the Eleatics, simply as being or essence. Or we could conclude from finite to infinite, or from real being to ideal being, or from parts (the many) to the whole (the One), or from selfless things to God as the power behind them, or from effects to cause.[18] Logic, however, focuses on the relationship of contingency and necessity since this is the one in which all the relations between finite and infinite are summed up and brought together. The most concrete determination of the finitude of being is "contingency" (Zufälligkeit), a term that suggests its tendency to collapse or "fall" (Proofs 10, 96–99).

The logical or syllogistic form of the proof is as follows: the contingent rests not on itself but on the absolutely necessary; the world is contingent; therefore the world presupposes an absolute necessity. The major premise follows from the definition of contingency as the collection of things that do not come from or proceed by themselves but are destined to pass away and are limited by other things; they are only *possible* (they can equally well not be as be). They must therefore rest on something that does not pass away, is not limited, and is not merely possible but necessary; otherwise their being is not accounted for. A form of relative necessity already appears within the sphere of contingency in the form of laws of cause and effect, but that upon which contingency rests is absolute necessity. The minor premise, that the world is contingent, seems obvious, but in fact, as we shall see, the word "is," predicated of the world, proves to be problematic (Proofs 11, 101–106).

Most of the remainder of Hegel's treatment of the cosmological proof in the *Lectures on the Proofs* focuses on defects in the proof. Above all it is Kant who criticizes the cosmological proof, but Hegel is critical of Kant's criticisms. This is the burden of the fragment "On the Cosmological Proof" that Hegel composed at an earlier time and that was inserted after the tenth lecture by the editors of the *Werke*.[19] Hegel makes several points in response to Kant: (1) The category of the most real is in fact deducible from that of the absolutely necessary, although the latter is inadequate as a definition of God. (2) Kant's critique depends on his doctrine of the inadmissibility of getting beyond the sensible by means of thought, his limitation of the categories to the world of sense, and his claim that the thing in itself cannot be grasped cognitively. (3) Reason, however, is independent of the world of sense, is autonomous in and for itself, and is able to grasp such ideas as those of a first cause and an absolutely necessary being. (4) The fundamental challenge is to show how it is that the infinite and absolutely necessary being starts from an other – the finite and contingent – and yet in doing so starts only from itself. A double movement occurs, from finite being to the concept of God as infinite being, and from the concept of God to being. Kant regards the second movement (the ontological proof) as specious and assumes that the first movement (the cosmological proof) depends on it; whereas Hegel argues that the two movements are valid but interdependent, each passing into the other. The mediated categories, finite and infinite, contingency and necessity, exist only in transition rather than as static entities. From Hegel's point of view, Kant fails to grasp the transition, the relational nature of the concepts, and thus is unable to do justice to the true nature of the proofs. "At the same time he laid the basis for the complete paralysis of reason, which has since his day been content to be nothing more than an immediate knowing."[20]

Hegel's critique of Kant provides clues to his own analysis of defects in the cosmological proof. He identifies two such defects: in its concept of God and in the argument

420

from contingency to necessity. As to the first, he emphasizes the inadequacy of the concept of absolute necessity, which is the only sort of God arrived at by the cosmological proof. Absolute necessity is abstract insofar as it depends on itself, does not subsist through an other, is not related to an other, has no finitude within it, is simply present to itself. Hegel wonders whether elevation to this sort of abstraction can truly satisfy spirit. What satisfaction did the Greeks find in subjection to necessity? The wills of its most noble heroes were annihilated by it, and no true reconciliation was accomplished (*Proofs* 12, 107–110).[21] In his concluding lecture, he elaborates at length on the religious and philosophical systems that have not gotten beyond the category of the absolutely necessary being or essence (*Wesen*), which "is not subject, and still less is it spirit." These include the Greek and Hindu religions and the Eleatic and Spinozistic systems, all of which tend toward pantheism – not atheistic but acosmic pantheism, an annihilation of the finite world in the absolute substance. Fortunately, the other proofs bring with them "further and more concrete determinations" of God (*Proofs* 16, 133–44).

The defect in the argument from contingency to necessity resides in the implication found in the customary form of it: "*Because* the worldly is contingent, *therefore* an absolutely necessary being or essence exists." This form of the argument seems to make necessity into a result that follows from contingency as its ground. This critique, however, is misleading in the sense that it is only our *knowledge* of the absolutely necessary being that is conditioned by the contingent starting point, not absolute necessity itself. But there is another aspect of the proof that is defective, namely, its attributing the quality of "having being" to contingency in the minor premise: "*there is* a contingent world," "the contingent world *exists*." The distinctive quality of the finite is to have an end, to collapse, to be the sort of being that is only *possible* and that can just as well not be as be. If it has a being, the being that it has cannot be its own being but only that of an other. It is, therefore, not because the contingent *is*, but rather because it is *not*, is nonbeing, is only self-sublating appearance, that absolute necessity *is*, and is not merely one side of a relation but the whole. In sum, the moment of the *negative* is not found in the ordinary form of the syllogism, that of the understanding (*Verstand*), whereas it is just the self-negation of the contingent that makes it a starting point (not a ground) of the elevation to the absolutely necessary. Thus in place of the false proposition of the understanding, "The being of the contingent is *only its own being* and not the being of an other," Hegel sets forth the true proposition of speculative thinking, "The being of the contingent is *not* its own being but *only* the being of *an other,* and indeed it is defined as the being of *its* other, the absolutely necessary" (*Proofs* 13, 111–117; "On the Cosmological Proof," 159–165).[22] Despite the defects, this is the element of validity in the cosmological proof.

It is said (by Lessing, Kant, Schelling, Jacobi) that there is no bridge or passage from finite to infinite; the finite is related simply to itself, not to its other. Finite knowledge cannot know an infinite content, and every relationship of mediation falls away. The gulf between finite and infinite is based on the assumption that the finite remains only with itself because it is only its own being, not in any sense the being of an other, least of all of *its* other, the infinite. Hegel's agenda is to affirm that there is in fact a bridge or passage, but it is based not on the *self-affirmation* or self-projection of the finite, but rather on its *self-negation* and the recognition that any connection with the infinite

421

derives from the infinite, not the finite (*Proofs* 13, 117–118; 15, 127–132). This rec-ognition is the speculative insight that lies at the heart of the ontological proof.

6.   The Teleological Proof

The teleological proof mediates between the cosmological and ontological proofs. With it a transition occurs to the categories of freedom, purpose, and wisdom. Kant criticizes this proof, too, but he also says that it deserves to be treated with respect, for it is the proof that is clearest to ordinary human beings. He formulates the proof as follows: the world is not simply an aggregate of contingent things but a mass of purposive connec-tions, which must have a cause full of power and wisdom, and this cause is God (*LPR* 2:703–706).[23] His chief criticism is that we cannot conclude from worldly purposive-ness to an absolute author. But, Hegel responds, what is involved is not really a leap from the relative to the absolute; rather the ground we start from (the world) is "undermined by ... the authentic ground." In the teleological proof as well as the cos-mological, the transition is not an affirmative passing over from finite to infinite but a self-negation of the finite and a self-actualization of the infinite. The awareness of worldly harmony arouses humanity to an astonishment that passes over into venera-tion of God. So what we have is not an argument to a wise creator from empirical evidence but a religious elevation with the quality of awe and self-negation (*LPR* 2:707–712). The proofs "probe" what is going on in this elevation and are not deductive proofs in the strict sense at all.

It is just as well that this is the case because the empirical evidence is highly ambigu-ous. Examples of the wise orderings of nature (such as providing mice for cats to feed upon, or cork trees to have bottle stoppers) are trivial, unworthy of God. Finite purposes are stultified and perish without issue; living things prey upon the death or decay of other life; the highest human purposes are sabotaged; the earth is covered with ruins; petty purposes are fulfilled while essential ones come to grief. "There is much good in the world, but also an infinite amount of evil." Finite, worldly purposiveness is negated by the ambiguity of good and evil (just as contingency is negated by its potentiality not to be), and it thereby passes over into the universal. The universal divine purpose is not to be found in *experience*; nonetheless it is fulfilled in the world by its own power. "The good is what is determined in and for itself by reason, and nature stands over against it – physical nature, on the one hand, ... but also the natural aspect of humanity, with all the private purposes that run counter to the good" (*LPR* 2:716–719).

At this point Kant introduces his theory of moral postulates, one of which is God. In face of the struggle between good and evil, God is needed as the guarantor of a final kingdom of the good. But belief in God is for Kant merely subjective and cannot be proved. Such belief serves a useful moral function by motivating people to act in accord with moral duties out of fear of punishment and promise of reward. Hegel likens such belief to children who make a scarecrow and then agree to pretend to be afraid of it. These utilitarian reasons for believing in God are unworthy of God and contradict the fact that morality consists in reverence for the law simply for its own sake.[24] For Kant the existence of God and the harmony of goodness with the world remain a *demand* of practical reason, not a *demonstration* of theoretical reason. "This deficiency arises," says

Hegel, "because, by the standard of Kant's dualism, it cannot be shown that the good as an abstract idea, as merely subjective in itself, consists in sublating its subjectivity; nor can it be shown that nature, or the world in itself, consists in sublating its external-ity and difference from the good, and in exhibiting as its truth something that appears as a third factor (with regard to nature and the good) but is at the same time defined as what is first."[25] With this twofold showing Hegel hints at the transition to the onto-logical proof.

The transition also occurs in the following way. The divinity at which the teleological proof arrives is the universal described by the ancients as "soul," *nous*, the organic life of the world, or what Plato called "world soul" or *logos*, the life principle. This is as far as the teleological proof can go; it does not reach spirit (*LPR* 2:713–716). To reach spirit, an inference such as the following is needed: "There are finite spirits. But the finite has no truth, for the truth of finite spirit and its actuality is instead just the abso-lute spirit. The finite is not genuine being; it is implicitly the dialectic of self-sublating or self-negating, and its negation is affirmation as the infinite, as the universal in and for itself. It is surprising that this transition was not specified in the proofs of God" (*LPR* 1:431; cf. 427–431). This transition starts not with the factors of contingency and purposiveness but with the presence of finite spirits, who pass over to absolute spirit through a self-negation that is at the same time the self-affirmation and self-manifestation of the absolute. It is the latter just because this is the way the absolute works in the finite. Finite and infinite are relative terms, each present in and passing over to the other. Hegel is surprised that this transition, which points the way from the cosmological and teleological proofs to the ontological proof, is not found in the traditional proofs of God.

7. The Ontological Proof

This proof, which constitutes the metaphysical foundation of Christianity, was first discovered, Hegel claims, by Anselm and then adduced by later philosophers. It is the "only genuine" proof (*LPR* 3:352[26]). The concept of God is normally regarded as some-thing subjective and opposed to objectivity and reality. But now the concept is the beginning, and what matters is to show that being also pertains to this concept. The point is to show not just that *concepts exist*, but that the *object* of the concept of God has being. The argument, in brief, is that the concept of God "cannot be grasped except as including being within itself; to the extent that being is distinguished from the concept, the concept exists only subjectively, in our own thinking." That the concept of God "is not just *our* concept but also *is*, irrespective of our thinking, has to be demonstrated." Anselm's version of the proof is that God is understood to be what is "most perfect," and we deem as perfect that which is not just a representation but possesses being as well. Therefore what is "most perfect" is also "most real": God is the essential sum of all reality (*LPR* 3:352–354).[27]

Kant objects that being is not a predicate or reality; it makes no difference to the concept whether its object is or is not. What I represent does not exist simply on that account: a hundred thalers remain the same whether I merely imagine them or have them. Hegel responds as follows: "It may be conceded that being is not a predicate; what is required, however, is not indeed to add anything to the concept ... but to remove from

423

it rather the shortcoming of being only subjective, of not being the idea. The concept that is only something subjective, separate from being, is a nullity" (*LRP* 3:354). Hegel is not denying that it is certainly possible to have subjective concepts, but they are figments of the imagination or hypothetical constructions without any reality-reference. While the understanding rigidly separates being and concept, the "ordinary view" held by people is that the concept devoid of being, or thought devoid of reality, is something one-sided and untrue. In any event, the antithesis between being and concept found in finitude cannot occur in what is infinite, God. While Kant's critique is not persuasive, there is another problem, however, which is that for Anselm and other defenders of the ontological proof the identity of the most perfect being with the most real being is merely a *presupposition*. What is needed is a *demonstration* that the true concept includes being or reality within itself. Hegel's demonstration unfolds in three steps.[28]

First, being in its immediacy is simple relation to self, the absence of mediation. The concept "is that in which all distinction has been absorbed, or in which all categorial determinations are present only in an ideal way. The ideality is sublated mediation, sublated differentiatedness," and in this sense the concept, like being, has an absolute self-relatedness, a sheer self-presence. "Thus the concept contains being implicitly" (*LPR* 3:355).

But in the second place, "the concept does not only have being within itself implicitly – it is not merely that we have this insight but that the concept is also being explicitly. It sublates its subjectivity itself and objectifies itself. Human beings realize their purposes, i.e., what was at first only ideal is stripped of its one-sidedness and thereby made into a subsisting being. ... When we look closely at the nature of the concept, we see that its identity with being is no longer a presupposition but a result. What happens is that the concept objectifies itself, makes itself reality and thus becomes the truth, the unity of subject and object" (*LPR* 3:356). The concept, like the human "I," is alive and active; its activity can be called a *drive*, and every satisfaction of a drive is a sublation of the subjective and a positing of the objective (*LPR* 1:438–439). [29]

Thus far the argument is based solely on the logic of the concept. If, in the third place, we turn to Christianity, Hegel believes that we find a concrete representation of this logical insight. Here the unity of concept and being is to be grasped "as an absolute process, as the living activity of God." As such God is self-differentiating and self-revealing (*LPR* 3:356–357). God is also self-incarnating. "As spirit or as love, God is this self-particularizing. God creates the world and produces his Son, posits an other to himself and in this other has himself, is identical with himself" (*LPR* 1:437). Incarnation, claims Hegel, is the "speculative midpoint of religion" (*LPR* 1:245). In the Christian narrative, God takes on finite, worldly existence in the form of a human being – an individual who lives, suffers, dies, and rises into the life of the community of faith in which God is spiritually present (*LPR* 3: 109–133, 211–223, 310–328). In this very concrete sense it is appropriate to speak of the *Dasein Gottes*.

8.   The Dialectic of the Proofs and the Speculative Reversal

When the proofs are taken together as a whole, we arrive at an adequate conception of God. God is absolute necessity (power, substance), absolute wisdom (knowledge, goodness), and absolute spirit (love, subjectivity). The attributes, like the proofs on which they are based, are mutually interdependent. The proofs are simply abstract philosophical ways of thinking about God. They prove in the sense of probing and purifying the meaning and truth of God-talk as it arises out of worldly experience and religious intuition. While they appear in a diversity of religions in seemingly random fashion, they are in fact logical components of a larger organic perspective.

We have seen that Hegel emphasizes the deficiencies of both the cosmological and teleological proofs, deficiencies that are resolved by their passing into the ontological proof. But does the ontological proof also have a deficiency? While Hegel avers that it is the "only genuine" proof, the matter is not so simple. Because it is God's very nature to bring godself down to humanity, to create a world and take on the form of a servant (*Proofs* 5, 67), the ontological proof requires a reference to the world and to the human self that is provided by the cosmological and teleological proofs. Otherwise God remains an abstraction, "that than which nothing greater can be conceived" in Anselm's formulation, the supremely necessary and perfect being, but not a loving, suffering, spiritual being. Thus we find a two-way passage occurring in the proofs: from nature through finite spirit to God, and from God into nature and finite spirit. The two passages belong to a single concept, a totality that is both foundation and result. The result of one movement becomes the foundation of the other. By its own dialectical nature each movement drives itself over to the other (*Proofs* 9, 89–92). Each shows itself as transient, as a transition into the other (*LPR* 3:174–175). In the strict sense there is no foundation but a dialectical mirroring of elements that are always in play.

What Hegel calls "the speculative" involves a relationship of double mirroring[30] – of consciousness by the object, and of the object by consciousness; or of the finite by the infinite, and of the infinite by the finite. In the fragment "On the Cosmological Proof" he says that the proposition of the ontological proof is not simply "the infinite *is*" but "the infinite is finite." "For the infinite, in resolving itself to become *being*, determines itself to what is *other* than itself; but the other of the infinite is just the finite." By contrast with a "silly idealism" that maintains that if anything is thought it ceases to be, a serious idealism "contains within itself the counterstroke [*Gegenschlag*] that is the nature of the absolute unification-into-one of the two previously separated sides, and that is the nature of the concept itself" (*Proofs*, 164–165). The "counterstroke" is the ontological transition from infinite to finite, from concept to being, that balances and incorporates the cosmo/teleological transition from finite to infinite, from being to concept. In the *Lectures on the Philosophy of Religion* (1:227 n. 115; 322) Hegel employs similar images of a "counterthrust" (*Gegenstoß*) or of "a stream flowing in opposite directions" to suggest the speculative reversal that lies at the heart of his thought: the rise of finite consciousness to the absolute is at the same time the return of absolute spirit to itself from its materialization and externalization in finitude. In becoming finite, the infinite raises the finite to the infinite. The infinite is the ground of the whole process in the sense of being the energy or power that pulses through it, but the pulsations move in two directions.

In the introduction to the *Encyclopedia*, the language of "reversal" occurs explicitly: "When we say, 'Consider nature, for it will lead you to God, and you will find an absolute final purpose,' this does not mean that God is mediated, but only that *we* make the

425

journey from an other to God, in the sense that God, being the consequence, is at the same time the absolute ground of what we started with, so that the process of the two is *reversed*: what appears as the consequence also shows itself to be the ground, while what presented itself as ground to start with is reduced to consequence."[31] God is *self*-mediated. Rational proof is not a deduction or demonstration of the infinite from the finite; rather it entails a reversal between ground and consequence; the infinite proves itself in being made the object of proof.[32]

9. Hegel's Proofs Today

Hegel offers a highly original interpretation and defense of the proofs of the existence of God. If one is drawn into the Hegelian way of thinking, it is difficult to challenge the cogency of the arguments. But of course it is possible to challenge his way of thinking and the presuppositions on which it is based. The principal presupposition is the speculative vision of the double mirroring and movement between infinite and finite, God and the world, that we have just discussed. For Hegel this vision is not just a presupposition but the result of the whole of philosophy; yet for many today the Hegelian whole has collapsed into fragments on the rocks of modernity and postmodernity. The principal presupposition of modernity is that, while the infinite may exist, the finite is cut off from it and cannot know it. God is not an object of cognition but a postulate of moral behavior or an axiom of faith. The result is agnosticism or religious positivism. The principal presupposition of postmodernity is that finitude (or nature) is the sole reality, that humans find themselves in an ultimately meaningless and purposeless (though "infinitely" extended) cosmos. The result is atheism and secularism. (These are of course sweeping judgments, and there are both modernists and postmodernists who disagree with them.)

Whether positivism, agnosticism, or atheism are better or truer worldviews than that of Hegelian holism is the question we face today. Do they take more adequate account of the complexity of human experience, history, and culture? Do they provide a more satisfactory guide to human activity? Do they satisfy the longings and intuitions of the human heart? Or do they represent barren reductions, intellectually, ethically, religiously, emotionally? Hegel foresaw this debate and for this reason he addressed the question of the proofs with a sense of urgency.

Kierkegaard said of Hegel that if only he had acknowledged that his philosophy is a thought-experiment he would have been the greatest of thinkers.[33] But Hegel in his own way made this acknowledgment. Certainly he knew that every philosophical system, every theological doctrine – even and especially that of God – is a thought-experiment, a construction of human imagination. In his lectures, a *thinking* was in play that did not cease to experiment with the materials at hand. As a student of the history of philosophy Hegel was familiar with the multiplicity and limitations of all such experiments, and he did not suffer the illusion that his own thoughts would escape the judgment of history. He added, however, that what gives legitimacy to the experiments is that absolute spirit is coming to self-consciousness in them, that our finite thoughts are expressions of the mind of God. The *itinerarium mentis in Deum* is God's own thought-experiment.

426

Notes

1   These additions (*Zusätze*) were included in the *Werke* edition of the *Encyclopedia of Philosophical Sciences*, edited by Leopold von Henning, and are translated by T. F. Geraets, W. A. Suchting, and H. S. Harris in *The Encyclopedia Logic* (Indianapolis, Ind.: Hackett, 1991). In the *Lectures on the Proofs of the Existence of God*, ed. and trans. Peter C. Hodgson (Oxford: Oxford University Press, 2007), 99, Hegel remarks that logic is "metaphysical theology" because it "treats of the evolution of the idea of God in the aether of pure thought, and thus it properly attends only to this idea, which is utterly independent in and for itself."

2   *Science of Logic*, trans. A. V. Miller (London: George Allen & Unwin, 1969), 705–706.

3   Ibid., 707–8.

4   *The Encyclopedia Logic*, §§36, 50–51 (an evaluation of the treatment of the proofs by rational theology and critical philosophy). The ontological proof is discussed in §193 in the context of the transition from the subjective to the objective concept.

5   *Lectures on the History of Philosophy*. In the translation of the *Werke* edition by E. S. Haldane and Frances H. Simson, vol. 3 (London: Kegan, Paul, Trench, Trübner & Co., 1896), 61–7, 233–238, 451–456, 462–464; in the translation of the critical edition (ed. Pierre Garniron and Walter Jaeschke) by Robert F. Brown, vol. 3 (Oxford: Clarendon Press, 2009), 43–45, 112–113, 186, 192–196.

6   *Lectures on the Philosophy of Religion*, 3 vols., ed. Peter C. Hodgson, trans. R. F. Brown, P. C. Hodgson, and J. M. Stewart (Berkeley and Los Angeles: University of California Press, 1984, 1985, 1987; reprinted Oxford: Oxford University Press, 2007), 1:414–441; 2:100–104, 127–134, 199–206, 250–266, 390–421, 703–719; 3:65–73, 173–185, 351–358.

7   The translations are based on the critical editions by Walter Jaeschke of the lectures on the proofs, the fragment on the cosmological proof, and appendices to the philosophy of religion lectures. The original manuscripts are lost and access to this material is available through secondary transmissions of the *Werke*. For details see the editorial introduction to *Lectures on the Proofs of the Existence of God*, 1–4, 21, 25. I draw upon this editorial material at various points in the present article. Used by permission of Oxford University Press.

8   References to the *Lectures on the Proofs of the Existence of God* are cited in-text with the abbreviation *Proofs* followed by the lecture number and page number. Page numbers of the German texts are in the margins of the English edition. Quentin Lauer notes that for Hegel with the introduction of "proof" thought moves from a mythical to a rational explanation of the world. *Hegel's Concept of God* (Albany: State University of New York Press, 1982), 204.

9   In *Proofs* 1, 40, and in the *Lectures on the Philosophy of Religion*, 1:154, Hegel quotes Anselm: "It seems to me negligence if, after we have been confirmed in the faith, we do not make an effort to understand [*intellegere*] what we believe" (*Cur Deus Homo*, 1.1).

10   The prefix *be-* is used in German to change an intransitive to a transitive verb.

11   The *Lectures on the Philosophy of Religion* are cited in-text with the abbreviation *LPR*. Page numbers of the German texts are in the margins of the English edition. The term "idea" always translates *Idee* and in this chapter always appears in lower case.

12   In a passage in *LPR* 3:174–175 the three terms, *Sein, Dasein, Existenz*, are used in apposition in reference to God.

13   See *Proofs* 10, 97 n. 8; 11, 105 n. 1.

14   Quentin Lauer prefers the term "reality" and translates the title of the lectures as *Lectures on Proofs for the Reality of God*; see *Hegel's Concept of God*, 211. However, Hegel does not speak simply of God's "reality" (*Realität*), which suggests a contrast with God's "ideality" (also to

be affirmed), but rather of God's "actuality" (*Wirklichkeit*), a term that encompasses both ideality and reality.

15 See Robert R. Williams, "Hegel's Concept of the True Infinite" (unpublished essay).

16 The transition from necessity to purposiveness and freedom is described in detail in the 1824 philosophy of religion lectures (*LPR* 2:391–392, 401–404).

17 In the *Encyclopedia*, §50, Hegel remarks that the Humean and Kantian critiques of the capacity of thought cannot cancel the elevation of the human spirit to God. This elevation is thinking as such and cannot be canceled without canceling thinking itself (*The Encyclopedia Logic*, 94–95).

18 In the 1821 and 1824 philosophy of religion lectures Hegel discusses the argument from finite to infinite in connection with the religions of nature, the argument from the many to the One in connection with Jewish religion, and the argument from contingency to necessity in connection with Greek religion (*LPR* 2:100–104, 127–134, 250–266, 390–404).

19 In the new edition of the *Proofs* this material is printed as an independent unit following Hegel's lectures.

20 *Proofs*, 149–159, 163. This is a very brief and inadequate summary of a complex set of arguments. A fuller summary is provided in the editorial introduction to the *Proofs*, 22–24. I do not attempt to evaluate the fairness of Hegel's portrayal of Kant or to judge the legitimacy of his critique.

21 In the *Encyclopedia*, §§36, 50, Hegel notes that such a God is the abstract essence of the understanding, the supreme being, "the dead product of the modern Enlightenment," an absolute substance but not a spiritual God (*The Encyclopedia Logic*, 73–75, 97–98).

22 Hegel offers a similar critique in *LPR* 1:417–425; 2:262–265.

23 The citations here are to the 1831 philosophy of religion lectures. This material is reproduced in the *Lectures on the Proofs of the Existence of God*, but the references are to the original source, the appendix to vol. 2 of *LPR*. Pagination of the German text appears in the margins. Hegel discusses the teleological proof in all of the philosophy of religion lecture series; reference is also made below to the 1827 version (*LPR* 1:427–432).

24 *Lectures on the History of Philosophy*, Haldane and Simson translation, 3:462–464.

25 *Lectures on the History of Philosophy*, Brown translation, 3:195.

26 The citations are to the 1831 philosophy of religion lectures, printed as an appendix to *LPR* 3:351–358 and reproduced in the *Lectures on the Proofs*. The 1827 version of the ontological proof (*LPR* 1:433–440) is very similar. Much of the limited critical literature on Hegel's proofs focuses on the ontological proof. See Dieter Henrich, *Der ontologische Gottesbeweis* (Tübingen: J.C.B. Mohr, 1960), 189–219; Louis Girard, *L'Argument Ontologique chez Saint Anselm et chez Hegel* (Amsterdam: Rodopi, 1995); Patricia Marie Calton, *Hegel's Metaphysics of God: The Ontological Proof as the Development of a Trinitarian Divine Ontology* (Aldershot: Ashgate, 2001).

27 Hegel summarizes Anselm's argument in categories used not by Anselm himself but by later philosophers (Descartes, Wolff, Baumgarten, Kant).

28 This demonstration is the unique contribution of the 1827 and 1831 versions of the ontological proof (in 1827 the order of the steps differs). It is not found in the 1821 and 1824 versions.

29 In Hegel's scheme the concept realizes itself in and through nature as well as humanity. Thus nature's contingent achievement of being and order is itself a form of the ontological proof prior to and apart from Christianity, although Hegel does not mention the proof in connection with nature. I am indebted to Hyo-Dong Lee for this observation.

30 *Speculum* in Latin means "mirror."

31 *Encyclopedia of the Philosophical Sciences*, §36 addition (*The Encyclopedia Logic*, 75).

32 Robert R. Williams, who read a draft of this chapter, suggests that Hegel's "elevation" and "speculative reversal" are heavily influenced by Spinoza's *amor intellectus Dei:* the love with which the human being loves God is but the love with which God loves godself. The proofs are not demonstrative arguments but articulations of this circular or spiraling movement of love.

33 Søren Kierkegaard, *Journals and Papers*, 7 vols., ed. and trans. Howard V. Hong and Edna H. Hong (Bloomington: Indiana University Press, 1967–1978), 2:217 (No. 1605). Strictly Kierkegaard is referring to Hegel's logic. Williams suggests that, while posing as anti-Hegel, Kierkegaard is in fact very close to Hegel in that for him too God alone provides human beings with the condition of possibility for knowing God. Perhaps this is why, with the proviso of the thought-experiment and a dose of irony, he regarded Hegel as the greatest of thinkers.

Part X

History of Philosophy

21

Hegel's Aristotle: Philosophy and Its Time

ALFREDO FERRARIN

1.   Introduction

Hegel's praise of Aristotle is quite extraordinary, especially for someone who does not normally pull any punches.[1] In the *Lectures on the History of Philosophy* Hegel reserves for no other philosopher such admiration and such an extended treatment. The texts he spends most time commenting on are the *Metaphysics*, the *De anima*, the *Physics*, and the *Nicomachean Ethics*. At the end of what is considered his system, the Berlin *Encyclopaedia*, Hegel simply cites one of the most famous passages from Aristotle's *Metaphysics* on the pure activity of divine thought thinking itself; he does not translate the text, which he quotes in Greek, let alone comment on it or explain it. One can hardly imagine a stronger endorsement, especially given the rarity of such unqualified approval in the Hegelian corpus. Perhaps even more striking, however, is what Hegel says about Aristotle's being the only writer who has anything important to say on the being and activity of spirit. Hegel prefaces his own philosophy of spirit with these words:

> Aristotle's books on the soul, as well as his treatises on its particular aspects and condi-
> tions, are still by far the best or even the sole work of speculative interest on this subject-
> matter. The essential purpose of a philosophy of spirit can be none other than re-introducing
> the concept into the cognition of spirit, and so re-interpreting the meaning of these
> Aristotelian books. (ENZ. §378, my trans.)

Such praise can be baffling, for how can Hegel endorse Aristotle's philosophy, and in particular his philosophy of spirit, if we consider Hegel's well-known theses that spirit's freedom was unknown to the ancients or that spirit makes progress in history? How can we avoid regarding Aristotle's philosophy as intrinsically immature and incomplete, if we consider that Hegel claims there is an identity between the development of logical categories and that of historically determined philosophical systems? Here are but a few examples of what appear to be obvious inconsistencies in Hegel's endorsement of Aristotle. What are we to make of the *Metaphysics* as an ontology of

---

independent substances, which seems to militate against any notion of dialectics? Or of the blank slate that the soul, which first gains its contents from perception, supposedly is in the "empiricist" epistemology of the *De anima?* How can we still profit from a reading of the *Physics,* the single work of Aristotle's that has attracted probably the most unanimous criticism in the modern age, with its final causes and unintelligible definition of motion? Or from a reading of the *Ethics,* with its confusing characterizations of virtue as the mean between two extremes or its old-fashioned appeals to high-minded but (in the eyes of some) ultimately vacuous notions such as "happiness," "the contemplative life," and haughty "magnanimity"?

No doubt Hegel would invite us to think again. What I have just sketched are some of the deep-seated preconceptions that he struggled all his life to clear from his students' minds. Hegel is in a particularly good position to liberate us from such prejudices insofar as his reading of Aristotle – whatever we think of its merits – is an example of a serious, unbiased, and, if I may add, ingenious approach to texts. Hegel, whose knowledge of Greek is astounding, is the first philosopher in modern times who engages in a thorough study of Aristotle in the original. He never relies on traditional interpretations, and by giving his own exegesis of what he is expounding, he thinks he is contributing to countering the oblivion and the mindless reception, which alternates with occasional piece-meal exploitation, of a philosophy that he takes to be the speculative peak of classical Greek thought.

The prejudices I have mentioned are not the only ones we are called upon to get rid of. Unless we also discard other passively received, or problematic, notions, we cannot make sense of Hegel's high regard for the Aristotelian soul or intellect. More to the point, unless we properly understand crucial Hegelian notions such as freedom and subjectivity, we cannot understand Hegel's Aristotle – for example, why Hegel says that Aristotle introduces the notion of pure subjectivity that was missing in Plato's ideas, and that *energeia* is subjectivity.[2] Unless we distinguish sharply between the ancient freedom of *thought* and the objective and historically determined realization of freedom in increasingly concrete *institutions,* we cannot understand why Hegel's speculative logic ascribes greater importance to Platonic dialectic or Aristotelian metaphysics than to the various forms of the modern philosophy of reflection.[3]

If the ancients thought more freely than the moderns, it is because they took their bearings from the identity of thought and being. This is what Hegel calls objective thinking, and within this standpoint of thought with regard to objectivity Aristotle represents the highest form of idealism, the speculative identity of thought and being. Notice that this idealism cannot be reduced to a determinate figure of consciousness, a definite method, a position of the will or a certain understanding of objects, because it is first and foremost a thesis about the *lack of separation and opposition between thought and being.*[4]

In Section 3 I will come back to the shape this idealism has for Hegel, and then turn in Section 4 to the question of whether or not Hegel's Aristotle is compatible with the principles of Hegel's historiography. I will then examine some problems regarding the relation between history and philosophy in Hegel and bring my conclusions on this point to bear on the limits Hegel identifies in Aristotle's philosophy (Section 5). In Section 6, finally, I will focus on some problems in Hegel's reading of Aristotle. But before I proceed, let me explain in Section 2 what is wrong with a different take on

Hegel's praise of Aristotle: an enthusiastic reading that takes such praise to be straightforward, unalloyed, and in need of no further interpretation.

2.   A "Retrieval" of Aristotle?

The interpretation which sees Hegel's praise of Aristotle as straightforward and unalloyed draws from it an impression which is in important ways misguided. When Hegel, speaking of the *De anima* and the *Nicomachean Ethics*, writes that it is just a matter of translating Aristotle's theses into our more elaborate language (VGPh II, W 19, p. 221), the last thing we should do is conclude that Hegel means simply to update, bring back to life or assimilate Aristotle into his own philosophy. First, there cannot be any question of *retrieving* Aristotle, as we will see in a moment. Second, this evaluation of Aristotle should not deceive us into thinking, in the words of Johann Eduard Erdmann (the first student of Hegel's to voice this preoccupation which seems again to be dominant among some Hegelians today), that Hegel intends to "restore" the old metaphysics, conservative politics, and dogmatic religion after Kant's revolution. In no way – political, metaphysical or religious – does Hegel understand his philosophy as a restoration; and he is adamant that we cannot be Aristotelians today (VGPh I, W 18, p. 65). Accordingly, Hegel's praise of Aristotle must be understood to reflect the stance he takes with respect to the scissions and separations of modern philosophy. For Hegel, the task is not to revert to the standpoint of Aristotle's day, but to discern in Aristotle a model of the unification of principles which can help us overcome the several forms of dualism in modern philosophy. What matters in the study of the ancients is thus not so much the degree of fidelity and authenticity with which we reconstruct past philosophies, but rather the relation between our own philosophy and its time.

In this sense, many of the trite and still common readings of the imagery introduced by Hegel need revisiting, beginning with that of the famous dictum that the owl of Minerva takes flight at dusk, according to which philosophy is merely a retrospective recognition of the objective forces that have shaped reality presumably without any contribution from the realm of thought. The editor of Hegel's lectures on the history of philosophy, Karl Ludwig Michelet, once wrote that philosophy cannot just be that owl: it should also be understood as the rooster's song announcing a new daybreak.[5] If Aristotle's philosophy is used by Hegel to show how to reconcile thought and being, we should not lose sight of the fact that, for Hegel, any such reconciliation is gained, if at all, only *after* the scissions of modernity: Hegel's philosophy arises precisely as the answer to this need to restore unity to our experience, and in particular to actualize a deeper form of thought that is striving to make our institutions conform to the deeper consciousness of our age. What Hegel's philosophy wants to show is the actuality of the Idea, the Greek identity of thought and being, in the new age he thought was dawning in his own time. And that means overcoming the modern opposition of subject and object.

As I have said, no retrieval is ever possible in philosophy, even of the most intelligent or speculative past philosophies. For the idea of a retrieval presupposes many problematic points. It presupposes that tradition is the preservation of truths as so many ready-made theses, bits of wisdom or knowledge that remain unaltered; and that such truths

435

to which we presume to have unmediated access are, like springs which quench our thirst and nurture us, inexhaustible and unmodifiable. It also presupposes that we, the retrievers, can bracket time as we presume to go back to some past, whereas in truth every going back to the past is a leap forward in one direction or other. The very repetition inherent in the idea of a retrieval is contradictory to begin with, for in philosophy to discuss the past thematically is to set thought in motion, and thought knows no boundaries and leaves nothing intact. Spirit's history is a constant re-elaboration which transforms its content as it assimilates it. All active assimilation cannot help being creative and productive, and in two ways: spirit transforms what it inherits, and it thereby transforms itself in this active reception (VGPh I, W 18, pp. 21–22). In the history of philosophy what we bear witness to is the self-finding of thought – and "in thought one finds oneself insofar as one produces oneself. Philosophies are just such productions" (VGPh I, W 18, p. 23 n.).

If finding and making are intertwined, it is because "the course of history does not show us the *becoming of things foreign* to us, but *our own becoming, the becoming of our science*" (VGPh I, W 18, p. 22). History shows us how we *transform* ourselves by discovering who we are. In the positive – nonphilosophical – sciences history comes down to the emergence of certain truths and the parallel rejection of what previously passed as true; we constantly correct and modify our cognitions based on experimental knowledge and the extension and refinement of our experience. Echoing Kant, Hegel says that progress in the sciences takes place through additions and juxtaposition (VGPh I, W 18, p. 27); the nature of the object itself is thereby left unaltered. By contrast, the history of philosophy replaces the category of juxtaposition with that of *development* (explicitly inspired by Aristotle's couple *dunamis-energeia*, VGPh I, W 18, p. 39), the development of the true as it is known, in the form in which we are conscious of it. Active involvement and appropriation in the history of philosophy take the shape of actualization, bringing out the potentialities inherent in a past figure of thought. No past philosophy is a fixed and unchangeable datum, because for us it is still alive, it belongs to us.

If the past qua simply past is dead and gone and our reading of past philosophies is a living engagement, if, that is, in the past we look for the one, living Idea latent in some particular system of thought, then the history of philosophy must be speculative; the past for the speculative philosopher is a living present.[6] Our most pressing task is that of distinguishing in past philosophies what is transient from what is a permanent, abiding acquisition that admits of different degrees of development. In other words, in a given philosophy we must be able to tell the difference between what is accidental and the new form of the Idea that comes to light and shapes the different aspects of its concreteness. The history of philosophy, for Hegel, is thus not a matter of retrieving givens, but of engaging in a living exchange with our predecessors. When we do so in a fruitful way, we bring out the potentialities of past forms of thought and further the development to greater concreteness and explicitness of the one living Idea in all true philosophy.

Let us draw some preliminary conclusions. History is either the recognition by thought of spirit's progress (what Hegel calls comprehended history, the *Erinnerung* or recapitulation of spirit's calvary in the *Phenomenology of Spirit*, W 3: 590–591), or it is no more than the observation of empirical singularity, contingency, and arbitrariness, which may not be considered a science in any sense (ENZ §16 A.). Either way, for Hegel, history is not ruled by laws. The historian of philosophy is not looking for laws but reawakening kindred spirits, for only a philosopher is in a position to rethink past philosophers and in their thought look for the one Idea in different stages of development. In words that Hegel himself never uses, the history of philosophy is the fruit of a sympathetic imagination guided by critical reason. It is guided by a certain empathy (or ability to identify with the point of view of others), which in turn is moderated by prudence and an effort at proper contextualization. Historical reconstruction and contextualization are as central to it as philological fidelity. There is no purely *passive* reception in the history of philosophy. The indifference of a supposed neutrality is neither possible nor desirable when what is at stake is our own highest interest.

3. Who Is Hegel's Aristotle?

To Hegel's eyes, Aristotle represents an example of a rational and viable overcoming of separation and opposition. Hegel thinks he finds in the concept of *energeia,* which he begins to interpret as purposive reason and self-realizing concept at the end of his Jena period, the concept of actuality as self-directed movement that he is looking for. In Hegel's reading, by understanding being as *energeia,* Aristotle makes room for movement and activity within being. Being is neither immobile and self-identical as for Parmenides, nor inwardly split into intelligibility and existence as it is according to Plato's theory of ideas. Movement, plurality, becoming do not fall outside of being, but define it as internally articulated. In Hegel's analysis, movement acquires for the first time with Aristotle the status of belonging to being itself, and conversely being is no longer a static givenness. Hegel takes Aristotle to have made nature, change, and all becoming intelligible in and of themselves. Thus we must not oppose substance as a passive substrate to movement, nor form or essence to becoming. In fact, Aristotle's progress beyond Plato (the notion of pure subjectivity I referred to above) lies specifically (and solely) in the concept of immanent form, in which Hegel finds an *archê* or cause that is not definable in abstraction and isolation. This cause does not just happen to be subject to change, in addition to and independently of its essence, but its very being consists in the *process* of its actualization.

Aristotle has discovered that being is fully act, its own actualization; reality is self-grounding actuality, a self-producing end. If substance is the actuality of some matter (Metaph. Theta 6, 1048b 9), and this actuality is its end (Theta 8, 1050a 9), so that substance and form are both act (1050b 2), then for Hegel this shows that Aristotle understands *ousia* as active, not inert or fixed; reality is an inner movement, being is activity. This movement is a development of and within the same and not a transition into something else: it is what Hegel calls the adequation of a being to itself. By this expression he means that being is inwardly divided: each being is the movement of fulfilling its concept, its end, its actuality, or its standard, which governs, and is prior to, its individual existence.

Hegel interprets *energeia* as the self-referential activity which he finds at work in its several manifestations: from the self-grounding of essence to the Concept, from the teleological process to natural life, from the essence of man to the forms of knowing and acting down to its most obviously free and self-determining dimension, absolute thinking which has itself as its object. This latter notion is for Hegel to be found in Aristotle's *noêsis noêseôs*, which prefigures absolute spirit and which is the subject of the closing quotation of the *Encyclopaedia* itself.

Hegel emphasizes the centrality of *energeia* in his reconstruction of the *Metaphysics*. Here Hegel finds three different types of substance: the sensible *ousia* (substance) as a substrate of change, the finite *nous* (intellect) as a formative principle of a given externality, and the divine *nous*, the absolute activity of thinking itself and of manifesting itself in nature and spirit. If *ousia* is identical with its concept, and this is the subject of its own actualization, Hegel finds in *phusis* (nature), in the theory of the form which has in itself the drive to actualize itself or the movement to reach its own *telos*, his own idea of natural subjectivity. But if the peak of the *Metaphysics* is for Hegel represented by its speculative Idea – God *qua* thought thinking itself, the complete identity of subject and object after which the entire cosmos strives – and yet the divine principle and substances in the sublunar world are mutually independent, then it is the *De anima* which represents for Hegel the Archimedean point allowing for the unification of natural subjectivity with spirit, from the latter's finite to its absolute forms.

For, as if to ward off any schematic application of the essential difference between ancient and modern philosophy according to which the ancient Greeks knew the objectivity of the Concept but not the depths of spirit, Hegel does not only understand Aristotle as the champion of objective thought; he also appropriates and transforms the meaning of *energeia* to *define spirit* itself. Spirit is actuosity, the self or subject containing in itself its own movement and purpose and expressing in the actualization of its potentialities its identity with itself and its permanence in its dealing with ever new and different contents.

For Hegel, in the *De anima* the subject of experience is understood as an active potency, an *Aufhebung* of externality. Hegel argues that in this work the different forms of life, knowing and acting, are conceived together as gradual moments in the actualization of the same process, the entelechy of living spirit. Thus in the *De anima* Hegel finds: the soul as life, an activity inseparable from its manifestations and a self-development in and through its relation to otherness (in the lexicon of the *Logic*, the immediate Idea); the negativity of spirit, for which each finite form becomes matter for the superior form of considering reality; the necessity for spirit to emerge from nature as the truth of the latter; sensation, *qua* identity of perceiver and perceived, as an activity within receptivity, and the actualization of the senses as spirit's shaping of its own receptivity in determinate directions; the notion of the I as an abiding and formed power (potency) or *hexis*, which preserves and idealizes givenness in memory, guaranteeing the continuity of experiences; the intellect which thematizes the inferior forms of knowledge, and in so doing comes to know itself; and finally, the unity of will and reason.

But it is in the theory of the intellect that Hegel locates Aristotle's real brilliance, specifically in Aristotle's thinking through of the relation between objective thought and subjective thought, between, it now turns out, passive and active *nous*. Here Hegel's reasoning is full of implicit moves that need to be unpacked. It can be reconstructed roughly as follows (to learn more, the reader can study the details of the transition from objective to subjective logic in Hegel's *Science of Logic* and the emergence of spirit out of nature in the *Encyclopaedia*). According to Aristotle as interpreted by Hegel, the several concepts with which we order and understand the world are our subjective concepts; but they can be our working concepts – they can be true – only insofar as they refer to laws, genera and species, and an order that we do not invent or impose on nature. The intelligibility of actuality is what Hegel calls thought's being, or objective thought. Still, there is a fundamental formal difference between the intelligible order that animates nature and our subjective concepts referring to it, between the essences that we identify in things and our conceptual elaboration of classes and universalities. In this sense, the Concept exists *realiter* in nature; and yet it is present in it only in a hidden form, in potentiality with respect to its existence as an object of actual thinking. If the universal is the essence of a natural being, of physical laws, and if it constitutes the objectivity of the living, it cannot at the same time be found *as such* in nature. In a very arbitrary interpretive move Hegel identifies the existing universal, the objective intelligibility of all that is, with the Aristotelian potential or passive *nous*, only to contrast these objectified thought-determinations with the active *nous*, the Concept that is the identity of subject and object.

In this relation between active and passive *nous*, the sensible is not opposed to reason; nature is not opposed to spirit. Nature is rather the immediate substance (*Grundlage*), the otherness of the Idea, out of which spirit emerges to attain to itself. This process of actualization in which spirit attains to itself is, as Hegel's logic purports to show, at the same time God's, that is, the self-thinking Idea's, gradual appropriation of itself. Stated differently, Hegel inverts the traditional understanding of thought: if subjectively speaking we rise to thought out of particular experience, absolutely speaking it is thought itself that runs the show.

In this movement spirit does not have to reach an end outside itself, for its end is internal to it; if spirit is the movement of positing itself as its other and of negating its otherness, then its activity is complete even when it is a production, for production, like theory and practice, is for Hegel spirit's *self*-production in reality. Aristotle himself would *oppose* production to theory and practice on account of the completeness of the activity, which in turn depends on whether the end is internal or external to it. If spirit for Hegel is being-at-home-with-itself, then we can say that Hegel makes a strikingly *un*-Aristotelian identification of *theôria*, *praxis*, and *poiêsis* as spirit's modes of self-relation. In the words of the *Nicomachean Ethics*, we can say that spirit's *energeia* is its own *eudaimonia* (happiness), its activity is its own flourishing. *"[D]ie ewige an und für sich seiende Idee sich ewig als absoluter Geist betätigt, erzeugt und geniesst,"* are the last words of the *Encyclopaedia* before the Aristotle quotation ("The eternal Idea that is in and for itself activates, produces and enjoys itself eternally as absolute spirit," ENZ §577, my trans.).

4. Is Hegel's Aristotle Compatible with His Idea of a History of Philosophy?

It is now time to step back for a moment and ask at least some of the many questions bound to arise from our discussion. I would like to start with some questions about the compatibility of Hegel's Aristotle with Hegel's procedure in the history of philosophy. Obviously Hegel does not present a method that can generate by itself the positions of the different figures he analyzes: if all confrontation with the past is a thinking and speculative examination, the texts being examined must be approached without any preconceived notions or the external imposition of methodological guiding principles. Yet it is a striking fact that some principles of Hegel's historiography seem to go against his practice, notably in his interpretation of Aristotle: namely, the idea of historical progress, and especially the thesis of the identity of the history of philosophy and the system of logical determinations as equally the "system in development" (VGPh I, W 18, p. 47; J 24–25). It is not in the untrustworthy notes of his students that this latter principle is affirmed, but in the very important Introduction to the *Encyclopaedia* (§14): "The same development of thinking that is presented in the history of philosophy is presented in philosophy itself, but freed from that historical outwardness, i.e., purely in the element of thinking."[7] If history is freed from what makes it accidental and arbitrary, it will show its systematic structure.

I find it puzzling that Hegel introduced such an identity when he did not practice it himself in his history of philosophy. I cannot go into a close criticism of this identity thesis; let me just mention a few of the reasons why I cannot take it seriously. Not only is a simple look at the particular succession of categories in the logic and of philosophical positions in the history of philosophy sufficient to doubt the plausibility of this identity. The more important fact is that different motives and criteria are at work in the logic and the history of philosophy, which differ with regard to teleology, necessity, inner development, presuppositionlessness, organic totality.[8] Finally, the very picture of Aristotle that Hegel presents in the lectures shows that Hegel does not follow the identity thesis when he reads Aristotle: for Aristotle's philosophy, as Hegel presents it, is clearly not reducible to any one of the categories expounded in Hegel's *Science of Logic*, but corresponds to several categories discussed at various points in Hegel's text.

I do not mean to contrast Hegel's presumed preoccupation with systematic considerations with an even more imaginary unencumbered reading of Aristotle, and thereby understand the system as a straightjacket vainly trying to contain a free approach to, in the case at hand, Aristotle's thought. A system is nothing other than the articulation of reasons; but the system's relation to history is what we must clarify now in order better to understand and evaluate Hegel's interpretation of Aristotle. We must shift from the thematic discussion of the several details of the picture of Aristotle presented by Hegel to its frame, so to speak – except that even this analogy may be misleading. For a picture is enclosed by its frame, which makes it visible and gives it its enclosed identity, but we may decide to change the frame at will. Here, by contrast, the frame is partly constitutive of the picture itself. That is to say, it is impossible to disentangle thoughts from their presentation. A "system" is not the external stitching together of thoughts acquired elsewhere, as if we were arranging or pasting materials together: a systematic exposition is the form that gives its several contents their meaning. When the systematic form is missing, a philosophy runs the risk of arbitrariness and contingency.

Hegel's notion of system is very close to Kant's, so that a detour through the Architectonic of Kant's first Critique is helpful to our understanding. Like Kant, Hegel thinks that all science needs to presuppose an idea which is constitutive for it. But what is the idea of a system for Kant? In reflecting on the system of cognitions of pure reason in the opening page of the Doctrine of Method (KrV A 707/B 735), Kant argues that after surveying the materials for the edifice in the Doctrine of Elements, he is now ready to clarify the plan of the building. The architect now replaces the mason in spirit; and he will do so literally in the Architectonic, which is the "the art of systems" (KrV A 832/B 860). Here we are told that only a system transforms cognitions into a science; failing that, cognitions remain an aggregate, whereas they must be conceived as an organism. Reason does not draw upon a model from the sciences; on the contrary, sciences can assume a systematic form only once reason has provided "the end and the form of the whole" (KrV A 832/B 860). Reason works independently of determinate cognitions: it is not instructed by the understanding, but projects or plans the thorough-going form of its cognitions and directs the understanding itself in its use.

Philosophy is understood as the science of the relation of all cognitions to human reason's essential ends (KrV A 839/B 867), and the philosopher is the legislator of human reason in both its fields of application (nature and morality). Reason promotes and determines an activity that is not merely moral – for *all* activity sets itself ends, beginning with the activity of philosophizing. In this *teleologia humanae rationis* the ends are understood in light of a cosmic concept of philosophy as an activity, which unites morality and metaphysics. This teleology is neither natural nor moral, but defines reason's activity itself.

If the parts of a system precede the whole, that unity is an aggregate and an accidental totality; if the idea of the whole precedes the parts, we obtain a science, in which the totality is internally articulated. The idea is then what makes possible the whole and constitutes the unity; this internal unity warrants the analogy with the organism, in which all growth is internal and is not the result of an external addition of parts. The system then is neither derived from experience nor made possible by a method imported from without: its idea rather precedes the construction of the edifice just as the architect's plan prescribes how to assemble the materials. If this excludes the possibility of a mathematical model for philosophy (the two species of rational knowledge follow different paths), it also means, more pertinently for our present purposes, that historical or empirical knowledge does not provide a model for philosophy either (KrV A 836/B 864). Rational knowledge is from principles alone, while historical knowledge is from facts. History and science seem mutually exclusive if science is an articulated systematic form of knowledge quite distinct from a tentative groping among concepts. To transcendental philosophy's gaze, the past offers just ruins (A 852/B 880).

Both in his system and in his idea of a history of philosophy, Hegel endorses many of these Kantian points, from reason as autonomous self-determination and internal finality to the analogy of reason with the organism. For example, the necessary priority of the Idea over the particular concepts becomes in the *Encyclopaedia* the principle that thought's free self-determination is the only way to validate in necessary form whatever cognitions we may gain from experience and the sciences and to show in them the immanent progression of logical determinations (ENZ §9); in the history of philosophy, Hegel argues that unless I know the Idea, I cannot recognize its develop-ment in history (VGPh I, W 18 p. 49) and find meaning in what I investigate. Hegel assumes, like Kant, that thought takes place in history, but he does not share the view of the past as a wasteland of ruins; philosophy and the appropriation of tradition are continuous, because different philosophies are all expressions of one, underlying, and developing truth.

The assumption behind Hegel's theory of the history of philosophy is that its object is truth; and truth is not a set of unchanging theses we must strive to grasp at all times, but is the underlying identity of thought and being in the different forms it acquires over time, articulated systematically according to ever new perspectives. In this sense truth is an abiding substance which actively takes on different forms. It is this idea of substance-that-becomes-subject, together with the superficiality of histories of philosophy that present a mere gallery of unrelated opinions, that leads Hegel to the "identity thesis", the thesis that the sequence of categories in logic is identical to the sequence of philosophical positions in the history of philosophy. This thesis, as I said, does not hold and is in my view a rhetorical exaggeration which is deployed polemically by Hegel against the loose collections of opinions which were passed off as "histories" by Hegel's contemporaries and predecessors.

Hegel's approach to his predecessors, and to Aristotle in particular, is speculative: we think along with past philosophers in the attempt to discern what in their philosophy still belongs to us. This speculative approach assumes that the truth – the one, living Idea – that is latent in past forms of thought admits of different degrees of development and, indeed, can be said to progress to greater concreteness and explicitness in history. It does *not*, however, presuppose that the history of philosophy constitutes the seamlessly continuous, linear, and irreversible progress of thought, for it recognizes that in history, as in life, there can be sudden breaks, unexpected turns or new directions. Contrary to popular belief, Hegel's reading of past philosophers is not guided by any preconceived idea of linearity or irreversible progress. Furthermore, as I suggested above, Hegel's speculative approach to past philosophers does not presuppose the identity of logic and the history of philosophy (even though he does advocate this identity). It would be tempting to conclude that this approach, for which neither the *Wirkungsgeschichte* of tradition nor the identity of logic and the history of philosophy provides an indispensable mediating condition is therefore ahistorical. The striking fact, however, is that Hegel calls precisely this procedure – thinking through what others have thought, from our perspective, carefully avoiding finding in them what did not belong to their time and superimposing on them later categories – *historical.*[9]

To be sure, Hegel is not Arnold Ruge, or a latter-day historicist. Unlike Bacon, Hegel thinks that the history of philosophy should not be consigned to mere memory, but is integral to philosophy; nor is truth simply *filia temporis*, the child of its time. Time itself is not just empty succession – relentless renewal and loss, Cronos devouring its children – because it is at the same time the changing concrete appearance of the same underlying truth, the manifestation of spirit's eternal essence. But philosophy is and remains for Hegel *its time grasped in thought*. It all comes down to understanding this phrase correctly. If it amounted to an expression of the historical relativity of our position, then thought would not determine itself but would be shaped by the epoch, and transcending one's age would be impossible.

But that is not the meaning of Hegel's phrase, or of the thought it expresses. Philosophy is neither "influenced" by its age, nor on the contrary does it constitute the supposed foundation of religion, politics, art, right (VGPh I, W 18, pp. 70–75). In this sense, balancing the supposedly historicist streak to Hegel's philosophy with other imagery from his work (such as the famous description of the logic as "the exposition of God ... before the creation of nature and of a finite spirit," WL 1, 44, SL 50, interpreted as a quasi-Platonic world of forms behind appearance) means reconciling aspects that we, in light of later interpretations of Hegel's philosophy, set up as opposed and project back onto Hegel. The question whether speculation and history are mutually independent is abstract and simplistic. The root common to philosophy, art, religion, and politics is the particular shape that *spirit* takes on in them. As a consequence, the surprising fact that Hegel makes so much of Aristotle as the teacher of Alexander the Great, thanks to whom the Greek principle is made effective where it was not known and philosophy pervades reality more deeply (or that Plato's philosophy is related to the crisis of the polis), is meant far more seriously than many would think. When many of us study Aristotle today, what we want to know is whether, say, abstracting from all questions external to the text, *Metaphysics* Z is internally coherent (and when we study Aristotle and Hegel, we confront both that question and its relation to Hegel's objective logic). Hegel would subordinate this question to that of the comprehensive unity of Aristotle's philosophy, and he would understand the latter in relation to Aristotle's epoch and to the particular shape of spirit that manifests itself therein.

It is no less important, however, to emphasize that by translating a particular shape of spirit into its language, philosophy *changes the very form* of its age. As it sets the substantial content of its age before its eyes, as it articulates it in thought, as it transforms it into knowledge, philosophy stands above its time. This superiority is only formal, as Hegel stresses, for the content remains the same.[10] But because the formal requisite of thought is that the moments hang together in a tight and necessary unity, the complete form that each philosophy is – as it articulates actuality in one totality and translates its content into a net of logical determinations – is, like the tortoise for Achilles, always one step ahead of reality. By its very being, philosophy – the epoch's self-understanding – introduces an ever new gap between itself and its age. The difference in form then becomes a fundamental difference in content; and that is not without consequences for actuality.

Hegel best expresses this thought in a letter to Niethammer: "I am daily ever more convinced that theoretical work accomplishes more in the world than practical work. Once the realm of representation is revolutionized, actuality will not hold out" (Oct. 28, 1808, in Briefe I, 253, Lett. 179). Every philosophy, not just his own and not just in relation to the Napoleonic wars, introduces a change into reality itself: it corrupts the world in which we used to find satisfaction, accelerates its collapse and brings it to dissolution. For every philosophy, as it produces a new form, destroys the ethical substance, the religious certainties, etc. of its age (VGPh I, W 18, p. 72). Hegel likens the gap between an age and its self-understanding to the difference between the ages of one and the same individual: In youth, fresh vitality is too busy sustaining institutions with its unstinting support and affirming itself in reality to reflect on what it does. In maturity, once we start feeling dissatisfied with the world we have produced, we collect ourselves and escape to the realm of pure thought; we thus corrupt our previous faith and end up undermining the world.

Why is that? Because philosophy is not contemplation, but the answer to the need for satisfaction that spirit has: to find itself at home in its world. This is yet another way to state the reason why we cannot consider any finite expression of spirit (including obviously Hegel's philosophy) definitive, or why we cannot be Aristotelians any more. In Hegel's strong phrase, "brought among the living, mummies do not endure" because spirit cannot rest content with "translations" (VGPh I, W 18, p. 66).

It is not out of love of paradoxes that in concluding this section we must reiterate that philosophy has no other object than reality and yet is always removed from it; and that – for all the qualifications I have clarified – Hegel considers Aristotle's philosophy to be the closest to his own.

5.   The Limits of Aristotle According to Hegel

If philosophy articulates its time in thought, what this means is that it isolates the logic of its own and its time's content: if the content (i.e., the several concrete appearances of the same eternal spirit) remains the focus in view, this change of form becomes philosophy's exclusive work. But if there is a logical articulation, then thought cannot but follow its own necessary course: the very idea that it may passively register data and import something from without, let alone that its order and logic be dictated by something other than it, is senseless. For only pure concepts are the object of thought, and thinking alone can shape and constitute such objects. Indeed, thought is nothing but the translation of contents into its own immanent logic. What thought finds – in the age, in the sciences and in all empirical realms – it now transforms into logical moments and endows with necessary form (ENZ §9).

Naturally, there is a direct (yet not causal) connection between the complexity of an epoch and the richness of its philosophy. The more complex the differences from which thought returns to itself, the deeper the thought that will result; the poorer and more abstract the content, the less internally articulated the philosophy. This is the only sense we can make of the vexed question of the relation between Hegel's logic and, say, the Reformation or the French revolution: if the Greeks had a higher conception of thought, still our age is more complex – and so is the logic that must comprehend it.[11] It is this greater complexity and this unprecedented depth that put us on a different level, according to Hegel – not the scientific revolution, the Lutheran Reformation, or the Kantian critical turn taken by themselves, as held by many contemporary Hegel inter- preters, who share Erdmann's fear. Where then does the greater complexity of our age lie? In none of those events taken singly, but in what Hegel dubs the necessity for spirit to overcome the alienation of inert forms toward which all those historical events push: to appropriate universals and bring life back to them. This contrast is expressed in a famous and important passage from the preface to the *Phenomenology*. While the ancients looked to complete the formation and development of natural consciousness, which philosophized about everything it came across, "in modern times instead the individual finds the abstract form ready-made," so that the task, rather than purging sensuous immediacy and turning it into an abstract universal, is now that of "freeing determinate thoughts from their fixity so as to give actuality to the universal."[12]

If this connection between philosophy and the historical concretization of spirit's eternal essence in the epoch concerned is not necessarily in contrast with Hegel's view of Aristotle's superiority over his successors, or with the fact that it is not one's date of birth that determines how important one's philosophy is, it does however compel us to ask how, under these circumstances, Hegel can affirm that "there is no higher idealism" than Aristotle's (VGPh II, W 19, p. 158, J/G 71). Is it possible that if Aristotle had lived in Hegel's age his philosophy would have been very close to Hegel's? What limits does Hegel find in Aristotle? And are these rooted in the structure of Aristotle's philosophy or in the spirit of Aristotle's age?

The simple answer is that, for Hegel, they depend on Aristotle's "external manner" (*äussere Manier*) of philosophizing. For curiously, after some introductory notes on Aristotle's life and work, Hegel begins his treatment of Aristotle in the lectures with some "methodological" remarks on Aristotle's manner of philosophizing in which he explains why we must not look for a system in Aristotle; and he returns to them in his conclusion, as if to round up his examination (VGPh II, W 19, 144–151, and 242–244). Still, this does not yet tell us whether that manner is peculiar to Aristotle's age or is a trait internal to his philosophy. In this section I want to focus on this point because the answer to that question is in my view quite instructive.

Hegel says that Aristotle leaves nothing outside his consideration; his genius is thoroughly comprehensive, but he does not proceed deductively (VGPh II, W 19, p. 145). Aristotle begins with the world of appearance; he thoroughly investigates the object in the richness of its details, establishes a series of particular truths, and finally grasps the essence of the object in its simplicity, in conceptual form. Aristotle gets speculative when he unites the empirical determinations of an object in a unitary concept. What results is a deep, speculative concept that is the product of the meticulous search of a thinking observer who leaves nothing outside investigation and holds fast to the particular.

Understanding the world of phenomena philosophically is all very good, but the form in which this is presented by Aristotle is not adequate for Hegel. Aristotle does not "bring particulars back to their universal principles" (VGPh II, W 19, p. 148). He does not affirm the universal as the truth of the particular or bring the speculative idea of thought thinking itself to bear on the particular objects of his investigation (VGPh 145–149). Aristotle's philosophy has an empirical side and no methodical *necessity* (ibid.).

For Hegel, the lack of systematicity in Aristotle's "manner" of philosophy depends on the historical circumstances of the development of the Concept in Greece (*"von dem Begriff der Philosophie damaliger Zeit,"* ibid.), rather than on any conscious theoretical resistance to the form of a system on Aristotle's part. *"Definition, Konstruktion usf."* (ibid.), *"Konstruieren, Beweisen, Deduzieren"* ("construction, proof, deduction," J/G 66), had not yet affirmed themselves in the concept of philosophy in Aristotle's time. This explains why Aristotle does not proceed from the identity of thinking and thought (*De anima* III, 5, and *Metaphysics* XII 7 and 9) to the truth of speculative idealism as Hegel conceives it. Aristotle expresses himself as if thinking were "some kind of state" (VGPh II, W 19, p. 164), one object among others. It is the most powerful and excellent form of being, but Aristotle does not give explicit expression to "the Concept" (VGPh II, W 19, p. 163–4) and say "that thinking is all the truth." And yet, for Hegel, all the several determinations are finally "united [by Aristotle] in a totally speculative concept" (VGPh II, W 19, p. 167), namely thought thinking itself. In this respect Hegel stresses that his fundamental vision is the same insofar as Aristotle considers everything in thought (VGPh II, W 19, p. 164) and transforms everything into thoughts: for Aristotle things

445

"are in their truth; this is their *ousia*" (ibid.). The problem is that this vision lacks conceptual necessity.

Why does this problem mar the greatness of Aristotle's philosophy? Actually, if we take seriously the passage from the *Phenomenology* quoted above, it does not: Aristotle could not have done any better, under the circumstances of his age. It does, though, mean that there is a gap in Aristotle's philosophy between the peaks of its speculative idealism and its overall presentation. And when there is a gap it is for Hegel inevitable that we try to fill it: it is a need we must face and respond to.

When Hegel says that Aristotle's thought lacks necessity and systematicity, the last thing he implies is that Aristotle needs a method to give his theories a logical cogency or a deductive proof-structure, possibly imported from his *Organon*. Hegel thinks that if Aristotle had followed his own "logic" – his theory of syllogism and judgment – he would never have been a speculative philosopher, for his logic is the finite logic of the understanding governed by the principle of identity. Aristotle's speculative philosophy, by contrast, works precisely insofar as it does not stop at fixed determinacies and stable essences but understands the concept as a self-determining universal: we could say that Aristotle is speculative insofar as he is a *phenomenologist* who only wants to grasp the thing while bracketing everything else, including his mind, which must be pure intentionality (the intellect is famously nothing before it thinks, and the soul is somehow all beings). The concept of immanent form as cause puts Aristotle beyond Plato as well as beyond all "intellectualistic" thinking dominated by the finite understanding.

In this sense what Aristotle is missing is not the movement or the dialectic of the concept; what he is missing is "the *unity* of the concept" (VGPh II, W 19, p. 244, emphasis added). Instead of presenting its logical categories one after another in a series, the system that Aristotle could have used is the subordination of all the several determinations to one overarching concept: the identity of thought and being. When a philosophy is not systematic it is not scientific because it is "contingent with regard to its content. A content has its justification only as a moment of the whole" (ENZ §14 A.). The true can only be expressed as a whole because only thus can we grasp the comprehensive totality of connections and see how they have the power to generate further determinations, which are not "found" as our examination goes forth but are produced by it.

If Aristotle cannot provide such a system, then the insights that his genius has opened up for us risk being forgotten. The grand synthesis offered by Aristotle is a self-enclosed form of thought, but as such (because, as we saw, all closed form cannot resist the attack of time) it points beyond itself to a greater comprehensiveness. It generates a need, the need to proceed to "pure self-consciousness," which will emerge in the Hellenistic age with Stoicism, Epicureanism, and skepticism (ibid.).

Yet given what we have just said, it is actually misleading to speak of Aristotle's "manner" in the way we have seen Hegel do: that manner is not external at all because it highlights the gap between form and content that pushes us beyond Aristotle. And the problem is that you cannot simply give a different form to the same content and thereby leave it unaltered. Stated differently, it is not the case that, if Aristotle had known a greater systematicity, his philosophy would have been improved; my point is that it would have been a *different* philosophy. In this sense it is not an "external manner" that gives Aristotle's philosophy the shape we know. And we seem

446

to be driven to the same conclusion if we now turn to a critical analysis of Hegel's Aristotle.

6.   The Limits of Hegel's Aristotle

What I intend to do in conclusion is not to denounce Hegel's supposed mistakes (critics of such errors, from Schelling to Heidegger to Aubenque and Gadamer, definitely abound). For Hegel does not – generally speaking, with a few minor exceptions – make mistakes: he translates and interprets very aptly the Aristotle edition he used.[13] Nor do I want to oppose my Aristotle to Hegel's, and based on that show what is "wrong" with Hegel's Aristotle. What I want to argue, rather, is that Hegel's Aristotle is defined against the backdrop of Hegel's historiography, and that whatever problems we find in this figure, Hegel's Aristotle, depend on the relation that Hegel sets up between history and philosophy. Let me explain what I mean.

With his keen historical sense, Hegel has taught us that the notion of system cannot be Aristotelian but only Hellenistic; he has also taught us not to look for concepts such as consciousness or will in Aristotle's philosophy.[14] But when he ascribes the lack of systematicity to the concept of philosophy in Aristotle's age, he treats this limitation as contingent. For him, it is a matter of fact, and not of principle, that Aristotle did not have an idealistic system and was rather more of a phenomenologist in the sense we have seen. What guides Hegel in this reading is the possibility of translating Aristotle's metaphysics into his own logic – not by arbitrarily imposing his categories on to Aristotle, but by bringing to fruition what he identifies as the core of Aristotle's idealism, thought thinking itself.

In my view, this reading has two problems. The general one is that by reducing different positions to a homogeneous continuum, it is not sensitive to, or is bound to downplay, conceptual differences that may simply constitute clear alternatives, and not variations on an underlying theme. The particular problem regarding Aristotle is that Hegel thinks, based on his selection of key concepts that comprehensively constitute his Aristotle, that Aristotle *happened* not to have a system – but *potentially* had one very close to his. We have seen that "system" means the articulation of reasons, necessity, subordination to one principle, truth as totality, as opposed to proceeding from object to object and from realm to realm, assuming what one in turn finds as *given*. This potential system, which only waits for a more complex concept of philosophy to actualize itself, stands or falls with Hegel's interpretation of the *nous* (intellect). In this regard, Hegel does impose his views on Aristotle until he eventually becomes blind to Aristotle's own views, especially to what it means for Aristotle to assume something as given. There are many respects in which Hegel obviously misunderstands the Aristotelian intellect, beginning with the supposed identification of passive *nous* and intelligibility, or the intellect's self-knowledge,[15] but here I am interested in what underlies this misunderstanding and how it is linked with Hegel's concept of philosophy.

When Hegel praises the identity of thinking and thought in the Aristotelian intellect, he takes it as the achievement of a stage in which subject and object are no longer separate. If all forms are internal to thinking, then the intellect knows itself in that it knows the *kosmos noêtos* it implicitly is. If all intelligible forms are the products of thought, then the intellect constitutes the principle of a dialectic of concepts, of a logic of the relations among essences. Hegel does not see, however, that for Aristotle the identity of thinking and thought is discrete and relative to each separate understanding of what is true in turn, and does not constitute the uniform ground for what Hegel calls science, the free thought not prejudiced by oppositions between itself and givenness or subject and object. The Aristotelian intellect finds rest in the *discontinuous* intellection of the several forms it thinks. This understanding is an act of seeing essences, the end of a process through which experience has led us; but as such the intellect takes on the form it understands, and is thus qualified and defined by its object. This means that in Hegel's terms the Aristotelian intellect is in principle finite, not infinite; and the identity of thinking and thought, which for Aristotle is our way of attaining a full and unimpeded vision of reality, should be considered by Hegel subjective, not beyond the subject-object separation. Essences are not the intellect's products: they are in the thing, as its causes, and the intellect "becomes" them once it thinks them in turn.

In the Preface to the *Phenomenology* (W 3, pp. 54 and 66, PhS 34 and 44), we find the first evidence of Hegel's Neoplatonic reading of the intellect that will become dominant later in the lectures: Hegel links the intellect as the origin of forms to Plato's *Parmenides* – and takes the skeptical and negative side of reason, the destruction of the independence of finite forms, as internal to the *nous*, which in knowing the finite knows itself as the one, infinite substance.

If we were to "defend" Aristotle from such an enthusiastic appropriation, we could turn to the *Metaphysics* and invoke as evidence of an opposite position Aristotle's criticism of the mathematization of the cosmos pursued by Plato, Aristotle's advocacy of the nongeneric universality of being, and the gaps he sees between the world and the divine, or between essence and substance, or between the grasp of intelligibles and discursive predication. But as Hegel has shown, the historian of philosophy is not an antiquarian intent on preserving its goods from contamination or aging: what alone counts is the testing of reasons, grounds, and principles. Those differences and oppositions are less fundamental than the principle upon which they hang: the conception of philosophy behind the respective positions.

When Aristotle writes that poetry is more philosophical than history because through its types it has at least a partially conceptual structure, his history is not Hegel's; nor is what he means by philosophy the same as what Hegel means by it. For there is no question for Aristotle of philosophy transforming reality; the most we can transform is our character, as we grasp an inwardly articulated reality that does not change. If, by contrast, philosophy is, as in Hegel, the answer to reason's need for satisfaction, then it is vitally related to history. And it cannot take anything for granted, beginning with inopportune divisions among separate realms. Differences are all immanent or internal to thought, and thoughts do not derive their status and objectivity from the objects to which they are relative, but from their systematic connection to other thoughts – for they are all moments of the self-articulation of the Idea.

What Hegel fails to take seriously is the possibility that for Aristotle philosophy sees reality as it truly is in and by itself, a form of contact that leaves things as they stand: Hegel fails to see that for Aristotle the intellect does not mediate, let alone constitute, our access to things, because its role is simply to bring the forms of things themselves to light. When we approach something what we require is, if I am allowed the expression, reason's sensitivity to the different modalities of givenness. We must be able to follow plastically the inner texture of things without a preceding method or rule. We start from what is given; and in our investigation this means we start from what is familiar, because the empirical is never something we try to overcome but is the appearance of whatever truth it is we are trying to bring to light. The very distinction between scientific and calculative intellect (Nicom. Eth. VI 2, 1139a 7–9) depends on the different modality of the respective object, what exists necessarily and what admits of being otherwise. We could say that for Aristotle thought is an act that must be declined in the plural, while for Hegel thought is the single, all-encompassing element in which we move: all thoughts are moments of thought's self-determination. It may, however, be more to the point to say that Hegel does not take seriously the possibility that for Aristotle being or nature are the criterion and standard from which we take our bearings.[16]

Regardless of whether we take our bearing from, and allow our thought to be governed by, being or reason, Aristotle's manner is not external, but an essential trait of his philosophy. In Hegel's words, the form is not without relevance for the content. In fact, it determines its meaning.

Notes

1   Hegel's works will be quoted with the following abbreviations:

Briefe = *Briefe von und an Hegel*, 4 Bände, ed. J. Hoffmeister, Hamburg: Felix Meiner, 1952, 1969³.

EL = *The Encylopaedia Logic*, trans. T. F. Geraets, W. A. Suchting, H. S. Harris. Indianapolis/ Cambridge: Hackett Publishing Co., 1991.

ENZ = *Enzyklopädie der philosophischen Wissenschaften* (W 8-9-10), followed by § (number of section), A. (Remark, Anmerkung), Z. (oral addition, Zusatz).

J = *Vorlesungen über die Geschichte der Philosophie*, Teil 1. Einleitung in die Geschichte der Philosophie. Orientalische Philosophie, neu ed. W. Jaeschke, Hamburg: Felix Meiner, 1993.

J/G 3 = *Vorlesungen über die Geschichte der Philosophie*, Teil 2. Griechische Philosophie 2, ed. P. Garniron und W. Jaeschke, Hamburg: Felix Meiner, 1996.

Lett. = *Hegel: The Letters*, trans. C. Butler and Ch. Seidler, with Commentary by C. Butler, Bloomington: Indiana University Press, 1984.

PhR = *Grundlinien der Philosophie des Rechts* (W 7); *Hegel's Philosophy of Right*, trans. with Notes by T. M. Knox, Oxford: The Clarendon Press, 1952.

PhS (= W 3) = *Phänomenologie des Geistes; Phenomenology of Spirit*, trans. A. V. Miller, with Analysis and Foreword by J. N. Findlay, Oxford: Oxford University Press, 1977.

VGPh = *Vorlesungen über die Geschichte der Philosophie* (W. 18-19-20, all translations from the lectures are my own).

W = G. W. F. Hegel, *Werke in zwanzig Bänden*, ed. E. Moldenhauer and K. M. Michel (Frankfurt am Main: Suhrkamp Verlag, 1969–1971) (followed by the number of the volume and of the page);

WL = *Wissenschaft der Logik* (= W 5–6); SL = *Hegel's Science of Logic*, trans. A. V. Miller, with Foreword by J. N. Findlay, London/New York: Humanities Press, 1969.

2   *"Das Prinzip der Subjektivität fehlt darin* [sc. in Plato]; *und dies Prinzip der Lebendigkeit, ... der reinen Subjektivität ist Aristoteles eigentümlich,"* VGPh II, W 19, p. 153. *"Energie ist konkreter Subjektivität,"* op. cit., p. 154.

3   We must keep separate what Hegel dubs the "metaphysics of the recent past," which collapses under Kant's blows, and the metaphysics of the ancients. Whereas the former proceeds thanks to the understanding's ascription of predicates to the supersensible substrates of special metaphysics, the latter is speculative and does not know this intellectualism. See ENZ §31 Z. (EL, p. 69): "Greek philosophy thought freely, but Scholasticism did not," and §36 Z. (EL, p. 76): "The understanding is one moment of speculative philosophy; but it is a moment at which we should not stop. Plato is not a metaphysician of this sort, and Aristotle still less so, although people usually believe the contrary." See also WL I, W 5, pp. 37–38 (Miller's translation, p. 45): "Ancient metaphysics had in this respect a higher conception of thinking than is current today. For it based itself on the fact that the knowledge of things obtained through thinking is alone what is really true in them, that is, things not in their immediacy but as first raised into the form of thought, as things *thought.* Thus this metaphysics believed that thinking (and its determinations) is not anything alien to the object, but rather is its essential nature, or that things and the thinking of them ... are explicitly in full agreement, thinking in its immanent determinations and the true nature of things forming one and the same content." Compare VGPh I, W 18, p. 129, and the lectures on Aristotle, VGPh II, W 19, p. 199.

On the relation between logic and history of philosophy (as well as on all aspects of Hegel's reading of Aristotle I cannot broach here) I refer the reader to my *Hegel and Aristotle* (Cambridge and New York: Cambridge University Press, 2001 and 2007); and "Hegels Idee einer Geschichte der Philosophie und Aristoteles," in *Die modernen Väter der Antike. Die Entwicklung der Altertumswissenschaften an Akademie und Universität im Berlin des 19. Jahrhunderts,* ed. Annette M. Baertschi and Colin G. King (Berlin: De Gruyter, 2009), pp. 277–302.

4   Such concepts as consciousness, method, will, object were hardly even familiar to Aristotle: they stem from post-Aristotelian philosophy, and it is only in modernity that they constitute the starting point of investigation. On how Aristotle's theory of causes differs from the post-Aristotelian, especially Stoic, universe of discourse, see Kenley Dove, "Logic and Theory in Aristotle, Stoicism, Hegel," *The Philosophical Forum* 37 (2006): 265–320; "Words and Things in Aristotle and Hegel: 'το ον λεγεται πολλαχως,'" *The Philosophical Forum* 33 (2002): 125–142; and "La trama della *Fenomenologia*," in *Lo spazio sociale della ragione,* ed. L. Ruggiu and I. Testa (Milano: Guerini, 2008).

5   K. L. Michelet, *Entwicklungsgeschichte der neusten deutschen Philosophie, mit besonderer Rücksicht auf den gegenwärtigen Kampf Schellings auf der Hegelschen Schule, Dargestellt in Vorlesungen an der Friedrich-Wilhelms Universität zu Berlin in Sommerhalbjahr 1842* (Berlin, 1843), 398.

6   What is at stake here "is the true, and this is eternal, ... the essence of spirit, into which neither moths nor thieves penetrate." Spirit's cognitions constitute spirit's being itself; and they cannot be an erudition relative to something dead and gone. "The history of philosophy has to with what does not pass, with what is now living" (VGPh I, W 18, pp. 57–58).

7   Trans. EL p. 38. See also VGPh I, W 18, p. 49; J 27; 115; 157; 220; 293.

8   See my *Hegel and Aristotle,* op. cit., 39ff., and "Hegels Idee," op. cit.

9   "We must proceed historically and ascribe to works only what they immediately [*unmittelbar*] give us" (VGPh I, W 18, p. 62). For example, Aristotle ascribed to Thales the idea that the principle of everything was water; but because we do not find the notion of *archê* before Anaximander, we cannot claim that Thales possessed it (op. cit., 63).

10 In the words of the preface to the *Philosophy of Right*, "Content is reason as the substantial essence of actuality, whether ethical or natural," while form is "reason as speculative knowing" (*als begreifendes Erkennen*; PhR, p. 27; Knox, p. 12). The entire first part of the Introduction to the *Encyclopaedia* is about this translation of form regarding the same content.

11 See Hegel's letter to Cousin of March 3, 1828: "As for Kant being so much lower than Plato, and the moderns so much below the ancients, in many connections this is undoubtedly true, but for depth and breadth of principles we are generally on a higher trajectory" (Briefe, 575; Lett. 666). Cf. also WL 1: 33, SL 42: if Plato revised the *Republic* seven times over, Hegel should have rewritten his logic seventy seven times because of the "profounder principle, a more difficult subject matter and a material richer in compass." It is once again Plato, who is admired by Hegel but who in his view does not go beyond the beautiful natural consciousness described in the dialogues, who provides a foil to the modern age in VGPh I, W 18, p. 68: "in Plato for example we find no philosophical solution to the problems of the nature of freedom, the origin of evil, providence etc." By contrast, "deeper ideas slumber in the spirit of the modern age."

   Christianity is one of the names for this greater depth and complexity, provided we understand by it less one religious faith among others than one (the highest) philosophical position on freedom and interiority. There is no question for Hegel of going back to the Greek soul after (these are my examples) Augustine, the discovery of conscience, freedom, the will. This is why I wrote earlier that the reconciliation can only occur for us as the modern individual's personal experience of the Greek identity of thought and being.

12 See W 3, p. 37, PhS pp. 19–20, Miller's translation corrected.

13 See *Hegel and Aristotle*, op. cit., chapter 3.

14 One example of a topic for a better grasp of which it seems almost inevitable to appeal to later notions (and the literature succumbs to the temptation) is Aristotle's "imagination." See my "Aristotle on *Phantasia*," in *Proceedings of the Boston Area Colloquium in Ancient Philosophy*, vol. 21, ed. J. J. Cleary and G. M. Gurtler (Leiden: Brill, 2006), 89–123.

15 For a textual analysis of Hegel's translation from *De anima* III 4–5, see my *Hegel and Aristotle*, op. cit., 308–25.

16 On this idea, which is at the root of the ancient natural right theories, see my *Artificio, desiderio, considerazione di sé. Hobbes e i fondamenti antropologici della politica* (Pisa: Edizioni ETS, 2001), chapters 3 and 4; and my *Saggezza, Immaginazione e Giudizio pratico. Studio su Aristotele e Kant* (Pisa: Edizioni ETS, 2004), chapter 2.

22

From Kant's Highest Good to Hegel's Absolute Knowing

MICHAEL BAUR

Hegel's most abiding aspiration was to be a *Volkserzieher* (an educator of the people) in the tradition of thinkers like Moses Mendelssohn (1729–1786), Gotthold Ephraim Lessing (1729–1781), and Friedrich Schiller (1759–1805).[1] No doubt, he was also deeply interested in epistemology and metaphysics, but this interest stemmed at least in part from his belief (which Kant also shared) that human beings could become truly liberated to fulfill their vocations as human beings, only if they were also liberated from the illusions and contradictions that plagued uncritical thinking about self, world, and God. Thus to appreciate Hegel's work in epistemology and metaphysics, one must first appreciate how he (following Kant) sought to think beyond the "special metaphysics" of self, world, and God as developed by Descartes and other pre-critical philosophers. The aim of this chapter is to analyze aspects of Hegel's critical appropriation and transformation of Kantian thought, shedding light not only on Hegel's own understanding of his move beyond Kant, but also on the philosophical reasons that might justify such a move.

1. Kant's Anti-Cartesianism

Kant's theory of knowledge is marked by three significant departures from Descartes's theory of knowledge. First, while Descartes held that our perception of ourselves as finite is to be explained by reference to our more primordial perception of the infinite,[2] Kant sought to show that our ideas of the infinite are – on the contrary – to be explained as products of our own reason as finite.[3] Second, while Descartes held that the knowing subject could come to know itself and its epistemic capacities in the absence of any knowledge about empirically given objects, Kant sought to show that the knowing subject could come to know itself and its epistemic capacities only through its knowing of empirically given objects.[4] Third, while Descartes held that any adequate justification of the reliability of our knowledge claims will depend on establishing the existence and interrelationship of three different kinds of being (namely, self, world,

A Companion to Hegel, First Edition. Edited by Stephen Houlgate and Michael Baur.
© 2011 Blackwell Publishing Ltd. Published 2011 by Blackwell Publishing Ltd.

and God), Kant sought to show that our talk of self, world, and God as three separate and theoretically knowable kinds of being will not only fail to deliver the desired justification, but will also lead our reason into irresolvable conflicts with itself. Indeed, the three central chapters of the Transcendental Dialectic in Kant's *Critique of Pure Reason* (i.e., the chapters on the Paralogisms of Pure Reason, the Antinomy of Pure Reason, and the Ideal of Pure Reason) correspond to the three kinds of being that play a pivotal role in the Cartesian project of epistemic justification (and in turn, these three kinds of being correspond to the three different branches of special metaphysics, namely: rational psychology, rational cosmology, and rational theology). In the Transcendental Dialectic, Kant argues that our ideas of self ("a simple substance that ... persists in existence with personal identity"; *CPR*, A672/B700), world ("the sum total of all appearances"; *CPR*, A672/B700), and God ("a highest being as the supreme cause"; *CPR*, A679/B707) do not refer to any independently existing, theoretically knowable entities or kinds of being, but only to the *rules* or *maxims* that we give to ourselves for the purpose of extending our empirical knowledge and bringing about the greatest possible systematic unity in such knowledge. Accordingly, the three central chapters in Kant's Transcendental Dialectic – taken together – can be understood as an implicit argument against the Cartesian attempt to make use of our ideas of self, world, and God (construed as referring to independently existing, theoretically knowable entities) for the purpose of demonstrating the reliability of our knowing.

It follows from Kant's account in the Transcendental Dialectic that it is a mistake to think that our idea of God refers to a theoretically knowable, independently existing entity whose supposed existence and goodness can provide an epistemic guarantee of the correctness of our judgments about an external world. For Kant, the pure concept or idea of God is merely a "schema" or "heuristic" that serves to show us how, under its guidance as a pure concept or idea, "we ought to *seek after* the constitution and connection of objects of experience in general" (*CPR*, A671/B699). In other words, the idea of God represents no theoretically knowable, independently existing reality, but only a certain kind of task or imperative that our own reason gives to itself. The task or imperative is to consider the sum total of all appearances within possible experience (that is, to consider the world of sense itself) *as if* it had "a single, supreme, and all-sufficient ground outside its range, namely an independent, original, and creative reason" (*CPR*, 672/B700); or to "consider every connection in the world according to principles of a systematic unity, hence *as if* they had all arisen from one single, all-encompassing being, as supreme and self-sufficient cause" (*CPR*, A686/B714). For Kant, in other words, the traditional metaphysical idea of God (just like the traditional metaphysical ideas of self and world) is "not a constitutive principle for determining something in regard to its direct object" (*CPR*, A680/B708), but a merely "regulative principle for the greatest possible empirical use of my reason" (*CPR*, A679/B707).[5]

Kant goes further and argues not only that it is a mistake to regard the idea of God as referring to "an actual thing to which one would think of ascribing the ground for the systematic constitution of the world" (*CPR*, A681/B709), but also that there is something self-defeating in any account that would seek to explain the systematic unity of the empirical world by reference to a theoretically knowable divine being that is thought to exist independent of and external to such a world. For Kant, the act of regarding God as an independently existing, theoretically knowable entity that allegedly

453

grounds the systematic unity of nature will actually end up undermining our attempts at appreciating this systematic unity. Kant writes:

> if I antecedently make a highest order being the ground [of the unity of nature], then the unity of nature will in fact be done away with. For then this unity is entirely foreign and contingent in relation to the nature of things, and it cannot be cognized from the universal laws thereof. (*CPR*, A693/B721)

The problem, in other words, is that the very act of regarding the divine being as something independent and beyond the scope of nature will inescapably lead one to think of this divine being "anthropomorphically," and this in turn will lead one to regard the systematic unity of nature as something that must be imposed on nature "forcibly" and "dictatorially" (*CPR*, A692/B720). But if systematic unity is something that must be imposed on nature in such a forcible, external manner, then this unity will become unintelligible and mysterious to us finite inquirers; for we can understand and appreciate the unity and coherence of nature only "on the path of physical investigation," by attending to nature's own (*internal*) universal laws.

For Kant, as long as we regard the systematic unity of the natural world as something that is imposed upon it from without (i.e., by a divine being conceived anthropomorphically), we will have to regard this systematic unity as something inaccessible and inscrutable to us. And as long as we regard nature's systematic unity as something inaccessible and inscrutable to us, we will be tempted to think that this unity can be explained only by reference to an independent divine being that exists beyond us and beyond nature. Thus, Kant suggests, we will find ourselves trapped in a "vicious circle" (*CPR*, A693/B721): the act of thinking that nature's systematic unity can be explained only externally (by reference to an independently existing divine being) will ensure that the systematic unity of nature appears mysterious and inscrutable to us; and in turn, this ongoing, obstinate inscrutability will incline us all the more vigorously to think that nature's systematic unity can be explained only externally (by reference to an independently existing divine being). We will be trapped not only in a vicious circle, but in a vicious circle *of our own making*. And as long as we fail to recognize this, we will continue to make theoretical claims that inescapably bring our reason into a state of internal contradiction, or into a state of war with itself (*CPR*, A751/B779).

When we find our reason entering into contradiction with itself, Kant acknowledges, it is tempting to think that the contradictions arise from accidental defects in our reason, or from some hidden causes lying in the "nature of things" outside us. Kant insists, however, that the contradictions are generated from the characteristic activities of our very own reason, and thus can be explained adequately by reference to the nature of our reason itself, without recourse to any talk about accidental defects or extrinsic causes in the "nature of things":

> [A]ll the concepts, indeed all the questions that pure reason lays before us, lie not in experience but themselves in turn only in reason, and they must therefore be able to be solved and their validity or nullity must be able to be comprehended. We are, also, not justified in repudiating these problems under the excuse of our incapacity, as if their solution really lay in the nature of things, and in rejecting further investigation, since reason has given birth to these ideas from its very own womb alone, and is therefore liable to give account of either their validity or their dialectical illusion. (*CPR*, A763/B791)[6]

With these remarks, Kant is elaborating a theme already suggested – though in a very rudimentary way – by his notion of a "Copernican revolution" in philosophy. As Kant argued in the Second Preface to his *Critique of Pure Reason*, the difficulties and contradictions that we encounter in metaphysics will continue to seem irresolvable to us, so long as we persist in thinking that their source lies in the nature of things outside us. And we will persist in thinking that their source lies in the nature of things outside us, so long as we adhere to a precritical or pre-Copernican stance that fails to recognize that our reason is legislative in relation to the things that it knows. In other words, the apparent obstinacy and intractability of the metaphysical difficulties and contradictions we encounter will only serve to confirm our (pre-critical or pre-Copernican) view that we ourselves have not generated such problems for ourselves, but are instead only the passive victims of mysterious forces or causes outside us. And in turn, as long as we continue to think that the metaphysical difficulties and contradictions we encounter have their source in things outside us, we will remain incapable of adopting a critical, Copernican stance, which alone is capable of illuminating our legislative activity in relation to the things that we know and liberating us from our self-made metaphysical difficulties. The problem, in short, is that the pre-Copernican stance that we ourselves uncritically adopt leads us into the difficulties that we encounter in metaphysics; and the obstinacy of these difficulties seemingly confirms the rightness of this pre-Copernican stance, according to which it is the nature of things outside us (rather than our very own stance) that is the cause of our ongoing metaphysical difficulties.

Hegel's own approach, especially in the 1807 *Phenomenology of Spirit*, can be understood as an implementation, for *all* shapes of insufficiently critical consciousness, of the basic strategy that Kant implemented in the Transcendental Dialectic of the *Critique of Pure Reason* regarding precritical, metaphysical consciousness. For Hegel, each shape of insufficiently critical consciousness takes a stance regarding the world within which it knows objects, and yet remains unaware of the extent to which its own stance-taking is responsible for the way in which objects in its world appear to it. When such insufficiently critical consciousness experiences difficulties and contradictions within its own experience, it naturally thinks that these problems have been caused – and can only be remedied – by some being or causality outside itself. The emergence of absolute knowing in the *Phenomenology* will coincide with the realization by consciousness that it is itself responsible for having generated such problems for itself, and thus is ultimately not the victim of an external causality, and not dependent on an alien, transcendent being for remedying them. A key shape of consciousness that eventually leads to the emergence of absolute knowing in the *Phenomenology* is the shape represented by Kantian "morality" and Kant's moral proof of the existence of God, to which we now turn.

2. Kant on the Highest Good and the Practical Necessity of Belief in God's Existence

Kant held that we cannot attain theoretical knowledge of God's existence or attributes; however, he argued that belief in God is not only rational, but also necessary from a moral point of view. Kant's argument – his so-called moral proof of God's existence[7] – depends on the notion of the "highest good."[8] For Kant, there are two different senses

455

of the "highest good": on the one hand, the highest good might mean the "supreme" good; on the other hand, the highest good might mean the "most complete" or "most perfect" good (*CPrR*, 5:110). A morally good will (one that acts out of pure duty or respect for the moral law) is supremely and unconditionally good; but a morally good will is not the only possible good. While moral virtue is the "supreme" good insofar as it is the unconditioned condition of all other goods, it does not follow that it is the "most complete" or "most perfect" good. What is required for the "highest good" in the sense of "completeness" and "perfection" is not just the morally good will, but also a proportionality between happiness and moral goodness (i.e., between happiness and worthiness to be happy).

Kant goes on to argue that we as finite rational human beings have a moral duty to promote the highest good (*CPrR*, 5:125). According to Kant, a world in which a person is "in need of happiness and also worthy of it," but still does "not partake of it" is a morally defective world, one that "could not be in accordance with the complete volition of an omnipotent rational being" (*CPrR*, 5:110). On Kant's account, to have a morally good or virtuous will is the same as to be worthy or deserving of happiness (*CPrR*, 5:110); accordingly, our moral duty to promote the highest good is at the same time a moral duty to promote a proportionality between desert and reward. But a proportionality between desert and reward is the same as justice (*CPrR*, 5:115, and 5:123). It follows, then, that our moral duty to promote the highest good is equally a moral duty to promote justice. Furthermore, since virtue is an effect of our freedom alone, and happiness is an effect of natural causes insofar as they relate to our desires and inclinations, it also follows for Kant that the duty to promote the highest good is also duty to bring about a harmony between freedom and nature. Kant thus speaks of the highest good as "the kingdom of God on earth"[9] and "the Kingdom of God in which nature and morality come into harmony with one another" (*CPrR*, 5:128).

On Kant's account, the fact that we have a moral duty to promote the highest good leads to a difficulty, and solving the difficulty leads us to the argument of the "moral proof." For Kant, we have a duty to promote the highest good; but the highest good involves a proportionality or harmony between two entirely heterogeneous elements, namely virtue and happiness; accordingly, any posited connection between these heterogeneous elements must be synthetic and not analytic (*CPrR*, 5:126–127). Now the synthetic connection between virtue and happiness can be conceived in only two possible ways: either the desire for happiness is the ground of virtue, or conversely the maxim of virtue is the ground of happiness (*CPrR*, 5:113). The first option, Kant argues, is impossible, for the first option (if true) would destroy the autonomy of practical reason by locating the determining ground of the will in the desire for happiness. But the second option is equally impossible: for a person's actual enjoyment of happiness does not depend only on the moral goodness of that person's will, but rather on (often unexpected) effects and consequences as they arise in the world of nature. While we have a moral duty to promote the highest good, there seems to be no ground that could possibly guarantee the requisite connection between virtue and happiness (or desert and reward, or freedom and nature). The world as we know it seems irremediably unjust: morally good people suffer, while morally bad people thrive.

Now Kant famously holds that an obligation that obliges us to do what is beyond our control cannot be an obligation at all.[10] Thus if it seems that we are morally obligated to promote the highest good, but nevertheless unable to do so through our own acts of willing, then any apparent moral obligation to promote the highest good must be null and void. In turn, the emptiness of this obligation would entail the invalidity of the moral law itself, since there is an intimate connection between the obligation to promote the highest good and the moral law. As Kant explains:

> no necessary connection of happiness with virtue in the world, adequate to the highest good, can be expected from the most meticulous observance of moral laws. Now, since the promotion of the highest good, which contains this connection in its concept, is an a priori necessary object of our will and inseparably bound up with the moral law, the impossibility of the first must also prove the falsity of the second. If, therefore, the highest good is impossible in accordance with practical rules, then the moral law, which commands us to promote it, must be fantastic and directed to empty imaginary ends and must therefore in itself be false. (*CPrR*, 5:113–114).

In the face of this difficulty, Kant holds that there must be some way in which we can think it possible to promote the highest good through our own moral agency; otherwise, the moral law itself would lose its binding force.

Kant begins to address this problem by pointing out that the initial absence of any guaranteed connection between virtue and happiness leads to an insuperable difficulty *only if* one first assumes that the ground of any such connection must reside in the moral activity of *finite* wills alone. The moral activity of such wills, as finite, necessarily presupposes the pre-existence of a given natural world *upon which* such activity is exercised. In other words, the finitude of such moral agents entails that the whole natural world upon which their moral activity is exercised is itself not *already* a product of their *own* moral activity (*CPrR*, 5:124). But since the natural world upon which such moral activity is exercised is itself not a product of this very moral activity, and since there seems to be no other source from which the natural world might acquire moral significance or direction, there seems to be no conceivable ground that can guarantee the complete harmony between virtue and happiness, freedom and nature. In other words, nature is at first simply "given" as indifferent and unrelated to the moral activity of finite rational agents. And because nature, so considered, is morally indifferent, there can be no guarantee that our finite moral activity can ultimately bring about the highest good as a harmony between virtue and happiness, freedom and nature. Accordingly, any obligation to promote the highest good seems to require something that is beyond our control, and so the obligation – along with the moral law connected to it – appears to be null and void.

Kant goes on to argue that this conclusion can be avoided only if one assumes the existence of a will that is not finite like our own, and thus not dependent on a pre-existing natural world – that is, only if one assumes the existence of a good and all-powerful God who created the natural world, and indeed created it such that it is not wholly indifferent to our moral purposes but completely conformable to them insofar as they are morally virtuous. Thus even though there is no necessary connection between *my* finite moral activity and the causes and effects that occur in the natural world, I can *think* of this connection indirectly, as mediated and guaranteed by the will of "an intelligible author of Nature" (*CPrR*, 5:115). For Kant, then, our belief in the existence of God is not only justified but also required as a matter of practical reason, insofar as we have an obligation to promote the highest good:

> Now, it was a duty for us to promote the highest good; hence there is in us not merely the warrant but also the necessity, as need connected with duty, to presuppose the possibility of this highest good, which, since it is possible only under the condition of the existence of God, connects the presupposition of the existence of God inseparably with duty; that is, it is morally necessary to assume the existence of God. (*CPrR*, 5:125).

Furthermore, Kant's "moral proof" justifies belief not just in the existence of a deistic, impersonal God, but in the existence of a God whose causality with respect to nature is "in keeping with the moral disposition" (*CPrR*, 5:125). In other words, the God that emerges in Kant's "moral proof" is a knowing and willing personal God who must possess the various attributes (omnipotence, omniscience, omnipresence, eternity, etc.) traditionally predicated of God by the Christian religion (*CPR*, A815/B843; see also *CPrR*, 5:140). Finally, Kant argues, this return to religion in general, and to the Christian religion in particular, does not in any way render our thinking heteronomous. For the kind of religious thinking that is justified through the "moral proof" involves the "recognition of all duties as divine commands" where these commands are not understood as the "arbitrary and contingent ordinances of a foreign will, but as essential laws of any free will as such" (*CPrR*, 5:129). Thus:

> the Christian principle of morality is not theological and thus heteronomous, being rather the autonomy of pure practical reason itself, because it does not make the knowledge of God and His will the basis of these laws but makes such knowledge the basis only of succeeding to the highest good on condition of obedience to these laws. (*CPrR*, 5:129)

For Kant, what we take to be divine commands are not binding on us simply because they are divine commands; rather, we regard certain imperatives as divine commands because they are already binding on us in accordance with the self-legislated imperatives of our own reason (*CPR*, A819/B847; *CPrR*, 5:131).[11]

3. The Moral Proof at the *Tübinger Stift* and Its Fate

Kant's moral proof garnered a great deal of attention at the Protestant seminary (the so-called *Tübinger Stift*) where Hegel, Schelling, and Hölderlin were not only fellow students and friends, but for a period in 1790 even shared accommodations together. On the one hand, Kant's moral proof was extremely suggestive and inspiring to the three young progressives, who – echoing Kant's own account of the highest good – shared excited thoughts about "the Invisible Church" and the "kingdom of God" on earth.[12] On the other hand, the three were also wary of the way in which some of the professors at the *Stift*, especially Gottlob Christian Storr (1746–1805) and Johann Friedrich Flatt (1759–1821), made use of Kant's critical philosophy in order to support some of their own conservative theological conclusions. Both Storr and Flatt argued, for example, that Kant's decisive critique of the pretensions of metaphysical reason allowed us to draw the conclusion that only revealed religion could save us from moral despair by providing us with answers to the speculative questions that we human beings can neither avoid asking, nor succeed in answering, on our own. Storr, furthermore, claimed that Kant's moral proof and his position on the postulates of practical reason might lead us not only to religion in general, but also to many positive doctrines of the Christian religion in particular (including even the doctrines of the Trinity, the Incarnation, and the Resurrection).[13]

To the young Hegel, Schelling, and Hölderlin, this reworking of Kant's critique of reason for the sake of adducing dogmatic conclusions amounted to the construction of an insidious Trojan horse whose attempted breach at the gates of the critical philosophy had to be vigorously resisted. And even after they had left the *Stift*, the three young progressives continued to complain to one another about the perversions of Kant's critical philosophy at the hands of the dogmatic theologians. In a letter to Hegel dated January 5, 1795, Schelling could hardly contain his disdain for the orthodox theologians' attention to the letter of Kant's philosophy at the expense of its spirit:

> I am firmly convinced that the old superstition of so-called natural religion as well as of positive religion has, in the minds of most, already once more been combined with the Kantian letter. It is a delight watching how keen they are at pulling the moral proof around on their string. Before you can turn around, the *deus ex machina* pops up, the personal individual Being who sits in heaven above![14]

Echoing his friend's sentiments, Hegel observes three weeks later that he is not surprised by the reactionary attitude of the orthodox theologians, since their clinging to orthodoxy is supported by powerful material and political interests. Anticipating his later notion of "immanent critique,"[15] Hegel suggests that the attempt to use Kantian materials in order to build a dogmatic theological fortress would be likely to undermine itself from within:

> Orthodoxy is not to be shaken as long as the profession is bound up with worldly advantages and interwoven with the whole of the state. This interest is too strong for orthodoxy to be given up so soon, and it operates without anyone being clearly aware of it as a whole. As long as this condition prevails, orthodoxy will have on its side the ever-preponderant herd of blind followers and scribblers devoid of higher interests and thoughts. ... I believe it would be interesting, however, to disturb as much as possible the theologians who in their antlike zeal procure *critical* building materials for the strengthening of their Gothic temple, to make everything more difficult for them, to block their every escape until they no longer find any way out and have no choice but to fully display their nakedness in the light of day. Yet, amidst the building materials they carry away from the funeral pyre of Kantianism in order to prevent the conflagration of dogmatics, they are carrying home with them some live coals. ...[16]

In spite of his suggestive observation about a possible immanent critique of the Tübingen orthodoxy, Hegel seemed not to have any clear sense about how such an immanent critique might proceed. Indeed, Hegel seemed to have overlooked some of the problems inherent in the moral proof itself, problems which had already led Schelling to doubt the proof as a whole. In a revealing passage from his letter of late January 1795, Hegel expresses his puzzlement over Schelling's suggestion that Kant's moral proof cannot, after all, justify belief in any personal God:

459

There is one expression in your letter concerning the moral proof that I do not fully understand: "which they know how to manipulate so that the individual, personal Being pops up." Do you think that we don't actually get so far [with the moral proof]?[17]

Schelling's response to Hegel, dated February 4, 1795, was prompt, direct, and illuminating:

Now for a reply to your question of whether I believe we cannot get to a personal Being by means of the moral proof. I confess the question has surprised me. ... Personality arises through the unity of consciousness. Yet consciousness is not possible without an object. But for God – i.e., for the Absolute Self – there is no object *whatsoever*; for if there were, the Absolute Self would cease to be absolute. Consequently there is no personal God. ...[18]

A week earlier, in a letter dated January 26, 1795, Hegel's other friend from the *Stift*, Hölderlin, had provided a similar explanation of the impossibility of belief in a personal God, referring directly to the thought of Fichte and Spinoza:

[Fichte's] Absolute Self, which equals Spinoza's Substance, contains all reality; it is everything, and outside of it, is nothing. There is thus no object for this Absolute Self, since otherwise all reality would not be in it. Yet a consciousness without an object is inconceivable; and if I myself am this object, then I am as such necessarily limited even if only in time, and thus am not absolute. Thus, in the Absolute Self, no consciousness is conceivable; as Absolute Self I have no consciousness; and insofar as I have no consciousness, to that extent I am – for me – nothing.[19]

With the help of the Fichte-inspired arguments from Schelling and Hölderlin, Hegel had become convinced by August 1795 that Kantian arguments about the highest good could not support belief in a personal God. For a personal God would have to be a God possessed of consciousness; but a being can be conscious only if it is conscious of something that counts as an object for it, and its consciousness of what counts as an object (or some "otherness") for it inescapably renders it finite or limited. Thus a personal, conscious God would have to be a finite God, which is to say that a personal, conscious God could not be a God at all. While rejecting the notion of a personal God, Hegel nevertheless told Schelling of his ongoing interest in discerning "what it might mean to approach God," and he thanked Schelling for helping to clarify "what previously floated before my mind darkly and in undeveloped form."[20] In the same letter, Hegel indicated his intention to proceed along the lines suggested by Kant's critical philosophy, according to which the failures of speculative reason are to be explained not by reference to any mysterious or ineluctable causes outside reason, but only by reference to "the very nature of reason" itself.[21]

4.   Self-Positing and the "Only True and Thinkable Creation Out of Nothing"

To followers of Fichte, Kant's attempt at demonstrating the necessity of belief in a personal God must have seemed like an unfortunate lapse into the sort of uncritical "special metaphysics" (of self, world, and an anthropomorphically conceived God) that Kant himself had criticized in the Transcendental Dialectic of the *Critique of Pure Reason*. For just as the Cartesian *Meditations* had relied on the notion of an all-knowing and all-benevolent (personal) God for the sake of establishing an epistemic connection between self and world, so too Kant's moral proof relied on the notion of an all-knowing and all-benevolent (personal) God for the sake of establishing a moral connection between the self and world. To some Kantians, it might have seemed possible to defend the moral proof's reliance on the triad of self, world, and God by saying that the triad in Kant's critical philosophy was not a triad of three separate and theoretically knowable entities (as it was in the Cartesian *Meditations*), but only a triad of regulative ideas that the self postulates for itself in order to make sense of its own moral aims. But to those who had imbibed Fichte's radical new philosophy, this possible defense of Kant – grounded on a firm distinction between theoretical and practical reason – was also untenable. To them, Fichte had shown that the distinction between theoretical reason and practical reason is not a fixed, unrevisable distinction that holds for all contexts or that is grounded in the very nature of reason itself. Rather, it is a contingent or relative distinction, and its relativity can be shown when one considers the founding act of all systematic philosophy: the act of self-positing.

According to Fichte, the act of self-positing is nothing other than the act through which the self both *is* itself and *is for* itself; that is, the act of self-positing is the act through which the self enacts both its *being* and its *being for itself* insofar as its being consists in nothing but its being for itself. Stated differently, what the self *is* and what the self *brings about* are identical in the act of self-positing; thus the act of self-positing can be characterized as an act of theoretical reason and an act of practical reason at once. As a result, the act of self-positing (which for Fichte is the founding act of all systematic philosophy) shows the untenability of any final or fixed distinction between theoretical reason and practical reason.

It is important to note that the act of self-positing, on Fichte's account, is the act of "being *for* self" where this "being for self" does not have the character of being any kind of "entity" or "content" that can be represented as an *object* for consciousness. For Fichte, the act of self-positing and the "content" of the act of self-positing fully coincide. In the act of self-positing, all that the self *is*, is simply its own act of being for self; and conversely, all that is *for* the self, is simply its act of being for self. In the act of self-positing, the act of *being a self* and the act of *being for self* fully coincide. And so in the act of self-positing, the self cannot have a conscious or object-like representation of the selfhood that it is; or (what amounts to the same thing) it cannot have a conscious or object-like representation of the selfhood that is its own act of self-positing. After all, such a conscious or object-like representation would require a distinction between the representer and represented; but if there were such a distinction, then the self doing the representing and the self being represented would not fully coincide. In the act of self-positing, however, the act of being a self and the act of being for self do fully coincide; but this is just to say that in the act of self-positing, the act of *being a self* (which is the same as the act of *being for self*) cannot be made into a representation or object for the self.

Fichte further explains: "*To posit oneself* and *to be* are, as applied to the self, perfectly identical. Thus the proposition, 'I am, because I have posited myself' can also be stated

461

as: '*I am absolutely* [*schlechthin*], *because I am.*' "[22] To say that the self "simply" or "absolutely" posits itself is to say that the self's act of self-positing, or its act of being the self that it is (whereby its act of being itself and its act of being for itself are identical) cannot be explained by reference to any represent-able or objectify-able cause or substance of which the self might become conscious. After all, if the self happens to have consciousness of any cause or substance whatsoever, then it has such (representational or object-like) consciousness only insofar as the self is also "for" itself in some non representational, non objective way. The self's act of *being itself* and (what amounts to the same thing) its act of *being for itself* is always presupposed by (and can never be explained by) its consciousness of some cause or substance that it might represent to itself. To say that the self "simply" or "absolutely" posits itself is to say that it is absolutely unable to explain itself or (what amounts to the same thing) it is unable to explain its being for itself by reference to any content, entity, or object that it might represent to itself. The presence to it of any represent-able content, entity, or object always already presupposes its own act of self-positing or its own act of being for self.

Fichte further observes that it would be a mistake to regard the self-positing self even as a kind of "thinking thing" or "thinking substance." The self-positing self is not a thing that also happens to think (a *res cogitans*); it is nothing but the activity of being for self that is non representationally present in (or presupposed in) all conscious thinking. In other words, the self "is an *act*, and absolutely [*absolut*] nothing more; we should not even call it an *active* something [*ein Thätiges*]."[23] Any attempt to think of the self-positing self as an underlying substance or substrate that sometimes does and sometimes does not include being for self, would mischaracterize what is meant by the act of self-positing. To think of the self-positing self as an underlying substance or substrate would be to think of it as a kind of independent "thing-in-itself" that allegedly has being or existence on its own, apart from the self's own activity of being for self.[24] But as we have already seen, the act of *being* and the act of *being for self* are perfectly identical in the act of self-positing. To say that the self-positing self might be an instance of being, but not being for self, would be a contradiction in terms.

From the foregoing analysis, it follows that the way in which the self-positing self is *for* itself, is very different from the way in which any represent-able entity or object can be for a conscious self. Recall the Fichtean argument by means of which Schelling and Hölderlin had shown Hegel in 1795 that a God possessed of personality and consciousness must be finite, and thus must not be a God at all. That Fichtean argument entailed that a being can be conscious, only if it is conscious of something that counts as an object for it, and its consciousness of what counts as an object for it inescapably renders the being finite or limited. Now, by contrast, the Fichtean notion of self-positing involves a self that is for itself, but not in the way that any object or representation can be for it. The self-positing self is for itself, but in an entirely non objective, non representational way; indeed, if the self-positing self were not for itself in this way, then no object or representation could ever be for it either.[25]

If the self-positing self is not for itself in the way that a representation or an object can be for a self, then how is the self-positing self for itself at all? We can give an initial answer to this question by observing that the self-positing self must be for itself in much the same way that an idea of pure reason, in Kant's system, is said to be for the self. For an idea of pure reason is for the self, not as any represent-able object or entity *within* the world of experience, but only as the implicit (non-represent-able) *criterion* or *maxim* for determining how one ought to think of objects within the world of experience, or how objects are to count as objects within the world of experience. Now based on this initial answer, one might be tempted to think that the self-positing self (like an idea of pure reason) is *for* the self, precisely to the extent that the self-positing self postulates for itself or gives to itself a kind of "template" or "framework" within which anything else that is given to the self might be regarded an object for the self. But to think in this way about the self-positing self's being for self would also be misleading. The being for self of the self-positing self cannot be regarded simply as the being for self (or the self-giving to the self) of a "template" or "framework" within which something else, as given to the self, might then count as an object for the self. After all, it would be wrong to think that the being for self of the self-positing self (or the self-positing self's act of giving to itself a kind of criterion or maxim for determining how objects are to count as objects) could somehow enable the self to become conscious of, or to regard as "objective," some sort of "raw material" that is known to exist somewhere, apart from the self's own activity. As Fichte had argued, the notion that there is some "raw material" that already exists somewhere, even though it does not exist for the self, is the same as the notion that there is an independent "thing in itself" that somehow exists apart from the self's knowing activity and yet nevertheless exercises a causal influence on the self's knowing activity. A truly critical philosophy (one that fully accepts the Kantian view that we cannot know of causal relations apart from the world of possible experience) must reject such a notion.

To make the same point differently: a truly critical philosophy will recognize that it is illicit to think that the being for self of the self-positing self (i.e., the self-positing self's act of giving to itself a kind of criterion or maxim) enables the self to bring objective "form" or "structure" to some independently existing material or content that is allegedly already present somewhere apart from the self-positing self's own activity. As Kant himself had argued (even though he did not do so with complete consistency), any given material that is thought to be present somewhere apart from the apperceptive (or self-positing) self's own activity, can only count as "nothing" for the self (*CPR*, B 131–132). Furthermore, the perspective of the critical (anti-Cartesian) philosopher must always remain the perspective of what is the case *for* the self, and not what might be the case for an external being (such as a God) who is imagined to hover above the self as a third-party guarantor of the self's epistemic claims. Accordingly, the critical philosopher must conclude that the self-positing self's being for self does not involve the *bringing-to-bear* of a criterion or maxim on some independent "raw material" that is thought already to exist somewhere, but rather the *bringing-into-being* of an entire world *for* the self. For apart from the self-positing self's own act of being for self, there simply is nothing that could count for the self as an existent thing at all. Apart from the self-positing self's own act of being for self, there is simply nothing for the self – no objects, no consciousness, and no world at all.

To illustrate this further, one might say that when the self-positing self ceases to be, the entire world that is *for* a self also ceases to be.[26] But even stating the matter in this way can be misleading, since the hypothetical ceasing-to-be of the world for a self (just like the self's own ceasing-to-be a self) can never be an actual event or happening *for* a self. It is for this reason that the world as it exists for a self will naturally appear to the

463

self as if it were a world that must have existed apart from the self's own activity. Stated more fully: the uncritical self will naturally regard the world as something that had already existed and will continue to exist, even apart from its own activity as a self, since the coming-to-be or ceasing-to-be of the world (just like the coming-to-be or ceasing-to-be of the self) can itself never be an actual event or happening *for* a self.[27] By contrast, we critical philosophers know that the world as it exists for the self *can* exist for the self only through the self's own activity which makes possible not only the being for self of the self, but also the being of the entire world for the self.

Along these lines, the young Hegel noted that the act of self-positing which actualizes not only *the being for self of the self* but also *the being for the self of an entire world*, is a kind of *creation out of nothing* – indeed, it is the only creation out of nothing that a critical philosopher can accept. In this act of "creation out of nothing," both the self-positing self *and* the entire world that exists for the self come to be "all at once," so to speak. In a fragment that has come to be known as the "Earliest System Programme of German Idealism," Hegel discusses such a "creation out of nothing," and he connects it with the Kantian claim that our talk about God can henceforth make sense only within the context of our own activity:

> Since the whole of metaphysics in the future falls under *morality* – of which Kant with his pair of practical postulates has given only an *example*, and has not *exhausted* – this Ethics will be nothing but a complete system of all Ideas or (what is the same thing) of all practical postulates. The first Idea is, of course, the presentation *of my self* as an absolutely free essence. Along with the free, self-conscious essence there simultaneously emerges an entire world – out of nothing – the only true and thinkable *creation out of nothing* [*die einzig wahre und denkbare Schöpfung aus Nichts*]. ...[28]

From this account of the activity of the self-positing self as a kind of creation out of nothing, we can draw the following important lesson: contrary to pre-critical "special metaphysics" and to Kant's moral proof, our ideas of self, world, and God do not pertain to three essentially separate things that can be understood as bearing some kind of external relation to one another. Rather, self, world, and God – understood most fundamentally – are coextensive with one another, since they are different aspects under which the same, originary activity of self-positing (or creation out of nothing) might be articulated discursively. In this activity of self-positing, there is no world that is not always already *for* a self; there is no self that is not always already mirroring the *entire* world[29]; and there is no external, transcendental God that is ultimately separable from the activity of self-positing (or "creation out of nothing") through which self and world come to be in the first place.

In his 1801 essay on *The Difference between Fichte's and Schelling's System of Philosophy*, Hegel no longer discusses the activity of self-positing as a "creation out of nothing" through which self and world come to be. But he gives expression to this same thought when he identifies the activity of self-positing as a "pure thinking" or "pure self-consciousness" that is neither subject nor object alone, but both at once: a "Subject-Object."[30] And in his 1802 essay on *Faith and Knowledge*, Hegel connects the notion of self-positing selfhood (whereby both self and world come to be in the first place) with Kant's thought about the highest good, which – if understood correctly, apart from

Kant's own anthropomorphizing tendencies – is nothing other than the thought of the identity of thought and being, self and world, freedom and nature:

> If we remove from the practical faith of the Kantian philosophy some of the popular and unphilosophical garments in which it is decked, we shall find nothing else expressed in it but the Idea that Reason does have absolute reality, ... that infinite thought is at the same time absolute reality – or in short we shall find the absolute identity of thought and being. ... This Idea of the absolute identity of thought and being is the very one which the ontological proof and all true philosophy recognize as the sole and primary Idea as well as the only true and philosophical one. Kant, to be sure, recasts this speculative Idea into humane form: morality and happiness harmonize. This harmony is made into a thought in its turn, and the realization of this thought is called the highest good in the world. ...[31]

5. The Way to Absolute Knowing in Hegel's *Phenomenology*

We have succeeded in distinguishing between two kinds of self. First, there is the conscious self that is conscious only insofar as it is confronted by, and thus limited or finitized by, that which counts as an object for it. It was on account of this notion of (finite) selfhood that Hegel became convinced in 1795 that God, as infinite, could not be possessed of personality or consciousness (in which case Kant's moral proof had to be rejected). But second, there is the self-positing self that is not finitized by any object of which it is conscious, but is rather an unbounded Subject-Object that is co-extensive with the world as a whole;[32] and the activity of the self-positing self is identical with a kind of "creation out of nothing" by means of which self and world come to be in the first place. Accordingly, we have (first) the always-finite self that is inescapably related to an other as to its object; and then we have (second) the self-positing self that is not related to or caused by anything outside itself, and so must be understood as unbounded and infinite.

For Hegel, every conscious self is necessarily both (a) a finite self that is conscious and represents to itself something that counts as an object for it, and (b) an infinite self that posits itself and in positing itself also posits an entire world that is coextensive with itself (thus it is neither subject nor object, but an unbounded Subject-Object). Furthermore, for Hegel, the (infinite) self's act of self-positing just *is* its act of instituting a world for itself; and in turn, its act of instituting a world for itself just *is* its act of giving to itself a (non objective, non representable) criterion or maxim for determining how objects are to count as objects within the world of experience, or for determining what may "show up" as an object of experience in the first place.

Significantly, Hegel holds that a conscious self can be finite only insofar as it is infinite, and infinite only insofar as it is finite. The reason for this is that a conscious, finite self can be conscious at all, only insofar as it regards something as an object for itself (for consciousness is always consciousness of an object); and it can regard something as an object for itself, only insofar as it (as infinite or self-positing) has instituted a world for itself and thereby given to itself a criterion or maxim for determining how something is to count as an object. But conversely, the conscious self can be an infinite self, only insofar as it is also a finite self. For only a finite self can be a conscious self; if infinite selfhood were infinite only, then there could never emerge any kind of consciousness or awareness. That is, an infinite self that was *only* infinite would not really be a self, since it would forever remain an unconscious, blind substance.[33]

On Hegel's account, we are to regard every conscious self as both a finite self and an infinite self at once; or perhaps better, we are to regard every conscious self as a self that is finite only insofar as it is infinite and as infinite only insofar as it is finite. The two moments (of being-infinite and being-finite) that constitute conscious selfhood are inseparable from one another and co-determine one another. Furthermore, for Hegel, the conscious self's moment of being-infinite (its moment of self-positing whereby it institutes an entire world for itself and thereby gives itself a criterion or maxim for determining how objects are to count as objects within the world of experience) is necessarily a moment that the self actualizes without any direct consciousness of its own activity in doing so. This is because the self, in its moment of (infinite, unbounded) self-positing, is not a self that stands over against anything that can be directly present as an object for it; and since *nothing* can be directly present to it as an object *for* it, it follows that it cannot *be* an *object* for itself.

In its moment of (infinite) self-positing, the self can have no direct consciousness of its very own activity of self-positing.[34] And yet even in its (infinite, non conscious) act of self-positing, the self is *for* itself in some fashion (for the self-positing self is still a self, and not just an infinite, blind substance). Since it cannot be for itself in the way that an object is directly for it, the (infinite) self-positing self can be for itself only as an idea or maxim that at first appears to the self under the guise of something that is regarded as external to itself.[35] It is for this reason that the uncritical self naturally mischaracterizes the infinite (self-positing, world-creating, criterion-instituting) moment of its own selfhood and thinks of this moment under the guise of some externally given being or personage (e.g., a transcendent God).

We can illustrate this by reference to the self that is observed in the "Unhappy Consciousness" section of the *Phenomenology of Spirit*. First of all, this self marks a genuine advance beyond the preceding forms of selfhood, since – unlike the preceding forms – it recognizes the imperative to bring about the unity of the Changeable Consciousness (the moment of finite selfhood) and the Unchangeable Consciousness (the moment of infinite selfhood). Furthermore, it recognizes that this imperative is not just a matter of external force; it is not an imperative imposed upon it by an alien master that aims only to serve his (the master's) own purposes. Rather, the self of the Unhappy Consciousness recognizes this imperative as essential to its own being or to its own vocation as a self. The problem, however, is that the self of the Unhappy Consciousness believes (a) that it cannot act so as to satisfy this imperative (to bring about the unity of the Changeable and the Unchangeable, or the unity of itself and God) without being pridefully sinful (even the act of self-renunciation for the sake of holiness and unity with God, is the self's own act, in which case it is really not an act of self-renunciation; see *PS*; 134); and therefore (b) that its unity with the Unchangeable can come about only through a kind of submission to God that is ultimately not its own doing. To the self of the Unhappy Consciousness, it lies in the very nature of things (and not in its own stance, or in its own act of self-positing) that justification (or unity with God) can never be achieved through its own actions, but only through an act of divine grace (*PS*; 137–138).

Like the self of the Unhappy Consciousness, the self of Kantian "morality" recognizes the imperative to bring about the unity of its own will and God's will (i.e., to promote the highest good, which is nothing other than "the kingdom of God on earth"). It also recognizes that this imperative is essential to its own vocation as a self. But unlike the self of the Unhappy Consciousness, the self of Kantian "morality" realizes that its own self-assertive activity aimed at bringing about this unity is not a prideful sin against a theoretically knowable, transcendent God; rather, it recognizes that its asserting itself with the aim of promoting the highest good is precisely what a God would command it to do. In addition, the self of Kantian "morality" enjoys a deeper (although not complete) appreciation of the intrinsic unity of the two moments (infinite and finite) of its own selfhood. On the one hand, it realizes that it could not regard itself as subject to the imperative to promote the highest good, if it were not an infinite self; for it realizes that it is bound by this imperative, not because the imperative is commanded by an external divine being, but only because it is an imperative that it gives to itself or legislates for itself. On the other hand, the self of Kantian "morality" also realizes that it could not regard itself as subject to the imperative to promote the highest good, if it were not also a finite self; for it realizes that it is bound by this imperative, only because it is confronted (and thus finitized) by an objective state of affairs in the world that it regards as morally deficient (as falling short of complete justice or the highest good), and thus in need of morally guided transformation. If the self of Kantian "morality" did not regard itself as thus confronted (or perhaps better, *affronted*) by a morally deficient or unjust world, then it would be incapable of apprehending any moral duty to do anything at all. Phrased differently: if the state of affairs that the self confronts were already morally perfected (if the highest good were already achieved), then the self could not possibly feel drawn or compelled by any moral "ought" to do anything at all. In fact, one might say: if the highest good were already achieved and the self nevertheless acted in some way to change things, then the self would be acting *immorally* (for in acting, it would be upsetting an already-achieved highest good). But even this way of stating the matter would be misleading; after all, if the highest good were already achieved, then the self would be incapable of apprehending *any* moral "ought" whatsoever – in which case all moral consciousness would disappear, and the self would be incapable of acting morally *or* immorally (all of the self's acts would be altogether *non*moral, in which case they would not really be the acts of a "self").

These observations allow us to begin to see why the self of Kantian "morality" cannot really be serious about the way that it talks about its own self-legislated moral imperative (to promote the highest good); and this, in turn, allows us to begin to see why Kantian "morality" is insufficiently self-critical. Recall that the self of Kantian "morality" can be the moral self that it is, only if it is confronted by a state of affairs that it regards as morally deficient, or as falling short of the highest good. If the self of Kantian "morality" were to succeed in bringing about the highest good, then a consequence of such success would be the complete elimination of all moral consciousness and therewith the complete elimination of itself as a moral self. But no moral self can seriously aim at a goal whose achievement would entail the elimination of itself as the moral self that it is. Stated differently, if (hypothetically) the moral self were to succeed in bringing about the highest good, then it would never "live to see" (or to have any conscious enjoyment of) its own success. For the achievement of the highest good would entail the elimination of all moral consciousness (it would entail the elimination of the consciousness of every moral "ought"), in which case the moral self would be incapable of consciously experiencing that its own moral "ought" (to promote the highest good) has actually been fulfilled (one must have consciousness of a moral "ought" in order to have consciousness that the "ought" has been fulfilled). But once again, this way of stating the matter would be misleading: for if there were no longer consciousness of any moral "ought," then there would no longer exist a "moral self" at all (see *PS*, 376–377).

Fichte was deeply sensitive to the difficulties in the moral world-view as articulated by Kant. For Fichte, Kant's fundamental mistake was to argue – as he did in his various contexts – that the nature upon which human beings exercise their moral agency is in the first instance simply given to them as unrelated to their own activity. According to Fichte, if nature were simply given in this external way, then it could never be regarded by humans beings as morally deficient (as falling short of complete justice or the highest good), and thus in need of morally guided transformation. Kant rightly observed that nature considered in itself lacks any moral significance whatsoever; but he was not entirely consistent in drawing out the fuller implications of this observation. Moral significance is not a function of the ways in which human beings relate to an externally given nature, but – Kant realized – of the ways in which they *relate to one another with respect to nature* (that is, the ways in which they relate to one another by manipulating nature and dividing it up amongst themselves). But if this is the case, then human beings can never be morally affronted by nature considered in itself, but only by nature insofar as it is a reflection of what human beings do to one another.

Aiming to develop a key point that Kant had touched upon but not sufficiently plumbed, Fichte insisted that consciousness that there is some moral deficiency in nature (that is, consciousness of any moral "ought" whatsoever, and thus moral consciousness in general) arises not on account of the way that human beings relate to nature as such, but only on account of the way that they relate to one another through nature.[36] Because of this, nature – considered on its own – can never provoke or awaken in human beings a sense of moral obligation or "oughtness." Thus the "gift" of moral consciousness (and thus of moral selfhood in general) is given to human beings by themselves alone, or through their own interactions with one another. Accordingly, we humans do not need to think of our moral selfhood as given to us by a transcendent God who also presents us with an external, indifferent nature upon which we are supposed to exercise our God-given moral agency. Furthermore (and contrary to Kant's moral proof), we do not need to rely on the thought of a transcendent God in order to make sense of how we might succeed in fulfilling our duties as moral beings. Just as we can make sense of how we give to ourselves our own duties as moral beings, so too we can (without relying on the thought of a transcendent God) make sense of how we are actually able to fulfill those duties.[37] As Fichte explains in his 1798 *System of Ethics*, we know that we are fulfilling our moral duties, not by undertaking action and then relying on the thought of a transcendent God to ensure the conformability of nature to our moral purposes (or to ensure that the consequences of our actions eventually contribute to justice or the highest good); rather, we know that we are fulfilling our moral duties simply by undertaking action with the genuine and immediately certain *conviction* that we are doing the right thing.[38] For Fichte, the God that ensures the success of our moral activity is not a transcendent God, but is an immanent one; it is the God that is immediately present to us and indistinguishable from the voice of our own conscience. Thus for Fichte, action in fulfillment of one's "pure duty" is not something beyond or opposed to action in fulfillment of one's particular duties; rather, "pure duty" is simply the uncompromising, compelling character of the way in which each individual (acting out of genuine conviction) is bound to abide by his or her own conscience in fulfilling particular duties.[39]

With his notions of conscience and conviction, Fichte has come close to articulating the fundamental unity of the infinite and finite moments of selfhood (or the Unchangeable Consciousness and Changeable Consciousness, or God's will and our will). But for Hegel, Fichte came close without quite succeeding. The problem, as Fichte himself acknowledges in his *System of Ethics*, is that the conscientious, conviction-driven individual is never able to know for certain whether or not his or her conscientious action might be taken as an infringement, offense, or affront to other conscientious individuals with differing convictions.[40] Hegel, by contrast, explains that we *can* have certainty, but certainty of a different sort. For Hegel, we can be certain that the conscientious, conviction-driven action of one individual *will* be taken as an infringement, offense, or affront to others. For as noted above, the condition of the possibility of moral consciousness and moral selfhood in general is that there is some awareness that things are not as they ought to be (and this awareness emerges only through the way in which human beings relate to one another, and not to nature considered in itself). And furthermore, according to Hegel: not only is it the case that the conscientious, conviction-driven individual's action will be an affront to others; it is also the case that the individual's very being (and continued being) as a moral agent depends on the fact that he or she has always already been offended and affronted by others. In other words, the individual owes his or her own moral consciousness, and indeed his or her own very being as a moral agent, to other individuals whose actions have served as a moral affront and thus as an awakening to moral consciousness. For Hegel, contrary to Fichte, the condition of the possibility of moral consciousness is not a pre-established harmony among conscientious, conviction-driven individuals,[41] but rather a pre-established (i.e., necessary) *disharmony* among them.

Because there is an inescapable disharmony, Hegel concludes that a conscientious, conviction-driven individual – in order to be fully self-critical – will recognize the need for reciprocal forgiveness between itself and other conscientious individuals with differing convictions. After all, a fully self-critical individual will recognize that he or she owes his or her own moral consciousness to the affronting, provoking actions of other individuals who were only acting conscientiously on the basis of their own genuinely held (but differing) convictions. Furthermore, a fully self-critical individual will also recognize that these other selves *had* to act as they did, since they were acting as they were inescapably bound to act, from within a seemingly self-validating circle of their own making. Finally, a fully self-critical individual will recognize that his or her own actions are not essentially different from the actions of these others who happen to have differing convictions. Just as the actions of these others *had* to appear as an affront to those with differing convictions, so too the fully self-critical individual will recognize that his or her own actions *must have* appeared as an affront to others. Thus the fully self-critical individual will seek forgiveness from others with differing convictions, and will at the same time recognize the need to offer forgiveness in turn. Engaged in this activity of reciprocal forgiveness, the individual will know that his or her own doing is in essence no different from the doing of those affronting-and-forgiving others, who stand on the other side of such reciprocal activity; that is, the individual will be engaged in the activity of universal or absolute knowing, or knowing "itself in its absolute opposite" (PS, 409).

According to Hegel, individuals within such a community of reciprocally forgiving and forgiven selves will recognize that there is no duty that is not fundamentally a duty given to individuals through the community itself, and that there is no affront or infraction by individuals that is not fundamentally forgivable through the community itself. And so this kind of community will be one whose members realize that there is no need to appeal to an external, transcendent personage in order to explain how they – as individuals – acquire moral duties and can fulfill their moral duties. Members of this community will realize that the appearing of God (the One alone who binds and looses sins) is possible only in and through a community of conscientious, conviction-driven, and reciprocally forgiving individual selves. Indeed, such a community will recognize itself as nothing other than the "kingdom of God on earth," or as "God manifested in the midst of those who know themselves in the form of pure knowing" (PS, 409).[42]

Notes

1   See H.S. Harris, *Hegel's Development*, vol. 1: *Toward the Sunlight (1770–1801)* (Oxford: Oxford University Press, 1972), chapters 1and 2.

2   Thus in his Third Meditation, Descartes tells us that we know of our own finitude only because we know that we are limited and imperfect in comparison with a being that is entirely unlimited and perfect: "Thus the perception of the infinite is somehow prior in me to the perception of the finite, that is, my perception of God is prior to my perception of myself. For how would I understand that I doubt and that I desire, that is, that I lack something and that I am not wholly perfect, unless there were some idea in me of a more perfect being, by comparison with which I might recognize my defects?" See René Descartes, *Philosophical Essays and Correspondence*, ed. Roger Ariew (Indianapolis, Ind./Cambridge: Hackett, 2000), 118.

3   Regarding the idea of God, Kant explains: "For it is always only an idea, which is by no means related directly to a being different from the world but rather referred to a regulative principle of the world's systematic unity, but only by means of a schema of that unity. ... This idea is therefore grounded entirely *respective to the use* our reason makes of it *in the world* ..." (emphasis in the original). See Immanuel Kant, *Critique of Pure Reason*, trans. Paul Guyer and Allen W. Wood (Cambridge: Cambridge University Press, 1997), 619–620. All subsequent references to Kant's *Critique of Pure Reason* will be based on this translation and cited parenthetically in the text in the following format: CPR, A697–698/B725–726 (referring to the pagination in the 1781 A edition and the 1787 B edition of the *Critique*).

4   Along these lines, Kant famously notes that the nonempirical conditions of the possibility of experience are at the same time the conditions of the possibility of the objects of experience (CPR, A111). For Kant, then, if we knew nothing about objects as given to us within experience, we would also know nothing about our capacity to know (see also CPR, A108).

5   Or stated differently: the idea of God is "nothing but a regulative principle of reason for attaining to the highest systematic unity by means of the idea of the purposive causality of

the supreme cause of the world, *as if* this being, as the highest intelligence, were the cause of everything according to the wisest aim." (*CPR*, A688/B716).

6   Here one is reminded of Jean-Jacques Rousseau's famous statement in Book I, Chapter 1, of the *Social Contract:* "Man is born free, and everywhere he is in chains." See Jean-Jacques Rousseau, *The Social Contract*, trans. Maurice Cranston (New York: Penguin Books, 1968), 49. As Rousseau goes on to argue, it is tempting to think that the human being's condition of servitude must be explained by reference to the "nature of things" outside us; but further analysis will reveal that this servitude arises not through any external cause, but only through the characteristic activities of our own reason.

7   But this label can be misleading. Kant's "moral proof" does not aim to demonstrate that we can know of God's actual, independent existence. It aims to demonstrate only that we are rationally justified (indeed, rationally compelled) to believe that God exists, on moral and not theoretical grounds.

8   Immanuel Kant, *Critique of Practical Reason*, in *Immanuel Kant: Practical Philosophy*, trans. Mary J. Gregor (Cambridge: Cambridge University Press), 227. All subsequent references to Kant's *Critique of Practical Reason* will be based on this translation and cited parenthetically in the text in the following format: *CPrR*, 5:108 (referring to the Akademie-edition volume and page number).

9   Immanuel Kant, *Religion within the Limits of Reason Alone*, trans. Theodore M. Greene and Hoyt H. Hudson (New York: Harper and Row, 1960), 87–89.

10   See, for example, Immanuel Kant, "Toward Perpetual Peace: A Philosophical Project," in *Immanuel Kant: Practical Philosophy*, trans. Mary J. Gregor (Cambridge: Cambridge University Press, 1999), 338. The Akademie-edition reference is 8:338 (referring to the volume and page number).

11   The argument presented in this section recounts part of the argument that I made in "Kant's Moral Proof: Defense and Implications," in *Philosophical Theology: Proceedings of the American Catholic Philosophical Association*, ed. Michael Baur (New York: American Catholic Philosophical Association, 2001), 141–161.

12   See, e.g., Hegel's letter to Schelling from late January of 1795. *Briefe von und an Hegel*, ed. Johannes Hoffmeister (Hamburg: Felix Meiner, 1952), I: 15–18. This letter is translated in *Hegel: The Letters*, trans. Clark Butler and Christiane Seiler (Bloomington: Indiana University Press, 1984), 30–32.

13   See G.C. Storr, *Bemerkungen über Kants philosophische Religionslehre* (Tübingen: Cotta, 1794).

14   *Briefe*, I: 14; Butler and Seiler, 29.

15   See, for example, *Hegel's Science of Logic*, trans. A.V. Miller (New York: Humanities Press, 1976), 580–581.

16   *Briefe*, I: 16–17; Butler and Seiler, 31.

17   *Briefe*, I: 18; Butler and Seiler 32.

18   *Briefe*, I: 21–22; Butler and Seiler, 32–33.

19   *Briefe*, I: 19–20; Butler and Seiler, 33.

20   *Briefe*, I: 29; Butler and Seiler, 41.

21   *Briefe*, I: 30; Butler and Seiler, 41.

22   J.G. Fichte, *The Science of Knowledge*, trans. Peter Heath and John Lachs (Cambridge: Cambridge University Press, 1982), 99.

23   J.G. Fichte, "First Introduction to the Science of Knowledge," *Science of Knowledge*, 21.

24   In his "Aenesidemus Review" of 1794, Fichte makes the same point when he says that we should not even think of the self-positing self as a kind of "faculty of representation" that exists on its own and somehow underlies our actual acts of representing. For to think of it in this way, is to think of it as a "thing in itself" which exists "independently of its being

represented." See J. G. Fichte, "Review of *Aenesidemus*," in *Fichte: Early Philosophical Writings*, trans. Daniel Breazeale (Ithaca: Cornell University Press, 1988), 66–67.

25   Kant makes a similar point when he says that the "I think" of pure apperception "must be able to accompany all my representations," even though the "I think" is not itself any kind of representation; if the self-positing self (the "I think" of pure apperception) were not for itself in this non objective, non representational way, then every possible representation "would be nothing for me" (*CPR*, B131–132).

26   Kant makes this point when he notes: "If I were to take away the thinking subject, the whole corporeal world would have to disappear. ..." (see *CPR*, A383).

27   Kant touches upon this point when he observes that a self's experience of any happening always presupposes that something else preceded the happening; but the self can never have experience of an empty time that allegedly preceded some happening (see *CPR*, A188/B231–A195/B240). Accordingly, the self can experience only the coming-to-be and the ceasing-to-be of things *within* the world, but never the coming-to-be or the ceasing-to-be of the world itself. In order to be able to experience the coming-to-be or the ceasing-to-be of the world itself, the self would have to be able to experience the world either as preceded by or as followed by an empty time – but such is impossible.

28   The text of this fragment is written out in Hegel's hand, and most likely dates back to 1796, when Hegel was living in Berne. Some scholars have argued that "The Earliest System Programme" was originally authored by Schelling (or by Schelling and Hölderlin) and that the surviving fragment is merely the result of what Hegel copied down from a now-lost original text. However, both Otto Pöggeler and H.S. Harris have argued convincingly that this fragment was not only written out in Hegel's own hand, but also originally authored by Hegel himself. See H.S. Harris, *Toward the Sunlight (1770–1801)*, 249–257; and Otto Pöggeler, "Hegel, der Verfasser des ältesten Systemprogramms des deutschen Idealismus," in *Hegel-Studien, Beiheft* 4 (1969): 17–32.

29   The relevant model for this claim is the Leibnizian monad, which perceives or reflects the entire world "all at once," so to speak, and is thus co-extensive with the entire world. Schelling makes this clear in his *System of Transcendental Idealism* from 1800: "For nobody, surely, who has once seen how the objective world, with all its determinations, develops out of pure self-consciousness without any affection from outside, will still find need for another world independent of this; which is approximately the view taken in misinterpretations of the Leibnizian theory of pre-established harmony." See F.W.J. Schelling, *System of Transcendental Idealism*, trans. Peter Heath (Charlottesville: University of Virginia Press, 1978), 35.

30   See G.W.F. Hegel, *The Difference between Fichte's and Schelling's System of Philosophy*, trans. H.S. Harris and Walter Cerf (Albany: State University of New York Press, 1977), 119.

31   G.W.F. Hegel, *Faith and Knowledge*, trans. Walter Cerf and H.S. Harris (Albany: State University of New York Press, 1977), 94.

32   And just as Kant had argued, the "world as a whole" is not a bounded extensive magnitude, and so it is never given as an object for conscious selfhood (only objects *within* the world are thus given). Nevertheless, the idea of the "world as a whole" is a non representable or non objective idea that the self necessarily gives to itself (this self-giving just *is* the act of self-positing), in order to determine how objects are to be regarded as objects of possible experience for it (see *CPR*, A505/B533; A508/B536–A510/B538; and A651/B679).

33   This observation helps to explain why, on Hegel's account, Spinoza's system was ultimately inadequate. Schelling, in his 1797 *Ideas for a Philosophy of Nature*, provides a helpful explanation of the matter: "[In Spinoza's system], I myself was only one of the Infinite's thoughts, or rather just a constant succession of presentations. But Spinoza was unable to make intelligible how I myself in turn become aware of this succession. ... For, generally speaking, as

it came from his hand, his system is the most unintelligible that ever existed. ... How affections are and can exist in an Absolute external to me, I do not understand. ..." See F.W.J. Schelling, *Ideas for a Philosophy of Nature*, trans. Errol E. Harris and Peter Heath (Cambridge: Cambridge University Press, 1988), 28.

34 Thus this activity of self-positing by means of which the self institutes a world for itself and thus makes it possible for objects to count as objects in the first place, must occur "behind the self's own back," so to speak. See *Hegel's Phenomenology of Spirit*, trans. A.V. Miller (Oxford: Oxford University Press, 1977), 56. All subsequent references to Hegel's *Phenomenology* will be based on this translation and cited parenthetically in the text, in accordance with the following format: *PS*, 56.

35 Or, as Kant had argued, the ideas of self, world, and God (which for Hegel are not three separate things but three aspects under which one might apprehend the self's own originary act of self-positing or "creation out of nothing") are given by the self to itself, even though the uncritical self continues to regard these as three separate, independently existing entities that are given to the self from outside itself and apart from the self's own activity.

36 Here one is reminded of Jean-Jacques Rousseau's observation (in Book II of *Émile*) that the dependence of human beings on things (in nature) involves no morality, and that morality pertains only to the dependence of human beings on one another. See Jean-Jacques Rousseau, *Émile*, trans. Barbara Foxley (London: J.M. Dent; North Clarendon, Vt.: Tuttle Publishing, 1993), 58.

37 From Fichte's point of view, Kant continued to think of nature as given apart from the activities of human moral agents, since he continued to think of the source of such nature (God) as an external and transcendent (even if not theoretically knowable) entity; and conversely, Kant continued to think of God as an external and transcendent entity, because he continued to think of nature as given apart from the activities of human moral agents. Thus for Fichte, Kant was caught in a seemingly self-validating "vicious circle" precisely of the kind that Kant himself had diagnosed and criticized in the Transcendental Dialectic of the *Critique of Pure Reason* (*CPR*, A693/B721).

38 See J.G. Fichte, *The System of Ethics*, trans. Daniel Breazeale and Günter Zöller (Cambridge: Cambridge University Press, 2005), 148 and 159–161. See also *PS*, 386–388.

39 In a similar vein, Fichte holds that the "thing in itself" is not something that is given apart from or beyond experience; rather, the "thing in itself" is simply the residual lack of determinacy or lack of intelligible (conceptual) unity that is given as a feature *within* all possible experience (and thus it is given as a task that reason gives to itself).

40 See Fichte, *System of Ethics*, 159 and 221–223.

41 See Fichte, *System of Ethics*, 230: "How then can one become aware of that upon which everyone agrees? This is not something one can learn simply by asking around; hence it must be possible to presuppose something that can be viewed as the creed of the community. ..."

42 I would like to thank Stephen Houlgate for his very helpful comments on an earlier version of this chapter. Of course, I am solely responsible for any remaining shortcomings or errors to be found in the account that I present here.

Part XI

Hegel and Post-Hegelian Thought

23

Hegel and Marx

ANDREW CHITTY

Hegel and Marx differ profoundly: one a philosophical and historical idealist (however exactly this idealism is to be understood) and the other a materialist; one a defender of some form of Christianity and the other a resolute atheist; one a modest political reformist who sees the contemporary social and political order as essentially rational and the other a revolutionary who aims at the complete overthrow of that order.[1]

Nevertheless, Hegel's influences on Marx's thought, both acknowledged and unacknowledged, are pervasive. They have generated a large literature, beginning with Marx's own enigmatic comments in the 1873 Afterword to *Capital* on "inverting" Hegel's dialectic, which is "standing on its head," and extracting its "rational kernel" from its "mystical shell" (C 103/27, cf. G 101) and Engels's attempt to develop them in his *Ludwig Feuerbach and the Outcome of Classical German Philosophy*, and continuing up to the present.[2] Yet although no one doubts that Hegel influenced Marx's thought, it remains disputed at what level, and in what periods of Marx's life, he did so.

With regard to level, it is uncontroversial that Marx was indebted to Hegel at the level of some very general orientations. Thus both shared a fundamental emphasis on change. Both conceived history as the gradual emergence of human freedom through a series of major stages, and also as driven in some way by "contradictions." Both saw human beings and their thinking as deeply formed by the historical epoch in which they lived, making every individual a "child of his time" (PR 21/26). Both rejected individualist conceptions of the good life and methodological individualism as a way of understanding social systems. Both forswore the idea of judging existing social and political institutions by a transcendent philosophical standard, and instead aimed at elucidating a rationality immanent in the existing social world or in its development: at "seeking the idea in the actual itself" (LF 18/8).[3] What is more controversial is whether they shared a single "dialectical method" and whether there are more specific parallels between particular parts of their thought: for example, between Hegel's conception of the "universal class" and Marx's of the proletariat, between Hegel's master–servant relation and Marx's capitalist–worker relation, or between Hegel's logic of

---

A Companion to Hegel, First Edition. Edited by Stephen Houlgate and Michael Baur.
© 2011 Blackwell Publishing Ltd. Published 2011 by Blackwell Publishing Ltd.

essence and Marx's value theory. The mere fact of common general orientations is no proof of a single shared method or of such specific parallels. Nor is Marx's use of Hegelian terminology, for it is quite possible to "coquette with" Hegel's terms, as Marx admits doing in chapter 1 of *Capital* (C 103/27), while expressing ideas that have nothing significant in common with Hegel's.

With regard to the periods of Marx's life, the best known debate is the one initiated by Louis Althusser, who argued that although there are strong parallels with Hegel in Marx's writings in 1844, there follows an "epistemological break" after which Marx retains from Hegel nothing more than the general idea of history as a "process without a subject," driven by contradictions.[4] In fact, there is *prima facie* evidence of Hegelian influence at virtually every stage in Marx's career, though from different parts of Hegel's works. He seems to draw on the *Essay on Natural Law* and the *Philosophy of Right* in his journalistic writings of 1842, on the *Phenomenology of Spirit* and the *Lectures on Aesthetics* in his 1844 manuscripts, on the *Philosophy of History* in the *German Ideology* of 1845–1846, and on the *Logic* as well as once more the *Philosophy of Right* in his economic writings of the 1850s and 1860s. The question in each case, though, is how far Marx really draws from Hegel and how far he merely seems to.

In this chapter I cannot hope to survey all the issues raised by this literature. In particular it will not be possible to investigate the question of whether Marx and Hegel share a "dialectical method" in their accounts of historical change, or of structures such as the modern state or the capitalist economy, a method that consists in tracing the emergence and resolution of contradictions. Perhaps it is enough to say that although Hegel does describe the dialectical (or speculative) method in this way (PhS 55; EL §§81–82), and although he often effects his transitions by identifying a contradiction in a historical epoch or a category and trying to show how this is resolved by the transition to a subsequent epoch or category, still the kinds of contradictions and ways of resolving them that he points to are so varied that it has proved impossible to say anything much more specific about Hegel's "method." Indeed on many occasions in the *Logic* he makes a transition from one category to the next without identifying a contradiction in the former at all. Meanwhile in Marx's *Capital* there are only a very few transitions between categories that can plausibly be construed as operating in this way. So the prospects do not look promising for discovering a specific dialectical method, based on identifying contradictions, which is common to Hegel and Marx.

Instead here I shall attempt to demonstrate that there are two specific parallels between Hegel's thought and that of Marx in 1843–1844, the two years in which he wrote almost all of his explicit comments on Hegel: a parallel between their philosophical anthropologies and another between their conceptions of the overall shape of history. With regard to the first, I shall argue that Marx's conception of humans as essentially "species-beings" is a direct descendant of Hegel's conception of humans as essentially "spirit." With regard to the second, I shall argue that both thinkers conceive history as a process in which human beings first realize (or actualize) their essence in an "estranged" form characterized by "abstract universality," making it possible for them to subsequently realize it in a non-estranged form. In terms of the above division into "general orientations," "method," and "specific parallels," these connections are of the third type. Nevertheless they relate to core elements of both Hegel's and Marx's thought.

1.   Humanity, Mutual Recognition, and the State in Hegel

Hegel equates humanity considered in its essentials, "the genuine nature of man," with "spirit" (ES, §377A/10, cf. §377).[5] Humans are essentially spiritual beings. His full philosophical account of human beings is therefore laid out in his *Encyclopedia Philosophy of Spirit*. There he gives a developmental account of spirit, although the development is meant to be "logical" rather than chronological. Arguably the most crucial stage in this development is the emergence of self-awareness, or the capacity to think and say "I": "the first and simplest determination of [spirit] is that it is I" (ES §381A/21).[6] It is by this capacity that humans genuinely distinguish themselves from other animals: "Thinking of oneself as an I is the root of human nature" (RH 50/57); "The animal cannot say 'I,' only the human being can" (EL §24A1/83, cf. ES §412A). So for Hegel "self-aware" and "human" are coextensive terms.

The idea that the capacity to think "I" distinguishes humans from animals goes back to Descartes, but Hegel goes on to tie this capacity to the ideas of both universality and freedom: "'I' is ... the existence of wholly abstract universality, that which is abstractly free" (EL §20R/75). Thus a human being is "essentially something universal" (PR §132R/247) or possesses an "inner universality" (PR §153/303, cf. §§5A, 90), and "man is in and for himself free, in his substance" (LHP1 49/18:68, cf. PR §18A).

Hegel derives freedom from the bare ability to think "I," in much the same way that Fichte did before him. Self-awareness is not awareness of an already-existing self but is rather constitutive of the self, or as Hegel calls it "the I": "the I cannot exist ... without being aware of itself [*ohne von sich zu wissen*], without having and being the certainty of itself," so it must be understood as "relating to itself alone," rather than depending on anything outside itself, and thus as purely self-determining (ES §413A/200). So the I is "pure abstract freedom for itself" (ES §413/199, cf. §412A). As far as universality goes, Hegel derives it from self-awareness in two ways.[7] First, as self-aware I am aware of myself as standing above all my single experiences and characteristics, and thus as universal with respect to them:

> "I," however, abstractly as such, is pure relation to itself, in which abstraction is made from representation and sensation, from every state as well as from every particularity [*Partikularität*] of nature, of talent, of experience, and so on. (EL §20R/74–75, cf. PR §4A)

Here Hegel closely follows Kant on pure apperception, as he acknowledges (EL §42A1). But he adds another point. Just because in self-awareness I abstract from the above-mentioned particularities "of nature, of talent, of experience," I also abstract from everything that defines me as this single individual. The word "I" refers to me, but it also refers to every self-aware being, that is, every human being. So when I utter it I am implicitly aware of myself as universal in a second way, as a member of the class of all human beings:

> [W]hen I say "I," I *mean* me *as this one* excluding all others; but what I say, "I," is precisely each one. ... "I" is the universal that is in and for itself, and communality [*Gemeinschaftlichkeit*] is also a form, although an external one, of universality. All other humans have this in

479

common with me, to be "I," just as all *my* sensations, representations etc. have in common that they are *mine*. (EL §20R/74, cf. ES §381A, PhS 62).

To be self-aware is therefore to be universal in two senses: an internal sense (universal with respect to each of one's own experiences) and an external sense (a member of the universal kind consisting of all self-aware or human beings). It is also to be *aware* of oneself, at least implicitly, as universal in these two senses. This is what Hegel means when he says that the I is "the relation of the universal to the universal" (ES §§412A/198, cf. ES §412, EL §24A1). In fact to be self-aware is to be implicitly aware of oneself as universal and *at the same time* as singular in both the internal and the external senses. I am aware of myself as singular in that at any one time I am always conscious of myself as experiencing this singular sensation as well as being the subject of all my other sensations, and also in that I am always conscious of myself as this singular self as well as of possessing an I-hood that is not tied to any one self. Thus the I is, both internally and externally, characterized at once by universality and singularity. Since Hegel's view of the Notion (or Concept, *Begriff*) is that it has this same double structure, he can connect the I with the Notion:

> This absolute universality which is also immediately an absolute singularisation,[8] ... constitutes the nature of the *I*, as well as of the *Notion*; neither the one nor the other can be comprehended at all unless the two indicated moments are grasped at the same time both in their abstraction and also in their complete unity. (SL 583/6:253, cf. ES §413A, LPS 167)[9]

In Hegel's full account of the Notion he says that it unites not only universality and singularity (*Einzelheit*) but also particularity (*Besonderheit*) (e.g., SL 603; EL §163), where particularity refers to features that are possessed by some members of a kind but not others.[10] So presumably the I must also be characterized by all three of these aspects. He expresses the idea that the Notion unites these three aspects by saying that it is not an "abstract" universal; that is, its universality is not separated off from particularity and singularity, but rather it is a "concrete" universal (SL 603–604/6:277–278), for "the concrete is the universal which particularises itself and in this particular, this becoming finite, yet remains infinitely with itself" (LHP2 381/19:412).[11] Therefore the I too must be characterized by concrete universality.

In a number of places Hegel contrasts the freedom and universality of humans with their absence in animals. Animals lack freedom: "the animal soul is still not free, for it always appears as one with the determinacy of the sensation or excitation, as bound to one determinacy" (ES §381A). Animals also lack internal universality. The animal

> exhibits only the spiritless dialectic of transition from one singular sensation filling up its whole soul to another singular sensation which equally exclusively dominates it; it is man who first raises himself above the singularity of sensation to the universality of thought, to awareness of himself, to the grasp of his subjectivity, of his I. (ES §381A/25, cf. §412A)

With regard to external universality, Hegel says that the animal possesses this kind of universality in that it is a member of a *Gattung* (genus, species, or kind). By the *Gattung* of a thing he sometimes just means the class to which it belongs (e.g., EL §§177, 177A), but in the *Philosophy of Nature* he means an organic kind, whose individual members he conceives as arising out of the kind when they are born and sinking back into it when they die in a continuous process, the *Gattungsprozess* (PN §§367, 374A, cf. SL 772–774, PhS 106–108). The genus and its members are therefore characterized by a kind of concrete universality (PN §366, cf. SL 649, 654). However, the animal is not aware of itself as a member of its genus and so as concretely universal. The animal "only senses the genus, it is not aware [*weiss nicht*] of it; in the animal ... the universal as such is not for the universal" (ES §381A/20, cf. PN §368A, PhS 108–109). To be more exact, the animal "senses" its genus insofar as it is attracted to another member of the genus, specifically to one of the opposite sex. In fact copulation is its unconscious attempt to make its own genus present to itself, although it succeeds only in producing further single members of the genus, namely its offspring (PN §§368–370A, SL 773, ES §381A).

By contrast, humans are free and both internally and externally universal, and (at least implicitly) aware of themselves as such. However, there is a contradiction inherent in this self-awareness, and in order to resolve this contradiction humans are driven into a certain form of community, which in the first instance is a community of mutual recognition or "universal self-consciousness" and finally is the political community of the modern constitutional state.

The logic of this process is set out in the first two parts of the *Encyclopedia Philosophy of Spirit*.[12] It revolves around the relation between the self-aware subject and its objects. To be aware of itself as the subject of all its experiences, this subject must construe its experiences as experiences of external objects, as Kant had also argued (ES §§412–413). Yet this contradicts the subject's freedom, or self-determination, for insofar as it is "burdened with an external object," it is limited by that object and so not purely self-determining (ES §425/213, cf. ES §385A, EL §24A2). To resolve this contradiction and so to actualize its freedom, the subject must find a way to see the object as numerically identical to itself while continuing to see this object as external, that is, as numerically distinct from itself, and this is only possible when, first, the object is another self-aware being (another "I"), and, second, these two beings have entered into relations of mutual recognition, in which each recognizes the other as free, or purely self-determining. In this mutual recognition, or "universal self-consciousness," each sees the other as independent of and so distinct from itself, and yet at the same time each sees both the other and itself as separate from their own desires and so from their own bodies, and thus as instances of a single freedom and even a single common self. "Each as a free singularity has absolute independence, but, through the negation of its immediacy or desire, does not distinguish itself from the other" (ES §436/226). Through the "universal mirroring of self-consciousness" of mutual recognition (ES §436R/226), subjects can see themselves as distinct individuals and yet at the same time as essentially numerically identical with each other:

> At this standpoint, therefore, the mutually related self-conscious subjects, by the supersession of their different particular singularity, have risen to the consciousness of their real universality, of their freedom befitting all, and hence to seeing [*Anschauung*] their determinate identity with each other. ... Here, therefore, we have the tremendous diremption of spirit into different selves which are, in and for themselves and for one another, completely

free, independent, absolutely unyielding, resistant, and yet at the same time identical with one another, hence not self-subsistent, not impenetrable, but, as it were, merged together. (ES §436A/227, cf. §425A)

With the achievement of universal self-consciousness we can now speak of "spirit" in the full sense of the word, spirit as Hegel defines it in the *Phenomenology of Spirit*: "*I* that is *We* and *We* that is *I*" (PhS 110/145, cf. PR §264) or "the awareness [*wissen*] of oneself in one's externalization" (PhS 459/552), and in fact in the *Encyclopedia Philosophy of Spirit* the section entitled "Spirit" almost immediately follows the discussion of universal self-consciousness (ES §440). With this achievement individuals become properly aware of themselves as at-once-singular-and-universal (i.e., as concretely universal) in the external sense, that is, properly aware of themselves as at once singular selves and members of their genus.[13] Thereby they actually *become* properly concretely universal in the external sense. In fact, we might take a community of mutual recognition, or of spirit, to be Hegel's paradigmatic example of concrete universality.[14]

At the same time, since individuals now see themselves as essentially identical to each other, neither experiences the other as a limitation on its own freedom. Therefore they have now resolved the above-mentioned contradiction and so become properly free for the first time, at least in their relations with each other. As Hegel says, contrasting mutual recognition with the master–servant relation that immediately precedes it:

[T]he master confronting the servant was not yet genuinely free, for he did not yet thoroughly see [*schaute an*] himself in the other. It is only by the servant becoming free that the master consequently also becomes completely free. (ES §436A/226–227, cf. §435A)

However, by the very fact that they see each other as identical, their freedom is of a new kind. If in general freedom means self-determination, then we now have a new kind of self, a self that is simultaneously distinct from and yet identical to other selves in a community of mutual recognition. So freedom becomes the self-determination of selves so conceived, therefore a freedom that can only be achieved jointly. This is what Hegel calls "concrete" freedom (EL §158A/303, cf. PR §7A, LPS 188–190). When he says that "formally the essence of spirit is freedom" (ES §382/25, cf. ES §482R, RH 47–48) or that "man as man is free, the freedom of spirit constitutes his very own nature" (RH 54/62), it is this concrete freedom that he has in mind.

Yet even universal self-consciousness does not fully resolve the contradiction posed for the freedom of the subject by the existence of external objects, for although participants in universal self-consciousness have resolved this contradiction with respect to each other as individuals, they have not done so with respect to the world of physical objects that surrounds them. The freedom of these participants remains contradicted, for they are still confronted by an external world that limits them. As Hegel says at one point, "Freedom is only present where there is no other for me that is not myself" (EL §24A2/84). To overcome this contradiction and so fully actualize their freedom, human beings have both to discover the essential features of their own spirit in physical reality itself and to objectify those essential features in the world around them, specifically through establishing the "system of right" culminating in the modern constitutional state. Insofar as they do the first, they engage in the various cognitive activities that culminate in "thinking" (ES §§445–468), and insofar as they do the second they exercise a "free will" (ES §§481–482, PR §§4–30).

Therefore, both "thinking" and exercising "free will" are activities in which humans engage only as members of a community of mutual recognition.[15] In fact, the concrete universality of this community is reflected in the structure of these activities. Thinking transforms "the objective content confronting it" into "a concrete universal" (ES §387A/42, cf. PN §368A), and the will possesses a combination of universality, particularity, and singularity (PR §§5–7), so that it is concretely universal (PR §§7R, 24R). Furthermore, the concrete universality of thinking and willing is not only internal, but also external. In thinking, I not only relate universal concepts to single objects; in addition, those concepts themselves are common to myself and other thinkers, even though I use them as a single individual. Likewise in willing, I not only abstract from all possible actions and yet will one particular action; in addition, I abstract from the standpoint of every particular subject (PR §5A) and yet differentiate myself from all others in my action (PR §6).

In the institutions successively described in the *Philosophy of Right*, the three different aspects of this concretely universal will are objectified, so that they have an "existence" (*Dasein*) for individuals. For example, the "person" of "Abstract Right" is both singular and universal (in the external sense) (PR §35). The singular aspect of the person's will is objectified in objects that are owned as that person's private property and recognized by others as such (PR §40), and the universal aspect is objectified in the contract, which is willed by two persons so that it is the objectification of a "unity of different wills" (PR §73/156) and so of a "common will" (PR §76/159). Similarly, in civil society particularity is objectified in the self-interested activities of private persons, and universality in the ways that these persons must conform to generalized market conditions and in institutions established to secure the self-interests that they all share (PR §§182–187). But whereas in personality singularity and universality are in "contradiction" (PR §35A/95), and in civil society "particularity and universality have come apart" (PR §184A/340–341), the modern state taken as a whole integrates all three of these aspects of the concretely universal will: "personal singularity," "its particular interests," and "the interest of the universal" (PR §260/406–407, cf. §264).

Thereby the modern state objectifies the freedom that is the essential characteristic of the will, so that it is "the actuality [*Wirklichkeit*] of concrete freedom" (PR §260/406, cf. PR §4, LHP3 401–402). Freedom is now actualized in that human beings no longer experience themselves as limited by anything that is external to them, for in the institutions in which they participate they find nothing but embodiments of their own freedom (PR §153, RH 97, LA1 98). But it is also actualized in that once their freedom is objectified in this way they can become properly *aware* of it: "the state is freedom which is rational, is aware of itself objectively [*sich objektiv wissende*] and is for itself" (RH 123/147, cf. ES §385A), and it is only by being properly aware of themselves as free that human beings actually become free: "It is the sensation of freedom alone which makes spirit free, although it is in fact always free in and for itself" (RH 48/56, cf. 55).

To summarize, for Hegel humans are essentially self-aware, and so essentially both free and universal. But they possess these characteristics only as a potential (PR §57R). They can actualize their freedom and universality only by establishing a community of mutual recognition and institutionalizing this community in an appropriately

483

structured state, namely the modern constitutional state, in which they can become properly aware of that freedom and universality. World history is the successive establishment and supersession of societies and states that better and better approximate to an institutionalized community of mutual recognition. So it is essentially "the progress of the consciousness of freedom" (RH 54/63), and thereby the process of the actualization of freedom. Since freedom and universality are the essential qualities of human beings, it is also the process of the actualization of humanity.

2.   Species-Being and Communism in Marx

After this survey it should be possible to demonstrate how indebted Marx was to Hegel for his early conception of humans as "genus-" or "species-beings" (*Gattungswesen*).[16] I shall argue that in Marx's 1844 writings the idea of humans as species-beings is modeled on Hegel's view of humans as free and universal beings who can properly actualize their freedom and universality only through mutual recognition, and that Marx's early idea of communist society is modeled on Hegel's conception of an institutionalized community of mutual recognition.

Although the term "species-being" and its cognates begin to appear in Marx's 1843 writings, he first explicitly characterizes humans as species-beings, and spells out what he means by the term, in the *Economic and Philosophical Manuscripts* (1844):

> Man is a species-being, not only because he practically and theoretically makes the species [*Gattung*] – both his own and those of other things – his object, but also – and this is simply another way of saying the same thing – because he relates to himself as the present, living species, because he relates to himself as a *universal* [*universellen*] and therefore free being. (EPM 327/515)[17]

As we have seen, *Gattung* can mean genus, species, or kind, so *Gattungswesen* could also be translated as "generic being" or even "universal being." In fact here Marx makes the idea of universality central to the concept. In the first part of the above passage he echoes Feuerbach, who begins *The Essence of Christianity* (1841) by saying that the essential difference between human beings and animals is that for a human being "his species [*Gattung*], his essentiality, is an object," and that in virtue of this he "can make the essential nature of other things or beings an object" (EC 1–2/1). The only difference is that Marx says that humans make the species their object *practically* as well as theoretically. But in turn both Feuerbach and Marx clearly borrow heavily from Hegel here. Like Hegel, they make the awareness of one's own *Gattung*, that is, awareness of one's external universality, distinctive to human beings, and like Hegel they connect this closely to the awareness of objects as members of their kinds, for such an awareness is an essential part of what Hegel calls "thinking." The difference is that Hegel spells out the rationale for this connection.

Even more significant is the idea contained in the last few words of the above quotation: "he relates to himself as a universal and therefore free being." Here Marx suggests that humans are aware of themselves as free *because* they are aware of themselves as (externally) universal. A passage a few lines later emphasizes this point even more strongly, at least if we read "species-being" as referring to the awareness of one's external universality: "Man ... is a conscious being, i.e. his own life is an object for him, just because he is a species-being. Only because of that is his activity free activity" (EPM 328/516). The implication is that human beings' freedom depends on their awareness of their external universality, that is, of themselves as members of their own kind. This is an idea that makes sense, I suggest, only if we read it in the context of Hegel's thought. For it is Hegel who says that universal self-consciousness, in which we become properly aware of our external universality, is the means whereby we first become genuinely free.[18]

Meanwhile, we need to notice that although Marx puts theoretical and practical universality on a par in the above quotation, he goes on to focus almost exclusively on *practical* universality. Combining Aristotle's thought that the "proper function" of an animal is "that which corresponds to its activity" (Aristotle 1962, 1176a 4–5) with the concept of labor that was at the heart of the political economy of his time, he asserts that the essential activity of human beings is *labor* or *production:*

> [L]abor, life activity, productive life itself ... is species-life. It is life producing life. The whole character of a species, its species-character, resides in its kind of life activity, and free conscious activity is the species-character of man. (EPM 328/516)

Labor is "free conscious activity," but it is also a universal activity. It is internally universal in that it can be applied to any object at all, so that through it the human being "makes the whole of nature his inorganic body" (EPM 328/516). It is externally universal in that it is oriented to the human species as a whole, for it produces goods that in principle any human being could use. I suggest that Marx is referring to this external universality of labor when he says that man "practically" makes his own species his object (EPM 327, quoted above). In tying his conception of the human essence so closely to labor, Marx departs from Hegel.[19]

Finally, Marx's account of human beings differs from Hegel's in his equation, for example in the last quotation, of labor with "life" and "life-activity." Taken together with the specifically biological connotations of the word *Gattung*, these suggest a naturalist strand in Marx's conception of human beings, perhaps derived from Feuerbach or Aristotle, that does not sit easily with the Hegelian emphasis on freedom and universality. For Marx, "man is a part of nature" (EPM 328/516), and "as a natural, corporeal, sensuous, objective being, he is a suffering, conditioned, and limited being, like animals and plants" (EPM 389/578).

However, despite these productionist and naturalist strands, Marx's concept of species-being is built on an essentially Hegelian framework. This becomes clear in passages in the *Notes on James Mill* (1844) where Marx speaks of the human essence as something that humans actualize through the establishment of social relationships between themselves, although where Hegel speaks of relationships of mutual recognition Marx speaks of relations of producing for each other:

> The *interchange* both of human activities in the course of production and of *human products* with each other is equal to the species-activity and the species-spirit[20] whose actual, conscious and true existence consists in *social* activity and *social* enjoyment. In that the

human essence is the *true community* [*Gemeinwesen*] of man, men, by activating their *essence, create,* produce the human community, the social essence, which is no abstract-universal power standing over against the singular individual, but is the essence of every individual, his own activity, his own life, his own spirit, his own wealth. (NJM 265/450–451)

In Marx's longest description of a communist society, one that fully realizes humans as species-beings, he construes mutual production in a similarly Hegelian way. If we had produced voluntarily for each other in the absence of private property, he says, then we would have jointly objectified and realized our own essence:

In my individual life-expression I would have immediately created your life-expression, thus in my individual activity I would have immediately *confirmed* and *actualized* my true essence, my *human essence*, my *community* [*Gemeinwesen*]. Our products would be so many mirrors in which we saw our essence reflected. (NJM 277–278/462–463, cf. CHDS 189–190, EPM 349)

Here voluntary mutual production for each other's needs takes the place of Hegel's mutual recognition of each other as free. Further, the products of this activity take the place of the institutions of the modern state as the medium in which the essential character of human beings (freedom and universality) is objectified so that humans themselves can be properly aware of it.[21]

Meanwhile Marx's community of production combines singularity and universality: genuine communism is "the true resolution of the conflict ... between individual [*Individuum*] and species" (EPM 348/536). It also realizes a freedom that, like Hegel's concrete freedom, can only be achieved jointly: as Marx and Engels later say in the *German Ideology*, "In the actual community [*Gemeinschaft*] individuals obtain their freedom in and through their association" (GI 78/74).

I conclude that the early Marx's conception of humans as species-beings, beings essentially characterized by a freedom and universality that they can only actualize socially, should be understood as a productionist and naturalist reworking of Hegel's philosophical anthropology. Whereas in Hegel the means by which humans can know and thereby actualize their freedom and universality is the community of mutual recognition as institutionalized in the modern state, in Marx freedom and universality are characteristics of humans as producers, and the means by which this freedom and universality can be known and actualized is a system of direct mutual production no longer mediated by private property, that is, communism. In both cases this is a medium produced by humans themselves, so that just as for Hegel "spirit produces and realises [*realisiert*] itself" (RH 48/55–56), so for Marx history is "the self-creation of man" (EPM 386/574).[22]

3. Hegel on the Roman World

For Hegel, the historical process through which humans become aware of, and so realize, their own freedom and universality is not a straightforwardly linear one. Successive peoples conceptualize this freedom and universality in quite different ways,

486

embodying their conceptions in their legal and political institutions, as well as in their religion, art, and philosophy. In chapter 6 of the *Phenomenology*, this process has three main stages: a first ("The Ethical World") in which individuals see themselves simply as instantiations of their own national community and its "ethical substance," a second ("Legal Status" and the start of "Self-Estranged Spirit") in which they distinguish themselves from this community and come to see themselves as separate and autonomous individuals, and a third (the remainder of chapter 6) in which they gradually come to unite these two self-conceptions. In the mature Hegel, these stages correspond respectively to the Oriental and Greek worlds, the Roman world, and the Germanic world (PR §353–354). In this section, I sketch Hegel's account of the Roman world, and in the next I argue that the Marx of 1843–1844 shares with Hegel a three-stage view of history, and that Hegel's Roman world forms a model for Marx's account in 1843–1844 of the modern "estranged" world, specifically of the modern state and of capital.

In the Roman world, according to Hegel, individuals experience themselves as "persons," self-sufficient atoms, and their sense of belonging to a community is reduced to a shared conviction that they are all equals:

> The universal unity into which the living immediate unity of individuality and substance withdraws is the spiritless community which has ceased to be the unconscious substance of individuals, and in which they now count in their singular being-for-self as self-essences [*Selbstwesen*] and substances. The universal is thus split up into atoms of an absolute multiplicity of individuals, and this lifeless spirit is an *equality* in which *all* as *such*, as *persons*, count. (PhS 290/355)

Individuals feel no inner connection with each other: "they are, as persons, for themselves, and exclude any continuity with others by their absolutely unyielding pointlikeness [*Punktualität*]" (PhS 293/358). Yet at the same time, they are part of a community. Therefore, this community can only take the form of a universal power that they experience as external and alien to them as individuals, thus the form of an "abstract universality" and an "abstract state" (PH 278–279/339–340, cf. PH 288), so that we have "the infinite tearing apart of ethical life into the extremes of *personal* or private self-consciousness and *abstract universality*" (PR §357/511). This abstract state holds individuals together through sheer domination (*Herrschaft*) (LPR2 296, 308; PH 308). Since the only status that individuals recognize is that of personhood, the power of this state must eventually be incarnated in one person, an "absolute person" (PhS 292/357) or "person of persons" (PH 320/387). This is the Roman emperor, who exerts his power over his subjects in the form of a universal domination (*Allherrschaft*) (PhS 293/359, cf. PH 316, LPR2 315).[23] Yet at the same time, the emperor is who he is only thanks to his subjects, without whom he would be a "non-actual, powerless self" (PhS 292/358).

For Hegel, the Roman world is a necessary stage in history because in it the "freedom of the I within itself" (PH 279/340), and the corresponding "principle of subjective freedom" (PR §185R/342), emerge for the first time. That is, individuals for the first time see themselves as individually self-determining and demand to be treated as such. As we saw above, this individual self-determination is an essential element of the full concept of concrete freedom. At the same time, in the Roman world for the first time individuals become aware of themselves as externally universal. The Roman empire crushes all national states and their gods (LPR2 321–323, PH 318), and each subject of this empire comes to think of him- or herself simply as a person among persons, regardless of nationality (PH 279, 316). Yet this universality of the person is again an abstract universality, one unconnected with the specific characteristics of the person as a single individual.[24] Therefore, in a sense, in the Roman world each person sees his or her own abstract universality incarnated, in an estranged form, in the emperor. In this world humans become aware of their universality, but in an abstract and estranged form. Hence Hegel calls the condition to which the Roman world immediately gives rise one of "self-estranged [*sich entfremdete*] spirit" (PhS 294/359). The Germanic world represents the replacement of this abstract and estranged universality by concrete universality, in that the modern state in which this world culminates is the objectification of a concretely universal will that unites universality, particularity, and singularity, and that each citizen knows as his or her own will.

In the *Phenomenology*, Hegel associates the Roman world with the philosophical schools of Stoicism and Skepticism, but also with the religious outlook he calls the "unhappy consciousness" (PhS 290–294, cf. LPR2 320–322), and in fact the unhappy consciousness replicates some central features of this world at the level of its metaphysics. In the unhappy consciousness, the subject divides itself into a singular "changeable self" and a universal "unchangeable self" that is common to all selves and is conceived as a universal and judgmental God alien to each changeable self, so that its relationship to the changeable self mirrors the relationship between the Roman emperor and his citizens (PhS 126–127, cf. LPR2 301–302, 308). In fact, in Hegel's account of Roman religion in the *Lectures on the Philosophy of Religion*, the God of this religion ends up incarnated in the emperor, so that "the emperor is divinity, the divine essence, the inner and universal that appears, is revealed, and exists as the singularity of the individual" (LPR2 320/181–182, cf. 308).

Just as the Roman state is a necessary stage in the emergence of the concretely universal state of the Germanic world, so the "unhappy" or Roman conception of God is a necessary stage in the emergence of the concretely universal (because triune) conception of God in Christianity. Christianity is the "resolution and reconciliation of the opposition" inherent in Roman religion (LPR2 320/182), so that the unhappiness of this religion is the "birth-pangs of the religion of truth" (LPR2 322/183, cf. PhS 456). In the unhappy consciousness, individual subjects conceive the communality between them in the form of a being that is alien to them all (PhS 126), but in Christianity subjects no longer conceive their communality in this estranged way.

4. Marx on the Modern State and Capital

In *The Essence of Christianity*, Feuerbach effectively adapts Hegel's critique of the Roman world to provide a critique of religion as such. As we saw, for Feuerbach human beings are essentially aware of their own external universality, that is, of themselves as members of their own kind, and thus of the features common to this kind, which for him are reason, will, and love (EC 3). Yet, just as for Hegel, this awareness is one that has to develop historically. In the first instance, we can only become aware of ourselves as possessing these features in common by first abstracting them from ourselves as socially interacting individuals and then projecting them onto another individual in whom they become incarnate, namely God: "God is the concept of the species as an individual ... he is the species-concept, the species-essence conceived immediately as an existence, a singular being [*Einzelwesen*]" (EC 153/185). As a result, religious thought separates human beings from their own essential features: "religion estranges [*entfremdet*] and steals our own essence from us" (EC 236/284). Yet this projection and resulting self-estrangement is a necessary stage toward human self-knowledge: "religion is the first, but indirect, self-consciousness of man," in which man "misplaces his essence outside himself before he finds it within himself" (EC 13/16, cf. 31, 206).

So, just as in Hegel's Roman world individuals conceive their own universality as an abstract universality incarnate in an individual whom they have endowed with power but who dominates them (the emperor), so in Feuerbach's account of religion they first conceive their essential features as incarnate in an individual whom they have invented but who dominates them (God). Furthermore, just as in Hegel's Germanic world individuals go on to overcome the separation between their own singularity and universality, so for Feuerbach the same thing will happen when we go beyond religion and recognize the essential human characteristics (including universality) that we have projected onto an alien being as characteristics of ourselves as single individuals.

In his 1843 and 1844 accounts of the modern state and capital, and of their prospective overcoming, Marx adopts the framework of Feuerbach's account of religion and its overcoming, frequently drawing analogies between state, capital, and religion (e.g., CHDS 87, OJQ 220, NJM 260, EPM 324).[25] But in these critiques he also draws directly on Hegel's account of the Roman world and its religion and their eventual supersession.

Thus in the *Critique of Hegel's Doctrine of the State* (1843) and *On the Jewish Question* (1843) Marx argues that the modern world is characterized by a fundamental separation between the political state, representing universality, and civil society, representing particularity.[26] In the modern world, "the opposition between state and civil society is ... fixed; the state resides not in civil society but outside it" (CHDS 111/252, cf. 137, 185). Therefore, the modern state is an "abstract political state" (CHDS 158/295, cf. 90, 145). Meanwhile, civil society is a realm of private persons, of atomism and egoism (CHDS 145, OJQ 232–233). Humans can realize themselves as species-beings only in the political state, therefore in a way that is estranged from their everyday lives as members of civil society. The human "leads a twofold life, a heavenly and an earthly life": life in the political state, where he "counts as a species-being," that is, as a universal being, and life in civil society, where he "is active as a private man," so that individuals actualize their universality as members of the political state only as a "nonactual [*unwirklichen*] universality" (OJQ 220/354–355), a universality from which they are estranged. Yet at the same time Marx portrays the emergence of this modern abstract state as a step forward in the realization of humans as species-beings. In it, human beings free themselves "through the medium of the state" and so only "in a roundabout way" (OJQ 218/353), but this is a decisive step toward human emancipation (OJQ 221).

Furthermore, a least in the *Critique of Hegel's Doctrine of the State*, Marx sees the power of the modern or political state as characteristically concentrated in a single individual. Since the sovereignty of the state, by which he means the unity of the political community, is detached from civil society, it ends up as incarnated in a single private person, the monarch (CHDS 97), so that "the ruler is the abstract person who has the state in himself" and "the essence of the state is the abstract private person" (CHDS 100/242). Meanwhile, the people is "subsumed under" and dominated by the monarchical constitution, and thus by the monarch himself, even though in fact they are the "true ground" of the constitution and so of the monarch, for "the people make the constitution" (CHDS 87/231, cf. 88–89).

Again, when Marx looks ahead to the condition that must replace the modern system of civil society and political state, what he calls "true democracy" in the *Critique of Hegel's Doctrine of the State* and "human emancipation" in *On the Jewish Question,* he describes this future condition in terms of the overcoming of the divide between civil society and the political state, and so between particularity and universality. True democracy means the "dissolution" of both the abstract political state and civil society (CHDS 191/326). It is the "first true unity of the universal and the particular" (CHDS 88/231). In human emancipation, "the actual individual man takes back into himself the abstract citizen, and as an individual man ... has become a species-being," who "no longer separates social power from himself in the shape of *political* power" (OJQ 234/370).

In all this, we can see Marx applying Hegel's account of the Roman world, its emperor, and its final supersession by the Germanic world, to the system of civil society and modern state, its constitutional monarch, and its future supersession by "true democracy" or "human emancipation."[27] Of course, Marx's conception of how the opposition between particular and universal is to be overcome is very different from Hegel's. While Hegel sees the solution in a socio-political system that institutionalizes separate spheres (civil society and the political state) for the particular and the universal and integrates them through a series of mediating institutions, Marx in 1843 sees this integration as a failure and calls for a more radical, although also radically underspecified, unity of particular and universal.[28] But the roots of this call lie in Hegel's idea of concrete universality.

In the *Economic and Philosophical Manuscripts* of 1844 Marx gives an account of capital as an estranged realization of species-being that parallels his 1843 account of the modern state.[29] At the heart of this account is the idea of "alienated labor," or more precisely "externalized" (*entäussert*) and "estranged" (*entfremdet*) labor (EPM 322–334/510–512).[30]

The verb *entäussern* means "to relinquish or renounce" or "to alienate" in the economic or legal sense of "transfer or give up an item of property or a right" (not in the interpersonal sense of "make unfriendly or hostile"), but it can also be translated as "externalize." It seems first to have been used in a philosophical way in Luther's Bible, in the so-called Philippian hymn where Paul writes that Jesus Christ "existing in the form of God ... emptied himself [*eauton ekenosen*], taking the form of a servant, being made in the likeness of men" (Philippians 2:6–7, American Standard Version). Luther translates the Greek *eauton ekenosen*, literally "emptied himself," as *entäusserte sich selbst*, using the verb *entäussern* for the only time in his translation of the Bible. In his *Attempt at a Critique of All Revelation* (1792), Fichte reverses the poles of Luther's usage. He uses *Entäusserung* to describe the act in which humans project their inner moral law outside themselves in the form of an all-powerful God, an act that he says is the "real principle of religion" (Fichte 1978, 73).[31] Hegel uses the term in a variety of ways, but most significantly for our purposes he uses it to describe God's incarnation in Jesus (PhS 324–325, 457–458, 470–472), the transition from the Logical Idea to nature (EL §18; PP 125), and the process in which the atomized persons of the post-Roman world renounce their singularity, give themselves a universal character, and thereby at once give objectivity to, and achieve a new kind of unity with, their own ethical substance (PhS 294–299, cf. ES §435).[32] Feuerbach, following Fichte's usage but perhaps also the third of Hegel's, uses the term to describe the process in which humans objectify their own essence in something outside themselves, the process that he, like Fichte, sees as central to all religious thought. Thus he says, "The personality of God is itself nothing other than the externalized [*entäusserte*], objectified personality of the human-being" (EC 226/273, cf. 31), and "The activity, the grace of God is the externalized [*entäusserte*] self-activity of man, objectified free will" (EC 239/287–288).

Marx's usage of the term is best interpreted as following Fichte's and Feuerbach's, but whereas in both of these *Entäusserung* describes a way of thinking, in Marx it describes a way of acting. Externalized labor is labor that objectifies the essence of human beings in something external and alien to them, namely first in private property and second in the accumulation of private property as capital. Thus in private property "man becomes objective for himself and at the same time in fact becomes to himself an alien [*fremder*] and inhuman object" (EPM 351/539), and capital (or wealth) is "the estranged [*entfremdete*] actuality of human objectification" (EPM 385/573). Since the human essence consists in part in universality, this means that capital, like the modern political state, is an objectification of human universality in an estranged form, therefore in the form of abstract universality. Furthermore, it is an objectification that dominates the very individuals who have produced it. The worker "falls under the domination of his product, of capital" (EPM 324/512, cf. 285–286). Marx speaks similarly of money in the *Notes on James Mill*:

> The essence of money is ... that the *mediating activity* or movement, the *human*, social act by which man's products mutually complement one another, is *estranged* [*entfremdet*] and becomes the property of a *material thing* outside man, of money. Since man externalizes [*entäussert*] this mediating activity itself, he is active here only as a man who has lost himself and is dehumanised; the *relation* itself between things, the human operation with them, becomes the operation of a being [*Wesen*] outside man and above man. (NJM 260/445–446, cf. OJQ 241)

In the modern economy, then, humans externalize their own essential universality, as an estranged and abstract universality, in the form of capital. By contrast in Marx's communism, by appropriating this externalized essence and overcoming their estrangement from it, humans will actualize their essential universality in such a way that it is no longer estranged from their particularity. Furthermore, the externalized and so estranged objectification of their essence in capital is a necessary stage toward the genuine non-estranged actualization of this essence in communism: "man's relating to himself as an alien being and activation of himself as an alien being" is in fact "the coming to be of species-consciousness and species-life" (EPM 395/584).

Again, then, Hegel's account of the Roman world and its supersession provides a framework (mediated by Feuerbach's account of religion) for Marx's 1844 account of capital and communism. Capital now replaces Hegel's Roman state as the estranged and dominating actualization of human universality, and communism replaces the modern system of right of the German world as the institutional form that reconciles particularity and universality.

5.   Marx on His Relation to Hegel

How does all this fit with Marx's own view in 1843−1844 of his relationship to Hegel? To answer this question we need to look briefly at Feuerbach's account of Hegel. Feuerbach fits Hegel into his general account of religious thought: Hegel is a religious thinker, and his speculative philosophy is a "rational theology" (PF 6/246). However, Hegel replaces the Christian God by "the essence of thinking, thinking abstracted from the I, from the thinker," that is, by the system of categories of the *Logic* or the Logical Idea, which he hypostatizes and makes the ground of everything (PF 36/280). So more specifically he is a kind of neo-Platonist (PF 47). More specifically still, for Feuerbach Hegel's Idea achieves its full reality only through its self-emanation in nature and humanity and then its coming to self-consciousness through the medium of human beings (PF 32–33). For according to Hegel, "man's consciousness of God is the self-consciousness of God" (PF 36/279, cf. PT 157, EC 226, 230), and yet self-consciousness is an essential feature of God (EC 226). So for Feuerbach, Hegel is what we might call a "realizatory emanationist."[33]

Thereby in Feuerbach's view, Hegel, like religion in general, "inverts" the real situation. For

> religious speculation ... makes what is derivative primordial and what is primordial derivative. God is the first, man the second. Thus it inverts the natural order of things! The first is precisely man, the second the essence of man made objective to himself: God. (EC 117–118/141)

In the same way, Hegel makes humans the product of the Logical Idea when in fact the Logical Idea is the product of humans. This is part of what Feuerbach means when he says that Hegel has inverted the truth, or has reversed subject and predicate in his propositions (PT 157).[34]

In the 1843 *Critique,* Marx adopts Feuerbach's view of Hegel as a neo-Platonic idealist who has inverted the relationship between empirical reality and the basic categories that describe it, so that the former is conceived as an emanation of the latter.[35] So, for example, Hegel presents the modern separation of civil society and the political state as "a necessary moment of the Idea, the absolute truth of reason" (CHDS 138/277). Thereby "the true way is turned on its head ... what should be a starting point becomes a mystical result and what should be a rational result becomes a mystical starting point" (CHDS 99–100/242). Hegel reverses subject and predicate: "Instead of conceiving them as predicates of their subjects, Hegel makes the predicates independent and then lets them be transformed in a mystical way into their subjects" (CHDS 80/224).

This neo-Platonic inversion is what Marx has in mind whenever he accuses Hegel of "mysticism."[36] He goes beyond Feuerbach only in arguing that through this inversion Hegel implicitly sanctifies and justifies existing institutions, for "while they are left just as they are, they nevertheless acquire the meaning of a determination of the Idea, of its result or product" (CHDS 62/206), so that whatever currently exists gains "a philosophical form, a philosophical certificate" (CHDS 99/241, cf. EPM 385, HF 61). Meanwhile, Marx does not acknowledge any debt to Hegel, beyond saying that he has identified the modern division between civil society and the political state (CHDS 138) and that he "describes the essence of the political state, as it is" (CHDS 127/266).

In 1844, Marx follows Feuerbach further, describing Hegel as a *realizatory* emanationist: in Hegel, we have "the absolute subject as a process, as a subject that externalizes [*entäussert*] itself and returns to itself from externalization, while at the same time re-absorbing this externalization" (EPM 396/584).[37] However, unlike Feuerbach, Marx applies this interpretation to the *Phenomenology of Spirit*. He reads this book as claiming that the whole of objective reality is generated by the self-externalization of "self-consciousness," so that it concludes in the knowledge on the part of self-consciousness that its objects are simply its own self-objectifications: in knowledge of "the objective being [*Wesen*] as its own self-externalization" (EPM 392/580).

At first sight, this is a highly implausible "subjective idealist" interpretation of the *Phenomenology*.[38] It seems to describe the standpoint reached at the beginning of the chapter on "Self-Consciousness," in which the self-conscious subject comes to conceive its objects as nothing but "moments of self-consciousness" (PhS 105/138), rather than the standpoint reached by the end of the book. The interpretation might be salvaged if we read Marx as meaning by "self-consciousness" the bare idea of I-hood in abstraction from any particular self, and claiming that the Absolute of the *Phenomenology* is a hypostatization of this bare idea. This would be close to Feuerbach's view of Hegel's Logical Idea as the hypostatization of the bare idea of thinking in abstraction from any thinker. However, for our purposes what is important is not so much the identity of "self-consciousness" in this passage as the fact that Marx here reads the metaphysics of the *Phenomenology* as a version of realizatory emanationism, in which an original entity of some kind externalizes itself in a world of physical objects and then comes to know itself through this externalization. This view sets the scene for Marx's account of how the *Phenomenology* is related to his own thought, namely that in it Hegel has anticipated Marx's account of the realization of humans as species-beings through the development of externalized labor and capital and their prospective abolition.

> The importance of Hegel's Phenomenology and its final result – the dialectic of negativity as the moving and producing principle – lies in the fact that Hegel conceives the self-creation of man as a process, objectification as loss of object, as externalisation [*Entäusserung*] and as supersession of this externalisation; that he therefore grasps the essence of *labor* and conceives objective man – true, because actual man – as the result of his *own labor*. The *actual, active* relating of man to himself as a species-being, or the activation of himself as an actual species-being – i.e., as a human being – is only possible if he actually employs all his *species*-powers, which again is only possible through the cooperation of mankind and as a result of history, and treats them as objects, which is at first only possible in the form of estrangement. (EPM 386/574, cf. 395)

Marx's implication is that in his metaphysical account of the self-realization of "self-consciousness" through its self-externalization and the overcoming of this self-externalization Hegel has grasped the general shape of human history. For history is essentially the story of humans' self-externalization of their own essence in products that they produce as private property and capital, and then their overcoming of this self-externalization by taking collective control over those products. Hegel has "merely discovered the abstract, logical, speculative expression of the movement of history" (EPM 382/570). For "humanity" he has substituted "self-consciousness," for "private property and capital" he has substituted "the objects of self-consciousness," and for "communism" he has substituted "self-consciousness's realization that these objects are its own externalization."[39]

It will be obvious from what has gone before that in my view Marx gives a seriously mistaken account of his real debt to Hegel here. Two points can immediately be made against it. First, the analogy he draws between Hegel's supposed metaphysics of self-consciousness and Marx's own vision of history is a very weak one, for even if we can somehow see the *Phenomenology* as expounding a metaphysics in which a hypostatized "self-consciousness" externalizes itself in the form of its objects, it is not plausible to see these objects as *dominating* this self-consciousness. Yet the fact that capital dominates the human beings who have produced it is central to Marx's account of it. Second, if Marx's view of the shape of human history is correct, then Hegel has grasped this basic shape in chapter 6 of the *Phenomenology*, even if he has misidentified the epoch of estrangement as the Roman world rather than the present. This makes it mysterious why he should also have expressed this shape in the coded form of a metaphysics of self-consciousness.

6. Conclusion

I have argued that the Marx of 1843–1844 is indebted to Hegel in two major ways: for his concept of humans as free and universal beings who can realize that freedom and universality only through an analogue of Hegel's institutionalized community of mutual recognition, and for his three-stage vision of history in which human universality must first be embodied in the modern state and capital as an abstract and estranged universality before it can finally be realized as a universality that is no longer counterposed to the particularity of human beings. Meanwhile, in these writings Marx himself gives a different and, I claim, mistaken account of his own debt to Hegel in these areas: in 1843 failing to acknowledge any debt at all, and in 1844 asserting that Hegel has grasped the overall shape of history as Marx conceives it, as the externalization of labor and its overcoming, but has misexpressed this insight in the form of a metaphysics of self-consciousness.

Of course, the indebtedness for which I have argued will be of little interest unless it can be shown that it extends to Marx's mature writings. There is no space to pursue this matter here, but it is worth pointing out that the threefold division of history into precapitalist, capitalist, and communist social forms that Marx sets out in the *Grundrisse* (1857–1858) clearly shows its ancestry in Hegel's sequence of the pre-Roman, Roman, and Germanic worlds:

Relations of personal dependence (to begin with entirely naturally arisen) are the first social forms, in which human productivity develops only to a slight extent and at isolated points. Personal independence based on *thinglike* [*sachlicher*] dependence is the second great form, in which a system of universal social metabolism, of universal relations, of all-round needs and universal capacities is formed for the first time. Free individuality [*Individualität*], based on the universal development of individuals and on their subordination of their communal, social productivity as their social wealth, is the third stage. The second stage creates the conditions for the third. (G 158/75–76, cf. 163–164, C 202–203)[40]

Meanwhile, the early chapters of *Capital* (1867) suggest the continuing influence of Hegel's account of the Roman world on Marx's thought. For Marx, the fact that individual labors in a commodity-producing society are carried out privately means that they can be connected to each other only in so far as their products acquire an abstractly universal character, value, which is counterposed to their particular character as use-values. Thereby the labor that produces these commodities must also acquire a double character. It is "concrete labor" insofar as it produces a particular product with a particular use-value, but "abstract labor" (or "abstract universal labor" as Marx calls it in the 1859 *Contribution to the Critique of Political Economy*) insofar as it produces products that have value (C 131–137).[41] As a result its universal or "social" character, its character of playing a role in the division of labor of society as a whole, is divorced from its character of producing a particular product with a particular use-value (C 160, 165–167). In turn, the value produced by labor as abstract labor has to become incarnate in one particular commodity, money (C 162, cf. G 221), and then (in its self-expanding form) in capital, which becomes an "automatic subject" or "self-moving substance" dominating the very workers who have produced it (C 255–256/169, cf. 1019–1038).

This account of isolated labors that can only be united by being given an abstractly universal character, which in turn is incarnated in a form that dominates the laborers themselves, clearly has structural similarities to Hegel's account of the Roman world. Meanwhile, in Marx's statement in the first edition of *Capital* that the combination of use-value and value in the commodity makes it "an immediate contradiction" (TC 40), with its implication that the same applies to labor insofar as it is both concrete (i.e., particular) and abstract labor, it is possible to detect the idea of a society in which human particularity and universality would no longer be separated: a society informed, therefore, by the idea of species-being, and behind it by Hegel's concept of concrete universality.

Bibliography

Primary Texts

For direct quotations the section number or English pagination is given first followed by a forward stroke and the German pagination; for other references the German pagination is omitted.

495

C   Karl Marx. *Capital*, Vol. 1, trans. B. Fowkes. Harmondsworth: Penguin, 1976 [1867/1873]; Karl Marx and Friedrich Engels, *Karl Marx Friedrich Engels Werke*. Berlin: Dietz Verlag, 1956- (hereafter MEW), Vol. 23.

CHDS   Karl Marx. "Critique of Hegel's Doctrine of the State." In *Early Writings*, ed. L. Colletti. Harmondsworth: Penguin, 1975 [1843]; MEW Vol. 1.

EC   Ludwig Feuerbach. *The Essence of Christianity*, trans. G. Eliot. New York: Prometheus Books, 1989 [1841]; Lúdwig Feuerbach, *Sämtliche Werke*, ed. Hans-Martin Sass. Stuttgart/Bad-Cannstatt: Frommann-Holzboog, 1960–1964 (hereafter FSW), Vol. 6.

EL   G.W.F. Hegel. *Encyclopedia Logic*, trans. T.F. Geraets, W.A. Suchting, and H.S. Harris. Indianapolis, Ind.: Hackett, 1991 [1817/1830]; G.W.F. Hegel, *Werke*, eds. E. Moldenhauer and K.M. Michel. Frankfurt am Main: Suhrkamp, 1986 (hereafter HW), Vol. 8.

ES   G.W.F. Hegel. *Philosophy of Mind*, trans. W. Wallace and A.V. Miller, ed. M. Inwood. Oxford: Clarendon Press, 2007 [1817/1830]; HW Vol. 10.

EPM   Karl Marx. "Economic and Philosophical Manuscripts." In *Karl Marx: Early Writings*, ed. L. Colletti. Harmondsworth: Penguin, 1975 [1844]; MEW Erganzungsband Teil 1.

G   Karl Marx. *Grundrisse: Introduction to the Critique of Political Economy*, foreword by Martin Nicolaus. Harmondsworth: Penguin, 1973 [1857–1858]; Karl Marx, *Grundrisse der Kritik der politischen Ökonomie (Rohentwurf) 1857–1858*. Berlin: Dietz, 1974.

GI   Karl Marx and Friedrich Engels. The German Ideology. In *Collected Works*, Vol. 5. London: Lawrence and Wishart, 1976 [1845–1846]; MEW Vol. 3.

HF   Karl Marx and Friedrich Engels. The Holy Family, or Critique of Critical Criticism. In *Collected Works*, Vol. 4. London: Lawrence and Wishart, 1975 [1844]; MEW Vol. 2.

LA1   G.W.F. Hegel. *Aesthetics: Lectures on Fine Art*, trans. T.M. Knox. Oxford: Clarendon Press, 1975. Vol. 1; HW Vol. 13.

LF   Karl Marx. "Letter to His Father." In Karl Marx and Friedrich Engels, *Collected Works*, Vol. 1. London: Lawrence and Wishart, 1975 [1837]; MEW Vol. 40.

LHP1-3 G.W.F. Hegel. *Lectures on the History of Philosophy*, trans. E.S. Haldane and Frances H. Simson. Lincoln: University of Nebraska Press, 1995. Vols. 1–3; HW Vols. 18–20.

LPR2   G.W.F. Hegel. *Lectures on the Philosophy of Religion*, Vol. 2, trans. E.B. Speirs and J.B. Sanderson. London: Kegan Paul, Trench Täubner, 1895; HW Vol. 17.

LPS   G.W.F. *Hegel. Lectures on the Philosophy of Spirit*, trans. R. R. Williams. Oxford: Oxford University Press, 2007 [1827–1828].

NJM   Karl Marx. "Excerpts from James Mill's Elements of Political Economy." In *Karl Marx: Early Writings*, ed. L. Colletti. Harmondsworth: Penguin, 1975 [1844]; MEW Erganzungsband Teil 1.

OJQ   Karl Marx. "On the Jewish Question." In *Early Writings*, ed. L. Colletti. Harmondsworth: Penguin, 1975 [1843]; MEW Vol. 1.

PF   Ludwig Feuerbach. *Principles of the Philosophy of the Future*, trans. M.H. Vogel. Indianapolis: Hackett, 1986 [1843]; FSW Vol. 2.

PH   G.W.F. Hegel. *The Philosophy of History*. New York: Dover, 1956; HW Vol. 12.

PhS   G.W.F. Hegel. *Phenomenology of Spirit*, trans. A.V. Miller. Oxford: Oxford University Press, 1977 [1807]; HW Vol. 3.

PN   G.W.F. Hegel. *Philosophy of Nature*. Oxford: Clarendon Press, 1970; HW Vol. 9.

PP   G.W.F. Hegel. *The Philosophical Propaedeutic*, trans. A.V. Miller. Oxford: Blackwell, 1986; HW Vol. 4.

PR   G.W.F. Hegel. *Elements of the Philosophy of Right*, ed. A. Wood. Cambridge: Cambridge University Press, 1991 [1821]; HW Vol. 7.

PT   Ludwig Feuerbach. "Preliminary Theses on the Reform of Philosophy." In *The Young Hegelians: An Anthology*, ed. Lawrence S. Stepelevich. Cambridge: Cambridge University Press, 1983 [1843]; FSW Vol. 2.

RH   G.W.F. Hegel. *Lectures on the Philosophy of World History. Introduction: Reason in History*, trans. H.B. Nisbet. Cambridge: Cambridge University Press, 1975; G.W.F. Hegel, *Die Vernunft in der Geschichte*, ed. Johannes Hoffmeister. Berlin: Akademie Verlag, 1966.

SL   G.W.F. Hegel. *Science of Logic*, trans. A.V. Miller. London: George Allen and Unwin, 1969; HW Vols. 5–6.

TC   Karl Marx. "The Commodity: Chapter One, Volume One of the first Edition of Capital." In *Value: Studies by Marx*, trans. Albert Dragstedt. London: New Park, 1976 [1867].

Secondary Literature

Albritton, Robert, and John Simoulidis (eds.). *New Dialectics and Political Economy*. Basingstoke: Palgrave Macmillan, 2003.

Althusser, Louis. *Politics and History: Montesquieu, Rousseau, Hegel and Marx*, trans. Ben Brewster. London: NLB, 1972 [1959–1970].

Althusser, Louis. *For Marx*. London: Verso, 1986 [1965].

Aristotle. *Nicomachean Ethics*. Indianapolis, Ind.: Bobbs-Merrill, 1962.

Arthur, Christopher J. *Dialectics of Labour: Marx and His Relation to Hegel*. Oxford: Basil Blackwell, 1986.

Avineri, S. *The Social and Political Thought of Karl Marx*. Cambridge: Cambridge University Press, 1968.

Burns, Tony, and Ian Fraser (eds.) *The Hegel–Marx Connection*. Houndmills: Macmillan, 2000.

Chitty, Andrew. "On Hegel, the Subject and Political Justification." *Res Publica* 2(2) (1996).

Chitty, Andrew. "First Person Plural Ontology and Praxis." *Proceedings of the Aristotelian Society* 97 (1997).

Chitty, Andrew. "Species-Being and Capital." In *Karl Marx and Contemporary Philosophy*, ed. Andrew Chitty and Martin McIvor. Houndmills: Palgrave Macmillan, 2009.

Colletti, Lucio. *Marxism and Hegel*, trans. Lawrence Garner. London: Verso, 1973 [1969].

Colletti, Lucio. *From Rousseau to Lenin*, trans. John Merrington and Judith White. London: NLB, 1972 [1969].

Duquette, David. "Marx's Idealist Critique of Hegel's Theory of Society and Politics." *Review of Politics* 51(2) (1989).

Engels, Friedrich. *Ludwig Feuerbach and the Outcome of Classical German Philosophy*, ed. C.P. Dutt. London: Martin Lawrence, n.d.

Fichte, Johann Gottlieb. *Attempt at a Critique of All Revelation*, trans. G. Green. Cambridge: Cambridge University Press, 1978 [1792].

Fichte, Johann Gottlieb. *The Science of Knowledge*, trans. Peter Heath and John Lachs. Cambridge: Cambridge University Press, 1970 [1794].

Hook, Sidney. *From Hegel to Marx*. Ann Arbor: University of Michigan Press, 1971 [1950].

Inwood, Michael. *A Hegel Dictionary*. Oxford: Blackwell, 1992.

Lobkowicz, Nikolaus. *Theory and Practice: History of a Concept from Aristotle to Marx*. Notre Dame and London: University of Notre Dame Press, 1967.

Lukács, Georg. *History and Class Consciousness*. London: Merlin Press, 1971 [1923].

Lukács, Georg. *The Young Hegel: Studies in the Relations between Dialectics and Economics*. London: Merlin Press, 1975 [1948].

McCarney, Joseph. *Social Theory and the Crisis of Marxism*. London: Verso, 1990.

McCarney, Joseph. "'The Entire Mystery': Marx's Understanding of Hegel." In *Karl Marx and Contemporary Philosophy*, ed. Andrew Chitty and Martin McIvor. Houndmills: Palgrave Macmillan, 2009.

McIvor, Martin. "Marx's Philosophical Modernism: Post-Kantian Foundations of Historical Materialism." In *Karl Marx and Contemporary Philosophy*, ed. Andrew Chitty and Martin McIvor. Houndmills: Palgrave Macmillan, 2009.

Marcuse, Herbert. *Reason and Revolution: Hegel and the Rise of Social Theory*. London: Routledge and Kegan Paul, 1986 [1941].

Margolis, Joseph. "Praxis and Meaning: Marx's Species-Being and Aristotle's Political Animal." In *Marx and Aristotle: Nineteenth-Century German Thought and Classical Antiquity*, ed. G.E. McCarthy. Savage, Md.: Rowman & Littlefield, 1992.

Meikle, Scott. *Essentialism in the Thought of Karl Marx*. London: Duckworth, 1985.

Rosenthal, John. *The Myth of Dialectics: Reinterpreting the Hegel-Marx Relation*. London: Macmillan, 1998.

Royce, Josiah. *The Spirit of Modern Philosophy*. Boston: Houghton, Mifflin, 1992.

Rubin, Isaak Illich. "Abstract Labour and Value in Marx's System." In *Debates in Value Theory*, ed. Simon Mohun. Basingstoke: Macmillan, 1994 [1927].

Sayers, Sean. "Creative Activity and Alienation in Hegel and Marx." *Historical Materialism* 11(1) (2003).

Schacht, Richard. *Alienation*. London: George Allen and Unwin, 1971.

Smith, Tony. *The Logic of Marx's Capital: Replies to Hegelian Criticisms*. Albany: State University of New York Press, 1990.

Stern, Robert. "Hegel, British Idealism, and the Curious Case of the Concrete Universal." *British Journal for the History of Philosophy* 15(1) (2007).

Taylor, Charles. *Hegel*. Cambridge: Cambridge University Press, 1975.

Westphal, Merold. *History and Truth in Hegel's Phenomenology*, 2nd edition. Atlantic Highlands, N.J.: Humanities Press International, 1990 [1979].

Wood, Allen W. *Karl Marx, Arguments of the Philosophers*. London: Routledge and Kegan Paul, 1981.

Notes

1 I am grateful to Georgios Daremas, Meade McCloughan, and Sean Sayers for comments on an earlier draft of this chapter. All errors remain my own.

2 Landmarks in this literature include Lukacs (1971, 1975), Marcuse (1986), Althusser (1986), and Colletti (1973). Among more recent contributions, see Avineri (1968), Schacht (1971), Arthur (1986), McCarney (1990), Smith (1990), Rosenthal (1998), Burns and Fraser (2000), and Albritton and Simoulidis (2003).

3 For an elaboration of some of these points, see Hook (1971, 41–56) and, for the last one, McCarney (1990, 91–145).

4 See Althusser (1972, 163–186; 1986, 31–38, 87–128, 161–218).

5 I have modified most translations from Hegel and Marx. In short quotations, I have generally omitted the emphases as distracting, but in all longer quotations I have retained them. Although I use "human" in my own commentary, I have not systematically modified traditional but sexist translations of *Mensch* as "man."

6 In this chapter, I use "self-awareness," rather than "self-consciousness" to refer to this general capacity, since Hegel appears to give the latter term a narrower meaning (PhS 101–104, ES § 424).

498

7   The following account of the universality of Hegel's "I" largely follows Inwood (1992, 121–123, 302–305).

8   *Vereinzelung.* In quotations from Hegel and Marx I always translate *einzeln* as "singular," and *individuell* or *Individuum* as "individual."

9   By "the Notion," I take Hegel to be referring to the structure that is inherent in all genuine concepts, where such concepts are thought of as immanent first in an unconscious form in nature and then in a conscious form in human minds.

10 See Inwood (1992, 303). Here I pass over Hegel's doctrine that singularity is a synthesis of universality and particularity (EL §163, PR §7).

11 For Hegel, "abstract" typically means "separated out from a larger whole," and "concrete" means "internally complex," as implied by their respective etymologies: *ab tractare,* "drag away from," and *con crescere,* "grow together." On concrete universality in Hegel, see also SL 58, 662, EL §163A1, and the discussions in Royce (1892, 222–226, 492–506) and Stern (2007).

12 For an attempt at an expanded version of what follows, see Chitty (1996).

13 Hegel hints at the idea that spirit is genus that has become self-aware at SL 780.

14 At one point, Hegel says that the relationship of mutual recognition is "thoroughly speculative in kind" and adds that the speculative consists in "the unity of the Notion, or the subjective, and the objective," implying that the relation of mutual recognition embodies the structure of the Notion (ES §436A/227). See also his references to spirit as the realization of the Notion (or of the Idea) at PN §376, ES §377A.

15 This is why Hegel can describe the will's freedom as implicitly present in "friendship and love" (PR §7A/57), which elsewhere he says have universal self-consciousness as their "substance" (ES 436R/226). See also his comparison between the will as he understands it and Rousseau's general will at PR §258R.

16 In discussing and quoting from Marx, I follow convention and translate *Gattung* as "species," rather than "genus." For fuller discussions of Marx's concept of species-being and its realization, see Chitty (1997, 2009), Margolis (1992), Lobkowicz (1967, 349–372), and Wood (1981, 16–30).

17 Cf. EPM 329/516–517: "Man is a conscious species-being, i.e. a being which relates to the species as its own essence or to itself as a species-being."

18 Feuerbach makes out a connection between human universality and freedom somewhat differently at PF 69.

19 However, even here he develops a theme that is implicit in Hegel's work. Labor plays a central role in Hegel's early account of spirit in the Jena systems of 1803–1804 and 1805–1806; it continues to feature in the development from self-awareness to universal self-consciousness in the *Phenomenology* (PhS 115–118, 132–133, 213); and there is a clear suggestion in the "system of needs" in the *Philosophy of Right* that humans realize their own universality through producing for each other's needs (PR §§190R, 194). For discussions of Hegel's concept of labor in relation to Marx's, see Lobkowicz (1967, 321–348) and Sayers (2003).

20 The *Marx-Engels Gesamtausgabe* (MEGA 2) 4/2 (Berlin: Academie Verlag, 1981), p. 452, gives *Gattungsgenuss* (species-enjoyment) instead of *Gattungsgeist* (species-spirit) here, and *sein eigner Genuss* (his own enjoyment) instead of *sein eigner Geist* (his own spirit) at the end of the passage. I am indebted to Meade McCloughan for pointing this out.

21 Here, too, Marx is drawing on suggestions in Hegel, for whom as we saw above (Section 1) items of private property are the first objectification of the concretely universal will and so of mutual recognition. However for Marx human products must precisely cease to be private property in order to serve this purpose.

22 On the "modernist" character of Hegel's and Marx's thought, see McIvor (2009). It should be said that although, as I have argued, Marx's connections between freedom and universality, and between their joint actualization and the establishment of something akin to a community of mutual recognition, parallel similar connections in Hegel, it is not clear how far Marx can avail himself of Hegel's *arguments* for these connections, given that he shows no sign of adopting the "idealist" conceptions of the self and freedom on which those arguments are premised.

23 Cf. Hegel's more elaborate explanation for why this state power must take the form of a single person, whom he there calls "the lord of the world," at PhS 292.

24 See Hegel's account of the "person" as a single individual who is also an "abstract I" at PR §35R.

25 In drawing such analogies, Marx is only following Hegel's lead in his lectures and the *Phenomenology* (see, e.g., the analogy between "state power" and "wealth" at PhS 301–316).

26 Unlike Hegel, Marx does not seem to distinguish systematically between particularity and singularity.

27 It should be mentioned that some of the features of Hegel's Roman world are also present in his account of civil society in the *Philosophy of Right*. For example, there too the universal is experienced as something external to and imposing itself upon the particular (PR §§182, 184A, 186), so that civil society is "the system of ethical life, lost in its extremes" (PR §184/339). So Marx may also have been drawing on Hegel's account of civil society in this work. See Duquette (1989, 219–225).

28 See Duquette (1989, 235–238).

29 The argument for this claim that follows is set out more fully in Chitty (2009).

30 The main English editions of Marx's early works translate *Entäusserung* as "alienation," but some instead translate *Entfremdung* as "alienation." For a survey, see Arthur (1986, 146–149). In what follows I translate *Entäusserung* as "externalization," *Entfremdung* as "estrangement," and *fremd* as "alien." I avoid the word "alienation" altogether.

31 Cf. Fichte (1970, 154), and for a brief discussion Lobkowicz (1967, 300–302).

32 For a discussion of Hegel's usage of *Entäusserung* in the *Phenomenology*, see Schacht (1971, 30–64).

33 For a contemporary version of this interpretation of Hegel, see Taylor (1975, 76–124).

34 In fact, Feuerbach means quite a lot more, but it is only this part of what he means that Marx takes up from Feuerbach.

35 For a careful investigation of the strands in the early Marx's view of Hegel's metaphysics, see McCarney (2009).

36 Cf. EPM 396, and for Marx's most extended version of this accusation, HF 57–61. Marx repeats the accusation in his passage on Hegel in the 1873 Afterword to *Capital*, mentioned at the start of this chapter.

37 As noted above (Section 4), Hegel himself uses *Entäusserung* to describe the transition from the Logical Idea to nature.

38 For a critique, see Westphal (1990, 214).

39 For a fuller account of Marx's 1844 view of the *Phenomenology*, see Arthur (1986, 59–76).

40 For a discussion of this view of history in Marx's later writings, see Meikle (1985, 94–104).

41 For further discussions, see Rubin (1994) and Colletti (1972, 76–92).

24

Kierkegaard and Hegel on Faith and Knowledge

JON STEWART

Hegel is well known for his claim that religion and philosophy share in some significant sense the same subject matter. Indeed, at the very beginning of the *Encyclopedia of the Philosophical Sciences*, he writes that philosophy "does, initially, have its objects in common with religion. Both of them have the *truth* in the highest sense of the word as their object, for both hold that *God* and God *alone* is the truth. Both of them also go on to deal with the realm of the finite, with *nature* and the *human spirit*, and with their relation to each other and to God as to their truth."[1] At the beginning of his *Lectures on the Philosophy of Religion*, he expresses this even more radically by speaking of philosophy and religion as a unity:

> Thus religion and philosophy come to be one. Philosophy is itself, in fact, worship; it is religion, for in the same way it renounces subjective notions and opinions in order to occupy itself with God. Philosophy is thus identical with religion, but the distinction is that it is so in a peculiar manner, distinct from the manner of looking at things which is commonly called religion as such.[2]

Hegel consistently claims that religion is a form of knowing and to this extent is continuous with philosophy. Similarly, he is consistently critical of all attempts to separate religion from philosophy and to isolate it in a sphere unto itself.

By contrast, Kierkegaard, working with an entirely different set of presuppositions, goes to great lengths to separate religion or specifically Christianity from all forms of knowledge. One of Kierkegaard's main objections to Hegel's philosophy is that it misunderstands the nature of religion by placing it on a par with various forms of scholarship and knowing. Through his pseudonymous authors, Kierkegaard stubbornly insists that faith is fundamentally different from knowledge, and Christianity from speculative philosophy. Kierkegaard's famous words from his early *Journal AA*, already from the year 1835, sound like a kind of battle slogan that anticipates much of his later polemics: "*Philosophy and Christianity can never be united.*"[3] All attempts at such a unification, in his view, result in a dangerous distortion of Christianity and its infinitely important

A Companion to Hegel, First Edition. Edited by Stephen Houlgate and Michael Baur.
© 2011 Blackwell Publishing Ltd. Published 2011 by Blackwell Publishing Ltd.

message. Of all the well-known aspects of Kierkegaard's criticism of Hegel or Hegelianism, this is certainly one of the most central and most significant. On its own it constitutes a large part of Kierkegaard's philosophy of religion generally and touches in one way or another on a number of related issues that are also of great importance to him, for example, the Incarnation, Revelation, and communication.

The positions of the two thinkers are grounded in two quite different sets of fundamental intuitions about the nature of religion. In the present chapter I wish to explore this issue from both sides. How did Hegel understand the relation of faith to knowledge? Why did he argue for the commensurability of the two? By contrast, why was Kierkegaard so insistent on keeping the two spheres absolutely separate and distinct? My goal is to bring the two thinkers into a dialogue with one another by capturing the basic premises and presuppositions that lie behind their respective positions. I will first explore Hegel's philosophy of religion with an eye toward this issue. Then I will give an account of the criticism of this and similar views as found in the works of Kierkegaard's pseudonymous authors. Finally, I will attempt to allow each to respond to the criticisms of the other on the key issues.

1. Hegel's Account of Faith

1.1. The Concept of Faith and Its Relation to Knowing

Hegel addresses the issue of the relation of faith to knowledge, understood as speculative cognition, in a number of places throughout his corpus: "The Spirit of Christianity and its Fate" from the *Early Theological Writings*,[4] the "Faith and Knowledge" essay,[5] the religion chapter in the *Phenomenology of Spirit*,[6] the section on religion in the *Encyclopaedia of the Philosophical Sciences*,[7] the foreword to Hermann Friedrich Wilhelm Hinrichs' (1794–1861) *Die Religion im inneren Verhältnisse zur Wissenschaft*,[8] the review of Karl Friedrich Göschel's (1781–1861) *Aphorismen über Nichtwissen und absolutes Wissen*,[9] and of course the *Lectures on the Philosophy of Religion*.[10] It would be impossible to give an exhaustive overview of all these works in this context. I will instead attempt to give a general account of Hegel's position based on scattered references to these different texts.

Hegel received his philosophical and theological education at a time when Kant's philosophy was the central object of discussion. Kant attempted to demonstrate the limits of reason by critically examining the faculties of the human mind. He argued that only those things that could be given in experience were possible objects of knowledge. By contrast, those things that were not possible objects of experience could not be known and remained forever cut off from us. These included God, immortality, and freedom, which could not be demonstrated since they transcend the sphere of experience.[11] The point of this critique of reason was then "to deny *knowledge* in order to make room for *faith*."[12] By knowing the limits of human reason, one could then properly identify what lay beyond its purview and was thus the proper object of faith.

With this approach Kant effectively created a dualism of phenomena and noumena (or things in themselves). The former were things that could be objects of possible experience and could thus be known, while the latter were objects not of possible experience but only of thought. We can think things as they are in themselves, that is, apart from our ways of perceiving them, but we can never know them as such. According to this scheme, the divine clearly falls on the side of the noumena. All attempts to gain knowledge of God are thus doomed to failure since such attempts always invoke something that transcends experience and thus what it is possible to know.

Given that God was not an object of experience, Kant argued that from a metaphysical point of view God is unknowable. However, Kant nonetheless attempted to save a belief in God by means of the so-called postulates of pure practical reason.[13] What was lost in the theoretical philosophy is won again in the practical philosophy. Although we cannot know God with certainty and can never demonstrate His existence metaphysically, we must nonetheless presuppose His existence in order for our moral universe to make sense. In other words, we must act on the assumption that there is a God and that we are free agents since without these assumptions our concepts of morality, responsibility, and so on would be meaningless.

This solution was problematic for many thinkers who were otherwise sympathetic to Kant's critical enterprise. To many it seemed that Kant had decisively demonstrated the limitations of reason and the fruitless nature of metaphysical speculation about the divine. However, they saw that his attempt to salvage the situation and escape the apparently agnostic conclusion by means of a postulate of practical reason was unsatisfying since it simply reduced God to a moral principle or, even worse, a presupposition for one. In other words, Kant's God seemed to be deprived of the usual characteristics attributed to Him in dogmatics and to have more or less exclusively the function of guarantor of the moral world. God was no longer the loving personal deity who could be the object of prayer and adoration but rather a moral or epistemological principle.

Hegel believed that Kant had a profound insight with respect to his theory of representations and the necessary structures of the human mind. However, he was critical of the conclusions that Kant drew from this with respect to religion. Hegel objected to the claim that we could only have knowledge of objects of possible experience. He argued that those objects that Kant had placed beyond experience can in fact be known as objects of consciousness. Hegel claims that we have knowledge of the divine through *faith* itself. Every country and people has traditional beliefs about the divine that can be analyzed and understood. The goal of the philosophy of religion, for Hegel, is to explore these beliefs and to discover the hidden reason in them. Given this, he regards it as absurd to claim that we cannot know the divine or that God dwells in an inaccessible sphere beyond our own. On the contrary, the collective human mind is full of stories and ideas about the divine. It is the task of the philosopher to make sense of them and to disclose the knowledge of the divine that they contain.

Some will argue that it is, on the contrary, the task of the theologian to make sense of these ideas, but Hegel notes that since religion is a part of human culture that develops throughout history, it thus overlaps with any number of other developments in different cultural spheres, such as history, politics, and philosophy. For this reason expertise is required that goes beyond that of a theologian or specialist in religion. What is required is someone who can grasp the wider movement of Spirit in the entire cultural sphere and then understand the religious phenomena in this sphere.

Hegel's initial intuition is the idealist claim that thinking is at the heart of the different human spheres of activity. Human beings are characterized by "Spirit," and every sphere of their lives is permeated by it: "it is through thought, concrete thought, or, to put it more definitely, it is by reason of his being Spirit, that man is man; and from man as Spirit proceed all the many developments of the sciences and arts, the interests of political life, and all those conditions which have reference to man's freedom and will."[14] In this sense he is quick to reject the view that in religion we are concerned with some unique or special faculty, for example, feeling or immediate knowing, whereas in philosophy we are concerned with thought. In the *Encyclopedia,* he refers to "the prejudice of our day and age, which separates feeling and thinking from each other in such a way that they are supposedly opposed to each other, and are even so hostile that feeling – religious feeling in particular – is contaminated, perverted, or even totally destroyed by thinking, and that religion and religiosity essentially do not have their root and their place in thinking."[15] Hegel attempts to refute this view as follows:

> Making a separation of this kind means forgetting that only man is capable of religion, and that the lower animals have no religion, any more than right and morality belong to them. ... Religion, right, and ethical life belong to man alone, and that only because he is a thinking essence. For that reason *thinking* in its broad sense has not been inactive in these spheres, even at the level of feeling and belief or of representation; the activity and productions of thinking are *present* in them and are *included* in them.[16]

This recalls Hegel's criticism of Schleiermacher's claim that faith is essentially a feeling, specifically the feeling of absolute dependency on God. Hegel believes that there is an element of *thought* in feeling, which must be developed and understood philosophically; faith, therefore, cannot be a matter of feeling alone. Hegel argues that the result of Schleiermacher's view would be that "a dog would be the best Christian for it possesses this [i.e., the feeling of dependence] in the highest degree and lives mainly in this feeling."[17] The point is obviously that only humans have religion; therefore, the cognitive faculty that is at work in religious belief must be one that is unique to human beings. To understand faith as mere feeling means devaluing the very concept of faith and reducing it to a base level.

Hegel further argues that the misunderstanding arises from the fact that when people hear the claim that religion, right, and ethics are essentially concerned with thought, they mistakenly take it to mean that conscious reflection is always at work in these different spheres. Instead, Hegel's thesis is that the necessary *logos* or reason is always present and developing in these different contexts, regardless of how reflective particular individuals may or may not be.

Reason in religion is not, however, an abstract or formal principle; instead, it takes different specific forms in relation to different specific contents in the various descriptions of the divine provided by the different world religions. For Christianity to be a determinate religion, therefore, it must have a determinate content. If it lacks this content, then an ostensible belief in Christianity could in effect be a belief in anything at all. Hegel explains this while criticizing what he takes to be a mistaken "philosophizing" view of his own age that he associates with Jacobi and some of the German Romantics:

> The Christian faith implies an authority that belongs to the church, while, on the contrary, the faith of this philosophizing standpoint is just the authority of one's own subjective

504

revelation. Moreover, the Christian faith is an objective content that is inwardly rich, a system of doctrine and cognition; whereas the content of this [philosophical] faith is inwardly so indeterminate that it may perhaps admit that content too – but equally it may embrace within it the belief that the Dalaï-Lama, the bull, the ape, etc., is God, or it may, for its own part, restrict itself to God in general, to the "highest essence."[18]

With these examples it is clear that content is not an indifferent part of a religion. The content is precisely what defines the individual religions and separates and distinguishes them from one another. Simply by saying that one believes is not enough to define one's religion. But this content is precisely the proof that belief is a matter of knowledge. One must *know* the content of one's belief in order to distinguish it from other beliefs.

Hegel argues that the advocates of religious feeling often make the mistake of confusing the object of belief in sense perception with that of religious belief. While one can believe in the truth of the senses, this is not what is at issue in religious faith. For the latter we are concerned with faith in God, not with some object of sense in any straightforward manner. Hegel illustrates this view by referring to Jacobi: "We *believe*, says Jacobi, that we have a *body*, we believe in the *existence* of *sensible things*. But, when we talk about faith in what is true and eternal, or about God being revealed, or given, in immediate knowing and intuition, these are not sensible things at all, but a content that is *inwardly universal*, i.e., objects that are [present] only to the *thinking* spirit."[19] Thus to know the divine one needs to think and to use philosophical cognition and not the senses.

This explains Hegel's polemic against belief based on the miracles of Jesus. These miracles are also the objects of sense. As pure particulars they do not capture the universal truth and message of Christianity. The latter is accessible only by means of thought. Hegel grants that there is an aspect of immediate knowing in Christianity, but this is not the final word and is in need of being supplemented with something higher. He writes, for example, "Although Christian baptism is a sacrament, it implies, of itself, the further responsibility of providing a Christian education. This means that, for all that religion and ethical life are a matter of *believing*, or *immediate* knowledge, they are radically conditioned by mediation, which is called development, education, and culture."[20] Therefore, the immediate elements in religion must be developed into the higher forms of cognition if they are to be understood correctly.

1.2. Christian Faith as Revelation

One of the key features of Hegel's view of the Christian religion is that it must have a concrete content. As has been seen, he is critical of a merely formal conception of belief that is not related to any specific content. Moreover, this content is revealed and for this reason is known. Hegel thus refers to Christianity as "the revealed religion." He claims that this feature of Christianity renders absurd those views that claim that humans cannot know the divine. God revealed Himself to humanity so that He could be known. Thus Revelation itself is a proof that faith is in fact a kind of knowing. It would be absurd to imagine that God revealed Himself and yet failed to reveal anything. If He revealed Himself, then there must be some content in that revelation.

Since religion is a kind of knowing, it follows the same structural form as the different kinds of knowing in other fields. As we know from Hegel's idealist metaphysics, the Concept *(Begriff)* constitutes the basic structure of the world and the human mind. The Concept consists of the dialectical movement from universality *(Allgemeinheit)* to particularity *(Besonderheit)* and then to their unity in individuality *(Einzelheit)*.[21] This is the basic structure of all human thinking and thus of the different conceptions of the divine as well. While other religions capture this truth only partially or inadequately, Christianity fulfills and completes it. It is by virtue of this doctrine that Christianity is continuous with speculative philosophy and philosophical knowing. The Trinity represents a speculative triad of thought and is thus not just the object of mere sense or feeling. In the Christian Trinity, the metaphysical Concept is embodied in one of its highest forms. Hegel writes in the *Encyclopaedia of the Philosophical Sciences*,

> the Absolute Spirit exhibits itself (α) as eternal content, abiding self-centered, even in its manifestation; (β) as distinction of the eternal essence from its manifestation, which by this difference becomes the phenomenal world into which the content enters; (γ) as infinite return, and reconciliation with the eternal being, of the world it gave away – the withdrawal of the eternal from the phenomenal into the unity of its fullness.[22]

(A) God the Father, dwelling in the beyond, represents the universal aspect of the Concept. (B) This universality must become particular and enter into actuality with Christ, the Son. (C) Finally, with the death of the particular, the Son is reunited with the Father in the unity of the Holy Spirit. Thus in this key Christian doctrine, when understood conceptually, one finds the necessary features of the metaphysical Concept.

A. God as universality: the Father.[23] God is initially conceived as an abstract idea or other in the beyond. The human mind abstracts from itself and posits another in opposition to itself. Self-consciousness is then externalized and placed in a sphere that is beyond the known realm of actuality. In time this other comes to take on an independent reality of its own. In the *Phenomenology* Hegel writes, "The element of pure thought, because it is an abstract element, is itself rather the *'other'* of its simple, unitary nature, and therefore passes over into the element proper to picture-thinking – the element in which the moments of the pure Concept obtain a *substantial* existence relatively to one another."[24] This conception of God is entirely abstract; the divine is merely conceived as a self-conscious other that dwells in the beyond. Due to this abstract nature, this first stage represents that of universality, for if the divine were in any way concrete, then this universality would give way to particularity.

According to Hegel's view, this purely universal conception cannot remain abstract and static for long. It is the nature of the Concept to develop and to be a part of a dynamic process: "Spirit ... is movement, life; its nature is to differentiate itself, to give itself a definite character, to determine itself."[25] The universal seeks to determine itself and make itself particular. The initial idea of God is that of a spirit "outside of or before the creation of the world."[26] Here God is indeterminate since there is no other by means of which He can distinguish Himself. He dwells, as it were, in a universe with only one object. For this reason He remains abstract. Hegel describes this as follows in the *Encyclopaedia*: "Under the 'moment' of *Universality* – the sphere of pure thought or the abstract medium of essence – it is therefore the Absolute Spirit, which is at first the presupposed principle, not, however, staying aloof and inert, but (as underlying and essential power under the reflective category of causality) creator of heaven and earth."[27] Thus, God's first attempt to externalize and particularize Himself is understood to be in the act of creation. By creating the world, God creates an other to Himself. But this distinction does not adequately reflect and thus determine the nature of God:

> When we say, God has created a world, we imply that there has been a transition from the Concept to objectivity, only when the world is here characterized as essentially God's Other, and as being the negation of God, outside of God, without God, godless. In so far as the world is defined as this Other, the difference does not present itself to us as being in the Concept itself or as contained in the Concept; i.e., being, objectivity must be shown to be in the Concept, must be shown to exist in the form of activity, consequence, determination of the Concept itself.[28]

The problem is that God is Spirit, but Spirit is not reflected in the world that He created. Thus in the dialectic of recognition and mutual determination, God stands opposite a thing and not another Spirit. The world itself is considered "godless," a sterile thing. Another form of externalization and particularization is required for God to be genuinely determined as Spirit.

B. God as Particularity: the Son.[29] What is required is for God to externalize Himself not as an object but rather as Spirit. Thus, at the second stage God is understood to make Himself particular in the form of His Son, Jesus Christ. Through the Son God enters the world of actuality in the form most appropriate to Him, Spirit. In this manner, an opposition arises between Father and Son, who mutually reflect and determine each other. God the Father is reflected in the Son in a way that He is not reflected in nature. Hegel explains that the divine "is, in fact, the negative in its own self and, moreover, the negativity of thought or negativity as it is in itself in essence; i.e. simple essence is absolute *difference* from itself, or its pure othering of itself."[30] At this stage God by means of Christ is understood to become "the self-opposed or 'other' of itself."[31] Universality then stands opposed to particularity and abstraction to concretion, with each term being the other of its opposite: the "*actuality* or self-consciousness [i.e., Christ], and the *in-itself* as substance [i.e., God, the Father], are its two moments through whose reciprocal externalization, each becoming the other, Spirit comes into existence as this their unity."[32]

The revelation of God in Christ is a key characteristic of the Christian religion for Hegel, and it is for this reason that he designates it "the revealed religion." The revelation is significant since it represents God showing Himself, revealing Himself or making Himself known to humanity. In the long story of the development of conceptions of the divine that Hegel has traced, he has shown that there is a movement from obscurity to clarity. It is only in earlier religions, where there is an alienation of humanity from nature and the world, that the gods are conceived as unknown, obscure, and impenetrable. By contrast, in Christianity the divine is revealed and humanity is thereby to be reconciled with it.

The other important dimension of the revelation is that God reveals Himself as a man, that is, as Spirit. Human beings can thus immediately relate to the divine in human form. Hegel writes in "The Spirit of Christianity and Its Fate," "Faith in Jesus means more than knowing his real personality, feeling one's own reality as inferior to his in might and strength, and being his servant. Faith is a knowledge of spirit through spirit, and only like spirits can know and understand one another; unlike ones can know only that they are not what the other is."[33] In this way, earlier forms of religious alienation – such as the revelation of the divine in Hinduism in the form of different animals – are overcome. Thus, the culmination of the story of different forms of revelation is Christianity in which God makes Himself known as a human being. Only in this way does the alien element of the divine disappear: "Spirit is known as self-consciousness and to this self-consciousness it is immediately revealed, for Spirit is this self-consciousness itself. The divine nature is the same as the human, and it is this unity that is beheld."[34]

According to the development of the Concept, Christ is the particular that has emerged from the universal. As a concrete particular, he has thus overcome the abstraction of the divine in the beyond of the previous stage. However, the particular, although being an advance in the development of the Concept, is still inadequate. The particular is empirical and transitory. Christ as a particular is not present to humanity forever. It is a mistake to think that one's faith should be fixed on the particular as such. This leads to a kind of fetishism, whereby the believer is fixated on the concrete and empirical: one collects bones of the saint, or splinters of the cross; one searches for the Holy Grail or the burial shroud of Jesus. It is, according to Hegel, a mistake to understand the meaning of Christ solely as a particular in this way. Christ rebukes those who believe only because they have seen miracles. The particular points beyond itself to something higher. But in order to reach this, the particular must perish. Only when the particular has disappeared can the new principle emerge.

C. God as Individuality: the Holy Spirit.[35] The third step in the development of the Christian Concept is the Holy Spirit, in which the universal God in the beyond is known to be united with the particular revealed God. The Holy Spirit is the spirit of the divine as it lives on in the community of religious believers. Hegel writes, "Spirit is thus posited in the third element in *universal self-consciousness; it is its community*."[36] The importance of this third and final stage is that the shortcomings of abstract universality and concrete particularity are overcome. With the death of Christ it is no longer possible to hang on fixedly to the particular; now one is compelled to contemplate the universal nature of the message, which is not some empirical thing but an idea. But it is no longer an abstract and empty idea as at the first stage of pure universality. Now in the Holy Spirit the Christian idea is full of content by virtue of the life and teachings of Christ that it contains. This is embodied in the spirit of the Christian community that is constantly contemplating and appropriating it in their specific context.

The particular, Christ, must therefore perish in order to establish an enduring truth for the religious community. In this way the sphere of nature is overcome and the revelation is completed as an idea. Only with his death is the idea of Christ truly realized: "The movement of the community as self-consciousness that has distinguished itself from its picture-thought is to make explicit what has been implicitly established. The dead divine man or human God is *in himself* the universal self-consciousness."[37] In the Holy Spirit the abstract God in the beyond and the particular incarnate God are unified, and the dualism ceases. Universal and particular are sublated in the individual. The individual believer is united with Spirit. Thus, Hegel regards the idea of the Holy

Spirit as reconciling any number of key dualisms and forms of alienation that have plagued earlier religions. Therefore, only in Christianity is the truth known and is humanity reconciled with the world and the divine.

According to Hegel, the Christian account of the movement from the abstract God in the beyond to the concrete God with the Incarnation and finally to the resurrected God in the Holy Spirit is religion's way of expressing the speculative truth of the Concept. As has been noted at the outset, Hegel's central claim is that philosophy and religion express the same truth or the same content but in different ways. Philosophical knowing is in a sense the same as religious knowing.[38] Speculative philosophy attempts to demonstrate the necessity of the Concept in the different spheres of thought. In so doing, it shows that certain phenomena originally thought to be separate and distinct are in fact necessarily related and constitute a single conceptual unit. In this way philosophy overcomes various forms of dualism that are stuck at subordinate levels of knowing. The speculative history of the forms of religions that Hegel traces performs a similar function. It shows the conception of the divine developing in such as way as to overcome the dualism of human and divine, and thus the alienation that humans feel from the divine. This dualism is just one of many forms of dualism that speculative philosophy attempts to sublate.

Despite these similarities, there is also a key difference in the way in which religious thinking and philosophical thinking understand their objects. Religious thinking sees the story of the Incarnation and the Resurrection as grounded in divine freedom, just as it saw the Fall as the result of human wilfulness. Thus, these events might or might not have happened, and in that sense are "contingent." By contrast, speculative philosophical thinking discerns the *necessity* of this development since it embodies the development of the Concept. If there is a universal, it is necessary that there be a particular. If there are both a universal and a particular, it is necessary that they be united in an individual. This is a necessary movement of thought. It is no mere contingency, but a necessary ontological movement found in all spheres of human thought. The Christian Trinity thus mirrors the three parts of the speculative Concept. But the Christian believer fails to see the necessary conceptual structure that lies at bottom in the Trinity. This is what constitutes the difference between religious thinking and philosophical thinking. The speculative philosopher can see the Concept as Concept, that is, in its pure conceptual form, whereas the religious thinker sees it only in its specific religious forms. The externalization of the universal in the particular is grasped in anthropomorphic terms as the birth of the Son of God in the world. Instead of speaking of the universal and the particular, the religious believer speaks of the Father and the Son.

In Hegel's hierarchy of knowing, religious thinking thus represents the penultimate form of thought, second only to philosophy. In the *Phenomenology of Spirit*, he explains that religion is still inadequate in its grasp of the truth:

> This form is not yet Spirit's self-consciousness that has advanced to its Concept *qua* Concept: the mediation is still incomplete. This combination of being and thought is, therefore, defective in that ... the *content* is the true content, but all its moments, when placed in the medium of picture-thinking, have the character of being uncomprehended [in terms of the Concept], of appearing as completely independent sides which are externally connected with each other.[39]

509

This is Hegel's way of saying that the different conceptions of the divine are considered separate and in their essence unrelated. Their relation is only contingent. Picture-thinking is thus limited and falls short of being a completely adequate and satisfying form of knowing.[40] It requires philosophy to discern the conceptual truth in religion and thus to distinguish it from the contingent.

2. Kierkegaard's Criticism: The Separation of Faith and Knowledge

Just as Hegel's statements about religious faith are strewn through a number of different texts, so also Kierkegaard's accounts of Christian faith encompass virtually his entire corpus. Thus, I will focus my analysis on what I take to be particularly significant accounts that he gives through his pseudonymous author Johannes Climacus in the *Concluding Unscientific Postscript.*

At the beginning of the *Postscript,* Kierkegaard has his pseudonymous author make a key distinction that will inform both the content and the structure of the work. He speaks of "the objective issue," which he defines as the issue "about the truth of Christianity."[41] By contrast, he continues, "The subjective issue is about the individual's relation to Christianity."[42] The work itself is then divided into two parts reflecting this distinction. Right away here one can see the knowledge/faith dichotomy reflected. The objective issue concerns the knowledge that one can have about Christianity, while the subjective issue concerns the individual's faith. Climacus clearly takes Hegel's philosophy to belong to the objective side, which is evidenced by the fact that it is the second main standpoint treated in part one of the book, which is dedicated to exploring the different forms of the objective approach to Christianity. In that short section, "The Speculative Point of View," he begins his polemic against those who confuse the objective and the subjective approach, and he makes his initial attempt to demonstrate that the objective approach has nothing to do with Christian faith. However, his polemic is by no means limited to this section. In fact, it appears repeatedly in the second part of the book, dedicated to "the subjective issue," as he attempts to develop his view of the subjective approach to Christianity. This view is worked out and defined in explicit contrast to the objective view.

In the introduction to the work Kierkegaard's pseudonymous author gives a useful preliminary sketch of the distinction that he will come to work out in the course of the next several hundred pages. He explains that "the issue is not about the truth of Christianity but about the individual's relation to Christianity, consequently not about the indifferent individual's systematic eagerness to arrange the truths of Christianity in paragraphs but rather about the concern of the infinitely interested individual with regard to his own relation to such a doctrine."[43] He then goes on to explain what the subjective approach means to him, specifically as an individual: "I, Johannes Climacus, born and bred in this city and now thirty years old, an ordinary human being like most folk, assume that a highest good, called an eternal happiness, awaits me just as it awaits a housemaid and a professor. I have heard that Christianity is one's prerequisite for this good. I now ask how I may enter into relation to this doctrine."[44] By "eternal happiness" here Climacus clearly makes reference to the doctrine of immortality or the resurrection of souls in Christianity. This is the guiding motivation for Climacus and, he argues, for everyone else, since every individual has an infinite personal interest in his or her own eternal happiness or salvation. (Given the centrality of this claim, it is odd that the Christian doctrine of immortality fills so little space in Kierkegaard's authorship as a whole.[45])

In any case, this is a key point of difference between the subjective and the objective approach. It is connected to the epistemological question of the degree of certainty that can be achieved by the objective approach. According to Climacus, even the best, most rigorous scholarly approaches to Christianity, whether historical, philological, or philosophical, will always fall short of certainty. There will always be something in them that can be called into doubt. For the objective approach this does not matter too much, since it lies in the nature of science to continually approach the truth as it gains new data and refines its own methods. This approach is always a kind of "approximation" of the truth that never reaches absolute certainty.[46] However, for the subjective approach this is a decisive shortcoming. Since what is at stake is one's eternal happiness, nothing less than absolute certainty will do. Thus, even the very best results of the scientific, objective approach will fall far short of what is required for one to risk one's eternal happiness.

Based on this point of departure, Climacus gives us several defining characteristics of the subjective approach. Among these one finds the following: passion, freedom and decision, becoming and striving, subjectivity, inwardness, absurdity and paradox, and indirect communication. Since these concepts are familiar to most Kierkegaard readers, I will touch on them only briefly.

(A) Passion. True Christian faith involves passion due to the fact that what is at issue is one's own eternal happiness. By contrast, the historian or the philologist who approaches Christianity in an objective manner may well have a certain limited passion that derives from an intellectual curiosity about the material, but this can in no way be compared to the infinite passion of Christian faith.

(B) Freedom and Decision. Unlike science, according to Climacus, Christian faith requires a free decision on the part of the believer. By contrast, the goal in science is to construct discursive theories and proofs such that there are no gaps and every conclusion follows necessarily from the premises. The objective approach thus works with necessity and requires no decision as such; one merely needs to follow each step in the argument in order to reach the conclusion. By contrast, there is no such discursive way to Christian faith. The believer must simply make a conscious and free decision to believe. Necessity plays no role in faith.

(C) Becoming and Striving. While the objective thinker reaches a definitive result, the subjective thinker is always in the process of becoming and thus never comes to a final solution. Faith is not a resting place but a fluid movement.[47] The subjective thinker is always striving, without reaching a goal.[48]

(D) Subjectivity and Inwardness. While the objective thinker is oriented outward toward his or her subject matter, the subjective thinker is oriented inward toward his or her own subjective relation to the divine: "Whereas objective thinking is indifferent to the thinking subject and his existence, the subjective thinker as existing is essentially interested in his own thinking, is existing in it."[49] This then leads to the concept of

511

inwardness. "Therefore, his thinking has another kind of reflection, specifically, that of inwardness, of possession, whereby it belongs to the subject and no one else."[50]

(E) Absurdity and Paradox. Kierkegaard's pseudonymous author invokes Tertullian's famous claim *"credo, quia absurdum est."*[51] He argues that only objective thinking can build on reasons, evidence, and plausible arguments. By contrast, Christian faith requires one to believe in the absurd, specifically, what Kierkegaard sketches as the contradiction of the Incarnation, namely, that God, the eternal, became temporal. This is a contradiction that no amount of argument or reasoning can get around. This is "the ultimate paradox of thought," which "thought itself cannot think."[52]

(F) Indirect Communication. While objective thinking can use direct communication, subjective thinking can be communicated only indirectly.[53] Since the content of faith is paradoxical and absurd, it cannot be communicated in a straightforward manner. Any attempt to do so will only result in distortions. The best one can do is attempt a form of indirect communication that enjoins one's interlocutors to look into themselves and examine their own faith.

3. Critical Evaluation

How might Hegel respond to the criticism of the union of faith and knowledge and the model of faith that Kierkegaard's pseudonymous author presents? Perhaps the most obvious objection is the charge of formalism: four of the five sets of characteristics of Kierkegaardian faith outlined in the previous section – passion, freedom and decision, becoming and striving, inwardness – fail to determine any specific content.

There are a number of passages in Kierkegaard's corpus where he, or one of his pseudonymous authors, seems to confirm that he is guilty of this charge of formalism. For example, Climacus' criticism of the historical point of view in the *Postscript* seems to point in this direction. Climacus invites his reader to assume first that "with regard to the Bible there has been a successful demonstration of whatever any theological scholar in his happiest moment could ever have wished to demonstrate."[54] Even if one imagines that this was the best possible demonstration, Climacus insists that this is wholly irrelevant for the faith of the individual. Such an iron-clad demonstration can in no way help the believer to faith. By contrast, he continues,

> I assume the opposite, that the enemies [i.e., of Christianity] have succeeded in demonstrating what they desire regarding the Scriptures, with a certainty surpassing the most vehement desire of the most spiteful enemy – what then? Has the enemy thereby abolished Christianity? Not at all. Has he harmed the believer? Not at all, not in the least. ... That is, because these books are not by these authors, are not authentic, are not *integri* [complete], are not inspired (this cannot be disproved, since it is an object of faith), it does not follow that these authors have not existed and, above all, that Christ has not existed. To that extent, the believer is still equally free to accept it.[55]

One can raise doubts and even definitively refute key points about Christianity, but as long as the existence of Christ is not disproved, there is no danger to faith. The point is clear: no truths that can be established by scholarship can ever have any relevance for

Christian faith. The problem here is that this seems to deprive Christianity of almost all of its doctrinal content since (with the exception of the idea of the Incarnation) no such content is needed for genuine faith.

The relative emptiness of Christian faith is shown even more clearly in the *Philosophical Fragments*, where Climacus states quite straightforwardly that all that is needed for Christian faith is to know that Christ is God incarnate or, indeed, that some people believed he was:

> Even if the contemporary generation had not left anything behind except these words: We have believed that in such and such a year the god appeared in the humble form of a servant, lived and taught among us, and then died – this is more than enough. The contemporary generation would have done what is needful, for this little announcement, this world-historical *nota bene*, is enough to become an occasion for someone who comes later, and the most prolix report can never in all eternity become more for the person who comes later.[56]

If only this minimal information is required, then it is clear that there is little of what we usually understand by way of Christian doctrine and dogma. If this statement is all that is needed for faith, then most all of the key questions of dogmatics remain open.

Another good example of this is Johannes Climacus' famous distinction between "what is said," which characterizes the objective approach, and "how it is said," which characterizes the subjective approach.[57] Climacus clearly places the focus on the "how" of faith. This would seem to imply that the key to faith is not its object or its content but rather the way in which one believes.

This seems to be confirmed in the striking passage that compares the purported Christian believer with the worshiper of idols:

> If someone who lives in the midst of Christianity enters, with knowledge of the true idea of God, the house of God, the house of the true God, and prays, but prays in untruth, and if someone lives in an idolatrous land but prays with all the passion of infinity, although his eyes are resting upon the image of an idol – where, then, is there more truth? The one prays in truth to God although he is worshipping an idol; the other prays in untruth to the true God and is therefore in truth worshipping an idol.[58]

This seems to imply that one can nonetheless be a Christian, although one worships an idol, provided that one does so correctly. For Hegel, this would of course involve a complete distortion and indeed destruction of Christianity, which has a necessary content, which it cannot do without.

Finally, in a draft of a response to what Kierkegaard regarded as the misappropriation of his works by his one-time friend and associate, the philosopher Rasmus Nielsen (1809–1884), he gives the following retrospective consideration of his intentions with his works: "In the pseudonymous writings the content of Christianity has been compressed to its least possible minimum simply in order to give all the more powerful momentum toward becoming a Christian and to keep the nervous energy all the more intensively concentrated so as to be able to master the confusion and prevent the intrusion of 'the parenthetical.' "[59] Here he states explicitly that it was the conscious goal, at least in the pseudonymous writings, to avoid entering into detailed points of dogmatics (as Nielsen had done). Kierkegaard seems to think that such discussions lead away from the true goal, which is to become a Christian. The idea is that such considerations, so to speak, introduce a parenthesis in the deeply personal process that is involved in the individual's consideration of his or her relation to Christianity. This seems again to be a clear indication that Kierkegaard intentionally avoids discussions about the concrete content of Christianity in favor of a focus on the form of belief.

One might argue on Kierkegaard's behalf that he does claim that the infinite passion of faith can have only one correct object, that is, God or the Incarnation. One cannot have infinite passion for finite things. But this response would not be enough to satisfy Hegel since the doctrine of the Incarnation *alone* is not enough to qualify faith as *fully* Christian and so to distinguish it properly from the faith of other religions. While Kierkegaard likes to return to the absolute demand that Christianity places on each individual believer by enjoining them to make a decision and believe, he seems to neglect the fact that other religions make a similar demand on their believers. How then is one properly to distinguish correct belief from incorrect belief if there is no fully articulated difference in content?

One might also argue that while Kierkegaard might appear to be a victim of formalism from Hegel's point of view, by the same token Hegel fails to do justice to Kierkegaard's unwavering demand for the recognition of the subjective dimension of faith. This question opens up the larger issue of whether or not Hegel and Kierkegaard are ultimately compatible in their general approaches. Since Kierkegaard's goal is the inward religious reform of the individual believer, he is not interested in understanding or knowing as such. Instead, his focus is on the irreducibly private and individual nature of faith. Given this goal, it is hardly surprising that he would find this aspect lacking in Hegel's account. By contrast, Hegel's goal is not individual religious reform but rather a philosophical, that is, speculative, conceptual understanding of religion. From this perspective the personal faith of the individual is not a relevant issue. The goal of speculative philosophy is to grasp the Concept in the different spheres of human thought and activity. But in these spheres there are also an infinite number of particular empirical entities that have nothing to do with the Concept. This is what Hegel refers to as the bad infinity of particularity. The irreducible, personal particular of the faith of the individual is not the object of philosophical inquiry for Hegel. Kierkegaard would be in perfect agreement with him on this point. Kierkegaard's objection would be that while Hegel rejects this sphere of private faith as irrelevant (from a philosophical perspective), it is, however, what is the most important thing from the truly religious perspective. Here one can easily see that the two thinkers are simply at cross-purposes. Although they can be brought into a dialogue, as I have attempted to do here, their goals are so completely different that this largely undermines a fair comparison since most of the criticisms on the one side or the other end up begging the question.

A couple of somewhat surprising or counterintuitive conclusions seem to follow from these considerations: (1) There is some irony here in Kierkegaard's repeated criticism of the abstraction of Hegel's philosophical system. Through his pseudonymous authors, he repeatedly charges Hegel with losing himself in vapid abstractions that have no connection to actuality and existence. Hegel is purportedly not interested in the burning truth for the individual. But here it is clear that the situation is just the reverse. It is Kierkegaard's view of faith that is overly abstract and lacking in real content, whereas Hegel has a clear view of what the content of Christianity is and should be in distinction from other religions. It is Kierkegaard who escapes to abstractions in his attempt to define Christian faith.

(2) A second counterintuitive point can be seen in the following observation. At least one branch of Kierkegaard studies sees the Danish thinker as a great Christian apologist, defending the faith against its detractors. He represents a great spokesman for the Christian religion in today's otherwise secular world. This same branch invariably sees him as the grand critic of Hegel's thought, which is regarded precisely as the epitome of modern secular reason in opposition to Christianity. However, when one looks at the matter more closely, one sees that Kierkegaard's statements about Christianity can hardly be taken as a defense or recommendation of the faith to non-Christians. Indeed, what he says about the impossibly high demands of Christianity almost seems designed to scare away potential new believers and alienate those who consider themselves old ones. Ironically, Hegel seems much better to fit the description of Christian apologist. He explicitly defends Christianity as the one true religion and indeed at times does so in a way that can be interpreted as offensive to modern sensibilities about ecumenism and religious tolerance.

Abbreviations of Hegel's Primary Texts

EL   *The Encyclopaedia Logic. Part One of the Encyclopaedia of the Philosophical Sciences*, trans. T. F. Gerats, W. A. Suchting, and H. S. Harris. Indianapolis, Ind.: Hackett, 1991.

EPS   *Encyclopaedia of the Philosophical Sciences in Outline and Critical Writings*, ed. Ernst Behler. New York: Continuum, 1990. (A translation of the *Encyclopaedia* from 1817.)

ETW   *Early Theological Writings*, trans. T. M. Knox, fragments trans. Richard Kroner. Chicago: University of Chicago Press, 1948; Philadelphia: University of Pennsylvania Press, 1975.

Jub.   *Sämtliche Werke. Jubiläumsausgabe in 20 Bänden*, ed. Hermann Glockner. Stuttgart: Friedrich Frommann Verlag, 1928–1941.

MW   *Miscellaneous Writings of G. W. F. Hegel*, ed. Jon Stewart. Evanston, Ill.: Northwestern University Press, 2002.

Phil. of Mind   *Hegel's Philosophy of Mind*, trans. William Wallace and A. V. Miller. Oxford: Clarendon Press, 1971.

Phil. of Religion I–III *Lectures on the Philosophy of Religion*, vols. 1–3, trans. E. B. Speirs and J. Burdon Sanderson. London: Routledge and Kegan Paul; New York: Humanities Press, 1962, 1968, 1972.

PhS   *Hegel's Phenomenology of Spirit*, trans. A. V. Miller. Oxford: Clarendon Press, 1977.

PR   *Elements of the Philosophy of Right*, trans. H. B. Nisbet, ed. Allen Wood. Cambridge and New York: Cambridge University Press, 1991.

TJ   *Hegels theologische Jugendschriften*, ed. Herman Nohl. Tübingen: Verlag von J. C. B. Mohr, 1907.

Abbreviations of Works by Kierkegaard

CA	*The Concept of Anxiety*, trans. Reidar Thomte in collaboration with Albert B. Anderson. Princeton, N.J.: Princeton University Press, 1980.
CD	*Christian Discourses: The Crisis and a Crisis in the Life of an Actress*, trans. Howard V. Hong and Edna H. Hong. Princeton, N.J.: Princeton University Press, 1997.
CUP1	*Concluding Unscientific Postscript*, vols. 1–2, trans. Howard V. Hong and Edna H. Hong. Princeton, N.J.: Princeton University Press, 1992, vol. 1.
JP	*Søren Kierkegaard's Journals and Papers*, vols. 1–6, ed. and trans. Howard V. Hong and Edna H. Hong. Bloomington and London: Indiana University Press, 1967–1978. Cited by volume number and entry number.
KJN	*Kierkegaard's Journals and Notebooks*, vols. 1–11, ed. Niels Jørgen Cappelørn, Alastair Hannay, David Kangas, Bruce H. Kirmmse, George Pattison, Vanessa Rumble, and K. Brian Söderquist, Princeton and Oxford: Princeton University Press, 2007– .
Pap.	*Søren Kierkegaards Papirer*, vols. 1–16, ed. P. A. Heiberg, V. Kuhr, and E. Torsting. Copenhagen: Gyldendal, 1909–1948; supplemented by Niels Thulstrup. Copenhagen: Gyldendal, 1968–1978.
PF	*Philosophical Fragments; Johannes Climacus, or De omnibus dubitandum est*, trans. Howard V. Hong and Edna H. Hong. Princeton, N.J.: Princeton University Press, 1985.
SKS	*Søren Kierkegaards Skrifter*, vols. 1–28, K1-K28, ed. Niels Jørgen Cappelørn, Joakim Garff, Jette Knudsen, Johnny Kondrup, and Alastair McKinnon. Copenhagen: Gad Publishers, 1997.

Notes

1　Hegel, *EL*, §1; *Jub.*, vol. 8, p. 41. *PhS*, p. 479; *Jub.*, vol. 2, p. 602: "Spirit itself as a whole, and the self-differentiated moments within it, fall within the sphere of picture-thinking and in the form of objectivity. The *content* of this picture-thinking is Absolute Spirit." *PR*, §270; *Jub.*, vol. 7, p. 349: "The content of religion is absolute truth, and it is associated with a disposition of the most exalted kind." *EL*, §45, Addition; *Jub.*, vol. 8, pp. 135–136: "absolute idealism can hardly be regarded as the private property of philosophy in actual fact, because, on the contrary, it forms the basis of all religious consciousness. This is because religion, too regards the sum total of everything that is there in short, the world before us, as created and governed by God." See *PhS*, p. 488; *Jub.*, vol. 2, p. 614: "The content of religion proclaims earlier in time than does Science, what *Spirit is*, but only Science is its true knowledge of itself."

2　Hegel, *Phil. of Religion*, vol. 1, p. 20; *Jub.*, vol. 15, p. 37. See also *Phil. of Mind*, §573; *Jub.*, vol. 10, pp. 458–474.

3　*KJN* 1, 25; *SKS* 17, 30, AA:13. See also *KJN* 1, 29; *SKS* 17, 34, AA:17. *KJN* 1, 29–31; *SKS* 17, 34–36, AA:18. See Hermann Deuser, " 'Philosophie und Christentum lassen sich doch niemals vereinen' – Kierkegaards theologische Ambivalenzen im *Journal AA/BB* (1835–37)," *Kierkegaard Studies Yearbook*, 2003, pp. 1–19. Andreas Krichbaum, *Kierkegaard und Schleiermacher. Eine historisch-systematische Studie zum Religionsbegriff* (Berlin and New York: Walter de Gruyter, 2008), pp. 46–52.

4 *Hegels theologische Jugendschriften*, ed. Herman Nohl (Tübingen, 1907). (In English as *Early Theological Writings*, trans. T. M. Knox, fragments trans. Richard Kroner (Chicago: University of Chicago Press, 1948; Philadelphia: University of Pennsylvania Press, 1975).)

5 "Glauben und Wissen oder die Reflexionsphilosophie der Subjektivität, in der Vollständigkeit ihrer Formen, als Kantische, Jacobische und Fichtesche Philosophie," *Kritisches Journal der Philosophie*, 2, no. 1 (1802): 1–188. (Reprinted in *Vermischte Schriften*, vols. 1–2, ed. Friedrich Förster and Ludwig Boumann, vols. 16–17 (1834–1835) in *Hegel's Werke*, vol. 16, pp. 3–157. In *Jub.*, vol. 1, pp. 277–433.)

6 Hegel, *System der Wissenschaft. Erster Theil, die Phänomenologie des Geistes* (Bamberg und Würzburg: Joseph Anton Goebhardt, 1807).

7 Hegel, *EPS*, §§465–471; *Jub.*, vol. 6, pp. 305–307. Hegel, *EL*, §§564–571; *Jub.*, vol. 10, pp. 453–458.

8 Hermann Friedrich Wilhelm Hinrichs, *Die Religion im inneren Verhältnisse zur Wissenschaft* (Heidelberg, 1822). Hegel's foreword appears on pp. i-xxviii of Hinrichs's text.

9 Hegel, *"Aphorismen über Nichtwissen und absolutes Wissen im Verhältnisse zur christlichen Glaubenserkenntniß. – Ein Beitrag zum Verständnisse der Philosophie unserer Zeit. Von Carl Friederich G ... l. – Berlin, bei E. Franklin. 1829,"* *Jahrbücher für wissenschaftliche Kritik*, vol. 1 (May-June 1829), nos. 99–102: 789–816; (June), nos. 105–106: 833–835.

10 *Vorlesungen über die Philosophie der Religion*, I-II, ed. Philipp Marheineke, vols. 11–12 [1832], in *Hegel's Werke*.

11 Kant, *Kritik der reinen Vernunft* (Riga: Johann Friedrich Hartknoch, 1781), 2nd ed., 1787, B xxix and f. *Critique of Pure Reason*, trans. Paul Guyer and Allen W. Wood (New York and Cambridge: Cambridge University Press, 1998), pp. 116f.

12 Kant, *Kritik der reinen Vernunft*, B xxx. *Critique of Pure Reason*, p. 117.

13 Kant, *Kritik der praktischen Vernunft* (Riga: Johann Friedrich Hartknoch, 1788), pp. 219ff. *Critique of Practical Reason*, trans. Lewis White Beck (Indianapolis, Ind.: Bobbs-Merrill, 1956), pp. 126ff.

14 Hegel, *Phil. of Religion* I, pp. 1f.; *Jub.*, vol. 15, p. 19.

15 Hegel, *EL*, §2; *Jub.*, vol. 8, p. 42.

16 Hegel, *EL*, §2; *Jub.*, vol. 8, pp. 42f.

17 Hegel, *MW*, pp. 347f.; *Jub.*, vol. 20, p. 19.

18 Hegel, *EL*, §63; *Jub.*, vol. 8, p. 168.

19 Hegel, *EL*, §63; *Jub.*, vol. 8, p. 167.

20 Hegel, *EL*, §67; *Jub.*, vol. 8, p. 173.

21 Hegel, *EL*, §163; *Jub.*, vol. 8, pp. 358–361.

22 Hegel, *Phil. of Mind*, §566; *Jub.*, vol. 10, p. 455.

23 Hegel, *Phil. of Religion* III, pp. 7–33; *Jub.*, vol. 16, pp. 223–247; *PhS*, pp. 466–469; *Jub.*, vol. 2, pp. 586–590.

24 Hegel, *PhS*, p. 467; *Jub.*, vol. 2, p. 587.

25 Hegel, *Phil. of Religion* III, p. 10; *Jub.*, vol. 16, p. 226.

26 Hegel, *Phil. of Religion* III, p. 7; *Jub.*, vol. 16, p. 223.

27 Hegel, *Phil. of Mind*, §567; *Jub.*, vol. 10, p. 455.

28 Hegel, *Phil. of Religion* III, p. 16; *Jub.*, vol. 16, pp. 231.

29 Hegel, *Phil. of Religion* III, pp. 33–100; *Jub.*, vol. 16, pp. 247–308. *PhS*, pp. 469–471; *Jub.*, vol. 2, pp. 590–592.

30 Hegel, *PhS*, p. 465; *Jub.*, vol. 2, p. 584.

31 Hegel, *PhS*, p. 467; *Jub.*, vol. 2, p. 587.

32 Hegel, *PhS*, p. 457; *Jub.*, vol. 2, p. 575.

33 Hegel, *ETW*, p. 239; *TJ*, p. 289.

34 Hegel, *PhS*, p. 460; *Jub.*, vol. 2, p. 578.

35 Hegel, *Phil. of Religion* III, pp. 100–151; *Jub.*, vol. 16, pp. 308–356. *PhS*, pp. 471–478; *Jub.*, vol. 2, pp. 592–601.

36 Hegel, *PhS*, p. 473; *Jub.*, vol. 2, p. 594.

37 Hegel, *PhS*, p. 473; *Jub.*, vol. 2, pp. 594f.

38 See "The Position of the Philosophy of Religion Relatively to Philosophy and Religion," *Phil. of Religion* I, pp. 18–35; *Jub.*, vol. 15, pp. 36–52. See Quentin Lauer, "Hegel on the Identity of Content in Religion and Philosophy," in *Hegel and the Philosophy of Religion*, ed. Darrel E. Christensen (The Hague: Martinus Nijhoff, 1970), pp. 261–278.

39 Hegel, *PhS*, p. 463; *Jub.*, vol. 2, pp. 581–582. Translation slightly modified. See also *PhS*, pp. 465–466; *Jub.*, vol. 2, pp. 585–586. *PhS*, pp. 477–478; *Jub.*, vol. 2, pp. 599–601.

40 Hegel, *PhS*, p. 412; *Jub.*, vol. 2, p. 520: "So far as Spirit in religion *pictures* itself to itself, it is indeed consciousness, and the reality enclosed within religion is the shape and the guise of its picture-thinking. But, in this picture-thinking, reality does not receive its perfect due, viz. to be not merely a guise but an independent free existence; and conversely, because it lacks perfection within itself it is a *specific* shape which does not attain to what it ought to show forth, viz. Spirit that is conscious of itself."

41 *CUP1*, p. 17; *SKS*, vol. 7, p. 26.

42 *CUP1*, p. 17; *SKS*, vol. 7, p. 26.

43 *CUP1*, p. 15; *SKS*, vol. 7, p. 24f.

44 *CUP1*, pp. 15f.; *SKS*, vol. 7, p. 25.

45 Kierkegaard, *CA*, pp. 139–141, pp. 151–154: *SKS*, vol. 4, pp. 439–443, pp. 451–453. *CUP1*, pp. 165–188: *SKS*, vol. 7, pp. 153–173. *CD*, 202–213: *SKS*, vol. 10, pp. 211–221. See Gregor Malantschuk, "The Problems of the Self and Immortality," in his *Kierkegaard's Way to the Truth*, trans. Mary Michelsen (Montreal: Inter Editions, 1987), pp. 79–96.

46 *CUP1*, p. 30; *SKS*, vol. 7, p. 36.

47 *CUP1*, p. 73; *SKS*, vol. 7, p. 73.

48 *CUP1*, p. 91; *SKS*, vol. 7, p. 90.

49 *CUP1*, pp. 72f.; *SKS*, vol. 7, p. 73.

50 *CUP1*, p. 73; *SKS*, vol. 7, p. 73.

51 See Pierre Buehler, "Tertullian: The Teacher of the *credo quia absurdum*," in *Kierkegaard and the Patristic and Medieval Traditions*, ed. Jon Stewart (Aldershot: Ashgate, 2008) (*Kierkegaard Research: Sources, Reception and Resources*, vol. 4), pp. 131–142.

52 *PF*, p. 37; *SKS*, vol. 4, p. 243.

53 *CUP1*, pp. 74ff.; *SKS*, vol. 7, pp. 74ff.

54 *CUP1*, p. 28; *SKS*, vol. 7, p. 35.

55 *CUP1*, p. 30; *SKS*, vol. 7, pp. 36f.

56 *PF*, p. 104; *SKS*, vol. 4, p. 300.

57 *CUP1*, p. 202; *SKS*, vol. 7, p. 185.

58 *CUP1*, p. 201; *SKS*, vol. 7, p. 184.

59 *JP* 6, 6574; *Pap.* X-6 B 121.

25

Thinking of Nothing: Heidegger's Criticism of Hegel's Conception of Negativity

DANIEL O. DAHLSTROM

In 1938–1939 Heidegger delivered a series of remarks to a group reading Hegel's *Science of Logic*. These remarks call into question the conception of negativity at work in Hegel's text, particularly as it bears on the treatment of the conception of nothingness on its opening pages. The published notes to these remarks are often exasperatingly fragmentary and aphoristic, which perhaps explains the relatively scant attention they have received.[1] Nonetheless in these remarks, through consideration of this core principle of Hegel's thinking, Heidegger mounts a significant challenge to its claims for completeness or absoluteness. The problem, Heidegger contends, is not that Hegel overlooks any particular matter but that he fails to entertain nothingness in a telling sense. Indeed, according to Heidegger, there is a way of thinking of nothing that is overlooked but presupposed by Hegel and is the origin of the most basic senses of negativity. Weighing the force of this criticism is a daunting task, given both the inherent difficulty of the topic and the vastly diverging conceptions of philosophy in play. The humbler aim of the following essay is simply to try to understand Heidegger's basic criticism. To this end in the first part of the essay, I introduce the general problems associated with the concepts in question by briefly presenting a standard interpretation of ordinary uses of "nothing" and the equivalent use of negatives. In part two after elaborating why and how Hegel's conceptions of nothing and negativity depart from such an interpretation, I sketch the central roles they play in his thinking. In part three I elaborate Heidegger's specific criticisms of these conceptions. Heidegger's argument for these criticisms is and, on his own terms, must be inconclusive from a metaphysical point of view. By way of conclusion, I attempt to identify what motivates Heidegger, nonetheless, to mount this criticism.

Nothing and Negativity from a Logical Point of View

Ordinary uses of "nothing" are usually equivalent to uses of negatives. For example, if someone asks, "What were you thinking?" after you've run a red light, you might say,

---

A Companion to Hegel, First Edition. Edited by Stephen Houlgate and Michael Baur.
© 2011 Blackwell Publishing Ltd. Published 2011 by Blackwell Publishing Ltd.

"Nothing," to indicate that you were not in fact thinking at all or, if you were thinking in some sense, that you were not thinking about what you were doing. In keeping with this equivalence to uses of negatives, "nothing" is typically a relative term, standing for the absence of something or other, not the absence of everything. Indeed, the very thought of the complete absence of everything seems patently self-contradictory: we can hardly sustain a claim to think the absence of everything given that thinking, if not the thought itself, is something.

Thus, when someone makes the assertion "I was thinking of nothing," the assertion can only be meaningful if we take the person making the assertion to be claiming that she was not in fact thinking. Nor is there anything objectionable about this way of talking. Thinking is a double-barreled concept, always including an act and a content. If there is no act, there's no content either and this explains the appropriateness of saying "Nothing" in reply to the question "What are you thinking of?" when we are not thinking. But, in that case, thinking of nothing would be a euphemism for not thinking or not thinking of this or that.

There is an analogous equivalence between "doing nothing" and "not doing any-thing," "hearing (seeing, eating, etc.) nothing" and "not hearing (seeing, eating, etc.) anything," and so on. Nor is this structural equivalence limited to these verbs of per-formance. When shoppers have cleared stocks of items from a store in anticipation of a storm, the report that "there is nothing on the shelves" simply means that there is no merchandise left. So, too, for intransitive verbs like "run" or "exist," when we say "nothing runs" or "nothing exists," we presumably can rewrite these expressions the way logicians do as "it is not the case that something runs or exists" without loss of meaning or truth. Accordingly, it would seem that practically every imaginable case/use of "nothing" can be adequately reformulated and understood as a matter of the *negation* of something or other.

This construal of the relation of negation and nothing corresponds to the ways logi-cians typically introduce and express negation and nothing in their notation, where negation is a truth function of a given proposition dependent upon there being a propo-sition (p, $-p$), and "nothing of the sort" is expressed by the negation of an existentially quantified sentence ("$-\exists x\,(Fx)$"), which says that "it is not the case that there is at least one x, such that x is F").[2] The notation for negation accordingly piggybacks on some-thing already entertained as being or possibly being the case (expressed by "p" or "Fx"), and the logical expression for saying that there is nothing of the sort is the negation of a sentence stating something to be the case (as expressed by the negation of an exis-tentially bound variable).[3]

Hegel's Conceptions of Nothing and Negativity

The foregoing analysis of nothing and its equivalence to negatives supposes the univo-cal and constant significance of the terms of the analysis or what might be termed the "ideal" or "sublimed" status accorded to what they signify. That status is ideal inasmuch as "real things" are in various stages of coming to be and passing away. Hegel attempts to express this fundamentally dynamic character conceptually by arguing for the primacy of the category of *becoming* over those of being and nothing. There are two stages of argument relevant here: first, that being and nothing entail each other, and second, that this mutual entailment entails their basic unity in becoming. In advancing the first stage of the argument, Hegel recites a variant of the above mentioned equivalence of "nothing" and "not thinking anything." However, instead of construing "not thinking anything" as equivalent to "not thinking," he glosses first being and then nothing as "empty thinking" (*das leere Denken*) or even "empty intuiting" (*das leere Anschauen*). Such empty thinking is not simply the absence of thought but is rather a thinking in which nothing – that is, *nothingness as such* – is brought to mind. "To intuit or think nothing thus has a meaning; both are distinguished, hence nothing *is* in our intuiting or thinking."[4] Yet at the same time both being and nothing by themselves lack content, determinacy, and therefore any basis for differentiation from something else (including from one another). The contradiction is patent: being and nothing both are and are not the same. But instead of taking this contradiction as a basis for dismissing the consideration of being and nothing, Hegel concludes that their true significance lies in the movement of the one category immediately disappearing into its opposite. In "becoming" being and nothing are distinguished "but by virtue of a distinction that has just as immediately dissolved itself" (WL, I, 83).[5] Such becoming, Hegel argues, itself leads logically to the further thought of "determinate being" (*Dasein*), in which being and nothing – now in the form of not-being or *negation* – remain utterly inseparable from one another in their very distinctness.

This mode of argument flies in the face of the ordinary language analysis of uses of "nothing" and "negatives," and the refinement of that analysis in formal or symbolic logic, where we are constrained to entertain something ("*p*," "*Fx*") or even posit its existence ("$\exists x (Fx)$") as a constant that underlies negation. But given Hegel's dynamic conception of what exists, he has good reason to refuse to give those analyses the last word. In the first place, for Hegel there is nothing, no component of reality, that is not inseparable from and suffused with negation, that is, a determinacy that essentially distinguishes it or in terms of which it distinguishes itself from something, even preeminently itself. So the formal logician's use of negation can be misleading if it is presumed to reflect or determine the nature of things in the final analysis.[6] That is to say, since there is no determinate proposition "*p*" to which negation of a certain sort does not *already* apply, we have to beware of thinking of negative aspects as somehow posterior or external to aspects that are affirmed.

In addition, analyses of "being," "nothing," and "negation" that cling to the parameters of quantification tend to give an ontological priority to individual denumerable entities over what is common or universal to them. This tendency prejudices the debate over the ontological status of universals in a nominalist direction since it confirms a habitus of thinking that the individual entities somehow obtain independently of the universal or even that the universal is reducible to them. By contrast, Hegel's own approach to logic looks to the universals themselves purely as determinations of thought (to the purely formal character of thinking), not in indifference to but explicitly in abstraction from entities permeated by them.[7] Confusion reigns, Hegel notes, when "consciousness brings along to such an abstract logical proposition [as that 'being and nothing are inseparable'] representations of a concrete something and forgets that we are talking not about this but only about the pure abstractions of being and nothing and that we need to fasten on these alone" (WL, I, 87). If we conceive "nothing" in contrast to something, i.e., in contrast to a determinate entity (*ein bestimmtes Seiendes*) distinguished from something else, we would be entertaining a determinate nothing – not "nothing in its indeterminate simplicity" (WL, I, 84).

Of course, the thought of nothing in its indeterminate simplicity immediately demonstrates not only its relatedness to the thought of being but also the embeddedness of that relation in a structured process, and that is precisely Hegel's point. When we think of nothing, we are led to see not simply its inherent relatedness to being but also that this relation is captured by the concept of becoming (and that of determinate being).

Negation continues to play a central role throughout Hegel's *Science of Logic*. In the introduction to the logic of essence, essence is said to have become what it is "through its own negativity," as opposed to an external negativity, and its own negativity is the reflection on the negation entailed by being, from which Hegel concludes that essence is "the initial negation of being" (WL, II, 14ff). Turning explicitly to the topic of "the positive and the negative" in the logic of essence, he argues that the negative lies in the very concept of the positive and vice versa since each has meaning only in relation to the other. "Each is only insofar as its *not*-being *is* [Nicht-*sein* ist] and, indeed, in an identical relation" (WL, II, 57). This meaning-enabling relation of negation is, however, anything but static. Each also "negates" its relation to the other (WL, II, 59). In what sounds very similar to Heidegger's notion of ecstatic existence, Hegel writes that the positive by virtue of the fact that it is in itself negativity "goes outside itself and undergoes alteration" (WL, II, 76). Analogous considerations apply to the negative.[8] Accordingly, Hegel concludes that each – positive as well as negative – is also in itself "the self-referring negation of being-merely-posited, of the negative, and thus is itself the absolute negation" (WL, II, 71). For this reason, Hegel adds, the construal of the positive as "objective" and the negative as "subjective" is a purely external reflection.[9]

Towards the conclusion of the logic of essence, this dynamic ontological character of negativity is prominent in Hegel's characterization of the category of substance insofar as it is for itself. Substance is the absolute in and for itself: "in itself" as the identity of possibility and actuality and "for itself" as "this identity as absolute power or *negativity* simply relating itself to itself" (WL II, 246). The shift from the logic of essence, culminating in this absolute relation, to the logic of the concept turns on the negativity at work also. Thus, although the substance's unity is only an inner necessity, it posits itself "by virtue of the moment of absolute negativity," in the process becoming "the posited identity and thereby the freedom that is the identity of the concept" (WL II, 251).

These instances of Hegel's appeal to forms of negativity are selective but paradigmatic. It comes as no surprise when in Hegel's review of the dialectical method on the final pages of the *Science of Logic*, he dubs negativity "the *turning point* of the movement of the concept" (WL, II, 563). What Hegel precisely has in mind here is the second moment of the dialectic, that is, "the first negative" that far from issuing in the "empty negative, the nothing," contains in itself and constitutes the determinacy of the first immediate moment of the dialectic (which is the concept "in itself") (WL, II, 561f). Because it contains in itself its opposite, this first negative is contradictory and accordingly dismissed by nondialectical thinking under the presumption that one should countenance no thought of anything not conforming to the law of purely formal identity, and that one should employ negation only in an abstract sense.[10] In fact, negativity is "the essential, dialectical moment" of thinking that by virtue of thinking's universal reach, applies to itself (WL, II, 565). There is accordingly, a "second" negative, the negation of this first negative. But this second negative does not mediate in a merely external formal way the first negation and the immediacy negated by it; this second negative is rather, in Hegel's words, "the absolute negativity ... the moment of absolute mediation, the unity that is subjectivity and soul."[11] This absolute negativity restores what was initially taken immediately but does so in the internally mediated fashion proper to thinking. The result of the dialectic, generated by absolute negativity, is not a static unity of immediacy and mediation but that unity as "the movement and activity mediating itself with itself" (WL, II, 565).[12]

Beyond the confines of Hegel's logic, that is, when he turns from pure determinations of thought to reality itself, there is a clear counterpart to his distinctive take on the equivalence of nothing and negation. In the Preface to the *Phenomenology of Spirit*, Hegel characterizes the subjectivity of the living substance as "sheer negativity," more precisely, the negation of simplicity and the negation of that negation. The idea of divine life and cognition as loving play degenerates into vacuousness, he adds, if it lacks the "seriousness, painfulness, patience, and labor of the negative."[13] Similarly, Hegel describes the life of spirit as the capacity to sustain itself in and through negations. The life of spirit consists in the patient and laborious process of countenancing, negating, and thereby superseding the dissolving analyses of the understanding ("the most astonishing and mightiest of powers"). So, too, a person comes to exist freely on her own through "the tremendous power of the negative," negating the very social differences to which she is nonetheless bound. Not least, the life of spirit is the capacity to look death in the eye, "this non-actuality ... of all things the most dreadful." Summing up these points, Hegel observes that "it [the spirit] is this power, not as something positive, which closes its eyes to the negative, as when we say of something that it is nothing or false, and then, having done with it, turn away and pass on to something else; on the contrary, spirit is this power only by looking the negative in the face and tarrying with it. This tarrying is the magical power that converts it into being."[14]

Such appeals to the fundamental roles played by negativity and nothingness in Hegel's thinking could easily be multiplied, but they suffice to demonstrate how radically Hegel opposes the tradition of formal thinking that refuses to waver from the constraints of formal logic even when the question turns to the grounds of thinking and logic itself. Whereas formal thinking clings to "abstract" or merely "formal negation" without countenancing the "positive in *its* negative," Hegel's dialectical thinking takes negativity seriously, not only as the negation of this formal negativity but as an "absolute negativity" or "negativity existing for itself." This absolute sense of negativity is the self-mediating negativity of the concept, which explains his contention on the final pages of the *Science of Logic* that negativity is "the essential, *dialectical* moment" (WL, II, 561–566).

Heidegger's Criticism

Heidegger is fully cognizant of the distinctiveness and central importance of Hegel's conceptions of negativity and nothing for his philosophy. He prefaces his 1938–1939 remarks on these conceptions by explaining his reasons for focusing on them. On the one hand, he notes there is no higher philosophical standpoint than Hegel's philosophy; his system subordinates every earlier philosophy (4, 56). As a result, the basis of any critical engagement with Hegel's philosophy cannot be something external to it (though Heidegger arguably fails to follow through in this regard). On the other hand, Hegel's philosophy is no less comprehensive than it is fundamental (*grundsätzlich*); indeed, by his own account its truth lies in its systematic sweep. Hence, a critical engagement with Hegel's philosophy must be directed at its fundamental determination (*Grundbestimmung*), the determinate conception underlying the system in its specific parts and as a whole. Negativity, Heidegger submits, is what fundamentally determines Hegel's philosophy; it is "the 'energy' of what is absolutely actual" for Hegel (27). Glossing how the negative for Hegel, precisely in the difference between thinking and what is thought, is the moving power (*das Bewegende*) of consciousness, Heidegger observes: "Everywhere, from the ground up, the *negative* of the *difference* dominates" (29).

The Senses of "Negativity" and Their Unquestioned Origin

Heidegger acknowledges not only the importance of negativity for Hegel but also his supple employment of the notion. In this connection Heidegger differentiates at least four sorts of negativity operative in Hegel's thinking. (For ease of reference, I enumerate the four in order.) The first sort of negativity (N1) abstracts from any entity or representation of an entity, thereby yielding the thought of being that is not any entity (*das Nicht des Seienden*).[15] (In Heidegger's early thinking, he stressed the importance of a basic sort of ontological difference, namely, the difference between being and beings. Inasmuch as this first sort of negativity differentiates being from beings, it expresses a sense of that ontological difference, albeit feebly, given the emptiness of the concept of being at the outset of the *Science of Logic*.) Heidegger refers to this conception of being at the outset of the *Logic*, yielded by N1, as Hegel's narrow sense of being.

The second sort of negativity (N2) is the negation of the foregoing sense of being (*das Nicht des Seins*). Heidegger also designates this second sense of negativity as the "completely abstract" negation expressed by "not-being" (*Nichtsein*) at the beginning of the *Logic* – completely abstract because it abstracts from the first abstraction, the conception of being and the "immediate, undetermined representing" that corresponds to it at the outset of the *Logic*. Positing, abstracting from and thereby negating this first abstraction, yields the conception of pure nothing. The first two senses of negativity glossed by Heidegger are then those at work at the outset of the *Science of Logic*.

According to Heidegger, Hegel also employs a third sense of negativity (N3), namely, a conditioned, abstract negativity, consisting of (a) a first negation (typically in the form of subject or object)[16] and (b) a second negation, presumably, the negation of the first. Heidegger does not elaborate these two senses of abstract negativity in any detail but he likely is referring to the implicit negation in the positing of any conditioned content or domain and its explicit negation as the second move of the dialectical process. Hegel's remark, noted above, regarding the positive and the negative, namely, that "each is only insofar as its *not*-being *is* [Nicht-*sein* ist]," exemplifies N3 as does the account (also mentioned above) that he gives at the end of the *Logic* of "the first negative" within the dialectical method.

The fourth sense of negativity (N4) employed by Hegel according to Heidegger is the negativity that is "concrete" and "unconditioned" as the negation of both senses of the conditioned abstract negativity (N3 [a] and [b]). N4 reproduces the sense of negativity expressed in Hegel's conclusion (cited above) regarding the positive and the negative, namely, that each is in itself "the self-referring negation of being-merely-posited, of the negative, and thus is itself the absolute negation." Since any instances of conditioned negativity are themselves posited by absolute thinking and in that sense not external to it, this sort of unconditioned negativity (N4) is also self-negating negativity – what at the conclusion to the *Science of Logic* Hegel calls, as noted above, "absolute negativity" and "the negativity for itself" through which the concept mediates itself. This fourth sense of negativity is inherent in what Heidegger describes as Hegel's "broader sense of being," namely, the sense of being that possesses and sustains nothingness – the negation of entities (*das Nicht 'des' Seienden*) – within itself.[17]

Yet despite the importance and plasticity of Hegel's notion of negativity, Heidegger contends that Hegel fails to put negativity itself in question. The concept allegedly goes without question, as something neither question-worthy nor questionable. More specifically, Heidegger charges that Hegel makes no attempt to explain its origin and at bottom does not take it seriously.[18] As a result, what goes by the name of "negativity" in Hegel's thinking has, Heidegger charges, already "sacrificed" (*darangegeben*) everything negative or everything with the character of "not" (*Nichthafte*) and "swallowed" it up in positivity from the outset (14f).

According to Heidegger, the question of negativity does not come up for Hegel because it is something already posited as part of the presupposed region of his questioning. That region is thinking, and Hegel can no more put negativity in question than he can put thinking – as he construes it – in question.[19] Heidegger attempts to support this startling charge by glossing what thinking allegedly means for Hegel. According to Heidegger, thinking is for Hegel the process of determining beings by way of our consciousness of them or, equivalently, our way of presenting or representing them to ourselves in general (37). Thinking as it is understood here says of entities what and how they respectively *are*. In other words, thinking provides the perspective within which being as such is determined. Thinking determines not only the respective entities in the course of representing them but "*above* all" (vor *allem*) the sense of being as "the unhidden presence" of entities (39f).

In this fundamental respect, Heidegger submits that Hegel follows the modern metaphysical tradition initiated by Descartes for whom the beingness of beings (*Seiendheit des Seienden*) is the presence of what can be thought or, equivalently, what can be presented or represented to the I or subject – including the I itself.[20] The beingness of beings is their status of being presented or represented (*Vor-gestelltheit*). In Heidegger's eyes, Hegel's conception of "subjectivity as an unconditioned subject-object-relation, thinking and encompassing everything in what is thought by it [*alles in ihrer Gedachtheit*]" consummates the history of metaphysics by completing the modern reversal of the relation from which ancient metaphysics began. At the inception of Western metaphysics, being is conceived as the primary being (*das Seiendste*), or better, its presence (*Anwesenheit*), that is, the ever-present *physis* as the reality of beings as a whole. At the end, or better, at the beginning of the end of this metaphysical tradition, entities as a

whole are resolved into what is thought, or equivalently, into subjectivity as the unconditioned subject-object-relation.[21]

Negativity and Difference

Precisely at this juncture, one might object that even on this truncated account of the
sort of thinking that Hegel presupposes, he has a perfectly acceptable explanation of
negativity's origin.[22] Is not every sense of negativity differentiated above, not least the
foundational absolute negativity, plainly entailed by thinking and consciousness even
on Heidegger's gloss of them? The Hegelian objection plays right into Heidegger's
hands. Heidegger acknowledges that difference is inherent in any sort of thinking or
consciousness (including self-consciousness) and indeed inherent in a way that is
directly relevant to the meanings of negativity. Yet difference can be understood in more
than one sense, and in each sense, the relation to negativity – and thus the origin of
negativity itself – remains underdetermined, thereby confirming Heidegger's complaint. To underscore this crucial point, Heidegger considers possible ways of understanding the notion of difference in Hegel's presupposition.

The pre-eminent difference is the difference already signaled by the structure of
the thinking that Hegel presupposes, namely, the difference between subject and
object. Consciousness as the "I representing something" is this difference. From the
vantage point of this difference, three alternatives present themselves: (a) negativity
may be the formal difference that enables the relation of opposition between subject
and object; (b) negativity may be abstracted from that opposition; or (c) negativity
may be the process of the subject differentiating itself from the object (entailing a difference between what is represented and what it is represented *as*) (22f, 29).[23]
Heidegger recognizes that neither of the first two alternatives can correspond to
Hegel's concrete sense of negativity (N4). The concrete sense of negativity is not the
external formal difference enabling opposition in consciousness qua thinking (the
first alternative), nor does it correspond to a difference abstracted (after the fact, as
it were) from the opposition between consciousness and its object (the second
alternative). In other words, that concrete sense of negativity corresponds not to the
difference of consciousness simply but to that of self-consciousness as it *sets itself* in
opposition to the object (the third alternative), or better, "the *self-differentiating* of absolute knowing" (26f).

In view of this location of the conception of negativity in difference as self-
differentiation, Heidegger's complaint can now be specified more sharply. Given that
negativity is supposed to be grounded in the self-differentiation proper to the absolute,
he asks: "In what sense and with what right and to what extent is the 'not' thereby
grounded [or justified: *begründet*]?" (27). I take the question to be largely rhetorical;
according to Heidegger, the sense of negativity in Hegel remains generally opaque, and
Hegel's conception of an absolute self-differentiating sheds no fundamental light on the
matter. Thus, after acknowledging that the abstract negativity (N3) must spring from
absolute negativity (N4) for Hegel, Heidegger observes that this leaves the question of
the latter's origin on the table. To be sure, he adds, the origin cannot be something
external to the absolute idea, but the question remains as to how it arises within the
absolute (22).

According to Heidegger, as we have been noting, Hegel's failure to explain negativity's origin is rooted in what Hegel ultimately presupposes and takes to be self-evident: thinking. Heidegger addresses the sense of this presupposition not only in terms of the subject-object structure of conscious (and self-conscious) thinking, but also in terms of its logical (predicational) structure (expressed by "*S is P*" or "*Fx*"). Heidegger moves too cavalierly between these two approaches. He no doubt does so because the difference in consciousness (not only between representing and represented but more importantly, between representing something and representing it as such-and-such) underlies the logical structure of judgments, and because Hegel, in Heidegger's view, regards that structure as mirroring (or at least capable of mirroring) the difference in consciousness. In any case, Heidegger reads Hegel as conflating the being of beings not only with being presented or represented (*Vor-gestelltheit*) but also with being asserted (*Ausgesagtsein*) and thus with being something "categorical" (14f, 28f, 37, 54f). For this reason, Heidegger makes the charge that Hegel does not depart radically enough from the parameters of traditional logic – a surprising charge, given the differences glossed at the outset between Hegel's approach and that of formal logic. Heidegger contends that Hegel construes negativity solely in terms of the use of 'not' in sentences, applying it to entities as a whole (*das Nicht des Seienden im Ganzen*) – N2 above – to yield the concept of "nothing" (*das Nichts*). Along with this usage, a family of terms is fatally taken to be as self-evident as thinking:

> On the basis of the self-evident character of thinking and that it must always have 'something' to think in order to be itself, there is, as a result, an utter lack of any question of negativity. ...[24]

Heidegger insists that to the contrary, "negativity" is the name precisely of a realm of questions about "the connection of *saying no, denial, being denied, not, nothing*, and *nihilitude [Nichtigkeit]*" (37).[25]

As a means of corroborating his charge that negativity goes without question for Hegel, Heidegger also appeals to the transition from the conclusion of the *Phenomenology of Spirit* to the beginning of the *Science of Logic*. Heidegger notes that the beginning of logic is to be made, as Hegel puts it, "in the element of the thinking existing freely for itself, in pure knowing," or equivalently, as "absolute knowing" – "the truth that has become certainty" – at the conclusion of the *Phenomenology of Spirit* (WL, I, 21). This absolute knowing gives way to "pure being" as the absence of determinacy because the subject of the knowing has become the object. All difference from something else has gone by the wayside, and this thinking of thinking, the unconditionedness of thinking, amounts to the emptiness captured by the concept of being at the beginning of the logic.[26]

Negativity and Nothingness at the Outset of the Science of Logic

One might expect, Heidegger observes, that the origin of negativity for Hegel is to be found in his account of nothingness. But if so, it cannot be the account given in the opening argument of the *Science of Logic*. According to that argument, as Heidegger reads it, the concept of being as the first category of the *Logic* amounts to the beingness of beings, that is, of beings as such or the universal set of beings, where each of them

527

may be determinate, but what they have in common (their *Seiendheit*) is not. In its immediate indeterminacy, this concept of being – the product of the first sort of negation (N1) mentioned earlier – amounts literally to "nothing," as Hegel points out at the beginning of the *Logic*. But this identity by no means illumines the notion of negativity. Nor can negativity be determined by appealing to Hegel's conception of nothing (at least as the result of N2 and as presented in the opening chapter of the *Logic*) since the putative difference between it and being (their mutual negation) collapses in favor of becoming. That is to say, they are ultimately undifferentiated, not differentiated (negated) in themselves or in relation to one another. From Hegel's inference that there is no difference between them, Heidegger concludes that Hegel countenances no genuine negativity here (13f, 17, 19f). [27] In other words, Heidegger may be said to construe the difference between being and nothing at the outset of Hegel's *Logic* as a merely verbal difference or, as is sometimes said, a distinction without a difference. As Heidegger observes, "No difference is at hand, namely, no difference even within the thought to be entertained [*innerhalb der zu denkenden Gedachtheit*] of the beingness of beings."[28]

The Forsaken Difference and the Abyssal Nothingness of Primordial Being (Seyn)

In certain respects, the criticism just glossed is plainly misguided and unfair. After all, as noted at the outset, it is by no means apparent that there is any meaningful – or at least *sustainably* meaningful – way to speak of thinking of absolutely nothing. Nothing, like the negatives to which it is equivalent, always proves to be a relative term, indicating the absence of something other than it, and as we shall see below, this observation is no less true for Heidegger's than it is for Hegel's way of thinking of nothing. Hegel's opening argument in the *Science of Logic* may be said to turn on this emerging relativity even as he argues that the truth of what we are thinking, when we come to think of nothing no longer as pure nothing but as nothing relative to being, is becoming. Strictly speaking, moreover, the place to look for the origin of negativity in Hegel's thought is not in the beginning but in the end of his system and its confirmation that the unconditioned and thus self-negating negativity (N4) is, in Heidegger's own words, the "energy" of the absolute.

As if expecting this riposte, Heidegger extends his criticism of Hegel's conceptions of negativity and nothingness to the relation between the outset of the *Logic* and the absolute (including the absolute thinking) presupposed from the outset. In this connection, Heidegger distinguishes the beginning that the *Logic* starts with and then leaves behind (*Beginn – womit das Ausgehen anhebt und was als solches verschwindet*) from what this thinking is caught up in from the outset and fastens on every step of the way (*Anfang...woran sich das Denken anhält*, worin es im voraus sich aufgefangen hat), until it is finally determined as what is absolutely actual (52, 56f). The difference between the beginning of the system and the grounding wellspring expressed in its conclusion corresponds to the difference, already alluded to, between the two senses of being: the narrow, abstract sense at the beginning of the *Logic*, and the broad, essential sense of what is "absolutely actual" – the "actuality" that corresponds to "unconditioned thinking" (14, 19, 50). (The latter, broad sense of "being" incorporates the concrete sense of negativity, labeled "N4" above.) Yet although Heidegger acknowledges the importance of this difference for Hegel, he contends that the same basic criticism that negativity is taken for granted without being itself explained is no less true for the idea of the absolute confirmed at the end of the system than it is for the outset of the *Logic*. Reciting the tautology that everything within absolute thinking that is not this thinking itself is determined by negativity, Heidegger notes that negativity is for Hegel – necessarily – but "a *privation* of the *absolute*."[29]

In explaining this more fundamental criticism, Heidegger notes that the first sense of negativity (N1) is common to both the system's beginning and its founding inception in the idea of the absolute. As noted earlier, N1 is equivalent to a feeble version of the difference between being and beings, the most salient "ontological difference" in Heidegger's writings (albeit where "being" has a far more robust meaning than it is given at the outset of the *Science of Logic*).[30] According to Heidegger, Hegel forsakes (*ab-sagt*) and ultimately forgets the ontological difference, not merely in the sense that the difference between being and beings is not thematized but more importantly in the sense that it cannot be thematized, that is, there is no content to thematize, given the narrow sense of being or, what is the same, its sameness with nothing at the outset of the *Science of Logic*. Heidegger submits that this obliviousness to the ontological difference – both to thinking that being is not beings and to entertaining the historical significance of this negation – is the essential presupposition for the pretension to absolute unconditioned thinking. It is thanks to this tacit presupposition, Heidegger submits, that Hegel presumes to be able to resolve, or in a sense ab-solve (*auflösen*) everything – including senses of nothingness and negation – into the positivity of the ab-solute. Though the beginning of the *Science of Logic* with the narrow sense of 'being' is the result of dismantling (*ab-bauen*) the broad, robust sense of 'being' as absolute actuality at the conclusion, both senses of being depend upon an ontological difference that Hegel does not thematize because it is not necessary for the designs of his thinking and because it is unfamiliar or even all too familiar to him (14, 20, 41).

Yet ultimately, Heidegger charges, Hegel's thinking must forsake any consideration of this ground or relinquish its claim to being unconditioned. Hegel supposes a difference between beings and being but in his hands, owing to his conception of thinking as a kind of representing, "being" is synonymous with "being presented or represented at all" (*Vorgestelltheit*) or, equivalently, "what is thought by unconditioned thinking" (*Gedachtheit des unbedingten Denkens*).[31] Hence, the difference between being and beings cannot, properly speaking, be represented, and so from the vantage point of representation, any consideration of its origin necessarily amounts to nothing.[32] In other words, it would amount to a category mistake to entertain the difference between being and beings or contemplate the source of it in the light of some conception or representation of being (*Seiendheit* or *Sein*).[33]

This obliviousness to the ontological difference is crucial for Heidegger's general argument. Even the first sense of negativity, adumbrating as it does the ontological difference (being is not a being or beings) originates, he submits, in *primordial* senses of nothing and being (*Seyn*).[34] To make this point, Heidegger is forced to have recourse to tropes and neologisms, though he introduces these senses by focusing again on the very structure of thinking that Hegel presupposes. He contends that thinking is for Hegel (as it is for Descartes and Kant) basically a matter of representing or presenting something as this or that "in the light of being" (*im Lichte des Seins*). Some conception of being – no doubt a conception with a family resemblance to its Greek ancestry – is at work in the representing of entities. As noted earlier, in contrast to the term for entities or beings (*Seiendes*), Heidegger designates this conception of being with the familiar modern German spelling of the word for "being," *Sein,* or with a technical term for "beingness," *Seiendheit.*[35] Heidegger designates the entire structure of thinking or representing as the clearing (*Lichtung*), that is, the representing of something as something in the light of being, but contends that this clearing is an "abyss" (*Ab-grund*), something necessarily removed from any ground in being or beings. To emphasize this aspect of the abyss, Heidegger places a hyphen between the first two syllables of the German word for "abyss"; thus, *Ab-grund* signifies literally *away from a ground.* Heidegger characterizes this abyss as a kind of nothingness that is "not nil but instead the genuine center of gravity, primordial being itself [*Seyn selbst*]" (15). The abyss characterizes the utter lack of a ground (in being or beings) of the clearing that forms the structure of thinking or representing. Since the abyss is unthinkable apart from that structure, thinking and representing may indeed be said to be constitutive of primordial being – only they do not do so by themselves, that is, they do not do so without the groundless clearing that forms their structure.

Whereas the thought of nothing at the outset of the *Science of Logic* is utterly empty and thus the same as the thought of being, Heidegger would have us think of a primordial nothing that by virtue of historically grounding the difference between being and beings and denying us any support or protection in either, is the same as being in a primordial sense (a sense Heidegger designates by using the archaic spelling of 'being': *Seyn*). What he means by their sameness is something less than a strict identity since he characterizes nothing in the primordial sense as "the first and supreme gift" of this primordial being.[36] In order to clarify this primordial sense of being and the sense in which it coincides with a primordial sense of nothing, it may be helpful to review in broad strokes Heidegger's criticism of traditional metaphysics and the development in his own thinking in this connection.

As early as *Being and Time* (1927), long before his excursions into Hegel-interpretation, Heidegger emphasizes the supposedly Greek legacy of understanding being as presence – presence not only in the sense of the temporal present but also in the sense of being present here and being present, that is, potentially available or accessible to a human subject (the modern emphasis given to this traditional understanding, as noted earlier).[37] When Heidegger turns to the study of Hegel, he finds no reason not to suppose that Hegel shares this same basic prejudice. In Heidegger's early attempts to raise the question of being, he insists on the need to articulate the ontological difference, and during this time, he thinks of the being (*Sein*) of beings as an interplay of their respective presences and absences or, equivalently, as temporal.[38] But by the time he focuses a critical eye on Hegel's concept of negation in the 1938–1939 remarks considered in this chapter, he has come to the conclusion that what it means to be, entailing the ontological difference, is a historical event, and this event, or more precisely, its unfolding or prevailing (*Wesung*), is the primordial sense of being (*Seyn*).[39] This event neither is a being nor falls under a concept or manner of being, and these negations, these "refusals" to be so countenanced, originate in the event of primordial being itself (*genitivus appositivus*). Being in the primordial sense is the event in which, as Heidegger figuratively puts it, *Seyn* "bestows" nothing with and as itself upon that "clearing" mentioned earlier that forms the structure of thinking or representing anything at all.[40] For Heidegger during this period (the late 1930s), the shortfall of Western metaphysics (exemplified in Hegel's thinking) lies not so much in its failure to investigate and ascertain the sense of the being of beings (*Sein des Seienden*) as in its failure to appreciate and think the historical groundless ground of that sense of being and its difference from beings – that abyss that he considers equivalent to the "identity" of primordial senses of nothing and being (*Seyn*). He accordingly thinks of nothing in that primordial sense, not as the negation of being (*Sein*) or beings, but as the ground of the ontological difference between them, a ground that cannot be equated with or itself grounded upon any being(s) (*Seiendes*), any set of beings (*Seiendheit*), or any conception of being (*Sein*).

As the source of the difference between being and beings (and thus also the source of N1), this primordial nothingness is obviously not to be confused with either the nothingness that is equivalent to being at the outset of the *Science of Logic* or the senses of nothingness that figure in the absolute's self-negation. Though the primordial nothing that Heidegger would have us think grounds thinking in general, even Hegel's own allegedly "unconditioned" thinking and its senses of negativity, it does so neither in the way one entity grounds another nor in the way that a conception of being grounds what it means to be or not. Negativity is grounded in a primordial nothing (quite literally, an abyss) that is itself grounded neither in anything else nor – importantly, when we think of the Hegelian absolute – in itself.

Conclusion

Heidegger's criticism of Hegel's conception of negativity may be said to operate on three levels. As we have seen, he charges (a) that Hegel fails to offer an explanation of the senses of negativity that he presupposes; (b) that he uncritically assumes senses of negativity inherent in a modern conception of thinking as representing, and as a result overlooks the ontological difference – or, better, the senses of the ontological difference, given Hegel's narrow and broad senses of 'being' – to which those senses of negativity correspond; and (c) that there is a another way of thinking of nothing (i.e., a primordial nothing coincident with primordial being) that underlies the senses of negativity. But has Heidegger even approximated an adequate argument – if an argument at all – for these criticisms? In what are admittedly only notes for his remarks in 1938–1939, one can hardly conclude that he has done so. Several issues and questions would require far more elucidation than one finds in these published notes. For example, even if Hegel does not offer an explanation of negativity in the sense that Heidegger demands, it remains unclear why one should accede to such a demand. Moreover, what, after all, does it mean to give an explanation (to determine the origin) of negativity? How can nothing – in any sense – explain it? Heidegger claims that negativity originates in primordial nothingness, but his own explanation of that claim is undeveloped at best, and at least on these pages, his account of what it means to think of primordial nothing is for the most part barely more determinate than Hegel's way of thinking of nothing on the opening pages of his *Logic*. Indeed, one might argue in Hegel's defense that there is no more basic way of thinking of nothing and of negativity than that exemplified on those opening pages. There can be no doubt that from a Hegelian point of view, Heidegger's argument is metaphysically inconclusive.[41]

But there is a sense in which these considerations are misguided since Heidegger's aim in addressing Hegel on negativity is not to defend an opposing metaphysical position but rather to move away from metaphysics altogether. But, then, even leaving aside the question of the possibility of addressing Hegel's thought critically without invoking an alternative metaphysical agenda, one has to wonder what motivates the criticism.[42]

Heidegger frequently chides the conventional wisdom that Hegel's philosophical vision collapsed shortly after his death. "In the 19th century," Heidegger contends, "this philosophy alone determined the reality of things," albeit not in the form of a heeded doctrine but "as metaphysics."[43] According to Heidegger, Hegel's failure to specify adequately or explain the notion of negativity at work in his thinking goes hand-in-hand with his pretensions to absoluteness, to a thinking to which allegedly nothing – quite literally – is alien.[44] Such pretensions allegedly correspond to the full development of a legacy of metaphysical thinking that presumes to have answered the very question of not only what there is but how to determine what there is and, indeed, what it means to be at all. As Heidegger puts it, "Hegel grasps this moment of the history of metaphysics in which absolute self-consciousness becomes the principle of thinking."[45]

By contrast, Heidegger would have us think of nothing in the primordial sense as the acknowledgement of the absence of any ground, be it in beings or a conception of being. Moreover, Heidegger contends that "this forsaking [*Versagung*] of any ground" – without the support or protection of any entity – is "the supreme guarantee of the dire need [*Not*] for decision and differentiation." (47f) In remarks such as these, we get a glimpse both of what fundamentally motivates Heidegger's criticism of Hegel's conceptions of nothing and negativity, and Heidegger's attempts to work out more primordial accounts of these concepts in supposedly nonmetaphysical terms. That motivation is a considered conviction that there is a realm of *decision* – and presumably responsibility for decisions – that needs cultivation, care, and sheltering that no metaphysical thinking, even or especially in the complete form that Hegel gives it, can provide.[46]

Notes

1   Martin Heidegger, *Hegel: 1. Die Negativität. Eine Auseinandersetzung mit Hegel aus dem Ansatz in der Negativität (1938/39, 1941), 2. Erläuterung der «Einleitung» zu Hegels «Phänomenologie des Geistes» (1942)*, ed. Ingrid Schüßler, *Gesamtausgabe*, Band 68 (Frankfurt am Main: Klostermann, 1993); all numbers appearing on their own within parentheses in the body of this paper refer to page numbers of this volume. In the text and endnotes, I cite this volume as "GA 68," followed by the page numbers. Valuable discussion of this volume can be found in Walter Biemel, "Heidegger im Gespräch mit Hegel," in *Metaphysisches Fragen*, ed. Paulus Engelhardt and Claudius Strube (Köln: Böhlau, 2008), 167–200; Karin de Boer, *Thinking in the Light of Time: Heidegger's Encounter with Hegel* (Albany: SUNY Press, 2000), 297–303; Otto Pöggeler, "Hegel und Heidegger über Negativität," *Hegel-Studien* 30 (1995): 145–166; and Annette Sell, *Martin Heideggers Gang durch Hegels "Phänomenologie des Geistes"* (Bonn: Bouvier, 1998), 126ff. For helpful criticisms of an earlier draft of this chapter, I am grateful to Timothy Brownlee, Klaus Brinkmann, and especially Stephen Houlgate.

2   Or, as the class, no member of which is identical to itself, i.e., the null class: "Λ" or { } or {z: z ≠ z}; see W.V.O. Quine, *Set Theory and its Logic* (Cambridge, Mass.: Harvard University Press, 1963), 19.

3   W.V.O. Quine, "On What There Is," in *From a Logical Point of View,* second, revised edition (Cambridge, Mass.: Harvard University Press, 1980), 12f.

4   G.W.F. Hegel, *Wissenschaft der Logik,* Erster Teil (Frankfurt am Main: Suhrkamp, 1969), 83 (hereafter "WL, I," followed by the page numbers).

5   Hegel's attempt to think the logical category of nothing is not unprecedented. As Heidegger points out (GA 68: 23, 25, 33, 49), in this respect he follows Kant's rundown of senses of nothing, corresponding to the four groups of logical forms of judgments; see Immanuel Kant, *Kritik der reinen Vernunft* (Hamburg: Meiner, 1930), A 290ff/B 346ff.

6   From a Hegelian point of view, claims to the ontological neutrality of the notation mistakenly suppose that the form (or way of taking up the content) does not make a difference to the content.

7   Thus, Hegel describes "pure being" as "the negation of everything finite" and, as such, is determined as essence; see G.W.F. Hegel, *Wissenschaft der Logik,* Zweiter Teil (Frankfurt am Main: Suhrkamp, 1969), 13f (hereafter "WL, II," followed by the page numbers).

8   However, Hegel also contrasts the positive as the contradiction in itself with the negative as the posited contradiction. Heidegger's criticism can be viewed as being directed precisely at the superseding of the negative that ensues from this posited contradiction; see WL, II, 66–70.

9   Hegel distinguishes negation in general from the negative (WL, II, 66), though Heidegger does not appear to take note of the distinction.

10 This presumption is not "factical," Hegel adds, employing a term that a younger Heidegger will exploit for his own purposes (WL, II, 563).

11 WL II, 564; Heidegger's criticism, reviewed below, takes aim at precisely the claim that *"Negativität ist daher zugleich Aufhebung"* (GA 68: 28).

12 The difference between Hegel and Heidegger may be said to come down to the extent to which this result subsumes or sustains this second sense of negativity, that is, to the manner in which absolute negativity is inherent in the absolute.

13 G.W.F. Hegel, *Phänomenonologie des Geistes,* ed. H.-F. Wessels and H. Clairmont (Hamburg: Meiner, 1988), 14f.

14 Ibid., 26.

15 Heidegger turns the participle for being, *seiend,* into the noun *Seiendes* to designate an entity or entities (beings) in contrast to the being (*Sein*) of the entity. In this way he expresses the poles of the central ontological difference, the difference between being and beings – in contrast to ontological differences between, for example, being-here (*Da-sein*) and being on hand (*Vorhandensein*). According to Heidegger, as discussed below, the sense of nothing that is understood in terms of the negation of being or beings is not the primordial sense of nothing, and that primordial sense is coeval with a primordial sense of being, which Heidegger expresses with the archaic word for being, namely, *Seyn,* in contrast to the traditional senses and contemporary uses of *Sein.*

16 Heidegger probably has in mind the following passages that acknowledge the negative in the first moment of the dialectic: WL, II, 555: "Selbst das abstrakte Allgemeine als solches, im Begriffe, d.i. nach seiner Wahrheit betrachtet, ist nicht nur das *Einfache,* sondern als *Abstraktes* ist es schon *gesetzt* als mit einer Negation behaftet"; WL, II, 562: "Weil das Erste oder Unmittelbare der Begriff *an sich,* daher auch nur *an sich* das Negative ist, so besteht das dialektische Moment bei ihm darin, daß der *Unterschied,* den es *an sich* enthält, in ihm gesetzt wird."

17 All passages cited in this paragraph are to be found in GA 68: 17f and 29, where Heidegger discusses senses of 'negativity' and of the "origin of the *not,*" respectively. I combine the two

discussions because they overlap so significantly. However, it bears noting that the former discussion leaves out the account of being as the negation of entities and the latter discussion makes no mention of the two sorts of negation involved in abstract negativity. Part of the discrepancy is based upon the fact that the account of senses of negativity concerns Hegel's operative uses throughout the system, and the focus of the account of the "origin of *the not*" is the outset of the *Logic*.

18   GA 68: 22: "So wesentlich und entscheidend durchgängig die Negativität ist, so fraglos sie *mit* der absoluten Idee 'ist,' so dunkel bleibt doch ihr Ursprung"; GA 68: 24: "Die Philosophie als *ab*-solute, als *un*-bedingte, muß in einer eigentümlichen Weise die *Negativität in sich schließen* und, d.h., doch im Grunde *nicht ernst* nehmen." Heidegger later downplays the question of negativity's origin for Hegel in favor of the question of "how it is itself conceived and projected" (GA 68: 29). In Hegel's defense, one might counter that Hegel's concern is to explain negativity, otherness, and determinacy precisely by locating their origin in being, construed as the potential for determinacy. The dialectical analysis of being demonstrates that this potential is initially indeterminate but determinable. I am grateful to Klaus Brinkmann for help clarifying this point.

19   GA 68: 14: "Die Fraglosigkeit der Negativität als Folge der Fraglosigkeit des Wesens des Denkens."

20   Sometimes Heidegger employs the term *Seiendheit*, which in contrast to the term *Sein*, clearly designates the abstract concept of being, as an abstraction of what all entities have in common, in contrast to being itself (in whatever sense the latter is understood). This set of contrasts – being (*Sein*), beings or entities (*Seiendes*), and beingness (*Seiendheit*) – corresponds to the Medieval Latin differentiation of *esse*, *ens*, and *ens commune*, respectively.

21   GA 68: 14f, 21, 28f, 37, 54f; see also Martin Heidegger, *Besinnung*, ed. Friedrich-Wilhelm von Herrmann, *Gesamtausgabe*, Band 66 (Frankfurt am Main: Klostermann, 1997), 128 (hereafter "GA 66," followed by the page numbers). According to Heidegger, Plato's conception of *eidos* inaugurates the Western metaphysical conception of being as a standing presence, in virtue of which entities can be present to someone. Modernity supposedly appropriates this conception into a form of idealism by equating the reality of things with the appropriate perception or representation of them that is certain of itself. Heidegger marks Hegel's conception of the idea as "the absolute self-appearing of the absolute" as the culmination of this development. Hegel's achievement, in Heidegger's grand narrative, is to have combined into a historical yet ever-present absolute both the ancient conception of objective nature and the modern appreciation of a subjectivity irreducible to nature. Yet, since being an object, a subject, or their union is dependent on in the presence of absolute subjectivity, the culprit for Heidegger remains the same: the stubborn refusal to grasp being as anything other than presence: "Die sich selbst gegenwärtige Gegenwart, die in der Anwesung sich spiegelnde Anwesenheit" (GA 68: 32). The contention that Hegel's philosophy marks the consummation (*Vollendung*) or at least the beginning of the consummation of Western metaphysics (where Nietzsche is the end or penultimate step of its consummation in "technology") is a familiar refrain of Heidegger's postmetaphysical period; see, for example, his 1935 essay, "Überwindung der Metaphysik," in *Vorträge und Aufsätze* (Pfullingen: Neske, 1954), 72ff, 76f; GA 66: 281–286.

22   One might also attempt to disestablish Heidegger's interpretation here by considering Hegel's way of distinguishing representation (*Vorstellung*) precisely from thinking (*Denken*); see G.W.F. Hegel, *Enzyklopädie der philosophischen Wissenschaften*, ed. F. Nicolin and O. Pöggeler (Meiner: Hamburg1969), 359–379.

23   These three alternatives might be glossed as follows: (a) the formal difference is a difference within thinking itself, for example, the difference between the act and content of thinking, that is presupposed by any difference between thinking and its object (not to be confused

with its content); (b) the abstract difference is a difference that is abstracted from the opposition between subject or consciousness and its object; and (c) the absolute difference is the process of self-differentiating where something is represented and thereby differentiated if and only if it is represented *as* such-and-such (requiring a conscious projection, i.e., taking the object *as* such-and-such). This gloss is an admittedly speculative attempt to fill out Heidegger's highly adumbrated account in this connection (GA 68: 22f).

24   GA 68: 38; see, too, GA 66: 294.

25   GA 68: 37. There is another side to Heidegger's argument in the 1938–1939 notes that I forego for the sake of keeping this paper to a manageable length. It concerns what he regards as the basic anthropomorphism of Western metaphysics that Hegel's thinking renders explicit. The notion that the being of entities is their presence and thus their potential presence to a subject goes hand-in-hand with both (a) the neglect of the ontological difference and the primordial abyssal sense of nothing inherent in it, and (b) an interpretation of humans as rational animals in possession of the logos and thus capable of coming into determinate possession in some sense of whatever can be thought or said about anything; see GA 68: 15, 19, 39ff.

26   GA 68: 56f. Without blinking, so to speak, in the brief but heady sequence glossed here ("»*Der logische Anfang* ('*das reine Denken*')«," Heidegger equates pure knowing with absolute knowing and absolute knowing with "thinking of thinking."

27   By equating nothing with being (i.e., in the narrow sense) at the outset of the *Science of Logic*, Hegel has in effect construed nothing as the privation of the absolute actuality (being in the broader sense). But Heidegger contends that nothing is in no way a privation of being, something that takes away or diminishes (*Abbruch tun*) being – but is precisely what being needs "as the ground of a possible diminishing [*Ab-brechung*]." In this oblique if not obscure manner, Heidegger gives some indication of what he understands as genuine negativity, namely, the negativity of a sense of nothing that is operative in being but is necessarily not derivative from or dependent upon being. See GA 66: 294; see, too, Martin Heidegger, *Beiträge zur Philosophie*, ed. Friedrich von Herrmann, *Gesamtausgabe* 65 (Frankfurt am Main: Klostermann, 1989), 266f (hereafter "GA 65," followed by page numbers).

28   GA 68: 20. Heidegger observes that Hegel's "negativity" differs from Plato's μὴ ὄν only by virtue of placing it on the ground of the absolute "I think something," a move that leaves it as indeterminate and unexplained as before; see GA 66: 293f.

29   GA 66: 293; see, too, GA 65: 264; as noted below, Heidegger thinks that a comparable criticism applies to Hegel's concrete sense of negativity (N4).

30   Martin Heidegger, *Grundprobleme der Phänomenologie*, ed. Friedrich-Wilhelm von Herrmann, *Gesamtausgabe*, Band 24 (Frankfurt am Main: Klostermann, 1975), 322. Later Heidegger adopts a more nuanced, often critical posture towards this ontological difference, given the ways in which it can mislead owing to its metaphysical nature. This ontological difference can mislead one not only into construing the difference between being and beings purely conceptually (where being is *Seiendheit*) but also into construing nothing on a par with being or beings, as something grounded in the like; see GA 68: 43–48 and GA 65: 258, 466ff.

31   GA 66: 376: "*Sein und Nichts sind dasselbe. Das 'Nichts' ist hier im Hegelschen Sinne, d.h. metaphysisch verstanden, am Leitfaden des vor-stellenden Entwurfs der Seiendheit als Gegenständlichkeit; ... Das Nichtende Nichts dagegen entspringt dem Wesen des Seyns als Verweigerung (Ereignung in die Verbergung). Aus der Verweigerung entspringt erst die Verneinung.*"

32   The difference between being and beings cannot be represented, conceived, or thought insofar as representation, conception, or thought are construed – again, from this traditional vantage point – as entailing the presence of what is represented, conceived, or thought. Accordingly, Heidegger's early construal of philosophical concepts as formal

indications and his later work on thinking are attempts to transform the traditional senses of these notions.

33 See note 15 above.

34 GA 68: 23ff; see GA 65: 266ff.

35 Early in his career, Heidegger emphasized the need to think of being (*Sein*) in contrast to beings – in other words, to think the ontological difference. However, he became increasingly suspicious that this emphasis led to focusing on a conception of being (hence, *Sein* as *Seiendheit*) at the expense of the primordial historical source of the difference. He accordingly introduces the archaic term *Seyn* to designate the historical unfolding of the difference within an epoch.

36 GA 66: 295.

37 Martin Heidegger, *Sein und Zeit* (Tübingen: Niemeyer, 1972), 25f.

38 Martin Heidegger, *Grundprobleme der Phänomenologie*, ed. Friedrich-Wilhelm von Herrmann (Frankfurt am Main: Klosterman, 1975), 322, 452–469.

39 In contrast to what Heidegger understands – rather monolithically, to be sure – as the traditional sense of "being" (*Sein*), that is the *presence* of beings or entities, the primordial sense of being is the active *absencing* of any ground in any presence.

40 Or, in other words, *Seyn* "is" the groundless (abyssal) origin of the difference between beings and being. Nothing (in the primordial sense) is not only distinct from anything merely not on hand, not effective, not being (*Un-seienden*) but must be said to "nihilate" from the abyss (*Ab-grund*); see GA 68: 47.

41 If, as Heidegger contends, Hegel's absolute thinking is grounded in *Seyn*/nothingness as the self-concealing condition of any emergence of beings and determinate thinking (or "representing"), the question of the nature of this grounding (this dependence) presents itself, especially since absolute thinking denies any such dependence or grounding and since Heidegger denies that the grounding in question is metaphysical. His argument is accordingly beset with all the difficulties and the promise of demonstrating that absolute thinking is not in fact absolute and that there is a plausible sense to talk of "a non-metaphysical grounding of metaphysics." Again, I am grateful to Klaus Brinkmann for helping clarify this issue.

42 My aim in moving to this level is not to adopt Heidegger's ground rules uncritically or exonerate his failure to demonstrate his case against Hegel on traditional philosophical grounds. I am interested in trying to determine why he is apparently so confident that his conceptions of primordial being and primordial nothing supply an explanation and, indeed, a postmetaphysical explanation at that for what Hegel's philosophy, given its unconditioned pretensions, is obliged to explain.

43 *Vorträge und Aufsätze*, 72; GA 65: 213ff; GA 66: 284.

44 Nihilism consists, Heidegger avers, not in thinking that there is nothing but in forgetting nothingness by virtue of being lost to the dominance of entities (*Seienden*) alone. In this respect, the equation of being and nothingness in the opening argument of Hegel's *Science of Logic* signals this nihilism. In writings in the late 1930s, Heidegger speaks of the "machination" (*Machenschaft*) of entities, and in this regard he adds that Hegel and Nietzsche make common cause; see GA 68:15f, 29f and GA 66: 279–286. Heidegger accordingly sees in Hegel's standpoint not only an "uncommon fruitfulness," but also "the complete boredom – that nothing more happens and can happen" (GA 68: 54).

45 *Vorträge und Aufsätze*, 95. For critical discussion of the points raised by Heidegger in this regard, see my "Heidegger and German Idealism" in *A Companion to Heidegger*, ed. Hubert L. Dreyfus and Mark A. Wrathall (Oxford: Blackwell, 2005), 76–79.

46 GA 68: 41; GA 65: 213f, 389–392.

26

Adorno's Reconception of the Dialectic

BRIAN O'CONNOR

Adorno's work contains a number of radical criticisms of Hegel that reveal deep philosophical differences between the two philosophers. He represents Hegel's philosophy as directed, ultimately, against particularity and individual experience. The core motivation of Hegel's philosophy, Adorno argues, is a concern with system and universality. Conceived in this way it is antagonistic to the idea of nonidentity, the very idea that lies at the center of Adorno's philosophical project.

In employing nonidentity as a critical concept – that is, in assessing the capacity of a philosophical system to meet the requirement of, and to do justice to, nonidentity – Adorno advances beyond the historical-materialist reaction against idealism (seen, e.g., in the work of Marx) in which the replacement of *Geist* with social labor returns philosophy to a concern with human action. Yet it would be mistaken to think of Adorno's engagement with Hegel as motivated by a purely hostile critical impulse. Rather, his many criticisms of Hegel have as their objective the retrieval from Hegel of what Adorno thinks of as important insights. Adorno acknowledges Hegel's discovery that there is a moment of nonidentity in conceptualization, an idea that might be said to define Adorno's "negative dialectic." He also refers often to the exemplary model of rationality implicit in Hegel's notion of experience. In essence, Adorno finds a range of revolutionary philosophical insights in Hegel that he himself goes on to develop. According to Adorno, however, these are insights that in Hegel's work come to be subordinated to a systematizing agenda. His criticisms of Hegel are designed to release these insights from the compromised roles they allegedly play in the Hegelian system. Adorno's engagement with Hegel is, for that reason, a process of critical appropriation. Central ideas in Adorno's philosophy, such as determinate negation, immanent critique, dialectic, and experience are taken from the Hegelian system and given a materialist transformation. The influence of Kantian and Marxian philosophy colors much of that transformation.

A great many issues, therefore, are involved in a consideration of Adorno's relation to Hegel. There is (1) the complex matter of specifying the influence of Hegel on Adorno.

A Companion to Hegel, First Edition. Edited by Stephen Houlgate and Michael Baur.
© 2011 Blackwell Publishing Ltd. Published 2011 by Blackwell Publishing Ltd.

We also need to understand (2) the nature of Adorno's disagreement with Hegel. This latter task involves analyzing the evidence for Adorno's contention that Hegel's philosophy is biased toward system and universality. Finally, since Adorno's critique of Hegel is also a critical appropriation, (3) we must assess the success and coherence of his redeployment of Hegelian ideas. These matters will be considered in turn.

1.   Hegel and Negative Dialectic

Adorno interprets Hegel's philosophy as "[o]scillating between the most profound insight and the collapse of that insight."[1] The insight at issue is a nexus of interrelated ideas, those of determinate negation, experience, and dialectic. Central elements of Adorno's position – his negative dialectic – are articulated through the process of retrieving that insight from Hegel who, Adorno contends, ultimately "violates his own concept of the dialectic."[2] Referring to the elements of the position he develops Adorno claims that "there is not a single one that is not contained, in tendency at least, in Hegel's philosophy,"[3] indeed in Hegel's "most profound insight."

1.1.   The Core Concepts of Adorno's Philosophy

Adorno argues that dialectic is essentially negative. This notion of dialectic is intended as a subversion of what he alleges is the positive dialectic of Hegel. It is, at the same time, a subversion that is facilitated by the resources of Hegel's philosophy itself, as we shall see. In the negative process (as Adorno conceives it) dialectic problematizes what is assumed to be the truth of the object through our experience of the inadequacy of our concepts. In that experience there is, as Adorno usually describes it, nonidentity, "the irremovable nonidentity of subject and object."[4] This experience of nonidentity intimates, without determining it, the complexity of the object itself. The subject seeks to grasp an object that it knows to be other than it. This otherness is irreducible, yet the subject strives to conceptualize this object in order to bring itself closer to it. At the same time the subject can never make the object identical with its concepts. But the failure of concepts does not mean that the effort to know – to conceptualize the object – is pointless. The complexity of the object is increasingly specified, albeit negatively, in each of those failures. This capacity for negative experience is the capacity, then, to recognize the failure of concepts to encapsulate objects, a failure that Adorno describes as "contradiction " (i.e., between the object in its complexity and the concept). "The less identity can be assumed between subject and object, the more contradictory are the claims made upon the cognitive subject."[5] Being responsive to contradiction, then, is the mark of rationality, since it is precisely the capacity for the persistent, self-conscious critique of truth claims. Dialectic stands in sharp contrast to manipulative forms of rationality in which, Adorno claims, the successful categorization of objects is the criterion of knowledge. This process of categorization is a procedure in which, supposedly, an effort is made to render the object identical with the concept. Adorno describes this as the imposed "subjective *adaequatio*."[6] That, however, limits our potential for the experience of objects, a potential that is realized in dialectical experience. As Adorno puts it: "Experience forbids the resolution in the unity of consciousness of whatever appears contradictory ... contradiction cannot be brought under any unity without manipulation, without the insertion of some wretched cover concepts that will make the crucial differences vanish."[7]

Adorno sees the negative dialectic as "a logic ... of disintegration," of the disintegration of the apparent identity between concept and reality.[8] It establishes that there are unrecognized contradictions between the two that are obscured by identity claims. In so doing it releases the thing or object from its forced and harmonizing identity or conceptualization, thereby bringing about a "confrontation of concept and thing."[9] According to Adorno this process is one in which critique immanently engages with these conceptualizations in order, as he describes it, "to grasp, through their form and meaning, the contradiction between their objective idea" – what it is that these conceptualizations describe – "and that pretension" – the claims to objectivity in the conceptualizations. This process does not simply end, however, with the rejection of the "pretension" of the concept. Rather, Adorno writes, it "seeks to transform this knowledge into a heightened perception of the thing itself."[10] The sense of the "thing," the "matter," the "object," is heightened by our experience of failure to encapsulate it. The thing appears more complex than our conceptualization seemed to allow. For Adorno, in fact, this experience contributes ultimately to a reconciliation of subject and object in that the subject's "heightened perception of the thing" means that it has become conscious of ways in which it has misrepresented the object. This is not reconciliation in the sense of identity between subject and object: "It is up to dialectical cognition to pursue the inadequacy of thought and thing, to experience it in the thing."[11]

The term Adorno gives to the structure of the subject-object relation is "mediation" (*Vermittlung*). Through this structure – in its unimpaired operation at least – the subject experiences the world and its objects in ever richer ways: this is transformative experience. At the same time, through the subject's increasing awareness of the object's complexities, which are intimated in nonidentical experience, the object is also understood as a dynamic element in the relation. Adorno describes the mediating role played by the subject as the "how" and the object as the "what" in this relation.[12] As the "how," the subject is in the business of articulating and conceptualizing the object, whereas the object, as the "what," is that to which the subject must adjust its concepts. Because of this process of articulation and adjustment the relation of subject and object cannot conclude in the identity of the two. Adorno describes it as follows: subject and object "constitute one another as much as – by virtue of such constitution – they depart from each other."[13]

1.2.   The Hegelianism of Adorno's Philosophy

These core concepts of Adorno's negative dialectic can be traced back, "in tendency at least," to Hegel. The logic of disintegration, as a process of heightened perception, is a version of Hegel's idea of determinate negation. As Adorno notes, "the negativity I am speaking about contains a pointer to what Hegel calls *determinate* negation. In other words, negativity of this kind is made concrete."[14] That is to say, negativity, as Hegel claims, can be informative. What Adorno is referring to is Hegel's characterization of the dynamic of experience as a determinate negation or "a *determinate* nothingness, one which has a *content*."[15] This dynamic is the productive negation of a belief, a process Hegel sees as a "labour of the negative."[16] Hegel contrasts the capacity for determinate negation – that is, the capacity to find something informative in the negation – with that of skepticism, since skepticism effectively holds that the failure of some particular mode of justifying a belief makes it impossible for us to be certain of our beliefs in general. Skepticism thus declares that there is a limit on our ability to gain knowledge of the world. Determinate negation, however, prompts reflection on the failure of justification and thereby a *revision* of the conceptual framework that brought us into the problem in the first place.

Contrary, then, to the logic of skepticism the possibility of determinate negation means that consciousness – the knowing agent – can correct its knowledge. It is not stuck with a fixed interpretation of the object or matter it is trying to understand, and furthermore the process of correction is not imposed by any external authority. In dialectical experience the subject can revise its criteria of knowledge through its engagement *with* objects. Adorno claims, speaking of Hegel, that "[d]ialectic is the unswerving effort to conjoin reason's critical consciousness of itself and the critical experience of objects."[17] This is a radical innovation: consciousness is not isolated in the space of its own self-certainty, because it has the capacity for self-correction through its dialectical interaction with objects.[18] As Hegel famously puts it: "consciousness suffers this violence at its own hands: it spoils its own limited satisfaction."[19] This advance beyond skepticism is based on a theory of experience in which the exercise of critical self-reflection means that consciousness is always in process. Furthermore, rationality is embedded in the process of subject-object interaction. It is a rational process in that the subject cannot be satisfied with a contradiction or negativity: reason compels it to go beyond contradiction. Of this rational dimension Adorno notes that "the concept of determinate negation ... sets Hegel off from Nietzsche's ... irrationalism."[20] The rather striking contrast that Adorno makes here is that between a process driven by the norms of reason and one – supposedly Nietzsche's – in which the relation of the subject to the object is one in which only the subject's evolutionary drives – never the object – play a role in the process.

Experience, with its dynamic of self-correction, has implications not only for the knowing subject and its inventory of beliefs and concepts. The object that is the focus of the experience is also changed, since it reveals new dimensions of itself in and through our increasingly sophisticated understanding of it. In this sense it becomes a changed object: "in the alteration of the knowledge," Hegel writes, "the object alters for it too, for the knowledge that was present was essentially a knowledge of the object: as the knowledge changes, so too does the object, for it essentially belonged to this knowledge."[21] When we alter our concept, then, we actually transform what we take the object under consideration to be since it is only through conceptualization that we can specify what an object is. Since the subject's beliefs are challenged and transformed in this process and the object in some respects comes to be grasped in new ways, Hegel's account is one in which the subject-object relationship is dynamic and both components are determined anew. Hegel, Adorno claims, "preserves the distinct moments of the subjective and the objective while grasping them as mediated by one another."[22] This idea of reciprocal mediation, as we have seen, is carried into Adorno's philosophy.

540

An important further feature of determinate negation is that it is, for Hegel, the path of progress. For Hegel determinate negation leads to a transformation of our understanding, forcing us into a distinctive new way of understanding what we do when we think we are making knowledge claims or expressing beliefs. From a perspective that lies *outside* that of experience itself – the perspective of the phenomenological observer – this can be represented as *progress*: "The necessary progression and interconnection of the forms of the unreal consciousness will by itself bring to pass the *completion* of the series."[23] As we shall see, Adorno's disagreement with Hegel essentially concerns this notion of progress, the notion that the dialectic leads in a conclusive direction, since that, for Adorno, reduces dialectic to system. Nevertheless, Adorno recognizes within this something of great philosophical significance: the idea of truth as *process*.[24] This idea is correlative, of course, to the notion of the dialectic as experience.

2. Adorno's Disagreement with Hegel

From the material just considered we can see that Adorno's professed indebtedness to Hegel is no exaggeration. Yet, as we noted at the outset, he is also deeply critical of Hegel. Where does the disagreement between them lie? As suggested, Hegel's commitment to the progressive character of the dialectic turns out to be the central point of contention. What Adorno rejects is the way in which Hegel, according to Adorno, turns away from his own insight into the negativity of the dialectic and ends up with a progressive dialectic that is placed at the service of the system. The evidence cited by Adorno to support this charge of forced progression needs to be examined. Adorno's comments on Hegel's philosophy of history provide an important point of departure for this examination. Hegel's normative commitments are, according to Adorno, instantiated in his socio-historical analyses. These commitments, in the end, drive the dialectic. And, in Adorno's interpretation, they drive the dialectic to follow an agenda, thereby prejudicing the process.

I want to consider separately the issues that motivate Adorno's disagreement with Hegel by examining, first, his critique of Hegel's notion of history and, second, his worries about Hegel's systematization of the dialectic.

2.1. Adorno's Disagreement with Hegel: History

The notion of "universal history" is the foundational idea of Hegel's philosophy of history. It signifies history understood as a narrative of progress that connects temporally separate cultures and societies. As such it is a speculative philosophical construction that gives expression to the idea of a historical continuity that cannot be discerned through empirical analysis. Kant also proposed a universal history, based on what he saw as the thesis of the unfolding of a providential design of nature. [25] It is, however, almost exclusively Hegel's version of the theory that stimulates Adorno's considerable analyses of the questions of history and progress.

The idea that history is nothing more than a disconnected series of events is denied by the theory of universal history. It is replaced by the idea that history as a whole is meaningful, "that Reason *does* exist there."[26] Universal history is not a narrative pieced together by the philosopher. Rather, this narrative captures (what are taken to be) the objective processes of progressive historical development. Progress, in turn, is specified as the increase of freedom. Hegel writes: "The History of the world is none other than the progress of the consciousness of Freedom, a progress whose development according to the necessity of its nature it is our business to investigate."[27] This notion may be historically disputable. It is certainly philosophically problematic. How is progress carried forward through a series of civilizations that are not connected to one another? How is a level of progress maintained as a new dominant civilization emerges to carry it forward? The contention that *Geist* is the ever evolving repository of progress – and so of continuity – brings history into the arena of metaphysics.

Adorno's response to the notion of universal history is not entirely critical. This is, perhaps, surprising, given that the notion can easily be conceived (a) as an ideological theory in its assumption of historical progress and (b) as essentially metaphysical in two respects: (i) its processes transcend the space of human decision and action and (b) its selective abstraction of human events produces an essentialization of aspects of material reality. Adorno does indeed agree with and elaborate on all of these criticisms. What makes Adorno's engagement with Hegel's theory interesting is that it is philosophically creative. Unlike conventional antimetaphysical critics of the theory, Adorno appreciates what Hegel is trying to do. What is required in his view, however, is the materialist transformation or what Adorno refers often to as a secularization of that theory. The allegation, then, is that Hegel understands historical meaning quasi-theologically to operate above the space of human agency.

In his lectures on the philosophy of history Adorno announced that "[i]f you wish to say anything at all about the theory of history in general, you must enter into a discussion of the construction of universal history."[28] Utter repudiation of the notion of universal history leads us to a theory that sees history as a series of disconnected events. But this is not, obviously enough, a thesis that critical theory – the theory espoused by Adorno – can endorse. After all, critical theory is in the business of critically analyzing the patterns of domination that have evolved, almost to the point of total control, with or through (the thesis is ambiguous) the development of capitalism. To see history merely as a series of disconnected facts is a kind of naïveté that serves only to obscure these patterns. At the same time, the theory of universal history is not satisfactory either. One of Adorno's most quoted lines conceals the true nature of his disagreement with that theory. "No universal history," he writes, "leads from savagery to humanitarianism, but there is one leading from the slingshot to the atom bomb."[29] This carelessly presents a simple reversal of the Hegelian historical trajectory, replacing a continuous narrative of progress with one of decline. Were that Adorno's actual position he would merely have substituted one telos for another, and the narrative would be no less metaphysical. That is, it too would be committed to the notion of an inexorable process that transcends human intervention: it would be, in that way, philosophical history. This would leave it open to the criticism of doing violence to historical reality in the name of narrative consistency, that is, of being undialectical.

What distinguishes Adorno's theory of history from Hegel's is not, in fact, a reversal of the historical narrative. It is, rather, his introduction of the notion of *historical discontinuity*. This is a complex idea, conceived as a direct criticism of universal history, though not as an outright rejection. What it attempts to capture is the idea that historical events do not simply belong to the historical process; that is, it is not sufficient to understand them simply as "moments" of that process. Rather, they possess a particularity, a specificity that is not to be subsumed under general narratives: "The truth is that, while the traditional view inserts facts into the flow of time, they really possess a nucleus of time in themselves, they crystallize time in themselves. What we can legitimately call ideas is the nucleus of time within the individual crystallized phenomena, something that can only be decoded by interpretation. In accordance with this we might say that history is *discontinuous* in the sense that it represents life perennially disrupted."[30] What this means, though, is not that historical events are simply disconnected but that discontinuity and disruption turn out to be part of the historical *process* itself. This, for Adorno, specifically calls into question the Hegelian position. Hegelian history, for Adorno, is a synthetic exercise in which historical events are subsumed under a general concept. By contrast, "the materialist turnabout [*Umwendung*] in dialectic cast the weightiest accent on insight into the discontinuity of what is not comfortingly held together by any unity of spirit and concept."[31]

It is important to note that, for Adorno, discontinuity does not stand on its own. History is a *process* made up of discontinuous events. History therefore, Adorno writes, "is the unity of continuity and discontinuity."[32] This is not a paradox: it means actually understanding historical events *as* events and not as moments. When events are conceived as mere moments, history is understood to sweep over the suffering they contain. Hegel situates this suffering within the overarching narrative of progressive history and thereby deprives it of its specificity. In this, Adorno claims, Hegel "transfigured the totality of historic suffering into the possibility of the self-realizing absolute."[33]

Rejection of the notion of progress is, however, no straightforward matter for Adorno. To abandon it means, minimally, (a) denying that progress is possible and, maximally, (b) arguing for its opposite, regression. Option (a) cannot be endorsed without further qualification by critical theory, since critical theory understands itself to be socially transformative and beneficent. And (b), as we saw, would simply be a reversal of Hegel's notion. What Adorno proposes instead, and against the thesis of universal history, is that progress is achievable but only once the narrative of progress itself is abandoned.

An implication of the progress thesis is that the historical situation in which we find ourselves is now the result of prior historical progress. When societies operate under this positive self-conception, however, they find no need for radical self-analysis. Their central challenge becomes, rather, that of continuing the project of societal amelioration that has already been well established by the historical process. The task of a critical theory is to bring into doubt settled questions about the deepest normative commitments of our society. It is, in this way, as Axel Honneth puts it, "evaluative world disclosure."[34] And the historically specific and concretely situated questions of what we are and what direction we need to take are pushed aside once we tie our analysis to the idea of progress framed within universal history. Adorno writes: "No progress may be supposed that implies that humanity already existed and could therefore be assumed to continue to progress. Rather progress would be the establishment of humanity in the first place.... the concept of universal history ... cannot be salvaged."[35]

These criticisms of Hegel's conception of progress stem from Adorno's quite different analysis of the historical condition of humanity. Adorno provides an explanation for why Hegel's theory falsely posits the notion of progress in spite of (what Adorno considers to be) the overwhelming evidence, evidence that Hegel himself dismissed. If Adorno is right that we are not yet in a position to think of the historical process as one marked by continuous progression, that it is a process of "unspeakable suffering,"[36] how could Hegel commit himself to a notion of historical harmony even while describing history as a "slaughter-bench"?[37] Adorno's thought is that so long as history is understood to be a metaphysical matter the painful details of material life will not significantly determine its course. And Hegel does indeed regard history as a matter of metaphysics. Adorno's position, however, is a historical-materialist one in a broadly Marxist sense, and that means that what Hegel has understood as the engine of history, namely *Geist*, must in fact be understood as *labor*. Adorno's concern is that when Hegel conceives of *Geist* as history as a whole he is, in fact, expressing a conception of society as a whole that determines every part within it (just as apparently contingent historical events turn out to be determined by the process of universal history). Hegel's metaphysical commitments reflect the same tendency as his social ones: to bring systematization to the whole (of history and society). Just as the historical narrative is distorted by Hegel to produce a system of history, so he effectively distorts the social totality. But to construe society under a system is to make it into a coercive whole. That is, Adorno believes, Hegel's social-normative commitment. The charge is this: Hegel's "idealism becomes false when it mistakenly turns the totality of labor into something existing in itself, when it sublimates its principle into a metaphysical one, into the *actus purus* of spirit, and tendentially transfigures something produced by human beings, something fallible and conditioned, along with labor itself, which is the suffering of human beings, into something eternal and right."[38] Whereas, then, Hegel presents history as the progress of *Geist* toward an ultimate path of self-realization, Adorno sees it as the ongoing process of social antagonism between the needs of individuals and the needs of the social totality: "full reconciliation through spirit in a world which is in reality antagonistic is a mere assertion."[39] The difference between Adorno and Hegel here is a substantial one in that it is a difference that Adorno thinks of as indicative of a difference between materialism and idealism. For Adorno materialism is attentive to individual moments of suffering and to the tangible effects of social arrangements on individuals, whereas idealism, in Hegel's case at least, involves the construction of narratives whose dialectical development transcends in significance the material beings whose lives are determined by that development.

Adorno further articulates it as a difference between particularism and universalism. Hegel's position drives history toward a system in which particularity is to be absorbed. This is not simply a dispute about "dialectic," that is, about whether the dialectic can produce further moments leading to a harmonious systematic culmination. Insofar as history is the social process, it has become, according to Adorno, a process of constant systematization. This systematization is conceived within modern societies as guided by the desire to coordinate and ultimately harmonize the lives of individuals. A systematized harmonization, however, will contradict this desire in that *qua* system its priority is not individual difference.

544

2.2. Adorno's Disagreement with Hegel: Dialectic and System

According to Adorno, the normative commitments that are manifest in Hegel's philosophy of history also have a bearing on his account of the operations of the dialectic in more abstract contexts. As we have seen, Adorno construes Hegel as committed to the systematization of historical events into a progressive narrative in which particularity (suffering) is explicated within, and thereby subordinate to, universal history. Adorno's argument is that Hegelian logic, which is supposed to be presuppositionless, is driven by just this synthesizing agenda. Before turning to Adorno's substantiation of this allegation we need to consider what is at stake philosophically, for Adorno, in Hegel's subversion of the dialectic.

For Adorno, the operation of determinate negation is characteristic of experience that is marked by rational responsiveness. Determinate negation, in this context, is an informative moment of experience not because it opens up the object to us directly, but because it indicates the limitation of our judgment about, or conceptualization of, that object. It unsettles our previous belief in the conceptualization of an object. Only indirectly can we read off anything about the object from that process. Adorno argues, however, that Hegel takes the wrong lesson from the process of negativity: he allegedly sees it as bringing us ever closer to the object, indeed to the point at which the object is fully conceptualized. What Hegel's account represents, though, is a subversion of the dialectic, since it is, in this way, an effort to make the latter positive. Against this Adorno argues that "[t]he non-identical is not to be obtained directly, as something positive on its part, nor is it obtainable by a negation of the negative. The negation is not an affirmation itself as it is to Hegel."[40] For Adorno dialectic – negative dialectic – articulates that nonidentity without attempting to carry it into a system as Hegel supposedly does in his pursuit of "absolute consistency."[41] It is for this reason that Adorno alleges that Hegel attempts to "dispute away the contradiction between idea and reality,"[42] that is, in effect, to overcome nonidentity. While the dialectic is the experience of nonidentity, it becomes, ultimately, a moment of the Hegelian system (a reconfiguration that parallels that of the philosophy of history): "Hegel actually takes cognizance of that dimension only for the sake of identity, only as an instrument of identity."[43]

Obviously enough, this charge of subversion is quite schematic, though it is hardly new or controversial to think of Hegel as a systematic thinker. What Adorno must make good on is the claim that Hegel's systematicity is actually distorting, that is, that it manipulates "the dialectic" in order to deliver outcomes required for the system. Adorno needs to do this not merely to establish the accuracy of his interpretation of Hegel, but also to justify his criticism of the rationality of Hegelian dialectic itself. Adorno insists that the negative character of the dialectic should mean that it cannot be part of a process that brings about "the completion of the series." What it truly is is the capacity for nonidentity. It therefore cannot be rendered into a procedure that converts moments of nonidentity into moments of a system. System implies the final ordering of the moments and resolution of the contradictions. In his published writings Adorno does not justify his criticism in any great detail. A useful corroboration of his interpretation is, however, provided in his posthumously published lectures on the idea of a negative dialectic.

In the lectures Adorno analyzes the most famous example of a "transition" in Hegel's work, that of being, nothing, and becoming. He argues that the dialectic is distorted to produce the transition required by systematization. That means that the transitions do not correspond to what Adorno takes to be the ideal of Hegel's philosophy – namely, that of "simply looking on" (as Hegel describes it in the *Phenomenology*) – in which things "themselves speak in a philosophy that focuses its energies on proving that it is itself one with them."[44] A transition that does not come about through "simply looking on" is forced and thereby driven not by reason, which presupposes no outcome, but rather by an unstated procedural imperative. The version of the transition that Adorno analyzes is that of the *Science of Logic*, to which we now turn.

Hegel justifies beginning the *Logic* with "pure being" on the grounds that it is "purely and simply *an* immediacy, or rather merely *immediacy* itself."[45] It is thus free of determinations, according to Hegel, which should not be presupposed at the start of philosophy. It is "indeterminate immediacy" (*unbestimmte Unmittelbarkeit*). Pure being is thereby "pure indeterminateness and emptiness" (*reine Unbestimmtheit und Leere*). Because it is empty "there is nothing to be thought in it." And this leads us to the thought that pure being "is in fact *nothing*, and neither more nor less than *nothing*." This transition from pure being to nothing seems quite unforced. "The second thought simply and immediately comes to mind," as one commentator puts it.[46]

The literature abounds with criticism of the very idea of "pure being": it might be dismissed as a pseudo-ontological concept that has no ontological reference, a collapsed concept. However, Adorno's concern is not with the concept itself but with its seemingly purely logical transition to nothing. The criticism is this: Hegel achieves the transition through a subtle substitution of terminology: he starts out with pure being as "the indeterminate," then without explanation recasts it as "indeterminateness." Whereas "the indeterminate" can mean *something* that is without determination, "indeterminateness" is the concept of indeterminacy, and as the concept of indeterminacy (a matter entirely different from *that which* is indeterminate) it facilitates the transition to nothing. "The indeterminate" refers to something – something announced by the definite article – whereas "indeterminateness" refers to nothing in particular.

Adorno picks up on Hegel's third remark following the presentation of the transition from being to nothing to becoming. There Hegel writes[47] (and is quoted by Adorno): "They [i.e., the thoughts of pure space, pure time, pure consciousness, or pure being] are the results of abstraction; they are expressly determined as *indeterminate* [*als Unbestimmte bestimmt*] and this – to go back to its simplest form – is being."[48] Hegel follows this claim – again quoted by Adorno – with a clarification which Adorno sees as actually introducing a further claim, though it is presented, by Hegel, merely as an elaboration on the first: "But it is this very *indeterminateness* which constitutes its determinateness [*diese Unbestimmtheit ist aber das, was die Bestimmtheit desselben ausmacht*]."[49] Adorno sees a crucial shift of significance here from "the indeterminate" to "indeterminateness." He writes: "'[t]he indeterminate' is in the nature of a substratum."[50] He argues then that "when Hegel substitutes 'indeterminateness' for this, the concept, namely, the absence of determinateness *as such* takes the place of what is undetermined."[51] And the transition of thought from being to nothing occurs thereby. Yet, Adorno contends, "the equality of being and nothing depends on thinking of being as indeterminateness; in other words, being is supposed from the outset to belong to the conceptual sphere. If it were still the indeterminate – as Hegel writes at first [...] it would not be possible to equate it with nothing. For a something can be undetermined, but it cannot be said of it that it is 'as good as nothing.'"[52]

Adorno's criticism does, at least, raise the issue of the apparent inconsistency of Hegel's terminology. Hegel uses two terms, but his initial framing of the idea of pure being is as "the indeterminate" which meets his criterion of being a simple immediacy. Indeterminateness, precisely as an abstract concept, cannot, however, be immediacy. A rather awkward defence of Hegel might be that, in fact, Hegel is ambiguous on the matter. His statement that pure being is "purely and simply *an* immediacy, or rather merely *immediacy* itself" refers both to the substratum idea and the concept. Nevertheless Adorno's critical analysis puts significant pressure on the text. And it is informative in relation to the broader issue of how Adorno actually roots his programmatic criticism of Hegel, whom he sees as distorting the dialectic, in specific analyses.

The allegation of distortion is not an end in itself. Adorno is not out simply to make a textual criticism, but a philosophical point about the fate of nonidentity within systematic thinking. He claims that Hegel's initial "manoeuvre" – from the indeterminate to indeterminateness – is indicative of a desire to conjure "away the non-conceptual."[53] For Adorno, Hegel's idea of "the indeterminate" indicates his recognition of the non-conceptual, since it is the idea of something that is not saturated with the concepts or "determinations" of the subject. The transformation of "the indeterminate" into "indeterminateness," however, conceptualizes it absolutely.

3. The Hegelianism of Adorno's Critical Theory: An Assessment

Having examined Adorno's general appropriation of Hegel as well as his specific criticisms of the dialectic, we should now consider whether that appropriation produces a coherent philosophical position. This consideration brings us to the critical employment that Adorno makes of the materialistically transformed notions of determinate negation and dialectic. These notions have specific roles within Hegel's philosophy, but can they be extracted from that context in order to produce the framework for a form of social critique?

The innovative ambition of critical theory – Adorno's in particular – is to develop modes of critique that do not operate from ideal or utopian perspectives. After all, those perspectives are easily characterized as arbitrary, ungrounded, and not at all compelling. We might describe utopian assertions as *extranormative*. They are extranormative in that they are a demand for transformed social arrangements and human relations that could not resonate with the conventional perspective of the individual for whose benefit the consciousness-raising exercise of progressive social theory is conceived. The demand, for example, for the abolition of private property would place in doubt a great many conventional assumptions about what society is while also bringing into question moral codes that support the preservation of private property. An extranormative claim seems to ask the individual to reject all of these assumptions and codes. The critic of extranormativity denies that such a rejection can come about just by referring individuals to higher values given that so much of an individual's social identity is invested in the conventional perspective. Adorno's term for extranormative criticism, in fact, is

547

"transcendent" in that it imagines itself to operate outside the influence of the conventional perspective. He writes: "The transcendent critic assumes an as it were Archimedean position above culture and the blindness of society."[54] This transcendent position or norm is known to the philosopher, thanks to some advanced perspective, but it is unknown otherwise. That is to say, it has no normative force – it is merely a philosophical construction – for the conventional perspective. The problem with extranormativity, clearly enough, is that as a tool of critique it actually cannot achieve the very thing it needs to achieve, namely, persuasiveness: it lies outside the space of persuasion precisely in being extranormative. Indeed, Adorno points out that the notion of a transcendent perspective is, in any case, illusory in that it falsely thinks itself free of the effects of reification and the other social conditions it seeks to expose. It congratulates itself on an imaginary purity: "The choice of a standpoint outside the sway of existing society is as fictitious as only the construction of abstract utopias can be."[55] For Adorno, the critique of society ought not to be guided by a transcendent moral preference: to set out a view of the right society with which to contrast the deficiencies of contemporary society simply begs the question.

But where do we go if current norms are compromised and extranormativity is simply transcendent? Adorno's proposal is *immanent critique*. Immanent critique involves an examination of the coherence of a position by assessing it through its own standards. Adorno writes: "If an assertion [*Behauptung*] is measured by its presuppositions, then the procedure is immanent, i.e. it obeys formal-logical rules and thought becomes a criterion of itself."[56] Hence arbitrary transcendence is avoided and no illusion of social detachment on the part of the critic is implied. The criterion of reasonableness is provided by whatever the position under examination normatively aspires to, so long, of course, as those holding the position are also committed to "formal-logical rules," that is, they can recognize the force of contradiction. In revealing the tensions between the reality of a position and what it takes itself to be, immanent critique, Adorno writes, "pushes with the latter's own force to where it cannot afford to go."[57] It is not simply that the position is shown to be contradictory, but rather that it is a contradiction alone that gives it its reality: it is essentially contradictory, though it claims to be rational.

Since immanent critique operates on the basis of the revelation of contradictions that might produce new perspectives on the supposed reasonableness of the social totality, it is, in fact, a process of determinate negation. As we saw when looking at this idea in Hegel, determinate negation is not driven by external norms. It proceeds through a rational response to the experience of contradiction, a contradiction that is not between a claim and a wholly different counter-claim, but rather between the claims that make up the phenomenon that is being examined (the complex of beliefs that can be judged true or false). The dimension of contradiction is central to both determinate negation – as the *productive* experience of contradiction – and immanent critique – as the *destruction* of a position once its inner contradictions are exposed (the logic of disintegration). And contradiction is proposed as something informative insofar as contradiction – immanently identified – points us toward what is problematic. Any individual committed to "formal-logical" thinking ought to be prompted to further reflection by the apparent contradiction that immanent critique uncovers. As Rahel Jaeggi notes: "In precisely this sense critique means the critique ('*bestimmte Kritik*,' linked to Hegelian 'determinate negation') of 'particular social moments' that 'have their standard in the constantly renewed idea of a right society.' The negative is then not only what *should not be*, but rather what cannot exist, what cannot be thought and lived, without contradiction."[58]

We have seen the features of determinate negation that might seem to provide the theoretical underpinnings of an immanent form of social critique: (i) it is situational (what needs to be negated is intelligible only in context) and (ii) it does not appeal to any predetermined standards of truth or excellence, but relies instead on the expectation of a facility in the individual who engages with the critique to act in the face of "contradiction." Immanent critique appears to be a promising alternative to the question-begging transcendent or extranormative critique of society, precisely because it seems to assume very little: it aims to understand a position merely on its own terms. Ultimately, however, it is subject to a serious difficulty: society is not a text that is set out in propositions and that would therefore be amenable to the kind of conclusive analysis in which contradiction appears. (Adorno offers some powerful instances of the immanent critique of philosophical texts. But texts are determinate in that their central claims can be identified.) Indeed, as Adorno frequently argues, society is a totality that does not reveal itself as such. It cannot be identified through "facts." He writes: "For while the notion of society may not be deduced from any individual facts, nor on the other be apprehended as an individual fact itself, there is nonetheless no social fact which is not determined by society as a whole. Society appears as a whole behind each concrete situation."[59] What makes society what it is, in other words, is not apparent; it is not encounterable in facts at least. This means that what we, as social theorists, identify as the defining claims and practices of society are not facts that speak for themselves. They are interpretations that can be quite easily disputed by opposing styles of social theory. The only tools we have in the task of clarifying the very notion of society are, after all, hermeneutic and not empirical.

We might analyze this difficulty more concretely through consideration of a typical instance of immanent critique from Adorno's social theory. Adorno claims that in modern society the individual defines him- or herself as free, yet is compelled to be something in particular by society. There is therefore a "contradiction" between the concept of freedom and the restricted life choices open to an individual: "a contradiction like the one between the definition which an individual knows as his own and his 'role,' the definition forced upon him by society."[60] This contradiction is one that allegedly sustains society. But the very formulation of this "immanent critique" is not neutral, since the notion that social roles are "forced" upon individuals is disputable. It is certainly not consistent with all reported experience. The significant point here, then, is that in the absence of texts the very idea of what comes to be seen, through immanent critique, as contradictory cannot draw any neutral reader into the argument. What happens, in fact, is that once neutrality is violated we fall into the same difficulty that nullifies the force of transcendent critique.

In view of this problem with neutrality there is a serious question about whether immanent critique can provide a foundation for the variety of critical theory that wishes specifically to avoid extranormativity. It is, however, unclear whether Adorno himself wanted immanent critique to be regarded as a foundational principle. A great number of Adorno's pronouncements about the "false life" of modern society are unapologetically based on his moral sensibility (and it is still a matter of dispute among Adorno scholars whether that sensibility is the articulation of a philosophically grounded position). To add to the complexity, Adorno occasionally warns us against an exclusively immanent critical approach. For instance: "The alternatives – either calling culture as a whole into question from outside under the general notion of ideology, or confronting it with norms which it itself has crystallized – cannot be accepted by critical theory. To insist on the choice between immanence and transcendence is to revert to the traditional logic criticized in Hegel's logic."[61] This is certainly confusing, as transcendent norms surely cannot be allowed to creep into the critique without undoing the alleged achievements of immanent critique. Yet it is clear that, for Adorno, immanent critique is merely one moment of social criticism that brings to light problems in society but does not provide constructive solutions to them. It is for this reason that immanent critique and determinate negation are placed together in a single theory: they are distinguishable moments of critique that capture both immanence and transcendence. Determinate negation provides the moment of transcendence in the Hegelian sense, since it takes us beyond what is merely given, through a process of concept revision (or at least through prompting society to reflect both on the *limits* of the concepts that structure its view of the world and on the possibility of revising those concepts). It is to an examination of the coherence of that single theory that we now turn.

As we have seen, determinate negation is, for Hegel, a form of negation, one that has a result. It is the result that emerges from the complication that consciousness experiences as it "suffers ... violence at its own hands." Precisely as a result, a determinate negation is posterior to the moment of complication in the sequence of experience: it is the moment when the need to reflect on the commitments that led to that complication becomes apparent to the consciousness undergoing the experience. Let us take two quite different examples. A racist consciousness must confront some of its commitments when it fails to understand why one or more particular members of the ethnic group that he or she denigrates is more talented, intelligent, virtuous than the allegedly superior group to which the racist belongs. A racist society persists, however, for as long as these contradictions are not thematized by the society itself. Or we can consider Hegel's analysis in the *Phenomenology* of the collapse of the epistemological explanation of knowledge as simple sense certainty. This explanation is built on the insight that the relation between a subject and an object is essentially a relation of a perceiver to a particular. However, dimensions of knowledge are not captured by this explanation. For instance, the sheer immediacy of simple sense certainty excludes conceptuality: concepts are both universals and are mediated. The exclusion of concepts, however, renders knowledge inexpressible. No doubt the theorist of simple sense certainty might want to reformulate the theory in order to accommodate the conceptual dimension without abandoning the priority of particularity. Nevertheless, the commitments that produced the theory in its original articulation are challenged by the *experience* of sense certainty itself.

The materials of immanent critique – the contents of its judgment – are differently arranged, I suggest. Immanent critique does not explore the complications that consciousness or society *itself* experiences, but it sets out what the *critic* of consciousness or society understands to be the contradictions inherent in the object of examination.

550

The social critic thus assembles evidence that critically undermines the supposed rationality of current arrangements (as we have just seen) by showing that they are by their own standards irrational. That is, the critic demonstrates that specific conventional social commitments that sustain society in its current form are, in fact, compromised by the very arrangements that supposedly guarantee those commitments (e.g., the freedom that capitalist societies value is undermined by capitalism itself). However, in order to be motivated to undertake an immanent critique of this kind the social critic must, in fact, be motivated by some *prior* intuition about the problematic society he or she is interpreting, that is, that it is contradictory. The process of immanent critique is thus not – like determinate negation – an unexpected problematization of society. The result of determinate negation is, precisely, the unexpected unsettling of what had seemed to be effective commitments. Immanent critique, by contrast, is that which emerges from what the critic identifies as – what we might call – the structured hypocrisy of society. Hence, if society is understood by its members as that which provides the context for rational (as opposed to natural) freedom and yet the obligation to undertake structured labor within the capitalist workplace is unavoidable, since it is the only means of self-preservation within capitalism, then society by its own standards is problematized. The social critic seems here to have revealed a point of fundamental significance without introducing theories from abroad. However, the social critic does not discover these problems serendipitously.

What is the outcome of immanent critique? The answer to this question reveals another key difference from the process of determinate negation. Immanent critique as a logic of disintegration sees the collapse of the positions it immanently criticizes. A logic of disintegration is certainly that: the collapse is supposedly undeniable. Although the social critic may wish to *use* this contradiction as a judgment on the falsehood of society, the contradiction does not, in fact, give rise directly to a logic of transformation. That is, the awareness of the apparent incoherence of society's beliefs is not the same thing as moving beyond them.

In this specific way immanent critique is quite a different matter from "determinate negation," which is newly informative about the *limits* of the criteria through which we know some given phenomenon and thereby implicitly points to the possibility of *revising* those criteria. In Hegel, as we have seen, determinate negation is, indeed, progressive for the phenomenological observer and contributes to "the completion of the series" of the forms of consciousness. In contrast, precisely as a disintegrating critique, immanent critique, if we deploy it more strictly than Adorno, does not point beyond itself. For example, the disintegration of the ideology of the allegedly free society is no more than just that. It cannot be rigorously interpreted as a demonstration of a dissatisfied demand for freedom or of the fact that freedom is in an unfinished condition any more than it can be read as a demand for total capitalism (the other part of the claim).

But could it not be that the outcome of immanent critique – revelation of contradiction – is informative and thus in some sense a determinate negation? It should be clear that the logic of the two processes does not allow for this synthesis. That is not to say that one could not use them both in a unified critical strategy. What one cannot do, however, is to conflate them, as Adorno does. This is a serious matter in that it is a synthesis of the two ideas that produces the distinctive form of social analysis offered by Adorno's critical theory. We can perhaps give greater sharpness to their divergence by looking at the distinction of perspectives that is crucial to the very structure of Hegel's *Phenomenology*. I suggest, indeed, that these two perspectives parallel those of social criticism. This can be explained as follows. The social critic occupies a vantage point different from that of the experiencer whose beliefs undergo the process of determinate negation. The social critic is aware of what she takes to be conflicting social beliefs, the necessary contradictions sustaining capitalist society. She knowingly assembles the evidence from the social totality. To move seamlessly between immanent critique and determinate negation is to commit the mistake of conflating these two perspectives.

The two perspectives parallel those of the perspectives of the *experiencer* and the *observer* in the *Phenomenology*. As Michael Rosen explains, Hegel "explicitly draws the distinction between the experience of the consciousness whose development the *Phenomenology* charts and the consciousness of the author and reader to whom it is displayed, observing that consciousness's progress is intelligible 'for us' in a way that it cannot be for itself whilst undergoing the process."[62] This crucial contrast for the *Phenomenology* captures the key differences between determinate negation and immanent critique. The beliefs of the experiencer undergo the process of determinate negation, but the full significance of determinate negation is nonetheless not transparent to the experiencer. She follows through on the commitments of his beliefs, though there is no predetermined path, which means that he will come to grasp, for example, the principle, to which critical theory is committed, that the bourgeois-individualist concept of freedom compromises the very possibility of freedom. While determinate negation is progressive within the structure of the completed system of knowledge, the individual undergoing this experience cannot see it as progress. The individual is prompted by her experience to reflect on the limits of the criteria that underlie her point of view (and, indeed, to consider the possibility that these criteria may have to be revised), but such reflection is simply *unsettling* for the individual, not liberating. It is for this reason that Hegel uses the term "violence": the individual's experience is not one of success but of loss, albeit one that has a significance. It is only the *observer*, therefore, for whom determinate negation (and the experience through which it results) constitutes a moment in the unambiguous *progress* of consciousness.

The perspective of the social critic, by contrast, is an external one for whom contradiction plays a key role in the critique of society. Although Rosen does not set out the distinction between immanent critique and determinate negation as I do, as a distinction between the perspectives of the social critic and that of the experiencer, he nevertheless shows how the distinction between the two perspectives of the *Phenomenology* cannot be crafted into a social-criticism version of Hegel. He takes issue with Habermas's redevelopment of the notion of determinate negation, which, he argues, "identifies it with the phenomenological path taken by self-consciousness."[63] The intention of Habermas's construction is to offer determinate negation as the knowledge of progress, whereas the dual perspective of the *Phenomenology* assigns that to the perspective of the observer. Rosen cites Habermas: "The figure of determinate negation applies not to an immanent logical connection but to the mechanism of the progress of a mode of reflection in which theoretical and practical reason are one.... A *form of life* that has become an abstraction cannot be negated without leaving a trace, or overthrown without practical consequences. The revolutionized situation contains the one that has been surpassed, because the insight of the new consists precisely in the experience of revolutionary release from the old consciousness."[64] And what Rosen charges against this is that Habermas's deployment of the notion of determinate negation "goes beyond what the model licenses." Rosen is arguing not against the idea that determinate negation produces a result, but rather against "the claim that it represents a model of rational progress."[65] Rosen is certainly correct here in that what Habermas actually does in seeing determinate negation as rational progress is to introduce the perspective of the social critic who understands it as a progressive immanent critique.

If we disentangle immanent critique and determinate negation – as we must – we are left with a significantly less potent form of social criticism. Immanent critique is, as we have seen, the privileged perspective of the observer, bearing witness, as it were, to the inner contradictions of society and imagining a society that is free of them. The revelation of these contradictions does not by itself point beyond what generates the contradictions – and in that sense does no more than *disintegrate* the society under examination – but it is nonetheless motivated by the desire for social progress (in the nuanced sense I attributed to Adorno; see p. 543). Determinate negation, by contrast, is the actual *experience* of contradiction, the full significance of which is not transparent to the experiencer. Conflating immanent critique and determinate negation, as Adorno's social critique does, seems to allow the experience of determinate negation in itself to be *progressive* (since it takes us beyond the contradictions of society) and immanent critique seems to be *unforced* (since it proceeds by working through the experience of determinate negation). It is, however, a conflation – of Hegelian theses – that falls apart on close analysis.

As we have seen, Adorno's appropriation of Hegel's dialectic generates significant philosophical ideas. Nonidentity, experience, and mediation – all of them materialist transformations of Hegelian notions – are distinctive and challenging philosophical proposals. At the same time, the extraction of Hegel's dialectic from its speculative context, in order to construct a new form of social critique, cannot, as the analysis shows, successfully proceed in the form that Adorno develops.

Notes

I am grateful to the editors of this volume for their many comments and suggestions, which helped greatly in the preparation of this chapter.

1   Theodor W. Adorno, *Negative Dialectics*, trans. E. B. Ashton (London: Routledge, 1973), 160; Theodor W. Adorno, *Gesammelte Schriften*, 6 (Frankfurt: Suhrkamp, 1973), 162.

2   Theodor W. Adorno, *Hegel: Three Studies*, trans. Shierry Weber Nicholsen (Cambridge, MA / London: MIT Press, 1993), 147; Theodor W. Adorno, *Gesammelte Schriften*, 5 (1970), 375.

3   Theodor W. Adorno, *Lectures on Negative Dialectics*, trans. Rodney Livingstone (Cambridge: Polity Press, 2008), 21; Theodor W. Adorno, *Vorlesung über Negative Dialektik, Nachgelessene Schriften*, IV/16 (Frankfurt: Suhrkamp, 2003), 39.

4   Adorno, *Negative Dialectics*, 85; *Gesammelte Schriften*, 6, 92.

5   Adorno, *Negative Dialectics*, 21; *Gesammelte Schriften*, 6, 41.

6   Adorno, *Hegel: Three Studies*, 39; *Gesammelte Schriften*, 5, 284.

7   Adorno, *Negative Dialectics*, 152; *Gesammelte Schriften*, 6, 152.

8   Adorno, *Negative Dialectics*, 145; *Gesammelte Schriften*, 6, 148.

9   Adorno, *Negative Dialectics*, 144; *Gesammelte Schriften*, 6, 148.

10 Theodor W. Adorno, *Prisms*, trans. Samuel and Shierry Weber (Cambridge, Mass., and London: MIT Press, 1981), 32; Theodor W. Adorno, *Gesammelte Schriften*, 10.1 (1977), 27.

11 Adorno, *Negative Dialectics*, 153; *Gesammelte Schriften*, 6, 156.

12 Theodor W. Adorno, "Subject and Object," trans. Andrew Arato and Eike Gebhardt, in *The Adorno Reader*, ed. Brian O'Connor (Oxford and Malden, Mass.: Blackwell, 2000), 142; Theodor W. Adorno, *Gesammelte Schriften*, 10.2 (1977), 746.

13 Adorno, *Negative Dialectics*, 174; *Gesammelte Schriften*, 6, 176.

14 Adorno, *Lectures on Negative Dialectics*, 25; *Vorlesung über Negative Dialektik*, 44.

15 G.W.F. Hegel, *Phenomenology of Spirit*, trans. A. V. Miller (Oxford: Oxford University Press, 1977), 51; G.W.F. Hegel, *Werke*, 3 (Frankfurt: Suhrkamp, 1970), 74.

16 Hegel, *Phenomenology of Spirit*, 10; *Werke*, 3, 24.

17 Adorno, *Hegel: Three Studies*, 9–10; *Gesammelte Schriften*, 5, 258.

18 It is, Adorno says, "the moment in which the intentions of the subject are distinguished in the object" (Adorno, *Hegel: Three Studies*, 7; *Gesammelte Schriften*, 5, 256).

19 Hegel, *Phenomenology of Spirit*, 51; *Werke*, 3, 74.

20 Adorno, *Hegel: Three Studies*, 77–78; *Gesammelte Schriften*, 5, 316.

21 Hegel, *Phenomenology of Spirit*, 54; *Werke*, 3, 78.

22 Adorno, *Hegel: Three Studies*, 7; *Gesammelte Schriften*, 5, 256.

23 Hegel, *Phenomenology of Spirit*, 50; *Werke*, 3, 73.

24 Adorno, *Hegel: Three Studies*, 38; *Gesammelte Schriften*, 5, 283.

25 Hegel highlights the difference in this way: "Even if they at the same time profess their faith in a higher power by references to *providence* and a providential *plan*, these remain empty ideas, for they also declare explicitly that the plan of providence is beyond their cognition and comprehension" (G.W.F. Hegel, *Elements of the Philosophy of Right*, trans. H. B. Nisbet (Cambridge: Cambridge University Press, 1991), §343n; G.W.F. Hegel, *Werke*, 7 [1970], §343).

26 G.W.F. Hegel, *The Philosophy of History*, trans. J. Sibree (New York: Dover, 1956), 10; G.W.F. Hegel, *Werke*, 12 (1970), 22.

27 Hegel, *The Philosophy of History*, 19; *Werke*, 12, 32.

28 Theodor W. Adorno, *History and Freedom*, trans. Rodney Livingstone (Cambridge: Polity Press, 2006), 81; Theodor W. Adorno, *Zur Lehre von der Geschichte und von der Freiheit, Nachgelessene Schriften*, IV/13 (Frankfurt: Suhrkamp, 2001), 119.

29 Adorno, *Negative Dialectics*, 320; *Gesammelte Schriften*, 6, 314.

30 Adorno, *History and Freedom*, 91; *Zur Lehre von der Geschichte und von der Freiheit*, 134.

31 Adorno, *Negative Dialectics*, 319; *Gesammelte Schriften*, 6, 313–314.

32 Adorno, *Negative Dialectics*, 320; *Gesammelte Schriften*, 6, 314.

33 Adorno, *Negative Dialectics*, 320; *Gesammelte Schriften*, 6, 314.

34 Axel Honneth, "The Possibility of a Disclosing Critique of Society: The Dialectic of Enlightenment in Light of Current Debates of Social Criticism," in *Disrespect: The Normative Foundations of Critical Theory* (Cambridge: Polity, 2007), p. 60.

35 Adorno, *History and Freedom*, 146; *Zur Lehre von der Geschichte und von der Freiheit*, 206–207.

36 Adorno, *Hegel: Three Studies*, 82; *Gesammelte Schriften*, 5, 320.

37 Hegel, *The Philosophy of History*, 21; *Werke*, 12, 35.

38 Adorno, *Hegel: Three Studies*, 23; *Gesammelte Schriften*, 5, 269.

39 Adorno, *Hegel: Three Studies*, 27; *Gesammelte Schriften*, 5, 273.

40 Adorno, *Negative Dialectics*, 158; *Gesammelte Schriften*, 6, 161.

41 Adorno, *Hegel: Three Studies*, 13; *Gesammelte Schriften*, 5, 261.

42 Adorno, *Negative Dialectics*, 335; *Gesammelte Schriften*, 6, 329.

43 Adorno, *Hegel: Three Studies*, 147; *Gesammelte Schriften*, 5, 375.

44 Adorno, *Hegel: Three Studies*, 6; *Gesammelte Schriften*, 5, 255.

45 G.W.F. Hegel, *Science of Logic*, trans. A. V. Miller (London: George Allen and Unwin, 1969), 70; G.W.F. Hegel, *Werke*, 5 (1969), 69.

46 John W. Burbridge, *On Hegel's Logic: Fragments of a Commentary* (Atlantic Highlands, N.J.: Humanities Press, 1981), 39.

47 Hegel, *Science of Logic*, 98–99; *Werke*, 5, 103–104.

48 Adorno, *Lectures on Negative Dialectics*, 60; *Vorlesung über Negative Dialektik*, 92.

49 Adorno, *Lectures on Negative Dialectics*, 61; *Vorlesung über Negative Dialektik*, 93.

50 Adorno, *Lectures on Negative Dialectics*, 61; *Vorlesung über Negative Dialektik*, 93.

51 Adorno, *Lectures on Negative Dialectics*, 61; *Vorlesung über Negative Dialektik*, 94.

52 Adorno, *Lectures on Negative Dialectics*, 62; *Vorlesung über Negative Dialektik*, 94.

53 Adorno, *Lectures on Negative Dialectics*, 62; *Vorlesung über Negative Dialektik*, 94.

54 Adorno, *Prisms*, 31; *Gesammelte Schriften*, 10.1, 26.

55 Adorno, *Prisms*, 31; *Gesammelte Schriften*, 10.1, 26.

56 Theodor W. Adorno, *Against Epistemology: A Metacritique*, trans. Willis Domingo (Cambridge, Mass.: MIT Press, 1983), 25; Theodor W. Adorno, *Gesammelte Schriften*, 5 (1970), 33.

57 Adorno, *Against Epistemology*, 5; *Gesammelte Schriften* 5, 14.

58 Rahel Jaeggi, "'No Individual Can Resist': *Minima Moralia* as Critique of Forms of Life," *Constellations*, 12, no. 1 (2005), 76.

59 Theodor W. Adorno, "Society," trans. Frederic Jameson, in *Salmagundi* 10–11 (1969–1970), 145; Theodor W. Adorno, *Gesammelte Schriften*, 8 (1972), 10.

60 Adorno, *Negative Dialectics*, 152; *Gesammelte Schriften*, 6, 155.

61 Adorno, *Prisms*, 31; *Gesammelte Schriften*, 10.1, 26.

62 Michael Rosen, *Hegel's Dialectic and Its Criticism* (Cambridge: Cambridge University Press, 1982), 41–42.

63 Ibid., 36.

64 Jürgen Habermas, *Knowledge and Human Interests*, trans. Jeremy Shapiro (London: Heinemann, 1972), 18, quoted in Rosen, *Hegel's Dialectic and Its Criticism*, 36.

65 Rosen, *Hegel's Dialectic and Its Criticism*, 37.

27

Hegel and Pragmatism

ROBERT STERN

The relation between Hegel and pragmatism is fraught and complex. On the one hand, a number of prominent classical and modern pragmatists have been happy to claim Hegel as an ally (Peirce in some moods; Dewey; Rorty in some respects; and Brandom, for example); on the other hand, he has also been identified by pragmatists as an enemy (Peirce in other moods; James; and Rorty in other respects, for example). Historically, the roots of American Hegelianism and the origins of pragmatism in the late nineteenth century are somewhat intertwined, and more recently the revival of interest in Hegel in the Anglo-American philosophical world has benefited from the interest taken in him by figures like Rorty and Brandom. At the same time, however, very few of the central interpreters of Hegel have been pragmatists or have shown much interest in this connection,[1] and I think it is fair to say that this approach has had nothing like the impact of readings of Hegel adopted by Marxists, existentialists, phenomenologists, deconstructionists, and others.

Although there is a fascinating historical story to be told here, in this chapter I want to concentrate more on conceptual issues and consider if there is some shared philosophical outlook between Hegel and the pragmatists or whether at some crucial point, these positions are always destined to diverge. This question could be prosecuted at several levels – metaphysical, ethical, and political, for example – but my main focus will be on epistemology because it is here (I will argue) that the heart of the pragmatist outlook lies, and also where it may appear that the greatest disagreement with Hegel is to be found.[2]

1

As with any complex school of thought that has evolved over time and been taken up by a number of different thinkers, it is impossible to reduce the outlook of pragmatism to any simple formula – even a formula proposed by the pragmatists themselves.

A Companion to Hegel, First Edition. Edited by Stephen Houlgate and Michael Baur.
© 2011 Blackwell Publishing Ltd. Published 2011 by Blackwell Publishing Ltd.

Nonetheless, if one tries to trace the web of pragmatist belief back to anything like a center, then it is arguable that there one finds a distinctively anti-Cartesian epistemology out of which all of the rest of the pragmatic outlook can be seen to develop. Anti-Cartesian epistemology has its antecedents – most particularly, perhaps, in the "constructive scepticism" of Pierre Gassendi and Marin Mersenne, and in the "commonsensism" of Thomas Reid – but the pragmatists were to develop its implications to the widest and furthest degree, and it is in following out those implications in different ways that the divergence between the pragmatist thinkers themselves can best be understood.

The first step in this direction is taken by Peirce, who challenged the Cartesian starting point of modern philosophy, encapsulated in Descartes's famous "method of doubt." At the heart of this method, as standardly conceived, is the thought that if philosophy is to reach anything like knowledge, then it must begin by suspending belief in whatever is not certain, which it turns out, according to Descartes, is most but not quite everything we believe. From out of the rubble some beliefs are said to survive (the belief in my own existence and the existence of God), based on which the edifice of knowledge can be rebuilt, this time on secure foundations. Descartes thus makes central a number of the ruling intuitions of epistemology, namely that knowledge requires foundations that are certain; that all our ordinary beliefs can be rendered doubtful by the skeptic; that each individual is required to look for secure foundations working on his own; that before it can be used, any faculty of knowledge must be shown to be reliable; and that the burden of proof on these matters lies with us and not the skeptic.

In a crucial early paper, "Some Consequences of Four Incapacities" of 1868, Peirce contrasts the Cartesian approach with that of the Scholastics and declares, "Now without wishing to return to scholasticism, it seems to me that modern science and modern logic require us to stand upon a very different platform from this."[3] First, in contrast to Descartes's view that "philosophy must begin with universal doubt," Peirce declares:

> We cannot begin with complete doubt. We must begin with all the prejudices which we actually have when we enter upon the study of philosophy. These prejudices are not to be dispelled by a maxim, for they are the things which it does not occur to us *can* be questioned. Hence this initial scepticism will be a mere self-deception, and not real doubt; and no one who follows the Cartesian method will ever be satisfied until he has formally recovered all those beliefs which in form he has given up. ... A person may, it is true, in the course of his studies, find reason to doubt what he began by believing; but in that case he doubts because he has a positive reason for it, and not on account of the Cartesian maxim. Let us not pretend to doubt in philosophy what we do not doubt in our hearts.[4]

Second, Peirce objects to Descartes's claim that the property of being clearly and distinctly conceived can be used as a criterion of truth because this leads to a kind of rationalistic intuitionism that is perniciously individualistic and immediate: if I claim to see clearly and distinctly that *p* is true, who are you to challenge me, and why should I provide any reasons for believing *p* beyond this experience of its clearness and distinctness as an idea? In fact, Peirce thinks the test of truth that science actually uses is agreement between inquirers, so we need to see ourselves as part of a community of investigators within which doubts arise and need to be answered through the challenges of people who see the world in a different way rather than through the questioning of an abstract skeptic who does not exist in real life at all.

Third, Descartes is also mistaken that a successful inquiry can be conducted in a foundationalist manner, by attempting to start from some unshakeable premise and arguing from there to further conclusions. In fact, Peirce claims, the sciences do not proceed in this way at all, but reach their conclusions by adopting a more holistic and coherentist approach: "Its reasoning should not form a chain which is no stronger than its weakest link, but a cable whose fibres may be ever so slender, provided they are sufficiently numerous and intimately connected."[5] Finally, Peirce argues that the Cartesian principle is inimical to science because certain facts remain unexplained, by being traced back to the inscrutable will of God.

There are, I think, a number of notable and fateful elements to Peirce's discussion here, including his distinction between real and artificial doubt; his claim that fallibilism is not the same as skepticism, in the sense that I can hold a belief and recognize that I might come to have reason to question it in the future as a result of further inquiries without on that basis being required to doubt that belief now; his claim that although Cartesianism may set out to oppose dogmatism, it in fact invites it by ending up with an individualistic criterion of truth that rules out reasonable disagreement between inquirers; and his claim that although Cartesianism claims to provide a foundation to the sciences and to therefore legitimate them, it is in fact at odds with the methods of communal and holistic inquiry that those sciences themselves actually employ. These elements are fateful because so much of what has come to be associated with pragmatism can be traced back to the central shift in perspective that they embody, where at the center of this shift lies the distinction between real and artificial doubt. Thus, there is plenty of room for divergence and disagreement within the pragmatist tradition on issues like the viability of metaphysics, the ambitions of philosophy, and truth as the goal of inquiry; nonetheless, these divergences are from a common starting point, which can be traced back to Peirce's anti-Cartesian conception of epistemology – which direction one takes from there is a matter of what one takes the full implications of that conception to be and thus, whether one thinks Peirce himself best understood these implications or whether they were better grasped by his successors.

2

If we therefore take Peirce's anti-Cartesianism to be the starting point of pragmatism, this gives us a clear way of gauging how far Hegel's position may be thought of in pragmatist terms: namely, did Hegel share this starting point? If he did not, it would seem hard to view the further details of his position in a pragmatist manner, and any similarities would be at best superficial (such as the conceptual realism he shares with Peirce, the antidualism he shares with Dewey, or the focus on historical change he shares with Rorty). At the same time, as we have noted, pragmatists who have shared this starting point have then gone in different directions, so the orientation of Hegel's thought could still be called pragmatist even if from here his thought differs from that of some of the pragmatists, as could also be said of the way in which the pragmatists diverge amongst themselves. The interpretative issue, then, is not whether Hegel was or was not a metaphysician, a realist about truth, or a believer in intellectual progress, for example, because these are all matters on which the pragmatists have disagreed. Whatever Hegel's views on these questions, the crucial issue is whether Hegel's stance here can be traced back to something resembling Peirce's distinctive response to Cartesian epistemology, and thus whether this Peircean approach is one he can be said to share with the pragmatist tradition as a whole.

It can be argued, however, that if we take Hegel's systematic claims and intentions seriously, and if we view him as the genuine heir to Kant, then it must be accepted that Hegel's position has a fundamentally Cartesian aspect; it would therefore follow that Hegel should be seen not as an ally of pragmatism but as one of its enemies, at least as I have presented it. We therefore need to look carefully at this sort of interpretation of Hegel in order to see whether a case can indeed be made for claiming that his approach is fundamentally at odds with pragmatism's guiding idea.

A reading of this kind, which sees Hegel's position in broadly Cartesian terms, has been presented in recent years by Stephen Houlgate.[6] Central to Houlgate's approach is the importance he attaches to Hegel's claims to *presuppositionlessness* in his philosophical work, where Houlgate understands these claims in a Cartesian manner. Houlgate thus places emphasis on passages such as the following:

> All ... presuppositions or assumptions [*Voraussetzungen oder Vorurteile*] must equally be given up when we enter into the Science, whether they are taken from representation or from thinking; for it is this Science, in which all determinations of this sort must first be investigated, and in which their meaning and validity like that of their antitheses must be [re]cognised... Science should be preceded by *universal doubt*, i.e., by total *presuppositionlessness* [*die gänzliche Voraussetzungslosigkeit*].[7]

According to Houlgate, what this shows is that Hegel was committed to questioning all assumptions because like Descartes he held that in a rational scientific inquiry (which is what Hegel means by 'Science' or *Wissenschaft*) none of these assumptions can be taken for granted, although also like Descartes, Hegel believed that this questioning had a limit. However, this limit is not that of the *cogito* but of thought having being. Thus, Houlgate writes, "The path of 'universal doubt' that leads into Hegel's science of logic is clearly very similar to that taken by Descartes. Hegel's conclusion, however, is not 'I think, therefore I am' but rather 'thinking, therefore *is*.'"[8] This Cartesian approach thus takes us, Houlgate argues, to the category of pure being, from which thought itself then proceeds to the further categories of nothing, becoming, determinate being, and all the rest. Such is Hegel's commitment to presuppositionlessness, on Houlgate's account, that Hegel doesn't even assume any particular method (dialectical or otherwise) in moving from one category to the next as to do so would be to make another unwarranted assumption; rather, his approach is just to "look on" and see what happens.[9]

In presenting Hegel as Cartesian in this way, Houlgate also offers an account of Hegel's motivations in which he argues that Kantian considerations made this Cartesian approach seem necessary to any philosophical outlook that considered itself fully modern; for Houlgate believes that from Hegel's perspective, it is Kant who held that it is only by engaging in a critical philosophy aimed at rooting out all unquestioned assumptions that we can be free as thinkers and fully self-determining in our view of the world in a way that is distinctive of a truly modern outlook that takes no tradition, authority, or givens for granted.[10] For Houlgate, therefore, after Kant the Cartesian project is seen to be more than just the rather narrow attempt to "provide solid foundations for the sciences"; it now becomes part of a much more ambitious agenda, which is to "liberate human consciousness," by developing "Descartes's idea that philosophy may take nothing for granted in its search for truth and that thought is the principle of doubt or criticism that frees us from the authority of habitual but unwarranted belief."[11]

Seen from this perspective, Houlgate argues, Hegel may be viewed as attempting to complete this Kantian project of radical self-criticism that Kant himself was unable to achieve insofar as he took too much for granted concerning the nature of thought and its categories, with the result that he failed to provide a proper deduction of them (as Fichte and others had also argued):

> Kant simply bases his understanding of the categories on the functions of judgment traditionally assumed in formal logic. ... Kant thus does not subject the categories themselves to critical examination but retains – without proving that it is necessary to do so – what Hegel regards as a quite traditional (Aristotelian) understanding of them. In this respect, Kant's critique of pure reason remains, for Hegel – like the thought of the "older metaphysicians," Leibniz and Wolff – "an *uncritical* thinking". ... A properly critical thinking, by contrast, would suspend the traditional conception of the categories and determine anew how the categories are to be understood.[12]

Houlgate argues, therefore, that just as much as Kant, and indeed Descartes, Hegel deserves to be seen as a thoroughly modern philosopher for whom self-critical thinking is a fundamental requirement not only for certainty and the kind of foundations needed by the sciences but also for human freedom and dignity; insofar as he took this project further and more deeply than even his predecessors managed to do, Houlgate believes that Hegel should be thought of as providing "*the* quintessentially modern philosophy."[13]

3

We have therefore explored Houlgate's claim that "[t]he best way to understand Hegel is to see him as exemplifying a Cartesian willingness to suspend his cherished beliefs and habits of thought, and to accept as true only what reason itself determines to be true,"[14] and we have also seen in the first section how pragmatism might be defined in terms of its suspicions concerning the need for any such "Cartesian willingness." Houlgate's reading of Hegel would therefore seem to render any pragmatist appropriation of Hegelian thought thoroughly misconceived, notwithstanding any superficial similarities that may be found between them.

And yet, there is a crucial place in Hegel's work where he appears to draw something very like the Peircean distinction between real and artificial doubt, which I have claimed is so central to pragmatism. This occurs in the Introduction to the *Phenomenology of Spirit*, and in a way that I believe makes clear his fundamental opposition to Cartesianism in any narrow epistemological sense and to that extent at least shows him to be anti-Cartesian. We therefore need to consider this text in some detail.

The Introduction begins by discussing what Hegel says may seem a "natural assumption," that before we begin our inquiries, we should investigate our cognitive methods and capacities, first because some capacities may be better for knowing about some things than others, and second because otherwise we may find ourselves being led astray; unless we proceed in this manner, "we might grasp clouds of error instead of the heaven of truth."[15] It is clear, I believe, that here Hegel has the outlook of thinkers like Descartes, Locke, and of course Kant in mind. In a passage that Hegel cites elsewhere,[16] Locke famously recommends this procedure, which requires that we "take a Survey of our own Understandings, examine our own Powers, and see to what Things they [are] adapted,"[17] and although Locke is referred to here, Descartes expresses a similar view when he writes, "Now, to prevent our being in a state of permanent uncertainty about the powers of the mind, and to prevent our mental labours being misguided and haphazard, we ought once in our life carefully to inquire as to what sort of knowledge human reason is capable of attaining, before we set about acquiring knowledge of things in particular."[18] Hegel equally sees Kant's critical project as sharing essentially the same outlook according to which we must start in philosophy by first examining the scope of our intellectual capacities: given that "[t]he very first [task] in the Kantian philosophy, therefore, is for thinking to investigate how far it is capable of cognition," this meant that "the faculty of cognition was to be investigated before cognition began."[19]

While allowing that there is something intuitive and appealing about this approach, Hegel nonetheless makes clear that he thinks it is potentially disastrous because in fact it leads inevitably to a focus not on the object of our inquiries, but on our cognitive capacities as a kind of instrument or medium by which we are put in touch with those objects; nevertheless, once we think of our cognitive capacities in this way, the suspicion then emerges that our cognitive capacities *stand between* us and reality as an instrument or medium that *distorts* how things are. Thus, starting from the "feeling of uneasiness" that perhaps we should put our cognitive capacities to the test before we begin our investigations, we end up believing that we can never really be confident that those capacities are not leading us astray. Hegel argues that it then becomes impossible to remedy this "evil," for example, by trying to dispel the effects of any distortion by trying to adjust for it, as unless we already knew what reality is like, how could any such adjustment be made? On the one hand, the critical philosopher cannot just allow that our cognitive capacities are accurate as this would render his investigation of these capacities superfluous; on the other hand, if he does not allow this, then there seems to be no prospect of determining what we should do to ensure that our inquiries succeed using those capacities, leading inexorably to a skeptical conclusion.

Hegel claims, therefore, that the worry with which we began – that without this investigation of our cognitive capacities "we might grasp clouds of error instead of the heaven of truth" – has in fact ended up seeming to put rational inquiry or "science" out of our reach. But, he argues, rational inquiry never in fact does grind to a halt in this way as in reality we just get on with trying to find out about the world without being much moved by this fear that perhaps we are going astray, which suggests that perhaps it is a worry that we can legitimately ignore:

> Meanwhile, if the fear of falling into error sets up a mistrust of Science, which in the absence of such scruples gets on with the work itself, and actually cognizes something, it

> is hard to see why we should not turn round and mistrust this very mistrust. Should we
> not be concerned as to whether this fear of error is not just the error itself?[20]

The point here does appear to be a Peircean one: The Cartesian philosopher insists on placing a burden on the inquirer to reflect on his capacities prior to inquiry (what Hume identified as Descartes's "antecedent" skepticism),[21] but in fact it is pointless to feel any such burden: we would do better to just get on with inquiring, and if this goes well, we will know our cognitive capacities are in order anyway, and if it goes badly, there is no reason to think this prior investigation would have helped. As the Cartesian cannot really tell us in advance either way or do anything to improve our prospects of success, it seems fruitless to be moved by his concerns and better to just "get on with the work itself."

However, it might perhaps be argued by the Cartesian philosopher that we should conduct this scrutiny of our cognitive capacities not in order to prevent us from wasting our time or going wrong in our investigations but in order to avoid the epistemic sin of making unwarranted presuppositions, namely the presupposition that our cognitive capacities are all in order and capable of getting us to the truth – for surely it would be highly presumptuous of us simply to assume that this is so. Hegel argues, however, that to motivate his investigations into our capacities, to make this a rational thing for us to undertake, the Cartesian philosopher *also* makes an assumption about how our capacities stand *between* us and the world in some way, raising the specter that they could easily cut us off from the way things are, and assumes that we could have knowledge merely of "appearances;" therefore, this position also involves some prior commitments that cannot be substantiated until we go ahead and begin our inquiries and see how far they get:

> Indeed, this fear [of error] takes something – a great deal in fact – for granted as truth, supporting its scruples and inferences on what is itself in need of prior scrutiny to see if it is true. To be specific, it takes for granted certain ideas about cognition as an *instrument* and as a *medium*, and assumes that there is a *difference between ourselves and this cognition*. Above all, it presupposes that the Absolute stands on one side and cognition on the other, independent and separated from it, and yet is something real; or in other words, it presupposes that cognition which, since it is excluded from the Absolute, is surely outside of the truth as well, is nevertheless true, an assumption whereby what calls itself fear of error reveals itself rather as fear of truth.[22]

Thus, although it may claim to be the most rational procedure because it is without presuppositions, Hegel argues that the critical approach is not the most rational and makes no fewer presuppositions than the sort of position that just "gets on with the work itself" rather than tarrying on the brink.

Moreover, elsewhere he argues that this Cartesian approach is of dubious coherence for on the one hand, it motivates its reflective investigation of our capacities with the concern that perhaps they might lead us astray, but on the other hand, in order to investigate those capacities, it must use these or other cognitive methods that either have their efficacy taken for granted at this second level (in which case why not take their efficacy for granted at the first level?) or themselves require another level of reflective scrutiny (in which case, how will the regress of reflection ever be brought to an end?). So, this approach is either redundant or impossible, and as absurd as someone who tries to learn to swim without getting into the water for fear of drowning, much as the critical philosopher who would try to learn how best to acquire knowledge without actually using any of his cognitive capacities for fear of making mistakes.[23]

Hegel makes plain in the *Phenomenology* that he sees a kind of bad faith in the Cartesian position, which instead of getting on with trying to find things out about the world and thus accomplish "the hard work of Science" or rational inquiry, just goes about "giving the impression of working seriously and zealously," while in actuality giving us "excuses which create the incapacity of Science." Hegel thus seems to think that the doubts raised by the Cartesian skeptic that motivate his investigation of our cognitive capacities are fraudulent and empty, and can be brushed aside in favor of actually getting on with the business of inquiry.

However, Hegel makes clear that this does not mean that even "Science" can assume it will simply be able to assert that its view of the world is the right one with no further ado, for any such position will have real competitors to deal with that see the world differently, and with which it must engage if it is not to be merely dogmatic and just insist on the correctness of its position without any satisfactory argument:

> For, when confronted with a knowledge that is without truth, Science can neither merely reject it as an ordinary way of looking at things, while assuring us that its Science is a quite different sort of cognition for which that ordinary knowledge is of no account whatever... By [this] *assurance*, Science would be declaring its power to lie simply in its *being;* but the untrue knowledge likewise appeals to the fact that *it is;* and *assures* us that for it Science is of no account. *One* bare assurance is worth just as much as another.[24]

Similarly, as Hegel makes clear elsewhere, we may find that our investigations actually *do* get into difficulties, in which case it will not be the empty Cartesian "fear of error" that motivates us to look at the way in which we think about the world but what seem to be genuine problems (such as Kant's antinomies, where these apparently intractable metaphysical questions make it reasonable to examine our ability to conduct inquiries of this sort). In such circumstances, Hegel allows, the critical project makes good sense by recognizing that traditional forms of philosophizing were unable to make any headway, which is what made "subjecting the determinations of the older metaphysics to investigation" in the Kantian manner "a very important step."[25]

Hegel fully understands, therefore, that reflection on the way we think and the categories we use can be shown to be necessary in a legitimate way when we are faced with others who think about the world differently, or when we come up against apparent obstacles to our inquiries, at which points Hegel's method of "immanent critique" is offered as a way of handling these challenges. Rather than dogmatically asserting that a given view is correct, it must be shown that its competitors have their own internal difficulties that this view can resolve, which is then established in a non-question-begging way.[26] For Hegel, therefore, once such an incoherence or aporia shows itself within a position, reflection on its categories must follow, a process aimed at arriving at a world view that is fully stable and is thus to be preferred to any of the alternatives against which it can lay claim to truth in a nondogmatic manner.

Now, it is at this point in the Introduction that Hegel contrasts the doubt we feel in these circumstances with the Cartesian doubt dismissed earlier. The doubt that motivates us to reflect on our cognitive capacities in a critical manner is now motivated by our experience of a *genuine* conflict between world views and *genuine* breakdowns in our investigations as opposed to the abstract "fear of error" he associates with Descartes, which because of its abstractness has little actual effect on our thinking. Thus, Hegel tells us that the kind of self-questioning our ordinary forms of thinking (or "natural consciousness") will be forced to go in for in the *Phenomenology* is grounded in the real difficulties it is forced to face in a way that the kind of questioning Descartes goes in for is not:

> Natural consciousness will show itself to be only the Notion of knowledge, or in other words, not to be real knowledge. But since it directly takes itself to be real knowledge, this path has a negative significance for it, and what is in fact the realization of the Notion [i.e., the view of the world adopted by philosophy], counts for it as the loss of its own self; for it does lose its truth on this path. The road can be regarded as the pathway of *doubt*, or more precisely as the way of despair. For what happens on it is not what is ordinarily understood when the word "doubt" is used: shilly-shallying about this or that presumed truth, followed by a return to that truth again, after the doubt has been appropriately dispelled – so that at the end of the process the matter is taken to be what it was in the first place. On the contrary, this path is the conscious insight into the untruth of phenomenal knowledge [i.e., the knowledge claimed by our ordinary ways of thinking], for which the supreme reality is what is in truth only the unrealized Notion [i.e., for which what appears to be true is not the final story].[27]

The doubt that Hegel expects to motivate our inquiries, therefore, and to cause consciousness to question its previous certainties is the doubt that comes about when we are confronted by the fact that what we thought about the world cannot be made to work coherently and forces us to change our minds; furthermore, because the problems we face are determinate, consciousness can also see how such a doubt might be resolved, in contrast to Cartesian doubt, which provides no way forward because the doubt it raises is too abstract to be amenable to resolution.[28] Unlike Cartesian doubt, which Hegel believes is inevitably paralyzing in its own terms and so only leads one to carry on much as before, the doubt in which Hegel is interested is one that is thrown up by seeing that something has gone wrong in what we have previously thought; it thus pushes us to try to right this wrong, and in so doing, helps determine a direction in which we might move forward, a way that offers a positive resolution to the doubt in question and a change in outlook rather than just a return to what we thought before.

Now, from what has been said previously in this chapter about Peirce, it should be clear that much of what Hegel argues for here should be viewed sympathetically by the Peircean, for as we have seen, Hegel is as keen as Peirce to distinguish between different kinds of doubt and to reject the sort of apparently groundless questioning of our beliefs that the Cartesian goes in for, which is claimed to be a necessary preliminary to any responsible form of inquiry. Like Peirce, Hegel holds that such questioning can be carried out intelligibly only if we are offered real grounds for doing so, which requires the doubter to provide some evidence of error, which will then leave us able to try to correct it as normally happens when we are made to realize we have made a mistake.

564

It turns out, therefore, that contrary to the way things seemed to be going in Section 2 of this chapter, there is considerable common ground between Hegel and pragmatism on these issues after all.

4

Thus, while Cartesian doubt can provide a motivation for the rejection of all assumptions, so that a concern with presuppositionlessness of the sort Houlgate identifies in Hegel may seem to indicate that he had a commitment to Cartesianism in some form, it is nonetheless wrong to take Hegel's demand for a presuppositionless philosophy to stem from any such Cartesian sympathies in epistemology and thus to see this demand as driving a wedge between Hegel and pragmatism: as we have shown, Hegel, like Peirce, sees little force in Cartesian "antecedent" skepticism, so it would be a mistake to think that this was the basis for Hegel's desire to construct a presuppositionless philosophy, as it was, arguably, for Descartes himself.

However, even if Hegel's focus on presuppositionlessness was not grounded in a distinctively Cartesian concern with skeptical doubt, it could still be argued that this focus sets him at odds with the pragmatist tradition because it was based instead on a conception of what it is for thought to be *free*, a conception that derives not from skeptical worries but from the way in which Kant developed Descartes's demand that we take nothing for granted because otherwise we would be following tradition, authority, or natural habit in a heteronomous manner. This, indeed, is how Houlgate sees Hegel's central concern rather than identifying it with any more narrowly Cartesian preoccupation with "antecedent" skepticism.[29] It is prima facie plausible to think that on the one hand, this, too, is an antipragmatist perspective but also, on the other, that this must be the motivation behind Hegel's talk of presuppositionlessness, given the apparently obvious link between the two.

In a recent discussion of the idea of "free thought," both these points have been emphasized by John Skorupski; in general, his discussion is very illuminating in relation to our concerns here. Skorupski argues that it is characteristic of everyone who adopts this idea to hold that "[f]ree thought is thought ruled by its own principles and by nothing else; in other words, by principles of thinking that it discovers by reflecting on its own activity."[30] However, there is an important further division along this path: "Down one route lies the idea of free thought as thought that is *unconstrained* by any authoritative source external to it. Down the other lies the idea of it as radically *presuppositionless*."[31] Skorupski identifies the latter idea with Descartes, and argues that it runs through to German Idealism in a way that resembles the sort of account also given by Houlgate:

> [T]he idea that free thought must be presuppositionless is highly plausible. If it rests on some presupposition or assumption, how can it be free? Must it not freely question that assumption? That has been an enormously influential modern conception of what it is to think really freely. Call it the Cartesian idea, after the French philosopher, René Descartes, who expounded it in his *Meditations*. ... One way of spelling out its shaping influence would be to tell the story of German philosophy from Kant to Nietzsche. This tradition takes the

565

ROBERT STERN

Cartesian idea with utmost seriousness, and then seriously tries to free itself from its clutch. Kant responds to Descartes' failure by a critique of free thought itself (the "Critique of Pure Reason"). Truly free thought, he says, must investigate the conditions of its own possibility. ... The story continues with Hegel. He finds fault with Kant's project because it imposes a basic cleavage of subject and object. So he tries to show how free thought itself literally generates everything: a kind of apotheosis of presuppositionless free thought. Nietzsche sees the failure of these high-wire heroics and diagnoses a crisis of Western values.[32]

In contrast with the Cartesian conception of free thought, Skorupski identifies a different approach,

according to which free thought does not start by refusing to make any assumptions at all, but instead maintains a continuing critical open-mindedness about everything we take ourselves to know, without any exemptions whatever. This "constructive empiricism" also goes back to the seventeenth century. It is naturalistic, in that it takes us to be a part of the world that we scientifically study. It is holistic, in that it works from within our convictions as a whole. It takes the fallibilistic attitude that *any* of the things we think we know, however seemingly certain, could turn out to be wrong in the course of our continuing inquiry. That includes our initial assumptions – but it does not follow that we cannot start from them.[33]

Skorupski calls this approach "thinking from within,"[34] and it should be clear from what we have already said that pragmatism can be seen as a development of this perspective rather than the Cartesian one. And yet, if this is so, and if by contrast it is the Cartesian conception of free thought that drives Hegel into radical presuppositionlessness, doesn't this show once again that Hegel and pragmatism must be taken to diverge?

However, though at first placing Hegel within the Cartesian camp, Skorupski also notes that "Hegel's method, incidentally, could also be described as thinking from within"[35] thereby putting him in the alternative tradition to which the pragmatists belong. Skroupski doesn't elaborate on this remark any further, but I take it he has in mind the historicist and communitarian side of Hegel's position, according to which a particular historical time and social place inevitably forms the horizon of our thinking. It is this aspect of Hegel's outlook that is encapsulated in his well-known comments that "[e]ach individual is the son of his own nation at a specific stage in this nation's development. No one can escape from the spirit of his nation, any more than he can escape from the earth itself";[36] and "[a]s far as the individual is concerned, each individual is in any case a *child of his time*; thus philosophy, too, is *its own time comprehended in thoughts*."[37] On this basis, then, it can be argued that Hegel no less than the pragmatists understood that inquiry must be conducted "from within."

We should be careful, therefore, in inferring that just because Hegel says that "we must make no presuppositions" is "a very great and important principle,"[38] this makes him a Cartesian in a way that would separate him from pragmatism. For, first, he makes clear that although the reason Descartes gives for this principle "in his own fashion" is that "we must make no presuppositions because it is possible to be mistaken," this is not the fundamental issue for Hegel because "[i]n the Cartesian form [of this position] the stress is not on the principle of freedom as such, but instead on reasons more

566

popular in tone," namely the possibility of error and the need for certainty;[39] second, even if we see "the principle of freedom" as what for Hegel really underlies the concern with presuppositionlessness, this need not mean that this commits him to the idea that free thought must begin with no assumptions and so be presuppositionless in this sense because thought can still be free as long as it is always able to reflect further on the presuppositions with which it starts, even though it cannot reflect on them all at once from a position that makes no assumptions whatsoever.

And indeed, when Hegel writes about the way presuppositions might pose a threat to "free thought," he does not seem to be going along with the idea which for Skorupski drives the Cartesian approach here, namely "that if [thought] rests on some presupposition or assumption, how can it be free?" Rather, the presuppositions Hegel identifies as posing a threat to the "principle of freedom" are those that are posited as prior to thought in a special sense, namely as things that thought cannot grasp or understand, and so are presupposed in the sense of "put before" (*voraus-gesetzt*) thinking. In the *Lectures on the History of Philosophy*, Hegel thus resists presuppositions not because he is concerned by Cartesian doubt or even because he is unwilling to "think from within" but because he objects to the idea of "something found already there [pre-posited] that thinking has not posited, something other than thinking," such as (in an example Hegel gives) F. H. Jacobi's God, which thought is unable to comprehend and which we can be aware of only through the nonintellectual means of "immediate intuition or inward revelation." In a presupposition of *this* sort, Hegel argues, "thinking is not present to itself" because it clearly has limits imposed on it by this prior positing, much in the way in which it does when told to believe things on an external authority that it cannot fathom.[40] Thus, for Hegel, presuppositions of the kind postulated by Jacobi as "pre-positings" violate the freedom of thought by setting up something that is alien to it. In contrast, Hegel holds that freedom for thought requires it to find nothing alien and so to be "at home with itself," a freedom that he believes constitutes the "greatness of our time."[41] I take it that this is what Hegel is getting at when he writes that "[w]hatever is recognized as true must present itself in such a way that our freedom is preserved in the fact that we think."[42] It seems, then, that Hegel can take presuppositions as his target here in this sense without this committing him to a tradition of "free thought" that is at odds with the one followed by the pragmatists or indeed his own historicist conception of the context of beliefs and assumptions that forms the background to any inquiry.

5

We have seen, then, that although there is indeed a deep concern with the issue of presuppositions in Hegel of the sort highlighted by Houlgate and others, it would be wrong to think that he should therefore be identified with a Cartesian approach in epistemology or with a Cartesian (or Kantian) conception of "free thought" – for to the extent that he is committed to free thought, we have seen that Hegel's idea of "free thought" (like the pragmatist's) does not take a form that commits him in itself to a demand to think presuppositionlessly and neither does his rejection of the Jacobian idea that there might be anything that thought cannot grasp. Yet, as Houlgate rightly emphasizes, Hegel nonetheless insists that the *Logic* must proceed *without presupposi-tions*. This, however, seems to leave us with a puzzle: if Hegel is not Cartesian in outlook, what motivation for "presuppositionlessness" does he have instead that leads him to insist on such thinking in the *Logic*, and is this also compatible with pragmatism? In fact, I will now argue that not only is Hegel's concern with presuppositionlessness compatible with pragmatism but also that this concern is one shared by the pragmatists themselves, so far from presenting an obstacle to a pragmatist reading of Hegel (as we initially feared), his claims about the need for presuppositionlessness in fact provide support for it. Hegel's commitment to presuppositionlessness arises, I will show, because of the way he views the nature of his *Logic*, and, I will claim, his reasons for viewing the *Logic* in this way are ones that are based on just the sort of real, non-Cartesian doubt that the pragmatists also endorse.

Hegel's *Logic* is the first part of his system (to which the *Phenomenology* is its "introduction" or "ladder") and has as its aim "[t]o exhibit the realm of thought philosophically, that is, in its own immanent activity or what is the same, in its necessary development."[43] Insofar as it is a philosophical investigation of thought in this manner, Hegel argues that it must be presuppositionless, for a variety of related reasons:

(a) Unlike other sciences, it cannot assume anything about the methods of thinking because these are part of what an investigation of thought should inquire into.[44]

(b) Again unlike other sciences, it cannot start with some experience or representa-tion of the object it is investigating because thought cannot be experienced or represented.[45] Other inquiries, Hegel suggests, must therefore presuppose their objects (such as space, or numbers, or God), but the *Logic* cannot and need not do so because it is an investigation of thought and so produces its objects simply through the process of inquiry itself, which involves thought:

> With regard to the *beginning* that philosophy has to make, it seems, like the other sci-ences, to start in general with a subjective presupposition, i.e., to have to make a par-ticular ob-ject, in this case *thinking*, into the ob-ject of thinking, just like space, number, etc., in the other sciences. But what we have here is the free act of thinking putting itself at the standpoint where it is for its own self, and where hereby it produces and gives to itself its ob-ject.[46]

(c) Although an inquiry into other matters can be empirical and so can legitimately involve claims that are contingent, a science of thought such as the *Logic* is not something that can be conducted in this way; rather, it must reveal thought to have a necessary structure, which it cannot do if the claims it makes about thought rest on groundless assumptions, for "[i]f the beginnings are immediate, found, or presupposed ... the form of necessity fails to get its due."[47]

(d) The *Logic* is concerned with the categories belonging to thought, which Hegel distinguishes from the representations [*Vorstellungen*] that belong to other facul-ties and are distinct from but related to the faculty of thought. As a result, the *Logic* cannot use these representations as a basis for determining the nature of the categories of thought since in fact the two behave in very different ways:

Since the determinacies of feeling, of intuition, of desire, of willing, etc., are generally called *representations*, inasmuch as we have *knowledge* of them, it can be said in general that philosophy puts *thoughts* and *categories*, but more precisely *concepts*, in the place of representations. Representations in general can be regarded as *metaphors* of thoughts and concepts. But that we have these representations does not mean that we are aware of their significance for thinking, i.e., that we have the thoughts and concepts of them. Conversely, it is one thing to have thoughts and concepts, and another to know what the representations, intuitions, and feelings are that correspond to them.[48]

This fundamental contrast between thought and the other faculties means that thought can and must be investigated on its own without any need to base that investigation into its categories on representations taken from elsewhere; indeed, if the attempt were made to do so, the result would be a distortion of those categories, so that presupposing representations in this way would prove disastrous for the *Logic*.

We can see, therefore, why it is that for Hegel philosophy can only conduct an investigation into thought in a presuppositionless manner and thus why the *Logic*, as the "science of thought" must proceed without presuppositions. It seems, then, that this has nothing to do with Cartesian doubts or Kantian aspirations to "free thought"; it just follows from the fact that the *Logic* has thought as its object, and this object (Hegel believes) can only be investigated presuppositionlessly or not at all. It can be argued, then, that Hegel's commitment to presuppositionlessness is driven by his conception of the *sui generis* nature of thought as the subject-matter of this "science" rather than the sorts of issues highlighted by Houlgate.

But, it might be asked, why does Hegel think we need to go in for this "science" at all? Why should we make thought into the object of our investigations? Until we know the answer to this question, the suspicion might remain that Hegel is still Cartesian in his approach after all, perhaps because he wants to investigate thought in order to avoid the possibility of error or to show that thought can be rendered free by being rendered presuppositionless.

However, I think this suspicion can easily be allayed, and that in fact when we examine the motivation that Hegel himself provides for the *Logic*, it is thoroughly compatible with pragmatism as we have envisaged it. Hegel makes plain that the reason we must conduct his "science of thought" is that we have found that much of our ordinary thinking is prone to error, confusion, and incoherence, which is just the kind of *real* doubt that he contrasts with the Cartesian one. He completely accepts, therefore, that until we perceive the failings in our ordinary thinking, we have no reason to go in for his "science of thought," and he uses the *Phenomenology* to show that without it, we will face the sort of genuine intellectual and practical difficulties that he documents so richly in that text.

Hegel thus allows that although the *Logic* is driven by "the resolve ... that we propose to consider thought as such," any such resolution "can only be regarded as arbitrary" unless we are shown why we must commit ourselves to it.[49] Hegel clearly holds that the only way to get us to "consider thought as such" and to make "thoughts themselves, unmixed with anything else, into ob-jects"[50] as we do in the *Logic* is by showing how problematic our view of the world will be if we fail to employ the categories of thought properly. According to Hegel, "[i]n its relation to ordinary consciousness, philosophy would first have to show *the need* for its *peculiar mode of cognition,* or even to awaken this need"[51] by showing ordinary consciousness that it will face real problems otherwise, the problems for ordinary consciousness that are documented in the *Phenomenology,* after which consciousness is ready to take seriously the *Logic* as a "science of thought."

It can therefore be said that the only grounds for the sort of investigation carried out by the *Logic* into thought (which must therefore be carried out presuppositionlessly insofar as thought is its object) is exactly the kind of "real doubt" championed by the pragmatists at the expense of the "artificial doubt" associated with Cartesianism. Hegel emphasizes that it is only when consciousness has been brought to a state of genuine despair that it will be ready for the *Logic,* a despair the "shilly-shallying" doubt of Descartes can never achieve, thereby providing no proper motivation for the kind of investigation into thought that Hegel believes must in the end be carried out.[52] The rationale for Hegel's presuppositionless inquiry is thus one with which the pragmatist can safely sympathize rather than an inquiry having an objectionable Cartesian (or Cartesian-cum-Kantian) basis.

Turning finally to the passage from the *Encyclopaedia Logic* that perhaps led Houlgate to his Cartesian reading of Hegel, we may now put it in a different light, but the passage requires more extensive quotation if this is to be seen:

> All ... presuppositions or assumptions must equally be given up when we enter into the Science, whether they are taken from representations or from thinking; for it is this Science, in which all determinations of this sort must first be investigated, and in which their meaning and validity like that of their antitheses must be [re]cognised.

I would read this as Hegel saying that the *Logic,* as the science of thought, cannot begin by presupposing anything about how various concepts relate to one another or should be understood because any investigation into thought is precisely an investigation into such concepts.

> Being a negative science that has gone through all forms of cognition, *scepticism* might offer itself as an introduction in which the nullity of such presuppositions would be exposed. But it would not only be a sad way, but also a redundant one, because, as we shall soon see,[53] the dialectical moment itself is an essential one in the affirmative Science. Besides, scepticism would have to find the finite forms only empirically and unscientifically, and to take them up as given.

Given that the *Logic* has to be presuppositionless, it might be felt that the way to proceed here is to adopt a skeptical approach. But this sort of prior skepticism is *not* needed as the categories themselves will show themselves to be inadequate in various ways through the dialectic, whereas the skeptical approach cannot ever be really systematic and exhaustive.

> To require a consummate scepticism of this kind, is the same as the demand that Science should be preceded by *universal doubt,* i.e., by total *presuppositionlessness.* Strictly speaking, this request is fulfilled by the freedom that abstracts from everything, and grasps its own pure abstraction, the simplicity of thinking – in the resolve of the *will to think purely.*[54]

What the skeptical position represents in its insistence on universal doubt is the requirement for presuppositionlessness; but the science of logic fulfils this requirement without the need for universal doubt because it sets out to think in a pure manner, which can only be done in a presuppositionless way. Thus no skeptical beginning for this project of presuppositionless inquiry is either called for or required – it is just part of the nature of the inquiry into thought itself. To this extent, therefore, Hegel can agree with all the pragmatist objections to skepticism, while still basing his project on a set of considerations that favor proceeding presuppositionlessly, considerations which (I have argued) should not in themselves trouble the pragmatist.

6

We have seen, therefore, that when it comes to the motivations underlying Hegel's commitment to presuppositionlessness in the *Logic*, there is no problematic Cartesianism either relating to some sort of Cartesian doubt or to the broader Cartesian/Kantian conception of "free thought." Is this enough, however, to show that Hegel and pragmatism can be unproblematically aligned with one another when it comes to the issue of presuppositions? For, even if I am right in saying that Hegel's *reasons for thinking* we should proceed presuppositionlessly in the *Logic* are not Cartesian or Kantian, and thus that his position need not raise any qualms with the pragmatist on this score, I am still nonetheless allowing that Hegel does think we are *able* to suspend our presuppositions when it comes to this "science of thought." Isn't *this* enough to render Hegel a "Cartesian" in a broad sense? And isn't this also something the pragmatist would deny, holding instead that we must always make some assumptions in any inquiry as Peirce seems to claim when he writes, "We must begin with all the prejudices which we actually have when we enter upon the study of philosophy," as if the having of such "prejudices" is just a necessary feature of what it is to be a thinking subject at all?

As Houlgate rightly notes, there *are* some critics of Hegel's approach in the *Logic* who do take this line, and so who claim not merely that presuppositionless inquiry is unwarranted in normative terms (by the "emptiness" of the Cartesian doubt that drives it, or whatever), but also that it is just an unrealizable project and so "an impossible demand to fulfil"[55] or "preposterous."[56] Houlgate works hard to show that in fact, it may not be as unrealizable as critics of this sort suppose.[57] The question for us here, therefore, is whether the pragmatist needs to be put among critics of *this* sort and thus whether there remains a significant point of difference between Hegel and the pragmatist tradition over the *feasibility* of presuppositionlessness inquiry, regardless of whether trying to conduct such an inquiry could ever be *justified* or warranted. Even if the Hegelian could convince the pragmatist that his Hegelian grounds for trying to inquire presuppositionlessly in the *Logic* are not in themselves objectionable, might not the pragmatist still commit himself to insisting, along with other critics of Hegel (such as Heideggerians and hermeneuticists), that it just cannot be done?

Now, one way to raise this kind of criticism of Hegel is to say that the *Logic* project is unrealizable because we are just unable to think or reason presuppositionlessly, given how thinking works for us, where Peirce may seem to be saying precisely this in insisting that our "prejudices" are something with which we "must begin." However, although this question is too large to be satisfactorily settled here, I would argue that Peirce's comment should *not* be taken as an attack on presuppositionlessness of this sort but rather that his position centers squarely on the normative issue of whether such an inquiry can be justified. That is, on my reading, Peirce is saying that "when we enter upon the study of philosophy" and thus begin an inquiry in this domain, the sense in which we "must" begin with the beliefs we find ourselves with at that point is that there is nothing the Cartesian can do to legitimately dislodge those beliefs by appealing to his "Cartesian maxim" that we should begin with universal doubt because at the start of this inquiry, no "real doubt" has been raised over them (though it might be so raised later). In my view, the "must" here has a normative basis grounded on the inadequacy of Cartesian doubt to put these beliefs legitimately into question, not a basis in any supposed fact about how the mind must work and what is required to make thinking possible.[58]

However, a further question may perhaps remain: even if Hegel were able to convince the pragmatist that he can give us good grounds on which to suspend our beliefs when it comes to the project being envisaged in the *Logic*, would the pragmatist not argue that from that sort of presuppositionless position, *no further inquiry is possible*, not because we must always operate with some assumptions which cannot be set aside, but because no inquiry can make progress when all such assumptions are put in abeyance, so that Hegel is bound to find that his "path of inquiry" in the *Logic* is blocked?[59]

Now, again, this is a large issue, but also harder to gauge both in terms of where the differences between the pragmatist and Hegel might lie and how important these differences ultimately are. To concentrate once more on Peirce, it is certainly correct that he believed that such a "blockage" would be the consequence of the *Cartesian* way of questioning our assumptions, and that this therefore would hinder our investigations when it comes to our everyday inquiries, natural science, and so on. But the *Logic* is rather different from these sorts of investigations, with a different kind of focus, so there are perhaps reasons to think that the Hegelian could convince Peirce that presuppositionless inquiry will work when it comes to the sort of investigation Hegel envisages here, particularly when (as Houlgate makes clear) the kind of presuppositionlessness Hegel is after and what he means by it is qualified in some respects.[60] Arguably, moreover, what Peirce takes to be stultifying about Cartesianism is not so much that it asks us to suspend all our beliefs but that the abstractness of its doubts makes it impossible for us to resolve them, with the result that the inquiry cannot continue or get anywhere. However, here, as we have seen, Hegel is in agreement with the Peircean but takes his inquiry *not* to be based on abstract doubt, and so to have a determinate way forward as a result. Thus, just as the pragmatist can perhaps be brought to accept the motivations for Hegel's project in the *Logic*, so, too, can he be brought to accept that no obstacles stand in the way of Hegel's actually achieving it and bringing that project to completion.

7

In this chapter we have considered how much common ground can be found between Hegel and pragmatism where I have argued that there is more than may initially have appeared. As we have seen, when it comes to the normative commitments underlying Hegel's justification for the *Logic*, there is nothing that need force him apart from the pragmatist once this work is seen in the right context. Whether, however, Hegel could convince the pragmatist that his goal of presuppositionless inquiry in the *Logic* is *achievable* is perhaps harder to establish as much will depend on how that project is conceived in more detail on the one hand, and on the other hand, what role in inquiry the pragmatist gives to the having of assumptions and whether that role would in fact apply to the *Logic* – where it is very likely that the pragmatists would disagree among themselves on precisely what their "Neurathian" outlook really amounts to and how far it should go. Nonetheless, even if in the end this question has to remain open, I hope to have cleared the way for seeing how deeply Hegel's position can be aligned with that of the pragmatist on certain fundamental issues once that position is understood along the lines that I recommend here.[61]

Notes

1 One honorable exception among Hegel commentators is Kenneth R. Westphal; see, e.g., "Hegel and Realism," in John Shook and Joseph Margolis (eds.), *A Companion to Pragmatism* (Oxford: Blackwell, 2006), pp. 177–183. The issue is also discussed in Terry Pinkard, "Was Pragmatism the Successor to Idealism?" in Cheryl Misak (ed.), *New Pragmatists* (Oxford: Oxford University Press, 2007), pp. 142–68.

2 References to the works of Peirce are given as follows:
CP: *Collected Papers of Charles Sanders Peirce*, vols. 1–6 ed. Charles Hartshorne and Paul Weiss, 1931–1935, vols. 7 and 8 ed. A. W. Burks, 1958 (Cambridge, Mass.: Belknap Press); references to volume and paragraph number.
EP: *The Essential Peirce: Selected Philosophical Writings*, 2 vols., ed. Nathan Houser and Christian Kloesel (Bloomington: Indiana University Press, 1992); references to volume and page number.
References to the works of Hegel are given as follows:
Werke: *Werke in zwanzig Bänden*, 20 vols. and index, ed. Eva Moldenhauer and Karl Markus Michel (Frankfurt: Suhrkamp, 1969–1971); references to volume and page number.

3 Peirce, CP 5.265, EP I: 28.

4 Peirce, CP 5.265, EP I: 28–29.

5 Peirce CP 5.265, EP I: 29.

6 See in particular *An Introduction to Hegel: Freedom, Truth and History*, 2nd edition. (Oxford: Blackwell, 2005), and *The Opening of Hegel's Logic* (West Lafayette, Ind.: Purdue University Press, 2006).

7 Hegel, *Logic: Part I of the Encyclopaedia of the Philosophical Sciences*, trans. T. F. Geraets, W. A. Suchting, and H. S. Harris (Indianapolis, Ind.: Hackett, 1991) (hereafter EL), §78, p. 124 (*Werke* VIII: 167–168). This passage is discussed by Houlgate in *Introduction to Hegel*, p. 30, and *Hegel's Logic*, p. 29. In this connection, Houlgate also cites Hegel, *Science of Logic*, trans. A. V. Miller (London: George Allen & Unwin, 1969) (hereafter SL), p. 70 (*Werke* V: 68–69): "the beginning must be an *absolute*, or what is synonymous here, an *abstract* beginning; and so it *may not presuppose anything*, must not be mediated by anything nor have a ground; rather it is to be itself the ground of the entire science"; and he refers to G.W.F. Hegel, *Lectures on the History of Philosophy*, 3 vols., ed. Robert F. Brown, trans. Robert F. Brown, J. M. Stewart, and H. S. Harris (Berkeley: University of California Press, 1990) (hereafter LHP),

III: 137–138 (*Vorlesungen über die Geschichte der Philosophie, Teil 4, Philosophie des Mittelalters und der neueren Zeit*, ed. Pierre Garniron and Walter Jaeschke (Hamburg: Felix Meiner, 1989) (hereafter VGP), p. 92).

8   Houlgate, *Hegel's Logic*, pp. 31–32. See also ibid., pp. 82 and 128, and *Introduction to Hegel*, pp. 31–32.

9   See Houlgate, *Hegel's Logic*, pp. 32–35, 51–53, 60–62.

10   Cf. Houlgate, *An Introduction to Hegel*, pp. 27–28.

11   Ibid., p. 27.

12   Houlgate, *Hegel's Logic*, p. 26. Cf. also *An Introduction to Hegel*, p. 31.

13   Houlgate, *Hegel's Logic*, p. 39.

14   Houlgate, *An Introduction to Hegel*, p. 39.

15   Hegel, *Phenomenology of Spirit*, trans. A. V. Miller (Oxford: Oxford University Press, 1977) (hereafter PS), p. 46 (*Werke* III: 68).

16   Hegel, *Faith and Knowledge*, translated by Walter Cerf and H. S. Harris (Albany: SUNY Press, 1977), pp. 68–69 (*Werke* III: 303–304).

17   John Locke, *An Essay Concerning Human Understanding*, ed. P. H. Nidditch (Oxford: Oxford University Press, 1975), chap. 1, §6, p. 47.

18   René Descartes, "Rules for the Direction of the Mind," in *The Philosophical Writings of Descartes*, trans. John Cottingham, Robert Stoothoff, and Dugald Murdoch, 2 vols. (Cambridge: Cambridge University Press, 1985), I: 30.

19   Hegel, EL, §41 Addition, p. 82 (*Werke* VIII: 114).

20   Hegel, PS, p. 47 (*Werke* III: 69).

21   Cf. David Hume, *Enquiries Concerning Human Understanding*, 3rd edition, ed. L. A. Selby-Bigge, revised by P. H. Nidditch (Oxford: Oxford University Press, 1975), Section XII, pp. 149–50.

22   Hegel, PS, p. 47 (*Werke* III: 69–70).

23   Cf. EL, §10, p. 34 (*Werke* VIII: 54); and also LHP III: 263 (VGP, p. 182).

24   Hegel, PS, pp. 48–49 (*Werke* III: 71).

25   Hegel, EL, §41 Addition, p. 81 (*Werke* VIII: 114).

26   This is a central part of Hegel's response to the challenge of *ancient* skepticism, which Hegel always took much more seriously than modern or Cartesian skepticism, because it was based around the equal force or equipollence of genuinely competing views. For further helpful discussion of this contrast in Hegel's attitudes, see Michael N. Forster, *Hegel and Skepticism* (Harvard: Harvard University Press, 1989), and Kenneth R. Westphal, *Hegel's Epistemological Realism* (Dordrecht: Kluwer, 1989).

27   Hegel, PS, pp. 49–50 (*Werke* III: 72).

28   Cf. Hegel, PS, p. 51 (*Werke* III: 74), and EL, §81 Addition, p. 131 (*Werke* VIII: 176).

29   Cf. Houlgate, *An Introduction to Hegel*, pp. 27–28.

30   John Skorupski, *Why Read Mill Today?* (London and New York: Routledge, 2006), p. 6.

31   Ibid., p. 7.

32   Ibid., pp. 7–8.

33   Ibid., p. 8.

34   Ibid., p. 9.

35   Ibid.

36   Hegel, *Lectures on the Philosophy of World History: Introduction*, trans. H. B. Nisbet (Cambridge: Cambridge University Press, 1975), p. 81 (*Vorlesungen über die Philosophie der Weltgeschichte*, vol. 1, ed. Johannes Hoffmeister (Hamburg: Meiner, 1955), p. 95).

37   Hegel, *Elements of the Philosophy of Right*, ed. Allen Wood, trans. H. B. Nisbet (Cambridge: Cambridge University Press, 1991), p. 21 (*Werke* VII: 26).

38   Hegel, LHP III: 138 (VGP, p. 92).

39   Hegel, LHP III: 139 (VGP, p. 93).

40   Hegel, LHP III: 138–139 (VGP, p. 93).

41   Hegel, LHP III: 257 (VGP, p. 178). Cf. also Hegel, *Philosophy of Mind: Part III of the Encyclopaedia of the Philosophical Sciences,* trans. William Wallace and A. V. Miller (Oxford: Oxford University Press, 1971) (hereafter EM), §440, pp. 179–180 (*Werke* X: 230): "Free mind...is determined as embracing within itself all objectivity, so that the object is not anything externally related to mind or anything mind cannot grasp."

42   Hegel, LHP III: 139 (VGP, p. 93).

43   Hegel, SL, p. 31 (*Werke* V: 19).

44   See Hegel, SL, p. 43 (*Werke* V: 35): "Logic ... cannot presuppose any of these forms of reflection and laws of thinking, for these constitute part of its own content and have first to be established within the science." Cf. also EL, §1, p. 24 (*Werke* VIII: 41).

45   Cf. Hegel, SL, p. 74 (*Werke* V: 74), and EL, §1, p. 24 (*Werke* VIII: 41).

46   Hegel, EL, §17, p. 41 (*Werke* VIII: 62–63); translation modified. The word "ob-ject" is used as a translation of *Gegenstand.*

47   Hegel, EL, §9, p. 33 (*Werke* VIII: 52).

48   Hegel, EL, §3, pp. 26–27 (*Werke* VIII: 44), translation modified. Cf. also ibid., §20, pp. 49–50 (*Werke* VIII: 72–74), and SL, p. 33 (*Werke* V: 22). For more on Hegel's distinction between these various faculties, see Hegel, EM, §§445–468, pp. 188–228 (*Werke* X: 240–288).

49   Hegel, SL, p. 70 (*Werke* V: 68).

50   Hegel, EL, §3, p. 27 (*Werke* VIII: 44).

51   Ibid., §4, p. 27 (*Werke* VIII: 45).

52   Cf. Hegel, PS, pp. 49–50 (*Werke* III: 72).

53   Hegel is referring here to the subsequent sections of EL: see §§79–82.

54   Hegel, EL, §78, p. 124 (*Werke* VIII: 167–168), translation modified.

55   Houlgate, *Hegel's Logic,* p. 28.

56   Ibid., p. 40.

57   See Houlgate, *Hegel's Logic,* esp. chapters 3 and 4.

58   Cf. Wittgenstein's remark in *On Certainty,* with which Peirce's position is often compared: "But what about such a proposition as "I know I have a brain"? Can I doubt it? Grounds for *doubt* are lacking! Everything speaks in its favor, nothing against it" (Ludwig Wittgenstein, *On Certainty,* trans. Denis Paul and G.E.M. Anscombe (Oxford: Blackwell, 1969), §4, p. 2). Wittgenstein is clearly saying here that I cannot doubt "I have a brain" not because there are some things that must be presupposed in thinking and this is one of them but because the Cartesian does not give us sufficient *grounds* for questioning this belief even though it could turn out to be false ("Nevertheless it is imaginable that my skull should turn out empty when it was operated on").

59   Cf. Peirce CP 5.416, EP II: 335–336.

60   See Houlgate, *Hegel's Logic,* esp. chapter 3.

61   I am particularly grateful for comments from Chris Hookway and Stephen Houlgate on this chapter. A longer version is published in my *Hegelian Metaphysics* (Oxford: Oxford University Press, 2009), pp. 209–238.

28

The Analytic Neo-Hegelianism of John McDowell and Robert Brandom

PAUL REDDING

The historical origins of the analytic style that was to become dominant within academic philosophy in the English-speaking world are often traced to the work of Bertrand Russell and G. E. Moore at the turn of the twentieth century and portrayed as involving a radical break with the idealist philosophy that had bloomed in Britain at the end of the nineteenth. Congruent with this view, Hegel is typically taken as representing a type of philosophy that analytic philosophy assiduously avoids. His writings are regarded as indirect, metaphorical, and "darkly Teutonic," whereas analytic philosophers usually think of themselves as prizing the clarity of plain speech except when making use of the precision of scientific logical notation. This analytic directness, furthermore, is usually seen as consonant with the increasingly "naturalistic" outlook of analytic philosophy, especially as practiced in the United States. In contrast, Hegel is seen as regarding philosophical thought as mysteriously engaging with a content that is somehow generated out of the mind's (or "spirit's") own activities, linking philosophy more to art and religion than natural science. Moreover, even if the details of his criticisms have been largely forgotten, it is usually accepted that Russell showed Hegel's bizarre metaphysical doctrines to be based on some fundamental logical mistakes.[1]

Analytic philosophers might then find it odd when members of its clan refer to Hegel in positive terms and indeed try to relate contemporary developments within analytic philosophy to Hegelian precedents. Nevertheless, in the last decade of the twentieth century this happened in the case of two important analytic philosophers, John McDowell and Robert Brandom. If nothing else, the claims of McDowell and Brandom suggest something of the complexity of the relation that analytic philosophy actually bears to its philosophical past and in particular to the idealist tradition of the nineteenth century. We are reminded that analytic philosophy was fed not only by earlier forms of empiricism and common sense realism but also by the rationalist and arguably Kantian orientation of the founder of the logic on which it has always drawn, Gottlob Frege.[2] Indeed, Frege and Wittgenstein are now sometimes spoken of in relation to

A Companion to Hegel, First Edition. Edited by Stephen Houlgate and Michael Baur.
© 2011 Blackwell Publishing Ltd. Published 2011 by Blackwell Publishing Ltd.

those distinctly "continental" roots of analytic philosophy that coexisted with those established in the soil at Cambridge by Russell and Moore.[3]

McDowell and Brandom both appeal to the Kantian heritage of analytic philosophy, but in extending this heritage to Hegel they go far beyond other more modest attempts to reconcile analytic philosophy with Kantian idealism. Kant has always maintained a certain authority within the analytic world – within moral philosophy, especially – but *Hegel?* In what follows I will sketch something of the respective paths that have taken McDowell and Brandom from issues at the center of analytic debates to the devil's lair and after that will offer some thoughts about the possibility of further reconciliation of these seemingly antithetical approaches to philosophy.

John McDowell: From the Problems of Empiricism to Hegel's Absolute Idealism

McDowell commences his major work of 1994, *Mind and World*, by alluding to a dilemma that has been at the center of many analytic philosophical disputes through-out the second half of the twentieth century. Analytic philosophy has been afflicted by an "interminable oscillation"[4] between two opposed and equally untenable positions. One attempts to secure thought about the world in some passively received "givens" of perceptual experience; the other, rejecting the idea of "the given," leaves the application of concepts in judgment seemingly unconstrained.

In 1956, the American philosopher Wilfrid Sellars had provided what many consider to be the definitive critique of the first position.[5] Empiricists had traditionally tried to justify perceptual judgments by grounding them in the mind's capacity to passively record the bare givens of experience – an idea found in both Russell and Moore with the notion of "sense-data." But Sellars argued that it was useless to try to base the justification of judgments on something that was nonconceptual: a judgment, having propositional content, can only be justified by something to which it bears the right logical relation – something that itself has propositional content. Later, Donald Davidson was to make the same point with the idea that the only thing capable of justifying a belief was another belief.[6] Any notion of nonconceptual bare presences known with certainty and capable of grounding knowledge has to be given up.

However, although McDowell endorsed Sellars's classic criticism, he nevertheless pointed to the inverse danger awaiting the critic of the given, one he saw threatening in the work of Davidson himself. Abandoning the idea of a nonconceptual given capable of rationally constraining the application of concepts in perceptual judgments can lead to the embrace of an equally implausible position in which concept application is simply unconstrained. Thus for the critic of the given, "exercises of concepts threaten to degen-erate into moves in a self-contained game."[7] Davidson had attempted to hold onto the idea of the world's constraining "friction" on thought by stressing the causal con-straints exercised by the world on judgment, but this, claimed McDowell, could not capture the normative role that experience plays in providing thought with its objective purport. What is needed is a way of maintaining the idea of experience as exercising rational and not simply causal constraint on belief. Hence McDowell appealed to a "minimal empiricism" free of the "mythical" interpretation of the given as some nonconceptual "ultimate ground" or "bare presence" to which we can gesture in justifying our claims. Experience, then, if it is to be capable of providing rational constraint on thought must be already thoroughly conceptual, and it was this idea that pointed McDowell in the direction of Hegel.

According to McDowell, Hegel's predecessor, Immanuel Kant, had been on the verge of a philosophy that would be free from the type of intolerable oscillation besetting contemporary analytic philosophy, but with his idea that a form of nonconceptual representation – "intuition" – was required to provide concepts with their empirical content, Kant was himself still ensnared in a version of the myth of the given. This was because he regarded empirical intuitions as issuing from the impact of a supersensuous reality beyond the mind – a reality to which concepts could not stretch. Hegel, however, following the critique of Kant by Fichte and Schelling, had rejected the dualism of intuition and concept, and along with this had "urged that we must discard the supersensible in order to achieve a consistent idealism."[8]

It is common for analytic philosophers to regard the German idealists' abandonment of Kant's idea that concepts must be constrained by some nonconceptual given as precisely the move that leads to the result that McDowell captures with the metaphor of thought's "frictionless spinning in a void,"[9] but on McDowell's account that reaction is indicative of an approach held hostage to the myth of the given. In fact, Hegel's approach shows just how thought can be responsive to the world in virtue of what is presented in experience. Following Hegel, claims McDowell, we must think of the world itself as "made up of the sort of thing that one can think,"[10] and to think of the world in this way requires us to reject the image found in Kant that "the conceptual realm has an outer boundary" beyond which concepts cannot stretch. This is just what Hegel did in his "Absolute Idealism," and when we grasp this philosophy as capable of showing us the way beyond the oscillation of analytic philosophy, "we have arrived at a point from which we could start to domesticate the rhetoric of that philosophy."[11]

Perhaps the most obvious parallel to the Sellarsian "critique of the myth of the given" that can be found in Hegel is the theme that runs through the first three chapters of his *Phenomenology of Spirit*, in which Hegel aimed to demonstrate the inadequacy of the idea that knowledge can be founded on the pure givenness to consciousness of "objects" of various kinds. In the first of these chapters, "sense-certainty," the particular object given to consciousness is meant to be a simple nonconceptualized singular item, perhaps something akin to Kant's idea of an empirical intuition considered in isolation from any concept or its early analytic equivalent, the "sense-datum" postulated by Russell and Moore and supposedly known immediately in "acquaintance."[12] Not surprisingly, Hegel's way of proceeding here was different to that of Sellars, but there are clear correspondences, with Hegel attempting to show that the very idea of a singular presence as knowable in its "singularity," and hence nonconceptually, collapses in contradiction, with the object of sense-certainty coming to be replaced by a more complex object purportedly given in experience. The epistemological outlook of sense-certainty had conceived of the pure "this" as given in an immediate way without the participation of any general concept, but effectively drawing on the rationalist idea of the difference between perception and *ap*perception, Hegel suggests that such a "this" is at the same time taken by the experiencing subject as an instance of a more general category – we might say, taken as an instance of "thisness." In the object that comes to replace it – the object of the shape of consciousness that Hegel calls "perception" (*Wahrnehmen*) – the fact that it instantiates some general kind is made explicit, and so this object is effectively conceived as an Aristotelian substance – what Aristotle had referred to as a "*tode ti,*" a "this such." The implicitly conceptual nature of the content of sense-certainty has been replaced by the explicitly conceptual nature of the content of perception.

In Hegel's account the concept of such a pure self-subsistent object of "perception" with its particular categorical constitution undergoes a similar collapse and is replaced by a conception of something much more like a theoretically posited object found in modern scientific explanations of the world – the notion of a "force," for example. This outlook Hegel calls "the understanding." Thus what ultimately exists for the understanding are no longer simply everyday things perceived as instances of kinds: the understanding's "objects" are not "perceived" directly at all but *posited* as explanations of certain observable effects. Indeed there seems something characteristically "modern" in Hegel's "understanding," and the contrast between "the understanding" and "perception" appears to align with the difference that Sellars talked of in terms of different "scientific" and everyday "manifest" images of the world.[13] Although the contents of both perception and the understanding are "conceptual," they are nevertheless conceived as conceptual in different ways. Perception is conceptual in that its object will be conceived as a "this such" – an instance of some conceivable *kind*. In contrast, the content of the understanding, I suggest, is primarily *propositional*.

One of the founding texts of analytic philosophy, Ludwig Wittgenstein's *Tractatus Logico-Philosophicus*, commences with the claim that the world is made up not of objects but of "states of affairs" or "facts,"[14] and this seems to signal at the level of logic a distinction similar to that which Hegel attempts to capture with his distinction between the contents of perception and the understanding. Aristotle had thought of the world as made up of objects ("primary substances") that instantiated "kinds" and that were individuated by differentiating attributes. Hence he employed a "subject–predicate" or "term" logic, the basic units of which referred to the kinds of things objects instantiated on the one hand and the attributes that distinguished those instances on the other. In contrast, the Stoics had thought of the basic units of logic as whole *propositions* (a content that could be true or false) rather than separate terms. By the end of the nineteenth century, however, Gottlob Frege managed to unify these hitherto separate "term" and "propositional" logics in his revolutionary predicate calculus, and Wittgenstein's conception of the world as basically one of "facts" or "states of affairs" reflects this logical revolution. In short, for Wittgenstein and Frege, the "objects" of the world are no longer conceived as "Aristotelian" (that is, instances of kinds) but as components of "facts" or "states of affairs."[15] Hegel was philosophizing well before the changes in logic from which the modern analytic movement emerged, but I suggest he signals the type of change that was in the air with his distinction between the objects of perception and the posits of the understanding. McDowell, following Frege and Wittgenstein in their approach to logic, fails to capture Hegel's distinction.

In accordance with the *Tractatus'* injunction, McDowell thinks of the components of "the world" as thinkable "facts," but he also thinks of such propositional contents as just what the mind is open to in *perceptual experience*. That is, McDowell follows Hegel's criticism of sense-certainty in affirming the *conceptual* nature of perceptual

579

experience, but he ignores the differences in the ways in which cognitive content can be conceptual that Hegel signals in the difference between perception and the understanding. For McDowell (but not Hegel) perceptual content is not only conceptual but also *propositional*.

Assuming the modern Fregean approach to logical form, McDowell requires that the contents of perceptual experience are propositional for his minimally empiricist attempt to retain some experientially given rational constraint on judgment. This need disappears, however, in Brandom's account, as in *his* Hegelian development of Sellars's thought, the constraining influence on thought played by the world via perceptual experience is replaced by constraints exercised by others when they hold one's utterances to socially instituted norms. At this point then we might switch our attention to Brandom's version of "Pittsburgh neo-Hegelianism" in order to pursue further the purported parallels between contemporary analytic philosophy and Hegel's idealism.

Robert Brandom: From the Problems of "Representationalism" to Hegel's "Inferentialism"

In 1994, the year of the publication of *Mind and World*, Robert Brandom, a colleague of McDowell's at the University of Pittsburgh, published a work, *Making It Explicit*, that also made strong claims as to the relevance of Hegel for analytic philosophy.[16] In developing his appeal to Hegel in that book, however, Brandom has invoked quite different aspects of Hegelianism and drawn on rather different consequences from Sellars's critique of the myth of the given than those leading to McDowell's "minimal empiricism."

Making It Explicit is fundamentally a work in philosophy of language and philosophical semantics, and among its heroes are the key thinkers of the "continental" roots of analytic philosophy, Gottlob Frege and Ludwig Wittgenstein. Influenced not only by Sellars but also by Richard Rorty's deployment of Sellars's ideas in his 1979 critique of analytic philosophy, *Philosophy and the Mirror of Nature*,[17] Brandom refers to Hegel as the forebear of his own attack on the dominant "representationalist" paradigm within analytic philosophy's attitude to meaning. Representationalists classically think of words as names for worldly things, events, or states of affairs. However, the representationalists' picture, claims Brandom, has been undermined within analytic philosophy along with the myth of the given, and in contrast he puts forward his so-called "inferentialist" approach to the semantic content of words.

Like McDowell, Brandom philosophizes in the wake of Frege's revolutionizing of logic in the late nineteenth century, finding the origins of his own inferentialist semantics in Frege's early approach to semantics from which Frege himself retreated in later work and which has been overlooked by most of his analytic followers. For an inferentialist the meaning of words is seen as coming not from any one-to-one "representational" relation existing either between the words and things or properties (as with Aristotle) or between the contents of judgments and "facts" (as with most followers of Frege), but from the patterns of inference within which asserted sentences stand. Brandom focuses on Frege's "context principle" – the principle that "the meaning of a word must be asked for in the context of a proposition, not in isolation"[18] – that had been exploited by Wittgenstein in the *Tractatus*.[19] Starting with this idea that the primary semantic units in language are not individual words but sentences with full propositional content, Brandom then, following Wittgenstein in his *later* writings,[20] thinks of sentences as in turn gaining their meanings by the roles they play in "language games." This move not only broadens the contexts appealed to in the "context principle" but makes it clearer that the meaning of structures such as sentences are to be thought of in terms of the pragmatics of language use and brings analytic philosophy into contact with the naturalistic pragmatism of American philosophy, a pragmatism that itself in its nineteenth-century form had been influenced by the thought of Hegel.

Sellars also had looked to the role played by sentences in language games, but his interest was in the somewhat rationalistically conceived language games involving the making of assertions and the asking for and giving of *reasons* for them. To give reasons for my assertion of sentence *S* is to place the content of *S* in an "inferential" relation to that of the sentence that I offer *as* its reason, an understanding that gives Brandom a way of widening the context of the "context principle." The word may have a meaning in the context of some *S*, but *S* itself has its meaning in the context of a wider slab of actual or potential discourse, the totality of linked sentences that stand in inferential relations to *S*. Not only do words not stand in one-to-one or one-to-many relations with objects, properties, or relations, neither do sentences stand in one-to-one or one-to-many relations with "facts" or "states of affairs." The network of meaning-giving relations connects words in virtue of the inferential relations standing between the sentences within which the words appear, an image found in Quine's widely influential image of the "web of belief."

This standpoint now provides a perspective from which the history of modern philosophy looks very different from standard accounts given within analytic philosophy. If one favors an inferentialist semantics over a representationalist one, then it will be the views of Leibniz rather than, say, Locke, that will appear as an early anticipation of the correct view. From among Leibniz's inheritors, Brandom points to Kant as the thinker who most clearly grasped the "primacy of the propositional" in semantics – the idea that the "fundamental unit of awareness or cognition, the minimum graspable, is the *judgment*."[21] But Kant's version of rationalism, in its appeal to the role of empirical intuitions, still held onto the idea of something (some mental equivalent of an independent subsentential unit of language) *given* – a notion in tension with Kant's insight into the primacy of the propositional. But from the inferentialist perspective, the idea of needing to secure the empirical content of a concept by appeal to something like the intuitions with which it is linked becomes redundant.

The idea that concepts gained empirical content in virtue of the fact that they were found in judgments that were inferentially linked within a network of judgments, thinks Brandom, had been implicit in Kant's notion of the unity of judgments within the "transcendental unity of apperception."[22] However, the inferentialist move was only made explicit by Hegel, who abandoned Kant's dualism of intuitions and concepts and so was able "to complete the inversion of the traditional order of semantic explanation by beginning with a concept of experience as inferential activity and discussing the making of judgments and the development of concepts entirely in terms of the roles they play in that inferential activity."[23] Such an inferentially mediated conceptual holism is just the outlook expressed in Hegel's classic claim that "the syllogism is the truth of the judgment."[24]

Once more the easiest way to initially align Brandom with Hegel is to appeal to the opening chapters of the *Phenomenology of Spirit*. As we have seen, Hegel's transition from sense-certainty to perception involved a radical change in the categorical structure of the very object supposedly "given" to a passively conceived receptive consciousness, and further changes are found between the objects of perception and the understanding. I have described the objects of Hegel's "perception" chapter as classically Aristotelian – a perceptual object is an instance of a kind about which some perceivable property is predicated in such a way that such a property is seen as excluding some contrary properties. Aristotelian "term" logic, however, is not so easily adapted to the sorts of judgments involved in the more mediated structures of the understanding. Rather than single contentful judgments being at issue as in perception, in the understanding what comes to the fore are the inferential relations between judgments, and here a propositionally based logic is more appropriate. (One should recall that the items connected in Aristotelian syllogisms are the terms into which propositions or judgments are resolved rather than those propositions or judgments themselves.[25])

As earlier noted, in Hegel's time there had been no simple way to formally represent the resolution of a proposition into its constituent parts such that "propositional" and "term" logics could be in some way unified. Unifying such traditionally opposed approaches was one aspect of Frege's later achievement in logic. But Frege's subsequent way of extracting something like the original subject–predicate structure out of a given proposition (by adapting the mathematical form of analysis into "argument" and "function") was to produce a purported subject–predicate structure that was wholly different to the one of traditional term logic. For Frege, argument terms were fundamentally conceived as *singular* terms, but singular terms, such as proper names, had officially been denied a role in Aristotelian syllogisms. In Aristotle's syllogistic logic, the subject term of a judgment must include some "sortal" term to capture the *kind* to which the object belonged, as can be seen in the fact that the two judgment forms permitted have subjects that in respect of "quantity" are either "universal" (as in "All Greeks are mortal") or "particular" (as in "Some Greeks are bearded"). Adapted to perceptual judgments about individual objects, one could use a form of judgment like, say, "*This Greek* is mortal" within a syllogism, but "officially" syllogistic reasoning excluded properly *singular* judgments as in "*Socrates* is mortal." Thus the object picked out by an argument term in Frege's analysis, when that term is thought of as a singular term, could not be thought of as of the same categorical type as the object of Hegel's "perception," which is to be treated as an instance of a universal, a "this such," but it was perfect for thinking of what was picked out in "the understanding" if we think of *its* constitutive structures as having a proposition based rather than term based logic. As Frege was to show, if one takes the proposition as semantically basic and then decomposes it into its parts, the resulting "subject" terms will be singular.

Brandom, however, challenges the standard *representationalist* understanding of Fregean argument terms as "singular terms" that can be mapped in a one-to-one relation to individual worldly entities. Following the dictates of the context principle, one can construe the semantic properties of singular terms in terms of the role they play in sentences. To talk of singular reference was, as Quine had put it, "only a picturesque way of alluding to the distinctive grammatical roles that singular and general terms play in sentences. It is by grammatical role that general and singular terms are properly to be distinguished."[26] One might think of the naming relation as absolutely fundamental to language, but Quine's radical critique of the primacy of the denoting of singular terms was in fact an extension of a challenge to our most basic assumptions about language that had been part of the analytic movement since its inception.

From the earliest application of Fregean logic to philosophy by Russell, analytic philosophers had used Fregean propositionally based "predicate calculus" to reinterpret ("regiment") the logical form of sentences of ordinary language. Russell had classically done this both for what in Aristotelian logic were treated as universally affirmative judgments (as in "*All Greeks* are mortal") and for sentences whose subjects were definite descriptions (as in "*The teacher of Plato* was mortal"). Especially with the latter case, Russell had been trying to address the problem of nonreferring terms, as with his celebrated example, the definite description "the present king of France."[27] But such a technique of reinterpreting the apparent "subject" term of the sentence was just what was later extended by Quine to include proper names like "Socrates" or "Pegasus," traditionally thought of as paradigm singular terms. For Quine, a proper name such as "Pegasus" was to be treated as a predicate, in this case, the verb "is-Pegasus" or "pegasizes."[28] In earlier cases of such regimentation, the point had been to show that a sentence such as "All Greeks are mortal" shouldn't really be thought as being "about" what the subject term apparently names, here *all Greeks*. Because Russell had schematized the sentence as a universally quantified *conditional* (roughly, for all things "*if* that thing is a Greek, *then* it is mortal"), the sentence itself should be thought of as "about" the totality of things (effectively, the whole universe, over which the quantifier "ranged"). Russell's original point had been that it was erroneous to think of "All Greeks are mortal" as structurally akin to "Socrates is mortal," but Quine was to undercut the very contrast by treating "Socrates is mortal" in just the same way! For Quine, "Socrates is mortal" was to be effectively treated in terms of a bound quantifier that "ranged" over a domain of discourse and as stating that if something is found that *socratizes*, then that thing is mortal. In fact, as Quine was well aware,[29] his move of treating proper names as predicates could be seen as having a precedent in the way that medieval scholastic logicians had got around Aristotle's prohibition on using singular judgments within syllogisms. In the context of syllogisms, the sentence "Socrates is mortal" could be treated as having the logical form of a universal judgment on the grounds that, like "All Greeks are mortal," it is exceptionless.[30] But as we have seen, treating something simultaneously as a singular and a universal was just what Hegel had claimed operated within "sense-certainty."

As proper names had provided the paradigm form of the way we think of ourselves as picking out or "representing" entities able to be "given," in Quine's hands post-Fregean logic came to disrupt radically the "representationalist" dimensions of language by attacking the basic referential notion of naming. As he put it, names were "altogether immaterial to the ontological issue."[31] Thus Quine could regard physical objects as "posits" that explain sensory experiences and are "comparable, epistemologically, to the gods of Homer."[32] Congruent with this, it would seem that the closest thing in natural language to what in Quine's logical language is a *referring term* is a relative pronoun, such as "who" or "which," serving merely to tie predicate terms together.[33]

Quine maintained the independence of this elimination of reference from the question of the actual ontology to which one subscribed, but it neatly fitted his strongly scientistic conception of the world in which one can secure the truth value of a sentence without committing oneself to the existence of things apparently referred to in that sentence.[34] For example, one might want to think of the sentence "the walls are bright yellow" as stating a truth even if one didn't include the terms "walls" and "yellow" among the terms of one's ultimate explanatory theories.

I have suggested that understood in this way, the reinterpretations of the nature of our referring terms going from Russell to Quine would give an analytic analog of the idea Hegel pursues with his account of the passage from the "shape of consciousness" called "perception" to that of "the understanding." With Quine, those apparently representational assumptions about the nature of what is given to consciousness in "perception" have now been thoroughly undermined: judgments might seem to be "about" the everyday things we consciously use them of, but they are really about some posited "whatever" it is (elements of our best scientific explanations) that ultimately secures the truth of those judgments. It was just this radical detachment of the ultimate references of our judgments from the experienceable objects that they are naively taken to be about that motivates McDowell's concern to find something that stops thought's "frictionless spinning in the void." In McDowell's account, however, it leads to the idea – problematic from both Hegelian and analytic perspectives – that the contents of *perceptual* experience are fundamentally *propositional*. In Brandom's account, by contrast, we find a solution to this problem that invokes ideas from Hegel's solution to the problems of "the understanding" not by retreating to any "minimal empiricism" but by moving forward to Hegel's treatment of self-consciousness in the next chapter of his *Phenomenology of Spirit*. Brandom thus appeals to the intersubjective pragmatic infrastructure that in his theory underpins what we might think of as the mind's capacity to be "about" the world, an account that he links to Hegel's famous "recognitive" account of "spirit [*Geist*]."

Hegel and Brandom on the Recognitive Infrastructure of Intentionality

In Hegel's account of *understanding* as a shape of consciousness, such a consciousness had come to the self-understanding that the object it had taken as given was in fact in no sense "given" at all but rather "posited" by itself – in Quinian terms, the value of a bound variable, some *whatever* that was responsible for the patterned events of one's experience. In Hegel's telling of this story, consciousness responds to the realization that what was previously thought to be "given" is actually an active posit, with the idea that such an object must be its creation. Thus in this new orientation, the assumption from which "consciousness" had started has been reversed: at the start of the series sense-certainty, perception, and the understanding, the "given" *object* was conceived as the "truth" of consciousness itself, but now consciousness has come to regard *itself* as "the truth" of its object.[35] This new cognitive state is thus properly understood as a form of *self*-consciousness, and as productive of its object, it is understood as a primarily *practical* rather than *theoretical* intentional state. This is the starting point from which Hegel commences in the *Phenomenology of Spirit*, in chapter 4 ("The Truth of Self-Certainty"), section B ("Self-Consciousness").

In this chapter the analysis becomes focused on the same internal contradictions of a now practical self-consciousness that had earlier plagued the shapes of consciousness in chapters 1 to 3. Self-consciousness takes its object to be really nothing more than that which it wills, and its immediate form, "self-certainty," is that of a type of immediately appetitive and devouring subject, but this form of self-consciousness also will be revealed to be self-contradictory. Consider a primitive appetitive subject who desires some singular "this" and, devouring it, satisfies its appetite. In annihilating the previously independent object (the "this"), it annihilates the very thing that allowed it to be conscious of itself as a desirer. From the failure of this, Hegel thinks, this self-consciousness will somehow come to see that the only stable "mediating" object for it would be one that maintains its independence in the relation, and the only thing capable of that, on this model, is another self-consciousness.

It is this lesson that is worked through in the now famous passage from a unitary *desiring* self-consciousness to the duality of *mutually recognizing* ones in the "master-slave" section of the *Phenomenology*.[36] In this section Hegel ultimately comes to focus on the nature of the relationship that holds between the two self-consciousnesses, the relationship of mutual "recognition" or acknowledgment (*Anerkennung*). It is in these passages that Hegel first suggests that definite patterns of such relationships of recognition actually constitute what he refers to as "Spirit" (*Geist*).[37] Recognition is by its very nature a reciprocal affair, but this is not at all at first apparent to the members of the relationship of master and slave. Thus the master regards his slave as a mere thing-like instrument of his will whose dependent nature stands in stark contrast to his own independence. However the master is in fact *dependent* upon his slave for that "free" recognition that he needs in order to be the properly "spiritual" (*geistig*) being that he takes himself to be. Both master and slave must eventually learn that the master's independence is equally dependent upon that passive material objectivity he recognizes in his slave, and that the slave's objectivity in truth harbors an active, independent subjectivity that he recognizes in his master. As the earlier instances of objective givenness, this particular instance of the recognitive relation will be shown to be self-contradictory: they will collapse and be replaced by some other, more complex form.

In Brandom's account, this idea of the fundamental nature of this intersubjective recognitive relationship is worked out within a theory of the pragmatics of language use. Within the Brandomian framework, we might then think of a problem analogous to McDowell's "frictionless thought" and the master's unilateral self-ascription of free agency. For example, a speaker might think, as did Lewis Carroll's Humpty Dumpty, that she could mean by her words whatever she wanted them to mean. Such a conception of verbal "mastery" would be in relation to one of total dependence or subservience on the part of that speaker's interlocutor. But drawing on ideas from Wittgenstein's later conception of "rule-following," Brandom *denies* the conceptual possibility of any isolated individual "instituting" of the type of semantic relation that we regard as relating words to world. In Brandom's account, interlocutors thus stand in the same relations of "reciprocal recognition" that Hegel finds at the heart of all human relations, even the apparently asymmetric ones of slavery. Although there is nothing simply "given" from the world to normatively constrain the semantic content of our claims,[38]

585

there are norms concerning the way words are put together and used in contexts that are beyond the "legislative" powers of any individual speaker. The "norm-instituting" practices responsible for the semantic relations that enable our words to bear on the world are necessarily social ones, at the heart of which are relations of reciprocal recognition.

Thus the way that I string words together and apply the resulting sentences is not answerable to things or facts in the world as commonly understood. In my speaking I am only answerable to my interlocutor as a recognized bearer of the social norms that we co-institute in the very process of conversing. When I utter, for example, "Socrates is ugly," my sentence does not confront some independently real "fact" in the world that determines its truth value. (A "fact" for Brandom is just a true proposition, the content of an utterance that is true, and its truth in turn is explained in terms of what is preserved in correct inferences. From Brandom's conceptually holistic point of view, to talk of something that makes the utterance true would be to talk of the world as a whole.) Rather, if it "confronts" anything in particular, it will be something like *your* disposition to give utterance to some *contrary* content, for example, "Socrates is beautiful"! Such a response will challenge my "entitlement" to my original words, and so challenge me to reveal their "title" by coming up with a reason backing up my state-ment. I might, for example, say something like "Socrates has an offensively snub nose," an assertion that is meant to stand in the appropriate inferential relation to my earlier one. But here the response will be appropriate only if there is consensus on the legiti-macy of the pattern of "material inference" from "Such and such has a snub nose" to "Such and such is ugly," and of course my entitlement to that assumption could be further challenged.

For Brandom, the discipline of logic is what results when we reflectively give chal-lengeable expression to the social norms that govern our inferential practices in a way analogous to that in which expression has here been given to our *aesthetic* norms. Making such norms "explicit" is, he thinks, ultimately what Hegel was doing in his massive *Science of Logic*.

We might then sum up some of the ways in which the so-called "Pittsburgh Neo-Hegelianism" of McDowell and Brandom approximates but remains distinct from the thought of the historical Hegel. McDowell, in his critique of the "myth of the given," takes over from Hegel the idea that the content of experience is fully conceptual, but McDowell departs from Hegel in equating the conceptual nature of perception with the thesis that perceptual content is propositional, thereby collapsing what Hegel distin-guishes as perception and the understanding. Like McDowell, Brandom's Hegelianism derives from Sellars's critique of the "myth of the given," but largely bypassing percep-tual experience, he concentrates more on the idea that the semantic contents of our judgments are derived from their inferential relations in the "space of reasons." And taking this "space of reasons" as grounded in historically changing social practices of assertion, questioning, and reason giving, he thereby interprets Hegel's key concepts of "recognition" and "spirit" or "Geist" in terms of his own "social pragmatics." However, the same objection that was raised for McDowell might be raised for Brandom: relying exclusively on the logic of Frege for his "inferentialist" approach to semantic content, Brandom seems also to have eliminated any structural distinction between perception and understanding as "shapes of consciousness."

586

Dialectical Logic and Ontology

In relation to the entirety of the systematic content of Hegel's philosophy, the work of the "Pittsburgh Neo-Hegelians" bears on relatively few aspects of Hegel's thought. Nevertheless, what they do bear upon are surely those parts that are central to his overall system, and this had certainly not been usual in cases where analytic philosophers had engaged with Hegel's work. In particular concrete areas of his philosophy, especially in the area of political philosophy, Hegel has not lacked analytically trained sympathetic readers, but this has usually been at the expense of those areas being detached from Hegel's systematic "logical" concerns. Hegel himself had insisted on the logic at the heart of his system, and that was the logic that Russell dismissed as antiquated and responsible for faulty metaphysical assumptions. The attempts of McDowell and Brandom, which draw on modern post-Fregean logic, to rehabilitate just those core logical areas of Hegel's thought for which he has been traditionally dismissed deserve to be taken seriously. This said, however, one does not find much in the work of either that engages with that aspect of Hegel's logic for which he is probably most well known – the so-called "dialectical" nature of his logic with its controversial claims about the nature of "contradiction."[39] We might therefore ask after the possibility of making sense of Hegel's dialectic within an otherwise analytic version of Hegel's logical thought. Indeed, it may be that the structural distinction between perception and the understanding that is largely effaced by McDowell and Brandom is particularly relevant here.

In *The Problems of Philosophy*, Bertrand Russell notes of the three self-evident logical principles, the laws of *identity*, *contradiction*, and *excluded middle*, that rather than being laws primarily pertaining to *thoughts*, they should be regarded as laws pertaining to *existence* – laws "that things behave in accordance with."[40] Perhaps nothing about Hegel's way of thinking here concerns analytic philosophers as much as his apparent denial of just these three laws. When Russell talks of the law of contradiction, he refers to what is often called the law of *noncontradiction*: "Nothing can both be and not be."[41] But when Hegel invokes the law of contradiction, he means it literally: it is the law that "*everything is inherently contradictory*,"[42] and with this he attacks the purported "first law of thought ... A = A."[43] This conception of identity and the associated law of non-contradiction are for Hegel characteristics of "reflection" and "the understanding" rather than speculative "reason," and are expressions of what he calls the "affirmative principle," which he attributes to Plato but from which he exempts Aristotle: "While ... with Plato the main consideration is the affirmative principle, the Idea as only abstractly identical with itself, in Aristotle there is added and made conspicuous the moment of negativity, not as change, nor yet as nullity, but as difference or determination."[44]

Among the most immediate roots of Hegel's dialectical logic is surely the subject matter that is covered in "Division Two" of Kant's *Critique of Pure Reason*, "The Transcendental Dialectic," in which contradiction is linked to the unfettered operations of inferential reason. Kant's basic argument there is well known: metaphysics had classically sought knowledge of the world as it is "in itself" on the basis of inferential reasoning from pure concepts alone, thus applying concepts beyond those limits that had been established earlier in "The Transcendental Analytic." Properly, concepts, both empirical and pure, should be thought of as applying to contents that are given in

587

PAUL REDDING

"intuition," a form of representation that in being both "singular" and "immediate" stands in contrast to the "general" and "mediated" nature of conceptual representation. For Kant, inferential reasoning can aid in the unification of knowledge, as when we posit entities that explain certain observable phenomena.[45] But there are definite limits to this: a potentially rational explanation of appearances can be extended to posit some ultimately nonappearing entity as in classical metaphysics. That something has gone wrong in such forms of thought, Kant thinks, is signaled in the fact that it falls into irresolvable "antinomies."

In chapter 2 of the "Transcendental Dialectic," the "Antinomies of Pure Reason," Kant tracks how attempts at achieving "absolute totality in the synthesis of appearances," an "allegedly pure (rational) cosmology," will fall into contradictorily opposed views that seem intrinsically resistant to any rational resolution.[46] Ultimately, Kant's diagnosis of such problems of metaphysics amounts to the claim that in all such metaphysical claims, the distinction between intuition and concept as different representational forms has been effaced. Although concepts and intuitions both in some sense unify manifolds, the modes of unification are clearly different. Traditionally, concepts have been conceived as unifying knowledge by grouping particulars under some general concept as when we bring particular cats under the genus "cat," or when we bring the genus itself under some higher one, such as "mammal." Certain features of the behavior of my cat, Socrates, might be explained by features possessed by cats in general, but in turn cats may share features with all other mammals, and so on. Here the unity achieved will be a "distributive" unity among *judgments* about cats and other things, and Kant warns us against confusing this type of conceptually mediated unity with the unity that we think of as given in intuition – the unity of some experienced spatio–temporal object: my cat Socrates, for example. We may not normally be tempted to think of the genus "cat" as a large cat-like empirical object, but this seems to be the type of error that, according to Kant, leads us to think of the world as a whole as a type of object about which we can have conceptual knowledge. Thus Kant distinguishes the "*distributive* unity of the use of the understanding in experience" from a "collective unity of a whole of experience,"[47] and thinks we are led to confuse these types of unity on the basis of what he calls "transcendental illusion"[48] or "transcendental subreption."[49]

Kant's warnings about these traps of reasoning using traditional syllogistic logic indeed seem to converge with Russell's critique of the faulty metaphysics that he saw resulting from traditional logic, the same critique that motivated his practice of reinterpreting the logical structure of traditionally conceived universal affirmative judgments. For Russell, we should not think of the logical structure of "all cats have two kidneys" on the model of "Socrates has two kidneys." "All cats" do not, in short, name or refer to some kind of thing that is considered as the object about which "has two kidneys" could be predicated. On Kant's diagnosis, traditional metaphysics seems to conceive of its task along these lines, and the result is its falling into contradiction. Moreover, Kant's diagnosis of the problems here seems close to Russell's concerns about confusing the apparent subjects of universal judgments with singular things. In "transcendental subreption," concepts are confused with intuitions; concepts, it will be remembered, are general representations, and intuitions are singular. In standard set-theoretic interpretations of Frege's logic, a concept corresponds to a class of entities, and singular

588

representations refer to members of such classes. Russell famously pursued the paradoxes and antinomies that resulted from confusing these two ideas.[50]

We have glimpsed something along the lines of this phenomenon already in Hegel's account of "sense-certainty." The singular "this" of experience was, at the same time, taken by the experiencing subject as an instance of a more general category, "thisness." The object of sense-certainty was meant to be irreducibly singular but at the same time it instantiated a type of universality and thus became embroiled in the type of dilemma that, according to Kant, affected metaphysical thought traditionally conceived. However, though Kant seemed to have regarded the self-contradicting thought of metaphysics as avoidable, Hegel considered this "dialectic" as an essential dimension to any self-reflecting thought at all; as an essential dimension of thought, it is thereby regarded as an essential dimension of the objects presented to us *in* thought.

To preserve something of this dialectical structure within analytic philosophy it would seem that we would need to make sense of at least three ideas: first, the idea that "objects" have not fixed but *variable* logical or categorical structures; next, that this variation is not random but in some way orderly; and finally, that this orderly variation is somehow bound up with the rational working out of the "contradictions" internal to each of these constitutive structures considered in isolation from the others. Making sense of these ideas from within the framework of analytic philosophy would undoubtedly be a challenge, but perhaps the same resources upon which McDowell and Brandom have drawn may still be useful here.

Hegel's idea in the opening chapters of the *Phenomenology of Spirit* of a succession of "shapes of consciousness," when translated into the framework of analytic concerns with issues of reference and meaning, suggests the idea of a plurality of ways of thinking and talking about objects such that grammatically distinct ways correlate with differently structured objects. I have suggested that Hegel's objects of "perception" are conceived basically as "Aristotelian" objects that might typically be thought of as expressed in everyday unreflective discourse with a traditional subject–predicate grammatical structure. But as we have seen, this discourse can be "regimented" into forms of discourse with overtly different grammatical forms. We might think, then, that when Russell paraphrases a sentence whose subject is a definite description as one whose form is given in terms of quantifiers and variables, those sentences have in some sense become "about" objects with a different categorical structure, the "posits" of the Hegelian "understanding." Of course on one way of thinking of this phenomenon, there has been no real change within the nature of the "objects" referred to. The most obvious way to take the activity of analysis is to think of the logical paraphrase as the sentence that truly captures the actual logical structure of the object it is about, and to think that the nonparaphrased sentence is not really at all about the purported object it appears to be about. Russell, after all, wanted to deny that the sentence "All Greeks are mortal" was in any way about some collectively conceived object, "all Greeks." Along these lines, many scientific eliminativists want to deny the reality of many of the objects we purport to perceive and talk about.

This attitude, however, is the attitude that idealism of the Kantian variety opposes. This idealism was, after all, developed on the basis of the idea that the "form" of objects of cognition, including their conceptual form, should not be thought of as something that belonged to the objects "in themselves." Within analytic philosophy, such a distinctly Kantian approach might be thought to be found in those critical of the Russellian view that the logical structure of our thought or talk is dictated by the logical structure of an independently considered world. Indeed, the very collapse of the idea of reference, initiated by Russell and made explicit in thinkers like Quine and Davidson, itself suggests a collapse of the classically Russellian view. Within analytic philosophy, however, the immediately resulting view is often like that found in Hegel's "self-certainty," the type of view McDowell diagnoses as "rebounding" from the myth of the given.

In the view that so rebounds, the objects of thought will be conceivable as capable of variation and change because they are mere reflections of the variable and changeable ways in which we talk about them, but McDowell is correct that Hegel was critical of any such "subjectively idealist" alternative to a precritical realism. Hegel's way of avoiding this type of subjectivism was to appeal to "reason," which he conceived of in a way resembling Aristotle's thought of a world-pervading "nous." Different types of objects, then, had to be linked in logical ways rather than simply juxtaposed relativistically, and this was achieved by the idea of the contradictory nature of objects themselves within any one shape of consciousness or *Geist* and the idea that these contradictions would be resolved with the passage to some succeeding shape. We return again, then, to the peculiar idea of the contradictory nature of such objects, but it should be kept in mind how Kant's resistance to the idea that the logical structure of thought reflects, even ideally, the logical structure of the world considered independently of thought (that is, considered "in itself") opens up the possibility of difference within the ways objects can be logically constituted and so the possibility of such objects themselves being "contradictory."

One way this might perhaps be approached within the analytic frame is to take up the theme of the intersubjective nature of language pursued by Brandom, the idea that links to the primacy of the idea of intersubjective recognition in Hegel. Think, for example, of a situation in which I am discussing with an interlocutor the color of some "object" we are both currently perceiving. Disagreement may lead us to reflectively place our opposing claims within the "space of reasons," and we start to bring diverse theoretical considerations to bear on each other's judgment (the quality of the ambient lighting and the possibility of color blindness, for example). Qua object of "perception," this object will have the particular logical structure of a substance whose color is thought of as an immediate perceivable attribute. However, this becomes replaced by the posit of a more theoretical discourse – the "whatever" that is responsible for our experience of color. We want to say that our simply talking about it couldn't have changed the object and that it is "the same" object discussed in different ways, but if as Wittgenstein held, "grammar tells us what kind of object anything is,"[51] and here our logical grammar has changed, then there seems something wrong with expressing our intuition in this way. We have no available unproblematic way of individuating the thing that is supposed to remain the same. From a Russellian perspective, this is surely irrational, but the reasons for this, the idea that there is an unproblematic, atomistically conceived, external self-identical referent for the sentence, is just what Quine's development of Russell's innovations seems to have eliminated.[52] Quine, we might say, had prised analytic philosophy away from Russell's Platonic "principle of affirmation," and put analytic philosophy on its path to Hegelianism, even perhaps one with a potential for some kind of "dialectical" logic intact.[53]

590

Notes

1   See, e.g., Bertrand Russell, *Our Knowledge of the External World* (London: Allen and Unwin, 1914), 48.

2   On the Kantian roots of Frege's philosophy see, e.g., Hans Sluga, *Frege* (London: Routledge, 1980), and Robert Hanna, *Kant and the Foundations of Analytic Philosophy* (Oxford: Clarendon Press, 2001).

3   See, e.g., Gottfried Gabriel, "Frege, Lotze, and the Continental Roots of Early Analytic Philosophy," in *From Frege to Wittgenstein: Perspectives on Early Analytic Philosophy*, ed. Erich Reck (Oxford: Oxford University Press, 2002).

4   John McDowell, *Mind and World*, second paperback edition with a new introduction (Cambridge, Mass.: Harvard University Press. 1996), 9 and *passim*.

5   Wilfrid Sellars, *Empiricism and the Philosophy of Mind*, with introduction by Richard Rorty and study guide by Robert Brandom (Cambridge, Mass.: Harvard University Press, 1997). This had been first delivered as "The Myth of the Given: Three Lectures on Empiricism and Philosophy of Mind" at the University of London in 1956.

6   "The trouble we have been running into is that the justification seems to depend on the awareness [of having the sensation], which is just another belief. ... The relation between a sensation and a belief cannot be logical, since sensations are not beliefs or other propositional attitudes." Donald Davidson, "A Coherence Theory of Truth and Knowledge," in *Kant oder Hegel?* ed. Dieter Henrich (Stuttgart: Klett–Cotta, 1983), 427–428.

7   McDowell, *Mind and World*, 5.

8   Ibid., 44.

9   Ibid., 11 and *passim*.

10 Ibid., 27–28.

11 Ibid., 44.

12 See, e.g., Bertrand Russell, *The Problems of Philosophy* (London: Oxford University Press, 1959), 12. Russell had believed that Kant's account of intuition was essentially in agreement with his position on sense-data. Ibid., 85.

13 Wilfrid Sellars, "Philosophy and the Scientific Image of Man," in *Science, Perception and Reality* (London: Routledge and Kegan Paul, 1963), 5 and *passim*.

14 Ludwig Wittgenstein, *Tractatus Logico-Philosophicus*, trans. C. K. Ogden (London: Routledge and Kegan Paul, 1922), §§1 and 1.1.

15 This is reflected in the so-called context principle, wherein names have a meaning only in the context of a proposition, as discussed in the next section.

16 Robert Brandom, *Making It Explicit* (Cambridge, Mass.: Harvard University Press, 1994). See also his *Articulating Reasons* (Cambridge, Mass.: Harvard University Press, 2000). Brandom develops his inferentialist reading of Hegel in *Tales of the Mighty Dead: Historical Essays in the Metaphysics of Intentionality* (Cambridge, Mass.: Harvard University Press, 2002).

17 Richard Rorty, *Philosophy and the Mirror of Nature* (Princeton, N.J.: Princeton University Press, 1979).

18 Michael Beaney, ed., *The Frege Reader* (Oxford: Blackwell, 1997), 90.

19 "[O]nly in the nexus of a proposition has a name meaning." Wittgenstein, *Tractatus Logico-Philosophicus*, §3.3.

20 Especially, Ludwig Wittgenstein, *Philosophical Investigations: The German Text, with a Revised English Translation*, trans. G.E.M. Anscombe (Oxford: Wiley-Blackwell, 2001).

21 Brandom, *Articulating Reasons*, 159–160.

22 "The subtlety and sophistication of Kant's concept of representation is due in large part to the way in which it is integrated into his account of the inferential relations among judgments." Brandom, *Making It Explicit*, 92.

23 Ibid. In particular, Brandom finds in Hegel's methodological use of the combination of "mediation" and "determinate negation" ideas about the implicit structuring of the linguistic practice of the asking for and giving of reasons that are at the heart of his own rationalist pragmatism. In this way, the post-Fregean inferentialist movement toward a type of conceptual holism found in Wittgenstein, Sellars, Quine, Davidson, Rorty, and others effectively reprised the move found within post-Kantian idealism away from Kant's focus on judgments toward Hegel's on inferences.

24 G.W.F. Hegel, *Science of Logic*, trans. A. V. Miller (London: Allen and Unwin, 1969), 669.

25 See Aristotle, *Prior Analytics*, Book 1, in Aristotle, *The Categories, On Interpretation, and Prior Analytics*, ed. and trans. H. B. Cooke (Cambridge, Mass.: Harvard University Press, 1938).

26 W.V.O. Quine, *Word and Object* (Cambridge, Mass.: MIT Press, 1960), 96, quoted in Brandom, *Making It Explicit*, 361. As Quine had earlier put it, a singular term "need not name to be significant." *From a Logical Point of View* (New York: Harper and Row, 1961), 9.

27 See Russell's classic paper from 1905, "On Denoting," in Bertrand Russell, *Logic and Knowledge: Essays 1901–1950* (London: Allen and Unwin, 1956).

28 Quine, *From a Logical Point of View*, 8.

29 Thus "logicians in past centuries ... commonly treated a name such as 'Socrates' rather on a par logically with 'mortal' and 'man,' and as differing from these latter just in being true of fewer objects, viz. one." Quine, *Word and Object*, 181.

30 Quine's move was, of course, more radical. For the medievals, this was a matter of *accommodating* singular judgments within the framework of a term logic. For Quine, it effectively amounted to the *elimination* of the distinction between singularity and universality.

31 Quine, *From a Logical Point of View*, 12.

32 Ibid., 44–45.

33 "To be assumed as an entity is, purely and simply, to be reckoned as the value of a variable. In terms of the categories of traditional grammar, this amounts roughly to saying that to be is to be in the range of reference of a pronoun. Pronouns are the basic media of reference; nouns might better have been named propronouns." *From a Logical Point of View*, 13. See the detailed discussion of this point in David S. Oderberg, "Predicate Logic and Bare Particulars," in *The Old New Logic: Essays on the Philosophy of Fred Sommers*, ed. David S. Oderberg (Cambridge, Mass.: MIT Press, 2005).

34 See, e.g., Quine's discussion of accommodation of "half-entities in a second-grade system" in *Ontological Relativity and Other Essays* (New York: Columbia University Press, 1969), 24.

35 "The *necessary advance* from the previous shapes of consciousness for which their truth was a Thing, an 'other' than themselves, expresses just this, that not only is consciousness of a thing possible only for a self-consciousness, but that self-consciousness alone is the truth of those shapes." G.W.F. Hegel, *Phenomenology of Spirit*, trans. A. V. Miller (Oxford: Oxford University Press, 1977), ¶164.

36 Ibid., chapter 4, "A. Independence and Dependence of Self-Consciousness: Lordship and Bondage."

37 Ibid., ¶177.

38 There will always, of course, be some *causal constraint* exercised by the world in our perceptually based verbal responses to it, but the conflation of this with the idea of *rational constraint* – i.e., that to which we could appeal in justification – was just what Sellars had attacked as the "myth of the given."

39 I have explored Brandom's approach to the role of contradiction in Hegel in *Analytic Philosophy and the Return of Hegelian Thought* (Cambridge: Cambridge University Press, 2007), chapter 7.

40 Russell, *The Problems of Philosophy*, 72–73.

41 Ibid., 72.

42 Hegel, *Science of Logic*, 439.

43 Ibid., 413.

44 Hegel, *History of Philosophy*, vol. 2, 140. It should be noted here that that aspect of Aristotle that Hegel has in mind here is his conception of God as *"noesis noeseos noesis,"* "thought thinking itself."

45 This happens, for example, when a physician posits the presence of some underlying aetiological agent causing the pattern of symptoms identified as a certain disease.

46 Kant, *Critique of Pure Reason*, A406–408/B432–435.

47 Ibid., A582/B610.

48 Ibid., A293–303/B349–359.

49 In the "Inaugural Dissertation," Kant had called a "metaphysical fallacy of subreption" a "confusion of what belongs to the understanding with what is sensitive." Immanuel Kant, *Theoretical Philosophy, 1755–1770*, ed. and trans. David Walford and Ralf Meerbote (Cambridge: Cambridge University Press, 1992), 408.

50 Thus, in 1902 Russell conveyed to Frege the bad news of the inconsistency afflicting one of the axioms of his attempt to ground arithmetic in logic. The axiom required that one think of a certain expression as containing a term that simultaneously played the role of *function* with a particular argument and *the argument* of that function. Russell's posed the problem in terms of a class of classes that could not be considered members of themselves.

51 Wittgenstein, *Philosophical Investigations*, §373.

52 One could say that there is an enduring "external" referent for our changing sentences, the world itself. (After all, once we have Russellized a sentence such as "all Greeks are mortal" into "if something is a Greek, then it is mortal," there is still *something* that makes the new sentence, if true, true: the world itself). I would suspect that Hegel could be satisfied with this. What we have to avoid is taking this thought any further and thinking that there was something to be said about *the way* the world is that is responsible for the truth. For this, we have to attribute to the world a form, and then we are back in the problem.

53 I would like to thank Stephen Houlgate for very helpful feedback on an earlier version of this chapter.

29

Différance as Negativity: The Hegelian Remains of Derrida's Philosophy

KARIN DE BOER

1. Introduction

Derrida's texts go against the grain of academic philosophy in many ways. Following in Kierkegaard's wake, Derrida employs all sorts of rhetorical devices to interrupt or defer the conceptual line of thought he wishes to put across. Whereas his provocative contributions to contemporary thought have earned him fame in circles of literary theory, they have been neglected or even despised by a considerable part of the philosophical world.[1] I believe that this latter assessment is not justified. Throughout his work, Derrida develops a radical critique of both metaphysics and the metaphysical assumptions informing modern culture, science, and politics. In this respect, his thought is more deeply akin to that of Kant and Hegel than may appear at first sight.

Evidently, Derrida's deconstructive readings target these two giants of modern thought as well. As far as his struggle with Hegel is concerned, Derrida clearly issues from the critical tradition forged by, among others, Marx, Kierkegaard, Adorno, and Heidegger. Yet it is far from clear at what point exactly Derrida departs from Hegel, or how his philosophical project is related to the many efforts at overcoming Hegel undertaken in the nineteenth and twentieth centuries. This chapter aims to provide a preliminary answer to these questions. For this reason, it focuses as much as possible on the philosophical strand of Derrida's work.

Notwithstanding the importance Derrida has often attributed to Hegel, only a few of his texts are in fact devoted to Hegel's work. The only essay that is uniquely concerned with Hegel is "The Pit and the Pyramid: Introduction to Hegel's Semiology" (1972). This text primarily addresses Hegel's conception of the sign in the third part of the *Encyclopaedia*.[2] Derrida draws on Bataille's reading of Hegel in "From Restricted to General Economy: A Hegelianism without Reserve" (1967). Although a number of essays from the same period – published in *Margins of Philosophy* and *Writing and Difference* – contain important references to Hegel, none of them discusses particular texts in any detail. The only book partly devoted to Hegel is *Glas* (1974).

A Companion to Hegel, First Edition. Edited by Stephen Houlgate and Michael Baur.
© 2011 Blackwell Publishing Ltd. Published 2011 by Blackwell Publishing Ltd.

Since *Glas* belongs among Derrida's most extravagant texts and, moreover, draws on a number of ideas put forward in earlier works, I will consider this text only after examining the implicit and explicit discussion of Hegel that Derrida undertakes in *Margins, Writing and Difference*, and other seminal texts. A passage from the interviews gathered in *Positions* – published in 1972 – may serve as a guiding thread for my interpretation of Derrida's relationship to Hegel:

> Since it is still a question of elucidating the relationship to Hegel – a difficult labour, which for the most part remains before us, and which in a certain way is interminable ... – I have attempted to distinguish *différance* ... from Hegelian difference, and have done so precisely at the point where Hegel, in the greater *Logic*, determines difference as contradiction only in order to resolve it ... into the self-presence of an onto-theological or onto-teleological synthesis.[3]

In this passage Derrida implicitly refers to the second part of Hegel's *Science of Logic*, entitled the *Doctrine of Essence*. Although he never elaborated on the concepts of difference, opposition, and contradiction that Hegel discusses in this part, nor on other parts of the *Science of Logic*, I will take up his suggestion that the concept of différance can be elucidated against the backdrop of the *Doctrine of Essence*.[4] More precisely, I will consider différance as a principle that concurs with the principle Hegel calls "absolute negativity," yet which, unlike the latter, does not necessarily yield the synthesis of contrary conceptual determinations. I thus hope to demonstrate that the principle of deconstruction relies on a modification of the negativity from which Hegel's speculative science derives its immense energy.

It might be objected that différance cannot possibly be called a principle, since philosophical principles have traditionally been used to develop comprehensive systems. I hold, however, that any philosophy presupposes a basic guiding thread that functions as a principle, if only to expose the purported one-sidedness of the principles that had been put forward until then. In what follows I will conceive of différance as such a critical principle, and treat it on a par with the Hegelian principle of absolute negativity. To discuss the affinity between Hegel and Derrida at the level of their "logic," I will keep a certain distance from Derrida's actual comments on Hegel. Even though this approach may run counter to Derrida's own writings, I hope it will allow me to point out the irreducible difference between his thought and Hegel's.

2. The Production of Arbitrary Differences

In the interview in *Positions* quoted above, Derrida unambiguously presents deconstruction as a critique of both metaphysics and the metaphysical assumptions that undergird other, more concrete modes of thought:

> [W]hat has seemed necessary and urgent to me, in the historical situation which is our own, is a general determination of the conditions for the emergence and the limits of philosophy, of metaphysics, of everything that carries it on and that it carries on. (Pos 69/51)

KARIN DE BOER

The Kantian spirit of this passage cannot be overlooked. Yet Derrida's critique of pure reason is more akin, I would argue, to the critique of metaphysics that Hegel elaborated in the *Doctrine of Essence* and elsewhere. Kant limited the domain of theoretical pure reason to the a priori principles constitutive of scientific knowledge. To achieve this self-limitation of pure reason, however, he had to oppose the sphere of sensibility to that of thought, *phenomena* to *noumena*, necessity to freedom. As is well known, Hegel's speculative science turns against any mode of thought that abides by fixed oppositions. I would argue that Derrida's critique of metaphysics bears a close resemblance to this negative dimension of Hegel's philosophy.

While Derrida thus implicitly aligns deconstruction with the task Hegel set himself in the *Doctrine of Essence*, he does not adopt the principle – absolute negativity – that Hegel here and elsewhere deployed to establish the *unity* of such contraries as identity and difference, the inner and the outer, form and matter, or spirit and nature. To criticize, in his turn, the fixed oppositions established by metaphysics, Derrida introduces a different principle, which in his early works he calls "différance." Since Derrida in *Of Grammatology* (1967) comments extensively on Saussure and other linguists to explain what he means by this notion, différance has often been considered a linguistic principle. I would contend, however, that Derrida uses the context of Saussure's linguistics – then at its height – for a purpose by no means limited to the element of language alone.[5]

According to Saussure, linguistic meaning is produced by the arbitrary difference between oral or written signifiers. Any language, he holds, is constituted by a network of differences, none of which can be traced back to a positive, self-identical element. Following Saussure's conception of linguistic meaning, Derrida argues that these linguistic differences should be conceived as effects of différance. He departs from Saussure, however, by suggesting that the latter failed to take into account the radical implications of this principle. Saussure, he contends, maintained a strict distinction between the signified, that is, the nonsensible meaning of a word, and the arbitrary play of sensible signifiers. For this reason, he remained indebted to the classical ontological opposition between inside and outside. This opposition presupposes that the outside (e.g., the body) is determined by the inside (e.g., the soul), whereas the inside determines itself from within. Derrida's criticism of Saussure is directed against this opposition:

> The signified face, to the extent that it is still originally distinguished from the signifying face, is not considered a trace; by rights, it has no need of the signifier to be what it is. ... This reference to the meaning of a signified thinkable and possible outside of all signifiers remains dependent upon the onto-theo-teleology that I have just evoked.[6]

Saussure held that signifiers owe their significance to their difference from other signifiers. Yet he assumed, at least according to Derrida, that the arbitrariness of the signifiers does not prevent the *meaning* of a word from being immediately given to the eye of the beholder. In contrast to Saussure, Derrida no longer reduces the differing force of différance to the element of external signifiers. On his view, a signified no less than a signifier owes its identity to the irresolvable difference between signifiers. Derrida turns against Saussure by maintaining that this latter difference might well infringe on the purportedly "proper" meaning of a word. Any such meaning, in other words, owes its identity to something the effects of which it does not control. If, as Derrida main-

596

tains, not just the production of external signifiers, but the very production of meaning results from the principle of différance, then no meaning is immune to the arbitrariness traditionally assigned to the element of exteriority alone.[7] This is not to say, however, that he completely eradicates the ontological distinction between inside and outside. He merely rejects the interpretation of this distinction as a hierarchical opposition in which one term *governs* the other.

According to Derrida, Saussure raised the production of arbitrary differences into a basic principle in order to liberate linguistics from a paradigm that had lost its pertinence. Derrida, in his turn, developed the implications of this principle – now called différance – to liberate philosophy from the ontological paradigm he held informed philosophy, science, and politics from Plato to Saussure himself. On this view, Derrida's criticism of Saussure is concerned not so much with his linguistics as with the hierarchical ontological oppositions on which it relies.

It is far from certain, however, whether the principle of différance such as it manifests itself in the element of language is well suited for the radical criticism of philosophy on which Derrida was embarked. Clearly, he did not conceive of différance as the principle or force that produces arbitrary differences alone. In line with Hegel, he would maintain that this is merely one of the ways in which différance manifests itself. Yet Derrida never seems to have elucidated the relation between, on the one hand, the process that yields arbitrary differences between, for example, linguistic signifiers and, on the other hand, the process that produces the irresolvable conflict between seemingly opposed determinations such as that between inside and outside. To shed light on this relation, the next section first examines Derrida's critique of ontological oppositions.

3. Conflictual Ontological Oppositions

In the seminal essay "La différance," published in 1968, Derrida explicitly claims that différance underlies the apparently fixed ontological oppositions that have shaped the history of philosophy (MP 12–13/36–37). Yet everything that has been achieved in this history results, he maintains, from the effort to discard the disturbing effects of this principle. Philosophy is said to have repressed différance by defining its object in terms of fixed oppositions such as those between inside and outside, spirit and nature, idea and experience, necessity and coincidence, or thought and extension. Moreover, by defining one of these contraries as the unique principle of both, philosophy effaced the struggle of *both* contrary moments to establish themselves as such a principle. On this view, the fixed, hierarchical, ontological oppositions produced by philosophy testify to its effort at annulling the primordial, nondialectical struggle between contrary conceptual determinations. Philosophy, Derrida notes with reference to Nietzsche, lives

> *in* and *on différance*, thereby blinding itself to the *same*, which is not the identical. The same, precisely, is *différance* (with an *a*) as an equivocal detour [*comme passage détourné et equivoque*] leading from one differing element to another, from one term of an opposition to the other. Thus one could reconsider all the pairs of oppositions on which philosophy is constructed ... and discover in them a necessity according to which each of the terms appears as the différance of the other ... (the intelligible as that which differs from the

sensible [*différant du sensible*], as the deferred sensible; the concept as deferred-differing intuition [*intuition différée-différante*]; culture as deferred-differing nature; all the others of *physis* – *tekhné, nomos, thesis*, society, liberty, history, spirit, etc. as a deferred or differing *physis* ...). Thus, *différance* is the name we might give to the "active," moving discord of differing forces. (MP 18–19/17)

This dense passage is worth examining in some detail. The principle of différance, I take Derrida to mean, both underlies *and undermines* such ontological oppositions as have informed the history of philosophy. By referring to this principle as "the same," he suggests that each of these oppositions testifies to the incapacity of philosophy to affirm the irresolvable difference between contrary determinations.[8]

To clarify this I will take the relation between nature and spirit as an example. Unlike Descartes and Kant, Derrida does not define the relation between nature and spirit as a clear-cut opposition. Unlike Hegel, however, he does not conceive of nature and spirit in terms of a unity that embraces both moments, either. He rather suggests that nature is from the outset divided against itself (*nature différée*) and occurs as the conflict between its contrary tendencies (*nature différante*). Now Hegel also conceives of nature as an "unresolved contradiction," for he considers nature, largely defined by arbitrariness, to be at odds with its ultimate principle, that is, with the concept as such (*der Begriff*).[9] Yet for Hegel the struggle between, on the one hand, the arbitrariness proper to nature and, on the other, the proper force of the concept, is such that the latter must necessarily prevail. Since the concept constitutes the absolute principle of *both* nature and spirit, the emergence of human consciousness out of nature testifies to the necessary actualization of the concept *qua* Idea.

Now Derrida would not contest the view that consciousness emerges from nature. Yet he attempts to trace back the classical opposition between nature and spirit to a struggle that is not necessarily resolved by the emergence of the latter. Seen from his perspective, this opposition rather appears as the result – or effect – of a struggle within nature that, for its part, cannot be resolved. Just as linguistic meaning is made possible by the production of differing signifiers, spirit originates, he suggests, from a differing process that occurs within the element to which Hegel would refer as exteriority.

According to Hegel, spirit actualizes itself by reducing the proper force of this exteriority to a necessary, yet subordinate moment of spirit itself. Derrida, by contrast, suggests that nature and spirit can come into their own only by means of a detour (*un passage détourné*) that leads from one to the other. Since Derrida suggests that nothing precedes the differing process within nature, he might seem to defend a Nietzschean naturalism. Yet this is only part of the story, and not the most interesting part.[10] For he also suggests that *both* nature and spirit can come into their own only by means of a detour. This means, if I am right, that he regards neither moment as more primordial than the other. If neither nature nor spirit constitutes the ultimate principle of its contrary moments, then *both* these moments might be regarded as struggling to actualize themselves at the expense of their contrary. If each moment seeks to subject its contrary to its proper end, in other words, then each may thwart the self-actualization of the other.

If, as Derrida suggests, a certain exteriority from the outset inhabits phenomena such as spirit, culture, reason, or thought, then the latter need not necessarily succeed in overcoming the proper force of this exteriority. On this view, the purported "purity" of thought, for example, would result from its utterly precarious struggle to establish itself as pure thought in the first place. To "repress" the threat posed by the exteriority with which it is entangled, it would attempt to reduce the latter to a contrary that lacks the power to infringe upon its alleged purity – whence its opposition to sensible intuition, will, body, nature, or the realm of arbitrary signifiers. In this way, philosophy would have established the opposition between the inner and the outer and, in its wake, the other ontological oppositions mentioned above. In each case the moment that constitutes a determination of pure thought, to use a Hegelian term, is defined as the principle of both itself *and* its contrary. Such oppositions thus affirm the power of pure thought to actualize *itself* by means of its contrary. Deconstruction calls all such oppositions into question. Yet it cannot be appropriated by "a dialectics of the Hegelian type," Derrida notes in *Positions*, since "Hegelian idealism consists precisely of a *relève* of the binary oppositions of classical idealism, a resolution of contradiction into a third term" (Pos 59/43). What Derrida calls a third term is precisely the unity of two contraries in which the one becomes a subordinate moment of the other.

This perspective throws a different light not merely on the classical concept of spirit, but on any conceptual determination that in the history of philosophy has been conceived as more primordial, pure, and powerful than its contrary. As I see it, Derrida's critique of reason comes down to the view that philosophy, assigning the production of arbitrary differences to the element of exteriority alone, has always shied away from the *precariousness* of whatever human beings strive to accomplish in the name of reason, the good, or freedom. Although Hegel showed that oppositions such as those between spirit and nature or the inner and the outer are untenable, he could do so only by *reaffirming the power of the former over the latter*. Hegelian dialectics therefore represents, in Derrida's eyes, just one more way of negating their irresolvable difference.

4. Negativity

So far I have argued that Derrida implicitly distinguishes between two forms of différance. Within the element of linguistic exteriority, différance functions as a principle that produces the arbitrary differences constitutive of linguistic meaning. Within the element of pure thought, conversely, différance generates the irresolvable difference between seemingly opposed determinations such as essence and appearance, inside and outside, freedom and necessity, spirit and nature, reason and will.

The distinction between these two forms bears an unmistakable resemblance to Hegel's distinction between *abstract* and *absolute* negativity. The mode of différance that produces arbitrary differences might well be compared to what Hegel calls abstract negativity (cf. L I, 124/115–116). According to Hegel, briefly put, abstract negativity produces external differences. Insofar as something is governed by abstract negativity, it is distinguished from itself in such a way that it cannot identify with this its contrary moment. Within the element of exteriority, abstract negativity manifests itself first and foremost as the sequence of temporal moments. Within the element of pure thought, it manifests itself as the principle that allows thought to distinguish things in a merely external way, for example, white roses from red ones. Absolute negativity, by contrast, pertains to the movement wherein something opposes its contrary so as to actualize itself through the latter. Whereas this negativity constitutes the principle of any mode of self-determination, it truly manifests itself only in the element of spirit. Since Hegel's speculative science is intended to comprehend any possible object of thought in terms of its attempt to determine itself from within, this negativity constitutes the ultimate principle of his philosophical method as well.

As is to be expected, Hegel did not simply oppose these contrary modes of negativity. Instead, he raised the negativity that informs processes of self-actualization into the absolute principle of thought and reduced abstract negativity to its subordinate moment. This decision allowed him, Derrida suggests, to comprehend the history of spirit as a history in which the sway of abstract negativity is increasingly overcome and, more generally, to develop an encompassing philosophical system.[11] In his essay on Bataille, Derrida suggests that Hegel thereby turned away from a differing negativity that makes possible and at the same time threatens to make impossible any process of self-actualization:

> Hegel, through *precipitation*, blinded himself to that which he had laid bare under the rubric of negativity. ... Therefore, he must be followed to the end, without reserve, to the point of agreeing with him against himself and of wresting his discovery from the too *conscientious* interpretation he gave of it.[12]

Even though Hegel was the first to comprehend the production of differences in terms of negativity at all, he could do so, Derrida suggests, only by raising the negativity that produces the *unity* of contrary determinations into the absolute principle of his philosophy.[13] In Derrida's view, Hegel thereby failed to take seriously the negativity that produces both arbitrary differences and the irresolvable difference between contrary ontological determinations.[14] Whereas he defined the negativity that produces the former as abstract negativity, he ignored that which produces the latter altogether.

Clearly, Derrida aimed to extricate this differing negativity from Hegel's dialectical determination of it. It is not quite clear, however, how Derrida himself conceives of the *relation* between the two forms of différance he apparently distinguishes. He seems to hold, I would suggest, that philosophy has always attempted to mitigate the proper force of this differing negativity by assigning the production of arbitrary differences to the element of exteriority alone, that is, to time, nature, the body, the will, or the signifiers. By doing so, philosophy at the same time purified its proper element, that is, the element of thought, from the element of exteriority. By determining the disturbing difference between inside and outside in such a way that the latter can no longer infringe upon the former, philosophy has always effaced the negativity at work in the initial struggle between inside and outside. For Derrida, the distinction between abstract and absolute negativity attests no less to this effacement.

5. Différance, Difference, and Contradiction

While the preceding section examined Derrida's relation to Hegel by comparing the concept of différance to Hegel's concept of negativity in quite general terms, the present section aims to clarify the relation between these principles in light of Hegel's *Doctrine of Essence*. In the passage from *Positions* quoted above, Derrida notes with regard to this text:

> I have attempted to distinguish *différance* (whose "a" marks, among other things, its productive and conflictual characteristics) from Hegelian difference (*Unterschied*), and have done so precisely at the point at which Hegel, in the greater *Logic*, determines difference as contradiction only in order to resolve it. ... [The] conflictuality of différance – which can be called contradiction only if one demarcates it by means of a long work on Hegel's concept of contradiction – can never be totally resolved. (Pos 59–60/44)

Derrida never accomplished the work he here parenthetically refers to. Yet this passage offers some clues as to the way he conceived of his relation to Hegel. To begin with, Derrida here distinguishes Hegel's concept of difference (*Unterschied*) from his own concept of différance. Now Hegel argues in the *Doctrine of Essence* that the concept of difference is a very poor ontological category. Determined by abstract negativity, this category is perfectly suited to articulate the difference between white and red roses and, hence, to be employed in empirical judgments. Yet it is ill-suited, in Hegel's view, as a genuinely philosophical principle. For if the concept of difference would be used to distinguish pure concepts such as infinity and finitude, for example, they could not be comprehended as contrary moments of the concept of infinity – that is to say, true infinity – that constitutes their unity (cf. L I, 149/137).

So Hegel would agree with Derrida that the concept of difference does not suffice to comprehend the *conflict* between contrary determinations. In his view, the concepts "opposition" and "contradiction" – which Derrida does not distinguish – are indeed more appropriate for this purpose. For only if philosophy becomes aware of the self-contradiction at work in pure concepts or forms of spirit can it achieve insight into their unity.[15] Yet Hegel comprehends the concept of difference as a particular form of the concept as such, that is, as an as yet abstract form of the absolute negativity that impels concepts to establish the unity of their contrary determinations. Derrida, for his part, might have argued that the concept of difference treated in the *Doctrine of Essence* is a one-sided determination of a negativity that itself cannot be reduced to absolute negativity. On this reading, the concept of difference need not necessarily develop into a category that allows thought to comprehend its object – whatever it is – in terms of resolvable oppositions. It might just as well develop into a category that allows thought to comprehend its object in terms of the irresolvable struggle between contrary determinations.

However, Derrida's scarce remarks on the concepts of difference and contradiction by no means suffice to confront Hegel's philosophy with its alleged blind spot (WD 380/259), let alone assign it its "rightful place" (396/269–270). To do so, Derrida should at least have accounted for the fact that the concepts treated in the *Doctrine of Essence* constitute one-sided, abstract determinations of the concept as such. He does not seem to acknowledge the similarity between this part of the *Logic* and his own way of deconstructing the oppositions established throughout the history of thought.

As we have seen, Derrida's critique of reason is directed, as much as Hegel's is, against the tendency of thought to interpret the world in terms of clear-cut ontological oppositions. Derrida turns against Hegel, however, by arguing that the difference between contrary determinations is such that it does not necessarily develop into their opposition, nor, consequently, into their resolvable contradiction. Whereas Hegel holds, in sum, that ontological oppositions result from the negation of their implicit *unity*, Derrida contends that apparent oppositions result from the negation of their *irresolvable difference*. As I hope to show in the next section, this largely implicit understanding of the relation between the principles constitutive of speculative science and deconstruction also informs *Glas*. This work might be considered the last – and longest – detour Derrida took in order not to write that "long work on Hegel's concept of contradiction" (Pos 59–60/44).

6.   *Glas*

Glas is one of Derrida's most experimental texts. Each page consists of two columns, set in different fonts, which are regularly interrupted by insertions in yet different fonts. Apart from a title now and then, bibliographical details are omitted.[16] While the right-hand column is concerned primarily with Jean Genet's work, the left-hand one offers a commentary on Hegelian texts, moving back and forth between the Jena writings, the *Philosophy of Right*, the *Encyclopaedia*, and various other texts. Derrida's commentary contains many long quotations and slightly distorting paraphrases, sometimes merely interrupted by a couple of open questions. The texts selected from Hegel's oeuvre often seem to resonate with passages from texts by or on Genet. As a result, the two columns seem to reflect one another, thus undoing their apparent contrast. In the section of *Glas* concerned with the discussion of flower religion in the *Phenomenology*, for example, Hegel no longer appears to be defending the power of reason at all costs.[17] However, in what follows I will abstract from the surplus of meaning generated by the interplay of the two columns and focus exclusively on the left-hand column.

Although the French term *glas* refers to the sound of the death knell, the work so entitled does not simply announce, it seems to me, that Hegel is dead once and for all. *Glas* rather undertakes to liberate a certain strand of Hegel's thought from a body of texts deemed to have become obsolete. Derrida's reading of Hegel might perhaps best be seen as a psychoanalysis of Hegel's oeuvre. The patient, detached attention he devotes to such parts of it as are often overlooked should allow these texts to speak for themselves – yet to tell a story that differs from the one that dominates Hegel's own discourse as well as that of his interpreters. Hegel's text, we are told, "lays itself open to the grip and weight of two readings, that is to say, lets itself be struck with indetermination by the impossible concept" (G 223/199). This "impossible concept" might well be another name for différance, that is, the principle that allows Derrida to read Hegel's text in light of elements it contains, but of which it cannot appropriate the implications. In this respect, Derrida's reading of Hegel follows Bataille's, which he earlier described as "a simulated repetition of Hegelian discourse," in the course of which "a barely perceptible displacement disjoints all the articulations and penetrates all the points welded together by the imitated discourse."[18]

While the content and outward appearance of *Glas* differ from Derrida's earlier discussions of Hegel, it rests, I would argue, on the same methodological principle. In the same vein as earlier texts, some passages of *Glas* indicate how this principle differs from Hegelian notions such as difference, opposition, contradiction, and absolute negativity. Now with regard to Hegel's alleged conception of the feminine and masculine, Derrida once again affirms that the opposition between these notions,

> like opposition in general, will have been at once the manifestation of difference ... and the process of its effacement or reappropriation. As soon as difference determines itself, it determines itself as opposition; it manifests itself to be sure, but its manifestation is at the same time ... the reduction of difference, of the remain(s). (G 263/235–236)

Even though Derrida in this context no longer writes difference with an "a," the term "difference" clearly refers to the principle that generates irresolvable differences. *Glas* relates the reduction of this principle not only to Hegelian thought, but also to the Christian doctrine of the immaculate conception (IC):

> As soon as difference is determined as opposition, no longer can the phantasm ... of the IC be avoided. ... All the oppositions that link themselves around difference as opposition (active/passive, reason/heart, beyond/here-below, and so on) have as cause and effect the immaculate maintenance of each of the terms, their independence, and consequently their absolute mastery. (250/223)

The idea of the immaculate conception – taken in a broad sense – implies that pure thought can generate contents without being dependent on matter, nature, or any other mode of externality. These contents themselves then affirm their alleged purity by reducing their contrary to a secondary moment. For Derrida, by contrast, opposite terms not only presuppose one another – as Hegel would be the first to affirm – but are related in such a way that the subjugated term first makes possible the emergence of the allegedly purely spiritual filiation. If, as Derrida suggests, the subjugated term is not secondary, then it does not necessarily yield to the term that attempts to establish itself as the pure principle of itself and its contrary. Seen from this perspective, the ensuing conflict between both terms is not necessarily resolvable. By ignoring the corrupting effects of the subjugated term, Christianity – and Hegel in its wake – allegedly took itself to have achieved "absolute mastery" over ontological oppositions such as that between soul and body or spirit and nature.

However, Derrida does not seem to acknowledge here that his critique of these oppositions shares common ground with Hegel's own. When he at one point quotes and paraphrases a passage from the *Differenzschrift* in which Hegel puts forward this critique, he does so without mentioning its similarity to his own project:

> To relieve the terms of the opposition, ... such would be the "interest of reason," the unique interest of philosophy. The progress of culture has led oppositions of the type spirit/matter, soul/body, faith/understanding, freedom/necessity, and all those deriving from these back to the great couple reason/sensibility or intelligence/nature. ... Reason is another name for the power of unification. (109–110/95)

Evidently, Derrida does not endorse Hegel's view of the negativity that establishes the unity of contrary determinations. In the following passage, however, he suggests that

Hegel's philosophy – notwithstanding the power it grants to absolute negativity – itself contains elements that resist this very power. For this reason, his reading need not oppose Hegel:

> So it is not certain that something more or different from Hegel is being said, that some-thing more or different from what he himself read is being read when the word castration and other similar things are put forward. It is not certain that one conceptually intervenes in his logic. To do that, ... one would have to make visible forces resistant to the *Aufhebung,* to the process of truth, to speculative negativity, and as well that these forces of resistance do not constitute in their turn relievable or relieving negativities. (53/43–44)

Sketching the program actually elaborated in *Glas,* this passage again obliquely refers to a negativity that does *not* turn the differences it brings about into oppositions, let alone into their unity. Once again, however, Derrida does not use this guiding thread to treat the text he consistently calls the "greater" logic – a logic too great, perhaps, to confront head on.[19]

Instead, he dwells on more concrete texts in order to lay bare such elements as do not comply with the prevailing tendency of speculative science. These "remains," Derrida suggests, can all be traced back to the differing force he formerly called dif-férance (cf. 7/1). Although this principle constitutes the ultimate "transcendental" of Hegel's system (183/162, 187/166), it cannot be appropriated by the latter. This dif-fering force makes possible the system, I take it, to the extent that the latter is erected against the threat posed by the former. Precisely by attempting to make itself immune to it, the Hegelian system would testify to the very force of différance. Considered in this light, absolute negativity is a reactive rather than an active principle.

It might be argued that *Glas* aims to expose the struggle between pure difference and absolute negativity such as it unfolds in Hegel's oeuvre, albeit behind his back. To this end, Derrida closely examines texts that deal with transitions that, for Hegel, testify to the power of spirit to overcome its self-externalization. Moving back and forth between early and later texts, *Glas* notably dwells on the transition from nature to spirit, from the family to civil society, from Judaism to Christianity, and from Christianity to absolute knowing. According to Derrida, Hegel purports to resolve the apparent opposition between these terms by treating one side – for example, nature, the family, or religion – as an abstract, external moment of its contrary, such that the latter emerges as its true essence or truth. For Derrida, this latter "truth" results from repressing the destruc-tive force exhibited by the purportedly abstract moments – a repression he holds can never completely succeed. A few examples must suffice to clarify this point. Although, in my opinion, Derrida's reading of Hegel is not necessarily convincing – if judged by rigorous scholarly standards – I will refrain from criticizing him at this level.

(1) *Glas* discusses Hegel's accounts of sexual difference in the *Phenomenology* and the *Philosophy of Right* at some length. Drawing on the *Antigone,* the *Phenomenology* conceives of the relation between brother and sister, in Derrida's words, as a "relation of consanguinity that breaks with (desiring) naturalness." The sister's recognition of her brother "is pure ... and yet passes through no conflict, no injury, no rape." Their "symmetrical relation ... needs no reconciliation to appease itself, ... does not know the horizon of war, the infinite wound, contradiction, negativity" (170/150). As Derrida

sees it, the very idea of a symmetrical relation, not haunted, moreover, by an internal contradiction, is at odds with Hegel's explicit conception of the negativity supposedly at work in any mode of human life. Such a relation would be something that "the greater logic cannot assimilate" and that is "inconceivable" from the perspective of speculative science as a whole (170/150).

Accordingly, Derrida suggests, sexual desire emerges for Hegel only once the symmetrical relation between brother and sister has been overcome. Whereas Hegel affirms that the relationship between brother and sister is without desire (169/149) or opposition (190/168), it nevertheless constitutes a first, as yet completely undetermined mode of sexual difference. This can only mean for Hegel, Derrida notes, that it must give way to a mode of sexual difference that actually is defined by opposition:

> In overcoming natural difference as diversity of the sexes, we pass on to difference as opposition. In *Sittlichkeit* sexual difference finally becomes a true opposition. ... The sexual difference has only just appeared. It has only just determined itself in ... *positing itself,* that is, in opening itself to negativity and in becoming opposition. (190/168)

Derrida here clearly draws on his earlier reflections on différance, difference, and opposition. In his view, Hegel's decision to assign desire to the oppositional, that is, "proper" mode of sexual difference alone (and to exclude it from the brother-sister relation) testifies to the incest taboo rooted in human culture as a whole:

> What is the position of desire in this passage from difference-diversity to difference-opposition? ... Must one wait for opposition or contradiction to see it upsurge?[20]

For Derrida, societies that restrict sexual desire to the monogamous, asymmetrical relationship between men and women not bound by blood ties do so in the attempt to stabilize ethical life, an attempt that has nothing to do with the allegedly necessary self-actualization of reason (cf. 222/198). Whereas Derrida, it seems to me, would not deny that such forms of self-protection are reasonable, he reinterprets them as a response to a threat that can never be completely warded off. "Pure difference" would be one way of naming the nature of this threat. Thus, Derrida seems to agree with Hegel that the relationship between brother and sister is symmetrical. He opposes Hegel, however, by suggesting that the negativity at work in sexual desire may well disturb the serenity that Hegel connects to this symmetry. This negativity does not necessarily let itself be tamed by the bonds of wedlock – that is, by a difference posited as hierarchical opposition – but already inhabits relationships other than the asymmetrical one between husband and wife. The difference that this negativity produces between brother and sister, for example, by no means precludes the presence of sexual desire. For Derrida, their relationship is marked not so much by the absence of desire as by the unconscious effort to repress its troubling effects. On this reading, *Glas* targets not so much Hegel's attempt to restrict the domain of sexual desire as the prevailing tendency of human culture that his speculative science – allegedly uncritically – reflects.

(2) Religion forms another important axis of *Glas*. It allows Derrida to elaborate on a number of topics treated by Hegel from *The Spirit of Christianity* onward, notably the relation between Judaism, Christianity, and speculative science itself. Seen from Derrida's perspective, Christianity tends to cover over its historical particularity by

opposing itself to its historical origin. Only by conceiving of Judaism as an abstract, immature form of religion could Christianity interpret itself as the "truth" of Judaism. According to Derrida, Hegel uncritically repeated this excluding gesture, thus betraying the lasting dependence of speculative science on the particular historical epoch defined by Christianity (40/32). This is, at least, what the following questions seem to imply:

> What is the function of this Christian model? In what sense is it exemplary for speculative onto-theology? Can this model be circumscribed and displaced as a finite and particular structure, bound to given historical conditions? Can a history different from the one represented here be interrogated? Can the horizon be changed? the logic? (41–42/33)

As is well known, Hegel considered his speculative science to translate the ultimate content of Christianity into the language of the pure concept. Derrida suggests, by contrast, that this language is anything but pure and universal, but takes over the particular content of Christianity while effacing its particularity. Thus, the Christian dogma of the Trinity would recur within speculative science as the assumption that an allegedly pure content necessarily has the force to distinguish itself from its contrary in such a way that it can actualize itself through the latter (cf. 253–254/227). This teleological pattern would betray the dependence of absolute knowing on a history defined by the effort to achieve mastery over pure difference.

(3) Toward the end of *Glas* Derrida approaches Hegel's account of religion from the angle of the *Phenomenology*. The first mode of natural religion that Hegel discusses here has light as such as its object of worship. "Pure and figureless," Derrida comments, "this light burns all" (266/238). Whereas Hegel affirms that this light "plays limitlessly," he cannot but regard it, in Derrida's view, as a moment that necessarily gives way to less indeterminate forms of religion. In this process of "mediation, of the hard-working negative," the pure play of difference "must pass into its contrary" (268/240). For Derrida, on the other hand, "the pure play of difference" (266/239) intimated by the all-burning light need not necessarily be interpreted from within an "onto-theo-teleological horizon" (266/238). It is far from evident, in his view, that the "consuming destruction without limit" that this light exemplifies can give rise to "the dialectical process" (268/240) according to which, I add, the various forms of religion emerge from one another until the stage of Christianity is reached.

These examples make clear, I hope, how Derrida time and again dwells on elements of Hegel's thought that, seen from the perspective of speculative science, must necessarily be overcome, and this in world history itself as well as in the text that comprehends the logic on which this history rests. By means of many detours, some of which do not seem to lead anywhere, he aims to show that moments that Hegel considers to be abstract – such as the cult of light – are "overcome" not because they would not yet adequately embody the pure concept, but because they still testify to a *differing force* the effects of which human history has always tried to suppress.

7. Conclusion

In contrast to Hegel, Derrida never elaborated a philosophical logic or a systematic account of the history of philosophy. Yet all his writings assume, in my view, that human culture – and philosophy in particular – has never been able to adopt différance as its ultimate principle. Had he written a history of philosophy, Derrida would have argued that both Hegel and post-Hegelian philosophers such as Nietzsche, Freud, Bataille, and Heidegger somehow tried to account for the disturbing implications of différance, but could only do so in a limited way.[21]

Hegel was the first, in his view, to raise negativity to the ultimate principle of philosophy and, hence, to deconstruct any mode of thought grounded on purportedly stable oppositions. According to Derrida, however, Hegel's critique of metaphysics continued to assume that reason possesses the force to resolve whatever oppositions it encounters. Whereas this assumption allowed Hegel to develop a comprehensive account of thought, nature, and history, it would not necessarily allow contemporary thought adequately to respond to the challenges posed by the contemporary world.

No more than Kant's or Hegel's is Derrida's critique of reason concerned with philosophy alone. Responding to the history of the twentieth century, Derrida questions above all the purported purity of reason and, hence, its capacity to control the proper force of the elements on which it depends to actualize itself. Whereas he thus turns against the optimism inherent in modernity, he does not defend a pessimism that would be merely its reverse. The perspective he brings into play is rather meant to account, I would contend, for the utter *precariousness* of whatever humans venture to undertake. If this is the basic impetus of Derrida's confrontation with Hegel, then the texts devoted to his work are directed not so much against speculative science itself as against the unbridled faith in reason that such science comprehends and reflects.

Derrida generally does not clearly distinguish these two levels. Neither does he distinguish the method Hegel deploys to develop a comprehensive philosophical system from the actual world he aims to understand. This vagueness makes it quite difficult, in my view, adequately to assess the significance of Derrida's reading of Hegel. Yet I believe that Derrida was right to point out that Hegel could not but interpret opposed moments in light of the unity contained in them, and that Hegel thus failed to grasp adequately those elements of human life, history, and thought that testify to irresolvable differences and conflicts rather than resolvable contradictions.

Even though Derrida's actual criticisms of Hegel are not always persuasive, I take it that the insight on which they rely challenges the prevailing paradigm of modernity in a forceful way. And insofar as Hegel's equally forceful criticism of modernity indeed remained entangled with essential elements of this very paradigm, this insight continues to pose a challenge to speculative science as well. By immunizing itself against such challenges, speculative science would risk reducing itself to a remnant of the past. That is why Derrida was right, I believe, when he remarked in *Positions* that the work to be done on Hegel "for the most part remains before us, and ... in a certain way is interminable" (Pos 59/43–44).

Notes

1   For important exceptions, see Rodolphe Gasché, *The Tain of the Mirror: Derrida and the Philosophy of Reflection* (Cambridge, Mass.: Harvard University Press, 1986), and *Hegel after Derrida*, ed. Stuart Barnett (New York: Routledge, 1998). Barnett rightly notes that Gasche's

important work on Hegel and Derrida paved the way for other investigations into the philosophical dimension of Derrida's texts in the United States. See also *Philosophie der Dekonstruktion. Zum Verhältnis von Normativität and Praxis,* ed. Andrea Kern and Christoph Menke (Frankfurt am Main: Suhrkamp, 2002).

2   Jacques Derrida, "The Pit and the Pyramid: Introduction to Hegel's Semiology," in *Marges de la philosophie* (Paris: Editions de minuit, 1972); *Margins of Philosophy,* trans. Alan Bass (Chicago, Ill.: University of Chicago Press, 1982), hereafter referred to as "MP." The essay is based on a paper delivered in 1968 at a seminar on Hegel's *Science of Logic,* which was directed by Jean Hyppolite. Derrida refers to this context as follows: "[I]nstead of remaining within the *Logic,* ... we will proceed chiefly by detours, following texts more appropriate to demonstrate the architectonic necessity of the relations between logic and semiology. Since some of these texts have already been examined by Jean Hyppolite in *Logique et existence,* most notably in the chapter 'Sens et sensible,' we will implicitly and permanently appeal to the latter" (MP 81/71). In 1957 Derrida had started working on a doctoral thesis on this subject under Hyppolite's direction. After the latter's death in 1968 Derrida definitively abandoned this project. See Jacques Derrida, "The Time of a Thesis: Punctuations," in *Philosophy in France Today,* ed. Alan Montefiore (Cambridge: Cambridge University Press, 1983). For a detailed exposition of Derrida's relation to Hyppolite, see Leonard Lawlor, *Derrida and Husserl: The Basic Problems of Phenomenology* (Bloomington: Indiana University Press, 2002), 88–104. Lawlor rightly claims, it seems to me, that Derrida's approach to Hegel owed a great deal to Hyppolite, who, as he notes, was the first to read Hegel in connection with Heidegger and Husserl, to oppose Kojève's influential anthropological reading of Hegel's *Phenomenology,* and to put Hegel's *Logic* central stage.

3   Jacques Derrida, *Positions* (Paris: Editions de minuit, 1972), 59–60; *Positions,* trans. Alan Bass (Chicago, Ill.: University of Chicago Press, 1981), 43–44, hereafter referred to as "Pos." Derrida here seems to refer to passages from the *Science of Logic* such as these: "Difference as such is already contradiction *in itself;* for it is the *unity* of sides which are, only insofar as they are not one – and it is the separation of sides which are only insofar as they are separated *in one and the same respect.*" See G.W.F. Hegel, *Wissenschaft der Logik* II, ed. Eva Moldenhauer and Karl Markus Michel (Frankfurt am Main: Suhrkamp, 1969), 65; *Hegel's Science of Logic,* trans. A. V. Miller (Amherst, N.Y.: Prometheus Books, 1997), 431, hereafter referred to as "L." Unless indicated otherwise, I refer to this edition of Hegel's work. It is no coincidence, I presume, that Hyppolite comments on this passage, and related ones, in *Logique et existence: essai sur la logique de Hegel* (Paris: Presses Universitaires de France, 1953), 156–157; *Logic and Existence,* trans. Leonard Lawlor (Albany: SUNY Press 1997), 120–121. The quoted passage from *Positions* – as well as many other passages – equally testifies to the influence of Heidegger's *Identity and Difference* (1957), even though Derrida in "Différance" and *Positions* does not explicitly refer to this text.

4   Heinz Kimmerle approaches the relation between Hegel and Derrida from a similar angle. In "Verschiedenheit und Gegensatz" (in *Hegels Wissenschaft der Logik,* ed. Dieter Henrich (Stuttgart: Klett-Cotta, 1986), 265–282), he suggests that Hegel's *Logic* cannot account for such forms of difference as cannot be overturned into oppositions and hence into resolvable contradictions: "Does not a comprehension of difference and variety require a type of thought that cannot be lodged within dialectical thought? Isn't it rather the case that [this comprehension] constitutes a broader type of thought, such that the comprehension of opposition retains a specific position within the former?" (275, cf. 274). His elaboration of these questions, as well as his references to Derrida, remain rather sketchy, however. In the context of this chapter I will not be able to discuss Hegel's own work in any detail. On this topic, see my article, "The Dissolving Force of the Concept: Hegel's Ontological Logic," *Review of Metaphysics* 57 (2004): 787–822, and *On Hegel: The Sway of the Negative*

(Basingstoke: Palgrave, 2010). Focusing on Hegel's conception of negativity, I argue here that Hegel failed to account for the entanglement of contrary determinations and, hence, for the tragic nature of conflicts occurring within the realm of world history. The present chapter draws on the interpretation of Hegel elaborated in this book.

5   A footnote added to the passage quoted above states this explicitly: "If I have chosen to demonstrate the necessity of this 'deconstruction' by privileging the Saussurian references, it is not only because Saussure still dominates contemporary linguistics and semiology; but also because he seems to me to hold himself at the limit: at the same time within the metaphysics that must be deconstructed and beyond the concept of the sign (signifier/signified) which he still uses." See Jacques Derrida, *De la Grammatologie* (Paris: Les éditions de minuit, 1967), 107; *Of Grammatology,* trans. Gayatri Chakravorty Spivak (Baltimore, Md.: John Hopkins University Press, 1974), 329 (hereafter referred to as "Gram").

6   Gram, 106–107/73. cf. also MP 3–29/3–27. Terms such as "onto-theo-teleology," frequently used by Derrida, are borrowed from Heidegger, who, in *Identity and Difference* and other texts, characterized the history of metaphysics – including Hegel's philosophy – as onto-theology. Derrida's critique of metaphysics clearly follows in the footsteps of Heidegger, who, from *Being and Time* onward, aimed to deconstruct the basic presuppositions of this tradition. Yet Hegel's philosophy cannot be dismantled, in my view, simply by pointing out its indebtedness to classical theological and teleological motives, for in this case one does not account for the critical – and radical – transformation of this legacy Hegel himself achieved.

7   In "The Pit and the Pyramid," Derrida also points out that Hegel's conception of language remains bound to the classical distinction between soul and body (MP 94/82). I do not think, however, that Hegel's philosophy can be deconstructed merely by referring to his indebtedness to classical metaphysics at this level. See Stephen Houlgate, "Hegel, Derrida, and Restricted Economy: The Case of Mechanical Memory," *Journal of the History of Philosophy* 34 (1996): 79–93, for a nuanced discussion of this text. I agree with Houlgate that Derrida tends to underestimate the extent to which Hegel accounts for the precariousness of human life. As Houlgate points out, Hegel does not simply interpret the emergence of new – finite – shapes of consciousness in terms of the return of spirit to itself (92). Houlgate values Derrida's effort, however, "to render meaning and intelligibility just a little more enigmatic than they have hitherto been held to be" (92).

8   Derrida here implicitly draws on Heidegger's distinction between "the same" and "the identical" in *Identität und Differenz* (Pfullingen: Neske, 1957), 41; *Identity and Difference,* trans. Joan Stambaugh (Chicago: University of Chicago Press, 1969), 45. Heidegger here notes that he intends to discuss with Hegel about "the same" matter the latter was concerned with, but in such a way that this sameness manifests precisely the difference between them. Derrida applies this distinction to the conflictual force that metaphysics has generally tried to annul.

9   G.W.F. Hegel, *Enzyklopädie der philosophischen Wissenschaften im Grundrisse II; Hegel's Philosophy of Nature,* ed. and trans. Michael J. Petry (New York: Humanities Press, 1970), § 248 remark. Derrida here apparently draws on Hyppolite's reflections: "Indeed, Nature is the negation of the Logos. ... Certainly, Nature is also what reflects its other; *it contains therefore this self-difference;* it points to the Logos, sense. ... There is therefore in nature this non-resolved contradiction that the Logos thinks; ... it is Nature and Logos at the same time." Jean Hyppolite, *Logic and Existence,* 132/102 (emphasis added). Only in the final chapter does Hyppolite distance himself from Hegel, who, as he claims in a Marxian vein "has misunderstood nature because, instead of starting from it, he has seen there a relative, non-originary term" (236/181). See Leonard Lawlor, *Derrida and Husserl: The Basic Problems of Phenomenology,* 99.

10 On the one hand, Derrida points out in *Positions,* "we must traverse a phase of *overturning.* ... [I]n a classical philosophical opposition we are ... dealing with ... a violent hierarchy. ... To

609

deconstruct the opposition, first of all, is to overturn the hierarchy at a given moment. To overlook this phase of overturning is to forget the conflictual and subordinating structure of opposition. ... This movement must be complemented by the irruptive emergence of a new 'concept,' a concept that can no longer be ... included in the previous regime" (Pos 56–57/41–42). These concepts "inhabit philosophical opposition, resisting and disorganising it, ... without ever leaving room for a solution in the form of speculative dialectics" (Pos 58/43).

11 "Indeed, nowhere is such a reconcilitory knowledge more urgently required than in world history. This reconciliation can be attained only by knowledge of the affirmative, such that the negative is dissolved into the latter as a subordinate and vanquished element." See G.W.F. Hegel, *Vorlesungen über die Philosophie der Geschichte*, 28; *The Philosophy of History*, trans. John Sibree (Buffalo, N.Y.: Prometheus Books, 1991), 15.

12 Jacques Derrida, "De l'économie restreinte à l'économie générale," in *L'écriture et la différence* (Paris: Editions du Seuil, 1967), 381; "From Restricted to General Economy," in *Writing and Difference*, trans. Alan Bass (London: Routledge and Kegan Paul, 1978), 259–260, hereafter referred to as "WD."

13 During the discussion of the paper that was published as "Différance," Derrida replied to one of the questions as follows: "You asked me when the word *différance* or the concept of *différance* took its place within metaphysics. I would be tempted to say: with Hegel, and it is not by chance that it is precisely the interest that Hegel took in the thought of *différance*, at the moment when philosophy was closing itself, completing itself, or, as we say, accomplishing itself, which obliges us today to connect the thought of the end of metaphysics and the thought of *différance*. It is not by chance that Hegel is fundamentally the one who has been the most *systematically* attentive within metaphysics to *différance*. And perhaps – but this is a question of reading – there is a certain irreducibility of *différance* in his texts." Quoted in *Derrida and Différance*, ed. David C. Wood and Robert Bernasconi (Evanston, Ill.: Northwestern University Press, 1988), 95, cf. Gram 41/26.

14 "[I]t could be shown ... that the immense revolutions of Kant and Hegel only reawakened or revealed the most permanent philosophical determination of negativity. ... The immense revolution consisted ... in taking the negative *seriously*. In giving *meaning* to its *labor*" (WD 380/259).

15 Speculative thought, Hegel notes in the *Logic*, "consists solely in holding on to the contradiction, and thus to itself. Unlike representational thought, it does not let itself be dominated by the contradiction, it does not allow the latter to dissolve its determinations into other ones or into nothing" (L II, 76/440–441).

16 See John P. Leavey, *Glossary* (Lincoln: University of Nebraska Press, 1986), for helpful clarifications of the text, including the location of the passages cited by Derrida.

17 Jacques Derrida, *Glas* (Paris: Galilée, 1974), 272; *Glas*, trans. John P. Leavey and Richard Rand (Lincoln: University of Nebraska Press, 1986), 245, hereafter referred to as "G." All page numbers refer to the left-hand column. For general interpretations of *Glas*, see Simon Critchley, "A Commentary upon Derrida's Reading of Hegel in *Glas*," in *Hegel after Derrida*, ed. Stuart Barnett, 197–226; Rodolphe Gasché, "Strictly Bonded," in *Inventions of Difference: On Jacques Derrida* (Cambridge, Mass.: Harvard University Press, 1994), esp. 180–198.

18 WD 382/260, cf. MP 15/14, 21/19, G 11/5, 123/107.

19 See, e.g., G 185/164, 189/168, 251/224.

20 G 190/168, cf. 214–215/191.

21 See, among many other places, MP 18/17.

30

You Be My Body for Me: Body, Shape, and Plasticity in Hegel's *Phenomenology of Spirit*

CATHERINE MALABOU AND JUDITH BUTLER

The following piece on the problem of the body in Hegel's *Phenomenology of Spirit* has a dialogical structure and a dialectical outcome, although it should become clear that neither dialogue nor dialectic is an easy notion here. Commentators have remarked that the subject of Hegel's *Phenomenology* either has no body (and is disembodied from the start) or seeks to renounce its body in the course of its trajectory (and so delegates its body to others or to objects). The title "you be my body for me" is one way of giving voice to the act of delegation, which involves an imperative substitution. It first appeared in an essay that Judith Butler wrote on Lordship and Bondage.[1] In that formulation, the body is something redoubled, occurring elsewhere, *as* or *in* another body. It calls into question whether the body is a finite particularity or, rather, *only* a finite particularity, or some other kind of vexed relation. To think of the body as a vexed relation, which is the aim of this chapter, is to suggest that it is of the structure of the body to be outside itself and that this imperative or demand – you be my body for me – can only ever be partially fulfilled. Indeed, the demand produces a perpetual bind: although there is no body that is mine without the other's body, there is no final expropriation of one's own body, and no final appropriation of another's body.

This chapter is coauthored in a specific sense. It contains two essays and two responses. Our first essays were written simultaneously, followed by a response by Catherine Malabou and then one by Judith Butler.[2] We each, however, had a chance to edit our pieces in light of the emergent debate and discussion that ensued between us. To approach the question of the body and its "outsideness," we moved in two directions.

Malabou sought initially to situate Butler's reading of Hegel in light of some key interpretative frames, and then to question whether the later Foucault ends up taking a position that implicitly involves a Hegelian structure. For Foucault, the subject who would oppose a form of power not only finds that he or she is conditioned by that power, but develops a practice of self-making on the basis of this constitutive paradox. And yet, which Hegel is it that Foucault recapitulates here? Is the Hegel of "self-attachment"

A Companion to Hegel, First Edition. Edited by Stephen Houlgate and Michael Baur.

(understood as attachment to the conditions of own's own formation) valued over another Hegel, one who takes detachment – and even the ecstatic meanings of detachment – as key?

Butler returns to the *Phenomenology* to consider how developing notions of life, shape, and desire circumscribe the site of the body in Hegel, focusing on the recurrent figure of the "shape" (*Gestalt*). As shapes encounter one another, the body yields its status as an object, becoming a vexed relation, at once outside itself and not. The debate that follows concerns the question of how and where to find the body in Hegel's work, and also how to understand the relation between life, shape, and self-shaping. Must the self remain attached to itself to shape itself? Must the self detach from itself to shape itself, and how are we to understand the resulting "plasticity" (Malabou's term) as a figure for absolute knowledge, but also, clearly, in relation to the body: to be this being here and to be that being elsewhere, partially both and fully neither, as the essential condition of becoming?

Catherine Malabou: "Unbind Me"

In the *Phenomenology of Spirit*, the two substantives "Lordship" and "Bondage" appear to be conceptual names for "detachment" and "attachment." To be able to prove itself to be a consciousness – and not a thing or an object – to another consciousness, consciousness will have to "show that it is not attached to any specific *existence*, not to the individuality common to existence as such, that it is not attached [*geknüpft*] to life."[3] Attachment to life means first of all attachment to one's body. What Hegel calls the "objective mode of existence" can only be understood as bodily life. The master is the one who is capable of such a detachment; the bondsman, on the contrary, is enslaved by his irretrievable attachment to life and consequently to his body.

The issues I would like to address here are the following: is (servile) attachment always the truth of detachment? Can dialectics both admit and produce the possibility of an absolute detachment from life and from the body?

In a sense, Hegel's answer to the last question is ambiguous. It is yes and no. Yes, because the master is not afraid of putting his own life at risk; no, because in the end, the master's position is unsustainable, and superseded by the bondsman's. Yes and no; yes or no?

The answer is difficult to determine. It appears that detachment is possible because one's body is, according to Hegel, always "out of itself" (*außer sich*).[4] This suggests that the body is always already evacuated, loaned out, and lived elsewhere. Detachment from the body has then always already taken place. That is why, in the life and death struggle, such a detachment is at the same time possible (it has taken place already, it is consciousness's structural relationship to its own body) and impossible (as a pre-existing structure, it cannot be performed anew).

It is remarkable, however, that Hegel never utters the word "body" in the section on Lordship and Bondage. Many readers of Hegel have tried to bring him to explain himself on that point. I would like to confront three fundamental readings of Lordship and Bondage, and consequently three ways of making Hegel speak, three kinds of ventriloquism. Ventriloquism – the presence of one's voice in the other's body, the conquest of one's own self as an act of robbery of the other's identity – is precisely what is at stake in Lordship and Bondage.

The three main interpretations I wish to put into play are Alexandre Kojève's *Introduction to the Reading of Hegel*, Jacques Derrida's *From General to Restricted Economy*, and Judith Butler's *The Psychic Life of Power*.[5] Each of these readings makes Hegel speak, forces him to specify what he understands by the notions of attachment and detachment. Each of them presupposes that Hegel must have understood both attachment and detachment as operations of *delegation* and *doubling:* to detach oneself from life would doom the other consciousness to be exceedingly attached to it – to be attached to life *for* the other, in its place.

For Kojève, the movement of attachment and detachment causes a split within self-consciousness. Attachment to life appears as the *animal* side of consciousness, and detachment as the *human* one. To show that one is not attached to life consists in liberating the human from its own animality. This liberation leads consciousness to make use of its *voice*, to ventriloquize its own flesh, to speak *through* it and *for* it. For Kojève, both consciousnesses in the life and death struggle necessarily speak when they fight. A silent struggle for recognition is unthinkable. Freedom is the voice of life, thus causing life to be displaced from the realm of the empirical to that of the *concept*. Consciousness frees or detaches itself from life by giving *voice* to life, by turning life into *language*, that is, by detaching life from life itself. Through speech, life and desire become their own concepts, "nonbiological" notions. Double life, double desire. The animal lives for the human, who speaks for it. For Kojève, however, the authentic symbolic detachment eventually occurs through the slave's labor. Labor appears to be the achievement of detachment, which preserves life.

Derrida performs a double ventriloquist operation in his interpretation of Lordship and Bondage. First, he reads Hegel through Bataille. Second, he pushes Hegel to the point where he would have contradicted himself had he spoken more lucidly about the ultimate meaning of detachment, which is death. Derrida uses Bataille as a surrogate to make Hegel speak *against* himself. The Hegelian notion of "mastery" is doubled by Bataille's notion of "sovereignty." According to Derrida's Bataille, sovereignty would be the genuinely detached attitude, whereas mastery would be only another name for a servile overattachment to life.

According to both Kojève and Derrida, attachment, for Hegel, would be the necessary regulation that eventually exercises its domination over detachment, consumption, expenditure, and loss. In the eyes of both, Hegel's slave would appear at last as the figure of power that gives the anonymous fluidity and *puissance* of life the form of subjectivity. In other words, for Hegel, *absolute* detachment would in no way be possible, since detachment and freedom are achieved by the slave who remains *attached to life*. Absolute detachment *without attachment* would play the part of a necessary but temporary fantasy.

Judith Butler for her part considers the issues of delegation, doubling, attachment, and detachment all through the sections on Lordship and Bondage and the Unhappy Consciousness as being one and the same: the issue of *bodily substitution*. The nonspeaking animal flesh that has to be sacrificed ("detached"), according to Kojève, the nondialectical voice that has to be split ("detached") from the dialectical one, according to Derrida, become for Butler, very simply, essentially, and strongly, the body. She

613

ventriloquizes Hegel by giving speech to the master: "the imperative to the bondsman consists in the following formulation: you be my body for me, but do not let me know that the body you are is my body."[6] Bodily substitution characterizes both detachment and attachment; detachment, because the master is the "I" who delegates his body (he detaches himself from his own flesh) to the bondsman. The lord's body is then to be found outside itself, in another being or consciousness. The body seems to be for Hegel the removable or detachable instance par excellence. At the same time, absolute detachment or total bodily substitution ("be my body for me, in my place") are not possible either. The lord's body to the extent that it is supported by the slave's – the laboring body – is not totally evacuated or delegated. Desire may be desire for a complete delegation of the body, for a total detachment from one's own body, but it appears that this detachment can be accomplished only partially. This implies that detachment always entails some attachment. Indeed, the very act of claiming that absolute detachment is necessary reveals an attachment to it; otherwise, why would it have to be claimed?

Butler asserts the impossibility of absolute detachment in Lordship and Bondage and in Hegel's philosophy in general. It is impossible, first, because the operation of bodily substitution is denied by the master. The master claims to be able to detach himself from his own body but denies, in so doing, that he is only transferring it to the slave, asking him to be his body *in his place* while disavowing this very demand. Butler writes:

> To disavow one's body, to render it "Other" as an effect of autonomy, is to produce one's body in such a way that the activity of its production – and its essential relation to the lord – is denied. This trick or ruse involves a double disavowal and an imperative that the "Other" become complicit with this disavowal. In order not to be the body that the lord presumably is, and in order to have the bondsman posture as if the body that he is belongs to himself – and not be the orchestrated projection of the lord – there must be a certain kind of exchange, a bargain or deal, in which ruses are enacted and transacted. In effect, the imperative to the bondsman consists in the following formulation: you be my body for me, but do not let me know that the body you are is my body.[7]

Second, absolute detachment is impossible because the slave places his body at the service of the lord and so, as it were, turns his own body into the *lord's* body, but disavows this operation as well, thus becoming "complicit" with the master's disavowal. The "contract" in which the bondsman substitutes himself for the lord is immediately "covered over and forgotten."[8] It is in this sense that bodily substitution characterizes attachment as well as detachment.

The first section of this part of the chapter seeks to situate Butler's reading of bodily substitution and the problematic of subjection vis-à-vis Kojève's and Derrida's understandings of detachment and servile attachment. We will see how the three voices artificially incorporated in (or introjected into) Hegel both form a harmonious whole and contradict each other. Each reader lends his or her body to Hegel, asking him to unbind the body itself from its spiritual enslavement in the *Phenomenology* – knowing at the same time that it is impossible. In the second section, I analyze Butler's demonstration according to which even Foucault is "stubbornly attached to Hegel" – as are we all.

1. Hegel Read and Spoken by ...

"To Live As a Man, to Die As an Animal." (Kojève)

Because Hegel says very little about the body or about bodies in general in the *Phenomenology*, anyone who intends to determine the meaning of this "very little" has to make Hegel speak more thoroughly about it, and consequently to confer an imaginary voice on the Hegelian body itself.

For Kojève, the "body proper" is what appears once the human has been split off from the animal. Through the struggle for recognition, the master's consciousness shows its detachment from life and acquires for that reason a symbolic and conceptual dimension of which the other consciousness, full of fear, is first deprived. In putting its life at risk, the master's consciousness disavows its animality and cuts itself off from its biological content, that is, from its natural body. Kojève writes: "Man will risk his biological *life* to satisfy his *nonbiological* [i.e., symbolic] desire. And Hegel says that the being that is incapable of putting its life in danger in order to attain ends that are not immediately vital – i.e. the being that cannot risk its life in a fight for *recognition*, in a fight for pure *prestige* – is *not* a truly *human* being."[9] "Biological life" is further identified with bodily life, and "nonbiological" desire is further identified with language.

The "properly human" is identified with that which is other than the body: the "concept" or the "meaning" as detached from any empirical content and therefore universal. Meaning is precisely what may be detached from any kind of context. Words can be unbound from the empirical and material things that they designate, they can be combined and recombined, they can be *substitutes* for one another. They become the genuine spiritual bodies, and accomplish Spirit's incarnation: "meaning incarnated in the word and in speech is no longer subject to necessity.... Thus, for example, the meaning incarnated in the word 'dog' can continue to subsist even after all the dogs on earth have disappeared."[10] Once the symbolic has been separated from the biological, separation exists for itself as the power of language. The body, as the locus of human animality, belongs to the "biological." Such an animality is what is at risk in the struggle, what has to be murdered as a proof of detachment. The attempt to rid the specificity of human being of the necessity of its own embodiment becomes, as a consequence, the very instance of the sacrifice of animality. Kojève needs here to make Hegel speak of the "human," the "animal," "meaning," and "language," all terms that are totally absent from the Lordship and Bondage scene. In the end, Kojève asserts that the genuine spirit's body is the "book" that the "wise man" (in Absolute Knowledge) has been able to write.

The empirical body, within Kojève's analysis, will have appeared and spoken for a brief moment, before it disappears again under the name of the *corpus* understood as a text – namely the "book" written by the wise man. The slave, or the bondsman, who incarnates attachment because of his attachment to incarnation (or bodily life), is laboring to perform his own detachment, not through the immediacy of desire, like the master, but through the long forming of phrases and chains of words of the absolute.[11] So Kojève thinks the becoming-*corpus* of the body.

It was maintained above that for Hegel, as understood by Kojève and Derrida, absolute detachment is impossible. We can now see, however, that, for Kojève (and for

Kojève's Hegel), absolute detachment from life and from the body is fact both possible and impossible. It is possible as the detachment of the symbolic from the biological, which is presented at the beginning of Lordship and Bondage as the pure affirmation of freedom which can only be obtained through risking one's life: "It is only through staking one's life that freedom is won."[12] It is impossible as the pure act of risking one's life, to the extent that, as Hegel says: the "trial by death, however, does away with the truth which was supposed to issue from it, and so, too, with the certainty of self generally. For just as life is the *natural* setting of consciousness, independence without absolute negativity, so death is the *natural* negation of consciousness, negation without independence, which thus remains without the required significance of recognition. Death certainly shows that each staked his life and held it of no account, both in himself and in the other; but that is not for those who underwent this struggle."[13] The direct consequence of this contradiction in the trial by death is that consciousness must remain attached to life if it is to enjoy the recognition it seeks. In this sense, absolute detachment is impossible.

"To Maintain Oneself in Life..." (Derrida)

Eventually, concludes Derrida reading Kojève, "through a ruse of life, that is, of reason, life has thus stayed alive. Another concept of life had been surreptitiously put in its place, to remain there, never to be exceeded, any more than reason is ever exceeded.... This life is not natural life, the biological experience put at stake in lordship, but an essential life that is welded to the first one, holding it back, making it work for the constitution of self-consciousness, truth, and meaning. Such is the truth of life."[14] The substitution of symbolic life for natural or biological life, the substitution of an "essential body" (book, corpus, meaning) for the living empirical one: this whole chain of delegations and surrogates proves the impossibility of absolute detachment when it is thought within dialectics. The truth of detachment would be for Hegel, in the end, servility: "The truth of the master is in the slave."[15]

The lord's consciousness is not truly independent because it requires the mediation of the slave's attachment to life. The slave works in order to fulfill his master's desire and provide him with pleasurable consumption. What happens through his very labor is that the slave works on the "Thing," "elaborates" it, and thus learns how to "inhibit" (*hemmen*) his own desire, to "delay" (*aufhalten*) his satisfaction and the disappearance of the thing. Maintaining oneself in life does not have the same meaning at the beginning and at the end of the account of Lordship and Bondage. First, it means that the slave is unable to risk his life. At the end, it means that the result of labor is the necessity of paradoxically preserving the truth of the master's gesture. The master desires to suppress his own life. The bondsman preserves this very suppression via his work and thus produces the truth of the master's consciousness. It opposes to "abstract negativity" "the negation characteristic of consciousness, which cancels in such a way that it preserves and maintains what is sublated, and thereby survives its being sublated.... In this experience self-consciousness becomes aware that *life* is as essential to it as pure self-consciousness."[16]

This "comedy" of detachment that ends in an excess of attachment is what makes Bataille *laugh*. To the voice that Kojève lends to the human against the animal, to this way of making Hegel speak, Derrida opposes Bataille's voice, a voice that does not speak, but laughs: ventriloquism versus ventriloquism.

Such laughter transgresses the horizon of meaning, of the preservation of life, of dialectics in general: it "makes the difference between lordship and sovereignty shine, without *showing* it however and, above all, without saying it.... What is laughable is the *submission* of meaning to self-evidence, to the force of this imperative: that there must be meaning, that nothing must be definitely lost in death, or further, that death should receive the signification of 'abstract negativity,' that a work must always be possible which, because it defers enjoyment, confers meaning, seriousness and truth upon the 'putting at stake.' This submission is the essence and element of philosophy, of Hegelian Ontologics."[17]

For Bataille, absolute detachment means first of all the necessary detachment from dialectics. To detach oneself from dialectics, and from the so-called Hegelian ontology in general, implies a strategy of supersession which has to imitate *Aufhebung* while *doubling* it. Sovereignty appears to be the mime or the simulacrum of lordship, which cannot be integrated, as a sham, within any system. What then remains unsublatable is what Derrida/Bataille call "the blind spot" or the "point of nonreserve" of dialectics, a site that Hegel would have indeed perceived, but to which he never dared venture. This point or spot, "which is attached to nothing and does not even want to maintain itself,"[18] is the immediacy of life, of pleasure, consumption, expenditure (*dépense*), of *erotism*: the body.[19]

The body is (the) sovereign, always lost in excessive desire, without any possible return to an intimacy or a home. It "has no identity, is not *self, for itself, toward itself, near itself*."[20] Being forever outside oneself – as only a body can be: this is what Hegel would have refused to think. It is also what renders all bodily substitution impossible. My body is forever outside itself and *I* have to bear it, to experience it: nobody can be my body in my place. Nobody can be my body for me. Death is my own. This irreplace-ability does not lead to the essentializing of the irreplaceable. On the contrary, the pos-sibilities of playing with one's life are kept wide open. We have to put meaning at risk and perform nonsense in language: "we must redouble language and have recourse to ruses, to stratagems, to simulacra. To masks ..."[21]

There is then another kind of writing, sovereign writing, which doubles and dis-places Kojève's conception of the "book." "The book of which Kojève speaks [is] the slave['s] language, that is, the worker['s] language."[22] The other, sovereign writing does not form a totality. Just like the body that it expresses, it is "subordinated to nothing or no one."[23] Further: "the sovereign renunciation of recognition enjoins the erasure of the written text."[24]

Bataille lends his voice to Derrida to say what Hegel would not or could not have said: that the body's constitutive "being outside itself" leads to the erasure of dialectics and consequently of Hegel himself.

"A Set of Consequential Erasures..." (Butler)

Butler's reading strategy orients Lordship and Bondage in a totally different way, even if it stresses the same fundamental issues as do Kojève and Derrida: attachment and detachment, ventriloquism and substitution. First, Butler seems to share Kojève's analysis of the body's sacrifice. The living body is what has to be denied. At the same time, there is in Hegel an "impossibility of a full and final reflexive suppression of what we may call loosely call the 'body' within the confines of life."[25] The lost or sacrificed body has to be preserved in some way. "In Hegel, the suppression of bodily life is shown to require the very body that it seeks to suppress."[26] This preservation of what is suppressed seems to bring Butler very close to Kojève's conclusion regarding the conferral of meaning through the bondsman's labor: "As the bondsman slaves away and becomes aware of his own signature on the things that he makes, he recognizes in the form of the artefact that he crafts the markings of his own labor, markings that are formative of the object itself. His labor produces a visible and legible set of marks in which the bondsman reads back from the object a confirmation of his own formative activity." In other words, the bondsman reads in the thing as in a book! Is not the slave's bodily expropriation of his own flesh (to the extent that he has to incarnate the master) followed directly by its reappropriation through the production, here again, of a corpus or a text?

At this very moment, the analysis changes direction and engages itself on another path. Butler asks: "Can, then, the labor reflected back be said finally to be the bondsman's own?"[27] The answer is negative. "The bondsman discovers his autonomy, but he does not (yet) see that this autonomy is the dissimulated effect of the lord's."[28] He does not see that he is the lord's disavowed body. Bodily substitution can only produce the bondsman as a surrogate and his autonomy as a "credible effect of this dissimulation."[29]

Being an other's body has definite effects, the substitution "becomes consequential" and "formative."[30] The bondsman learns how to read his signature on the thing on which he labors. But because this signature is in fact the lord's one, the thing or the artefact belongs to the lord, "at least nominally."[31] At the very moment at which it becomes the act of reading a book, the slave's relationship to meaning through his own formative behavior *immediately deconstructs itself*. There is no need for any "sovereignty" to double, from outside, domination or mastery; there is no need for a nondialectical act of erasure of meaning or traces. The marks that the bondsman learns how to read erase themselves as soon as they are deciphered. The "signature is erased when the object is given over to the lord, who stamps it with *his* name, owns it, or consumes it in some way. The working of the slave is thus to be understood as a marking which regularly unmarks itself, a signatory act which puts itself under erasure at the moment in which it is circulated, for circulation here is always a matter of expropriation by the lord.... The signature is always already erased, written over, expropriated, resignified.... What emerges is less a palimpsistic object – like Kafka's topographies – than a mark of ownership produced through a set of consequential erasures."[32]

The writing on the thing does not then constitute an essential or spiritual inscription, as Derrida asserts. On the contrary, this writing, proceeding from a substitute, from another body, another hand, another voice – those of the lord – that activate and ventriloquize the bondman's body, the bondsman's hand, the bondsman's voice, consists in a set of traces that never come to presence, permanence, or substantiality.

The way in which Butler makes Hegel speak short-circuits both Kojève's and Derrida's readings. The book and the trace obliterate one another. The book is always already deconstructed. Deconstruction, or the operation of the trace, appears then to be dialectically foreseen or foreseeable.

Does it mean that bodily substitution comes to no result, that it cannot be superseded, that the erasure and remarking of the signature have to be endlessly repeated? In fact, Butler distinguishes two steps in Lordship and Bondage, which correspond to a genuine dialectical evolution of the bodily substitution. These two steps correspond to a double relationship to death. "In the earlier version," Butler writes, meaning the very beginning of the chapter, that is, the life and death struggle, "death happened through the violence of the other; domination was a way of forcing the other to die *within* the context of life."[33] Death first appears as a threat coming from an *other* (the master). Once the slave discovers himself as a laboring consciousness that forms itself as it forms the thing, death appears to be the slave's *own* fate and not, as it used to be, an external hazard. It is only in the end that the bondsman becomes a finite, mortal consciousness. Hegel declares: "the formative activity has not only this positive significance that in it the pure being-for-self of the self-consciousness acquires an existence; it also has, in contrast with its first moment, the negative significance of *fear*. For, in fashioning the thing, the bondsman's own negativity, his being-for-self, becomes an object for him through his setting at nought the existing *shape* confronting him. But this objective *negative* moment is none other than the alien being before which it has trembled. Now, however, he destroys this alien negative moment, posits *himself* as a negative in the permanent order of things, and thereby becomes *for himself,* someone existing on his own account."[34]

Butler comments on this passage: "The laboring body which now knows itself to have formed the object also knows that it is *transient*. The bondsman not only negates things (in the sense of transforming them through labor) and is a negating activity, but he is subject to a full and final negation in death. ... The failure of domination as a strategy *re*introduces the fear of death, but locates it as the inevitable fate of any being whose consciousness is determined and embodied, no longer as a threat posed by another."[35]

We see here all the subtlety of such a reading. The scene produces in the end its dialectical truth, which is the *bondsman's finitude*. Far from ending in the supersession of the finite empirical consciousness through the substitution of the signifying body for the biological one (Kojève), or in the displacement of mastery by sovereignty (Derrida), which would introduce finitude from outside, the end of Lordship and Bondage brings to light the truth of "being towards death." Bodily substitution teaches the bondsman the unsubstitutable character of his mortality. "No one can take the other's dying away from him,"[36] we can hear from another voice ventriloquizing Hegel. Substitution ends in unexchangeability. Is this not what Hegel suggests in the end: "In the lord, the being-for-self is an 'other' for the bondsman, or is only *for* him [i.e., is not his own]; in fear, the being-for-self is present for the bondsman himself; in fashioning the thing, he becomes aware that being-for-self belongs to *him,* that he himself exists essentially and actually in his own right"?[37]

Instead of developing a theory of the essential and symbolic body (the signifying body substituting for the biological one), as Kojève does, Butler displaces what is for Kojève the *telos* of servility: the paradoxical *possibility* of detachment through language incorporated into the labored thing as a meaningful "signature," that is, through the markings or imprint of spirit on the object. For Butler, the bondsman discovers his own body as an erased set of traces, and in consequence as the locus of deconstructed ownership. This adventure of meaning as a process of erasure leads the bondsman to interiorize his finitude. This means also that successful detachment (even if mediated by attachment) and sovereignty are not possible. Butler is calling into question not only *absolute* detachment (which is also called into question by Kojève), but also the detachment-mediated-by-attachment in which Kojève believes.

In opposition to the theory of sovereignty, Butler shows that finitude is discovered at the end of Lordship and Bondage as a definitive (but deconstructed) *attachment* of the self to itself or to its "own" and unsubstitutable meaning. This is true not only of the bondsman but also of the lord. In the lord and bondsman section, it is the laboring body that is elsewhere, and that is a body for the lord; the lord still consumes, and so maintains some bodily activity in relation to what his exteriorized body provides. So in the end the lord's body is never fully evacuated, which suggests that the very process of evacuating the body or loaning it out is inevitably partial and, hence, partially impossible.

2.   Foucault and Stubborn Attachment

Such an orientation displaces the political issues that are held to be at stake in this moment of the *Phenomenology*. For Butler, it is not a matter of emancipating humanity through and by labor (Kojève), or of freeing meaning, speech, and writing from the domination of absolute knowledge (Derrida). Freedom is examined here within the Foucaultian frame of "subjection" ("*assujettissement*: the simultaneous *forming* and *regulating* of the subject"[38]): "Foucault suggested that the point of modern politics is no longer to liberate a subject, but rather to interrogate the regulatory mechanisms through which 'subjects' are produced and maintained."[39] Butler shows that Foucault's theory of the subject's formation is indebted to Hegel even if Foucault rejects any kind of relation to Hegel in his account of this genesis.

Hegel ventriloquized by Butler appears to be the thinker of "stubborn attachment." She reminds both Derrida and Kojève that detachment is irreducibly inseparable from attachment and is therefore *impossible* in the way that Kojève and Derrida conceive it. Kojève thinks that *attachment* eventually dominates detachment, in so far as freedom and power are achieved by the slave; nonetheless the Hegelian slave achieves definitive *detachment*, insofar as the symbolic is detached from the biological in the slave's activity (though such detachment is made possible by the slave's *attachment* to labor). For Butler, by contrast, the slave does not end up as definitively detached as Kojève thinks.

Derrida for his part thinks that *attachment* eventually dominates detachment for Hegel, but that this domination appears to be the result of a failure, the failure to grasp philosophically the glimpse that Bataille offers us of a more profound *detachment* that he calls "sovereignty." Again, Butler casts doubt on the idea that detachment can have the last word.

At the end of Lordship and Bondage, the bondsman knows himself as a transient being, subject to death. The duality of self-consciousness is no longer figured by two existing and struggling consciousnesses: it is now interiorized and recognized as the very structure of self-consciousness. To interiorize finitude is to become aware of one's bodily existence. For the slave to know and interiorize his transience thanks to "fear" implies that he has now reincorporated his own body, which reintroduces a *new kind of bodily substitution*. Butler writes: "The bondsman takes the place of the lord by recognizing its own formative capacity, but once the lord is displaced, the bondsman becomes lord over himself, more specifically, lord over his own body; this form of reflexivity signals the passage from lordship and bondage to unhappy consciousness. It involves splitting the psyche into two parts, a lordship and a bondage internal to a single consciousness, whereby the body is again dissimulated as an alterity, but where this alterity is now interior to the psyche itself."[40]

Bodily substitution does not come to an end with the bondsman's emancipation from the master's external threat. The disavowal of the body now becomes the very shape of the bondman's consciousness: "No longer subjected as an external instrument of labor, the body is still split off from consciousness [at the same time as this splitting appears to be the structure of consciousness itself]. Reconstituted as an interior alien, the body is sustained through its disavowal as what consciousness must continue to disavow."[41]

The interiorization of the denied body, that is, also of the site of pleasure, produces this very denial as an *ethical norm*. The ethical injunction may be considered as the dialectically sublated version of the injunction to incarnation ("you be my body for me"): the disavowal and obliteration of the body has now become self-consciousness's own operation. Fear thereby creates the further injunction, for consciousness, to cling to its *own* body, since it needs that very body in order to disavow it. This new form of attachment to oneself through disavowal of oneself becomes a moral and regulatory norm.

"Subjection," for Foucault, presupposes the suppression of the body as well as the denial of this very suppression, both operations creating the norm or the set of norms as such. According to Butler, the Foucaultian concept of subjection is prefigured in Hegel's analysis of the bondsman's final ethical self-incarceration. For Foucault, "a certain structuring attachment *to* subjection becomes the condition of moral subjectivation."[42]

As we just saw in the discussion of Hegel, this attachment presupposes a disavowal of the body: the subject splits itself from its body, but requires this suppressed body in order to maintain this splitting operation. Are we allowed, however, to bring together Hegel's and Foucault's conceptions of this disavowal? We know that Foucault disagrees with Hegel on an essential point: according to Foucault, such a "maintaining disavowal," which preserves what it denies and is very close to the Freudian concept of sublimation, is not possible. Butler admits it: "For Foucault, the repressive hypothesis, which appears to include within its structure the model of sublimation, fails to work precisely because repression *generates* the very pleasures and desires it seeks to regulate. ... Repression *produces* a field of infinitely moralizable bodily phenomena in order to facilitate and rationalize its own proliferation" (emphasis added).[43] This nonsublatable proliferation is, for Foucault, what is lacking in Hegel's account. For Foucault, it is not a matter of denial *preserving* what is denied, but of repression first *generating* what is regulated.

This lack marks a very serious failure to the extent that the proliferation of regulatory regimes appears paradoxically for Foucault to be the site of resistance to regulation itself. "This proliferation both marks off Foucault's theory from Hegel's and constitutes the site of potential resistance to regulation."[44]

Foucault brings to light the possibility of resisting regulation from within, this resistance amounting here again to a certain type of *detachment*, that of pleasure(s). Every kind of bodily attachment would be doubled by a possible and pleasurable bodily detachment. This bodily detachment may be understood as the multiplicity of "body pleasures" (the plural is essential here), as the variety of multiple unrelated and nonunified sexual functions that Foucault talks about in the first volume of *The History of Sexuality*.[45] Pleasures would detach themselves from the norm, like "grins [that have] hung about without the cat."[46]

Butler declares: "Foucault appears to presume precisely this detachability of desire in claiming that incitements and reversals are to some degree *unforeseeable*, that they have the capacity, central to the notion of resistance, to *exceed* the regulatory aims for which they were produced."[47] For Foucault, a norm tends to cause the proliferation of what it forbids or regulates. It is impossible to foresee and predetermine in what way a body will respond to its own regulation, and in this sense the body's possible responses are *detached* from the regulatory norms that produce them. This gap between the injunction and the response constitutes the site of the resistance to power.[48] Such a gap would not appear at all, according to Foucault, in Hegel's account of Lordship and Bondage.

Acknowledging these disagreements between the two philosophers, Butler, in a quite "Hegelian" way, nevertheless points out the contradictory meaning of the Foucaultian version of detachment: such a detachment remains stubbornly *attached* to itself. It becomes a norm in its turn. This attachment to detachment generates a further attachment to the very rule of subjection that produces the proliferation of detached, unforeseeable pleasures. She writes: "Although Foucault criticizes [Hegel's] and Freud's hypothesis of repression, he is indebted to this theorization in his own account of the production and proliferation of the regulated body. In particular, the logic of subjection in both Hegel and Freud implies that the instrument of suppression becomes the new structure and aim of desire, at least when subjection proves effective. But if a regulatory regime requires the production of new sites of regulation and, hence, a more thoroughgoing moralization of the body, then what is the place of bodily impulse, desire, and attachment? Does the regulatory regime not only produce desire, but become produced by the cultivation of a certain attachment *to* the rule of subjection?"[49]

Attachment would then always play a major role in both the subversion *and the production* of norms. "A regulatory regime" seems always to "exploit this willingness to attach blindly to what seeks to suppress or negate that very attachment."[50] Such would be Hegel's response to Foucault!

3. Conclusion: Plasticity and Hetero-affection

Absolute detachment seems then definitely impossible. We see that all theories of absolute detachment, however different – and even theories, such as Kojève's, that understand detachment to be mediated by attachment but nonetheless to be successful – develop a stubborn attachment to detachment, a stubbornness that marks their frailty and failure. Absolute (or any other successful or definitive) detachment can only be exceedingly attached to itself. To claim such detachment amounts to revealing a philosophical attachment to detachment.

In consequence, absolute detachment *from Hegel* becomes also unthinkable. Sovereignty or proliferation-that-resists would forever be indebted to dialectics. The "capacity of desire to ... reattach will constitute something like the vulnerability" of any anti-Hegelian discourse concerning freedom and pleasure. This inevitability of attachment and reattachment does not lead Butler to share Kojève's conclusions, either. For Kojève, the attachment of meaning to itself – which results from the detachment of meaning from biological life – is achieved in the book once and for all. For Butler, there is no permanent attachment – or permanent detachment – but a series of withdrawals and reattachments. Butler's Hegel is thus the thinker not only of "stubborn attachment," but also of repeated, ultimately *unsuccessful* attempts at detachment. In the end I would like to challenge this conception.

The infinite separation between body and consciousness that seems to structure the whole *Phenomenology of Spirit* corresponds to the impossibility of *auto-affection*. Contrary to Kant, Hegel does not conceive the individual subject as a *unity* differentiated into its transcendental and its empirical (and bodily) forms. He does not consider consciousness to be the site of the permanence of self-identity within the changing flow of succession, permanence that generates the basic sense of *ipseity*. Ipseity or auto-affection is not given as a necessary pre-existing structure of subjectivity. The transcendental and empirical forms of the "I" are alien to each other, and the body appears as an other self within the self. No "I" can ever affect or touch itself. Consciouness is an originary hetero-affected structure, always "out of itself."

I have characterized this hetero-affected structure as the subject's *plasticity*.[51] "Plasticity," like the substantive "plastics" and the adjective "plastic," are derived from the Greek *plassein*, which means "to model," to "mold." "Plastic" means two things: on the one hand, to be "susceptible to changes of form" or malleable (clay is a "plastic" material), and on the other hand: "having the power to bestow form, the power to mold," as in the expressions "plastic surgeon" and "plastic arts." This twofold signification is met again in "plasticity," which describes the nature of what is "plastic," being at once capable of receiving and of giving form.

Plasticity's range of meanings is not yet exhausted, and it continues to evolve in the language. "Plastic material" is a synthetic material that can take on different shapes and properties according to the functions intended. "Plastic" also describes an explosive material with a nitroglycerin and nitrocellulose base that can set off violent detonations. The plasticity of the word itself draws it to two extremes, both to those concrete shapes in which form is crystallized (sculpture) and to the annihilation of all forms (the bomb). When Hegel, in the Preface of the *Phenomenology*, says that the subject is plastic, he means that it is both capable of shaping itself (of bestowing form on itself) and of receiving the very shape that it gives to itself as if it came from outside.[52] There is then a noncoincidence between the given and received shape. That is why shaping one's own body always amounts to disavowing this very operation, as if this shaping were somebody else's operation. Plasticity expresses the contradictory nature of hetero-affection.

Such a motif appears in the Anthropology of the *Encyclopaedia Philosophy of Spirit*. The origin of individual identity is a paradoxical disjunction of the self that leads the soul to madness. Originally, the self is not identical to itself; the mind and the body are definitely split. This doubling of the self is intolerable and maddening. The "feeling of self" in its immediate form is a "mental derangement." The "body is a foreign being" that contradicts the unity of the self.[53] All through the *Phenomenology of Spirit*, this splitting of individual identity will change form and evolve, but will never be sublated as such. The body, being obliterated as the empirical side of consciousness, is always transferred to a site other than the one of self-identity. Self-consciousness always asks somebody else "to be its body in its place," always tries to detach itself from its own incarnation. At the same time, this detachment always comes to fail, revealing the impossibility of a constant, pure, and permanent mastery over things and laboring bodies.

Nevertheless, at the very end of the *Phenomenology of Spirit*, a supreme detachment, presented as the "absolute" itself, occurs. Plasticity acquires here its definitive meaning. The "Self" is not attached to the form of self-consciousness any longer; it loses the form of the "I" and it loses as well the form of its disjunction. The form of the "I" explodes and dissolves itself. This explosive detachment is presented by Hegel as an *Aufgeben*, a letting-go. This *Aufgeben* is not exactly a sublation but a free release, or a giving up. Hegel writes: "Thoughts become fluid when pure thinking, this inner immediacy, recognizes itself as a moment, or when the pure certainty of self abstracts from itself – not by leaving itself out, or setting itself aside, but by giving up [*aufgeben*] the fixity of its self-positing."[54]

The anonymous self of Spirit emerges, which gives up forever its own struggling essence. This abandonment will never give way to a reattachment. Neither a book nor a sovereign, this new form of self without inwardness, without externality, is *subjected* neither to anyone nor to anything. It is not even attached to itself. Shall we see in this absolute detachment a form of stubborn *attachment* to infinite and ideal desire? Or shall we regard it as an impersonal, silent, and so pleasurable ecstatic indifference, which, erasing the limits of what used to be "our" bodies, *unbinds* us from the chain of continuation?

Judith Butler: What Kind of Shape Is Hegel's Body in?

At stake in this joint exploration is the question of what it means to be bound up with another. The question seems to presuppose a dyad and a relation between these two terms, living, conscious, bounded, and yet not. Are they bound to one another and, if so, in what way? If this "being bound" is part of what each of them "is," then how do we rethink the ontological status of each term as both separable and not? Moreover, if the individuated life of each term is not fully exhausted in this relational structure, then how do we understand this persistent, individuated life? Is there an attachment to life itself (one's own life, and life more generally, including the life of the other) that is countered by a detachment from this life and, indeed, from the persistence and particularity of one's "own" life? For Malabou, the concept of plasticity is crucial to understanding the particular dynamic of space and time that characterizes absolute knowledge for Hegel. Plasticity involves the making and unmaking of shapes, but also the condition of being given over to being made by forces outside oneself – a condition that paradoxically grounds the possibility of what we might call "self-making." A few questions follow from this predicament. First, does the attachment to life imply an attachment to one's own life, or does the fact of being shaped by exterior means, of being a shape among shapes, imply a detachment from one's own life in the name of life itself? Second, if life implies an attachment to one's own body, how do we find the body in Hegel? Is it not precisely what must be evacuated, found, and located elsewhere, in order to be understood as one's "own"? Last, does the body find or lose itself when it is bound up with other living bodies in this way?

By the time we arrive at the Lordship and Bondage chapter in the *Phenomenology of Spirit*, it would appear that consciousness discovers another consciousness outside itself as a kind of scandal: how did it get there? How is it possible that this is "me" over there? And how can I account for this apparent distance between the "me" over there and the "I" who regards this me? At first it seems to be a question of comprehension, but it is hardly a dispassionate moment. If I have come "outside myself," then I am no longer localized, and this tells me something new about who I am, my relation to space in particular. I am not a fully or exclusively bounded sort of being, since whatever I am, I have the capacity to appear elsewhere. I am a kind of being who is here and there, apparently at once. I can, as it were, face myself, and this involves a certain measure of self-loss ("I have become other to myself"); it also entails a surprising recurrence of myself at a spatial distance from where I thought I was. I am, then, not quite bounded in space as I apparently assumed, and this unboundedness by which I am now characterized is one that seems bound up, as it were, with a redoubling of myself. The "I" seems to have become two. Of course, the problem is that the "other" whom I face is in some sense me, and in some sense "not me" – and this means that the redoubling of myself that happens in this initial encounter is one that establishes some "other" who is not me. So I encounter myself at a spatial distance from myself, redoubled; I encounter, at the same time, and in the same figure, the limit to what I can call "myself." These two encounters happen simultaneously, but this does not mean that they are reconciled; on the contrary, they exist in a certain tension and this "other" who appears to be me is at once me and not me. So what I have to live with is not just the fact that I have become two, but that I can be found at a distance from myself, and that what I find at that distance is also – and at once – not myself.

The sudden appearance of the "Other" has confused commentators on the *Phenomenology* for some time. Why is it that the Other appears, and why is it that the Other appears as another shape? Let us remember that prior to this sudden event at the outset of chapter 4, the reader has been exposed to a discourse on life, desire, and the way in which shapes come into being and cease to be. Does this prior discourse in some sense set the stage for what appears to be a sudden encounter at the outset of chapter 4? If so, in what way? And is the "suddenness" of this appearance simply arbitrary, or is there a certain significance to the unexpectedness with which this shape appears? The appearance of the other is a "scandal" for a certain way of thinking, one that persists in assuming that the certainty of the "I" is grounded in this specific determinate existence that it is – a position that suggests that this specific body is the basis of whatever certainty the "I" might have about itself.

In an earlier section of the *Phenomenology*, space, time, and distance are conceptualized in relation to "force" (*Kraft*) and "understanding" (*Verstand*). Understanding is differentiated from perception (*Wahrnehmung*). In perception, the determinateness of a thing is known, along with its distinct and determinate qualities. We might understand this way of linking perception to determinateness as prefiguring the "bounded" and distinct sense of the "I" as it first comes face to face with its *redoublement* (*die Verdopplung*) in or as the Other. Of course, what happens in the domain of perception is to some extent analogous with what happens in the domain of understanding, consciousness, and unconsciousness (*das Unbewusste*), even as there are progressive and qualitative distinctions among these domains. For the moment, let us consider the analogy, since this structure is less negated than recapitulated in later chapters. For a "thing" to be determinate, it must be distinguished from other determinate things, and there has to be a way of accounting for that distinction. If one thing is only determinate to the extent that it is not some other, determinate thing, then it follows that part of the very definition of the first thing – as, indeed, of the second – is that it is "not" the other, at which point the distinction between them is revealed as a determinate negation. "Determinateness" not only characterizes the various "things," but the ways in which these things gain their separateness, indeed, their shape, by virtue of the specific ways they are *not* other things. It thus follows that a shape is assumed and maintained to the extent that it is not some other shape – specifically not "this" other, and furthermore "not this other in a specific way."

When Hegel refers earlier to "the Thing," he considers the conceit of self-sufficiency that characterizes its understanding. The thing is independent, it is defined in opposition to other things,[55] and its independence depends on this sustained opposition. This proves to be impossible, as the formulation already suggests ("its independence depends on ... x"), but this particular impossibility is essential to what it is at this stage of development. Hegel writes, "But it is only a Thing, or a One that exists on its own account, insofar as it does not stand in this relation to others; for this relation establishes rather its continuity with others, and for it to be connected to others is to cease to exist on its own account [*und Zusammenhang mit Anderem ist das Aufhören des Fürsichseins*]." The thing "ceases to exist on its own account," but what precisely does this mean? It means first of all that whatever determinate shape it takes ceases to appear determinate when it comes to take stock of itself not as a bounded being, but as a relation to other bounded beings. In general, the notion of relation (*Zusammenhang*) seems to trump the idea of determinateness, at least provisionally. But, of course, this particular inversion will not hold. For the moment, though, let us consider that relationality upends the conviction that this shape derives its specificity and independence from its determinate character.

I have used the concept of "shape" here perhaps proleptically, since what happens in this key transition between perception and understanding does not yet make use of the concept of shape. But it seems clear that once we are referring to the determinate ways in which a thing is bounded, we are, at least implicitly, referring to its shape, or so I would like to argue. As the sections of the *Phenomenology* proceed, this conviction that the thing is a self-sufficient truth gives way to a conception of "differences" as an ultimate truth. The text considers the ways in which differences are gathered or grouped, and asks what holds them together. The principle or rule according to which a unity is made and recognized is then regarded either as inherent to a determinate series or as belonging to a subjective cognitive sphere, or "internal" world, separated from that

series. Ultimately, the mediation between the principle that unifies the series characterizing external realities and the internal principle that unifies the series gives way to an
"inverted world" that then poses a new challenge: what mediates between these two
ostensible worlds? Without rehearsing all of the important transitions that give rise to
this question of mediation, let us underscore that what is at stake at this moment is no
less than the relation between what appear to be two worlds: sensible and supersensible.
The difference between the two turns out to be, in Hegel's terms, "inner difference, a
repulsion of the self-same, as selfsame, from itself, and likeness of the unlike as unlike"
(*Gleichsein des Ungleichen als Ungleichen rein darzustellen und aufzufassen*). This rendition
of difference is not exactly a static formulation, since it turns out that the two worlds
are constantly regenerating each other in their separateness and in their interrelation.
To think this "difference" between the two worlds is to be transformed by the thought
itself, since thought *itself* must now participate in two worlds (sensible and supersensible). What do we call this thought that comes to understand itself as partitioned in this
way? Hegel introduces the notion of self-consciousness precisely on the occasion when
this configuration of partitioned thought becomes thinkable. In other words, this
apprehension is of the way in which the difference between those two worlds not only
defines them as objects of thought but regenerates them – and this proves to be an
infinite process. At the same time, and through this very process, this "apprehension"
alters consciousness, giving it a new form or, indeed, giving it a "shape" (*Gestalt*) in the
domain of appearance — paradoxically, as an infinity that takes on a new, determinate
shape.

Indeed, it is at this juncture that the notion of "shape" becomes important for Hegel's
exposition. He writes, "consciousness, in the way that it *immediately* has this Notion [of
infinity], again comes on the scene as a form belonging to consciousness itself, *or as a
new shape of consciousness* [emphasis added], which does not recognize in what has gone
before its own essence, but looks on it as something quite different."[56] Let us consider
then how "consciousness comes on the scene as a form." What is this scene? How does
consciousness "come on the scene"? It seems to come on the scene at the same time
that it assumes a form or a new shape. It does not arrive on the scene and *then* take on
a new shape; rather, its arrival is the very act by which a new shape is assumed. In
other words, to arrive on the scene, which must be a new scene (after all, consciousness
is *just* arriving somewhere), is also to assume a new shape. Scene and shape thus
emerge at once. To enter onto a scene is to assume a shape, and to assume a shape is,
indeed, to enter onto a scene.

But for infinity to take on a shape, or for self-consciousness itself to take shape, we
have to understand that "shape" itself is no simple matter: it cannot be identified with
bounded and static form. Shape comes into being (is both the process and end result of
shaping) and passes from being (in dissolving, it loses its shape). Moreover, shape is, as
Hegel remarks, "divided within itself,"[57] a way of describing shape that calls into question its stable, spatial appearance. Shape appears "as something determinate, for an
other"; it is not simply self-subsisting, but defined in relation to an infinite series of
shapes. The idea of a relation and a process of differentiation defining what shape "is"
calls into question the notion of shape as restrictively spatial and static. There seems to
be an operation of time in "shape" and also a set of relations that entail thinking the
interstices among shapes as part of what defines shape itself. Hegel understands that

627

this calls into question a certain common sense approach to shape, one that tends to regard shape as self-subsisting or existing. Only when we take the determinate existence of a shape as definitive of what shape is do we understand shape as "for itself." However, there remains an "infinity of difference" in which and through which this existent shape takes shape. That infinity is thus central to what shape is, since not only does it form the necessary background to every existent shape, it constitutes an essence that is not fully reducible to that existence. This open and limitless time seems to be as definitive of shape as any determinate spatial existence. Just as shape cannot be reduced to its particular existence, so shape cannot be reduced to the infinity to which it belongs. Shape thus vacillates between particular existence and infinity, and this vacillation becomes its defining characteristic and action.

Can we assume that by referring to shape Hegel is also referring to the *body?* The body has a shape and may even be one of the key models we have for thinking about shape in general. But before we can make the link between the two, we have to follow a few more transitions in the text: the relation of shape to life, to desire, and then to the two emergent self-consciousnesses whose particular mode of desire leads them to threaten each other's life – something that can hardly be done if there are no bodies that can fight and die. Yet even later, Hegel will refer to the two self-consciousnesses that encounter one another as "independent shapes."

Significantly, this discussion of the apparent contradiction that defines and motivates "shape" leads Hegel to a discussion of "Life" – and so, we might say, the scene is being set for the emergence of a set of "shapes" onto the scene of life, a scene that will turn out, in the next section, to be characterized by death as well as life – death as part of life. "Shape" seems sometimes to "preserve itself" and sometimes to be "dissolved"; it preserves itself as "existing," but it is dissolved in what Hegel calls a "universal substance" or "element." To preserve itself, it must separate itself from the universal substance to which it belongs.[58] This process of "separating off" (*die Absonderung*), which seems to secure a determinate existence against dissolution, is equated at one point with "consumption" (*das Aufzehren*). A certain parsing or "separating out" of shapes takes place, quietly or calmly (*ruhig*), characterizing a process by which shapes appear in a certain movement with one another. As with other transitions in the *Phenomenology*, a new term is introduced or, indeed, a new term "appears on the scene" at the moment that a new conceptualization takes place. A new word, "Life," describes this dynamic of preserving oneself and becoming dissolved, of shapes that are not fully self-sufficient but bound up with one another.[59] It is, interestingly, a quiet medium, distinct then from the *"Unruhigkeit"* or disquiet that characterizes the dramatic trajectory of the desiring subject (cf. the preface to the *Phenomenology*). But here we are introduced to a concept of life, and even of a living being (*das Lebendige*), that is conceived as a medium. This life is a quiet movement of shapes, but what precisely does this mean? It is not just any movement, but the specific movement of giving and dissolving shape, one that characterizes not only this or that shape, but all shapes. Determinate lives come into being and pass away, but "Life" seems to be the name for the infinite movement of imparting and dissolving shape. No determinate life is all of Life, and Life cannot be grasped through reference to this or that life. Life itself is characterized as the process through which shape is imparted or instituted (*Gestaltung*) and overcome (*das Aufheben*). This process is clearly not linear: "It is the whole round [*Kreislauf*] of this activity that constitutes Life."[60]

628

However infinite, "Life" is still a quiet process. Disquiet only emerges once something called consciousness arrives on the scene. Consciousness is first called the "genus" in the Miller translation,[61] but might be better called the "species" (*die Gattung*), prefiguring what will become for Feuerbach and Marx the "species-being" (*Gattungswesen*). As a species, it would seem that the one life is linked with others, and that this shared or common life becomes specified as one that belongs to self-consciousness. That term is introduced to describe the scene in which the "I" takes itself as a simple universal. There is life in general, but then there is the understanding of life as differentiated into species, including the one to which the "I" belongs. What precisely circumscribes this species we do not know, but what becomes clear[62] is that the idea of life as simple – and as a presumptively "quiet" medium – is disrupted by the existence of an "independent life." Of course, the notion of "independent life" was already presupposed by the very idea of the species, since a species is a way of grouping or collecting such independent lives; but if life is understood as the universal element that groups or collects, then life cannot easily be understood as any of the independent existences collected by the term. We could say that the idea of the species logically implies an internally differentiated group, but Hegel may also be implying that the idea of the species is bound up with the reproduction of the species. It is difficult to know what accounts for the arrival of this other life, but an independent life does appear on the scene, and this happens before the beginning of the Lordship and Bondage section.

The "I" who simply instantiates the universal is "simple" and even "quiet," but disquiet seems to enter precisely when consciousness seeks to become *certain* of itself, certain of its truth. As an instance of universality, it is but one of many shapes coming into being and passing out of being. But it turns out that it will be disquieted precisely by its *substitutability*, on the one hand, and its *finitude*, on the other. Surely, the idea of the species implies substitutability: the "I" is one shape among others, subject to a process of coming into and passing out of existence. The condition of differentiation defines the species, but the idea of the species would itself dissolve if this were a differentiation without limit. At least two dimensions of bodily life are presupposed by this account: first, one is a body among bodies; second, the body involves a process of being formed or being dissolved. The species outlives the existing individual, even as the species requires existing individuals to reproduce it. So what is it about the idea of "certitude" that makes this condition of being substitutable and transient so disquieting? Why not simply remain quiet and content with this *Kreislauf* that is Life?[63]

To become certain of itself as singular and determinate, this consciousness, which is already aware of being redoubled, must overcome or supersede the other and reachieve its self-certainty. And if it cannot reachieve self-certainty on that basis, it must find it on another. Once this action is under way, another term, "self-consciousness," arrives on the scene whose effort to supersede the other is characterized as desire (*Begierde*). Duplication appears insurmountable within this scene. If the process of overcoming (desire) is essential to self-consciousness, it would seem that desire requires that the other self-consciousness survive and persist (it will turn out that this independent life has to be overcome again and again, infinitely). To overcome the independent life of the other is to overcome one's own independent life as well – at least potentially. The "I" becomes redoubled and, as that redoubling, becomes bound up in a scene of desire and fear: it requires the other, but it also requires the obliteration of that other.

At the outset of "Lordship and Bondage," the independent and living shape that belongs to another existence proves to be a problem, a disquieting challenge, since how am "I" to be certain of myself if I find myself redoubled there? The problem is not simply that there is an unequivocally independent life over there, emphatically not-me. Rather, the problem, the offense, the scandal, is that the independent life over there is also me, and yet is not. The logic of noncontradiction is not working precisely at the moment when the "I" seeks to know and affirm itself with unequivocal certainty. It would seem that this redoubling cannot itself be overcome, and that the "I" who would know its truth with certainty will have to know its own redoubling as its certain truth. In what way does this imply a problem pertaining not only to desire – a term (*Begierde*) that preserves a sense of animality – but to embodied life more generally?

In what sense exactly is the "I" redoubled? First, it would appear that there is another shape over there, self-subsisting, and that it is also an "I" and so of the same species as me, co-instantiating a universal form of life. Second, it would appear that even as this "I" *is* this determinate shape, and takes this shape to be the basis of its life, its life belongs to a life that is neither "this" or "that" life, but the very process of coming into being and dissolving of shape. So to speak of "my life" is already to refer to my own persistent shape, and determinateness is surely part of the picture; but life also refers to nonpersistence, to the time when this life did not yet exist, to the alterations that have formed the trajectory of its existence, and to the time in which this life will no longer exist. Not even the "this" of "this life" belongs to me. The fact that there is this defining shape *over there*, characterizing an opposing and similar "I," links the sense of my expungibility to that of my substitutability. But how do we understand the interrelation of finitude and substitutability? It is not only that there is a time before and after I exist, and that this time is part of Life, conceived precisely as a differentiating process. There are others who precede and exceed this "I," who survive this life, or prevail when this "I" has not. And even within this life, there are these independent lives that are not the same as my own, which challenge this "I" to find the truth of itself in its desirous (also then, fearful, murderous) relation to others. This "I" is bound to others, but also, as shape, unbound.

Hegel has come to establish through these steps the constitutive sociality of this self-consciousness. The first few paragraphs of the "Lordship and Bondage" chapter explain how this works at an abstract level, but in paragraph 185 (in the Miller translation) Hegel turns specifically to the question of how "this pure Notion of recognition, of the duplicating of self-consciousness in its oneness, appears to self-consciousness."[64] And it is only within this more strictly phenomenological development that we learn that, "appearing immediately on the scene," these two self-consciousnesses "are for one another like ordinary objects, independent shapes." These shapes are considered living, and life, accordingly, is understood as something that belongs to this or that living thing. The medium of Life – the process of imparting and dissolving shape – has not yet been apprehended, since the one self-consciousness understands life to be *this* or *that* life. In other words, the shape defines and contains the life; to destroy the shape would be to negate the duplication of shape, and so to eradicate the scandal of substitutability itself. But it will turn out, as we all know, that the living consciousness can return to its absolute singularity only by risking its own life. And yet in dying, that living consciousness could not achieve the self-certainty it seeks.

This opens up the larger question of how certainty is to be achieved on the basis of substitutability. Who is this "I" who is, on the one hand, substitutable, and yet, on the other, also singularly alive? If this "I" is to register its substitutability, it has to survive as *this* life to do precisely that. In other words, its singularity is the precondition of its understanding of substitutability, and is presupposed, logically, by the idea of substitution itself (one term is replaced by another). It is in this sense that the *non*substitutable is the persistent logical and existential condition of substitutability. The one can seek to assert its singularity only by substituting itself for the other. Through destroying that other and taking its place (indeed, taking up all the places that there are), the one can try to establish its singularity. But there may be other others who may seek to destroy that one for the same purpose, so how does one survive in such a world, without avowing an interdependent sociality? As much as the "I" is threatened by negation – or threatens the other with negation – so it is clear that the life of the one is dependent on the life of the other. This interdependency becomes a new way of conceiving of life as sociality. Sociality cannot be reduced to the existence of this or that group, but is the open temporal trajectory of interdependency and desire, struggle, fear, and murderous dispositions (a clear way in which Hegel prefigures the psychoanalytic work of Melanie Klein).

Of course, much more could be said about why the encounter with finitude follows from the encounter with substitutability. The absent and mediating term seems to be the body itself. One might simply conclude that the other self-consciousness becomes the site where the "I" encounters its finitude. I am not only exchangeable or substitutable by the other, but I encounter my death there at the site of substitutability. Yet I can only die if the "I" is animal, part of an *organic* nature, and this is everywhere assumed but rarely acknowledged in Hegel's language. This ellipsis functions as a kind of persistent and legible disavowal, since the body is everywhere assumed, though nowhere named. We are solicited by the text to assume this body, to understand that it functions as the necessary condition of any argument he makes about shape, life, desire, and death. But if it is to remain known and yet unspeakable, what does this tell us about how the body is to comport itself in this process?

One might rightly remark that the body does not appear in Hegel's text or that the body is simply absent. To maintain such a view, however, is not yet to explain how this "nonappearance" makes itself known in the realm of appearance. After all, if the discussions of life, shape, desire, and pleasure all presuppose the body, then the body is logically presumed, even if not overtly thematized. From the above analysis, there are already some conclusions to be drawn: the "I" is a bounded shape, but it finds itself reduplicated, at which point substitutability counters the specificity of this body here as the defining characteristic of the "I." Both seem to be true, and paradoxically so: this body here constitutes my life; but that body there is also me. This means that I am at once here and there, and that whatever certainty I may gain about the truth of this "I" will be one that accepts this spatial vacillation as its precondition. That other shape is not me, if "I" am understood only as this body here. But it turns out that my shape only gains its shape through being differentiated from that other shape, and so I am bound to that other. *For a body to be a body, it must be bound to another body.* This being bound might be understood as an "attachment," but it would be wrong to see that attachment as "my" attachment. It is not that "I" am attached, or attach myself, to

631

another body, but that without such an attachment, there is no "I" and there is no "you." When the two self-consciousnesses ready themselves for their fight, they are described as seeking to show that they "are not attached to life." When they grasp the necessity of living, they grasp the necessity of living together; the substitutability essential to sociality becomes essential to individual survival. So these bodies must be bound together before they can emerge as bodies: there is no singular shape that exists outside of this differentiated relation to other shapes. And just as it was established that, logically and phenomenologically, substitutability requires the survival of the singular life, understood as nonsubstitutable, so it appears that singularity cannot survive without this substitutability.

How does this relate to our effort to find the body in Hegel? And what is its specific relation to desire as the means through which one body becomes bound up with another? The encounter between the two self-consciousnesses is a mute one. No one addresses the other, but is there a form of address that implicitly takes place in the life and death struggle, and then again in the lordship and bondage relation? Is it not possible, or even necessary, to ventriloquize the voice of direct address that implicitly takes place in this encounter? "You, you seem to live, but if I am the one who lives, then life cannot take place over there as well, without you having taken away my life!" And then, "You, you have to live, since I do not want to have my life threatened by you, and I see now that threatening your life also puts my own life at risk. This seems to be true since we mirror each other, duplicate each other, at some level, but this is still in some ways unbearable to me, for where is my singularity?" In resolving on domination as a way to handle the problem of (a) needing to live as this singular life and (b) accepting substitutability as a constitutive condition of sociality, the Lord emerges as a figure who will seek to control the body of the other through a specific instrumentalization of substitutability. "You, you be my body for me."

Attributing a direct address to the phenomenological scene is interesting for all kinds of reasons, since it references first an "I" who would delegate its body to another, but also a form of desire that turns on that delegation. The body can only be delegated if it first belongs to the one who delegates it. And yet the body is already delegated, understood as a shape among shapes, outside itself, bound to others. Of course, in Hegel, the "body" does not appear as such, which could mean that Hegel, at least in this context, seeks to elaborate a conception of desire, life, shape, without explicit recourse to the body. We can read this as a suppression, a structural somatophobia, but it might be more productive to ask how the body is always leaving its trace, even when it operates without being named explicitly. Maybe there is something about the body that cannot be named as such, or that is always conceptualized exclusively as a determinate shape, and so misrecognized, when it becomes "the body." After all, we have already seen how for Hegel shape does not derive its truth from its specificity; shape is defined as much by infinity as by space; life gives and dissolves shape, and so shape is part of this larger, indeed infinite, process; substitutability thus seems to be another way of recasting both shape and desire in open temporal terms. This is not to say that the spatial or determinate character of shape is transcended through the shapeless trajectory of infinity; rather, it is to suggest that shape cannot be thought apart from its constitutive temporality, and that that temporality both conditions and exceeds its determinate existence.

632

One question then emerges: Is it a trace of infinity that happens when the body finds itself redoubled? The scene is dyadic, but does it turn out to be part of a limitless series of substitutions? But a second question emerges: How are we to understand that "doubling" at the level of the body? If "you" are my body for me, then you are my body in my place, and I am relieved of having to be a body. You take it over and live it for me, and I am able to stay in relation to that my-body-as-another. This suggests that the body is not precisely redoubled, but that it is evacuated, loaned out, and lived elsewhere. This is a different sense of being *"hors de soi"* or *"ausser sich gekommen."* In the Lord and Bondsman section, it is the laboring body that is elsewhere, that is a body for the lord, but the lord still consumes and in this way remains a body in relation to what his exteriorized body provides. The lord's body is thus never fully evacuated, and it follows that nobody's living body fully is: the very process of evacuating the body or loaning it out is inevitably partial and, hence, partially impossible. How do we want to think about the "partial impossibility" of that substitution? If the act of "loaning out" is itself part of the trajectory of desire, to what extent does desire rely on that always partial evacuation of the body into and as the other body? The logic of redoubling is part of the trajectory of desire, understood as the desire to overcome and to preserve another. As a negation that must keep happening, that cannot fully negate what it requires, desire is always a partial overcoming – not just of the body of the other, but of one's own body. If desire is always a desire to overcome bodily existence, it is equally bound by the necessity of preserving it. Modes of mock murder, failed efforts at full instrumentalization, constant efforts to evacuate the bodies that one is and that one requires all return us to the bind of being bound. To be redoubled is thus not fully to be vanquished, nor fully to vanquish, but to reenact, without end or resolution, the evacuation of the body in the midst of its persistence.

Catherine Malabou: What Is Shaping the Body?

Judith, I would like to focus on one sentence of your beautiful text. This sentence is in fact a question, which appears to me to be the hinge, or the cornerstone, of your analysis. You ask: "Can we assume that by referring to shape Hegel is also referring to the *body?*" This question I would like to question in turn myself. I do not think that you are addressing the possibility of identifying *shape* and *body* in Hegel. I think that, through your powerful reading of Lordship and Bondage ("You be my body for me"), you are addressing the problem of *shaping the body,* which is quite different. Bodies that matter are for Hegel bodies that take shape, to the extent that, as you say: "To enter onto a scene is to assume a shape, and to assume a shape is, indeed, to enter onto a scene." How could such a structure – shape-taking/shape-giving – characterize something other than the very economy of bodily plasticity?

"Can we assume that by referring to shape Hegel is also referring to the *body?*" What makes me hesitate to consider this question as being *your* question here is that Hegel himself answers it very clearly. Yes, by referring to shape, Hegel refers (also) to the body in the discussion of shape. You insist on the fact that the body seems to be absent not only from the Lordship and Bondage scene, but from the whole *Phenomenology of Spirit.* I think that this is only an approximation. Leaving aside the discussion of Christianity in the account of the Unhappy Consciousness (with its developing ideas of sacrifice and extreme suffering), there is a very explicit and thematic section devoted to the body in "Observing Reason" (more precisely: "Observation of the Relation of Self-Consciousness to Its Immediate Actuality: Physiognomy and Phrenology").

In this section, we see clearly that the body is a shape, both shaped and unshaped (both a natural gift – an unshaped shape – and the result of a formative process – a shaped shape). The individual's activity of shaping its own body, of giving a form to it (or of "making" it), is understood to include both the process of "work" and of "language." "This being, the body of the specific individuality, is the latter's original aspect, that aspect in the making of which it has not itself played a role. But since the individual is at the same time only what he has done, his body is also the expression of himself which he has himself *produced;* it is at the same time a sign, which has not remained an immediate fact, but something through which the individual only makes known what he really is, when he sets his original nature to work."[65] Further: "the body is the unity of the unshaped and of the shaped being, and is the individual's actuality permeated by his being-for-self."[66]

I do not have time to expound on the fascinating movement of this section, devoted to organs and expression, flesh and signs, the originary nature and cultural transformation of the body. I just wish to insist on the plastic relationship between the individual and his or her body, between the natural, unshaped and animal part of it, on the one hand, and the labored and spiritually sculpted part of it, on the other.

Again, the assumption of the identity between shape and body in Hegel is perfectly legitimate and justified. There is an explicit thought of the body in Hegel, which asserts that the body is and has a shape, and defines the very activity of consciousness (material as well as symbolic) as the process of forming the body.

Therefore, it appears that your genuine interrogation concerns less the body/shape identity than the conditions of possibility for this identity itself: how are we to understand the *shaping* of the body? More specifically, what exactly is shaped through this activity?

Before I make myself clearer, I would like to confide that the difficulty I intend to explore is also *my* difficulty, a constant source of reflection that remains wide open. What I will now say is for that reason only tentative.

It concerns the Hegel/Foucault relationship. Here now is my question to your question: "Can we assume that by referring to shape and to the body (or to the body considered as a shape) Hegel refers in advance to the self as Foucault will define it?" More exactly: "Can we assume that, under the name of plasticity, Hegel describes in advance what Foucault will present as the cultivated relation of the self to itself, that is, as a self-transformation or stylization?" Is there any other valid conception of the shaping of oneself (of one's own body, identity, mind, etc.) outside the one that Hegel presents as the very structure of subjectivation, the subject's plasticity?

Even if Foucault clearly rejects dialectics, are we not led to regard his definitions of self-transformation and stylization as being very close to Hegel's conception of plasticity? If we stress the notions of form, shape, taking shape, dissolving shape, and so on in our readings of Hegel, if we grant plasticity a privilege over ontology,[67] how can we then avoid considering the Foucaultian notion of the cultivation of the self, in all its aspects, as the truth of the *Phenomenology of Spirit,* as being the phenomenology of spirit itself?

If we consider that the master's disavowal of his own body in Lordship and Bondage becomes a relation of the bondsman's self-consciousness to its own body, then we must admit that the result of the plastic operation of shaping one's body as Hegel presents it is very close to what Foucault describes as the stylization of oneself, as the transformation of oneself (one's self) into a work of art.

I would like to point out that, while you argue with Foucault about resistance and emancipation all through your interpretation of Lordship and Bondage, you do not specify the difference between Hegel's and Foucault's conceptions of bodily shaping. Even if Foucault strongly refused to consider Lordship and Bondage as an archetype for subjectivation, it seems that we are allowed to consider a posteriori this moment of the *Phenomenology* as a chapter of *The History of Sexuality,* or as a preface to *What Is Critique?*[68] In this text, we know that Foucault shows that a subject is constituted by its assimilation of a set of regulatory norms (it is formed, or shaped by them), and by its singular interpretation of these norms (it forms the norms in return). This constitutes both the subject's enslavement and its "practice of liberty." You argue that one can be enslaved *by* one's own practice of liberty, you reintroduce conflict and sublimation (dialectics and psychoanalysis) within the Foucaultian self, but it seems that the issue of a possible *plasticity* of this self is left aside.

I do share your understanding of shape. I totally agree with the claims (which are one and the same): (1) that "'Shape' itself is no simple matter: it cannot be identified with bounded and static form. Shape comes into being (is both the process and end result of shaping), and passes from being (in dissolving, it loses its shape)," (2) that "'shape' seems sometimes to 'preserve itself' and sometimes to be 'dissolved,'" and (3) that "the body involves a process of being formed or being dissolved." Again, my own insistence on the motif of plasticity in Hegel confirms the attention I pay to shape, and to the double process of bestowing and receiving form as being constitutive of both power relationships and the experience of freedom. But it is true (that is why I mentioned that the issues I am addressing to you here are also addressed to my own work) that I constantly wonder what exactly the difference is between Hegel's conception of self-making and Foucault's concept of self-formation.

Why would this crossing between Hegel and Foucault be a matter for debate at all? one might ask. What is so puzzling in the assimilation of dialectical bodily shaping to self-transformation or self-stylization? Why should there be a dramatic difference between both processes of self-shaping? There is, perhaps, no reason, except insofar as the meaning of the *self* is concerned. The plastic operation of shaping one's body, as Hegel presents it, is, indeed, very close to what Foucault describes as the stylization of oneself, but the two processes are not precisely the same.

Let's recall that for Foucault, "critique" is "an instrument, a means for a future or a truth that it will not know nor happen to be; it oversees a domain [the body?] it would not want to police and is unable to regulate."[69] Because of this lack of control, this freeing from its own mastery, "critique is akin to virtue."[70] It seems, therefore, that the critical self that Foucault is defining can always become aware of the kind of transformation in which it is involved. Even if it is not able to master what is happening to it, it can "oversee" transformation, it can be willingly involved in it and make it a virtuous process, the process of "care." The Foucaultian self seems then to be constantly auto-affected by its own form, even when this form is to come and is still unknown. The self

635

affects itself even with what it does not know about itself. This nonknowledge is included in self-transformation, and is in a way its condition of possibility. In all cases, the self never loses itself; it is bound to itself, even if not reflectively, within the critical frame. Repetition, exercise, practice, self-modeling realize the synthesis of the well-known and the unknown aspects of one's subjectivity. This synthesis occurs precisely at the level of the body.

We can understand at that point why Hegel himself was so defiantly critical of critique that in fact never loses control of itself. The critical soul is affected by its bodily shaping. As Hegel powerfully demonstrates, critique can only be the critique of the subject by itself as being other than itself. This activity of critique is both a shaping and a dissolving of the subject: the subject exists (has a form) by virtue of its own critique, but this critique dissolves the conceit of its self-sufficiency. However, for Hegel, critique is never negative enough, it is never critical enough to challenge the auto-affective structure of subjectivity, according to which a subject is an "I," an individual self, a self subject to self-critique. The structure of auto-affection, that is, of *attachment*, involves a determined relationship between me and the other, my soul and my body, my current bodily shape and the form into which it will soon be transformed. If the notion of self-transformation is to be genuinely *critical*, it has to transform itself conceptually and to provoke the *explosion* of the traditional notion of the "I." Hegel is the thinker of such an explosion (we saw that *plastic* also names an explosive).

Again, it is not that "in Hegel, the 'body' does not appear as such, which could mean that Hegel … seeks to elaborate a conception of desire, life, shape, without explicit recourse to the body." We saw that several passages from the *Phenomenology* contradict this statement. The problem is that, for Hegel, when self-consciousness interiorizes its own bodily and mortal condition, when it understands that it forms its own mortality, that finitude is a plastic process, this interiorization and understanding cause a dissolution of self-consciousness itself. In this way, I think, Hegel challenges the structure of auto-affection.

The self that transforms itself does not coincide with itself; it becomes alien to its own body, to its own "I." This is not a single event, but a structure. Self-transformation is always a hetero-affection. Such is the meaning of this "letting go," of this absolution, this *Aufgeben*, I was talking about in my section above, "Unbind Me." A plastic subject can only be detached from its own form.

I wonder if the Foucaultian self is capable of such an explosive detachment from itself. Is it not exceedingly attached to its transformation?

In the end, this is "my" critique, which, of course, is not a critique, but a malicious tribute to your beautiful text: To what extent are you attached yourself to the Foucaultian articulation of self-transformation, that is, to his possible stubborn attachment to (self-) attachment?

Judith Butler: A Chiasm between Us, but No Chasm

It seems to me that we agree on certain points and that our disagreement perhaps illuminates a certain agonism at the heart of Hegel's text. It is true, as you claim, Catherine, that there is an impossibility of an absolute detachment from the body, but this opens the question of what kind of detachment there might be. I want to add to this a contrary claim, equally true, that there is no absolute attachment, either. I take it that this last claim is the one you want to press in these pages, and I think it is an important one. If there is no absolute attachment, then what kind of attachment might there be?

I can see that my own position is one that could be construed as asserting self-attachment as a primary and insuperable truth. But even if there is no absolute or complete escape from self-attachment, it does not immediately follow that self-attachment is thus more primary than detachment. In fact, if it proves true that absolute detachment is impossible as well, then we have two fundamental truths, each of which seems to limit and condition the other and to produce a recurring tension within Hegel's text.

I think there are ways of reading Hegel that draw him close to Spinoza and, indeed, to Freud, such that we read a kind of *conatus* at work, a desire that attaches to existence presupposed by every act of the subject. That would be an attachment to persistence that would support the attribution of a "life-drive" to Hegel or perhaps a kind of auto-affection that Freud reflects on in the opening paragraphs of his essay "On Narcissism." It seems true that Hegel draws on Spinoza in his formulation of desire, and he may be seen to prefigure Freud by showing how every effort at absolute self-disavowal carries the seeds of its own final failure. You are clearly right, however, to remind us that in Hegel, there is "hetero-affection" from the start, since to attach oneself to one's own life turns out to be impossible without a certain dispossession of the self. I take it that even Hegel's concept of life includes the necessary dissolution of shape as well as the understanding of life as exceeding each and every finite and particular life. To be alive or, indeed, to be "attached" to life would mean to be attached to one's own dissolution or, indeed, to discover that life is never exclusively one's own. In this instance as in many others, "ownness" undergoes a certain constitutive crisis, so I simply confirm your point that self-attachment cannot be understood as any more insuperable or absolute than detachment from the self. But there are two further points I would like to make in this context.

The first is that if we can fully escape neither attachment nor detachment, then perhaps we are referring to a chiasm that gives shape, as it were, to the problem of life. This figure might be important, might be, in fact, the ultimate shape, since it suggests that attachment and detachment are bound by "life" at the same time that they exceed and oppose one another. In other words, there is a zone of encounter and repulsion, which we might actually call *the life of the body,* understood as propulsion to and away from persistence as such. This would allow something like the "death drive" to enter into our conception of Hegel's notion of life; it would differentiate Hegel from Spinoza and his more Spinozistic readers; and it would explain the irreducible tension between these two movements (attachment, detachment) as constitutive of life itself.

The second is that in Hegel and Foucault alike, there is no way to "attach to the self" without mediation, and so self-attachment can function neither as a metaphysical ground nor as a form of self-certainty. The life I would embrace is not prior to the social and linguistic formulation of life: sociality conditions and interrupts each and every apparently intimate and immediate relation I might have to my existence. This does not mean that each and every relation I have to my existence is reflective or conscious, since

637

the social and linguistic terms by and through which I become conscious of myself are not fully available to me, nor can I reflexively grasp the full range of historical processes that condition my emergence as a subject and the relations that presupposes. My sense is that critique is not a practice of hyper-reflexivity, but the necessary encounter with the limits that make any knowledge possible. In a way, the self that is supported by available ontologies reaches its limit precisely there, and so cannot be attached to itself; it rather becomes attached to a future that is defined by its negative relation to what exists. What interests me most about Foucault is how he casts those limits as discursive ones, established by modes of rationality and power understood as historically variable. If critique is a virtue, it is perhaps the virtue of courage that is required in that exercise of liberty that challenges the limits of those schemes of intelligibility that limit who will be a recognizable subject, and who will not. I would add that critique involves risking and even losing that form of recognizability that allows for self-attachment: how can I be attached to myself, if I do not yet know what self it is I am becoming and can become? To be attached to one's self is thus to be attached to what I am not and cannot yet know, and can never fully know.

Of course, your way of linking the problem of shape to the conception of plasticity is most pertinent. I wonder if there is not a specific ontology of plasticity or if, in your view, plasticity always exceeds ontology. How can that be? If finitude is a plastic process, as you insist, and if self-dissolution is the result of that process, then perhaps we can return to this double movement of attachment and detachment, persistence and desistance, as Derrida once put it, in order to understand how plasticity is another name for absolute knowledge. The alienation from the body that follows from receiving and bestowing form entails, in your words, "a dissolution of self-consciousness itself." I would agree that whatever contingent "self" it is to which I seek to attach myself will have to exceed and confound my efforts at self-attachment, if that self is a living body. It is a body among other bodies, but also one that is fundamentally dependent on those other bodies to receive and impart shape. If it attaches to itself at the expense of that process, then it fails to live, and if it detaches from itself completely, it follows a different route toward death. Both specters of nonlife constitute its own life, but what persists, we might say, is not persistence or even attachment to self, but an internally repelling movement — a dynamic state of being "attached/not attached" without resolution or harmony. In this sense, perhaps the agonism between us can be better understood as the constitutive chiasm of Hegel's text. An overlapping set of movements propelling toward and away from one another, in other words, a figure that is not quite a settled image — is apparently "the shape" the body is in.

Notes

1   Judith Butler, "Stubborn Attachments" in Judith Butler, *The Psychic Life of Power: Theories in Subjection* (Palo Alto, Calif.: Stanford University Press, 1997).

2   For some of our previous publications on Hegel, see Catherine Malabou, *L'avenir de Hegel*, published in English as *The Future of Hegel: Plasticity, Temporality and Dialectic*, trans. Lisabeth During (London: Routledge, 2005); Judith Butler, *Subjects of Desire: Hegelian Reflections in*

   Twentieth-Century France (New York: Columbia University Press, 1987), and Butler, "Stubborn Attachments."

3   Hegel, *Phenomenology of Spirit*, trans. A. V. Miller (Oxford: Oxford University Press, 1977), 113.

4   Ibid., 111.

5   Alexandre Kojève, *Introduction à la lecture de Hegel* (Paris: Gallimard, 1947), and *Introduction to the Reading of Hegel*, trans. Allan Bloom (Ithaca, N.Y.: Cornell University Press, 1969); Jacques Derrida, "From Restricted to General Economy," in *Writing and Difference*, trans. Alan Bass (Chicago: University of Chicago Press, 1978); Butler, *Psychic Life of Power*.

6   Butler, *Psychic Life of Power*, 35.

7   Ibid., 35.

8   Ibid. Further: "Hence, it is as a substitute in the service of disavowal that the bondsman labors; only by miming and covering the mimetic status of that labor can the bondsman appear to be both active and autonomous" (36–37).

9   Ibid., 41.

10 Kojève, *Introduction to the Reading of Hegel*, 544.

11 Ibid., 376.

12 *Phenomenology of Spirit*, 114.

13 Ibid., 114.

14 Derrida, "From Restricted to General Economy," 255.

15 Ibid., 255.

16 Ibid.

17 Ibid., 256–257.

18 Ibid., 264.

19 Ibid., 273.

20 Ibid., 265.

21 Ibid., 263.

22 Ibid., 276.

23 Ibid., 255.

24 Ibid., 255.

25 Butler, *Psychic Life of Power*, 57.

26 Ibid., 57. See also the development on the dialectical sublation of animal functions in the analysis of Unhappy Consciousness, 50ff.

27 Ibid., 36.

28 Ibid., 37.

29 Ibid., 37.

30 Ibid., 36.

31 Ibid., 37.

32 Ibid., 38–39.

33 Ibid., 41.

34 *Phenomenology of Spirit*, 118 and 256–257.

35 Butler, *Psychic Life of Power*, 41.

36 Heidegger, *Being and Time*, trans. Joan Stambaugh (Albany: State University of New York Press, 1996), §47, at 223.

37 *Phenomenology of Spirit*, 118.

38 Butler, *Psychic Life of Power*, 32.

39 Ibid., 31–32.

40 Ibid., 42.

41 Ibid.

42 Ibid., 33.

43 Ibid., 58.

44 Ibid., 60.

45 Michel Foucault, *The History of Sexuality*, Vol. 1: *The Will to Knowledge* (London: Penguin, 1992), 154, and all of chapter 3.

46 Michel Foucault, *Herculine Barbin: Being the Recently Discovered Memoirs of a Nineteen Century Hermaphrodite*, trans. Richard McDongall (New York: Colophon, 1980), 13.

47 Butler, *Psychic Life of Power*, 60.

48 Butler gives the following examples: "Impulse is continually fabricated as a site of confession and, hence, of potential control, but this fabrication exceeds the regulatory aims by which it is generated. In this sense, criminal codes which seek to catalogue and institutionalize normalcy become the site for a contestation of the concept of the normal; sexologists who would classify and pathologize homosexuality inadvertently provide the conditions for a proliferation and mobilization of homosexual cultures" (*Psychic Life of Power*, 59).

49 Butler, *Psychic Life of Power*, 60.

50 Ibid., 62.

51 Malabou, *Future of Hegel*.

52 *Phenomenology of Spirit*, 39.

53 *Philosophy of Mind*, part 3 of the *Encyclopaedia of the Philosophical Sciences* (1830), trans. A. V. Miller (Oxford: Clarendon Press, 1971), §407.

54 *Phenomenology of Spirit*, 20.

55 Ibid., 75 (para. 125).

56 Ibid., 102 (para. 164).

57 Ibid., 107 (para. 170).

58 Ibid., 107–108 (para. 171).

59 Ibid.

60 Ibid., 108 (para. 171).

61 Ibid., 108 (para. 172).

62 Ibid. 109, (para. 174).

63 One might similarly ask how this *Kreislauf* sets the stage for the bacchanalian revel described in the Preface.

64 *Phenomenology of Spirit*, 112 (para. 185).

65 Ibid., 185–186.

66 Ibid., 186.

67 I mean the privilege of making, shaping, and fashioning over being.

68 Michel Foucault, *What Is Critique?* (1968), in *The Essential Foucault: Selections from the Essential Works of Foucault 1954–1984*, ed. Paul Rabinow and Nikolas Rose (New York:New Press, 2003), 263–278.

69 Ibid., 263.

70 Ibid., 264.

Index

Absolute Knowing, 48, 59, 61, 68, 77, 116, 251, 327, 452, 455, 465, 470, 526–27, 535n26, 604, 606. *See also* Absolute Knowledge

Absolute Knowledge, 66n55, 612, 615, 620, 624, 638. *See also* Absolute Knowing

Adorno, Theodor W, 14, 537–51, 553, 594

Agency, 25, 27–28, 38, 48, 77, 105, 232–33, 239–40, 277, 300, 394, 542, 585; Artistic, 366n4; Moral, 23, 25, 30, 36, 361, 457, 468; Rational, 25–26, 28–30, 35–36, 277; Socialized, 30–31, 38; Tragic, 30

Agnosticism, 426

Alexander, Samuel, 218n27

Alexander the Great, 443

Alienation, 28, 31, 99, 257, 282–84, 295n3, 296n5, 389–91, 393, 444, 500n30, 507–9, 638

Altenstein, Karl Siegmund von, xvi, 5–6, 298

Althusser, Louis, 478, 498n2, n4

Anselm, 412n101, 414–15, 423–25, 427n9, 428n27

Aristotle, 1, 9, 14, 165, 174n24–6, 200n83, 217n21, 220n46, 232, 240n18, 241n19–20, 245, 396, 398, 433–51, 485, 579–80, 582–83, 587, 590, 593n44

Art, 1, 10, 12–14, 18n93–95, 34, 48, 63n4, n7, 93, 105, 173n7, 244, 246, 253, 258, 288, 353–65, 366n4, n7–8, 367n13, n 20, n22, 368n34–35, 369–82, 384n29, 399, 412n116, 441–43; Classical, 13, 363–64, 366n4, 367n13; the Death of, 14; History, 1, 333–34, 347n11, 363, 366n7; Mimetic,

373, 381; Modern, 14, 376; Romantic, 13–14, 363–64, 366n4, 367n13, 373, 379; Symbolic, 13, 363, 366n4, 367n13;

Atheism, 7, 400, 404, 406, 419, 421, 426, 477

Aubenque, Pierre, 447

Bach, Johann Sebastian, 372–74, 379

Bacon, Francis, 82, 442

Barnett, Stuart, 607n1

Barth, Karl, 1

Bataille, Georges, 594, 600, 602, 607, 613, 616–17, 620

Baumgarten, Alexander Gottlieb, 416, 428n27

Bayen, Pierre, 220n45

Beautiful Soul, 103–4, 359, 362, 367n22

Beethoven, Ludwig van, xiv, 5, 371, 377

Begriff, 7, 10, 80, 153, 159–60, 173n3, n7, 208, 210, 212, 217n22, 288, 480, 506, 598. *See also* Pure Concept

Böhme, Jakob, 14

Brandom, Robert, 1, 69, 94, 107n21–22, 556, 576–77, 580–87, 589–90, 592n23, 593n39

Buber, Martin, 409n53

Buhl, Ludwig, 326

Burckhardt, Christiana Charlotte, xvi, 4

Burckhardt, Jacob, 332–33

Butler, Clark, 4

Butler, Judith, 1, 611–14, 617–24, 640n48

Carlsbad Decrees. *See* Karlsbad Decrees

Carové, Friedrich Wilhelm, 6

A Companion to Hegel, First Edition. Edited by Stephen Houlgate and Michael Baur.
© 2011 Blackwell Publishing Ltd. Published 2011 by Blackwell Publishing Ltd.

Blackwell Companions to Philosophy

This outstanding student reference series offers a comprehensive and authoritative survey of philosophy as a whole. Written by today's leading philosophers, each volume provides lucid and engaging coverage of the key figures, terms, topics, and problems of the field. Taken together, the volumes provide the ideal basis for course use, representing an unparalleled work of reference for students and specialists alike.

Already published in the series: